INTERIOR
GRAPHIC
STANDARDS

MARYROSE McGOWAN, AIA

EDITOR IN CHIEF

KELSEY KRUSE, AIA

GRAPHICS EDITOR

WILEY

JOHN WILEY & SONS, INC.

This book is printed on acid-free paper. ♾

Copyright © 2003 by John Wiley & Sons, Inc. All rights reserved

Published by John Wiley & Sons, Inc., Hoboken, New Jersey

Published simultaneously in Canada

For general information on our other products and services or for technical support, please contact our Customer Care Department within the United States at (800) 762-2974, outside the United States at (317) 572-3993 or fax (317) 572-4002.

Wiley also publishes its books in a variety of electronic formats. Some content that appears in print may not be available in electronic books. For information about Wiley products, visit our website at www.wiley.com

Library of Congress Cataloging-in-Publication Data:

McGowan, Maryrose.
    Interior graphic standards / Maryrose McGowan.
        p. cm.
    Includes index
        ISBN 0-471-40568-X (Cloth)
        1. Building—Details—Drawings. 2.
    Building—Details—Drawings—Standards. I. Title.
        TH2031 .M34 2003
        721'.028'4—dc21
                                    2002153261

Printed in the United States of America

10 9 8 7 6 5 4 3 2 1

CONTENTS

2 INTERIOR BUILDING COMPONENTS 177

FOREWORD

I am delighted to celebrate with our partners The American Institute of Architects and John Wiley & Sons, Inc., the publication of the first edition of *Interior Graphic Standards*.

Ada Louise Huxtable has observed that this is a terribly important period in architecture—the greatest since the Renaissance—in terms of creativity and change. "Traditionally," she has noted, "buildings were conceived as the shape of exterior things; they are now being designed from the inside out in a radical way, starting with interior function and space." The process of creating space in a contemporary context involves deconstructing and reconstructing a building starting with the interiors.

The RISD Department of Interior Architecture has a rich history of exploring, adapting, and creating truly inspired spaces. It was in the late 1940s that the head of the department, Ernst Lichtbau, redirected the program. As a student of Otto Wagner's, Lichtbau emphasized a more rigorous approach to the design of space. Today, the Department of Interior Architecture, headed by Brian Kernaghan, continues this tradition with innovative programs, which re-create and challenge our notion of interior architecture. Kernaghan's firmly held belief that good design is essential to the fabric of society is evident in the student work and pervades the atmosphere of the department.

The heart and soul of this ambitious project has been the Interior Architecture students. Student research is included in the discussion of construction and finish materials in Part 2—"Interior Building Components"—of this book. Part 3— "Interior Typologies"—was developed under the mentorship of the *Interior Graphic Standards* Advisory Board in an innovative seminar class sponsored by John Wiley & Sons, Inc. The board members worked with the students both on campus and at a distance, tirelessly sharing the benefit of their professional experience. The RISD community was honored to host these industry leaders, and our students were privileged to work under their tutelage. I would like to thank the gifted designers who formed the advisory board: Eric Alch, SOM, New York; Stephen Apking, AIA, SOM, New York; Sarah Bader, Gensler, Chicago; Jan Bishop, AIA, The Hillier Group, Princeton; Jane Clark, AIA, Zimmer Gunsul Frasca Partnership, Seattle; John L. Hogshead, AIA, Perkins and Will, Atlanta; Ted Kollaja, AIA, lauckgroup, Dallas; Elizabeth Niedzwiecki, AIA, The Hillier Group, Princeton; and Tim Shea, AIA, Richard Meier & Partners, Los Angeles.

This year marks the 125th anniversary of the founding of Rhode Island School of Design college and museum. It is fitting that in this year we offer this landmark publication to the design and the art community, to empower and inspire them in their efforts to enrich the fabric of society through innovation and excellence. It is our rich legacy to the future of the profession.

RISD graduates are world-renowned for creating works of art that open the eye and mind, and for advocating solutions to issues of contemporary life that enhance our man-made environment. We are pleased that *Interior Graphic Standards* will offer guidance to such noble efforts for many years to come.

ROGER MANDLE
President
Rhode Island School of Design
Providence, Rhode Island

PREFACE

Based in professional practice and inspired by the artists who create solutions to contemporary life by enhancing the built environment, *Interior Graphic Standards* is the first comprehensive source of design data and project management information for all aspects of commercial interiors practice. *Interior Graphic Standards* aims not only to instruct but also to inspire architects, interior designers, interns, construction specifiers, facility managers, construction contractors, and students in all these fields. In the process of creating this first edition, we have codified the current state of Interiors practice.

This ambitious project was conceived by Amanda Miller, Associate Publisher at John Wiley & Sons, Inc. With each new edition of *Architectural Graphic Standards* (it is currently in its tenth edition with more than 1 million copies sold in over 70 years), the inclusion of design criteria and detailing for Interiors has steadily increased. In acknowledgment of this burgeoning practice area, Amanda brought together the talents and foresight of The American Institute of Architects and the Department of Interior Architecture at Rhode Island School of Design (RISD) and entrusted them with the mission to create an indispensable guide to the art and craft of commercial interior design. Drawing upon her professional education in architecture, Julie Trelstad, Senior Editor, has executed this vision and expanded the basic premise of this project into areas that will help to revolutionize the way buildings are designed and the way those designs are documented.

The planning, designing, detailing, finishing, and decorating of commercial spaces from the programming to the project closeout phases can be found in these pages. The book is organized to present three areas of practice information: general design criteria, finish material selection and construction assembly detailing, and building typology design criteria. Some of the more than 170 topics include: accessibility, color theory, acoustic and lighting design, project management checklists, casework, architectural concrete, cabinet construction and joinery, countertops, interior architectural woodwork, finishes for architectural hardware, glass-fiber-reinforced gypsum, textiles and leather, systems furniture, and design criteria for office, museum and exhibition, entertainment, health care, hospitality, and educational facilities.

Interior Graphic Standards contains more than 3,000 illustrations, 100 color plates, and—for the first time—construction details appropriate for adaptation and use in contract documents. The construction details include those that are familiar and suitable for forming the basis of any office library of standard details, in addition to truly inspired design solutions from Sir Norman Foster; Kohn Pedersen Fox Associates PC; Venturi, Scott Brown and Associates; and Reg Hough, FAIA, to mention only a few. The vitality and integrity of the first edition of *Interior Graphic Standards* has been established by the expert advice of the more than 200 contributors under the guidance of an advisory board of leading designers from all over the country.

John Wiley & Sons, Inc., Rhode Island School of Design, and The American Institute of Architects are proud to offer the international design and construction community this first edition of *Interior Graphic Standards*. Our hope is that it will become a source of design inspiration to all who seek its guidance.

MARYROSE McGOWAN, AIA
Editor in Chief
Cambridge, Massachusetts

ACKNOWLEDGMENTS

JOHN WILEY & SONS, INC.

ROBERT C. GARBER
Vice President and Group Executive Publisher

AMANDA L. MILLER
Associate Publisher

JULIE M. TRELSTAD
Senior Editor

DIANA CISEK
Production Director

EILEEN G. CHETTI
Production Manager

MICHAEL OLIVO
Senior Production Editor

JENNIFER ACKERMAN
Assistant Developmental Editor

ROSANNE KONEVAL
Editorial Assistant

LAUREN LaFRANCE
Editorial Assistant

ELIZABETH CEPEDA
Production Assistant

JANICE BORZENDOWSKI
Copy Editor

LISA STORY
Proofreader

JENNIFER RUSHING-SCHURR
Indexer

LUCINDA GEIST
Graphic Designer

RHODE ISLAND SCHOOL OF DESIGN

ROGER MANDLE
President

DAWN BARRETT
Dean, Division of Architecture & Design

BRIAN KERNAGHAN
Department Head, Interior Architecture

WENDY ABELSON
Department Assistant, Interior Architecture

SCHEME DETAILING STUDENT CONTRIBUTORS
Mia Alwen
Elizabeth Aukamp
Pyinerl S. Chang
Winnie Cheng
Jason Dickerson
Carl Henschel
Yon-Hwa Jang
Min Kyeng Kang
Tonu Lensment
Tanya Nachia
Manami Nakabayashi
Lerlux Sophonpanich
Merve Yoneymen
Thitapa Youngcharoen

INTERIOR TYPOLOGIES STUDENT CONTRIBUTORS
Lalana Assawamunkong
Michael Blankenship
Pyinerl S. Chang
Leonor De Lope Friedeberg
Mayura Dhume
Douglas Flandro
Meryl Grant
Natasa Jelic
Sunyoung Kwon
Ted Milligan
Tanya Nachia
Natasza Naczas
Betty Ng
Shawn Parks
Soyploy Phanich
Sukamorn Prasithrathsint
Heidi Rhodes
Anna Rosete
Mette Shenker
Lerlux Sophonpanich
Perry Sye
Brian Tan
Nancy Vayo
Thitapa Youngcharoen
Ji-Seong Yun

INTERIOR GRAPHIC STANDARDS

ADVISORY BOARD
Eric Alch
SOM, New York

Stephen Apking, AIA
SOM, New York

Sarah Bader
Gensler, Chicago

Jan Bishop, AIA
The Hillier Group, Princeton

Jane Clark, AIA
Zimmer Gunsul Frasca Partnership, Seattle

John L. Hogshead, AIA
Perkins and Will, Atlanta

Ted Kollaja, AIA
lauckgroup, Dallas

Elizabeth Niedzwiecki, AIA
The Hillier Group, Princeton

Tim Shea, AIA
Richard Meier & Partners, Los Angeles

MARYROSE McGOWAN, AIA
Editor in Chief

KELSEY KRUSE, AIA
Graphics Editor

KAREN LINDBLAD
Assistant Editor

GLENN HAMILTON
Assistant Graphics Editor

CONTRIBUTING EDITORS
Faith Baum, AIA, IIDA
Susan Hardiman
Trey Klein, AIA
Margery Morgan
Sean Solley

EDITORIAL ASSISTANTS
Ted Milligan
Betty Ng
Sukamorn Prasithrathsint

CONTRIBUTING GRAPHICS EDITORS
Thea Hahn, AIA
Denie McLaren
Gloria Mikolajczyk
Chuck Richter
Gary Trakas
Fernando Zúñiga-Pflücker, AIA

PART 1

GENERAL PLANNING AND DESIGN DATA

Human Factors

Design Principles

Color Theory

Principles of Perception

Acoustics

Interior Lighting Design

Programming

Contract Administration

Security

Interior Landscape Design

Environmental Quality

Stair Design

Life Safety Considerations

Building Systems

HUMAN FACTORS

Human factors information refers to the variables that affect human performance in the built environment, such as human physiology and human psychology. Data accumulated from the fields of engineering, biology, psychology, and anthropology are integrated in this multidisciplinary field.

Fit describes a design that uses human factors information to create a stimulating but nonstressful environment for human use. Some areas of fit are physiological, psychological, sensual, and cultural.

ANTHROPOMETRICS AND ERGONOMICS

The field of anthropometrics provides information about the dimension and functional capacity of the human body. *Static anthropometrics* measures the body at rest; *dynamic anthropometrics* measures the body while performing activities defined as "work." Dimensional variation occurs in anthropometric data because of the large range of diversity in the human population. To utilize anthropometric charts effectively, a designer must identify where a subject user group falls in relationship to these variables. The factors that cause human variations are gender, age, ethnicity, and race. Patterns of growth affected by human culture cause variation in human measure as well. Percentiles that refer to the frequency of occurrence describe dimensional variation on anthropometric charts: that is, the mean percentile (50%), the small extreme percentile (2.5%), and the large extreme percentile (97.5%).

Ergonomics is the application of human factors data to design. This term was coined by the U.S. army when it began to design machines to fit humans, rather than trying to find humans to fit machines.

HUMAN BEHAVIOR

Human behavior is motivated by innate attributes such as the five senses and by learned cultural attributes. Each human has a unique innate capacity to gather sensual information. How that information is understood is determined by personal and cultural experience.

Proxemics is the study of human behavior as it relates to learned cultural behavior. Human behavior is motivated by the innate nature of the animal, and this behavior is expressed and modified by each person's learned culture and traditions.

Innate Human Attributes

The five senses determine human comfort levels in the environment and are a part of human factors studies.

- *Sight.* Behavioral scientists agree that, for human beings, seeing is the most engaged sense for gathering information. Physical form is perceived when visual data is organized into patterns, and that data is integrated with memories and emotions. Visual form is perceived as having a context with boundaries. Visual form can be understood to be a dynamic system of directional lines of forces that are innate, kinetic, and independent of the representational content of a form. Once a form's attributes have been perceived, humans tend to give the perceived form symbolic meaning. This meaning is cultural and personal, resulting from associations and past experiences.

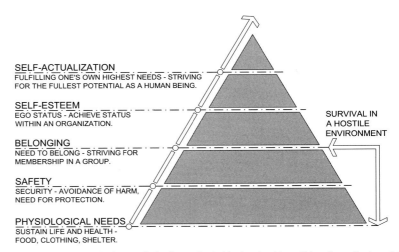

Maslow's diagram attempts to explain human behavior motivated by innate drives. It is a theoretical model that describes human needs and motivations. This "need hierarchy system" is presented as a constantly evolving process, such that when a person satisfies one need, another presents itself, and the individual will be driven to satisfy that set of needs. This is a nonlinear process. Most building programming efforts focus on human behavior that addresses the areas of belonging, self-esteem, and self-actualization.

HIERARCHY OF NEEDS (AFTER MASLOW) *Source: Forrest Wilson,* A Graphic Survey of Perception and Behavior for the Design Professions; *New York: Van Nostrand Reinhold, 1984 (p.163).*

- *Touch.* Touch is essential to human development and growth. Texture is learned most completely through skin contact. Human skin is sensitive to temperature, pain, and pressure. Vision and touch are interwoven in sighted humans. Memory of tactile experiences allows humans to understand their environment through visual scanning.
- *Hearing.* Humans can use hearing to determine distances. Sound moves in concentric circles and in horizontal and vertical planes. The ear transmits these airborne vibrations to the brain where it is processed and assigned meaning. The ability to focus hearing is called *sensory gating.* The ability to gate sound varies, and diminishes with aging.
- *Smell and Taste.* Research about smell is difficult to conduct because human sensitivity to smell is highly variable over time and from person to person. A person's sense of smell to an odor can fatigue quickly during exposure. Smell is defined in terms of commonly perceived odors such as flowery, putrid, burned, resinous, and spice. Taste and smell are closely related in human experience.

UNIVERSAL DESIGN

Good design that works with respect to human factors issues can result in *universal design.* Principles of universal design are:

- Equitable use
- Perceptible information
- Flexibility
- Tolerance of error
- Simple and intuitive use
- Low physical effort

Universal design differs from *accessible design.* Universal design functions equally well for as inclusive a group of users as is possible; accessible design addresses the requirements of only one user group, people with disabilities. By limiting the user group description, accessible design can be exclusive and can segregate people with disabilities from others.

DISTANCE RELATIONSHIPS AMONG PEOPLE

DISTANCE RELATIONSHIPS

Some aspects of human behavior related to territoriality are cultural. The space between objects has form but the space between people is kinetic. The dimension of human territoriality varies in dimension due to cultural forces.

- *Defensible space* occurs when designed form reinforces meaning for the user and where boundary and ownership are visible in public space.
- *Intimate space* is where lovers, family, small children, and close friends are allowed to enter.
- *Personal space* is a protected area where strangers are not welcome.
- *Social space* is a range of space in which most public interactions occur. Speech and expression are clear and communications are efficient and accurate.
- *Public distance* is the range of space where it is not considered rude to ignore someone; and it does not allow interaction.

Faith Baum, AIA, IIDA; Faith Baum Architect; Lexington, Massachusetts

MOTOR DEVELOPMENT ● EXPRESSION OF EMOTIONS ◆ (TIME OF EMERGENCE) SOCIAL DEVELOPMENT ■ LANGUAGE MILESTONES ▲ COGNITIVE DEVELOPMENT ○

MEASURE AND DEVELOPMENT OF INFANTS—BIRTH TO 11 MONTHS

MEASURE AND DEVELOPMENT OF INFANTS—12 TO 23 MONTHS

1 □   **HUMAN FACTORS**

Henry Dreyfuss Associates, The Measure of Man & Woman (Alvin R. Tilley, Ed.). John Wiley & Sons, Inc., New York. 2001.

● MOTOR DEVELOPMENT   ■ SOCIAL DEVELOPMENT   ▲ LANGUAGE MILESTONES   ○ COGNITIVE DEVELOPMENT

2.5 - 3 YEARS

4 YEARS
GIRLS TALLER THAN BOYS

● CANNOT TURN OR STOP SUDDENLY OR QUICKLY

● MORE EFFECTIVE CONTROL OF STOPPING, STARTING, AND TURNING

● CAN JUMP A DISTANCE OF 15 TO 24 INCHES

● CAN JUMP A DISTANCE OF 24 OR 33 INCHES

● CAN ASCEND STAIRWAYS UNAIDED, ALTERNATING THE FEET

● CAN DESCEND LONG STAIRWAYS ALTERNATING THE FEET, IF SUPPORTED

BEGINNINGS OF CONVERSATION; BREAKTHROUGH IN ATTENTION TO COMMUNICATION.

CHILD THINKS THAT HIS OR HER POINT OF VIEW IS THE ONLY ONE POSSIBLE

▲ NEW WORDS ARE LEARNED ALMOST EVERY DAY.
COMPREHENSION IS EXCELLENT, ALTHOUGH CHILD
STILL MAKES MANY MISTAKES IN GRAMMAR.

▲ VOCABULARY REACHES 1,000 WORDS, ABOUT 80% ARE INTELLIGIBLE.
GRAMMAR IS CLOSE TO ADULT SPEECH, AND SYNTACTIC MISTAKES ARE FEWER.

GROUNDWORK FOR LOGICAL THINKING: CHILDREN CAN THINK ABOUT OBJECTS, PEOPLE, OR EVENTS IN THEIR ABSENCE
BY USING MENTAL REPRESENTATIONS OF THEM, BUT THEY CANNOT YET MANIPULATE THESE REPRESENTATIONS.

MEASURE AND DEVELOPMENT OF TODDLERS—2.5 TO 4 YEARS

5 YEARS

6 YEARS

● CAN START, TURN, AND STOP EFFECTIVELY IN GAMES

● GIRLS ARE SUPERIOR IN ACCURACY OF MOVEMENT.
BOYS ARE SUPERIOR IN FORCEFUL, LESS COMPLEX ACTS.

● CAN MAKE A RUNNING JUMP OF 28 TO 38 INCHES

● CAN DESCEND LONG STAIRWAYS UNAIDED, ALTERNATING THE FEET

● CAN THROW WITH PROPER WEIGHT SHIFT AND STOP

CHILD THINKS THAT HIS OR HER OWN POINT OF VIEW IS THE ONLY ONE POSSIBLE

CHILD LEARNS NOT ONLY BY SENSING AND DOING, BUT BY THINKING AS WELL.
BASIC UNDERSTANDING OF CAUSE AND EFFECT.

MEASURE AND DEVELOPMENT OF YOUTHS—5 TO 6 YEARS

Henry Dreyfuss Associates, The Measure of Man & Woman
(Alvin R. Tilley, Ed.). John Wiley & Sons, Inc., New York. 2001.

● **MOTOR DEVELOPMENT**   ■ **SOCIAL DEVELOPMENT**   ○ **COGNITIVE DEVELOPMENT**

7 YEARS

● BALANCING ON ONE FOOT WITHOUT LOOKING BECOMES POSSIBLE
● CAN HOP AND JUMP ACCURATELY INTO SMALL SQUARES
● CAN ACCURATELY PERFORM JUMPING JACK EXERCISES

8 YEARS

● GRIP STRENGTH PERMITS STEADY 12-POUND PRESSURE
● GIRLS CAN THROW A SMALL BALL 40 FEET

CHILD REALIZES THAT OTHERS MAY INTERPRET A SITUATION IN A WAY DIFFERENT FROM HIS OR HER OWN

CHILDREN CAN THINK LOGICALLY ABOUT "HERE & NOW", BUT NOT YET ABOUT ABSTRACTIONS

AVG WT: 50.4 LB - 22.9 KG

AVG WT: 56.1 LB - 25.5 KG

MEASURE AND DEVELOPMENT OF YOUTHS—7 TO 8 YEARS

9 YEARS

● GIRLS CAN JUMP VERTICALLY TO A HEIGHT OF 8 1/2 INCHES; BOYS, 10 INCHES
● BOYS CAN RUN 16 1/2 FEET PER SECOND
● BOYS CAN THROW A BALL 70 FEET

10 YEARS

● CAN JUDGE AND INTERCEPT PATHWAYS OF SMALL BALLS THROWN FROM A DISTANCE
● GIRLS CAN RUN 17 FEET PER SECOND

CHILD HAS RECIPROCAL AWARENESS, REALIZES OTHERS HAVE A POINT OF VIEW AND THAT OTHERS ARE AWARE THAT HE OR SHE HAS A PARTICULAR POINT OF VIEW.

CHILD UNDERSTANDS IMPORTANCE OF LETTING OTHERS KNOW THAT THEIR REQUESTS HAVE NOT BEEN IGNORED OR FORGOTTEN.

GAINING PROFICIENCY AT CLASSIFYING, MANIPULATING NUMBERS, DEALING WITH CONCEPTS OF TIME AND SPACE, AND DISTINGUISHING REALITY FROM FANTASY

AVG WT: 62.9 LB - 28.6 KG

AVG WT: 70.2 LB - 31.9 KG

MEASURE AND DEVELOPMENT OF YOUTHS—9 TO 10 YEARS

1 □ HUMAN FACTORS

Henry Dreyfuss Associates, The Measure of Man & Woman *(Alvin R. Tilley, Ed.). John Wiley & Sons, Inc., New York. 2001.*

MOTOR DEVELOPMENT   ### SOCIAL DEVELOPMENT   ### COGNITIVE DEVELOPMENT

11 YEARS
GIRLS TALLER THAN BOYS

12 YEARS
GIRLS TALLER THAN BOYS

STANDING BROAD JUMP OF 5 FEET IS POSSIBLE FOR BOYS;
4 1/2 FEET FOR GIRLS.

STANDING HIGH JUMP OF 3 FEET IS POSSIBLE

CHILD CAN IMAGINE A THIRD PERSON'S PERSPECTIVE, TAKING INTO ACCOUNT SEVERAL DIFFERENT POINTS OF VIEW

10 YR

ABILITY TO THINK ABSTRACTLY.
CAPABABLE OF HYPOTHETICAL-DEDUCTIVE REASONING.

CAN BRING TO BEAR WHAT HAS BEEN LEARNED IN THE PAST TO SOLVE
THE PROBLEMS OF THE PRESENT, AND PLAN FOR THE FUTURE.   ADULTHOOD

BOYS SHOW SLIGHT MATHEMATICAL AND SPATIAL SUPERIORITY.
GIRLS SHOW SLIGHT VERBAL SUPERIORITY.

WT: 77.4 LB - 35.2 KG

WT: 86 LB - 39.1 KG

MEASURE AND DEVELOPMENT OF YOUTHS—11 TO 12 YEARS

13 YEARS
GIRLS TALLER THAN BOYS

14 YEARS

ADOLESCENCE: PERSON REALIZES THAT COMMUNICATION AND MUTUAL ROLE THINKING DO NOT ALWAYS RESOLVE DISPUTES OVER RIVAL VALUES   ADULTHOOD

WT: 97.2 LB - 44.2 KG

WT 110 LB - 50 KG

MEASURE AND DEVELOPMENT OF YOUTHS—13 TO 14 YEARS

Henry Dreyfuss Associates, The Measure of Man & Woman
(Alvin R. Tilley, Ed.). John Wiley & Sons, Inc., New York. 2001.

MEASURE OF YOUTHS—15 TO 16 YEARS

MEASURE OF YOUTHS—17 TO 18.5 YEARS

Henry Dreyfuss Associates, The Measure of Man & Woman
(Alvin R. Tilley, Ed.). John Wiley & Sons, Inc., New York. 2001.

MEASURE OF MAN—FRONT VIEW

MEASURE OF MAN—SIDE VIEW

Henry Dreyfuss Associates, The Measure of Man & Woman
(Alvin R. Tilley, Ed.). John Wiley & Sons, Inc., New York. 2001.

MEASURE OF WOMAN—FRONT VIEW

MEASURE OF WOMAN—SIDE VIEW

Henry Dreyfuss Associates, The Measure of Man & Woman
(Alvin R. Tilley, Ed.). John Wiley & Sons, Inc., New York. 2001.

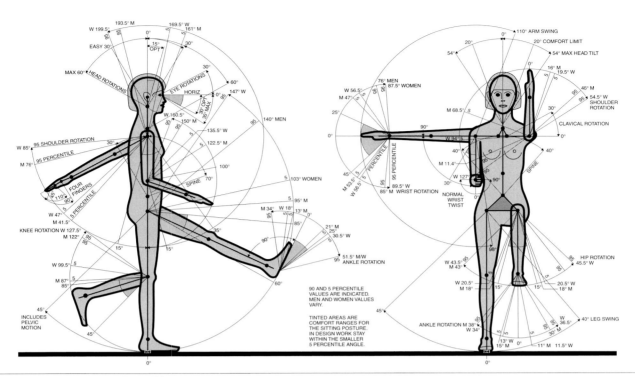

ANGLE MOVEMENTS OF BODY COMPONENTS

ANGLE MOVEMENTS OF BODY COMPONENTS—TOP VIEW

Henry Dreyfuss Associates, The Measure of Man & Woman
   (Alvin R. Tilley, Ed.). John Wiley & Sons, Inc., New York. 2001.

ACCESSIBILITY

DEFINITION

Accessible is a design term that was first introduced in the 1950s to describe elements of the physical environment that can be used by people with disabilities. Originally, the term described facilities that could be accessed by wheelchair users, but it has evolved to include designs for a wider group of people with more diverse functional requirements.

Society's need for accessible design has increased as a result of continuing medical advances. Concurrently, the development of new building technologies, such as residential elevators, wheelchair lifts, and power door operators, has made the provision of accessible facilities more practical and less expensive.

From a designer's perspective, there is a difference between appropriate accessible design for public facilities and the best approach for private, custom-accessible projects. Public accessibility standards establish general design specifications that broadly meet the targeted population's needs. By contrast, custom-accessible design should address the specific needs of an individual user.

REGULATORY HISTORY

The American National Standards Institute (ANSI) published the first national standards for accessible design in 1961. After its initial publication, many state and local jurisdictions began to adopt ANSI A117.1, *Accessible and Usable Buildings and Facilities,* as their accessibility code, although they often modified selected standards to suit their communities. ANSI has periodically revised the A117.1 standard since it was first published. In 1980, it was expanded to include housing standards focused primarily on the needs of wheelchair users (specifically paraplegics).

The 1968 Architectural Barriers Act was the first federal legislation that required accessible design in federal facilities. To address the absence of federal accessibility standards and the lack of an enforcement mechanism, Congress enacted the 1973 Rehabilitation Act. In addition, the act required facilities built with federal funds, and facilities built by entities that receive federal funds, to be accessible.

Section 502 of the 1973 Rehabilitation Act created a new federal agency, the Architectural and Transportation Barriers Compliance Board (ATBCB) to develop and issue minimum guidelines for design standards to be established by four standard-setting agencies. In 1984, the ATBCB issued the Uniform Federal Accessibility Standards (UFAS), which were established by the Department of Defense (DoD), the Department of Housing and Urban Development (HUD), the General Services Administration (GSA), and the U.S. Postal Service (USPS). UFAS is similar to the format and content of ANSI A117.1, 1980.

In 1988, Congress enacted the Fair Housing Amendments Act (FHAA). Although the act's guidelines include design requirements, it is a civil rights law, not a building code. Two years later, in 1990, President George Bush signed the Americans with Disabilities Act (ADA). This landmark legislation provided new civil rights protections for people with disabilities, and its guidelines included new federal accessibility stan-

FHAG: FAIR HOUSING ACCESSIBILITY GUIDELINES

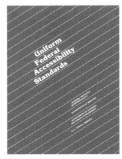

UFAS: UNIFORM FEDERAL ACCESSIBILITY STANDARDS

ADAAG: AMERICANS WITH DISABILITIES ACT ARCHITECTURAL GUIDELINES (TITLE III)

CABO/ANSI: AMERICAN NATIONAL STANDARDS INSTITUTE A117.1

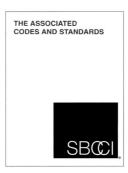

SBCCI: SOUTHERN BUILDING CODE CONGRESS INTERNATIONAL

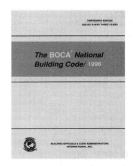

BOCA: BUILDING OFFICIALS AND CODE ADMINISTRATORS INTERNATIONAL

dards. ADA addresses the design and operation of privately owned public accommodations and state and local government facilities and programs. ADA design standards are very similar to the 1986 ANSI standards. ADA did not include housing design requirements because they were addressed in the earlier Fair Housing Amendments Act.

CIVIL RIGHTS LAWS AND BUILDING CODES

Enactment of the 1988 Fair Housing Amendments Act and 1990 Americans with Disabilities Act created a complex relationship between federal laws and the local building codes that already existed throughout the United States. Although many of the accessible design requirements in the civil rights laws and the codes are similar, there are major differences.

Building codes are specific to a legal jurisdiction, such as a state, county, township, or city. These state/local regulations are usually based on national model codes (BOCA, UBC, SBCCI, IBC) that a jurisdiction elects to adopt. The state and local jurisdictions typically modify the model codes and, as part of their review and enforcement process, make administrative rulings and interpretations. Over time, these modifications and interpretations make the design requirements of each municipality unique even though the underlying code is based on a national model.

Building officials use local codes to review architectural and engineering plans before they permit construction.

They also perform on-site inspections to verify that the completed construction is in compliance.

Unlike municipal officials, federal agencies do not issue building permits and typically do not inspect construction. Neither does the federal government issue rulings or interpretations for individual projects. Civil rights law enforcement is a "complaint-based process" that HUD administers for Fair Housing, and the Department of Justice administers for ADA. These agencies may choose to act on a citizen complaint, or a complainant may elect to seek direct relief through federal courts.

As civil rights laws, Fair Housing and ADA include both provisions both for facility design and construction and for facility operation and management. Provisions that address operation and management create new legal responsibilities that are shared between facility designers and facility operators.

Terminology common to both civil rights law and building code standards can be confusing because the same words often have different meanings. The term *dwelling,* for example, has a much different meaning in the Fair Housing design guidelines than it does in building codes. Similarly, building use and occupancy categories such as *transient lodging* and *assembly areas* (places of assembly) are not consistent between ADA and the building codes. Because designers must deal with both types of standards, they should carefully review the definitions included in each.

ADA AND FHAA DESIGN REQUIREMENTS

The Americans with Disabilities Act (ADA) and the Fair Housing Amendments Act (FHAA) are the two broad federal civil rights laws that address accessible design and construction of both public and private facilities. The Fair Housing Amendments Act covers multifamily housing. The Americans with Disabilities Act is applied to a wide range of public accommodations offered by private entities (Title III) and municipal facilities (Title II). Other federal laws, such as the 1973 Rehabilitation Act, may also apply to some projects. Designers should be aware that, in many aspects, federal civil rights laws are different from building codes. Therefore, receiving a building permit does not indicate that a project design complies with these federal laws.

The Americans with Disabilities Act includes design requirements for new facility construction and for additions to and alterations of existing facilities that are owned, leased, or operated by both private entities and local governments. However, design standards and management responsibilities differ between the two owner groups.

Owners and operators of existing private facilities that serve the public have ADA construction responsibilities under what is called "barrier removal." Local governments also have the responsibility of making all their new and existing programs accessible. Meeting this ADA responsibility for municipal programs may sometimes require new construction or physical modifications to existing facilities. ADA also prescribes employer responsibilities for changing their policies or modifying their facilities to accommodate employees with disabilities (Title I).

Several ADA concepts determine design requirements, such as "path-of-travel" components for renovation projects and the "elevator exception" for small multistory buildings. It is imperative that designers familiarize themselves with all aspects of the law, as well as with the design standards.

The Fair Housing Amendments Act addresses new multifamily housing constructed either by private entities or local governments. Generally, it covers apartments, dormitories, and other lodgings included in projects with four or more total dwelling units that are built for sale or lease. Existing housing structures and any remodeling, conversion, or reuse projects are not covered by FHAA.

The Fair Housing guidelines allow the exclusion of certain dwelling units because of site considerations such as steep topography and floodplains. The guidelines include site practicality tests for analyzing site constraints.

APPLICABLE ACCESSIBILITY STANDARDS FOR SAMPLE PROJECTS

PROJECT DESCRIPTION	FEDERAL LAWS	BUILDING CODES
Federally owned project of any type	1968 Architectural Barriers Act 1973 Rehabilitation Act Other standards as described by the agency	Building codes may or may not be applicable.
Project that utilizes federal funds or is built by the recipient of federal funds (private or government)	1968 Architectural Barriers Act 1973 Rehabilitation Act Other standards appropriate with ownership use and type	State and/or local building codes may apply.
Local government-owned commercial or public facility	ADA Title II 1973 Rehabilitation Act	State and/or local building codes may apply.
Local government-owned multifamily housing	ADA Title II 1973 Rehabilitation Act 1988 Fair Housing Amendments Act	State and/or local building codes may apply.
Privately owned public accommodation or commercial facility	ADA Title III	State and/or local building codes may apply.
Privately owned multifamily housing	1988 Fair Housing Amendments Act (Public accommodation spaces must meet ADA.)	State and/or local building codes may apply.
Privately leased, government-owned public accommodation	ADA Title III-Tenant ADA Title II-Owner	State and/or local building codes may apply.
Government-leased, privately owned public accommodation	1973 Rehabilitation Act-Tenant ADA Title II-Tenant ADA Title III-Owner	State and/or local building codes may apply.
Church-operated, church-owned facility	None	State and/or local building codes may apply.
Privately operated, church-owned facility	ADA Title III-Tenant None-Owner	State and/or local building codes may apply.
Church-operated, privately-owned facility	None-Tenant ADA Title III-Owner	State and/or local building codes may apply.

Note: Temporary facilities must meet the same federal standards as similar permanent facilities.

FEDERAL RULE-MAKING PROCESS

FEDERAL LEGISLATIVE PROCESS

To help them understand current civil rights law design requirements and monitor the publication of new standards, designers should familiarize themselves with the federal legislative process. Information on federal design standards is available within specific acts, in the resultant regulations, and in published guidelines. Additional information is available in the legislative history of an act and in the numerous documents issued during the rule-making process.

The administrative process for implementing federal laws requires public notice (in the *Federal Register*) and a public comment period for any proposed new regulations or guidelines. Designers should monitor this ongoing process in order to track the new standards that are periodically added to the existing accessibility guidelines. The architectural guidelines for laws like ADA are also periodically revised through the same rule-making process. Technical Assistance Manuals (TAMs) are another design information source. Administering agencies such as the Department of Justice and HUD periodically publish these manuals in order to clarify existing guidelines or standards.

Kim A. Beasley, AIA, and Thomas D. Davies, Jr., AIA; Paralyzed Veterans of America Architecture; Washington, D.C.

ACCESSIBILITY COMPLIANCE

These flowcharts address only the architectural aspects of the following federal laws that govern accessibility: the Architectural Barriers Act of 1968 (ABA), Section 504 of the Rehabilitation Act of 1973 (Section 504), the Fair Housing Amendments Act of 1988 (FHA), and Title II and Title III of the Americans with Disabilities Act (Title II ADA and Title III ADA). Other accessibility laws and standards may apply.

Many conditions apply to the decision points in the flowcharts, and occasionally the appropriate outcome may differ from what is illustrated. Consult relevant standards, regulations (e.g., GSA leasing regulations), and your client to ensure accuracy.

Federal agencies periodically update their accessibility standards; always make sure you are working with the most current copy of any federal law.

Terms Used in the Charts

ALTERATION: Any change that affects usability. This includes remodeling, renovation, rearrangements in structural parts, and changes or rearrangement of walls and full-height partitions.

COMMERCIAL FACILITIES: This category includes nonresidential facilities whose operations affect commerce.

CONTINUING OBLIGATION: Barriers must be removed whenever it becomes readily achievable to do so.

MULTIFAMILY HOUSING: As defined by the ABA, FHA, ADA, and Section 504 of the Rehabilitation Act of 1973, multifamily housing is a "building with four or more dwelling units." Further, they state that "dwelling units within a single structure separated by fire walls do not constitute separate buildings."

PATH OF TRAVEL: This is a continuous route connecting an altered area to the entrance and point of arrival. It can include sidewalks, lobbies, corridors, and elevators, as well as telephones, restrooms, and drinking fountains serving the altered area.

PLACE OF PUBLIC ACCOMMODATION: This set of facilities has retroactive requirements. There are 12 categories:

 Places of lodging (e.g., inns, hotels, motels, except for owner-occupied establishments renting fewer than six rooms)

 Establishments serving food or drink (e.g., restaurants and bars)

 Places of exhibition or entertainment (e.g., motion picture houses, theaters, concert halls, stadiums)

 Places of public gathering (e.g., auditoriums, convention centers, lecture halls)

 Sales or rental establishments (e.g., bakeries, grocery stores, hardware stores, shopping centers)

(Continues on next page)

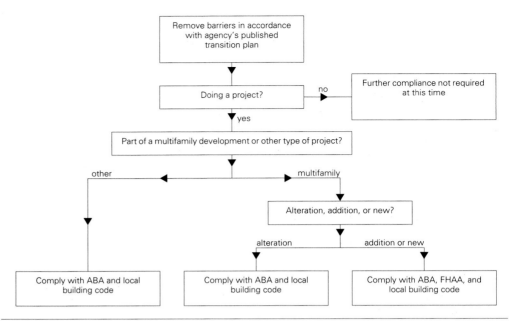

OWNED OR LEASED BY THE EXECUTIVE BRANCH, FEDERAL GOVERNMENT

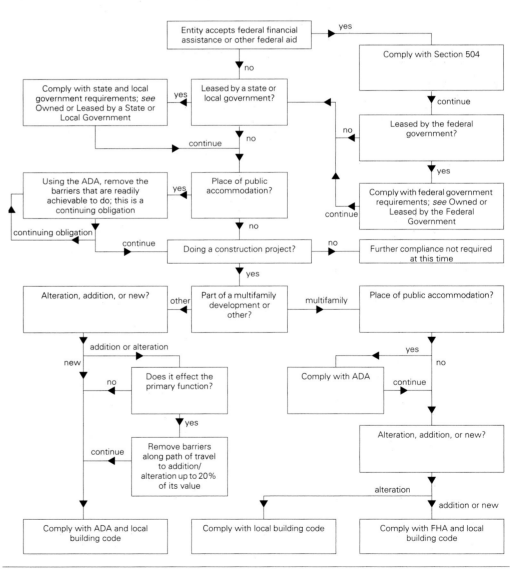

OWNED OR LEASED BY A PRIVATE ENTITY

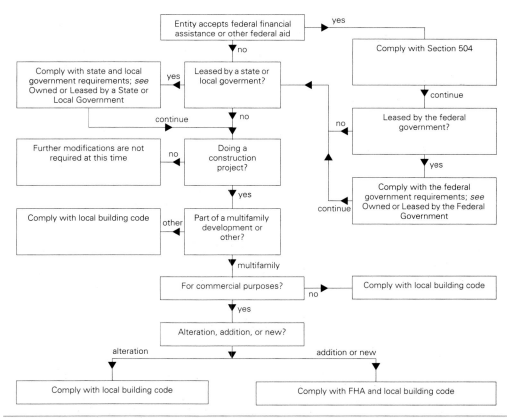

OWNED BY A RELIGIOUS ORGANIZATION OR PRIVATE CLUB

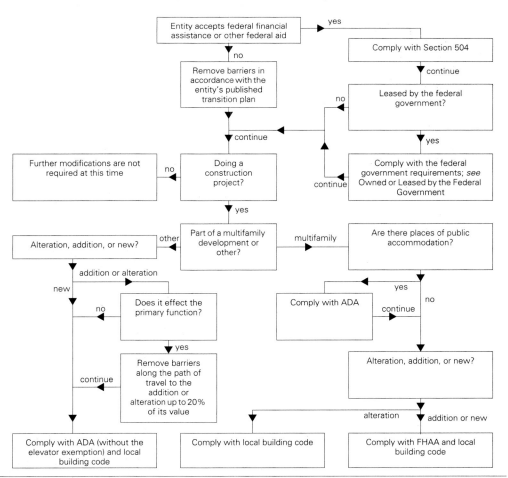

OWNED OR LEASED BY A STATE OR LOCAL GOVERNMENT

Terms Used in the Charts (continued)

Service establishments (e.g., shops, professional offices, hospitals)

Public transportation terminals, depots, or stations (not including facilities relating to air transportation)

Places of public display or collection (e.g., museums, libraries, galleries)

Places of recreation (e.g., parks, zoos)

Places of education (e.g., nursery schools; elementary, secondary, undergraduate, or postgraduate schools)

Social service center establishments (e.g., day care centers, senior citizen centers, homeless shelters, food banks, adoption agencies)

Places of exercise or recreation (e.g., gymnasiums, health spas, bowling alleys, golf courses)

PRIMARY FUNCTION: Any area in which a major activity takes place. It does not include mechanical rooms, boiler rooms, supply storage rooms, employee lounges or locker rooms, janitorial closets, entrances, corridors, or restrooms.

PRIVATE CLUB: To qualify, these organizations must meet the following criteria: Members exercise a high degree of control over club operations; the membership selection process is highly selective; substantial membership fees are charged; the entity is operated on a nonprofit basis; the club was not founded specifically to avoid compliance with federal civil rights laws.

READILY ACHIEVABLE: According to the laws, this means "easily accomplishable and able to be carried out without much difficulty or expense." The Department of Justice lists examples of what is readily achievable, including:

Installing ramps; making curb cuts in sidewalks and entrances

Repositioning shelves; rearranging tables, chairs, vending machines, display racks, and other furniture; repositioning telephones

Adding raised markings on elevator control buttons

Installing flashing alarm lights

Widening doors; installing offset hinges to widen doorways; installing accessible door hardware

Eliminating a turnstile or providing an alternative, accessible path

Installing grab bars in toilet stalls; rearranging toilet partitions to increase maneuvering space; insulating lavatory pipes under sinks to prevent burns; installing a raised toilet seat; installing a full-length bathroom mirror; repositioning the paper towel dispenser in a bathroom

Installing an accessible paper cup dispenser at an existing inaccessible water fountain

Removing high-pile, low-density carpeting

Mark J. Mazz, AIA, P.A.; Hyattsville, Maryland

MANEUVERING CLEARANCES

FORWARD APPROACH—ALCOVE

30" X 48" (762 X 1219) CLEAR FLOOR SPACE

ALCOVE

FORWARD

PARALLEL APPROACH—ALCOVE

PARALLEL

MANEUVERING CLEARANCES

EQUIPMENT PERMITTED IN SHADED AREA

SAMPLE MANEUVERING CLEARANCES—DRINKING FOUNTAIN

Knee and toe clearance can be included as part of the wheelchair turning space and clear floor space at accessible elements. However, the extent and location of knee and toe clearance can affect the usability of the space.

Knee and toe clearance that is included as part of a T-shaped turning space should be provided only at the base of the T or on one arm of the T. In some configurations, the obstruction of part of the T-shape may make it impossible for a wheelchair user to maneuver to the desired location.

WHEELCHAIR TURNING SPACE

THIS AREA MAY BE USED AS PART OF MANEUVERING CLEARANCE OR WHEELCHAIR TURNING SPACE

25" (635) MIN. TOE AND KNEE CLEARANCE

KNEE CLEARANCE

TOE CLEARANCE

MAXIMUM CLEARANCE
Additional space can be provided beneath the table, desk, or other element, but that space is not considered knee and toe clearance.

THIS AREA MAY BE USED AS PART OF MANEUVERING CLEARANCE OR WHEELCHAIR TURNING SPACE

17" (430) MIN. TOE AND KNEE CLEARANCE

8" MAX. (205)

11" MIN. (280)

6" (150) MAX. TOE CLEARANCE

KNEE CLEARANCE

TOE CLEARANCE

MINIMUM CLEARANCE
Clearances shown are required at specific accessible elements. Knee and toe clearance must always be at least 30 in. (762 mm) wide.

THIS AREA MAY BE USED AS PART OF MANEUVERING CLEARANCE OR WHEELCHAIR TURNING SPACE

6" (150) MAX. TOE CLEARANCE

TOE CLEARANCE ONLY

KNEE AND TOE CLEARANCES

1 ☐ **HUMAN FACTORS**

Lawrence G. Perry, AIA; Silver Spring, Maryland

HIGH AND LOW SIDE REACH LIMITS

UNOBSTRUCTED FORWARD REACH

PERSON WITH DISABILITY, TYP.

UNOBSTRUCTED SIDE REACH

MAXIMUM SIDE REACH OVER OBSTRUCTION

20" (510) MAX. COUNTER DEPTH

10" (255) MAX.

CLOSET

UNOBSTRUCTED HIGH FORWARD REACH

ANSI A117.1 provides exception for existing elements located 54 in. (1,372 mm) maximum above the floor or ground.

A117.1 provides exception for elevator car controls, allowing buttons at 54 in. (1,372 mm) maximum, where the elevator serves more than 16 openings.

A117.1 does not apply the 48-in. (1,219-mm) restriction to tactile signs. Tactile signs must be installed so

OBSTRUCTED SIDE REACH

the tactile characters are between 48 and 60 in. (1,219 and 1,524 mm) above the floor.

FHAG allows inaccessible controls in covered dwelling units if "comparable" accessible controls are provided.

Floor outlets are permitted if an adequate number of accessible wall outlets isare provided.

Electric outlets above kitchen counters can be located in corners, provided additional outlets are located within reach.

SHELVES

Accessible controls and operating mechanisms should be operable with one hand and not require tight grasping, pinching, or twisting of the wrist, with the following exception: FHAG does not regulate the operating force or type of operation required for controls and operating mechanisms in dwelling units.

PARALLEL/SIDE REACH LIMITS

REACH RANGES

SPECIFICATIONS FOR WATER CLOSETS SERVING CHILDREN

DIMENSION	PRE-K–K (AGES 3 AND 4) IN. (MM)	GRADES 1ST–3RD (AGES 5-8) IN. (MM)	GRADES 4TH–7TH (AGES 9-12) IN. (MM)
Water closet centerline	12 (305)	12–15 (305–380)	15–18 (380–455)
Toilet seat height	11–12 (280–305)	12–15 (305–380)	15–17 (380–430)
Grab bar height	18–20 (455–510)	20–25 (510–635)	25–27 (635–685)
Dispenser height	14 (355)	14–17 (355–430)	17–19 (430–485)

CHILDREN'S REACH RANGES FROM A WHEELCHAIR

FORWARD OR SIDE REACH	AGES 3 AND 4 IN. (MM)	AGES 5-8 IN. (MM)	AGES 9-12 IN. (MM)
Maximum	36 (915)	40 (1,015)	44 (1,120)
Minimum	20 (510)	18 (455)	16 (405)

Lawrence G. Perry, AIA; Silver Spring, Maryland

CANE HITS POST OR PYLON BEFORE PERSON HITS OBJECT

HIGHER THAN 27" (685)

12" (305) MAX.

12" (305) MAX.

THIS OVERHANG CAN BE GREATER THAN 12" (305) BECAUSE THE OBJECT CANNOT BE APPROACHED FROM THIS DIRECTION

OBJECTS MOUNTED ON POSTS OR PYLONS

FREESTANDING OBJECTS

27" (685) OR LESS

12" (305) OR GREATER

ELEVATION

HIGHER THAN 27" (685)

12" (305) MAX.

ELEVATION

HIGHER THAN 80" (2030)

12" (305) OR GREATER

ELEVATION

12" (305) OR GREATER

PLAN

POSTMOUNTED PROTRUDING OBJECTS

PROTECT SHADED AREA FROM PEDESTRIAN TRAFFIC

80" (2032)

CANE DETECTION AREA

OVERHEAD HAZARDS—EXAMPLE

27" (685) OR LESS

PLANTER

27" (685) OR LESS

RAILING POST GROUTED IN PLACE

RAILING

2" MIN. (51)

CURB

OVERHEAD HAZARD PROTECTION—EXAMPLES

4" MAX. (102)

80" MAX. (2030)

HIGHER THAN 27" (685)

WALKING PARALLEL TO A WALL

ANY AMOUNT   CLEAR WIDTH

27" (685) OR LESS

WALKING PARALLEL TO A WALL

ANY AMOUNT

27" (685) OR LESS

CANE RANGE

WALKING PERPENDICULAR TO A WALL

DIMENSIONS OF PROTRUDING OBJECTS

PROTRUDING OBJECTS

Wall sconces, fire alarm appliances, environmental controls, door hardware, signs, and suspended lighting fixtures are examples of protruding objects.

Some standards specify the extent to which doorstops and door closers may protrude into the 80-in. (2,032-mm) vertical clearance, generally allowing a 2-in. (51-mm) maximum projection.

Protruding objects are not permitted to reduce the required width of an accessible route (36 in. (915 mm), with this exception: a 32-in. (813-mm) width is permitted for a 24-in. (6,100-mm) length).

Lawrence G. Perry;, AIA; Silver Spring, Maryland

TWO WHEELCHAIRS | ONE WHEELCHAIR AND ONE AMBULATORY PERSON

SINGLE WHEELCHAIR

CHANGES IN LEVEL

Changes in level greater than ½ in. (13 mm) must be ramped. Some standards prohibit changes in level in clear floor space, maneuvering clearances, wheelchair turning space, and access aisles.

CLEAR WIDTH OF AN ACCESSIBLE ROUTE

CARPET ON FLOOR OR GROUND SURFACES

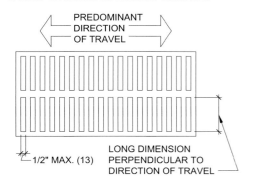

OPENING IN FLOOR OR GROUND SURFACES

All surfaces must be firm, stable, and slip-resistant. Other openings, such as in wood decking or ornamental gratings, must be designed so that a ½-in. (13-mm) diameter sphere cannot pass through the opening. The potential for wood shrinkage should be considered.

FLOOR AND GROUND SURFACES

42" MIN. (1067) X 42" MIN. (1067)

U-TURN AROUND AN OBSTRUCTION

90 ° TURN

Dimensions shown apply when X is less than 48 in. (1,219 mm).

TURNS

REQUIREMENTS FOR INTERIOR ACCESSIBLE ROUTES

Accessible routes are generally required as follows:

Multilevel buildings and facilities: Required between all levels, including mezzanines, in multistory buildings, unless exempted.

- *ADA elevator exception:* Buildings with only two floors are exempt from providing an accessible route to the upper or lower level. Buildings with less than 3,000 sq ft (279 sq m) per floor, regardless of height, are exempt from providing an accessible route to upper or lower floor levels. Neither exception applies to shopping centers, offices of professional health care providers, public transportation terminals, or state and local government facilities.
- *Building code elevator exception:* Model building codes generally exempt a maximum aggregate area of 3,000 sq ft (279 sq m), regardless of the number of levels. Similar to the ADA restrictions, this exception cannot be used in offices of health care providers, passenger transportation facilities, or mercantile occupancies with multiple tenants. Consult the applicable local code.

FHAG elevator requirements: Required for buildings containing dwelling units, and not public or common-use spaces, FHAG does not require accessible routes to all levels. Instead, the existence or lack of an elevator determines the extent of units covered. When elevators are provided, they generally must serve all floors; an exception is provided for elevators serving only as a means of access from a garage to a single floor. When elevators are not provided, only the "ground floor" units are subject to the FHAG requirements. In mixed-use construction, an accessible route is required to the first level containing dwelling units, regardless of its location. Consult FHAG for specific requirements.

Levels not containing accessible elements or spaces: For facilities in which only a percentage of the spaces provided are required to be accessible (assembly, residential, institutional, and storage), the model codes do not require an accessible route to serve levels not containing required accessible spaces. Separate requirements for dispersion of accessible elements and spaces may still require multiple accessible levels. Consult the applicable local code.

Accessible spaces and elements: To all spaces and elements that are required to be accessible.

- *Toilet rooms and bathrooms:* ADA generally requires that all toilet and bathing rooms be accessible. This does not trigger a requirement for accessible routes if the floor level is not otherwise required to have an accessible route.
- *Alterations:* ADA and the model building codes generally do not require that altered elements trigger a requirement for accessible routes to the elements, unless covered under specific "primary function" requirements. Consult ADA and the applicable local code.

COMPONENTS OF ACCESSIBLE ROUTES

Accessible routes are permitted to include the following elements: (1) walking surfaces with a slope of less than 1:20, (2) curb ramps, (3) ramps, (4) elevators, and (5) platform (wheelchair) lifts. The use of lifts in new construction is limited to locations where they are specifically permitted by the applicable regulations. Lifts are generally permitted to be used as part of an accessible route in alterations.

Each component has specific technical criteria that must be applied for use as part of an accessible route. Consult the applicable code or regulation.

LOCATION OF ACCESSIBLE ROUTES

Accessible routes must be located as follows:

Interior routes: Where an accessible route is required between floor levels, and the general circulation path between levels is an interior route, the accessible route should also be an interior route.

Relation to circulation paths: Accessible routes should "coincide with, or be located in the same area as, a general circulation path." Avoid making the accessible route a "second- class" means of circulation. Consult the applicable regulations for additional specific requirements regarding location of accessible routes.

Where the accessible route departs from the general circulation path, and is not easily identified, directional signs should be provided as necessary to indicate the accessible route.

Lawrence G. Perry, AIA; Silver Spring, Maryland

ACCESSIBLE RAMPS

COMPONENTS OF A RAMP

RAMP

RAMP AND RAMP LANDING EDGE

RAMP LANDINGS

Handrails are required on both sides when rise is greater than 6 in. (152 mm).

Edge protection is required at ramps and landings that drop off.

RAMPS AND LANDINGS—SECTIONS

CIRCULAR

NONCIRCULAR

Provide continuous handrails at both sides of ramps and stairs and at the inside handrail of switchback or dogleg ramps and stairs. If handrails are not continuous at bottom, top, or landings, provide handrail extensions as shown in the ramp and stair example; ends of handrails must be returned smoothly to floor, wall, or post.

HANDRAIL DESIGN

LOW RAILING

RAILING WITH BALUSTERS

CURB

RAMP AND RAMP LANDING EDGE PROTECTION DETAILS

---

1   ☐   **HUMAN FACTORS**

Lawrence G. Perry, AIA; Silver Spring, Maryland

LOBBY PANEL PROVIDES INFORMATION FOR SECURITY AND EMERGENCIES

HALL SIGNALS

DOORS AND FRAMES OF HEAVY-GAUGE METAL

TACTILE AND BRAILLE FLOOR SIGN AT BOTH JAMBS

72" (1830) MIN.

60" (1524)

HALL CALL BUTTONS

HOISTWAY ACCESS (BY KEY)

48" (1219) MAX.

35" (890) MIN.

29" (735)

5" (125)

AUTOMATIC DOOR REOPENING SENSOR, TYP.

ELEVATOR LOBBY

35" MIN. (890)

48" MAX. (1219)

A117.1 (SEE TEXT)

An exception is provided for elevator cars serving 16 or more openings, for which controls as high as 54 in. (1,372 mm) are allowed. Other standards generally allow controls up to 54 in. (1,372 mm) when a side reach is possible.

CONTROL PANEL HEIGHT

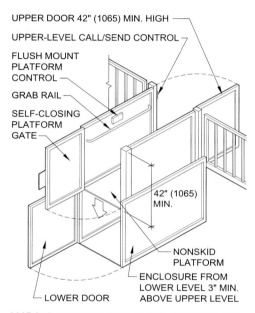

UPPER DOOR 42" (1065) MIN. HIGH

UPPER-LEVEL CALL/SEND CONTROL

FLUSH MOUNT PLATFORM CONTROL

GRAB RAIL

SELF-CLOSING PLATFORM GATE

42" (1065) MIN.

NONSKID PLATFORM

ENCLOSURE FROM LOWER LEVEL 3" MIN. ABOVE UPPER LEVEL

LOWER DOOR

A117.1 allows manual doors or gates on lifts with doors or gates on opposite sides (a roll-through configuration). Other lifts must have low-energy, power-operated doors or gates that remain open for at least 20 seconds. Doors/gates located on the ends of lifts must provide 32 in. (813 mm) clear width; doors/gates located on the side of a lift must provide 42 in. (1,067 mm) clear width.

ASME/ANSI standard, A18, *Platform Lift and Stair Chair Lift Safety Standard*, replaces the portions of A17.1 that address lifts.

TYPICAL VERTICAL WHEELCHAIR LIFT

ELEVATORS

Elevator doors must open and close automatically and have a reopening device that will stop and reopen the car and hoistway door if the door is obstructed.

Tactile designations at each jamb of hoistway doors should be 2 in. (51 mm) high. Include a five-pointed star at the main entry level.

Audible hall signals should sound once for cars traveling in the up direction and twice for cars traveling down.

Destination-Oriented Elevator Systems

Destination-oriented elevator systems assign passengers to specific cars by requiring them to enter their destination floor at a keypad or by other means, such as use of a coded identification card.

Destination-oriented elevator systems must provide both an audible signal/announcement and a visible signal to indicate the car assigned. Therefore, the elevators in the bank must be audibly and visibly differentiated, and the signals/announcements provided at the point of input must be the same as those provided at the car upon arrival.

A visible display is required in the car to identify the registered destinations for each trip, and an automatic verbal announcement is required to announce the floor as the car stops. Tactile signs at hoistway jambs are required to identify not only the floor level but also each car.

Elevator Emergency Communications

Elevator cars must provide an emergency two-way communication system between the car and a point outside the hoistway. Controls must be located within accessible reach ranges. When the system includes a handset, the cord must be at least 29 in. (737 mm) long. The system must provide both audible and visible signals; it cannot be limited to voice communication.

Elevator Car Position Indicators

Within elevator cars, audible and visible signals are required to identify the location of the car. Visible signals at least ½ in. (13 mm) high must be provided for each floor the car serves; these signals must illuminate to indicate the floors at which the car stops or passes.

Audible signals for new elevators must be automatic verbal announcements that indicate the floor at each stop.

Lifts are generally permitted to be used as part of an accessible route in new construction only to reach performing areas in assembly occupancies; wheelchair spaces in assembly occupancies; spaces not open to the public with an occupant load of no more than 5; and spaces within a dwelling unit.

When lifts are used in new construction, accessible means of egress may be required from the spaces served by the lifts.

Lifts are not permitted to be used as part of an accessible means of egress; therefore, in nonsprinklered buildings, horizontal exits or areas of refuge may be required in spaces served by lifts.

Lifts are generally permitted as part of an accessible route in alterations to existing buildings.

Lawrence G. Perry, AIA; Silver Spring, Maryland

Elevator Cars

ANSI A17.1, *Safety Code for Elevators and Escalators Elevator Safety Standard*, covers general elevator safety and operational requirements. It has been adopted in virtually all jurisdictions. Consult the applicable accessibility regulations for elevator exceptions. Model codes, the Fair Housing Act, the Americans with Disabilities Act, and the Architectural Barriers Act all have a different thresholds for requirement of elevators.

OFF-CENTERED DOOR LOCATION

CENTERED DOOR LOCATION

EXISTING CAR CONFIGURATION
The existing car configuration requires a person in a wheelchair to either enter or exit by maneuvering backward.

ANY DOOR LOCATION
A ⅝-in. (16-mm) tolerance is permitted at 36-in. (915-mm) elevator doors, allowing the use of industry-standard 900-mm clear-width doors.

ANY DOOR LOCATION
Any other car configuration that provides a 36-in. (915-mm) door and either a 60-in. (1,524-mm) diameter or T-shaped wheelchair turning space within the car, is permitted.

INSIDE DIMENSIONS OF ACCESSIBLE ELEVATOR CARS

This type of elevator is permitted per A117.1 as part of an accessible route within dwelling units.
Doors must be located on the narrow end of the car.

PRIVATE RESIDENCE ELEVATOR

NEW
LULA elevators must comply with Part XXV of ANSI A17.1 and are permitted to be used as part of an accessible route in certain conditions. Check applicable accessibility regulations for permitted installations.

EXISTING LIMITED-USE/LIMITED-APPLICATION (LULA)
LULAs move more slowly than other passenger elevators and may not be appropriate when large numbers of people must be served.

LIMITED-USE/LIMITED-APPLICATION (LULA) ELEVATOR

POWER UNIT

TOP LANDING GATE

SOLID SMOOTH
PANEL REQUIRED

NONSLIP SURFACE

HINGED OR FIXED RAMP,
OR LOWER LANDING GATE

CONTROL OR CALL BOX

OVERALL VIEW—WHEELCHAIR LIFT

COVER PLATE

GUIDE RAILS

DRIVE SCREW

3'-6" (1067) PANEL

ACCESS
RAMP

3" (76)   PLATFORM

CUT-AWAY SECTION
Screw- driven lift platform is lifted along a threaded rod, which is rotated by the power unit.

POWER UNIT

CONTROL BOX

HINGED RAMP

3'-0" TYP. (915)

NONSLIP
PLATFORM
AND RAMP

18" (457)   4'-0" TYP. (1219)

GATE

RAIL

LANDING

TYPICAL PLAN

WHEELCHAIR LIFT

WHEELCHAIR LIFTS

Wheelchair lifts are suitable for retrofits of buildings that are not barrier-free. Verify applicable regulations before selecting a specific type of lift.

Eric K. Beach, Rippeteau Architects, PC; Washington, D.C.

WHEELCHAIR LIFT REQUIREMENTS

TYPICAL ANSI A17.1, SECTION 2000.1B	PRIVATE RESIDENCE ANSI A17.1, SECTION 2100.1
42-in. (1,066-mm) door for top and bottom landings, mechanical/electrical interlock, solid construction	36-in. (914-mm) for top landing; bottom landing can have guard (other requirements similar to 42-in. (1,066-mm) door)
Platform sides: 42-in. (1,066-mm) solid construction	Platform: 36 in. (914 mm) solid construction
Grab rails	Same
Enclosure or telescoping toe guard	Obstruction switch on platform
Maximum travel 12 ft (3,657 mm)	Maximum travel 10 ft (3,048 mm)
	Automatic guard 6 in. (152 mm) at bottom landing in lieu of door
Key operation	Key operation

POWER UNIT

TRACK FOR RAIL

CHAIR (CONTROL BUTTON UNDER ARMREST)

MOUNTS

OPTIONAL POWER UNIT LOCATION

The compact size of this Cchair lift's compact size may make this lift type more feasible than others for residential use.

CHAIR LIFT—SECTION

AUTOMATIC OR MANUAL DOWN-SWING SAFETY BAR

POWER UNIT

CONTROL BOX, FIXED OR HANDHELD

OPTIONAL FOLD-DOWN CHAIR

NONSLIP PLATFORM

STEEL GUIDE RAIL BOLTED TO WALL OR SUPPORTED BY POSTS ALONG RUN

CALL BOX

CUSTOM-DESIGNED SUPPORT RAILS MAY TURN CORNER. FOLD-UP PLATFORMS ALSO AVAILABLE

STAIR LIFT OR PLATFORM (STRAIGHT RUN)

INCLINED WHEELCHAIR LIFT REQUIREMENTS

TYPICAL RESIDENCE ANSI A17.1, SECTION.2001	PRIVATE ANSI A17.1 SECTION.2100
42-in. (1,066-mm) self-closing door: solid construction, mechanical/electrical interlock, lower landing	36-in. (914-mm) self-closing door: solid construction, mechanical/electrical interlock, upper landing
42-in. (1,066-mm) platform side guard: not used as exit; solid construction	36-in. (914-mm) platform side guard: not used as exit; solid construction
6-in. (152-mm) guard: permitted in lieu of side guard	6-in. (152-mm) guard: permitted in lieu of side guard
6-in. (152-mm) retractable guard: to prevent wheelchair rolling off platform	6-in. (152-mm) retractable guard: to prevent wheelchair rolling off platform
Door required at bottom landing	Underside obstruction switch bottom landing
Travel: 3three floors max.	Travel: three floors max.
Key operation: attendant operation is push button	Key operation: attendant operation is push button and requires door at bottom landing

SUPPORT POST

CALL BOX

POWER UNIT

PLATFORM SET FOR ENTRY AT LEVEL 3

PASSENGER SEAT

CALL BOX

LEVEL 3

PLATFORM CONTROL

CALL BOX

LEVEL 2

6" - 8" MIN. (153 - 203)

PLATFORM

SET FOR EXIT TO LEVEL 1

LEVEL 1

STAIR LIFT OR PLATFORM SECTION

CONTROL PANEL AT EACH LANDING

4'-8" (1422) REQUIRED FOR 90° OR 180° TURN

PLATFORM SIZE APPROX. 2'-6" X 3'-4" (762 X 1016)

7"

UP

OPTIONAL POWER UNIT LOCATION

LOWER LEVEL

180° TURN

90° TURN

POWER UNIT

STAIR LIFT OR PLATFORM PLAN WITH TURNS

RAISED CHARACTERS, TYP.

BRAILLE, TYP.

Tactile signs with raised characters and Braille are required on signs provided as permanent designations of rooms and spaces. A117.1 allows either combined tactile/visual characters or separate tactile characters with redundant visual characters. Room numbers, room names, exit stairs, and restrooms are examples of spaces with "permanent" designations. Tactile characters must be located between 48 in. (1,219 mm) and 60 in. (1,524 mm) above the floor or ground.

Tactile signs at doors must be located so that a person reading the sign will not be hit by a door that is being opened. A117.1 allows door-mounted tactile signs on the push side of doors with closers, which do not have hold-open devices. Tactile signs located on the pull side of doors should be located so that an 18-in. x 18-in. (457-mm x 457-mm) "safe" zone, centered on the sign, is provided beyond the arc of any door swing between the closed position and the 45° open position.

Signs that provide directional information to, or information about, permanent spaces are required to comply with specific requirements for visual characters. Minimum character heights are regulated both by the height of the sign above the floor and the intended viewing distance. Consult the applicable regulations for signs required to identify specific accessible features, spaces, or elements.

SIGNS

AUTOMATIC TELLER MACHINES AND FARE MACHINES

Where ATMs or fare machines are provided, generally at least one machine is required to be accessible. A117.1 provides extensive criteria addressing the input and output requirements of these machines and is intended to make them usable by someanyone with a vision or hearing impairment.

Detectable warnings are required at passenger transit platforms whose edges border a drop-off where no screen or guard is provided. The detectable warning should be a 24-in.- (610-mm-) wide strip of truncated domes, contrasting with the adjacent walking surface.

DETECTABLE WARNINGS

Stadiums, theaters, auditoriums, lecture halls, and similar fixed-seating assembly areas are required to provide assistive listening systems if these locations have a capacity of more than 50 persons or if an audio amplification system is provided. Portable systems may be acceptable.

Signs should be provided at ticketing areas or other clearly visible locations to indicate the availability of the assistive listening system.

ASSISTIVE LISTENING SYSTEMS

FIRE ALARMS

Fire alarm systems are not required by accessibility regulations, but they are required to include accessibility-related features, primarily visible-alarm-notification devices. Criteria for the placement and intensity of visible alarms and the cumulative effect of multiple appliances are regulated to ensure that the signal is immediately noticed, without creating light patterns that could trigger seizures.

VOLUME-CONTROLLED TELEPHONE　　**INTERNATIONAL TTY SYMBOL**

Wheelchair-accessible telephones are required where public telephones are provided. One wheelchair-accessible phone is required on each floor or level where phones are provided; where more than one bank (three or more phones) is provided on a floor or level, at least one phone at each bank must be wheelchair-accessible. At least one phone per floor or level must allow forward approach. Federal regulations require all new telephone equipment to be hearing-aid compatible.

Volume-controlled: All wheelchair-accessible telephones, plus an additional 25% of telephones, must provide volume control. Check the applicable standards for required amplification requirements, as they vary. Telephones with volume control must be identified by signs, unless all telephones have volume control.

Text telephones (TTYs): Consult the applicable standards for the required number and location of TTYs. Recent model codes, based on the recommendations of the ADAAG Review Committee, provide for an increased number of TTYs.

Public TTYs should be identified by the international TTY symbol. Directional signs to TTYs should be provided at banks of public telephones not providing TTYs. In addition, there may be requirements for shelves and outlets at banks of telephones without TTYs, to allow use of a portable TTY.

ACCESSIBLE TELEPHONES

A117.1 introduced a new approach to visible alarm criteria for dwelling units. While previous editions and the model codes have required visible alarms only in wheelchair-accessible units, the new approach requires that all units be capable of adding visible alarms (on an as-needed basis), with the capability to use a single set of visible notification appliances for notification of both unit smoke detector activation and building fire alarm activation.

Lawrence G. Perry, AIA; Silver Spring, Maryland

SIDE REACH POSSIBLE ELEVATION

SIDE REACH POSSIBLE PLAN

FORWARD REACH REQUIRED PLAN

FORWARD REACH REQUIRED PLAN

WHEELCHAIR-ACCESSIBLE TELEPHONES

STANDARD HANDLE

OFFSET CURVED HANDLE

STRAIGHT HANDLE

ADJUSTABLE FROM 24" - 41"
(610 - 1041)

Canes provide support by shifting some body weight to the user's arm and shoulder and by helping the user to maintain balance.

AMBULATING CANES

16" - 18"
(406 - 457)

32" - 36"
(813 - 915)

2'-0"
(610)

1'-2"
(356)

Walkers can provide some support for users, but primarily they are used to help maintain balance. Folding walkers are generally made of lightweight aluminum tubing and collapse to a width of approximately 4 in. (102 mm). Basket, or rolling, walkers are 27 to 28 in. (686 to 711 mm) wide and have three or four wheels and hand brakes.

WALKER

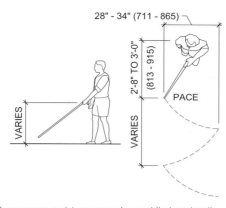

28" - 34" (711 - 865)

2'-8" TO 3'-0"
(813 - 915)

PACE

VARIES

VARIES

Long canes assist persons who are blind or visually impaired to detect obstructions in their path of travel.

Long canes are typically 36 to 48 in. (915 to 1,219 mm) long; they may fold, telescope, or be rigid.

Long canes may be used in either the "touch" technique (the cane is moved side to side, touching the floor surface 6 to 8 in. (152 to 203 mm) outside each shoulder) or the "diagonal" technique (the angled cane is held stationary with the tip just above the ground surface).

LONG CANE

ADJUSTABLE FROM 37" - 60" (940 - 1524)

CRUTCH
Crutches reduce body weight stress on lower extremities by transferring force to either the user's shoulders or forearms.

CRUTCHES

HANDLE

DESK ARMREST

36" (915)

30" (762)

19" (483)

27" (685)

8" (203)

26" (660)

18" (457)

42" (1067)

6" (152)

Manual chairs are hand-propelled using rims mounted on large front or rear drive wheels. Armrests are usually "cutaway" to allow closer access to tables and counters.

Specialized wheelchairs are available for daily activities such as bathing and for athletic competitions such as basketball and tennis.

MANUAL WHEELCHAIR

2'-6"
(762)

2'-8"
(813)

AXILLARY CRUTCH
Axillary crutches have an underarm support to transmit forces to the user's shoulder. Nonaxillary crutches have handgrips and a forearm or upper-arm cuff to distribute weight to the user's forearm.

45" (1143) UP
38" (965) DOWN

27" (685)

3'-7" TO 4'-0"
(1092 - 1219)

27" (685) UP
21" (535) DOWN

THREE-WHEELED

ELECTRIC SCOOTERS

50" (1270)

40" (1016)

FOUR-WHEELED

Individuals with impaired mobility or with stamina insufficient to travel relatively long distances often use electric scooters.

When operated indoors, scooters are often used differently than from wheelchairs. Some compact scooters, however, can turn and maneuver within parameters similar to those of wheelchairs.

The scooter seat may swivel to facilitate its use in stationary positions, such as in front of a desk. Seat heights are typically adjustable to suit the rider.

16" - 19"
(406 - 483)
TO SEAT

MOTORIZED WHEELCHAIRS

22" - 24"
(559 - 610)

40" - 44"
(1016 - 1118)

Motorized wheelchairs are usually controlled by a hand mechanism, or joystick, mounted on the chair arm. The joystick restricts access to tables, desks, and so on. Some motorized wheelchairs are controlled by sip-and-puff operators.

Motorized wheelchairs are similar in overall size to manual wheelchairs, but they are heavier and generally less maneuverable. The frames are not collapsible, although they can be partially disassembled.

Users often need assistance transferring out of their wheelchairs onto a seat, bed, or toilet fixture.

Kim A. Beasley, AIA, and Thomas D. Davies, Jr., AIA; Paralyzed Veterans of America Architecture; Washington, D.C.

RESIDENTIAL BEDS

For wheelchair users who can independently transfer themselves between bed and chair, bed heights should facilitate their access from a sitting position.

Quadriplegics or other wheelchair users who cannot independently transfer themselves between bed and chair are typically assisted by attendants, who use a portable lift mounted on a metal stand. The lift base typically requires approximately 8 in. (203 mm) of clearance under the bed.

DRESSERS, CHESTS, AND CABINETS

Dressers and chests for wheelchair users should be situated so there is a clear access aisle of approximately 42 in. (1,067 mm) in front.

Cabinets, tables, stands, and other furniture with doors should have relatively narrow leaves so the arc of the swing when they are opened is small. This makes the leaf easier to operate without moving the wheelchair as the door is opened.

DESKS, TABLES, AND WORKSTATIONS

Knee space is integral to the use of desks, tables, and workstations. Furniture must offer knee space that can accommodate the wheelchair in a position that places the user's legs fully beneath the horizontal surface and his or her upper body close to the front edge of the top.

The recommended minimum width for a knee space of 2 ft 6 in. (762 mm) requires an aisle of approximately 3 ft 4 in. (1,016 mm) in order for most wheelchairs to easily complete a 90° turn.

CHAIRS

For ambulatory people who have difficulty maintaining their balance, chairs should be stable in order to provide support. Chairs equipped with armrests help ambulatory users to sit and rise, and are generally more comfortable to sit in. Chair leg supports and cross-bracing should not obstruct kick space below the seat. Kick space allows the chair occupant to position his or her feet partially beneath the body in order to rise.

Ergonomic work chairs allow many aspects of the chair, such as seat height and angle of incline, to be adjusted to suit each individual. Wheelchair users who transfer diagonally can use chairs with armrests, while those who transfer from a parallel position must have clear side access without fixed armrests.

PLAN

SECTION

BEDS

CABINETS	CABINETS
CHESTS	CHESTS
DESKS	DESKS
DIFFICULT TO OPERATE	**EASY TO OPERATE**

FURNITURE OPERATION FOR ACCESSIBILITY

ACCESSIBLE DRAWER PULL

ADJUSTABLE HEIGHT WORK SURFACE

For knee space below a tabletop with a minimum width of 2 ft 6 in. (762 mm) between obstructions (e.g., table legs), the approach clearance should be 3 ft 6 in. (1,067 mm). A knee space width of 3 ft 0 in. (915 mm) or more should have an approach clearance of 3 ft 0 in. (915 mm).

TABLE CLEARANCES

CHAIR FOR DINING OR DESK

ERGONOMIC WORKSTATION CHAIR

Kim A. Beasley, AIA, and Thomas D. Davies, Jr., AIA; Paralyzed Veterans of America Architecture; Washington, D.C.

TOILET PARTITION
URINAL (ELONGATED TYPE)
URINAL PARTITION
MIRROR

6" MAX. (150)
1'-0" MAX. (300)
4'-6" MIN. (1370)
3'-6" MIN. (1065)
1 1/2" (38)
1 1/2" (38) CLEAR
1 1/4" TO 1 1/2" (30 TO 38)
1 1/2" (38)
3'-0" MAX. (915)
3'-6" (915)
1-7" MIN. (480)
2'-9" TO 3'-0" (890 TO 915)
3'-4" MAX (1015) TO REFLECTING SURFACE
6" MIN. (150)
1'-6" (460)
1'-5" MAX. (430)
3'-8 1/2" MAX. (1120)
5'-0" MIN. CLEAR (1525)
9" MIN. (230)
2'-3" MIN. (685)
2'-5" MIN. (760)
2'-10" MIN. (865)
CLEAR FLOOR SPACE 2'-6" X 4'-0" MIN. (760 X 1220)
1'-5" MIN. (430)
BOWL AND PIPES MUST BE CONTAINED WITHIN THIS AREA

The particular configuration of clear floor space affects the maximum and minimum heights of the controls. If the partition is greater than or equal to 2 ft 0 in. (610 mm) deep, urinal clear floor space must be 3 ft 0 in. (915 mm) wide. If less than 1 ft 5 in. (430 mm) deep, it may be 29 in. (737 mm) wide.

LOCATION OF ACCESSIBLE FIXTURES AND ACCESSORIES

1'-6" (460)
2'-0" (610)
8 1/2" (215)
2'-4" (710)
2'-8" (810)
SWING-UP GRAB BAR

These configurations do not comply with UFAS or ADAAG.

OPTIONAL GRAB BAR CONFIGURATIONS

1'-0" MAX. (305)
2'-0" MIN. (610)
4'-0" MIN. (1219)
MOUNT CONTROLS IN THIS AREA ONLY
2'-9" TO 3'-0" (888 - 915)
9" (230)
2'-6" MIN. (762) PARALLEL APPROACH
REMOVABLE SEAT
5'-0" MIN. (1524)
4'-0" MIN. (1219) PERPENDICULAR APPROACH

FIXED SHOWER HEAD
HANDHELD SHOWER HEAD
3'-6" MIN. (1065)
1'-6" (480)
GRAB BAR 1 1/2" (38) DIAMETER
1'-2" TO 1'-7" MAX. (430 TO 480)
1'-3" MAX. (380)
3'-6" MIN. (1065)
FOLDING SHOWER SEAT
2'-9" TO 3'-0" (890 TO 915)
3'-7" +/- 5" (1040 +/- 125)
CONTROL AREA 5'-1" (1550)
3'-0" (915)
3'-0" MIN. (915)
3'-0" (915)
SLOPE DOWN 1:50 TYP.
4'-0" (1220)
1'-0" MIN. (300)

ACCESSIBLE BATHTUB AND SHOWER

EXPANSION BOLT, TYP.
MASONRY WALL
MOUNTING PLATE
GRAB BAR
COVER PLATE, TYP.

MASONRY WALL

2X WOOD STUD
2 X 6 MIN. CONTINUOUS WOOD BLOCKING, CUT INTO STUD
MOUNTING PLATE FASTENED WITH THREE WOOD FASTENERS, TYP.
GRAB BAR
COVER PLATE, TYP.

WOOD CONSTRUCTION

MOUNTING PLATE
CONCEALED FLANGE COVER
APPROPRIATE FASTENER FOR WALL CONSTRUCTION
THREE STAINLESS-STEEL CONE POINT SET SCREWS
GRAB BAR

CONCEALED FLANGE

Size: 1½ in. (38 mm) or 1¼ in. (32 mm) O.D. with 1½ in. (38 mm) clearance at wall.

Material: Stainless steel or chrome-plated brass with knurled finish (optional).

Installation: Concealed or exposed fasteners; return all ends to the wall, intermediate supports at 3 ft 0 in. (915 mm) maximum. Use heavy-duty bars and methods of installation.

Other grab bars are available for particular situations.

Consult ANSI and ADAAG requirements, as well as applicable local and federal regulations.

GRAB BAR ATTACHMENT DETAILS

Mark J. Mazz, AIA; Hyattsville, Maryland

ACCESSIBLE TOILET ROOMS

All dimensional criteria on this page are based on ANSI A117.1, and on adult anthropometrics.

In new construction, all public and common- use toilet rooms are generally required to be accessible. Where multiple single-user toilet rooms or bathing rooms are clustered in a single location, and each serves the same population, only 5%, but not less than one, of the rooms must be accessible. The accessible room(s) must be identified by signs.

Single-user toilet and bathing rooms provided within a private office are permitted to be adaptable. Making the room accessible is permitted to involve replacement of the water closet and lavatory, changing the swing of the door, and installing grab bars in previously reinforced walls.

Doors are not permitted to swing into the required clear floor space at any fixture, except in single-user rooms, where a clear floor space is provided beyond the swing of the door.

Unisex Toilets

Recent model codes require accessible unisex toilets in certain assembly and mercantile occupancies. These unisex rooms are beneficial for parents with small children and for persons with disabilities who require personal assistance in using toilet facilities. This requirement applies when a total of six or more water closets (or water closets and urinals) is provided in the facility.

Unisex facilities must be located within 500 ft (152 m), and within one floor, of separate-sex facilities. Doors to unisex toilet and bathing rooms must be securable from within the room.

Accessible unisex toilet and bathing rooms are permitted in alterations in lieu of altering existing separate-sex facilities in certain conditions. Unisex rooms must be located in the same area and on the same floor as the existing inaccessible facilities.

Toilet Room Layouts

Some of the toilet room layouts shown are similar. Variations are in the direction of the door swing and based on whether the width or depth is the more constraining dimension. Dimensions show comfortable minimums and preferred dimensions.

Overall room dimensions include a 2-in. (51-mm) construction tolerance.

Each layout shows the required clear floor space for the fixtures and the doors.

For door maneuvering clearances, see ADAAG (Section 4.13.6 and Figure 25) for various requirements and conditions. Variables include direction of swing, direction of approach, size of door, and door hardware.

Doors to bathrooms are assumed to be 36 in. (915 mm) wide, with a closer and latch for privacy.

Maneuvering clearances at the base of water closets and below lavatories may vary due to fixture design. Confirm actual water closet and lavatory dimensions for other makes and models.

SHORT AND COMPACT—OUTSWINGING DOOR

OUTSWINGING DOOR   **INSWINGING DOOR**   **OUTSWINGING DOOR**

LAVATORY ON OPPOSITE WALL

LAVATORY ON SIDE WALL

PLAN CLEARANCE

SIDE WALL ELEVATION

REAR WALL ELEVATION

ANSI 117.1-1998 requires the water closet clearance to be unobstructed by lavatory or other fixtures. Other regulations allow configurations with a lavatory within the water closet clearance.

The dashed area indicates the allowable location of the toilet paper dispenser. Dispensers should allow continuous paper flow and not control delivery.

WITHOUT PERMANENT SEAT

WATER CLOSETS

END-OF-ROW WHEELCHAIR ACCESSIBLE

MID-ROW

AMBULATORY ACCESSIBLE

Toe clearance 9 in. (230 mm) high and 6 in. (152 mm) deep is required at the front and at least one side of accessible toilet compartments. Toe clearance is not required when the compartment size exceeds the minimum dimension by 6 in. (152 mm) or more.

WITH PERMANENT SEAT

Bathtub controls, other than drain stoppers, must be located on an end wall between the tub rim and grab bar and between the open side of the tub and the midpoint of the tub width. A 59-in. (1,500-mm) minimum-length shower spray unit is required.

Tub enclosures must not obstruct controls, interfere with transfer from a wheelchair to the tub, or have tracks mounted on the tub rim.

TOILET COMPARTMENTS

BATHTUBS

TRANSFER-TYPE COMPARTMENT

STANDARD ROLL-IN TYPE

ALTERNATE ROLL-IN TYPE

A fixed, folding, or removable seat is required in transfer-type compartments. Seats in roll-in showers, where provided, should be folding-type and located on the wall adjacent to the control wall.

Shower compartment thresholds are not permitted to exceed ½ in. (13 mm). A 59-in. (1,500-mm) minimum-length shower spray unit is required.

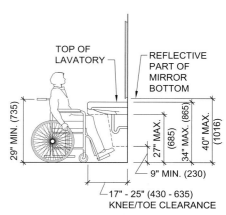

Exposed pipes and water supply pipes located beneath accessible lavatories must be insulated or located so as to protect users from contact.

SHOWERS

LAVATORIES

Lawrence G. Perry, AIA; Silver Spring, Maryland

BATHROOM LAYOUTS
For alternate B, reverse the plumbing at the tub.

ACCESSIBILITY STANDARDS FOR BATHROOMS

Residential bathrooms and single-use toilet rooms can be divided into two general categories: *private facilities* such as those located in single- or multifamily dwellings, and *public or institutional facilities* such as those located in nursing homes, hospitals, dormitories, or hotels.

Wheelchair bathroom standards for private dwellings were first included in the 1981 edition of ANSI A117.1. Four years later, the Uniform Federal Accessibility Standard (UFAS) published nearly identical bathroom standards for dwellings included in federal projects. In most multifamily projects, whether privately or publicly funded, between 1% and 5% of the total dwellings must meet the ANSI or UFAS standards for full wheelchair accessibility.

In 1988, the Fair Housing Amendments Act (FHAA), a federal civil rights law that addressed private multifamily housing design, was enacted. FHAA guidelines included new and different standards for residential bathrooms. The Fair Housing guidelines include two alternative bathroom design standards. In covered dwellings with two or more full bathrooms, the more strict standards can be used for one bath; more minimal standards can be applied to the second bathroom.

In 1991, the Americans with Disabilities Act (ADA) included new design standards called the Americans with Disabilities Act Accessibility Guidelines (ADAAG). ADAAG standards are not typically applied to private residential facilities because the previously issued Fair Housing standards already apply. However, bathrooms located in "transient lodging" facilities, such as hotels, or public institutional facilities, such as hospitals, may be required to meet both ADA and Fair Housing standards.

Maneuvering Space

Bathrooms that comply with Fair Housing must be "usable" rather than "accessible" and therefore have lower maneuvering space standards. According to FHAA, if the entry door swings into the bathroom, there must be enough clear space to position a wheelchair clear of the door swing.

All of the standards permit required floor space for fixtures to overlap with required maneuvering space. Current ADAAG standards, however, do not permit the bathroom door (even in single-user facilities) to swing into any fixture clearance.

Bathroom Entry Doors

Fair Housing permits a 2-ft-10-in. (864-mm) door to provide a "nominal" 32-in. (813-mm) clear opening. ANSI, UFAS, and ADAAG require installation of at least a 3-ft-0-in. (915-mm) door to provide the full 32-in. (813-mm) clear opening.

Grab Bars

Grab bar arrangement can influence the floor plan of an accessible bathroom. FHAA grab bar standards are less strict, and this permits the design of smaller bathrooms.

Adaptable Features

In residential bathroom design, *adaptability* was a new term when introduced in the 1980 ANSI edition. Adaptability in this case is defined as "the capability of certain elements to be altered or added so as to accommodate the needs of persons with or without disabilities, or to accommodate the needs of persons with different types or degrees of disabilities." Some codes and civil rights laws require provisions in certain bathrooms for "adaptable" features.

For single-family custom homes or remodeling projects, bathroom designs should be specially tailored to the individual homeowners. If a master bathroom is planned for a wheelchair user, for example, the design should reflect that person's individual capabilities and preferences.

Kim A. Beasley, AIA, and Thomas D. Davies, Jr., AIA; Paralyzed Veterans of America Architecture; Washington, D.C.

WATER CLOSET SPACE REQUIREMENTS

ANSI A/B, UFAS, ADAAG, FHAG (EITHER APPROACH)

ANSI A, UFAS, ADAAG (FRONT APPROACH)

ANSI A, UFAS, ADAAG (SIDE APPROACH)

ANSI B, FHAG (EITHER APPROACH)

ANSI B, FHAG (SIDE APPROACH)

LAVATORY AND SHOWER SPACE REQUIREMENTS

ANSI A, UFAS, ADAAG (WITH KNEE SPACE)

ANSI B (NO KNEE SPACE)

ANSI A, UFAS, ADAAG (STALL SHOWER)

ANSI B, FHAG (STALL SHOWER)

ANSI A, UFAS, ADAAG (ROLL-IN SHOWER)

ADAAG (ALTERNATE ROLL-IN SHOWER)

OPTIONAL SHOWER HEAD LOCATION

BATHTUB SPACE REQUIREMENTS

ANSI A, UFAS, ADAAG (PARALLEL APPROACH)

ANSI A, UFAS, ADAAG (PERPENDICULAR APPROACH)

ANSI A, UFAS, ADAAG (TUB/SHOWER WITH SEAT)
For a tub/shower with seat, an additional 1 ft (305 mm) of clear space beyond the seat is required.

ANSI B, FHAG (ALTERNATE A)

ANSI B, FHAG (ALTERNATE B)

PLUMBING FIXTURE STANDARDS

Water Closets

The major differences between FHAA and the other standards are the minimum space required behind the water closet and the configuration of the lavatory or vanity that may be located adjacent to the toilet. In order to meet FHAA standards, an adjacent lavatory does not have to include knee space, whereas knee space is an important ANSI/UFAS and ADAAG requirement.

Lavatories and Vanities

FHAA does not require knee space, but the other standards do. In some instances, the knee space height

required by ADAAG is greater than that required by ANSI or UFAS. All accessibility standards except Fair Housing include requirements for a maximum sink depth. ADAAG, ANSI, and UFAS also include requirements for faucets, mirrors, and medicine cabinets.

Bathtubs and Tub/Showers

The ADAAG, ANSI (pre-1998), and UFAS accessible bathtub standards also have subtle differences. The bathtub clear floor space requirements are similar to those for water closets in that an approach direction is indicated (either perpendicular or parallel).

FHAA offers two different clear space requirements; the designer may choose to comply with either. Of these alternatives, Alternate B is stricter because it requires clear space adjacent to the foot of the tub.

Stall Showers and Roll-in Units

Accessible showers include both transfer stalls (where a bather moves from a wheelchair to a bench or portable seat) and roll-in stalls (where a bather remains seated in a special shower chair and is either pushed by an attendant or self-propelled into the stall). All accessibility standards require either wall reinforcing or grab bars inside a shower.

Lawrence G. Perry, AIA; Silver Spring, Maryland

ACCESSIBILITY GUIDELINES FOR KITCHENS

The 1980 American National Standards Institute (ANSI) A117.1 and the 1984 Uniform Federal Accessibility Standards (UFAS) were the first to include kitchen design standards that focused on the needs of wheelchair users. The kitchen standards in the 1988 Fair Housing Amendments Act (FHAA), a federal civil rights law, include less specialized wheelchair design features for multifamily housing.

Designers should carefully verify which kitchen requirements are appropriate for their specific project because accessibility codes and civil rights laws have very different design standards.

Accessible kitchens should reflect conventional layout principles with regard to proper workflow and functional adjacencies.

Fixture and Appliances

The three general types of wheelchair standards for residential kitchens are:

- General kitchen maneuvering space
- Individual fixture and appliance maneuvering space
- Other fixture specifications such as basin depths, switch locations, and faucet configurations

Sufficient clear floor space must be provided at fixtures and appliances to accommodate either a parallel or front approach, depending on the applicable design standard requirements.

The 1998 ANSI appliance clearances are more sophisticated than previous standards. For example, oven clearances depend on whether the unit is a self-cleaning model and the door is side- or bottom-hinged.

ANSI and UFAS require either adjustable height counters or fixed counters at a height of 34 in. (865 mm). FHAA does not address counter heights.

Adaptable Features

The term *adaptability* is defined as "the capability of certain elements to be altered or added so as to accommodate the needs of persons with or without disabilities." For accessible kitchens, adaptable elements might include removable base cabinets that can be eliminated to provide knee space below countertops, or adjustable-height countertop sections that can be raised and lowered.

Lawrence G. Perry, AIA; Silver Spring, Maryland

APPROACH DIAGRAM FOR FIXTURES OR APPLIANCES

FHAA guidelines require a 5-ft-0-in. (1,524-mm) clearance if a sink, range, or cooktop is installed in the base leg of the U. If the base leg fixture includes a knee space or removable base cabinets, the 5-ft-0-in. (1,524-mm) clearance is not required.

U-SHAPED KITCHEN PLAN

ANSI and UFAS require a 40-in. (1,016-mm) clearance between kitchen cabinets and opposing walls, cabinets, or appliances *where the counters provide knee space*. Otherwise, an accessible route is required. The FHAA guidelines, however, require a 40-in. (1,016-mm) clearance in all cases.

GALLEY KITCHEN PLAN

FLOOR SPACE AND KNEE SPACE REQUIREMENTS FOR FIXTURES AND APPLIANCES

APPLIANCE	REQUIRE-MENT	FAIR HOUSING	ANSI/ UFAS
Sink	Approach	Parallel	Parallel or front
	Knee space	No	Yes
Range/ cooktop	Approach	Parallel	Parallel or front
	Knee space	No	Optional
Workspace	Approach	Not required	Front
	Knee space	No	Yes
Refrigerator	Approach	Parallel or front	Parallel or front
	Knee space	No	No
Dishwasher	Approach	Parallel or front	Parallel or front
	Knee space	No	No
Oven (self-cleaning)	Approach	Parallel or front	Front
	Knee space	No	No
Oven (non-self-cleaning)	Approach	Parallel or front	Front
	Knee space	No	Yes (off-set)
Trash compactor	Approach	Parallel or front	Parallel or front
	Knee space	No	No

Note: HUD interpretations of FHAA guidelines require clear floor space to be centered on the appliance or fixture. In a kitchen plan, this can have significant design impact.

4'-0" X 2'-6" (1219 X 762) SIDE APPROACH AREA

The sink should be a shallow unit with easy-to-operate faucets. A tall spout and a pullout spray attachment are also recommended. Garbage disposals must be offset in order to provide full knee space under the sink.

KITCHEN SINK AND DISHWASHER

The design of kitchen storage space for wheelchair users should provide both visual and physical access to wall and base cabinets, drawers, and pantries. Base cabinets, for example, can be specified to include pullout shelves or drawers that will provide easy access to items stored in the back of the cabinets.

KITCHEN STORAGE

A range or cooktop should have front- or side-mounted controls so the seated user does not need to reach over the heated surfaces. A smooth cooktop surface allows pots to be slid rather than lifted on and off the burners.

STOVES AND COOKTOPS

Side-by-side models offer the user both freezer and refrigerator storage at all height levels from the floor to the top shelf.

REFRIGERATORS

WAYFINDING

Wayfinding refers to the way people orient themselves in a given environment and find their destination. The ability to orient oneself is based on many pieces of information—visual clues, memories, knowledge of a place—and the ability to reason. Environmental psychology terms the ability to acquire, code, store, recall, and decode information about the physical environment *cognitive mapping*. Successful wayfinding is the ability to naturally orient oneself in the environment and to easily locate a destination without experiencing stress.

HIGHLY IMAGEABLE SPACES

The work of Kevin Lynch, presented in *The Image of the City* (1960), was based on studies that found three components for the analysis of environmental imaging:

IDENTITY, or objects in background

STRUCTURE, or objects in relationship to each other

MEANING, or personal, societal, or figurative belief

Lynch focused on the identity and structure of spaces to discern what makes cities imageable or known. He notes: "[Imageability is]… that quality of a physical object which gives it a high probability of evoking a strong image in any given observer. It is that shape, color, or arrangement which facilitates the making of a vividly identified, powerfully structured, highly useful mental image of the environment. It might also be called legibility."

A highly imageable space has components that relate in a well-structured manner. The way a space is mapped for an individual varies, depending on the person. Certain images and visual clues are perceived similarly by groups of people who share similar backgrounds, activities, or routines, and recurrent features in their environment. For example, a group of schoolchildren may be of a similar age, share the learning and play activities of a school, and be aware of the physical features of the school building.

MAPPING ELEMENTS

Lynch's research resulted in the identification of five categories of elements that people use to map an environment:

PATHS: Channels of movement

EDGES: Boundaries that break, contain, or run parallel to the forms

DISTRICTS: Areas of recognizable identity

NODES: Places of intense activity

LANDMARKS: Points of reference that are visually distinguishable

COGNITIVE MAPS

Cognitive maps are psychological impressions or representations of individuals' ability to understand space and the organizing elements by which they orient themselves. Cognitive maps usually combine several of the mapping elements. These elements are not formed simply in the floor plan, but the three-dimensional characteristics of a space, the material choices, the colors, and the lighting can all impact the formation of edges, districts, or nodes.

Where the boundaries of the districts meet, an edge may be formed, providing a sense of having exited one area and entered another. A node may occur at an intersection of activities or along paths where activity is concentrated. Landmarks may be used by the designer to mark entrances or points of interest.

WAYFINDING AND AGE

The process of learning involves an increase in perception of detail as a person develops. The following reference systems, proposed by Gary Moore (1976), relates the phases of development to the progress of perception from early childhood to the adult years:

1. An egocentric reference system; that is, one organized around the child's own position and actions in space.
2. Several different possibilities of fixed reference systems organized around various fixed, concrete elements, or places in the environment.
3. An abstract or coordinated reference system organized in terms of abstract geometric patterns including—in special cases—the cardinal directions (north, south, east, and west).

As adults, people tend to rely on maps, diagrams, and more highly abstract information for orientation and finding their way within a new area. An adult who is visiting an unfamiliar city will use a city map to reach a destination (reference system 3 on the preceding list). Adults navigate wide-reaching, complex environments on a daily basis, whereas children's environments are more limited in overall range and tend to be perceived on the basis of reference points. The adolescent child's orientation system (reference system 2) may be based on a local hang-out, the path of travel between home and school, local landmarks within the community, and similar points of reference. The designer of environments for small children should be aware that children are naturally oriented in relation to their own positions (reference system 1).

Children see the world always in relation to themselves. For example, an especially enjoyable piece of equipment at the playground and its relationship to the toilet facility a child uses while at the playground may be the elements by which he or she organizes and understands that environment. A child's cognitive map will likely include detailed aspects of a space with which he or she is directly involved.

SIGNAGE

Signage is an important part of directing people through a space. Building signage can include building identification, building layout illustration, directional signs, and place signs.

Signs should be designed and placed consistently throughout the facility. The overuse of signage and cluttered signage, which becomes ineffective, should be avoided. Signs should be placed strategically at decision-making areas.

WAYFINDING CLUES

In addition to signage, visual clues can be utilized to help orient the user. Architectural elements like lobbies, stairs, elevators, and areas of special use can create a framework into which users can place themselves. The following interior treatments typically used for aesthetic effect can also assist the designer in creating a highly understandable environment:

- Change of wall color, type, or texture
- Change in flooring
- Use of lighting to highlight or minimize areas
- Change of ceiling treatments
- Furniture arrangement or type

The extent of wayfinding clues incorporated in the environment should vary from public to private spaces. Public areas require more information to be presented to aid visitors in locating their destinations. As the spaces become more private, fewer clues will be needed because of the occupants' knowledge of the environment.

Source: Bradford Perkins (Stephen Kliment, Ed.), Building Type Basics for Elementary and Secondary Schools, *(New York: John Wiley & Sons, Inc.), 2001, pp. 193-200.*
Source: Kevin Lynch, The Image of the City, *(Cambridge: MIT Press), 1960.*
Source: Gary T. Moore, "The Development of Environmental Knowing: An Overview of an Interactional-Constructivist Theory and Some Data on Within-Individual Development Variations," In Psychology and the Built Environment, *David Carter and Terrence Lee, Eds. (London: Architectural Press), 1976.*

PATH   NODE   EDGE   DISTRICTS   LANDMARK

MAPPING ELEMENTS

CLASSICAL ARCHITECTURE AND DECORATION

HISTORY

With a 2,500-year history, classical architecture and decoration is the primary architectural language in the West. After being developed by Greek architects over a 500-year period, the forms and rules for Classical architecture and decoration were reformulated by the Romans. This legacy was revived and further developed over another half-millennium, from the advent of the Renaissance to the Second World War. Classicism is currently being reinvestigated by a group of architects and designers who believe that contemporary design issues can be solved by using its formal vocabulary and theoretical principles.

Classical theoretical principles assist in achieving a sense of strength, function, and beauty in a structure or an interior. The designer's basic premise is that models from past productions can be imitated for development, and adapted with invention, to solve current problems. This belief is key to the paradigmatic method articulated in about 20 B.C. by the Roman architect, Vitruvius, in his *Ten Books on Architecture.* His work synthesized the ideas of Greek treatises for a revival of Greek-inspired architecture under the Emperor Augustus. Vitruvius's text was honored throughout the Middle Ages by being copied for intense revival and development from the Renaissance to the present. *The Ten Books on Architecture* was essential to Andrea Palladio, for example, who called Vitruvius his "master and guide."

Both today and historically, the application of classical elements and ideals are at once consistent with core principles, yet diverse. The variety of interpretation stems from different cultural perspectives, from access to diverse models for imitation, and from the effects of the varying temperaments of the individuals who have successfully reestablished classicism over two millennia.

COLUMN TYPES

Vitruvius considered columns and their entablatures, or beam structures, to be the fundamental concept of what classical architecture entails. Vitruvius did not refer to column "orders," as they came to be called in the Renaissance; instead he referred to them more generally as types, or kinds, because he considered columns and beam structures to be components of a large collection of elements, including doors, windows, and railings.

DORIC

IONIC

ATTIC
"Attic" refers to the Attica region of Athens.

VITRUVIAN PORTALS *Source: Mati Rosenshine; Mati Rosenshine Architect; Jerusalem, Israel*

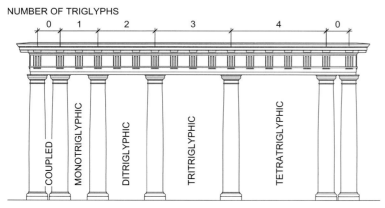

NUMBER OF TRIGLYPHS

0   1   2   3   4   0

COUPLED
MONOTRIGLYPHIC
DITRIGLYPHIC
TRITRIGLYPHIC
TETRATRIGLYPHIC

ROMAN DORIC INTERCOLUMNIATION

NUMBER OF MODULES

2   3   5   5   7   8

COUPLED
PYCNOSTYLOS (TIGHTLY COLUMNED)
SYSTYLOS (CLOSELY COLUMNED)
EUSTYLOS (CORRECTLY COLUMNED)
DIASTYLOS (OPENLY COLUMNED)
AEROSTYLOS (WIDELY COLUMNED)

ROMAN IONIC INTERCOLUMNIATION

INTERCOLUMNIATION

COLUMN CAPITAL

VOLUTE

VOLUTE PROPORTIONS

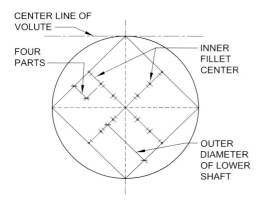

VOLUTE CONSTRUCTION

Below the centerline of the volute, draw a circle with a diameter of one-eighth the height of the volute. Inscribe a rotated, quartered square within this circle, or "eye." The six divisions of the centerline of this square give the centers for a series of diminishing arcs. From center 1 draw arc 1, from center 2, arc 2, and so on. Successive arcs meet at a line defined by their centers.

VOLUTE PLACEMENT AND CONSTRUCTION

IONIC ELEVATION

DORIC ELEVATION

PLAN

SALON ELEVATION WITH SUPERPOSED PILASTERS

DESIGN PRINCIPLES □ 1

CLASSICAL INTERIORS

Many systems of proportion for rooms have been proposed since ancient times. Vitruvius provided interrelated ratios for the width and length of atria and ratios for the height of their ceilings and the size of the roof opening. Andrea Palladio provided similar ratios for the principal rooms of a house.

Room Proportions

One rule of thumb is to have a 2:3 ratio of width to length in plan. The ceiling height could be the same as the width, creating a square interior elevation, or the height could be achieved by dividing the width into four parts and multiplying the result by five. Thus, an ideal room of 20 by 30 ft (6 by 9 m) would have a ceiling height of 20 or 25 ft (6 or 7.5 m). It is rare to be able to work with such volumes today, but even when we do, other factors must often be accommodated. These include preexisting structural conditions, the functional requirements of adjacent rooms, or the modules of building systems.

Classical Salon

The salon illustrated on the following two pages has a roughly 2:3 plan with a ceiling height of just over 2, similar to the width ratio. The ceiling is divided into three squares on each side with two rectangles flanking an open shaft for a skylight. On one of the short elevations, the equal ceiling coffers correspond to the central portal and adjacent cabinet doors. A Doric entablature surrounds the room at the height of the door lintel. The frieze has triglyphs and metopes with traditional cow skulls. The entablature is projected forward along with the door jambs. The adjacent friezes are adjusted to achieve two full-size triglyphs meeting at the corners. The proportions of the architrave, frieze, and cornice are different from the other model shown here. This demonstrates the variety of proportions that are possible. Working within the established geometries of Doric and Ionic architecture is one of the stimulating challenges of engaging the classical language in interior design. Making subtle and inventive variations in response to many constraints is one of the rewards of learning to "speak" and manipulate the classical vocabulary and its rules of "grammar."

CLASSICALLY PROPORTIONED SALON—PLAN

CLASSICALLY PROPORTIONED SALON—REFLECTED CEILING PLAN

DORIC ENTABLATURE

CORNICE

5/8" GYPSUM BOARD

3/4" MDF TRIM

9"

7/8"

1"

WOOD TRIM, TYP.

4 1/2"

1 1/2"

1 5/8"

5/8" GYPSUM BOARD

CABINET SECTION

CLASSICALLY PROPORTIONED SALON—ELEVATION

This illustrates a parallel comparison based on Vignola proportions with a constant lower diameter. The proportional relationships of the column types and their entablatures are based on a modular system, usually based on the lower diameter of the column shaft. This module is multiplied or divided to obtain the measurements of both large and small components.

TUSCAN   DORIC   IONIC   CORINTHIAN   COMPOSITE

THE FIVE CLASSICAL ORDERS—RENAISSANCE PROPORTIONS

MOLDINGS—TYPES, PATTERNS, AND DECORATION

PLAN OF SOFFIT

SECTION - TRIGLYPH

SECTION - TRIGLYPH GUTTAE

PLAN AND SECTION - GUTTAE

PLAN AT NECK

PLAN AT BASE

NECK

COLUMN

PILASTER

BASE

DORIC ORDER (MUTULAR)

PLAN OF SOFFIT

ENTABLATURE

FACE OF CAPITAL/SECTION-ROLL

PLAN SECTION OF CAPITAL

PLAN AT NECK

PLAN AT BASE

NECK

COLUMN

PILASTER

BASE

IONIC ORDER

DESIGN PRINCIPLES ☐ **1**

APPROPRIATE CHOICE OF COLUMN TYPES

The tradition of classical interiors is as diverse as the parallel architectural developments. The concept that Vitruvius called *decor* describes the need to make appropriate choices of which column type to use to convey the correct meaning for the function of an interior. The selected architectural armature must then be deliberately interpreted in a spectrum from the most articulate detail through successive levels of abstraction. These choices can convey different nuances of meaning even within one kind, such as Doric. These decisions also respond to varying levels of expenditure. Since the "language of architecture" is relatively mute by nature, sculpture, painting, and decorative embellishment can be incorporated within rooms to convey specific ideas through iconographic programs.

Thomas Gordon Smith, AIA; Thomas Gordon Smith Architects; South Bend, Indiana
Scot C. McBroom, AIA; Alexandria, Virginia

PLAN OF SOFFIT

ENTABLATURE

NECK

COLUMN   PILASTER

PLAN AT NECK

PLAN AT BASE

BASE

PEDESTAL

CORINTHIAN ORDER

DIVIDE UPPER 2/3 OF SHAFT INTO EQUAL NUMBER OF PARTS

LOWER 1/3 OF SHAFT IS STRAIGHT

1 DIA

1

2

3

Lay out column height, centerline, and upper and lower diameters at one-third point on column; draw a half circle equal to lower diameter. Drop a line from the upper diameter to the semicircle (1). Divide the resulting minor arc and upper two-thirds of the shaft into an equal number of equal parts. Draw vertical lines from the arc divisions to the horizontal shaft divisions (2). The resulting points define the curved profile of the column shaft (3).

ENTASIS

KEY WIDTH = IMPOST HEIGHT

MAX. HEIGHT OF KEY IS TWICE KEY WIDTH

IMPOST HEIGHT 1/9 W TO 1/7 W

2/3 W MAXIMUM PIER WIDTH

W

WILLIAM CHAMBERS' GUIDELINES FOR SETTING OUT ARCHES

ARCHED DOORWAY CONSTRUCTION

1 ☐ DESIGN PRINCIPLES

PROPORTIONING SYSTEMS

IDEAL PROPORTIONS

Geometric methods have been developed to determine the ideal proportions. These systems attempt to establish an aesthetic rationale for design.

GENERATIVE GEOMETRY

The archetypal circle and square can geometrically generate many forms. Ancient cultures recognized these forms and relationships as essential and sacred, a metaphor of universal order. The circle and square in the act of self-division gives three generative roots: the square roots of 2, 3, and 5 (Figures 1A and 1B). These root relationships are all that are necessary to form the five regular (Platonic) solids that are the basis for all volumetric forms (Figure 1C). Also, 2, 3, and 5 are the only numbers required to divide the octave into musical scales.

THE SQUARE ROOT OF 2

In seeming paradox, the half of a square produces its double; this is analogous to biological growth from cell division and the generation of musical tone. In Figure 2A, the diagonal of square ABCD (square 1, Figure 2A) is exactly equal to the side of square ACFG (square 2). The area of square 2 is exactly twice that of square 1. The side of a square is called its *root*. The side of square 1 equals 1; the side of square 2 equals the square root of 2. The diagonal of square 2 equals 2, exactly twice the side of the primary square. The division of the square by the diagonal yields three seemingly contradictory, yet geometrically true, relationships:

$$\frac{\text{root}}{\text{diag}} \; : \; \frac{\text{root}}{\text{diag}} \; :: \; \frac{1}{\sqrt{2}} : \frac{\sqrt{2}}{2} \qquad \frac{\text{root}}{\text{diag}} \; : \; \frac{\text{diag}}{\text{root}} \; :: \; \frac{1}{\sqrt{2}} : \frac{\sqrt{2}}{2}$$

The square root of 2 represents the power of multiplicity through the geometric progression a:b::b:c (Figure 2B). The relationship of the side to the diagonal may be written:

$$\frac{1}{\sqrt{2}} \; : \; \frac{\sqrt{2}}{2} \; : \; \frac{2}{2\sqrt{2}} \; : \; \frac{2\sqrt{2}}{4} \; : \; \frac{4}{4\sqrt{2}}, \text{ and so on}$$

THE VESICA PISCIS AND THE SQUARE ROOT OF 3

The Vesica Piscis is a form generator of the triangle, square, and pentagon—the basic planar elements of the five Platonic solids. The overlapping circles are an excellent representation of a cell or any unity in the midst of becoming dual. Medieval churches and cathedrals incorporated the fish-shaped geometry as a symbol of Christ.

To construct the Vesica Piscis, draw a circle of any radius about center A; at any chosen point on the circumference, draw another circle of equal radius (B). The area and shape defined by the two centers and the overlap of the two circumferences is known as the Vesica Piscis (Figure 3A).

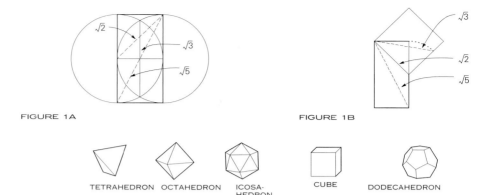

FIGURE 1A

FIGURE 1B

TETRAHEDRON   OCTAHEDRON   ICOSA-HEDRON   CUBE   DODECAHEDRON

FIGURE 1C

GENERATIVE GEOMETRY

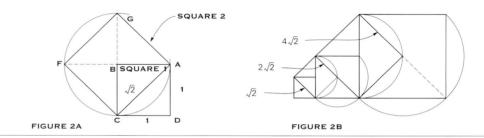

FIGURE 2A

FIGURE 2B

THE SQUARE ROOT OF 2

FIGURE 3A

FIGURE 3B

FIGURE 3C

THE SQUARE ROOT OF 3

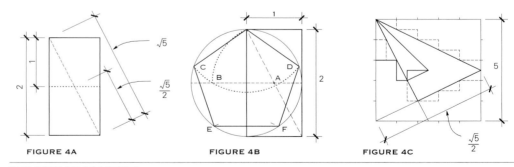

FIGURE 4A

FIGURE 4B

FIGURE 4C

THE SQUARE ROOT OF 5

Figure 3B shows the generation of equilateral triangles.

In Figure 3C, we see that if AB=1, then DG=1, CG=2, and, by the Pythagorean Theorem ($a^2 + b^2 = c^2$), the major axis:

$$CD = \sqrt{(CG^2 - DG^2)} = \sqrt{3}$$

THE SQUARE ROOT OF 5

The square root of 5 may be generated from a 1:2 rectangle (a double square); see Figure 4A. Figure 4B demonstrates the relationship of the square root of 5, both with the number 5 (as the square of its root) and with the fivefold symmetry of the pentagon. The 3, 4, 5 "Pythagorean" triangle (Figure 4C) is derived from the crossing of three semidiagonals (square root of 5 divided by 2). The square root of 5 is the proportion that opens the way for the family of relationships called the Golden Proportion.

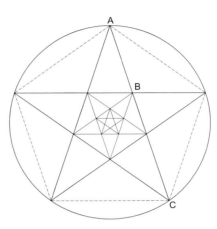

$$\frac{\sqrt{5}}{2}$$

$$1$$

$$\frac{1}{2}$$

$$\frac{\sqrt{5}}{2}$$

$$\frac{1 + \sqrt{5}}{2} = \phi$$

FIGURE 5A

$$\frac{1 + \sqrt{5}}{2} = \phi$$

$$\phi$$

$$\frac{1}{\phi}$$

$$\frac{1}{\phi}$$

$$\frac{1}{\phi^2}$$

$$\phi$$

FIGURE 5B

$$\frac{1 + \sqrt{5}}{2} = \phi$$

$$\frac{-1 + \sqrt{5}}{2}$$

$$1$$

$$\frac{1 + \sqrt{5}}{2}$$

$$\sqrt{5}$$

FIGURE 5C

THE GOLDEN PROPORTION

A   B   A + B

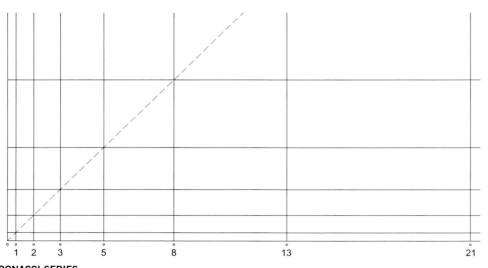

FIBONACCI SERIES
1   2   3   5   8   13   21

FIBONACCI SERIES
The Fibonacci Series is a sequence of numbers where the first two terms are 1 and 1, and each subsequent term is the sum of the two preceding numbers; 1, 1, 2, 3, 5, 8, 13, 21, and so on. The ratio between consecutive terms approximates the Golden Proportion.

GOLDEN PROPORTION CONSTRUCTION METHODS

RATIO AND PROPORTION

Ratio is the relation in magnitude, quantity, or degree between two or more similar things.

A:B   A/B

Proportion is the comparative, harmonious relation of one part to another or to the whole with respect to magnitude, quantity, or degree.

A:B:C   A/B=B/C

THE GOLDEN PROPORTION

The Golden Proportion can be found in nature, where it governs plant growth patterns and human proportions. Its presence can be found in the sacred art and architecture of Egypt, India, China, Greece, Islamic countries, and other traditional cultures. It was hidden in Gothic cathedrals, celebrated in Renaissance art, and used by modernist architects such as Le Corbusier (pseudonym of Charles-Edward Jeanneret) and Frank Lloyd Wright.

Discontinuous proportions contain four terms (a:b::c:d). Geometric relationships are of a three-term proportional type (a:b::b:c). There is only one proportional division that is possible with two terms; this is written a:b::b:(a + b). The unique two-term proportion (designated by the Greek letter ø was called "golden" by the ancients because the original unity is always represented in its division, written

$$\frac{1}{\phi^3} : \frac{1}{\phi^2} : \frac{1}{\phi^2} : \frac{1}{\phi} : \frac{1}{\phi} : 1 :: 1 : \phi :: \phi : \phi2 :: \phi2 : \phi3,$$ and so on

Figure 5A shows the construction of the Golden Proportion from the 1:2 rectangle. Figure 5B demonstrates the relationship of three squares related by f. Figure 5C reveals an important pentagonal relationship: the side of a pentagon is in relation to its diagonal as:

$$(1 + \sqrt{5}) \, \emptyset \, 2 \quad \text{or} \quad 1 : \emptyset,$$ the golden section

where ø represents a coinciding of the processes of addition and multiplication called the Fibonacci Series, which manifests itself in some biological growth patterns.

LE MODULOR
Le Corbusier developed Le Modulor proportioning system based on a standard human height of 1,829 mm (6 ft). (Dimensions shown are millimeters.)

Scott C. McBroom, AIA; Alexandria, Virginia

COLOR

DESCRIBING COLOR

The three universal, measurable characteristics of color are as follows:

- *Hue:* The spectral category to which the color belongs; hue is the basic name of a color, such as "red."
- *Value:* The lightness or darkness of the color; high-value samples are light, low-value samples are dark.
- *Saturation:* The brilliance or dullness of the color; the amount of hue in a color. For example, vermilion has a great deal of red, but pink has very little.

INDETERMINATE ATTRIBUTES OF COLOR

More than 90% of what we know of the world comes to us through our vision. The eye's retina absorbs the light and sends a signal, or sensation, to the brain. This sensation makes us aware of a characteristic of light—color. The National Bureau of Standards estimates that the human eye can distinguish more than 10 million different colors.

Indeterminate attributes are assigned to our perceptions of colors—to the way they make us feel. They cannot be measured; rather, they arise from our intuitive experience of color. These indeterminate attributes provide the mystery of color and range from the poetic language we use to express our perceptions of color to the psychological effects of color on our mood.

DETERMINATE ATTRIBUTES OF COLOR

Determinate attributes of color can be measured by various instruments. Optics is the branch of science that analyzes the mechanisms we use to perceive color—the rods and cones on the eye's retina. Colorimetry measures the color systems developed to precisely communicate color. The mystery and the mechanics of color are tightly entwined. We seldom see a single color in isolation, completely independent from the influence of other colors or other external factors, such as the light source, the surface of the object, and the surrounding objects. Neither do we perceive color without the modifying influences of psychological and symbolic factors. Our response to color depends on who we are and what our culture tells us certain colors should mean.

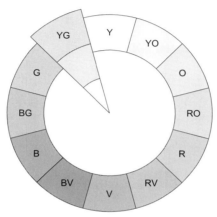

THE COLOR WHEEL
The color wheel displays the visible hues. The color wheel acts as a synopsis of the basic spectrum available to the designer; there are too many hues in the range of human vision to include.

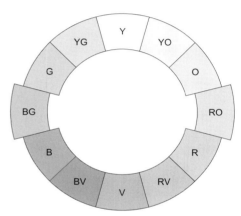

MONOCHROMATIC COLOR SCHEMES
Monochromatic schemes use one hue with variations on its value; for example, beige, taupe, and mustard yellow, or white, black, and gray (silver). These schemes are often used in professional offices or high-end retail spaces, and suggest sophistication, even elegance. (See Figure C-2 in color insert.)

COMPLEMENTARY COLOR SCHEMES
Complementary schemes use two hues that are situated opposite each other on the color wheel; for example, yellow and purple, or red-orange and blue-green. These energized schemes are the boldest and popular for use in sales offices and shopping malls. (See Figure C-3 in color insert.)

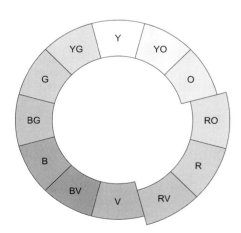

ANALOGOUS COLOR SCHEMES
Analogous schemes use two or more hues that sit within a 90° arc of each other on the color wheel. These schemes can be energized when warm and cool colors are mixed, such as red-orange, red, and red-violet. Analogous schemes are popular choices for facilities supporting high-energy activity such as grade schools, child care centers, and sports facilities. (See Figure C-4 in color insert.)

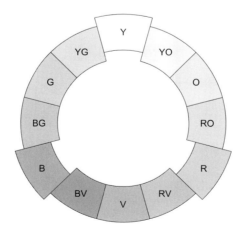

CONTRASTING COLOR SCHEMES
Contrasting schemes use colors whose location on the color wheel create an equilateral triangle, such as red, blue, and yellow. These schemes are bold and are often used in large spaces such as sports arenas and entertainment facilities.

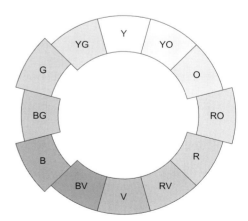

SPLIT COMPLEMENTARY COLOR SCHEMES
Split complementary schemes use one hue from one side of the color wheel and the two hues adjacent to its complementary color; for example, red-orange, blue, and green. The complement contrasts vibrantly against the harmonious adjacent colors. These schemes are used to create impact and can often be seen in businesses specializing in innovation, bars, and dance clubs.

THE COLOR WHEEL

DESIGNING A COLOR SCHEME

The design of a color palette for an environment involves a different process from that of creating a palette for a static two-dimensional graphic format. Three approaches have emerged:

- Combining color selections due to their location on the color wheel.
- Making color selections based on form, function, and spatial effect.
- Selecting specific colors because of their cultural or historic significance.

Form, Function, and Spatial Effect

The illusions of color perception, such as depth, weight, temperature, and figure-ground relationships, can be implemented to create a desired spatial reading. Form, space, and color are considered congruently. Program, site, and design concept drive the color selections. Space-shaping elements are layered and sculpted using color. Changes in color are used to create spatial focus. The work of Jorge Luis Barrigan and Richardo Legorreta are examples of this use of color. (See Figure C-5 in color insert.)

Culture and History

Color schemes can be designed based on specific hue, value, and saturation combinations derived from historical sources. These palettes carry symbolic meanings due to the learned tradition of the culture in which they are used. Examples of three palettes that speak to Western culture are the *natural scheme*, the *white scheme*, and the *polychromatic scheme*.

Natural Color Scheme

The natural scheme leaves materials in their natural state. Generally, applied colors are neutrals and earth tones except where highly saturated accents are used to symbolize a special focus, such as "factory-made" materials, rather than those found in nature. This type of scheme can be found in the work of Frank Lloyd Wright.

White Color Scheme

The white scheme uniformly applies the color white to almost all surfaces. That which is not white has a specific meaning, such as furniture that is movable. Human occupants of the architecture provide color as well. The architecture of the International Movement is a good example of this type of scheme. The white interior flattens cultural differences. Highly saturated color is applied to movable objects such as furniture in order to highlight, through contrast, the universality of the architecture.

Polychromatic Color Scheme

The polychromatic scheme uses many colors in one scheme. The colors are experienced simultaneously on all surfaces. Color and color change are used to define structure, surface composition, and the decorative motif. Victorian architecture is an example of a polychromatic scheme that carries learned cultural meaning for American interiors.

SENSING COLOR

Light allows us to sense color. Sensing color depends on four factors:

- *Spectral energy distribution of the light;* that is, the conditions under which the color is perceived.

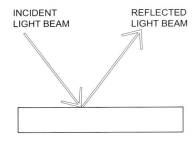

SMOOTH SURFACE
Light reflecting off a high-gloss surface reflects back to the eye directly.

ROUGH SURFACE
Light reflecting off a rough surface scatters the light in many directions, making the surface appear darker.

REFLECTION AND SCATTERING

- *Sensitivity of the eye in registering light* and then turning it into electrochemical impulses and sending them via the optical nerve to the brain.
- *Spectral characteristics of the object* in terms of how much light it absorbs, reflects, and transmits.
- *Psychological factors;* that is, the experiences and the personality of the viewer affect how color is perceived.

Spectral Energy Distribution of the Light

Light is a form of radiant energy or, more precisely, electromagnetic energy, a category of energy that includes gamma rays at one end of the spectrum and radio waves at the other. The light our visual system responds to in the experience of seeing, called "visible radiant energy," is a very small portion of the spectrum, falling between infrared and ultraviolet radiation. Bands of visible radiant energy appear to us as color, and we call them light.

Sensitivity of the Eye

Light, whether from a luminous object or reflected from the surface of a nonluminous object, enters our eyes and photochemically activates key nerve cells on the retinas known as *rods* and *cones*. Rods operate at low light levels—for example, at night or in a darkened, windowless room—and sense blacks, whites, and grays (also called *achromatic colors* because they have no hue). The cones in our eyes operate at higher light levels—for example, during the daytime or in a lighted room—and sense chromatic color, or hues. When the cones are active during the day, the rods are dormant. At night, the rods take over and the cones rest.

Three types of reception systems produce the colors we see: red/green, yellow/blue, and black/white. These systems operate from three types of cone photorecep-

tors: red-, blue-, or green-making. Because we create all the colors we see from red-, blue-, and green-sensing cones, humans are known as *trichromats*. When one set of color-sensing cones fails or is missing, a form of color blindness occurs—either *monochromatism* (when only one of the three photoreceptors works) or *dichromatism* (when two of the three work). These dysfunctions are a genetic trait occurring mostly in men. About 8 of every 100 men suffer from some type of color blindness, while only 1 in every 200 women does.

Color Terminology

ACHROMATIC: Having no discernible hue or color.

AFTERIMAGE: A "ghost" image generated by the eye in response to stimulation by a single color in the absence of its complement.

BEZOLD EFFECT: An effect in which all colors in a composition appear lighter by the addition of light outline, or darker by the addition of dark outline; also, an effect in which a colored ground appears lighter because of a carried linear design in light line, or darker because of a carried linear design in dark line.

METAMERISM: The phenomenon that occurs when two objects that appear to match under one set of light conditions do not match under a different set of light conditions.

PRIMARY COLORS: The simplest colors of the artist's spectrum: red, yellow, and blue; those that cannot be reduced or broken down into component colors.

SHADE: A pure color made darker, or with black added.

SIMULTANEOUS CONTRAST: Changes in either the lightness or hue of a target produced by its surround; or our tendency to perceive colors differently depending on what is around them.

TINT: A pure color made lighter, or with white added.

Spectral Characteristics of Objects

The spectral characteristics of objects are sometimes called "surface" and "surround." How a surface reflects, absorbs, or transmits light, and how the colors and textures surrounding the surface influence its color, give us the information we need to understand the objects we perceive. They help us know an object's shape and location, although the interaction of surface and surround can also distort our perceptions—as when an office painted yellow makes the faces of the people who work in it appear jaundiced.

The different visual sensations we get from viewing two tabletops—one with a gloss finish, the other with a matte finish—illustrate the influence texture has on the character of color. Even though the color of the two tabletops may be identical, the gloss on one will create an internal refraction, or bending of the light waves, making its color appear more brilliant than the color on the matte-finished top. Surface color can also be the result of a material's structure. Polar bear fur, blue jay feathers, and a kitten's blue eyes are actually clear. Their structures refract, or bend, the light that illuminates them to cause the colors we see.

Psychological Factors

Symbolic ways of sensing color are almost always tied to specific objects—white mourning clothes in Japan, white wedding dresses in the United States—which is why one color may have widely different connotations from one culture to another or even within the same culture. In the latter case, for example, to Americans, black is a symbol of death, yet a chair upholstered in black leather suggests affluence and sophistication.

Gestalt psychologists describe our inclination to select and order what we see as the principle of *figure-ground perception*, or our tendency to regard any kind of pattern or form we see as a figure against a background. Most people need the psychological and physical moorings of a high figure-ground organization in order to make sense of their environments. They become disoriented in environments where figure-ground relationships aren't apparent, such as those in which carpet, furniture, and walls all have the same pattern or are the same color.

On the other hand, the tendency to see figure-ground relationships means our brains often supply information that is missing from what we see. When we see a square table with three chairs around it, we automatically look for the fourth, sometimes supplying it in our minds even though it's not there. This is the principle of *closure*—our tendency to see incomplete patterns as complete or unified wholes. In a related way, we tend to see furniture of different styles but the same color as a unified group.

COLOR PERCEPTION PHENOMENA

At the same time that our brains are sensing color on a conscious level, they are also responding to it with phenomena that operate so quickly and effortlessly they seem unconscious. The phenomena that have an impact on how our brains perceive color are:

- Color constancy
- Simultaneous contrast
- Optical mixture
- Spatial dimension

Color Constancy

Color constancy involves our tendency to compensate for the effect of various light sources on the color of the objects we see. For example, a company's logo is displayed prominently just outside its corporate headquarters building. Here, we see its color in daylight. Just inside the building, we see the logo again, this time illuminated by fluorescent lamps. That evening, we leave the building and see the outdoor logo illuminated by spotlights. Without the proper filter for each viewing situation, a camera would register dramatic shifts in the logo's color because of the various light sources. Our brains, however, rapidly compensate for each situation, and we perceive the color of the logo as the same in all three cases.

Our minds prefer the psychological equilibrium that results from accepting the logo colors as the same. By doing so, we free ourselves to focus on the differences we perceive in the environment that are of greater importance to us.

Simultaneous Contrast

Simultaneous contrast involves our tendency to perceive colors differently depending on what is around them. Designers are well aware of how gray carpets seem to shift in color, depending on the surrounding

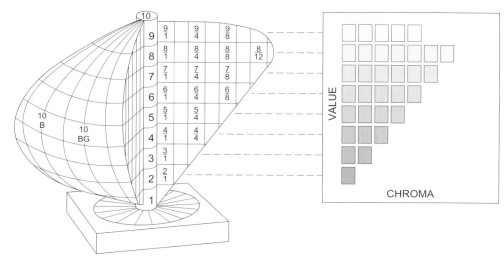

The American art educator Albert Munsell (1858–1918) developed the widely used Munsell Color System, which arranges all colors on the basis of their appearance. Munsell's system describes color in three dimensions.

MUNSELL COLOR SYSTEM

wall color. This occurs because our perception of one color becomes tinged toward the complement (the color directly opposite another on a color wheel) of the color around it. For example, a gray square looks reddish on a green background and greenish on a red background.

When complementary colors of equal intensity are next to each other, the afterimages (the ghostly tinges of color we see when we look away) heighten our experience of both colors. That is why red/green, yellow/purple, or orange/blue color combinations are the most startling. It is also why, when we study a painting, the afterimage of one patch of color influences the next patch of color we look at. The same thing happens when a worker stares up at a magenta flipper door and then looks down at a light-toned work surface, which appears to have a greenish cast. (See Figures C-6, C-7, C-8, and C-9 in color insert.)

Optical Mixture

Optical mixture is the opposite of simultaneous contrast. When an object's patches of color are so small that they pass below the threshold of conscious perception, we see the colors as optically mixed. Sometimes, as when the two colors on a top spin too fast to be seen individually, we perceive a third color. This also happens when viewing a multicolored brick building from a distance. The building appears to be one color, optically mixed.

Understanding optical mixture in interiors is necessary for determining where best to use patterns, especially in regard to their scale and location in a room. Colored patterns should only be used after an evaluation of it in the position it will occupy in a space. A tackboard covered in a fabric with a small pattern may look red and blue close up; but from a distance, the red and blue can mix and the tackboard will look purple among the other red and blue elements in the space. That combination may not be what the designer intends, or it can be a way of achieving a new color without actually using it in the scheme.

Spatial Dimension

Spatial dimension, the fourth of these internal phenomena, occurs when our brains add or subtract distance, depending upon the colors perceived. We

tend to perceive warm-colored objects, for example red, orange, and yellow, as closer than cool-colored ones, such as green, blue, and purple. (See Figure C-5 in color insert.)

Red, orange, and yellow may be "warmer" in the sense that they are closer to us, since red has a longer wavelength and therefore a closer focal point than blue does. The shorter wavelength of blue and its longer focal point result in the perception of distance. Thus the selection of greens, blues, or purples for ceilings and walls can make these surfaces appear to recede, giving the space a more open feeling.

Munsell was the first to refer to the three main characteristics of color—hue, value, and saturation—likening them to a musical note's pitch, tone, and intensity. The Munsell Color System, which arranges all colors on the basis of their appearance, does not incorporate methods to evaluate the effects of a surface's shininess or dullness on the perceived color. A quarter of the solid is removed to show color notation scales for hue, value, and saturation.

CIE STANDARD FOR COLOR NAMING

In the 1920s, the scientists of the Commission Internationale d'Eclairage (CIE) developed a system for measuring the bands of color in light waves based on standards for daylight and artificial illumination. This precise measurement of the electromagnetic waves reflecting from the surface of an object enables the precise communication of hue. For example, when a designer specifies the tristimulus values of 0.5375, 0.3402, and 0.2078, the vendor knows which color is meant: cadmium red.

As exact as the CIE standards are, they are cumbersome to use. Most people prefer to use color maps, such as the one Munsell developed. Whatever their limitations, these color maps enable us to communicate color to anyone, anywhere, who has the same map. However, most U.S. furniture manufacturers refer to CIE standards.

Faith Baum, AIA, IIDA; Faith Baum Architect; Lexington, Massachusetts
Herman Miller, Inc.; Zeeland, Michigan

VISUAL DEVICES

A visual illusion is a misperception; it is an interpretation of visual sensations that contradicts the reality of what a person sees. When the human eye receives electromagnetic energy, sensations are transmitted to the brain, and the brain translates these stimuli into meaningful images. This is vision. Visual perception is influenced by prior knowledge of the focal objects and the context of those objects. Since specific visual stimuli are understood in specific conditions, designers are able to devise a wide range of spatial configurations that simulate these conditions and create impressions that defy the physical character of space.

The human eye seeks order over chaos. Often, the brain will edit difficult visual information to clarify its understanding of the world around it, resulting in selective perception. Sometimes the brain is unable to distinguish elements due to ambiguity or camouflage, or it misunderstands what it sees because of intellectual expectations for conditions such as symmetry or constancy. By becoming familiar with these types of visual phenomena, the designer is able to manipulate a scene, intentionally altering the viewer's perception.

Commonly used visual devices include the manipulation of surfaces, light, form, and space.

SURFACE MANIPULATION

Color and Texture
Color and texture are two of the easiest-to-use and most powerful tools in the design of interior space. Surface coverings, material finishes, and furnishing selections are fundamental to creating the ambiance of a room or a space. Color can be used to compress a space or extend the perceived dimensions of a room. Texture can make a solid surface dematerialize or give a sense of stability to a lightweight object. Dark colors make spaces appear smaller, and light colors make spaces seem larger; but there are other applications of surface color and texture that can alter the appearance of an interior.

The muscles in the human eye respond differently to the various wavelengths of the visible spectrum, creating a relationship between color and the impression of spatial depth. These muscular reactions cause warm hues (red, orange, yellow) to appear as though they are advancing, and cool hues (blue, green, gray) to appear to be receding. In addition, distant objects appear cooler the farther they are from an individual because dust particles in the air obscure the purity of their color waves as they meet the human eye. These physical properties combine to create the illusion that objects identical in size, shape, and distance from the viewer, but differing in color and/or texture, will appear to be in different locations. Color *value*, the amount of lightness or darkness in a color, also impacts the perception of objects in space. High contrast makes objects appear to advance and low contrast makes areas look as though they recede. A textured object lit to articulate high contrast will appear to have deep relief.

Using these principles, the vertical space of a room can appear taller if the ceiling is white or a light color, while a dark ceiling can lower the perceived height of a room. A ceiling height can appear even more compressed by lowering the crown molding from its typical position at the intersection of the wall and the ceiling to a height along the upper part of the wall. The illusion can be reinforced by painting the wall plane above the molding the same color as the ceiling. This phenomenon is achieved through the designer's combined understanding of the effects of using a continuous hue on adjacent surfaces and of defying the expectation that a crown molding marks the height of a room.

The horizontal dimensions of a room can be affected by color as well. By painting one wall of a room in contrast to the others, a room can grow deeper or shallower in perception and feel. A room will seem cozier with the introduction of warm tones, and will open up with cool tones.

Faux Finishes
Faux finishes are surfaces painted to appear as though they were made from another material, such as a column painted to look like marble, a wainscot painted to look like wood, or a floor painted to look like mosaic tile.

The grand lobby of the USG Building in Chicago's Loop, designed by Skidmore, Owings, and Merrill, is a rich interior, with a dynamic floor pattern in marble tile, and walls faced with a white marble block—or so it appears. In actuality, only the lower portion of the wall is faced in marble tile; the upper portion of the wall is painted to appear as though it were.

Faux finishing can be brought into the third dimension, as well. In 1867, Baron Georges Haussmann designed *Parc des Buttes-Chaumont,* a romantic garden in northeast Paris. The then-new material portland concrete was used to imitate the look of rocks, unpolished stone, and even wood in the design of cliffs, a grotto, a classical colonnaded temple, handrails, and benches. Concrete's plasticity and ability to absorb color made it a perfect material for "fooling" the parkgoer.

Faux finishing techniques are often used in conjunction with *trompe l'oeil* perspectives to create both spatial and material deception.

Trompe l'Oeil Perspective
The development of *trompe l'oeil* perspective during the Renaissance corresponded with the rediscovery of linear perspective. Literally meaning the "fooling of the eye," tromp l'oeil perspective employs mathematical principles and painting techniques to translate depth onto a two-dimensional surface, thereby altering the viewer's understanding of distance.

Leon Battisa Alberti (1404–1472) and Filippo Brunelleschi (1377–1446) are credited with making the techniques for creating linear perspective comprehensible. Brunelleschi gave public demonstrations of perspective in his "Peepshows," and Alberti described his discoveries in his 1435 treatise *Della Pitura (On Painting)*. Both explained the nature of visual depth perception and the mechanics of portraying what the eyes see: parallel lines, both horizontal and vertical, appear to converge at a vanishing point, and objects of equal size appear reduced in inverse proportion to their distance from the viewer. Since that time, Western artists and designers have used the principles of perspective to create the illusion of deep, proportionally correct space on a two-dimensional picture plane.

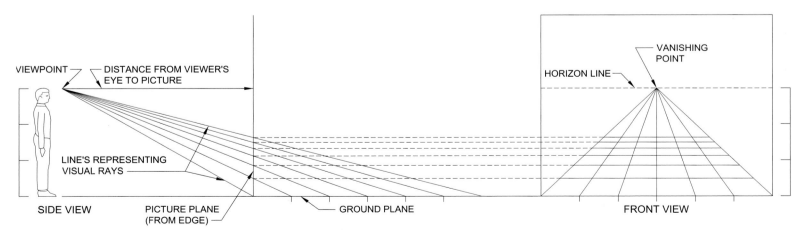

Depth perception and the mechanics of portraying what the eyes see: parallel lines, both horizontal and vertical, appear to converge at a vanishing point, and objects of equal size appear reduced in inverse proportion to their distance from the viewer.

LINEAR PERSPECTIVE

TROMPE L'OEIL PAINTING

The great hall of the *Villa Farnesina* in Rome is an early example of trompe l'oeil. Appropriately named the *Salone delle Prospective,* it was painted in 1517 by Baldassare Peruzzi (1481–1526) who was an architect, painter, and stage-set designer. He drew on his theatrical expertise and his knowledge of classical wall painting to create the illusion that the *Salone* extended beyond the dimensions of its floor plate. He painted dramatic porticoes on all four sides of the salon, each leading to low "stone" balconies, which in turn overlooked beautiful imagined landscapes.

Trompe l'oeil continues to be a favorite device in the design of interiors. Architect Beverly Willis used the technique in her design for the Greenwich Apartment, situated on the steep eastern side of San Francisco's Telegraph Hill. With an exquisite view of the bay, Willis created an illusion by painting a scene on the living room wall that used the same horizon line as the exterior view, which terminates with a view of the exterior itself. The water level is the same inside and out, blurring the edges between the interior of the residence and the exterior.

Muralist Richard Haas has enhanced many urban settings with his masterly trompe l'oeil painting. His *112 Prince Street* façade in New York City depicts a masonry wall with punched windows on a surface previously blocked from view by an adjacent building. Complete with a cat sitting on a window sill, Haas's composition is a convincing continuation of the building's rhythm of pilasters and openings. Haas used his photorealistic painting art in interior space as well.

Placement of Paintings

Mural paintings and frescos can greatly enhance an interior space, but careful planning must be used in the placement of these elements in order to achieve the best effect.

As part of the Iowa Art in State Buildings program, Richard Haas was commissioned to create paintings for the end walls of the long corridors of the Agronomy Building. Haas incorporated the hallway's existing architectural details, such as floor tiles, window moldings, and columns, into the ground floor corridor's composition. The mural plays with the illusionary effects of the horizon line and one-point perspective, depicting a view of Iowa's rolling landscape through a painted window. Included in the landscape are fields, farm buildings, livestock, and the skyline of Iowa's state buildings in the distance, a convincing view of what might be seen if there was fenestration at the end of the hall.

Arguably one of the world's most mysterious illusions, Leonardo da Vinci's *The Last Supper* (15 ft × 22 ft –10 in. (4.5 m × 6.9 m)) occupies the north wall of the refectory (monastic dining room) of the Convent of Santa Maria delle Grazie, Milan. The fresco sits high on the wall directly over the entrance to the refectory and is designed to look like a deep upper room overlooking the dining room. Da Vinci painted the scene's coffered ceiling in deep perspective, suggesting that the upper room is located adjacent to the dining room, behind the architectural cornice and the lunettes. The abbot and monks of the convent ate on the lower level at the other end of the refectory, perhaps imagining themselves to be sharing their meal with 13 others. The unusual perspective of *The Last Supper* lifts the viewer's eye from the floor to the correct viewpoint.

Mirrors

Mirrors are commonly used in public places to give the illusion of space. Restaurants and hotel lobbies use reflective surfaces to imply greater patronage as well. Mirrors bring light into dark spaces and bring reflected views into a room. Mirrors set across from one another create an effect of infinite reflection.

The traditions of the Chinese art of placement, *feng shui,* include the use of mirrors for their illusionary properties as much as for their capabilities to bring good *ch'i* (life force) into a living space and deflect bad *feng shui* spatial configurations. For example, mirrors are used to create a healthy visual sense of distance when walls are too close together or a room is too crowded.

The Hall of Mirrors *(Gallerie des Glaces)* at Versailles is an extreme example of how mirrors can extend the perceived space of a room. In 1684, interior designer Charles Le Brun designed the grandiose hall in Louis XIV's country home, which included 17 arched windows opening out toward the great gardens of the chateau. On the wall opposite the fenestration, he designed a series of 17 arched recessed panels, each faced with a Venetian mirror, "mirroring" the size and shape of the windows, themselves. This dynamic composition succeeds in bringing the outside in as well as visually enlarging the space for the festivities of the kings of France.

At the other end of the scalar spectrum, mirrors have been incorporated in the design of furniture, as well. For example, pier tables were popular pieces of furniture in the American colonies of the late eighteenth and nineteenth centuries. Typically placed with their backs flat against a wall, these tables were curved in the front (both on the tabletop and the lower surface). The back panel between these surfaces is mirrored, and the reflections complete the curvilinear form of the table while subtly suggesting an extension of the volume of the room. Located below the tabletop, the viewer is less aware that the surface is reflective, making the discovery of the device that much more rewarding.

Light

The ethereal quality of light makes it a wonderfully deceptive element for interior design. In its close connection to the properties of color, bright light can make a space expand, and the absence of light can make a space contract.

A more obscure characteristic of light is that shadows cast by light are the complementary color of the source of the light. Outdoors, shadows are black because the light from the sun is white; indoors, the possibilities differ. Architect Luis Barragon used this phenomenon in the Chapel for the *Capuchinas Sacramentarias del Purisimo Corazon de Maria* in Tlalplan, Mexico. He placed a cross in front of a yellow-tinted glass window. When direct sunlight shines through the window, it becomes a yellow light, and the shadow cast by the cross is purple.

The right eye of Jesus occupies both foreground and background simultaneously. In the foreground, the eye is part of the painting's story; in the background, it is the vanishing point. In both cases, that point is about 15 ft (4.5 m) above the floor level.

In order for the painting to appear like an extension of the refectory, the vanishing point should be lower, at the spectator's eye level; instead, the intensity of the perspective seems to lift the viewer from the floor to the correct viewing point, creating a spiritually uplifting phenomenon.

LEONARDO DA VINCI'S *THE LAST SUPPER*

Standing at the entry to Borromini's garden colonnade, a figure's height is less than half that of the barrel vault above.

Standing at the rear of the colonnade, the same figure is much taller and wider compared to the surrounding barrel vault.

A false impression of depth is created by proportionally diminishing the architectural details toward the rear of the colonnade.

FRANCESCO BORROMINI, PALAZZO SPADA: GARDEN PERSPECTIVE COLONNADE

FORM

Principles of scale and proportion are useful in creating visual illusions. Scale, the relationship of the size of objects to the size of people, can be easily manipulated to make individuals feel much smaller or much larger. Proportion, the internal relationship of one part of an object or collection of objects to itself, can be manipulated to deceive individuals into misunderstanding the dimensional qualities of space.

Michelangelo experimented with both concepts in the design of the vestibule to the Laurentian Library, in 1525, in Florence. By giving the entrance staircase a monumental scale, visitors to the library are made to feel small compared to the importance of the library they are about to enter. The extraordinary stair rises to the library door in three flights, although only the center flight has treads that are easy to climb. It is set in a small square space, potentially too small for such a staircase. In order to balance the composition, Michelangelo manipulated other details to open the space of the vestibule. He de-emphasized the double columns by placing them in niches and integrating their presence into the surface of the wall, and he proportionally enlarged the brackets to match the size of the stair instead of the columns. Through this play of scale, and by changing proportional relationships among the elements of the classical composition, patrons of the library are convinced that the monumental stair is suited for the space in which it sits.

Sir John Soane (1753–1837) was another proponent of visual manipulation. In his home at 13 Lincoln's Inn Fields in London, he played with scale to impact the impression his spaces convey. Visitors to the home's crypt are made to feel like Titans—eye level with the capitals of the space's columns. On the upper floors, Soane exaggerated the perceived monumentality of the rooms by narrowing their vertical features, such as the doors and cabinets. He used cast-iron to create thin columns in rooms, such as the dining room, to reinforce the vertical expression.

Japanese designs are detailed with small-scaled objects to provide a sense of space that is otherwise difficult to find on the densely populated island nation. Bonsai trees are strategically placed in gardens to suggest that they are at a great distance from the viewer, although they are a mere yard (meter) or two.

Space

Forced perspective is based on the same principles of Renaissance perspective that are used in trompe l'oeil, but extended into the third dimension. Often accompanied with trompe l'oeil painting and faux finishes, the designer can achieve an artificial sense of dimension through the deliberate manipulation of objects in space. Since parallel lines converge, and objects in space appear smaller, actually converging parallel elements and reducing the size of the objects will deepen a shallow space or, in reverse, foreshorten a deep space, despite the actual dimensions of a place.

In designing the church of *Maria presso S. Satiro* in Milan, Donato Bramante (1482–1492) used forced perspective with trompe l'oeil to masterly affect. The site for the church was not long enough to include the choir required to complete the traditional cruciform plan. In a mere 6-ft- (2-m-) deep space, Bramante created the illusion of a full choir. He created the impression of deep space beneath a barrel vault by narrowing and slanting elements of the vault toward the vanishing point. The ceiling's coffers, the lines of columns, and the full suite of architectural details diminish in size and shape to imitate the effects of perspective, suggesting that the area beyond the altar is a full, deep choir. The visual device is not evident to a visitor to the church until he or she is close to the altar, delighting the visitor with an understanding of Bramante's clever design solution.

Francesco Borromini (1599–1667) created a false impression of great depth in the inner courtyard of Rome's *Palazzo Spada* in 1652. The elements of the apparently lengthy arcade mimic perspective effects; the columns literally get smaller the farther back they go, and they are thicker at the front than the back; the floor slopes upward, and the cornices downward; and the ceiling coffers and the squares on the pavement pattern are actually trapezoids. Despite appearances, the perspective arcade is only 28 ft- 2 in. (8.5 m) long.

Of course, when seen from the opposite end, the arcade foreshortens, suggesting that the arcade can be traversed in just a few paces.

Forced perspective and trompe l'oeil are popular techniques used in theatrical scenic design. In *Teatro Olimipco,* 1580, Andea Palladio (1508–1580) built a system combining both techniques into the architecture of the theatre. Built in Vicenza, Italy, Palladio designed five narrow tunnels at perspectival angles behind arched openings in the far wall (upstage) of the stage. Set designer Vincenzo Scamozzi created his vision of the "ideal city," a permanent series of urban street scenes built in accelerated perspective, visible to the audience through the openings. He painted the walls of the streets in a forced perspective along a narrow backstage area. He used trompe l'oeil to simulate the marble and stucco façades, and he incorporated the effects of light and color to reinforce the deep three-dimensionality of the image.

Landscape architects have incorporated forced perspective in their designs as well. Andre le Notre denies the great distance of a statue of Hercules in the garden of *Vaux le Viscomte* by lowering the topography below the horizon line in the expanse of the garden and by raising the focus of the statue high on a hill above the vanishing point. By contrast, the great lawn behind the Federalist-style mansion at Dumbarton Oaks in the Georgetown area of Washington, DC, appears longer than it is by the symmetrical trapezoidal shape leading to the wooded valley below.

FORCED PERSPECTIVE

Combining Effects

The Arthur M. Sackler Gallery at Harvard University, designed by James Sterling in 1987, combines two effects, forced perspective and a scale shift. The monumental, single-directional staircase narrows as it moves upward, exaggerating the visual phenomenon of a one-point perspective. The perceived distance is increased again by the placement of the torso of a Roman statue of Aphrodite, dating from the second century B.C. The viewer anticipates that the torso is a larger-than-life marble sculpture, appearing smaller because of its great distance from the bottom of the staircase. The deception is revealed when the visitor reaches the destination more quickly than anticipated and then discovers that the torso is a mere 38 in. (970 mm) high.

Venturi, Scott Brown and Associates used a number of illusionary principles in their 1981 design of the Sainsbury Wing addition to the National Gallery located in London's Trafalgar Square. Walking toward the new galleries, the viewer is confronted with a series of four arched entries. The arches recede in actual size, proportionally, the way they would appear in perspective, forcing the view to appear longer than its measured length. This distance is given even greater depth by the placement of a painting, the *Incredulity of Saint Thomas* by Cima (c. 1504): its arched top continues the visual rhythm created by the forced perspective and leads the eye beyond the back wall on which the painting is placed.

Sally Levine, AIA; Cleveland, Ohio

VIEW FROM POINT "B"

SECTION THROUGH MAIN STAIR *Sainsbury Wing, National Gallery, London; Venturi, Scott Brown and Associates*

LOCATION OF PAINTING, *THE INCREDULITY OF SAINT THOMAS* *Sainsbury Wing, National Gallery, London; Venturi, Scott Brown and Associates*

ROOM KEY
A. Galleries
B. Bridge to existing galleries
  a. Passenger elevators
  b. Entrance area to gallery

PLAN *Sainsbury Wing, National Gallery, London; Venturi, Scott Brown and Associates*

PARALINE AND PERSPECTIVE DRAWINGS

DRAWING METHODS

Perspective and paraline drawing methods are used to create three-dimensional drawings. Three-dimensional modeling software is available to generate such drawings. These computer programs are based on the basic principles of handdrawn perspectives. Paraline drawings differ from perspective drawings, in that the projection lines remain parallel instead of converging to a point on the horizon.

PARALINE DRAWINGS

Paraline drawings are sometimes referred to as axonometric (Greek) or axiometric (English) drawings. These drawings are projected pictorial representations of an object, which portray a three-dimensional quality. They can be classified as *orthographic projections,* as the plan view is rotated and the side view is tilted. The resulting "front" view is projected at a 90° angle to the picture plane.

Paraline drawings are useful for interior spaces and objects, particularly for cabinet and furniture design drawings. Exploded drawings of this type are often used to convey how various components can be made into a whole. Manufacturer's product literature often uses exploded isometrics to illustrate how to assemble a product or to create a component list. Designers can use these drawings to convey a design idea or show a contractor how an intended installation should be assembled.

In paraline drawing, parallel lines are used to create three-dimensional drawings that have a true measured or proportional scale in three principal axes: width, depth, and height. These drawings are typically easier to construct than perspective drawings and can convey a proportional three-quarter view of an object or space.

ORTHOGRAPHIC DRAWING

Two-dimensional, scaled orthographic drawings are used to develop three-dimensional paraline and perspective drawings. Orthographic drawings include:

- plan, or top view
- section, or crosssection, cutaway view
- elevation, facade, or side view

OBLIQUE DRAWING

In an oblique drawing one face (either plan or elevation) of the object is drawn directly on the picture plane. Projected lines are drawn at a 30° or 45° angle to the picture plane. The length of the projecting lines varies according to the angle chosen.

Plan Oblique

An axonometric drawing, also referred to as a *plan projection,* is projected and generated from plan. The plan remains in scale and perpendicular to the line of sight. The vertical components of an object or wall are projected vertically from the plan.

Elevation Oblique

An elevation oblique, also referred to as an *elevation projection,* is an axonometric drawing projected and generated from the elevation or sides. The elevation remains in scale and perpendicular to the line of sight. The horizontal components of an object or wall are projected from the elevation.

Planometric

A planometric is a combination of the plan oblique and the elevation oblique. The plan and elevation are both used in scale and in relationship to each other when constructing the drawing so that both the plan and elevation remain in scale.

Dimetric

A dimetric drawing is similar to oblique, with one exception: the object is rotated so that only one of its corners touches the picture plane. In dimetric drawings, two different scales are used to draft an object. Two of the width:depth:height scale ratios remain equal, such as 1:1:⅝.

The most frequently used angle for the projecting lines is an equal division of 45° on either side of the leading edge. A 15° angle is sometimes used when it is less important to show the "roof view" of the object.

Isometric

The isometric, a special type of dimetric drawing, is the easiest and most popular paraline drawing, and is generated from the dimensions of the object. All axes of the object are simultaneously rotated away from the picture plane and kept at the same angle of projection (30° from the picture plane). All legs are equally distorted in length at a given scale and therefore maintain an exact w:d:h proportion of 1:1:1.

Trimetric

The trimetric drawing is similar to the dimetric, except that the plan of the object is rotated so that the two exposed sides of the object are not at equal angles to the picture plane. Three different w:d:h scale ratios are used, such as 1:¾:⅝. The plan is usually positioned at 30/60° angle to the ground plane. The height of the object is reduced proportionately as illustrated (similar to the 45° dimetric).

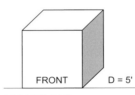

CAVALIER 50%

FRONT   D = 5'

PROJECTED 75%

FRONT   D = 7.5'

CABINET 100%

FRONT   D = 10'

Given:
Width = 10 ft   If front elevation is drawn at scale, ¼ in. = 1 ft 0 in.
Depth = 10 ft   Depth is ¾ × ¼ = ³⁄₁₆ in.
Height = 10 ft   Use scale ³⁄₁₆ in. = 1 ft 0 in.

OBLIQUE ELEVATION

30° ELEVATION OBLIQUE

45° ELEVATION OBLIQUE

45° DIMETRIC (PLAN OBLIQUE)

15° DIMETRIC

ISOMETRIC

TRIMETRIC

AXONOMETRIC—MEASURED METHOD

ADJUSTING THE OBLIQUE DIMENSION TO REDUCE DISTORTION

Dimetric and trimetric adjustments can be made to correct distortions to the image caused by the optical illusion when an object is rotated from view. Adjusting the proportional factor in computer programs allows the adjustment of the angle of view to compensate for distortion.

0° PLANOMETRIC

PLAN

ELEVATION

1:½:1

ISOMETRIC 1:1:1

1:¾:1

45° PLAN OBLIQUE

ELEVATION OBLIQUE 1:½:1

75° PLAN OBLIQUE

1:1:1

The width/depth/height ration has been adjusted in these illustrations by a factor of ½ and ¾, respectively. Adjusting the scale of the depth of an oblique drawing will result in a more believable proportion.

ORTHOGRAPHIC DRAWINGS

DIMETRIC ADJUSTMENT OF DEPTH

PRINCIPLES OF PERCEPTION ☐ **1**

PERSPECTIVE DRAWINGS

The major types of perspective drawings include:

- one-point perspectives
- two-point perspectives
- three-point perspectives
- multipoint perspectives

ONE-POINT INTERIOR PERSPECTIVES

A one-point perspective typically presents one face of a room or space perpendicular to the viewer and parallel to the picture plane. The primary face of the room or object is turned fully toward the viewer. This will appear in plan as a 0° relationship to the picture plane. All objects that are oriented in this manner will appear to be in an orthographic, flat, or an end-on view relationship to the viewer. All of the perpendicular planes to this plane will appear to converge toward the central vanishing point, which can be either in front of or behind the picture plane. The vanishing point is usually located at the sitting or standing height of an average person within the space (eye level can be located at 5 ft 4 in (1,626 mm) from the floor). In most cases, the vanishing point is located within the confines of the enclosed space being represented in the drawing. In one-point perspectives, the true height line can coincide with the entire measured plane that is in scale. Therefore, horizontal as well as vertical scale measures can be used to project the proportions of an intended subject.

CONSTRUCTION OF A ONE-POINT INTERIOR PERSPECTIVE

Construction of a one-point interior perspective is as follows:

1. Draw the primary elevation, or section, to scale. Locate the horizon line and vanishing point (VP) within the confines of the interior space. Locate the 45° measuring point (45° MP), which is also the station point (SP) in section. Strike an arc from the most remote corner of the room to a vertical line drawn from the VP. From this intersection draw a line upward at 60° (to the vertical) to meet the horizon. This intersection shall be the 45° MP.
2. Determine the room depth by starting at point 0 on the ground line and measuring to the right. Connect this point to the 45° MP on the horizon. The back wall is located where the line intersects the vertical base line drawn from the vanishing point to the ground line.
3. Complete the back wall as illustrated. Note that all lines occurring at a 45° angle in the elevation remain parallel in perspective. All surfaces that are parallel to the picture plane will remain parallel in perspective.

TWO-POINT PERSPECTIVES

Two-point perspectives allow for a wide variety of drawing angles. They are more dynamic and more widely used to depict three-dimensional space and objects. Traditional hand-constructed projections as well as computer-generated images can be used to develop quick sketch models, which can be used to further refine design elements by freehand sketch overlay techniques.

LOCATE HORIZON 1/3
UP FROM GROUND LINE
AND VP 1/3 OVER
FROM ONE WALL

HORIZON

VP

2/3

1/3

2/3   1/3

DRAW FRONT ELEVATION
TO DESIRED SCALE

FRONT ELEVATION

HORIZON

45° MP   VP

30°   RADIUS

GROUND LINE

MOST REMOTE
CORNER FROM VP   60°

LOCATE 45° MEASURING POINT

CONNECT ALL
CORNERS TO VP   HORIZON

45° MP   VP

0 1 2 3 4

GROUND LINE

LOCATE BACK WALL

HORIZON

45° MP   VP

COMPLETE

ONE-POINT DIRECT MEASURED INTERIOR PERSPECTIVE

TWO-POINT PERSPECTIVE USING THE MEASURING POINT METHOD

This is a simplified alternative to the conventional method of laying out the plan picture plane and projecting the vanishing lines. The measuring point method of drawing a two-point perspective eliminates the necessity of the preliminary layout of the plan. One of the obvious advantages of this method is the ease with which the size of the drawing can be adjusted. A perspective can be made larger by simply increasing the scale of the drawing.

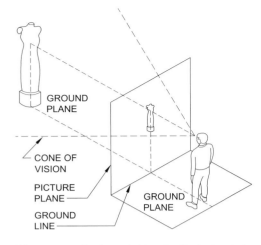

GROUND PLANE

CONE OF VISION

PICTURE PLANE

GROUND PLANE

GROUND LINE

A linear perspective is created by using the basic principles of ground plane and picture plane. The perceived object, in this case a sculpture, is plotted on a plane (referred to as the *picture plane*) parallel to the stationary viewer. A scale image is produced this way.

PERSPECTIVE PRINCIPLES

PERSPECTIVE
Terminology and Concepts

HORIZON LINE: A line drawn on the picture plane to represent the horizon. It is usually located at the point where all parallel lines recede away from the viewer and finally converge.

PICTURE PLANE: An imaginary, transparent plane, onto or through which the object is perceived in a perspective rendering. The picture plane is a curved plane for a wide angle perspective view.

STATION POINT: The point from which the object is viewed. The location of this point will be the factor that determines the width of the drawing. A 30° cone of vision is drawn from the station point. A common way of determining the distance between the station point and the picture plane is by referring to the following parameters:

- Minimum – 1.73 times the width of the image
- Average – 2.00 times the width of the image
- Maximum – 2.5 times the width of the image

VANISHING POINT: A specific point or points located on the horizon line, where all parallel lines, drawn in perspective, converge or terminate. The location of the vanishing points varies with the type of perspective drawing. In the two-point perspective, the distance between the vanishing point left and the vanishing point right is estimated as being approximately four times the overall size of the object being rendered.

TWO-POINT PERSPECTIVE USING 30°/60° DIRECT MEASURED SYSTEM

Two-point perspectives using the 30°/60° direct measured system are constructed as follows:

1. SETUP: Draw a horizon line and locate vanishing point right (VPR) and vanishing point left (VPL) separated at a distance that is approximately 4 to 4.5 times the maximum width of the image. Follow the illustration to locate the station point and leading corner of the image.

2. LENGTH: Measure, to scale, the length of the image along length line L. A perpendicular line is drawn from these designated points to the ground line. The vanishing perspective lines are then drawn directly from these points to the appropriate vanishing point (VPL). In this way the correct length of the line can be determined. Note what happens when equally spaced points are projected from the ground line to the vanishing point. The visual distance (length) between them, as they get closer to the vanishing point, is progressively foreshortened.

3. WIDTH: The width is measured along the width line at double scale. That is, if the perspective is drawn at a scale of ⅛ in = 1 ft, and a particular line is to be drawn at 5 ft, measure 5 ft at ¼ in. scale starting at the corner, and measure to the left of the corner horizontally. A line is drawn from each point on the width line to the appropriate vanishing point (VPR). The intersections of the length and width vanishing lines will define the "plan" in perspective.

4. HEIGHT: Since the leading corner of the image is placed directly on the picture plane, the height is measured, to scale, directly on the horizon line. It is then carried to VPL and VPR, as illustrated.

TWO-POINT PERSPECTIVE USING 45° DIRECT MEASURED SYSTEM

Two-point perspectives using the 45° direct measured system are constructed as follows:

1. SETUP: Similar to the method used in the 30°/60° setup, the vanishing points are placed on the horizon line and separated by 3 times the diagonal width.

2. LENGTH: Measure, to scale, the length of the image along the length line L. Connect the points directly to VPL.

3. WIDTH: In this setup, the width is the same as the length scale. Measure the width of the image along the width line W. The length and width lines will form an outline of the "plan" in perspective.

4. HEIGHT: The height line is positioned at a 45° angle and marked off to scale. A line representing the leading corner of the image is drawn perpendicular to the ground line. Connect or draw a line from the measurement points along the height line horizontally to the vertical corner line. As in the 30°/60° setup, these points are then carried to VPR and VPL.

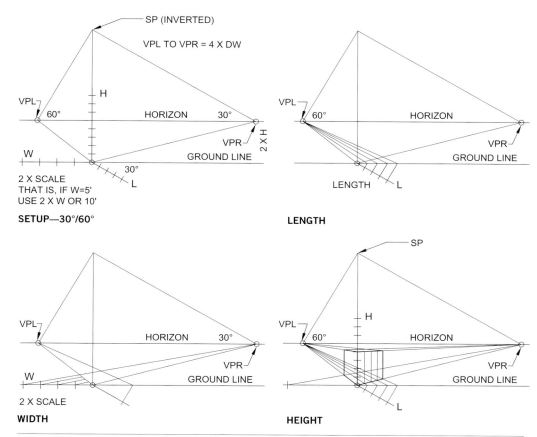

TWO-POINT PERSPECTIVE—30°/60° DIRECT MEASURED SYSTEM

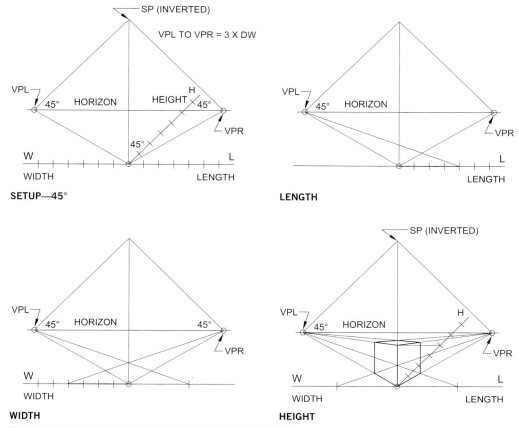

TWO-POINT PERSPECTIVE—45° DIRECT MEASURED SYSTEM

THREE-POINT PERSPECTIVES

Three-point perspectives are used to develop a third orientation and vertical diminution of form. In one- and two-point perspectives, objects are shown to converge toward vanishing points that are located on the horizon line or at eye level. All vertical dimensions are drawn to scale relative to one another. Vertical lines do not become more diminutive in a one- or two-point perspective, since many interior spaces are one or few stories high and rarely does the dominant view exceed the normal cone of vision. In the perspective drawing of taller and larger interior spaces and buildings, a third vanishing point is introduced somewhere along the vertical visual axis of the center of vision located by the station point. In the three-point perspective, the picture plane, which is assumed to be perpendicular to the center of vision, is rotated vertically from the station point creating a vertical as well as a horizontal component of the picture plane.

Three-point perspectives are constructed as follows:

1. LENGTH: The length line is drawn at the same scale as the line connecting points 1 and 2 (which is four times the maximum length of the object). Measured points are projected perpendicularly from the length line L to the ground line. From the ground line, the measured points are connected to vanishing point left (VP1).

2. WIDTH: The width should be double the scale used for length. For example, if the length is at a ¼ in. scale, use ½ in. scale for the width. Locate the distances along the width line, and connect these points directly to the vanishing point right (VP2).

3. HEIGHT: Using the original scale, mark off the measuring points along the height line (H). These points are projected perpendicularly to the line labeled "vertical plane." From these points a line is drawn to VP2, thereby cutting the vertical lines vanishing to VP2.

4. 45° POINT: This point on the horizon is determined by projecting a line from the upside-down station point so that it will meet the horizon line at a 75° angle. All lines occurring at a 45° angle to the picture plane (in viewing) will converge to this point; it is, therefore, often convenient to use this as a reference point when converting exact width to length, or vice versa, in plan.

MULTIPLE VANISHING POINT DRAWINGS

Multiple vanishing point perspectives are a combination of two or more perspectives in one space. When an object in the room depicted is rotated from the parallel planes of the room, that object or series of objects will have its-their own corresponding vanishing points on a common horizon line. Each orientation or parallel plane will have its own vanishing point. For example, in a one-point perspective, a chair that has been turned from view may have its own vanishing points.

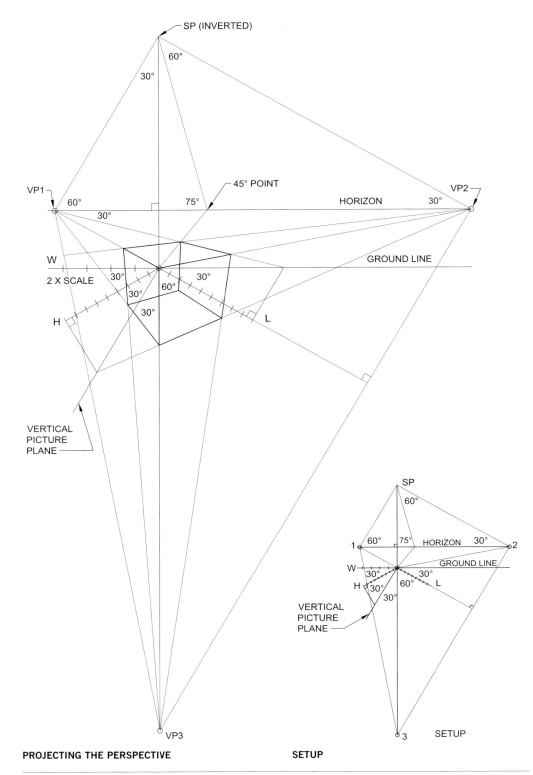

PROJECTING THE PERSPECTIVE   **SETUP**

PROJECTING THREE-POINT PERSPECTIVES

PLAN PROJECTION METHOD OF PERSPECTIVE CONSTRUCTION

Before the drawing can be laid out, the following information must be obtained:

1. An approximation of the overall dimensions of the interior space.
2. The location of the interior space in relation to the picture plane.
3. The orientation of the interior space, either in front of or behind the picture plane.

While the interior space can be located anywhere in the drawing—in front of, behind, or at any angle to the picture plane—the simplest approach is to place the interior space at the picture plane. The horizontal lines of the interior space would be parallel to the picture plane in a one-point perspective or placed at an angle to the picture plane. Usually this will be a 30°/60° or 45° angle in a two-point perspective.

ONE-POINT PERSPECTIVE

45° TWO-POINT PERSPECTIVE

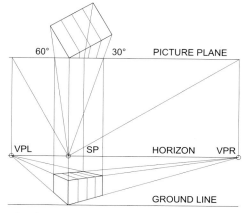

30°/60° TWO-POINT PERSPECTIVE

PERSPECTIVE CONSTRUCTION—PROJECTION METHOD

USING THE PLAN PROJECTION METHOD OF PERSPECTIVE CONSTRUCTION

The following steps are taken to construct a perspective using the plan projection method:

1. Consider the most important features of the room or object. Identify the location in plan from which the subject is viewed. This is the station point (SP).

2. Rotate and arrange the plan, slightly above where the perspective will be drawn. Conventional orientations could include a 30°/60° or 45° for two-point perspectives and 90° for one-point perspectives. Orientations such as a 15°/75° and others are possible. This allows the layout of two-point perspectives that have two vanishing points.

3. Establish a cone of vision (COV). The average person has an approximately 60° normal cone of vision, with additional peripheral vision. Typically, a maximum of 90° is used.

4. Establish the picture plane (PP). The picture plane is an imaginary plane, represented as a line in plan, onto which the intended subject will be drawn. Visual rays will be drawn from the viewer at the station point to the object. Where they intersect, the picture plane will determine their graphic position in the perspective layout. The picture plane should be drawn through some known and measurable point in the plan. Later, this point will be used as a scale measure line or true height line.

5. Establish the vanishing point locations on the picture plane. In a one-point perspective, there is only one vanishing point. When two or more vanishing points are used in one drawing they can be labeled with a subscript such as vanishing point left (VPL); vanishing point right (VPR). The vanishing points are determined by extend-

ing visual rays from the station point to the picture plane parallel to the object being drawn. In order to properly lay out and draft a perspective drawing, the drawing area should be arranged parallel to the picture plane.

6. Establish the direction of the angle of view. Once the direction of view is established, the SP should be at least 30° away from the furthest point of the intended subject. This will ensure the incorporation of a 60° cone of vision.

7. Identify the 60° cone of vision, which is an imaginary angle of view that closely approximates normal vision. The station point should be far enough away from the intended subject to view it within the normal cone of vision. Objects that are drawn outside of the normal cone of vision will become distorted in shape. Some computer programs will allow the adjustment of the cone of vision. In most interior perspectives a 90° maximum cone of vision is typical.

8. Establish the ground line (GL). The ground line ordinarily corresponds to either the floor level of the space or object being drawn.

9. Draw the horizon line at the appropriate eye level above the ground line. The eye level would be approximately 5 ft to 5 ft 6 in. (1,524 mm to 1,676 mm) above the ground level in a conventional perspective. If a higher view is desired, for example, from the top floor of an atrium space, the eye level would be 5 ft 6 in. (1,676 mm) plus the floor-to-floor height.

10. Locate the true height line (TH). The true height line is a line which begins at the ground line and extend upward and will serve as a point of reference or scale, from which all of the vertical elements and measurements in the perspective drawing will be derived. The true height line is usually a point of known scale that intersects the picture plane. It is helpful to place the picture plane within the interior space or touching

or intersecting an object being drawn. This primary true height line will be in the same scale as the plan.

11. Locate the lines of convergence that correspond to the major design elements in the plan. These will include the walls, large-scale planes and surfaces, including rugs or floor patterns as well as dominant architectural elements such as doors, window openings, or columns.

12. Locate the "leading edge" or nearest edge of the closest object to be drawn and its corresponding major coordinates (four corners, in the case of a rectangular object) by extending visual rays from the station point to the object and through or to the picture plane. These intersecting points will establish the vertical connection or relative position along the eye level of the perspective drawing.

13. Locate the major furnishings or other architectural elements in the plan by extending the vertical edges to the perspective drawing. Reduce complex forms to their simplest shapes prior to adding detail. Such shapes may include rectilinear and cubic solids.

14. Determine the depth of the drawing by extending the location of each object's footprint along the ground plane. Determine the height of the objects by lines from the vertical dimensions or the elevation to the true height line and following the perspective proportional height through the perspective space.

15. Extend the lines of a footprint, such as a sofa to the wall, to find the alignment of the sofa to that wall in perspective by extending the visual rays from the station point to the picture plane and back down to the perspective. By extending lines of convergence from the vanishing point forward into the room, the intersecting lines with the vertical extension lines will determine the four corners of the sofa.

PROJECTION SETUP
Locate major floor and ceiling elements. Locate footprint of major furniture elements and sketch out basic volumes in perspective.

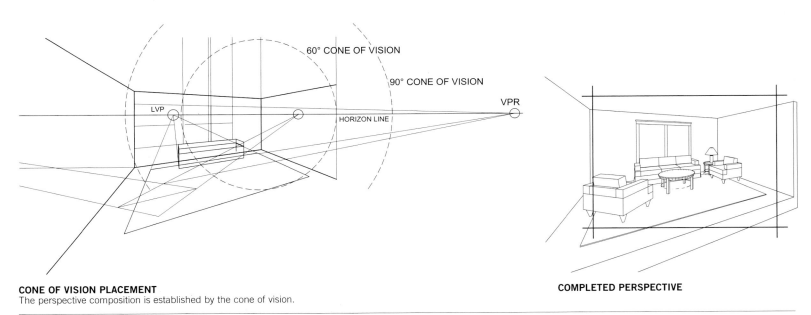

CONE OF VISION PLACEMENT
The perspective composition is established by the cone of vision.

COMPLETED PERSPECTIVE

PLAN PROJECTION METHOD OF PERSPECTIVE CONSTRUCTION

1   □   PRINCIPLES OF PERCEPTION

IMAGINARY PICTURE PLANE

PROJECTION LINES

VPR

PERSPECTIVE LAYOUT AREA

DRAWING SURFACE

HL

VPL

ELEVATION

SCHEMATIC DIAGRAM OF PLAN PROJECTION METHOD OF PERSPECTIVE CONSTRUCTION

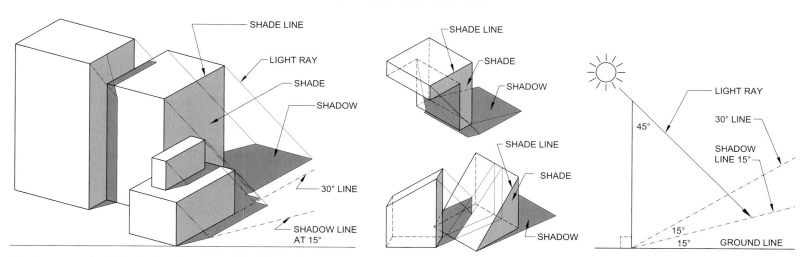

SHADE LINE

LIGHT RAY

SHADE

SHADOW

30° LINE

SHADOW LINE AT 15°

SHADE LINE

SHADE

SHADOW

SHADE LINE

SHADE

SHADOW

LIGHT RAY

30° LINE

SHADOW LINE 15°

45°

15°

15°

GROUND LINE

Shadows are constructed by drawing a line, representing a light ray, from a corner of the lighted surface at a 45° angle to the ground plane. The 45° light ray is extended until it meets the shadow line, and this point determines the length of the shadow for any given vertical height of the object. The shade line is the line (or the edge) that separates the light area from the shaded areas of the object. Shadow lines of all vertical edges of the object are drawn parallel to one another.

AXONOMETRIC SHADES AND SHADOWS

The one-point perspective grid tends to be more formal in appearance than a two-point perspective. This can be used to advantage in some presentation schemes. It is relatively easy to master the use of this grid.

ONE-POINT PERSPECTIVE GRID

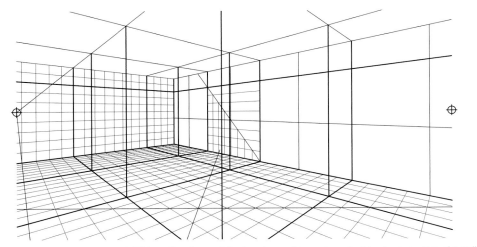

This spatial grid has been rotated 45° from the view and the imaginary picture plane. In this view two sides of a wall or object can be seen, depending upon its orientation to the viewer.

45° TWO-POINT PERSPECTIVE GRID

This spatial grid has been rotated 30°, allowing the viewer to see an entire room within a slightly expanded cone of vision. When extending the spatial grid in these drawings, ensure that unnecessary distortion is avoided at the extremes of the drawing layout.

30°/60° TWO-POINT PERSPECTIVE GRID

1 ☐ **PRINCIPLES OF PERCEPTION**

PERSPECTIVE CHARTS

Perspective charts can be used for quick sketches of interior space and furnishings. The use of these charts requires a basic understanding of the concepts of convergence and vanishing points. The three basic charts shown can be extended, rotated, or mirrored to facilitate compositions and views that will more clearly convey design ideas.

USING THE CHART METHOD OF PERSPECTIVE CONSTRUCTION

When using the chart method of generating perspectives, the projected perspective of the chart serves as a gridwork to locate and define architectural form and space. The following steps are taken to construct a perspective using a chart:

1. Determine the station point or point from which a viewer will be observing the space. A preliminary thumbnail sketch may be advantageous. Imagine what the space may look like from the preferred view.
2. After choosing an appropriate angle of view, choose the appropriate chart and chart orientation.
3. Identify the furthest distances from the viewer.
4. Determine the perimeter, enclosures, or wall elements on the chart.
5. Find and trace along the charted lines or grids the appropriate heights for ceilings, door, and windowsills and heads.
6. Along the gridded ground plane, locate the intended architectural objects, furnishings, and other items such as major accessories. Lesser accessories and details can be added later.
7. Using either the known dimensions or elevation drawings and other information, determine the major vertical dimensions of all the objects to be drawn. Most manufacturers publish product dimensions, including height, width, depth, and seat height and arm height of a piece of furniture.
8. Simplify complex shapes to the simplest geometric forms such as cubes, or cylinders, or intersecting patterns. A sofa or armchair can be reduced to a composition of several rectangular forms. A coffee table can be reduced to its simplest geometry.
9. Using reference photos, magazine cuts, catalog information, or repeat pattern dimensions, fill in and refine the layout.

THREE-POINT PERSPECTIVE GRIDS

Three-point perspective grids can be used to produce drawings that have the appearance of looking up or down into a space. Since a three-point perspective may be difficult to layout using the plan projection method, an adequate perspective can be achieved by adding detail using the vanishing points that are established by the chart or a rough wire frame computer model.

Robert Bernier, AIA; Somerset, Massachusetts

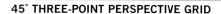

Eye level is 20 ft (6100 mm) above ground line. The center of view (CV) is 5 ft (1525 mm) above ground line.

45° THREE-POINT PERSPECTIVE GRID

Eye level is 20 ft (6 m) above ground line. The center of view (CV) is 5 ft (1.5 m) above ground line.

30°/60° THREE-POINT PERSPECTIVE GRID

ACOUSTICS

SOUND

Sound is energy produced by a vibrating object or surface and transmitted as a wave through an elastic medium. Such a medium may be air (airborne sound) or any solid common building material, such as steel, concrete, wood, piping, gypsum board, and so on (structure-borne sound). A sound wave has *amplitude* and *frequency*.

AMPLITUDE (DECIBELS)

Difference between sound levels (in dB)	0–1	2–3	4–9	>10
Add this number to higher sound level	3	2	1	0

For example, 90 dB + 20 dB = 90 dB; 60 dB + 60 dB = 63 dB.

The amplitude of sound waves is measured in decibels (dB). The decibel scale is a logarithmic scale based on the logarithm of the ratio of a sound pressure to a reference sound pressure (the threshold of audibility). The values of a logarithmic scale, such as the decibel levels of two noise sources, cannot be added directly. Instead, use the simplified method described in the table entitled "Decibels."

FREQUENCY

The frequency of sound waves is measured in Hertz (Hz; also known as cycles per second) and grouped into octaves (an octave band is labeled by its geometric center frequency). An octave band covers the range from one frequency (Hz) to twice that frequency (f to 2f). The range of human hearing covers the frequencies from 20 to 16,000 Hz. Human hearing is most acute in the 1,000- to 4,000-Hz octave bands.

The human ear discriminates against low frequencies in a manner matched by the A-weighting filter of a sound-level meter, measured in dBA, or A-weighted decibels. This is the most universally accepted single-number rating for human response to sound.

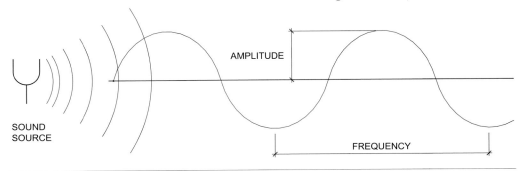

SOUND AND FREQUENCY

TYPICAL SOUND LEVELS

SOUND LEVEL (DBA)	SUBJECTIVE EVALUATIONS	ENVIRONMENT	
		OUTDOOR	INDOOR
140	Deafening	Near jet engine and artillery fire	—
130	Threshold of pain	Jet aircraft departure (within 500 ft (152 m)	—
120	Threshold of feeling	Elevated train	Hard-rock band
110		Jet flyover at 1,000 ft (305 m)	Inside propeller plane
100	Very loud	Power mower, motorcycle at 25 ft, auto horn at 10 ft	Crowd noise in arena
90		Propeller plane flyover at 1,000 ft, noisy urban street	Full symphony or band, food blender, noisy factory
80	Moderately loud	Diesel truck at 40 mph (18 m/s) at 50 ft (15 m)	Inside auto at high speed, garbage, disposal, dishwasher
70	Loud	Heavy urban traffic	Face-to-face conversation, vacuum cleaner, electric typewriter
60	Moderate	Air-conditioning condenser at 15 ft (4.5 m), near freeway auto traffic	General office
50	Quiet	Large transformer at 100 ft (30 m)	Large public lobby, atrium
40		Bird calls	Private office, soft radio music in apartment
30	Very quiet	Quiet residential neighborhood	Bedroom, average residence without stereo
20		Rustling leaves	Quiet theater, whisper
10	Just audible	Still night in rural area	Recording studio
0	Threshold of hearing	—	—

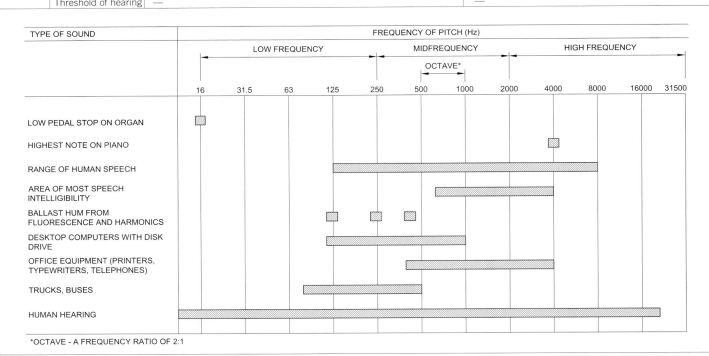

FREQUENCY OF COMMON SOUNDS

SOUND ABSORPTION PROPERTIES OF MATERIALS

All materials and surfaces absorb some sound greater than 0% and less than 100%. The percentage of incident sound energy that is absorbed by a material, divided by 100, equals the coefficient of absorption, designated α, which ranges from 0 to .99. The coefficient varies as a function of frequency, Hz.

Any material can be tested in a proper laboratory to determine its α values, as per ASTM C423, *Standard Test Method for Sound Absorption and Sound Absorption Coefficients by the Reverberation Room Method*. Some tests give values greater than 1.0, but this is an anomaly caused by the testing procedure; such values should be corrected to be not more than 1.0, since no material can absorb more than 100% of the incident energy that strikes its surface.

Sound Energy Absorption Mechanisms

There are three mechanisms by which sound energy is absorbed or dissipated as it strikes a surface. In all cases, sound energy is converted to heat, although never enough heat to be felt.

- *Porous absorption* entails the use of soft, porous, "fuzzy" materials such as glass fiber, mineral wool, and carpet. The pressure fluctuations of a sound wave in air cause the fibers of such materials to move, and the friction of the fibers dissipates the sound energy.
- *Panel absorption* involves installation of thin lightweight panels such as gypsum board, glass, and plywood. Sound waves cause panels to vibrate. Sound absorption for a panel is greatest at its natural or resonant frequency.
- *Cavity absorption* entails the movement of air pressure fluctuations across the narrow neck of an enclosed air cavity, such as the space behind a perforated panel or a slotted concrete masonry unit, also called a Helmholtz resonator. Friction of the resonating air molecules against the wall of the neck converts sound energy to heat. If there is also insulation within the cavity, additional energy is extracted via the porous absorption mechanism.

Sound Absorption Average (SAA)

The method for determining the sound absorption average (SAA) is defined by ASTM C423. *Pink noise* is generated by a computer-controlled sound system and

FREQUENCY

RANGE OF OCTAVE (HZ)	OCTAVE BAND CENTER FREQUENCY (HZ)
22-44	31.5
44-88	63
88-175	125
175-350	250
350-700	500
700-1,400	1,000
1,400-2,800	2,000
2,800-5,600	4,000
5,600-11,200	8,000

TYPICAL VALUES FOR POROUS ABSORPTION

it is emitted from two loudspeakers in the receiving room. While the sound is triggered on and off, 50 decay rates (from 80 to 500 Hz) are measured with (referred to as *full room*) and without (referred to as *empty room*) the test specimen installed in the chamber. The decay rate data is used to calculate the empty and full room absorption. The empty and full room absorption is used to calculate the SAA rating.

Noise Reduction Coefficient (NRC)

Noise reduction coefficient (NRC) is obsolete; however, references to these values may continue to be made. Usually, the numerical value of NRC is almost the same as that for SAA.

SUBJECTIVE REACTIONS TO CHANGE IN SOUND LEVEL

CHANGE IN SOUND LEVEL*	CHANGE IN APPARENT LOUDNESS
1 to 2	Imperceptible
3	Barely perceptible
5 or 6	Clearly noticeable
10	Significant change—twice as loud (or half as loud)
20	Dramatic change—four times as loud (or a quarter as loud)

Measured in decibels (plus or minus)

TYPICAL VALUES FOR PANEL ABSORPTION

Sound-Absorbing Coefficients

The sound-absorbing coefficients for a given material may vary depending on the thickness of the material, how it is supported or mounted, the depth of the air space behind the material, and the facing in front of the material. In general, thicker, porous materials absorb more sound. The air space behind a material will increase the absorption efficiency, especially at low frequencies. Thin facings degrade high-frequency absorption.

Mounting Assemblies

For consistency in comparing test results, standards have been set for the mounting assembly used in testing absorbent materials. These mounting conditions should be reported along with test data so that the data accurately reflect field conditions.

SOUND-ABSORBING COEFFICIENTS FOR VARIOUS MATERIALS

TYPICAL DATA/MATERIAL	125 Hz	250 Hz	500 Hz	1,000 Hz	2,000 Hz	40,000 Hz	NRC
Marble	.01	.01	.01	.01	.02	.02	.00
Gypsum board, ½ in.	.29	.10	.05	.04	.07	.09	.05
Wood, 1 in. thick, with air space behind	.19	.14	.09	.06	.06	.05	.10
Heavy carpet on concrete	.02	.06	.14	.37	.60	.65	.30
Acoustical tile, surface-mounted	.34	.28	.45	.66	.74	.77	.55
Acoustical tile, suspended	.43	.38	.53	.77	.87	.77	.65
Acoustical tile, painted (est.)	.35	.35	.45	.50	.50	.45	.45
Audience area: empty, hard seats	.15	.19	.22	.39	.38	.30	.30
Audience area: occupied, upholstered seats	.39	.57	.80	.94	.92	.87	.80
Glass fiber, 1 in.	.04	.21	.73	.99	.99	.90	.75
Glass fiber, 4 in.	.77	.99	.99	.99	.99	.99	.95
Thin fabric, stretched tight to wall	.03	.04	.11	.17	.24	.35	.15
Thick fabric, bunched 4 in. from wall	.14	.35	.55	.72	.70	.65	.60

Note: This table gives representative absorption coefficients at various frequencies for some typical materials. To determine values not provided here, refer to manufacturer's data or extrapolate from similar constructions. All materials have some absorption values that can be determined from proper test reports.

ROOM ACOUSTICS

The total sound-absorbing units (a) provided by a given material are a function of the absorptive properties (α) and surface area (S) of that material, as defined by the formula:

$$a = S\,\alpha$$

where a = sabins (units of sound absorption), S = surface area (measured in sq m or sq ft), and α = the coefficient of absorption.

The total sabins in a room can be determined by adding together the sabins of all the surfaces, which vary as a function of frequency. Since most materials absorb more high-frequency sound waves than low-frequency ones, it is typical to find more sabins in a room at high frequencies than at low frequencies.

In general, sound energy that is not absorbed will be reflected; thus, surfaces with low coefficients of absorption can be used to encourage sound reflection when appropriate.

PROPERTIES OF SOUND

Distance and time comprise the two properties of sound. Outdoors, sound drops off 6 dB each time the distance from a source is doubled (Inverse Square Law). Indoors, the reflecting sound energy in a room reaches a constant level as a function of the sound-absorbing units (sabins) in the room.

Outdoors, sound ceases when the source stops. Indoors, sound energy lingers; this decay is called *reverberation*. The reverberation time (RT) is defined as the length of time, in seconds, it takes for sound to decay by 60 dB. Reverberation time is directly proportional to the volume of a space and inversely proportional to the units of absorption (sabins) in it, as expressed in this formula:

$$RT = KV/a$$

where RT = reverberation time in seconds, K = .161 (if volume is in m^3) or .049 (if volume is in cu ft), V = volume in m^3 or cu ft, and a = total absorption in sabins (metric or English units).

Shorter reverberation times greatly enhance speech intelligibility and are imperative in listening environments for people with hearing impairments and for rooms with live microphones for teleconferencing.

USE OF SOUND-ABSORPTIVE MATERIALS

Sound-absorptive materials (such as acoustic tile, glass fiber, wall panels, carpet, curtains, etc.) can be added to a room in order to control or reduce noise levels or shorten reverberation time. Noise control is especially helpful when the noise sources are distributed around a room, as in a gymnasium, classroom, or cafeteria.

While sound-absorptive materials can be added to any surface in a room, the greatest area available for coverage is usually the ceiling. Because many soft, porous materials are fragile, they should not be located on surfaces that are susceptible to abuse. For these reasons, sound-absorptive materials are often installed on ceilings. However, it is well known that limiting absorption to one surface or to two parallel surfaces may not effect as great a change as calculated, since an assumption of the reverberation and noise reduction formulas is that the absorption is rather evenly distributed among the surfaces of the space.

GUIDELINES FOR USE OF SOUND ABSORPTION

ROOM TYPE	TREATMENT
Classrooms, corridors and lobbies, patient rooms, laboratories, shops, factories, libraries, private and open-plan offices, restaurants	Ceiling or equivalent area; add additional wall treatment if room is quite high
Boardrooms, teleconferencing rooms, gymnasiums, arenas, recreational spaces and meeting and conference rooms	Ceiling or equivalent; add wall treatments for further noise reduction and reverberation control and to eliminate flutter or echo
Auditoriums, churches, etc.	Special considerations and complex applications

Average Coefficient of Absorption

One measure of the quality of sound in a room is the average coefficient of absorption (or average noise reduction coefficient—NRC) for all surfaces combined, as determined by this formula:

$$à = a/S$$

where à = the average coefficient (at a given frequency or average NRC), a = the total sabins (sound-absorbing units), and S = the total surface area in the room (metric or English units; be consistent).

As determined by using the average coefficient of absorption, the quality of sound in a room can be evaluated as .1, .2, or .3. A room with an average coefficient of .1 is rather "live," loud, and uncomfortably noisy; one with an average coefficient of .2 is comfortable, with well-controlled noise; and one with .3 is rather "dead," suitable for spaces in which the emphasis will be on amplified sound, electronic playback, or a live microphone for teleconferencing.

INDOORS
Indoors, sound waves reflect off surrounding surfaces, building up energy so sound drops off less quickly over distance or time.

SOUND PATTERNS

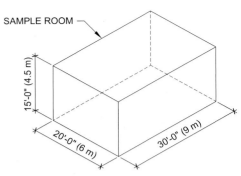

SAMPLE ROOM
Volume of sample room is 9,000 cu ft (255 cu m).

SAMPLE CALCULATION 1

SURFACE	MATERIAL	AREA	ALPHA	A
Floor	Carpet	600 sq ft (55 sq m)	.37	222
Ceiling	Gypsum board	600 sq ft (55 sq m)	.01	6
All four walls	Gypsum board	1,500 sq ft (139 sq m)	.01	15
Total	—	2,700 sq ft (250 sq m)	—	243

The reverberation time for the sample room with a gypsum board ceiling is calculated as follows:

$$RT = .049\ V/a = .049 \times 9{,}000\ \text{cu ft}/243 = 1.8\ \text{sec}$$

SAMPLE CALCULATION 2

SURFACE	MATERIAL	AREA	ALPHA	A
Floor	Carpet	600 sq ft	.37	222
Ceiling	Acoustical tile	600 sq ft	.77	462
All four walls	Gypsum board	1,500 sq ft	.01	15
Total	—	2,700 sq ft	—	699

The reverberation time for the sample room with an acoustical tile ceiling is calculated as follows:

$$RT = .049V/a = .049 \times 9{,}000\ \text{cu ft}/699 = .63\ \text{sec}$$

The average coefficient of absorption (α) in the sample room changes significantly from sample 1 to sample 2. The room with a gypsum board ceiling is rather live and noisy, while the room with an acoustical tile ceiling is comfortable, with well-controlled noise. The calculations that show this follow.

Before: $\alpha = a/S = 243/2{,}700 = .09$

After: $\alpha = a/S = 699/2{,}700 = .26$

CALCULATION OF AVERAGE COEFFICIENT OF ABSORPTION (SAMPLE AT 1,000 Hz)

OUTDOORS
Outdoors, sound waves expand spherically, becoming more dispersed, that is, quieter, over distance and time.

TRANSMISSION LOSS PROPERTIES OF MATERIALS

The property of a material or construction system that blocks the transfer of sound energy from one side to another is transmission loss (TL), which is measured in decibels (dB). Specifically, TL is the attenuation of airborne sound transmission through a construction during laboratory testing, according to ASTM E90, *Method for Laboratory Measurements of Airborne-Sound Transmission Loss of Building Partitions*. Transmission loss values range from 0 to 70 or 80 (or higher). A high TL value indicates a better capability to block sound; that is, more sound energy is "lost" as the sound wave travels through the material.

Sound transmission class (STC) is a single-number rating system designed to combine TL values from many frequencies. STC values for site-built construction range from 10 (practically no isolation; e.g., an open doorway) to 65 or 70 (such high performance is only achieved with special construction techniques). Average construction might provide noise reduction in the range of STC 30 to 60.

It is very difficult to measure the STC performance of a single wall or door in the field because of the number of flanking paths and nonstandard conditions. Field performance is measured with Apparent Sound Transmission Class (ASTC) ratings, which cover effects from all sound transfer paths between rooms. ASTC ratings, previously referred to as the Noise Isolation Class (NIC), is derived by using the STC procedure (ASTM E413, *Standard Classification for Determining Sound Transmission Class*) to rate the uncorrected sound-level difference spectrum without correction or normalization factors.

Derivation and Use of the STC Curve

To determine the STC rating for a particular construction, the STC curve shown in the accompanying figure is applied over the transmission loss (TL) curve for a laboratory test of the construction. The STC curve is then manipulated in accordance with prescribed rules to obtain the highest possible rating. The procedure states that the TL curve cannot be more than 8 dB less than the STC curve in any one-third octave band, nor can the TL curve be more than a total of 32 dB less than the STC curve (average of 2 dB for each of 16 one-third octave band frequencies). Any values from the TL curve that are above the STC curve are of no benefit in the rating. The object is to move the STC curve up as high as possible and to read the STC rating number from the point at which the STC curve at 500 Hz crosses the TL curve.

The STC curve has three segments: the first segment, from 125 to 400 Hz, rises at the rate of 9 dB per octave (3 dB per one-third octave); the second segment, from 400 to 1,250 Hz, rises at the rate of 2 dB per octave (1 dB per one-third octave); and the third segment, from 1,250 to 4,000 Hz, is flat.

Transmission Loss

Design of construction and materials for high transmission loss builds on three principles:

- *Mass:* Lightweight materials do not block sound. Sound transmission through walls, floors, and ceilings varies with the frequency of sound, the weight (or mass) and stiffness of the construction, and cavity absorption. Theoretically, the transmission loss increases at the rate of 6 dB per doubling of the surface weight of the construction. A single solid panel behaves less well than the mass law would predict, since the mass law assumes a homogeneous, infinitely resilient material/wall.
- *Separation:* Improved TL performance without an undue increase in mass can be achieved by separation of materials. A true double wall with separate unconnected elements performs better than the mass law predicts for a single wall of the same weight. The transmission loss tends to increase about 5 dB for each doubling of the airspace

If two layers of dense material are separated by an airspace (rather than being continuous), they create two independent walls. The improvement in transmission loss depends on the size of the airspace and the frequency of sound. Avoid rigid ties between layers in all double wall construction. The accompanying graph indicates the approximate improvement in TL when a wall of a given weight is split into two separate walls.

BENEFIT OF AIRSPACE IN IMPROVING TRANSMISSION LOSS (TL)

between wythes (minimum effective space is approximately 2 in.). Resilient attachment of surface skins to studs or structural surfaces provides a similar benefit, as do separate wythes.
- *Absorption:* Use of soft, resilient, absorptive materials in the cavity between wythes, particularly for lightweight staggered or double stud construction, increases transmission loss significantly. Viscoelastic (somewhat resilient but not fully elastic) materials, such as certain insulation boards, dampen or restrict the vibration of rigid panels such as gypsum board and plywood, increasing transmission loss somewhat. Follow manufacturer-recommended installation details.

NOISE REDUCTION

Noise reduction (NR) depends on the properties of a room and is the actual difference in sound pressure level between two spaces. It is the amount of sound blocked by all intervening sound paths between rooms, including the common wall, but also the floor, ceiling, outside path, doors, and so on.

Noise reduction also depends on the relative size of a room. If the noise source is in a small room next to a large receiving room (e.g., an office next to a gymnasium), the noise reduction will be greater than the TL performance of the wall alone because the sound radiating from the common wall between office and gym will be dissipated in such a large space. On the other hand, if the noise source is in a large room next to a small one (as from a gym to an office next door), the noise reduction will be far less than the TL of the wall alone because the common wall, which radiates sound, is such a large part of the surface of the smaller room. An adjustment for this ratio, plus the contribution of the absorptive finishes in the receiving room, enters into the calculation of actual noise reduction between adjacent spaces.

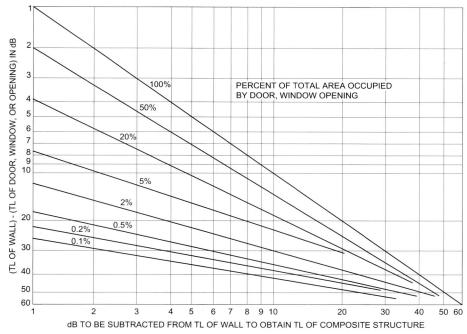

When a wall or surface of a room is made up of two or more different structures (e.g., a window in an outside wall or a door in an office), the TL performance (or STC) of the composite construction should be evaluated by combining the TL (or STC) values of the components, in accordance with the accompanying chart. Note that small gaps and cracks such as the perimeter of an ungasketed door can dramatically degrade the performance of a high TL construction.

GRAPHIC TECHNIQUE TO DETERMINE COMPOSITE TRANSMISSION LOSS (COMBINING TWO DIFFERENT CONSTRUCTION ELEMENTS)

SOUND ISOLATION AND NOISE REDUCTION

One of the most common goals in the design of sound isolation construction is achievement of acoustical privacy from a neighbor. This privacy is a function of whether the signal from the neighbor is audible and intelligible above the ordinary background noise level in the environment.

Privacy index = noise reduction + background noise

Noise reduction is measured as a field performance, where it is evaluated and given an STC value.

Normal privacy, in which you are aware of a neighbor's activity but not overly distracted by it, can usually be achieved with a privacy index of 68 or higher. Confidential privacy, in which you are unaware of the neighbor, usually requires a privacy index of 75 or higher.

A quiet environment with little or no natural background sound (from HVAC systems) between neighbors requires a higher degree of sound-separation construction to achieve the same privacy as that in a noisier environment with louder background sound.

IMPACT NOISE RATING

Floors are subject to impact or structure-borne sound transmission noises such as footfalls, dropped objects, and scraping furniture. Parallel to development of laboratory sound transmission class (STC) ratings for partition constructions is the development of an impact insulation class (IIC). This is a single-number rating system used to evaluate the effectiveness of floor construction in preventing impact sound transmission to spaces beneath the floor. The current IIC rating method is similar to the STC rating.

Testing for IIC ratings is a complex procedure using a standard tapping machine. Because the machine is portable, it cannot simulate the weight of a person walking across a floor; therefore, the creak or boom that footsteps cause in a timber floor cannot be reflected in the single-figure impact rating produced from the tapping machine. The correlation between tapping machine tests in the laboratory and field performance of floors under typical conditions may vary greatly, depending on the construction of the floor and the nature of the impact.

Impact Noise Reduction Design

Often the greatest annoyance caused by footfall noise is the low-frequency sound energy it generates, which is beyond the frequency range of standardized tests. Sometimes this sound energy is near or at the resonant frequency of the building structure. Whenever possible, to stifle unwanted sounds, use carpet with padding on floors in residential buildings, and resilient, suspended ceilings with cavity insulation. For especially critical situations, such as pedestrian bridges or tunnels, hire an acoustical consultant.

Slamming doors or cabinet drawers are other sources of impact noise. If possible, bureaus should not be placed directly against a wall. Door closers or stops can be added to cushion the impact of energy from a door so it is not imparted directly into the structure. Common-sense arrangements can help minimize problems in multifamily dwellings. For example, kitchen cabinets should not be placed on the other side of a common wall from a neighbor's bedroom.

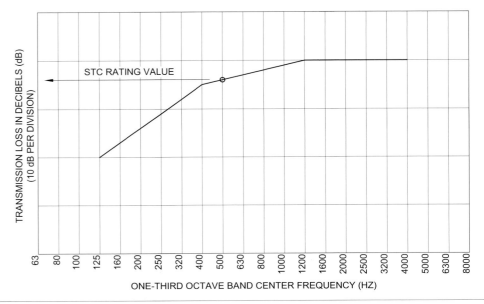

SOUND TRANSMISSION CLASS (STC) RATING CURVE

DOUBLE STUD WALL

DOUBLE WALL—CMU AND STUD

FLOOR/CEILING CONSTRUCTION—CONCRETE

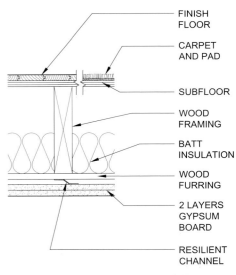

FLOOR/CEILING CONSTRUCTION—WOOD

TYPICAL HIGH SOUND ISOLATION CONSTRUCTION

MECHANICAL SYSTEM NOISE AND VIBRATION CONTROL

Mechanical system noise, as a major component of acoustics in modern buildings, must be addressed in developing mechanical design and acoustical goals.

Room Criterion (RC) Rating

Background sound levels from mechanical systems are measured and evaluated by means of Room Criteria (RC) ratings, as well as by actual A-weighted decibel levels. Though the widely used (since 1957) Noise Criterion (NC) rating method for HVAC systems was discontinued by ASHRAE in 1995, NC ratings continue to be referenced. Like NC, RC uses the octave band spectrum of air conditioning sound as the basis for the assessment. Instead of finding the point of tangency to a family of curves, the numeric RC rating is the integer average (arithmetic mean) of the sound levels at 500, 1,000, and 2,000 Hz.

This number corresponds to the Preferred Speech Interference Level, which is a good guide to the interfering or masking effect of the noise on speech communication. The numeric values of the RC ratings correspond closely to the earlier NC ratings, in the sense that if a value of 30 to 35 is recommended for a particular occupancy, then that would be the acceptable range for either the NC or the RC rating of the noise. RC incorporates an additional quality or designator, which characterizes the calculated or measured noise spectrum as *rumbly* (R), *neutral* (N), or *hissy* (H). This is found by first plotting a sloped line (which drops at a rate of 5 dB per octave) through the RC value of the curve.

If any of the low-frequency portion (31.5 to 250 Hz) exceeds this line by 5 dB, the sound is termed rumbly, and (R) is added to the RC rating. If the high-fre-quency portion of the curve (1,000 to 4,000 Hz) exceeds this line by 3 dB, it sounds hissy, and (H) is added to the RC rating. Otherwise, the sound is judged to be bland or neutral, and (N) is added.

The RC rating consists of three parts:

- The average of three sound levels, as in RC.
- The calculation of the perceived character, or Quality Assessment Index (QAI), of the sound (now extended to include LF for low-frequency rumble, MF for midfrequency roar, and HF for high-frequency hiss). Two other characterizations are added if sound-level information is available down to 16 Hz: LFB, indicating moderate but perceptible sound-induced wall/ceiling vibration, and LFA, indicating a noticeable degree of sound-induced wall/ceiling vibration.
- A subjective occupant satisfaction estimate based on the QAI value and its frequency characteristic. This can result in *acceptable*, *marginal*, or *objectionable* degrees of satisfaction with the sound of the noise spectrum.

Mechanical System Noise Sources

Mechanical equipment creates noise and vibration from the rotary or reciprocating motion of its moving parts, and their effect on air or a working fluid. Four aspects of the noise and vibration to be addressed are *machine noise*, *fan noise*, *air noise*, and *vibration noise*.

Machine Noise

Sound isolation requirements for the walls and floors of a mechanical equipment room depend on the type of equipment to be housed and the sensitivity of adjacent spaces. Chillers can be extremely loud, requiring double walls and extra-thick floor slabs. Air-handling units may only require regular wall construction, perhaps STC 50 systems. Major secondary sound paths are duct penetrations, open curbs under rooftop units, and doors; all potential sound paths must be controlled.

Fan Noise

Rotation of the fan motor and the fan itself generates noise, which is transmitted along the duct path (both supply and return) to the listening space. Typical fan noise control elements include package silencers (inserted into a straight run of duct, often at the wall of the mechanical equipment room) and internal acoustical duct lining (glass fibers adhered to the duct walls). The degree of fan noise attenuation can be determined by calculations based on the size and sound power levels of the fan, the length and configuration of duct runs, the attenuation of the duct systems, the number and type of diffusers, and the room finishes in the listening space.

Air Noise

Movement of air through a duct generates turbulence, which creates noise. For sensitive spaces and quiet noise levels, the airflow must be at low velocity (hence the need for large ducts) with smooth inlet and outflow conditions. For extremely quiet noise levels, air velocities at diffusers or terminal devices may need to be below 400 fpm (2 m/s). Volume dampers to control flow for such spaces are critical; keep dampers 10 ft (3 m) from diffusers, and avoid opposed blade dampers at diffusers. A simple duct layout that provides even distribution of air to all diffusers in a room can eliminate many problems. Round and square ducts are best for decreasing noise created by moving air and turbulence. As rectangular ductwork is flattened out to save headroom (and the aspect ratio of width to height increases) ductwork is increasingly prone to vibrate and create rumble. This can be difficult, expensive, or impossible to fix.

SOUND ISOLATION CRITERIA

SOURCE ROOM OCCUPANCY	RECEIVER ROOM ADJACENT	SOUND ISOLATION REQUIREMENT (MIN.) FOR ALL PATHS BETWEEN SOURCE AND RECEIVER
Executive areas, doctors' suites, personnel offices, large conference rooms: confidential privacy requirements	Adjacent offices and related spaces	STC 50-55
Normal offices, regular conference rooms for group meetings: normal privacy requirements	Adjacent offices and similar activities	STC 45-50
Large general business offices, drafting areas, banking floors	Corridors, lobbies, data processing; similar activities	STC 40-45
Shop and laboratory offices in manufacturing laboratory test areas: normal privacy	Adjacent offices: test areas, corridors	STC 40-45
Mechanical equipment rooms	Any spaces	STC 50-60+[1]
Multifamily dwellings	Neighbors (separate occupancy)	
Bedrooms	Bedrooms	STC 48-55[2]
	Bathrooms	STC 52-58[2]
	Kitchens	STC 58-58[2]
	Living rooms	STC 52-57[2]
	Corridors	STC 52-58[2]
	Living rooms	STC 48-55[2]
Living Rooms	Bathrooms	STC 50-57[2]
	Kitchens	STC 48-50[2]
School buildings	Adjacent classrooms	STC 50
Classrooms	Laboratories	STC 50
Large music or drama area	Corridors	STC 45
Music practice rooms	Adjacent music or drama area	STC 60[3]
	Music practice rooms	STC 55[3]
Interior occupied spaces	Exterior of building	STC 35-60[4]
Theaters, concert halls, lecture halls, radio and TV studios	Any and all adjacent	Use qualified acoustical consultants to assist in the design of these critical occupancies

[1] Use acoustical consultants when designing mechanical equipment rooms to house equipment other than that used for air handling (e.g., chillers, pumps, and compressors) and heavy manufacturing areas that house equipment that generates noise at or above OSHA-allowable levels or generates high-vibration levels.

[2] Ratings depend on nighttime, exterior background levels and other factors directly related to the location of a building. Grades I, II, and III are discussed in "Guide to Airborne, Impact, and Structure-borne Noise Control in Multifamily Dwellings," HUD TS-24 (1974).

[3] The STC ratings shown are guidelines only. These spaces typically require double-layer con-struction with resilient connections between layers or, preferably, structurally independent "room-within-a-room" construction. The level of continuous background noise, such as that provided by the HVAC system or an electronic masking system, has a significant impact on the quality of construction selected and must be coordinated with the other design parameters.

[4] Ratings depend on the nature of the exterior background noise—its level, spectrum shape, and constancy—as well as thermal considerations and the client's budget. Use qualified acoustical consultants for analysis of high noise outdoor environments such as airports, highways (especially those with heavy truck traffic), and industrial facilities.

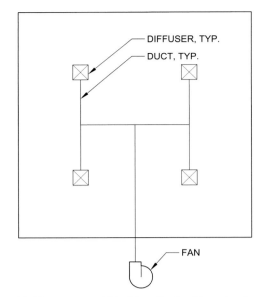

All diffusers are equidistant from the fan. The system is self-balancing. The duct layout does not need volume dampers.

PREFERRED DUCT LAYOUT

VIBRATION NOISE

Rotating equipment generates vibration, which can travel through a structure and be radiated as noise in a distant location. Vibration isolation may entail use of neoprene pads, spring isolators, or inertia bases, depending on the size and power of the rotating equipment, the proximity of sensitive spaces, and the stiffness of the supporting structure. Piping attached to rotating equipment, especially chilled water piping, must also be isolated from the structure to prevent transmission of sound energy. The effectiveness of a vibration isolator depends on the static deflection of the isolator under load. Lower-frequency mechanical equipment rotation requires greater static deflection isolation to be effective. Pneumatic isolators, sometimes termed *air bags*, offer good vibration isolation with relatively little deflection and optional automatic leveling. These require a source of compressed air and control pneumatics. Optical isolation tables employ this methodology to assure extremely stable platforms.

IMPACT DESIGN CRITERIA

STANDARD	PURPOSE
ASTM E492: *Standard Test Method for Laboratory Measurement of Impact Sound Transmission through Floor-Ceiling Assemblies Using the Tapping Machine*	For lab tests of the impact sound levels in the receiving room
ASTM E1007: *Standard Test Method for Field Measurement of Tapping Machine Impact Sound Transmission through Floor-Ceiling Assemblies and Associated Support Structures*	For field tests of the impact sound levels in the receiving room
ASTM E989: *Standard Classification for Determination of Impact Insulation Class*	To determine Impact Insulation Class

Jim Johnson; Wrightson, Johnson, Haddon & Williams, Inc.; Dallas, Texas
Doug Sturz; Acentech, Inc.; Cambridge, Massachusetts
Carl Rosenberg, AIA; Acentech, Inc.; Cambridge, Massachusetts

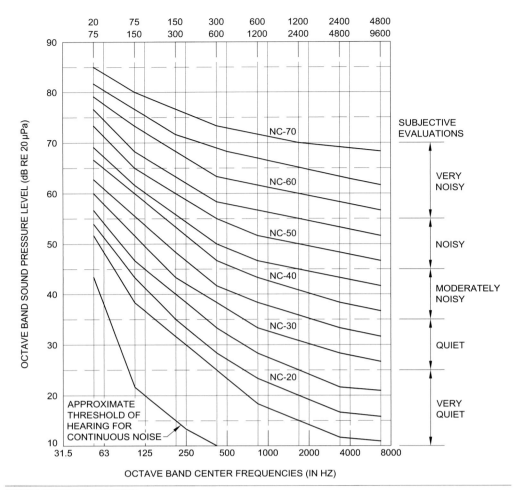

NOISE CRITERIA CURVES

NOISE CRITERIA SOUND PRESSURE LEVEL TABLE*

NC CURVE	SOUND PRESSURE LEVEL (DB)							
	63 Hz	125 Hz	250 Hz	500 Hz	1,000 Hz	2,000 Hz	4,000 Hz	8,000 Hz
NC-70	83	79	75	72	71	70	69	68
NC-65	80	75	71	68	66	64	63	62
NC-60	77	71	67	63	61	59	58	57
NC-55	74	67	62	58	56	54	53	52
NC-50	71	64	58	54	51	49	48	47
NC-45	67	60	54	49	46	44	43	42
NC-40	64	57	50	45	41	39	38	37
NC-35	60	52	45	40	36	34	33	32
NC-30	57	48	41	36	31	29	28	27
NC-25	54	44	37	31	27	24	22	21
NC-20	50	41	33	26	22	19	17	16
NC-15	47	36	29	22	17	14	12	11

For convenience in using noise criteria data, the table lists the sound pressure level (SPL) in decibels for each NC curve.

RECOMMENDED BACKGROUND NOISE CRITERIA FOR TYPICAL OCCUPANCIES

TYPE OF SPACE	USES	NC RATING RANGE	A-WEIGHTED DECIBELS
Sensitive listening spaces	Broadcast and recording studios, concert halls	NC-15 to NC-20	25 dBA
Performance spaces	Theaters, churches (no amplification), video and teleconferencing (live microphone)	NC-20 to NC-25	30 dBA
General presentation spaces	Large conference rooms, small auditoriums, orchestral rehearsal rooms, movie theaters, courtrooms, meeting and banquet rooms, executive offices	NC-25 to NC-30	35 dBA
Quiet areas	Offices, small conference rooms, classrooms, private residences, hospitals, hotels, libraries	NC-30 to NC-35	40 dBA
Public spaces	Restaurants, lobbies, open-plan offices and clinics	NC-35 to NC-40	45 dBA
Service and support spaces	Computer equipment rooms public circulation areas, arenas, convention floors	NC-40 to NC-45	50 dBA

INTERIOR LIGHTING

FUNCTIONS OF LIGHTING

Light is one of many tools available to design a space. Considering the basic functions of lighting at the beginning of a project can help ensure the desired design effect:

- *Performance of tasks:* Lighting to perform work, whether it is reading, assembling parts, or seeing a blackboard, is referred to as task lighting. Visual work is a primary functional reason for providing lighting.
- *Enhancement of space and structure:* It is only through the presence of light that spatial volume, planes, ornament, and color are revealed. For centuries, structural systems evolved partly in response to aesthetic as well as functional desires for light of a certain quality. The progress from bearing wall to curtain wall was driven by the push of newly discovered technologies (both in materials and in technique), by evolving cultural desires for certain spatial characteristics, and by a desire to admit light of a particular quality. These developments are reflected in the Gothic church window, the baroque oculus, and the Bauhaus wall of glass. With the advent of electric lighting systems, this connection of structure to light was no longer entirely necessary, but most architects continue to pay homage to this historical tie.
- *Focusing attention:* The quality of light in a space profoundly affects people's perception of that space. The timing and the direction of an individual's gaze are often a function of the varying quality and distribution of light through the space. Lighting draws attention to points of interest and helps guide the user of a space.
- *Provision of safety and security:* Lighting can enhance visibility and thereby engender a sense of security. Lighting can also be used to illuminate hazards, such as a changing floor plane or moving objects.

ILLUMINANCE

Most lighting standards discuss the quantity of light in terms of incident light or light that falls onto a surface. This light, called *illuminance*, is measured in footcandles (fc) or lux. Although convenient to calculate, illuminance is not, of course, what actually enters our eyes.

Light that reaches our eyes is usually reflected either off the details of the task (typed letters), the immediate background (e.g., paper), and the surround (e.g., desktop and room). Important exceptions are electronic visual displays using cathode ray tubes (CRTs) and light-emitting diodes (LEDs), which emit their own light. In these visual tasks, light reflected off their surfaces generally reduces their legibility, and much attention needs to be given to the lighting of the surround.

LIGHT SOURCE SELECTION

When selecting a light source, the designer should consider several important issues including *color, size, efficiency, life,* and *maintenance.*

Color

Each lamp family has its own inherent color characteristics. The different light sources render color qualities differently and create varying perceived color effects (see color plate C-11).

Size

It is useful to think of sources and source/fixture combinations classified into *point, line,* or *area sources.* Point sources—for example, bare incandescent lamps, recessed incandescent, or high-intensity discharge (HID) fixtures with small apertures and specular reflectors—can be precisely controlled in terms of where light is and is not and can provide sparkle in a space by means of reflections off polished room surfaces. Line sources—bare fluorescent tubes and linear fluorescent fixtures—can be controlled in their transverse axis of output, but not longitudinally. This makes them useful for lighting large open areas where repetitive rows of fixtures are suitable. Area sources—for example, a window—are arrays of line sources covered by a diffusing element. These sources usually provide medium to high levels of light with little directional control.

Efficiency

A source's inherent efficiency can be crucial to its acceptability for energy conservation. Some sources such as incandescent and tungsten halogen possess desirable color, size, and cost advantages, but are relatively inefficient. Most high-intensity discharge sources are very efficient but might require sacrifices of other attributes.

ILLUMINANCE VALUES FOR VARIOUS INDOOR ACTIVITIES

| TYPES OF ACTIVITY | ILLUMINANCE CATEGORY | RANGES OF ILLUMINACE | | REFERENCE WORK PLANE |
		LUX	FOOTCANDLES	
Public spaces with dark surroundings	A	20-30-50	2-3-5	General lighting throughout spaces
Simple orientation for short, temporary visits	B	50-75-100	5-7,5-10	
Working spaces used only occasionally for visual tasks	C	100-150-200	10-15-20	
Performance of visual tasks of high contrast or large size	D	200-300-500	20-30-50	Illuminance on task
Performance of visual tasks of medium contrast or small size	E	500-750-1,000	50-75-100	
Performance of visual tasks of low contrast or small size	F	1,000-1,500-2,000	100-150-200	
Performance of visual tasks of low contrast and very small size over a prolonged period	G	2,000-3,000-5,000	200-300-500	Illuminance on task, provided by a combination of general and local (supplementary) lighting
Performance of very prolonged and exacting visual tasks	H	5,000-7,500-10,000	500-750-1,000	
Performance of very special visual tasks of extremely low contrast and small size	I	10,000-15,000-20,000	1,000-1,500-2,000	

Note: Standards for lighting and illumination in North America are established by the Illumination Engineering Society of North America (IESNA). These recommendations are summarized in the IESNA Lighting Handbook, *8th edition, from which this table is taken.*

LIGHT SOURCE SELECTION GUIDE

	APPLICATION
LAMP CCT[1] (KELVINS OR K)	
<2500	Bulk industrial and security (HPS) lighting
2,700–3,000	Low light levels in most spaces (<10FC); general residential lighting; hotels, fine dining and family restaurants, theme parks
2,950–3,200	Display lighting for retail and galleries; feature lighting
3,500–4,100	General lighting in offices, schools, stores, industry, medicine; display lighting; sports lighting
4,100–5,000	Special application lighting when color discrimination is very important; not commonly used for general lighting
5,000–7,500	Special application lighting when color discrimination is critical; uncommon for general lighting
MINIMUM LAMP CRI[2]	
<50	Noncritical industrial, storage, and security lighting
50–70	Industrial and general illumination when color is of minor important
70–79	Most office, retail, school, medical, and other work and recreational spaces
80–89	Retail, work, and residential spaces when color quality is important
90–100	Retail and work spaces when color rendering is critical

[1]*CCT: correlated color temperature*
[2]*CRI: color rendering index*

LIGHT SOURCE COMPARISON

LIGHT SOURCE CHARACTERISTICS	INCANDESCENT	TUNGSTEN HALOGEN	FLUORESCENT	COMPACT FLUORESCENT	NEON/ COLD CATHODE	DELUXE MERCURY	METAL HALIDE	HIGH-PRESSURE SODIUM	WHITE SODIUM	CERAMIC METAL HALIDE	LOW VOLTAGE HALOGEN
Ballast/transformer	No	No	Yes	Yes	Yes	Yes	Yes	Yes	Yes	Yes	Yes
Operating position Restrictions	None to few	None to few	None	None to few	None	None	Some	None	None	None to some	None
Color rendition	Very good	Good to very good	Fair to very good	Very good	N/A	Fair	Fair to good	Poor to fair	Good	Good	Good to very good
Efficacy (lm/W)	Low	Low	High to very high	High	Moderate	Moderate	High	High to very high	High	Moderate to high	Low
Life	750–1,000 hours	2,000–3,000 hours	18,000–24,000 hours	10,000–20,000 hours	25,000+ hours	24,000+ hours	10,000–20,000 hours	24,000+ hours		10,000–20,000 hours	2,000–4,000 hours
Lumen maintenance	Good	Very good	Fair to good	Good	Good	Fair	Poor to fair	Fair to good	Good	Fair to good	Very good
Optical control	Good	Very good	Fair to good	Fair to good	Poor	Poor	Good	Good	Good	Good	Very good
Starting time (to full output)	Instant	Instant	Instant to fast	Fast	Fast	7 to 9 minutes	5 to 10 minutes	3 to 5 minutes	3 to 5 minutes	5 to 7 minutes	Instant

[1]CCT: correlated color temperature
[2]CRI: color rendering index

Lamp Life

Lamp life varies significantly from source to source and is an important operational factor for most projects. Short-lived sources should be avoided whenever possible in hard to reach areas. Shorter life lamps may offer some first-cost advantages, but trade-offs in long-term maintenance must be explored.

Lumen Maintenance

An electric light source degrades in output over its life. Some lamps, such as metal halide and mercury vapor, may lose 30% to 50% of their light prior to failing. Conversely, incandescent and most fluorescent sources maintain their light producing levels to with just a few percentage points of their original output. Lighting system designs must account for these losses to assure functional illuminance levels over time.

ESTABLISHING LIGHTING DESIGN CRITERIA

Lighting design requires the definition of the following criteria for each application: *quantity of illumination, quality of illumination, color of light,* and *suitable luminaire styles.*

Quantity of Illumination

Standards for illumination are set by the Illuminating Engineering Society of North America (IESNA). Illumination is generally measured in the horizontal plane 30 in (760 mm) above the floor. The units of illumination are footcandles (lumens per sq ft) and lux (lumens per sq m). IESNA-recommended levels are summarized on the following page (Lighting and Lighting Systems)—more detailed and specific information is given in the *IESNA Lighting Handbook* and in other IESNA publications.

Specific lighting levels are also established by codes, such as life safety and health codes. For instance, NFPA 101, *National Fire Protection Association Life Safety Standard,* recommends an average illumination of 1 fc (10 lux) along a path of emergency egress with an emergency power source. Some owners establish their own lighting level requirements for specific areas.

Choosing lighting levels involves thoughtful application of IESNA recommendations to meet the goals of the project. Too much light will lead to excessive energy use and failure to meet energy code limits.

The uniformity of interior lighting levels is also identified in IESNA recommendations. For interior lighting, IESNA generally recommends the following ratios of illumination for comfort:

Task-to-immediate surround: 1:3 to 3:1

Task-to-distant surround: 1:10 to 10:1

When light is designed to maintain these relationships, the human eye continually adapts to the light level and responds quickly to visual stimulus. However, visual interest is caused by contrast in which ratios between task and surround might be 100:1 or even greater. This is one of the greatest paradoxes of lighting design: The most appealing visual scenes are often uncomfortable.

Guidelines for Illumination

- *Eliminate flicker:* Light sources should minimize or eliminate flicker caused by AC power or other influences.
- *Eliminate or minimize glare:* Shield lamps from view. Minimize very bright and very dark surfaces. Illuminate walls and ceilings.
- *Use light sources with good color rendering:* Halogen, high CRI (color rendering index) full-size and compact fluorescent, and high CRI metal halide and white high pressure sodium (HPS) lamps should be used whenever possible.

Color of Light

Both the correlated color temperature (CCT) and color rendering index (CRI) for light sources should be used in choosing light sources. In general, try to match CCT when mixing sources, such as halogen and fluorescent.

Suitable Luminaire Styles

Many design problems have reasonably obvious solutions determined by a combination of budget, energy code, and industry standards. For instance, most office lighting designs utilize recessed troffers because they are cost-effective and energy-efficient and they meet the standard expectations of owners and tenants.

Choices among troffers require further consideration, although at that point style is a lesser issue.

Some situations call for uncommon or creative designs. In these cases, the distribution of the luminaire and its physical appearance become critical. In particular, luminaires that enhance the architecture are desired for residences, hotels, restaurants, and other nonwork spaces. Decorative styles range from contemporary to very traditional; lamp options may permit a choice between incandescent and more energy-efficient light sources, such as compact fluorescent or low-watt high-intensity discharge (HID) luminaires. In fact, energy-efficient decorative lighting fixtures, both interior and exterior, are one of the fastest growing parts of the lighting fixture industry as the market expands for attractive luminaires that comply with energy codes.

Lighting Terms

LUMINAIRE: A structure that holds an electric lamp and its socket, wiring, and auxiliaries, such as ballasts.

PORTABLE LUMINAIRE (LAMP): A luminaire equipped with a cord and plug and designed to be moved from space to space.

LIGHTING FIXTURE: A luminaire that is permanently attached ("hard wired") to a building.

LIGHTING SYSTEM: The lighting fixtures in a building, sometimes including portable lights, subdivided into smaller systems (e.g., the lighting system in a room or all luminaires of a particular type in a room or building).

ILLUMINANCE: The measure of light striking a surface, in footcandles (lumens per square meter). Illuminance can be measured and predicted using calculations; also illumination.

LAMP: The electric bulb or tube within a luminaire.

PHOTOMETRY: The measure of light, especially with respect to a luminaire.

PHOTOMETRIC REPORT: A report that describes the manner in which light is emitted from a luminaire, presented in an industry standard format.

CONTRAST

Without contrast, the environment produced has the quality of a cloudy, overcast day. If all objects and surfaces in a room receive equal emphasis from light, contrast is lost. Patterns of luminance contrast evoke positive emotions in much the same way as background music. Lighting contrast can affect the performance of tasks, the behavior of people, and the degree of contentment and pleasure.

Over time, a lack of contrast can cause feelings of listlessness and even depression. To establish patterns of luminance contrast, the lighting designer must first evaluate the activities or tasks that will occur in the space. Some activities and tasks benefit from a high degree of contrast, to encourage participation and stimulate enjoyment. Other activities and tasks benefit from a minimum of contrast, to help a person feel contented, comfortable, and relaxed. Although individuals react differently to the same environment, there is a high degree of similarity in people's reactions to light.

After the activity or task has been identified, luminance contrast is established by developing patterns of light and shade. The relationship between foreground and background is determined by selecting specific surfaces and objects to receive lighting emphasis while leaving others in comparative darkness.

In addition to altering our perception of space, the direction and distribution of light affect the perception of surfaces and objects in a room.

THREE-DIMENSIONAL FORMS

Three-dimensional forms are seen as a pattern of luminance contrasts, often consisting of highlights and shadows. A change in this pattern, caused by a change in the direction and distribution of light, alters visual impressions of form and surface.

LUMINANCE CONTRAST

Use the high end of the level ranges for older people, where finishes are especially dark, or where the work is particularly important or requires great speed.

LIGHTING LEVELS FOR TYPICAL RECEPTION AREA

DIFFUSE WASH LIGHT
Diffuse wash light reduces the likelihood that surface flaws will be noticed, and strengthens an impression of surface smoothness. This is more suitable for a gypsum board wall or an acoustical tile ceiling. Diffuse wash light from the front is particularly successful in reducing or removing shadows and small luminance variations.

GRAZING LIGHT
Grazing light from luminaires located close to the lit surface strengthens highlights and shadows. It enhances the perception of depth by emphasizing the textures and sculptural relief of the surface. It is also used for inspection to detect surface blemishes and errors in workmanship. Grazing light is appropriate for lighting heavily textured surfaces such as rough plaster, masonry, or concrete. It is not appropriate for smooth surfaces because minor surface imperfections such as trowel marks, tape, and nail-head depressions are magnified by the shadows that result from grazing light.

THE PERCEPTION OF TEXTURE Source: Gordon and Nuckolls, Interior Lighting for Designers, 3rd Ed., John Wiley & Sons, Inc., 1995.

Design Guidelines for Material Transmission
Most direct transmission materials, such as clear or tinted glass, clear acrylics, and open mesh, maintain visual transparency, permitting a view through the apposite side.

When attempting to rear-illuminate a semidiffuse material such as most fabrics, translucent acrylics, and frosted glass, pay special attention to the light source location and its intensity. Remove it from the normal line of sight to the material so that a fuzzy, intense image is not seen through it.

The more diffuse a material is, the easier it is to softly backlight it.

When working with light through perforated metals, it is often advisable to place a secondary translucent material as a backing.

REFLECTION AND TRANSMISSION

Design Guidelines for Material Reflectance

Materials of high gloss or mirror appearance reflect their surroundings. Be conscious of the influence of other light sources and surfaces in the space on the material's final rendition.

Light sources that have been mounted close to a polished or specular wall surface in an attempt to wash it with light are relatively ineffective. The extreme angle at which the light strikes the surface causes most of that light to reflect downward to the floor at the base of the wall.

Semispecular materials such as brushed metals, vinyl wall coverings, many woods, and some stones, will look different when lighted, depending on the angle from which they are viewed.

Diffuse materials, such as drywall, matte paints, rough stone, unfinished brick, and some wood finishes, can offer the softest and, sometimes, richest reflections (lighted uniformly from a distance) or very dramatic returns (highlighted by sources placed very close to the surface).

Diffuse materials may exhibit changes in their reflectance characteristics over time due to the wearing down of textures or finish. A surface's reflectance characteristics—specular, semispecular, or diffuse—are independent considerations from its reflectance value, or percentage. For example, a marble wall can be highly polished and specular, yet reflect vastly different quantities of light depending on whether it is predominantly dark- or light-colored.

Always select the materials using the light source under which it will normally be viewed. Conduct informal mock-ups of how the material is rendered when illuminated in different ways.

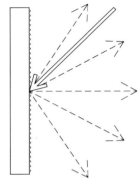

SPECULAR REFLECTION
A smooth, highly polished surface like a mirror alters the direction of a beam of light without changing its form. The angle of reflection is equal to the angle of incidence, a property that makes specular materials ideal where precise beam control is desired. Because these surfaces are virtually mirrors, their own surfaces are almost invisible; they may appear dark or bright, depending on the observer's position and on the luminance of the reflected image.

SEMISPECULAR (SPREAD) REFLECTION
Irregular surfaces, such as those that are corrugated, hammered, brushed, sandblasted, or etched, partially disperse the reflected beam. The greatest intensity, however, is still reflected at an angle near the angle of incidence. Semispecular materials appear with highlights or streaks of higher luminance on a background of lower luminance. In interiors, they are often used as elements of sparkle. In luminaires, semispecular materials produce a moderately controlled beam that is smooth and free from striations.

DIFFUSE REFLECTION
Rough or matte surfaces neutralize the directional nature of the incident beam. Light is reflected from each point in all directions, with maximum intensity perpendicular to the surface. Sand on the beach is an example of a diffuse reflecting surface. There are no bright spots; the surface appears the same from all angles of view. In interiors, this quality is often desirable for walls, ceilings, and work surfaces. In luminaires, diffuse reflection materials are used to produce wide distributions of light.

Reflection is the return of light from a surface; it occurs when a portion of the light falling on a surface is thrown back by that surface, just as a ball bounces back from the floor. Three kinds of reflection are involved in the control of light: *specular, semispecular,* and *diffuse. Source: Gordon and Nuckolls,* Interior Lighting for Designers, *3rd Ed., John Wiley and Sons, Inc., 1995.*

REFLECTION

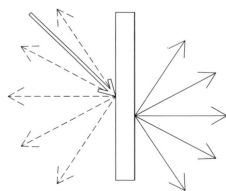

DIRECT TRANSMISSION
Transparent materials leave the light distribution unchanged. They are used as protective covers for absorbing or reflecting infrared or ultraviolet radiation or where change in the color of light is desired while maintaining the light distribution produced by reflecting contours. Because the light remains visible, materials such as clear glass and plastic are ineffective for glare control.

SEMIDIFFUSE (SPREAD) TRANSMISSION
Translucent materials emit light at wider angles because of configurations on at least one side of the material. A slight redirection of the transmitted beam is achieved by minor surface irregularities, such as shallow facets or flutes, which smooth out imperfections and striations. A greater degree of diffusion is achieved by etches, sandblasts, and matting aerosol sprays. Semidiffuse materials provide lamp concealment and glare control.

DIFFUSE TRANSMISSION
Diffuse transmission disperses light in all directions and eliminates the directional quality of the beam. Full diffusion is achieved by using opal glasses and plastics that incorporate microscopic particles and remove all directionality from the transmitted beam.

Transmission is the propagation of light through a medium. The transmission of light is effected by two conditions: the reflections at each surface of the material and the absorption and reflection within the material. *Source: Gordon and Nuckolls,* Interior Lighting for Designers, *3rd Ed., John Wiley and Sons, Inc., 1995.*

TRANSMISSION

1 ☐ INTERIOR LIGHTING DESIGN

PSYCHOLOGICAL ASPECTS OF LIGHTING

Pioneering lighting research efforts in the early 1970's lead by the late professor John Flynn, demonstrated that as patterns of luminance contrast change in the environment, the strength of visual stimuli changes, altering our impressions of space. As a part of this important work, evidence was uncovered that lighting changes alone can elicit significantly different reactions from people. It was found that alterations in lighting cues could induce consistent and predictable responses in three areas: spaciousness, perceptual clarity, and pleasantness.

Impressions of Spaciousness

An impression of largeness or smallness is affected by the intensity and uniformity of the room perimeter. Differences in the quantity of horizontal illuminance from overhead systems have negligible influence on impressions of pleasantness. Differences in quantity of illuminance significantly alter impressions of perceptual clarity and spaciousness. The higher illuminance values are often described as clear, bright, distinct, large, and more spacious.

Impressions of Perceptual Clarity

The appearance of people's faces is of critical importance to the lasting impression made by an interior. Lighting schemes that are rated high in facial clarity are considered more public; schemes that are rated low in facial clarity are considered more private.

The importance of lighting as an influence on one's subjective impression of space should not be overlooked. From workplaces to restaurants, lighting can either enhance or detract from the designer's ultimate vision for the environment. By considering these influences during the lighting design process, it is possible to predict and control these effects for the betterment of the project.

Public space implies intermingling and bringing people together. The potential for visual contact improves as the intensity of general illuminance is increased. Increasing intensities reduce anonymity and bring people together because facial expressions and gestures are more clearly perceptible.

Private space suggests separating people and keeping them apart. Shadow and silhouette strengthen feelings of detachment and privacy because these lighting techniques inhibit the ability to perceive precise facial detail; even nearby individuals become more anonymous.

In a crowded space, when it is impossible to separate people physically by distance, it is possible to separate them visually by lighting. This technique is used in cocktail lounges, fine restaurants, and reception rooms.

Impressions of Pleasantness

The nonuniform luminance produced by the downward-concentrating system rates more favorably than the uniform luminance produced by the diffuse system. The nonuniform luminance is often perceived as more friendly, pleasant, sociable, and interesting.

When wall lighting is added, ratings shift to the positive for all three categories of impression. Lighted vertical surfaces strengthen feelings of spaciousness, clarity, and pleasantness.

OVERHEAD DOWNLIGHTING—LOW INTENSITY

OVERHEAD DOWNLIGHTING WITH LIGHTED END WALLS

PERIPHERAL WALL LIGHTING—ALL WALLS

OVERHEAD DIFFUSE—HIGH INTENSITY

OVERHEAD DIFFUSE—LOW INTENSITY

OVERHEAD DOWNLIGHTING WITH OVERHEAD DIFFUSE

LIGHTING EFFECTS Source: *Gordon and Nuckolls,* Interior Lighting for Designers, *3rd Ed., John Wiley & Sons, Inc., 1995.*

CALCULATIONS: LUMEN METHOD

Lighting design involves determining how many luminaires are needed for a particular application and where to locate them. The most accurate means of determining illumination performance is by computer; a number of point-by-point lighting programs are available (see the annual computer issue of *Lighting Design and Application,* an IESNA publication, for a current list of commercially available programs). It is also possible to estimate illumination results from a proposed lighting design using the lumen method and photometric reports from candidate luminaires.

The lumen method, also known as the *zonal cavity system,* is a calculation method that can be used to determine the horizontal illuminance that will result from a proposed lighting fixture selection and layout or the number of fixtures required by a proposed fixture selection and its horizontal illuminance value.

The lumen method is based on the definition of average footcandles over an area. The method modifies the fundamental equation of 1 fc = 1 lumen/sq ft (10 lux/sq m) to account for room size and proportion; reflectance from walls, ceiling, and floors; fixture efficiency; and reduction in output over time due to dirt accumulation, deterioration of reflecting surfaces, and reduction of lamp lumen output.

The lumen method requires the following information:

- Room dimensions (to compute wall area and floor area)
- Height of fixtures above work plane
- Reflectance values of major surfaces (ceiling, walls, floor)
- An estimate of the light loss factor (LLF)
- Initial lamp lumens
- A target illuminance level
- Lighting manufacturer's photometric test report

COEFFICIENT OF UTILIZATION

The coefficient of utilization (CU), found in the photometric test report, is the percentage of total lamp lumens generated within the fixture that actually reaches the work plane. As such, it has nothing to do with the intensity of the fixture but rather with the efficiency of the fixture (lumens emitted from the fixture divided by lamp lumens and the direction of the lamp output—this direction of output is graphically represented by the candlepower distribution curve). For purposes of this procedure, the plane of interest is invariably a horizontal plane (typically either the floor or desk level), therefore a fixture that distributes the greatest percentage of its lumens downward will have a higher CU (room cavity ratio and reflectance values being equal) than one that distributes light in any other direction. A higher CU is not necessarily a virtue; it only ranks fixtures according to their ability to provide horizontal illuminance.

The lumen method/zonal cavity system is limited by the following:

- It is based on a single number, average value.
- It assumes a uniform array of lighting fixtures.
- It assumes all room surfaces have a matte finish.
- It assumes the room is devoid of obstruction, at least down to the level of the work plane.

Formulas for Average Lighting Calculations

$$\text{NUMBER OF LUMINAIRES} = \frac{\text{footcandles desired} \times \text{room area}}{\text{CU} \times \text{LLF} \times \text{lamps/luminaire} \times \text{lumens/lamp}}$$

$$\text{AVERAGE FOOTCANDLES} = \frac{\text{lumens/lamp} \times \text{lamps/luminaire} \times \text{CU} \times \text{LLF}}{\text{area of room (sq ft)}}$$

$$\text{POWER DENSITY (W/sq ft)} = \frac{\text{design watts (including ballast)}}{\text{area of room}}$$

Where:
CU = coefficient of utilization (percentage of light that actually reaches task)
LLF = light loss factor (time-dependent depreciation factors)

Note: *See the Illuminating Engineering Society's* Lighting Handbook *for manufacturer's photometric tables of values for CU, LLF, lumens/lamps, and others.*

$$\text{NUMBER OF FIXTURES} = \frac{50 \times 25 \times 40}{0.67 \times 0.7 \times 4 \times 2,850} = 9.35 \text{ luminaires (use 9 or 10)}$$

$$\text{POWER DENSITY (W/sq ft)} = \frac{9 \times 111}{25 \times 40} \text{ or } \frac{10 \times 111}{25 \times 40} = \begin{array}{l} 0.999 \text{ W/sq ft (9 luminaires) or} \\ 1.111 \text{ W/sq ft (10 luminaires)} \end{array}$$

Typical Examples
Room size 25 × 40 ft (7.6 × 12 m); ceiling height 9 ft; illumination level 50 fc (500 lux) (IESNA category 10); 2 × 4 ft (2.7 m) recessed troffers with four 32-watt T8 lamps (2,850 lm) each.

CU = 0.67 (plastic lens)
Electronic ballast input watts = 111
LLF = 0.7

LIGHT LOSS FACTOR

The light loss factor (LLF), also known as the *maintenance factor,* is used to calculate the illuminance of a lighting system at a specific point in time under given conditions. It incorporates variations from test conditions in temperature and voltage, dirt accumulation on lighting fixtures and room surfaces, lamp lumen output depreciation, maintenance procedures (mainly frequency of cleaning and relamping), and atmospheric conditions.

To use a CU table, assumptions must first be made about the reflectance of major room surfaces. If surface finishes have been selected for the space, these assumptions can be made more reliably. Then the room cavity ratio (RCR) can be determined according to one of the following formulas:

For rectangular rooms: RCR = [5 × H(L + W)] / (L × W), in which H is the cavity height

For odd-shaped rooms: RCR = 2.5 wall area/floor area

LIGHT FIXTURE

H

H

POTENTIAL PLANES OF INTEREST

H

H

Any one of these dimensions may be the cavity height (H), which is the distance from the light fixture to the work plane of interest.

CAVITY HEIGHT DIAGRAM

LIGHTING ENERGY CODES

Most codes presently calculate allowable lighting power based on building type and area. Codes generally determine allowed interior lighting watts in one of these three ways:

- ROOM BY ROOM: Determine the specific use of each room and its net area. Multiply the area of each room by the allowed power density (watts/sq ft) adjusted for the room cavity ratio (RCR). Add the wattage for all rooms together; for example, private office, open office, coffee room, copy room, and toilet rooms.
- AREA: Determine the use of major portions of a building or renovation and the gross lighted area of each. Multiply the gross lighted area by the allowed power density (watts/sq ft) for each group of rooms by type. Add the figures for all areas together; for example, all offices, all storage rooms, and general support areas.
- WHOLE BUILDING: Determine the building type and the gross lighted area for the entire building. Multiply the gross lighted area by the allowed power density (watts/ sq ft) for the entire building by type; for example, all habitable square footage within the building or project.

To find the total allowable lighting power for the interior of a building, start with the total wattage as determined by one of the three methods above. Then subtract "credit" watts for lighting controlled by advanced automatic devices, such as daylighting or motion sensing and add other allowed watts, if any.

An allowed lighting load can also be determined by using a building energy simulation program like DOE-2. However, because the program's algorithm is based on the same power density assumptions as the allowed amount given above, it is unlikely the value for lighting determined in this manner will be significantly different, only more accurate.

LIGHTING ENERGY CODE COMPLIANCE STRATEGY

To realize design compliance with local energy codes without significant redesign, observe the following guidelines:

- Choose a general lighting system that uses one of these sources predominantly: fluorescent T-8 or T-5 with electronic ballasts, compact fluorescent with electronic ballast, or metal halide or high-pressure sodium (HPS).
- Make certain the luminaire and room combination are reasonably efficient. Use localized direct lighting for tasks whenever possible, and make room finishes light, especially ceilings.
- Design to meet IESNA minimum recommendations for each space, unless it is absolutely necessary to use higher levels.
- For downlighting, wall-washing, and other traditional incandescent applications, use compact fluorescent or high-intensity discharge (HID) sources when possible.
- Use incandescent and halogen sources sparingly, confining them to applications where color, precise control, or the lighting's decorative characteristics are critical.
- Add advanced controls such as motion or occupancy sensors and daylight photocells with in-line dimming. These allow the reduction of actual lighting watts and can help bring a design into compliance with energy efficiency requirements.

LIGHTING CONTROLS

Most energy codes require readily accessible switching for all electric lights. The National Electric Code requires switching at specific locations in residential settings. Traditional switches meet these requirements.

TYPICAL APPLICATIONS FOR LIGHTING CONTROLS

Office buildings schools	Motion sensors in private offices, classrooms, and conference rooms
	Time scheduling systems for open office areas, corridors, halls, and lobbies
	Motion sensors in toilet rooms and storage
	Daylighting in areas adjacent to windows, skylights or clerestories
	Combined systems (e.g., motion and daylighting) whenever logical
Retail	Time scheduling for store windows, general and display lighting
	Motion sensing for storage dressing rooms and restrooms
	Daylighting and lumen maintenance near skylights and clerestories
	Adaptation compensation for general lighting
Industrial, institutional	Time scheduling in most areas
	Daylighting near windows, skylights and clerestories
	Motion sensing in restrooms, little used storage areas

ENERGY-EFFICIENT LIGHTING CONTROLS

DEVICE OR METHOD	OPERATION	TYPICAL CREDIT
Time, clock (with manual override readily accessible)	Turns lights on and off at scheduled times	0–10%
Wallbox Dimmer	Reduces lighting power by manual adjustment	0%
Motion (occupancy) sensor	Turns lights on and off based on space	15% (>250 sq ft) to 30% (<250 sq ft)
Daylighting controls	Reduces interior lighting power based on amount of daylight in space	20% (stepped) to 30% (continuous dimming)
Preset (scene) dimming	Reduces average power by dimming combinations of lighting systems	10–20%
Tuning	Reduces lighting power by hidden adjustment	10–15%
Lumen maintenance	Reduces interior lighting power based on age of lamps and cleanliness of space	10–15%
Combined systems	Combinations of the above are not necessarily directly additive	Up to 45%

The credit offered varies from code to code and may not be available everywhere.

Other lighting controls choices are discussed in the following subsections.

Switching

Standard single-throw (toggle) switches are the most commonly used lighting controls. Three-way and four-way switches permit control from several locations. Examples include on/off "toggle" switches, electronic touch-switches, and so on.

Wall Box Dimming

Manual dimming is popular in residential applications and commercial spaces where flexibility in illumination levels is desired. Incandescent dimming is inexpensive and simple to apply. The dimming of fluorescent lighting should make use of electronic high-frequency dimming ballasts and associated dimming controls. An energy credit may be available for using manual dimming under some conditions.

Preset Dimming

Preset dimming or multichannel scene-dimming systems are increasingly being used for spaces with four or more independent dimming channels, such as restaurants, conferencing facilities, auditoriums, hotel lobbies, and custom-built homes. Preset dimming systems are similar in function to modern theatrical dimming in that there is a cross-fade between specific scenes, which are combinations of preset dimming levels for the channels controlled by the system. By establishing these scenes in advance, the user need only push a single button to bring all lighting in the space to the desired level for a specific function.

Time Scheduling

Lighting controls that use clocks to operate lighting systems on predictable schedules are the most commonly used form of automatic lighting controls. Some energy codes require automatic controls of this type as a minimum standard. Controls may vary from individual time clock switches to electronic programmable timers and large-scale energy management systems.

LINEAR SLIDE CONTROL   ROTARY OR PUSH ON/OFF CONTROL   TOUCH-PLATE CONTROL

DIMMING CONTROL DEVICES

Occupancy Sensing

Motion sensors can be used to control lights according to space occupancy. Passive infrared sensors are the most commonly used; ultrasonic sensors are also popular and work better in spaces with partitions. Sensors possess sensitivity and time-out adjustments to fine-tune the controller to the peculiarities of the space. For small rooms, choose wall box sensors with internal switches or dimmers; for larger rooms, choose ceiling-mounted sensors with remote relays. Multiple sensors are needed in larger spaces to ensure adequate area coverage and detection.

Energy credits for using motion sensor systems are fairly substantial, as these systems save significant energy in most applications. The payback on these devices is relatively short, especially in retrofit situations.

Daylighting And Related Controls

Daylighting systems use dimming or switching to reduce interior lighting when adequate daylight of sufficient quality is present. In buildings with windows near the work area, savings can be significant, and most codes permit a substantial controls credit for daylighting.

Lumen-Maintenance Controls

Lumen-maintenance controls allow lighting to be dimmed automatically when it is new and, through photoelectric sensing, to be increased gradually over time as lamps age and luminaires get dirty. The equipment for these controls is similar to that for daylighting, and most systems can be programmed to do both.

Adaptation Compensation Controls

Adaptation compensation controls (the opposite of daylighting) increase interior light as exterior light increase levels. Tunnels are classic applications for adaptation compensation, but the same principles can be used to save energy in interior lighting situations where the daylight tends to overpower the electric light during the day, while at night this additional light intensity may not be necessary.

Demand Management

Lighting can be gradually dimmed up to 20% with little effect on productivity but a profound impact on overall building load. By sensing incoming electric service for peaks, lighting can be dimmed when other building systems are peaking in load. The result is a "flattening" of the energy use curve, which lowers electric energy cost, normally computed using peak demand values.

LUMINAIRE DESIGN

Luminaires

A luminaire is any device that includes a lampholder, a means of electrification, and a support. Lighting fixtures are luminaires that are permanently attached to a building. Luminaires are characterized by the manner in which light is distributed.

Luminaire Characteristics

Direct luminaires tend to be the most efficient because they distribute light directly onto the normal task areas. They generally result in darker ceilings and upper walls, which can be dramatic but may create discomfort from high-contrast conditions.

Indirect luminaires produce comfortable low-contrast soft light when appropriately spaced, which psychologically enlarges space. Though they tend to be less efficient for delivering light to a traditional horizontal task, the appealing nature of their light compensates for this deficiency .

Diffuse luminaires create broad general light that often is considered glaring due to the lack of shielding at the critical angles at which the luminaire is viewed. Their decorative architectural or ornamental appropriateness is often the principal reason for their selection.

LUMINAIRE TYPES

TYPE		LIGHT DISTRIBUTION
Direct		Emits over 90% light downward. Most recessed lighting types, including downlights and troffers, are direct luminaires.
Indirect		Emits over 90% light upward, so it bounces from a ceiling into the space below. Many styles of suspended luminaires, sconces, and some portable lamps provide indirect lighting.
Diffuse		Emits light in all directions uniformly. This type includes most bare lamps, globes, and chandeliers and some table and floor lamps.

Direct/Indirect luminaires are often a good compromise between the efficiency of direct lighting and the comfort of indirect lighting.

INDIRECT AND DIRECT/INDIRECT LIGHTING SYSTEMS

Most indirect and direct/indirect lighting systems are designed to illuminate offices and similar finished spaces. In most cases, the ceiling should be finished in white paint or white acoustical tile, as the reflectance of the ceiling plane is critical.

Indirect Lighting Systems

Indirect lighting systems only produce uplight. Generally they should be mounted at least 15 to 18 in. (381 to 457 mm) below the ceiling; longer suspension lengths can improve uniformity but potentially will decrease efficiency. To maintain adequate clearance, ceilings should be at least 9 ft (2.7 m) high.

Direct/Indirect Lighting Systems

Direct/indirect lighting systems are intended to produce some indirect lighting for its comfort and balance, and some direct lighting, for efficient production of task lighting. Similar suspension length and ceiling height considerations apply. The percentage of uplight to downlight varies; generally, the higher the ceiling, the greater the downlight percentage recommended.

TYPE		LIGHT DISTRIBUTION
Direct/Indirect		Emits light upward and downward but little to the side. Many types of suspended luminaires, and some table and floor lamps, offer this type of lighting. These luminaries can offer mostly direct or mostly indirect lighting.
Asymmetric		For special applications. For instance, asymmetric uplights are indirect luminaires with a stronger distribution in one direction, such as away from a wall. Wall washers are a form of direct luminaire with stronger distribution to one side to light a wall.
Adjustable		Luminaires with inherent, usually flexible, adjustable mechanisms to permit the principal focus of the distribution to be altered for specific effects or functions. Examples are track lights, floodlights, and accent lights.

INDIRECT, DIRECT/INDIRECT, AND DIRECT LUMINAIRES

1   □   **INTERIOR LIGHTING DESIGN**

LIGHTING FIXTURES (LUMINAIRES)

Troffers

Troffers are widely used in offices, stores, schools, and other commercial and institutional facilities for general lighting in work and sales areas. They are the most common type of fluorescent luminaire.

Most troffers are recessed and designed to be laid into acoustic tile ceilings, with the fixture face matching the size of the tile. The most common troffer sizes are 2 × 4 ft (610 × 1220 mm), although 2 × 2 ft (610 × 610 mm) and 1 × 4 ft (305 × 1220 mm) are also readily available. Other sizes exist, often to match a specific ceiling (such as 20 × 60 in. (508 × 1524 mm) fixtures for a 5-ft (1,524-mm) ceiling grid system). Different mounting types are made, including the following identified by the National Electrical Manufacturers Association (NEMA):

NEMA "G": For fixtures in a standard exposed inverted T-grid.

NEMA "F": For fixtures furnished with a flange and designed to be installed in an opening in plaster or gypsum board.

NEMA "SS": For fixtures in a screw-slot inverted T-grid.

NEMA "NFSG": For fixtures in a narrow face slot T-grid.

NEMA "Z": For fixtures in a concealed Z-spline ceiling.

NEMA "MT": For fixtures in a metal pan ceiling system.

Some recessed troffers are also designed to interface with the building HVAC system: *Heat extraction troffers* have vents in the top of the fixture to allow return air to be pulled into the troffer, past the lamps, and into the ceiling plenum. *Air-handling fixtures* have slots around the lens or louvers to supply air to a room (by means of a special boot that can transfer air to the supply air system) or to remove it (by connection to a return duct).

Troffers can also be equipped with emergency battery packs to power some or all of the lamps during a power outage or emergency condition.

Lensed Troffers

Lensed troffers use an acrylic or polycarbonate lens to refract light and distribute it into useful zones. Lenses can contain internal Radio Frequency Interference (RFI) shields for use in hospital operating and laboratory rooms. Lens troffers equipped with highly polished internal reflectors can offer very high efficiency.

Parabolic Troffers

Parabolic troffers have parabolically shaped aluminum or plastic louvers that shield the lamp from direct view to improve visual comfort. These troffers offer sharp cutoff, which makes some of them suitable for use in computer work spaces. "Parabolics" generally refer to deep-cell louvers 6 in. (152 mm) or larger across; "paracubes" are shallower louvers with smaller cells. Larger cells are more efficient, but smaller cells possess a more extreme cutoff angle.

Troffer Ratings

Most troffers are rated for standard dry indoor applications and must not touch insulation. Some special types include

GASKETED: Can be damp or even wet-rated.

PARABOLIC LOUVRED — ALUMINUM LOUVER

LENSED — ACRYLIC LENS

TROFFERS

FIRE-RATED: Can maintain up to one-hour ceiling rating in certain rated ceilings.

VANDAL-RESISTANT: Equipped with vandal-resistant lens and latching hardware.

RFI: Lens troffers that are shielded from radio frequencies.

Troffers can be equipped with most fluorescent technologies, including dimming, magnetic or electronic ballasts, and T-12, T-8, or T-5 lamps. Special troffers are made for ceiling systems like the linear metal slat system (4 in. (100 mm) wide). Recessed troffer depth varies from 3½ (89 mm) to more than 7 in. (177 mm), so troffers must be coordinated with other elements above the ceiling.

PAR LAMP DOWNLIGHT

PAR LAMP WALL WASHER

PAR LAMP ADJUSTABLE ACCENT

DOWNLIGHTS

Downlights

Downlights are used principally for general illumination in a wide range of residential and commercial applications, especially in lobbies, halls, corridors, stores, and other finished spaces. Downlights can be equipped with incandescent, halogen, low-voltage, compact fluorescent, or high-intensity discharge (HID) lamps. There are several major types of downlights, which accommodate varying sources, ceiling heights, plenum heights, room types, and beam spreads. These include the following:

OPEN REFLECTOR: The reflector of this type of downlight shields the lamp from direct view and forms a beam pattern.

OPEN BAFFLE: Ridged baffles, usually black, shield the lamp from direct view and minimize glare.

OPEN ELLIPSOIDAL: An elliptical reflector allows a small aperture; this beam spread is highly efficient.

LENSED PRISMATIC, ARTICULATED, OR FRESNEL: Often used outdoors or in wet locations, the lens protects and seals the lamp compartment; some lens types are used to provide additional beam shaping.

DIFFUSER: A diffuser distributes light broadly, which is especially useful in closets and showers.

ADJUSTABLE: An adjustable downlight can be used as a downlight or as an accent light.

PULL-DOWN: This feature allows the light to be used as a downlight or an accent light, and permits higher aiming angles.

Downlight Ratings

Choice of a downlight depends on the applications for which it is listed. The primary rating types are as follows:

THERMALLY PROTECTED (T): These downlights are suitable for all applications except direct concrete pour.

INSULATION PROTECTED (IP): These downlights are used when the fixture may come in contact with insulation. They are designed to prevent fixture overheating.

INSULATION CEILING (IC): These fixtures are used when the fixture is intended to be in contact with insulation.

AIRTIGHT INSULATION CEILING AIC): These downlights are for applications in which the fixture is in contact with insulation and air leaks in the ceiling must be prevented.

DAMP LOCATION FIXTURES: These fixtures can be exposed to moist air but not to direct water spray or rain.

WET LOCATION FIXTURES: These can be exposed to direct water spray or rain.

SPA OR SHOWER FIXTURES: These are designed to be used in a shower stall, over a spa, or in a locker room.

CONCRETE-POUR FIXTURES: These are designed to be installed in direct contact with concrete.

EMERGENCY FIXTURES: These are equipped with a backup battery to produce light for at least 90 minutes during a power outage (generally available only for compact fluorescent luminaires).

Architectural and Decorative Lighting Fixtures

Wall washers come in several types. *Eyelid wall washers* essentially are downlights with an eyelid-shaped shield on the room side. *Recessed lens wall washers* resemble downlights but use an angled lens to throw light more to one side. *Surface and semi-recessed lens and open wall washers,* which throw light onto an adjacent wall, generally work best; they can also be mounted to track. *Downlight/wall washers* are designed to illuminate rather than scallop an adjacent wall, although the light they provide may not be intense enough for display purposes.

Linear Wall Grazing Fixtures

Linear wall grazing fixtures, sometimes called *wall slots,* are used to illuminate walls in lobbies, corridors, and core areas. They are especially suited for textured or polished surfaces.

Accent Fixtures

Accent fixtures focus light on specific targets such as art, retail displays, lecterns and building façade features. *Recessed accent lights* appear as downlights but internally permit rotation and elevation of the light beam. *Eyeballs and pull-down* accents resemble downlights, but can be adjusted. Track lighting systems are specifically designed for accent lighting of art and retail displays, with easy relocation of lamp holders along the track.

Commercial Fluorescent Fixtures

Several types of fluorescent direct luminaires appropriate for general and utility lighting are employed as commercial fixtures. Most utilize wraparound lenses or diffusers in which the lamp is surrounded by the lens; the lamp is hidden from direct view while radiating light downward and to the sides. Commercial luminaires are among the lowest-cost lighting fixtures and are typically used for general and utility and back-of-house lighting in modest projects.

Industrial Lighting Fixtures

These fixtures generally have a utilitarian or functional appearance. Fluorescent industrials incorporate strip lights in open fixtures, with simple reflectors that are designed to be surface-mounted or hung by chains or rods. HID industrials include high-bay and low-bay downlights. Industrial fixtures are generally used in factories and warehouses, and increasingly in schools and retail stores where a less finished appearance is desired.

Linear Cove Lights

Linear cove lights provide asymmetric uplighting from coves or other architectural elements more efficiently than strip lights, and without socket shadows.

Task Lights

Task lights are specifically designed to illuminate a task area while minimizing veiling reflections (reflected glare).

Chandeliers

Chandeliers are ornate luminaires that generally comprise many small incandescent lamps to simulate the effect of candle flames. Chandeliers are hung from the ceiling and are used for decorative-only applications or, occasionally, general illumination in areas such as dining rooms, foyers, and other formal spaces where few demanding visual tasks are performed.

WRAPAROUND FLUORESCENT WITH ACRYLIC DIFFUSER   **FLUORESCENT STRIP**

HIGH BAY HID LAMP   **INDUSTRIAL FLUORESCENT**

COMMERCIAL AND INDUSTRIAL FIXTURES

Pendant Fixtures

Pendants are also ceiling-hung decorative fixtures. In general, the term is used for luminaires that are less formal than chandeliers, such as those used in offices or restaurants. Some pendant luminaires also use incandescent lamps, although most modern variations are available with HID or compact fluorescent sources.

Close-to-Ceiling Fixtures

Close-to-ceiling luminaires are similar to pendants but are mounted close to the ceiling to allow use in rooms with lower ceiling heights.

ROUND [4 TO 9 IN (101 TO 228 MM) DIAMETER]
Up, down, or up/down

OVOID
Up, down, or up/down

RACETRACK OVAL
Up, down, or up/down

ELONGATED OCTAGON
Up, down, or up/down

"V" OR WEDGE
Up only

OPTIMAL FOR USE WITH VIDEO TERMINAL
Up/down

SUSPENDED LIGHTING SHAPES

Sconces

Sconces are usually decorative wall-mounted luminaires. Often they are used in concert with an adjacent chandelier; in other cases, they are the sole decorative lighting element. Most commercial sconces use compact fluorescent sources, while in hospitality and residential applications, wide use of traditional incandescent continues.

Lamps

Lamps are traditional portable luminaires generally used for table or floor mounting. *Torchères* are floor lamps designed for uplighting. Most portable lighting uses incandescent or halogen sources, although compact fluorescent options should be considered for commercial and hospitality applications.

GENERAL LIGHTING SYSTEM ALTERNATIVES

FLUORESCENT STRIP LIGHTS AND LENSED TROFFERS provide adequate light for the lowest cost, are the easiest to install, and tend to be the most efficient. These systems also are accompanied by a significant amount of glare and may appear to the consumer as a budget-driven choice.

HID INDUSTRIAL-STYLE FIXTURES provide good basic light at relatively low cost, but also appear to be a budget-conscious choice and may be a glare source if not properly shielded. They can be used to help create a warehouse look and feel. Perimeter valances or display lighting may can enhance these systems.

PARABOLIC LOUVERED SYSTEMS produce inherently less offending glare and may suggest the presence of higher-quality merchandise. They should be used in conjunction with valances and/or other perimeter and display lighting to avoid the darker wall appearance that often accompanies parabolic systems.

SUSPENDED DIRECT, DIRECT/INDIRECT, AND INDIRECT SYSTEMS work best in ceilings greater than 8 ft (2.4 m). These lighting types play a major role in the appearance and style of a space and are generally chosen to reinforce a specific marketing motif.

TROFFER SYSTEMS, lensed or parabolic fluorescent, provide good, acceptable light at low cost; they are commonly used in schools. Recessed lighting minimizes vandalism and is efficient.

SUSPENDED DIRECT/INDIRECT AND INDIRECT SYSTEMS are favored for better visual comfort and are generally suited for spaces with ceilings higher than 9 ft (2.7 m).

INDUSTRIAL-STYLE HIGH-INTENSITY DISCHARGE (HID) LIGHTING SYSTEMS are often used in industrial education, arts, gymnasium, and other spaces requiring plentiful, relatively inexpensive, durable lighting. If using HID sources, provide quartz auxiliary lamps in some fixtures for emergency backup lighting during power loss.

SPECIAL APPLICATION LUMINAIRES come in hundreds of different types, each optimized for a specific job, workstation, environment, or hazard. Examples include explosion-proof, vapor tight, and paint-booth luminaires. Consult the IESNA *Lighting Handbook* for a comprehensive outline of industrial specialty luminaires.

DAYLIGHT MEDIA GUIDELINES FOR WORKSPACES

	ORIENTATION	CONTROL TECHNIQUES	SURFACE REFLECTANCE GUIDELINES		MOST APPROPRIATE ELECTRICAL LIGHTING	APPLICATION NOTES
			WALLS	CEILINGS		
Monitors	North East West South	Moderate transmission glass (30% to 50%) Architectural baffles or louvers (exterior) Architectural setbacks Overhangs Light shelves	Medium to light (30% to 50%)	Very light (90%)	Indirect Semi-indirect Direct/indirect	Avoid small, intermittent, punched openings. Assess time-of-day occupancy to establish best orientation(s).
Clerestories	North East West South	Moderate transmission glass (30% to 50%) Architectural baffles or louvers (exterior) Architectural setbacks Overhangs Light shelves	Medium to light (30% to 50%)	Very light (90%)	Indirect Semi-indirect Direct/indirect	Avoid small, intermittent, punched openings. Assess time-of-day occupancy to establish best orientation(s).
Skylights	(Controllable only on sloped roofs) North East West South	Very low transmission glass (2% to 10%) Architectural baffles or louvers (exterior) Deep skylight wells Frit patterns Solar shades, blinds	Medium (30% to 50%)	Very light (90%)	Indirect Semi-indirect Direct/indirect Direct	Avoid large-area, shallow openings. Assess time-of-day occupancy to establish best orientation(s).
Windows	North East West South	Low transmission glass (5% to 15%) Significant overhangs Architectural baffles or louvers (exterior) Frit patterns Solar shades, blinds	Light (30% to 50%)	Light to Very light (80% to 90%)	Indirect Semi-indirect Direct/indirect Direct	Avoid small, intermittent, punched openings. Assess time-of-day occupancy to establish best orientation(s).

DAYLIGHTING

Health

Exposure to daylight offers significant health benefits, which include the physiological aspects of circadian rhythms that are important for minimizing seasonal affective disorder (SAD) and for the production of vitamin D.

Illuminance

Daylight can provide much of the light needed to perform many home and work-related tasks. Because daylight is highly variable and has limited availability, designing the daylighting system in any building to meet illuminance targets requires an immense team effort and typically entails greater initial and maintenance costs. While this should certainly not eliminate daylighting from consideration, it indicates the degree of care, finesse, integration, and user education that is necessary a successful daylight-integrated installation. Illuminance from daylight, when correctly implemented, should result in reduced energy use.

Luminance

Luminance balancing (from surface to surface) can be achieved with daylight. However, the variability and intensities of daylight will present a serious challenge for the design team. In effect, daylight is not a free energy source. Successfully implementing daylight raises the following issues: initial capital expenditures that are higher than most clients or users may be expecting, an ongoing maintenance requirement, sophisticated controls, and a team whose members all must be equally experienced with installing successful, effective electric lighting.

Sustainabiltiy

The success of daylighting as a sustainable practice is very sensitive to the integration and interaction of the various building materials and systems. The sun (also called the solar disc) and the sky are the two most significant daylight sources readily available to designers. Reflected daylight from other surfaces is secondary. Any of these daylight sources can introduce lumi-

nances of such significance that one or several of the following may occur:

- Distraction
- Direct glare
- Reflected glare
- Veiling reflections
- Transient adaptation

The key to successful design using daylighting requires managing daylight to provide at the least a view, and at the most a view, illuminance, and luminance. To achieve cost and occupant effective sustainable daylighting, it is necessary to use such daylight media as monitors, clerestories, skylights, and windows with appropriate orientation, shading control, and room surface finishes along with proper electric lighting.

Randy J. Burkett, FIALD, IES, LC; Burkett Lighting Design, Inc.; St. Louis, Missouri
James Robert Benya, PE, FIES, IALD; Pacific Lightworks; Portland, Oregon
Robert Sardinsky; Rising Sun Enterprises; Basalt, Colorado

PROGRAMMING

Architectural programming is the process of identifying and defining user requirements before proceeding with design development. The goal is to develop and document the client's business system and his or her needs. During the process, the analyst also gathers information on what is, and is not, currently working, and what exists, or needs to exist, for the client to carry out his or her purpose or mission. In the field of architecture, these needs are related to space requirements, which, when completely defined, are referred to as the *architectural program*.

Architectural programs have several fundamental components:

- Summary of the project scope and program results (answers who, what, why, where, and how,)
- Program support analysis, including projections for headcount, conference room utilization, cafeteria, and so on
- Business and building analysis, including adjacency diagrams and supporting analysis
- Program document, program summary reports, and interview notes
- Appendices, containing supporting information provided by the client or from related research

Architectural programming is the first step in the design process and is, perhaps, the most important phase. Meaningful communication is required to assess, review, refine, and document a client's space requirements. During the programming process, the client's problems are identified and clarified in order to develop a solution for today and for the future. Programming promotes an understanding of the whole problem, as opposed to symptoms or pieces or parts of the client's problem.

Unless the designer completely understands the needs and uses of a space, the resulting design will fall short of the needs of the client and the users of the space. Also, more often than not, an incomplete understanding of client needs results in project cost overruns, and unidentified or misunderstood needs result in design changes. Changes made late in the design process or during implementation are much more expensive than changes made early in the programming or schematic phase of the design. A thoughtful architectural program supports the designer and his or her design by fully capturing the needs of the client. The result is a more effective design that is implemented on time and within budget parameters.

PROGRAMMING EFFECT ON COST

Changes made as a project design is being implemented increase the overall cost of the project. Effective programming—that is, fully identifying and defining client needs at the beginning of the project—enables design projects to better meet budget and schedule goals.

ADDITIONAL PROGRAMMING SERVICES

Some clients may have needs that are more complex than simple space planning; for example, the need to move or lease more space Clients want to use space more effectively; want to tailor workspace to their employees' needs; are dealing with space standards for the first time; feel the space they have is not being used effectively; are changing their culture; want to be more competitive; have staff recruitment and retention issues; or have any number of other business circumstances that impact space. For clients with these types of needs, additional services are often provided.

Typical additional services provided in support of developing a program are:

- *Work methods analysis,* to identify individual workspace requirements; for example, to support developing new space standards for a client.
- *Alternative office solutions analysis,* to identify nontraditional solutions to workspace needs; for example, to increase the utilization of real estate.
- *Benchmarking studies,* to identify how a client's competitors are meeting their workspace and environmental needs; for example, by comparing workspace standards.

PROGRAMMING TRENDS

Driving current trends are client needs for space efficiency, flexibility, and economy. The goal of many real-estate-savvy firms is to reduce overall real estate costs as well as costs and time associated with *churn,* the movement of, or change in, people and groups of people. *Churn rate* is used as a measure of the level of dynamics of an organization. Churn costs have historically been high, and timeframes have been too long. As business product life cycles and development times become shorter and shorter, the need to shift and move people or whole organizations increases. Loss of time in today's business environment equates directly to loss of profit and leadership in competitive markets. The insightful programmer working to meet the client's real estate goals must keep abreast of current design solutions and thinking associated with client needs.

PROGRAMMING PROCESS

Reducing the programming process to its most elementary level results in three steps, as follows:

1. *Information gathering,* which involves research, listening, and learning about the client's needs.
2. *Analyzing and synthesizing,* which involves consolidating the acquired information for a full understanding of the client's problems, needs, options, and potential costs, as well as proposing options and making recommendations.
3. *Documentation and validation,* which involves documenting the findings, reviewing the findings and recommendations with the client, then getting feedback, modifying the program, and reissuing the program document.

ARCHITECTURAL PROGRAMMING AND DESIGN

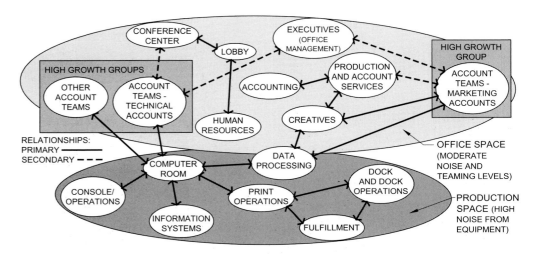

ADJACENCY DIAGRAM FOR TYPICAL OFFICE WITH PRODUCTION FACILITY

Step 1: Information-Gathering Process

The first step in the programming process, information gathering, consists of three primary activities: the *initial meeting*, the *goal-setting session*, and the *needs and requirements interviews*.

Active Listening

During this initial programming step, and throughout the process, active listening is critical to the success of the programmer. Active listening involves quieting the mind and focusing completely on the information being presented. If questions arise, they are quickly asked, then documented in your notes when the speaker has completed all his or her thoughts associated with the previous question. Repeating back to the speaker what was heard, using the listener's own words, is also a critical part of active listening. It accomplishes two primary goals: first, it gives the speaker confidence that he or she was heard and understood; second, it gives the speaker the opportunity to clarify ideas or points that may have been misunderstood.

Advance preparation of questions frees the mind to focus on the speaker and his or her comments. The program is only good if the gathered information is complete and accurate. If we listen well, we increase the probability of generating an effective program.

Initial Meeting

The initial, or "kickoff," meeting is a forum for discussing the logistics of the project and for gaining an understanding of the timeline and the client's role. If not established prior to this meeting, the following are identified: the members of the project's decision-making team and the organization members to be interviewed. A tour of the site with the client enables a deeper understanding of the project and associated issues.

Goal-Setting Session

The goal-setting, or "vision," session is held with the members of the project decision-making team. The programmer facilitates this meeting. During this session, the goals of the business, environment, and project—what the client wants to achieve and why—are discussed. The objective of the session is to identify, understand, and document the goals of the client for both the project and the new environment. It is important to devise questions in advance that will facilitate the brainstorming process and ensure that required issues are exposed and discussed.

Needs and Requirements Interviews

The final activity in this step is to conduct the needs and requirements interviews. Interviews can take two forms: *face-to-face question-and-answer sessions* or *questionnaires*. The most effective means of gathering information is to hold either individual or focus group interviews. Information gained in interviews is less open to interpretation and can be clarified on the spot. That said, there are situations where interviewing personnel is neither feasible nor acceptable to the client, in which case questionnaires are in order. Regardless of the method by which the information is gathered, the programmer must prepare clear, well-bounded, nonleading questions. When developing the questions, the programmer considers how to construct the question so as to extract the required information, given the specifics of the project. Interviews are also useful for testing concepts proposed by management or the facility team. Questions are developed in advance and used for each interview to ensure that consistent information is gathered from each group. Ideally, interview sessions also include a walk-through of the spaces currently occupied by the department or group interviewed.

Step 1: Information-Gathering Process: Activities and Products

Activities

- Research client.
- Acquire floor plans, client organization chart, and current personnel report.
- Prepare questions for "vision-image" and interviews.
- Walk through site.
- Facilitate vision-image or goal-setting session.
- Develop mission statement.
- Conduct interviews.
- Gather space demand/utilization information for conference rooms, cafeterias, training rooms, and so on.

Products

- Client background and an understanding of who/what the client is today.
- Documented project goals and vision with mission statement.
- Interview notes.
- Marked-up floor plate drawings with notes and updates.
- Client data, including current personnel report and space utilization reports for conference rooms, cafeterias, training rooms, and so on.

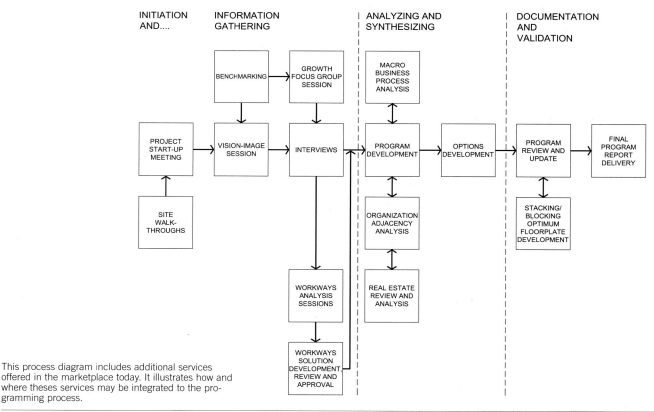

This process diagram includes additional services offered in the marketplace today. It illustrates how and where theses services may be integrated to the programming process.

STRATEGIC PROGRAMMING PROCESS

Step 2: Analysis and Synthesis Process

After gathering and organizing a comprehensive review of the information, quantitative and qualitative specifics about each required space are extracted, to include the following:

- Space types
- Sizes
- Quantities
- Design characteristics

The result is a fundamental set of space types for both individual organizational groups and common or shared spaces. Space standards (standard workplace sizes to be applied throughout the program) that meet the needs of individual work processes and the building module are developed at this time. Space sizes for all of the various space types are also identified and documented. Generic space diagrams are included to illustrate how space sizes are developed and what they mean to the user in terms of functionality.

Space quantities are developed next. Analyzing headcount projections, support space utilization statistics, and any other quantifiable data available enables the programmer to understand the quantities required for specific spaces. The result of quantifying both the size and number of each space required by the client is the net square footage (NSF) of the space requirement. Circulation factors must be selected and applied at both micro and macro levels in the program to develop both initial total usable and total rentable square footage (RSF) results. Total usable square footage and total rentable square footage are two key products of the programming process. At this point, a draft program should be nearing completion.

Statistics and other analytical tools are required to

Step 2: Analysis and Synthesis Process: Activities and Products

Activities

- Analyze interview notes.
- Develop flow diagram of business process.
- Identify themes and potential conflicts in needs.
- Resolve conflicts or open issues with client.
- Analyze headcount and develop projections.
- Analyze space utilization reports for conference rooms, cafeterias, training rooms, and so on.
- Develop program, space list, and quantities.
- Analyze interactions and develop adjacency diagram.
- Acquire rentable square footage (RSF) and rentable factors for buildings being examined, or desired factors for potential shell designs.
- Develop stacking and blocking diagrams.
- Perform cost analysis.
- Develop options with associated costs.

Products

- Base program.
- Headcount projections.
- Conference rooms, cafeteria, and training room demand/utilization projections.
- Adjacency diagram and other potential diagrams.
- Process flow diagram (optional, based on client need).
- Stacking and blocking diagrams.
- Program options and costs.
- List of conflicts or issues requiring resolution.

SECONDARY CIRCULATION FORMULA AND TABLES: RULES OF THUMB

Secondary Circulation Factor is used to calculate the Usable Square Footage from the programmed Net Square Footage.

The Secondary Circulation Factor is calculated using the following formula:

$$\text{CIRCULATION FACTOR} = \frac{1}{(1.0 - \% \text{ circulation})}$$

The Usable Square Footage (USF) is equal to the Net Square Footage (NSF) multiplied by the Secondary Circulation Factor.

USF written as an equation is:

$$\text{USF} = \text{NSF} \times \frac{1}{(1.0 - \% \text{ circulation})}$$

Example: Given the NSF is 50,000 square feet and the appropriate Secondary Circulation is identified as 35%, then:

$$\text{USF} = 50,000 \times \frac{1}{(1.0 - 0.35)}$$

$$\text{USF} = 50,000 \times 1.54$$
$$\text{USF} = 77,000 \text{ Usable Square Feet}$$

% SECONDARY CIRCULATION	SECONDARY CIRCULATION FACTOR
50%	2.00
45%	1.82
40%	1.67
35%	1.54
30%	1.43
25%	1.33
20%	1.25
15%	1.18
10%	1.11

Note: Typical circulation percentage assumed for typical office space is 35%.

DESIGN DEPARTMENT SECONDARY CIRCULATION

SPACE TYPES	DESIGN DEPENDENT PERCENTAGES
Break Spaces	25%-40%
Executive Briefing Centers	10%-25%
Copy Center	25%
Fitness Spaces	25%
Kitchen Spaces	25%-40%
Large Meeting Spaces	25%
Loading Dock	10%
Mail Room	25%
Site Amenities	40%
Support Spaces	35%
Training Spaces	25%-40%
Visitor Reception	25%-50%
Workspace – Open	35%-40%
Workspace – Open – Call Centers	50%-55%
Workspace – Closed Intermingled with Open	35%-40%
Workspace – Closed – Traditional Layout (for example, law firm)	25%-35%

Note: The Design Department Secondary Circulation Numbers in the above chart assume a standard rectangular building with good planning efficiencies.

Circulation factors vary depending on type of business and other factors.

understand the meaning and implications of some of the data gathered. Data projection is required during this process. It is typical, for example, to project headcounts at least three years into the future for a program. Clients do not always have the information required to program future needs, especially those beyond three years. Statistics can provide information that enables the programmer to project data into the future when the data available from the client is incomplete.

The program is the synthesis of the client information and the specification of the client's needs. Outcomes of the synthesis of the information include the program document, adjacency diagrams, and stacking diagrams.

Step 3: Documentation and Validation

The final step in the process is to document and validate the program. Once the program is complete, a program review meeting is scheduled. The program review may be held at various levels of detail, depending on the client's personality and project complexity. Each page may be examined in detail; or an overview of the results, assumptions, and key issues may be provided to the client. Regardless, all fundamental assumptions, such as projections of headcount, conference usage, and so on, must be reviewed in detail, agreed to, and signed off by the client.

Once the assumptions and draft program have been reviewed and signed off, the final program can be completed and the program report developed. The completed program report is a "stand-alone" document that communicates to the client all required information about the environment, its functions, and the space needs; it should not require additional explanation. A good-quality program fills the individual and unique needs, or answers the questions, of everyone in the process. When a program is well conceived and executed, it becomes a useful tool for the real estate broker, the design team, and the client.

Acceptance Statement

The final step in the process is twofold: delivering the final program report and getting a signed program acceptance statement from the client. The acceptance statement is a critical, and often overlooked, part of the process. Sign-off is an important step, both to confirm that a client agrees with the fundamental assumptions and the resulting program as well as to provide documentation that reduces future liability to the design firm. The program is only as good as the information provided and gathered. Given economic ups and downs and other changes, tomorrow's headcount could be very different from the level projected. Programmers are given information by the client that is processed in order to identify the space implications. Those implications and solution options are reported to the client, who then selects the direction and desired solution.

Step 3: Documentation and Validation: Activities and Products

Activities
- Summarize findings.
- Document findings in report format.
- Review findings, program, and options with client.
- Identify program direction and document program changes.
- Update program and documentation.
- Get client sign-off on program and projections.

Products
- Draft of program report.
- Options analysis.
- Program review meeting notes.
- Revised and final program report.
- Signed program acceptance statement.

SAMPLE PROGRAM WITH INTERVIEW NOTES FOR A SMALL DEPARTMENT

AREA TYPE POSITION	SPACE/STD.	AREA	STAFF/QTY/AREA (SQ.FT.)								
			YE 2003			YE 2008			YE 2012		
			STAFF	QTY	AREA	STAFF	QTY	AREA	STAFF	QTY	AREA
Workplaces											
1 Shareholder	PO.01	225	2	2	450	2	2	450	2	2	450
2 Shareholder Growth	PO.01	225	1	1	225	2	2	450	2	2	450
3 Other LC Growth	PO.02	150	3	3	450	3	3	450	4	4	600
4 Paralegals	PO.03	100	1	1	100	1	1	100	1	1	100
5 Paralegal Growth	PO.03	100	2	2	200	3	3	300	3	3	300
6 Secretary	WS03	65	1	1	65	1	1	65	1	1	65
7 Secretary Growth	WS03	65	2	2	130	3	3	195	3	3	195
SUBTOTAL NET (USF) Workplaces				12	1,620		15	2,010		16	2,160
Secondary Circulation		43%			697			864			929
SUBTOTAL (USF) Work places			12	12	2,317	15	15	2,874	16	16	3,089
Support Areas											
1. Local Files-Attorney	FILE 01	9	0	24	216	0	32	288	0	32	288
2. Secretarial file cabinets	FILE 01	9		6	54		8	72		8	72
SUBTOTAL NET (USF) Support Areas				30	270		40	360		40	360
Secondary Circulation		43%			166			155			155
SUBTOTAL (USF) Support Areas			0	30	386	0	40	515	0	40	515
SUBTOTAL NET (USF) Area Types				42	1,890		55	2,370		56	2,520
Total Secondary Circulation		43%			813			1,019			1,084
TOTAL (USF) Financial Institutions			12	42	2,703	15	55	3,389	16	56	3,604

Space standards are developed in response to the program. Individual space requirements are developed from the needs defined by the client and what is known about the potential furniture solution.

INFORMATION INDEX

CONSIDERATIONS	GOALS	FACTS	CONCEPTS	NEEDS	PROBLEM
Function	Mission	Statistical data		Space requirements	Unique and important
People	Maximum number	Area parameters	Service grouping	Parking requirements	Performance requirements
	Individual identity	Manpower/workloads	People grouping	Outdoor space	that will shape
	Interaction, privacy	User characteristics	Activity grouping	requirements	building design
	Ranking of values	Community characteristics	Priority		
	Exercise of authority	Authority structure	Hierarchy		
Activities	Security	Value of potential loss	Security controls		
	Progression	Time-motion study	Sequential flow		
	Segregation	Traffic analysis	Separated flow		
	Encounters	Behavioral patterns	Mixed flow		
	Efficiency	Space adequacy	Relationships		
Relationships	Information exchange	Type/intensity	Communication		
Form	Bias on site elements	Site analysis	Enhancement	Site development costs	Major form considerations
Site	Sound structure	Soil analysis	Special foundations		that will affect building design
	Efficient land use	F.A.R. (floor area ratio)	Density		
	Physical comfort	Climate analysis	Environmental controls	Environmental	
	Life safety	Code survey	Safety precautions	influences on costs	
Environment	Sociality	Surroundings	Neighbors		
	Individuality	Psychological implications	Home base		
	Encoded direction	Point of reference	Orientation		
	Direct entry	Entry symbols	Accessibility		
	Projected image	Generic nature	Character		
Quality	Building quality level	Cost/sq ft	Quality control		
	Spatial quality level	Building efficiency		Building cost/sq ft	
	Technical quality level	Equipment costs		Building efficiency	
	Functional quality level	Area per unit		Equipment costs	
Economy	Extent of funds	Cost parameters	Cost control	Cost estimate analysis	Attitude toward the initial
Initial Budget	Cost-effectiveness	Maximum budget	Efficient allocation		budget and its influence
	Maximum return	Time-use factors	Multifunction		on the fabric and geometry
	Return on investment	Market analysis	Merchandising		of the building
Operating Costs	Minimize operating costs	Energy source-costs	Energy conservation	Energy budget (if req'd)	
	Maintenance and operating costs	Activities and climate factors	Cost control	Operating costs (if req'd)	
Life-Cycle Costs	Reduce life-cycle costs	Economic data	Cost control	Life-cycle costs (if req'd)	
Time	Historic preservation	Significance	Adaptability		
Past	Static dynamic activities	Space parameters	Tolerance		
	Change	Activities	Convertibility		
Present	Growth	Projections	Expansibility		
	Occupancy date	Durations	Linear/concurrent scheduling	Time schedule	
Future	Cost-controlled growth	Escalation factors	Phasing	Time/cost scheduling	

This matrix represents typical programmatic issues and provides an information index. The index can be used by the programmer as a reference tool to aid in collecting the information relevant to the project at hand. *Source:* Problem Seeking, *William Pena, John Wiley & Sons, Inc., New York, 2001.*

INFORMATION INDEX

Problem Seeking, by William Pena, defines a five-step process for gathering and organizing programming information. The process provides a methodology for capturing, organizing, and processing information. The five steps of the process are:

- *Establish goals.* "What does the client want to achieve and why?"
- *Identify facts.* "What is it all about?"
- *Uncover concepts.* "How does the client want to achieve the goals?"
- *Determine needs.* "How much space, money, and quality?"
- *State the problem.* "What are the significant conditions and the general directions that the design should take?"

Information gleaned and developed during each step of the process is organized into the following categories:

- *Function,* which relates to people, activities, and relationships.
- *Form,* which relates to the site, the environment, and the quality of construction, finishes, and furnishings.
- *Economy,* which relates to the initial budget, operating costs, and life-cycle costs.
- *Time,* which relates to past, present, and future considerations.

Anne Mott; lauckgroup; Dallas, Texas

CONTRACT DOCUMENTS FOR COMMERCIAL INTERIORS

Contract documents describe the proposed construction of furniture, furnishings, and equipment installation. They include written specifications and graphic documentation, such as drawings, which communicate the design of the project. The two sets of contract documents that a designer must prepare for a complete commercial interiors project are the *construction contract documents*, and the *furniture, furnishings, and equipment (FF&E) contract documents*

THE CONTRACT FOR CONSTRUCTION

The agreement between the owner and the construction contractor is the contract for construction. The construction contractor's responsibilities are described in AIA A201, *The General Conditions of the Contract for Construction*. The construction contractor is responsible for supervising and directing the construction of the project. This includes providing labor, materials, equipment, tools, water, heat, utilities, and other facilities and safety features. The *construction contractor* employs the various trades required to accomplish the work of the contract, or makes agreements with subcontractors. The *general contractor* coordinates the work of these specialty contractors, such as electricians, plumbers, painters, carpenters, and carpet installers.

In addition to orchestrating various construction activities, construction contractors perform a variety of administrative tasks. The general contractor is usually responsible for securing and paying for the building permit and other permits required for completion of the project. The general contractor is also generally responsible for the preparation of a construction schedule, and must prepare and submit shop drawings and samples for the architect's approval.

Shop drawings illustrate specific situations or details of a project. They are prepared by the construction contractor, one of the subcontractors, the product manufacturer, or the supplier. These drawings are then submitted to the designer for approval (for example, samples of the materials or workmanship); these are used to verify selections and to establish standards by which the completed work will be judged. Shop drawings and samples are not contract documents. They are submitted to demonstrate the way in which the construction contractor intends to accomplish the design expressed by the contract documents.

CONSTRUCTION PROJECT TYPES

The traditional approach to a construction project is the design-award-build sequence of events. The designer fully documents the project in the contract documents, which include the construction drawings and specifications. Proposals to build the project are requested from construction contractors. These bids are evaluated, a contractor is selected, and a construction contract between the successful bidder and the owner is signed. The "owner" in most cases is the tenant, but, depending on the terms of the lease and work letter, the owner may also be the landlord. The architect is usually retained to administer the contract for construction between the owner and the construction contractor.

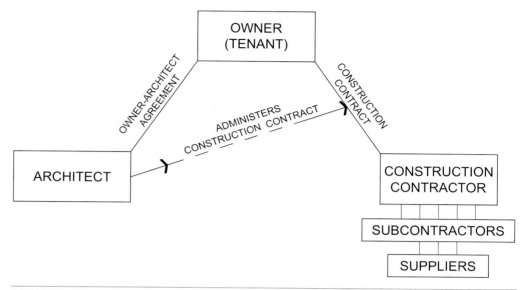

CONSTRUCTION CONTRACT

It is often necessary to begin construction as soon as possible because of accelerated occupancy schedules or the high cost of financing a project. In the fast-track approach to construction, building begins before the project design is complete. Separate construction contracts are defined, and contract documents are prepared for each phase. Items that are last to be installed or constructed, such as custom casework, will be the last to be fully designed and bid. The design schedule extends into the construction schedule, reducing the duration of the project. Fast-tracking often increases construction costs due to decreased labor efficiency.

In design/build projects, one party is responsible for both the design and the construction of the interior. The design/build firm may be a construction company with in-house designers or one that has hired a design firm consultant. The advantage of this method of con-

struction contracting is that the contractor is involved with the project from the initial stages. Costs, material availability, and scheduling can be estimated much more accurately.

Construction for commercial interiors on leased properties is referred to by various names, including *tenant build-out work, tenant fit-up,* or *tenant improvements*. Lease provisions often require that the landlord approve the prime, or general, contractor and the subcontractors. In some cases, landlords retain contractors to build all tenant spaces in their buildings.

FURNITURE, FURNISHINGS, AND EQUIPMENT (FF&E) CONTRACTS

The FF&E contractor is responsible for procuring, delivering, and installing the goods described in the FF&E contract. The designer typically administers the agreement between the owner and the FF&E contractor. The FF&E contractor is often a furniture dealer but may also be a furniture manufacturer or a design professional.

FF&E Contractors

The furniture dealer is the local or regional presence of the manufacturer. The dealer processes the sale and provides various support and follow-up services to the owner. In this way, the manufacturer concentrates on product development and production, and the dealer focuses on sales and service. One of the services a dealer typically offers is warehousing the goods between the time manufacturing has been completed and the point at which the project site is ready to receive them for installation.

A direct sales force represents the manufacturer, not the manufacturer's dealer. Equipment is commonly procured directly from the manufacturer through a direct sales force. For example, a hospital bed manufacturer may not require a showroom to market a relatively expensive product with a limited user base. The sale may be effectively accomplished by sending a sample bed to the hospital on a trial basis or by arranging a tour of the factory showroom.

DESIGN/BUILD CONTRACT

Construction documents diagram, reprinted from the Construction Specifications Institute's *Manual of Practice*.

COMPLETE CONTRACT DOCUMENTS FOR A COMMERCIAL INTERIORS PROJECT

1   ☐   **CONTRACT ADMINISTRATION**

COMPARISON OF CONSTRUCTION CONTRACT AND FF&E CONTRACT BY PROJECT PHASE

CONSTRUCTION CONTRACT FOR INTERIORS	FF&E CONTRACT	DESIGNER	TENANT	FF&E OR CONSTRUCTION CONTRACTOR
PREDESIGN				
Programming		P	A	
Select Building	N/A	R	P	
Work Letter/Lease Negotiation	Space Planning or Test Layouts	P	R, A	
Site Survey	FF&E Inventory	P		
Building Standards	Work Station Standards		R	
SCHEMATIC DESIGN				
Conceptual Design		P	A	
Initial Plans		P	A	
Conceptual Elevations		P	A	
Outline Specifications		P	A	

Consultant Coordination
  Acoustical
  Electrical
  Mechanical
  Structural
	Consultant Coordination
	  Planting (Indoor Landscaping)
	  Signage
	  Furniture Project Manager
		P		

Preliminary Pricing		P	R, A	
Meetings/Presentation		P	R, A	
DESIGN DEVELOPMENT				
N/A	Research FF&E	P	R, A	
Construct Mockups	Install Mockups/Manufacturer Presentation	R, A	A	P
Definitive Construction Documents	Definitive FF&E Documents	P	R, A	
Definitive Construction Specifications	Definitive FF&E Specifications	P	R, A	
Develop Budget for Construction	Develop Budget for FF&E	R	P	
CONTRACT DOCUMENTS				
Final Construction Drawings	Final FF&E Drawings	P	R, A	
Final Construction Specifications	Final FF&E Specifications	P	R, A	
Prepare Bid Documents UNIT PRICES (adjustment to contract made by change order during contract administration): These prices are determined by bidder. ALTERNATES (options are priced separately): Alternates are accepted by tenant. ALLOWANCES (monies reserved in contract): Tenant allows for work not determined at time of bid.	Prepare Bid Documents UNIT PRICES: Bids are itemized as unit prices. Cost per item is determined by contractor's discount price. ALTERNATES: Less commonly used. Costs are known during design phase and are factored in item selection. ALLOWANCES: Less commonly used. Tenant can use allowances for budgeting purposes.	P	R, A	R
BIDDING OR NEGOTIATION				
Prequalification of Bidders		A		
Issue Addenda		P	A	R
Receive Bids		R	P, A	
Bid Review/Analysis		P	R	
Confirm Performance Bond			P	
Confirm Insurance			P	
Award Contracts		R	P	
Submit Construction Schedule	Submit P.O. Tracking Report	R		P
CONTRACT ADMINISTRATION				
CONSTRUCTION	**INSTALLATION**			
Determine Deposits/Orders for Long Lead Items	Determine Deposits for FF&E Orders	R	P	
Set up Temporary Facilities	Determine Staging Area		A	P
Project Coordination Contractor responsible for subcontractors.	Project Coordination: Tenant coordinates FF&E contractors and their work with construction contractor.	R		P
Construction Meetings	Job Progress Meetings	R, A	A	P
Submittal Review		R, A		P
Review Project Progress		P	A	
Product Substitutions; proposed by contractor	Typically not permitted. Contractor points out reason why substitution must be made. Designer proposes substitute to tenant.	R, A	A	P
Authorize Payments	P.O.s may not be submitted to designer for approval.	R, A		P
Issue Certificate of Payments	Tenant pays P.O. invoice.	R, A		P
Contract Document Revision		P	A	
Issue Change Orders	Issue, revise, or cancel P.O.s	R, A	A	P
Determine Substantial Completion	Tenant pays P.O. invoice.	A		P
Not Applicable	P.O. Coordination	R, A		P
Prepare Punchlist		P	A	R
Not Applicable	Move Coordination	P	A	
Determine Final Completion	Tenant pays final P.O. invoice.	A		P

P = Performs task

R = Reviews

A = Approves

American Institute of Architects; Washington, D.C.

FF&E Contractor Roles

The FF&E contractor prepares purchase orders based on the FF&E contract. A purchase order is the form used to obtain the required goods for the project. It contains a description of the goods, the supplier's catalog number, the number of items required, and the price. Separate purchase orders are prepared for each supplier involved in the project.

An *acknowledgment*, also referred to as a *purchase order acknowledgment*, is prepared by the supplier as confirmation of the purchase order. The acknowledgment must be verified by the FF&E contractor to make sure it is an accurate interpretation of the purchase order. If the purchase order acknowledgment is correct, the order is placed and the manufacturing process begins.

The FF&E contractor coordinates the requirements for customer's own material (C.O.M.), material that is not supplied by the product manufacturer. C.O.M. is purchased separately from the product and supplied to the product manufacturer for application. "Customer" in this case does not refer to the designer's customer, the owner, but to the manufacturer's customer, the party placing the order, which is the FF&E contractor. It is the FF&E contractor who is responsible for the acquisition and coordination of C.O.M.

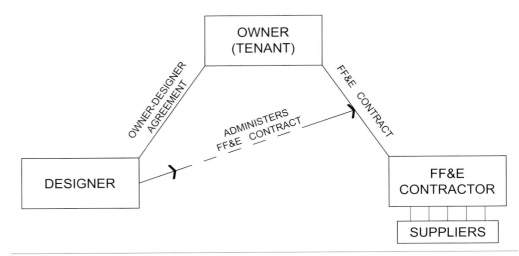

FF&E CONTRACT FOR INTERIORS PROJECT

The owner can also procure the required goods through their in-house purchasing departments. Large corporations can purchase products—for example, carpet, furniture, fabric, and light fixtures—and supply them to the contractor for installation. This allows a business to establish national accounts with vendors and to reduce costs by buying in volume.

After the goods have been manufactured, they are packaged for delivery. An invoice, a bill requesting payment for the goods, is prepared by the manufacturer and sent to the FF&E contractor, typically at the same time the goods are shipped.

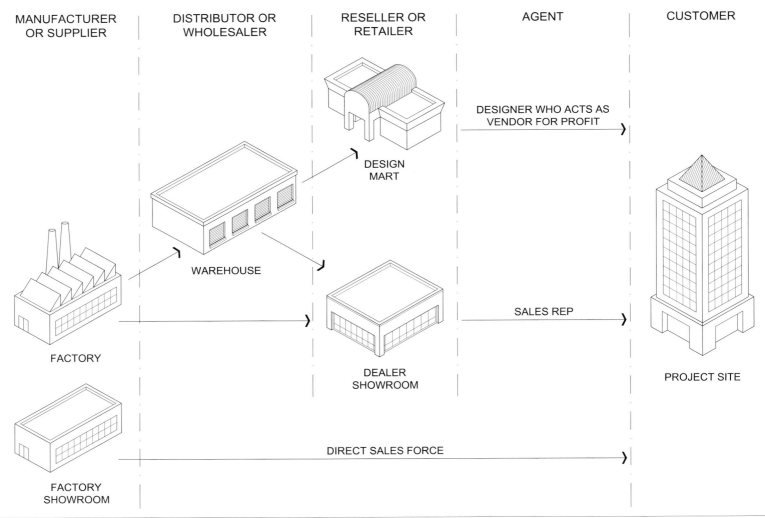

THREE COMMON METHODS OF FF&E DISTRIBUTION

DELIVERY AND INSTALLATION OF FF&E

The Uniform Commercial Code (UCC) defines many of the terms, and sets forth the procedures, used in the delivery of goods. Delivery is defined by the UCC as voluntary transfer of possession (UCC 1-201). Delivery does not necessarily indicate ownership. Title means ownership. If you have title to goods, you own them. For example, a manufacturer delivers furniture to a carrier for transportation to its destination. The manufacturer is not transferring title to the goods; therefore the carrier does not own the furniture. Receipt is defined as taking physical possession of goods (UCC 2-103).

A carrier is a transportation company. Carriers that operate in interstate commerce are regulated by the Interstate Commerce Commission (ICC). Common carriers offer transportation services to the general public. They are usually responsible for the goods they are shipping, whether or not they have been negligent. Contract carriers provide transportation only to those with whom they choose to do business. They do not insure the goods they transport unless they are contracted to do so. Private carriers are not in the transportation business. They own and operate trucks to transport their own goods. The ICC does not regulate private carriers.

With few exceptions, such as when goods are picked up by the buyer (see UCC 2-509), whoever has title to the goods bears the risk of their being lost, stolen, damaged, or destroyed. The risk of loss is commonly indicated by the abbreviation F.O.B., defined by the UCC as "free on board" (UCC 2-319).

F.O.B. at a named place indicates where title to the goods and risk of their loss or damage pass from the seller to the buyer, which is typically the FF&E contractor. The buyer pays the transportation costs from the point named in the F.O.B. "place."

F.O.B. Designations

When goods are sent *F.O.B. place of shipment*, the buyer owns the goods at the place of shipment (typically, the manufacturer's factory loading dock). The goods are given to the carrier (typically, a truck), and the seller is no longer responsible for the delivery of the goods or their condition upon arrival. The buyer pays for shipping. If the goods are stolen, damaged, or destroyed in transit, it is the buyer's responsibility to recover damages from the carrier. When the terms of shipment do not specify shipping point or destination, it is assumed to be F.O.B. place of shipment.

F.O.B. place of destination means the seller is responsible for delivering the goods. The cost of the goods includes shipping charges. If the goods are stolen, damaged, or destroyed in transit, it is the seller's responsibility to recover damages from the carrier (UCC 2-319).

F.O.B. factory—freight prepaid means that the buyer has title to the goods during transit but that the supplier pays the transportation charges to the destination. In this way, the buyer has the convenience of not having to arrange for transportation, and the supplier reduces its liability.

Shipment Tracking

A *drop shipment* means the goods will be shipped to a destination different from that of the party who ordered and paid for them. A *bill of lading* is defined

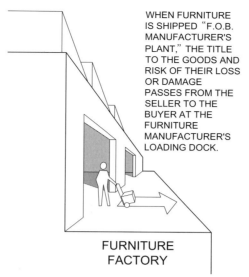

WHEN FURNITURE IS SHIPPED "F.O.B. MANUFACTURER'S PLANT," THE TITLE TO THE GOODS AND RISK OF THEIR LOSS OR DAMAGE PASSES FROM THE SELLER TO THE BUYER AT THE FURNITURE MANUFACTURER'S LOADING DOCK.

FURNITURE FACTORY

F.O.B. MANUFACTURER'S PLANT

WHEN FURNITURE IS SHIPPED "F.O.B. PROJECT SITE," THE TITLE TO THE GOODS AND RISK OF THEIR LOSS OR DAMAGE PASSES FROM THE SELLER TO THE BUYER AT THE PROJECT SITE LOADING DOCK.

PROJECT SITE

F.O.B. PROJECT SITE

F.O.B. "FREE ON BOARD"

PASSAGE OF TITLE

	SELLER ASSUMES EXPENSE AND RISK OF...	PASSAGE OF TITLE OCCURS AT...	PRICE OF GOODS...
F.O.B.: Place of shipment	Putting goods into the possession of the carrier place of shipment	Place of shipment (typically manufacturer's factory loading dock)	Does not include shipping charges
F.O.B.: Place of destination	Transporting the goods to the destination	Destination (typically the project site's loading dock)	Includes shipping charges

by the UCC as a document confirming the receipt of goods for shipment issued by a person engaged in the business of transporting (UCC 1-201).

The supplier prepares the bill of lading. The carrier verifies that the goods loaded on its vehicle match those listed on the bill of lading. The bill of lading lists the number of boxes, crates, or packages. It is not intended to verify that the goods being transported are the goods that were ordered. A packing list is a detailed list of quantities and descriptions of the goods being delivered. It is used to check the items, and it cross-references the bill of lading. The packing list is typically attached to the outside of the shipping package in a clear plastic envelope.

LAWS GOVERNING CONTRACTS FOR INTERIORS PROJECTS

A contract is an agreement between two or more parties that is based on mutual promises to do (or refrain from doing) something that is neither illegal nor impossible. A contract is basically a promise that the law will enforce. U.S. laws must conform to the U.S. Constitution and can originate from any of the three branches of government: executive, legislative, or judicial. Laws governing interiors projects stem from a variety of sources. These sources include *constitutional law*, *statutory law*, *common law*, and *administrative law*, as well as *contract and commercial law*.

Constitutional Law

A constitution is the basic law of a nation or state. Constitutional law is the supreme law of a nation. All forms of law must conform to the constitution. The

U.S. Constitution establishes the organization of the federal government.

Statutory Law

Laws passed by a legislature are known as *statutes*. At the federal level, these are the laws that are passed by Congress and signed by the president. At the state level, statutes are enacted by state legislative bodies. Statutory law also includes ordinances passed at the local level by cities and counties.

Because many different statutes are passed each year by each state's legislative body, there are significant differences in statutory law throughout the United States. This may present problems when parties from different states and subject to different laws try to do business. The most important development in uniform legislation among the states has been the Uniform Commercial Code (UCC), the group of statutory laws governing sales transactions in the United States. The UCC governs contracts for FF&E.

Common Law

Common law is based on the outcome of previous court cases under comparable circumstances. The tradition of common law dates back to the early English kings' attempts at establishing a fair system of rules that all courts in the kingdom could hold in common. Consistency was maintained by relying on previous legal decisions. These previous decisions, known as *precedents*, became model cases for the courts to follow when facing similar situations. Common law, as modified by statute, governs contracts for construction.

Administrative Law

Contemporary society often presents problems so complex that neither legislators nor judges have the expertise to provide adequate counsel. To assist in this effort, legislators commonly delegate their power to others by creating administrative agencies, boards, and commissions. The rules made by administrative agencies comprise administrative law.

Contract Law and Commercial Law

All contracts contain agreements, but not all agreements are contracts. An agreement may or may not be legally enforceable. To be enforceable, an agreement must conform to the law of contracts. Contract law is the framework for all commercial law. It serves as the basis for much of the law described in more specialized areas, such as the sale of goods.

SALES CONTRACTS AND SERVICES CONTRACTS

If the subject of a contract is real estate or services, common law and certain statutory provisions govern. If the subject of a contract is goods, then the UCC applies. Goods are defined as all things (except money, stocks, and bonds) that are movable. When a contract includes both goods and services, the dominant element of the contract determines whether it is a sales contract or a services contract.

A contract for construction, which is between the owner and the construction contractor, is essentially an agreement to provide expertise and service, and includes the purchase of construction materials. It is regulated by common law as modified by statute. A contract for FF&E, which is between the owner and the FF&E contractor, includes services such as warehousing, delivery, and installation, but it is primarily a sale-of-goods contract. A contract for FF&E is regulated by the UCC.

Uniform Commercial Code

The Uniform Commercial Code (UCC) is the set of statutes that governs the commercial transactions of all 50 states (except Louisiana, which has adopted only Articles 1, 3, 4, and 5, and the District of Columbia and the Virgin Islands). For practical purposes, the rules governing commercial transactions are consistent throughout the country because of the UCC.

In cases in which the UCC is silent, the common law of contracts and applicable state statutes govern. Common law rules and UCC provisions are quite often the same. The UCC simplifies the law governing commercial transactions by making the fundamental rules of contract law less rigid. UCC provisions are more appropriate than common law for a variety of circumstances typical of sales transactions. Although many common law rules and UCC provisions are the same, there are some significant differences.

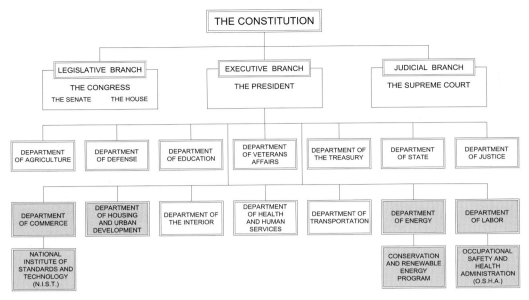

Shaded departments are involved in building regulations.

THE U.S. GOVERNMENT

Differences between Contract Law and Commercial Law: Warranties

Offer and Acceptance in Formation of Contract (UCC 2-206)

Rules of commercial law regarding the way an offer is made and accepted are not as strict as those of contract law. In many cases, an enforceable sales contract can be made in any way—written, oral, or by conduct that shows an agreement has been reached. Unless the original agreement is in writing with a stipulation that it may not be modified except by a signed contract, mutual promises are not required to modify a contract for the sale of goods. In a sale-of-goods contract, the purchase price may be omitted and the amount of goods to be sold need not always be defined.

UCC Warranty Definitions

The UCC is the primary source for rules regarding warranties in commercial transactions. It defines two important types of warranties: *express* and *implied*.

An express warranty is a representation about the quality of a product. There are three different ways to make an express warranty: by a statement of fact or promise, by a description of the goods, or by a sample or model (UCC 2-313).

An implied warranty is inferred from the nature of the transaction. The seller does not offer an implied war-

ranty; it is imposed by law. Implied warranties are designed to promote fairness and honesty. There are two types of implied warranties: an *implied warranty of merchantability* and an *implied warranty of fitness* for a particular purpose.

An implied warranty of merchantability assures the buyer that the goods are fit for the ordinary purpose for which they are to be used. This warranty type applies only to sales made by merchants who deal in goods of the kind sold (UCC 2-314). For example, a furniture dealer makes an implied warranty of merchantability every time it sells a desk, but a neighbor selling the same desk at a yard sale does not. For a claim to be made for a breach of this type of warranty, a defect must exist at the time the goods are purchased.

When a buyer relies on a seller's judgment to select the goods, it is implied that the seller warrants that the goods will be fit for the purpose for which they are to be used. This creates the implied warranty of fitness for a particular purpose. This warranty type applies to both merchants and nonmerchants. If the seller knows how the buyer will use the goods and knows the buyer is relying on the seller's skill in selecting the goods, there is an implied warranty of fitness (UCC 2-315).

DIFFERENCES BETWEEN THE UCC AND CONTRACT LAW

UCC	CONTRACT LAW
Not all terms have to be included in the contract (UCC 2-204).	An offer must be definite enough for the parties (and the courts) to ascertain its essential terms when the contract is accepted.
Firm written offers by merchants for three months or less cannot be revoked (UCC 2-205).	An offer can be revoked any time before acceptance.
The price does not have to be included to have a contract (UCC 2-305).	Price must be included.
Variation in terms between the offer and the acceptance may not be a rejection (UCC 2-207).	Variation in terms between the offer and the acceptance act as a rejection of, and a counteroffer to, the offer.
A modification for the sale-of-goods contract does not require mutual agreement (UCC 2-209).	Modification of common law contract requires mutual agreement.

REGULATORY ANALYSIS CHECKLIST FOR COMMERCIAL INTERIORS

This checklist can be used to verify that all aspects of regulatory requirements, including building codes, fire codes, and other authorities having jurisdiction have been addressed. Many of the requirements in this checklist are discussed in detail in *Building Code Overview*.

REGULATORY ANALYSIS CHECKLIST FOR COMMERCIAL INTERIORS

STEP	PROCEDURE	IBC SECTION	P—Performs Task: Verification, Determination, or Calculation / R—Reviews / A—Approves / S—Support NAME	NAME	NAME	NAME	NAME	NAME	REGULATORY REQUIREMENTS AND COMMENTS
Determine Building Occupancy Classifications and Loads									
1.	Determine occupancy classification(s). Determine incidental and accessory uses (Sections 302.1.1 and 302.2).	Sections 302–312							
	Are high-hazard areas present?								
2.	Review specific requirements for certain occupancies.	Chapter 4							
3.	Calculate occupant load (the allowed number of people).	1003.2.2 and Table 1003.2.2.2							
4.	Determine mixed-occupancy separations required, if applicable. (Fire separations between mixed occupancies are not required if the building is designed for the most restrictive occupancy (see Section 301.3.2).)	302.3 and Table 302.3.3							
	Maximum compartment size								
Determine Construction Type and Building Size									
5.	Verify whether construction-type information will be applicable (e.g., new column covers). If available, new interior construction must conform to fire-resistive requirements in Table 601.	Chapter 6 and Table 601							
	Maximum allowed stories (building height)								
	Maximum allowed area								
Determine Means of Egress									

Exit Access: The portion of a means of egress that leads to the entrance of an exit. It includes any room or space occupied by a person, doorway, aisle, corridor, stair, or ramp traveled on the way to the exit. It leads an occupant to an exit.
Exit: The portion of a means of egress that is protected and fully enclosed. It is between the exit access and the exit discharge.
Exit Discharge: The portion of a means of egress between the termination of an exit and the public way.

STEP	PROCEDURE	IBC SECTION							
6.	Check for common path of egress travel. (If the common path of egress travel distance is exceeded in a space that would normally only require one exit, additional exits may be required.)	1004.2.5							
7.	Determine number of exits required.	1004.2; 1005.2.1							
8.	Verify that maximum distance to exits has not been exceeded.	1004.2.4 and Table 1004.2.4							
9.	Determine arrangement of exits. (In odd-shaped spaces, be conservative and measure the distance that is greatest.)	1004.2.2							
10.	Determine width of exits.	1003.2.3; Table 1003.2.3; 1004.2.4; 1005.3.3.1							
11.	Check for dead-end corridors, exits through adjoining rooms, and special exiting requirements of Sections 402–415.	1004.2.3; 1004.3.2.3; Chapter 4							
12.	Verify special exiting requirements for A and R occupancies at the end of Chapter 10.	1008; 1009							
13.	Determine required extent and construction of corridors.	1004.3.2.1 and Table 1004.3.2.1							
	Maximum distance between rated exit doors								
	Maximum distance to nearest exit								
	Requirements for unsprinklered corridors								
	Requirements for sprinklered corridors								
	Requirements for at-grade corridors								
	Maximum dead end								
	Occupant per exit unit								
	Minimum width								
	Clear headroom								
	Maximum glass area in corridor wall 1-hour or 2-hour								
14.	Verify exit door rating, size, hardware, and swing.	1003.3.1							
	Minimum width								
	Maximum width								
	Units of exit width								
	Occupants per exit unit								
	Swing of corridor door								
	Rating/glass size:								
	• Fire doors								
	• Smoke doors								
	• Horizontal exit door								
	• Stair door								
	• Corridor doors								
	Special hardware requirements								
	Minimum height								
	Direction of swing								
	Maximum height for required rating								
	ADA requirements								

REGULATORY ANALYSIS CHECKLIST FOR COMMERCIAL INTERIORS *(continued)*

STEP	PROCEDURE	IBC SECTION	P—Performs Task: Verification, Determination, or Calculation / R—Reviews / A—Approves / S—Support (NAME × 6)						REGULATORY REQUIREMENTS AND COMMENTS
Determine Means of Egress *(continued)*									
15.	Verify stairway requirements, if applicable.	1003.3.3; 1005.3.2							
	Unit of exit width								
	Occupants per unit								
	Minimum exit width								
	Minimum landing width								
	Maximum landing reduction by door								
	Maximum vertical distance between landings								
	Minimum headroom								
	Stair formula								
	Tread and riser dimensions								
	Maximum handrail projection								
	Handrail height								
	Handrail length at landing								
	Smokeproof tower								
	Exit-level barrier								
	OSHA requirements								
16.	Check requirements for ramps, if applicable.	1003.3.4							
Determine Fire-Resistive Ratings									
17.	Determine maximum flame spread requirements for interior finishes.	Chapter 8 and Table 803.4							
	Determine fire-resistive rating of other construction:								
	• Exterior bearing walls								
	• Exterior nonbearing walls								
	• Exterior doors and windows								
	• Interior bearing walls								
	• Interior nonbearing walls								
	• Permanent partitions								
	• Shaft enclosures								
	• Floor construction								
	• Roof construction assembly								
	• Structural frame								
	• Exterior columns								
	• Interior columns supporting roof or other floors								
	• Occupancy separation walls								
	• Smoke baffles								
	• Interior court								
	• Stair enclosures								
Determine Interior Environment Requirements									
18.	Check required light, ventilation, and sanitation requirements for occupancy, if applicable. (Chapter 12 also contains requirements for sound transmission in R occupancies, minimum interior space dimensions, and requirements for surrounding finish materials in toilet and bathing rooms.)	Chapter 12; Chapter 29							
	Room size								
	Maximum ceiling height								
	Natural light and ventilation								
	• Window requirement								
	• Maximum sill height								
	Sound control								
	Pest control								
Determine ADA Requirements									
19.	Verify accessibility requirements for type of use. (The IBC adopts ICC/ANSI A1171.1, *Accessible and Usable Buildings and Facilities*, as the standard for accessibility. The ADA Accessibility Guidelines should also be consulted.	Chapter 11 and ADAAG							

REGULATORY ANALYSIS CHECKLIST FOR COMMERCIAL INTERIORS *(continued)*

STEP	PROCEDURE	IBC SECTION	P—Performs Task: Verification, Determination, or Calculation / R—Reviews / A—Approves / S—Support						REGULATORY REQUIREMENTS AND COMMENTS
			NAME	NAME	NAME	NAME	NAME	NAME	
Other Requirements									
20.	If glass is used, verify glazing requirements.	714.3.6; 2406							
21.	If guards are used, check requirements. ("Guards" is the new terminology for guardrails used in previous codes.)	1003.2.12							
22.	Determine Fire and Smoke Protection Requirements:								
	Are sprinklers required?								
	Are sprinklers present?								
	Heat detectors								
	Smoke detectors								
	Alarm systems								
	Special fire-suppression systems								
	Fire district provisions								
	Firefighter access								
23.	Determine Mechanical, Electrical, Plumbing, and Conveying System Requirements:								
	Mechanical requirements								
	Electrical requirements								
	Lighting standards								
	Plumbing fixture requirements								
	Elevator requirements								
	Escalator requirements								
24.	Determine Structural Load and Construction Material Requirements:								
	Roof								
	Floor								
	Special live-load requirements								
	Earthquake requirements								
25.	Determine Energy Efficiency Requirements:								
	Environmental restrictions								
	Percent glass requirements								
	U-factor wall requirements								
	Roofs								
	Cooling criteria BTU h/sq ft requirements								
	• Walls								
	• Roofs								

PROJECT MANAGEMENT CHECKLIST FOR COMMERCIAL INTERIORS

PROJECT MANAGEMENT CHECKLIST FOR COMMERCIAL INTERIORS

REQUIREMENTS AND COMMENTS	P—Performs Task: Verification, Determination, or Calculation / R—Reviews / A—Approves / S—Support (NAME ×6)	CONSTRUCTION CONTRACT	FF&E CONTRACT	P—Performs Task: Verification, Determination, or Calculation / R—Reviews / A—Approves / S—Support (NAME ×6)
Predesign				
		Programming		
		Work Letter/Lease Negotiation	Space Planning or Test Layouts	
		Site Survey	FF&E Inventory	
		Building Standards	Work Station Standards	
Schematic Design				
		Conceptual Design		
		Initial Plans		
		Conceptual Elevations		
		Outline Specifications		
		Consultant Coordination	Consultant Coordination	
		• Acoustical	• Furniture Project Manager	
		• Electrical	• Signage	
		• Mechanical	• Interior Landscaping	
		• Structural	• Specialized Equipment	
		• Other	• Other	
		Preliminary Pricing		
		Present Schematic Design to Owner		
		Written Approval from Owner of Schematic Design		
Design Development				
		Review Schematic Design		
		• Project Budget	• Furniture Budget	
		• Scope of work, so that additional services can be established	• Scope of work, so that additional services can be established	
		• Regulatory Analysis, including:		
		• Fire marshall		
		• Zoning Commission		
		• Planning Commission		
		• Department of Health, Department of Education, etc., if applicable		
		Establish Project Documentation		
		• Project file		
		• Directory of in-house and out-of-house team members		
		• Finish sample binders	• Cut sheet binders	
		• Product information binders	• FF&E information binders	
		• Outline specifications (coordinate format with consultants)	• Equipment specifications	
		• List of drawings	• List of drawings	
		• Cartoon set of drawings	• Cartoon set of drawings	
		Mock-ups		
		• Construct mock-ups for Owner verification.	• Install mock-ups/manufacturer presentation for Owner verification.	
		• Approval of construction assembly mock-ups	• Approval of furniture mock-ups	
		Prepare Definitive Contract Documents		
		Design Development Closeout		
		• Confirm construction budget.	• Confirm furniture budget.	
		• Provide cost estimate to Owner, if in Scope of Work.	• Provide cost estimate to Owner, if in Scope of Work.	
		• Confirm Owner's signed approval of DD drawings, product data, and finishes manual.	• Confirm Owner's signed approval of DD drawings and furniture selections.	
		• Provide consultants with DD drawings for coordination.	• Provide consultants with equipment specifications and requirements.	
		• Archive DD construction drawings in preparation for Contract Documents phase.	• Archive DD FF&E drawings in preparation for Contract Documents phase.	

1　☐　**CONTRACT ADMINISTRATION**

PROJECT MANAGEMENT CHECKLIST FOR COMMERCIAL INTERIORS *(continued)*

REQUIREMENTS AND COMMENTS

P—Performs Task: Verification, Determination, or Calculation
R—Reviews
A—Approves
S—Support

NAME	NAME	NAME	NAME	NAME	NAME	CONSTRUCTION CONTRACT	FF&E CONTRACT	NAME	NAME	NAME	NAME	NAME	NAME
						Contract Documents							
						Final Construction Drawings	Final FF&E Drawings						
						Final Construction Specification	Final FF&E Specifications						
						Prepare Bid Documents							
						• Unit Prices (adjustment to contract made by change order during contract administration)—These prices are determined by bidder.	• Unit Prices—Bids are itemized as unit prices. Cost per item is determined by Contractor's discounted price.						
						• Alternates (options that are prices separately)—Alternates are accepted by tenant.	• Alternates—Less commonly used. Costs are known during the design phase and are a factor in item selection.						
						• Allowances (monies reserved in contract)—Tenant allows for work not determined at time of bid.	• Allowances—Less commonly used. Owner can use allowances for budgeting purposes.						
						Bidding or Negotiation							
						Prequalification of Bidders							
						Issue Addenda							
						Receive Bids							
						Bid Review and Analysis							
						Confirm Performance Bond							
						Confirm Insurance							
						Award Contracts							
						Review construction schedule.	Review Purchase Order Tracking Reports.						
						Contract Administration							
						CONSTRUCTION	INSTALLATION						
						Verify deposits.	Verify deposits.						
						Verify orders for long lead times.	Determine orders for long lead items.						
						Review submittals							
						Review project progress							
						Review substitutions							
						Review payment requests.	Review purchase orders, if in Scope of Work						
						Review change orders.	Review, revise, or cancel purchase orders, if in Scope of Work.						
						Respond to Requests for Information (RFIs)							
						Initiate bulletins							
						Review payment applications and compare with schedule of values. Request subcontractor lien waivers with each application and make sure that they are notarized.	Review purchase orders, if in Scope of Work.						
						Prepare Punchlist							
						Determine Substantial Completion Initiate certificate of substantial completion when work is sufficiently complete in accordance with the Contract Documents, to the extent that the Owner can occupy the project for the use for which it was intended. Attach punchlists to the application if any items are outstanding.							
						Move Coordination							
						Determine Final Completion							
						Project Closeout							
						Review Contractor's Punchlist							
						Ensure Owner receives as-built drawings; review as-built drawings, if in Scope of Work.							
						Submit record drawings to Owner, if in Scope of Work.							
						Review final application for payment.							
						Request subcontractor lien waivers with application.							
						Ensure Owner receives warranty and O&M (owner and maintenance manuals)							
						Ensure Owner receives spare parts and materials, as well as keys and keying schedule.							
						Archive CAD files, specifications, etc.							

The right-side columns also carry the legend:

P—Performs Task: Verification, Determination, or Calculation
R—Reviews
A—Approves
S—Support

COORDINATION CHECKLIST FOR CONSTRUCTION DRAWINGS AND SPECIFICATIONS

This checklist can be used to verify that all aspects of the project are described either in the Specifications or on the construction documents. It is organized by engineering and other disciplines that are often assigned to consultants. By locating relevant information in one place only, modifications and project coordination can be simplified.

Modify this checklist to suit the specific requirements of your practice or of a project.

COORDINATION CHECKLIST FOR CONSTRUCTION DRAWINGS AND SPECIFICATIONS

MECHANICAL COORDINATION

	CONFIRMED
General	
What type of heating and cooling system is specified, and which devices will be visible?	
Coordinate space requirements or ceiling devices, shafts, duct runs, and connections.	
Consider requirements for supplemental air (e.g., equipment rooms, after-hours work).	
Provide equipment specifications to engineer.	
Ductwork and Piping	
Verify that ductwork is sized logically.	
Verify that mechanical ducts and pipes do not conflict with architectural features, light fixtures, or structural members.	
Verify that adequate ceiling height exists at worst-case duct intersection or largest beam.	
Provide ventilation at stairwells, elevator/dumbwaiter, shafts, and at all toilet rooms.	
Ventilation	
Indicate structural supports for mechanical equipment on structural drawings.	
Verify that only required ductwork penetrates special acoustical partitions.	
Provide sound liners as required.	
Verify that air transfer ducts are included and occur above door.	
Indicate dampers at smoke partitions and fire walls.	
Provide exhaust fans as required:	
• Toilet rooms	
• Smoking rooms	
• Copy centers	
• Kitchen areas	
Diffusers and Grilles	
Confirm specification trim and finish of diffusers.	
Design supply and return grilles, considering the following:	
• Coordinate location with mechanical engineer's drawings.	
• Review specifications to assure mechanical engineer has specified desired grille type.	
• Long-term maintenance of interior finishes, art, and so on: verify that air diffuser location will not accumulate dirt/soot that will be visible on or damaging to an adjacent surface.	
Locate Young's regulators (a sort of "keyhole" for manually adjusting dampers in gypsum wallboard ceilings) and specify if concealed or exposed.	
Equipment	
Verify that equipment is located at accessible ceiling locations to avoid or minimize access panels in gypsum wallboard ceilings. Where required, access panels are frameless type.	
Verify working space around equipment required for use and servicing.	
Verify that mechanical equipment will fit in spaces allocated and that there is room for maintenance such as for removing filters or replacing parts.	
Verify that supplemental 24-hour air-handling units are located in computer rooms and rooms used after hours and on weekends.	
Verify that horsepower ratings, phases, and voltages of major items of equipment shown on drawings match that which is specified.	
Verify that cutsheets of all visible mechanical equipment have been received from consultants and have been reviewed (baseboard heat, fan coil units).	
Coordinate outdoor equipment on rooftop units with roof design, areas served, and views to buildings. Locate pads as required and coordinate with building design.	
Coordinate with mechanical engineer for items that require wall access panels, such as plumbing in an adjacent room.	
Coordinate wall heaters with mechanical engineer's drawings. Show them on interior elevations.	
Thermostats	
Note: Generally, thermostats operate better when located in the center of the room, away from direct sunlight, and out of the path of air movement. If the thermostat is located on a column in open office space, assure it will not conflict with furniture panels or be subject to damage if facing into a high-traffic corridor.	
Specify finishes for thermostat and provide instruction to Owner for HVAC controls.	
Review thermostat options with mechanical engineer and review again on shop drawings.	
Verify that thermostat type reinforces the design concept of the space.	
Note: The type of thermostat may be determined by the Owner's prescribed system for HVAC controls.	
Discuss with the mechanical engineer and the Owner whether the occupants of the space should have access to adjust the thermostat. If not, select a thermostat that prevents user access. Avoid the use of locking plastic covers over thermostats, applied after the fact, to prevent thermostat adjustment by room occupants.	

ELECTRICAL COORDINATION

	CONFIRMED
General	
Verify that the finishes of cover plates, switchplates, and so on are specified or that architectural color has been modified to match backsplash, fabric panel, and wall paint.	
Power receptacles: Coordinate locations with electrical engineer's drawings and others whose work requires electrical outlets (e.g., A/V equipment, coffeepots, copiers, microwaves, fax machines, printers, other equipment, outlets required within casework, etc.).	
Data and phone jacks: Coordinate locations with electrical engineer's drawings, A/V designer's drawings, and others for jacks for phones, computers, other computer network devices, fax machines, and so on.	
What is the Owner standard regarding power/data provisions? Refer to the approved program.	
Are emergency power provisions required?	
Define and coordinate furniture systems requirements. How many circuits? How many wires? How are they fed?	
Determine "clean" and "dirty" power requirements.	

1 ☐ **CONTRACT ADMINISTRATION**

COORDINATION CHECKLIST FOR CONSTRUCTION DRAWINGS AND SPECIFICATIONS *(continued)*

CONFIRMED

Is a conduit required for data or security?

Has Owner provided specifications for all Owner-provided equipment?

Establish size allowances for all equipment.

Is a public address system required? Coordinate device locations.

What are the audiovisual requirements?

Is CATV required?

Are lighting controls systems (dimmers) required? Who will provide systems? Coordinate switch locations.

Coordinate with electrical engineer and/or lighting designer for energy code, emergency lighting, and other technical requirements for lighting.

If the fixture is located in rated ceiling, determine if it requires rated construction around it (e.g., above ceiling).

Verify that emergency light fixtures are indicated.

Verify that occupancy sensors are provided, if required.

Verify that dimming systems have been provided where required.

Verify that engineer has been provided with the latest architectural background.

Power Supply

Verify that all equipment power has been provided and that dedicated circuits have been provided as required.

Verify that systems furniture power requirements are provided and coordinated with manufacturers' requirement. Verify that whips are not concealed behind panels if not allowed by jurisdiction.

Address clean/dirty power requirements with Owner.

Verify that electrical circuits are appropriate for:

- Computers
- Printers
- Copiers
- Other equipment

Verify that electrical shades and motorized projection screens are powered and that their switch locations are logical.

Verify that electrical power is provided for high-density storage systems.

Light Fixtures

Location

Coordinate with electrical engineer's or lighting designer's drawings.

Coordinate with other ceiling items on mechanical engineer's and architectural drawings.

Determine that pendant fixtures do not conflict with operable items such as door swings, projection screens, and so on, and will not obstruct views (e.g., view to signage or projection screen beyond, view of art on wall beyond) or increase "clutter" in small spaces.

Verify that mounting heights are coordinated with architectural drawings

Verify that task lighting is provided at workstations and that override switches are provided.

Fixture Type

Determine who selects and specifies fixtures and whether lamps need to be energy-efficient. Verify that trim colors, other accessories, and color of lamp are specified.

Determine whether maintenance will be done from above or below the fixture. Account for servicing the fixture (cleaning, lamp replacement, access to ballasts).

Assure that fixture location does not prohibit access for lamp replacement.

Review specifications for coordination with drawings of fixture type, size, finish, housing, voltage, lamp, lamp color (temperature), and so on.

Meet with electrical engineer and/or lighting designer to review catalogue cuts and specifications.

Verify that light fixtures are scheduled to mount in scheduled ceiling finish (suitable to gypsum wallboard, acoustical ceiling tile, or exposed regular edge).

Lighting Controls

Determine if dimming or multilevel switching is required.

Locate lighting controls and coordinate with electrical engineer's and lighting designer's drawings.

Other Electrical Equipment

Verify that equipment has electrical connections and that horsepower ratings, phases, and voltages are consistent with other discipline schedules.

Verify that the equipment layout matches other discipline floor plans and that there are no conflicts with columns.

Verify that equipment is connected to utility systems.

Verify that outdoor equipment is coordinated with building design and views and that the required pads are provided.

Verify that cable tray locations are coordinated with other trades.

Pantry Equipment

Verify that pantry equipment matches architectural equipment list.

Indicate outlet mounting heights above millwork, counters, and backsplashes.

Locate ventilating fans.

Verify if garbage disposal is required.

Verify if coffeepot timer is required.

Data and Telephone

Verify that data/telephone locations are designated to ring and string to ceiling above.

Verify data/telephone locations in floor.

Verify if A/V equipment is required.

Verify that junction boxes are provided in ceiling for AV or other equipment.

Verify if ATM is required.

Panels

Verify that locations of panel boards are consistent with architectural, mechanical, and plumbing floor plans, and that panel boards are indicated on the electrical riser diagram.

Verify that there is sufficient space for electrical panels to fit.

Verify that electrical panels are not recessed in fire-rated walls; provide plywood backboard if required.

Verify that locations of electrical conduit, runs, floor trenches, and openings are coordinated with structural plans.

Security Systems

Security systems, such as switches to disable the system when opening for business: Coordinate with Owner's security staff and hardware consultant.

Switches for "panic alarms"

Switches for autolocking of doors

Switches to disarm card reader door locks for patient/customer entry, and so on.

COORDINATION CHECKLIST FOR CONSTRUCTION DRAWINGS AND SPECIFICATIONS *(continued)*

Automatic Door Operators	CONFIRMED
Require push buttons on the wall or on separate bollards, and sometimes require bulky equipment located at the door head.	
Coordinate with hardware consultant for type, size, style, and with ADA requirements for push button height and proximity to door, and so on.	
Controlled entry devices	
Intercoms	
Door chime buttons	
Door chime speakers	
Cameras	
Motion detectors	
Occupancy sensors (for energy management of lighting)	
Card reader doors (if required as "request to exit" device)	
Theft detection or metal detection devices (floor- or wall-mounted)	

Life Safety	
Fire pull stations: Locate according to fire code and ADA-compliant heights.	
Coordinate with other wall-mounted devices (switches, thermostats, etc.) for attractive grouping of items.	
Fire extinguishers: Locate according to fire code.	
Select type appropriate to design, such as wall-mounted or in a cabinet (cabinet type includes wall mount, semi-recessed, fully recessed, and fire-rated for recessed installation in fire-rated walls).	
Locate for ADA-compliant height. Review Owner's policy for signage; some require signage on the wall above the cabinet for distant viewing over furniture and people.	
Fire horn/strobes: Locate per ADA and fire code.	

Other Concerns	
Review locations with art or other wall features (refer to discussion above about thermostats).	
Switches for lighted signage	
Locations of electrical signage	
"White noise" or other continuous audio systems (includes volume controls)	
Switches for operation of Owner's equipment	

PLUMBING COORDINATION

General	CONFIRMED
Plumbing fixtures match plumbing schedules, cutsheets, and architectural locations; verify color and finish.	
Pantry equipment is plumbed, including refrigerators with icemakers, dishwashers, and coffeemakers; include drain lines at icemakers.	
Sanitary drain system pipes have been sized and connect all fixtures.	
Verify floor penetrations required by plumbing lines do not conflict with structural member locations.	

Sprinklers	
Note: Sprinklers are appropriate in rooms including closets under 50 sq ft (4.6 sq m), under stairs, soffits, where required, computer/equipment rooms, kitchens, and atria.	
Specify if heads are to be in the center of the tile, centered on corridor, or other.	
Verify that run does not conflict with other plenum elements. Provide cutouts at structural members.	
Coordinate with other ceiling items and consider conflicts with sprinkler pipe.	
Specify recessed, concealed, or exposed.	
Verify finishes.	
Review specifications to assure mechanical engineer has specified type desired (be aware that there are often requirements by the Owner's insurance coverage that dictate sprinkler head type).	

Fire Hose Valves	
Verify that requirements for locations of fire hose valves (lengths of hose) and fire extinguisher cabinets are met.	
Verify that valves and cabinets are not located in rated partitions, where possible (provide rated cabinet if required), and coordinate with architectural drawings.	
Verify that cabinets are recessed type.	

Water Heaters	
Identify concealed water heaters.	
Provide plastic drip pan at overhead water heater.	
Provide access to water heater in lower cabinets as required.	

Waterlines and Filters	
Provide filters as needed for:	
• Tap water	
• Ice machines	
• Coffee lines	
Provide waterline for equipment as required:	
• Ice machines in refrigerators	
• Freestanding coffee stations	
• Mechanical equipment	
• Dishwashers	
• Clothes-washing machines	

Toilet Room Fixtures	
Coordinate sinks, lavatories, restrooms, and shower doors with wall depth and fire rating, if recessed.	
Consider method of trimming out recessed items, if not self-trimming.	
Verify that plumbing ducts and pipes do not conflict with architectural features, light fixtures, or structural members.	

STRUCTURAL COORDINATION

General	CONFIRMED
Verify expansion joint locations.	
Fireproofing is coordinated with architectural drawings per code requirements.	
Slab openings, sizes, and locations; reframing around existing conditions is indicated on drawings.	
Reinforcing for heavy equipment (including mechanical) or furniture is provided.	

1 ☐ **CONTRACT ADMINISTRATION**

COORDINATION CHECKLIST FOR CONSTRUCTION DRAWINGS AND SPECIFICATIONS *(continued)*

	CONFIRMED
Equipment pads are provided if required.	
Structural supports for mechanical equipment are provided.	
Depressed or raised slabs are indicated and match architectural drawings.	
Note location, size, and configuration of lateral bracing that may impact openings in walls.	
Columns	
Columns, floor beams, and roof beams are listed in column and beam schedules.	
Roof framing plan column lines and column locations match foundation plan column lines and column locations.	
Length of columns in column schedule match the length shown in section and the elevation on drawings.	
Verify if ATM is required. Existing floor loading may be inadequate.	

OTHER COORDINATION ISSUES	
Verify acoustic ratings and requirements of partition types.	
Do certain areas require special acoustic consideration? Sound attenuation?	
Will floor penetrations affect spaces below? Is there exposed structure below?	
Audiovisual	
Food service	
Furniture	
Graphics	
Lighting	
Security	
Specialized equipment	
Telecommunications	

CONSTRUCTION DRAWING CHECKLIST

This checklist lists items that should appear in construction documents if they occur in a project. The checklist is organized by drawing type to help ensure that each sheet of the construction documents is complete. Modify this checklist to suit the specific requirements of your practice or of a project.

CONSTRUCTION DRAWING CHECKLIST

FLOOR PLAN, SMALL SCALE	
ARCHITECTURAL ISSUES	
Area of Work	**CONFIRMED**
Differentiation between new and existing construction	
Structural grid	
Elevator shafts for new elevator sizes per manufacturer	
Doors with swing	
Fire extinguisher, hose, and valve locations	
Casework location (show hatched)	
Partition height; that is, ceiling height or extend to structure above	
Partition rating indication	
Partitions drawn accurately with nominal (not actual) thickness; that is, 5 in. for steel stud, 8 in. for CMU	
Room names and numbers	
Penetrations coordinated with floor/ceiling below	
Systems furniture requirements and layout	
Communications room and LAN room requirements (including raised flooring and ramps)	
Verify toilet rooms have required fixture count and ADA clearances.	
Mechanical Issues	
Verify mechanical floor plans match architectural floor plans.	
Coordinate thermostat locations with architectural drawings (e.g., at doors, above outlets, away from dimmers, away from accent walls).	
Electrical Issues	
Verify that electrical floor plans match the latest architectural and mechanical drawings. Check that the location of the floor-mounted equipment is consistent between the disciplines.	
Power and telecommunications plans	
Equipment location, including copier and fax machines	
Pantry equipment locations: Verify ADA requirements.	
Electric water cooler locations: Verify ADA requirements.	
Confirm clearances and power requirements for Owner equipment.	
Determine space requirements for electrical closets and equipment rooms.	
Life Safety	
Verify that exit signs have been installed and do not conflict with door swings.	
Verify that strobes/pull stations are provided, meet ADA requirements, and do not conflict with architectural and furniture elements.	
Plumbing Issues	
Plumbing floor plans match architectural floor plans.	
Plumbing fixtures match architectural floor plans.	
Wall chases are provided to conceal vertical piping.	
Dimension fittings and chases accommodate carriers for wall-hung toilets.	
Sanitary drain system pipes have been sized and connect all fixtures.	
Verify that fire hose valves and cabinets are not located in rated partitions, where possible (provide rated cabinet if required), and coordinate with architectural drawings.	
Verify that plumbing ducts and pipes do not conflict with architectural features, light fixtures, or structural members.	

CONSTRUCTION DRAWING CHECKLIST (continued)

Structural Issues	
Structural grid	
Size of existing structural columns	
Locations of columns, bearing walls, and overall building dimensions	

FLOOR PLAN, LARGE-SCALE

Architectural Issues	
Dimensioned building core	
Dimensioned elevator shafts, stairs	
Exit corridors, life safety, ADA-required clearances marked	
Dimensioned toilet rooms	
Entry lobby	
Other special, unusual, or complex areas	

FINISH PLANS

Architectural Issues	
Floor patterns	
Floor transition accessories	
Wall finishes	
Finish schedules	

MILLWORK AND CASEWORK PLANS AND DETAILS

Architectural Issues	
Plans	
Elevations	
Sections	
Edge profiles	
Joinery methods	
Veneer grain pattern	
Veneer matching	
Operating hardware	
Electrical Issues	
Outlets in casework	
Under-cabinet light fixtures in casework	
Plumbing Issue	
Sinks in casework	

INTERIOR ELEVATIONS

Architectural Issues	
Special or complex areas, such as a lobby	
Walls with finishes	
Walls requiring coordination information	
Toilet room fixture heights:	
• Mirrors	
• Soap dispensers	
• Lotion dispensers	
• Paper towel dispensers (for folded towels or on a roll)	
• Waste receptacles	
• Shower soap dispensers	
• Shower curtains	
• Grab bars	
• Towel bars	
• Towel heaters	
• Feminine product dispensers and disposal	
• Seat cover dispensers	
• Toilet paper dispensers	
• Automatic air freshener dispensers	
• Hooks	
• Shelves	
• Baby changing tables	
• Hair dryers	
• Hand dryers	
Toilet rooms showing generic wall finishes, partition mounting (overhead or floor mount)	
Verify that wall-mounted diffuser locations match mechanical drawings and are located exactly in gypsum wallboard ceilings.	

Mechanical Issues	
Show wall heater locations.	
Coordinate thermostat locations with architectural drawings (e.g., at doors, above outlets, away from dimmers, away from accent walls).	
Verify that mounting height of thermostat is ADA-compliant, especially if operable by room occupants.	

1 ☐ CONTRACT ADMINISTRATION

CONSTRUCTION DRAWING CHECKLIST (continued)

Electrical Issues

Verify that mounting heights for wall-mounted light fixtures are shown and coordinated with electrical drawings.

Power receptacles:
- A/V equipment
- Coffeepots
- Copiers
- Microwaves
- Fax machines
- Printers
- Outlets required within casework

Phone jacks

Data jacks

Switches, general:
- Light fixtures
- Electrical shades
- Motorized projection screens
- Task lighting
- Switches for operation of Owner's equipment
- Switches for lighted signage

Security:
- Security systems disable switch
- "Panic alarm" switch
- Switches for automatic locking of doors
- Switches to disarm card reader door locks for patient/customer entry, and so on

Automatic door operator push buttons
Note: Coordinate with hardware consultant for type, size, style, and with ADA requirements for push button height and proximity to door, and so on.

Controlled entry devices

Intercoms

Door chime buttons

Door chime speakers

Cameras

Motion detectors

Occupancy sensors (for energy management of lighting)

Card reader doors (if required as "request to exit" device)

Theft detection or metal detection devices (floor- or wall-mounted)

Life Safety

Fire pull stations: Locate according to fire code and ADA-compliant heights.

Fire horn/strobes: Locate per ADA and fire code.

Other Concerns

Review locations with art or other wall features.

REFLECTED CEILING PLANS

Architectural Issues

Acoustic ceiling grids, with set-out points

Ceiling materials

Lighting fixtures: Coordinate with depth of ceiling plenum and with door and cabinet door swings.

HVAC register and diffusers

Sprinklers

Exposed structure locations

Ceiling heights

Soffits, coves, drapery pockets

Mechanical Issues

Verify that diffuser locations match mechanical reflected ceiling plans and are located exactly in gypsum wallboard ceilings.

Show ceiling access doors and panels.

Electrical Issues

Show light fixtures to scale and verify that there is adequate space above ceiling for fixture.

Show junction boxes if required in ceiling for AV or other equipment.

Plumbing Issues

Show sprinkler heads in design-sensitive spaces.

Position sprinkler heads in center of tile, located exactly in gypsum wallboard ceilings.

CONSTRUCTION DETAILS

Architectural Issues

Typical door head, sill, jamb

Blind door and other atypical head, sill, jamb conditions

Typical partition types, keyed to plan

Casework and millwork

Stair details, including tread, stringers, and railings

Special ceiling conditions, keyed to Reflected Ceiling Plan

Transitions between elements

Transitions between planes

Special, unusual, or complex conditions

BUILDING SECURITY

DESIGN PRINCIPLES

The protection of persons and property is an essential function of built space. While the client is ultimately responsible for implementing a security program, it is the responsibility of the design professional to incorporate physical security principles into the design. This section serves to familiarize the designer with the basic security design principles and technologies in use today. While the examples focus on the security considerations specific to high-rise office buildings as the predominant form of interior renovation, the basic security concepts identified here can be applied to the security program of any built space.

SECURITY PROGRAMMING

As with architectural programming and planning, security design requires the same process to achieve an accurate problem statement. The goal of programming for security is as follows:

- Establish goals and objectives.
- Collect data.
- Develop security concepts.

Goals

Although each project may have other specific goals, the primary goals of any security program are as follows:

- To protect the persons and property within a defined space, during a defined time.
- To mitigate threats to security.
- To promptly detect and respond to a threatening event, should it occur.

Data

Sources of relevant security data are widespread. Consider review of, or consultation with, each of the following:

- Client security department
- Client policies and procedures
- Client security incident history reports
- Client asset inventory
- Federal and local law enforcement
- Qualified security consultant
- Similar facility types
- Publications on security of similar facilities
- Nearby facilities
- Local American Society for Industrial Security (ASIS) chapter

PRINCIPLES OF SECURITY

The basic principles of security are as follows:

- Know what is being protected.
- Provide a defensible perimeter with limited and clearly defined access points.
- Provide layers of defense for increasingly secure spaces.
- Provide means to surveil the perimeter or area of protection.
- Provide for response to events.
- Keep accurate and detailed records of events.

ARCHITECTURAL STRATEGIES

Architectural measures are generally the least expensive to implement; electronic measures are more expensive; and operational measures are the most

LOSS PREVENTION: EXAMPLE PROGRAM

OBJECTIVE	ARCHITECTURAL	ELECTRONIC	OPERATIONAL
Monitor laptops.	Make company laptops easy to differentiate from other equipment	Outfit laptops with electronic article surveillance (EAS) tags.	Take inventory regularly. Adopt laptop checkout policy.
Establish defensible perimeter.	Limit doors, windows, and openings.	Monitor all openings with sensing devices.	Instruct all employees in security access policy.
Provide means to surveil perimeter.	Design open space plans free from viewing obstructions.	Install cameras at access points.	Station personnel at access points.
Provide for response.	Plan security post near exits.	Provide autodialer or security communication.	Foster good relations with civil authorities.
Keep records of laptop incidents.	Provide secure space for storage of records.	Use security system with automated history generator.	Use standard report forms and periodically review for abnormalities.

Loss of laptops is a common problem in today's office environment, hence they provide a good example of the combination of the principles of loss prevention. This table illustrates the various means of improving security for laptops.

expensive. Optimizing building security through architectural means, where feasible, minimizes the required electronic security measures.

The basic principles incorporated in the defense of medieval castles are still applicable in security today. The process of designing security into architecture is known as *crime prevention through environmental design (CPTED)*. CPTED originally focused the application of these principles on low-income multifamily residential facilities, which were plagued with high crime rates. Subsequently, they have been more broadly applied to all facility types. The concepts of CPTED emphasize the use of natural or passive means to achieve security objectives. The primary concepts of CPTED are as follows:

- Create defensible space.
- Develop a sense of territoriality among users.
- Increase opportunities for natural surveillance.

ARCHITECTURAL SECURITY STRATEGIES

Defensible Space

Defensible space can be created not only through the provision of a hardened perimeter of physical barriers but also through the use of architectural transitions used to define spaces. In transitioning from a public to private space, the following architectural devices can be implemented:

- Setbacks surrounding perimeter
- Flooring material change
- Floor height increase
- Ceiling height decrease
- Narrowing passage

The arrangement of furnishings within a space can promote a sense of defensible space on the interior in the same manner that landscaping can on the exterior. Walls surrounding secured spaces should be installed deck to deck. Mechanical shafts or chases may provide an unprotected means of access between floors. Consider protection of exterior glass where accessibility through the exterior is a concern, particularly when adjacent to other buildings, trees, or other structures. Glazing less than 20 ft (6,096 mm) from a grade-accessible level or from shared balconies is of primary concern. Penetration-resistant grating can be provided at openings as required to ensure a defensible space.

Territoriality

There is an instinct in many species to gain and defend exclusive rights to territory. Where humans have a sense of ownership in the property they occupy, and outwardly express this instinct through care and defense of that property, less crime is perpetrated against them. Good maintenance and upkeep are the hallmarks of a well-cared-for property. Where this is lacking, crime and vandalism are likely to follow. This can be a challenge to the design professional in a program that also calls for openness and a great deal of public or community space. The design professional can promote the territorial instinct by incorporating the following into a design:

- Creating a sense of the unique for a place's occupants
- Selecting materials that are wear- and vandal-resistant
- Erecting signage to indicate that the area is protected and that access is allowed for authorized users only

Surveillance

Natural surveillance is most affected by the layout of walls, windows, and furnishings, and the amount of light.

To increase surveillance opportunities, the following should be considered:

• Clear lines of sight (open space plans)
• Windows for viewing outside the perimeter, particularly at access points
• Elimination of hiding places
• Adequate lighting

The lighting levels for certain periods of operation are often overlooked. Emergency lighting should be used to maintain appropriate minimum levels. Areas under closed circuit television (CCTV) surveillance should be sufficiently illuminated at all times. Most security cameras can capture good images with less than 1 fc (10 lx) of scene illumination.

The lighting levels should be even throughout. The ratio of average to minimum levels should be less than 6 to 1. Security lighting standards vary widely.

MINIMUM INTERIOR LIGHTING LEVEL RECOMMENDATIONS FOR SAFETY

SPACES	FC	LX
General	0.5	5
Elevation change (e.g., loading dock)	1.0	10
Entrances and stairs	2.0	20
Hazardous areas (e.g., machine room)	5.0	50

OPERATIONAL STRATEGIES

Operational security strategies typically include providing staff where critical thinking skills are necessary; that is, at critical access points, monitoring and dispatch stations, and where roving response is necessary. Training and testing staff regularly on security procedures must be included in any operational security strategy.

ELECTRONIC STRATEGIES

Electronic security strategies include providing equipment that can reduce staffing needs or operational costs; creating a database of activity, including access and alarm events and video records; and providing a means to centrally monitor and administer the system equipment.

Electronic security systems are divided into three types: *field devices*, *multiplexing and processing equipment*, and *administration and monitoring equipment*. Understanding the components of the security system will help to meet the spatial requirements of each.

Field Devices

Field devices consist of switches, sensors, card readers, locks, cameras, and communications devices. Most devices are manufactured to be concealed within standard building products or mounted onto standard electrical boxes. Most devices will mount in a standard 2⅛-in. (54-mm) deep box. Where a 2⅛-in. (54-mm) deep box may not be mounted (e.g., a glass curtain wall), or where devices require extra depth, special construction is required.

Defensible space can be created with physical barriers such as water features, planters, and benches.

CRIME PREVENTION THROUGH ENVIRONMENTAL DESIGN (CPTED)

ELECTRONIC EQUIPMENT TYPES

FLUSH-MOUNT   PINHOLE

Security cameras may be mounted behind a plate or with a pinhole lens. A sizable wall cavity is required for both scenarios. The cavity should be accessible from either the front or the rear for installation and service.

CONCEALED CAMERAS

The designer must ensure that a suitable pathway is available for wiring security devices. The pathway should be considered from field device to processing equipment to headend equipment. Full conduit systems are not frequently required, but some means to install and protect the cabling must be provided.

Many security devices, particularly emergency duress, access control, and communications devices, are provided for public use.

ADA MOUNTING HEIGHTS FOR SECURITY DEVICES

Multiplexing and Processing Equipment

Most access control, intrusion, and CCTV equipment connects to intermediary processing equipment; however, some security equipment connects directly to remote annunciators. Access control field devices (switches, detectors, and readers) connect to data-collection panels, which are typically wall mounted. A 4 ft by 8 ft (1,219 mm by 2,438 mm) plywood backboard painted with fire retardant should be supplied.

SECURITY BACKBOARD EQUIPMENT DETAIL

SECURITY EQUIPMENT CLOSET—PLAN

TYPICAL SIZES OF RACK-MOUNTED SECURITY EQUIPMENT

EQUIPMENT	RU
16-input video multiplexer (MUX)	1
Videocassette recorder (VCR)	3
16-input digital recorder (DVR)	4
32-input video switcher	6
(2) 9 in. (228 mm) CCTV monitors	6
14 in. (355 mm) CCTV monitor	8
20 in. (508 mm) CCTV monitor	10
24-input fiber optic (4:1) video transmission devices	4

Vertical dimensions are measured in rack units (RU). One RU equals 1.75 in. (44 mm). A typical loaded equipment rack will weigh less than 500 lbs (453 kg) but may weigh up to 2,000 lbs (907 kg), creating concentrated loads of 100 to 500 psf (4,788 to 23,940 Pa).

Data Collection Panels

Data collection panels may be dispersed throughout the facility. A dedicated closet is preferred, but frequently space is shared within a telecomm/data closet. One closet should be provided for every 10,000 to 150,000 sq ft (929 to 13,935 sq m) of office space, depending on device quantity, density, and arrangement. In high-security facilities, more closets are required. In high-volume spaces, such as auditoriums and convention centers, possibly fewer are necessary. Typically, one closet is required per floor in a high-rise building.

Dedicated closets should be not less than 1 ft by 6 ft (305 mm by 1,828 mm). Less space is required when the service space can extend into a hallway or be shared with the service space of other equipment. Doors and ceiling heights should be sized to accommodate the installation of notably large equipment racks and 4 ft by 8 ft (1,219 mm by 2,438 mm) plywood sheets.

Each closet will likely require a 120-VAC power circuit. Where emergency generator or UPS power is available, it may be used. If fail-safe locks are powered from the closet, an additional nonemergency circuit and a connection to the fire alarm system will also be required. Adequate lighting and a convenience outlet should be located within close proximity for servicing.

Most security equipment has a broad operating range of 20% to 80% RH, noncondensing at 50º to 100ºF (10º to 37ºC). Equipment on a typical 4 ft x 8 ft (1,219 mm by 2,438 mm) panel will dissipate less than 500 W. An equipment rack may dissipate twice as much heat. These factors should be considered in designing closet ventilation.

Cameras generally connect to signal processing equipment, including multiplexers, recorders, and switchers. Most CCTV monitoring and recording equipment is mountable in 19-in.- (482-mm-) wide Electronic Industries Alliance (EIA) standard racks. Though the equipment varies in height and depth requirements, most equipment can be accommodated in a 26-in.- (660-mm-) deep rack.

PLAN

ELEVATION

SECURITY EQUIPMENT CLOSET

ADMINISTRATION AND MONITORING EQUIPMENT

An important decision to make early in the design process is how to monitor and administer the security equipment. A typical site should be monitored 24 hours a day, 7 days a week. The primary question is: Will the site have a 24-hour on-site presence, or will an off-site monitoring company provide services after normal business hours? Whatever the facility size, it is often most prudent to provide one location for centralized monitoring and administration.

The aggregate size of security systems administration and monitoring equipment varies greatly from the partial floor tenant to the large multiuse facility. In the smallest of facilities, the equipment should be placed in a secured location that is readily accessible to its administrator on a daily basis. Common locations are within the LAN room or facility administrator's office. Where a regular security presence justifies a dedicated room, it should be located on the primary access level, near the core or main access point of the facility.

The smallest console rooms are about 80 sq ft (7 sq m). The average console room and adjacent equipment room is several hundred square feet (meters). Larger facilities will have a control room approaching 1,000 sq ft (92 sq m) and perhaps a security suite of several thousand square feet (several hundred square meters).

SECURITY DESK DESIGN

There are three common options for security desk design: *standard equipment racks*, a *custom desk*, or a *hybrid* (custom surfaces built around standard modules). Standard equipment is recommended for the typical console; custom and hybrid designs can be expensive and should be reserved for special high-end applications.

Whether the operator will stand or sit will determine the overall dimensions of the console. In lobbies, the operator should be able to view the lobby area over the console. It is also preferable that the operator be at or above eye level with the public when interaction is expected. A dais may be used to raise the console; or, if the operator will sit, an adjustable chair can be used. These factors generally require that the portion of the console above the counter be less than 18 in. (457 mm) high.

Custom Security Desk Design

Some common pitfalls to avoid in the design of a custom security desk include:

• Misunderstanding of EIA standard dimensions
• Inadequate construction tolerances
• Insufficient depth
• Inadequate wireways
• Inadequate ventilation

Using EIA standard rack rails allows for easy replacement of the equipment in the future. Air intake should be filtered. Exhaust fans should be located to maximize flow throughout the console. Exhaust may be directed into knee space for operator comfort in colder climates. Each bay within the wire space should be provided with 120V power. A wireway connecting each bay should also be provided. A conduit connection, typically in the floor, is required to connect to security devices.

The lobby security desk is a typical application requiring a custom-designed desk. Dimensions should conform to EIA standards. Working in 19-in. wide × 7-in. high (482-mm wide × 177-mm high) increments is recommended. Some equipment measures up to 20 in. (508 mm) deep or more. Consoles, like equipment racks, generally measure 26 in. (660 mm) or more in depth. Slope-faced consoles have greater depth requirements. When considering spatial requirements for consoles, remember to include a 12-in. (304-mm) counter where necessary.

SECURITY CONSOLE DESIGN CONSIDERATIONS

Radial arrangements for security consoles are generally preferred for easy viewing of monitors and access to equipment. Excessively tall consoles contribute to eye and neck strain. A low-profile desk with a video wall can provide more ergonomic viewing angles. An accessible raised floor provides an easy means for wiring low-profile desks. Windows and lighting should be configured so as to prevent glare. Task lighting may be provided at desk level. Room lighting should be placed on dimmer switches.

CUSTOM DESK—SECTION

CUSTOM DESK—ELEVATION

SMALL SECURITY DESK LAYOUTS

MODERATE-SIZE SECURITY DESK LAYOUTS

Ideally, a separate equipment room behind the console should be provided. This is desirable for several reasons:

• Rear access to console enables ease of service and installation of equipment.
• The HVAC system can be zoned separately to provide for the comfort of the security operator and cooling for the equipment.
• Equipment noise can be isolated from the operator.
• Equipment to which the operator should not have access, or that is infrequently accessed, can be stored in a separate equipment room.

SECURITY CONTROL ROOM DESIGN

Designing the security control room requires review of all aspects of architectural design. The number of individuals and quantity of equipment that the room will be required to house will govern its overall size. Most control rooms are designed for one or two operators. Provisions for the following equipment should be considered:

- Security monitor and keyboard
- Security printer
- Card enrollment workstation with card supply
- Key control cabinet
- Door controls
- CCTV monitors
- CCTV control keyboard
- CCTV switchers
- CCTV multiplexers and recorder
- Video review workstation
- Security intercom

- Elevator intercom
- Radio base station
- Telephones
- Auxiliary system monitoring and control equipment for: fire alarm, elevator, HVAC, lighting, and so on
- Files and binders for security policies and procedures, guardpost orders, shift schedules, event logs, system and equipment operating manuals
- Lost and found
- First-aid equipment
- Traffic cones and temporary barriers

SECURITY DOOR HARDWARE

The appropriate door hardware is essential to effective access control because, frequently, problems occur when inappropriate hardware is provided. The hardware specifier should coordinate carefully with the security system specifier to ensure that access concepts are compatible. Many lock options are available,

some of which may require a specialized preparation of the door or frame; however, not all electronic hardware options are available for each door. Door hardware must first meet life safety codes for egress.

Fail-Safe and Fail-Secure Hardware

Fail-safe door hardware is required on doors that are controlled in the direction of egress. Fail-safe door hardware unlocks on loss of power, whereas fail-secure door hardware remains locked on loss of power. Fail-secure door hardware should be used where fail-safe door hardware is not required. Electric latch retraction required on automatic doors is not recommended. Fire-rated doors require fire-rated hardware.

Position Switches

The most common type of position switch is the concealed magnetic switch. Switches should be concealed whenever possible. Door stiles and frames should be of sufficient size and construction to accommodate the switches. A hole 1 in. (25 mm) in diameter and 2 in. (50 mm) deep is typical for hollow metal doors. While many devices are unobtrusive, designers generally have concerns about the appearance of card readers and cameras. At some expense, solutions are available that may improve the appearance. Proximity readers make it possible to conceal the reader to some extent. This application is frequently used in elevators and may be utilized elsewhere.

180 SQ FT (17 sq m)

SECURE SPACE

125 SQ FT (12 sq m)

FILES

CABINETS ABOVE

250 SQ FT (23 sq m)

EQUIPMENT ROOM

SUPERVISOR'S OFFICE

375 SQ FT (35 sq m)

MODERATE-SIZE CONSOLE ROOM LAYOUTS

CONDUIT
FINISHED WALL
BACKBOX (FOR GROUTED FRAMES)
HOLLOW FRAME
SWITCH
MAGNET
HOLLOW STEEL DOOR

CONCEALED MAGNETIC SWITCH IN HOLLOW STEEL DOOR

VIDEO WALL

FOV

RAMP   RAISED FLOOR

MODERATE-SIZE CONTROL CENTER LAYOUT

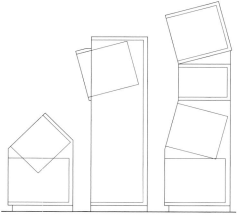

A wide variety of standard console profiles are available. Different profiles can be combined in one console. Console manufacturers provide 30° and 45° wedges to fill the gaps in nonlinear console plans.

STANDARD CONSOLE SECTIONS

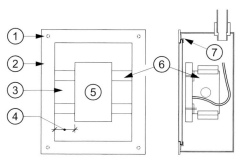

1. Tamper-resistant screws
2. Trimplate
3. Nonmetallic, break- and scratch-resistant, translucent plate
4. Two in. (50 mm) minimum recommended offset from metal
5. Proximity card reader
6. Adjustable reader mounting bracket
7. Removable clip

CONCEALED PROXIMITY READER

ELECTRIC MORTISE

Electric mortise locksets operate like standard mortise locks. An electric signal to the lock determines whether the latch is secure or operable. Storeroom function locksets may allow free egress. These locksets are often recommended for use because of their high reliability and security.

ELECTRIC STRIKE

Electric strikes release a door, allowing the unretracted latch to be pulled through a breakaway portion of the strike. An electric signal to the strike determines whether the strike is secure or operable. Electric strikes do not provide latching and are not acceptable for fire stairwell use. They are cost-effective and reasonably reliable.

ASTRAGAL
ELECTRIC STRIKE

ELECTROMAGNETIC LOCK

Electromagnetic locks secure a door by creating an electromagnetic bond between an armature plate on the door and an electromagnetic lock on the frame. Loss of power to the lock releases the door. These locks do not provide latching and are inherently fail-safe. However, they are not allowed in some jurisdictions and should not be used with lever sets.

2'-0" MAX
(610)

3'-6"
(1067)

COMMON ELECTRICAL SECURITY DOOR HARDWARE

Door Hinges

Out-swinging doors are more susceptible to tampering than in-swinging doors. Nevertheless, out-swinging doors are required at many exterior locations. At these locations, protection of the hinges and latches must be considered. Exterior hinges should not have hinge pins that are easy to remove. Where possible, use concealed hinges or fix the hinge pins by welding or other means.

Locksets

All locksets should incorporate a deadlatch pin or similar device to prevent "loiding," or forcing, of the door latch. Certain installations, electrified strikes in particular, may warrant the application of an astragal over the strike plate to prevent latch tampering.

Key-Controlled Doors

Access-controlled doors should have a key override feature in case of malfunction. All key-controlled doors can incorporate interchangeable core lock cylinders and be part of a grand master keying system. These measures minimize exposure time and expense in the event of lost keys.

High-Security Keys

High-security installations may warrant consideration of high-security keys, which have a special shape or cut, or incorporate other means to thwart attempts at unauthorized duplication.

Lock Options

Cylindrical electric
- Less costly than mortise locksets
- Not as secure as mortise locksets

Shear
- Type of magnetic lock
- Concealed within door header
- Requires precise installation and more frequent adjustment than other lock types

Delayed egress
- Available in panic or electromagnetic variety
- Not allowed in all jurisdictions
- Provides up to a 30-second delay before opening

Closers

Closers should be provided on all controlled or monitored doors. The closers should be adjusted such that the doors cannot be left ajar without a stop.

ACCESS CONTROL

Access control can be accomplished with standard nonelectric architectural products, electronic products, or operational measures. Standard products may include combination locks or keyed locks. A popular access control product is the mechanical pushbutton combination lock. The pushbutton lock provides a low level of access control and can be used effectively when its features and limitations are understood. No power source or wiring is required and no activity record is kept. The pushbutton lock is frequently used in shared-office toilet rooms and community tennis courts to discourage access by the general public.

Another popular stand-alone product is the battery-powered keycard lock, which is frequently used in the hotel industry. The power source is self-contained and no wiring is required. In general, battery changes are required, though some units recharge during use. Battery-powered keycard locks require visiting the unit to obtain reports and reconfigure.

PUSHBUTTON LOCK   **BATTERY-POWERED KEYCARD LOCK**

ELECTRIC DOOR LOCKS

MAGNETIC STRIPE
Typically found on credit/ATM cards. Duplication is not difficult.

EMBEDDED MAGNETIZED WIRES

WIEGAND
Magnetically polarized wires are embedded in the card. Duplication is difficult.

PROCESSOR
ANTENNA

PROXIMITY (PASSIVE)
It is the most ADA-compliant option as it does not require insertion. A microchip and antennae are embedded in the card. Duplication is difficult.

BAR CODE
The bar code is the UPC standard. Lines of variable width are printed on the card. Duplication is not difficult, though a mask can be applied to hinder duplication.

HOLES

HOLLERITH/PUNCH CARD
Only mechanical keycard option. Holes are punched in the card. It is frequently used as a hotel card. Duplication is not difficult.

MAGNETS

BARIUM FERRITE
Frequently used in parking lot access control. An array of magnets are embedded in the card, making duplication difficult.

CONTACT

SMART CARD
Among the newest technologies, in a smart card, a microchip with memory is embedded. Available in contact or contactless varieties.

A common means of security access control is the keycard. Keycards can provide a unique access credential for each user. While anyone may possess the keycard, only one person may have the card at one time. This is a substantial advantage over input codes.

KEYCARDS

ELECTRONIC IDENTIFICATION

There are two primary techniques for identifying valid users with electronic security access control equipment: *user input code* and *biometric evaluation*. Both of these techniques may be used alone or in combination.

User Input Codes

A keypad is the primary device that requires user input codes. There is a distinct advantage to having a unique identifying code or credential for each user; that said, a primary failing of user input codes that while many keypad systems today can accommodate unique codes for each user, the same code can be utilized by multiple individuals

Biometric Evaluation

Where a higher degree of control is required, biometric devices may be considered. Currently, biometric devices are used primarily as verification tools in conjunction with card readers or keypad access. When used together, a high degree of identity authentication is achieved. Two important concepts to review when considering biometric devices are the accuracy of identification and the access processing time. Available technologies include:

- Fingerprint recognition
- Hand geometry recognition
- Retinal scan
- Face recognition
- Voice recognition
- Signature recognition

ALARM MONITORING

A great number of facilities requiring protection are not occupied 24 hours a day. These facilities without on-site security depend on off-site services for alarm response. To provide for off-site monitoring, at least one phone line termination should be provided adjacent to the security system alarm processing equipment. Ideally, this line will not be dependent on the building phone exchange. Where tampering of the phone lines is likely, additional redundancy is warranted. A wireless (cellular or digital) dialer may be provided. Ensure that the dialer is compatible with the security equipment.

FALSE ALARMS

Some statistics suggest that more than 90% of all alarms are false.

In some situations, supplementing alarm equipment with access control and communications equipment can reduce false alarms. For all access-controlled doors, remote release should be considered for exceptional access, that is, for visitors and staff without credentials. In this case, intercom systems are recommended as an alternate means of identification.

Intrusion Sensor Types

A variety of intrusion sensor types and technologies are available. They can be classified by the manner in which they protect space.

Point
- Magnetic switches (most commonly, sensors that are used to monitor position of operable doors and windows)
- Mechanically actuated switches
- Duress buttons

Linear
- Photoelectric
- Tapes
- Wires

Planar
- Glass break
- Vibration sensor
- Capacitance
- Curtain passive infrared (PIR)

Volumetric
- Passive infrared (PIR)
- Microwave
- Ultrasonic
- Audio

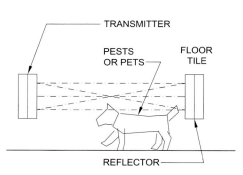

PHOTOELECTRIC BEAM
Photoelectric beam devices function by transmitting and collecting a continuous light beam. The device may have a separate transmitter and receiver pair or may be a transceiver with a reflector. An alarm is created when an object interferes with the beam path. These devices are a good means of providing linear protection over great ranges. Beam devices can protect a perimeter up to 500 ft (152 m). A multiple beam array is generally recommended. Indoors, false alarms can be caused by animals or particulate matter.

CORRECT

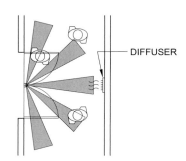

INCORRECT

PASSIVE INFRARED SENSORS
Passive infrared (PIR) sensors detect warm bodies. They detect best when the body is moving across the detection field. They are best utilized as request-to-exit (RTE) sensors, such as found at automatic doors. While the range required to function as an RTE sensor is generally small, some devices have ranges up to 100 ft (30 m). Vestibules on the interior of controlled doors should be created so that incidental cross-traffic does not activate the sensor. False alarms are caused by heat sources. Avoid placement near HVAC diffusers.

CORRECT

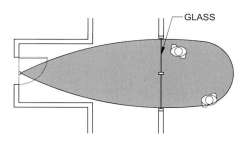

INCORRECT

MICROWAVE MOTION SENSORS
Microwave motion sensors emit energy pulses. They offer the best detection when objects are moving toward them. Ranges are similar to PIR sensors for indoor sensors. In outdoor applications they can be used to detect at much greater distances. Microwave radiation can penetrate glass and light construction. They should not be placed so that they will likely be activated by legitimate activity outside the desired area of protection.

INTRUSION SENSORS

LOBBY SECURITY

In general, building lobbies represent semipublic spaces. Visitors and deliveries are received here; and in some high-rise facilities, the lobby level is occupied by retail establishments. Security in the main lobby serves to control access to the upper floors and restricted areas of the building.

A 24-hour security desk within the lobby provides excellent means for security monitoring and response. In smaller buildings, this may serve as the primary monitoring location. The lobby and security desk location should be designed to allow for simultaneous monitoring of security equipment and surveillance of all building access points. A fire command room is often required near the firefighters' point of entry to the building. Location of the security desk in close proximity to this room is also desirable.

While any means of access to the upper floors, which might circumvent security, requires monitoring (escalators, dumbwaiters, low balconies, a scalable exterior skin, etc.), the primary means of access to the upper floors are the elevators and stairs.

ELEVATORS

Access to all elevators should funnel past the security desk. Elevators should be grouped to enable optimum visibility by the lobby security guard of all traffic between the elevators and outside of the building. Elevator bank lobbies may be closed on one end to force all traffic past the guard's view. Parking garage elevators should be separate from office tower elevators.

High traffic associated with typical day usage of the elevators makes access control within elevators ineffective. Tailgating is easily executed and generally goes unchallenged. However, where elevators are accessible after hours, access control of elevators can be an effective tool for controlling floor access.

Some elevator manufacturers have access control features integral to their operation. By using the floor-select buttons to enter an access code, access to floors is granted. Implementation of this feature is, however, less effective than card-reader control. Proximity card readers may be flush-mounted in the

cab-operating panel. Duress and stop alarms should report to the security desk which car has a problem.

Intercoms should be provided between the cabs and the 24-hour staffed location; in buildings without 24-hour staff, telephones with automatic dialers to off-site monitoring service should be used. CCTV cameras in elevators can provide both effective deterrence and detection of criminal activity. Cameras may be concealed within an upper corner of the cab. Installation of security items in the elevator cab should be coordinated with the elevator specifier.

STAIRS

Stairs can cause significant security problems in multi-tenant buildings. Stairs accessible from an unsecured space (for instance, the exterior) may act as shelter for the homeless or as a hiding place for criminals, or may provide an unprotected means of access between floors and an avenue for removing property from the

building. To mitigate these problems, stair access should be carefully controlled and monitored.

Access to the stairs should be controlled at the exit level. Stair doors to the exterior may be established as exit-only or outfitted with delayed-egress devices to discourage use. Stairs below and above the exit level should not directly connect, if the lower levels are not secure. Stairs used for access to service spaces should be separate from fire stairs, where possible.

Cameras and motion sensors may also be desirable for monitoring activity in the stairs. They should be positioned to enable security personnel to, first, identify perpetrators and, second, give them sufficient time to reach the exit before the intruders can escape.

Jeff Schroeder; Kroll Security Services Group; Bastrop, Texas

TYPICAL SMALL LOBBY LAYOUT

OPTICAL TURNSTILES
5 X 32" (812) LANES = 160"
(4064) EGRESS WIDTH

MECHANICAL TURNSTILES
5 X 18" (457) LANES / 2 +
42" (1066) ADA GATES =
87" (2209) EGRESS WIDTH

LOBBY WITH TURNSTILES

SECURE LOBBY LAYOUTS

EA EGRESS ACCESS
AC ACCESS CONTROL

TYPICAL ACCESS FLOOR LAYOUT

EA EXIT ALARM DEVICE
AC ACCESS CONTROL DEVICE
AM ALARM MONITORING DEVICE

Z CORRIDOR LAYOUT

EA EXIT ALARM DEVICE
AC ACCESS CONTROL DEVICE
AM ALARM MONITORING DEVICE

FULL CORRIDOR LAYOUT

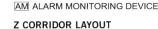

ACCESS FLOOR LAYOUT *Source:* Protection of Assets Manual; *Los Angeles, POA Publishing, 1999.*

INTERIOR LANDSCAPING

CONSIDERATIONS

Thriving indoor plants are dependent on the successful integration of the requirements of the plant material and the interior environmental conditions. Typically, plant materials tolerant to existing interior conditions must be selected. However, in projects in which plants are a significant part of the design statement, or when an interior landscape designer is involved early in the design process, the environmental conditions can be adjusted to accommodate the needs of plants. The primary considerations for supporting plant growth indoors are light, temperature, humidity, and irrigation.

Light

The intensity, duration, and quality of both natural and artificial light affect plant life. These three attributes must be addressed for plants to thrive.

Light Intensity

It is a popular misconception that some plant species thrive on low light; in fact, they merely tolerate low light better than other species. Very few species can be successfully sustained for an extended period of time under less than 50 foot candles (fc) (500 lx) of light.

LIGHT INTENSITY FOR PLANTS

SPECIMENS	WILL TOLERATE
"Low-light" plants	35–100 fc (350–1,000 lx)
"Medium-light" plants	90-400 fc (900–4,000 lx)
"High-light" plants	More than 300 fc (3,000 lx)

Direct sunlight outdoors during the summer may vary from 8,000 to 12,000 fc (80,000 to 120,000 lx).

Light Duration

Like outdoor plants, indoor plants benefit from light available during daylight hours, or from approximately 8 hours a day during the winter to 16 hours a day during the summer in temperate climates. Skylights alone rarely provide high levels of light for more than a few hours a day. Lack of intensity can be somewhat compensated for by increasing duration, but a well-defined day/night cycle (or *photoperiod*) is essential to plant health. Plants lighted 24 hours a day will be placed under stress and will experience shorter life spans. A maximum of 16 hours a day of available light year round is recommended.

Light Quality

Daylight provides outdoor plants with a full range of light, from infrared through the entire visible light spectrum to ultraviolet. Indoor plants are lighted either from electric sources whose light spectrum is limited or from daylight that has been altered as it passes through glazing. Neither artificial light nor natural light through glazing provides the full spectrum of light. Optimal spectral energy for plants occurs at two peak frequencies for both chlorophyll synthesis and photosynthesis. Ideal lighting for indoor plants will utilize either electric lamps or glazing that offers peaks in those frequencies.

Electric Light. Metal halide is generally considered the best electric light source for plant growth. Because it is a high-intensity discharge (HID) source, its beam can be altered by the shape of its reflector to focus on a wide or narrow target and it can effectively light plants from a distance. Many fluorescent lamps are similarly capable of providing acceptable spectral quality for plant growth, but the characteristics of fluo-

rescent lights and their fixtures require the lamps to be within 18 in. to 8 ft (457 mm to 2,438 mm) from the foliage. Halogen can also be used successfully for plant growth, though its spectral quality is not as ideal as metal halide or fluorescent.

Daylight. Clear, single-pane glass is optimal for plant growth; however, it is not used in commercial buildings because of the associated heat gain and heat loss. Interior landscape designers must ascertain the percentage of light transmittance of glazing systems used to provide plant growth lighting or obtain a daylighting analysis of the space to determine anticipated lighting levels.

TEMPERATURE

Plants available for indoor use thrive in room-temperature conditions (68ºF to 72ºF (20ºC to 22ºC). Temperatures may vary substantially within a room, most notably near windows or exterior doors, where nighttime lows during winter in a northern temperate climate could reach as low as the mid-50sºF (10sºC), and daytime highs in summer could exceed 100ºF (37ºC). Such temperature extremes will damage, and even kill, plants. Locating plants close to air supplies should also be avoided or otherwise addressed. Forced-air movement can cause plants to desiccate (dry out). This can occur even when room-temperature air is discharged.

HUMIDITY

Virtually all plants prefer higher humidity than will be found in a typical interior environment. It is not unusual for an interior space in a northern temperate climate during the winter to have a relative humidity as low as 10% to 15%. Most subtropical and tropical plants used indoors prefer a relative humidity of 50% or more. Because of potential problems in introducing higher humidities to interior spaces (generation of molds and mildew, condensation, rust, human discomfort, etc.), successful indoor plants are those that can adapt to lower humidity levels.

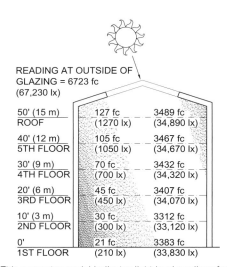

READING AT OUTSIDE OF
GLAZING = 6723 fc
(67,230 lx)

50' (15 m) ROOF	127 fc (1270 lx)	3489 fc (34,890 lx)
40' (12 m) 5TH FLOOR	105 fc (1050 lx)	3467 fc (34,670 lx)
30' (9 m) 4TH FLOOR	70 fc (700 lx)	3432 fc (34,320 lx)
20' (6 m) 3RD FLOOR	45 fc (450 lx)	3407 fc (34,070 lx)
10' (3 m) 2ND FLOOR	30 fc (300 lx)	3312 fc (33,120 lx)
0' 1ST FLOOR	21 fc (210 lx)	3383 fc (33,830 lx)

This computer model indicates light level readings for direct sunlight passing through glazing into an atrium space at the latitude of Detroit, Michigan (42°–20′ N), at noon on March 21. Direct sunlight loses only 3% of its intensity from skylight to the atrium floor, while indirect light loses 83%.

LIGHT LEVELS IN ATRIUM SPACE

THE GREENHOUSE EFFECT

Multistory atrium spaces that are skylighted or sidewall glazed can experience an unusual environmental condition called the *greenhouse effect* that can be extremely dangerous to plants. Solar gain in a well-lighted multistory space will cause the air temperature at upper levels of the space to heat more quickly than at lower levels. Tall plants located on the ground floor of skylighted atria can be badly damaged by high temperatures, unless the warmer air can be recirculated into the lower portions or vented outside the building. *See also* Interior Plantings, for irrigation methods.

Nelson Hammer; Hammer Design, Landscape Architecture; Boston, Massachusetts

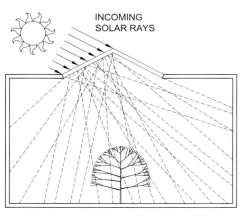

INCOMING
SOLAR RAYS

TRANSLUCENT GLAZING
Translucent glazing has the capability to disperse even low-angle, early-morning, and late-afternoon sunlight into useful plant growth lighting.

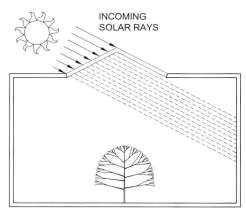

INCOMING
SOLAR RAYS

TRANSPARENT GLAZING
In winter, midday, the low angles of the sun may preclude direct sunlight passing through clear glazing from reaching an atrium floor.

Glazing systems incorporating fiberglass or other similarly translucent materials can be highly advantageous for plants because the dispersion of light will result in a net increase in brightness without increasing heat gain.

DISPERSED SUNLIGHT

SUSTAINABLE DESIGN CRITERIA

CONTEXT

For thousands of years people have been creating structures that, out of necessity, have been specific to a given region and its climate. These structures were, by nature, "sustainable" within their local landscapes. Design strategies had to work with climate conditions as well as within the limitations of local materials.

Since the late nineteenth century, advances in technology have enabled a shift from this model, allowing nature to be simply overpowered. But as widespread concern is raised over the limitations of natural resources, as well as the planet's finite ability to absorb pollutants, the role of technology is being reconsidered. Today, technology is increasingly being employed to augment natural processes rather than outdo them, and materials are being utilized with greater efficiency and more in harmony with the Earth's ecology.

In 1987, the World Commission on Environment and Development described sustainable development as that "which meets the needs of the present without compromising the ability of future generations to meet their own needs." Many viable sustainable design models provide guidance in implementing this overarching goal. The four primary areas of investigation required for sustainable design are *energy, resources, water,* and *health.* Energy, water, and resources revolve primarily around efficiency and pollution prevention; health deals primarily with maintaining the environment.

ENERGY

The Worldwatch Institute, a nonprofit public policy research organization, estimates that buildings are responsible for 40% of total energy use worldwide. Thus energy consumption accounts for a majority of the environmental impacts associated with buildings. Energy generation and use has been linked to air pollution, acid rain, reduced water quality, ozone depletion, risk of global warming, and depletion of nonrenewable resources. Energy conservation is a high priority and serves to improve a building's overall environmental performance while reducing operating costs.

Systems Approach

When designing with environmental and health impacts in mind, all elements of a project necessarily become interrelated. For example, energy systems design should not be isolated from site selection or building design; both have an effect on energy efficiency and conservation. This systems approach is most effective when begun early in the design process.

Renewable and Alternative Energy

Renewable energy systems provide nonpolluting power for building-scale applications without depleting nonrenewable natural resources. Alternative energy systems, which provide cleaner, less polluting options for power generation, can be implemented as follows:

- Incorporate wind, photovoltaic (solar), and/or hydro-generation systems.
- Incorporate net metering, which eliminates battery systems and allows direct offset of utility costs

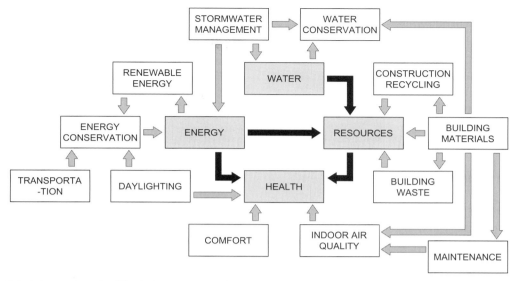

Links between elements of the design process are shown.

SYSTEMS THINKING MODEL

- Choose "green power" from utility company.
- Supplement with fuel cells and desiccant cooling systems.

Energy Conservation and Efficiency

Reduction in energy use associated with buildings involves many interrelated actions. Passive techniques involve simple design choices integrated during schematic design, and are achieved through building orientation, form, and layout. Energy efficiency focuses on minimizing overall heating, cooling, and electrical loads, and may be implemented as follows:

- Align building with solar orientation.
- Utilize shading devices to reduce heat gain.
- Provide passive ventilation.
- Incorporate vestibules at main entrances.
- Install vegetated roofs to reduce energy flow through roof envelope and reduce urban heat island effect.
- Superinsulate the building envelope and eliminate thermal bridging.
- Use high-performance glazing (such as low-e).
- Specify Energy Star appliances (see "Programs," below).
- Reduce energy for hot water with solar or tankless "on demand" water heaters, or utilize waste heat from air conditioning systems.
- Use energy-modeling software.
- Install energy-efficient mechanical systems, such as geothermal with heat recovery ventilators (HRVs).
- Specify mechanical systems that are free of chemicals with ozone-depleting potential such as fluorocarbons.

Lighting and Daylighting

Electrical lighting not only requires energy, but also generates unwanted heat, which subsequently increases the load on cooling systems. Utilizing available sunlight as an additional resource reduces energy consumption while providing high-quality light. The U.S. Department of Energy (DOE) estimates that total lighting costs in commercial buildings can be cut by 30% to 60% through efficient lighting and daylighting strategies. Additionally, sunlight produces positive physiological and psychological effects for occupants, thus improving overall indoor environmental quality. The following lighting strategies are commonly employed in lighting design:

- Design glazing to capture available daylighting.
- Utilize window treatments to control glare and heat gain without eliminating views.
- Utilize automatic daylight-dimming sensors.
- Specify energy-efficient, low-mercury lighting.
- Provide occupant-controlled task lighting.
- Ensure that all exterior lights focus downward.
- Enroll in a fluorescent light recycling program.
- Specify LED exit signs.

ECOSYSTEM RESOURCES

The construction and operation of buildings accounts for an estimated 40% of the Earth's extracted raw materials and half of all waste generated, according to the Worldwatch Institute. The result is destruction of landscapes, air and water pollution, deforestation, depletion of nonrenewable resources, and overburdened landfills. By reducing the total resource burden through preservation and conservation strategies, the health and balance of the Earth's ecosystems can be preserved.

Building Reuse

Existing buildings are themselves a resource, with aesthetic, historical, and cultural value. Reusing an existing building promotes resource efficiency in two ways: demolition materials are not sent to landfills, and fewer virgin materials are used in construction. Consider building reuse in site selection, salvaging and recycling demolition waste, and retrofitting the existing thermal envelope to increase energy efficiency.

Building Materials

Often the most visible element of sustainable design is the selection of finish materials. Materials frequently are removed and discarded before their useful life is over. Dealing with such high rates of renovation magnifies the overall environmental and health impacts of materials selection. It also creates a unique opportunity to promote healthy and sustainable building materials in a visible setting.

Healthy resources are those that do not:
- Threaten human health
- Negatively impact natural ecosystems

Sustainable resources can be defined as:
- Renewable or regenerative
- Acquisitioned without ecological damage
- Used at a rate that does not exceed the natural rate of replenishment

Resource conservation can ultimately result in "closed-loop" acquisition streams, where existing "waste" is viewed as valuable raw material for new products. Closed-loop models are economically sustainable, as they do not rely on nonrenewable resources. Specifying environmentally preferable building materials involves establishing the following eight health and sustainability criteria:

REDUCED: lower total burden
- Create smaller compact plans.
- Use structural elements as finishes.
- Optimize material use.

REUSED: longer life span
- Incorporate salvaged materials.
- Design for dismantling and reuse.
- Create flexible designs (that don't need to be redesigned as often).

RENEWABLE: replenished by natural systems
- Specify agriculture-based products.
- Specify certified sustainably harvested wood.

RECYCLED: waste becomes a resource
- Specify products with a minimum of 25% post-consumer or 40% postindustrial waste.

HEALTHY: nontoxic
- Avoid products with ozone-depleting or global-warming potential.
- Avoid toxic chemicals or minerals.
- Avoid products that support pathogens or bio-contaminants (such as mold/mildew, fungi, bacteria).
- Create details that protect materials from water damage.
- Select materials that are easy to maintain.

LOCAL: less transportation energy
- Give preference to locally manufactured materials.

DURABLE: longer life span
- Specify high-quality, long-lasting products.
- Specify materials that can be partially replaced as needed (such as carpet tiles).
- Create details that protect materials from premature damage.

POSTUSE: avoid disposal
- Select materials that can be salvaged, reused, or recycled (with no downgrading).
- Select materials that are biodegradable.

Building Waste Management

Commercial operations realize savings on disposal expenses by maximizing waste recycling efforts. In a typical office, wastepaper is the predominant component of the waste stream, representing an average of 70% of total waste. Categories of recyclable building waste include white paper, mixed paper, cardboard; mixed containers of metal, glass, or plastic; food; and landscaping. The remaining 30% of waste includes glass, metal, plastics, food, and miscellaneous trash. To conserve building waste, consider the following:

- Outline items to be separated for recycling.
- Identify local haulers or recycling facilities for each waste category.
- Provide convenient, centralized recycling containers and/or chutes.
- Participate in programs that assist in educating all building occupants on reducing and recycling waste.

Construction Waste Recycling

Recyclable waste materials are generated during demolition, construction, and remodeling. The key element of successful construction waste recycling is on-site separation. Categories of recyclable construction waste include: land-clearing debris, concrete and masonry, metals (steel, aluminum, copper, iron), untreated wood, gypsum board, insulation, paints, cardboard, paper goods, plastic, glass, and salvaged goods. Once separation methods are established, recycling can be accomplished with little effort. Most job sites experience increased materials-use efficiency with the act of separation, ultimately resulting in increased profits. Consider the following:

- Include a construction waste recycling specification with construction documents.
- Outline separation, salvage, and recycling strategies.
- Identify categories of recyclable and salvageable waste.
- List local recycling purchasers and salvage organizations.

Product Labeling

Several organizations and agencies provide product labeling to help identify environmentally preferable choices:

Green Seal: Nonprofit organization that evaluates material categories and awards a "Green Seal of Approval" to products.

Energy Star: Federal energy-efficient product labeling program through the EPA and DOE.

Certified Forest Products Council (CFPC): Nonprofit organization that promotes use of responsible forest products through an online database listing suppliers of certified wood products.

Forest Stewardship Council (FSC): Member of CFPC that certifies wood for sustainable forest management and chain-of-custody.

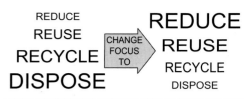

RECYCLING MODEL

WATER

The Worldwatch Institute estimates that U.S. buildings alone use 17% of all freshwater flows. Growth in development has been linked to lower water tables worldwide. Rainwater is diverted along impervious surfaces and prevented from replenishing groundwater tables and aquifers. Increased runoff flows promote erosion and contribute to nonpoint source pollution. Water treatment facilities are responsible for introducing environmental pollutants such as chlorine and phosphorous into natural bodies of water in unnatural quantities. Sustainable sites encourage natural water filtration processes and reduce overall use of potable water.

Stormwater Management

The primary goal of stormwater management initiatives is to promote the absorption of normal rainwater flows. Consider the following:

- Reduce impervious surfaces with pervious paving and vegetated roof systems.
- Place vegetated swales and infiltration strips to absorb excess stormwater runoff (especially from parking areas).
- Utilize native plant species that are appropriate to climatic conditions for all landscaping.
- Collect rainwater in cisterns for irrigation or toilet flushing.

Water Conservation

Water conservation results in savings in operating costs while reducing the burden on local water processing facilities. Potable water resources are most efficiently used when limited to applications where it is reasonable that a person may ingest water, such as drinking fountains, sink faucets, and showers. Nonpotable uses of water, such as irrigation and toilet flushing, can utilize site-processed graywater or collected rainwater. Consider the following:

- Specify ultralow-flow faucets with aerators and automatic shutoff sensors.
- Specify toilets that meet or exceed *Energy Policy Act of 1992* (EPACT) specifications. Specify waterless urinals.
- Specify water-efficient appliances.
- Do not use potable water for irrigation.

HEALTH

The term *indoor environmental quality* (IEQ) is commonly used to encompass all conditions that potentially affect occupant well-being in a given space. This includes thermal comfort, light quality, and indoor air quality (IAQ). Thermal comfort is addressed by code for all public spaces, but should be designed for efficient and flexible delivery. Diffused natural daylight provides the highest-quality light. IAQ deals with indoor pollutants that have the potential to cause negative health impacts.

The EPA has consistently ranked indoor air pollution in the top five environmental risks to public health. EPA studies have shown that indoor levels of pollutants can be 2 to 5 times, and in some cases more than 100 times, higher than outdoor levels. Indoor air pollution has been linked to Building Related Illness (BRI) and Sick Building Syndrome (SBS), with symptoms such as chronic fatigue, burning eyes, dry coughs, headaches, dizziness, rashes, and temporary loss of memory. Research indicates that people spend approximately 90% of their time indoors, thus increasing risk of exposure to pollutants.

Indoor Air Quality (IAQ)

Sources of indoor pollution include combustion gases, airborne chemicals, particulates, and microbes (such as mold). Some of these sources release pollutants constantly while others are related to specific activities. Inadequate ventilation and high humidity can compound problems. Consider the following:

- Specify building materials that are nontoxic and do not support microbial growth.
- Control moisture to prevent mold and mildew growth.
- Specify that materials with off-gassing potential be installed prior to absorptive materials (with a flush-out period between).
- Require a final flush-out period when construction is complete.
- Provide ample ventilation and monitor CO_2.
- Place building air intake away from sources of combustion gases.
- Design air distribution systems to be easily cleaned and maintained.
- Incorporate interior plants that filter pollutants from air.
- Eliminate smoking indoors.

Maintenance

Harmful chemicals such as benzene, butyl carbitol, chlorine, and formaldehyde are found in the solvents, fragrances, and degreasers of cleaning products. Many of these chemicals are known or suspected human carcinogens; others are narcotic and target the central nervous system. In addition, disposal of chemical cleaning agents can pose a serious threat to environmental health. While some of these chemicals legitimately improve product effectiveness, few are vital. A growing number of products are available that are safer to use yet provide the same performance at similar cost. Consider using maintenance products that are nontoxic, biodegradable, and contain zero VOCs.

SUSTAINABLE DESIGN COST CONSIDERATIONS

When sustainable design principles are addressed throughout the design process, many decisions serve to reduce environmental impacts with no associated cost penalty, and possibly to generate cost savings. Also, when first costs are assessed for complete systems, certain strategies may show an increased line-item cost, but it will be offset by a cost reduction for some other component. (For example, an increase in first costs for lighting fixtures and daylighting strategies may reduce the size and cost of mechanical systems, resulting in a net decrease in costs.) Implementing such measures should be automatic, and can be incorporated into standard specification documents.

Other decisions may increase first costs, but will save money over time. Many energy strategies fall into this category. If building costs are evaluated utilizing a 10- to 20-year life cycle, these costs can be justified by showing how long it will take for the savings to pay off.

Finally, buildings that are constructed using sustainable design principles are generally higher quality and have increased value to owners and occupants. "Green" projects also tend to receive more media attention, thus increasing the marketing potential for developers and owners. Making sustainable projects visible and publicly accessible helps to educate others on what is possible with respect to so-called green buildings.

Programs

The following programs assist in sustainable design efforts:

WasteWise: A free waste-reduction program through the EPA. Local recycling programs are also available throughout the country.

Energy Star: An energy-efficiency labeling program of products, homes, and buildings through the EPA and DOE.

Fluorescent lamp recycling programs: Several national and regional programs provide recycling and mercury recovery for fluorescent lamps. Contact local/regional department of waste management, or search for "fluorescent lamp recycling" on the Internet.

Leadership in Energy and Environmental Design (LEED™) Green Building Rating System: A comprehensive rating system applied to completed buildings; developed by the U.S. Green Building Council.

Cost Benefits of Daylighting

Lack of adequate daylighting has been associated with elevated stress levels, calcium deficiency, and Seasonal Affective Disorder (SAD). Natural daylighting provides high-quality light that has been documented to increase productivity and reduce absenteeism.

Daylight Zones

Rooms can be arranged within the building so that activities that need higher lighting levels are near the windows, while activities that don't need as much light are farther from daylight sources.

Areas nearest the skin of the building have the greatest opportunity for daylight at the highest illumination levels. If activities are zoned so that those that need the light are placed near openings in the skin and those that don't are placed in the interior, then the amount of relatively expensive skin and glazed openings can be reduced because of a smaller skin-to-volume ratio. The rate of electric light use, and thus heat gains, are also reduced. In dense urban areas with narrow streets or tall buildings, there is more light available on upper floors than at street level.

Light Shelves

Light shelves can be used to shade view glazing, evenly distribute light, and reduce glare. Compared to an ordinary window of equal size and height, a window divided into upper and lower sections by a horizontal light shelf performs better in several ways. If the light shelf extends beyond the exterior surface of the glazing on sunny exposures, it can be used to shade the view glazing. At the same time, it can reflect light off its top surface through the upper glazing to the ceiling, where it is then reflected deeper into the space. The light shelf section that extends into the space also reflects light from the upper part of the window deeper into the space while decreasing the light levels immediately adjacent to the window, thereby evenly distributing the light throughout the space. The interior portion of the light shelf also blocks the occupants' view of the sky, which is a potential source of glare.

The optimum size of light shelves is governed by several considerations. They should be as low as possible without interfering with views through the lower part of the window. If reducing solar gain is an important concern, the light shelves should extend beyond the building far enough to shade the view glazing during the cooling season. They should extend inside the building enough to block the view of the bright sky, thus reducing glare. To prevent excess heat gain, the upper glazing above a light shelf should be shaded on the south exposures during the cooling season. This can be accomplished with reflective louvers or by recessing the upper glazing to the back of the shelf.

The upper surface of the light shelf should be white or, if heat gain is not an issue, mirrored. Ceiling reflectance should be high. The top surface of the light shelf should never be seen by occupants because of its glare potential. Tilting the external part of a light shelf above horizontal can increase the light reflected onto the ceiling. Remember that sloping the shelf reduces its effectiveness at shading the lower glazing, so it should be lengthened or thickened.

Daylight-Enhancing Shades

Daylight-enhancing shades can protect windows from solar gain while preserving sky view, reflecting daylight, and reducing glare. Carefully designed perforations or louvers in overhangs and fins allow them to maintain the same shading characteristics but still reflect light into the space. A perforated shade allows a small amount of light to penetrate the shading surface, lightening the appearance of the underside while still blocking most of the solar radiation.

SUSTAINABLE BUILDING MATERIALS

The standard product selection process involves weighing a variety of criteria, including aesthetics, performance, and cost. Environmental and health impacts present additional criteria when specifying green materials.

Evaluation Tools

Two primary methods are used to evaluate building materials for environmental impacts: *embodied energy* and *life-cycle analysis* (LCA). Embodied energy calculations establish energy expenditures; LCA assesses environmental and health impacts.

Embodied Energy

Embodied energy calculations quantify the total energy consumption embedded in a particular material, from raw material acquisition and manufacturing processes through transportation to point-of-use. The more processing associated with a given material, the greater its embodied energy. The total energy associated with all materials in a typical building is estimated to equal 20 years of operating energy. Selecting materials with lower embodied energy values saves energy costs and reduces environmental impacts related to the use of fossil fuels.

EMBODIED ENERGY

PROS	CONS
Quantitative results are easily compared (if calculated by single source).	Limited available data.
	Calculation assumptions vary.
Provides a useful relative indicator.	No consideration of health or nonenergy impacts.
	No differentiation between sources of energy (natural gas vs. coal vs. solar).
	Evaluation ends with delivery to site.

Life-Cycle Analysis (LCA)

LCA is a qualitative evaluation tool that provides context for material selection. LCA examines environmental and health impacts from "cradle to grave": from acquisition of raw materials through end-of-use recovery. (A cradle-to-cradle approach closes the acquisition loop.) Analyzing the entire life cycle provides a complete, transparent assessment of impacts on health and the environment.

LIFE-CYCLE ANALYSIS

PROS	CONS
Reflects total impacts through entire life cycle.	Evaluation is subjective.
Evaluation is "transparent."	Involves educating the end user.
Allows prioritization.	
Can be updated.	
Embodied energy data can be included.	

Evaluation Process

In order to specify healthy and sustainable materials, it is necessary to define pertinent criteria. Rarely are there products that meet all green criteria as well as requirements for suitability and cost. Therefore, the relative importance of each issue is prioritized depending on the client, region, and project goals. For example, indoor air quality might be of primary concern where sensitivity to air pollutants is an issue; energy conservation might be prioritized if long-term energy costs are an issue.

Embodied energy is a useful indicator of one aspect of environmental impact; that is, the total energy required to produce and deliver a material. Calculation methods are, however, complicated, and require data that is often difficult to quantify. Resulting values are useful primarily on a relative basis. For example, one can say that "wood has lower embodied energy than steel" or "a product imported from overseas has higher embodied energy than a local equivalent." When using embodied energy values, it is recommended to note the source and date that the calculations were developed, as well as the margin of error.

LCA is a more broadly applicable tool for evaluating building materials. Since the entire life cycle of the material is evaluated, results present a more global picture of environmental and health impacts. LCA also allows for differences between products and lends itself to prioritization of issues. Embodied energy data can be included in LCA evaluations.

Performing Analysis

Analyzing a material throughout its life cycle involves gathering research data. The entirety of this research comprises the LCA for that material. Data can include embodied energy values, other published LCA evaluations, and supporting data on health and environmental issues. Specific product data is acquired by questioning manufacturers.

A product questionnaire can provide useful information from manufacturers on life-cycle impacts of their products. Ask for substantiation of all test results (through independent labs) and for a material safety data sheet (an MSDS) to support claims regarding safety and toxicity. Life-cycle categories include:

Raw Material Acquisition

Manufacturing Process

Packaging

Shipping

Installation

Indoor Air Quality

Durability

Resource Recovery

Recovery of materials at end-of-use provides raw material for new products.

LIFE-CYCLE ANALYSIS—CLOSED LOOP MODEL

The results of LCA are typically in the form of a report or a comparative matrix. Information is transparent and therefore easily updated to reflect changes in environmental and health priorities, as well as innovations in manufacturing.

Interpreting Results

Determining the health and sustainability of a material involves subjective evaluation. Ultimately, materials are judged relative to the typical application and through the weighted priorities for a given project.

MATERIALS GOALS

MATERIAL ATTRIBUTE	GOAL
Raw Materials	Safe, low-impact
Manufacturing Process	Safe, closed-loop, and nonpolluting systems
Packaging	Minimal waste
Shipping	Minimal transportation
Installation	Safe; minimal waste
Indoor Air Quality	No negative health impacts
Durability	Suited to use; long-lasting
Resource Recovery	Reusable, recyclable, biodegradable

Environmental Quality Glossary

carcinogen   A substance identified as causing cancer. A carcinogen is classified as "known," "probable," "presumed," or "suspected," depending on test study data.

downcycling   Recycling into a product that has less value or is considered more disposable than the original.

EPA 33/50 Program   Voluntary EPA program targeting 17 priority chemicals for reduction.

EPACT (Energy Policy Act of 1992) Comprehensive legislation to improve conservation and efficiency in energy and water use.

NIOSH (National Institute for Occupational Safety and Health)   Part of the U.S. Department of Health and Human Services that conducts research and makes recommendations on health and safety standards.

ODP (ozone-depleting potential)   A relative measure of the ability of a substance to break down the stratospheric ozone layer.

off-gassing   The vaporization of chemical compounds into surrounding air.

postconsumer   Waste material that has served an intended use.

postindustrial Waste material from manufacturing processes.

teratogenic   A substance that has been directly linked to birth defects during human fetus development.

toxicity   The degree to which a material causes or threatens to cause adverse health effects to living organisms. Expressed in exposure limits.

VOC (volatile organic compound)   Chemical compounds that contain carbon and that partially vaporize at normal room temperature. VOCs are a group of chemicals that have varying degrees of toxicity and effects.

PRODUCT QUESTIONNAIRE

LIFE CYCLE	QUESTIONS TO ASK MANUFACTURERS	CRITERIA FOR EVALUATION
RAW MATERIALS ACQUISITION	Is the product made up of salvaged materials?	Material is reused with minimal processing/refinishing.
	Does the product contain rapidly renewable resources or agricultural waste?	Materials such as straw, soy, cornhusks, bagasse (sugar cane husks), etc.
	If the product contains wood, is the wood certified as being sustainably harvested?	Certified by the Forest Stewardship Council or equivalent.
	Does the product contain significant recycled content?	Minimum of 30% postconsumer or 50% postindustrial content.
	Are there toxic constituents in the product?	Products contain noVOCs and chemicals targeted for reduction by the EPA; verify information with an MSDS.
	Are highly energy-intensive raw materials avoided?	Materials such asrecycled aluminum are used instead of virgin aluminum made from mined bauxite.
	Does raw material acquisition for this product negatively impact the ecosystem?	Materials should not be acquired using methods such as strip mining, dredging, clear cutting, and so on.
MANUFACTURING PROCESS	Is the manufacturing facility local to raw material acquisition?	Facility should be wthin 200 miles of the job site.
	Does the manufacturing process recycle all in-plant waste back into product?	Manufacturing process uses a closed-loop material (no scrap is generated in manufacture).
	Is the manufacturing process highly energy-intensive?	Manufacturer should be able to quantify energy use without unusual difficulty
	Is power for manufacturing generated with renewable sources?	A percentage of power for manufacturing is generated by a source such as wind, solar orhydroelectric.
	Is all water used in manufacturing a closed-loop system?	All water is filtered and reused on-site or water use is minimized by verifiable water-reduction strategies.
	Has manufacturing eliminated environmentally harmful emissions?	Harmful emissions include greenhouse gases, chemicals that have ozone-depleting potential, or chemicals that contribute to acid rain (such as CO_2, SOX, and NOX, CFCs, HCFCs, HFCs)
PACKAGING AND SHIPPING	Is packaging for this product eliminated or minimized?	Items bundled for shipping instead of wrapping individually.
	Is packaging reusable? (Reuse strategy must be plausible.)	Packaging is accepted bythe manufacturer for reuse?
	Does packaging contain 100% postconsumer recycled materials? (Does it contain any recycled content?)	Recycled packaging materials include cardboard, plastics, peanuts
	Is packaging easily recyclable?	Standard local facilities exist for recycling
	Are manufacturing facilities local to the project?	Facility or regional distributor should be wthin 200 miles of the job site.
	Are products shipped using energy-efficient methods?	Shipping methods should be full loads only and direct delivery.;
INSTALLATION	Does installation pose any health risk to installers?	Verify with the MSDS if protective clothing or equipment isrequired for installation
	Does installation require any materials that emit VOCs (such as adhesives)? (Are there nontoxic alternatives, such as mechanical fasteners or nontoxic products?)	Installation materials should be zero –VOC and nontoxic
	Does installation involve large amounts of waste material?	Materials such as tile produce less waste material than sheet goods.
	Can installation waste be readily recycled locally?	Installation waste should be accepted for recycling by the manufacturer or at standard local facilities
	Are any special tools or methods required for installation?	Materials should be able to be installed with conventional tools and methods.
INDOOR AIR QUALITY	Does this product or any material required to install it contain or emit VOCs?	VOC Emission can be verified with the MSDS, and/or third-party IAQ testing data (such as ASTM, or CA or WA state IAQ testing).
	Does this product or any material required to install it contain any toxic compounds?	Verify with the MSDS that VOCs and chemicals should not be targeted for reduction by the EPA (see list)
	Is this type of product known to support microbial growth?	Materials should not be used in an application that will encourage the growth of mold, mildew or other microbes.
	Can this product be cleaned and maintained with non-toxic cleaning methods and materials?	Verify that the use of nontoxic cleaning materials and methods will not affect warranty coverage.
DURABILITY AND PERFORMANCE	Is this product suitable in the intended application?	Verify product limitations in specific used such as wet applications or structural requirements
	Is the product as long- or longer-lasting as industry standards?	Support product durability with warranty information and/or product testing data.
	Is the product line available in patterns and colors that outlast style fads?	Faddish styles or colors would potentially cause replacement before the product's useful life is over.
	Can elements of the product be replaced individually?	Materials such as carpet tile can be individually replaced, whereas products such as broadloom cannot.
	Does the product facilitate some other aspect of sustainability?	Such as energy or water efficiency, natural daylighting, recycling, etc.
RESOURCE RECOVERY	Do recommended installation techniques allow this product to be easily removed without damage?	The product be reasonably removed with the intention of reusing it (for example solid surface goods attached with mechanical fasteners are removable whereas laminates cannot be removed)
	Is product inherently reusable?	The product is long-lasting and durable
	Is product biodegradable after its useful life?	Theroduct shouldcompletely breakdown into benign, organic components
	Is product recyclable (with no downcycling)?	The product should be recyclable into a similar product.
	Does disposal pose an environmental health risk?	Disposal should not harm the environment with any disposal technique, including landfill, incineration and so on.
COMPANY PROFILE	Does company have any overall environmental policy?	A copy of the company's written environmental policy should be available on request.
	Does company meet ISO 14000 criteria "Environmental Management System Standard Certification?"	Verify that the company has participated in ISO 14000 in the past
	Are products third-party-certified as being environmental?	Environmental certification comes from organizations such as Green Seal, Forest Stewardship Council, Energy Star, etc.
	Do company facilities have recycling program for all waste?	Companies should recycle office paper, cans and so on.
	Are company facilities constructed such that they are themselves examples of sustainable design?	Facilities should be energy- and water-efficient; using such techniques as filtering and absorbing stormwater and providing easy ways for employees to commute via mass transit or bicycle

Sigi Koko; Down to Earth; Arlington, Virginia

ROLE OF THE U.S. GREEN BUILDING COUNCIL (USGBC)

The U.S. Green Building Council (USGBC) was established in 1993 as a national nonprofit organization, with a voluntary, diverse membership that operates on consensus principles. The heart of the USGBC are committees that provide a forum for members to resolve differences, build alliances, and find solutions that add value to the existing membership.

USGBC works with members to incorporate their ideas into the overall organization. The consensus of USGBC members is to work together to promote green building and help to foster greater economic vitality and environmental health. USGBC accomplishes this by working with the industry to help bridge ideological gaps, thus providing benefits for the entire construction communiity.

Leadership in Energy and Environmental Design (LEED) Rating System

One of the many achievements of USGBC is the establishment of the Leadership in Energy and Environmental Design (LEED) rating system. Launched in 1995, LEED is a voluntary point-based rating guideline that establishes consistent criteria for sustainable design projects. LEED serves as a tool to aid integrated sustainable design and to help owners and design teams obtain the benefits in the overall health and efficiency of building design. LEED is based on accepted energy and environmental principles, and strikes a balance between known effective practices and emerging concepts.

During the development of LEED, committee members carefully reviewed existing green building rating systems such as Building Research Establishment Environmental Assessment Method (BREEAM) and Building Environment Performance Assessment Criteria (BEPAC). The committee determined that these existing systems involved a costly infrastructure for which the U.S. market was not ready to follow.

LEED Rating System Categories

LEED has five categories:

Sustainable Sites

Water Efficiency

Energy and Atmosphere

Indoor Environmental Quality

Materials and Resources

Each category is composed of individual points and prerequisites that, in aggregate, allows a participant to achieve one of four levels of certification of sustainability as defined by USGBC.

Of the five LEED categories, Materials and Resource (MR) specifically addresses interior finishes and specifications. This category has one prerequisite that must be met before any points can be obtained: for each building, an area specifically located on a ground floor must be dedicated to the separation, collection, and storage of materials for recycling paper, glass, plastic, and metals.

In addition to the recycling prerequisite, the following specifically address interior finishes and specifications:

MR Credit 3—Resource Reuse: Specifically addresses the percentage of salvaged or refurbished materials that are required for building materials. One point is available for using 5% of building materials; another point is available for using salvaged or refurbished materials for 10% of the total building materials. The intent of this credit is to divert material from the solid waste stream and avoid environmental impacts of producing new construction and product materials.

MR Credit 4—Recycled Content: Specifies the percentage of postconsumer recycled content and postindustrial recycled content in building materials. Recycled content in a product has a significant effect on reducing the solid waste stream by recycling material rather than disposing of it in a landfill. USGBC provides one point for providing 25% of the building materials that contain in aggregate a minimum weighted average of 20% postconsumer recycled content material or 40% postindustrial recycled content. An additional point can be earned by improving from 25 to 50% of the building materials. Through the voluntary LEED rating system, USGBC has managed to alter the way in which many manufacturers produce products, providing both financial and environmental benefits.

MR Credit 5—Local/Regional/Materials: Sets a radius of 500 miles from a project site for the purchase of building materials. The intent of this credit is to support the local economy and reduce transportation costs and environmental impacts on moving goods across the country.

MR Credit 6—Rapidly Renewable Materials: Requires the specification of alternative materials that substantially replenish themselves faster than traditional extraction. In addition, the materials must not result in significant biodiversity loss, increased erosion, or air quality changes. One point is available for specifying rapidly renewable building materials for 5% of the total building materials. Such materials include cork, linoleum, and bamboo.

MR Credit 7—Certified Wood: Encourages the use of forest products that are certified as sustainably harvested building materials; specifically, they must be in compliance with the Forest Stewardship Council Guidelines (FSC). One point is available for specifying 50% or more of the wood-based materials compliant with FSC guidelines.

In aggregate, 8 out of 13 points are dedicated to interior finishes in the Materials and Resources category. By selecting materials carefully and reducing waste, the result is the use of materials with less environmental impact, which creates a healthier environment for the end user and future generations.

LEED RATING SYSTEM

LEVEL	POINTS PERCENTILE
LEED Certified	32–38 (50–60%)
Silver Level	39–45 (61–70%)
Gold Level	46–51 (71–80%)
Platinum Level	52+ (81% or better)

MATERIAL SAFETY DATA SHEETS (MSDS)

A material safety data sheet (MSDS) provides information about the physical and health hazards of a chemical product. The United States Occupational Safety and Health Administration (OSHA) requires all manufacturers to issue an MSDS with the first shipment of any hazardous (or even potentially hazardous) chemical product. OSHA also requires that MSDSs must be accessible to employees.

Limitations

MSDSs are an important source of health and safety information, but they should not be the only source of information used to evaluate chemical hazards. While MSDSs discuss short-term chemical exposure, they do not describe possible effects from low levels of carcinogens or toxins that may affect a chemically sensitive person. They also do not consider the effects of materials on the environment.

MSDS Content

An MSDS lists the manufacturer's information and identification of the substance. This includes the name, address, and contact numbers of the company that produced the material. The MSDS's date of issue or most recent revision and the name of the material are also given. The latter must be spelled exactly as it is seen on the container; if it is not, it may be the wrong MSDS, as many chemical names appear to be similar. If one generic MSDS is used to cover various grades of a material, all grades must be listed, as well as any known synonyms.

Source: "Material Safety Data Sheets"; Washington, DC, U.S. Department of Labor, OSHA, 1977.
Source: "Preparing, Understanding, and Using Material Safety Data Sheets," Lab Safety Supply, 1988.
Source: The MSDS Pocket Dictionary, 3rd Ed.; Schenectady, NY, Genium Publishing Corp., 1999. (This pamphlet explains how to read an MSDS and defines commonly used terms.)
Source: Spiegel, R., and Meadows, D., Green Building Materials: A Guide to Product Selection and Specification; John Wiley & Sons, Inc., 1999, pp. 67–70. Michelle Scurfield, AIA; Scurfield Architects, LLC; Washington, D.C.

Margery Morgan; Symmes Maini & McKee Associates; Cambridge, Massachusetts
Heidi Rhodes; Rhode Island School of Design; Providence, Rhode Island.

INDOOR AIR QUALITY

INDOOR AIR POLLUTION

Over the past few decades, office building construction has increasingly focused on meeting both the demands of climate control and the need for energy efficiency. As a result, the nearly across-the-board adoption of central heating and cooling systems has also prompted the development of airtight buildings that reduce energy consumption by minimizing air loss. Though energy efficiency has increased markedly, such sealed environments can at times pose serious health risks, which are aggravated by the simultaneous use of more complex chemicals and compounds in the furniture, clothing, cleaners, detergents, and other products that fill them. Combined, these trends have created workplaces where exposure to harmful particles and gases has created indoor air pollution.

According to the World Health Organization (WHO), 40% of all buildings pose significant health hazards from indoor pollution; and according to the Environmental Protection Agency (EPA), indoor air in the United States is now on average 2 to 10 times more contaminated than the air outside. As a result, a reported 20% of all workers suffer from related irritations or illnesses. Poor indoor air quality—and its role in Sick Building Syndrome (SBS) and Building-Related Illness (BRI) has been declared by the EPA as the country's number-one environmental health problem.

Indoor Air Quality (IAQ) Defined

Indoor air quality, or IAQ, refers to the quality of air inside buildings where people work or live. Air quality is essential for comfort and productivity, but, most importantly, good air promotes good health. IAQ can be compromised under the following four conditions:

- Inadequate ventilation doesn't provide enough outside air.
- Chemicals used in cleaning and office products get trapped inside a building.
- Outdoor pollutants enter and are trapped inside.
- Mold or other microorganisms grow, multiply, and disperse particles through heating, air conditioning, and ventilation systems.

Sick Building Syndrome (SBS)

When IAQ is poor, often what results is SBS and BRI. SBS describes a wide range of physical afflictions, often similar to mild allergic reactions, that usually result from exposure to contaminants in indoor air (although noises and other environmental factors can contribute, as well). The specific causes are not identified, but the symptoms coincide with time spent in a particular building and disappear once the sufferer leaves. A BRI describes the same range of ailments, from mild allergic reactions to more serious infections such as pneumonia, except it applies in cases where the specific cause is known. Both SBS and BRI are largely the result of poor indoor air quality.

PARTICULATE IRRITANTS

Microorganisms

The most prevalent particles in the air that can cause problems are microorganisms, dust, and pollen. Though bacteria and fungi are present everywhere, in both outdoor and indoor environments, office buildings are especially vulnerable, as they provide areas of high humidity and standing water in circulation and air conditioning ducts, ceiling tiles, insulation, and even ice machines. These intruders release what are called *bioaerosols,* which include the tiny spores from molds and other fungi that float through the air, causing skin and mucous membrane irritation and coughing. Such allergic reactions are also induced by dust, pollen, and endotoxins from certain bacteria that circulate throughout the air. Sensitive people, such as the elderly, very young, or those with weaker immune systems, can be at risk of serious infection.

Respirable Particles

Respirable particles are defined as particles less than 10 microns in diameter (the diameter of a human hair is about 100 microns). In humans, larger particles are usually caught in the nose before they reach the lungs. Because of their minute size, however, respirable particles flow easily through the nasal passage and can be inhaled deeply into the lungs to cause coughing, wheezing, and even respiratory tract infection. In an office, respirable particles are given off by everything from human skin to the carbon from copy machines.

GASEOUS IRRITANTS

Volatile Organic Compounds (VOCs)

The use of strong office cleaning products, paints, glues, and photocopiers intensifies the IAQ problem. At room temperature, synthetic organic chemicals release vapors and gases that are known as volatile organic compounds (VOCs). Consistently found at higher levels indoors, VOCs come from many different sources including building materials, consumer products, and combustion sources such as car engines and heating systems. Many VOCs are toxic, including benzene and carbon tetracycline, and can induce a host of health problems, from eye irritation to fatigue and dizziness. Some VOCs have been determined to be carcinogens, so long-term exposure could possibly cause cancer. Though not all are as seriously harmful, many do cause discomfort and are found nearly everywhere in offices: one major VOC irritant is formaldehyde, a pungent gas that exists in nearly 3,000 different products, including certain floor adhesives, wallcoverings, particleboard, and furniture.

Carbon Monoxide

Carbon monoxide (CO) is an odorless, colorless gas. It is a dangerous pollutant that is regulated outdoors, making it an even greater hazard if found indoors. Carbon monoxide is given off by fuel-burning engines such as those in cars, and though the highest interior concentrations are usually found in underground or indoor garages, adjacent buildings can be contaminated if not properly ventilated. In these cases, the gas seeps into the building and its offices, where the prolonged exposure of employees decreases the oxygen-carrying capacity of their blood, resulting in shortness of breath, fatigue, and nausea.

Other Pollutants

Some office equipment releases ozone, which is a respiratory irritant that at high concentrations can cause serious harm to people. And despite the fact that smoking has been all but eliminated in office buildings over the past decade, it can still pose a threat to nonsmoking workers. If, for example, outside air vents are located in close proximity to smoking areas, the smoke—and its carbon monoxide and harmful particles—can get sucked inside.

IRRITANT PARTICLE SIZES (IN MICRONS)

DETERMINING INDOOR AIR QUALITY

Currently, methods of air pollution detection are complicated, time-consuming, and costly. Air-quality consulting agencies may be brought in if a building's management suspects an air problem. These agencies start with a lengthy question-and-answer session to help occupants determine which health effects are being felt, how long they have persisted, and what, if any, preexisting issues may be causing them. The agency will then conduct a walk-through of the office to see if there are any obvious sources of contamination, and to check air temperature, humidity levels, and airflow. All these are factors in the spread of indoor pollutants and can give clues to their presence; for instance, if humidity is at a high level, it would be reasonable to suspect that bacterial contamination could be the problem. If a definitive cause still eludes these efforts, air sampling is usually the next step.

FIGHTING POOR INDOOR AIR QUALITY

Once the pollutant has been identified, there are two primary ways of fighting it: *ventilation* and *air cleaning*. As both are usually components of integrated systems, they are not mutually exclusive.

Ventilation

According to most experts, including the American Society of Heating, Refrigerating, and Air-Conditioning Engineers (ASHRAE), increasing ventilation and air distribution is the best and most cost-effective way of freshening the air inside most buildings. Air enters office buildings through both mechanical ventilation systems and natural circulation. The latter occurs, primarily in older buildings, largely by way of leaks around windows and doors and other openings. Newer, larger, and highly energy-efficient buildings with sealed windows and heavy insulation depend primarily on mechanical ventilation.

In a modern office building, the HVAC system is designed to keep occupants comfortable and healthy by controlling temperatures and bringing outside air into the internal environment, simultaneously filtering both incoming and recirculated air. Ventilation is thus an integral part of HVAC systems, and is accomplished by blowers and fans that move the air, ductwork that delivers it to the building's rooms, and vents that distribute it. A good ventilation design will distribute supply air uniformly—except in areas with heat- and vapor-producing office machines that require added airflow—and place supply and exhaust vents sufficiently apart to allow fresh air to circulate more freely. ASHRAE has established a general guideline of 20 cu ft (.56 cu m) of outside air per minute/per person for an office environment to sufficiently dilute building contaminants and maintain a healthy environment.

Cleaning Air with Filtration

Following the energy crisis of the 1970s, the trend toward airtight buildings resulted in the widespread installation of HVAC systems that recirculate already-temperature-adjusted air rather than bringing in untreated air from the outside. Consequently, these buildings rely heavily on filtration to preserve air quality. The most widely used methods of filtering out gases and particles are lower-efficiency filters, High-Efficiency Particulate-Arresting (HEPA) filtration, and adsorption with activated carbon.

MAJOR CONTAMINANTS, THEIR SOURCES, AND HEALTH EFFECTS

TYPE OF CONTAMINANT	SOURCES	HEALTH EFFECTS
PARTICLES		
Microorganisms, bioaerosols, and other biological contaminants: Animal dander Molds and fungi Dust mites Viruses Bacteria Pollen	Areas of high humidity or condensation Damp organic materials Porous wet surfaces Humidifiers Animals and insects Food and food products Plants Human respiration	Exacerbation of asthma Sneezing/runny nose Recurrent fever Malaise Sore throat Muscle aches Tightness of chest Cough Eye irritation Infectious diseases (rare)
Respirable particles (<10 microns): Any particles or particle fragments less than 10 microns Some molds Viruses Bacteria	*Same as above, and:* Tobacco smoke Unvented combustion appliances (e.g., gas stoves, kerosene heaters)	*Same as above*
GASES		
Volatile organic compounds (VOCs): Formaldehyde Benzene Carbon tetracycline Trichloroethylene Toluene Methyl ethyl ketone Alcohols Methacrylates Acrolein Polycyclic aromatic hydrocarbons Pesticides	Personal products (fragrances and hair sprays) Cleaning products Office equipment (photocopiers and printers) Office products (permanent markers, correction fluids, carbonless copy paper) Glues and adhesives (including those used in carpeting, textiles, furniture, wallcoverings, etc.) Asphalt Paints Insecticides and herbicides Gasoline vapors Tobacco smoke Combustion products	Nose, throat discomfort Headache Allergic skin reactions Eye, respiratory tract, mucous membrane irritation Nausea Epistaxis (for formaldehyde) Fatigue Dizziness Possibly cancer
Carbon monoxide	Tobacco smoke Fossil-fuel engine exhausts Improperly vented fossil-fuel appliances	Dizziness Headache Nausea Cardiovascular effects Death (in extreme cases)

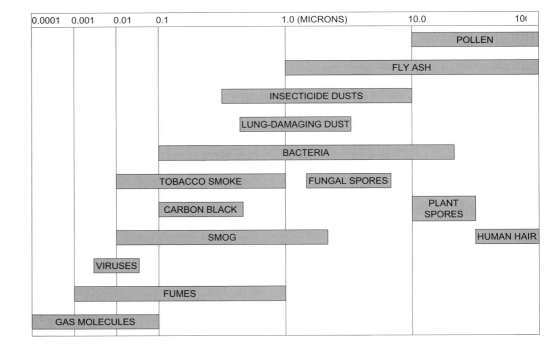

Particle Filtration

When air is being circulated in an HVAC system, it passes through filters installed at various points to stop particles from passing through. Based on economic constraints, either lower-efficiency filters or HEPA filters are used. Most buildings use lower-efficiency filters that employ woven fiberglass strands to catch particles. These filters are less expensive; and with a lower density weave, air flows more freely through them so smaller fans and less energy are needed. However, they can trap only larger particles—and fewer of them. They tend to catch only between 10% and 60% of particulates.

On the other hand, HEPA filters are generally made from a single sheet of water-repellent fiber that is pleated to provide more surface area with which to catch particles, making them much more effective. HEPA filters are able to catch 99.97% of all particles, including those that are respirable. But because they are more densely woven, they require larger and more energy-intensive fans, making their greater expense economically undesirable in most buildings—not to mention the added noise from the bigger motors. Accordingly, HEPA filters are usually reserved for hospital operating rooms, manufacturing clean rooms (such as those for computer chips), and other spaces especially sensitive to contamination.

Gas and Vapor Filtration

The most widely used and cost-effective vapor and gas removal technique is called *adsorption* (as opposed to absorption). Whereas absorption describes a process in which one substance mixes evenly into another, adsorption is the physical attraction and adherence of a gas to the surface of a solid, usually activated carbon in the case of filtration. Once the gas is on the activated carbon, it moves down into the carbon particle, eventually condensing into a liquid. Though effective, these filters capture only a small percentage of certain gases and vapors.

Independent Air Purification Units

Personal Air Filters

Particle and gas filtration systems are not only used in HVAC systems, but are also employed in personal or room air purifiers; the small size of the units makes use of HEPA filters more economically feasible. Personal or room HEPA purifiers, specifically designed for respirable particle removal, are able to capture up to 99.97% of all particles larger than 0.3 microns in spaces up to 400 sq ft (11.3 sq m). Personal or desktop purifiers can be effective ways of cleaning the air in a limited workspace to at least create a "comfort zone" of clean air for the worker. In addition to the more traditional filtration methods discussed above, these machines can also use two to three different types of purification techniques not available in buildingwide systems, including negative ionization, ozone, and ultraviolet light.

Negative Ionization

In personal air purifiers using negative ionization, air and any accompanying particles pass through an electrical field within the purifier, which charges the particles. These particles are then attracted to and trapped on oppositely charged collector plates within the unit, much like a magnet would attract metal dust. While personal air purifiers using this technology can have a beneficial effect on airborne particles, they may also require frequent maintenance and cleaning.

Ozone

Although it is harmful in high concentrations, ozone may also help reduce pollutants. When oxygen (O_2) is broken down with an electrical discharge, the molecules end up coming back together in groups of three to form ozone (O_3) molecules. Once released into the air, ozone actively seeks out pollutants, attaching itself to a wide range of contaminants—including chemical gases, bacteria, mold, and mildew—and destroying them by cracking their molecular membranes. Because ozone has a very short life span—between 20 and 30 minutes—it is easy to avoid achieving the high concentrations that can be detrimental to people's health.

Ultraviolet Light

Personal air purifiers may also use ultraviolet (UV) light, which is believed to be one of nature's own methods of purifying the air. The light rays are germicidal and effectively destroy the DNA structure of viruses, bacteria, and fungi. UV has been used for years in hospitals to sanitize rooms and equipment, and is also effective in eliminating many odors and the spread of colds and flu viruses. However, it can be more expensive than other purification techniques.

Strategies for Improving Indoor Air Quality

1. ASSESSMENT. Determine which contaminants are in the air through inspection and testing by outside consulting firms or in-house facilities managers.
2. VENTILATION. Bring in sufficient air from the outside by opening windows and doors (where possible); using mechanical systems (HVAC); or passively, through cracks and leaks in exterior walls and windows (usually only possible in older buildings).
3. AIR CLEANING. Clean interior air through particle, gas, and vapor filters installed in HVAC systems and/or in freestanding personal units.
4. PRODUCT SPECIFICATION. Source low-emitting products that are certified to contribute minimal levels of pollutants into the air.

Tom Revelle; Humanscale; New York

STAIR DESIGN

Stairways are an essential component in the circulation and egress systems of most buildings. In the United States, they are also the site of accidents that, annually, result in approximately 4,000 deaths and 1 million injuries requiring hospital treatment. For these reasons, stairway design is strictly controlled by building regulations.

The information contained in this section summarizes most International Building Code (IBC) and access regulation requirements. Check authorities having local jurisdiction for additional requirements.

MINIMUM REQUIREMENTS

Consult the IBC for stairway requirements to determine dimensional limits for treads, risers, landings, and stair width. Verify that local codes are not more restrictive. Refer to the Americans with Disabilities Act (ADA) for accessibility requirements regarding stairs.

Stair Details

Treads and risers within a flight must be uniform in size within close tolerances. Treads must be slip-resistant. Carpeting or other stair coverings should be applied securely and should not create a nosing radius greater than permitted. Handrails, guardrails, and stairways themselves must meet structural load requirements.

Access regulations in some localities require that floor material strips of contrasting color be located at the top approach to a stair and at the lowest tread. These markings are intended to aid the visually impaired in identifying the limits of the stair. The application of such markings may be appropriate even where not required, particularly where a high proportion of elderly or visually impaired users are anticipated.

DIRECT FLIGHT

STRAIGHT RUN

L-SHAPED

WINDERS

Z-SHAPED

ALTERNATIVE STEP

DIVIDED RETURN

WIDE-U, RETURN FLIGHT

SPLIT-U

T-SHAPED

O-SHAPED

CIRCULAR

SPIRAL

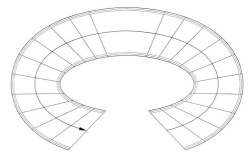

CURVED OVAL

STAIR TYPES

Stair Types

Stair type refers to its design and plan layout. Stair types vary, and are subject to code requirements. Stair type selection depends on the space available, the starting and ending points required of the stair, and the appearance desired.

Egress stairs must be enclosed as required by building codes, but the designer can vary the openness of nonegress stairs.

Layout refers to the overall horizontal and vertical dimensions required to meet functional and building code requirements. This includes determining the width, total rise, and run of the stair, and space for landings.

Tread and riser dimensions are proportionally related to each other. The tread and riser proportion, or pitch, affect safety as well as the comfort of using the stair. Code requirements are minimums.

Minimum stair widths are defined by building and accessibility codes, based on occupancy, tread and riser dimensions, handrail dimensions and positions, headroom requirements, and distance between landings.

Details of construction include how the treads and risers are supported, handrail profiles and construction, materials used, and other finish considerations, including slip resistance.

Stair Layout

Maintain minimum headroom of 6 ft 8 in. (2,032 mm) for nonresidential, and 6 ft 6 in. (1,981 mm) for residential stairs.

Avoid flights with fewer than three risers, to minimize tripping hazards. If one or two risers are used, increase tread depth and clearly mark the level changes.

The use of door alcoves is recommended to prevent stairway doors from obstructing the egress travel path.

Stair Width

The minimum width of any straight stair is 36 in. (914 mm) when the occupant load is 50 or fewer. The minimum width is 44 in. (1,118 mm) when the occupant load is more than 50. Handrails may encroach no more than 4½ in. (114 mm) on each side. For large occupancies, calculate the minimum width according to the exit width provisions of the IBC. When the stair serves an area of evacuation assistance, the minimum clear width between handrails must be 48 in. (1,219 mm).

In residential occupancies, wider stairways allow for easier movement of furniture. For commercial occupancies, wider stairways allow for more comfortable circulation when two people are passing or carrying objects.

RETURN STAIR PLAN LAYOUT

RETURN STAIR SECTION LAYOUT

Horizontal Stair Layout

Steps involved in sizing the horizontal layout of the stair are as follows:

1. **Determine riser height.** The number of risers required determines the number of treads required. For standard straight stairs, begin the calculation by taking the total rise of the stairway, in inches, and dividing by 7 in. (179 mm). This is a comfortable riser height and is the maximum allowed for most commercial stairways. If the result is not an even number, select the next-highest even number and divide that number into the total rise. This establishes a riser height of less than 7 in., which is a whole number and is the number of risers required. The number of treads is one less than this number for a straight-run stair and two less for a return or L-shaped stair (the landing takes the place of one tread). For straight-run residential stairways where allowed by code, divide by 7.75 in. (197 mm). This is the maximum allowable riser height for Group R-3 occupancies and within dwelling units in Group R-2 occupancies.

2. **Determine the proportion between the riser and tread dimensions.** Stair dimensions are based on the normal stride of a person while ascending and descending a stair. Several formulas relating rise and tread have been proposed through the years, but one of the most common is:

$$2R = T = 25 \text{ or } T = 25 - 2R$$

where R is the riser height and T is the tread depth. The IBC identifies the minimum tread depth of 11 in. (279 mm) for commercial stairs and 10 in. (254 mm) for residential stairs. For straight-run, L-shaped, T-shaped, and wide-U stairs, the total run is the number of treads multiplied by the tread depth. For return stairs, an unequal number of risers and treads in the lower and upper flight is recommended, to allow the first riser of the upper landing to lead the last riser of the lower landing by one tread depth. The handrail can then make a clean switchback without having to offset vertically.

HORIZONTAL LAYOUT

LANDINGS

HANDRAIL DIMENSIONS

HANDRAILS

Handrail requirements are governed by building and accessibility codes. Typically, handrails are required on both sides of stairs. Exceptions include dwelling units and private dwellings where there is a change of only one step at an entrance or egress door. In these cases, only one handrail is required. Handrail gripping surfaces must be continuous, without interruption by newel posts or other obstructions. Handrails in dwelling units are allowed to have newel posts at landings and volutes at the lowest tread.

For wide stairways used as a means of egress, intermediate handrails are required so that all portions of the stairway width are within 30 in. (762 mm) of a handrail. On monumental stairs, handrails must be located along the most direct path of egress travel.

Handrail Mounting Height

Handrails must be mounted with their top surface from 34 to 38 in. (864 to 965 mm) above the nosings. Some research studies have shown that the higher end of the range is best for safety, especially when descending a stair. For open stairways more than 30 in. (762 mm) above the floor, the IBC also requires a guard 42 in. (1,067 mm) above the nosing in addition to a handrail.

Handrail Extensions

Handrails must extend beyond the top and bottom treads as required by codes. At the inside turn of return stairs, the handrail must be continuous. The ends of the handrail must return to the wall or a guard, or the floor or must be continuous to the next handrail of an adjacent stair flight.

AREA OF RESCUE ASSISTANCE

The ADA and building codes identify requirements for Areas of Rescue Assistance. Areas of Rescue Assistance are stairway clear widths that allow for easier maneuverability of rescue personnel and physically challenged persons, as well as the clear dimensions at specified areas on landings provided as waiting areas for a person in a wheelchair.

STEEL STAIR HANDRAILS

STEEL STAIR HANDRAIL AT FLOOR

HANDRAILS

IBC and ADA require handrails to be a circular cross-section, with a dimension between 1½ in. (32 mm) and 2 in. (51 mm).

Other shapes are allowed if the perimeter dimension is between 4 and 6½ in. (102 and 159 mm) and the maximum cross-sectional dimension does not exceed 2½ in. (57 mm).

Edges must have a minimum radius of ⅛ in. (3.2 mm).

HANDRAIL GRASPABILITY

The IBC and ADA require a minimum clearance of 1½ in. (38 mm) between the inside of the handrail and the wall. Some studies have suggested that a better dimension is 2 in. (51 mm). This larger dimension is good for general graspability and works better for a person wearing gloves. For children, an additional handrail should be 1⅛ to 1½ in. (29 to 32 mm) in diameter and mounted 22 to 24 in. (559 to 610 mm) above the nosing line.

RAILINGS AT WALLS

PLAN SHOWING HANDRAIL EXTENSIONS

PLAN DIMENSIONS REQUIRED FOR RESCUE ASSISTANCE (ADA)

TREADS, RISERS, AND NOSINGS

Treads

The minimum dimensions for stair treads are indicated in the building codes. If space permits, research has shown that slightly deeper treads than the minimum are more comfortable and safer to use.

Tread material should be nonslip, but not so rough that feet may be caught on the nosing. Traditionally, a coefficient of friction of 0.5 or greater has been a widely accepted standard for slip resistance. In areas where slip resistance is a concern, it is recommended that tread materials be selected with a greater coefficient of friction than the minimum requirements.

Risers

Straight, vertical risers are permitted by the IBC and the ADA; however, treads with nosings are more comfortable for the user. Treads must be designed to follow requirements that prevent sharp or abrupt edges, which may catch a person's foot and present a safety hazard.

Open risers may not be used in most situations. The IBC limits the amount of nosing overhang to 1¼ in. (32 mm), while the ADA limits the amount to 1½ in. (38 mm). A 1-in. (25-mm) overhang is usually sufficient.

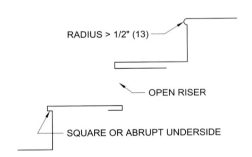

RADIUS > 1/2" (13)

OPEN RISER

SQUARE OR ABRUPT UNDERSIDE

STAIR PROPORTIONING GRAPH

(graph: RISER HEIGHT, FLOOR-TO-FLOOR HEIGHT, TREAD DEPTH)
OPTIMUM TREAD DEPTH (READ RIGHT TO LEFT) 2R + T = 25" (635 mm)

UNACCEPTABLE NOSINGS AND RISERS

1/2" (13) RADIUS MAXIMUM

60° MINIMUM

FLUSH RISER

1/2" (13) RADIUS MAXIMUM

60° MINIMUM

1-1/4" (32) MAX.

ANGLED NOSING

1/2" (13) RADIUS MAXIMUM

60° MINIMUM

1-1/4" (32) MAX.

ROUNDED NOSING

NOSINGS

1 ☐ **STAIR DESIGN**

WOOD STAIRS

Wood stairs used in private, residential applications usually are not governed by the ADA; however, wood stairs in commercial facilities and places of public accommodation must conform to ADA Accessibility Guidelines (ADAAG).

Verify requirements that may differ from the general recommendations provided here. In general, a minimum interior stair width of 36 in. (914 mm) should be provided.

Minimum headroom is 6 ft 8 in. (2 m) as measured vertically from a diagonal line connecting tread nosings to the underside of the finished ceiling or stair landing directly above the stair run. Recommended headroom is 7 ft (2.1 m).

Only handrails and stair stringers may project into the required width of a stair. Use the following guidelines:

- The maximum handrail projection is 3½ in. (89 mm).
- The maximum stringer projection is 1½ in. (38 mm).
- For a stair to comply with ADAAG, no projections are allowed into the minimum required stair width.
- The width of a landing or platform should be at least as wide as the stair.
- The maximum vertical rise of a stair between landings is 12 ft (3.6 m).
- Riser height should be 4 in. (102 mm) minimum and 7 in. (178 mm) maximum.
- Tread depth should be 11 in. (279 mm) minimum, measured from riser to riser.
- Variation in adjacent treads or risers should not exceed ³⁄₁₆ in. (4.8 mm). The maximum variation allowed in the tread depth or riser height within a flight of stairs is ⅜ in. (9.5 mm). ADAAG requires uniform treads and risers.
- Nosings project 1½ in. (38 mm) max. Verify that building codes and ADAAG don't require other restrictions.

WOOD STAIR SECTION

HEAVY TIMBER STAIR

CLOSED RISER STAIR/WOOD FINISH

CLOSED RISER STAIR/CARPET FINISH

Open riser stairs do not comply with Americans with Disabilities Act Accessibility Guidelines.

OPEN RISER STAIR

HOUSED STRINGER AT SOLID
RAIL AND WALL BEYOND

HANDRAIL

BALUSTER

NEWEL POST

ADAAG
ACCEPTABLE
RAILING EXTENSION
(NO NEWEL POST)

ROUNDED
END

SOLID RAIL

OPEN

1'-0"

ONE
TREAD
WIDTH

OPEN STRINGER/
OPEN RAIL

CLOSED STRINGER/
SOLID RAIL

CLOSED STRINGER/
OPEN RAIL

ELEVATION OF FACE STRINGER

NOTE
HANDRAIL COMPLIES WITH
ADAAG IF DIMENSIONS
ARE MAINTAINED.

1-1/2" MIN.
1 1/4" - 1 1/2"

SPACER

BLOCKING

CARRIAGE

SPACER

NO STRINGER

NOTE
HANDRAIL COMPLIES WITH
ADAAG IF DIMENSIONS
ARE MAINTAINED.

1-1/2" MIN.
1 1/4" - 1 1/2"

METAL
BRACKET

BLOCKING

STRINGER

CARRIAGE

SPACER

FULL STRINGER

HANDRAIL DOES
NOT COMPLY
WITH ADAAG

DOWEL
LET INTO
HANDRAIL
AND
FRAMING

STRINGER

FINISH
FLOOR

PLYWOOD
TREAD

CARRIAGE

BLOCKING

WALL
FINISH

WALL OR
SOLID RAIL

NOTCHED STRINGER

CLOSED RISER STAIRS AT WALLS AND SOLID RAILING WALLS

WOOD STAIR HANDRAILS

Per ADAAG, the height of a handrail above stair nosings should be 30 to 34 in. (762 to 864 mm) or 34 to 38 in. (864 to 965 mm). Guardrail height at landings should be 36 or 42 in. (914 or 1067 mm); check local code.

Design handrails that are easy to grip and fit the hand. Recommended diameter is 1¼ to 1½ in. (32 to 38 mm) for round handrails and a similar size for an elliptical or rounded square-edge section. Handrails should be structurally designed so that both downward (vertical) and lateral (horizontal) thrust loads are considered.

Extensions of handrail at top and bottom of stair may affect total length of required run. Verify extensions required by local codes or ADAAG when designing a stair.

METAL STAIRS

Metal stairs are normally constructed of steel, and fabricated in the shop to fit the dimensions required by the opening in which they are used.

Treads and landings are typically filled with 1½ to 2 in. (38 to 51 mm) of concrete. Any finish material can then be applied over the concrete. Balusters are anchored by welding, bolting, or screwing to the stringers, as shown in the diagrams. Glass balusters are anchored into a special U-shaped channel, which is attached to the edge of the stringer. A similar detail can be used for glass railings.

Design Guidelines for Metal Stairs

1. Width of stair:
   a. Dwelling stairs: minimum 36 in. (914 mm) treads
   b. Public exit stairs: minimum 44 in. (1,118 mm) treads
   c. Rescue assistance area (ADA): 48 in. (1,219 mm) between handrails
2. Treads:
   a. Dwellings: 9 in. (229 mm) minimum (nosing to nosing)
   b. Other (ADA): 11 in. (279 mm) minimum (nosing to nosing)
   c. Uniform depth within one flight
3. Risers:
   a. Dwellings: 8¼ in. (206 mm) in maximum
   b. Other (ADA): minimum 4 in. (102 mm), maximum 7 in. (178 mm)
   c. Uniform height within one flight
4. Nosing: maximum 1½ in. (38 mm) with 60° under nosing; maximum ½ in. (13 mm) radius at edge.

Design Guidelines for Metal Stair Handrails

1. Stair rails:
   a. Height in dwellings: 36 in. (914 mm)
   b. Height in exit stairs: 42 in. (1,067 mm)
   c. Arrange rails so that a sphere 4 in. (102 mm) in diameter cannot be passed through.
   d. Arrange rails to discourage climbing.
   e. Concentrated load nonconcurrently applied at the top rail must be 200 lbf (1,156 N) in vertical downward and horizontal direction. The test loads are applicable for railings with supports not more than 8 ft (2.4 m) apart.
2. Handrails:
   a. Dwellings: on one side only, required
   b. Other (ADA): required on both sides
   c. Height: 34 to 38 in. (864 to 965 mm)
   d. Grip surface: 1¼ to 1½ in. (32 to 38 mm)
   e. Clearance at wall: 1½ in. (38 mm)
   f. Projecting or recessed
   g. Extension at top of run: 12 in. (305 mm)
   h. Extension at bottom of run: 12 in. (305 mm) plus depth of tread
   i. When a guardrail more than 38 in. (965 mm) high is used, a separate handrail should be installed.
   j. Nothing should interrupt the continuous sliding of hands.
3. Regulators and standards: building codes, ADA, ASTM, ANSI, NFPA, and OSHA

METAL STAIR SECTION

STRINGER DETAILS

RAILING DETAILS

ALTERNATE STAIR TYPES

Alternate stair types include *winding stairs*, *circular stairs*, and *spiral stairs*. Generally, the IBC does not allow these types of stairs to be used for egress except within private dwelling units. Spiral stairs may also be used as egress from a space not more than 250 sq ft (23 sq m) and serving not more than five occupants. When these alternate stair types are allowed, they must meet the minimum dimensional requirements of the codes. Riser heights for circular and winding stairs must meet the code maximums of 7 in. (178 mm) for commercial stairs and 7¾ in. (197 mm) for residential stairs. Riser heights for spiral stairs must be such that clear headroom of 78 in. (1,981 mm) is provided, but in no case can the riser height be greater than 9½ in. (241 mm).

Spiral Stairs

Spiral stairs are composed of wedge-shaped treads supported from a central column, usually 4 in. (102 mm) in diameter. Prefabricated spiral stairs are commonly made from steel.

Spiral stairs are available in custom sizes. To meet building code requirements as a means of egress, stairs must be at least 5 ft (1.5 m) in diameter to meet the 26 in. (660 mm) clear width requirement, assuming a 4-in. (102-mm) center post. Larger diameters increase perceived comfort, ease of use, and safety. Treads are available with 22½°, 27°, and 30° angle treads. The most common are 27° and 30° tread angles because these can maintain at least a 7½ in. (190 mm) dimension 12 in. (305 mm) from the center pole. Tread selection depends on the riser height desired, the total rise, the headroom clearance requirements, and the top and bottom riser orientation.

Critical minimum headroom dimensions should be calculated based on a three-quarter turn of the stair, even if a full 360° turn is being used to travel the full rise.

David Ballast, AIA; Architectural Research Consulting; Denver, Colorado
Sukamorn Prasithrathsint; Rhode Island School of Design; Providence, Rhode Island
David W. Johnson; Washington, D.C.
The Bumgardner Architects; Seattle, Washington
Janet B. Rankin, AIA; Rippeteau Architects; Washington, D.C.
Charles A. Szoradi, AIA; Washington, D.C.

ELEVATION

PLAN

Design considerations for circular stairs are similar to those for spiral stairs. A fabricated steel tube serves as a one-piece stringer to which treads are bolted or welded. Risers can be open or closed.

CIRCULAR STAIRS

Note: For clarity, only one baluster per tread is shown.

ELEVATION SPIRAL STAIR

PLAN VIEW SPIRAL STAIR

WINDING STAIRWAY

CIRCULAR STAIR

SPIRAL STAIR

SACKLER GALLERIES STAIR, ROYAL ACADEMY, LONDON

DESIGNER: FOSTER AND PARTNERS, LONDON, ENGLAND

SHOT-BLASTED
STAINLESS STEEL
HANDRAIL

GLASS BALUSTRADE

25 mm
SAND-BLASTED
GLASS TREAD

SHOT-BLASTED
STAINLESS STEEL
ANGLE FRAME

ROLLED
STEEL PLATE
STRINGER

CANTILEVERED
HOLLOW STEEL
BEAM BEYOND

SECTION AT LANDING

SHOT-BLASTED
STAINLESS STEEL
HANDRAIL

GLASS
BALUSTRADE

25 mm
SAND-BLASTED
GLASS TREAD

SHOT-BLASTED
STAINLESS STEEL
ANGLE FRAME

ROLLED
STEEL PLATE
STRINGER

CANTILEVERED
HOLLOW STEEL
BEAM BEYOND

SECTION AT INSIDE LANDING RAIL

HOLLOW STEEL
COLUMN

25 mm
SAND-BLASTED
GLASS TREADS

SHOT-BLASTED
STAINLESS STEEL
ANGLE FRAME

ROLLED STEEL
PLATE STRINGER

CANTILEVERED
HOLLOW
STEEL BEAM

SECTION AT COLUMN

STAIR DESIGN ☐ **1**

FIRST-FLOOR PLAN

PLAN AT LANDING

SECOND-FLOOR PLAN

SECTION THROUGH LIGHT-WELL AT GLASS-TREAD STAIR

NASDAQ STAIR, NEW YORK

DESIGNER: KOHN PEDERSEN FOX ASSOCIATES PC; NEW YORK, NEW YORK

3" 1" 1 1/2"

CONTINUOUS RAIL
BELOW

HANDRAIL BELOW

3 3/4"

GLAZING CHANNEL
BELOW

GLASS PANEL

TREADS BELOW

①

PLAN DETAIL AT TOP RAIL

COUNTERSINK DOWEL
THROUGH BAR STOCK
POST CONNECTING
GLAZING CHANNEL
SUPPORT

TREAD SUPPORTS
BELOW

②

PLAN DETAIL AT GLASS PIN CONNECTION

TREADS AND
RAILS ABOVE

BAR STOCK POST

3" 3" 4"

1"

1 3/4"
1/2"

TREAD SUPPORT
T-BLADE

CLAD STRINGER

1/4"-DEEP REVEAL

③

PLAN DETAIL AT TREAD SUPPORT

BAR STOCK POST
WELDED TO END PLATE
BOLTED THROUGH
STRUCTURAL TUBE

CLAD STRINGER.
COVER ALL BOLTED,
WELDED CONNECTIONS

TREADS AND
RAILS ABOVE

④

**PLAN DETAIL AT STRINGER/POST
CONNECTION**

GLASS PANELS

HANDRAIL AND
EXTENSION

GLASS
TREADS

2'-10" A.F.F.

6 1/2"

FLOOR
STRUCTURE

STONE BASE

Ⓐ

DETAIL AT BOTTOM LANDING

GLASS TREAD
SHOWN DASHED

1/4" STEEL-T
TO SUPPORT
TREAD

OUTLINE OF
CLAD STRINGER

TREAD T-SUPPORT

①

3/8"
2"
8"

3 3/4"

HANDRAIL

2'-10"

GLASS PANEL

4'-7"

②

GLASS TREADS

1"

③

④

1/2"

CLAD STEEL
TUBE STRINGER

10"

1/2" 4"

Ⓑ

SECTION THROUGH STAIR

COVE LIGHTING

FINISH CEILING

SUSPENSION HANGER

BRIDGE

C

E

F

B

D

TOP OF GUARDRAIL

GLASS GUARDRAILS

UPPER FIN. FLR.

3'-6"

6'-0"

12 EQUAL RISERS

℄ OF STEEL

℄ OF STEEL

UPPER LANDING

3'-0"

6 EQUAL RISERS

LOWER LANDING

3'-0"

6 EQUAL RISERS

LOWER FIN. FLR.

TOP OF SLAB

6"

3/8"

METAL-CLAD STRINGER

6'-8" CLEARANCE AT START OF CANE DETECTION RAIL

CANE RAIL

2'-3"

A.F.F.

A

STONE BASE

1/2" REVEAL

METAL-CLAD POST

ELEVATION

℄ SUSPENSION HANGER

30'-8"

1"   3'-5"   3'-6"   3'-6"   3'-6"   1'-9"   1'-9"   3'-6"   3'-6"   4'-1"   2'-10"

1'-10 1/2"

℄ STEEL BELOW

3"   3"

1'-1"   1'-5"

℄ POST

8"

DN

11 TREADS AT 1'-2" EA. = 12'-10"

4'-8" LANDING 4 PLANKS AT 1'-2" EA.

DN

5 TREADS AT 1'-2" EA. = 5'-10"

7'-0" LANDING 6 PLANKS AT 1'-2" EA.

5'-5"

℄ POST

4'-9"

GLASS TREADS AND LANDINGS

9"

1'-7"

℄ POST

2'-3"

13'-1"

STONE BASE AND BOTTOM TREAD

4'-10"

6 TREADS AT 1'-2" EA. = 7'-0"

DN

5'-5"

TREAD WIDTH

5'-10"

℄ POST

4'-8"

4'-9"

9"

℄ POST

8"

1'-3"   7"   2'-11"   3'-6"   4'-1"   2'-1"

1'-10 1/2"

13'-2"

PLAN

1 ☐ **STAIR DESIGN**

C — SECTION AT ATRIUM OPENING

E — ENLARGED ELEVATION

D — SECTION AT STEEL HANGER

F — SECTION AT BRIDGE

BUILDING CODES

CODES AND REGULATIONS AFFECTING INTERIORS

There are many types of codes and regulations that affect interior design. These include requirements at the local, state, and national level. Building codes are usually adopted at the local level, either by a city or, in sparsely populated area, a county. Some states have adopted a statewide code. The legal entities that have adopted the code are commonly referred to as the *authorities having jurisdiction*.

Although some jurisdictions write their own codes, most adopt one of the model codes promulgated by code-writing organizations that write, update, and publish a code and related material. The local jurisdiction may add local amendments to the model code to account for regional differences.

Until 2000, there were three main model codes used in the United States: the Uniform Building Code (UBC), the Building Officials and Code Administrators (BOCA) National Building Code, and the Standard Building Code. The three organizations responsible for writing these codes worked together as the International Code Council (ICC) to create the International Building Code (IBC), which was first published in 2000. In addition, the ICC publishes other related international codes, including the International Mechanical Code, the International Plumbing Code, and others. Some jurisdictions have adopted the IBC while others are still using various versions of one of the other model codes.

The National Fire Protection Association (NFPA) is in the process of developing an alternate building code, which may be adopted by some authorities having jurisdiction. This section describes the IBC, as the NFPA code has yet to be published.

OTHER REGULATIONS

In addition to the IBC (or whichever code is applicable in the jurisdiction of the project), the following regulations may also affect your project:

- *Local agency requirements such as municipal health department rules and regulations.* For example, a local health department may have rules governing finishes for restaurants.
- *State or federal agency requirements that govern specific building types.* These may include codes for schools, prisons, and health facilities, as well as regulations governing federal facilities built for the Department of Defense, General Services Agency, Federal Housing Authority, and the Department of Justice.
- *Energy codes.* These are usually adopted at the state level, but the authorities having jurisdiction may require energy conservation measures as part of the local amendments to the code used.
- *Flammability regulations.* In addition to model code requirements for interior finish flammability, cities or states may adopt standards regulating flammability for furniture, draperies, and finishes.

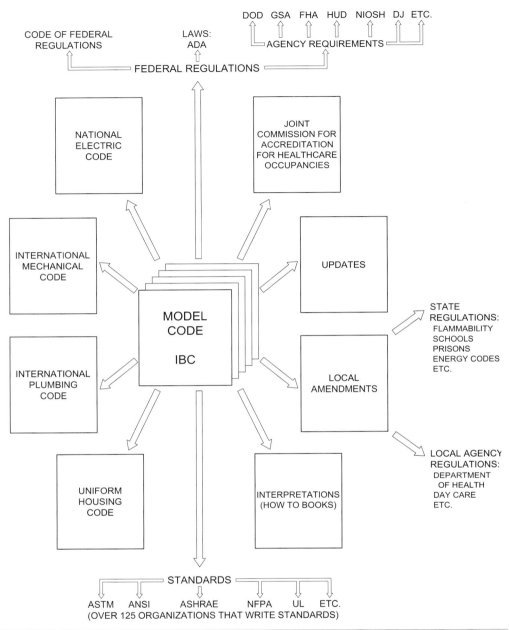

REGULATIONS AFFECTING INTERIOR DESIGN

- *Federal regulations.* These include federal laws, such as the Americans with Disabilities Act (ADA), as well as regulations published in the Code of Federal Regulations, such as the regulation for safety glazing.
- *Standards adopted by reference.* All model codes adopt, by reference, standards developed by hundreds of trade associations, testing agencies, and standards-writing groups. For example, the American Society for Testing and Materials (ASTM)

publishes thousands of standards and test methods for a wide variety of materials that are referred to by the IBC.
- *Indoor air quality.* Local or state agencies may adopt requirements for indoor air quality. These requirements may limit the amount of outgassing or certain materials, limit the use of materials with volatile organic compounds (VOCs), or require certain levels of ventilation.

COMMERCIAL PROJECT CODE REVIEW CHECKLIST FOR INTERIOR DESIGN

STEP	PROCEDURE	IRC SECTION
1.	Determine occupancy group(s). Also determine incidental and accessory uses (Sections 302.1.1 and 302.2).	Sections 302–312
2.	Check specific requirements for certain occupancies.	Chapter 4
3.	Calculate occupant load(s).	1003.2.2 and Table 1003.2.2.2
4.	Determine mixed-occupancy separations required, if applicable. (Fire separations between mixed occupancies are not required if the building is designed for the most restrictive occupancy (see Section 301.3.2).	302.3 and Table 302.3.3
5.	Verify if construction-type information will be applicable (e.g., new column covers). If available, new interior construction must conform to fire-resistive requirements in Table 601.	Chapter 6 and Table 601
6.	Check for common path of egress travel. (If the common path of egress travel distance is exceeded in a space that would normally only require only one exit, additional exits may be required.)	1004.2.5
7.	Determine number of exits required.	1004.2; 1005.2.1
8.	Verify that maximum distance to exits has not been exceeded.	1004.2.4 and Table 1004.2.4
9.	Determine arrangement of exits. (In odd-shaped spaces, be conservative and measure the distance that is greatest.)	1004.2.2
10.	Determine width of exits.	1003.2.3; Table 1003.2.3; 1004.3.2.2; 1005.3.3.1
11.	Check for dead-end corridors, exits through adjoining rooms, and special exiting requirements of Sections 402–415.	1004.2.3; 1004.3.2.3; Chapter 4
12.	Verify special exiting requirements for A and R occupancies at the end of Chapter 10.	1008; 1009
13.	Determine required extent and construction of corridors.	1004.3.2.1 and Table 1004.3.2.1
14.	Verify exit door rating, size, hardware, and swing.	1003.3.1
15.	Verify stairway requirements, if applicable.	1003.3.3; 1005.3.2
16.	Check requirements for ramps, if applicable.	1003.3.4
17.	Determine maximum flame spread requirements for interior finishes.	Chapter 8 and Table 803.4
18.	Check required light, ventilation, and sanitation requirements for occupancy, if applicable. (Chapter 12 also contains requirements for sound transmission in R occupancies, minimum interior space dimensions, and requirements for surrounding finish materials in toilet and bathing rooms.)	Chapter 12; Chapter 29
19.	Verify accessibility requirements for type of use. (The IBC adopts ICC/ANSI A1171.1, *Accessible and Usable Buildings and Facilities,* as the standard for accessibility. The ADA Accessibility Guidelines should also be consulted.	Chapter 11 and ADAAG
20.	If glass is used, verify glazing requirements.	714.3.6; 2406
21.	If guards are used, check requirements. ("Guards" is the new terminology for guardrails used in previous codes.)	1003.2.12

See also *Regulatory Analysis Checklist for Commercial Interiors—Building Codes and Other Authorities Having Jurisdiction.*

RESIDENTIAL PROJECT CODE REVIEW CHECKLIST FOR INTERIOR DESIGN

STEP	PROCEDURE	IRC SECTION
1.	Check minimum sizes and heights for rooms.	R304 and R305
2.	Check spacing of plumbing fixtures, if applicable.	R307
3.	If glass or glass block is used, check requirements.	R308 and R610
4.	If remodeling sleeping areas, verify requirements for emergency escape windows.	R310
5.	Verify requirements for stairs and other exit components.	R311; R312; R313; R314; R315; and R316
6.	Verify requirements for finish flame spread.	R319
7.	Verify requirements for interior wall finishes.	R702
8.	Check requirements for plumbing fixtures, if applicable.	Chapter 27
9.	Verify requirements for electrical outlets. Also verify requirements for alarm devices, e.g., smoke alarms.	E3801 and E3802
10.	Verify requirements for lighting.	E3803; E3903; and E3905

OCCUPANCY (IBC CHAPTER 3)

Occupancy refers to the use of the building or interior space. Occupancies are based on occupant- and content-related hazards and the life-safety characteristics of the building. Occupant-related hazards include considerations such as the number, density, age, and mobility of the occupants. Buildings or portions of buildings may also consist of more than one occupancy, in which case the code may require fire separation between the occupancies.

Because many other requirements of building codes are based on occupancy, one of the first steps in code-conforming design is to determine the occupancy classification. If the classification of a project is unclear, consult the local building officials.

Incidental and Accessory Uses (IBC 302.1.1; 302.2)

An incidental use area is a room or area that poses a risk not typically addressed by the provisions of the occupancy group under which the main building or space is classified but that does not qualify as a different occupancy, creating a mixed-use condition. Incidental use areas may apply to all occupancy groups. Incidental use areas require fire-rated separation from other areas. For example, a furnace room presents a special hazard, and will require a separation from other occupied areas.

An accessory use is a minor use necessary to the function of a building's major use, but that has few characteristics of the major occupancy. For example, a small office area (B occupancy) is required for the administration of a large warehouse (S-2 occupancy). In these cases (except for H-occupancies), where the accessory use does not exceed 10% percent of the floor area of the major use, no fire separation is required.

Mixed Occupancies (IBC 302.3)

When a building or portion of a building contains two or more different occupancies, it is considered a mixed occupancy. The code requires that particular combinations of adjacent occupancies be separated with fire barrier walls or horizontal assemblies, or both, with an hourly rating defined by the code. Hourly ratings range from one hour to four hours.

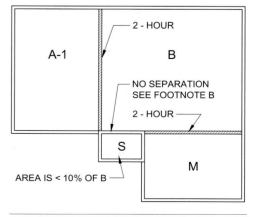

OCCUPANCY SEPARATION

OCCUPANCY CLASSIFICATION. (IBC 303; 312)

OCCUPANCY	DESCRIPTION	EXAMPLES
A-1	Assembly with fixed seats for the viewing of performances or movies	Movie theaters, live performance theaters
A-2	Assembly for food and drink consumption	Restaurants, bars, clubs, banquet halls
A-3	Assembly for worship, recreation, and similar activities not classified elsewhere	Libraries, art museums, churches, conference rooms for more than 50 people, lecture halls
A-4	Assembly for viewing of indoor sports	Arenas, swimming pools
A-5	Assembly for outdoor sports	Stadiums, bleachers
B	Business for office or service transactions	Offices, educational functions above 12th grade, doctor's offices, banks, TV stations
E	Educational used by more than five people for grades 12 and lower	Grade, middle, and high schools, day care if >5 children and >2.5 years old
F-1	Factory of moderate-hazard uses that is not classified as an H occupancy	Manufacturer of metals, photographic film, millwork, etc.
F-2	Factory and industrial low-hazard uses, which include the use of noncombustible materials and uses which that do not cause a significant fire hazard.	Manufacturer of nonalcoholic beverages, ceramics, glass, and similar products
H	See code for groups and complete requirements	Flammable liquids, explosives, etc.
I-1	Residential buildings housing more than 16 ambulatory people	Assisted living facilities, group homes, alcohol and drug centers, halfway houses
I-2	Medical care facilities used on a 24-hour basis by people who are not capable of self-preservation	Hospitals, skilled care nursing homes
I-3	Facilities of more than five people who are under restraint or security	Jails, prisons, reformatories
I-4	Day care for five adults or infants under 2.5 years, for less than 24 hours per day	Day care for infants or adults
M	Mercantile for the display and sale of merchandise	Department stores, retail stores, sales rooms, markets
R-1	Residential for transient lodging (<30 days)	Hotels and motels
R-2	Residential with three or more units where residents are primarily permanent	Apartments, dormitories, convents
R-3	One or two dwelling units with attached uses or child care for fewer than six on less than a 24-hour basis	Houses, duplexes, small child-care; see the International Residential Code
R-4	Residential assisted living where the number of occupants exceeds 5, but is less than 16	Small assisted living center
S-1	Storage not otherwise classified as H occupancy	See IBC
S-2	Low-hazard storage	See IBC
U	Buildings or structure of accessory character	Carports, private garages

CONSTRUCTION TYPES (IBC 602)

Every building is classified into one of five types of construction, based on the fire resistance of certain building components. Four of the types are further subdivided into two groups, using the suffixes A and B. The building components include the structural frame, interior and exterior bearing walls, floor and roof construction, and exterior walls.

- Type I and II buildings must be constructed of non-combustible materials.
- Types III, IV, and V are considered combustible.
- Type I buildings are the most fire-resistive.
- Type V buildings are the least fire-resistive.

Construction type can affect the required fire ratings of structural element coverings, floor and ceiling assemblies, and openings in rated walls. Generally, interior, nonbearing partitions require one-hour construction unless otherwise noted in the code. The fire-resistance rating of the building elements is governed by the type of construction as defined in IBC Chapter 6.

BUILDING ELEMENTS

EXTERIOR NONBEARING WALLS — ROOFS — NONBEARING INTERIOR PARTITIONS — FLOORS — EXTERIOR BEARING WALLS — STRUCTURAL FRAME

EGRESS (IBC CHAPTER 10)

Designing an egress system requires the following:

- Planning the spaces and components that allow an occupant to safely exit a building during an emergency.
- Detailing the individual parts of the system to meet the requirements of the code.

A means of egress is a continuous and unobstructed path of vertical and horizontal egress travel from any point in a building to a public way. Once the overall exiting plan is developed, the following must be done:

- Determine occupant load.
- Determine the number of exits required.
- Verify the length of the common path of egress travel.
- Verify the maximum travel distance.
- Determine the arrangement of exits.
- Calculate the width of exits.
- Check for dead-end corridors.

Egress Components

Exit Access

The exit access is that portion of the means of egress that leads to the entrance to an exit. It is generally the most distant part of the building from safety. Exit access areas may or may not be protected, depending on the specific requirements of the code based on occupancy and construction type. They may include components such as rooms, spaces, aisles, intervening rooms, hallways, corridors, ramps, and doorways. In some cases in the IBC, the exit access is required to be a protected path of travel. The exit access is the portion of the building where travel distance is measured and regulated.

Exit

The exit is the portion of the egress system that provides a protected path of egress between the exit access and the exit discharge. Exits are fully enclosed and protected from all other interior spaces by fire-resistance-rated construction with protected openings (doors, glass, etc.). Exits may be as simple as an exterior exit door at ground level or may include exit enclosures for stairs, exit passageways, and horizontal exits. Exits may also include exterior exit stairways and ramps. Depending on building height, construction type, and passageway length, exits must have either a one- or two-hour rating.

Exit Discharge

The exit discharge is the portion of the egress system between the termination of an exit and a public way. It is usually not a consideration in the design of interiors. Exit discharge may also include building lobbies of multistory buildings if one of the exit stairways opens onto the lobby and certain conditions are met. The exit door in the lobby must be clearly visible, and the level of discharge must be sprinklered. The entire area of discharge must be separated from areas below by the same fire-resistance rating as for the exit enclosure that opens onto the area of discharge.

Public Way

A public way is any street, alley, or similar parcel of land essentially unobstructed from the ground to the sky that is permanently appropriated to the public for public use and having a clear width of not less than 10 ft (3 m).

Accessible Egress Route

If components of the egress system are part of an accessible route, they must conform to all the requirements of the ADA Accessibility Guidelines (ADAAG), which may be more stringent than the IBC requirements. For example, accessible egress stairways must be a minimum of 48 in. (1,219 mm) wide between handrails instead of 44 in. (1,117 mm).

OCCUPANT LOAD (IBC 1003.2.2)

The occupant load is the number of people that the code assumes will occupy a building or portion of a building for egress purposes. Occupant load is dependent on the occupancy classification of the building or space and assumes that certain types of use will be more densely occupied than others, and that exiting provisions must respond accordingly.

Occupant load is determined by the largest number established by one of the following conditions:

- The number of occupants calculated using the occupant load factors given in the code based on the intended use and size of the space. (This is the method most commonly used.)
- The actual number of occupants a space is designed to serve.
- The number of occupants, by combination, used when occupants from adjoining spaces egress through an area.

The IBC provides Occupant Load Factor Tables to determine the maximum floor area allowed per occupant, based on building and occupancy type.

OCCUPANT LOAD IN SEATING AREAS

For areas with fixed seating, the occupant load is the number of fixed seats installed. When the fixed seating does not have dividing arms (such as church pews), the occupant load is determined by dividing the length of the seating by 18 in. (457 mm). If there are multiple rows of such seating, the length should be multiplied by the number of rows before dividing by 18 to avoid rounding problems.

For areas with booths, the occupant load is calculated by taking the length of the booth measured at the backrest of the seat and dividing by 24 in. (610 mm). When a mezzanine is used in a room or space, the occupant load of the mezzanine must be added to the occupant load of the room or space.

GROUND-LEVEL EGRESS

UPPER-LEVEL EGRESS

COMMON PATH OF EGRESS TRAVEL

D = 20' (6100) MAX. BASIC
D = 50' (15,240) MAX. SPRINKLERED
   B AND F OR 2.5 X W

DEAD-END CORRIDOR CONDITION

SPACES WITH ONE MEANS OF EGRESS

OCCUPANCY	MAXIMUM OCCUPANT LOAD
A, B, E, F, M, U	50
H-1, H-2, H-3	3
H-4, H-5, I-1, I-3, I-4, R	10
S	30

MINIMUM NUMBER OF EXITS FOR OCCUPANT LOAD

OCCUPANT LOAD	MINIMUM NUMBER OF EXITS
1–500	2
501–1,000	3
More than 1,000	4

COMMON PATH OF TRAVEL

OCCUPANCY	COMMON PATH OF TRAVEL	
	NONSPRINKLERED FT (M)	SPRINKLERED FT (M)
A, E, I-1, I-2, I-4, M, R, U	≤ 75 (22.8)	≤ 75 (22.8)
B, F, S	≤ 75 (22.8)	≤ 100 (30.4)
H-1, H-2, H-3	—	≤ 25 (7.6)
H-4, H-5	—	≤ 75 (22.8)
I-3	≤ 100 (30.4)	≤ 100 (30.4)

COMMON PATH OF TRAVEL

OCCUPANCY	OCCUPANT LOAD	COMMON PATH OF TRAVEL	
		NONSPRINKLERED FT (M)	SPRINKLERED FT (M)
B, S, U	≤ 3075	≤ 100 (30.4)	≤ 100 (30.4)
B, S,	> 30	≤ 75 (22.8)	≤ 100 (30.4)
U	> 30	≤ 75 (22.8)	≤ 75 (22.8)

NUMBER OF EXITS (IBC 1004.2; 1005.2.1)

The number of means of egress required from a room or area depends on the occupant load and the occupancy. Rooms or areas are permitted to have only one exit or exit access doorway until they exceed a certain occupant load. (Reference Table 1004.2.1 of the IBC.)

The reason for requiring two or more means of egress is to allow alternate means of egress in case one exit is blocked by fire. However, when there are small spaces or areas with limited occupant load, the code recognizes that two exits are not necessary. Factors that contribute to the different numbers include concentration and mobility of occupants and the presence of hazardous materials.

When the occupant load becomes very large, additional exits may be required in very large spaces. (Reference IBC Table 1005.)

DEAD-END CORRIDORS (IBC 1004.3.2.3)

A dead end is a corridor or exit path that has only one way to exit. Generally, dead ends are limited to 20 ft (6 m). Exceptions for building occupancies may be granted if the building is entirely sprinklered, and dead-end corridors do not exceed prescribed lengths.

COMMON PATH OF EGRESS TRAVEL (IBC 1004.2.5)

The common path of egress travel is the portion of an exit access that the occupants are required to traverse, before either there is a choice of exits, or two paths merge to become one. The length of the common path is measured from the most remote point of a room or area to the nearest point where more than one exit path is available. Common paths of egress travel must be included within the permitted travel distance.

If furniture or equipment is located in the area, it may be necessary to measure the common path of travel around the furniture instead of on a straight path.

Even if two exits are not required based on occupant load, if the common path of travel exceeds the allowable distances, then two exits from a space are required.

In most cases, the common path is limited to 75 ft (22.9 m). For B, F, and S occupancies, if the building is sprinklered, the distance may be increased to 100 ft (30.5 m). In tenant spaces in B, S, and U occupan-

cies, when the occupant load is 30 or fewer, the distance may be increased to 100 ft (30.5 m).

ARRANGEMENT OF EXITS (IBC 1004.2.2)

When two exits or exit access doorways are required, they must be separated enough so that if one becomes blocked, the other is available for use. In non-sprinklered buildings, two exits or exit access doorways must be placed a distance apart equal to not less than one-half of the length of the maximum overall diagonal dimension of the room or area to be served. In sprinklered buildings, the minimum distance is one-third the diagonal dimension of the room or area to be served. If the room or area is irregular in shape, the dimension that gives the greatest length should be used.

When exit enclosures are connected with a one-hour fire-resistance-rated corridor, the required exit separation is measured along a direct line of travel in the corridor. The walls of the exit enclosures must be a minimum of 30 ft (9.1 m) apart at any point in a direct line of measurement.

When three or more exits or exit access doorways are required, at least two must be placed a distance apart equal to not less than one-half of the length of the maximum overall diagonal dimension of the area served. Additional exits or exit access doorways must be arranged a reasonable distance apart so that if one becomes blocked, the others will be available.

The code requires that the exits be located so that they are obvious and unobstructed at all times. There is no definitive statement about where the measurement between doors should be made; different officials measure differently. Often, this distance is measured to the centerlines of the doors.

COMMON PATH OF EGRESS TRAVEL WITH FURNITURE

EXITS THROUGH INTERVENING SPACES (IBC 1004.2.3)

Egress paths may pass through an adjoining room or area only if the adjoining room or area is accessory to the area served, is not a high-hazard occupancy, and provides a discernible path of travel to an exit.

Egress paths may not pass through kitchens, storerooms, closets, or spaces used for similar purposes, nor may they pass through rooms that can be locked to prevent egress.

Egress from dwelling units or sleeping areas may not pass through other sleeping areas, toilet rooms, or bathrooms. There are two exceptions:

- Egress path may pass through a kitchen area that serves adjoining rooms that are part of the same dwelling unit or guest room.
- Egress through high-hazard occupancies is permitted where the spaces involved are the same occupancy group.

WIDTH OF EXITS (IBC 1003.2.3; 1004.3.2.2)

The minimum required width of exits is determined by multiplying the occupant load of the area served by a factor identified in IBC Table 1003.2.3. The factors vary depending on the exit component and whether the building is sprinklered. Stairways require slightly wider dimensions because people tend to slow down when descending a stair. However, in no case may exit width be less than the minimum requirements for corridors, as shown in the Minimum Exit Component listing.

When multiple exits are required, they must be sized so that the loss of one will not reduce the required exit width by more than 50%. Also, the maximum capacity from any area or floor must be maintained to the exit discharge or public way.

When exit widths are calculated for several areas, each area must be checked individually to determine the exit widths for that area; then the occupant load for all the areas must be added to calculate the widths for exits serving the combined areas.

DOOR ENCROACHMENT (IBC 1003.2.3.1)

When doors open onto the path of egress, they cannot reduce the required width by more than one-half during the course of the swing and cannot project more than 7 in. (178 mm) when fully open. These restrictions do not apply to doors within a dwelling unit.

EXIT SEPARATION IN A ROOM

$d \geq 1/2$ D NONSPRINKLERED
$d \geq 1/3$ D SPRINKLERED

MINIMUM 30'
(9144)

EXIT SEPARATION ON FLOOR OR GROUP OF ROOMS

≤ TO 1/2 REQUIRED EGRESS WIDTH

7" (178) MAX.

EGRESS WIDTH

4" (102) MAX.

HANDRAIL

7" (178) MAX.

DOOR ENCROACHMENT

EXIT ACCESS TRAVEL DISTANCE[1]

OCCUPANCY	WITHOUT SPRINKLER SYSTEM FT (M)	WITH SPRINKLER SYSTEM FT (M)
A, E, F-1, I-1, M, R, S-1	200 (61)	250 (76.2)
B	200 (61)	300 (91.4)
F-2, S-2, U	300 (91.4)	400 (121)
H-1	Not permitted	75 (22.8)
H-2	Not permitted	1100 (30.4)
H-3	Not permitted	150 (45.7)
H-4	Not permitted	175 (53.3)
H-5	Not permitted	200 (61)
I-2, I-3, I-4	150 (45.7)	200 (61)

Source: International Building Code; International Code Council; Falls Church, Virginia, 2001

Note:
See the following sections for modifications to exit access travel distance requirements:
Section 402: For the distance limitation in malls
Section 404: For the distance limitation through an atrium space
Section 1004.2.4.1: For increased limitation in Groups F-1 and S-1
Section 1008.6: For increased limitation in assembly seating.
Section 1008.6: For increased limitation for assembly open-air seating
Section 1005.2.2: For buildings with one exit
Chapter 31: For the limitation in temporary structures

Buildings equipped throughout with an automatic sprinkler system in accordance with Section 903.3.1.1 or 903.3.1.2 See section 903 for occupancies where sprinkler systems according to Section 903.3.1.2 are permitted.

Buildings equipped throughout with an automatic sprinkler system, in accordance with Section 903.3.1.1

EGRESS WIDTH PER OCCUPANT SERVED

OCCUPANCY	WITHOUT SPRINKLER SYSTEM		WITH SPRINKLER SYSTEM	
	STAIRWAYS (INCHES (MM) PER OCCUPANT)	OTHER EGRESS COMPONENTS (INCHES (MM) PER OCCUPANT)	STAIRWAYS (INCHES (MM) PER OCCUPANT)	OTHER EGRESS COMPONENTS (INCHES (MM) PER OCCUPANT)
Occupancies other than those listed below	0.3 (7)	0.2 (5)	0.2 (5)	0.15 (3)
Hazardous: H-1, H-2, H-3	0.7 (17)	0.4 (10)	0.3 (0.7)	0.2 (5)
Institutional: I-2	0.4 (10)	0.2 (5)	0.3 (0.7)	0.2 (5)

Source: International Building Code; International Code Council; Falls Church, Virginia, 2001

Note: 1 inch = 25.4 mm

Buildings equipped throughout with an automatic sprinkler system, in accordance with Section 903.3.1.1 or 903.3.1.2, where allowed.

RESIDENTIAL EXITING (IBC 1009; IRC R310)

Both the IBC and the International Residential Code (IRC) require emergency escape and rescue openings in Group R occupancies. The IBC also requires such openings in Group I-1 occupancies. The IRC requires basements with habitable space and every sleeping room, as well as basements and sleeping rooms below the fourth story, to have at least one such opening. These openings must open directly into a public street, public alley, yard, or court. In the IBC, exceptions include:

- Fully sprinklered buildings except R-3.
- Sleeping rooms with a door to a fire-resistant-rated corridor having access to two remote exits in opposite directions, except R-3.

Openings may open onto a balcony within an atrium if the balcony provides access to an exit and the dwelling unit or sleeping room has a means of egress that is not open to the atrium. When the emergency escape opening is below grade level, both the IBC and IRC allow window wells, if minimum dimensional requirements are met.

TRAVEL DISTANCE (IBC 1004.2.4)

Because exit access areas are not protected, the code limits how far someone must travel to safety. Exit access travel distance is the distance that an occupant must travel from the most remote point in the occupied portions of the exit access to the entrance of the nearest exit. Maximum travel distances are based on the occupancy of the building and whether the building is sprinklered.

Travel distance is measured in a straight line from the most remote point through doorways, unless furniture or equipment requires a measurement along an actual path of travel. When the path of travel includes unenclosed stairways, the distance is measured along a plane parallel and tangent to the stair tread nosings in the center of the stairway.

MAXIMUM TRAVEL DISTANCE

NET CLEAR OPENING 9 SQ FT (0.84 SQ M) MINIMUM

PERMANENT LADDER OR STEPS REQUIRED IF BOTTOM OF WINDOW WELL IS MORE THAN 44" (1118) BELOW ADJACENT GRADE

36" (914) MINIMUM

36" (914) MINIMUM

WINDOW WELL

20" (508) MINIMUM

24" (610) MINIMUM

44" (1118) MAXIMUM

CLEAR OPENABLE AREA = 5.7 SQ FT, MINIMUM (0.53 SQ M). IF WINDOW IS LOCATED ON GRADE FLOOR, THE MINIMUM AREA = 5 SQ FT (0.46 SQ M)

EMERGENCY ESCAPE WINDOW

RESIDENTIAL EMERGENCY EXIT

WIDTH AT TABLES AND SEATING (IBC 1004.3.1.3)

Aisles are required from all occupied portions of exit access areas, which contain seats, tables, furnishings, displays, and similar fixtures and equipment. Aisles serving assembly areas, other than seating at tables, must comply with Section 1008 of the IBC.

Aisle access ways for table seating must provide a minimum of 12 in. (305 mm) of width plus 0.5 in. (13 mm) of width for each additional 1 ft (305 mm), or fraction thereof, beyond 12 ft (3.6 m) of aisle length measured from the center of the seat farthest from an aisle.

EXITS THROUGH ADJOINING ROOMS

AISLE ACCESSWAY WIDTH:
12" + 0.5" (X - 12) WHERE "X" IS THE DISTANCE IN FEET AS SHOWN ABOVE, FROM 12'-0" (3658) TO A MAXIMUM OF 30'-0" (9144).
[305mm + 12.7mm(X - 3658) METRIC]

AISLE ACCESSWAY WIDTH:
NO REQUIREMENT WHEN DISTANCE FROM AISLE TO CENTERLINE OF FARTHEST CHAIR IS 6'-0" (1829) OR LESS; AND SERVING FOUR OR FEWER PERSONS.

AISLE ACCESSWAY WIDTH:
12" (305) MINIMUM CLEAR WHEN DISTANCE FROM AISLE TO CENTERLINE OF FARTHEST CHAIR IS BETWEEN 6'-0" (1829) AND 12'-0" (3658).

WIDTH AT AISLES (IBC 1004.3.1.1)

PUBLIC AREAS IN GROUP B AND M

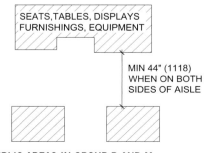

PUBLIC AREAS IN GROUP B AND M

NONPUBLIC AREAS

WIDTH AT AISLES

CORRIDORS (IBC 1004.3.2)

A corridor is an exit access component that defines and provides a path of egress travel to an exit. They may or may not be fire-resistance-rated, but they must be enclosed. IBC Table 1004.3.2.1 stipulates conditions when a corridor must be rated. Fire-resistance-rated corridors are not required, under the following circumstances:

- The corridor is within a dwelling unit or a guest room in Group R occupancy.
- The corridor is in a Group B occupancy, within a space requiring only a single means of egress.
- The corridor is in a Group E occupancy where each classroom has at least one door directly to the exterior and each assembly room has at least one-half of its doors opening directly to the exterior.

The minimum width of corridors is determined by multiplying the occupant load by the factors identified in IBC Table 1003.2.3; but in no case can they be narrower than the allowable corridor width.

Corridors must be continuous from the point of entry to an exit. Fire-resistance-rated corridors cannot be interrupted by intervening rooms with the following exceptions:

- Foyers, lobbies, or receptions rooms constructed as required for corridors are not considered intervening rooms.
- In fully-sprinklered Group B buildings, corridors may lead through an enclosed elevator lobby if all areas of the building have access to at least one required exit without passing through the lobby.

CORRIDOR WIDTH (IBC 1004.3.2.2)

Corridor width must be unobstructed, but doors may project a maximum of 7 in. (178 mm) when fully open, and handrails may project up to 4 in. (102 mm) on either side.

RATED CORRIDOR OPTIONS (IBC 1004.3.2.1; 708)

Fire-resistance-rated corridors require full separation from adjoining spaces.

GLAZING IN CORRIDORS (IBC 714.3.6)

When corridor walls are required to have a one-hour fire-resistive rating, any glazing in the corridor wall must meet the requirements for interior fire window assemblies. The allowable amount of glass depends on which type of glass is used—fire-protection-rated glazing or fire-resistance-rated glazing:

- *Fire-protection-rated glazing* includes ¼ in. (6 mm) wire glass set in steel frames and approved glass block. When this type of glazing is used, the total area of glass cannot exceed 25% of the area of the common wall separating two spaces or rooms.
- *Fire-resistance-rated glazing* includes products such as clear ceramics, tempered glass, and insulated glass. These products carry various fire-ratings of up to two hours and are tested as part of a wall assembly. The 25% limitation does not apply to these types of products, although each manufacturer's product may have size limitations based on the fire rating of the product.

Both types of glazing must have a label or other identification permanently affixed showing the manufacturer's name, test standard, and fire protection rating.

ACCESS TO ELECTRICAL, MECHANICAL, OR PLUMBING EQUIPMENT

OCCUPANT LOAD LESS THAN OR EQUAL TO 50, OR WITHIN A DWELLING UNIT

GROUP E OCCUPANCY WITH OCCUPANT LOAD OF 100 OR MORE

GROUP I CORRIDORS SERVING SURGICAL AREAS AND HEALTH CARE CENTERS, FOR AMBULATORY PATIENTS RECEIVING OUTPATIENT CARE, WHICH CAUSES PATIENTS TO BE NOT CAPABLE OF SELF PRESERVATION

CORRIDOR WIDTH CONDITIONS

CORRIDOR FIRE RESISTANCE RATING

| OCCUPANCY | OCCUPANT LOAD SERVED BY CORRIDOR | REQUIRED FIRE RESISTANCE RATING (HOURS) | |
		WITHOUT SPRINKLER SYSTEM	WITH SPRINKLER SYSTEM[3]
H-1, H-2, H-3	All	1	1
H-4, H-5	Greater than 30	1	1
A, B, E, F, M, S, U	Greater than 30	1	0
R	Greater than 10	1	1
I-2[1], I-4	All	Not Permitted	0
I-1, I-3	All	Not Permitted	1

Source: International Building Code; International Code Council; Falls Church, Virginia, 2001

For requirements for occupancies in Group 1-2, see Section 407.3.

For a reduction in the fire-resistance rating for occupancies in Group 1-3, see Section 408.7.

Buildings equipped throughout with an automatic sprinkler system, in accordance with Section 903.3.1.1 or 903.3.1.2.

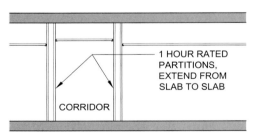

1 HOUR RATED PARTITIONS, EXTEND FROM SLAB TO SLAB

CORRIDOR

FULL-HEIGHT CORRIDOR PARTITIONS

CEILING AS REQUIRED FOR A 1-HOUR FLOOR SYSTEM

CORRIDOR

FIRE RESISTANT PROTECTION

RATED CORRIDOR CEILING

RATED CORRIDORS

ROOM WITH GLAZING

MAXIMUM 25% OF AREA OF COMMON WALL

COMMON WALL

GLASS

WHEN CEILING HEIGHT VARIES LOWER CEILING IS USED TO CALCULATE COMMON WALL AREA

RATED CORRIDOR GLAZING

DOORS (IBC 1003.3.1; 714.2.7)

When doors are part of a means of egress, they must meet the requirements of Sections 1003.3.1 and 714 of the IBC.

Building code requirements apply to doors as part of an opening assembly, including the door, its hardware, and the frame. When designing and specifying doors, consider all three components.

Fire-rated doors must be readily distinguishable from adjacent construction and be easily recognizable as an egress door. Fire-rated doors cannot be concealed with curtains, drapes, or similar materials.

Doors must be sized for the occupant load required, but in no case canmay they provide a clear width of less than 32 in. (813 mm). In practical terms, this means a 36-in.- (914-mm-) wide door must be used to allow for the decrease in width due to the stop and the thickness of the door when open.

Egress doors must be of the side-hinged swing type (with some exceptions found in IBC Section 1003.3.1.2) and must swing in the direction of travel when serving an occupant load of 50 or more or in a high-hazard occupancy.

Force Required to Operate Doors

The maximum force required to operate doors is as follows:

Opening force for interior, side-swinging doors with no closer: 5 lbf (22 N) maximum

Door latch release force for other side-swinging, sliding, and folding doors: 15 lbf (67 N) maximum

Force to set door in motion: 30 lbf (133 N) maximum

Force to open door completely: 15 lbf (67 N) maximum

Egress doors must be fire-rated and tested in accordance with NFPA 252, *Methods of Fire Test of Door Assemblies* or Underwriters Laboratories (UL) 10C, *Standard for Positive Pressure Fire Tests of Door Assemblies*. Either wood doors or metal doors and frames may be used if they meet the requirements of these tests. Doors and frames must be labeled, which means that they must bear the label of an approved testing agency, such as (UL). Doors must be installed according to NFPA 80, *Standards for Fire Doors and Windows*.

Glazing in Doors

Requirements for glazing in doors are as follows:

- If wire glass is used, size limitations apply, based on fire door rating. Fire-resistance-rated glazing may be used, which includes ceramic, special-tempered, and insulated glass. These products do not have size limitations except for those developed during manufacturer's test.
- For most interiors work, a 20-minute-rated door is required when used in a one-hour fire-resistance-rated partition used as an exit access corridor wall; and a ¾-hour-rated door is required when used in a one-hour partition other than a corridor wall. Both doors require gasketing for draft and smoke control.

ADA Doors

ADA design considerations for doors are as follows:

- There must be maneuvering clearances at swinging doors.
- There must be a clear opening of 32 in. (815 mm) minimum.
- No projections are permitted into the clear opening below 34 in. (865 mm).
- Lever handles must be used.
- All hardware must have shape that is easy to grasp with one hand.
- Maximum opening forces must be maintained.
- Required closing speeds must be maintained.
- Bottom of vision lights must be 43 in. (1,090 mm) above the floor.

Door, Frame, and Hardware Labels

Doors, frames, and hardware are required to be labeled or listed. A label is a permanent identifying mark attached to the door or frame by an approved testing organization that indicates the door or frame is in compliance with the standard tests for fire door assemblies and with NFPA 80, which governs the installation of fire doors.

A listed *device*, the term commonly used for "hardware," means that the component has been shown to meet applicable standards for use in fire-rated assemblies. When a product is successfully tested, it is listed as *approved*.

Door Hardware

Door hardware design considerations are as follows:

- Exit doors must be operable from the inside without the use of a key or any special knowledge or effort.
- Hinges must be ball-bearing and made of steel or stainless steel.
- Panic hardware is required for Group A occupancies, Group E occupancies with occupant loads greater than 100, and for Groups H-1, H-2, H-3, and H-5 occupancies. Panic hardware must be mounted between 34 and 48 in. (864 and 1,219 mm) high.
- Exit doors must have closers or other approved self-closing or automatic-closing devices; any device that holds open a door must release upon activation of a smoke detector or power failure.
- Doors must be provided with a latch that secures the door when it is closed.
- Hardware must meet the requirements of the ADA, including the use of lever handles and maximum opening forces.
- Thresholds must meet the slope and height requirements of the ADA.

DOOR ENCROACHMENT

EXIT DOOR SIZE

FIRE DOOR CLASSIFICATIONS

FIRE DOOR RATING (HRS)	USE OF WALL	RATING OF WALL	MAXIMUM GLAZING SIZE FOR WIRE GLASS	PREVIOUS OPENING CLASS DESIGNATION
3	Fire wall or fire-barrier wall	3- or 4-hr.	Not allowed	A
1½	Fire walls, fire barriers, and two-hour shaft walls	2-hr.		B:1½ hr.
1	Shaft and exit enclosure walls	1-hr.	100 sq in. (0.0645 sq cm)	B:1 hr.
¾	Fire barriers other than shafts and exit enclosure walls	1-hr.	1,296 sq in. (8,361 sq cm)	C
⅓	Exit access corridor wall	1-hr.	Not limited	None

Labeled wire glass ¼ in. (6.35 mm) in steel frames can be used for ¾-hr. assembly rating without label (714.3.2).

GLAZING (IBC 2406)

In addition to the requirements for the use of glazing in fire-resistance-rated assemblies, the use of safety glazing is required in hazardous locations. Hazardous locations are those subject to human impact, such as glass in doors, shower and bath enclosures, and glass sidelights in partitions.

Safety glazing is defined as glazing that meets the test requirements of Consumer Products Safety Commission (CPSC) 16 CFR 1201, Category II. Generally, tempered and laminated glass are considered safety glazing.

The most common situations where safety glazing is and is not required are shown in the diagram on this page. The IBC should be consulted for other conditions and exceptions.

SOUND TRANSMISSION (IBC 1206)

The IBC requires sound transmission control in residential buildings. It applies to common interior walls, partitions, and floor and ceiling assemblies between adjacent dwelling units or between dwelling units and adjacent public areas such as corridors, stairs, or service areas.

These are the sound transmission class numbers of building assemblies when tested in accordance with ASTM E90, *Test Method for Laboratory Measurement of Airborne Sound Transmission Loss of Building Partitions,* and Impact insulation class (IIC) ratings for floor/ceiling assemblies when tested accordance with ASTM E492, *Test Method for Laboratory Measurement of Impact Sound Transmission through Floor-Ceiling Assemblies Using the Tapping Machine.*

The requirements do not apply to dwelling entrance doors, which must be tight-fitting to the frame and sill.

SURROUNDING MATERIALS (IBC 1209)

Except for dwelling units, floors in toilet and bathing rooms must have a smooth, hard, nonabsorbent surface that extends upward onto the walls for at least 6 in. (152 mm).

Walls within 2 ft (610 mm) of urinals and water closets must have a smooth, hard, nonabsorbent surface, to a height of 4 ft (1.2 m) above the floor. The material used cannot be a type that is adversely affected by moisture. The exceptions include dwelling units, guest rooms, and toilet rooms that are not accessible to the public and do not contain more than one water closet.

Shower compartments must have floor and wall finishes that are smooth and nonabsorbent and that are not affected by moisture. Wall finishes must extend to at least 70 in. (1,778 mm) above the drain inlet.

GLAZING CONDITIONS

MINIMUM SOUND TRANSMISSION RATINGS

REQUIRED NONABSORBENT SURFACES

FIRE DETECTION AND SUPPRESSION (IBC 903, 904, 907)

Fire detection and suppression refers to any fire alarm or fire-extinguishing system that is designed and installed to detect, control, or extinguish a fire, or to alert the occupants or the fire department that a fire has occurred. For dwelling units, the system may be limited to smoke detectors. In commercial buildings, the system may include many elements, such as smoke and heat detectors, sprinklers, portable fire extinguishers, standpipes, smoke control systems, manual alarms, and smoke and heat vents.

Chapter 9 of the IBC specifies under which conditions fire detection and suppression systems are required. The IBC also cites many instances where sprinklers may be used as equivalent protection to other code requirements. If installed, but not required, sprinkler systems are still required to conform to NFPA standards.

The design and installation of sprinkler systems is governed by NFPA 13, *Installation of Sprinkler Systems*, published by the National Fire Protection Association. Sprinkler systems for residential occupancies are governed by NFPA 13R or 13D.

The IBC also refers to the International Fire Code (IFC) for many provisions. For examples, portable fire extinguishers must be provided in occupancies and locations in accordance with the IFC. Refer to Section 907 of the IBC for those occupancies that require fire alarm and detection systems and how they must operate.

Although the design and layout of a sprinkler system is the responsibility of the mechanical engineer or fire protection contractor, the preferred location of the heads is often based on the designer's reflected ceiling plan.

Types of Sprinkler Heads

Sprinkler heads are available in many styles, including recessed, pendant, upright, and sidewall.

- *Recessed heads* are completely or partially recessed above the level of the ceiling. Completely recessed heads have a metal cover, which conceals their appearance. When there is a fire, the cover falls away and the sprinkler activates.
- *Pendant sprinklers* are the traditional types for finished ceilings, where the head extends a few inches below the ceiling. The sprinkler heads are visible at the ceiling plane.
- *Upright heads* sit above exposed plumbing in rooms with high, unfinished ceilings.
- *Sidewall heads* are used for corridors and small rooms where one row of sprinklers will provide adequate coverage for narrow spaces, or where it is more practical to run pipe along the wall rather than in the ceiling.

Locating Sprinkler Heads

For light-hazard occupancies such as offices, stores, and restaurants, one sprinkler head is required for each 225 sq ft (21 sq m) of floor area if the system is hydraulically designed.

If obstructions are present, such as beam enclosures, dropped ceilings, tall bookshelves, or high office system partitions, certain horizontal and vertical dimensions must be maintained.

Refer to NFPA 13, *Installation of Sprinkler Systems*, NFPA 13R, *Installation of Sprinkler Systems in Residential Occupancies up to and Including Four Stories in Height*, or NFPA 13D, *Installation of Sprinkler Systems in One- and Two-Family Dwellings and Manufactured Homes,* as required, for complete descriptions of all occupancy classifications and detailed design and installation requirements.

INTERIOR FINISHES (IBC 803)

The IBC limits the use of interior finish materials based on their flammability, the occupancy group, and the areas of the building in which they are used. Materials and finishes are classified according to their flame spread and smoke-developed characteristics when tested according to ASTM E84, *Test Method for Surface-Burning Characteristics of Building Materials* (Steiner Tunnel Test).

Interior finish materials include the exposed surfaces of walls and ceilings including partitions, wainscoting, paneling, and other finishes applied structurally or for decoration, acoustical correction, surface insulation, or for similar purposes. However, it does not include trim such as baseboards, window and door casing, or similar materials used in fixed applications. Trim cannot exceed 10% of the area in which it is located.

Interior finish requirements also do not apply to finishes less than 0.036-in.- (0.9-mm-) thick applied directly to the surface of walls or ceilings or to the exposed portions of structural members complying with Type IV construction requirements.

When walls or ceilings are required to have a fire-resistance rating or to be noncombustible, finishes must be applied directly to the construction element or to furring strips not greater than 1¾-in.- (44-mm-) thick applied directly to the construction element. If the finishes project greater than this amount or are suspended from the structure above, then it must be a Class A material or have sprinklers on both sides.

Material less than or equal to ¼-in.- (6-mm-) thick must be applied directly against a noncombustible backing unless it is a Class A material or it has been tested in a suspended or furred out position.

SPRINKLERS NEXT TO OBSTRUCTIONS

MAXIMUM DISTANCE OF DEFLECTOR ABOVE BOTTOM OF BEAM OR OBSTRUCTION

DISTANCE FROM NEAR SIDE OF BEAM OR OTHER OBSTRUCTION

SPRINKLERS ABOVE OBSTRUCTIONS

MINIMUM VERTICAL DISTANCE

HORIZONTAL DISTANCE

OBSTRUCTION CONDITIONS

MAXIMUM 15'-0" (4572)

MAXIMUM 7'-6" (2286)

MAXIMUM 7'-6" (2286)

SPRINKLER HEADS

MINIMUM 24" (600)

VERTICAL OBSTRUCTION

LARGER THAN 4" (100)

MINIMUM 4" (100)

SPRINKLER HEAD LOCATIONS

Definitions

Noncombustible: A material that meets the requirements of ASTM E136, *Standard Test Method for Behavior of Materials in a Vertical Tube Furnace at 750°C*. This means that the material will not ignite or burn when subjected to fire. Noncombustible also includes composite materials, such as gypsum wallboard, that are composed of a surfacing not more than 0.125- in.- (3-mm-) thick that has a flame spread index not greater than 50, as long as the structural base is noncombustible.

Flame-resistant: A material that restricts the spread of flame in accordance with NFPA 701, *Standard Methods of Fire Tests for Flame-Resistant Textiles and Films*. This test is commonly referred to as the Vertical Ignition Test.

Trim: Picture molds, chair rails, baseboards, handrails, door and window frames, and similar decorative or protective materials used in fixed applications.

Combustible: A material that will ignite and burn, either as a flame or glow, and that undergoes this process in air at pressures and temperatures that might occur during a fire in a building.

INTERIOR FINISHES

Textile Wall and Ceiling Coverings (IBC 803.5)

Textiles include materials having woven or nonwoven, napped, tufted, looped, or similar surface. Textile wall coverings must meet either of the following conditions:

- They must have a Class A flame spread index and be protected by automatic sprinklers. When used to limit the spread of fire, sprinklers in this instance only have to be installed where the textile wall coverings are used.
- They must meet the criteria of NFPA 265, *Standard Methods for Evaluating Room Fire Growth Contribution of Textile Wall Coverings,* when tested in the manner intended for use, using the product mounting system, including adhesive. NFPA 265 is the Room Corner Test and simulates conditions of the contribution of wall coverings to room fire growth.
- Textile ceiling finishes must have a Class A flame spread index and be protected by sprinklers.

Acoustical Ceilings

If an acoustical ceiling is part of a fire-resistance-rated construction, it must be installed in the same manner used in the assembly tested and comply with the requirements of IBC Chapter 7.

Decorations and Trim (IBC 805)

Curtains, draperies,, and decorative materials suspended from walls or ceilings in Ooccupancies of Groups A, E, I, R-1, and dormitories in Group R-2 must be flame-resistant or noncombustible. In Groups I-1 and I-2, combustible decorations must be flame-retardant, unless they are of such limited quantities that a hazard of fire development or spread is not present. In Group I-3 occupancies, only noncombustible decorations are permitted.

Flame-resistant decorative material is limited to 10% of the aggregate area of walls and ceilings except for auditoriums in Group A, where the permissible amount is 50% and the building is sprinklered.

Flame-resistant material must conform to Tests 1 or 2 of NFPA 701, *Standard Methods of Fire Tests for Flame-Resistant Textiles and Films.*

Floor Finish Requirements (IBC 804)

Floor finishes regulated by the IBC include carpet, combustible materials installed in or on floors of Type I or Type II buildings, and flooring in certain exit and exit access areas of particular occupancies. Floors of traditional materials including wood, vinyl, linoleum, terrazzo, and resilient floor covering are composed of fibers that are not regulated.

FLAMMABILITY TESTS

Steiner Tunnel Test

ASTM E84, *Standard Test Method for Surface-Burning Characteristics of Building Materials,* also known as the Steiner Tunnel Test, is used to rate the surface-burning characteristics of building materials and interior finishes and to provide data on smoke density. Materials are rated from 0 to 200 for flame spread and from 0 to 800 for smoke density. Materials with ratings from 0 to 25 are Class A; from 26 to 75 are Class B; and from 76 to 200 are Class C. Class A has

the lowest flame spread. The test is also known as NFPA 255 and UL 723.

Vertical Ignition Test

NFPA 701, *Standards Methods of Fire Tests for Flame-Resistant Textiles and Films,* commonly referred to as the Vertical Ignition Test, defines two test procedures that are used to assess the propagation of flame beyond the area exposed to an ignition source. The tests are appropriate for testing materials, such as draperies, curtains, or other window treatment, that are exposed to air on both sides. This test method also includes multiple layers of fabrics, for example, lined draperies. Test 1 provides a procedure for assessing the response of fabrics lighter than 21 oz/sq yd (712 g/ sq m) individually and in multiple layer composites used as window treatments. Test 2 is for fabrics weighing more than 21 oz/sq yd (712 g/ sq m). Rating is either pass or fail. The test is also known as ASTM D6413.

Smoke Density Test

Smoke generated by fire inhibits vision and breathing, making escape more difficult. ASTM E622, *Standard Test Method for Specific Optical Density of Smoke Generated by Solid Materials,* the Smoke Density Test, measures the density of smoke that affects visibility during egress from a fire. It does not measure the

effect of eye irritants, which can significantly limit the visual range. This test measures the transmission of light through smoke generated from a cube of solid material.

Room Corner Test

NFPA 265, *Standard Methods of Fire Tests for Evaluating Room Fire Growth Contribution of Textile Wall Covering,* commonly referred to as the Room Corner Test, was developed exclusively for textile wall-coverings. It was designed to simulate more realistic circumstances than the Steiner Tunnel Test, which mounts materials on the ceiling of the test chamber. The wall substrate, adhesive, and textile wallcovering to be used are installed in a near full-scale room and tested. This test determines the contribution to a room fire made by a wall finished with a textile wallcovering.

CLASSIFICATION OF FINISHES

CLASS	FLAME SPREAD	SMOKE DEVELOPED
A	0–25	0–450
B	26–75	0–450
C	76–200	0–450

STEINER TUNNEL TEST

SMOKE DENSITY TESTING DEVICE

ROOM CORNER TEST

NFPA 701 TEST 1 APPARATUS

NFPA 701 TEST 2 APPARATUS

FABRIC APPLICATION AND FLAMMABILITY REQUIREMENTS

APPLICATION	APPLICABLE FLAMMABILITY TEST
Attached to Wall	
Stretched-fabric wall systems Freestanding furniture panels Tackboards Acoustic panels	Steiner Tunnel Test
Wallcoverings	Room Corner Test
Free Hanging	
Window treatments Banner and flags	Vertical Ignition Test
Seating	
Upholstery	Cigarette Ignition Resistance Test of Furniture Components
Floor Covering	
Carpet in corridors Carpet tile in corridors	Flooring Radiant Panel Test
Area rugs	Methenamine Pill Test

Methenamine Pill Test

ASTM D2859, *Standard Test Method for Flammability of Finished Textile Floor Covering Materials,* prescribes the standard for testing carpet flammability with a methenamine tablet for carpets larger than 6 ft (1,830 mm) in one dimension and greater than 24 sq ft (2.23 sq m) in area offered for sale in the United States. The test is also known as CPSC 16 CFR, Part 1630, *Standard for the Surface Flammability of Carpets and Rugs.*

Flooring Radiant Panel Test

Floor coverings are not usually regarded as the primary cause of flame spread during a fire. However, flooring material in corridors has been observed to present problems in full-scale tests and actual building fires. In a fully developed fire, the combination of heat, flame, smoke, and gases emanating from burning rooms surrounding a corridor can make a substantial contribution to flame spread.

ASTM E648, *Standard Test Method for Critical Radiant Flux of Floor Covering Systems Using a Radiant Heat Energy Source,* known as the Flooring Radiant Panel Test, exposes the floor covering sample to radiant heat and igniting flames. This test was designed to simulate more realistic circumstances than the Steiner Tunnel Test, which mounts materials on the ceiling of the test chamber. The Flooring Radiant Panel Test is different from most other flammability test methods because it measures an actual property of the carpet system. It is not based on an arbitrary scale.

Full Seating Test

ASTM E1537, *Test Method for Fire Testing of Real-Scale Upholstered Furniture Item,* evaluates the response to an open flame of an actual sample of furniture. During the test several measurements are made, including the rate of heat and smoke release, total amount of heat and smoke released, concentration of carbon oxides, and others. The most important measurement is the rate of heat release, which quantifies the intensity of the fire generated. It is one of the strictest tests for furniture and is required in several states. The test is also known as CAL Tech 133, NFPA 266, and BFD IX-10.

Cigarette Ignition Resistance Test for Furniture Components

ASTM E1353, *Standard Test Method for Cigarette Ignition Resistance of Components of Upholstered Furniture,* evaluates individual components (fabric and fillings) of upholstered furniture to cigarette ignition as well as flame. Separate fill materials, such as expanded polystyrene beads, cellular materials, feathers, nonartificial filling, and artificial fiber filling are tested separately for a variety of characteristics. The test is essentially the same as the Fabric Standard Classification Test by the Upholstered Furniture Action Council. The test is also known as CAL Tech 117, NFPA 260, and UFAC FSCTM.

Cigarette Ignition Resistance Test for Furniture Composites

ASTM E1352, *Standard Test Method for Cigarette Ignition Resistance of Mock-Up Upholstered Furniture Assemblies,* is used to evaluate the cigarette ignition resistance of upholstered furniture by using a mock-up. It determines how the composite material (padding and covering) reacts to a lighted cigarette. A mock-up includes vertical and horizontal surfaces meeting at a 90° angle. The cushion fails the test if the cushion breaks into flames or if a char develops more than 2 in. (50 mm) long. It is not intended to measure the performance of upholstered furniture under conditions of open flame exposure. The similar Business and Institutional Furniture Manufacturer's Association (BIFMA) test allows a 3 in. (76 mm) char length before the sample fails. The test is also known as CAL Tech 116, NAPA 261, and BIFMA X5.7.

David Kent Ballast, AIA; Architectural Research Consulting; Denver, Colorado
Bob Pielow; Pielow Fair Associates; Seattle, Washington

METHENAMINE PILL TEST

FULL SEATING TEST

FLOORING RADIANT PANEL TEST

THE CIGARETTE IGNITION TEST FOR FURNITURE COMPOSITES

LIFE SAFETY CONSIDERATIONS □ **1**

SEISMIC CONSIDERATIONS

PLATE TECTONICS

According to the theory of plate tectonics, the Earth's crust is divided into constantly moving plates. Earthquakes occur when, as a result of slowly accumulating pressure, the ground slips abruptly along a geological fault plane on or near a plate boundary. The resulting waves of vibration within the Earth create ground motions at the surface, which, in turn, induce movement within buildings. The frequency, magnitude, and duration of the ground motion, physical characteristics of the building, and geology of a site determine how these forces affect a building.

DESIGN JUDGMENT

In an earthquake, buildings designed to the minimum levels required by model codes often sustain damage. Early discussion with an owner should explore the need to limit property loss in an earthquake and the desirability of attempting to ensure continued building operation immediately afterward. To achieve these results, it may be necessary to make design decisions based on the seismic conditions of a site rather than on code requirements.

SEISMIC CODES

The minimum requirements for the structural design of buildings are set by locally adopted and enforced building codes. The four referenced building codes in use in the United States are: the International Building Code (IBC), the National Building Code (NBC), Standard Building Code (SBC), and Uniform Building Code (UBC). These codes are developed and published by industry associations representing building officials. The earthquake design provisions contained in these model codes are similar and are based on recommendations developed by the Structural Engineers Association of California and the Building Seismic Safety Council. In the most seismically active regions of the United States, design has been based on the UBC for many years.

UBC Design Philosophy

The UBC has adopted a seismic design philosophy intended to protect life safety; it addresses some structural and potentially significant nonstructural damage for earthquake levels as severe as can be expected at a site. The code implicitly sets forth the following three-level earthquake performance criteria: minor, moderate, and major earthquakes.

Minor Earthquakes

In a minor earthquake, a structural site resists minor levels of earthquake ground motion with no structural damage and with only minor damage to nonstructural features such as glazing, architectural finishes, and suspended ceilings. Such ground motion may occur many times during the economic life of a building and typically lasts only a few seconds.

Moderate Earthquakes

In a moderate-level earthquake, buildings resist moderate levels of earthquake ground motion with minor repairable structural damage and, possibly, some extensive nonstructural damage. Such ground motion could occur once or twice during the economic life of a building. The 1994 Northridge earthquake produced this level of ground motion throughout the Los Angeles area.

Major Earthquakes

In major earthquakes, buildings resist a level of earthquake ground motion that has an intensity equal to the strongest that has either been experienced or forecast for the building site without collapse but possibly with some major structural as well as extensive nonstructural damage. Such ground motion may or may not occur during the economic life of a building. The 1906 San Francisco earthquake produced motions of this intensity throughout northern and central California.

Lateral Forces

The lateral force design regulations are primarily for building components and connections subjected to strong shaking during an earthquake. They do not address the effects of potential ground failures, such as liquefaction, consolidation, landslides, and ground surface rupture. Any of these types of ground failures can result in excessive damage to a building, regardless of how well the building is constructed.

INTENT OF THE CODES

Life Safety

The intent of the seismic design provisions of the UBC is to prevent injuries and loss of life, *not* to minimize property damage. These minimum criteria are considered to be prudent and economically justified for the protection of life safety.

Additional Protection for Some Use Groups

Selected buildings are sometimes designed to improve performance during an earthquake. Such buildings are designed to substantially exceed the detailing, strength, and stiffness requirements specified by the building code as a minimum design basis. In some jurisdictions, schools, hospitals, fire and police stations, buildings containing hazardous materials, communications centers, and structures having essential facilities that are required for postearthquake recovery are required to be designed to such enhanced criteria. However, most buildings are designed for the code minimums.

The information in this section is based, in part, on the requirements in the 1997 National Earthquake Hazards Reduction Program (NEHRP) provisions, which are expected to appear in subsequent issues of all model codes. Detached one- and two-family dwellings will be exempt from seismic regulations in areas other than those with high seismicity. Seismic codes are constantly evolving, and designers should always consult the relevant code before beginning a project.

Elimination of Seismic Zones for Design Purposes

A significant change in the seismic codes was the elimination of seismic zones as a basis for establishing design acceleration. Seismic maps now show building response periods as a percentage of gravity.

The map shown below, based on a building response period of 0.2 of a second, gives accelerations to be used for low buildings. A similar map based on a building response of 1.0 second is proposed for taller buildings. Before determining what level of ground shaking applies to a project, a designer must find out the type of earth on which the building will be constructed. The maps are based on buildings built on soft rock, but note that ground motion increases with soil softness.

SEISMIC ACCELERATION FOR LOW BUILDINGS EXPRESSED AS A PERCENTAGE OF GRAVITY

TERMINOLOGY

Following is a short list of the terms used to describe common seismic conditions:

Base isolation: A foundation system that uses isolators to separate the building from ground motion. Base isolators operate in a manner analogous to the suspension system of an automobile. Isolators are generally located in a subbasement.

PERIMETER CLOSURE

BASE ISOLATOR

SECTION

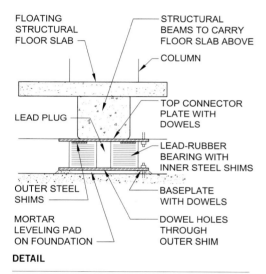

FLOATING STRUCTURAL FLOOR SLAB

STRUCTURAL BEAMS TO CARRY FLOOR SLAB ABOVE

COLUMN

LEAD PLUG

TOP CONNECTOR PLATE WITH DOWELS

LEAD-RUBBER BEARING WITH INNER STEEL SHIMS

OUTER STEEL SHIMS

BASEPLATE WITH DOWELS

MORTAR LEVELING PAD ON FOUNDATION

DOWEL HOLES THROUGH OUTER SHIM

DETAIL

BASE ISOLATION

Base shear (static analysis): Calculated total shear force acting at the base of a structure. Also referred to as *equivalent lateral force,* base shear is used in codes as a static representation of lateral earthquake forces.

DRIFT

STORY DRIFT

BASE SHEAR

DRIFT

BASE SHEAR AND DRIFT

Braced frames: Diagonal braces that resist lateral forces. Most braces limit the number of openings possible in a wall.

BRACED FRAMES

Design earthquake: Earthquake ground motion for which a building is designed.

Diaphragm: Horizontal elements, usually floors, roofs, or bracing that transfer seismic loads to the vertical elements of the lateral load-resisting system. Diaphragms can be viewed as deep horizontal beams turned on their sides that resist horizontal loads by spanning between the vertical lateral load-resisting elements. Diaphragms can consist of plywood nailed to the floor framing, concrete slab, metal decking, or concrete topping over metal decking.

GLASS

DIAPHRAGM

SHEAR WALL

FOUNDATION

GROUND MOTION

SHEAR WALLS AND DIAPHRAGMS

Drift: Lateral deflection of a building or structure. *Story drift* is the relative movement between adjacent floors.

Ductility: The capability of a structural frame to bend but not break. Its ductility is a major factor in establishing the capability of a building to withstand earthquakes. Ductile materials (steel in particular) fail only after permanent deformation has taken place. Good ductility requires special detailing of the joints.

Dynamic analysis: A structural analysis based on the vibration motion of a building. Dynamic analysis is time-consuming and normally reserved for complex projects.

Forces, in-plane: Forces exerted parallel to a wall or frame.

Forces, out-of-plane: Forces exerted perpendicular to a wall or frame.

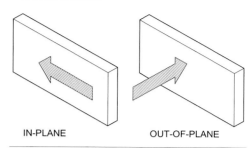

IN-PLANE

OUT-OF-PLANE

FORCE DIAGRAMS

Ground fault rupture: The direct manifestation of the movement that has occurred along a fault, projected to the ground surface. It consists of a concentrated, permanent deformation of the ground surface; in major earthquakes, it can extend along the trace of the fault for many miles. This deformation can be in a horizontal and/or vertical direction. A ground-surface rupture involving more than a few inches of movement within a concentrated area will cause major damage to structures that cross it. Fault displacements produce forces so great that the best method of limiting damage to structures is to avoid building in areas close to ground traces of active faults.

GROUND RUPTURE

Ground shaking: The primary and best-known hazard associated with earthquakes, ground shaking is the mechanism by which most energy released in an earthquake is dissipated. Ground shaking includes both horizontal and vertical motions that can last up to several minutes during major earthquakes. Generally, sites located remotely from the zone of fault rupture experience less severe ground motion than do sites located close to the fault. However, local soil conditions can amplify and modify the character of ground motion to produce more intense effects at individual sites. It is estimated that ground shaking causes more than 90% of all earthquake-related damage to buildings.

GROUND SHAKING

Liquefaction: The sudden loss of bearing strength that can occur when saturated, cohesionless soils (sands and silts) are strongly and repetitively vibrated in a seismic event. The consequences of liquefaction can include lateral spreading, landslides, a quick condition (loss of soil-bearing capacity or tilting), and differential settling of the ground. Buried structures, such as tanks, may even float to the surface. *Site liquefaction* typically occurs in loose sand deposits within 15 ft (4.5 m) of the ground surface when there is subsurface groundwater above a depth of 20 ft (6 m). Shallow groundwater and loose soil are usually localized conditions, resulting either from natural or human-made causes. As a result, site-specific data are necessary to accurately determine if liquefaction may occur at a location.

Lateral spreading: A secondary effect of liquefaction. When soils located on a sloping site liquefy, they tend to flow downhill in an uneven manner. A site that has experienced lateral spreading will typically exhibit a series of parallel cracks in the ground, oriented along the sloping face. Buildings or other structures located on sites experiencing lateral spreading are likely to be severely damaged, and sometimes may collapse.

LIQUEFACTION

Load path: The path that seismic forces take from the roof to the foundation of a structure. Typically, the load travels from the diaphragms through connections to the vertical lateral force-resisting elements and on to the foundation by way of additional connections. This path should be direct and uninterrupted. Seismic design begins with, and codes require, the establishment of a continuous load path.

Maximum considered earthquake: The greatest ground shaking expected to occur during an earthquake at a site. These values are somewhat higher than those of the design earthquake, particularly in areas where seismic events are very infrequent. The code maps are based on earthquakes of this magnitude.

Moment frame: A lateral load-resisting system utilizing beams and columns with special connections designed to resist bending and shear forces. Typically, moment frames are constructed of either monolithically placed reinforced concrete or structural steel. Building codes require special detailing for structures utilizing moment frames to ensure that they can behave in a ductile manner. They must be designed to absorb substantial amounts of seismic energy and sustain extensive distress before failing and collapsing.

Reentrant corner: The inside building corner of an L-, H-, X-, or T-shaped plan.

Shear wall: A lateral load-resisting system with walls designed to resist lateral loads. Shear walls in buildings are composed of reinforced concrete, reinforced or unreinforced masonry (concrete block or brick), or wood stud walls sheathed with plywood or gypsum board.

TYPICAL SHEAR-ONLY CONNECTION

TYPICAL MOMENT CONNECTION   **TYPICAL WELDED MOMENT CONNECTION**

CONNECTIONS

CONSIDERATIONS FOR BUILDING DESIGN

The seismic framing system selected for a structure must meet both architectural and seismic design requirements. Although most buildings can be made seismic-resistant, some architectural configurations interrupt the load path or otherwise interfere with seismic performance, increasing construction costs and making the seismic restraint system less effective. The examples that follow contrast configurations that probably would cause problems in areas with high levels of seismicity with variations that should avoid these problems.

Vertical Geometry Irregularity

Vertical geometric irregularity is considered to exist where the horizontal dimension of the lateral-force-resisting system in any story is more than 130% of that in an adjacent story. One-story penthouses need not be considered.

The base should not be too much larger than the tower above.

PREFERRED

Diaphragm Discontinuities

Diaphragms with abrupt discontinuities or variations in stiffness include those having cutout or open areas greater than 50% of the gross enclosed area of the diaphragm or changes in effective diaphragm stiffness of more than 50% from one story to the next.

PREFERRED

DISCOURAGED

Horizontal diaphragms (floors and roofs) can more readily transfer earthquake loads to the vertical force-resisting system when the size and number of holes in the diaphragm are limited.

DIAPHRAGM DISCONTINUITIES

Torsion in Plan

Torsional irregularity should be considered when the maximum story drift at one end of the building transverse to an axis is more than 1.2 times the average of the story drifts of the two ends of the building.

The lateral force-resisting system for a symmetrical building is much easier to design than that of an asymmetrical building. Because the source of an earthquake cannot be known, symmetry in both directions should be considered.

TORSION IN PLAN

Out-of-Plane Vertical Offsets

A building has out-of-plane vertical offsets when major elements, such as shear walls, are shifted from floor to floor within the building. This arrangement creates discontinuities in the lateral force path within the structure.

PREFERRED

DISCOURAGED

OUT-OF-PLANE VERTICAL OFFSETS

Reentrant Corners

Plan configurations of a structure and its lateral load-resisting system contain reentrant corners when a projection of the structure beyond a corner notch subtracted from a theoretically rectangular building form is greater than 15% of the plan dimension of the structure in the given direction.

PREFERRED   DISCOURAGED

This is a variation of the symmetry issue. When the notch gets too large, the building tends to tear at the inside corner.

REENTRANT CORNERS

Mass Irregularity

Mass irregularity occurs when a floor is substantially heavier than the adjacent floors (e.g., swimming pools within a building, equipment, etc.). For seismic analysis, mass irregularity is considered to exist where the effective mass of any story is more than 150% of the effective mass of an adjacent story. A roof that is lighter than the floor below need not be considered.

PREFERRED   DISCOURAGED

While all floors do not have to be the same, it is important that no floor have too much more mass than those adjacent.

MASS IRREGULARITY

Nonparallel Systems

Nonparallel systems occur within a building when the vertical lateral-load-resisting elements are not parallel to or symmetrical about the major orthogonal axes of the lateral-force-resisting system. This asymmetry may complicate seismic analysis, increase construction cost, and make the seismic restraint system less effective.

Soft Story

A soft story is inherently weaker (e.g., taller, longer structural spans, more widely spaced structural system) than the floor(s) above. It is one in which the lateral stiffness of a particular floor within a building is less than 70% that in the story above or less than 80% of the average stiffness of the three stories above.

PREFERRED   DISCOURAGED

When a taller (inherently weaker) first floor is desired, anticipate using much heavier first-floor framing to equalize the stiffness with that of the floors above.

SOFT STORY

In-Plane Discontinuity

In-plane discontinuity refers to an in-plane offset of the elements of the lateral-load-resisting-system, wherein the distance of the offset is greater than the length of the element.

PREFERRED   DISCOURAGED

Although both drawings illustrate shear walls in the same plane, one arrangement is discouraged because the load path is not direct.

IN-PLANE DISCONTINUITY

Weak Story

A weak story is one in which the strength of a particular floor is less than 80% that in the story above. The story strength is the total strength of all seismic-resisting elements sharing the story shear for the direction under consideration.

PREFERRED

While it is best to have uniform stiffness, some variation is acceptable.

PREFERRED

SEISMIC DETAILING FOR DESIGNERS

When detailing architectural and mechanical elements for seismic resistance, the designer's primary concerns are to minimize falling hazards and to maintain a normal egress route. Features such as masonry chimneys, parapets, light fixtures, suspended mechanical equipment, large ductwork, and heavy pipes are potential falling hazards. Cabinets and bookcases can block exits if they fall. An additional concern for designers working with sites in earthquake-prone areas is the need for a building to remain in operation after an earthquake.

Many resources that offer detailed solutions for seismic design only address areas with high seismic activity. However, no single detail is appropriate for all areas. The sections that follow are meant to help guide designers through the philosophy of seismic design.

LIFE SAFETY CONSIDERATIONS ☐ **1**

MASONRY SYSTEMS

Empirical rules and formulas for the design of masonry structures resulted from the long history of masonry use, and thus predate engineering and analysis. Empirical design is a method of sizing and proportioning masonry elements that depends on centering gravity loads over bearing walls, neglecting the effect of steel reinforcing.

For most masonry work, empirical design is conservative. It is generally appropriate for smaller buildings with interior masonry partitions and stiff floors, as well as buildings in lower seismic exposure areas and walls not part of the lateral resisting system (even when other walls are engineered). Buildings that are in higher-exposure areas or that have walls that are part of the lateral resistance system require engineering design that conforms to local codes.

There are specific limits on masonry as to height, wind, or other horizontal loads and seismic loads. In many cases, design for wind, and industry recommendations for crack control due to shrinkage or expansion, may govern building reinforcement in areas with lower seismic activity.

This detail allows transfer of out-of-plane forces but isolates in-plane forces from the structure.

NONBEARING WALL ISOLATION DETAILS

SHEAR WALL SPACING RATIO— EMPIRICAL DESIGN

Bearing Walls	Solid Units	$l/t < 20$
	Fully grouted	$l/t < 20$
	Others	$l/t < 18$
Nonbearing Walls	Interior	$l/t < 18$

l = wall length; t = wall thickness

Standard construction practice for masonry crack control requires W1.7 at 16 in. (410 mm) o.c., which would cover seismic requirements as well. W1.7 steel reinforcement at 8 in. (205 mm) o.c. should be used in parapet locations.

WALL REINFORCING FOR MASONRY WALL (EMPIRICAL DESIGN FOR MODERATE SEISMIC AREAS)

INTERSECTING WALL DETAIL

Preformed, hot-dipped galvanized tees (W1.7 wire at 8 in. (205 mm) o.c., vertical for bearing; 16 in. (410 mm) o.c. for nonbearing) are used for reinforcing intersecting walls.

INTERSECTING WALL REINFORCING

1   ☐   **LIFE SAFETY CONSIDERATIONS**

GROUT CELL AT ANCHOR ONLY

FLOOR JOIST PARALLEL TO WALL 16" O.C.

1/2" HEADED BOLT AT MAX. 6'-0" O.C.

CONTINUOUS BOND BEAM WITH #4 REBARS

CMU WALL

THROUGH WALL REINFORCING (W 1.7 16" O.C., VERTICAL)

PARALLEL TO WALL
Anchors should also be placed at cross bracing for joists.

GROUT CELL AT ANCHOR ONLY

FLOOR JOIST OR RAFTER PERPENDICULAR TO WALL AT 16" O.C.

METAL JOIST HANGER

3" LEDGER

1/2" HEADED BOLT AT MAX. 6'-0" O.C. (OR 1/2" THREADED ROD HOOKED)

CONTINUOUS BOND BEAM WITH #4 REBARS

THROUGH WALL REINFORCING (W 1.7 16" O.C., VERTICAL)

PERPENDICULAR TO WALL

GROUT CELL AT ANCHOR ONLY

JOIST/RAFTER PARALLEL OR PERPENDICULAR TO WALL

1/2" DIAMETER THREADED ROD, HOOKED TO BOND BEAM REBAR

CONTINUOUS BOND BEAM

THROUGH WALL REINFORCING (W 1.7 16" O.C., VERTICAL)

ALTERNATE CONNECTION

DIAPHRAGM CONNECTIONS FOR WOOD JOIST/RAFTER

GROUT CELL AT DOWEL ONLY

#3 DOWEL AT 16" O.C. (TURN DOWN 16" INTO BOND BEAM)

CONCRETE ON METAL DECK

4" X 4" X 5/16" CONTINUOUS STEEL ANGLE (ANCHOR WITH EXPANSION BOLT)

CONTINUOUS BOND BEAM (GROUT SOLID)

CMU WALL

THROUGH WALL REINFORCING (W 1.7 16" O.C., VERTICAL)

PARALLEL TO WALL

THROUGH WALL REINFORCING (W 1.7 16" O.C., VERTICAL)

CONCRETE ON METAL DECK

WELD JOIST TO PLATE

BEARING PLATE WITH #3 HOOK TO BAR

CONTINUOUS BOND BEAM (GROUT SOLID)

CMU WALL

STEEL JOIST

PERPENDICULAR TO WALL

DIAPHRAGM CONNECTIONS FOR STEEL JOISTS

WOOD TRUSS AT 24" O.C.

PRESSURE-TREATED WOOD PLATE

1" X 12" STEEL STRAP, EACH TRUSS

1/2" DIAMETER HEADED BOLT AT 6'-0" O.C.

CONTINUOUS BOND BEAM, GROUT SOLID

CMU WALL

WOOD TRUSS AT 24" O.C.

3" X 3" X 3/16" STEEL ANGLE AT 48" O.C.

PRESSURE-TREATED WOOD PLATE

1/2" DIAMETER HEADED BOLT AT 6'-0" O.C.

CONTINUOUS BOND BEAM, GROUT SOLID

CMU WALL

ROOF TIE DETAILS FOR MODERATE SEISMIC AREAS

AS ALTERNATE TO BRACE, USE #4 STEEL REBAR AT 48" O.C.; CAVITIES FILLED WITH GROUT

USE BRACE IF H/T > 3

ROOF STRUCTURE

HORIZONTAL JOINT REINFORCEMENT

Empirical design for masonry parapets should be used only for low seismicity. Engineering analysis is required when a height-to-thickness ratio of 3:1 is exceeded and in areas of higher seismicity.

MASONRY PARAPET DETAIL FOR SEISMIC AREAS

LIFE SAFETY CONSIDERATIONS ☐ 1

WOOD SYSTEMS

Wood frame structures with a variety of solid wood and engineered wood products can be designed to resist seismic forces using many of the same principles used to resist wind forces. Wind-resistant design involves resolving loads assumed to be applied to the structure in one direction for a short time (monotonic loads). Wind load can induce shear that is both perpendicular and parallel with the structure, resulting in an overturning motion as well as uplift on the structure. In contrast, seismic loads are cyclical, moving in different directions over a short period.

Reference Codes

Seismic loading conditions on conventional construction are referenced in four main sources, which also provide information about the capacity of various materials: American Society of Civil Engineers 7-95, Section A9.9.10; the Uniform Building Code, Section 2320; the Standard Building Code, Sections 2308.2.2 and 2310; and the National Building Code, Section 2305.8. In general, these provisions are limited to buildings with bearing walls not exceeding 10 ft (3 m) in height and gravity dead loads not exceeding 15 psf (718.2 Pa) for floors and exterior walls, and 10 psf (478.8 Pa) for floors and partitions.

Standards

Wood construction standards for all seismic areas include the following:

- Walls must be capped with double top plates.
- End joints in double top plates must be offset by at least 4 ft (1 m).
- Bottom plates must be 1½ in.- (38.1-mm-) thick (2 in. (50 mm) nominal) and be at least the width of the studs.
- Sheathing for braced walls must be at least 48 in. (1,220 mm) wide over studs spaced not more than 24 in. (610 mm) o.c.
- Forces must be transferred from the roof and floor(s) to braced walls and from the braced walls in upper stories to the braced walls in the story below, then into the foundation. Transfer must be accomplished with toe nails using three 8d nails per joist or rafter where not more than 2 ft (610 mm) o.c. or with metal framing devices capable of transmitting the lateral force.
- Roof-to-wall connections must be made at the exterior walls when the building is 50 ft (15 m) or less in length. A combination of exterior and interior bearing walls is necessary when the building length exceeds 50 ft (15 m).

Connections

Connections designed for both lateral and vertical (uplift or overturning) loads must be used in conventional wood frame structures designed for seismic areas. Traditional nailing schedules are often adequate to handle lateral forces. Vertical forces can be addressed by lapping structural sheathing and/or strapping the roof, walls, and floors together at appropriate intervals. In addition, the overturning loads in walls must be restrained by anchoring the ends of the shear panels (whether traditional or perforated) to the structural wall below.

Nontraditional Materials

Nontraditional materials such as Laminated Veneer Lumber (LVL), I-joists, and structural composite lumber can be used in seismic design; the capacities and applicable connection types of these products are available from the manufacturers.

Each diaphragm in a building must resist the seismic effects in both directions of all the mass above it, as well as of its own mass. The seismic loads caused by the roof mass must be transferred to the wall, and the wall must be designed to resist both the effect of the mass of the roof and the mass of the wall. These combined loads must then be transferred to the floor below, which must be designed to resist the effect of both its mass and the load applied by the wall above. In turn, walls below must resist these loads, until the force reaches the foundation, which must be able to resist the combined loads from the rest of the building.

SEISMIC LOAD TRANSFER

Use ¹⁵⁄₃₂ in. (11.9 mm) sheathing for the outside of shear panels, with 10d nails in 2× framing.

Capacities are based on structural I-panels of Douglas fir, larch, or southern pine. For additional thicknesses or alternative wood species, consult the American Plywood Association (APA).

The aspect ratio (the ratio of the longer dimension to the shorter) of a floor or roof diaphragm is limited to L2/L1≤4. Openings in the diaphragm are limited to either 12 ft (3.6 m) or half the length of the diaphragm, whichever is smaller.

FLOOR AND ROOF DIAPHRAGM

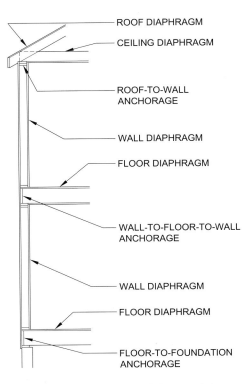

Diaphragms (the roof, floor(s), and shear panels in walls) must be designed to resist forces created by the dead-load mass of the structure and applied seismic loads. In wood frame construction, a diaphragm is typically a structural "panel" made of a skin (sheathing) stretched over and fastened to ribs (wood members such as two-by-fours). The resulting construction is stiff and strong enough to transmit forces to resisting systems such as the foundation. Connections must be designed to transfer lateral forces and restrain overturning motion. Lateral forces can be either perpendicular or parallel to the structure. The load from each part of a building that it creates as the building shifts from the movement of the Earth must be transferred to adjoining elements (roof sheathing to rafters to wall sheathing, and studs to bottom plates to floor sheathing and framing, and so on, until the lowest level of floor framing, from which the load moves to the foundation; in slab-on-grade construction, the load moves finally from the wall sheathing and studs to the bottom plates.)

The roof diaphragm comprises roof sheathing, roof framing, (rafters, top chord of truss, etc.), and blocking. The ceiling diaphragm comprises ceiling finish material (e.g., gypsum wallboard) and ceiling framing (joists, lower chord of trusses, etc.)

Roof-to-wall anchorage consists of hold-down anchors to resist uplift forces and nailing to resist shear forces. The wall diaphragm comprises wall sheathing, wall framing, and sheathing fasteners.

The floor diaphragm comprises floor sheathing, floor framing (joists, trusses, etc.), blocking, and so on. Wall-to-floor anchorage consists of hold-down anchors and shear connectors (e.g., nails).

Floor-to-foundation anchorage consists of hold-down anchors to resist overturning forces and anchor bolts [½ in. (13 mm) diameter at 6 ft (1.8 m)] to resist shear forces.

TYPICAL WALL SECTION FOR CONVENTIONAL WOOD FRAMING

WOOD STUDS AT 16" O.C., MAX.

4'-0" DOUBLE TOP PLATE JOINT OFFSET, TYP.

4' X 8' MIN. SHEAR PANEL

15/32" SHEAR PANEL, ATTACHED DIRECTLY TO STUDS BOTH SIDES

Shear panels that consist of framing members and sheathing panel(s) or diagonal sheathing members provide the principal lateral resistance to shear loads. Building codes require a maximum aspect ration of H/L≤2 or 3½ in. (50 or 90 mm) for the panel.

Sheathing panels are made of plywood or oriented strand board (OSB) (for structural panels), gypsum sheathing, or fiberboard. Diagonal wood sheathing boards or strapping can also be used.

The shear capacity of the material depends on the quality of the framing and sheathing materials and on the connections. Sheathing both sides with the same material doubles the capacity of the shear panel. Tests have shown that sheathing each side with a different material adds capacity, although this concept is not accepted by all codes.

Use 10d nails at all edges and in field (center area) as follows: for edge-nailing, 6 in. (150 mm) o.c. for 280 lb/ft (416 kg/m); 4 in. (100 mm) o.c. for 430 lb/ft (640 kg/m); 3 in. (75 mm) o.c. for 550 lb/ft (818 kg/m); 2 in. (50 mm) o.c. for 730 lb/ft (1086 kg/m); and 12 in. (305 mm) o.c. for field-nailing.

The illustration shown above is based on the use of structural I-panels of Douglas fir, larch, or southern pine. For additional thicknesses or alternative wood species, consult the American Plywood Association (APA).

WOOD WALL SHEAR PANEL

MINIMUM LENGTH OF BRACED WALL

STORY	SHEATHING TYPE*	LOW RISK			HIGH RISK
Top or only story	G-P	8 ft (2.4 m)	12 ft (3.7 m)	16 ft (4.9 m)	20 ft (6.1 m)
	SW	4 ft (1.2 m)	8 ft (2.4 m)	8 ft (2.4 m)	12 ft (3.7 m)
Story below top	G-P	12 ft (3.7 m)	16 ft (4.9 m)	20 ft (6.1 m)	—
	SW	8 ft (2.4 m)	8 ft (2.4 m)	12 ft (3.7 m)	29 ft (8.8 m)
Bottom of three stories	G-P	16 ft (4.9 m)	—	—	—
	SW	8 ft (2.4 m)	Not permitted as conventional		

*G-P = Gypsum; SW = Structural Wood

SHEAR PANEL, TYP.

LOCATION OF HOLD-DOWNS (AT EACH END OF SHEAR PANELS, TYP.)

In traditional shear wall design, parts of the wall that are sheathed from top to bottom without openings are considered individually as shear panels. Hold-down anchors are required at both ends of these panels. Each segment must be restrained against the overturning motion and the shear to which it will be exposed.

The capacity of a traditional shear wall is the sum of the capacities of the individual shear wall segments, which are determined by multiplying the length of each segment by the capacity of the sheathing (lb/ft (kg/m)). For example: Use $^{15}/_{32}$ in. (12 mm) sheathing for the outside of the shear panel, with 10d nails spaced 6 in. (150 mm) o.c. for 280 lb/ft (416 kg/m). The capacity of this shear wall would be equal to 280 × (A + B + C); 280 × H = uplift (hold-down capacity).

TRADITIONAL SHEAR WALLS

NAIL SPACING FOR BLOCKED DIAPHRAGM*

BOUNDARY PANELS IN (MM)	OTHER PANELS IN (MM)	CAPACITIES LB/FT (KG/M)
4 (102)	6 (152)	425 (59)
2½ (64)	4 (102)	640 (88)
2 (51)	3 (76)	730 (101)

*$^{15}/_{32}$-in. (12-mm) panel sheathing; 10d nails into 2x framing (Douglas fir, larch, southern pine).

BRACED WALL SPACING

SEISMIC PERFORMANCE CATEGORY	DISTANCE BETWEEN BRACED WALLS	MAXIMUM NUMBER OF STORIES
A	35 ft (10.7 m)	3
B	35 ft (10.7 m)	3
C	25 ft (7.6 m)	2
D	25 ft (7.6 m)	1*

*Two stories for detached one- and two-family dwellings.

6'-8" MAX. OPENING HEIGHT

HOLD-DOWNS AT ENDS OF WALL

For perforated shear walls, the whole wall is considered as a single shear panel without regard to wall openings. Hold-down anchors are required only at the ends of the wall. To determine the capacity of the wall, the lengths of the full-height sheathed areas are added together and the sum is multiplied by the capacity of the sheathing.

Perforated shear walls may require higher-capacity sheathing than traditional shear walls to compensate for the lack of intermediate hold-down anchors.

The sheathed walls above and below the openings in a perforated shear wall increase the capacity of the wall. The capacity of the shear wall must be adjusted by a factor derived from two variables: the maximum opening height and the percentage of full-height sheathing on the shear panel. In the following example, a factor of 0.49 is applied. The Wood Frame Construction Manual gives more examples. Use $^{15}/_{32}$ in. (12 mm) sheathing for the outside of the shear panel, with 10d nails spaced 6 in. (152.4 mm) o.c. for 280 lb/ft (416 kg/m). Shear = 280 × (A + B + C) x 0.49; 280 × 8 = 2,240 lb (1,016 kg) uplift (hold-down capacity).

PERFORATED SHEAR WALLS

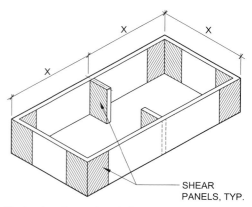

SHEAR PANELS, TYP.

The bracing element is typically a shear panel that is anchored against both shear and overturning.

BRACED WALL SPACING

CONNECTIONS

Connections are an important element of the lateral force-resisting framing system. Wood connections come in a variety of types, many of which are not appropriate for seismic or wind loading conditions. End-grain nailing performs poorly and should be avoided; and toenailing as the sole means of attachment is inadequate.

Positive connections using appropriate fasteners are necessary to establish a continuous load path. Shear walls must be fastened securely to the foundation. Diaphragms should be properly attached to the lateral force-resisting system. Connector design and detailing should include proper use of connectors to achieve required load capacity and code compliance. Adequate size and placing of nails is necessary to minimize splitting and to optimize the load-carrying capability of the frame.

ANCHORS

Anchors are either cast-in-place or drilled after placement of the concrete. When anchors can be precisely located before the concrete is poured, cast-in-place anchors are typically used. Postinstalled anchors are usually employed when anchor locations cannot be predetermined with accuracy.

Spacing between anchors, the distance to the edge of the concrete, embedment depth, stiffness characteristics, and the type of loading (e.g., dead, live, dynamic, seismic) all must be considered. For structural elements that require seismic design, only anchors tested under dynamic loading should be used.

The preferred anchor types for seismic performance include cast-in-place bolts and inserts. Acceptable postinstalled anchors are undercut anchors, heavy-duty sleeve (torque-controlled expansion) anchors, and chemical anchors. J-bolts and L-bolts are unreliable for uplift resistance.

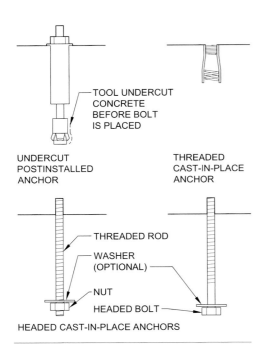

TOOL UNDERCUT
CONCRETE
BEFORE BOLT
IS PLACED

UNDERCUT
POSTINSTALLED
ANCHOR

THREADED
CAST-IN-PLACE
ANCHOR

THREADED ROD
WASHER
(OPTIONAL)
NUT
HEADED BOLT

HEADED CAST-IN-PLACE ANCHORS

ANCHORS

METAL CHANNEL
FASTENED TO
STRUCTURE ABOVE
PERMITS PARTITION
TO SLIDE AT TOP BUT
RESTRAINS IT FROM
LATERAL MOVEMENT

SEALANT REQUIRED
FOR ACOUSTIC
ISOLATION

METAL OR WOOD STUD

FASTEN BASE TO
STRUCTURE

PARTITION DETAIL FOR SEISMIC AREAS

SEISMIC REHABILITATION

Seismic rehabilitation (or *seismic retrofit*) refers to improving the seismic performance of existing buildings designed under early seismic codes or before such codes were introduced.

A number of typical building types have been identified as hazardous because of their generally poor performance in earthquakes:

URMS: This refers to bearing wall buildings with unreinforced masonry walls—URMS—usually brick.

Nonductile concrete frame: Typical of buildings constructed in the United States before about 1975, when new codes came into effect that recognized the problems caused by underreinforced concrete frame structures subject to brittle failure.

Concrete or steel frame with unreinforced masonry walls (often hollow tile): Popular for buildings constructed in the early twentieth century.

Precast concrete tilt-up construction: Common industrial building type that relies on the exterior concrete walls to act as shear walls against earthquake forces. Unless correctly detailed, the roofs may pull away from the walls and collapse.

Although the unique characteristics of each building must be considered when devising a rehabilitation strategy, some fundamental concepts have been developed from experience. They are: add strength; alter building stiffness; create structural continuity; add structural containment; rationalize existing capacity; isolate the building from the ground; add energy-dissipating details.

HVAC, ELECTRICAL, AND PLUMBING COMPONENTS

HVAC equipment is often heavy, with large inertial forces; therefore, securely attaching such equipment greatly reduces damage. Piping systems and ductwork generally perform well during seismic activity but are vulnerable at equipment connections. Bracing should be provided for larger piping, larger ductwork, and hazardous piping (such as gas lines) to prevent sway.

Heavy electrical equipment such as switchgear, transformers, and batteries are the parts of the electrical system most vulnerable to seismic activity. Emergency systems depend on electrical power for fuel or control and so may fail even though the equipment remains functional.

Plumbing distribution systems are relatively flexible and can withstand a fair amount of shaking. Piping and equipment should be anchored so it will move with the structure, limiting differential movement at the joints.

ELEVATORS

Traction elevators cause the most concern in regard to seismic activity. The main problem is that the counterweights may come loose and strike the cab. Current elevator standards address this problem, but older elevators may need to be upgraded.

SPRINKLER SYSTEMS

To brace sprinkler systems, designers must address three main problems: the falling hazard of heavy mains, separation of the mains at the joints (property loss is critical here), and breaking of the pipes where the heads pass through the ceiling. The latter problem is solved by enlarging the hole (with up to 1 in. (25 mm) clearance) and covering it with a large escutcheon plate. An alternative is to detail a swing joint in the sprinkler drop that will provide 1 in. (25 mm) movement in all directions. Another solution is to detail the grid and sprinkler drops as a single integral unit. (See NFPA 13, *Standard for the Installation of Sprinkler Systems,* for information on sprinkler bracing.)

WATER HEATERS

When a water heater overturns, a gas line can rupture. Depending on the level of seismicity, the common solution for residential water heaters is to use a flexible gas connection and/or a simple steel strap wrapped around the tank and securely anchored to a stud or solid wall.

FLEXIBLE
WATER
CONNECTIONS

STRUCTURAL
WALL
MAMBER

1/4" X 3"
LAG OR
EXPANSION
BOLT

2'-6"
MAXIMUM

4" +/- DISTANCE
FROM WALL

FLEXIBLE GAS
CONNECTION

3/4" X 24-GA.
PLUMBER'S TAPE

Fill space between water heater and wall with 2x blocking with cushioned face.

WATER HEATER SEISMIC REINFORCING

LIGHT FIXTURES

Suspend the light fixture from the structure above with two to four wires (if two wires, they should be in opposite corners), or brace the ceiling and clip the light fixtures to the grid (not used in areas with high seismicity). Pendant-mounted fixtures should not be able to swing into other building components.

12-GA. WIRES AT EACH CORNER OR AT LEAST AT DIAGONALLY OPPOSITE CORNERS; ANCHOR WIRE TO STRUCTURE ABOVE (MINIMUM THREE TIGHT TURNS IN 1 1/2" AT EACH END OF WIRE)

LAY-IN-LIGHT FIXTURE

LIGHTING FIXTURE DETAIL FOR SEISMIC AREAS

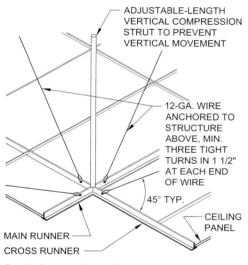

ADJUSTABLE-LENGTH VERTICAL COMPRESSION STRUT TO PREVENT VERTICAL MOVEMENT

12-GA. WIRE ANCHORED TO STRUCTURE ABOVE, MIN. THREE TIGHT TURNS IN 1 1/2" AT EACH END OF WIRE

45° TYP.

CEILING PANEL

MAIN RUNNER

CROSS RUNNER

Provide four-way diagonal bracing and struts approximately every 12 ft (3.6 m) each way.

STIFF SPACER, OR OTHER SUITABLE SYSTEM, TO KEEP PERIMETER COMPONENTS FROM SPREADING APART

WALL ANGLE

CEILING GRID

3/8" FOR LOW TO MODERATE SEISMIC, (3/4" FOR HIGH SEISMIC)

7/8" FOR LOW TO MODERATE SEISMIC, (2" FOR HIGH SEISMIC)

WALL ATTACHMENT DETAIL
Refer to the Ceilings and Interior Systems Construction Association standards.

CEILING DETAILS FOR SEISMIC AREAS

FURNITURE

Furniture located in buildings in seismic areas should be reviewed for potential hazards during the occurrence of seismic activity.

Heavy or large units with drawers or doors should be attached to the walls, if possible, to minimize movement of the furniture. Some codes require furniture with drawers (such as filing cabinets) to be weighted to prevent overturning. Furniture should not be placed where seismic activity may cause the furniture to block exit paths.

SHELVING AND CABINETS

Shelves and racks can slide and/or overturn during seismic activity, injuring building occupants or blocking exits. The hazard increases with the occupancy

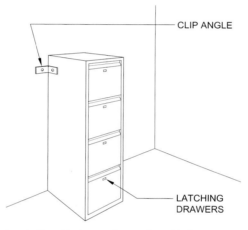

CLIP ANGLE

LATCHING DRAWERS

Locate file cabinets away from exits and hallways.

FILE CABINETS WITH CLIP ANGLE

METAL ANGLE WITH BOLTS

SHEET METAL SCREWS

If lockers or cabinets cannot be anchored, locate away from exits, hallways, and doors.

LOCKERS

density and the height of the equipment. The center of gravity of a fixture (for example, cabinet, shelf unit, or partial height partition) rises with the height of the unit, thus increasing the possibility of overturning in an earthquake. Fixtures should be bolted onto heavy-gauge studs above their center of gravity.

Jane Clark, AIA; Zimmer Gunsul Frasca Partnership; Seattle, Washington
Dan Fenton, PE; EQE International; Seattle, Washington
Edgar Glock; Masonry Institute of St. Louis; St. Louis, Missouri
David S. Collins, FAIA; American Forest and Paper; Cincinnati, Ohio
William W. Stewart, FAIA; Stewart-Schaberg Architects; Clayton, Missouri

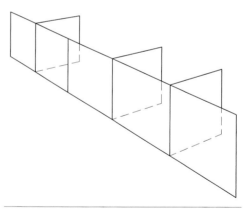

HIGH SHELVING NOT RECOMMENDED

SINGLE PARTITION

ANCHOR TO FLOOR

SINGLE PARTITION

T-SHAPED PARTITION ARRANGEMENT

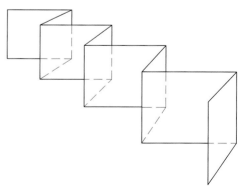

To ensure multiple partition stability, arrange in a zigzag or T-shaped pattern.

ZIGZAG PARTITION ARRANGEMENT

LIFE SAFETY CONSIDERATIONS   □   1

ATRIUM SMOKE MANAGEMENT

REGULATION

Atrium smoke management is regulated by building codes. Currently, most codes prescribe atria smoke protection that is based on the zone fire model concept. Consult with a fire and smoke consultant and mechanical engineer to review project conditions relating to atrium smoke management.

TERMINOLOGY

Smoke control is reserved for systems that provide smoke protection by use of pressurization, such as a pressurized stairwell.

Smoke management refers to systems that use any technique, including compartmentalization, pressurization, airflow, and buoyancy of hot smoke. Using this terminology, atrium exhaust systems are smoke management systems because they rely upon the buoyancy of hot smoke.

For smoke management purposes, smoke consists of the airborne products of combustion plus the air that is mixed with them. The airborne products are combustion gases, solid, and liquid particulates. The smoke being generated, exhausted, or vented is actually air mixed with relatively small quantities of particulates and combustion gases. Because the concentrations of these other quantities are relatively small, engineering design analysis for these smoke management systems considers the specific heat, gas constant, and other properties of smoke to be the same as those of air.

An atrium can be considered a large space of two or more stories. Other large open spaces include enclosed shopping malls, arcades, sports arenas, exhibition halls, and airplane hangers. The term *atrium* is used in a generic sense to mean any of these large spaces.

ZONE FIRE MODEL CONCEPT

All conventional approaches to atrium smoke management are based on the zone fire model concept. Zone fire models were originally developed for room fires. In a room fire, hot gases rise above the fire, and these gases form a plume. The plume entrains air so the diameter and mass flow rate of the plume increase with elevation. Accordingly, the plume temperature decreases with elevation. The fire gases of the plume flow upward and form a hot stratified layer under the ceiling. Hot gases in this smoke layer can flow through openings in walls to other spaces; such flow is referred to as a *doorjet*. The doorjet is similar to a plume in that air is entrained with similar effects on mass flow and temperature.

The concept of zone modeling is an idealization of room fire conditions. For this idealization, the temperature of the hot upper layer of the room is uniform, as is the temperature of the lower layer. The height of the discontinuity between the two layers is the same everywhere in the room. The dynamic effects on pressure are considered negligible, so that pressure is treated as hydrostatic. Other properties are considered uniform for each layer.

Some computer zone fire models allow exhaust from the upper layer, and this capability is essential for simulation of atrium smoke exhaust systems. Many zone fire models estimate heat transfer by methods ranging from a simple allowance as a fraction of the heat release of the fire to more complicated simulation of conduction, convection, and radiation.

ROOM FIRE

ZONE MODEL IDEALIZATION

ATRIUM FIRE

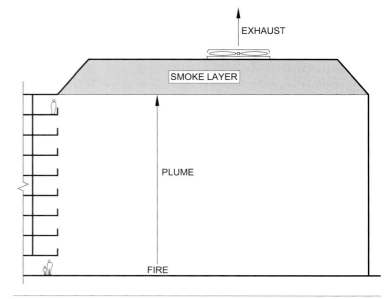

ZONE MODEL IDEALIZATION OF ATRIUM FIRE

AXISYMMETRIC PLUME MODELS

Axisymmetric plume models analyze the time-averaged flow of plumes. For a height above the plume source, the air entrained at the plume edge is considered to be proportional to some characteristic velocity of the plume at that height. The plume is determined to be coming from a *point source* that may be either above or below the surface of the fuel.

The mass flow of a plume depends on the height and heat release rate. The plume temperature decreases with elevation. This temperature drop is dramatic, and the concern with sprinkler performance for high ceiling spaces becomes apparent.

BALCONY SPILL PLUMES

National Fire Protection Association (NFPA) standard NFPA 92B *Guide for Smoke Management Systems in Malls, Atria, and Large* Areas refers to balcony spill plumes and window plumes. A balcony spill plume can be from any size fire, such that smoke flows under a balcony ceiling and into an atrium; a window plume is from a post-flashover fire, such that the smoke flows from the fire room through an opening to an atrium.

The balcony spill plume condition only applies when there is a doorway lintel between the fire room and the balcony. This lintel must be enough below the ceiling so that the momentum of the ceiling jet in the fire room does not directly contribute to the flow out the opening. A ceiling jet consisting of smoke flowing radially under the ceiling forms where a fire plume impacts the ceiling. The depth of the ceiling jet is about 10% to 20% of the height from the base of the fire to the ceiling.

For narrow balconies, smoke can curl inward toward the structure and move into portions of any balconies above. Experiments have shown that such inward-curling smoke can occur for balconies less than 2 m (6.6 ft) wide.

WINDOW PLUMES

A window plume is generated from a post-flashover fire. A post-flashover fire is one in which every object in the fire room that can burn is burning. The heat release rate of a post-flashover fire depends on the amount of air available for combustion, and the airflow into the room depends on the size and shape of the opening. Because of the common use of sprinklers, consideration of window plumes generally is reserved for unusual designs.

SMOKE MANAGEMENT SYSTEMS

Three types of smoke management systems can be designed for a steady fire or an unsteady fire:

- Fan-powered smoke exhaust
- Smoke filling
- Gravity venting

The three system types are based on the objective of preventing smoke from contacting occupants. An alternative objective is a system designed to provide tenable conditions even when smoke comes into contact with people.

SECTION VIEW

BALCONY SPILL PLUME

FRONT VIEW WITH DRAFT CURTAINS

FRONT VIEW WITHOUT DRAFT CURTAINS

Smoke Exhaust

Smoke can be exhausted near the top of an atrium through the use of exhaust fans to prevent smoke contact with occupants during evacuation. There are two approaches to design of smoke exhaust systems:

- Size the smoke exhaust to maintain a constant clear height.
- Size the smoke exhaust so that a descending smoke layer does not contact occupants during evacuation.

Smoke Filling

While smoke exhaust is probably the most common form of atrium smoke management in the United States, some atriums are of such size that no smoke exhaust is needed to keep the occupants from contacting smoke throughout a fire evacuation. This form of smoke management is called *smoke filling* and requires no exhaust capabilities.

Without smoke exhaust, the smoke layer that forms under the ceiling grows thicker, and the bottom of that smoke layer drops downward. The time it takes for the smoke to drop to a level that is above the heads of all the people in the atrium during a fire evacuation can be calculated. If this smoke-filling time is greater than the evacuation time, smoke filling is a viable form of smoke protection.

Gravity Venting

In the United Kingdom and Australia, smoke exhaust is achieved through a *gravity venting* system. In the United States, fan-powered smoke exhaust is used. This natural gravity venting method consists of opening vents in the atrium ceiling or high on the atrium walls to let the smoke flow out without the aid of fans. The flow rate through a gravity vent depends on the size of the vent, depth of the smoke layer, and the temperature of the smoke. When smoke is detected, all the vents need to be opened at one time. Thermally activated vents like those often used for industrial heat and smoke venting are inappropriate for gravity venting of atria, because of the time delay in opening the vents.

The applicability of gravity venting depends primarily on the size of the atrium, outside design temperatures, and wind conditions. Gravity venting is simpler and less costly than fan-powered exhausting. Because loss of power is common during fire situations, there is a significant advantage to a smoke management system that requires no power for fans.

Make-Up Air for Smoke Exhaust Systems

For smoke exhaust systems and gravity venting systems, air must be supplied to the atrium to make up for the smoke exhaust. Make-up air is essential for all smoke exhaust systems and gravity venting systems. Make-up air can be either fan-powered or nonpowered.

Velocity Limit

There is a concern that air velocity could disrupt the structure of the plume, resulting in failure of the smoke management system. The best current information available is that a velocity of 1 m/s (200 fpm) or less will not cause such disruption. For this reason, NFPA 92B indicates that velocities should not exceed 1 m/s (200 fpm) in the atrium where there could be a plume. This applies to any air velocity, whether it is for make-up air or for some other purpose.

OCCUPANT EVACUATION FACTOR

People movement calculations are used to determine the evacuation time for a space. When a fire alarm sounds, most people have a tendency to wait to see if there really is a fire or to see if conditions are threatening. This decision time needs to be factored in any calculation of evacuation time.

STRATIFICATION AND DETECTION

Often a hot layer of air forms under the ceiling of an atrium, the result of solar radiation on the atrium roof. The temperature of such layers may be in excess of 120°F (50°C). When the temperature of the smoke plume is less than that of the hot-air layer, the smoke cannot reach the ceiling. In this situation, the smoke cannot activate ceiling-mounted smoke detectors.

Beam smoke detectors can be used to overcome this detection difficulty, and the proposed NFPA 92B describes three methods of using beam detectors for this purpose. Two of the methods employ horizontal beams with the intent of either detecting the smoke layer or detecting the plume.

The third method uses upward-angled beams with the intent of detecting the development of a smoke layer at whatever stratification conditions exist. In this third approach, one or more beams are aimed at an upward angle to intersect the smoke layer regardless of the level of smoke stratification. For redundancy, when using this approach, more than one beam smoke detector is recommended.

NUMBER OF EXHAUST INLETS

When the smoke layer depth below an exhaust inlet is relatively shallow, a high exhaust rate can lead to entrainment of cold air from the clear layer. This phenomenon is called plugholing. To prevent plugholing, more than one exhaust inlet point may be needed.

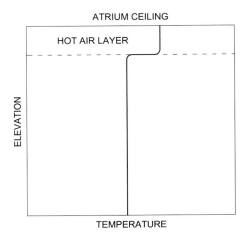

Hot layer of air under atrium ceiling and the resulting temperature profile.

HOT-AIR LAYER

Separation between Inlets

When the exhaust at an inlet is near this maximum flow rate, adequate separation between exhaust inlets must be maintained to minimize interaction between the flows near the inlets.

Smoke Layer Depth

The depth of the ceiling jet is about 10% to 20% of the height from the base of the fire to the ceiling. The proposed NFPA 92B clearly indicates that the smoke layer must be designed to be deep enough to allow for this ceiling jet.

ATYPICAL SITUATIONS

Due to the variety and complexity of building atria, situations may occur when the standard calculations for smoke management systems are not applicable. Scale modeling and computational fluid dynamics (CFD) may be used to determine the most appropriate method of smoke management.

SUMMARY

For some atria, a smoke-filling system can be built that eliminates the need for atrium exhaust.

There are many types of fire plumes; two of the most common for atrium design are axisymmetric plumes and balcony spill plumes. Window plumes are from post-flashover fires in rooms, and are less common for atrium design.

The plugholing of fresh air into the smoke exhaust has the potential of exposing occupants to smoke, and a method of preventing plugholing has been developed.

In the United Kingdom and Australia, gravity venting is often used where fan-powered smoke exhaust would be used in the United States. This approach has some advantages, and it could gain a level of acceptance in the this country.

A hot-air layer under an atrium ceiling can prevent activation of ceiling-mounted smoke detectors. Beam smoke detectors can be used to overcome this problem.

Scale modeling and computational fluid dynamics (CFD) can be used when the usual design equations for atria smoke management are not appropriate due to project conditions.

Review project conditions with a fire and smoke consultant and the mechanical engineer to determine smoke exhaust requirements.

John H. Klote; John H. Klote, Inc.; McLean, Virginia

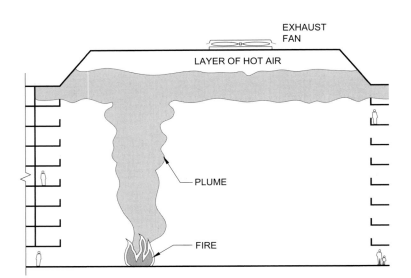

Stratified smoke in an atrium with a hot layer of air under the ceiling.

STRATIFIED SMOKE

Plugholing of air into smoke exhaust inlets can result in failure of a smoke exhaust system.

PLUGHOLING

HAZARDOUS MATERIALS

Asbestos, lead-based paint, and polychlorinated biphenyls (PCBs) are the hazardous materials commonly encountered in interior renovations.

ASBESTOS

Asbestos is a mineral that is mined from the ground like iron or copper. Asbestos comes in many varieties, the most common in the United States being chrysotile. Less common are amosite, crocidolite, and others. Unlike most minerals that turn to dust when crushed, asbestos breaks down into tiny fibers, often too small to be seen by the human eye.

Health Hazards Associated with Asbestos Exposure

Asbestos is a known human carcinogen and represents the greatest threat when inhaled. Risk of contracting an asbestos-related disease is directly dependent upon exposure. Ingestion can also cause problems, but the consequences for this type of exposure have not been clearly documented. The greatest risk to the public occurs during building renovation or demolition, when visible emissions or airborne asbestos fibers are released and proper containment and abatement (which means to reduce, not remove) procedures are not followed.

According to the Environmental Protection Agency (EPA), while some people exposed to asbestos develop asbestos-related health problems, others do not. Once inhaled, asbestos fibers can easily penetrate body tissues. Their microscopic size and inertness to acid are what make asbestos fibers a carcinogen. And because asbestos fibers remain in the body, each exposure increases the likelihood of developing an asbestos-related disease. Cigarette smoking has the symbiotic effect of increasing the likelihood of developing an asbestos-related disease by as much as 90 times. Asbestos-related disease may not appear until years after exposure.

"Safe" or threshold levels for exposure to airborne asbestos have not been established. However, current standards for workers, under Occupational Safety & Health Administration (OSHA), set 0.1 f/cc (fibers per cubic centimeter) as a Permissible Exposure Level (PEL). Federal and state standards for clearance air testing following a nonschool asbestos abatement project are 10 times higher, or 0.01 f/cc.

Illnesses associated with asbestos exposure include asbestosis, a serious, chronic, noncancerous respiratory disease; mesothelioma, a rare form of cancer, directly linked to asbestos exposure, which attacks the thin membrane lining of the lungs, chest, abdomen, or (rarely) the heart; lung cancer, which is responsible for the greatest number of asbestos-related deaths; and other cancers, including cancer of the esophagus, larynx, oral cavity, stomach, colon, and kidney.

Asbestos in Commercial Interiors

It is highly likely that asbestos is present in commercial, industrial, and institutional buildings built before 1978. Asbestos has been incorporated into more than 3,000 different products for a variety of reasons. It has been used for fireproofing, thermal insulation, acoustic control, moisture control, and a variety of decorative purposes. Asbestos is strong, flexible, and has high tensile strength; it is incombustible, inert to acids, and has high corrosion and friction resistance; it is a good insulator and a poor conductor of electricity.

Asbestos-containing material (ACM) falls into three categories:

- *Thermal system insulation* (TSI), such as pipe lagging, tank and boiler insulation, or duct insulation and building insulation.
- *Surfacing material*, such as spray fireproofing, acoustic plaster, and decorative plaster. Surfacing material by definition has been applied by trowel or spray-on application.
- *Miscellaneous material*, such as floor tile, resilient sheet goods, cloth, paint, ceiling tile, mastics, roofing, siding, cement board, wallboard, spackle, caulking compound, glazing putty, laboratory countertops, window stools, chalkboards, building papers, and ceramic tile grout.

The EPA banned the spray application of asbestos in 1973. Most other uses of asbestos in construction, such as in the manufacturing of vinyl floor tile, have been voluntarily ceased by U.S. manufacturers. However, some ACMs, such as mastics, plumbing pipe, and siding, are available in the United States and in other countries.

Asbestos Regulation

Owners and operators of facilities being renovated or demolished are required to test for asbestos, and to notify appropriate federal and state agencies, before work starts. The EPA National Emissions Standards for Hazardous Air Pollutants (NESHAP) is a strict liability standard.

Federal Regulations under EPA, OSHA, and state laws require that suspect ACMs be sampled and analyzed prior to being disturbed. The EPA NESHAP is part of the Clean Air Act, and requires that all suspect ACM be assumed positive for asbestos unless proven otherwise in all structures except for private residences and apartment buildings with four or fewer units. State laws require the asbestos inspector to be specially trained and licensed and that the lab engaged in the material analysis be accredited. The EPA requires a procedure called Polarized Light Microscopy (PLM) to determine if the suspect ACM contains asbestos and, if so, the amount of asbestos in the sample.

Federal and state regulations expressly forbid the grinding, drilling, sawing, crushing, or sanding of ACM. Operations such as renovation or demolition, which would cause the release of asbestos fibers, are not allowed.

Removal and Disposal of Asbestos

There are no federal or state regulations requiring the removal of ACM in good condition. However, if the ACM is being disturbed, appropriate abatement measures must be taken to remove, encapsulate, or enclose the ACM, or place it under appropriate operations and maintenance procedures. A 10-day written notice to federal and state regulatory agencies is required before asbestos abatement can commence.

The EPA advises that ACM greater than 1% be regulated with reference to removal and disposal. OSHA sets the PEL of 0.1 f/cc as the allowable amount of asbestos fiber in the air of a worker without personal protection equipment (PPE), such as a respirator. Friable (crushable by hand pressure) ACM requires special handling. Pipe lagging (insulation) or spray-applied acoustical ceilings (sometimes referred to as "popcorn" ceilings) would be considered friable, whereas floor tile and cement asbestos board in good condition would not. OSHA requires that all suspect TSI and surfacing materials be Presumed Asbestos-Containing Material (PACM) until proven otherwise.

Federal regulations require work sites to be sealed, workers to wear PPE suited for the task, specific work practices to be followed to protect the workers and the public, and monitors to inspect the work and declare the work site and the air clean at the completion of the abatement activities. Federal and state regulations typically require that the ACMs and asbestos-contaminated materials, such as personal protection suits and polyethylene used during the construction of containments, be transported off-site to a licensed waste disposal site for burial. The regulations for the waste disposal site are set forth in the NESHAP standards.

PERSONAL PROTECTION EQUIPMENT (PPE)

Exhaust duct is vented to a window. Arrows denote direction of airflow. Circled numbers indicate progression of removal sequence.

NEGATIVE PRESSURE SYSTEMS FOR THE REMOVAL OF ASBESTOS

LIFE SAFETY CONSIDERATIONS ☐ 1

LEAD AND LEAD-BASED PAINT

Lead occurs as an element in nature and is naturally bluish in color. It is mined from the ground, and historically was recovered as a by-product of silver smelting. Once lead has been mined and processed, it is a potential threat to human health. No known or foreseeable technology will destroy or render lead harmless.

Health Hazards Associated with Lead Exposure

Unlike iron, there is no biological need for lead in the body. Lead is a heavy metal and is a poison, like arsenic or cadmium. Too much lead in the body can cause damage to vital organs such as the kidneys, red blood cells, the central nervous system, and the brain. High levels of lead can cause retardation, convulsions, coma, and sometimes death. Children absorb a higher percentage of lead than do adults. Lead can be absorbed through the gastrointestinal tract (eating) and through the lungs (inhalation); the organic forms (for example, leaded gasoline) can be absorbed through the skin. Lead poisoning among children is normally through ingestion. Lead poisoning among adults is normally due to occupational exposure through inhalation.

Lead in Commercial Interiors

Lead is most commonly found in building exterior and plumbing components, where it has been formed into sheets and pipes. It is especially common in roofing, cornices, flashing, waterproofing pans, and solder. In the past, in building interiors, lead was often used as an additive to paint. As much as 50% of the content of enamel paint used through the mid-twentieth century was white lead.

Testing for Lead-Based Paint

There are several ways to test for lead paint; the most common is with an X-ray fluorescence gun. This method calculates the amount of lead on the component in micrograms per square centimeter. Other methods include lab testing of paint chips and chemical testing.

Lead Regulation

Different states have different lead regulations, but all states have them. In addition:

- *The Federal 1992 OSHA Title X Worker Protection Act* applies to all types of renovation and demolition projects, not just residential properties with children under the age of seven. Residential properties with children must have all painted surfaces intact. Mouthable surfaces must have the lead paint removed, covered, or encapsulated.
- *The OSHA Lead in Construction Standard, Title X,* mandates that airborne lead exposure in the breathing zone of a worker be limited to less than 50 micrograms per cubic meter.
- *The EPA Disposal Regulations and Toxic Substances Control Act (TOSCA)* is also applicable to renovation work where lead paint is located. Lead is classified under TOSCA as a hazardous material.

The amount of lead on the surface of a component being removed or disturbed is not as great a threat as the amount of lead in the air. Prior to performing renovation work, all surfaces should be tested for lead

paint. The federal standard for lead removal in facilities with children present (for example, a day care center or an apartment building) is 1.0 micrograms per square centimeter. Almost by definition, the renovation projects of existing spaces will involve the demolition or cutting or drilling of components that may contain lead paint, and thereby release lead dust.

Disposal of lead paint debris can be expensive, depending upon the percentage of lead in the waste stream. The Federal Resource Conservation Recovery Act (RCRA) allows lead paint debris to be disposed in a landfill, if the amount of lead is less than five parts per million. Percentage of lead is determined by doing representative samples of the waste stream and analyzing it using the Toxicity Characteristic Leaching Procedure (TCLP).

One of the most successful environmental efforts undertaken in recent years was to ban the use of leaded gas in automobiles. This federal effort has yielded dramatic results in lowering the blood lead level of children, especially inner-city youth. Also, the amount of lead in paint was restricted by federal regulation in 1976. Today, all paint found in housing built before 1980 must be considered lead-based and be tested before being disturbed. The same guidelines should be applied to any interiors project that disturbs painted surfaces, for the protection of the workers, owners, owners' employees, or visitors. If a project contaminates the work area, adjacent spaces, or the exterior with lead dust, the liability issues can be significant.

Polychlorinated Biphenyls (PCBs)

PCBs belong to a broad family of chemicals known as *chlorinated hydrocarbons*. PCBs range in consistency from heavy oily liquids to waxy solids. Prior to 1979, PCBs were widely used in electrical equipment, such as transformers, capacitors, switches, and voltage regulators, for their cooling properties because they do not readily burn or conduct electricity and boil only at high temperature. PCBs commonly have the appearance and texture of tar.

Health Hazards Associated with PCBs

PCBs released into the environment do not easily break apart. They persist for many years and bioaccumulate and bioconcentrate in organisms such as fish. Laboratory data shows PCBs to be carcinogenic to animals, and the EPA considers PCBs to be possible human carcinogens. Exposure to PCBs can cause chloracne (a painful disfiguring skin ailment), liver damage, nausea, dizziness, eye irritation, and bronchitis. Liver damage can occur from dermal contact and inhalation, not just from ingestion. Most PCBs are readily absorbed through the skin.

PCBs in Commercial Interiors

Fluorescent light ballasts are typically composed of a transformer (to reduce the incoming voltage), a small capacitor (which may contain PCBs), and possibly a thermal cut-off switch and/or safety fuse. In the past, these components were commonly surrounded by a PCB for sound-deadening purposes. All ballasts manufactured since 1978 that do not contain PCBs should be marked by the manufacturer with the statement "No PCBs." A ballast will contain approximately 1 to 1½ ounces of PCB in the capacitor itself. Additionally, fluorescent light fixtures and HID lamps contain mercury

and other metals that should be recycled, rather than disposed of in landfills. Transformers that contain PCBs are liquid-cooled, and normally are located in a vault.

Leaking oils from equipment should be reported immediately to the building owner. If fluorescent light ballasts are found leaking, the EPA recommends turning off the light fixture and vacating and ventilating the room. Since PCBs are readily absorbed through the skin, wear rubber gloves that will not absorb PCBs. Cleanup should be performed by appropriately trained persons.

PCB Regulation

The EPA regulates PCBs through the TOSCA regulations, which control the use, marking, storage, records, and disposal of PCBs.

Removal of PCBs

Arrangements may be made with various PCB transporters for shipment of ballasts, PCB-soiled items, or fluorescent fixtures containing PCBs to an EPA-approved chemical waste processing site.

Common Asbestos-Containing Materials Found in Buildings

Acoustical plaster
Adhesives
Asphalt floor tile
Blown-in insulation
Cement asbestos pipes, siding, shingles, wallboard
Ceramic tile-setting beds and mastic
Construction mastics (floor tile, ceiling tile, carpeting, paneling, etc.)
Ceiling tiles and lay-in panels
Cooling towers
Chalkboards
Caulking and putties
Decorative plaster
Ductwork insulation
Ductwork-flexible collars
Electrical panels
Elevator brake shoes
Flooring backing
Fire door cores
Fireproofing on steel
Gypsum wallboard
Heating and electrical ducts
Joint compound
Laboratory hoods and tabletops
Window stools
Mortar
Pipe insulation
Plaster
Roofing materials
Waterproofing and dampproofing materials
Spray-applied insulation
Spackling compound
Thermal paper products
Taping compounds
Textiles
Textured paints and coatings
Resilient floor tile and base
Resilient sheet flooring
Vinyl wallcovering

Peter Blaisdell, AIA, SFPE, NAA; Kendall, Taylor and Company; Billerica, Massachusetts

WOOD ROOF TRUSS AND WOOD FLOOR TRUSS

Legend
A: Shingles and roofing felt with metal flashing
B: Wood roof truss and plywood sheathing
C: Acoustical tile
D: Wood frame
E: Batt insulation
F: Gypsum board
G: Wood floor truss and plywood subfloor
H: Ducts and diffusers
I: Lapped wood siding
J: Window assembly
K: Slab on grade, concrete masonry foundation wall, and concrete footing
L: Carpet
M: Below-slab perimeter ducts

STRUCTURAL

In this example, a standard wood framing system is employed with prefabricated roof and floor trusses and exterior sheathing. The trusses are built at the factory to engineering specifications. The exterior panels act in concert with wall studs as a structural skin and weathering surface. The wood frame system unifies envelope and structure when this external skin acts as a diaphragm over the studs, joists, and rafters. Because trusses are made from commonly available dimension lumber, there is little chance that supply shortages will delay projects.

Bridging between floor trusses may be eliminated, depending on the depth of the truss and the application and rigidity of subflooring and ceiling finishes. When such bridging is used, it should not block possible transverse duct runs. Most floor truss systems allow for a continuous-edge ribbon at the truss ends in lieu of a header. Before truss units are lifted into place, it is wise to inspect them for uniformity of depth and camber and for general tightness. If substantial field-work is contemplated, it may be desirable to use plywood I-trusses, which can be cut to length and drilled to allow threading of pipes and wires.

Envelope

Wood components treated with fire retardants can now be used in many applications for which untreated wood is unsuitable. Some fire-retarding treatments may discolor wood, accelerate corrosion of metal fasteners, or alter the structural properties of the wood. For example, plywood can become delaminated, a particularly difficult problem when the plywood sheathing itself acts as the exterior finish surface.

Mechanical

Open web trusses allow threading of wiring, piping, and ductwork without on-site drilling or cutting, thus greatly speeding and easing the installation of heating, plumbing, and electrical systems.

Interior

The open web wood trusses permit longer clear spans than conventional timber framing, leaving greater flexibility for the location of interior partition walls that need not be load-bearing.

WOOD ROOF TRUSS AND WOOD FLOOR TRUSS

SYSTEM SUMMARY

Prefabricated roof and floor trusses eliminate much field labor, thus speeding on-site construction; help ensure dimensional stability; and may eliminate the need for intermediate load-bearing partitions. Longer clear spans are possible with floor trusses than with generally available dimension lumber, and recent advances in manufacturing techniques make it possible to specify many special features. Open web trusses are lighter in weight than dimension lumber and can be lifted easily in gangs by a small crane or lift. Trusses are available in standard configurations 12 to 24 in. (305 to 610 mm) deep; they allow threading of mechanical systems without cutting the members, which speeds installation. The smaller wood components used in these trusses are more readily available, from sustainable forests, as opposed to the older-growth trees harvested for larger standard lumber sections.

Richard J. Vitullo, AIA; Oak Leaf Studio; Crownsville, Maryland
Based on Richard D. Rush, AIA, The Building Systems
    Integration Handbook *(John Wiley & Sons, 1986).*

LAMINATED WOOD POST AND BEAM

Legend
A: Rigid conduits run through decking
B: Standing seam roof, roofing felt, and rigid insulation
C: Plywood sheathing and wood roof, tongue-and-groove wood decking
D: Ducts, supply and return system
E: Incandescent light fixtures
F: Window assembly
G: Wood siding
H: Heavy glued laminated wood beams
I: Carpeting
J: Exposed wood frame and plywood sheathing
K: Wood stud framing
L: Drywall
M: Clay tile flooring
N: Slab on grade and concrete foundation
O: Vapor barrier under slab

STRUCTURAL

Heavy glued and laminated beams and columns, which define the interior of the building, make up the frame in this example. The roof structure is laminated tongue-and-groove decking, nominally 2¼ in. (50 mm) thick, laid over the beams.

Considerable flexibility is available in selecting structural modules and bay sizes in heavy timber construction by varying the depth of beams and increasing the thickness of decking to span between beams. Columns are frequently overdesigned to give an appropriate appearance. If sized only to carry the loads transferred from above, they may appear too spindly in proportion to other framing elements.

Glued laminated beams, columns, and decking are generally preferred over dimensioned sawcut lumber because appearance is easier to specify and ensure. A variety of custom shapes, sizes, and presawn joints can be obtained in glued laminated pieces, and they are drier and more resistant to twisting, checking, and shrinkage. All pieces should remain factory-wrapped until in place and out of the weather, as rain and snow will stain them.

Envelope

Lower portions of perimeter walls are framed conventionally with wood studs between main timber columns; a vapor barrier is placed toward the occupied side, and the voids are filled with batt or rigid insulation. The exterior is sheathed in plywood and finished with diagonal wood siding. The roof deck is covered with a moisture barrier and insulated on top with rigid insulation board between sleepers. A standing seam metal roof is applied over the sleepers, which also provide diagonal bracing.

Mechanical

Space heating and cooling is provided by air supply-and-return ducts. Kitchens, lavatories, and other areas requiring both odor removal equipment and greater amounts of fresh air are separated by walls and covered by suspended or furred ceilings.

Interior

The underside of the laminated tongue-and-groove decking is exposed to interior view and should be specified for appearance grade.

LAMINATED WOOD POST AND BEAM

SYSTEM SUMMARY

Although used historically for larger buildings, post-and-beam construction is now generally confined to buildings of three stories or fewer. Its main advantages are simplicity of elements and details, combined with the potential for visual integration and bold structural and architectural forms.

Structure and interior are unified in post-and-beam construction. Because the structural elements in this system are exposed to view, as are portions of the mechanical system, care is required in the visual integration of these components and in the design and appearance of hardware used to join the wood members. Certain parts of the mechanical system can be concealed within interior partitions and exterior walls. The sizing of structural members and joinery details may be influenced more by considerations of visual proportion and appearance than strictly by the loading and stress conditions involved.

Source: Based on Richard D. Rush, AIA, The Building Systems Integration Handbook *(John Wiley & Sons, 1986).*

LIGHTWEIGHT STEEL FRAME AND BRICK VENEER

Legend

A: Ridge flashing
B: Shingles and roofing felt
C: Metal roof frame (C-stud brace, C-rafter, C-channel, C-joist)
D: Ducts with diffusers
E: Suspended acoustical tile
F: Gypsum board
G: Brick veneer
H: Window assembly
I: Carpet
J: Ceramic floor tile
K: Batt insulation
L: Metal floor frame (C-joist), steel deck, and concrete topping
M: C-stud assembly, wiring threaded through wall assembly
N: Resilient floor tile
O: Dampproofing
P: Slab on grade with concrete foundation

STRUCTURAL

The lightweight cold-formed steel members are load-bearing, and beams, columns, channels, headers, and other elements can be built up from standard steel shapes and sections. The frame's rigidity depends on crossbracing, the distance from exterior corner to exterior corner, and the type and layout of fasteners used. Sheathing both sides of the frame also provides some lateral stability. Steel studs used for masonry backup should be crossbraced with steel straps. Horizontal and diagonal bracing increase the frame's rigidity. Welded connections are stronger than self-tapping screws. The method of attachment can affect costs substantially. The positioning and types of fasteners for affixing both interior and exterior sheathing should be carefully specified, because these factors significantly affect lateral stability.

Cold-rolled steel framing is detailed and fastened quite differently from wood framing, so special noncarpentry tools and equipment are required. Advantages of cold-formed steel framing include its light weight, dimensional stability, speed and ease of assembly, resistance to moisture and decay, and, in some cases, readier availability than wood framing members. Also, steel framing members are frequently made from recycled scrap and can be endlessly recycled.

Envelope

Deflection in lightweight steel frame construction can be several times greater than deflection in exterior masonry veneer; such differentials must be accommodated in anchoring details, or overcome by adding structural rigidity to the wall frame. The masonry ties that anchor the veneer to the steel frame should permit free and independent movement of the two materials. Where the veneer depends on the steel frame for lateral stability, anchors should be flexible and should not resist shear; wire ties that allow independent movement are recommended. The framing design and method of fastening windows and doors should account for the differences in movement. In general, fenestration components should be attached to either the framing or the veneer, but not attached rigidly to both. When filled with batt insulation and fully sheathed, the lightweight steel frame wall is thermally isolated from the single wythe of masonry veneer. This

LIGHTWEIGHT STEEL FRAME AND BRICK VENEER

results in greater differential thermal movement in the veneer than would occur with solid double-wythe masonry construction; the interior heat is not transferred as readily to the exterior masonry.

Mechanical

Prepunched holes in the studs provide easy routing of plumbing and electrical lines. Most codes require the use of electrical conduit or sheathing of the prepunched stud opening to avoid stripping the insulation as wires are drawn through.

Interior

Interior gypsum board, along with exterior sheathing, applied to steel studs provides additional lateral bracing.

SYSTEM SUMMARY

Lightweight steel frame-bearing wall construction is often used in low-rise commercial and residential buildings. The long-term performance of lightweight steel framing in structures over three stories is a con-

cern. To date, its use in medium- and high-rise buildings has been mainly for exterior partitions or as nonbearing backup for exterior veneers.

Speed of construction, noncombustibility, and relative light weight are key advantages of this system. The space between studs eases insulation and accommodates piping and electrical distribution. Because the framing can be completed independent of the masonry veneer, the interior is out of the weather quickly and can be finished while the exterior brick veneer is laid. In nonresidential construction, which is likely to have fewer bracing walls and longer vertical spans and horizontal runs, added cold-formed bridging or bracing to the frame increases lateral stability. This can also be accomplished by decreasing the stud spacing or increasing the stud gauge.

*Richard J. Vitullo, AIA; Oak Leaf Studio; Crownsville, Maryland
Based on Richard D. Rush, AIA,* The Building Systems Integration Handbook *(John Wiley & Sons, 1986).*

STEEL BAR JOIST WITH BEARING WALL

Legend
A: Rooftop mechanical unit
B: Built-up roofing and rigid insulation
C: Steel decking and open-web steel joists
D: Exterior insulation and finish system (EIFS)
E: Suspended acoustical tile, sprinkler system suspended from structure in ceiling plenum
F: Fluorescent light fixture in ceiling
G: Ductwork
H: Concrete masonry bearing wall and concrete footing
I: Glazed interior face on concrete masonry unit (CMU)
K: Canopy assembly
J: Resilient tile
L: Vapor barrier and dampproofing
M: Slab on grade
N: Window assembly

STRUCTURAL

Bearing wall and bar joist roof building systems employ masonry walls bearing on a turndown slab on grade or conventional spread footings. The walls support a roof structure of open-web steel bar joists, through which mechanical distribution systems are threaded. Spans for J- and H-series open-web joists generally may not exceed more than 20 times the joist depth, or more than 50 to 60 ft (15 to 18 m). Long-span joists are available, as are a wide variety of special shapes. By their nature, open-web joists spaced at even intervals are best suited to relatively light, uniform loads; joists may be doubled or tripled to accommodate heavier, concentrated loads or may be combined with other steel framing for roof openings and rooftop mechanical equipment. The roof deck may be precast concrete plank, tongue-and-groove wood decking, or, more commonly, steel decking. Small openings in the roof area can be framed between joists by means of specially designed headers.

In buildings with masonry bearing walls, each joist should be anchored to the masonry by means of a joist anchor embedded in the masonry. Steel joists can be designed to cantilever beyond the edges of the bearing walls. Continuous horizontal bracing of both top and bottom joist chords is possible with spot-welded connections at each joist and with the ends of the bracing members anchored to a bearing wall; this type of system is well suited to seismic risk zones.

Envelope

The concrete masonry unit (CMU)-bearing walls are insulated on the exterior to take better advantage of the wall's thermal mass by placing it toward the occupied side. Long-span open-web steel joist roofs can deflect substantially, and the camber of the joists alone is often not sufficient to maintain the necessary slope to roof drains.

Interior

Suspended interior ceilings are nearly always preferred to directly attached interior ceilings. Finished ceilings attached directly to the bottom joist chord are not only difficult to alter but must be designed to accommodate the high degree of deflection the roof assembly will experience.

STEEL BAR JOIST WITH BEARING WALL

Mechanical

If ductwork is to be housed within the depth of the joist, headers or branches must be fed through the joist webs, perpendicular to the spanning direction.

SYSTEM SUMMARY

Steel open-web joist and bearing wall construction yields buildings that have relatively large interior clear spans and flexible interior layouts. The open webbing of the joist provides a lightweight structure that is easily penetrated by mechanical systems. The bottom chords of the joists are used for suspension of interior finishes, lighting fixtures, and air diffusers in finished areas, although they may be left uncovered. Masonry bearing walls and metal joist roofs are among the simplest and easiest to design and build. The relatively low cost of the system makes it attractive for speculative projects,

as does the fact that contractors find this construction method familiar and easy to erect. Retail commercial facilities often require flexibility in lighting, partitioning, and mechanical systems and large expanses of column- and wall-free space; the envelope and structural systems chosen often reflect these demands.

The height to which masonry bearing walls can be built without resorting to lateral bracing is limited, so they are used most frequently in one-story structures. Roof spans up to 60 ft (18 m) can generally be accommodated. The spacing and depth of joists is related to the spanning capability of the roof decking material and the requirements for loads on the roof structure.

Richard J. Vitullo, AIA; Oak Leaf Studio; Crownsville, Maryland
Based on Richard D. Rush, AIA, The Building Systems Integration Handbook *(John Wiley & Sons, 1986).*

STEEL FRAME WITH CURTAIN WALL

Legend

A: Steel decking welded to frame
B: Built-up roofing or single-ply membrane on rigid insulation
C: Suspended acoustical tile
D: Ducts, with diffusers, either suspended from structure in ceiling plenum or placed in floor plenum beneath access floor
E: Curtain wall units
F: Steel with welded and bolted connections
G: Fluorescent light fixture in ceiling
H: Electrical wires and cables placed in structural/electrified floor
I: Insulated spandrel panels
J: Gypsum wallboard
K: Systems furniture
L: Carpeted access floor system
M: Steel decking welded to primary frame members, with cast-in-place concrete topping
N: Waterproofing and protective board with foundation drain
O: Slab on grade with concrete foundation
P: Vapor barrier under slab

STRUCTURAL

Core shear walls add rigidity to frame; composite action of structural steel framing and a steel and concrete floor diaphragm result in relatively long, uninterrupted clear spans with smaller depth of construction. Heights can range from 1 to more than 100 stories. System allows for off-site fabrication of frame components, easy shipping to site, and rapid assembly. The corrugated steel deck becomes a working surface as soon as it is placed and provides formwork for concrete topping.

Envelope

The envelope is structurally independent of the steel frame, providing flexibility in weight, size, and configuration of the envelope system. Curtain wall units preassembled at the factory must be designed with shipping, storage, installation, and general handling in mind, emphasizing protection from damage at all stages.

Mechanical

Mechanical systems, hidden in floor or ceiling plenums or both, can be accessed through removable panels in ceiling or floor systems.

Interior

Suspended ceiling provides space for distribution of internal services, but it tends to be used principally for overhead lighting and ductwork. Structural/electrified floors and access floor systems keep all wires and cables in the space below the finish floor, which are easily accessible by removing floor panels. This allows for a high degree of flexibility for the interior environment. Buildup of static electricity and the ensuing risk of equipment damage and shocks must be considered. Access floors are not suited to situations involving heavy point loads or shifting heavy equipment. Stringerless systems are among the most flexible and least costly varieties, but they lack the stability of fully gridded systems and depend on perimeter walls for restraint. Use of access floors to create an air plenum, requiring tight and uniform joints between access panels, may hinder access to wires, cables, and pipes; ductwork in floor plenums may

STEEL FRAME WITH CURTAIN WALL AND ACCESS FLOOR

eliminate the advantages of access floors by blocking the path for wiring, cables, and pipes.

SYSTEM SUMMARY

Steel frame and curtain wall construction allows for off-site fabrication of frame and envelope components, easy shipping to the site, and rapid assembly at the site. The steel and concrete in the floors are designed to act as a composite diaphragm, providing a thin, lightweight structural element with or without an access floor. The access floor is advantageous in office environments that need especially flexible interior layouts. This system keeps all wires and cables in the space below the finish floor (generally not less than 4 in. (100 mm) deep) and out of wall cavities. Although access floors may add to overall floor-to-floor heights, the access floor conceals the most visually obtrusive distribution elements.

Richard J. Vitullo, AIA; Oak Leaf Studio; Crownsville, Maryland
Based on Richard D. Rush, AIA, The Building Systems Integration Handbook (John Wiley & Sons, 1986).

STAGGERED STEEL TRUSS

Legend

A: Rigid insulation under single-ply roofing and ballast

B: Ducts, with diffusers, and sprinkler system; underside of concrete planks, either painted or covered with acoustical ceiling tile

C: Precast hollow-core concrete plank deck

D: Staggered story-high steel trusses

E: Tile

F: Gypsum board

G: Window assembly

H: Precast shear panels

I: Steel columns

J: Conduit fed through vertical chases in outer walls

K: Joints at floor planks grouted; tops carpeted

L: Precast exterior wall panels that support floor slabs on both top and bottom chords

M: Slab on grade with concrete foundation

N: Vapor barrier and waterproofing with protective board

O: Precast stiffener beams

STRUCTURAL

This system is best suited to multiunit residential or hotel buildings of 7 to 30 stories with repetitive floor plans. Floor-height Pratt trusses are placed atop every other column in a staggered pattern, strengthening the structural system while reducing overall weight; precast hollow-core concrete planks serve as the floor without a topping slab, allowing for bays of approximately 60 x 60 ft (18 x 18 m) (twice the truss spacing). A fire-resistant membrane, such as drywall, is usually added to each side of a truss to provide protection; these walls also serve to divide individual units. Lower floors in this system can be finished and trimmed while upper-level structural members are still being laid; the structure becomes rigid as soon as the precast exterior wall panels and the outer concrete deck elements have been installed.

Envelope

Precast concrete wall members act as an envelope system as well as a structural system.

Mechanical

Because the Pratt-type trusses extend from floor to ceiling, with openings for corridors and elevator doors only, horizontal running of pipes, wiring, and ductwork can be difficult. For this reason, separate unit-by-unit heating and air-conditioning systems are often preferable. Also, unitary HVAC systems offer economic and maintenance advantages in multifamily residential construction. Utilities are typically fed upward through chases and risers on outer walls, with service or supply units placed to either side on each floor; end-wall stair enclosures are also used for this purpose. Most sprinkler systems are laid out in this fashion as well.

Interior

The smooth surface of concrete deck planks can provide interior ceiling finishes, if desired.

STAGGERED STEEL TRUSS

SYSTEM SUMMARY

Staggered truss construction is most often used for double-loaded residential-type occupancies, including hotels, high-rise apartments, nursing homes, and hospitals. Such building types usually have highly repetitive floor plans and can benefit from systems that integrate objectives regarding structure, interior unit separations, fire compartmentalization, and acoustical privacy. The system is not generally considered economical for low-rise buildings due to the manufacturing costs of the jigs for the trusses and the forms for the spandrel precasting. The system easily allows for long structural bays, permitting a high degree of flexibility in unit interiors. The ground floor is free of trusses and interior columns and thus is suitable for parking or retail commercial use. The system's light weight reduces foundation size.

Richard J. Vitullo, AIA; Oak Leaf Studio; Crownsville, Maryland Based on Richard D. Rush, AIA, The Building Systems Integration Handbook (John Wiley & Sons, 1986).

SPACE FRAME

Legend
A: Built-up roofing and rigid insulation
B: Space frame and metal deck
C: Ducts suspended from hubs of the frame
D: Light fixtures
E: Glass block panel
F: Concrete masonry unit (CMU) bearing wall
G: Brick veneer and rigid insulation
H: Wood flooring
I: Slab on grade and concrete foundation
J: Vapor barrier

STRUCTURAL

Space frames serve as both structural and interior systems, while providing a structure for envelope connections and space for meshing of mechanical distribution elements. A metal deck and built-up roof cover the space frame shown. Space frames may appear in horizontal, vertical, domed, vaulted, stepped, sloped, or tower configurations. In this example, the edges of the space frame are glazed to permit perimeter clerestory lighting of interior areas. Tubular high-strength extruded aluminum struts are joined by means of solid aluminum hubs, also designed to accommodate the hardware for fastening of clerestory glazing.

Space frames are commonly used as atrium covers; they have also been used as structures for entire building envelopes. In perimeter-supported applications, truss depth-to-span ratios of up to 1:30 are practical. In addition to their light weight and economy of materials, space frames have the quality-control advantages of factory production.

Envelope

Structure and envelope are connected in this example, with the exposed nature of the space frame requiring a high degree of visible integration between the frame's structural components and parts of the mechanical system.

Mechanical

Because the space frame is a highly regular structure and is exposed to view in most applications, the coordination of service systems with patterns in the frame is essential for visible integration. Piping can be suspended from the hubs of the frame and should correspond to the patterns of the frame. Fireproofing of space frames generally destroys their appearance, so sprinkling is usually a consideration unless the exposed frame is 20 ft (6 m) or more above floor level.

Interior

The ceiling unifies interior and structural systems and meshes them with unified mechanical and interior systems. The solid hubs in the frame serve to join the struts and can also accommodate mountings for the envelope system and various types of interior equipment.

SYSTEM SUMMARY

The triangulated space frame network is one of the strongest and most efficient structural configurations, permitting long column-free spans. Slender structural members make space frames advantageous where high light permeability is sought, yet where significant live structural loading may also occur. Typical applications include spans above entries, sports arenas, and convention centers.

SPACE FRAME

Based on Richard D. Rush, AIA, The Building Systems Integration Handbook, *John Wiley & Sons, Inc., 1986.*

STEEL FRAME SYSTEMS

The most commonly used framing systems for steel construction include open-web steel joists, rigid frames, framed tubes, braced cores, space frames, and moment-resisting frames.

OPEN-WEB STEEL JOISTS

Open-web steel joists are usually covered by 2½ to 3 in. (60 to 75 mm) of concrete on steel decking. Concrete thickness may be increased to accommodate electrical conduit or electrical/communications raceways. Precast concrete, gypsum planks, or plywood can also be used for the floor system.

SECTION THROUGH JOIST BEARING

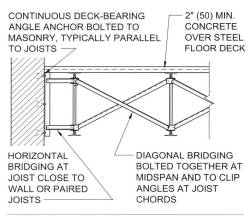

SECTION THROUGH LONG-SPAN STEEL JOISTS

SECTION THROUGH STEEL JOIST

Ceiling supports can be suspended from or mounted directly to the bottom chords of joists, although suspended systems are recommended because of dimensional variations in actual joist depths.

RIGID FRAME

Rigid frame construction combines columns and a beam or girder welded together to make a rigid connection. Such a frame can carry vertical loads and resist horizontal forces, either wind or seismic. Rigid frame buildings are usually single-story. The roofs are generally sloped, usually at least 1 in 12.

RIGID STEEL FRAME

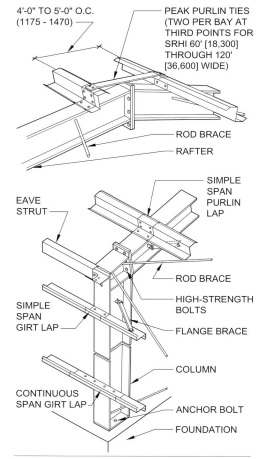

RIGID STEEL FRAME DETAILS

Because they span fairly long distances relatively cheaply (widths range between 30 and 130 ft (9 and 39 m)), rigid frame structures are used for recreational buildings; warehouses; light industrial buildings; and commercial buildings, such as supermarkets, automobile dealer showrooms, and garages. Bay sizes are usually 20 to 24 ft (6 to 7 m) but may be extended to 30 ft (9 m). The roof profile is most often configured as a symmetrical gable, but such a profile is not a structural necessity. Some manufacturers offer precast concrete and masonry siding. Preengineered buildings most often use rigid frames for roof and wall supports.

FRAMED TUBE

In the framed tube system, structural steel members form the load-bearing exterior perimeter wall; this wall is designed so the entire building becomes, in effect, a structural steel tube. The tubular strength is achieved in two ways: the exterior columns are spaced closely together (perhaps 6 ft (2 m) on center) and connected to spandrel beams, and the structure is stiffened by the floors to form a torsionally rigid tube. The spandrel beams are generally very deep, in units of feet as opposed to inches. The columns and spandrel beams are welded together to create a moment-resisting connection. Often this system is referred to as a pierced tube, the pierced areas being the window openings.

The framed tube system is most economical for very tall buildings. The World Trade Center Towers in New York were framed tube construction. The Sears Tower in Chicago is the most conspicuous existing example of this construction system. Systems like that at the Sears Tower, a combination of nine framed tubes in a 3 × 3 array, are sometimes called *bundled tubes*.

FRAMED STEEL TUBE

PERIMETER FRAMED TUBE WALL DETAIL

BRACED CORE

In the braced core system, walls around elevator shafts and stairwells are designed to act as vertical trusses that cantilever up from the foundation. The chords of each truss are building columns; the floor beams act as ties. Diagonals placed in a K-pattern (occasionally in an X-pattern) complete the truss. A system employing knee braces is used in seismic areas because of its greater capability to dissipate earthquake energy. Braced core systems can be used efficiently in single-story buildings as well as in buildings over 50 stories.

SPACE FRAMES

A space frame is a three-dimensional truss with linear members that form a series of triangulated polyhedrons. It can be seen as a plane of constant depth that can sustain fairly long spans and varied configurations of shape. The prime attributes of space frame structural systems are their light weight; inherent rigidity; their wide variety of form, size, and span; and compatible interaction with other building support systems,

primarily HVAC. Most systems are designed for specific applications, and a structural engineer with space frame experience should always be consulted. Manufacturers can provide the full range of capabilities—loading, spans, shapes, specific details—for their products. Standardized systems in 4- and 5-ft (1,220 and 1,525 mm) modules are available.

Metal space frames are classified as noncombustible construction and can usually be exposed when 20 ft (6 m) above the floor. However, an automatic fire-extinguishing system or a fire-rated ceiling may be required.

Moment-Resisting Frame

A moment-resisting frame's lateral stability and resistance to wind and seismic forces depend on a fixed connection of beams and columns. A moment-resisting connection is achieved when the top and bottom flanges of each beam are welded to the flanges of the connecting columns with full-depth welds. By directly welding the beam web to the column flange, the beam's horizontal reaction to wind forces is transferred to the column. (A connection using web angles and

high-strength bolts is also permitted.) The building's floors are designed to act as diaphragms that connect all of the columns and beams, enabling the building to react as a unit.

Moment-resisting frames are uneconomical in tall steel buildings because the larger lateral forces in such buildings can be handled more efficiently by diagonal members, as found in braced frames. To save costs, often the upper stories of a braced frame building use moment-resisting beam-column connections to resist wind loads.

Donald J. Neubauer, P.E.; Neubauer-Sohn, Consulting Engineers; Potomac, Maryland
Richard J. Vitullo, AIA; Oak Leaf Studio; Crownsville, Maryland

BRACED CORE

SPACE FRAME SUPPORT TYPES

MOMENT-RESISTING STEEL FRAME

BRACED CORE DETAILS

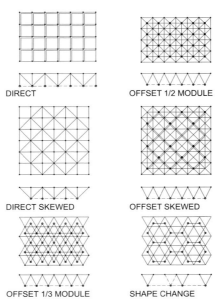

COMMON SPACE FRAME PATTERNS

Many proprietary systems are available for specific applications and budgets.

MOMENT-RESISTING STEEL DETAILS

CONCRETE FLOOR SYSTEMS

A flat plate is best for moderate spans because it is the most economical floor system and has the lowest structural thickness. Penetrations for piping and ductwork through the slab near columns must be avoided. Spandrel beams may be necessary.

Advantages: Inexpensive formwork; ceilings may be exposed; minimum slab thickness; fast erection; and flexible column location.

Disadvantages: Excess concrete for longer spans; low shear capacity; greater deflections.

Appropriate Building Types: Hotels, motels, dormitories, condominiums, and hospitals.

FLAT PLATE

A banded slab has most of the advantages of a flat plate, but permits a longer span in one direction. It can resist greater lateral loads in the direction of the beams.

Advantages: Longer spans; typically posttensioned; minimum slab thickness.

Disadvantages: Must reuse formwork many times to be economical.

Appropriate Building Types: High-rise buildings; same use as flat plates if flying forms can be used more than 10 times.

BANDED SLAB

DROP PANEL DIMENSIONS: 1/16 OF SPAN FOR EACH DIRECTION

OPTIONAL COLUMN DESIGN

Flat slabs are most commonly used today for buildings supporting very heavy loads. When live loads exceed 150 psf (7,182 Pa), flat slabs are by far the most economical.

Advantages: Economical for design loads greater than 150 psf (7,182 Pa).

Disadvantages: Formwork is costly.

Appropriate Building Types: Warehouses, industrial structures, parking structures.

FLAT SLAB

This is the best scheme if slabs are too long for a flat plate and the structure is not exposed. The slab thickness between joints is determined by the fire requirements. Joists are most economical if beams are the same depth as the joists.

Advantages: Minimum concrete and steel; minimum weight, thus reduced column and footing size; long spans in one direction; accommodates poke-through electrical systems.

Disadvantages: Unattractive for an exposed ceiling; formwork may cost more than flat plate.

Appropriate Building Types: Schools, offices, churches, hospitals, public and institutional buildings, buildings with moderate loadings and spans.

JOIST SLAB

Russell S. Fling, P.E.; Consulting Engineer; Columbus, Ohio Based on Richard D. Rush, AIA, The Building Systems Integration Handbook, *John Wiley & Sons, Inc., 1986.*

For large projects, a skip joist slab should be less expensive than a joist slab, and it permits lights and equipment to be recessed between joists.

Advantages: Uses less concrete than joist slab; incurs lower steel rebar placing costs; joist space is used for mechanical systems; permits lights and equipment to be recessed between joists.

Disadvantages: Similar to joist slab; joists must be designed as beams; forms may require special order.

Appropriate Building Types: Same as for joist slabs; especially for longer fire ratings.

SKIP JOIST

This scheme is most favored for parking garages, but the long span of about 60 ft (18 m) must be prestressed unless beams are quite deep. Shallow beams will deflect excessively.

Advantages: Long span in one direction.

Disadvantages: Beams interfere with mechanical services; more expensive forms than flat plate.

Appropriate Building Types: Parking garages, especially with posttensioning.

ONE-WAY BEAM AND SLAB

Column spacing should be multiples of pan spacing to ensure uniformity of drop panels at each column. Drop panels can be diamond-shaped, square, or rectangular.

Advantages: Longer two-way spans; exposed ceiling pattern; heavy load capacity.

Disadvantages: Formwork costs more and uses more concrete and steel than a joist slab.

Appropriate Building Types: Prominent buildings with exposed ceiling structure; same types as are suitable for flat slab, but with longer spans.

WAFFLE SLAB

The high cost of formwork and structural interference with mechanical systems make this scheme unattractive unless heavy concentrated loads must be carried.

Advantages: Long span in two directions; small deflection; can carry concentrated loads.

Disadvantages: Same as for one-way beams, only more so.

Appropriate Building Types: Portions of buildings in which two-way beam framing is needed for other reasons; industrial buildings with heavy concentrated loads.

TWO-WAY SLAB AND BEAM

Russell S. Fling, P.E.; Consulting Engineer; Columbus, Ohio
Based on Richard D. Rush, AIA, The Building Systems
   Integration Handbook, *John Wiley & Sons, Inc., 1986.*

FLAT-PLATE CONCRETE

Legend

A: Elevator equipment in penthouse
B: Rigid insulation and ballast
C: Protected roof membrane
D: Window assembly
E: Cast-in-place concrete flat plate
F: Suspended acoustical tile
G: Ducts with diffusers suspended from structure in ceiling plenum
H: Power and communication supplied to furniture by overhead poles or under carpet flat cable
I: Batt insulation
J: Gypsum board and metal stud assembly
K: Cast-in-place concrete column
L: Carpeting
M: Precast concrete spandrel panels
N: Slab on grade and concrete pile foundation
O: Waterproofing and protective board at foundation, with vapor barrier under slab

STRUCTURAL

Combines cast-in-place concrete columns with two-way concrete slab plates of uniform thickness. Two-way flat-plate concrete floors are among the simplest concrete structures for reinforcing, formwork, and detailing. Exterior precast concrete plates can be attached on lower floors, even with flat-plate shoring still in place, while concrete is being poured for upper-floor columns and plates. When crane hoists are used to lift concrete buckets or large equipment, a hole is generally left in a section of each plate to allow for passage of the hoist; this hole is filled later, when large components have been moved and concrete pouring is complete.

Flat-plate concrete construction permits more stories to be fitted into a given building height than any other system. This is because its floor structure has minimum thickness, especially when posttensioned. In addition, in many building types the underside of the floor plate can serve as the finish ceiling.

Envelope

Exterior precast concrete panels can be attached on lower floors, even with flat-plate shoring still in place, while concrete is being poured for upper-floor columns and plates. Window-framing elements and glazing are installed after the spandrels have been set.

Mechanical

Centralized core permits relatively uniform, short horizontal runs for power, plumbing, lighting, and other systems.

Interior

Workstations in unpartitioned interior offices can be serviced unobtrusively by ceiling height power and communications poles, in furred-out areas around columns, and in corridor partition walls. Office workstations require daylight exposure and views. Because the central core is farthest from perimeter zones, usable floor area in the perimeter can be maximized. On constrained urban sites, the central core may be moved against an unfenestrated wall and still retain this advantage.

SYSTEM SUMMARY

The drawing "Flat-Plate Concrete" combines cast-in-place columns and two-way concrete flat plates of uniform thickness, with precast concrete spandrel

FLAT-PLATE CONCRETE

panels. The system usually has a central core for vertical circulation and services, and it is typically employed for low- to medium-rise construction because of the costs and difficulties associated with placement of materials and labor in higher buildings. The central core also permits consolidation of vertical service risers, increasing fire protection by reducing or eliminating through-floor penetrations in office areas.

Flat-plate concrete construction is especially applicable to apartments, hotels, and dormitories, in which no suspended ceiling is required. Story height can be minimized in these applications by using the undersides of the slabs as finish ceiling.

Richard J. Vitullo, AIA; Oak Leaf Studio; Crownsville, Maryland
Based on Richard D. Rush, AIA, The Building Systems Integration Handbook *(John Wiley & Sons, 1986).*

POSTTENSIONED CONCRETE

Legend

A: Built-up roofing or single-ply membrane on rigid insulation
B: Concrete slab with reinforcing steel bars
C: Ducts, with diffusers, suspended from structure in ceiling plenum
D: Fluorescent light fixture in ceiling
E: Suspended acoustical tile ceilings
F: Resilient floor
G: Operable partitions
H: Metal stud and gypsum wallboard assembly
I: Window assembly
J: Concrete
K: Brick and concrete masonry with rigid insulation
L: Slab on grade and concrete foundation
M: Vapor barrier under slab
N: Waterproofing and protective board at foundation

STRUCTURAL

Posttensioning is a highly sensitive integration of the compressive strength of concrete with the tensile strength of steel. Plastic-sheathed, high-strength steel tendons are cast in the slab and, after curing, are placed in the tubes, anchored, and jacked into tension from one end. After stresses are applied, the tendon channels may be grouted to bond the tendons to the slab. For lengths greater than 100 ft (30 m), stresses must be applied simultaneously from two ends. Integration of mechanical services is influenced greatly by the positioning of tendons, which controls the locations of through-slab penetrations. Posttensioning permits the use of shallower beams and slabs, reducing overall building height and permitting longer spans with thinner structural members. The structure is quite rigid and less subject to movement and creep, allowing use of masonry infill envelope. Alterations and demolition can be difficult due to potential forces latent in posttensioned tendons.

Envelope

The building skin rests on the concrete frame by means of steel shelf angles attached to spandrel beams.

Mechanical

Mechanical systems hidden in ceiling plenums can be accessed through removable panels. This system is optimal for additions to hospitals and other medical facilities, which often require floor-to-floor heights that match those of the existing structure. Although contemporary standards for servicing and mechanical equipment require deeper interstitial spaces than are found in many older buildings, the shallower slabs and beams of posttensioned concrete construction can conserve such space.

Interior

A suspended ceiling provides space for distribution of internal services but tends to be used only for overhead lighting and ductwork.

SYSTEM SUMMARY

Posttensioned concrete construction is virtually identical to flat-plate concrete construction. The major difference lies in the thickness of the concrete slab, which is slightly reduced in this type of construction.

Posttensioning is a method of reinforcing concrete by stretching steel-reinforcing tendons after placement and

POSTTENSIONED CONCRETE

curing of the concrete structure. This prestressing reduces or eliminates tensile stresses on the concrete under use loading and strengthens the slab without increasing its thickness or adding the dead loads introduced by additional steel-reinforcing rods. Posttensioning is useful when slab thickness is important to economical or functional design aspects or when concentrated live loads are high and the building height must be kept to a minimum. It is also effective when project conditions require minimal floor-to-floor heights but maximum ceiling heights with generous space above the ceilings.

Richard J. Vitullo, AIA; Oak Leaf Studio; Crownsville, Maryland Based on Richard D. Rush, AIA, The Building Systems Integration Handbook (John Wiley & Sons, 1986).

PRECAST CONCRETE FRAME

Legend
A: Concrete topping as floor finish
B: Prestressed precast concrete double-T
C: Fluorescent light fixtures attached to structure
D: Prestressed precast concrete columns and span-
  drel beams
E: Cast-in-place concrete vertical circulation
F: Slab on grade, with cast-in-place concrete piles
G: Elevator equipment for hydraulic elevator

STRUCTURAL

This system is most commonly used for parking garages. Double-T joists are generally 8 or 12 ft (2 or 3.5 m) wide, at a depth of 18 to 36 in. (460 to 915 mm), depending on the spanning requirements. Spans of 60 ft (18 m) are considered maximum, due to the constraints of shipping and lifting the pieces, but longer spans and deeper sections are possible. It is advantageous to use as many similar elements as possible; that is, floors, inverted T-girders, and columns should all be of the same length and design. Off-site precasting can conserve time and materials for concrete forming, and on-site erection time is considerably faster than for cast-in-place construction. Cast-in-place core provides lateral stability to the frame. Adding final finishes and installation hardware to prestressed components before erection helps reduce on-site construction time. Temporary shoring and bracing may be required during construction, particularly until the toppings have cured to service strength (if the structure is composite). Lifting loops are generally embedded in the precast pieces and then covered with the topping or cut off after installation.

Envelope

For parking garages, the most common application of precast concrete frame, a weathertight condition is not needed; therefore, structural components can be directly exposed to the elements. Some aesthetic treatments can be cast in or applied to surfaces, but are not needed for moisture protection.

Mechanical

In parking structures, the requirements for through-floor penetrations are minimal. However, holes or sleeves can be cast in the stems and flanges of the Ts, to allow for passage of conduit and piping. These holes and openings can be as great as one-third of the stem's total depth but must avoid the reinforcing tendons; openings toward the top of the stem in midspan and toward the bottom at the ends are most common. Preplanning of all openings is essential to minimize sitework and to realize the inherent economies of the system. Ts may be notched at the ends to permit passage of conduit along girders or bearing walls. Also, channels can be formed by chamfering mated edges of adjacent Ts at the upper surface, setting the conduit, then pouring a concrete topping slab.

Interior

Most typical interior elements are not needed because of the open-air nature of the building type; however, all elements provided are attached directly to the exposed structure. In parking garages, the depth of the structural Ts and concerns for minimizing floor-to-ceiling height present special challenges for the integration of lighting and signs.

PRECAST CONCRETE FRAME

SYSTEM SUMMARY

Precast concrete components are usually pretensioned. Pretensioning is a method of prestressing concrete in which steel tendons are stretched prior to placement of concrete and maintained in tension until the concrete is cured. The external tension on the tendons is then released to compress the concrete. This example employs prestressed columns, inverted T-girders, ledger girders, and double-T joists, all of the same length and design. Once the floor and roof Ts are set, the surface is covered with a thin concrete topping that provides the finished, weather-exposed surface and a horizontal structural diaphragm. The precast components are fabricated off-site and lifted into place by crane. Various finished surfaces are possible, and the unity of materials presents an opportunity for natural visible integration of elements. Thin brick or tile can also be used as a surface material.

Richard J. Vitullo, AIA; Oak Leaf Studio; Crownsville, Maryland
Based on Richard D. Rush, AIA, The Building Systems
  Integration Handbook *(John Wiley & Sons, 1986).*

FLYING FORM

Legend
A: Concrete masonry parapet backup
B: Built-up roofing and rigid insulation
C: Concrete
D: Ducts and diffusers
E: Suspended acoustical tile ceiling
F: Fluorescent light fixture
G: Window assembly
H: Metal stud and drywall assembly
I: Carpet tile
J: Under-carpet flat cable
K: Flat plate
L: Precast concrete spandrel panels
M: Slab on grade and concrete
N: Vapor barrier

STRUCTURAL

Flying-form construction requires almost total regularity in structural bay widths. Flying forms can be used to construct flat slabs, pan-joist slabs, waffle slabs, and various types of beams-in-slabs. They are also used to form spandrels of varying configuration. Flat-plate or flat-slab construction is preferred, as this eases movement of the flying-form "table" and minimizes special additional forming. For flying forms to be economical, the building structural layout must be uniform, and the beams and spandrels should be very shallow.

There are three principal types of flying forms: *adjustable postshoring, manufactured truss forms, and column-supported forms.* Adjustable postshoring uses scaffolding that rests on a wood sill and blocking, which is raised by jacks. The forms are moved horizontally, usually by means of rollers, and are generally suitable for pours of up to 40 ft (12 m) in length.

Envelope

As in the case of conventionally cast-in-place flat-plate concrete construction, the structural and mechanical systems are concealed from view, with the precast concrete envelope spandrel and glazing units connected to the structural frame. Flying-form construction, which requires relatively uniform bay widths, can have an effect on visible integration because it produces regularity in the rhythm of structural elements.

Mechanical

In office applications, the high quality of the slab's finished surface lends itself readily to the use of flat wiring for power, lighting, electronics, and communications. Extra fire protection measures are unnecessary, as there are no through-slab penetrations to be sealed.

Interior

Flying-form construction permits great flexibility in interior layouts and furniture arrangements. The use of flat wiring frees the electrical system from restraints imposed by the structure, permitting the furniture layout and power needs to remain variable until very late in the construction process.

SYSTEM SUMMARY

Speed of construction, the economies realized through reuses of the forms, and the high quality of finished surfaces are among the most attractive features of this construction method. The systems employed with flying-form construction do not differ substantially from those found in other types of reinforced concrete con-

FLYING FORM

struction; the difference lies in the method of forming slabs and spandrels and in the sequencing of pours. A disadvantage of the flat-plate construction system is the relative difficulty of punching through the slab or plate. An important consideration with the use of flying forms is the regularity of bay spacing and the absence of deep beams or spandrels.

During construction, the forms are placed and removed in a sequence of related operations, with temporary shoring used after form removal under the slabs until they have cured. The repetitive use of the forms can lead to conservation of both time and, of course, the materials used in forming. Mechanical and interior systems are meshed in the suspended ceiling assembly. The use of flat wiring atop the floor slabs for internal distribution of power, lighting, electronics, and communications dictates the use of removable carpet tiles and yields a set of requirements for interfaces with furnishings and equipment.

Source: Based on Richard D. Rush, AIA, The Building Systems Integration Handbook *(John Wiley & Sons, 1986).*

TILT-UP CONCRETE

Legend
A: Skylights
B: Built-up roofing and rigid insulation
C: Steel deck and open-web steel joists
D: Ductwork in open-web bar joists
E: Radiant heat panels in suspended ceiling
F: Fluorescent light fixture
G: Window assembly
H: Precast concrete panels
I: Resilient tile flooring
J: Slab on grade and concrete footing
K: Rigid insulation

STRUCTURAL

Load-bearing tilt-up wall panels provide a unified vertical envelope, structure, and interior. The panels are precast on-site, generally using the floor slab or grade as the casting surface, and tilted or lifted into position. The floor slab used as a form must be level, smoothly finished, and treated with a bond-breaking agent to permit easy separation of the cast pieces. The wall panels, usually 6 in. (150 mm) in nominal thickness, may extend from one to several stories in height, and must be designed to withstand the bending loads involved in tilting and lifting, as well as loads that will be encountered once in place. They may be plain, reinforced, or prestressed, and are often provided with temporary timber or steel "strongbacks" for tilting, particularly when there are large window openings.

The panels must be braced during construction until all wall and roof structural members are in place. Columns are usually cast in place following installation of the panels. In load-bearing tilt-up wall systems, the roof and floor members are bolted or welded to plates, and angles are cast into a continuous ledge beam. Roofing systems may be steel open-web joists, precast concrete Ts, or hollow-core planks. Flashing reglets and other roofing connection details can be cast with the panels.

Envelope

Joints between panels should be designed to be concealed. This is easily accomplished where cast-in-place columns are designed to lap the panel edges or where the panels insert into a precast column channel.

Mechanical

Because the slab on which the panels are cast must be smooth, utility raceways, pipes, and conduits that will penetrate the slabs must be stubbed below the finish slab level, covered during wall panel casting, and then uncovered for final connections.

Interior

The site-cast panels are the load-bearing elements for the roof members and provide both interior and exterior finish. The building shell can be erected quickly, permitting interior work to proceed along with final joining and sealing of the envelope panels.

The clear spans produced by the bar joist roof structure and option for hung ceiling allow interior partitions to be placed virtually anywhere.

SYSTEM SUMMARY

Tilt-up walls have been used routinely in a variety of building types and heights, especially for single-story buildings with large, uncomplicated exteriors. The sys-

TILT-UP CONCRETE

tem is also increasingly used for multistory low-rise projects. Significant savings in time and formwork costs can be achieved, and long lead times required for precast or structural steel components are often averted. Because most of the forming and erection work is done within the floor slab area, tilt-up systems work well in confined construction sites.

Conservation of time and forming material is realized when there is uniformity in panel design and when the

floor surface can be used for forming. Careful planning of the forming, storage, and lifting sequence is essential, and early consultation with manufacturers and contractors is advisable. Regular inspection of casting and lifting operations is essential.

Based on Richard D. Rush, AIA, The Building Systems Integration Handbook, John Wiley & Sons, Inc., 1986.

PART 2

INTERIOR BUILDING COMPONENTS

Concrete

Masonry

Metals

Expansion Control

Wood

Plastics

Finish Carpentry

Custom Casework

Countertops

Architectural Woodwork

Custom Architectural Woodwork

Thermal and Moisture
  Protection

Fire and Smoke Protection

Doors

Windows

Plaster and Gypsum Board

Tile

Terrazzo

Ceilings

Flooring

Wall Finishes

Paints and Coatings

Visual Display Boards

Compartments and Cubicles

Wall and Corner Guards

Access Floors

Interior Signage

Lockers

Prefabricated Partitions

Toilet and Bath Accessories

Equipment

Fabrics

Task Lighting

Window Treatments

Furniture

Interior Plantings

Special Construction

Fire Suppression Systems

Conveying Systems

Mechanical Systems

Electrical Systems

CONCRETE SUBFLOOR PREPARATION

CONSIDERATIONS

A *subfloor* (the floor to which the finish floor is attached) must be free from oil, grease, wax, old floor finishes, paint, dust, dirt, old adhesives, and other coatings that adversely affect the flooring or the adhesive. Flooring manufacturers must be relied on to specify the requirements for subfloors to ensure the performance of their finish flooring. Typically, the moisture emission rate and the alkalinity level of the slab are of concern.

LEVELING A SUBFLOOR

Depending on the condition of the subfloor, an underlayment may be required before the finish flooring can be installed. An underlayment is used to level the floor and to cover cracks, and is either a board product or a liquid or cementitious compound. Exterior grade plywood is the most commonly used board product underlayment. Particleboard and ceramic tile backerboard are also used, depending on the application, but are not recommended for use under resilient flooring. Leveling compounds smooth subfloor irregularities. These are typically cementitious mixtures and can be trowel-applied or poured on. The poured compounds are referred to as *self-leveling*.

Self-Leveling Underlayments

The two types of self-leveling underlayments are cement-based or gypsum-based.

- *Cement-based underlayments* generally have a higher compressive strength, adhere to concrete substrates better, and have a higher internal strength than gypsum-based products. Higher compressive strengths increase indentation resistance. Increased bonding with substrates accommodates heavier traffic applications. Underlayments may break apart when the bond between the underlayment surface and adhesive-applied finish flooring is greater than the underlayment's internal strength. Cement-based underlayments are less susceptible to the effects of moisture than gypsum-based products.
- *Gypsum-based underlayments* soften when they absorb moisture and may become more brittle after redrying. These underlayments generally weigh less and cost less than cement-based products, but are usually not explicitly recommended by flooring manufacturers.

MOISTURE EMISSION

Moisture is the single greatest cause of adhesive bonding failures. It is a particular problem in new concrete slabs because of the naturally higher moisture content resulting from the curing process. A slab that is laid on or below grade can present a problem because of the natural moisture migration from the earth up through the slab into the building. Flooring manufacturers may require that new slabs cure for a minimum amount of time to reach an acceptable dryness. But even existing above-grade concrete floors can demonstrate unacceptable moisture conditions.

Flooring manufacturers must be relied on to specify the conditions under which moisture tests are con-

ducted, as the temperature can have a significant impact on the validity of the test results. Low temperatures can present inaccurate test data because moisture migration is retarded by the cold. Tests should not be performed on slabs where the temperature is below 50°F (10°C).

To avoid floor-covering failures caused by moisture problems from concrete slabs, subsurface-water migration through slabs on grade must be eliminated, and moisture-vapor transmission through slabs must be minimized. ASTM F710, *Practice for Preparing Concrete Floors to Receive Resilient Flooring*, "Appendix X1," includes specific recommendations for concrete slab design to prevent resilient floor covering failures.

Calcium Chloride Test

A calcium chloride moisture test can be used to determine the moisture emission rate of a concrete slab. A precise determination of the moisture content can be determined according to ASTM F1869, *Test Method for Measuring Moisture Vapor Emission Rate of Concrete Subfloor Using Anhydrous Calcium Chloride*. A clear plastic dish containing calcium chloride, a white powder, is placed under a sealed, clear plastic dome. A small amount of moisture will cause the calcium chloride powder to darken or cake. Larger amounts of moisture will cause drops to form on the powder; and if moisture conditions are severe, the calcium chloride will dissolve. The calcium chloride sample is weighed and compared to the pretest dry weight. A precise measurement is required and is best done in a laboratory by the manufacturers of the test kit or by using a pharmacist's scale. A safe maximum moisture-emission level of 3 to 5 lb of water/1,000 sq ft (1.36 to 2.27 kg of water/92.9 sq m) of slab in a 24-hour period is the accepted range for most resilient floor coverings.

Hygrometer

Another, less precise, method involves the use of a hygrometer, a device that measures relative humidity. The hygrometer is laid on the floor and covered with a

2-ft- (600-mm-) square sheet of clear plastic film. The plastic film is sealed around the edges with a plastic moisture-resistant tape, such as duct tape. The hygrometer measures the moisture being emitted from the slab. A rough estimate of the moisture emission level can be obtained in 15 to 30 minutes. For a more accurate reading, 24 hours is required.

Polyethylene Film Test

The easiest and most practical, but least precise, way to determine whether moisture is a problem is the polyethylene film test, described by ASTM D4263, *Test Method for Indicating Moisture in Concrete by the Plastic Sheet Method*. An 18-in- (450-mm-) square sheet of clear plastic film is sealed to the slab with tape and left for 16 hours. If there is no "sweating" or clouding on the underside of the plastic, then the slab may be considered dry enough by some flooring manufacturers for installation of their finish floor.

ALKALINE LEVEL

Diluted alkaline salts can migrate from a concrete slab to the floor surface. These salts can cause adhesive failures and can be absorbed into the flooring materials. The test for pH levels is relatively quick and inexpensive. pH levels are expressed by a simple numeric scale with values from 0 to 14, indicating how acidic or basic (alkaline) a solution is: 0 represents a very acidic condition, 7 indicates neutrality, and a pH level of more than 7 shows alkalinity. Alkalinity can be determined by wetting the floor slightly and applying pH test paper or litmus paper. The color of the paper will change, indicating the nature of the solution—increasingly blue for rising levels of alkalinity and increasingly pink for rising levels of acidity. A pH range of 6 to 10 is satisfactory. A reading above 10 usually requires corrective measures if adhesives are involved in the flooring installation.

MASTERSPEC®; published by ARCOM; Salt Lake City, Utah, and Alexandria, Virginia

CONCRETE SURFACE TEMPERATURE AT DEWPOINT

RELATIVE HUMIDITY	AIR TEMPERATURE °F (°C)												
	40 (4)	45 (7)	50 (10)	55 (12)	60 (15)	65 (18)	70 (21)	75 (24)	80 (26)	85 (29)	90 (32)	95 (35)	100 (38)
10%	5 (-15)	5 (-15)	6 (-14)	8 (-13)	9 (-13)	10 (-12)	13 (-10)	17 (-8)	20 (-6)	24 (-4)	27 (-3)	30 (-1)	34 (1)
20%	8 (-13)	9 (-13)	13 (-10)	16 (-8)	20 (-6)	24 (-4)	28 (-2)	31 (-.5)	35 (2)	40 (4)	43 (6)	48 (8)	52 (11)
30%	14 (-10)	16 (-8)	21 (-6)	25 (-4)	29 (-1)	33 (0.5)	37 (3)	42(5)	46 (8)	50 (10)	54 (12)	59 (15)	62 (16)
40%	18 (-17)	23 (-5)	27 (-3)	31(-.5)	35 (2)	40 (4)	45 (7)	49 (9)	53 (11)	58 (14)	62 (16)	67 (19)	71 (21)
50%	24 (-4)	28 (-2)	33 (.5)	36 (2)	41 (5)	46 (8)	50 (10)	55 (12)	60 (15)	64 (17)	69 (20)	73 (23)	78 (25)
60%	28 (-2)	32 (0)	36 (2)	41 (5)	46 (8)	51 (10)	55 (12)	60 (15)	65 (18)	69 (20)	74 (23)	79 (26)	83 (28)
70%	31 (-.5)	36 (2)	40 (4)	45 (7)	50 (10)	55 (12)	60 (60)	64 (17)	69 (20)	74 (23)	79 (26)	84 (29)	88 (31)
80%	34 (1)	39 (4)	44 (6)	49 (9)	54 (12)	58 (11)	64 (17)	68 (20)	73 (23)	78 (25)	83 (28)	88 (31)	93 (34)
90%	37 (3)	42 (5)	47 (8)	52 (11)	57 (14)	62 (16)	67 (19)	72 (22)	77 (25)	82 (28)	87 (30)	92 (33)	97 (36)
100%	40 (4)	45 (7)	50 (10)	55 (12)	60 (15)	65 (18)	70 (21)	75 (24)	80 (26)	85 (29)	90 (32)	95 (35)	100 (38)

Dewpoint is the temperature at which humidity in the air begins to condense in and on a substrate. Floor coverings and adhesives should not be installed when the air temperature or concrete subfloor surface temperature is within 5°F (-15°C) above dewpoint.
Source: National Flooring Trends; *Woodland Hills, California*

ARCHITECTURAL CONCRETE

Architectural concrete is a handcrafted, cast-in-place finish material. It differs in composition and quality level from conventional structural concrete. Architectural concrete requires coordination and quality control in the design and fabrication process. It is available in a wide variety of textures, colors, and finishes. Interior applications include walls, stairs, and other areas of monolithic exposed concrete.

Considerations for architectural concrete installations include:

- Alignment and layout of architectural concrete formwork
- Consistency of surface texture
- Consistency in color
- Monolithic appearance without cracks

Consult the American Concrete Institute for architectural concrete design recommendations and information.

ARCHITECTURAL CONCRETE DESIGN

Successful architectural concrete installations rely on the coordination of the designer, engineer, and contractor. Architectural concrete must be fabricated with as much precision as possible, as it is almost impossible to correct once installed. Issues to be considered in the design and fabrication of architectural concrete surfaces include:

- Design of architectural concrete within material fabrication restrictions
- Formwork quality and tighter tolerances on bracing of formwork
- Planned locations for control and construction joints, for function and appearance
- Defined formwork panel layout to determine locations of all joint lines, tie-rod locations, devices, and fastening
- Consistency in concrete mixes and concrete placement, in successive pours
- Finishing of hardened concrete to a consistent desired texture

Design drawings for architectural concrete should show form details, including openings, joints (contraction, construction, and rustication), and other important elements. Specify formwork type and quality, to create the tightness necessary to avoid leakage of the concrete. Specify a field mock-up, to evaluate the appearance of the concrete panel and the quality of workmanship.

The consideration of the actual construction process should also be reviewed in the design process to determine whether the architectural concrete surface can be built without undue difficulty. Economy of fabrication and sequencing of the installation can be reviewed by the contractor. Other factors that affect concrete surfaces are mixing and placing techniques, slump control, curing methods, and release agents.

The three methods of modifying the appearance of a concrete surface finish are:

- *Material variation,* which involves changing the size, shape, texture, and color of the coarse and fine aggregate, particularly in exposed aggregate concrete, and choosing white or gray cement.
- *Form variation,* which involves changing the texture or pattern of the concrete surface by means of form design, form liners, or joint edge treatments.
- *Surface treatment,* which involves treating or tooling the surface after the concrete has cured.

JOINT TYPES

Construction joints occur where concrete work is interrupted during construction, but they do not affect the structural integrity of the system.

Form joints occur where formwork joins or meets.

Control joints are placed to ensure that the concrete, which shrinks as it cures, will crack in predetermined locations. A number of factors influence the location of cracks, including the size and shape of the concrete member, steel reinforcement, and protection as the concrete cures. Members longer than 10 or 15 ft (3 or 4.5 m) will crack randomly unless control joints are provided.

EXPOSURE METHODS FOR ARCHITECTURAL CONCRETE SURFACES

METHOD	FINISH EFFECT	COLOR SOURCE	FORM SURFACE	CRITICAL DETAILS
As cast	Remains as-is after form removal; usually exhibits board marks or wood grain.	Cement first influence; fine aggregate second influence	Smooth and textured	Slump: 2½–3½ in. (64–89 mm) Joinery of forms Proper release agent Point-form joints to avoid marks
ABRASIVE BLASTED SURFACES				
Brush blast	Uniform scour cleaning	Cement and fine aggregate have equal influence.	All smooth	Scouring after seven days Slump: 2½–3½ in. (64–89 mm)
Light blast	Blasted to expose fine and some coarse aggregate (sandblast, water blast, air blast, ice blast)	Fine aggregate primary; coarse aggregate and cement secondary	All smooth	10% more coarse aggregate Slump: 2½–3½ in. (64–89 mm) Blasting between 7 and 45 days Water and air blasting used where sandblasting prohibited. 1,500 psi (10,342 kPa) concrete compressive strength, min.
Medium exposed aggregate	Blasted to expose coarse aggregate (sand blast, water blast, air blast, ice blast)	Coarse aggregate	All smooth	Higher-than-normal coarse aggregate Slump: 2–3 in. (51–76 mm) Blast before seven days
Heavy exposed aggregate	Blasted to expose coarse aggregate (sand blast, ice blast) 80% visible	Coarse aggregate	All smooth	Special-mix coarse aggregate Slump: 0–2 in. (0–51 mm) Blast within 24 hours Use high-frequency vibrator
Chemical retardation of surface set	Chemicals expose aggregate Aggregate can be adhered to surface	Coarse aggregate and cement	All smooth; glass fiber best	Chemical grade determines etch depth. Stripping scheduled to prevent long drying between stripping and washoff.
Mechanically fractured surfaces, scaling, bush-hammering, jackhammering, tooling	Varied	Fine and coarse cement and aggregate	Textured	Aggregate particles ⅜ in. (10 mm) for scaling and tooling 2½ in. (64 mm) minimum concrete cover over reinforced steel 4,000 psi (27,579kPa) concrete compressive strength, minimum
Combination/fluted	Striated/abrasive blasted/irregular pattern Corrugated/abrasive Vertical rusticated/abrasive Blasted Reeded and bush-hammered Reeded and hammered Reeded and chiseled	The shallower the surface, the greater the influence of fine aggregate and cement	Wood or rubber strips, corrugated sheet metal, or glass fiber	Depends on type of finish desired
Grinding and polishing	Terrazzo-like finish	Aggregate and cement	All smooth	Patch surface blemishes if possible. 5,000 psi (34,473 kPa) concrete compressive strength, minimum

SUBMITTAL REVIEW

Shop drawings and submittals should be carefully checked to determine concrete formwork quality and steel reinforcement placement. All elements, including joints, tie-rod size and spacing, cleanout panels, devices, and fastenings should be described on the shop drawings. Review details, including backup and hardware, to show methods of how forms and form joints are aligned and held tight under the pressure of the wet concrete.

Approval of shop drawings and sample submittals should relate to the designer's design intent and scope of responsibility. Approval of shop drawings still requires the contractor to perform the work as specified, to be responsible for the structural capability and safety of the formwork, and for the erection of acceptable architectural concrete work.

FORMWORK

The quality of the architectural concrete finish is dependent on the quality and tightness of the formwork. Tightly clamped, sealed forms improve the alignment, edge, and corner quality of the finished concrete. Shifting and leakage of the wet concrete should be anticipated, and formwork detailed accordingly. Corners and edges of the finished concrete are vulnerable to damage from spalling when the formwork is stripped away from the finished surfaces.

Formwork guidelines include the following:

- Provide aligned forms and tight formwork connections.
- Provide screw tie rods outside the contact area at corners, as close to the meeting joint as possible.
- Provide gaskets in joints as required to prevent leakage.
- Place formwork for successive pours tight to in-place concrete to minimize offsets.

Formwork is typically fabricated from ¾-in.- (19-mm-) thick plywood, and is available with plastic coatings. Other formwork materials may be employed if they are sufficiently rigid and strong enough to withstand the high hydraulic pressures of the rapid filling of the wet concrete and subsequent vibration movement.

For architectural concrete finishes that are smooth or blasted, formwork should be prepared to minimize visibility of screw holes and fasteners.

CONCRETE INSTALLATION

Choosing a placing technique (pumping versus bottom drop or other bucket type) is an important step toward achieving a desired architectural concrete surface and finish.

Verify that the vibrators used are of the proper size, frequency, and power.

Release agents are chemical treatments applied to the liner or face of the form that react with the cement to prevent it from sticking to the form. The safest way to select a release agent is to evaluate several products on a test panel under actual job conditions. The curing compound, used to retard or reduce evaporation of moisture from concrete or to extend curing time, is typically applied immediately after final finishing of the concrete surface. Consult manufacturers and the American Concrete Institute for more detailed information about the compatibility of these treatments and the form surface material or other finishes and surfaces to be applied to the concrete.

MINIMIZING DISCOLORATION

Sequencing of concrete placement is critical to the success of the architectural concrete appearance. Concrete discoloration is often caused by an excessive amount of elapsed time between deposited lifts of concrete. Discussion with the contractor regarding quality expectations may clarify how to sequence the concrete placement in a manner that will minimize discoloration.

AGGREGATE

Aggregate greatly affects the final appearance of the concrete surface. Aggregate should be selected on the basis of color, hardness, size, shape, gradation, method of exposure, durability, availability, and cost. Aggregate hardness and density must be compatible with structural requirements and weathering conditions. Sources for coarse and fine aggregates should be kept the same for an entire job to avoid variations in the final surface appearance, particularly in light-toned concrete. Following are the common types of aggregate and colors available:

- *Quartz* is available in clear, white, yellow, green, gray, and light pink or rose. *Clear quartz* is used as a sparkling surface to complement other colors and pigmented cements.
- *Granite* is known for its durability; it is available in shades of pink, red, gray, dark blue, black, and white. Traprock, such as basalt, can be used for gray, black, or green.
- *Marble* offers the widest selection of colors—green, yellow, red, pink, gray, white, and black.
- *Limestone* is available in white and gray.
- *Miscellaneous gravel*, after being washed and screened, can be used for brown and reddish-brown finishes. Yellow ochers, umbers, buff shades, and pure white are abundant in riverbed gravels.
- *Ceramic* exhibits the most brilliant and varied colors when vitreous materials are used.
- *Expanded lightweight shale* may be used to pro-

duce reddish-brown, gray, or black aggregate. Porous and crushable, this shale produces a dull surface with soft colors. It should be tested for iron-staining characteristics and must meet ASTM C330, *Standard Specification for Lightweight Aggregates for Structural Concrete* requirements.

Exposed Aggregate

An exposed aggregate surface is a decorative finish for concrete work achieved by removing the surface cement to expose the aggregate. Aggregates suitable for exposure may vary from ¼ in. (6 mm) to a cobblestone more than 6 in. (152 mm) in diameter. The extent to which the pieces of aggregate are revealed is largely determined by their size. Size is generally selected on the basis of the distance from which it will be viewed and the appearance desired.

Aggregates with rough surfaces have better bonding properties than those with smoother surfaces. A strong bond is important, particularly when small aggregate is used. For better weathering and appearance, the area of exposed cement matrix between pieces of aggregate should be minimal, which makes the color of cement in exposed aggregate concrete less important.

SURFACE TEXTURE/FORM LINER

Patterned forms and liners make it possible to simulate in concrete the textures of wood, brick, and stone. The texture and resulting shadow patterns conceal minor color variations or damage that would be conspicuous and unacceptable on a smooth surface. Use of rustication strips at joints in textured liners simplifies form assembly.

INTEGRALLY COLORED CONCRETE

Colored concrete can provide a cost-effective simulation of natural stone or other building materials. Two standard types of cement are available, offering different shades of color: *standard gray portland cement* and *white cement*. Integrally colored concrete is made by adding mineral oxide pigments to concrete mixes made with one of these two types. Fine aggregates should be selected carefully, since they can enhance the color effect. The amount of coloring material should not exceed 10% by weight of the cement; any excess pigment may reduce concrete strength, and strong colors can be achieved with less than 10% pigment. White cement is used when lighter, more delicate shades of concrete are desired, although it is more expensive; darker hues can be produced using gray cement.

Reginald D. Hough, FAIA; New York, New York
D. Neil Rankins; RGAA/Virginia; Richmond, Virginia

CONCRETE FLOOR TOPPINGS AND FINISHES

CONCRETE TOPPINGS

Concrete floor toppings are used where greater thickness, strength, abrasion resistance, and impact resistance are required than can be obtained from a medium-strength, normal-weight aggregate concrete floor slab. Toppings are placed in thin overlays, ¾ to 2 in. (19 to 50 mm) thick.

Typically, toppings are used over base slabs for heavy-duty, industrial-type applications where floors are subject to extensive abrasion and impact loads from heavy, steel-wheeled traffic. Uses include waste transfer stations, loading docks, heavy-equipment service centers, and steel mills. These toppings are made from either emery or iron aggregates and a proprietary blend of fast-setting portland or blended hydraulic cement, and superplasticizers for water reduction and for plasticizing the mix. They are designed to form a dense, very high-strength finish of low permeability. Regardless of aggregate type, whether emery or iron, to function effectively, such high-strength toppings should be placed over a base slab that has been designed for heavy loading and has a minimum compressive strength of 4,000 psi (27.6 MPa).

Metallic-Aggregate Toppings

Metallic-aggregate toppings are generally used in interior applications and areas not subject to deicing chemicals or mild chemical attack. Surface oxidation or rusting of the aggregate may occur when exposed to water and salts. Toppings made from metallic aggregates exhibit greater malleability than emery-aggregate toppings, but may be gouged. These toppings may not be suitable over concrete containing calcium chlorides, chloride-containing admixtures, saltwater-contaminated aggregates, or more than 3 percent air entrainment.

Emery-Aggregate Toppings

Emery-aggregate toppings may be used in interior and exterior applications and may exhibit reasonable resistance to mild chemical attack. Toppings made from emery aggregate exhibit higher abrasive resistance than iron-aggregate toppings, but may display some brittleness under impact loads. These toppings may not be suitable over concrete containing calcium chlorides, chloride-containing admixtures, saltwater-contaminated aggregates, or more than 3 percent air entrainment.

SURFACE PREPARATION

The preparation of concrete slabs that form the base for toppings differs depending on the age of the concrete. New monolithic concrete slabs require no supplemental bonding material. The concrete is still in a plastic state when the topping is placed.

Deferred topping applications refer to toppings that will be applied to hardened concrete, usually within 72 hours of finishing. Concrete in the base slab must receive a coarse profiled finish from a serrated float, rake, or wire broom. If the topping will be delayed until the base slab is dry, an epoxy adhesive should be used; and a broomed finish is needed.

Aged or existing concrete that requires a topping needs further surface preparation. Project conditions and the state of repair or soundness of the base slab must be evaluated. A failed heavy-duty topping or deteriorated conventional concrete overlay must be removed to a sound concrete base. To remove loosened and fractured paste and surface aggregates, the exposed surface must be textured by chipping, scarifying, or scabbling, followed by water blasting or milder cleaning methods. The last step is to clean the profiled surface to remove contaminants that would reduce the bond.

CONCRETE FINISHES

Concrete floor finishes include performance, decorative, and textured applications Textures can be achieved by stamping patterns into the uncured concrete surface.

Jennifer Davis; MBT; San Francisco, California

CONCRETE FLOOR FINISHES

TYPE OF TREATMENT	DESCRIPTION	CONSIDERATIONS
Veneer Concrete	Thin cementitious topping ranging from ³⁄₁₆ to 2 in. (5 to 50 mm) may be colored and stamped.	Veneer coatings can be susceptible to chipping. Use a thicker coating in high-traffic areas.
Integral Color—Liquid and Dry Pigments	Provides uniform color throughout; nonfading and weather-resistant.	Usually available in pastels and earth tones. Color cannot be saturated without compromising the structural integrity of the concrete. Light colors work best if white sand and aggregate are used. Use the same concrete supplier for consistency, and make sure the same batch of concrete is used for the entire load. Batch color at plant if possible. A test slab should be poured and approved prior to starting a job.
Acrylic Stain (methylmethacrylate copolymer)	Mar-, scratch-, stain-, and water-resistant.	Can be used on vertical surfaces. May be used to restore color to an older structure.
Acrylic Sealer (as above, except clear)	Antigraffiti; provides a clear protective film, which prevents the penetration of spray paint, etc.	Can be used on vertical surfaces.
Nonyellowing Oxidized Acrylic	Sealer with a "wet look."	Used for washed aggregate, ground face block, split block, or sand-blasted concrete.
Stamped Concrete	Texture is stamped into concrete to mimic patterns of brick, slate, stone, tile, etc.	Control and pour joints must be handled very carefully. Plan them to work with the stamped pattern selected. Control joints should be saw cut at least one-third of the slab thickness and should be installed once every 12 to 15 ft (3.6 to 4.5 m).
Stamped Concrete with Colored Release Agents (synthetic iron oxides for color)	Gives additional color and serves as a stamping tool release agent.	Can be used in conjunction with integral color or dry shake when imprinting the concrete.
Dry Shake Color Hardeners	Powdered cementitious material containing hard aggregates. When in-service conditions require concrete slabs with improved surface hardness, shake-on hardeners may be applied, floated, and troweled into the plastic concrete surface. Lightfast and weather-resistant. Not classified as a topping.	Hand-broadcast across the concrete surface and floated into the slab after the bleed water has evaporated.

CONCRETE MASONRY UNITS

CHARACTERISTICS

Concrete masonry units (CMU) are modular building units composed of aggregate particles embedded in a cementitious matrix. Concrete masonry units, with high compressive strength, conform to ASTM C90, *Specifications for Loadbearing Concrete Masonry Units*. Load-bearing units and concrete brick are commonly used in building core and shell construction. Nonload-bearing units may be specified for partitions and are commonly used for fire protection of steel columns and fire-rated partitions.

CONCRETE MASONRY UNIT TYPES

Type I, or moisture-controlled units, are specified to obtain a uniform degree of volume change due to moisture loss in a particular climate. The specification of Type I units facilitates the location of control joints. Type II, or nonmoisture-controlled units, may be more economical but will typically require closer spacing of control joints.

In addition to type, concrete bricks are specified by grade. Grade N is intended for use as architectural veneer and facing units in exterior walls and where high strength and resistance to moisture penetration and severe frost action are desired. Grade S is intended for general masonry where moderate strength and resistance to frost action and moisture penetration are required. Grade S is appropriate for use in interior construction.

Concrete masonry units are available in a variety of colors, sizes, textures, configurations, and weights, to accommodate design, detailing, and construction. Colors are now provided with lightfast metallic oxide pigments conforming to ASTM C979, *Standard Specification for Pigments for Integrally Colored Concrete*. The textures may be smooth, ground, split, ribbed, or otherwise prepared to maximize design versatility. Smooth finishes and more color options are available with prefaced, "integral glazed" concrete masonry units.

SIZES AND WEIGHTS

Concrete masonry units are specified as width by height by length. They are manufactured in both English and metric modular sizes. English-size CMU is nominally 8 × 8 × 16 in., and actually 7⅝ × 7⅝ × 15⅝ in. with a ⅜-in. grout joint. Metric size CMU is nominally 200 × 200 × 400 mm, and actually 190 × 190 × 390 mm with a 10-mm grout joint.

The weight of the units also varies. Depending on the aggregate used, concrete masonry units are typically made using concrete with densities ranging from 85 to 140 pcf (1,362 to 2,243 kg/m³). The lighter units tend to provide more fire resistance and have an improved noise reduction coefficient; they often are more economical to place in the wall. Heavier units tend to provide increased compressive strength, better resistance to sound penetration, higher water penetration resistance, and greater thermal storage capabilities.

Concrete masonry walls should be designed and constructed with modular coordination, to maximize efficiency. Concrete masonry unit sizes should be considered when building a wall; the use of full- or half-length masonry units is desirable when constructing a concrete masonry wall.

SINGLE WYTHE MASONRY

Single wythe masonry wall construction is common for many applications, both load-bearing and nonload-bearing and interior and exterior walls. These single wythe masonry systems are frequently used as interior partitions for fire protection.

Single wythe walls may be insulated on the interior or exterior. The insulation may be adhered or mechanically fastened directly to the masonry, or it may be installed in conjunction with conventional furring or studding systems.

TYPICAL CONCRETE MASONRY UNIT SHAPES

DIMENSIONING CMU WALLS

Concrete masonry unit construction should be dimensioned and detailed to minimize cutting and fitting on the site. The module established for concrete masonry design is 4 in. (100 mm) vertically and horizontally. Maintaining this module reduces waste and provides ready coordination with other masonry products, as well as window and door openings.

Standard dimensions for concrete masonry units are equal to the nominal dimension less the thickness of one mortar joint of ⅜ in. (English) or 10 mm (metric). The nominal 8-in.- (200-mm-) high, 16-in.- (400-mm-) long concrete masonry unit has an actual height of 7⅝ in. (190 mm) and an actual length of 15⅝ in. (390 mm). When laid into a wall with a ⅜-in. (10-mm) mortar joint, the unit always occupies an area of 8 by 16 in. (200 by 400 mm).

Outside Corner to Outside Corner Measurement

From the outside corner to the outside corner, a CMU wall has one fewer mortar joint than it has blocks. To calculate the actual length of the wall, the width of a mortar joint (⅜ in. (10 mm)) must be deducted from the nominal length of the wall.

Outside Corner to Inside Corner Measurement

Between an outside corner and an inside corner, a CMU wall has the same number of mortar joints and blocks. The length of the wall will be an exact multiple of 8 in. (200 mm) and the actual length is the same as the nominal length of the wall.

Inside Corner to Inside Corner and Opening Measurements

From inside corner to inside corner, a CMU wall has one more mortar joint than it has blocks. The actual dimension is ⅜ in. (10 mm) more than the nominal dimension.

CMU WALL SECTION

CMU WALL PLAN

SINGLE WYTHE CONCRETE MASONRY UNIT WALL

OUTSIDE TO OUTSIDE
(6) BLOCKS + (5) JOINTS

[N BLOCKS + (N-1) JOINTS]

OUTSIDE CORNER TO OUTSIDE CORNER MEASUREMENT

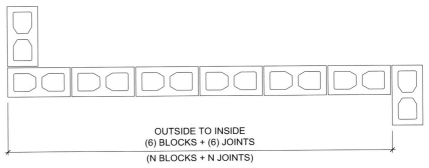

OUTSIDE TO INSIDE
(6) BLOCKS + (6) JOINTS

(N BLOCKS + N JOINTS)

OUTSIDE CORNER TO INSIDE CORNER MEASUREMENT

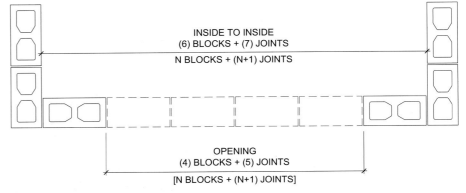

INSIDE TO INSIDE
(6) BLOCKS + (7) JOINTS

N BLOCKS + (N+1) JOINTS

OPENING
(4) BLOCKS + (5) JOINTS

[N BLOCKS + (N+1) JOINTS]

INSIDE CORNER TO INSIDE CORNER MEASUREMENT

CALCULATING CMU WALL LENGTHS

ACTUAL SIZE

NOMINAL SIZE

CONCRETE MASONRY UNITS (CMU)

HORIZONTAL SUPPORT FOR NONLOAD-BEARING WALLS—STEEL FRAME

HORIZONTAL SUPPORT FOR NONLOAD-BEARING WALLS—METAL DECK

STANDARD CMU WALL SECTIONS

ELECTRICAL OUTLET BOX IN CMU WALL

MASONRY ☐ **2**

REINFORCEMENT

In many applications, single wythe walls are reinforced. The term *partially reinforced* is erroneous. Reinforcement schedules are designed for a particular application, and all the required reinforcement is necessary. Nonreinforced single wythe walls are used in interior construction where no loads, including lateral loads, or other forces are anticipated. Consult with the National Concrete Masonry Association and engineers to determine wall construction requirements.

Concrete masonry unit walls are often partially grouted; that is, only the cells or cavities of the wall containing reinforcement are grouted. When walls are partially grouted, special units or construction fabric are used for vertical containment of the grout. Horizontal containment is usually provided by mortaring the webs of the masonry units. When steel placement is frequent, it may become economical or necessary to fully grout the walls.

Structural components of a building using reinforced masonry combine the tensile strength of reinforcement with the compressive strength of the masonry to resist design loads. The benefits of incorporating reinforcement are improved ductility, structural integrity, and resistance to flexural and shear stresses. Reinforced masonry provides economical construction, especially when a high degree of resistance to lateral loads is necessary.

Seismic performance categories A and B require no special provisions. In many instances, the wind loads will govern the minimum reinforcing levels in seismic performance category C and above. For designs in seismic performance category C, vertical reinforcement of at least 0.20 in. (5 mm) in cross-sectional areas must be provided continuously from support to support at each corner, at each side of each opening, and at the ends of walls. Horizontal reinforcement of not less than 0.20 in. (5 mm) must be provided at the bottom and top of all openings and extend not less than 24 in. (610 mm) nor less than 40 bar diameters past the opening. Horizontal reinforcement should be installed continuously at structurally connected roof and floor levels, at the tops of walls, and at the bottom of the wall or at the top of the foundation; maximum spacing is 10 ft (3 m), unless uniformly distributed joint reinforcement is provided.

For designs in seismic performance categories D and E, walls must be reinforced both vertically and horizontally. Requirements in addition to those for seismic performance category C include that spacing cannot exceed 4 ft (1,219 mm), except for designs using moment-resisting space frames, where the spacing of principal reinforcement must not exceed 2 ft (6 m). Also, the diameter of the reinforcement cannot be less than ⅜ in. (10 mm), except for joint reinforcement. Consult with an engineer and the National Concrete Masonry Association for information on specific project requirements for reinforcing.

Grace S. Lee; Rippeteau Architects, PC; Washington, D.C.
Stephen S. Szoke, P.E.; National Concrete Masonry
  Association; Herndon, Virginia
Brian E. Trimble; Brick Institute of America; Reston,
  Virginia
MASTERSPEC®; published by ARCOM; Salt Lake City, Utah,
  and Alexandria, Virginia

INTERIOR BOND BEAM
Source: National Concrete Masonry Association; Herndon, Virginia

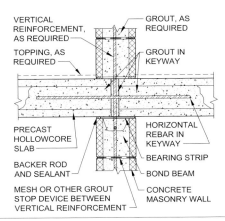

CMU WALL/CEILING INTERSECTION
Source: National Concrete Masonry Association; Herndon, Virginia

INCORRECT
Cut CMU units required.

CORRECT
No cut CMU units required.

CMU WALL DESIGN AND CONSTRUCTION *Source: National Concrete Masonry Association; Herndon, Virginia*

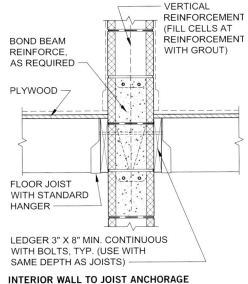

INTERIOR WALL TO JOIST ANCHORAGE

CMU WALL TO STEEL JOIST ANCHORAGE

WALL ANCHORAGE DETAILS

GLASS UNIT MASONRY ASSEMBLIES

CHARACTERISTICS

Glass unit masonry, commonly referred to as *glass block*, is a diverse building material whose many applications exhibit its multifaceted characteristics. The varying forms of glass block—type, thickness, size, shape, and patterns—along with the methods of installation can be combined to create unique design solutions.

Applications range from entire facades, windows, interior dividers, and partitions to skylights, floors, walkways, and stairways. In all applications, glass block units permit the control of light, both natural and artificial, for function or drama. Glass block also allows for control of thermal transmission, noise, dust, and drafts. With the use of thick-faced glass block or solid 3-in. (76-mm) bullet-resistant block, security can also be achieved.

An optimum mortar mix for installing glass block units is 1 part portland cement, ½ part lime, and 4 parts sand.

GLASS BLOCK SUPPORT

When specifying supports and shelf angles, the installed weight and deflection limitation of the glass block should be considered. Local building codes should be consulted for limits on panel sizes or installation details.

GLASS BLOCK

The basic glass block unit is made of two halves fused together with a partial vacuum inside. Faces may be clear, figured, or with integral relief forms.

Glass block is available in thicknesses ranging from a minimum of 3 in. (75 mm) for solid units to a maximum of 4 in. (100 mm) nominal for hollow units. Metric thicknesses range from 76 to 98 mm.

SQUARE GLASS BLOCK
4½ in. × 4½ in.
6 in. × 6 in. (5½ in. × 5½ in. actual)
½ in. × 7½ in.
8 in. × 8 in. (7¾ in. × 7¾ in. actual)
9½ in. × 9½ in.
12 in. × 12 in. (11¾ in. × 11¾ in. actual)
115 mm × 115 mm
190 mm × 190 mm
240 mm × 240 mm
300 mm × 300 mm
Metric sizes are available from foreign manufacturers through distributors in the United States.

GLASS MASONRY UNIT TYPES

THICK BLOCK

Some manufacturers provide thick blocks for critical applications where a thick-faced, heavier glass block is needed. These blocks have superior sound transmission rating properties. Their faces are three times as thick as regular glass block units.

SOLID AND COATED UNITS

Solid glass block units (glass bricks) are impact-resistant and allow through vision.

SURFACE DESIGN

Surface decoration may be achieved with fused-on ceramic, etching, or sandblasting. Glass block units may be split or shipped in halves if special decoration is to be applied to the interior of the unit. Blocks must then be resealed. Resealed blocks will not perform the same under various stresses as factory-sealed units. Placement in walls or panels should be limited to areas receiving minimum loading.

MORTAR		SEALANT AND BACKER (TYP.)
ASPHALT EMULSION		STEEL MULLION
SEALANT		SEALANT AND BACKER (TYP.)
PANEL ANCHOR		EXPANSION STRIP

MORTAR		SEALANT AND BACKER (TYP.)
ASPHALT EMULSION		STEEL MULLION
GLASS BLOCK UNIT		SEALANT AND BACKER (TYP.)
		EXPANSION STRIP

SHELF ANGLES IN MULTIPLE VERTICAL PANELS

PANEL ANCHORS ATTACHED TO STEEL PLATE		SEALANT
		PACKING
		EXPANSION STRIP
STEEL PLATE		PANEL REINFORCING

SUPPORT IN MULTIPLE HORIZONTAL PANELS

Panels with an expansion joint stiffener incorporating a concealed vertical plate should be limited to a 10 ft (3 m) maximum height.

SECTIONS AT SUPPORTS

EXPANSION STRIP

End block units have a rounded, finished surface on one edge. These units may be used to terminate interior partitions or walls, or, when installed horizontally, as space dividers.

END BLOCK

3 7/8"
1 1/4"
PANEL REINFORCING
45° BLOCK
2 1/4"
2 1/4"

45° BLOCK

SPECIAL CORNER SHAPES

5 3/4"
1/4"
5 3/4"
3 7/8"
PANEL REINFORCING
CORNER BLOCK
3 7/8"

CORNER BLOCK

Selected manufacturers provide special shapes to execute corner designs. These units may also be placed together for varying patterns and forms.

SOUND TRANSMISSION

STC	SIZE IN. (MM)	PATTERN	ASSEMBLY CONSTRUCTION
31	8 × 8 × 3 (203 × 203 × 76)	All patterns	Silicone system
37	8 × 8 × 4 (203 × 203 × 102)	All patterns	Mortar
40	8 × 8 × 4 (203 × 203 × 102) with LX fibrous filter	All patterns	Mortar
50	8 × 8 × 4 (203 × 203 × 102) thick faces block	Thick block	Mortar
53	8 × 8 × 3 (203 × 203 × 76) solid units	Solid block	Mortar

Sound transmission tested in accordance with ASTM E90, *Test Method for Laboratory Measurement of Airborne Sound Transmission Loss of Building Partitions and Elements.* STC rating value in accordance with ASTM E413, *Classification for Rating Sound Insulation.* Test method and STC rating value in accordance with ASTM E90 and ASTM E413, accordingly for mortar assembly construction.

PERMANENTLY ELASTIC SEALING COMPOUND

MANUFACTURER'S EXPANSION JOINT MATERIAL

DO NOT BRIDGE EXPANSION JOINT WITH PANEL REINFORCING

Expansion joints should be installed at every change of direction of a multicurved wall, at points of curved wall intersection with straight walls, and at center of curvature in excess of 90°.

GLASS BLOCK EXPANSION JOINT

METAL ANCHORS SECURE GLASS BLOCK PANEL TO ADJACENT CONSTRUCTION (BEND WITHIN EXPANSION JOINT)

EXPANSION STRIP TO ALLOW FOR DIFFERENTIAL MOVEMENT

HORIZONTAL JOINT REINFORCING, AS REQUIRED FOR EACH INSTALLATION

CLEAN SURFACES AFTER ERECTION WITH ORDINARY HOUSEHOLD SCRUB BRUSH WITH STIFF BRISTLES

GLASS BLOCK PANEL COMPONENTS

GLASS BLOCK DETAILS

Glass Block Panel Dimensions

Area of unbraced panel should not exceed 144 sq ft (13 sq m).

Area of interior unbraced panel should not exceed 250 sq ft (23 sq m).

Glass block panels are designed to be mortared at the sill, with head and jambs providing for movement and settling. Deflection of lintel at the head should be anticipated.

Consult manufacturers for specific design limitations of glass block panels. Thickness of block used also determines maximum panel size.

25'-0" MAX. (7.6)

20'-0" MAX. (6)

GLASS BLOCK PANEL DIMENSIONS

RADIUS MINIMUMS FOR CURVED PANEL CONSTRUCTION

BLOCK SIZE IN. (MM)	INSIDE RADIUS IN. (MM)	NUMBER OF BLOCKS IN 90° ARC	JOINT THICKNESS IN. (MM)	
			INSIDE	OUTSIDE
4 × 8 (102 × 203)	32 (813)	13	⅛ (3)	⅝ (16)
6 × 6 (152 × 152)	48½ (1,232)	13	⅛ (3)	⅝ (16)
8 × 8 (203 × 203)	65 (1,651)	13	⅛ (3)	⅝ (16)
12 × 12 (305 × 305)	98½ (2,502)	13	⅛ (3)	⅝ (16)

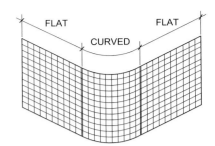

FLAT   FLAT
CURVED

INTERMEDIATE EXPANSION JOINTS AND SUPPORTS

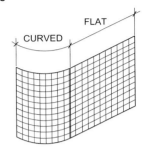

FLAT
CURVED

INTERMEDIATE EXPANSION JOINTS AND SUPPORTS

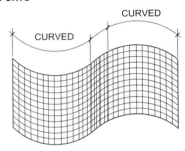

CURVED
CURVED

INTERMEDIATE EXPANSION JOINTS AND SUPPORTS

Curved areas should be separated from flat areas by intermediate expansion joints and supports.

When straight, ladder-type reinforcing is used on curved walls, the innermost parallel wire may be cut periodically and bent to accommodate the curvature of the wall.

CURVED PANEL CONSTRUCTION

(32" MIN. RADIUS 4" X 8" BLOCK)

90° ARC

(48 1/2" MIN. RADIUS 6" SQUARE BLOCK)

(65" MIN. RADIUS 8" SQUARE BLOCK)

(98 1/2" MIN. RADIUS 12" SQUARE BLOCK)

PANEL REINFORCING

RADIUS MINIMUMS

TYPICAL PARTITION WITH HORIZONTAL REINFORCING

- 1" MIN.
- 4-1/4"
- HEAD
- SILL
- SUPPORT FRAME
- PACKING
- SEALANT
- EXPANSION STRIP
- WIRE TIE
- GLASS UNIT MASONRY
- MORTAR
- CARPET EACH SIDE

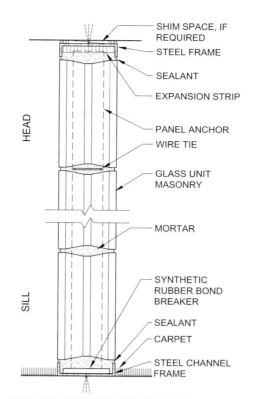

PARTITION REQUIRING VERTICAL PANEL ANCHORS FOR LATERAL BRACING

- SHIM SPACE, IF REQUIRED
- STEEL FRAME
- SEALANT
- EXPANSION STRIP
- PANEL ANCHOR
- WIRE TIE
- GLASS UNIT MASONRY
- MORTAR
- SYNTHETIC RUBBER BOND BREAKER
- SEALANT
- CARPET
- STEEL CHANNEL FRAME
- HEAD
- SILL

PLAN SECTION—PARTITION WITH STRUCTURAL STEEL T-SECTION

- SHIM SPACE IF REQUIRED
- SEALANT IF REQUIRED
- PACKING
- SEALANT
- EXPANSION STRIP
- WIRE TIE
- GLASS UNIT MASONRY
- MORTAR
- PANEL ANCHOR
- SEALANT AND PACKING
- 1" MIN.
- STEEL T-SECTION OR OTHER APPROPRIATE STRUCTURAL ANCHOR
- EXPANSION STRIP
- SEALANT
- 1" MIN.
- HEAD
- SILL

GLASS BLOCK PARTITIONS

HEAD AT DOOR FRAME SECTION/ELEVATION

- EXPANSION STRIP (TYP.)
- SEALANT (TYP.)
- STEEL BAR LINTEL
- PANEL ANCHOR (TYP.)
- HOLLOW METAL DOOR HEAD
- CONTINUOUS STEEL BAR; SECURE TO STRUCTURE ABOVE

PLAN SECTION ABOVE JAMB

- CONTINUOUS STEEL BAR; SECURE TO STRUCTURE ABOVE

JAMB AT DOOR FRAME

- JAMB ANCHOR; SECURE TO STEEL BAR
- STEEL BAR; SECURE TO STRUCTURE ABOVE
- PANEL ANCHOR
- GLASS BLOCK UNIT
- HOLLOW METAL DOOR AND JAMB
- HORIZONTAL PANEL REINFORCING
- SEALANT (TYP.)
- EXPANSION STRIP

DOOR FRAME DETAILS

HEAD AT SUSPENDED CEILING

- STEEL BRACE; SECURE TO STRUCTURE ABOVE
- SUSPENDED CEILING
- DEFLECTION SPACE
- PANEL ANCHOR
- SEALANT (TYP.)
- EXPANSION STRIP

HEAD AT INTERIOR PARTITION

- METAL STUD FRAMING
- DEFLECTION SPACE
- PANEL ANCHOR
- GYPSUM BOARD
- SOLID BLOCKING
- SEALANT (TYP.)
- EXPANSION STRIP

INTERIOR CONNECTION DETAILS

JAMB AT INTERIOR PARTITION

- METAL STUD FRAMING
- DEFLECTION SPACE
- SOLID BLOCKING
- SEALANT, TYP.
- PANEL ANCHOR
- GLASS BLOCK UNIT
- HORIZONTAL PANEL REINFORCING
- EXPANSION STRIP

JAMB AT PERPENDICULAR PARTITION

- METAL STUD FRAMING
- GYPSUM BOARD
- SOLID BLOCKING
- PANEL ANCHOR
- GLASS BLOCK UNIT
- HORIZONTAL PANEL REINFORCING
- EXPANSION STRIP
- DEFLECTION SPACE

Grace S. Lee; Rippeteau Architects, PC; Washington, D.C.

STONE

New technologies in stone quarrying and fabrication, including the creation of thinner-dimension stone and stone tile products, have made this material widely used in interior applications.

Dimension stone is defined as quarried stone with usually one or more mechanically dressed surfaces. These are thick slabs of stone that are marked as they are cut for matched-pattern installations, such as book-match or end-match configurations.

Dimension stone tiles are less than ¾ in. (19 mm) thick. They provide the natural beauty of a stone surface without the weight, depth, and expense of dimension stone. However, their thinness makes stone floor tiles more prone to cracking from impact or normal floor deflection. Stone tiles are installed by either the thick-bed or the thin-set installation methods.

North American and European dimension stones are cut to different thickness standards. North American stone is sawn to nominal inch thicknesses. European stone is sawn to nominal metric thicknesses measuring 20, 30, 50, 80, and 100 mm (approximately $1^{3}/_{16}$, $1^{3}/_{16}$, 2, $3^{3}/_{16}$, and $3^{15}/_{16}$ in.). If standard European thicknesses are used for stone wall facing, standard North American wraparound door hinges may not fit accurately and may require modification or shimming. If imported stone is required, final cuts and finish work are generally performed by local fabricators.

TYPES OF STONE

Granite is a hard, durable, low-maintenance stone. It is a grainy igneous rock (formed by volcanic action) that imparts a visual strength. Granite is relatively uniform in color and texture.

Marble is a metamorphic stone, identified by its variegated, veined surface, and is valued for its range of colors and luxurious surface. Marbles are comparatively soft, easily scratched stones that require dedicated maintenance, especially if a polished finish is selected. Marbles can be polished, honed, sawn, sandblasted, bush-hammered, split-faced, tumbled, and acid-washed.

Limestone is a sedimentary stone, which varies in hardness, density, and porosity from one type to another. Limestones are available in *oolitic*, *calcitic*, and *dolomitic*

types. Color range is limited to a neutral palette of buff and gray. More commonly used as exterior cladding for buildings, limestone is susceptible to staining and should not be exposed to excessive soil. Limestone finishes are available in polished, honed (some varieties can receive a high-honed (satin matte) finish, with a higher degree of reflectivity than the standard honed finish), sandblasted, flamed, bush-hammered, tumbled, and acid-washed.

Slate is a metamorphic stone, formed from shale and clay. Slate splits easily into thin sheets. The finish resulting from the natural face is referred to as a *cleft finish*. Slate can also be sand-rubbed to a smooth finish or honed.

Travertine is a sedimentary stone, distinguished by its natural cavities, formed by plants embedded during the rock's formation, which must be filled to achieve a smooth surface. Filling materials are typically portland cement, epoxy resins, or polyester resins. Though travertine is a type of limestone, some types that take a polish are classified as marble. It is popular for use as a flooring material because its visual texture conceals dirt much better than most other stones.

Onyx is a decorative stone, prized for its unique characteristics, including colored and banded patterns. Onyx is formed from quartz crystals, and the appearance can be enhanced by chemical treatment. Onyx is typically translucent, is relatively soft, and is brittle in its natural state. Treatment with resins can improve its performance and durability.

Quartzite is a metamorphic stone, formed from recrystallized sandstone. Quartzite contains silica, which contributes to this stone's density and durability. Quartzite is available in honed, sandblasted, and split- or cleft-faced finishes. Due to its composition, quartzite is easily split; and bullnose or ogee-type details may be difficult to fabricate.

Sandstone is a coarse-grained sedimentary stone. It is composed of quartz and is bonded with silica, calcium carbonate, or iron oxide. Different iron oxides provide variation in colors, ranging from yellow, buff, and brown to reds. Related stone types include bluestone, brownstone, and flagstone. Sandstone can be honed, sawn, and split-faced. Interior uses for sandstone include wall panels, interior paving, furniture, and casework.

STONE FINISHES

The stone finish affects the perception of the color, texture, and the slip resistance of stone flooring.

Polished finishes are the most reflective. They provide a mirror gloss with sharp reflections, which brings out the stone's full depth of color and pattern.

Honed finishes have a satin or dull sheen with little or no gloss. These surfaces are often good choices for commercial floors because of their slip resistance; however, they are susceptible to stain absorption.

Sawn finishes are textures that are not processed after the slab has been sawn from the block of stone. The texture is typically nondirectional, and consists of circular markings and grooved surfaces.

Sandblasted finishes are achieved by blasting the stone surface with sand to create a coarse, nondirectional texture. Depending on the size of the grains of sand used in this surface treatment, fine, medium, or coarse textures are created. Interior paving stone with a sandblasted finish is inherently slip-resistant, although the texture will be worn down to a honed finish under heavy pedestrian traffic.

Acid-washed finishes are produced by the application of acidic solutions to the stone surface to create a rustic texture. This texture is applied to calcium-based stones, such as marbles and limestones; quartz-based stones such as granite are resistant to this finish.

Thermal, also known as flamed, finishes are achieved by the application of intense flaming heat to the surface of the stone. The finish texture is coarse and irregular, following the crystal structure of the stone. A thermal finish is generally lighter in color and the stone characteristics are less pronounced than in polished or honed finishes. Thermal finishes are typically applied to granite.

Waterjet, or hydro, finishes are created by the use of high-pressure water forces, which texturize the surface and highlight the color of the stone. Waterjet finish textures are between honed and thermal finishes.

Cleft-face finishes are natural textures produced from cleaved, naturally foliated stones, including slate and quartzite. Textures vary according to the density of the stone; very dense stones will cleave in flatter planes than less dense stones, which will have a more irregular texture when split.

Tumbled finishes impart an antique appearance to the stone. Typically used on small stone blocks, the tumbling process softens edges and corners and rusticates the surface of the stone.

Bush-hammered and tooled finishes are created by striking the stone surface with tools to create surface texture. Stones receiving a bush-hammered or tooled finish must be of a sufficient density and thickness to withstand the impact of the tools.

Split-faced textures are similar to cleft-faced stone, but are used on stones that are not naturally foliated. Split-faced textures are created using either a guillotine or wedges, the latter which are power-driven into the stone. Surfaces created range from fairly flat, consistent textures, to textures similar to rougher thermal finishes.

ARCHITECTURAL STONE TYPES

GEOLOGY	SEDIMENTARY	METAMORPHIC			IGNEOUS
DEFINITION				Travertine (sedimentary form of marble)	SOLIDIFIED MOLTEN ROCK
Stone	Limestone	Slate	Marble		Granite
Quarry Locations	NY to AL, IN to MS, IA, NE, KS, MO, OK, AR, TX, WI, CO, SD, WY, CA, MN	MA to GA, CA, AR	NY to AL, IN to MS, NE, KS, MO, OK, AR, TX, CO, SD, WY, CA, MN, WI		MA, NH, VT, RI, CT, NY, NJ, MD, VA, NC, SC, GA, WI, MN, MO, OK, CA, SD, ME, PA
Colors	White, cream, gray, rust, pink, black, buff, tan, ivory, blue, rose	Blue, green, black, purple-gray	White, gray, red, pink, buff, rose, gold, green, yellow, black, brown, tan		Pink, brown, gray, white, blue, black, green, red
Finishes	Polished, smooth, honed, natural cleft, sand-rubbed	Polished, fine abrasive, textured			Polished, honed, fine-rubbed, thermal

Source: Marble Institute of America, Inc.; Westlake, Ohio

METALS

PROPERTIES OF METALS

Metals are generally categorized by iron content. Ferrous (from the Latin *ferrum*, meaning "iron") metals consist mostly of iron. Steel is a ferrous metal. Nonferrous metals contain little or no iron, generally have good corrosion resistance, and are nonmagnetic. Nonferrous metals include copper and aluminum. Desirable properties of different metals can often be combined by mixing metals together to form alloys.

METALS

FERROUS (CONTAIN IRON)	NONFERROUS (CONTAIN LITTLE OR NO IRON)
Steel	Copper
Stainless Steel	Aluminum
Iron	Tin
	Magnesium

FERROUS METALS

Steel

Steel comprises the various alloys of iron and carbon. More than 90% of the steel manufactured into finished products is carbon steel.

Carbon steel is iron that contains low to medium quantities of carbon. A higher carbon content increases metal strength and hardness but reduces its ductility and weldability. It is reasonably strong but has poor resistance to corrosion. Galvanizing is the application of zinc to the surface of carbon steel or steel alloys to prevent corrosion. The coating can be applied in one of two ways: *hot-dipped* or *electroplated*. Carbon steel is used in structural shapes such as welded fabrications or castings, metal studs and joists, fasteners, wall grilles, and ceiling suspension systems.

High-strength, low-alloy (HSLA) steels have better corrosion resistance than carbon steels, and they are chosen when weight is a consideration and higher strength is specified.

Typical elements used to modify steel include:

- *Aluminum* for surface hardening.
- *Chromium* for corrosion resistance.
- *Copper* for atmospheric corrosion resistance.
- *Manganese* in small amounts for additional hardening, in larger amounts for better wear resistance.
- *Molybdenum*, combined with other metals such as chromium and nickel, to increase corrosion resistance and raise tensile strength without reducing ductility.
- *Nickel* to increase tensile strength without reducing ductility; in high concentrations, nickel improves corrosion resistance.
- *Silicon* to strengthen low-alloy steels and improve oxidation resistance; larger amounts produce hard, brittle castings that are resistant to corrosive chemicals.
- *Sulfur* for free machining.
- *Titanium* to prevent intergranular corrosion of stainless steels.
- *Tungsten, vanadium, and cobalt* for hardness and corrosion resistance.

STAINLESS-STEEL ALLOYS

SERIES DESIGNATION	STRUCTURE	ALLOYING ELEMENTS
400	Martensitic (hardenable by heat treatment; ferromagnetic)	12–18% Chromium
	Ferritic (nonhardenable; ferromagnetic)	12–27% Chromium
300	Austenitic (hardenable by cold-working; nonmagnetic)	16–26% Chromium and 6–22% Nickel
200	Austenitic (hardenable by cold-working; nonmagnetic)	16–19% Chromium, 3.5–6% Nickel, and 5.5–10% Manganese

STANDARD DESIGNATIONS FOR STAINLESS-STEEL FINISHES

FINISH DESIGNATION	DEFINITION	TYPICAL USES
Unpolished or Rolled Finishes		
No. 1	A rough, dull surface that results from hot-rolling to the specified thickness, followed by annealing and descaling.	Furnace stacks, kiln liners
No. 2D	A dull finish that results from cold-rolling, followed by annealing and descaling and perhaps a final light roll pass through unpolished rolls. A 2D finish is used where appearance is of no concern.	Institutional kitchen equipment, furnace parts
No. 2B	A bright, cold-rolled finish resulting from the same process used for a No. 2D finish, except that the annealed and descaled sheet receives a light final roll pass through polished rolls. This is the general-purpose cold-rolled finish that can be used as-is or as a preliminary step to polishing.	Cookware, flatware
Polished Finishes		
No. 3	An intermediate polished surface obtained by finishing with a 100-grit abrasive. Generally used where a semifinished polished surface is required. A No. E finish usually receives additional polishing during fabrication.	Institutional kitchen equipment
No. 4	A polished surface obtained by finishing with a 120–150 mesh abrasive, following initial grinding with coarser abrasives. This is a general-purpose bright finish with a visible "grain" that prevents mirror reflection.	Column covers, wall panels, furniture, sinks, storefronts
No. 6	A dull satin finish having lower reflectivity than a No. 4 finish. It is produced by Tampico brushing a No. 4 finish in a medium abrasive and oil. It is used for architectural applications and ornamentation where a high luster is undesirable, and to contrast with brighter finishes.	Furniture (finish not generally available from stainless-steel producers, but can be obtained from metal finishers and may be applied to a product after manufacturing.)
No. 7	A highly reflective finish that is obtained by buffing finely ground surfaces, but not to the extent of completely removing the "grit" lines. It is used chiefly for architectural and ornamental purposes.	Furniture (finish not generally available from stainless-steel producers, but can be obtained from metal finishers and may be applied to a product after manufacturing.)
No. 8	The most reflective surface, which is obtained by polishing with successively finer abrasives and buffing extensively until all grit lines from preliminary grinding operations are removed. It is used for applications such as mirrors and reflectors.	Furniture (finish not generally available from stainless-steel producers, but can be obtained from metal finishers and may be applied to a product after manufacturing.)

Source: Finishes for Stainless Steel, AMP 503, National Association of Architectural Metal Manufacturers (NAAMM), Chicago, Illinois, 1988, p. 5.

Stainless Steel

Stainless steel is an iron alloy that is inherently corrosion-resistant because of the addition of chromium. The self-healing chromium-oxide forms a transparent film on the surface of the steel, preventing oxidation (rust). Stainless steels contain at least 11.5% chromium. Nickel or molybdenum is added when maximum corrosion resistance is required. Stainless steel is used in construction of handrails, floorplates, wall panels, hardware, fasteners, and anchors. Decorative shapes and statuary can be cast in stainless steel.

Stainless steel is not affected by mortar or concrete and does not stain adjacent surfaces. It is popular for use in commercial interiors as column covers and railings, hardware, wall panels, and numerous other products. Its durability, finish retention, and other properties also make it useful for equipment used in food preparation and other commercial equipment, furniture, accessories, and fine eating utensils.

There are three series designations for stainless-steel alloys:

- *Series 200* alloys contain magnesium in addition to chromium and nickel.
- *Series 200 and 300* alloys are austenitic (normally nonmagnetic).
- *Series 300* is more corrosion-resistant and is easier to fabricate and weld than any other type of stainless steel.
- *Series 400* does not contain nickel and is therefore less corrosion-resistant.

Although stainless steel is available in approximately 60 different alloys, Types 302 and 304 are most frequently used for both interior and exterior architectural applications. Sometimes referred to as *18–8*, these alloys contain approximately 18% chromium and 8% nickel. Types 302 and 304 are very similar in performance and appearance. The specification of Type 302/304 indicates that either alloy is acceptable.

IRON

Iron and steel, and their alloys, are usually the most cost-effective metal choices for structural applications.

Iron that contains no trace of carbon is soft, ductile, and easily worked, but it rusts in a relatively short time and is susceptible to corrosion by most acids. A higher carbon content increases metal strength and hardness but reduces its ductility and weldability.

Gray irons are high in carbon and silicon content and are rather brittle; however, they are excellent for damping (absorbing vibrations). Applications include decorative shapes, such as fences and posts, gratings, and stair components.

Malleable iron, which is more expensive than gray iron, has been used for decades in applications that require great toughness and high ductility. This low-carbon white iron is cast, reheated, and slowly cooled, or annealed, to improve its workability.

Ductile iron is made by adding magnesium to molten iron shortly before the metal is poured into molds. The magnesium alters the surface-tension mechanism of the molten iron and precipitates the carbon out as small spheres instead of flakes, which make the iron casting more ductile. Ductile iron is less brittle, stiffer, stronger, and more shock-resistant than gray iron. Ductile iron is the fastest-growing segment of the metal casting industry.

Ductile castings using a special austempering heat-treating process offer much higher tensile strengths. Called *ADI castings,* they rival or surpass certain alloy steel castings in tensile and yield strengths.

White-iron castings, which are extremely hard and brittle, are used primarily in industrial machinery parts that experience high wear and require abrasion resistance.

Compacted graphite iron characteristics fall between those of gray and ductile iron. The properties of this metal are so difficult to control during production that very few metal casters manufacture it.

High-alloy irons are gray, ductile, or white irons with an alloy content of 3% to more than 30%. Their properties are significantly different from those of unalloyed irons.

Wrought iron is made from iron ore that is heated until it is soft but not melted. Wrought iron or steel is relatively soft, corrosion- and fatigue-resistant, and machinable. It is easily worked, making it ideal for railings, grilles, fences, screens, and various types of ornamental work. It is commercially available in bars, rods, tubing, sheets, and plates.

Cast iron contains a large amount of carbon, making it so hard and brittle that it cannot be worked into the required shape but must be cast into molds. The characteristics of the many types of cast iron vary widely among six basic groups: gray, malleable, ductile, white, compacted graphite, and high-alloy iron. Cast iron is relatively corrosion-resistant. Plumbing drainage pipes and ornamental rails for exterior applications are often made from cast iron.

NONFERROUS METALS

Aluminum

About 8% of the Earth's crust is composed of aluminum, making it the world's most plentiful metal. Unlike the ores of gold and silver, aluminum ore is not found free in nature. It is always chemically combined with other elements and must therefore be extracted.

A unique combination of properties make aluminum the most versatile metal. Aluminum is soft and flexible, allowing it to be easily fabricated. It is light in weight yet remarkably strong. Some aluminum alloys have greater strength than structural steel. Unlike steel, it is highly resistant to corrosion. Aluminum is an excellent thermal and electrical conductor; electrical wiring is often made of aluminum. Aluminum is used for door frames and hardware, interior window frames, horizontal louver blind slats, and contemporary furniture.

Aluminum Finishes

Because it is inherently corrosion-resistant, aluminum often requires no special finish. A protective oxide film forms rapidly and naturally on the surface when exposed to air. Aluminum is, however, susceptible to attack by alkaline chemicals such as those found in concrete and masonry mortar.

Finishes are frequently applied to aluminum for decorative purposes. Conversion coatings are generally used to prepare the metal for painting, but can also be used as final finishes. Because aluminum's natural oxide film does not always provide a good bonding surface for coatings, the surface is "converted" to one with improved adhesion if a coating is desired.

The most common finish that is applied principally to aluminum and its alloys is the anodic coating. Anodizing involves passing an electrical current across a solution (most commonly sulfuric acid) in which the aluminum is immersed. The resulting coating is much thicker than the naturally formed aluminum oxide coating—as thick as 0.0012 in. (0.030 mm)—providing increased corrosion resistance. Anodized coatings can be transparent, translucent, or opaque, and can increase surface abrasion resistance without changing the surface texture.

SUMMARY OF STANDARD DESIGNATIONS* FOR ALUMINUM FINISHES

MECHANICAL FINISHES (M)

As Fabricated	Buffed	Directional Textured	Nondirectional Textured
M10–Unspecified M11–Specular as fabricated M12–Nonspecular as fabricated M1x–Other	M20–Unspecified M21–Smooth specular M22–Specular M2x–Other	M30–Unspecified M31–Fine satin M32–Medium satin M33–Coarse satin M34–Hand-rubbed M35–Brushed M3x–Other	M40–Unspecified M41–Extra-fine matte **M42–Fine matte** **M43–Medium Matte** **M44–Coarse matte** M45–Fine shot blast M46–Medium shot blast M47–Coarse shot blast M4x–Other

CHEMICAL FINISHES (C)

Nonetched Cleaned	Etched	Brightened	Conversion Coatings
C10–Unspecified **C11–Degreased** **C12–Chemically cleaned** C1x–Other	C20–Unspecified C21–Fine matte C22–Medium matte C23–Coarse matte C2x–Other	C30–Unspecified C31–Highly specular C32–Diffuse bright C3x–Other	C40–Unspecified C41–Acid chromate-fluoride C42–Acid chromate-fluoride-phosphate C43–Alkaline chromate C44–Nonchromate C45–Nonrinsed chromate C4x–Other

COATINGS—ANODIC (A)

General	Protective and Decorative	Architectural Class II	Architectural Class I
A10–Unspecified anodic coating A11–Preparation for other applied coatings A12–Chromic acid anodic coating A13–Hard coating A1x–Other	A21**–Clear (natural) A22**–Integral color A23**–Impregnated color A24**–Electrolytically deposited color A2x–Other	A31–Clear (natural) **A32–Integral color** **A33–Impregnated color** **A34–Electrolytically deposited color** A3x–Other	A41–Clear (natural) A42–Integral color **A43–Impregnated color** **A44–Electrolytically deposited color** A4x–Other

*All designations are to be preceded by the letters AA, to identify them as Aluminum Association designations. For example, AA-M12C22A31 specifies a nonspecular mechanical finish as fabricated; an etched, medium matte, chemical finish, with a clear anodic coating 0.01 mm (0.4 mil) or thicker.

**Third digit (1, 2, or 3) added to designate minimum thickness in 1/10 mils.

Note: Finishes printed in boldface type are those most frequently used on architectural work.

Note: The Aluminum Association (AA) and NAAMM use the same designation system for aluminum and its alloys.

Source: Finishes for Aluminum, *AMP 501, from the National Association of Architectural Metal Manufacturers (NAAMM), Chicago, Illinois, 1988, p.16.*

Copper

Copper is readily available, easily fabricated, and corrosion-resistant under a wide range of conditions. Copper is not affected by alkaline chemicals and so is often used where metal-to-masonry contact is required. In interior applications, the greatest use of copper is in electrical wiring; it has the second highest conductivity of any material (silver is only slightly higher). Copper is also popular for use in plumbing supply pipes and fittings. Copper can be made harder and stronger by adding small amounts of tin.

Prolonged exposure of an untreated copper surface results in a brown and, eventually, green patina. A patina is a thin layer of corrosion resulting from oxidation. Polishing the surface to remove the oxide film can restore copper's appearance. The metallic surface can also be preserved by the application of a transparent coating.

Bronze and Brass

Bronze was originally a copper-tin alloy, but the term today is used to identify other alloys with a bronze color, including aluminum bronzes, silicon bronzes, and leaded phosphor bronzes. Phosphor bronze is a copper-tin- phosphorus alloy; and leaded phosphor bronze is composed of copper, lead, tin, and phosphorus.

Brass, a copper-zinc alloy, is commonly used for door hardware and upholstered furniture tacks. Good thermal and electrical conductivity, corrosion resistance, and easy forming and joining all make copper and its alloys useful in construction. Some brass alloys may be called bronzes even though they have little or no tin in them. Common nonbronze brass alloys are commercial bronze (90% copper, 10% zinc), naval brass (60% copper, 29% zinc, and 1% tin), muntz metal (60% copper, 40% zinc), and manganese bronze (58% copper, 39% zinc, and 1% tin and iron). When a metal is identified as bronze, the alloy cannot contain zinc or nickel; if it does, it is probably brass. Architectural brasses and bronzes are actually all brasses; they are used for doors, windows, door and window frames, railings, trim and grilles, and finish hardware. Muntz metal, also called malleable brass, is a bronze alloy resembling extruded architectural bronze in color. Available in sheet and strip, it is used in flat surfaces in architectural compositions in connection with extruded architectural bronze.

Copper-based alloys characteristically form adherent films that are relatively impervious to corrosion and protect the base metal from further attack. Lacquer coatings can help retain the original alloy color.

Lead

An extremely dense metal, lead is corrosion-resistant and easily worked. Alloys are added to it to improve properties such as hardness and strength. Typical applications of lead include waterproofing, sound and vibration isolation, and radiation shielding. Lead can be combined with tin alloy to plate iron or steel, which

is commonly called *terneplate*. Care should be taken as to how and where lead is used because lead vapors and lead dust are toxic if ingested.

Zinc

Although it is corrosion-resistant in water and air, zinc is brittle and low in strength. Its major use is in galvanizing (dipping hot iron or steel in molten zinc), although zinc is also used to create sandcast or diecast components. Major building industry uses are roofing, flashing, nails, plumbing hardware, structural parts, and decorative shapes.

Tin

Key properties of tin are its low melting point (450°F (232°C)), relative softness, good formability, and readiness to form alloys. Principal uses for tin are as a constituent of solder, a coating for steel (tinplate, terneplate), and an alloy with other metals that can be cast, rolled, extruded, or atomized. Tin is most popular as an alloy for copper, antimony, lead, bismuth, silver, and zinc. Pewter alloys contain 1% to 8% antimony and 0.5% to 3% copper. Alloy metal in tin solders ranges from 40% lead to no lead and 3.5% silver.

SUMMARY OF STANDARD DESIGNATIONS FOR COPPER ALLOY FINISHES

MECHANICAL FINISHES (M)

As Fabricated	Buffed	Directional Textured	Nondirectional Textured
M10–Unspecified M11–Specular as fabricated M12–Matte finish as fabricated M1x–Other (to be specified)	M20–Unspecified M21–Smooth specular* M22–Specular* M2x–Other (to be specified)	M30–Unspecified M31–Fine satin* M32–Medium satin **M33–Coarse satin** **M34–Hand-rubbed** M35–Brushed* M36–Uniform M3x–Other (to be specified)	M40–Unspecified M41–(Unassigned) M42–Fine matte* M43–Medium matte M44–Coarse matte M45–Fine shot blast M46–Medium shot blast M47 Coarse shot blast M4x–Other (to be specified)

CHEMICAL

Nonetched Cleaned	Conversion Coatings
C10–Unspecified C11–Degreased C12–Cleaned C1x–Other (to be specified)	**C50–Ammonium chloride** (patina) **C51–Cuprous chloride-hydrochloric acid** (patina) **C52–Ammonium sulfate** (patina) C53–Carbonate (patina) C54–Oxide (statuary) **C55–Sulfide*** (statuary) C56–Selenide (statuary) C5x–Other (to be specified)

COATINGS—CLEAR ORGANIC (O)

Air Dry (General Architectural Work)	Thermoset (Hardware)	Chemical Cure
060–Unspecified 06x–Other (to be specified)	070–Unspecified 07x–Other (to be specified)	080–Unspecified 08x–Other (to be specified)

COATINGS—LAMINATED (L)

L90–Unspecified
L91–Clear polyvinyl fluoride
L9x–Other (to be specified)

COATINGS—VITREOUS AND METALLIC

Since the use of these finishes in architectural work is rather infrequent, it is recommended that they be specified in full, rather than being identified by number.

COATINGS—OILS AND WAXES

These applied coatings are primarily used for maintenance purposes on-site. Because of the broad range of materials in common use, it is recommended that, where desired, such coatings be specified in full.

Note: In this listing, finishes printed in boldface type are those most frequently used for general architectural work; those marked with an asterisk (*) are commonly used for hardware items.

The Copper Development Association (CDA) and NAAMM use the same designation system for copper and its alloys.

Source: Finishes for the Copper Alloys, AMP 502. Reprinted with the permission of the National Association of the Architectural Metal Manufacturers (NAAMM); Chicago, Illinois, 1988.

Nickel

Whitish in color, nickel is used for plating other metals or as a base for chromium plating. Nickel polishes well and does not tarnish. It is also widely applied as an additive in iron and steel alloys as well as other metal alloys. Nickel-iron castings are more ductile and more resistant to corrosion than conventional cast iron. Adding nickel makes steel more resistant to impact.

Chromium

A hard, steel-gray metal, chromium is commonly used to plate other metals, including iron, steel, brass, and bronze. Plated cast shapes can be brightly polished and do not tarnish. Several steel alloys, such as stainless plate, contain as much as 18% chromium. Chromium does not rust, which makes chromium alloys excellent for exterior uses.

Magnesium

Lightest of all metals used in construction, pure magnesium is not strong enough for general structural functions. Combining other metals such as aluminum with magnesium results in lightweight alloy materials used in ladders, furniture, hospital equipment, and wheels for automobiles.

DISSIMILAR METALS

When dissimilar metals are connected by an electrolyte, a current, called a *galvanic current,* flows from one to the other. An electrolyte is any liquid that conducts electricity, for example, water. The current causes one of the metals to deteriorate, and this reaction is called *galvanic corrosion*. The threat of galvanic corrosion is greatest in exterior applications where materials are exposed to rain or high humidity. However, even in interior applications, galvanic corrosion is of concern. Dissimilar metals in contact with each other, including nails, screws, and bolts, must be coated with or separated by a nonabsorbent, nonconductive material.

GALVANIC SCALE

CORRODED (ANODIC) END/MORE NOBLE
Zinc
Aluminum
Galvanized Steel
Cadmium
Mild Steel, Wrought Iron
Cast Iron
Stainless Steel, Types 304 and 316 (active)
Lead-Tin Solder
Lead
Brass, Bronze
Copper
Stainless Steel, Types 304 and 316 (Passive)

Source: Sheet Metal and Air Conditioning Contractors' National Association (SMACNA); Architectural Sheet Metal Manual, 5th ed.; Chantilly, Virginia, 1993.

Metals that are higher on the galvanic scale will corrode when electrolytically connected to metals that are lower on the scale. The metal that is more anodic will corrode, or lose material to, the metal that is more cathodic. The farther apart metals are on the scale, the more rapid the corrosion.

In addition to the dissimilarity of metals, the amount of metal also plays a part in galvanic corrosion. The less "noble" (inactive or inert) metal will more likely corrode severely if its surface area is small in comparison with the more noble metal. For example, aluminum (more noble) screws used to fasten a sheet of stainless steel (less noble) to a wall would present a serious corrosion problem in the presence of an electrolyte. But stainless-steel screws in an aluminum sheet most likely would perform acceptably.

METAL FINISHES

There are two primary references for metal finishes: one for metal sheets and shapes and one specifically for hardware. Metal finishing for aluminum, copper alloys, stainless steel, carbon steel, and iron is described in the *Metal Finishes Manual* published by the Architectural

Metal Products Division (AMP) of the National Association of Architectural Metal Manufacturers (NAAMM). The Builders Hardware Manufacturers Association (BHMA) sponsors ANSI A156.18, *American National Standard for Materials and Finishes*, which establishes finishes for metal hardware.

A third reference for metal finishes is still in use by some manufacturers. The Department of Commerce, Commercial Standard CS22-40, used the designation "US" to define metal finishes. However, this standard was discontinued after World War II. For easy comparison, ANSI A156.18 lists the nearest U.S. equivalents to the BHMA designation.

FINISHING PROCESSES

AMP 500, *Introduction to Metal Finishing,* describes the three basic finish types—mechanical, chemical, and coating—for various metals. Application environments, service requirements, and aesthetics together determine which metal finish or coating is best to specify. Finishes are usually selected for both appearance and function. Chromium plating on metal bathroom water faucets and handles or baked enamel on sheet metal lighting fixtures, for example, must be attractive as well as functionally protective.

Mechanical Finishes

Mechanical finishes are accomplished by buffing, grinding, polishing, or otherwise texturing the metal surface for a specific appearance.

As-fabricated finishes comprise the texture and surface appearance given to a metal by the fabrication process.

Buffed finishes are produced by successive polishing and buffing operations using fine abrasives, lubricants, and soft fabric wheels. Polishing and buffing improve edge and surface finishes and render many types of cast parts more durable, efficient, and safe.

Patterned finishes are available in various textures and designs. They are produced by passing an as-fabricated sheet between two matched-design rollers, embossing patterns on both sides of the sheet, or between a smooth roll and a design roll, embossing or coining on one side of the sheet only.

Directional textured finishes are produced by making tiny parallel scratches on the metal surface using a belt or wheel and fine abrasive or by hand-rubbing with steel wool. Metal treated this way has a smooth, satiny sheen.

Peened finishes are achieved by firing a stream of small steel shot at a metal surface at high velocity. The primary aim of shot peening is to increase the fatigue strength of the component; the decorative finish is a by-product. Other nondirectional, textured finishes are produced by blasting metal, under controlled conditions, with silica sand, glass beads, and aluminum oxide.

GUIDELINES FOR SELECTION OF FASTENERS BASED ON GALVANIC ACTION

FASTENER METAL BASE METAL	ZINC AND GALVANIZED STEEL	ALUMINUM & ALUMINUM ALLOYS	STEEL AND CAST IRON	BRASSES, COPPER, BRONZES, MONEL	MARTENSITIC STAINLESS TYPE 410	AUSTENITIC STAINLESS TYPES 302/304, 303, 305
Zinc and Galvanized Steel	A	B	B	C	C	C
Aluminum and Aluminum Alloys	A	A	B	C	Not recommended	B
Steel and Cast Iron	AD	A	A	C	C	B
Terne- (Lead-Tin-) Plated Steel Sheets	ADE	AE	AE	C	C	B
Brasses, Copper, Bronzes, Monel	ADE	AE	AE	A	A	B
Ferritic Stainless Steel (Type 430)	ADE	AE	AE	A	A	A
Austenitic Stainless Steel (Type 302/304)	ADE	AE	AE	AE	A	A

KEY:
A. The corrosion of the base metal is not increased by the fastener.
B. The corrosion of the base metal is marginally increased by the fastener.
C. The corrosion of the base metal may be markedly increased by the fastener material.
D. The plating on the fastener is rapidly consumed, leaving the bare fastener metal.
E. The corrosion of the fastener is increased by the base metal.
Note: Surface treatment and environment can change activity.
Source: Nickel Development Institute; Design Guidelines for the Selection and Use of Stainless Steel; Toronto, Ontario, 1991.

Chemical Finishes

Chemical cleaning cleans the metal surface without affecting it in any other way. This finish is achieved with chlorinated and hydrocarbon solvents and inhibited chemical cleaners or solvents (for aluminum and copper) and pickling, chlorinated, and alkaline solutions (for iron and steel).

Etched finishes produce a matte, frosted surface with varying degrees of roughness by treating the metal with an acid (sulfuric and nitric acid) or alkali solution.

The bright finish process, not used widely, involves chemical or electrolytic brightening of a metal surface, typically aluminum.

Conversion coating is typically categorized as a chemical finish, but since a layer or coating is produced by a chemical reaction, it could be considered a coating as well. Conversion coatings typically prepare the surface of a metal for painting or for receiving another type of finish but are also used to produce a patina or statuary finish. They can be applied either by spray or immersion and provide temporary resistance to a mildly corrosive environment. They can be specified for gray, ductile, and malleable iron castings as well as for steel castings, forgings, or weldments, such as railings and outdoor furniture.

Coatings

Organic coatings on metal can provide protection and serve decorative purposes. Protective coatings include primers or undercoats, pigmented topcoats in hidden areas, and clear finish protective coatings. General categories of organic coatings include paints, varnishes, enamels, lacquers, plastisols, organisols, and powders. Application techniques include dipping and spraying.

Electrodeposition, an increasingly popular alternative to spraying, is similar to electroplating, except that organic resins are deposited instead of metal. The coating builds up to a uniform thickness without runs or sags and can be deposited into the deeply recessed areas of a complex shape. The process of electrodeposition does not waste paint and emits low levels of volatile organic compounds (VOCs); however, it has limited coating thicknesses, and after the first coat, subsequent coats must be sprayed.

Powder coating is perhaps the best known, environmentally acceptable painting process. The paints are solventless, and therefore safer. Powdered paints are formulated in much the same way as solvent-based paints, with the same pigments, fillers, and extenders. Heat-reactive or "heat-latent" hardeners, catalysts, or cross-linkers are used as curing agents. Powder coatings are either thermoplastic or thermosetting. Thermoplastic coatings, which include vinyl, polyethylene, and certain polyesters, are melted by heat during application. Thermosetting paints undergo a chemical change; they cannot be remelted by heat. The thermosets do not require a primer. Coating powders include epoxies, polyurethanes, acrylics, and polyesters.

All three coating types are used extensively on aluminum. Carbon steel and iron require finishes to stabilize the metal surface. Copper alloys are commonly finished with both mechanical and chemical methods. Stainless steel is most frequently finished by mechanical means.

METAL TUBING AND PIPES

Rectangular and square tubing is typically fabricated with from steel and aluminum. The metal tubing fabricated with sharp corners is typically used for miscellaneous architectural metalwork.

Round tubing is measured by the outside diameter and the wall thickness by gauge, fractions, or decimals of an inch. Round tubing is used where a high-grade finish is required and exact diameters are necessary. Round tubing is available in steel, aluminum, copper, stainless steel, and other metals. Consult manufacturer's data for availability of materials and sizes.

Round pipe is made primarily in three weights: standard, extra strong (or extra heavy), and double-extra strong (or double-extra heavy). Outside diameters of the three weights of pipe in each size are always the same: extra wall thickness is always on the inside and therefore reduces the inside diameter of the heavy pipe. All sizes are specified by "nominal inside diameter." Round pipe is available in steel, aluminum, and stainless steel. Consult manufacturer's data for availability of materials and sizes.

METAL ANGLES, T'S, Z'S, AND CHANNELS

Miscellaneous metal angles, t's, z's, and channels are available in steel and aluminum. Consult manufacturer's data for availability of sizes and metal types for each shape.

Betty Ng; Rhode Island School of Design; Providence, Rhode Island
Robert C. Rodgers, P.E.; Richmond Heights, Ohio
MASTERSPEC®; published by ARCOM; Salt Lake City, Utah, and Alexandria, Virginia

COMPARATIVE APPLICABILITY OF VARIOUS FINISHES FOR ARCHITECTURAL APPLICATIONS

TYPE OF FINISH OR TREATMENT	METAL			
	ALUMINUM	COPPER ALLOYS	STAINLESS STEEL	CARBON STEEL AND IRON
MECHANICAL FINISHES				
As-fabricated	Common to all of the metals (produced by hot-rolling, extruding, or casting)			
Bright-rolled	Commonly used (produced by cold-rolling)			
Directional grit textured	Commonly used (produced by polishing, buffing, hand-rubbing, brushing, or cold-rolling)			
Nondirectional matte textured	Commonly used (produced by sand- or shotblasting)			
Bright polished	Commonly used (produced by polishing and buffing)			
Patterned	Available in light sheet gauges of all metals			
CHEMICAL FINISHES				
Nonetch cleaning	Commonly used on all of the metals			
Matte finish	Etched finishes; widely used	Seldom used	Not used	Not used
Bright finish	Limited uses	Rarely used	Not used	Not used
Conversion coatings	Widely used as a pretreatment for painting	Widely used to provide added color variation	Not used	Widely used as a pretreatment for painting
COATINGS				
Organic	Widely used	Opaque types rarely used; transparent types common	Sometimes used	Most important type of finish
Anodic	Most important type of finish	Not used	Not used	Not used
Vitreous	Widely used	Limited use	Not used	Widely used
Metallic	Rarely used	Limited use	Limited use	Widely used
Laminated	Substantial uses	Limited use	Not used	Substantial uses

For more information, see the Metal Finishes Manual for Architectural and Metal Products, *published by the Architectural Metal Products Division of the National Association of Architectural Metal Manufacturers.*

METAL DECK

INSTALLATION AND DESIGN

All metal floor decks must be secured to all supports, generally by means of puddle welds made through the deck to supporting steel. Steel sheet lighter than 22-gauge (0.0295-in.-thick) should be secured by use of welding washers. Shear studs welded through the floor deck also serve to secure the deck to supporting steel.

Side laps between adjacent sheets of deck must be secured by button-punching standing seams, welding, or screws, in accordance with the manufacturer's recommendations.

Decks used as lateral diaphragms must be welded to steel supports around the entire perimeter to ensure development of diaphragm action. More stringent requirements may govern the size and/or spacing of attachments to supports and side lap fasteners or welds.

When lightweight concrete is used in the construction, galvanized deck material should be used. In a fire-resistant assembly, metal components should be unprimed.

FIRE-RESISTANCE RATINGS

Floor deck assembly fire-resistive ratings are available both with and without spray-applied fireproofing and with regular weight or lightweight concrete fill. Ratings from one to three hours are possible using only concrete fill; consult Underwriters Laboratories (UL) Fire Resistance Index for assembly ratings. Consult the manufacturer's literature and technical representatives for additional information. Consult the *Steel Deck Institute Design Manual for Floor Decks and Roof Decks*, and the *Tentative Recommendations for the Design of Steel Deck Diaphragms*, issued by the Steel Deck Institute.

Metal Deck Types

- Floor deck (noncomposite)
- Composite floor deck interacting with concrete
- Permanent forms for self-supporting concrete slabs
- Cellular deck (composite or noncomposite)
- Acoustical cellular deck (composite or noncomposite)
- Electric raceway cellular deck

ROOF DECK TYPES

TYPES	PROFILE	REMARKS	SPAN (FT-IN.)	WIDTH IN. (MM)	MAX. LENGTH (FT-IN.)
Economy		Most economical decks for shorter spans; use with 1 in. or more insulation	2'-6" to 8'-0" (0.76–2.44 m)	32 to 33 (810 to 840)	42'0" (12.8 m)
Narrow rib (1 in. wide)		Use with ½ in. insulation; max. surface area on top for adhering insulation	4'-0" to 8'-0" (1.2–2.4 m)	36 (914)	42'0" (12.8 m)
Intermediate rib (1½ in wide)		Use with 1 in. insulation	4'-0" to 11'-0" (1.2–3.3 m)	36 (914)	42'0" (12.8 m)
Wide rib (2½ in wide)		Use with 1 in. insulation	5'-0" to 12'-0" (1.5-3.6 m)	36 (914)	42'0" (12.8 m)
Acoustical deck		Perforated type for sound absorption only	10'-0" to 20'-0" (3-6.1 m)	24 (610)	42'0" (12.8 m)
Cellular		For use as electrical raceway or as acoustical ceiling; bottom plate is perforated for sound absorption	9'-0" to 12'-0" (2.7–3.6 m)	24 (610)	40'0" (12.2 m)
Cellular			10'-0" to 13'-0" (3-3.9 m)	24 (610)	30'0" (9.1 m)
Cellular			20'-0" to 30'-0" (6.1–9.1 m)	24 (610)	30'0" (9.1 m)

COMPOSITE AND NONCOMPOSITE CELLULAR FLOOR DECK WITH CONCRETE FILL

TYPES	PROFILE	SPAN FT (M)	WIDTH IN. (MM)	CELL CROSS-SECTIONAL AREA
3 × 12 in. cellular deck (for steel frames requiring studs)		12–15 (3.6–4.5)	24 (610) 36 (914)	17.7 sq in./cell (114 sq cm) (35 sq in./sheet) (226 sq cm/sheet)
3 × 8 in. cellular deck (not suitable for structural studs)		12–15 (3.6–4.5)	24 (610)	17.4 sq in./cell (112 sq cm) (52.2 sq in./sheet) (337 sq cm/sheet)
1.5 × 6 in. cellular deck (for thinner total slabs)		4–8 (1.2–2.4)	24 (610) 30 (762) 36 (914)	6 sq in./cell (39 sq cm) (24 sq in./sheet) (155 sq cm/sheet)

COMPOSITE FLOOR DECK WITH CONCRETE FILL

TYPES	PROFILE	REMARKS	SPAN FT-IN. (M)	WIDTH IN. (MM)	MAX. LENGTH FT-IN. (M)
Shallow deck		Convex embossments bond with concrete fill; reverse deck for concave embossments	5'-0" to 12'-0" (1.5–3.6)	36 (914)	42'-0" (12.8)
Intermediate deck		Convex embossments	6'-0" to 13'-0" (1.8–3.9)	24 to 36" (610 to 914)	42'-0" (12.8)
Deep deck		Convex embossments	7'-0" to 14'-0" (2.1–4.2)	24" to 36" (10 to 914)	42'-0" (12.8)

NONCOMPOSITE FLOOR DECK WITH CONCRETE FILL

TYPES	PROFILE	REMARKS	SPAN FT-IN.	WIDTH IN. (MM)	MAX. LENGTH FT-IN.
Shallow deck		Narrow rib	2'-0"– 5'-6" (0.61–1.6 m)	30 (760) 35 (890) 36 (914)	42 (12.8 m)
Intermediate deck		Narrow rib	3'-0" to 10'-0" (0.9–3 m)	32 (810) 33 (840)	42 (12.8 m)
Intermediate deck		Narrow rib	4'-0" to 11'-0" (1.2–3.3 m)	32 (810)	42 (12.8 m)
Intermediate deck		Narrow rib	4'-0" to 11'-0" (1.2–3.3 m)	30 (760) 36 (914)	42 (12.8 m)
Deep deck		Wide rib	5'-6" to 14'-0" (1.6–4.2 m)	24 (610) 36 (914)	42 (12.8 m)

MAX. LOAD: 60 LBS. PER TAB

PIERCING-TYPE HANGER TAB

INTEGRAL HANGER TAB
A convenient, economical means of supporting lightweight acoustical ceilings is attaching a suspension system to hanger tabs at side laps, piercing tabs driven through the deck, or prepunched tabs in the roof deck. Do not use this tab-and-metal deck arrangement to support plaster ceilings, piping, ductwork, electrical equipment, or other heavy loads. Such elements must be suspended directly from structural members or supplementary subframing.

FLOOR DECK ACCESSORIES

CONCRETE COVER
PRESET INSERTS
SEPARATE TROUGH FOR POWER LINES
ACCESS HOLE
CELLULAR METAL DECK
TRENCH SET

Electric raceways may be built into floor slabs by using cellular deck or special units that are blended with plain deck. Two-way distribution is achieved by using trench ducts that sit astride the cellular units at right angles.

Using trench ducts with composite floor deck may reduce or eliminate entirely the effectiveness of composite action at the trench duct. This is also true for composite action between steel floor beams and concrete fill. Trench duct locations must be taken into account in deciding whether composite action is possible.

ELECTRICAL TRENCH DUCT

Advantages of Metal Floor Deck
- Metal floor decks provide a working platform, eliminating temporary wood planking in high-rise use.
- Composite decks provide positive reinforcement for concrete slabs.
- Both noncomposite and composite decks serve as forms for concrete, eliminating the need for forming and stripping.
- Consult the Underwriters Laboratories directory for specific fire-rating requirements.
- Acoustical treatment is possible.
- Electric raceways may be built into the floor slab.
- Metal floor decking provides economical floor assemblies.

Donald Neubauer, P.E.; Neubauer Consulting Engineers; Potomac, Maryland
Walter D. Shapiro, P.E.; Tor, Shapiro & Associates; New York, New York

INTERIOR EXPANSION JOINT COVERS

A large selection of prefabricated assemblies to cover interior expansion joints is available. Fire-rated barrier-type inserts are available and applicable to most assemblies.

Expansion joint covers that will respond to differential movement, both laterally and horizontally, should be provided at joints in structures, located where seismic action may be expected or where differential settlement is anticipated.

Paul Bonsall and Robert D. Abernathy; J.N. Pease Associates; Charlotte, North Carolina

EXPANSION JOINT COVER AT FLOOR AND WALL

SEISMIC JOINT COVERS

JOINT COVERS AT WALL OR CEILING

JOINT COVER AT FLOOR

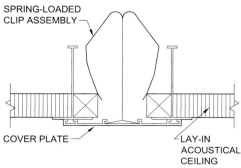

JOINT COVERS AT SUSPENDED CEILING

JOINT COVERS AT WALL

ELASTOMERIC JOINT COVER (REMOVABLE)

WOOD

WOOD CLASSIFICATION

Tree species are divided into two classes—softwood and hardwood—but these terms do not describe a wood's hardness or density. Basswood, for example, is classified as a hardwood but is actually relatively easy to cut or scratch. Softwoods are defined as coniferous trees, evergreens that have needles instead of leaves. Softwoods, by far the more widely used type of wood, are used as framing lumber and in decorative moldings. Hardwoods are from deciduous trees, which have broad leaves that are shed each winter; these include fruit and nut trees. Hardwoods are often used as flooring and furniture components.

WOOD HARVESTING

In response to environmental and lumber availability concerns, wood harvesting of many tree species has undergone change. Some woods, such as teak, are grown on regulated tree farms. Pine trees have been specifically grown for lumber for decades. If wood sources are of concern, an investigation of the source and related lumber practices may be useful.

SOLID WOOD AND WOOD COMPOSITE PANELS

Several different wood products are available for use in interior construction and furniture manufacturing. The traditional solid wood is giving way to the consistency and affordability of a variety of wood composite panels such as particleboard, plywood, medium-density fiberboard, and hardboard.

Solid Wood

Solid wood is used where durability and strength are of concern, for example, in countertop or table edges and chair legs. Unlike veneers or plastic laminates, which must be replaced when damaged, solid wood can be sanded down and refinished. The method by which wood is sawed affects its appearance and usability.

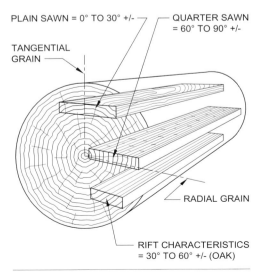

METHODS OF SAWING WOOD
Source: Architectural Woodwork Institute; Reston, Virginia

CONIFEROUS TREE   **DECIDUOUS TREE**

CONIFEROUS NEEDLES   **DECIDUOUS LEAF**

CONIFEROUS (SOFTWOOD) AND DECIDUOUS (HARDWOOD) TREES

Plain-sawn is the most common type of sawn lumber. It produces the least waste and requires the least labor. The cuts are made tangentially to the annual growth rings, which, when viewed from the end of the board, are 30° or less to the face of the board.

Quarter-sawn lumber, available in certain species, is more costly to produce than plain sawn. The growth rings, when viewed from the end of the board, are 60° to 90° to the face of the board. Quarter-sawn lumber is often preferred for wood flooring; because of its uniform surface, it tends to wear more evenly.

Rift-sawn lumber is cut with the growth rings at 30 to 60 degrees to the face of the board. In certain species, primarily oak, rift sawing produces flecks on the surface of the board.

Wood Composite Panels

Decreasing supplies of prime timber may continue to increase the popularity of wood composite panels. These boards are known not for their appearance, but for their performance and affordability.

Particleboard

Particleboard is manufactured from wood particles or fibers, which are bonded under heat and pressure with an adhesive resin. The wood particles can be viewed easily by examining a piece of particleboard. Its surface is relatively smooth and hard and can hold a shaped edge fairly well. It is one of the most dimensionally stable of the cellulosic boards. Exposed particleboard edges are usually covered, often with a solid wood edging, to improve their appearance. The edges offer poor screw-holding capability.

Particleboard is the most commonly specified substrate for decorative laminates. It is also popular for use as kitchen cabinet shelving and as a flooring underlayment. ANSI A 208.1, *Wood Particleboard,* sponsored by the National Particleboard Association (NPA), establishes the minimum performance requirements for particleboard.

HARDWOODS AND SOFTWOODS

SPECIES	SOFT-WOOD	HARD-WOOD	HARD-NESS
Ash		—	Hard
Basswood		—	Soft
Beech		—	Hard
Birch, Yellow		—	Hard
Cedar, Western Red	—		Soft
Cherry, American Black		—	Hard
Fir, Douglas	—		Medium
Hickory		—	Very hard
Maple, Hard		—	Very hard
Maple, Soft— "Natural"		—	Medium
Oak, English Brown		—	Hard
Oak, Red		—	Hard
Oak, White		—	Hard
Pecan		—	Hard
Pine, Ponderosa	—		Medium
Pine, Southern Yellow	—		Medium
Redwood	—		Soft
Teak		—	Hard
Walnut, American Black		—	Hard

Source: AWI, Architectural Woodwork Institute; Reston, Virginia

PARTICLEBOARD INTERIOR APPLICATIONS

APPLICATION	GRADE (ANSI A208.1)	PRODUCT REFERENCES
Floor Underlayment	M-1	ICBO, SBCCI, BOCA, One- and Two-Family Dwelling Code
Shelving	M-1 M-2 M-3	
Countertops	M-2 M-3	ANSI A161.1
Kitchen Cabinets	M-S M-2	ANSI A161.1
Door Cores	LD-1	MWWDA Industry Series IS 1 (*Wood Flush Doors*)
Stair Treads	M-3	HUD/FHA UM 70a
Moldings	M-3	WWMMP Standard WM 2

Source: National Particleboard Association; Buyer's and Specifier's Guide to Particleboard and MDF, 1994–95.

PARTIAL LIST OF REQUIREMENTS IN ANSI A 208.1, *WOOD PARTICLEBOARD*

REQUIREMENTS FOR GRADES OF TYPE 1 WOOD PARTICLEBOARD (FOR INTERIOR APPLICATIONS)

GRADE	HARDNESS	GENERAL USES
1-H-1	500	High-density industrial products
1-H-2	1000	
1-H-3	1500	
1-M-1	500	Underlayment, commercial
1-M-2	500	Industrial
1-M-3	500	Industrial
1-M-S	500	Commercial, industrial
1-LD-1	NS	Door core
1-LD-2	NS	Door core

H—High nominal density (above 50 lbs/sq ft (240 kg/sq m))
M—Medium nominal density (40 to 50 lbs/sq ft (200 to 240 kg/sq m))
LD—Lower nominal density (less than 40 lbs/sq ft (200 kg/sq m))

Plywood

Plywood is a sandwich of wood or wood products between two layers of wood veneer, top and bottom. Particleboard and medium-density fiberboard (MDF) are commonly used as a core for plywood. Layers of wood veneer or solid lumber can also be used. There are generally two categories of plywood: that which is faced with hardwood and used for decorative purposes and that which is used for underlayment or other concealed construction applications.

Construction-grade plywood is graded and marked according to product standard PS 1, *Construction and Industrial Plywood,* promulgated by the U.S. Department of Commerce, National Institute of Standards and Technology (NIST), in cooperation with the American Plywood Association (APA). Construction-grade plywood is rated and marked according to application, exposure (whether appropriate for interior or exterior use), and thickness.

Hardwood veneer plywood is used extensively in the manufacturing of furniture and decorative wall paneling. The Hardwood Plywood Manufacturers Association (HPMA) sponsors ANSI HP-1, *Hardwood and Decorative Plywood.* This standard classifies hardwood veneer plywood by species, grade of veneers, type of plywood, composition of the plywood panel, and size and thickness.

Medium-Density Fiberboard (MDF)

Medium-density fiberboard (MDF) is manufactured by breaking down wood particles into fibers through the use of steam pressure. The resulting fibers are mixed with an adhesive resin and pressed into MDF panels. The fineness of the fibers used in MDF determines its homogeneous appearance and very smooth surface. The panel edge allows intricate machining, and the face can be embossed to produce three-dimensional cabinet door fronts and moldings. MDF is also used as a substrate for decorative laminates.

ANSI HP CLASSIFICATION CATEGORIES FOR HARDWOOD AND DECORATIVE PLYWOOD

SPECIES	
Seventy-one species are classified in four categories (A, B, C, and D), based primarily on their modulus of elasticity and specific gravity.	
GRADES OF VENEERS	
Face Grades (Grade AA permits the fewest number of natural characteristics; more and larger flaws are permitted in each successive grade.)	Grades AA, A, B, C, D, E
Specialty Grade	SP
Back Grades	1, 2, 3, and 4
Inner Ply Grades	J, K, L, and M
TYPES OF PLYWOOD	
(Listed in descending order of the bond water-resistance.)	
Technical (Exterior)	
Type 1 (Exterior)	
Type 2 (Interior)	
CONSTRUCTIONS (BASED ON THE KIND OF CORE)	
Hardwood veneer core	
Softwood veneer core	
Hardwood lumber core	
Softwood lumber core	
Particleboard core	
Medium-density fiberboard (MDF) core	
Hardboard core	
Special core	

THREE-PLY VENEER CORE CONSTRUCTION

FIVE-PLY VENEER CORE CONSTRUCTION

THREE-PLY PARTICLEBOARD OR MDF CORE CONSTRUCTION

PLYWOOD TYPES

ANSI A 208.2, *Medium-Density Fiberboard,* sponsored by the NPA, describes the requirements for the strength and dimensional stability of MDF. MDF is available in different thicknesses and is classified by density and use (interior or exterior). There are four product grades: high-density; two medium densities, one for thicknesses greater than ⅞ in. (21 mm) and another for those of ⅞ in. (21 mm) or less; and low-density. As much as 95% of the MDF manufactured in the United States is medium-density grade.

Hardboard

Hardboard is essentially a high-density fiberboard. It is made from the same type of fibers used in MDF but is bonded under higher pressure, often without an adhesive. Hardboard is commonly known by the trade name Masonite. The familiar pegboard is made of hardboard. Two types of hardboard are available: smooth on one side or smooth on both sides. ANSI A 135.4, *Basic Hardboard,* sponsored by the American Hardboard Association (AHA), defines five classes of hardboard. Class 4 Service panels are recommended as underlayment for resilient flooring.

CLASSIFICATION AND MARKING OF HARDBOARD IN ANSI A135.4, *BASIC HARDBOARD*

CLASS NUMBER	NAME	MARKING (NUMBER AND COLOR OF STRIPES ON BOARD'S EDGE)
1	Tempered	1 red
2	Standard	2 red
3	Service tempered	1 green
4	Service	2 green
5	Industrialite	1 blue

WOOD FINISHING

Finishing operations include the application of stains and a protective topcoat. Finishing protects the wood surface from permanent staining by sealing the pores; it also guards against damage to the wood surface caused by heat, dirt, and spills, and enhances the beauty of the wood grain and color.

Concerns regarding volatile organic compounds (VOCs) have led to the development of water-based finishes. Recent improvements have increased the clarity and durability of the newer wood finishes.

Stains

Stains are transparent or opaque coatings that penetrate and color a wood surface without masking its inherent grain. Stains can be used to change the color of a piece of wood. For example, mahogany is usually stained a deep red-brown to modify its natural light-orange color. Sometimes wood is stained to resemble a different species.

Lacquers

Lacquers dry by the evaporation of their strong solvents. The solvents evaporate so fast that lacquers are typically spray-applied, rather than brushed on. Lacquers may or may not contain pigments and are the most popular commercial furniture and casework finishes. Acrylic and vinyl lacquers are available, which do not have a nitrocellulose base as do noncatalyzed and catalyzed lacquers.

Standard, or noncatalyzed, lacquers can be touched up easily or recoated, because the solvent in each coat slightly dissolves the previous coat, forming a monolithic finish. They are the most popular furniture finishes.

Catalyzed lacquers, like noncatalyzed lacquers, contain nitrocellulose. They dry faster than standard lacquers, so dust is even less likely to settle on the curing coat and contaminate the finish. Catalyzed lacquers are harder than standard lacquers and are moderately easy to touch up. They are very hard and brittle, and tend to splinter and spiderweb.

Varnishes

Varnishes cure by evaporation of the solvents, oxidation of the oil, or both. Polyurethane, added to make varnish resistant to water and alcohol, is popular as a wood floor finish. Conversion varnishes, like the lacquers, are very durable and fast drying, forming thick coats. They have superb resistance to a variety of common chemicals.

Polyester and Polyurethane Finishes

The contemporary, high-tech polyester and polyurethane coatings are known for their excellent chemical resistance and incredibly durable, dense, and smooth finishes. When pigmented, they resemble high-pressure decorative laminates. They require special skill and equipment for application and are expensive. Spectacularly shiny gloss levels can be achieved with these coatings. Polyesters are basically 100% solids when applied and are extremely difficult to touch up. Like polyesters, polyurethanes exhibit hardness and excellent resistance to chemicals but are much easier to apply.

PLASTICS

Plastics comprise a widely diverse group of materials; worldwide, there are about 15,000 different plastic formulas available. Like metals, plastics can be alloyed (mixed) with other such materials to improve performance characteristics. Many plastics have long, multisyllable chemical titles, and manufacturers often devise trade names for better marketability. For example, polytetrafluoroethylene is best known by the trade name Teflon.

All plastics share three common traits:

- First, with few exceptions (silicone is one), plastics are based on the carbon atom.
- Second, plastics are derived from petrochemicals.
- Third, all plastics are *polymers,* which are giant molecules, composed of up to millions of relatively light, simple molecules. *Polymerization,* the formation of these giant chains, is basic to the formation of plastics. Polymers are characterized by high molecular weight, outstanding stability, and a strength of intermolecular force that prevents easy destruction.

COMPONENTS OF PLASTICS

Resin (like polymer, an alternative term used for *plastic*) is the basic ingredient of plastic. Resins are combined with fillers, stabilizers, plasticizers, pigments, and other components to form plastics.

- *Fillers* are added to impart a certain characteristic property, such as durability or heat resistance. Some fillers, called *extenders*, may be added to decrease the amount of relatively expensive plastic required and to increase the mass of the product.
- *Stabilizers* lend protection against degradation of the plastic resulting from exposure to environmental conditions such as ultraviolet rays and even oxygen.
- *Plasticizers* are mixed with the resin to increase flexibility, resiliency, and impact resistance. The addition of plasticizers lends the required flexibility to sheet vinyl so that it can be rolled without cracking.

Plastics are commonly categorized as either thermoplastic or thermosetting materials.

- *Thermoplastics* become soft when heated and can be remolded repeatedly without affecting the properties of the plastic. Thermoplastics harden when cooled and require the addition of plasticizers to increase their flexibility.
- *Thermoset plastics* are permanently hardened after undergoing an irreversible chemical change during processing. Once they are set, they cannot be softened and remolded.

THERMOPLASTICS

Thermoplastics generally offer higher impact strength, easier processing, and better adaptability to complex designs than thermosets. Thermoplastics commonly used in construction materials and furniture include acrylonitrile-butadiene-styrene, acrylics, cellulosics, fluoroplastics, nylons, polyolefins, polystyrenes, and vinyls.

Acrylonitrile-Butadiene-Styrene (ABS)

Introduced in the late 1940s, acrylonitrile-butadiene-styrene (ABS) is very tough, but not brittle, and is resistant to chemicals and to impact. ABS is used in construction for plumbing drain, waste, and vent pipes. Outdoor furniture, drawer liners, and chair shells are common furniture applications for ABS.

Acrylics

Acrylics have the clarity of glass, good weatherability, surface hardness, and chemical resistance. This material is lightweight and colorfast; it does not yellow with age. Acrylics are used for skylight glazing, safety glazing, and paint resins. Lucite and Plexiglas are popular trade names.

Cellulosics

Developed in 1868, cellulose nitrate was the first synthetic plastic material. One of its early uses, in response to an ivory shortage, was in hair combs and billiard balls. Celluloid (photographic film) and cellophane (packaging material) are in the cellulosic family of plastics. The breakage resistance of cellulosics makes them ideal for table edging, venetian blind wands, signage, and store fixtures.

Fluoroplastics

Common characteristics of fluoroplastics are outstanding chemical resistance, resistance to temperatures from 425°F (220°C) to 500°F (260°C), low coefficient of friction, and practically no moisture absorption. Polyvinyl fluoride (PVF) and polytetrafluoroethylene (commonly known by the trade name Teflon) are the most commonly used fluoroplastics in architectural applications.

Nylon

Nylon was originally developed by DuPont in the 1930s and was first used as a high-strength fiber for women's stockings. Nylons offer high strength, toughness at low temperatures, and good wear and abrasion resistance. Nylon is probably best known as an extruded fiber in textiles and carpet. It is commonly used for chair caster rollers and drawer glides because of its low friction characteristic.

Polyolefins

The family of polyolefins includes many popular plastics used in commercial interiors products, such as polybutylenes, polyethylenes, and polypropylenes.

- *Polybutylenes* (PB) exhibit good retention of mechanical properties at elevated temperatures and high tensile strength. The largest markets for PB are plumbing supply pipe, hot-melt adhesives, and sealants.
- *Polyethylenes* are known for their strength and flexibility. They are tough materials, have excellent chemical resistance, offer a low coefficient of friction, and are easy to process. Polyethylene is commonly used for electrical wire insulation. In clear sheet form, it is used as a vapor barrier. It is also used as molded seating, drawer glides, and door tracks.
- *Polypropylenes* are among the most versatile plastics and are employed in many fabrication methods. They are semitranslucent or milky white in color and have excellent colorability and chemical resistance, a high melting point, and are moderately priced. Fiber is a major market for polypropylenes. They are commonly used in upholstery fabric, carpet backing, and indoor/outdoor carpet fiber.

Polystyrenes

Polystyrenes are inexpensive and easy to process. They are noted for their sparkling clarity, hardness, and extreme ease of processing. They have excellent colorability and are widely used for disposable fast-food packaging and cups. In the construction industry, polystyrenes are used for light fixture diffusers in sheet form and as the core material for doors in foamed, or expanded, form. For furniture, they are commonly used for wood-grain-patterned chair parts and mirror frames.

Vinyls

Vinyls encompass a large group of plastics, including polyvinyl chloride (PVC) and polyvinyl butyral (PVB). PVC has good impact resistance and dimensional stability and may be best known for its application as plumbing pipe. PVCs constitute perhaps the largest volume of plastics consumed worldwide.

Since 1938, PVB has been used as an interlayer in safety glass; it is also popular for use as a textile coating. Within the interiors industry, materials such as floor coverings, window blinds, upholstery material, and wallcoverings are largely made of vinyl.

THERMOSETS

Thermosets generally resist higher temperatures and provide greater dimensional stability than thermoplastics. Thermosets include alkyds, epoxies, furans, melamines, thermoset polyesters, and polyurethanes.

Alkyds

Alkyds are classified as polyesters. Alkyd plastics are actually by-products of the alkyd coating industry. Offering moderately high heat resistance, alkyds have a rapid cure cycle and good mold flow characteristics, which allow them to be molded into relatively complicated shapes. Their most prevalent use in commercial interiors is as a paint coating.

Epoxies

Epoxy resins react with curing agents or hardeners to form an exceptionally durable plastic. Epoxies have superior adhesion and excellent resistance to chemicals and corrosion. Their application in the construction industry is mainly as adhesives or protective coatings for floors and walls. Epoxy ester coatings are often used in floor and gymnasium finishes. Powder coatings, based on heat-cured epoxy resins, are increasingly popular as metal furniture finishes. Epoxies are an important component of solid surfacing materials such as Corian.

Furans

Furan resins are naturally dark in color and turn black when catalyzed to cure. Their most common use is in corrosion-resistant cements and grouts. The floors and walls of such structures as manholes and processing tanks can be protected by furan cement.

Melamines

Hardness, clarity, and stain resistance characterize the melamine family of plastics. Melamine surfaces are difficult to scratch or cut and they do not yellow with age. Most laminating resins for both low- and high-pressure laminates are melamines.

Thermoset decorative laminates, sometimes referred to as *low-pressure laminates,* are made by impregnating laminating paper with melamine resin and then applying it to a substrate (usually particleboard) under low pressure and low heat. The substrate is cut to the required size and shape, and the thermoset decorative laminate is applied, effectively sealing in the substrate. Polyester-impregnated paper is also used on thermoset decorative laminates. These panels are often used as interior panels and shelves in casework. They are not as durable as high-pressure decorative laminates, but they are far less expensive.

High-pressure decorative laminates (HPDLs) consist of a sandwich of melamine-impregnated overlay and decorative surface papers, over phenolic resin-impregnated

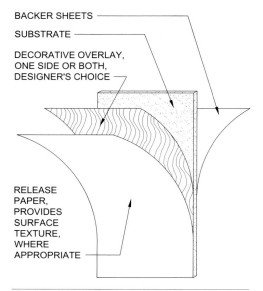

BACKER SHEETS

SUBSTRATE

DECORATIVE OVERLAY, ONE SIDE OR BOTH, DESIGNER'S CHOICE

RELEASE PAPER, PROVIDES SURFACE TEXTURE, WHERE APPROPRIATE

LOW-PRESSURE LAMINATE

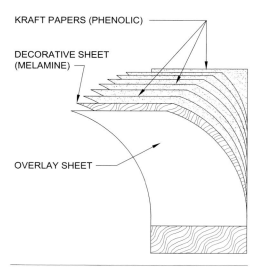

KRAFT PAPERS (PHENOLIC)

DECORATIVE SHEET (MELAMINE)

OVERLAY SHEET

HIGH-PRESSURE DECORATIVE LAMINATE

papers. These layers are pressed under temperatures exceeding 265°F (130°C) and high pressure. HPDLs are known by the common trade name Formica. Unlike thermoset decorative laminates, sheets of HPDLs are adhered to the surface of substrates, such as particleboard, which can then be trimmed and edge-banded.

The National Electrical Manufacturers Association (NEMA) publishes the standard for HPDLs—NEMA LD 3 *High-Pressure Decorative Laminates*. Before World War II, laminates were produced primarily for

electrical insulation. Although HPDLs today are used in a much greater variety of decorative applications, NEMA still promulgates the standard.

The four most common types of HPDL sheets are:

HGS, formerly GP (General Purpose). Used for most horizontal surfaces, for example, countertops. This type can be bent to a radius of approximately 6 in. (152 mm).

CLS, formerly CL (Cabinet Liner). A thin sheet used for vertical applications, typically inside casework, that will not be required to withstand heavy wear. (The cabinet liner should not be used as a balancing/backer sheet for countertops.)

BKL, formerly BK (Backer). Economical, nondecorative sheets used on the side of the substrate hidden from view to prevent warping as a result of changes in temperature or humidity.

HGP, formerly PF (Postforming). Used for tightly radiused curves, for example, at the edge of a formed countertop.

Polyesters

Thermoset polyesters include a very large family of plastics. Polyester is commonly used with glass fibers to form *fiberglass. Alkyds,* used in paints and other coatings, are oil-modified polyesters. A *gel coat* is a pigmented polyester coating that is applied to the inside surface of a mold and becomes an integral part of the finished piece. Cultured marble countertops are fabricated with a polyester gel coat.

Polyurethanes

Polyurethanes are available in a multitude of forms with an extensive variety of physical properties. Rigid polyurethane foam is widely used as a building insulation material. However, the most common application of polyurethane is for cushioning in seating and mattresses. Polyurethane foam can be molded for a preformed chair seat or back, or foam slabs can be cut into the desired shape.

Silicones

Silicones are unique among plastics because they are based on the silicon atom, rather than the carbon atom. The raw material for silicone is one of the most abundant on the Earth's surface—sand (quartzite). Silicone is still obtained by a process developed by General Electric in the 1940s. Similar to the way in which iron is reduced from iron ore, silicone is obtained by the reduction of silicon dioxide in a furnace. Silicones are known for their stability through a wide range of temperatures, ultraviolet radiation, and harsh weather. They are used in commercial interior applications as water-repellent fabric finishes and joint sealants.

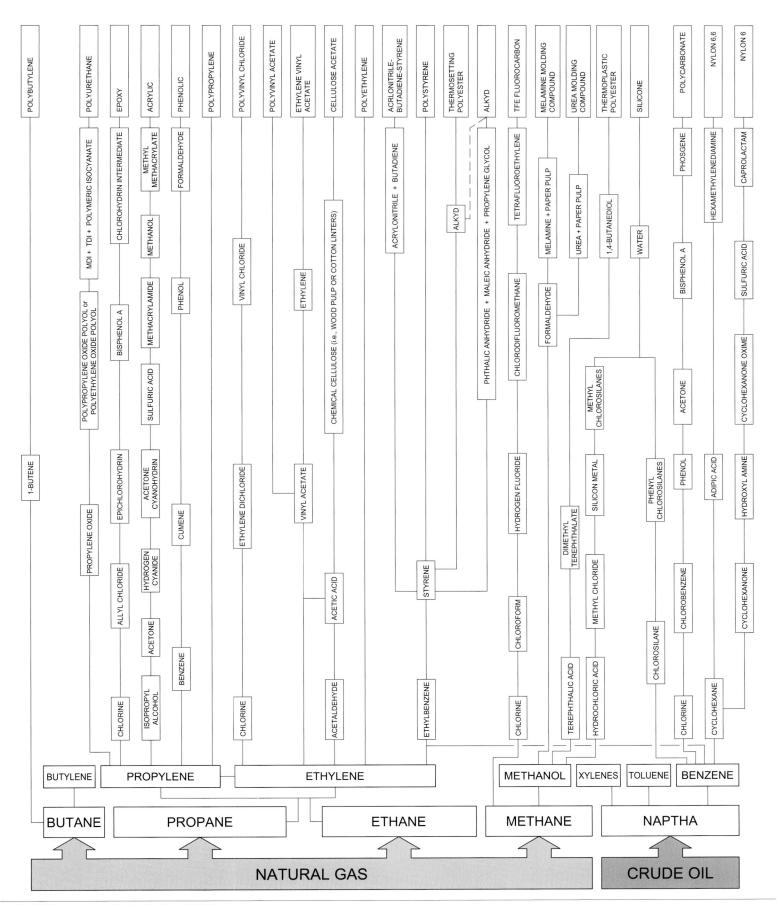

DERIVATION OF MAJOR PLASTIC RESINS

CLOSET AND UTILITY WOOD SHELVING

WOOD SHELF NO EDGE REINFORCEMENT NECESSARY

2" MIN. OVERHANG

16" OR 24" O.C. TYP. (ALIGN AT STUDS)

METAL STANDARDS GENERALLY SURFACE MOUNTED WITH SCREWS

METAL BRACKETS

STANDARDS AND BRACKETS

SHELF SUPPORT STANDARDS RECESSED IN SIDE WALL

ADJUSTABLE SHELF SUPPORT

STANDARDS AND CLIPS

STANDARDS SHELVING SYSTEM

WOOD CLEAT

WOOD BLOCKING, TOP AND BOTTOM

CLEAT ATTACHED TO SHELF UNIT

HANGING BRACKET HOUSING

CLEAT ATTACHED TO WALL AT STUD

HANGING RAIL

CLEAT

WOOD BLOCKING

HANGING CLEAT

HANGING BRACKET

All details except hanging bracket and rail must also be floor-supported.

BOOKSHELF WALL ATTACHMENT METHODS

PLYWOOD BACK

WOOD CROWN MOLD

EDGE BANDED SHELF

WOOD FACE FRAME

WOOD TOE BOARD

FIXED-SHELF

SHELF

SHELF

WOOD CLEAT

CLEAT

THROUGH DADO

WOOD FACE

SHELF

BLIND DADO

SHELF SUPPORT DETAILS

FIXED-SHELF SYSTEM

8 mm DIAMETER WOOD DOWELS SPACED 32 mm APART

ADJUSTABLE SHELF

NOTE: ALL DIMENSIONS AND SPACING ARE BASED ON A 32 mm MODULE

BOX FRAME

PLASTIC OR METAL HOUSING SET INTO BOTTOM OF SHELF; HOUSING FITS OVER FIXING SCREW

8 mm DIAMETER HOLES FOR BOX FRAME CONSTRUCTION

32 mm O.C.

32 mm O.C.

SHELF SUPPORT PINS

FIXING SCREW

5 mm DIAMETER HOLES FOR REMOVABLE SHELF PINS

32-MM SHELF SUPPORT SYSTEM

METAL CAM INSERTED INTO FRAME WALL

METAL EXPANSION SUPPORT PIN SCREWED INTO SHELF

CAM SCREW

WOOD SHELF

SEMIFIXED SHELF DETAIL

BOX FRAME SHELF SYSTEM

WOOD VENEER OR PLASTIC LAMINATE

PLYWOOD

MEDIUM DENSITY PARTICLEBOARD OR FIBERBOARD

WOOD EDGE BAND

EDGE BAND

BUTT JOINT

SOLID WOOD

BULLNOSE

RABBET JOINT

SHELF EDGE DETAILS

STANDARD CASEWORK AND CLOSET SHELVING DIMENSIONS

WALL-HUNG AND BASE CABINETS

ADA-COMPLIANT WALL-HUNG AND BASE CABINETS

Source: Architectural Woodwork Institute; Architectural Quality Standards, 7th Ed. (Version 1.2); Reston, Virginia, 1999

Kelsey Kruse, AIA; George Vaeth Associates, Inc.; Columbia, Maryland

CLOTHES CABINET

TELLER COUNTER

RECEPTION COUNTER

CLOSET AND UTILITY SHELVING

SHELF

SHELF WITH CLOTHES ROD

SHELF WITH INTERMEDIATE SUPPORT

SHELF WITH APPLIED DROP APRON

CABINET CONSTRUCTION

SOFFIT

WALL CABINET

PLASTIC LAMINATE
COUNTERTOP ON MDF OR
INDUSTRIAL PARTICLEBOARD

HARDBOARD
BACKING, TYP.

KILN-DRIED
SOLID LUMBER
OR PANEL
PRODUCT

BASE CABINET

FLUSH OVERLAY CONSTRUCTION

HARDBOARD BACKING, TYP.

SCRIBE TO WALL, TYP.

MELAMINE, WOOD VENEER,
OR PLASTIC LAMINATE SURFACE
ON MDF OR INDUSTRIAL
PARTICLEBOARD, TYP.

OPTIONAL BLOCK
FOR PIVOT HINGE

WALL CABINET AT DOOR

SCRIBE TO WALL, TYP.

SOLID HARDWOOD FACE PANEL

DRAWER FRONT

CABINET DOOR

BASE CABINET AT DRAWER

Flush overlay construction offers a clean, contemporary look because only the doors and drawer fronts are visible in elevation. When specified, grain matching between doors and drawer fronts can be achieved by having all pieces cut from the same panel. This style lends itself well to the use of plastic laminate for exposed surfaces. Conventional as well as concealed hinges are available for a variety of door thicknesses.

SOFFIT

WALL CABINET   REVEAL, TYP.

PLASTIC LAMINATE
COUNTERTOP ON MDF OR
INDUSTRIAL PARTICLEBOARD

FACE
FRAME,
TYP.   DRAWER

HARDBOARD
BACKING, TYP.

KILN-DRIED
SOLID LUMBER
OR PANEL
PRODUCT

BASE CABINET

REVEAL OVERLAY CONSTRUCTION

HARDBOARD BACKING, TYP.

SCRIBE TO WALL, TYP.

MELAMINE, WOOD VENEER,
OR PLASTIC LAMINATE SURFACE
ON MDF OR INDUSTRIAL
PARTICLEBOARD, TYP.

OPTIONAL BLOCK
FOR PIVOT HINGE

REVEAL, TYP.

REVEAL, TYP.

WALL CABINET AT DOOR

SCRIBE TO WALL, TYP.

SOLID HARDWOOD

DRAWER FRONT

CABINET DOOR

BASE CABINET AT DRAWER

Reveal overlay construction accents the separation between doors and drawer fronts by a reveal. This style is equally suited to either wood or plastic laminate construction. Although the detail shown here incorporates a reveal at all horizontal and vertical joints, this can be varied by the designer. A reveal over ½ in. (13 mm) requires the addition of a face frame, which will change the hinge requirements. With or without a face frame, this style allows the use of conventional or concealed hinges.

Source: Architectural Woodwork Institute; Architectural Quality Standards, 7th Ed. (Version 1.2), Reston, Virginia, 1999.

SOFFIT

WALL CABINET

PLASTIC LAMINATE
COUNTERTOP ON MDF OR
INDUSTRIAL PARTICLEBOARD

DRAWER

FACE
FRAME,
TYP.

HARDBOARD
BACKING, TYP.

KILN-DRIED
SOLID LUMBER
OR PANEL
PRODUCT

BASE CABINET

HARDBOARD BACKING, TYP.

SCRIBE TO WALL, TYP.

MELAMINE, WOOD VENEER,
OR PLASTIC LAMINATE SURFACE
ON MDF OR INDUSTRIAL
PARTICLEBOARD, TYP.

WALL CABINET AT DOOR

SCRIBE TO WALL, TYP.

SOLID HARDWOOD

DRAWER FRONT

CABINET DOOR

BASE CABINET AT DRAWER

Flush inset construction without a face frame is a highly functional style that allows the use of different thicknesses of door and drawer fronts. Door and drawer faces are flush with the face of the cabinet. This is generally an expensive style due to the increased care required in fitting and aligning the doors and drawers. This style does not lend itself to the economical use of plastic laminate covering finishes.

FLUSH INSET CONSTRUCTION WITHOUT FACE FRAME

SOFFIT

WALL CABINET

PLASTIC LAMINATE
COUNTERTOP ON MDF OR
INDUSTRIAL PARTICLEBOARD

DRAWER

FACE
FRAME,
TYP.

HARDBOARD
BACKING, TYP.

KILN-DRIED
SOLID LUMBER
OR PANEL
PRODUCT

BASE CABINET

HARDBOARD BACKING, TYP.

MELAMINE, WOOD VENEER,
OR PLASTIC LAMINATE SURFACE
ON MDF OR INDUSTRIAL
PARTICLEBOARD, TYP.

SOLID WOOD FACE FRAME, TYP.

WALL CABINET AT DOOR

SOLID WOOD FACE FRAME, TYP.

DRAWER FRONT

CABINET DOOR

BASE CABINET AT DRAWER

Flush inset construction with a face frame is a highly functional style that allows the use of different thicknesses of door and drawer fronts. Door and drawer faces are flush with the face of the cabinet. This is generally the most expensive of the four styles due to the increased care required in fitting and aligning the doors and drawers, in addition to the cost of providing the face frame. Conventional butt hinges should be avoided where hinge screws are attached to the edge-grain of panel products. This style does not lend itself to the economical use of plastic laminate covering finishes.

FLUSH INSET CONSTRUCTION WITH FACE FRAME

Source: *Architectural Woodwork Institute; Architectural Quality Standards, 7th Ed. (Version 1.2), Reston, Virginia, 1999.*

CABINET JOINERY

Spline joints are used to strengthen and align faces when gluing panels in width or length, including items requiring site assembly.

SPLINE JOINT

Stub tenant joints are commonly used for assembling stile and rail frames that require additional supports, such as web or skeleton case frames.

STUB TENON

Haunch mortise and tenon joints are commonly used for assembling paneled doors or stile and rail-type paneling.

HAUNCH MORTISE AND TENON JOINTS

Conventional mortise and tenon joints are commonly used for assembling square-edged surfaces such as case face frames.

CONVENTIONAL MORTISE AND TENON JOINT

Dowel joints are an alternative joinery method serving the same function as the conventional mortise and tenon joint.

DOWEL JOINT

French dovetail joints are used to join drawer sides to fronts when fronts conceal metal extension slides or overlay the case faces.

FRENCH DOVETAIL JOINT

Dovetail joints are the conventional method for joining drawer sides to fronts or backs. Usually limited to flush- or lipped-type drawers.

CONVENTIONAL DOVETAIL JOINT

Drawer lock joints are another joinery method for joining drawer sides to fronts. It is usually used for flush-type installations but can be adapted to lip- or overlay-type drawers.

DRAWER LOCK JOINT

Butt joints can be used at exposed finished ends for an economical treatment.

BUTT JOINT

Lock miter joints can be used at exposed finished ends.

LOCK MITERED JOINT

Through dado joints are conventionally used for the assembly of case body members. The dado is usually concealed by application of the case face frame.

THROUGH DADO

Blind dado joints are a variation of conventional dado joints, with applied edge "stopping" or concealed dado groove. They are often used when the case body edge is exposed.

BLIND DADO

Stop dado joints are another method of concealing dado exposure. They are applicable when veneer edging or solid lumber is used.

STOP DADO

Dowel joints are fast becoming an industry standard assembly method. This joint is often based on a 32 mm (1¼ in) spacing of dowels.

DOWEL JOINT

Screwed joints can be used where exposed fasteners are appropriate.

SCREWED JOINT

Architectural Woodwork Institute; Reston, Virginia

2   □   FINISH CARPENTRY

Source: *Architectural Woodwork Institute;* Architectural Quality Standards, *7th Ed. (Version 1.2), Reston, Virginia, 1999.*

CABINET HINGES AND CATCHES

CABINET HINGES

Hinge Type	BUTT	WRAPAROUND	PIVOT (KNIFE)	EUROPEAN (CONCEALED)	FACE-MOUNT
Elevation of Cabinet Face					
Door Swing	180°	180°	180°	95°, 125°, or 170°	180°
Easily Adjusted after Installation	No	No	No	Yes	Yes
Strength	High	Very High	Moderate	High-Moderate	Moderate
Requires Mortising	Yes	Occasionally	Usually	Yes	No
Cost of Hinge	Low	Moderate	Low	High	Low
Ease of Installation	Moderate	Easy	Moderate	Very Easy	Easy
Adjustability	No	One-Way	Two-Way	Three-Way	No
Easily Adjusted after Installation	No	No	No	Yes	No

Self-closing hinges spring-close the cabinet door when it is within 28° from being closed. When it is opened beyond 30°, the self-closer does not function, allowing the door to be left open. The self-closing feature eliminates the need for catches. Butt hinges are the only listed hinges not available with the self-closing feature.
After: Architectural Woodwork Institute; Reston, Virginia

BUTTON CATCH WITH STRIKE

TOUCH LATCH CATCH WITH STRIKE

BALL CATCH

BAR CATCH WITH STRIKE

BAR CATCH WITH STRIKE

DOUBLE ROLLER CATCH WITH C-CLIP STRIKE

MAGNETIC CATCHES

FRICTION CATCHES

DRAWER GLIDES

TRI-ROLLER GLIDE

CENTER-MOUNT GLIDE

SIDE-MOUNT GLIDE WITH THREE-FOURTHS EXTENSION

FULL-EXTENSION BALL BEARING GLIDE

EUROPEAN SIDE-MOUNT GLIDE WITH THREE-FOURTHS EXTENSION

EUROPEAN BOTTOM-MOUNT GLIDE WITH THREE-FOURTHS EXTENSION

STANDARD BASE CABINETS

2'-3"

OUTLET LOCATION, TYP.

6"

3/4" ADJUSTABLE SHELF CLAD IN PLASTIC LAMINATE WITH 1 1/2" FRONT LIP ON STANDARDS AND BRACKETS (RECESSED INSIDE PANELS)

1/2" PLYWOOD BACK ON 1 X 4 CLEATS

1 1/2"

3/4"

3'-0"

4"

3"

3/4" FULL-HEIGHT BACKSPLASH CLAD IN PLASTIC LAMINATE

3/4" COUNTERTOP CLAD IN PLASTIC LAMINATE

INTERIOR OF CABINET CLAD IN WHITE MELAMINE

3/4" SUBSTRATE CLAD IN PLASTIC LAMINATE (FRONT AND BACK)

BASE AS SCHEDULED

BASE CABINET WITH SINGLE DOOR

2'-6"

OUTLET LOCATION, TYP.

6"

3/4" ADJUSTABLE SHELF CLAD IN PLASTIC LAMINATE WITH 1 1/2" FRONT LIP ON STANDARDS AND BRACKETS (RECESSED INSIDE PANELS)

1/2" PLYWOOD BACK ON 1 X 4 CLEATS

1 1/2"

3/4"

1 1/2"

3'-0"

1 1/2"

4 3/4"

2 1/4"

3/4" FULL-HEIGHT BACKSPLASH CLAD IN PLASTIC LAMINATE

3/4" COUNTERTOP CLAD IN PLASTIC LAMINATE

PLASTIC LAMINATE ALL EXPOSED SURFACES

PLASTIC LAMINATE INTERIOR

BASE AS SCHEDULED

OPEN BASE CABINET WITH SHELF

2'-3"

OUTLET LOCATION, TYP.

6"

3/4" ADJUSTABLE SHELF CLAD IN PLASTIC LAMINATE WITH 1 1/2" FRONT LIP ON STANDARDS AND BRACKETS (RECESSED INSIDE PANELS)

1/2" PLYWOOD BACK ON 1 X 4 CLEATS

1 1/2"

6"

3/4"

3'-0"

4"

3"

3/4" FULL-HEIGHT BACKSPLASH CLAD IN PLASTIC LAMINATE

3/4" COUNTERTOP CLAD IN PLASTIC LAMINATE

INTERIOR OF CABINET CLAD IN WHITE MELAMINE

3/4" SUBSTRATE CLAD IN PLASTIC LAMINATE (FRONT AND BACK)

BASE AS SCHEDULED

BASE CABINET WITH PENCIL DRAWER AND SHELF

2'-3"

OUTLET LOCATION, TYP.

6"

1 1/2"

EQ.

EQ.

EQ.

3'-0"

EQ.

EQ.

4"

3"

1/2" PLYWOOD BACK ON 1 X 4 CLEATS

3/4" FULL-HEIGHT BACKSPLASH CLAD IN PLASTIC LAMINATE

3/4" COUNTERTOP CLAD IN PLASTIC LAMINATE

INTERIOR OF CABINET CLAD IN WHITE MELAMINE

3/4" SUBSTRATE CLAD IN PLASTIC LAMINATE DRAWER FACES

BASE AS SCHEDULED

BASE CABINET WITH DRAWERS

2'-3"

EQ.   10"   EQ.

3/4" FULL-HEIGHT
BACKSPLASH CLAD
IN PLASTIC LAMINATE

10" DIAMETER X 3" HIGH
STAINLESS-STEEL
TRASH CHUTE

3/4" COUNTERTOP
CLAD IN PLASTIC
LAMINATE

1 1/2"

INTERIOR OF
CABINET CLAD
IN FLAT BLACK
PLASTIC
LAMINATE

REFERENCE ELEVATION

30" TALL MAX.
WASTE
RECEPTACLE

3/4" SUBSTRATE
CLAD IN PLASTIC
LAMINATE (FRONT
AND BACK)

1/2" PLYWOOD BACK
ON 1 X 4 CLEATS

BASE AS
SCHEDULED

4"

3"

BASE CABINET WITH TRASH CHUTE

2'-3"

EQ.   10"   EQ.

3/4" FULL-HEIGHT
BACKSPLASH CLAD
IN PLASTIC LAMINATE

10" DIAMETER X 3" HIGH
STAINLESS-STEEL
TRASH CHUTE

3/4" COUNTERTOP
CLAD IN PLASTIC
LAMINATE

1 1/2"

INTERIOR OF
CABINET TO BE
PAINTED FLAT
BLACK

1'-0" TO CENTER
OF OPENING

REFERENCE ELEVATION

WASTE
RECEPTACLE

1/2" PLYWOOD BACK
ON 1 X 4 CLEATS

3/4" SUBSTRATE
CLAD IN PLASTIC
LAMINATE (FRONT
AND BACK)

BASE CABINET WITH TRASH CHUTE; WASTE RECEPTACLE ON FLOOR

2'-3"

3/4" FULL-HEIGHT
BACKSPLASH CLAD
IN PLASTIC LAMINATE

3/4" COUNTERTOP
CLAD IN PLASTIC
LAMINATE

4 1/2"

INTERIOR OF
CABINET TO BE
PAINTED FLAT
BLACK

8" OPG.

REFERENCE ELEVATION

WASTE
RECEPTACLE

1/2" PLYWOOD BACK
ON 1 X 4 CLEATS

3/4" SUBSTRATE
CLAD IN PLASTIC
LAMINATE (FRONT
AND BACK)

BASE AS
SCHEDULED

4"

3"

BASE CABINET WITH WASTE RECEPTACLE AND OPEN FACE

2'-3"

SINK, 6 1/2" MAX.
DEPTH

SHAPE TOP OF
PANEL WITH 1/8"
TOLERANCE
AROUND SINK

3/4" FULL-HEIGHT
BACKSPLASH CLAD
IN PLASTIC LAMINATE

3/4" COUNTERTOP
CLAD IN PLASTIC
LAMINATE

5"

2"

2'-3" MIN.

2'-10" A.F.F.

1/2" PLYWOOD
BACK ON
1 X 4 CLEATS

8" MIN.

PLASTIC LAMINATE
PANEL; PROVIDE
CLIP ANCHORS FOR
EASY REMOVAL

CLEAR SPACE
REQUIRED FOR
ACCESSIBLE
SINK SHOWN
DASHED

9" MIN.

SIDEWALL CLEAT
WITH ROLLER
CATCH, TYP.

6" MAX.

1'-7" MIN.

BASE CABINET AT SINK

STANDARD BASE AND WALL-HUNG CABINETS

1'-3"

1/2" PLYWOOD BACK ON 1 X 4 CLEATS

1 1/2"

7'-4" A.F.F. TYP. U.N.O.

3/4"

3/4" SUBSTRATE CLAD IN PLASTIC LAMINATE (FRONT AND BACK)

3/4" ADJUSTABLE SHELF CLAD IN PLASTIC LAMINATE WITH 1 1/2" FRONT LIP ON STANDARDS AND BRACKETS (RECESSED INSIDE PANELS)

INTERIOR OF CABINET CLAD IN WHITE MELAMINE

LIGHT FIXTURE

PLASTIC LAMINATE ON UNDERSIDE OF 3/4" PLYWOOD

3/4" FULL-HEIGHT BACKSPLASH CLAD IN PLASTIC LAMINATE

2 1/4"

1'-8" CLR. ABOVE COUNTERTOP

WALL-HUNG CABINET WITH SINGLE DOOR

1'-3"

GYPSUM BOARD

1/2"

ALIGN

1/2" PLYWOOD BACK ON 1 X 4 CLEATS

3/4"

3/4" SUBSTRATE CLAD IN PLASTIC LAMINATE (FRONT AND BACK)

3/4" ADJUSTABLE SHELF CLAD IN PLASTIC LAMINATE WITH 1 1/2" FRONT LIP ON STANDARDS AND BRACKETS (RECESSED INSIDE PANELS)

INTERIOR OF CABINET CLAD IN WHITE MELAMINE

2 1/4"

LIGHT FIXTURE

PLASTIC LAMINATE ON UNDERSIDE OF 3/4" PLYWOOD

3/4" FULL-HEIGHT BACKSPLASH CLAD IN PLASTIC LAMINATE

1'-8" CLR. ABOVE COUNTERTOP

WALL-HUNG CABINET WITH TOP PANEL

1'-3"

1/2" PLYWOOD BACK ON 1 X 4 CLEATS

5"

LIGHT FIXTURE

7'-0" A.F.F. TYP. U.N.O.

3/4"

3/4" SUBSTRATE CLAD IN PLASTIC LAMINATE (FRONT AND BACK)

3/4" ADJUSTABLE SHELF CLAD IN PLASTIC LAMINATE WITH 1 1/2" FRONT LIP ON STANDARDS AND BRACKETS (RECESSED INSIDE PANELS)

INTERIOR OF CABINET CLAD IN WHITE MELAMINE

2 1/4"

LIGHT FIXTURE

PLASTIC LAMINATE ON UNDERSIDE OF 3/4" PLYWOOD

3/4" FULL-HEIGHT BACKSPLASH CLAD IN PLASTIC LAMINATE

1'-8" CLR. ABOVE COUNTERTOP

WALL-HUNG CABINET WITH COVE LIGHTING

2'-3"

OUTLET LOCATION, TYP.

6"

1 1/2"

6"

6"

6"

3'-0"

3/4" FULL-HEIGHT BACKSPLASH CLAD IN PLASTIC LAMINATE

3/4" COUNTERTOP CLAD IN PLASTIC LAMINATE

INTERIOR OF CABINET CLAD IN WHITE MELAMINE

1/2" PLYWOOD BACK ON 1 X 4 CLEATS

3/4" SUBSTRATE CLAD IN PLASTIC LAMINATE DRAWER FACES

BASE AS SCHEDULED

4"

3"

BASE CABINET WITH PENCIL AND FILE DRAWERS

1 1/4"   1 1/4"

1 1/4"

1 1/4"

1 1/4"   1 1/4"

DRAWER OR CABINET PULL LOCATION

EQ.   EQ.   EQ.   EQ.

1 1/4"   1 1/4"

1 1/4"

1 1/4"

1 1/4"

1 1/4"

1 1/4"

COUNTERSINK PULL ANCHORS BEHIND DOORS AND DRAWERS

CABINET PULL LOCATIONS

Ted Kollaja, AIA; lauckgroup; Dallas, Texas

BOOKCASE WITH CREDENZA AND DESK

DOWNLIGHT LOCATION

ELECTRICAL OUTLET LOCATION AT UNDERSIDE OF SOFFIT

WALLCOVERING ON BACK WALL

3" COL.

1/4" REVEAL EACH SIDE

FINISHED END EACH SIDE

ADJUSTABLE SHELVES

FINISHED END

GRAIN

3" COL.

GRAIN

1/2" SCRIBE

4 1/2"   1'-6"   2'-11 3/4"   1'-6"   2'-11 7/8"   2'-11 7/8"   3'-0" CABINET

3 1/2"

16'-0 1/4"

4 1/2"

ELEVATION—BOOKCASE WITH CREDENZA

1'-11 1/2"   3/4"

4"

3/4" SOLID WOOD BACK

ADJUSTABLE GLASS SHELF

2'-6"

1'-9 1/4"

SOLID WOOD CROWN

1"-THICK WOOD STILE AND RAIL GLASS DOOR

HALF-ROUND COLUMN BEYOND

8'-0"

2'-0"

WALL COVERING ON BACK WALL

2'-8"

TWO EQUAL FILE DRAWERS WITH BARS AND CLIPS FOR LETTER-SIZE FILES RUNNING FRONT TO REAR

SIM.

1 1/4"

SOLID WOOD SKIRT

2'-2"

1'-9 1/4"

1'-7 3/4" DRAWER

SOLID WOOD BASE

4"

1'-11 1/2"

Ⓐ **SECTION AT CREDENZA**

1'-11 1/2"   3/4"

4"

3/4" SOLID WOOD BACK

ADJUSTABLE GLASS SHELF

5'-2"

1'-9 1/4"

SOLID WOOD CROWN

1"-THICK WOOD STILE AND RAIL GLASS DOOR

HALF-ROUND COLUMN BEYOND

8'-0"

2'-0"

CONTINUOUS HOLES ON 32 MM SYSTEM FOR SHELF CLIPS

1 1/4"

SOLID WOOD SKIRT

2'-2"

1'-9 1/4"

CABINET DOOR

ADJUSTABLE SHELF

SOLID WOOD BASE

4"

1'-11 1/2"

Ⓑ **SECTION AT BOOKCASE**

SOLID WOOD CROWN

1"   3/4"   1"

2 1/4"

1/8"

3/4"

3"   2 1/4"

1/8"   1"

1"-THICK WOOD STILE AND RAIL GLASS DOOR

Ⓒ **DETAIL AT CEILING**

1"   1 1/2"   1 1/4"

3"

1/8"

1 1/4"

SOLID WOOD SKIRT

3"

1/2"

1 1/2"   3/4"   1/2"

HALF-ROUND COLUMN

Ⓓ **DETAIL AT SKIRT**

CABINET DOOR

3/4"   1 1/2"   3/4"

2 1/4"

SOLID WOOD BASE

4"

Ⓔ **DETAIL AT BASE**

Project: St. Louis Rams Training and Administration Complex; Earth City, Missouri
Designer: O'Toole Design Associates; St. Louis, Missouri
Woodworker: Classic Woodworking; St. Louis, Missouri
Source: Design Solutions, Winter 2000

DESK

CENTRAL GANGING LOCK
PENCIL DRAWER
6'-6"
1"
2'-6"
GRAIN
A
1'-4 1/2"   3'-4"   1'-4 1/2"
3/4"   1 1/2"   1 1/2"   3/4"

ELEVATION—DESK

6'-6"
GRAIN
3'-6"   3'-0"
R 10'-9 3/4"
6"
A

PLAN

3"
1 1/4"

B **EDGE DETAIL**

VARIES
2'-6"
3 1/2"
3 1/2"
2"
9 5/8"
2'-2"
DRAWER
FILE DRAWER: INSTALL BARS AND CLIPS FOR HANGING FILES RUNNING FROM FRONT TO BACK
B
2'-8 1/2"

A **SECTION**

Project: St. Louis Rams Training and Administration Complex; Earth City, Missouri
Designer: O'Toole Design Associates; St. Louis Missouri
Woodworker: Classic Woodworking; St. Louis, Missouri
Source: Design Solutions, Winter 2000

BOARDROOM TABLE

3'-6"
GRAIN   GR.   GRAIN   GRAIN   GR.   GRAIN
SHOP JOINT
START OF RADIUS
1/4" ACCENT INLAY, TYP.
FIELD JOINT
GRAIN   GR.
1'-2"   GR.
R = 10'-4"
R = 13'-2"
GRAIN
GR.
10'-7 3/4"
START OF RADIUS
R = 43'-2"
R = 40'-4"
FIELD JOINT
FIELD JOINT
GRAIN
GR.
GRAIN
A
3'-6"
GRAIN   GR.   GRAIN   GRAIN   GR.   GRAIN
SHOP JOINT

PLAN

3'-6"
4"   WOOD VENEER PARTICLEBOARD   1/4" ACCENT INLAY   4"
SOLID WOOD TRIM
BULLDOG CATCH
REMOVABLE 3/4" WOOD VENEER PARTICLEBOARD PANEL WITH VENEER-BANDED EDGES
CONTINUOUS PAINT-GRADE HARDWOOD TRIM, PAINTED BLACK, NOTCHED INTO SUPPORT STUD
PAINT-GRADE HARDWOOD TRIM, PAINTED BLACK, ATTACHED TO PANEL
NOTCH STUD FOR TRIM
BLOCKING TO MAINTAIN 1/8" REVEAL
1/8" REVEAL   6"   WOOD TRIM
1'-1 1/2"
2'-6"

A **SECTION AT REMOVABLE PANEL**

Project: Pentair Corporate Offices; Minneapolis, Minnesota
Designer: BWBR Architects; St. Paul, Minnesota
Woodworker: Wilkie Sanderson; Sauk Rapids, Minnesota
Source: Design Solutions, Spring 2001

CURVED FRONT RECEPTION DESK

Project: AFLAC Customer Service Center; Columbus, Georgia
Designer: Hecht, Burdeshaw, Johnson, Kidd & Clark; Columbus, Georgia
Woodworker: Columbus Cabinet Company; Columbus, Georgia
Source: Design Solutions, Winter 2000

POLISHED STONE LEDGE

QUARTERED FIGURE WOOD
VENEER WITH SKETCH PATTERN
FACE-BOX MATCH

QUARTERED FIGURE
WOOD VENEER

8"
3'-8"
3'-0"

1'-8"   2'-2"   4'-4"   2'-2"   1'-8"

POLISHED STONE BASE

FRONT ELEVATION

SOLID WOOD NOSING

PLASTIC LAMINATE
ON 3/4" MDF

FABRIC-COVERED PANEL

POLISHED STONE LEDGE

8"
8"
2 1/2"
3'-8"
2'-4"

2'-0"

DRAWER
DRAWER
FILE
DRAWER
ON FULL
EXTENSION
GLIDES

PLASTIC LAMINATE
ON 3/4" PARTICLEBOARD

2 X 4 SILL PLATE;
FASTEN TO FLOOR

3/4" HORIZONTAL
PLYWOOD BRACES

TWO LAYERS 1/4" PLYWOOD

POLISHED STONE BASE

WOOD VENEER ON 1/4" MDF

3/4" VERTICAL PLYWOOD
BRACES AS REQUIRED

(A) **SECTION**

POLISHED STONE INSERT

12'-0"
2'-0"   8'-0"   2'-0"

1 1/2"
2'-4"
4"
2'-5 1/2"
VERIFY
R 12'-6"
R 12'-9"
3"

1'-8"   8'-8"   1'-8"

POLISHED STONE LEDGE
FACE OF DESK BELOW

PLAN

RECEPTION DESK

REAR ELEVATION

16'-6"
2'-6"   11'-6"   2'-6"

2'-8"

ELEVATION

GRAIN

R 8'-7 5/8"

PLASTIC LAMINATE
LOWER WORK TOP

UPPER GLASS LEDGE

GRAIN

WOOD
VENEER
CABINET
PIER, EA.
END, TYP.

GLASS SEAM

CHROME
SUPPORTS
FOR GLASS
LEDGE

11 9/16"   14'-6 7/8"   11 9/16"

PLAN

PLASTIC LAMINATE
LOWER WORK TOP

UPPER GLASS
LEDGE

GRAIN

3'-8"

2'-5"

GRAIN

4'-6"

PLASTIC LAMINATE
SUPPORT PANEL

WOOD
VENEER
CABINET
PIER, EACH
END, TYP.

6"   2'-0"

A **REAR ELEVATION**

PLASTIC LAMINATE
SUPPORT PANEL

2'-8"

GRAIN

4'-6"

3'-8"

2'-5"

GANG
LOCKS

FILE
DRAWERS

B **ELEVATION AT CABINET**

CHROME SUPPORTS
WITH FINISHED
CAPS

1/2" GLASS LEDGE

WOOD VENEER
CABINET FACES

SOLID WOOD
EDGE TRIM

SOLID WOOD
SUPPORT PANEL

PLASTIC LAMINATE
WORK TOP
AND EDGE

1'-3"

1 1/2"   1/2"

3'-8"   3'-2"

6"

1'-6"

2'-5"

PLASTIC LAMINATE
SUPPORT PANEL
CENTER BELOW TOP

REMOVABLE
PLASTIC LAMINATE
BACK PANEL

4"

3/4"

SOLID WOOD BASE

C **SECTION AT COUNTER**

SOLID WOOD
TRIM WITH
1/8" RADIUS

WOOD VENEER
CABINET FACES, TYP.

1/4" EDGE BAND WITH
1/8" RADIUS

ADJUSTABLE
SHELF

CONTINUOUS
HOLES ON 32 MM
SYSTEM FOR
SHELF CLIPS

4'-6"

4"

4"

1'-7 3/4" DRAWER

FILE DRAWER WITH
BARS AND CLIPS
FOR LETTER-SIZE
FILES RUNNING
FRONT TO REAR

6"   1'-9"   3"
2'-6"

SOLID WOOD BASE

D **SECTION AT CABINET**

*Project: St. Louis Rams Training and Administration
  Complex; Earth City, Missouri*
Designer: O'Toole Design Associates; St. Louis, Missouri
Woodworker: Classic Woodworking; St. Louis, Missouri
Source: Design Solutions, Winter 2000

LECTERN

SECTION AT A/V RACK

Project: Pentair Corporate Offices; Minneapolis, Minnesota
Designer: BWBR Architects; St. Paul, Minnesota
Woodworker: Wilkie Sanderson; Sauk Rapids, Minnesota
Source: Design Solutions, *Spring 2001*

JEWELRY DISPLAY CASE

Project: Carleton Varney; White Sulphur Springs, West Virginia
Designer: Dorothy Draper Co.; New York, New York
Woodworker: Architectural Wood; Roanoke, Virginia
Source: Design Solutions, *Spring 1997*

JEWELRY CASE SECTION

HOTEL RECEPTION DESK

FRONT ELEVATION

MARBLE GLOVE LEDGE

3"

4"

METAL VENEER TOEKICK AND RECESSED TRIM

WOOD VENEER PANELS

FRONT ELEVATION

A — FOR KEYCARD MACHINE

B — KEYBOARD SHELF

PRINTER

C

BROCHURE SHELVES

CASHIER DRAWER WITH LOCK

FORMS SHELVES

3'-6"   3'-4 1/2"

BACK ELEVATION

COMPUTER NICHE

METAL VENEER TRIM

WOOD VENEER CASEWORK

METAL VENEER PANEL

BACK ELEVATION

EQ   VARIES (MIN. 15'-0")   EQ   1'-1 1/2"

3"   EQUAL   3 1/4"   EQUAL   3 1/4"   EQUAL   3 1/4"   EQUAL

2'-0"

A   WOOD VENEER KEYBOARD SHELF AND COUNTERTOP

B   MARBLE GLOVE LEDGE

C   1 1/2"   9"   3'-8" MIN.

EQUIPMENT TABLE

PLAN VIEW   BACK OFFICE, COPY, AND STORAGE ROOM

PLAN

MARBLE GLOVE LEDGE

BROCHURE SHELVES

3'-6"   3'-0"

PRINTER NICHE

(A) **SECTION AT STORAGE**

KEYBOARD SHELF

3'-6"

MONITOR

WIRE AND CABLE RACEWAY, TYP.

COMPUTER DECK

(B) **SECTION AT KEYBOARD SHELF**

CASHIER DRAWER

DRAWERS

3'-6"   3'-0"

FILE DRAWER

(C) **SECTION AT DRAWERS**

CAFETERIA SERVERY STATION

Project: Spiegel Corporate Headquarters; Downers Grove, Illinois
Designer: ISI; Chicago, Illinois
Woodworker: Mielach/Woodwork Midwest; Elgin, Illinois
Source: Design Solutions, Winter 1993

PIN/BLOCK CASTER TO
LOCK WHEEL PERPENDICULAR
TO GATE FACE

PIN BLOCK CASTER DETAIL

RAIL
ABOVE

HINGE

ACCESS DOOR IN
OPEN POSITION

BALL CATCH

CASTER
BELOW

ACCESS DOOR SECTION

STAINLESS-STEEL
RUNNERS

CONTINUOUS METAL RAIL

COVED FLOOR BASE

COUNTER SECTION

STAINLESS-STEEL
RUNNERS

REMOVABLE TRAY SLIDE

HINGE

BALL CATCH

CONTINUOUS METAL RAIL

HINGE

CASTER BEYOND

SECTION AT DOOR

PATIENT ROOM HEADBOARD

Project: Christus Park St. Catherine Health and Wellness Center; Katy, Texas
Designer: FKP Architects; Houston, Texas
Woodworker: Quality Woodwork Interiors; Stafford, Texas
Source: Design Solutions, Spring 2001

GYPSUM BOARD BULKHEAD

RADIUSED WOOD TRIM TYPE 2

1/2" REVEAL

1/8"

3/4"

WOOD TYPE 2 AT PANEL FRAMES AND INTERIOR FACES

ADJUSTABLE SHELF WITH WHITE CABINET LINER

2'-10"

3'-6"

WOOD TYPE 1 AT PANEL FACES, TYP.

3" WIRE PULL

FIXED EQUIPMENT SHELF, WOOD TYPE 2

5 3/4"

1/8"

3/4"

7'-0"

GYPSUM BOARD WALL CONSTRUCTION

1'-0"

CUT-OUT FOR EQUIPMENT

1"

WOOD TYPE 2

EQ.

6 3/32"

1'-8"

1/8"

EQ.

2'-6"

1/8"

EQ.

WOOD TYPE 1 AT PANEL FACES, TYP.

4"

1'-9"

3"

RESILIENT BASE

2'-0"

(A) **SECTION**

RADIUSED GYPSUM BOARD BULKHEAD AND WOOD TRIM INSET

CROWN MOLDING

R = 10'-2"

(A)

FINISHED ENDS, WOOD TYPE 2, TYP.

RADIUSED WOOD TRIM

SOLID SURFACE COUNTERTOP

WIRE PULLS, TYP.

RADIUSED WOOD TRIM TYPE 2

WOOD TYPE 1 AT PANEL FACES, TYP.

GYPSUM BOARD AT BACK WALL OF EQUIPMENT NICHE

WOOD TYPE 2 AT PANEL FRAMES, TYP.

3/4"

3/4"

3'-6"

1 1/2"

1'-2"

2'-6"

3/4"

7'-2"

6'-10"

4"

1"   1"

10 3/4"

2'-3 3/4"

4'-6"
HEADWALL FOR BED

2'-3 3/4"

1"

2'-5 3/8"

1"

12'-5 5/8"

ELEVATION

LIBRARY CASEWORK

- 2" X 4" HARDWOOD POST
- MITER AT CORNERS
- 1/2" FIXED PLYWOOD SHELVES WITH HARDWOOD VENEER AND HARDWOOD EDGE
- WOOD SUPPORT BRACKET WITH VENEER TO MATCH
- 3/4" PLYWOOD COUNTERTOP WITH HARDWOOD VENEER
- HARDWOOD EDGE
- SOLID BLOCKING FOR POST SUPPORT AND FINISH WITH HARDWOOD VENEER
- BETWEEN POSTS, EXTEND CENTER PANEL TO UNDERSIDE OF COUNTERTOP
- 3/4" ADJUSTABLE PLYWOOD SHELVES WITH HARDWOOD VENEER AND HARDWOOD EDGE
- FINISHED END PANELS, TYP.
- LINE BORING WITH SHELF PINS AT 2" SPACING
- WOOD BASE

NEWSPAPER DISPLAY AND CABINET

- REMOTE BALLAST WITH 3/8" FLEXIBLE METAL CONDUIT
- WOOD VENEER OVER 3/4" PLYWOOD CORNICE
- WOOD VENEER OVER 3/4" PLYWOOD
- T2 SUBMINIATURE FLUORESCENT LIGHT
- ARCHITECTURAL GRILLE FOR PASSIVE AIR CIRCULATION
- WOOD VENEER AT EXPOSED CABINET INTERIOR AND ADJUSTABLE SHELVES
- PASSIVE AIR CIRCULATION TO RARE BOOKS
- CABINET DOOR PULL
- AIR SLOTS FOR AIR CIRCULATION
- FRAMED 1/4" GLASS DOORS ON CONCEALED HINGES
- PAINT BACK PANEL FLAT BLACK
- INTERMEDIATE BLOCKING BEYOND, CONCEALED BEHIND GRILLE AT BASE
- ARCHITECTURAL GRILLE AT BASE

SECTION

RARE BOOK STORAGE CASE

A FRONT VIEW

- POST BEYOND
- ANGLED DISPLAY SHELF
- BRACKET BENEATH

B TOP VIEW

- HARDWOOD POST
- BRACKET BENEATH
- ANGLED DISPLAY SHELF

- PAINTED T-PLATE CONNECTOR
- L-SHAPED BRACKET WITH PAINTED CLOSER AT SINGLE FIXTURE
- TUBESTEEL SLEEVE
- LIBRARY SHELF STANDARD AND CROSS-MEMBER
- STEEL PLATE WELDED TO UNDERSIDE OF TOP UNISTRUT, THROUGH-BOLT TO SHELF STANDARD
- UNISTRUT SUPPORT SYSTEM
- PAINTED CLOSURE STRIP
- FLUORESCENT FIXTURE
- AISLE SHIELD WHERE OCCURS

STACK LIGHT

2   □   CUSTOM CASEWORK

Jane Clark, AIA; Zimmer Gunzul Frasca Partnership; Seattle, Washington

COUNTERTOPS

COUNTERTOPS

Countertops for commercial and residential applications are fabricated from a number of different materials and finishes, ranging from high-pressure plastic laminate to stone, tile, wood, stainless steel, and manufactured materials. Function, appropriateness for the application, economy, and aesthetics should be considered when selecting a countertop material. Countertops are commonly supported by base cabinets, but can be installed as freestanding or supported units.

CONSTRUCTION

Countertop construction varies with the type of surface material selected and the type of support required. Some surface materials such as stone rest directly on a support system, while other finish surfaces require lamination to a substrate. All countertops require support, either on an architectural woodwork base cabinet or other undercounter support such as wall brackets or steel outriggers when no base cabinet is provided, or the countertop can be mounted on legs. When the countertop is not supported by a base cabinet or other similar unit, a careful review of the countertop support system is recommended. Anticipated loads should be reviewed, including the possibility of the countertop being used as a seat if it is mounted at a lower height.

SUBSTRATES

For laminated countertops such as HPDL, substrates include particleboard or medium density fiberboard (MDF), usually ¾ in. (19 mm) thick, as the surfaces are smooth and consistent. When moisture is a concern, exterior grade plywood is used, although the surface is not as fine as the particleboard or MDF. Plywood is not commonly used as an HPDL substrate, as the imperfections may telegraph through to the surface. Exterior grade plywood is used as a substrate under stone, tile, and other materials requiring a rigid substrate with resistance to moisture.

COUNTERTOP MATERIALS

Some of the most prevalent countertop types are laminated countertops, which include high-pressure decorative laminates (HPDL), wood veneers, linoleum, and some metal sheets such as zinc, with or without edging of different materials. Stainless steel, stone, tile, concrete, solid wood, and other finish surfaces may be used for countertop units.

Countertop should extend to or beyond the cabinet's pulls.

COUNTERTOP CLEARANCE

COUNTERTOP MATERIALS COMPARISON

MATERIAL	FEATURES	CONCERNS
Concrete	Durable Custom colors possible Objects can be recessed Tactile surface Acquires patina from use	Qualified installers required Sealer recommended Subject to staining and cracking Hot elements will damage sealer
Engineered Composite Stone (Silestone®, Zodiaq™)	Requires no sealing Nonporous Abrasion, stain and impact resistant	Not as heat-resistant as natural stone Resinous feel and appearance
Epoxy resin	Used for laboratory countertops Extremely durable Resistant to chemicals	Costly Qualified installers required
Granite (polished, honed, flamed)	Durable Stain resistant when sealed Water and heat resistant Natural stone features	Expensive to install Qualified installers required Avoid ammonia products
Laminates, Plastic (HDPL)	Moderate cost Dark edge on standard laminate Color through laminates offer less visible scratch marks Waterproof, stain resistant Easily cleaned	Not heat resistant Seam lines Joints susceptible to damage, delamination Scratches cannot be repaired
Lavastone, glazed (Pyrolave)	Water and heat resistant	Costly Easily scratched
Limestone	Dolomitic limestone preferred Heat resistant Neutral and soft colors	As porous as marble Sealer required Qualified installers required
Linoleum	Inexpensive "Green" product Water, stain, and heat resistant Antibacterial surface	Edge trim required
Marble (polished or honed)	Heat resistant Natural stone features Tactile feel on honed finish	Costly Qualified installers required Sealer required Susceptible to staining
Quartzite	Iridescent, crystalline appearance Cool, pale colors Water and heat resistant	Sealer required Qualified installers required
Slate	Available in honed finish Water and heat resistant Stainproof and antibacterial	Costly Qualified installers required Avoid ammonia products
Soapstone	Soft, satiny, tactile feel Water, heat, and stain resistant	Bimonthly oil treatment required to prevent chipping Qualified installers required Costly
Solid Surface (DuPont Corian, Wilsonart Gibraltar, Nevamar Fountainhead)	Water and stain resistant Light stains, scratches, and scorch marks can be buffed out Integral sinks available	Not heatproof Costly to fabricate and install Avoid acetone
Stainless Steel	Water, heat, and stain resistant Used in commercial food service Integral sinks available	Subject to water spots Qualified installers required Plywood backup recommended to reduce noise
Tile, Ceramic	Heat and stain resistant Water resistant when properly grouted Durable	Costly to install Glaze may be damaged by grit Grout requires maintenance Tile can be chipped from impact
Tile, Stone	Less costly than dimension stone Water, heat, and stain resistant Natural stone features in tile form	Labor-intensive to install Grout requires maintenance
Travertine	Heat resistant	Qualified installers required Natural stone features Filled travertine recommended Sealer required
Wood (Veneer and Solid Laminated)	Forgiving surface; does not dull knives	Susceptible to water damage Monthly application of mineral oil required Scorch marks and light stains can be sanded
Zinc	Warm metal appearance Zinc surface laminated similar to plastic laminate Many surface finishes available	Qualified installers required Easily maintained Protect from corrosive materials Large sheet sizes

WALL CONSTRUCTION AS SCHEDULED

3/4" GRANITE TOP AND SKIRT WITH 1/8" BEVELED EDGE

2" DIAMETER BLACK GROMMET

1'-6"

1/4"

3/4"

3/4"

STEEL ANGLE WELD TO VERTICAL CHANNEL

ADJUSTABLE SHELF ON METAL STANDARDS

3'-0"

WOOD VENEER FINISH EXTERIOR & INTERIOR FACE OF CABINET DOOR

VERTICAL STEEL ANGLE TO STRUCTURE ABOVE @ 32" O.C. LENGTH OF COUNTER

WALL-HUNG CREDENZA WITH GRANITE TOP

WALL CONSTRUCTION AS SCHEDULED

3/4" GRANITE TOP AND SKIRT WITH 1/8" NOTCH AT JOINT

1'-6"

1/4"

1/8"

1/8"

5"

3/4" PLYWOOD SUBSTRATE

STEEL ANGLE WELDED TO VERTICAL ANGLE WITHIN WALL

PLYWOOD SUBSTRATE

2'-6"

VERTICAL STEEL ANGLE TO STRUCTURE ABOVE @ 32" O.C. LENGTH OF COUNTER

PROVIDE CLIP ANGLE FOR ATTACHMENT TO SLAB

WALL HUNG GRANITE COUNTERTOP

BULLNOSE

STRAIGHT EDGE

COVE

OGEE

DEMI-BULLNOSE

STAIR TREAD

DOUBLE COVE

OGEE ROUNDOVER

DOUBLE BULLNOSE

RADIUS

COVE-DUPONT

COVE OGEE

FULL BULLNOSE

PLATNER

DUPONT

BEVEL

COMMON COUNTERTOP EDGE PROFILES

WOOD AND PLASTIC LAMINATE COUNTERTOP WORKMANSHIP CRITERIA

CRITERIA	PREMIUM	CUSTOM	ECONOMY
Selection at field joints on exposed surfaces	Selected for uniformity of grain, color, and/or pattern	Selected for pleasing blend of grain or pattern	No selection required
Selection for solid laminated (butcher block) components	Selected for pleasing blend of grain or pattern	No selection required	No selection required
End joints for solid (butcher block) components	Shall meet joint tolerances for exposed components, and no more than 1 per 4 sq ft (.4 sq m)	Shall meet joint tolerances for exposed components, and no more than 1 per 2 sq ft (.2 sq m)	Shall meet joint tolerances for exposed components, and no more than 1 per 1 sq ft (.1 sq m)
End matching of veneers on exposed surfaces	Leaves individually book matched and end matched	Selected for pleasing blend of grain or pattern	No selection required
Balancing sheet requirements for HPDL overlay	Standard .020" phenolic backer minimum required in all cases	Paper backer required wherever unsupported area exceeds 6 sq ft (.6 sq m) and core is ¾" (19 mm) thick; 8 sq ft (8 sq m) and core is 1" (25 mm) thick; 10sq ft (1sq m) and core is 1⅛: (28 mm) or thicker	No backer required
Edge application for HPDL	Edge laminated before top	Edge laminated before top	Edge laminated after top
Flatness (after installation) is a defect when maximum deviation exceeds	¹⁄₁₆" (1.6 mm) in any 4" × 8" (1,220 mm × 2,440 mm) segment	⅛" (3 mm) in any 4" × 8" (1,220 mm × 2,440 mm) segment	¼" (6 mm) in any 4" × 8" (1,220 mm × 2,440 mm) segment
Field joints	More than 48" (1,220 mm) apart, and shall not occur within 48" (1,220 mm) of the end of any top	More than 36" (914 mm) apart, and shall not occur within 36" (914 mm) of the end of any top	No requirement
Sealing of substrate at sink cuts	Required	Required	Not required
Maximum allowable separation between factory assembled splash and top components	¹⁄₆₄" (.4 mm) x 3" (76 mm) and no more than 1 per 4' (1,220 mm) section of top	³⁄₃₂" (.8mm) x 5" (127 mm) and no more than 1 per 4' (1,220 mm) section of top	¹⁄₁₆" (1.6 mm) × 8" (203 mm) and no more than 1 per 4' (1,220 mm) section of top
Application of silicone sealant to factory assembled joint between HDPL top and splash	Required	Not required	Not required
Use of thermoset decorative overlay as backer material	Not allowed	Allowed	Allowed
Joint in HDPL or substrate at factory sink cut	Not allowed	Not allowed	Not allowed

The Architectural Woodwork Institute's Quality Standards identify three levels of construction: premium, custom, and economy grades. It is recommended that both the countertops and base cabinets be fabricated with the same grade of construction for functional compatibility.
Source: Architectural Woodwork Institute; Reston, Virginia

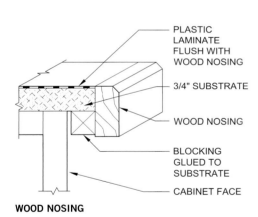

PLASTIC LAMINATE FLUSH WITH WOOD NOSING
3/4" SUBSTRATE
WOOD NOSING
BLOCKING GLUED TO SUBSTRATE
CABINET FACE

WOOD NOSING

METAL OR SOLID SURFACE PREFABRICATED NOSING
CABINET FACE

METAL OR SOLID SURFACE NOSING

Applied nosings can be wood, metal, or solid surface, adhered to the countertop substrate. Depending on the nosing detail, the applied edge can protect the plastic laminate surface from damage.

APPLIED NOSINGS

2 X VERTICAL BLOCKING AT BACKER PLATE ANCHOR POINTS
GROMMET ABOVE OUTLETS, TYPICAL
3/4" COUNTERTOP CLAD IN PLASTIC LAMINATE, SCRIBE TO WALLS
2'-6"
3"
1 1/2"
3"
2'-6" AFF
45°
3"
2 1/2" SQUARE OPENING IN SUPPORT PANEL FOR WIRE MANAGEMENT
1 1/2" PLASTIC LAMINATE-CLAD ANGLED SUPPORT PANELS AT 48" O.C., WITH PLASTIC LAMINATE BACKER PLATES
WOOD PLUGS, PAINT TO MATCH LAMINATE
2/3 DEPTH OF COUNTERTOP

WALL-HUNG OPEN COUNTER

PLASTIC LAMINATE

High-pressure decorative laminate (HPDL), commonly known as *plastic laminate,* is one of the most economical countertop materials. It is available in numerous colors and textures, performs well, and is easily fabricated, installed and maintained. ANSI A162.2 *Performance Standard for Fabricated High Pressure Decorative Laminate Countertops,* defines the standards for performance of HPDL countertops. HPDL is formed from a sandwich of a melamine-impregnated overlay sheet, and decorative or colored surface paper over phenolic resin-impregnated kraft papers bonded together under high pressure and heat.

The four most common types of HPDL sheets are as follows:

HGS, formerly GP–General Purpose: Used for most horizontal surfaces, for example, countertops. This type can be bent to a radius of approximately 6 in. (152 mm).

CLS, formerly CL–Cabinet Liner: A thin sheet used for vertical applications, typically inside casework that will not need to withstand heavy wear. (The cabinet liner should not be used as a balancing or backer sheet for countertops.)

BKL, formerly BK–Backer: Economical, nondecorative sheets used on the side of the substrate hidden from view to prevent warping as a result of changes in temperature or humidity.

HGP, formerly PF–Postforming: Used for tightly radiused curves, for example, at the edge of a formed countertop.

COLORTHROUGH LAMINATES

Colorthrough laminates are a solid color through the thickness of the sheet. This eliminates the problem of the HPDL's brown kraft paper core showing when the cut edge is exposed. Colorthrough HPDL is manufactured in thicknesses from 0.050 in. to 0.060 in.(1.3 mm to 1.5 mm) and must be carefully adhered to the substrate. Because of their high melamine resin content, colorthrough HPDLs can buckle when temperature or humidity shifts.

PLASTIC LAMINATE COUNTERTOP FABRICATION

HPDL countertops are fabricated by adhering plastic laminate to a substrate. Particleboard is often preferred as a substrate because it has a fine, smooth face without imperfections that could telegraph through the plastic laminate. Exterior grade plywood is preferred for

countertops exposed to liquids or high humidity because of its increased resistance to moisture. A backer sheet is applied to the unexposed, underside of the substrate to prevent warping and dimensional instability in changing temperature or humidity.

HPDL countertops are fabricated with three edge, or nosing, types: *self-edge, postformed edge,* and *applied*

edge. Plastic laminate is adhered to the counter substrate under uniform pressure and is trimmed flush with a router. Because seams are susceptible to water penetration, if possible, do not locate seams where water will be present, such as at a sink area. Plastic laminate countertops should be fabricated using balanced construction (backer sheet applied to underside of countertop) to minimize possibility of warping.

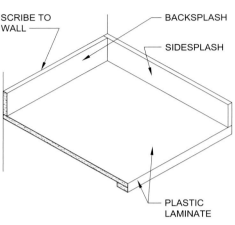

COUNTERTOP WITH BACKSPLASH AND SIDESPLASH

HPDL HGS COUNTERTOP

BACKSPLASH

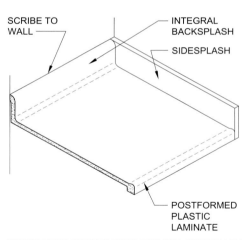

COUNTERTOP WITH BACKSPLASH AND SIDESPLASH

HPDL HGP COUNTERTOPS

BACKSPLASH

SELF-EDGE NOSING

NO-DRIP NOSING
No-drip edge contains spills.

HPDL POSTFORMED NOSING TYPES

WATERFALL NOSING

SOLID LAMINATE WOOD COUNTERTOPS

Solid laminated wood tops are constructed of narrow strips of wood that are face-glued together. The appearance is similar to "butcher block." The wood species preferred for this type of countertop is maple, due to the density of the wood. Expansion and contraction of wood countertops is to be expected, so the installation must allow for movement of the top. Solid wood tops are constructed of boards that are edge-glued to a desired width. Typically there is no matching of wood grain or color.

WOOD VENEER COUNTERTOPS

Wood veneer countertops require maintenance to preserve their appearance. Veneered countertops can be used where moisture is not present. Wood veneer is installed over a stable substrate and is edged with wood or other materials.

SOLID WOOD LAMINATED COUNTERTOPS

WOOD VENEER COUNTERTOPS

MATERIAL GRADES AND SIZE REQUIREMENTS FOR WOOD AND HPDL COUNTERTOPS

TYPE	PREMIUM	CUSTOM	ECONOMY
Solid wood	Grade I	Grade II	Mill option
Solid laminated	Grade I	Grade II	Mill option
Panel products	"AA" Face veneer	"A" Face veneer	Mill option
HPDL overlay	HGS - .048" nominal	HGS - .048" nominal	HGS - .048" nominal
WIDTH AND MATCH			
Solid wood—max width of individual boards in glue-up: Hardwood: 4¼" (108 mm) Softwood: 7¼" (185 mm)	Well matched for grain and color	Compatible for color	No match required
Solid wood, face laminated	Well matched for grain and color	Compatible for color	No match required
Solid wood & Veneer combined and/or adjacent.*	Well matched for grain and color	Compatible for color	No match required
Panel products—If width exceeds 48" (1,220 mm), shall have shop assembled joint	Sequence matched	Compatible for color	No match required
HPDL overlay—If width exceeds 60" (1,524 mm), shall have shop assembled joint (some limited to 48", determined by pattern selected or specified)	No match required	No match required	No match required

*It is recognized that the grain and color of solid lumber and the same species and cut of veneer will appear different. The cutting and pressing of the veneer often modifies the surface cells. These natural differences are acceptable in any grade.

MINIMUM THICKNESS			
Solid wood	1" (25 mm)	1" (25 mm)	¾" (19 mm)
Solid laminated	1⅛" (28 mm)	1⅛" (28 mm)	¾" (19 mm)
Panel products	¾" (19 mm)	¾" (19 mm)	¾" (19 mm)
HPDL overlay	¾" (19 mm)	¾" (19 mm)	¾" (19 mm)
CARE AND SUBSTRATE			
Panel product for HPDL	Industrial grade medium density particleboard or medium density fiberboard		
Premium and custom grade tops and backsplashes in which sinks occur	Shop sanded exterior grade veneer core plywood: or industrial grade particleboard or fiberboard with a 24 hr. thickness swell factor of 5% or less and a 24 hr. water absorption factor of 10% or less.		Industrial grade medium density particleboard or medium density fiberboard.

Source: Architectural Woodwork Institute; Reston, Virginia

SOLID SURFACE COUNTERTOPS

Solid surface countertops are formed from a polymer composition material that is easily shaped and molded into numerous edge profiles. Their integral uniform color and texture provide visual concealment of slight imperfections such as scratches. Each proprietary type of solid surface material is susceptible to different staining agents. Solid surface countertops can be fabricated with integral sinks.

CERAMIC AND STONE TILE COUNTERTOP INSTALLATION

Tile modules provide strength, abrasion, heat and water resistance, and are available in ceramic tile and stone tile units. Both types are installed with ceramic tile installation methods. Cement grout is most commonly used for countertops. Epoxy grout is stain-resistant, expensive, and difficult to work with. Colored grouts are available, but may be susceptible to bleeding and staining adjacent tiles.

There are three types of setting methods for ceramic tile countertops: the traditional *thickset cement mortar method,* the more common *thinset method,* and *adhering to a plywood substrate.*

Thickset Method

A portland cement mortar bed [¾-in.- to 1-in.- (19-mm- to 25-mm-)] thick is applied over a substrate, typically ¾ in. exterior-grade plywood. The thick-set method is highly durable, labor intensive, and expensive. The tile is set in a thick bed of mortar and the joints grouted.

Thinset Method

Cementitious backer board ¼-in.- to ¾-in.- (6- mm- to 19-mm) thick is adhered to a ¾ inch (19 mm) plywood substrate. The tile is adhered to the substrate and the joints grouted.

Adhering Method

The tile is adhered to a substrate and the joints are grouted. This method is appropriate for use in low-moisture, low-wear applications.

SINGLE THICKNESS NOSING

LAMINATED NOSING

SOLID SURFACE COUNTERTOP NOSINGS

SOLID SURFACE BACKSPLASH

INTEGRAL

UNDERMOUNT

SOLID SURFACE SINKS

THICK-SET

THIN-SET

ADHERED

CERAMIC TILE COUNTERTOPS

STONE COUNTERTOPS

Stone countertops are elegant, durable, and resistant to heat and water. Other properties vary with the type of stone selected, such as scratch resistance. Stone countertops are fabricated from dimension stone, ranging from ¾-in. (2 cm) to 1¼-in. (3 cm) thick, in large slabs which vary in size. Stone is one of the heaviest countertop materials.

Stone counters require substantial, rigid substrates to minimize the possibility of cracking. Very thick stone slabs may be installed without a substrate. Consult with the stone supplier or fabricator for information on specific installation recommendations for a particular stone. Stone can be set on a substrate with a thin-set epoxy or a silicone adhesive, based on the installer's recommendations for the stone. Stone seams are typically butt joints, bonded with colored epoxy adhesives, which match the stone. Built-up front nosings are also fabricated with colored epoxy, which minimizes the appearance of any joints. Stone countertops should be sealed to protect the surfaces.

GRANITE COUNTERTOPS

Granite is one of the most popular stones for countertops, due to its strength, numerous varieties, and hardness. Granite countertops are typically highly polished, but smooth-honed and flamed finishes perform well.

MARBLE COUNTERTOPS

Marble is a porous stone, and typically is not as strong as granite. It is easily damaged by acids, and chips easily due to the structure of the stone. However, the aesthetic qualities of marble make it a popular choice, and marble can be successfully used in countertop applications if properly prepared and supported with an appropriate substrate. Marble finishes are typically honed or highly polished and the colors and textures vary widely.

LIMESTONE COUNTERTOPS

Limestone is available in two basic types: *dolomitic* and *oolitic*. While dolomitic limestone is generally preferred for interior flooring and wall surfacing, both types can be used for countertops, if hard wear is not anticipated. Limestone is a sedimentary stone and is porous, so it is susceptible to damage and staining. Limestone is generally honed and is available in light and neutral colors.

SLATE COUNTERTOPS

Slate is a split finish stone that appears rougher than other stone countertop materials and is fairly porous. Slate is available in a range of colors. Slate countertops should be sealed.

ENGINEERED COMPOSITE STONE COUNTERTOPS

Engineered composite stone is a recent development; it typically consists of finely crushed stone aggregate, usually quartz. The stone is bound together by a resin and is formed into large sheets of specified thicknesses. Thinner sheets of engineered stone are installed similar to thin-bed ceramic tile.

MIRROR

STONE AT BACK SHELF, BACKSPLASH, TOP, AND SIDESPLASH

WOOD BLOCKING ONLY. LEAVE STONE EXPOSED AT UNDERSIDE OF COUNTER

STEEL ANGLE LOCATED AT THE FRONT REAR AND SIDES OF COUNTERTOP

STEEL PLATE; WELD TO BOTH SIDES OF VERTICAL STEEL TUBES

STEEL TUBE BETWEEN EACH LAVATORY, TYPICAL; STEEL TUBE SECURED TO FLOOR, TYPICAL.

2'-6"

WALL HUNG STONE COUNTERTOP WITH LAVATORY

SILICONE SEALANT

STONE BACKSPLASH

ADHESIVE

SILICONE SEALANT

STONE SLAB

SETTING MATERIAL

OPTIONAL SEALED PLYWOOD

CABINET FRAME

BACKSPLASH

SILICONE SEALANT

STONE CAP

STONE BACKSPLASH

SETTING MATERIAL

SEALED PLYWOOD

SILICONE SEALANT

STONE SLAB

SETTING MATERIAL

OPTIONAL SEALED PLYWOOD

CABINET FRAME

BACKSPLASH WITH LEDGE CAP

STONE SLAB WITH SHAPED NOSING, PROFILES VARY

SETTING MATERIAL

OPTIONAL PLYWOOD

CABINET FACE

SLAB EDGE NOSING

SETTING MATERIAL

STONE STRIP LAMINATED TO STONE SLAB

OPTIONAL SEALED PLYWOOD

CABINET FACE

LAMINATED NOSING

STONE SLAB COUNTERTOPS

SHEET METAL COUNTERTOPS

Galvanized steel, zinc, copper, and other metals can be used for countertops, but are not suitable for contact with food. Stainless steel countertops are used in food service areas and in locations where sanitation, stain, water, and heat resistance are critical. Stainless steel countertops provide strength and functionality in a durable surface. Fabrication and installation of stainless steel countertops by qualified companies is critical.

Stainless steel should be 16 gage or thicker to avoid denting. Substrates are typically ¾ in. (19 mm) plywood, but MDF is also used if no water will be present during use. Metal tops are shop-fabricated, and are bent and welded or soldered together and ground smooth. A No. 3 satin polished finish is commonly used on stainless steel countertops, although the finish may vary based on the intended use of the countertop. The materials used in the countertop surface must be nontoxic to avoid contamination, especially in food service areas. Nosings and backsplashes are formed by bending the metal, and integral sinks, if used, are welded to the counter surface. The metal top is attached to the substrate with a setting material, similar to a ceramic tile setting bed. Fabrication of stainless steel countertops is generally not done by architectural woodworkers, but by sheet metal and specialty metal shops.

CONCRETE COUNTERTOPS

Concrete countertops are durable and inexpensive units, and are fairly heat, stain, and abrasion resistant. They are monolithic, cast-in-place, or precast units.

- SILICONE SEALANT
- STAINLESS-STEEL COUNTERTOP WITH INTEGRAL BACKSPLASH
- SETTING ADHESIVE
- SUBSTRATE

BACKSPLASH

- SETTING MATERIAL
- STAINLESS-STEEL COUNTERTOP WITH INTEGRAL NOSING
- SUBSTRATE HELD BACK TO ALLOW COUNTERTOP TO FIT
- CABINET FACE

NOSING

STAINLESS STEEL COUNTERTOP

Appearance varies, due to the variety of colored pigments and aggregate types that may be added to the concrete mixture.

Cast-in-Place Countertops

Cast-in-place countertops are fabricated from cement, sand, aggregate, additives, and water, and are cast in place over a moisture resistant substrate, such as exterior grade plywood. A sheet moisture barrier should be placed on top of the substrate prior to casting the countertop. To shape the countertop, formwork must be installed and reinforcing placed where stresses will be greatest. The concrete is poured into the formwork and the surface texture is applied to finish the concrete. The concrete must be cured for the appropriate length of time to develop its strength, and should be sealed to protect the concrete upon completion. When installing cast-in-place concrete, care should be taken to not damage adjacent work.

Pre-cast Concrete Countertops

Precast concrete is typically factory-fabricated. However, large countertops may need to be formed

- BACKSPLASH FORMED OR SCRIBED TO CONFORM TO IRREGULARITIES IN COUNTERTOP
- SILICONE SEALANT
- 2" PRECAST CONCRETE WITH WIREMESH REINFORCING
- CABINET CASE

PRECAST CONCRETE

- BACKSPLASH (INSTALLED BEFORE CONCRETE IS PLACED)
- SILICONE SEALANT
- MOISTURE BARRIER; TRIM TO TOP OF CONCRETE OR TO CABINET FACE WHEN FORMWORK IS REMOVED
- 2" CONCRETE WITH WIREMESH REINFORCING
- 3/4" EXTERIOR-GRADE PLYWOOD
- CABINET CASE

CAST-IN-PLACE CONCRETE COUNTERTOP

from more than one precast section, due to manufacturing limitations, and seams may be quite visible.

Coordination of cutouts for sinks and other openings in countertops is critical to ensure proper placement and to allow adequate support for the units mounted within or on the countertop.

ACCESSIBLE COUNTERTOPS

Other concerns regarding countertops include coordination with adjacent architectural woodwork, such as base cabinets. Compliance is mandatory with Americans with Disabilities Act (ADA) requirements for accessible counters, when applicable. Partition construction, such as a gypsum board alcove that receives a countertop, may affect the final size of the countertop. Field verification of such conditions is recommended, as may be the use of reveals, which are scribed to fit the opening.

The ADA also establishes overall heights of accessible counters from 28 to 34 in. (711 mm to 864 mm) above the finish floor. A minimum clear height of 29 in. (737 mm) must be maintained for accessible lavatory countertops. The need for accessible countertops may affect the counter nosing dimension, undercounter support, and the installed height of the unit in areas under the accessibility requirements.

Food Service

Where food or drink is served at counters exceeding 34 in. (865 mm) in height for consumption by customers seated on stools or standing at the counter, a portion of the main counter which is 60 in. (1,525 mm) in length minimum shall have at least one accessible route or service shall be available at accessible tables within the same area.

Sales, Service, and Information Counters

In areas used for transactions where counters have cash registers, at least one of each type shall have a portion of the counter which is at least 36 in. (915 mm) in length with a maximum height of 36 in. (915 mm) above the finish floor. It shall be on an accessible route.

In areas used for transactions that may not have a cash register but at which goods or services are sold or distributed, for example, ticketing counters, teller stations, registration counters in transient lodging facilities, information counters, box office counters, and library checkout areas, there are three options:

- A portion of the main counter, which is a minimum of 36 in. (915 mm) in length, shall be provided with a maximum height of 36 in. (915 mm).
- An auxiliary counter with a maximum height of 36 in (915 mm) in close proximity to the main counter be provided.
- If a separate counter can't be provided, an equivalent facility must be provided for use by persons with disabilities. For example at a hotel registration counter, equivalent facilitation might consist of either a folding shelf attached to the main counter on which an individual with a disability can write, and use of the space on the side of the counter or at the concierge desk, for handing materials back and forth.

Ted Kollaja, AIA; lauckgroup; Dallas, Texas
Sarah Bader; Gensler; Chicago, Illinois

WOOD VENEERS

Monumental woodwork projects encompass widespread application of custom-selected wood veneers, either throughout a contiguous space or across broad elevations. In order to create large areas of matching wood panels, *flitches* are matched and applied to an appropriate substrate. A flitch is a part of a log created by slicing the trunk longitudinally, while keeping the sequence of individual leaves in the order they were created. When spliced together, flitches cut from the same log offer a uniform and continuous appearance of wood grain and character. No waste is generated in this process because the logs are sliced with long blades, not sawn, and so no sawdust is generated.

Of the more than 15,000 species of trees, only about 150 are normally sliced into veneer, and only about 25 are of suitable use for monumental woodworking. No more than 10% of any individual species cut and sliced for veneer yields material that meets even the minimum standards of the Architectural Woodwork Institute (AWI) for premium grade.

SELECTION CRITERIA

Environmental, market, and political factors affect the availability, cost, log size, and other factors that determine the suitability of a veneer to be used for large-scale interior architecture. There are four principal factors: availability, size of log, appearance, and physical properties.

The following species are currently readily available for use as "architectural" veneers:

Anegre
Ash, European
Avodire
Beech (steamed and unsteamed), European
Bubinga
Douglas fir
Etimoe
Eucalyptus
Mahogany (African and Honduras)
Makore
Moabi
Movinque
Oak, American red (various cuts)
Oak, American white (various cuts)
Oak, European white
Okoume
Pommele (Makore, Sapele, Moabi)
Sapele
Sycamore, American
Sycamore, English
Teak
Tigerwood
Walnut, American
Wenge
Zebrawood

Commonly specified veneers such as American cherry and maple are omitted because of their wide inconsistencies within the species and relative scarcity of high-grade flitches.

EIGHT-PIECE SUNBURST

BOX MATCH

PARQUET MATCH

REVERSE OR END GRAIN BOX

HERRINGBONE

SWING MATCH

DIAMOND

REVERSE DIAMOND

SKETCH FACE

SPECIAL WOOD VENEER MATCHING OPTIONS

COMMON FACE VENEER PATTERNS OF SELECTED COMMERCIAL SPECIES

PRIMARY COMMERCIAL HARDWOOD SPECIES	FACE VENEER PATTERNS[1]			
	PLAIN-SLICED (FLAT-CUT)	QUARTER-CUT	RIFT-CUT AND COMB GRAIN	ROTARY-CUT
Ash	Yes	Yes	—	Yes
Birch	Yes	—	—	Yes
Cherry	Yes	Yes	—	Yes
Hickory	Yes	—	—	Yes
Lauan	—	Yes	—	Yes
Mahogany (African)	Yes	Yes	—	Yes
Mahogany (Honduras)	Yes	Yes	—	Yes
Maple	Yes	Yes	—	Yes
Meranti	—	Yes	—	Yes
Oak (red)	Yes	Yes	Yes	Yes
Oak (white)	Yes	Yes	Yes	Yes
Pecan	Yes	—	—	Yes
Walnut (black)	Yes	Yes	—	Yes
Yellow poplar	Yes	—	—	Yes
Typical methods of cutting[2]	Plain slicing or half-round on rotary lathe	Quarter-slicing	Offset quarter on rotary lathe	Rotary lathe

[1]*The headings below refer to the face veneer pattern, not to the method of cutting. Face veneer patterns other than those listed are obtainable by special order.*

[2]*The method of cutting for a given face veneer pattern must be at mill option unless otherwise specified by the buyer in an explicit manner to avoid the possibility of misunderstanding. For example, plain-sliced veneer cut on a vertical slicer, or plain-sliced veneer cut on a half-round rotary lathe, could be specified.*

Source: Hardwood, Plywood, and Veneer Association

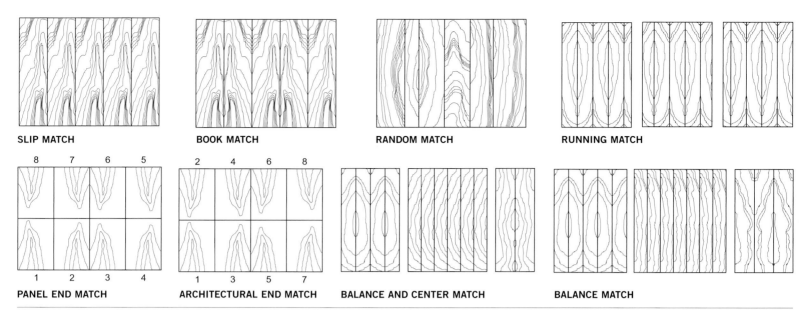

SLIP MATCH

BOOK MATCH

RANDOM MATCH

RUNNING MATCH

PANEL END MATCH

ARCHITECTURAL END MATCH

BALANCE AND CENTER MATCH

BALANCE MATCH

NEED SFG

CHARACTERISTICS OF WOOD VENEER SPECIES

SPECIES	TYPE OF CUT	WIDTH (FROM–TO) IN. (MM)	LENGTH (FROM–TO) FT (M)	LOG SIZE	COST	AVAILABILITY
Anegre	Quartered—nonfigured	6–14 (150–355)	9–12 (2.7–3.6)	Large	Low	Good
	Quartered—figured	4–20 (100–510)	9–12 (2.7–3.6)	Medium/large	Moderate/high	Good
	Quartered—fiddleback figure	4–16 (100–405)	9–12 (2.7–3.6)	Medium/large	High	Limited
	Plain-sliced—nonfigured	9–24 (230–610)	9–12 (2.7–3.6)	Medium	Low	Good
	Plain-sliced—figured	9–24 (230–610)	9–12 (2.7–3.6)	Medium	Moderate/high	Limited
Avodire	Quartered	4–8 (100–200)	9–12 (2.7–3.6)	Medium	Moderate	Good
Ash, European	Quartered/plain-sliced—figured	4–10/10–26 (100–255/255–660)	9–14 (2.7–4.2)	Medium	Moderate	Good
European beech (steamed)	Quartered/plain-sliced	4–10/10–26 (100–255/255–660)	9–12 (2.7–3.6)	Small/medium	Low	Good
European beech (unsteamed)	Quartered/plain-sliced	4–8/8–22 (100–200/200–560)	9–12 (2.7–3.6)	Small/medium	Low	Limited
Bubinga	Quartered/plain-sliced	6–12/12–30 (150–305/305–760)	9–12 (2.7–3.6)	Large	Moderate	Good
Douglas fir	Quartered	5–12 (130–305)	9–13	Medium/large	Moderate	Good
Etimoe	Quartered—figured	6–14 (150–355)	8–11	Large	Moderate	Good
Eucalyptus	Quartered—figured	6–12 (150–305)	9–14 (2.7–4.2)	Medium/large	Moderate	Good
Mahogany	Quartered	6–24 (150–610)	9–15 (2.7–4.5)	Large	Low	Good
(African; aka Khaya)	Quartered—figured	4–12 (100–305)	9–12 (2.7–3.6)	Medium/large	Moderate	Limited
	Plain-sliced	8–26 (200–660)	8–11 (2.4–3.3)	Small/medium	Low	Good
Mahogany (Honduras)	Quartered/plain–sliced	6–10/9–20 (150–250/230–510)	9–12 (2.7–3.6)	Small/medium	Low	Good
Makore	Quartered—nonfigured	6–18 (150–460)	9–14 (2.7–4.2)	Large	Low	Good
	Quartered—figured	6–24 (150–610)	9–14 (2.7–4.2)	Large	Moderate	Good
	Quartered—fiddleback figure	6–18 (150–460)	9–14 (2.7–4.2)	Large	Very high	Very limited
	Plain-sliced—nonfigured	9–24 (230–610)	9–14 (2.7–4.2)	Medium	Low	Limited
	Plain-sliced—figured	9–24 (230–610)	9–14 (2.7–4.2)	Medium	Moderate	Limited
Moabi	Quartered	4–14 (100–355)	9–12 (2.7–3.6)	Large	Low	Good
	Quartered—figured	4–12 (100–305)	9–12 (2.7–3.6)	Large	Moderate	Good
Movinque	Quartered—figured	6–16 (150–405)	9–12 (2.7–3.6)	Large	Moderate	Good
Oak, American white	Quartered	5–10 (130–250)	9–12 (2.7–3.6)	Small	Low	Good
	Plain-sliced	8–20 (200–510)	9–12 (2.7–3.6)	Small	Low	Good
	Rift-cut	4–9 (100–230)	9–12 (2.7–3.6)	Small	Moderate	Limited
Oak, American red	Quartered	5–10 (130–250)	9–12 (2.7–3.6)	Small	Low	Good
	Plain-sliced	8–24 (200–610)	9–12 (2.7–3.6)	Small	Low	Good
	Rift-cut	6–12 (150–305)	9–12 (2.7–3.6)	Small	Moderate	Limited
Oak, European white	Quartered	4–9 (100–230)	9–11 (3.3–3.3)	Small/medium	Moderate	Good
Okoume	Quartered—figured	7–14 (180–355)	9–12 (2.7–3.6)	Large	Moderate	Good
Pommele (Makore, Sapele, Moabi)	Rotary-cut	6–30 (150–760)	9–12 2.7–3.6)	Large	High	Good
Sapele	Quartered	5–14 (130–355)	9–14 (2.7–4.2)	Large	Low	Good
	Quartered—figured	5–14 (130–355)	9–14 (2.7–4.2)	Large	Moderate	Good
	Plain-sliced	10–22 (250–560)	9–14 (2.7–4.2)	Medium/large	Low	Good
Sycamore, American	Quartered	3–9 (75–230)	9–12 (2.7–3.6)	Medium	Moderate	Limited
Sycamore, English	Quartered/plain-sliced—figured	4–10/8–22 (100–250/200–560)	9–14 (2.7–4.2)	Medium	High	Limited
Teak	Quartered/plain-sliced	4–8/8–22 (100–200/200–560)	9–14 (2.7–4.2)	Small/medium	Moderate/high	Limited

Size of Log

The diameter and length of the log determine two key aspects of the veneer produced from it. The diameter directly determines the width of the veneer leaves. It is important to determine if a flitch will yield the square footage, leaf width, and length that a project requires.

Tropical species such as Anegre, Makore, and Sapele can provide very large quantities of wide veneer from a single log, often enough to complete a substantial project. Temperate species, on the other hand, are generally not available in such large flitches and leaf widths. In order to execute a very large project using these species, it is necessary to match up many flitches, "marrying" appearances including grain structure, natural color, and degree and type of figure.

Appearance

The appearance of wood is determined by naturally occurring characteristics that include grain, figure, color, heartwood or sapwood, knots and pin knots, and mineral and sap deposits. *Grain* is an expression of the annual growth ring structure of the tree that is revealed upon the cutting of the wood. *Figure* is caused by the convoluted growth of the wood fiber in the tree at a cellular level. Some trees grow quite regularly and therefore have an even orientation of wood fiber; once revealed, this wood shows a *nonfigured* appearance. When an irregular or aberrant growth pattern is established in the tree, the resulting wood shows figure. Bird's-eye maple and fiddleback Anegre are two such woods.

There are many figure types, but it is important to know that they are not found universally in all woods; and in many cases, they occur rarely or on a one-of-a-kind basis. The natural color of a particular species can vary greatly depending on various factors, including the growing area of the tree, the time of year the log was cut, and the length of time the log was steamed prior to slicing. Knots, pin knots, and mineral and sap deposits are all naturally occurring features that either diminish or enhance one's appreciation of the wood depending on the aesthetic at hand.

Physical Properties

All commercially available veneer is sliced, not sawn. A veneer-slicing machine uses a very sharp knife that contacts the flitch and cleanly slices off one piece of veneer without the waste inherent in sawdust. The log must first be "steamed." Steaming is a process whereby the log, after debarking, is soaked in large tanks of very hot water for up to three days. How much time a log is steamed, and at what temperature, depends on the species and size of the log. Steaming softens the wood within the log and allows the knife to slice through cleanly.

Combined, steaming and slicing affect the wood in several ways. First, the raw wood color is affected by steaming, and the veneer manufacturer must control this to provide a uniform wood color. In addition, slicing affects the very nature of the wood fiber. As the knife enters the wood, it puts the leading edge of the cut in compression, and the trailing surface (the back of the leaf being created) in tension. Thus, the two sides of every leaf of wood veneer created by a veneer slicer have opposite wood fiber properties, called *tight face* and *loose face*.

CATHEDRAL PATTERN / KNIFE / LOG OUTLINE

This is the slicing method most often used to produce veneers for high-quality architectural woodworking. Slicing is done parallel to a line through the center of the log. A combination of cathedral and straight-grain patterns results, with a natural progression of pattern from leaf to leaf.

PLAIN-SLICED (FLAT-SLICED) VENEER

NARROW STRIPED PATTERN / KNIFE / LOG OUTLINE / QUARTER LOG FLITCH

Quarter slicing, roughly parallel to a radius line through the log segment, simulates the quarter-sawing process used with solid lumber. In many species the individual leaves are narrow as a result. A series of stripes is produced, varying in density and thickness among species. "Flake" is a characteristic of this slicing method in red and white oak.

QUARTER-SLICED VENEER

NARROW STRIPED PATTERN / KNIFE / LOG OUTLINE / QUARTER LOG FLITCH

Rift veneers are produced most often in red and white oak, rarely in other species. Note that rift veneers and rift-sawn solid lumber are produced so differently that a "match" between them is highly unlikely. In both cases the cutting is done slightly off the radius lines, minimizing the "flake" associated with quarter slicing.

RIFT-SLICED (RIFT-CUT) VENEER

VERY BROAD PATTERN / KNIFE

To create rotary-cut veneers, the log is center mounted on a lathe and "peeled" along the path of the growth rings, like unwinding a roll of paper. This provides a bold, random appearance. Rotary-cut veneers vary in width, and matching at veneer joints is extremely difficult. Almost all softwood veneers are cut this way. Rotary-cut veneers are the least useful in fine architectural woodwork.

ROTARY-CUT VENEER

PARTICLEBOARD / FACE VENEER / PARTICLEBOARD CORE / FACE VENEER

MEDIUM-DENSITY FIBERBOARD / FACE VENEER / MEDIUM-DENSITY FIBERBOARD CORE / FACE VENEER

VENEER / FACE VENEER / VENEER CORE / FACE VENEER

LUMBER / FACE VENEER / CROSSBAND / LUMBER CORE / FACE VENEER

HARDWOOD PLYWOOD CORE TYPES

SOLID WOOD REVEAL—VENEERED EDGE

VENEER-FINISHED REVEAL—VENEERED EDGE

SOLID WOOD REVEAL

VENEER-FINISHED REVEAL—SOLID EDGE

MDF core recommended for incised reveals. MDF not readily available as fire-rated panels.

VENEER PANEL JOINTS
Source: Architectural Woodwork Institute; Architectural Quality Standards, 7th Ed. (Version 1.2), Reston, Virginia, 1999.

LOCK MITER

SPLINED MITER

SOLID WOOD CORNER

CUT-TO-FIT

SOLID WOOD REVEAL OUTSIDE CORNER

SOLID WOOD REVEAL INSIDE CORNER

VENEER PANEL CORNER JOINTS AND TRANSITIONS *Source: Architectural Woodwork Institute;* Architectural Quality Standards, *7th Ed. (Version 1.2), Reston, Virginia, 1999.*

CHARACTERISTICS* OF CORE MATERIAL PERFORMANCE

PANEL TYPE	FLATNESS	VISUAL EDGE QUALITY	SURFACE UNIFORMITY	DIMENSIONAL STABILITY	SCREW-HOLDING STRENGTH	BENDING STRENGTH	AVAILABILITY
Industrial particleboard core (medium density)	Excellent	Good	Excellent	Fair	Fair	Good	Ready
Medium-density fiberboard core (MDF)	Excellent	Excellent	Excellent	Fair	Good	Good	Ready
Veneer core—all hardwood	Fair	Good	Good	Excellent	Excellent	Excellent	Ready
Veneer core—all softwood	Fair	Good	Fair	Excellent	Excellent	Excellent	Ready
Lumber core—hardwood or softwood	Good	Good	Good	Good	Excellent	Excellent	Limited
Standard hardboard core	Excellent	Excellent	Excellent	Fair	Good	Good	Ready
Tempered hardboard core	Excellent	Good	Good	Good	Good	Good	Limited
Moisture-resistant particleboard core	Excellent	Good	Good	Fair	Fair	Good	Limited
Moisture-resistant MDF core	Excellent	Excellent	Good	Fair	Good	Good	Limited
Fire-resistant particleboard core	Excellent	Fair	Good	Fair	Fair	Good	Limited

Characteristics of core material performance are influenced by the grade and thickness of the core and specific gravity of the core species. Visual edge quality is rated before treatment with edge bands or fillers and, for lumber core, assumes the use of "clear edge" grade. Surface uniformity is directly related to the performance of fine veneers placed over the surface. Dimensional stability is usually related to exposure to wide variations in relative humidity. Screw-holding and bending strength are influenced by proper design and engineering.

FLITCH SELECTIONS

Veneer companies specializing in architectural veneer inventory their flitches for the designer's selection and specification. Every flitch of veneer carries a flitch number that identifies it, and this number can be included in the construction documents. Because there are so many variables to getting the desired results, flitches are identified and secured at the time a job is being specified.

Dan Meyerson; R.S. Bacon Veneer Company; New York, New York

PANELED PORTAL WITH ACCESS DOORS

Project: National Gallery of Art; Washington, D.C.
Designer: Vitetta Croup/Studio Four; Philadelphia, Pennsylvania
Woodworker: Washington Woodworking Company, Inc.; Landover, Maryland
Design Solutions, *Summer 1990*

7 1/4"

7 1/2"   1/4"   5'-6"   1/4"   7 1/2"

1/4"

10'-3" FINISH FLOOR TO FACE OF FINISH SOFFIT PANEL

DOOR ELEVATION

11/16"   8 5/8"   2'-0 7/8"   8 5/8"

2"

3"

3"

7 1/2"

1/4"

1/8"

- 5/8" GYPSUM BOARD
- 1/2" PLYWOOD
- 3/4" PLYWOOD
- METAL STUD FRAMING
- BLOCKING
- 1-3/4" SOILD CORE DOOR
- BEVEL

DOOR IN OPEN POSITION

PLASTER

SOLID WOOD TRIM, TYP.

WOOD PANEL DOOR

3/4" PLYWOOD PANEL

MARBLE BASE INSET BELOW

LINE OF MARBLE BASE

DOOR IN OPEN POSITION

1/8"   5 3/4"   1 5/8"

EQ.   2'-9 1/16"   EQ.

2 9/16"

3'-0 5/8"

DOOR JAMB

5'-6"

3'-5 1/8" AT JAMB

PLAN AT DOOR

BACK-LIGHTED PILASTERS

Project: Cinergy; Cincinnati, Ohio
Designer: Champlin/Haupt Architects Inc.; Cincinnati, Ohio

5/8" GYP. BD. OVER METAL STUDS
PAINT INTERIOR OF LIGHT BOX
COMPACT FLUORESCENT STRIP LIGHT
WOOD BLOCKING
PAINTED VENEER HARDWOOD OVER PARTICLEBOARD
1/8" STAINED GLASS WITH 10" RADIUS
2" RAD. WOOD TRIM, PTD.
BRONZE ANGLE WITH SOLID STEEL AT SCREW LOCATIONS
1/2" TH. X 1" W. BRONZE STRAP
6 1/2"   9"
2 1/2"   4 1/2"   10"   4 1/2"   2 1/2"
2'-0"

Ⓐ PILASTER AT BACK-LIGHTED STAINED GLASS

5/8" GYP. BD. OVER METAL STUDS
1/2" CEMENTITIOUS TILE BACKER BOARD
WOOD BLOCKING
PAINTED VENEER HARDWOOD OVER PARTICLEBOARD
WOOD BASE BELOW
MARBLE TILES
2" RADIUS HARDWOOD TRIM, PAINTED
1/2" WOOD QUARTER ROUND TRIM
6 1/2"   9"
2 1/2"   4 1/2"   10"   4 1/2"   2 1/2"
2'-0"

Ⓑ PILASTER AT MARBLE TILE TRIM

2'-0"   16'-0"   2'-0"   7'-0"   2'-0"
6"   6"   6"   4'-0"   6"
4"   7"
WOOD CAP, PAINTED
4"
2'-8"
30'-11" RADIUS TO FINISHED EDGE OF BULKHEAD
SOLID BRONZE STRAP
STAINED GLASS
VENEER HARDWOOD, PAINTED
HARDWOOD TRIM, PAINTED
MARBLE TILES
WOOD BASE, PAINTED
NOTE: RADIUS TO FINISHED FACE OF GYPSUM BOARD IS + 1/2"
APPLIED PIER, TYP.
5'-2"   9'-0"   5'-6"
6"   1'-8"   3"
6"
Ⓐ
Ⓑ
EQ.   EQ.
LAYOUT FOR PAINT PATTERN

ELEVATION

2 ☐ CUSTOM ARCHITECTURAL WOODWORK

CURVED PANELED WALL

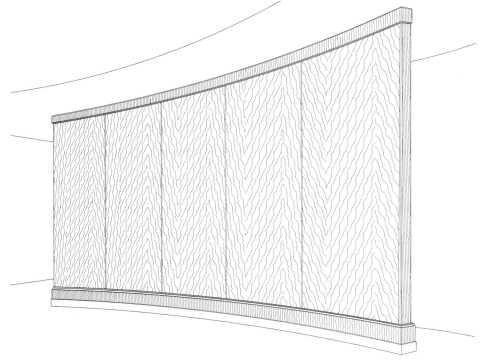

Project: AFLAC Customer Service Center; Columbus, Georgia
Designer: Hecht, Burdeshaw, Johnson, Kidd & Clark; Columbus, Georgia
Woodworker: Columbus Cabinet Company; Columbus, Georgia
Design Solutions, *Winter 2000*

A **DETAIL AT REVEAL**

- METAL STUDS
- GYPSUM BOARD
- VERT. CLEAT
- TWO LAYERS 1/4" PLYWOOD
- VENEER ON 1/4" PLYWOOD
- WOOD TRIM
- VENEER EDGEBANDING

4"
5/8"
1 1/2"
3/4"
3/8"
1/2"

B **DETAIL AT END WALL**

- VENEER ON 1/4" PLYWOOD
- TWO LAYERS 1/4" PLYWOOD
- METAL STUDS
- GYPSUM BOARD
- SOLID WOOD TRIM

3/8"
3/4"
5/8"
3 5/8"
5/8"
3/4"
3/4"
3 1/4"
3/8"
6 3/8"
7 7/8"
3/8"

- SOLID WOOD TRIM
- QUARTERED FIGURED WOOD VENEER PLYWOOD PANELS
- PANEL REVEALS
- PAINTED MDF TRIM
- POLISHED STONE BASE

C
A
B
D

6"
10'-7"
12'-0"
7"
4"

ELEVATION

A
B

VERIFY
4'-0"
4'-0"
4'-0"
VERIFY
VERIFY
R 40'-0"

PLAN

C **DETAIL AT CEILING**

- METAL STUDS
- GYPSUM BOARD
- SOLID WOOD TRIM
- HANGING RAILS
- VENEER ON 1/4" PLYWOOD
- TWO LAYERS 1/4" PLYWOOD

3/8"
1/2"
5"
6"
1/2"

D **DETAIL AT BASE**

- TWO LAYERS 1/4" PLYWOOD
- VENEER ON 1/4" PLYWOOD
- SOLID WOOD TRIM
- PAINTED UV-FILLED MDF TRIM
- HANGING RAILS
- POLISHED STONE BASE
- GYPSUM BOARD

5/8"
3/4"
1"
3/8"
1/4"
1"
1"
1/4"
7"
12"
N.T.S.
4"

PANELED LOBBY WITH CONCEALED DOOR JAMB

Project: Lobby, Second & Seneca Building; Seattle, Washington
Designer: Zimmer Gunsul Frasca Partnership; Seattle, Washington

DOOR ELEVATION

GYPSUM BOARD
ON METAL STUDS

HOLLOW
METAL
FRAME

SHIM AT METAL
STUDS

1/4" PLYWOOD

METAL CLEATS

HINGE

WOOD VENEER
PANEL

1/4"   1 1/2"   5/16"

SOLID HARDWOOD TRIM
AT HEAD AND JAMB

DOOR WITH
MATCHING
WOOD
VENEER

(A) CONCEALED DOOR JAMB

CONTINUOUS EDGEBAND
AT PANEL PERIMETER

SOLID WOOD AT REVEAL

METAL CLEATS

WOOD VENEER PANEL

1/4" PLYWOOD

GYPSUM BOARD
ON METAL STUDS

(C) INSIDE CORNER DETAIL

1 3/8"
1/4"   5/8"

GYPSUM BOARD
ON METAL STUDS

1/4" PLYWOOD

METAL CLEATS

SHIM AT CLEATS,
SECURE TO METAL
STUD AT CORNER

CONTINUOUS
EDGEBAND
AT CORNER

WOOD VENEER
PANEL

(B) WALL AT OUTSIDE CORNER

GYPSUM BOARD CEILING

SOLID WOOD AT REVEAL

CONTINUOUS EDGEBAND
AT PANEL PERIMETER

METAL CLEATS

WOOD VENEER PANEL

1/4" PLYWOOD

SHIM AT CLEAT

GYPSUM BOARD

(D) WALL AT CEILING DETAIL

1 3/8"
1/4"   5/8"

1/4" PLYWOOD

METAL CLEATS

SHIM AT REVEAL

CONTINUOUS EDGEBAND
AT PANEL PERIMETER

SOLID WOOD SPACER
AT REVEAL

WOOD VENEER PANEL

GYPSUM BOARD

(E) REVEAL DETAIL

1 3/8"
1/4"   5/8"

GYPSUM BOARD

METAL CLEATS

WOOD VENEER PANEL

CONTINUOUS EDGEBAND
AT PANEL PERIMETER

SOLID WOOD SPACER
AT REVEAL

SHIM AT REVEAL

1/4" PLYWOOD

NONSTAINING CEMENT

3/4" STONE BASE

GYPSUM BOARD
ON METAL STUDS

SHIM AT METAL
FLOOR TRACK

FINISH FLOOR

(F) WALL BASE

INTERIOR JOINT SEALANTS

Joint sealants occur at transitions between dissimilar materials and at junctures within long runs of similar materials to control cracking. They are applied by being extruded under pressure through a nozzle. In exposed locations, the resulting bead is tooled to a concave shape. Selection of the proper sealant material depends on the type of substrate, the amount of movement expected, if any, the location of the joint, and whether it will be visible in the finished space.

Four sealant types are popular for use in interiors:

- *Silicone* sealants are the most expensive, most durable, and have the best movement capability, but they are too soft for use in floor joints.
- *Urethane* sealants have good movement capability and cure harder than silicone. They resist penetration when used in floor joints.
- *Latex* sealants are inexpensive and are often used in applications with little movement or exposure to moisture.
- *Synthetic rubber* sealants are inexpensive, have good adhesion, and remain permanently tacky. They have little movement capability.

COLOR

Only latex sealants are paintable. Urethane and silicone come in a variety of colors. Silicone is also available as a translucent formulation. Sanitary sealant is white. Synthetic rubber acoustical sealant is dark gray and is not intended to be visible in the finished space.

MOVEMENT

If movement is expected in the joint, a bond breaker rod or tape should be inserted under the sealant to prevent three-sided adhesion.

Margery Morgan; Symmes Maini & McKee Associates; Cambridge, Massachusetts

APPLICATION SCHEDULE

LOCATION	PURPOSE	SEALANT TYPE	JOINT DESIGN
Vertical control and expansion joints on exposed interior surfaces of exterior walls	Close gaps to prevent air and vapor infiltration and insect migration.	Silicone, nonsag urethane, or paintable latex sealant	Butt joint
Perimeter and expansion joints in tile or stone flooring	Allow movement to avoid cracking.	Pourable urethane	Butt joint
Joints between plumbing fixtures and adjoining walls, floors, and counters	Close gaps to prevent leaks, water penetration, and mold growth.	Mildew-resistant silicone sanitary sealant	Fillet joint
Perimeter joints between interior wall surfaces and frames of interior doors, windows, and elevator entrances	Close gaps to prevent air infiltration and insect migration.	Paintable latex sealant	Butt joint, if feasible; otherwise, fillet joint
Interior perimeter joints of exterior openings	Close gaps to prevent air and vapor infiltration and insect migration.	Silicone, nonsag urethane or paintable latex sealant	Butt joint, if feasible; otherwise, fillet joint
Perimeter of sound-rated gypsum wallboard partitions and at penetrations in those partitions	Maintain acoustical barrier.	Latex sealant for concealed or exposed application; synthetic rubber for concealed application	Continuous bead
Joints between acoustical ceiling edge trim and wall	Eliminate air movement and light and sound leaks.	Synthetic rubber or latex	Continuous bead on back of vertical legs of trim pieces before they are installed
Joints between glass block units on interior faces	Eliminate air, water, and sound leaks.	Silicone	Butt joint
Interior joints in glass unit masonry assemblies	Eliminate air and water leaks; cover panel reinforcement.	Silicone or nonsag urethane	Butt joint
Intersections of components in cleanroom ceiling	Eliminate air leaks.	Silicone	Continuous bead on upward-facing surface of all flanges

BUTT JOINT WITH TAPE

BUTT JOINT WITH BACKER ROD

BUTT JOINT

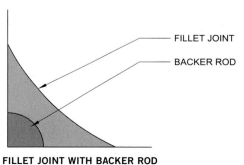

FILLET JOINT WITH TAPE

FILLET JOINT WITH BACKER ROD

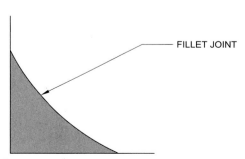

FILLET JOINT

SEALANT JOINT TYPES

APPLIED FIRE PROTECTION

FIRE-RESISTANT DESIGN

Several methods, both active (sprinklers) and passive, are possible for protecting building structures from fire. Designing for fire protection might include dividing a building into isolated modules with a limited number of penetrations for fire-rated doorways, electrical conduits, and ducts. Modules could be protected with sprayed fire-resistive materials, sprinklers, or both, depending on use, occupancy, potential exposure to abusive environments and individuals, and requirements of authorities having jurisdiction. Costs of sprinkling may be offset by savings from less-restrictive requirements for construction and finishes. Avoiding fire-rated doorways reduces costs for doors, hardware, and signs. Avoiding penetrations for electrical and mechanical work reduces the need for and expense of through-penetration firestop systems, fire-safing insulation, and fire dampers.

SPRAY-APPLIED FIRE-RESISTIVE COATINGS

Sprayed fire-resistive materials protect structural steel in both concealed and exposed applications. They include low-density cementitious and sprayed-fiber products, used predominantly for concealed locations, and a variety of medium- and high-density products, used for exposed locations that require a more finished appearance and greater resistance to physical abuse, air erosion, high humidity, and deterioration from weather, UV light, and chemical exposure.

Fire-resistance design decisions can affect the cost, scheduling, and complexity of sprayed fire-resistive material applications. For example, to forestall problems with warranty limitations and with the vulnerability of roof assemblies protected by applied sprayed fire-resistive materials when subject to construction, maintenance, or repair activities on the roof, roof-ceiling designs might be limited to those assemblies protected by materials other than sprayed fire-resistive materials applied to the underside of steel deck or to those not requiring additional protection. On a project-by-project basis, floor-ceiling assemblies, which are usually stiffer than roof-ceiling assemblies, may or may not require protection by sprayed fire-resistive materials applied on the underside of steel deck. It may be possible to eliminate the need to directly apply fire-resistive materials to the underside of steel deck by comparing design options with the same ratings, then selecting a design that results in thicker concrete slabs and requires no other protection of steel deck. The resulting stiffer floors will have the additional benefit of being better substrates for thin, rigid flooring, such as tile for restrooms.

If constraints, such as weather, aesthetic appearance, construction scheduling, environmental concerns, or the design program, make using sprayed fire-resistive materials inappropriate, alternative methods of protection may eliminate or reduce their extent. Alternative methods can include protecting structural steel with concrete; masonry; fire-safing insulation; mineral-fiberboard fire protection; sprinklers; and assemblies of gypsum plaster, portland cement plaster, gypsum board, veneer-plaster gypsum board, and rated acoustical ceiling panels.

Exposed Applications

For exposed applications, sprayed fire-resistive materials are higher in density, compressive strength, bond strength, and hardness than those for concealed applications. Suggestions for high-density products include exposed interior areas protected by deluge sprinkler systems and areas subject to contact, physical abuse, high impact, chemical exposure, high humidity, air, and erosion. Examples of areas where denser sprayed fire-resistive materials might be considered are parking garages, loading docks, piers, cargo facilities, warehouses, manufacturing plants, mechanical rooms, elevator machine rooms, shafts, air-handling plenums, stairwells, clean rooms, gymnasiums, and swimming pools.

The following products are used for exposed applications:

- Exposed cementitious sprayed fire-resistive materials
- Exposed sprayed-fiber fire-resistive materials
- Foamed magnesium oxychloride fire-resistive materials
- Intumescent mastic fire-resistive coatings, including water-based formulations, nonwater-based formulations, and thin films

Cementitious Coatings

Cementitious mixtures are sometimes referred to as *wet-mixed materials*. They are factory-mixed formulations consisting of dry ingredients including aggregates or fibers, gypsum cement, portland cement, and other binders. The dry ingredients are first mixed with water to form a slurry or mortar that is normally conveyed by pumping and then dispersed onto building structures by compressed air at the spray nozzle. Certain products for concealed applications require adding an accelerant at the job site. Cementitious formulations for concealed applications contain either gypsum or portland cement and either lightweight synthetic or mineral aggregates.

Sprayed-Fiber Coatings

Sprayed-fiber coatings, sometimes referred to as *dry-mixed materials*, consist of a dry formulation of mineral fibers, cement, and binders, conveyed by low-pressure air to a spray nozzle, mixed with atomized water, and then sprayed onto building structures.

Foamed Magnesium Oxychloride

Foamed magnesium oxychloride fire-resistive products are actually special types of plaster that are easily spray-applied for interior use. They react to fire exposure differently from ordinary gypsum or portland cement plasters and are much better protectors. However, they cost more and are not considered thermal insulators or sound absorbers. Compared to aggregate-based products, they are heavier, stronger, and less affected by moisture, and can be applied in lesser thicknesses to obtain the same protection. These products also bond strongly to substrates, similar to plasterbond. Spray application is a clean operation, and freshly placed materials are troweled, screeded, or leveled with a smooth paint roller. They are frequently used with metal lath boxing and corner beads as screeds, resulting in a finish-plaster appearance. Conditions requiring exterior exposure may require applying topcoats over foamed magnesium oxychloride products. These are more expensive than other cementitious products but are durable enough to replace thicker cast-in-place concrete for many applications, and provide savings in weight, space, and cost.

Magnesium oxychloride formulations are reputed to be corrosive. They must be prevented from contacting nonferrous metals, such as stainless steel, aluminum, and copper alloys. Their use must be limited to substrates whose compatibility with specific formulations has been proven by testing and field experience.

Intumescent Mastic Coatings

Intumescent mastic coatings foam or expand to form a thick, inert, carbonaceous insulator on substrates when exposed to heat. They are appropriate for exposed structural-steel members where a thin, durable, impact- and abrasion-resistant coating is desired. Some formulations also release moisture or gases that suppress combustion.

Intumescent mastic coatings may be used where a finished appearance is desired or where tight dimensional tolerance or lack of available space is critical. Because they provide fire protection by expanding, clearance for expansion must be considered.

Some systems consist of a base coat and a mandatory sealer/topcoat that provide decoration and protection from chemicals, abrasion, impact, and substrate deflection. Other systems allow, but do not require, aesthetic topcoats. Brush or trowel applications are allowed for some products with certain fire-resistance designs. Sprayed coats may need to be roller-leveled or applied in several thin layers for a smooth finish.

Thin-film intumescent mastic coatings may be used where a highly finished appearance and color are desired. Rigorous surface preparation may be required under thin-film intumescent mastic coatings because thin coatings do not hide defects in substrates.

ENCAPSULANTS

Encapsulants include materials that are spray-applied either over previously applied fire-resistive fibrous and cementitious formulations or to structural members from which previously applied materials have been removed. The latter are called *lockdown encapsulants*. Typically, encapsulants are part of a separate asbestos-abatement contract.

SEALERS AND TOPCOATS

Sealers and topcoats, mandatory or optional, are offered by some manufacturers to enhance product performance and to improve specific physical property limitations of individual formulations, such as resistance to chemicals and to growth of bacteria, fungus, mildew, and mold. Sealers and topcoats must be compatible with the manufacturer's formulation for sprayed fire-resistive materials. They should be applied at rates that maintain fire-resistance ratings; the saturation of sprayed fire-resistive materials with sealers and topcoats would probably negate fire-resistance performance.

COATING SELECTION

The primary consideration in selecting products for both concealed and exposed applications is anticipating which exposure conditions will prevail during the life of the structure.

Concealed Applications

Applications whose removal is unlikely during the life of the building, or in locations not requiring access for servicing of building environmental systems, appreciably reduce the risk of abrading or damaging the sprayed fire-resistive material. This type of application contrasts with spaces over accessible ceilings where frequent maintenance of wiring, air ducts, and piping exposes the sprayed fire-resistive material to possible damage. Because the future is difficult to predict, unanticipated exposure or removal of concealed applications may be required in a building subject to maintenance and remodeling efforts during its lifetime.

Exposed Applications

Exposed applications present considerations that differ from those for concealed applications. For interior applications, select products that have not only the desired finished appearance but also the appropriate physical properties needed to resist deterioration from physical abuse, high humidity, air erosion, and corrosive atmospheres. A sealer or a topcoat may be recommended or required by manufacturers to protect exposed products. For exterior applications and for interior applications exposed to moisture from high humidity or other causes, prime steel substrates to avoid corrosion. Detailing is important where appearance is concerned. For columns and beams, indicate whether to box out with a metal lath or to follow the contour of the individual member. Where sharp corners are required, indicate corner beads if they are permitted but not required for the fire-resistance rating.

Considerations other than the degree of exposure and durability may include appearance, ability to accept a topcoat, suitability for unconditioned interior use, fire-resistance life cycle, surface-burning characteristics, abrasion resistance, impact resistance, friability, erodibility, resistance to cracking and spalling, thickness/fire-resistance efficiency, seismic vulnerability, possibility of shop application, anticipated ambient conditions during and after application, potential health and nuisance hazards during and after application, repairability, environmental concerns, and initial and life-cycle costs.

Conditions Affecting Product Choice

Five specific conditions affect the choice of coating products.

1. *Where the ceiling space is either supply- or return-air plenum,* air movement may erode the sprayed fire-resistive material, which may not only lessen the fire-resistive material's effectiveness but also introduce unwanted dust or particles into the HVAC system.
2. *Clips, hangers, straps, and other support* for overhead suspended ceiling systems, signs, projection screens, blinds, shades, ducts, pipes, lighting fixtures, conduits, and other items are ideally placed before spraying most sprayed fire-resistive materials. This precaution is unnecessary for thin-film intumescent sprayed fire-resistive materials. If spaces above ceilings are tight or complex, sprayed fire-resistive materials may be damaged by subsequent installations. The penetration of fire-resistive materials for the installation of forgotten or unanticipated supports will compromise the performance of the materials and should be avoided. If systems are redesigned and rerouted after applications of sprayed fire-resistive materials, repositioned supports will penetrate the protective coating. Damage and penetrations will have to be patched.
3. *In elevator shafts and mechanical rooms,* vibrations from machinery, air pressures, and other causes may warrant using products with increased resistance to these forces.
4. *Certain surfaces, such as the underside of metal floors and roof decks,* may undergo continuous changes in loading or vibration from heavy traffic that could damage sprayed fire-resistive materials. Excessive deflection and impact forces on steel deck from construction activities and traffic have been identified by manufacturers of sprayed fire-resistive materials as the leading causes of lack of cohesion and adhesion and bond failure when sprayed fire-resistive materials are applied to steel deck. Problems with roof decks surpass problems with floor decks because floor decks are usually stiffer than roof decks and less susceptible to impact loads. Manufacturers of sprayed fire-resistive materials recommend that roofing and penthouse construction be completed, HVAC roof equipment be placed, and construction roof traffic be stopped before applying sprayed fire-resistive materials. Excessive construction loads on roof decks can dent and distort the decks and cause damage to applied fire-resistive materials.
5. *Interior applications in dry, humidity-controlled, conditioned spaces* in buildings with ducted HVAC systems that will be continuously maintained are more likely to endure and less likely to provide a growth medium for contamination by biological agents.

ENVIRONMENTAL CONSIDERATIONS

Many of the raw materials used in making sprayed fire-resistive materials are obtained by mining, often from open pit mines. Mines, especially open pit mines, and mining operations are environmentally costly. They cause erosion; pollute water, air, and soils; and negatively alter and destroy ecosystems over large areas. Mining operations and transportation of mined raw materials are fuel-energy–consumptive. Wastes generated by mining, such as quantities of excavated soils and rocks, tailings, and toxic leachate, are difficult to dispose of. Tailing ponds, toxic leachate, and mine runoff may need long-term containment and monitoring, and are potential causes of pollution disasters.

Indoor air-quality issues related to sprayed fire-resistive materials include particulate inhalation, particulate eye and dermal irritation, VOC emissions and absorption, and contamination by biological agents. Sensitive environments may have stringent requirements for the control of particulate matter in indoor air, VOC emissions, and potential pathogens. The removal and replacement of sprayed fire-resistive materials can be a significant source of indoor air pollution.

The content of sprayed fire-resistive material formulations, such as aggregate, fiber, cement, and other binders, is proprietary information, making it difficult to predict potential problems with particulate matter in indoor air. Formulations with high-fiber or potential dust content represent more particulate risk than low-fiber content and dustless formulations. Products that are denser, harder, more durable, and more abrasion- and impact-resistant are less likely to release particles. Bond failure, abrasion, impact, excessive substrate deflection, deterioration of the binder, or penetrations by subsequent work can cause dusting, flaking, cracking, and delaminating, and can generate airborne glass fibers, mineral wool fibers, and gypsum and other types of dust. Air-erosion tests, such as ASTM E859, *Standard Test Method for Air Erosion of Sprayed Fire-Resistive Materials (SFRMs) Applied to Structural Members,* are intended to measure the effect of an airstream in plenums during "normal service conditions" on sprayed fire-resistive materials, and to "evaluate the resistance to dusting, flaking, spalling, and delamination" of the sprayed fire-resistive materials. Some formulations of thin-film intumescent mastic coatings are reported to be free of fiber and dust.

Sprayed fire-resistive materials may emit VOCs and odors and, if wetted or exposed to humid conditions, may serve as a medium for microbial, mold, mildew, and fungal growth. Absorbed gases, moisture, humidity, and the presence of organisms may also affect a sprayed fire-resistive material's performance, durability, and serviceability. According to some manufacturers, products with a high content of gypsum binder are not recommended for wet or humid conditions.

BOARD FIRE PROTECTION

Board fire protection includes calcium silicate and slag-wool-fiberboards, and is used for fire protection of steel columns, steel beams, metal- and wood-framed walls, and solid walls. These materials form the encasing material for various assemblies with fire-resistance ratings. Another use for mineral-fiber board fireproofing is the protection of HVAC ducts.

The use of board protection instead of sprayed fire-resistive materials eliminates the cleanup of a wet residue and possible delays for drying that result from using sprayed material. Board fire protection is also less likely to corrode metal substrates.

Calcium Silicate Boards

Calcium silicate board is manufactured either from xonotlite or a combination of xonotlite and tobomorite. Xonotlite differs from tobomorite in crystalline structure and in physical properties. Xonotlite is designed for continuous service at 1700°F (926°C), and tobomorite at 1200°F (650°C), although both must withstand higher temperatures during testing per ASTM E119, *Standard Test Methods for Fire Tests of Building Construction and Materials,* to attain UL-listed fire-resistance ratings. Most, if not all, board fire protection systems are typically concealed behind other construction; however, the higher-density forms of calcium silicate can be left exposed and even painted.

Slag-Wool-Fiberboards

Slag-wool-fiberboard consists of fibers made from slag, which is a by-product of the production of steel, copper, and lead. (Slag is the mineral waste that rises to the top of molten metal.) Its uses include thermal insulation, curtain-wall insulation, and safing insulation (to establish fire barriers in the space between floor edges and curtain-wall spandrel panels). Slag-wool-fiberboards are more subject to damage and deterioration than calcium silicate units; they are softer, lighter, more absorbent, and more compressible.

THROUGH-PENETRATION FIRESTOP SYSTEMS

Fire-test-response characteristics of through-penetration firestop systems are measured in terms of F- and T-ratings. These are determined by testing systems per ASTM E814, *Standard Test Method for Fire Tests of Through-Penetration Fire Stops.*

- *F-ratings* indicate that the firestop system withstood the fire test for the rating period without the following taking place: flames passing through openings; flaming of any element on the unex-

posed side of the firestop system; and the development of any openings that permit water from the hose stream to project beyond the unexposed side.
- *T-ratings* signify that heat transmitted through the firestop system during the rating period did not raise the temperature of any thermocouple on the unexposed firestop system surface or on any pen-

etrating item by more than 325°F (180°C) above its initial temperature.

When selecting through-penetration firestop systems, the designer has to understand both what the local building code requires and how authorities having jurisdiction will interpret and enforce its provisions.

GYPSUM BOARD WALL PENETRATION
F-rating: 1 and 2 hour
T-rating: ¾ and 1½ hour

CONCRETE OR CMU WALL PENETRATION
F-rating: 1½ hour
T-rating: ½ hour

WALL-PENETRATION FIRESTOPS

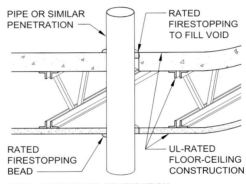

STEEL JOIST FLOOR PENETRATION
F-rating: 1 hour
T-rating: 1 hour

CONCRETE FLOOR PENETRATION
F-rating: 3 hour
T-rating: 2 and 3 hour

FLOOR-PENETRATION FIRESTOPS

FIRST COMPONENT

LETTER	CONSTRUCTION PENETRATED
F	Floor penetrations
W	Wall penetrations
C	Either floor or wall penetrations

An alpha character describes the type of surface penetrated.

SECOND COMPONENT

LETTER	DESCRIPTION
A	Concrete floors with a minimum thickness of less than or equal to 5 in. (125 mm)
B	Concrete floors with a minimum thickness greater than 5 in. (125 mm)
C	Framed floors
D	Steel decks in marine vessels
E–I	Not used now
J	Concrete or masonry walls with a minimum thickness less than or equal to 8 in. (200 mm)
K	Concrete or masonry walls with a minimum thickness greater than 8 in. (200 mm)
L	Framed walls
M	Bulkheads in marine vessels
N–Z	Not used now

An alpha character describes the construction material being penetrated.

THIRD COMPONENT

NUMBER RANGE	DESCRIPTION
0000–0999	No penetrating items
1000–1999	Metallic pipe, conduit, or tubing
2000–2999	Nonmetallic pipe, conduit, or tubing
3000–3999	Electrical cables
4000–4999	Cable trays with electrical cables
5000–5999	Insulated pipes
6000–6999	Miscellaneous electrical penetrants such as bus ducts
7000–7999	Miscellaneous mechanical penetrants such as air ducts
8000–8999	Groupings of penetrations including any combination of items listed above
9000–9999	Not used now

A four-digit number identifies the type of penetrating items.

UL-classified through-penetration firestop systems are identified in UL's *Fire Resistance Directory* under product Category XHEZ by an alphanumeric identification system.

UL-RATED FIRESTOP SYSTEMS

SELECTION CONSIDERATIONS

Consider the following when selecting the appropriate firestop system:

- *Fire ratings* required for each firestop system application based on the analysis of building code requirements. If this analysis does not provide a clear answer, obtain interpretations of authorities having jurisdiction. For through-penetration firestop systems, the minimum F-rating generally equals the fire-resistance rating of the construction penetrated. T-ratings are also usually required where heat transmission through the firestop system could ignite combustible items on the unexposed side. Typically, items penetrating through floors contained within wall cavities are not required to have T-ratings, but this should always be verified.
- *Extent of cyclic movement* that firestop system materials will undergo during normal use, as exerted by self-straining forces of materials forming openings and joints, by external forces, and by penetrating items.
- *Substrates* that firestop systems will contact.
- *Extent and type of penetrating items.* This involves indicating numbers, sizes, configurations, and locations of items and openings, and limitations on the sizes of openings in the different types of construction involved.
- *Frequency of changes* that through-penetration firestop systems are likely to undergo during building occupancy. If changes occur, this will require

installing firestop system products capable of enduring periodic reentry to add or remove penetrating items.

- *Exposure* of firestop systems during construction and after occupancy. Firestop systems may have to resist degradation from continuous or intermittent exposure to moisture from leaks, condensation, and other causes; high or low temperatures or both; chemicals; abrasion; and vibration.
- *Environmental considerations* as they relate to how firestop systems may affect building occupants during installation and reuse. Environmental regulations may prohibit products containing volatile organic compounds (VOCs) or other potentially harmful substances.
- *Other functions, if any, that firestop systems must perform.* Ascertain whether firestop systems must seal against the passage of sound, water, and radiation. For firestop systems not concealed by other construction, determine the kind of finished surface required and whether a paintable or integrally colored material is required. For systems installed in floors, find out whether cover plates or other means are needed to support loads from pedestrian traffic.

The lack of standard test methods for measuring the performance of through-penetration firestop systems for other than fire-test-response performance makes it difficult to evaluate products for durability, smoke-sealing capability, shrinkage, cyclic movement capability, and moisture solubility.

FIRE-RESISTIVE JOINT SYSTEMS

Fire-resistive joint systems are liquid-applied sealants, or caulks, that fill voids or cavities. By establishing the following, the proper fire-resistive system can be selected:

- *Fire ratings required* for each fire-resistive joint system as determined from the analysis of building code requirements. If this analysis does not provide a clear answer, obtain the interpretations of authorities having jurisdiction.
- *Extent and type of cyclic movement* of fire-resistive joint systems.
- *Types of fire-resistance-rated floor or wall assemblies* listed for use with the fire-resistive joint systems.
- *Other functions, if any, that fire-resistive joint systems must perform.* Ascertain whether fire-resistive joint systems must seal against the passage of sound, water, or radiation. For joint systems not concealed by other construction, determine the kind of finished surface required and whether a paintable or integrally colored material is required. For systems installed in floors, determine whether cover plates or other means are needed to support loads from pedestrian traffic.

MASTERSPEC®; published by ARCOM; Salt Lake City, Utah, and Alexandria, Virginia
Grace Construction Products; Cambridge, Massachusetts

FIRST COMPONENT

ALPHA CHARACTERS	DESCRIPTION OF JOINT SYSTEM
FF	Floor to Floor
WW	Wall to Wall
FW	Floor to Wall
HW	Head of Wall

Two alpha characters are used to describe the type of joint system.

SECOND COMPONENT

ALPHA CHARACTER	MOVEMENT CAPABILITY
S	No movement capability
D	Has movement capability

An alpha character describes joint movement.

THIRD COMPONENT

NUMBER RANGE	NOMINAL JOINT WIDTH
0000–0999	Less than or equal to 2 in.
2000–2999	Greater than 6 in. and less than or equal to 12 in.
3000–3999	Greater than 12 in. and less than or equal to 24 in.
4000–4999	Greater than 24 in.

A four-digit number identifies joint size.

UL-classified, fire-resistive joint systems are identified in UL's *Fire Resistance Directory* under product Category XHBN by an alphanumeric identification system.

UL-RATED JOINT SYSTEMS

INTERIOR DOORS

INTERIOR DOOR TYPES AND MATERIALS

Basic interior door types include hinged swinging, sliding pocket, folding, pivoted, bipass, and accordion doors. Standard materials for interior doors include solid core and hollow wood, hollow metal (steel), aluminum, and glass.

Special-Purpose Doors

There are many types of special-purpose doors. Performance-based interior door types that are integrated into openings of compatible performance include fire-rated, acoustic, security, and ballistic threat-resisting doors. Other types of special-purpose doors include heavy insulated cold storage doors; radio-frequency-shielded doors, which are lined with copper foil; and X-ray shielding doors, which are lead-lined.

Door Systems

Storefront, automatic opening, and overhead coiling doors are commonly provided as complete systems that are integrated into the design.

Selection and Specification of Interior Doors

Interior doors can be sophisticated, complicated pieces of equipment. For example, automatic doors require power mechanisms and controls; acoustic doors often use automatic door bottoms that seal the door undercut as the door is closed; a coordinator may be required to ensure that the inactive leaf of a pair of doors closes before the active leaf. Consultants are often required to ensure the proper selection and specification of interior doors.

Other Types

Other door types include overhead coiling, sound-retardant, blast-resistant, security, revolving, and radiation-shielding. Refer to manufacturers' catalogs for specific door types and details of construction and installation.

HINGED SWINGING DOOR
- Most common type of door; easy to install and most convenient to use. Requires space for swing.
- Fire rating available.
- Edges easily sealed to prevent passage of smoke, light, or sound.
- Available in wide range of materials and finishes, with multiple hardware options.

VERIFY MINIMUM PARTITION THICKNESS REQUIRED

RECESSED PULL

SLIDING POCKET DOOR
- Door is hung on track and slides into space within width of partition.
- No operating space is required.
- Relatively inexpensive.
- Awkward for frequent use.
- Difficult to seal against light or sound.
- Cannot be used as an exit door.

TRIM REQUIRED AT HEAD OF DOOR

CASED OPENING OR FRAMELESS

FOLDING DOOR
- Consists of hinged door panels that slide on overhead track.
- Uses minimum operating space.
- Often used as closet doors or as visual screen to other spaces.
- Awkward to use.
- Cannot be used as an exit door.

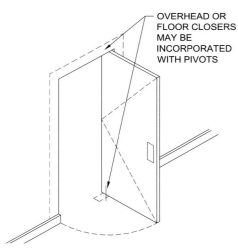

OVERHEAD OR FLOOR CLOSERS MAY BE INCORPORATED WITH PIVOTS

PIVOTED DOOR
- Center- or offset-hung; or balanced pivot hardware required.
- Center-hung pivots allow door to swing in both directions.
- Minimizes appearance of hardware, especially if center-hung pivots are used.
- Large, heavy door capacity.
- Balanced doors require less space to operate and take less effort to open.
- May be used for concealed doors.

CASED OPENINGS OF FRAMES

GUIDE ON FLOOR

BIPASS DOORS
- Doors are hung on track; heavy doors may slide on track in floor.
- No operating space required.
- Generally used for closet doors.
- Difficult to seal.
- Awkward for frequent use.
- Cannot be used as an exit door.
- Surface sliding doors, like barn doors, slide on surface of partition; not often used but may be applied for special effect.

CASED OPENINGS OF FRAMES

WOOD OR VINYL-COATED FABRIC

ACCORDION DOOR
- Used for subdividing space or as a visual screen.
- Is poor sound barrier.
- Cannot be used as an exit door.

TYPICAL INTERIOR DOOR TYPES

DOOR HANDING

The *hand*, or the *handing*, of a door refers to the standard method of describing the way a door swings. Handing is used in the industry to communicate how a door swings and the kind of hardware that must be supplied for a specific opening. Some hardware is specific to the hand of the door due to the bevel on the strike side of the door. Hardware that works on any hand of door is called *reversible* or *nonhanded*.

Handing is determined by standing on the outside of the door looking at the door. If the door hinges on the left and swings away, it is a left-hand door.

The corridor side is considered the outside of a room door, as is the lobby side of a door opening into a room or the room side of a closet door. When the distinction between outside and inside is not clear, the outside is considered the side of the door where the hinge is located.

DOOR-OPENING COMPONENTS

DOOR NOMENCLATURE

FRAME AND STOP TYPES

OPENING TYPES

MEETING EDGE TYPE FOR DOUBLE-DOOR LEAVES

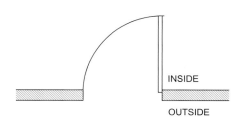

LEFT-HAND DOOR

RIGHT-HAND DOOR

DOOR HANDING

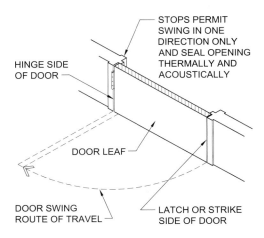

SINGLE-ACTING DOOR
The single-acting door, the most common door type, has a leaf that operates in a swinging or sliding motion in only one direction.

DOUBLE-ACTING DOOR
Double-acting doors have a leaf that operates in two directions. There is usually no stop present to restrict the motion of the door, but when the door can be stopped, it can be released mechanically to permit access in an emergency.

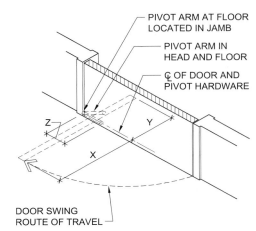

BALANCED DOOR
A balanced door is a single-action swinging door mounted on offset pivots. The leaf operates independently of the jamb, and the elliptical trajectory of the leaf requires less clear floor space than a conventional swinging door.

SINGLE-DOOR LEAF TYPES

PARTS OF A DOOR

Definitions

Active leaf: The primary operating leaf of a door pair.

Air curtain: A mechanically produced downward stream of air across a door opening intended to prevent transmission of heat and weather.

Automatic closing: A door that is normally open but that closes without the necessity for human intervention and is activated as a result of a predetermined temperature rise, rate of temperature rise, or combustion products.

Automatic door bottom: A device applied to the back side of a door at the bottom or mortised into the bottom edge of a door, which seals the undercut of a door as it is closed.

Balanced door: A door equipped with double-pivoted hardware designed to cause a semicounterbalanced swing action when opening.

Buck: A subframe of wood or metal set in a wall or partition to support the finish frame of a door.

Casing: The finished, often decorative framework around a door opening, especially that which is parallel to the surrounding surface and at right angles to the jamb.

Coordinator: A device used on a pair of doors to ensure that the inactive leaf is permitted to close before the active leaf.

Door bevel: The slight angle given to the lock stile (vertical edge) of a door, which prevents the door from touching the lock jamb as it swings. Typical bevels are: 1⅜ in. (35 mm) door—none; 1¾ in. (44 mm) door—⁷⁄₆₄ in. (3 mm); 2¼ in. (6 mm) door—⁹⁄₆₄ in. (3.5 mm).

Double-egress door: A pair of doors within a single special frame that swing in opposite directions to allow emergency egress from either side. Typically used where a fire or smoke partition crosses a corridor.

Flush bolt: A door bolt set flush with the face or edge of the door.

Fire-door assembly: Any combination of a fire door, frame, hardware, and other accessories that together provide a specific degree of fire protection.

Fire exit hardware: Panic hardware that is listed for use on fire-door assemblies.

Head: The horizontal portion of a door frame above the door opening.

Jamb: The vertical members at the sides of a door opening.

Labeled: Equipment, products, or materials marked with the label, symbol, or other identifying mark of an approved testing organization that indicates compliance with standards for manufacture and testing.

Listed: Equipment, devices, materials, or services included in a list published by a testing agency that have been shown to meet applicable standards for use in fire-rated assemblies or that have been tested and found suitable for use for a specified purpose.

Panic hardware: A door-latching assembly incorporating a device that releases the latch upon the application of a force in the direction of egress travel.

Power-assisted door: A door with a mechanism that helps to open the door or to relieve the opening resistance of the door.

Prehung door: Door and frame combination fabricated and assembled by the manufacturer and shipped to the site.

Sill: The horizontal members at the bottom of a door opening.

Subcasing: The finish frame components that support and guide the door.

Undercut: The space between the bottom edge of a door and the sill or threshold.

ACCESSIBILITY REQUIREMENTS

Door accessibility requirements are outlined below. For more information, consult the ADA Guidelines and ICC/ANSI A117.1, *Accessible and Usable Buildings and Facilities,* for additional requirements

- For opening width compliance, use doors 3 ft (914 mm) wide.
- Kickplates are recommended outdoors along accessible routes.
- Maximum opening force for interior hinged doors, sliding, and folding doors is 5.0 lb (22.2N). Minimum opening force for fire doors is regulated by the local authority having jurisdiction.
- Door closing speed must be a minimum of five seconds from an open position of 90° to an open position of 12°.

32" MIN. (815) CLEAR OPENING

CLEAR OPENING IS MEASURED FROM FACE OF STOP TO FACE OF DOOR WHEN OPEN 90°

MINIMUM MANEUVERING CLEARANCE VARIES BASED ON APPROACH DIRECTION, TYPE OF DOOR, AND WHETHER THE DOOR HAS A LATCH. SEE ANSI A117.1.

NO PROJECTIONS INTO THE CLEAR OPENING WIDTH ARE ALLOWED BELOW 34" (865) ABOVE FLOOR LINE. PROJECTIONS INTO THE CLEAR OPENING WIDTH FROM 34" - 80" (865 - 2020) MAY BE A MAXIMUM OF 4" (102)

CLEAR WIDTH OF ACCESSIBLE DOORWAYS

BOTTOM OF GLAZING MAXIMUM 43" (1090) A.F.F.

OPERABLE HARDWARE BETWEEN 34" AND 48" A.F.F. (865 - 1220)

34" (865) MINIMUM

BOTTOM 10" (255) OF MANUAL DOORS MUST BE SMOOTH, UNINTERRUPTED SURFACE ON PUSH SIDE. SEE ANSI A117.1 FOR EXCEPTIONS.

MAXIMUM THRESHOLD HEIGHT: 1/2" (13) WITH MAXIMUM SLOPE OF 1 VERTICAL TO 2 HORIZONTAL. RISE OF 1/4" (6) MAY BE VERTICAL; RISES GREATER THAN 1/2" (13) MUST BE MADE WITH 1:12 RAMP.

ACCESSIBLE DOOR FEATURES

DOOR AND FRAME DETAILING

SELECT DOOR WIDTH TO ACCOMMODATE FUNCTIONAL REQUIREMENTS, EXITING NEEDS, AND ACCESSIBILITY

PROVIDE MINIMUM 1/4" (6) SHIM SPACE AT JAMBS AND HEAD FOR OUT-OF-PLUMB ROUGH OPENING

VERIFY FRAME STRENGTH IF HINGES ARE USED OR DOOR WILL RECEIVE HEAVY USE

VERIFY FLOOR THICKNESS AND STABILITY IF FLOOR CLOSER IS USED

PROVIDE ADEQUATE ANCHORAGE IN PARTITION OR ABOVE CEILING IF OVERHEAD CLOSER USED

SPECIFY ADEQUATE FRAME ANCHOR AND ROUGH OPENING TO AVOID PARTITION SHAKE WHEN DOOR IS CLOSED

PROVIDE FOR FRAME AND ROUGH OPENING STRENGTH FOR SECURITY LEVEL NEEDED

PROVIDE FOR UNLEVEL FLOORS BY FILLING OR SPECIFYING ADEQUATE UNDERCUT

THRESHOLD THAT MEETS ACCESSIBILITY REQUIREMENTS IF NEEDED FOR FLOOR MATERIAL CHANGE OR AUTOMATIC DOOR BOTTOM

These detailing considerations for frames and partitions apply to the design of openings for doors of all types and materials.

DOOR DESIGN AND DETAILING CONSIDERATIONS

WIDTH (FRAME OPENING)

NET DOOR WIDTH

1/8"

1/8"

1/8"

THREE HINGES REQUIRED ON 1 3/8" TO 6'-8" LABELED UNITS AND UNLABELED ON REQUEST. THREE HINGES STANDARD ON ALL OTHER UNITS TO 7'-6".

TO SUIT HINGE

EQUAL

EQUAL

EQUAL

NET DOOR HEIGHT

NOMINAL HEIGHT (FRAME OPENING)

FINISHED FLOOR AS SPECIFIED

STANDARD DOOR AND DOOR CLEARANCE

Door Design Checklist

- For doors in corners, the hinge jamb must allow at least a 90° opening (with space for hardware).
- For doors serving a large number of people, use doors (and hardware) that will open at least 110°.
- Recess doors so they do not interfere with traffic or obstruct the required exit width.
- Verify that the door will swing clear of carpeting, uneven floors, and other obstructions.
- Verify the required maneuvering space and the maximum force requirements for accessibility.
- Include vision panels in double-acting and double-egress doors.
- Include required protection on the door such as armor plates, kickplates, edge guards, and so on.
- If used, verify that gaskets and sound seals are readjusted after a period of use.
- For wood doors, verify design compatibility with adjacent wood trim, woodwork, and furniture.
- For concealed doors, verify that the doors will operate after the application of finish material.
- Verify whether door tolerances need to be specified differently from industry standards.

WOOD DOORS

Face Material

Wood doors are available with face materials of wood veneer, composite veneer, high-density plastic laminate, medium-density overlay, and hardboard. Wood veneer on manufactured doors is available in the species offered by the manufacturer. Custom doors may be faced with any veneer available on the world market. Both reference standards listed below require face veneers of at least ⅟₅₀ in. (0.5 mm), but thicker veneers may be specified. Veneers may be rotary-cut, plain-sliced, quarter-sliced, or rift-cut, and may be matched with random, slip, and bookmatched methods.

- *Composite veneers* are manufactured by slicing sustainably grown hardwoods, then vat-dying and pressing them into new, composite "logs." The composite logs are then sliced to form new veneers that replicate other natural woods. By using various colors of natural veneers and slicing angles of the composite log, a nearly unlimited number of simulated wood species and veneer patterns can be created. These veneers can be applied to doors in the same way as natural veneers.
- *Plastic laminate veneers* provide a durable surface with hundreds of available colors and patterns.
- *Medium-density overlay (MDO) faces* are used to provide a smooth, paintable surface that resists grain raising and moisture. For this reason, they are often used for exterior doors.
- *Hardboard* is used with three-ply construction for interior doors that are to be painted and as a lower-cost option for MDO.

Wood Door Standards

The two main wood door standards are WDMA, I.S. 1-A, *Architectural Wood Flush Doors,* published by the Window and Door Manufacturers Association, and the *AWI Architectural Woodwork Quality Standards,* published by the Architectural Woodwork Institute. Generally, the WDMA standard is used to specify standard manufacturers' doors, while the AWI standards are used to specify custom doors. The Woodwork Institute of California also publishes standards in its *Manual of Millwork.*

Wood Door Grades

Both WDMA and AWI standards classify doors into three grades: Premium, Custom, and Economy. There are, however, some differences between the WDMA and AWI standards, and these should be verified before specifying.

- *Premium grade* is specified when the highest level of materials, workmanship, and installation is required.
- *Custom grade* is suitable for most installations and is intended for high-quality work.
- *Economy* is the lowest grade and is intended for work where price is a primary factor.

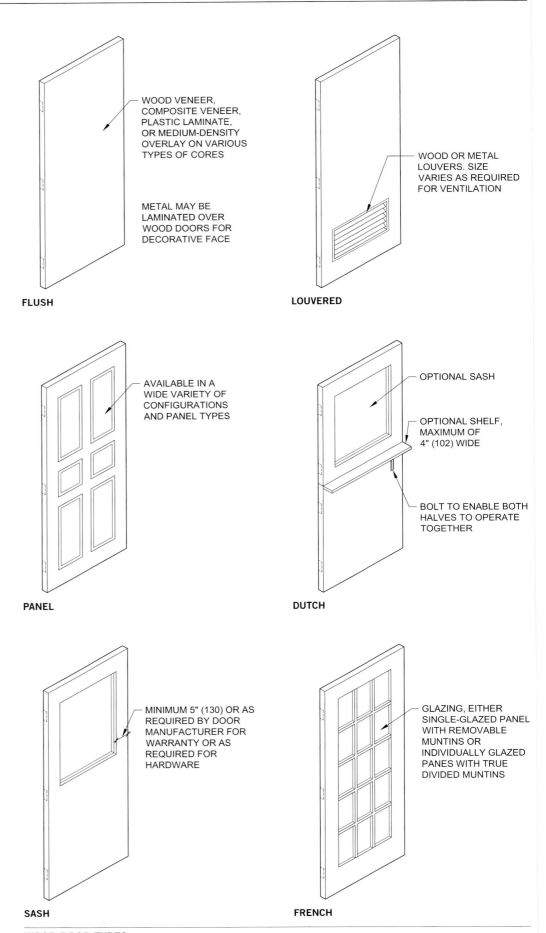

WOOD VENEER, COMPOSITE VENEER, PLASTIC LAMINATE, OR MEDIUM-DENSITY OVERLAY ON VARIOUS TYPES OF CORES

METAL MAY BE LAMINATED OVER WOOD DOORS FOR DECORATIVE FACE

FLUSH

WOOD OR METAL LOUVERS. SIZE VARIES AS REQUIRED FOR VENTILATION

LOUVERED

AVAILABLE IN A WIDE VARIETY OF CONFIGURATIONS AND PANEL TYPES

PANEL

OPTIONAL SASH

OPTIONAL SHELF, MAXIMUM OF 4" (102) WIDE

BOLT TO ENABLE BOTH HALVES TO OPERATE TOGETHER

DUTCH

MINIMUM 5" (130) OR AS REQUIRED BY DOOR MANUFACTURER FOR WARRANTY OR AS REQUIRED FOR HARDWARE

SASH

GLAZING, EITHER SINGLE-GLAZED PANEL WITH REMOVABLE MUNTINS OR INDIVIDUALLY GLAZED PANES WITH TRUE DIVIDED MUNTINS

FRENCH

WOOD DOOR TYPES

STANDARD   **INSTITUTIONAL**

STILES AND RAILS
LOCK BLOCK
CROSSRAIL
FACE VENEER

HOLLOW CORE

THREE-PLY WITH LAMINATE   **SEVEN-PLY**   **FIVE-PLY**

CROSSBAND
FACE VENEER

PARTICLEBOARD CORE

FIVE-PLY   **SEVEN-PLY**

GLUED BLOCK CORE
THREE-PLY PREMANUFACTURED HARDWOOD SKIN

STAVED LUMBER CORE

FIVE-PLY

MINERAL CORE
CROSSBAND
FACE VENEER

MINERAL COMPOSITION CORE

These are the most common core types. Other options are available, including structural composite lumber (or laminated strand lumber). These alternate types of cores are replacing the traditional staved lumber core doors:

Sound insulating core: A special core available in thicknesses of 1¾ in. (44 mm) and 2¼ in. (57 mm). The 1¾-in. (44-mm) core can provide a Sound Transmission Class (STC) rating of 36; the 2¼-in. (57-mm) core can achieve an STC of 42. Barrier faces are separated by a void or damping compound to keep the faces from vibrating in unison. Special stops, gaskets, and threshold devices are also required.

Lead-lined core: A special core consisting of ¹⁄₃₂-in. (.8-mm) to ½-in. (13-mm) continuous lead sheeting edge to edge inside the door construction. This material may be reinforced with lead bolts or glued. See Underwriters Laboratory requirements.

CORE TYPES

Hollow Core versus Solid Core Doors

Hollow core doors are typically used in residential construction and for commercial doors subject only to light use. Institutional hollow core doors, with heavier stiles and rails and with additional blocking, have increased strength and resistance to warping, but may cost as much as some solid core doors.

Solid core doors are more secure, more durable, more resistant to warping, and allow less acoustical transmission. They are used in most institutional and commercial projects.

Door Bevel

Doors are beveled to allow the door to open past the jamb without binding. The standard bevel is ⅛ in. in 2 in. (3 mm in 51 mm) (3½°). Generally, unit locksets are only available with the standard bevel; cylindrical locksets are available with either flat or standard bevel, and mortise locksets are available with bevels adjustable from flat to standard.

Bonded versus Nonbonded Cores

Solid core doors can either be bonded or nonbonded. With a bonded core, the stiles and rails are glued to the core material and the whole assembly is sanded as a unit before the faces are applied. This reduces the likelihood of telegraphing. With a nonbonded core, the elements can vary slightly in thickness and can telegraph through the faces noticeably. Five-ply doors are typically made with a bonded core, while seven-ply doors are made with a nonbonded core.

DOOR SIZES

Both wood and hollow metal doors are available in a variety of standard widths. Custom doors can be made in any size, but in general it is best to specify standard width doors and vary the height when ordering custom sizes.

Most door manufacturers do not offer a warranty if maximum heights are exceeded.

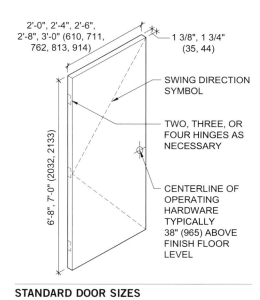

2'-0", 2'-4", 2'-6", 2'-8", 3'-0" (610, 711, 762, 813, 914)

1 3/8", 1 3/4" (35, 44)

SWING DIRECTION SYMBOL

TWO, THREE, OR FOUR HINGES AS NECESSARY

6'-8", 7'-0" (2032, 2133)

CENTERLINE OF OPERATING HARDWARE TYPICALLY 38" (965) ABOVE FINISH FLOOR LEVEL

STANDARD DOOR SIZES

TOP RAIL — — **RAIL (HORIZONTAL MEMBERS)**

HINGE STILE — **STILE (VERTICAL MEMBERS)**

GLAZING PANEL

LOCK STILE

MEETING STILE (PASSIVE/ STATIONARY LEAF)

LOCK (CROSS) RAIL PANEL (DISTINCT SECTION ENCLOSED BY FRAMEWORK)

FLAT PANEL

RAISED PANEL

MUNTIN (NONSTRUCTURAL MEMBER WITHIN FRAME OF DOOR)

BOTTOM RAIL

6'-8", 7'-0", AND 8'-0" (STORM/SCREEN DOOR, ADD 1")

INTERIOR: 1 3/8", 1 3/4"; EXTERIOR: 1 3/4", 2 1/4"; STORM/SCREEN DOOR: 1 1/8", 1 3/8"

INTERIOR: 1'-0", 1'-4", 1'-6". 2'-0", 2'-4", 2'-8", 3'-0"; EXTERIOR: 2'-6", 2'-8", 3'-0"

STILE AND RAIL TERMINOLOGY

VENEERED WOOD PANEL

SOLID STILE/RAIL FRAME WITH INTEGRAL OR APPLIED MOLDING

SOILD MOLDED FRAME WITH FLAT VENEERED PANEL

1/8" MIRROR (TEMPERED AS REQUIRED)

APPLIED MOLDING, EACH SIDE

VENEERED FLAT PANEL

VENEERED BUILTUP FRAME

MIRRORED PANEL

BEAD STOP MOLDING FOR INTERIOR USE

GLAZING (TEMPERED, INSULATING, ETC., AS NECESSARY)

MOLDED MUNTIN

PUTTY STOP FOR EXTERIOR USE

SOLID FRAME WITH INTEGRAL MOLDING STOP

GLAZED DOOR

STILE AND RAIL DOOR DETAILS

VENEERED BEVELED RAISED PANEL

MOLDING

VENEER/ FINISH PLY

STILE OR RAIL

CROSSBANDING PLY

HARDWOOD CORE

FINISH WOOD EDGE

STILE AND RAIL—RAISED PANEL

METAL CHEVRONS AND METAL FUSIBLE- LINK LOUVERS ALSO AVAILABLE FOR FIRE- RATED DOORS

WOOD SLATS

WOOD TRIM; PROFILE VARIES

WOOD CHEVRONS

STILE AND RAIL DOORS

Panel doors consist of a framework of vertical (stile) and horizontal (rail) members that hold solid wood or plywood panels, glass lights, or louvers in place.

The doors are made of solid or built-up stiles, rails, and vertical members (*muntins*), typically doweled per applicable standards. Stock material includes ponderosa pine, fir, hemlock, or spruce and hardwood veneers. Hardboard, metal, and plastic facings are available in various patterns.

GLAZING

Most building codes require all glass in doors to be safety glazed. Insulated safety glazing is available for increased thermal or acoustical performance.

BUILT-UP MEMBERS

The core and edge strip materials are similar to those used in flush doors. Face veneer is typically hardwood at 1/8 in. (3 mm) minimum thickness.

GLASS STOPS AND MUNTINS

Typical profiles used for trim work include cove, bead, or ovolo.

PANELS

Flat panels are typically three-ply hardwood or softwood. Raised panels are constructed of solid hardwood or softwood built up of two or more plies. Doors 1 ft 6 in. (457 mm) wide or less are one panel wide.

WOOD DOOR FRAMING

RABBET FOR 1 3/8" DOOR: 1 9/16" (39.7)
RABBET FOR 1 3/4" DOOR: 1 15/16" (49.2)

STOP TO END OF HINGE
LEAF: 5/16" (7.9)

FRAME CLEARANCE:
1/8" (3.2)

HINGE BACKSET:
1/4" (6.4)

DOOR
THICKNESS

CLEARANCE
FOR HINGE
BARREL:
1/4" - 3/8"
(6.4 - 9.6)

INSET:
1/8" (3.2)

FRAME
CLEARANCE:
1/8" (3.2)

STANDARD DOOR FRAME AND HINGE-SETTING DIMENSIONS

GYPSUM
BOARD

DOUBLE HEADER

CASING TRIM;
SHAPE AND SIZE
OF PROFILE
OPTIONAL

FRAME

HEAD

SHIM SPACE, TYPICALLY 1/4" (25)

ROUGH OPENING

DOUBLE
STUDS

JAMB

STOP; MAY BE SEPARATE
(AS SHOWN) OR INTEGRAL
WITH FRAME

DOOR

BASE

TYPICAL DOOR AND FRAME IN WOOD STUD PARTITION

METAL RUNNER:
2 1/2" OR 3 5/8"
(63.5 OR 92.1)

SHIM SPACE

SINGLE-RABBET
FRAME SHOWN

HEAD

DOUBLE METAL STUDS
AT JAMB 2 1/2" OR
3 5/8" (63.5 OR 92.1)

WOOD BLOCKING INSIDE
OF METAL STUD

JAMB

DOOR

PLINTH BLOCK
SHOWN WITH
WIDE TRIM

TYPICAL DOOR AND FRAME IN METAL STUD PARTITION

ALUMINUM
REVEAL TRIM

FINISH WOOD
FRAME

HEAD

SHIM AND WOOD BLOCKING

END OF DOOR ROUNDED

CENTER PIVOT POINT

JAMB

ALUMINUM
REVEAL
TRIM

BASE BEVELED OR
RETURNED ON ITSELF

1/2" (12)

ALUMINUM REVEAL TRIM

WOOD FRAME WITHOUT CASING FOR DOUBLE-ACTING DOOR

WOOD DOOR FRAMING

HEAD

GYPSUM BOARD
"L" TRIM, OPTIONAL:
"LK" TRIM CAN BE
FIT INTO KERF IN
WOOD SUBFRAME

WOOD BLOCKING AND SHIM
WITH METAL STUD PARTITION

JAMB

EXPOSED WOOD SUBFRAME
INSIDE REVEAL; OPTIONAL
FILLER STRIP MAY BE USED

SINGLE-RABBET FRAME

GYPSUM BOARD
"L" OR "LK" TRIM

BASE BEVELED OR
RETURNED ON ITSELF

SINGLE-RABBET FRAME WITHOUT CASING

HEAD

CONTINUOUS
WOOD STOP
(SHOWN) OR
METAL ANGLE
STOP IN HEAD

JAMB

ROLLER LATCH USED ON
STRIKE SIDE OF DOOR

RECESSED PULL
OR EDGE PULL

KERF CUT IN EDGE
OF DOOR TO ACCEPT
WALLCOVERING

DOOR AND WALL
COVERED IN VINYL OR
FABRIC WALLCOVERING

BASE
CONTINUES
ON DOOR

CENTER-HUNG PIVOT
USED ON HINGE JAMB

DOOR SWINGS OUT

HIDDEN DOOR

HEAD

FRAMING AS
REQUIRED

METAL TRACK
MAY BE
RECESSED
(AS SHOWN) OR
MOUNTED ON
HEAD FRAME

JAMB

INTERNAL FRAMING FOR DOOR UNIT
COMES PREASSEMBLED WITH DOOR

1 3/8" (35)
DOOR

OPTIONAL RECESSED
TRACK AND ROLLER
FOR HEAVY DOORS

ENLARGED VIEW OF TRACK

SLIDING POCKET DOOR

WOOD TRIM

HEAD

TRACK
ATTACHED
TO BLOCKING
IN HEAD

JAMB

FRAMELESS
OPENING (SHOWN)
OR CASED OPENING

BASE STOPS AT
OPENING OR RETURNS
TO DOOR POSITION

DOOR GUIDES
AT CENTER OF
DOOR OPENING

BIPASS DOORS

HOLLOW METAL DOORS

Door Types

Hollow metal doors are doors constructed from sheet steel attached to various types of cores. They are used in steel frames, also constructed of sheet steel bent into various profiles.

There are several types of steel doors. The Steel Door Institute uses a standard door design nomenclature to identify each type. Many of these are shown in the diagrams below. Refer to SDI 106, *Recommended Standard Door Type Nomenclature,* for a complete listing and for more information on door nomenclature.

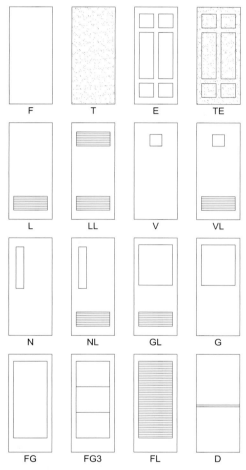

F   T   E   TE

L   LL   V   VL

N   NL   GL   G

FG   FG3   FL   D

Nomenclature Letter Symbols

F	Flush
T	Textured
E	Embossed
TE	Textured and embossed
L	Louvered (top or bottom)
LL	Louvered (top and bottom)
V	Vision lite
VL	Vision lite and louvered
N	Narrow lite
NL	Narrow lite and louvered
GL	Half glass and louvered
G	Half glass (several options available)
FG	Full glass
FG3	Full glass, three panes
FL	Full louver
D	Dutch door

DOOR TYPES

1 3/8", 1 3/4" (35, 44)

SEE TABLE

SEE TABLE. BASED ON DOOR THICKNESS.

Custom doors can be manufactured to nearly any practical size; however, standard widths should be used whenever possible.

Standard Widths

2 ft 0 in. (610 mm)	3 ft 4 in. (1,016 mm)
2 ft 4 in. (711 mm)	3 ft 6 in. (1,067 mm)
2 ft 6 in. (762 mm)	3 ft 8 in. (1,118 mm)
2 ft 8 in. (813 mm)	3 ft 10 in. (1,168 mm)
2 ft 10 in. (864 mm)	4 ft 0 in. (1,219 mm)
3 ft 0 in. (914 mm)	

Standard Heights

1¾-in.-doors	1⅜-in.-doors
6 ft 8 in. (2,032 mm)	6 ft 8 in. (2,032 mm)
7 ft 0 in. (2,134 mm)	7 ft 0 in. (2,134 mm)
7 ft 2 in. (2,184 mm)	7 ft 2 in. (2,184 mm)
7 ft 10 in. (2,388 mm)	
8 ft 0 in. (2,438 mm)	

STANDARD HOLLOW METAL DOOR SIZES

MAY HAVE FLUSH TOP OR INVERTED CHANNEL (FLUSH TOP SHOWN)

EXPOSED SEAM

FACE SEAMLESS

FULL FLUSH

MAY HAVE FLUSH TOP OR INVERTED CHANNEL (SHOWN)

NO VISIBLE SEAM ON VERTICAL EDGE

14-, 16-, 18-, OR 20-GA. STEEL FACE

SEAMLESS

HOLLOW METAL DOOR CONSTRUCTION

STANDARD STEEL DOOR GRADES AND MODELS

LEVEL	MODEL		FULL FLUSH OR SEAMLESS			CONSTRUCTION
			GAGE	IN.	MM	
I	Standard Duty	1	20	0.032	0.8	Full Flush
		2				Seamless
II	Heavy-Duty	1	18	0.042	1.0	Full Flush
		2				Seamless
III	Extra Heavy-Duty	1	16	0.053	1.3	Full Flush
		2				Seamless
		3				Stile and Rail*
IV	Maximum Duty	1	14	0.067	1.6	Full Flush
		2				Seamless

Stiles and rails are 16-gage; flush panels, when specified, are 18-gage.
Source: Steel Door Institute, SDI-108; Cleveland, Ohio

SDI DOOR LEVELS

SDI 108, *Recommended Selection and Usage Guide for Standard Steel Doors,* provides recommendations for levels of doors within a variety of building types and usages. In general, the following levels should be used:

Level 1: Doors for interior use in residences, dormitories, and hotels, except for entrances; individual office doors in office buildings and other commercial structures; and closets in most buildings.

Level 2: Doors for entrances to apartments, dormitories, and hotels, stairways, toilet rooms, hospital patient and operating rooms, and school classrooms.

Level 3: Entrance and stairwell doors in most buildings; in commercial and industrial buildings and schools, except closets; and in hospital kitchens.

Level 4: Doors for high-traffic entrances and stairwells in commercial and industrial buildings and entrances requiring increased security. Entrance and gymnasium doors in schools.

If doors are used in severe, humid environments or in humid areas such as pools or kitchens, a galvanized coating should be specified using either the hot-dip or electrolytic process.

REINFORCING PROVIDED FOR LOCK, CLOSER, HINGES, AND OTHER HARDWARE

STEEL EDGE FRAME

KRAFT PAPER HONEYCOMB CORE

HONEYCOMB

STEEL EDGE FRAME

POLYSTYRENE OR POLYURETHANE FOAM

METAL FACE PLY

FOAM-FILLED

Z-SHAPED OR C-SHAPED STEEL STIFFENERS, 4" - 6" APART

FIBERGLASS OR OTHER INSULATION

METAL FACE PLY

STEEL-STIFFENED

REINFORCING PROVIDED FOR LOCK, CLOSER, HINGES, AND OTHER HARDWARE

METAL FACE PLY

MINERAL CORE

CORE TYPES

Core Construction

Four types of cores are commonly used for hollow metal doors: honeycomb, steel stiffeners, foam plastic, and mineral board:

Honeycomb cores: These cores are made from heavy kraft paper formed into hexagonal cells ranging from ½ in. (13 mm) to about 1 in. (25 mm) in size. The core is impregnated with phenolic resin to resist moisture, mildew, and vermin.

Steel-stiffened cores: These doors use vertical stiffeners spaced between 4 in. (102 mm) and 6 in. (152 mm). The cavities in between are usually filled with fiberglass insulation. These types of cores are used primarily for exterior doors, where high rigidity is important.

Foam plastic cores: These may be filled with either polystyrene or polyurethane, materials used for their high insulative values. Polystyrene is used for typical exterior doors, and polyurethane is used where extreme protection from frigid cold is important. Both of these insulation types melt at relatively low temperatures, which may prevent using a hot baked-on paint system applied in the factory.

Mineral cores: These cores are constructed with a fire-resistive material similar to gypsum board. They are used on labeled doors where a temperature-rise limit is required.

HOLLOW METAL FRAMES

Frame Material Thickness

The thickness for frames is governed by the level of door installed, as shown in the table below. For each of the levels, except level 2, two options are provided. The option selected depends on security needs, width of opening, whether the door is for interior or exterior use, expected frequency of use, severity of service, availability, and cost.

Frames may be welded, knockdown, or gypsum board slip-on.

Hollow metal door frames are available in various steel gages according to where and how they will be used. Local codes and governing authorities establish minimum gages, which should always be consulted. Some manufacturers make custom moldings for a specific design, as long as a sufficient quantity is required.

For security, the exterior moldings on exterior doors should be welded into the frame, and exposed fasteners should be tamperproof.

RECOMMENDED THICKNESS FOR STEEL FRAMES BASED ON DOOR LEVEL

LEVEL	GAGE	THICKNESS IN. (MM)
1	18 or 16	0.042 (1) or 0.053 (1.3)
2	16	0.053 (1.3)
3	16 or 14	0.053 (1.3) or 0.067 (1.6)
4	14 or 12	0.067 (1.6) or 0.093 (2.3)

Source: Steel Door Institute, SDI-100; Cleveland, Ohio

Frame Types

Door frames can be factory- or field-assembled. All frames must be adequately anchored at the jambs and floor according to the manufacturer's specifications.

Light-gage metal frames are constructed of head and jamb members, with or without a transom panel, of aluminum (45-minute maximum rating) or light-gage steel (1.5-hour maximum rating). They consist of a single frame that slips over the partition. Separate casing trim pieces are then snapped onto the edges of the frames. These frames are available in 18-, 20-, and 22-gage thicknesses.

Pressed steel (hollow metal) frames have head and jamb members, with or without solid or glazed transoms or sidelights, of 18-gage or heavier steel (3-hour maximum rating). This frame is required for most metal doors.

Steel frames are generally made from one piece of sheet steel bent into the required profile in either a double-rabbet or single-rabbet configuration. These frames are available in 12-, 14-, 16-, and 18-gage thicknesses.

FRAME GAGES

GRADE	DUTY	MINIMUM GAGE
I	Standard	18
II	Heavy	16
III	Extra heavy	14

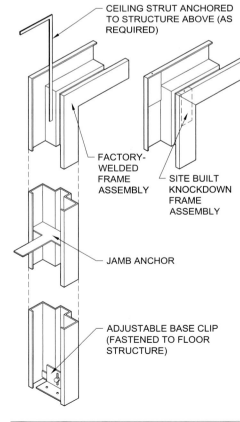

CEILING STRUT ANCHORED TO STRUCTURE ABOVE (AS REQUIRED)

FACTORY-WELDED FRAME ASSEMBLY

SITE BUILT KNOCKDOWN FRAME ASSEMBLY

JAMB ANCHOR

ADJUSTABLE BASE CLIP (FASTENED TO FLOOR STRUCTURE)

HOLLOW METAL FRAME COMPONENTS

Hollow Metal Frame Finishes

Hollow metal frames should receive at least one shop coat of rust-inhibitive primer before delivery to the job site. In very corrosive atmospheres, such as saltwater beach locations, is it advisable to have doors and frames hot-dipped-galvanized for additional protection.

Frames with factory-applied paint finishes in various colors are available from several manufacturers.

TAB AND SLOT

SET-SCREW

KNOCKDOWN FRAME CORNER CONSTRUCTION

TRIM (OPTIONAL)

B

A

3/16" NOMINAL

WALL LINE   SEALANT

Use anchors appropriate for the type of wall construction; a minimum of three per jamb is required.

Grout frame with mortar or plaster as used in wall.

Caulk frame at wall.

Dimension A is minimum 3 in. in area of pull or knob hardware.

Trim may be used to cover joint at wall line.

Check dimension B on hinge side for door swing greater than 90°.

BUTT FRAME/FLUSH FRAME

FINISHED WALL

1/16" NOMINAL   1/16" NOMINAL

WALL THICKNESS

THROAT OPENING

Basic wall dimension is less than throat opening dimension.

Use anchors appropriate for the type of wall construction; a minimum of three per jamb is required.

Fill frame with mortar or plaster as used in the wall.

Grout frame at masonry wall.

WRAPAROUND FRAME

FLOOR KNEES

BACKBEND 1/2" (12.2) TYPICAL
3/8" (9.5) MINIMUM
3/4" (19) MAXIMUM

BACKBEND RETURN FOR DRYWALL SLIP ON FRAMES

THROAT

STOP

5/8" (15.8) TYPICAL

DIMENSIONS VARIES BASED ON WALL THICKNESS

RABBET

1 9/16" (39.6) FOR 1 3/8" DOOR
1 15/16" (49.2) FOR 1 3/4" DOOR

FACE

SOFFIT

DIMENSION VARIES

2" (50.8) TYPICAL
1" (25.4) MINIMUM

Door and frame thicknesses should be indicated in minimum thickness of uncoated steel rather than by the older method of gages. Common frame thicknesses include the following:

Inches	mm	Gage
0.042 in.	(1.0)	18
0.053 in.	(1.3)	16
0.067 in.	(1.6)	14
0.093 in.	(2.3)	12

SINGLE-RABBET

STANDARD HOLLOW METAL FRAMES

FRAME WIDTH

CEILING STRUT

JAMB FACE

OPENING WIDTH

HEAD FACE

HEAD

CLOSER REINFORCEMENT

RUBBER BUMPERS

PLASTER AND GUARD

PLASTER AND GUARD

1", TYP.

DOOR OPENING HEIGHT

MASONRY COURSING WITH WRAPAROUND FRAME

MASONRY COURSING WITH BUTT FRAME

FRAME HEIGHT

HINGE REINFORCEMENT

HINGE JAMB

STRIKE JAMB

STRIKE REINFORCEMENT

WALL ANCHOR CLIPS, THREE REQUIRED MINIMUM

FINISH FLOOR

SUBFLOOR

FRAME EXTENSION

SPREADER BAR

BASE CLIP

STANDARD STEEL FRAME

HOLLOW METAL FRAME STOPS AND SEALS

METAL RUNNER
AT HEAD

HEAD

DOUBLE-RABBETED
FRAME

DOUBLE STUDS
AT JAMB

JAMB

METAL FRAME ANCHORS
NOT SHOWN, FOR CLARITY

NOTE:
GYPSUM BOARD
MUST EXTEND
A MINIMUM OF
1/2" (12) INTO
FRAME TO
MAINTAIN
FIRE RATING

OPTIONAL
THRESHOLD IF
REQUIRED

HOLLOW METAL FRAME IN METAL STUD PARTITION

HEAD

1/4" (25)
GLASS, TYP.

GLAZING TAPE OR SEALANT

REMOVABLE
STOPS

JAMB

BASE CAN
BE THE SAME
HEIGHT AS
MULLION OR HIGHER,
AS REQUIRED

HOLLOW METAL FRAME WITH SIDELITE

HEAD

GYPSUM BOARD
L-ANGLE TO FINISH
EDGE OF GYPSUM
BOARD AT REVEAL

JAMB

CUSTOM HOLLOW
METAL PROFILE
PROVIDES REVEAL

2" (50)

BASE STOPS
AT REVEAL

HOLLOW METAL FRAME FLUSH WITH PARTITION

HEAD

MASONRY
BOND BEAM

STRAP T-ANCHOR
IN MASONRY JOINT

JAMB

ROUGH OPENING,
MODULAR MASONRY
OPENING

1/4" (25) JOINT
FILLED WITH
SEALANT

HOLLOW METAL FRAME IN MASONRY WALL

ALUMINUM SYSTEMS

Door Frames and Partitions

Aluminum door frames and partition systems are often used in place of wood or hollow metal frames because of their crisp, sharp corners and available finishes or because they can match the shape and finish of exterior storefront or curtain wall systems. Aluminum door frames can be used alone, but are most typically used as part of a partition system that includes sidelite framing, partition supports, and base trim.

Aluminum door frames and interior window framing can be used in standard metal-stud-framed walls. Some manufacturers integrate them into a demountable or movable partition system where prefinished gypsum wallboard panels are attached to aluminum tracks and connectors.

Materials

Interior aluminum door and window frames are commonly 0.062 in. (1.6 mm) thick. This thickness compares with typical storefront systems that use 0.125-in.- (3.2-mm-) thick sections. Some manufactures provide members with slightly larger thicknesses.

Finishes

Finishes are available in standard Architectural Class II anodized coatings. They can also be finished with electrostatically applied thermoset powder coatings of acrylic, polyester, and urethane. Also available are liquid-sprayed and baked acrylics, polyesters, and urethanes, in many colors.

PLAN

SILL OF WINDOW

BASE AND CEILING TRIM

TYPICAL ALUMINUM FRAMES

TRIM VARIATIONS

TYPICAL ALUMINUM FRAME

Storefront Framing

Storefront framing consists of extruded aluminum sections assembled to form door and glazed openings. It is similar to aluminum door frames and partition systems except it is designed for exterior applications and does not accommodate gypsum wallboard partitions. It is often used for interior applications if exterior framing has to be matched or when partition system framing does not provide the necessary size, finish, or profiles available in storefront systems.

Manufacturers offer screw-spline, shear-block, and head- and sill-receptor storefront framing systems. Prefabricated or site-built assemblies are fit within an opening with the gap between the framing system and opening filled with sealant.

The height of entrance doors is typically 7 ft (2 m). Typical door widths are 3 ft (1,828 mm), pair of 2 ft 6 in. (1,524 mm), pair of 3 ft (1,828 mm).

A wide variety of finishes are available, including standard anodized colors as well as powder coatings and baked acrylics. Consult individual manufacturers for available finishes.

Structural analysis for deflection and wind load may require steel-reinforcing inserts or heavier mullion profiles.

Aluminum storefront systems generally cannot be used where a fire rating is required.

STOREFRONT HEAD PROFILE
VERTICAL MULLION PRIMARY MEMBER
SNAP-IN FILLER MEMBER

The head, intermediate horizontals, and sill pieces are screwed to vertical members at predrilled locations.

SCREW-SPLINE STOREFRONT ASSEMBLY

VERTICAL MULLION
FASTENER, TYP.
STOREFRONT HEAD PROFILE
SHEAR BLOCK FASTENED TO VERTICAL MULLION

SHEAR-BLOCK STOREFRONT ASSEMBLY

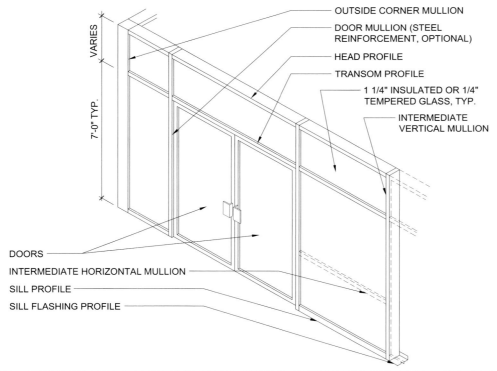

OUTSIDE CORNER MULLION
DOOR MULLION (STEEL REINFORCEMENT, OPTIONAL)
HEAD PROFILE
TRANSOM PROFILE
1 1/4" INSULATED OR 1/4" TEMPERED GLASS, TYP.
INTERMEDIATE VERTICAL MULLION
VARIES
7'-0" TYP.
DOORS
INTERMEDIATE HORIZONTAL MULLION
SILL PROFILE
SILL FLASHING PROFILE

TYPICAL STOREFRONT

4 1/2" TYP.
SHIM
1/2" TYP.
1 3/4", 2", 2 1/4", TYP.
WALL STRUCTURE
SEALANT
ALUMINUM STOREFRONT PROFILE, TYP.
1 1/4" INSULATING GLASS

HEAD OR JAMB

ALUMINUM STOP FOR GLAZING
ALUMINUM STOREFRONT PROFILE, TYP.

INTERMEDIATE HORIZONTAL MULLION

ALUMINUM STOREFRONT PROFILE, TYP.
STEEL-REINFORCING MEMBER, AS NECESSARY
HEAVIER END SECTION, AS NECESSARY

INTERMEDIATE VERTICAL MULLION

1 1/4" INSULATING GLASS
ALUMINUM STOREFRONT CORNER MULLION (WITH THERMAL BREAK)

CORNER MULLION

CORNER MULLION PROFILE
ALUMINUM STOP FOR GLAZING
ALUMINUM STOREFRONT PROFILE
SILL FLASHING
SEALANT

SILL

SHIM
FLOOR STRUCTURE

WALL SECTION AT STOREFRONT

GLASS DOORS

Glass doors are constructed primarily of glass, with fittings to hold the pivots and other hardware. Their strength depends on the glass rather than the framing. Glass doors are generally constructed of ½-in. (13-mm) or ¾-in. (19-mm) tempered glass.

Glass doors may be installed within an opening or as part of an all-glass entrance system. If used alone, glass doors may be set within a wall opening with or without a frame, or they can be installed between glass sidelights. The same type of fitting used on the door is generally used for sidelights. Although jamb frames of aluminum, wood, or ornamental metal can be used, they are not necessary and the glass sidelights can be butted directly to the partition.

The minimum configuration for a glass door requires some type of door pull and a corner fitting at the top and bottom (sometimes called the *shoe*) to hold the pivots. Some manufacturers provide hinge fittings that clamp on the glass and support the door in much the same way as a standard hinged door.

If the door is used for egress, the local building code may require the use of special hardware that allows the door to be locked from the outside, but still allows the door to be unlatched and opened from the inside with a single push on a push bar. Glass doors are heavy and may require a power operator or a balanced door system.

GLASS DOOR SECTION

GLASS DOOR PARTS

All-Glass Entrances

All-glass entrances, commonly used for interior storefronts, include glass doors and surrounding glazing that does not use visible framing members. Instead, special fittings are used to clamp adjacent glass pieces together and to support the glass doors. The glass, typically ½-in.- (13-mm-) or ¾-in.- (19-mm-) thick, is installed in channels set in the floor and above the ceiling. Glass fins, for additional lateral support, may be placed perpendicular to the main glass plane and attached with silicone sealant.

GLASS DOOR CONFIGURATIONS

GLASS DOOR INSTALLATIONS

TYPICAL ALL-GLASS ENTRANCE

FIRE-RATED OPENINGS

Code Requirements

Building code requirements apply to any door that occurs at any location in the means-of-egress system. These requirements include criteria for size, swing, opening force, and hardware, among others.

In addition to these requirements, when an egress door serves as an opening in a rated partition, it is an *opening protective,* also called a *fire door assembly,* or *fire-rated assembly.* An opening protective is a rated assembly that prevents the spread of fire or smoke through an opening in a rated wall. For doors, this assembly includes the door, the frame, hardware, and accessories, including gasketing. Each component is crucial to the overall performance of the assembly as a fire barrier. Choices to be made regarding the enclosure of openings in fire-rated walls include the following:

1. Fire-rated wall requirements
2. Size of opening
3. Means of egress
   a. Required size per occupancy
   b. Quantity and location
   c. Direction of egress flow and operation of enclosure
   d. Hardware requirements
   e. Window egress requirements
4. Materials and finishes
5. Security
6. Visibility and glazing

Fire Protection Criteria

National Fire Protection Association (NFPA) 80, *Standard for Fire Doors and Fire Windows,* is a consensus standard that establishes minimum criteria for installing and maintaining assemblies and devices used to protect openings in walls, ceilings, and floors from the spread of fire and smoke. The degree of fire protection (in hours) required for a given opening is referenced in the model building codes and the *Life Safety Code* (NFPA 101). Fire doors are classified by hourly references determined by testing done in accordance with NFPA 252, *Standard Method of Fire Tests of Door Assemblies* (also known as UL 10B). Further information is available in Chapter 6, Section 6 of the NFPA's *Fire Protection Handbook.*

Positive Pressure Testing

The IBC requires that fire door assemblies be tested under conditions that simulate actual fire situations. For positive pressure testing, the IBC references UL 10C, *Standard for Positive Pressure Fire Tests of Door Assemblies,* and NFPA 252, *Standard Methods of Fire Tests of Door Assemblies,* but local jurisdictions may have their own requirements.

When a door is required to meet the requirements of positive pressure fire testing, it must have approved gasketing or intumescent material along the edge of the door or frame.

Doors in corridors and smoke barriers must meet the requirements for a smoke- and draft-control door assembly tested in accordance with UL 1784. Local jurisdictions may require that they carry an S-label.

Definitions

Automatic: Providing a function without the necessity of human intervention.

Fire barrier: A continuous membrane, either vertical or horizontal (for example, a wall, floor, or ceiling assembly), that is designed and constructed with a specified fire-resistance rating to limit the spread of fire and restrict the movement of smoke.

Fire resistance: The property of materials or their assemblies that prevents or retards the passage of excessive heat, hot gas, or flames under conditions of use.

Fire-resistance rating: The time, in minutes or hours, that materials or assemblies have withstood fire exposure in accordance with the test procedure of NFPA 252, *Standard Methods of Fire Tests of Door Assemblies.*

Labeled: Equipment or materials marked with the label, symbol, or other identifying mark of an organization concerned with product evaluation that is acceptable to the local jurisdiction. This organization must periodically inspect production of labeled equipment, and the manufacturer, by labeling the product to indicate compliance in a specified manner with appropriate standards or performance.

Noncombustible: A material that, in the form in which it is used and under the conditions anticipated, will not aid combustion or add appreciable heat to an ambient fire.

Self-closing: As applied to a fire door or other protective opening, self-closing means the door is normally closed and is equipped with an approved device that will ensure closure after the door has been opened.

Smoke barrier: A continuous membrane, either vertical or horizontal, such as a wall, floor, or ceiling assembly, that is designed and constructed to restrict the movement of smoke. A smoke barrier may or may not have a fire-resistance rating.

Types of Openings

The hourly protection rating for openings depends on the use of the barrier, as in exit enclosures, vertical openings in buildings, building separation walls, corridor walls, smoke barriers, and hazardous locations. In most codes, class designations have been replaced by hour classifications:

4-hour and 3-hour openings: Located in fire walls or in walls that divide a single building into fire areas.

1½-hour and 1-hour openings: Located in multistory vertical communication enclosures and in two-hour-rated partitions providing horizontal fire separations.

¾-hour and 20-minute openings: Located in walls or partitions between rooms and corridors with a fire-resistance rating of one hour or less.

FRAME LABEL

DOOR LABEL

TESTING LABELS

RATINGS OF DOORS BASED ON PARTITION TYPE

TYPE OF PARTITION	RATING OF PARTITION	REQUIRED DOOR ASSEMBLY RATING
Corridors Smoke barriers	1 hour or less	20 minutes
Fire partitions Exit passageways	1 hour	¾ hour
Exit stairs Occupancy Separation Vertical shafts	1 hour	1 hour
Exit stairs Fire separations	2 hours	1½ hour

TYPES OF FIRE-RATED FRAMES

Fire-rated door frames can be assembled at the factory or in the field. Frames must be adequately anchored at the jambs and floor according to the manufacturer's specifications. Codes require doors to be installed in accordance with NFPA 80. Section 2-5, *Frames,* indicates that only labeled frames are to be used.

Light-gage metal frames have head and jamb members with or without transom panel made from aluminum (45-minute maximum rating) or light-gage steel (1½-hour maximum rating) and are installed over a finished wall.

Pressed steel (hollow metal) frames have head and jamb members with or without solid or glazed transoms or sidelights made from 18-gage or heavier steel (3-hour maximum rating). They are required for most metal doors.

Wood frames may be used if they meet the testing standards used by the code. Some manufacturers supply wood frames that have fire ratings of 20, 45, 60, and 90 minutes. Verify availability with individual manufacturers.

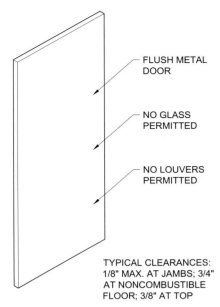

FLUSH METAL DOOR

NO GLASS PERMITTED

NO LOUVERS PERMITTED

TYPICAL CLEARANCES: 1/8" MAX. AT JAMBS; 3/4" AT NONCOMBUSTIBLE FLOOR; 3/8" AT TOP

4-HOUR/3-HOUR CLASSIFICATION

All hinges or pivots must be fabricated from steel. Two hinges are required on doors up to 5 ft (1,524 mm) in height; an additional hinge is required for each additional 2 ft 6 in. (762 mm) of door height or fraction thereof. The same requirement applies to pivots.

10" MAX.

GLASS LIGHT 100 SQ. IN. MAX. OF 1/4"-THICK WIRE GLASS

33" MAX.

24" MAX.

LOUVERS: 576 SQ. IN. MAX.

24" MAX.

1½-HOUR/1-HOUR CLASSIFICATION

While wired glass ¼-in.- (6-mm-) thick is the most common material used for glass lights, other materials have been listed and approved for installation. Refer to the UL fire protection directory.

54" MAX.

GLASS LIGHT 1296 SQ. IN. MAX. OF 1/4"-THICK WIRED GLASS IN 3/4-HOUR DOOR; UNLIMITED AREA IN 20-MIN. DOOR

54" MAX.

LOUVERS: 576 SQ. IN. MAX.

24" MAX.

24" MAX.

¾-HOUR/20-MINUTE CLASSIFICATION

Consult all authorities with jurisdiction before installing glass lights and louvers.

Fusible-link/automatic closing louvers are permitted in fire-rated doors with restrictions, but they are not permitted in smoke-barrier doors.

FIRE-RATED DOOR CLASSIFICATIONS

40 SQ. FT. MAX. OPENING

CLEAR HEIGHT: 6'-8" MIN. (10'-0" MAX.)

CLEARANCE BOTTOM OF FRAME TO FLOOR 3/4" MAX.

CLEAR WIDTH, (4'-0" MAX.)

The minimum width of each door opening must be sufficient for the occupant load it serves. Consult applicable building codes.

DOOR OPENINGS FOR MEANS OF EGRESS

MAXIMUM DOOR SIZES (HOLLOW METAL, ALL CLASSES*)

Single door	4 × 10 ft (1,219 × 3,048 mm) with labeled single-point or three-point latching device
	4 × 8 ft (1,219 × 2,438 mm) with fire exit hardware
Pair of doors	8 × 10 ft (2,438 × 3,048 mm) active leaf with labeled single-point or three-point latching device
	8 × 10 ft (2,438 × 3,048 mm) inactive leaf with labeled two-point latching device or top and bottom bolts
	8 × 8 ft (2,438 × 2,438 mm) with fire exit hardware

*Wood door size requirements are similar.

SWINGING FIRE DOORS

Types of swinging fire doors include:

Composite fire doors: Wood, steel, or plastic sheets bonded to and supported by a solid core material.

Hollow metal fire doors: Flush or panel design with a steel face of not less than 20-gage steel.

Metal-clad fire doors: Flush or panel design consisting of metal-covered wood cores or stiles and rails and insulated panels that are covered with steel of 24-gage or lighter.

Sheet metal fire doors: Steel of 22-gage or lighter of corrugated, flush sheet, or panel design.

Tin-clad fire doors: Wood core with a terne metal plate or galvanized steel facing (30- or 24-gage).

Wood core doors: Wood, hardboard, or plastic face sheets bonded to a woodblock or wood particleboard core material with untreated wood edges. Wood doors are available in fire ratings up to 90 minutes from some manufacturers, while hollow metal doors are required for ratings higher than 90 minutes.

Door Operation

Doors that swing in the direction of egress are preferred for fire-rated doors. Horizontal sliding and revolving doors are permitted with restrictions.

Hardware

Door hardware is provided by the builder, independent of the assembly, or furnished by the manufacturer with the door assembly. In either case, the manufacturer prepares the door and frame to receive hardware to ensure the integrity of the fire-rated assembly.

Fire doors are hung on steel ball-bearing hinges and must be self-closing. Labeled automatic latches and door closers can be self-operated or controlled by fail-safe devices that activate in a fire.

Pairs of doors require coordinators with astragals to ensure that both doors close. Heads and jambs should be sealed with gaskets when smoke control is required. Panic hardware may be required when space occupancy is greater than 100 people.

SPECIAL DOORS USED AS EGRESS DOORS

Doors which can be used as a means of egress include the following:

Revolving doors: May be used if they do not supply more than 50% of the egress capacity and if the leaves collapse under opposing pressures with a resulting exit path of at least 36 in. (914 mm). At least one exit door must be located in close proximity.

Power-operated doors: May be used if they can be opened manually in the event of a power failure with a maximum force of 50 lb (222 N).

Horizontal sliding doors: May be used if they comply with eight criteria, including the capability to be operated manually in the event of a power failure with no special effort or knowledge.

Access-controlled doors: May be used if they comply with six criteria. Refer to the IBC for additional information.

Security grilles: May be used if they do not provide more than 50% of the required egress and if they remain open during the time the space is occupied.

ACOUSTIC DOORS

Acoustic doors block the transmission of sound through an opening and include the door, frame, and gasketing material.

Solid Core Doors

A moderate amount of sound transmission loss can be achieved using swinging, solid core doors with standard perimeter sealing materials and automatic door bottoms. Sound Transmission Class (STC) ratings up to about 44 can be achieved using individual component parts in this manner.

Sound Control Doors

If a higher STC rating is required for critical applications such as recording studios, performing arts theaters, and the like, special manufactured sound control doors should be used similar to those shown in the diagram. These are assemblies designed and installed as complete assemblies that use thicker doors, special hardware, and gasketing to achieve the desired STC rating. STC ratings up to about 55 are available from many manufacturers, and ratings as high as 64 are available from some suppliers.

Other Acoustic Door Types

In addition to swinging doors, manufacturers can provide pairs of doors, oversized swinging, sliding, vertical lift, and multifolding doors to meet special applications.

ACCORDION DOORS

Accordion doors are multipaneled units of relatively narrow wood or fabric that are hinged together. Track-guided hangers/trolleys and optional jamb-side pivots allow the entire assembly to fold together like an accordion. Accordion doors may be used singly or in pairs for very large openings. The stacking distance of the panels when open may encroach upon the clear opening dimension or be concealed in a recessed pocket. Sizes vary from traditional doorways to room dividers. Accordion doors require less floor space than swing doors.

Acoustic accordion doors can provide an STC of about 40. They should be used only where sound control is not a primary consideration.

3'-0", 5'-0", 6'-0", 10'-0", TYP.

6'-8", 7'-0", 8'-0"

ACCORDION DOOR (WOOD, METAL, FABRIC-COVERED, PLASTIC, ETC.)

TYPICAL ACCORDION DOOR

RECESSED METAL TRACK

2"

WOOD BLOCKING AS NECESSARY

ACCORDION DOOR HEAD

AUTOMATIC DOORS

Automatic door operators open and close doors upon activation of a manual or automatic device. They are commonly used for accessible entrances and other doors where a hands-free operation is desired. They can control swinging, sliding, and folding doors.

Manual Activation

Manual activation devices include push buttons, push plates, pull cords, radio controls, and elbow switches. These are available as an inset- or surface-mounted control. Elbow switches should be mounted 43 in. (1,092 mm) above the floor.

Automatic Activation

Automatic devices use photocells, contact mats, or motion detection equipment. Photocells detect the interruption of a light beam near the door and direct the controls to open the door. Contact mats are surface- or recess-mounted on the floor in front of the door. Pressure exerted on the mat activates the door-opening controls. When mats are used for double doors, a safety mat should be used on the swing side of the doors. Motion detection equipment uses microwaves or infrared beams to detect movement and the presence of people.

Automatic door operators may be used to open standard wood or metal doors provided by another manufacturer, or may be supplied as a complete package that includes doors, operators, controls, and other accessories.

FRAME FILLED WITH FIBER OR GROUT

DOUBLE-COMPRESSION SEALS AT JAMBS AND HEAD OF DOOR WITH SOUND ENERGY ABSORBER IN CASE

NONHARDENING CAULK TO SEAL JOINT BETWEEN FRAME AND PARTITION

AUTOMATIC DOOR BOTTOM WITH DOUBLE BAND OF DROP SEAL

SOLID CORE WOOD DOOR OR FIBER-FILLED HOLLOW CORE METAL DOOR

OPTIONAL BRONZE SPRING-TYPE SEAL AT ALL FOUR EDGES OF DOOR

NEOPRENE COMPRESSION SEAL IN THRESHOLD

ACOUSTIC DOOR

LOCATION OF OPTIONAL RADAR UNIT

GUARD RAIL

CONTACT MAT

AUTOMATIC DOOR

OVERHEAD COILING DOORS

Overhead coiling doors are used to close large openings for fire separation or security. The doors can be open grille or solid slats of aluminum or steel. They are not intended for frequent passage, but to close off an opening for an extended period of time or to automatically close an opening during a fire. They are also used to close service counters. Because an overhead coiling door is not intended for passage, under most circumstances it cannot be used in an exit corridor or as a means of egress unless it meets certain criteria set forth in the code.

Space Requirements

Overhead coiling doors require a large space above the ceiling for the housing and motor and steel tracks on each side of the opening. The jamb tracks may be concealed with furred-out wall finish material, as shown in the diagram.

Operation

Overhead doors can be manually operated or motor-driven. For interior design applications, a motor-driven door should be used with a fail-safe feature so it will close during a fire even if power is interrupted.

Motor operators vary from 1/3 to 2 HP and may be wall-mounted alongside a curtain hood bracket or bracket-mounted alongside or behind a curtain hood, depending on building conditions. Consult manufacturers for all requirements and clearances.

COILING FIRE DOORS

Coiling fire doors and counter shutters are typically rated up to UL Class A (3-hour-rated). Automatic door closure and hood smoke and flame baffle activation

GUIDE RAIL JAMB DETAILS

OVERHEAD COILING DOOR GUIDES

are initiated when fusible link melts or when electromechanical devices are activated by heat detector, smoke detector, or building alarm system.

Jamb guides for fire-rated coiling doors are required to have ¾-in. (19-mm) clearance below the bottom of guide to allow for heat expansion in case of fire.

Standard coiling doors are designed to withstand a wind load of 20 lb/sq ft (96 kg/sq m).

SECTION AT HEAD

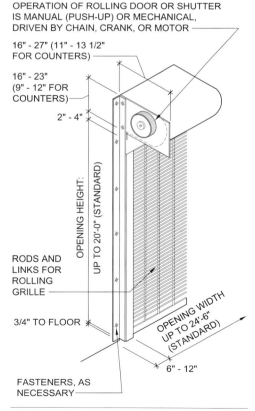

TYPICAL ROLLING DOOR, COUNTER SHUTTER, AND GRILLE

ROLLING GRILLE DOOR TYPES

Electric or pneumatic sensor edges stop or reverse motor-operated doors if they are obstructed.

BOTTOM BAR TYPES

Acrylic vision slats may be inserted within standard slats for light transmission and visibility.
Counter shutters are available in standard heights up to 7 ft (2.1 m) and widths up to 11 ft (3.3 m).

CURTAIN DOOR AND COUNTER SHUTTER SLAT TYPES

SECURITY DOORS

Security doors provide protection from forced entry and penetration that cannot be achieved with standard wood or hollow metal doors in standard steel frames. As with any security construction, the expected level of threat must be defined before the door opening is designed and specified. This may range from simple forced opening to high explosives.

Security Threats

There are three general types of security threats: forced entry, penetration with tools or firearms, and destruction with explosives or other types of blasts.

Low-security construction may be as simple as using heavy-gage hollow metal doors with steel frames securely anchored in hardened partitions to sophisticated assemblies supplied by a manufacturer specializing in security doors.

Security Glazing

Security glazing is composed of multiple layers of glass and/or polycarbonate plastic laminated together. Depending on the degree of security protection required, thickness can range from ⅜ in. (10 mm) to approximately 2½ in. (64 mm). Security glazing is subject to size limitations.

Layout

To maximize resistance to forced entry, security doors must swing outward (toward the attack side).

Walls must be constructed to meet the same level of resistance as the windows and doors installed in them. The doors must be anchored in accordance with the manufacturer's instructions to attain the standard of resistance.

Certification

Security doors should be certified as bullet-resistant by an independent testing laboratory.

ONE-PIECE GLAZING WITH DEAL TRAY

THREE-PIECE GLAZING WITH DEAL TRAY

ONE-PIECE GLAZING WITH TRANSACTION DRAWER

SECURITY TELLER WINDOWS

GUIDE SPECIFICATIONS FROM THE HOLLOW METAL MANUFACTURERS ASSOCIATION (HMMA)[5]

	860[1] HMMA	861[2] HMMA	862[3] HMMA	863[4] HMMA
DOORS				
Face sheets interior	20-ga.	18-ga.	14-ga.	14- or 12-ga.
Face sheets exterior	8-ga.	16-ga.	14-ga.	14- or 12-ga.
Minimum thickness	1¾ in. (44 mm)	1¾ in. (44 mm)	1¾ in. (44 mm)	2 in. (50 mm)
Stiffeners	22-ga.	22-ga.	18-ga.	18-ga.
Vertical edges	Continuous weld or interlocking seam welding at top and bottom of door	Continuous weld	Continuous weld	Reinforced by 10-ga. continuous steel channel, continuous weld
Top and bottom edges	Closed with 16-ga. continuous recessed steel channel	Closed with 16-ga. continuous recessed steel channel, spot-welded to face sheets	Closed with 12-ga. continuous recessed steel channel, spot-welded to face sheets	Reinforced by 10-ga. continuous steel channel, 10-ga. spot-welded to face sheets 4 in. (101 mm) on center
Glass molding and stops	Fixed moldings welded to door on security side; loose stops, 20-ga.	Fixed moldings welded to door on security side; loose stops, 20-ga.	Fixed moldings welded to door on security side; loose stops, 16-ga.	Fixed moldings, 12-ga. spot-welded to face sheets 5 in. (127 mm) o.c.; removable glass stops, 14-ga. pressed steel channel
FRAMES				
Interior openings	16-ga. (18-ga. for wood doors; 20-ga. for hollow core wood doors)	16-ga.; 14-ga. for openings over 4 ft (1219 mm) in width	12-ga.	12-ga.
Construction	Welded or knocked down with integral stop and trim	Welded units with integral stop and trim	Welded units with integral stop and trim	Welded units with integral stop and trim
Floor anchors	16-ga. welded inside jambs	14-ga. welded inside jambs	14-ga. welded inside jambs	Same gage as frame, welded inside jambs with at least four spot welds per anchor
Jamb anchors	In masonry walls, 16-ga. steel or 0.156-in. (3.9-mm) diameter steel wire. For stud partitions, 18-ga. steel anchors welded inside jambs	In masonry walls, 16-ga. steel or 0.156-in. (3.9 mm) diameter steel wire. For stud partitions, 18-ga. steel anchors welded inside jambs	In masonry walls, 14-ga. steel or 0.156-in. (3.9-mm) diameter steel wire. For stud partitions, 16-ga. steel anchors welded inside jambs	Same gage as frame
Loose glazing stops	20-ga. cold-rolled steel	20-ga. cold-rolled steel	16-ga. cold-rolled steel	10-ga. cold-rolled steel

[1]HMMA 860: For use in building projects where traffic is relatively light and hard usage is not anticipated.

[2]HMMA 861: For use in commercial and industrial applications where rigorous use is anticipated, such as schools, hospitals, industrial buildings, office buildings, hotels, nursing homes, airports, and convention centers.

[3]HMMA 862: For use in applications where security is paramount due to high susceptibility to vandalism, break-in, and theft, such as entrances and back doors of businesses, storerooms, warehouses, strip stores, apartments, and condominiums. HMMA 862 incorporates testing procedures and performance requirements promulgated by National Institute of Law Enforcement and Criminal Justice (NILECJ) for Class IV doors (ASTM F476) including jamb/wall stiffness test, jamb/wall stiffness performance, door impact test, and door and glazing panel impact-resistance performance.

[4]HMMA 863: For applications in jails, prisons, detention centers, and secured areas in hospitals or courthouses. HMMA 863 requires five tests: static load test, rack test, impact load test, removable glazing stop test, and bullet resistance test.

[5]Reprinted with permission from the Hollow Metal Manufacturers Association, division of National Association of Architectural Metal Manufacturers (NAAMM).

Ballistic Threat Design

Several standards are used to rate construction assemblies. One of the most common is Underwriters Laboratories UL 752, *Standard for Bullet-Resisting Equipment,* which sets eight ballistic threat levels from UL-Level 1 (lowest) to UL-Level 8 (highest). Ballistic threat level 8 provides protection from a 7.62 mm NATO round fired from a combat rifle at a velocity of 2,750 ft/sec (838 m/sec). Similar types of performance requirements have been established by the National Institute for Justice, the U.S. Department of Defense, and the U.S. Department of State.

Sliding Security Doors

Sliding glass doors are a particular concern in securing a building.

Locking Devices

The lock should be heavy-duty with a hook-type hardened-steel dead bolt. The locking system should include vertical rods, or level bolts, at top and bottom.

BLAST-RESISTANT DOOR

Frame

The sliding door frame should be solid or reinforced at the locking points; the stile must also be reinforces at the locking points.

Panel Design

The operating panels should be designed so that they cannot be lifted out of their tracks when in the locked position. Glazing and other components shoudl be installed from the inside so that entry cannot be gained by disassembly.

TYPICAL SECURITY DOOR HARDWARE AND ACCESSORIES

LOW-RANGE BLAST-RESISTANT DOOR DETAIL

MID- AND MAXI-RANGE BLAST-RESISTANT DOOR DETAIL

BALLISTICS/FORCED-ENTRY DOOR—DETAILS

BALLISTIC/FORCED-ENTRY TELLER WINDOWS

HEALTH-RELATED INSTITUTIONAL HARDWARE

DOOR OPENING REQUIREMENTS

To permit reverse opening of a door in an emergency, a foldable or collapsible stop, in conjunction with a center-hung pivot, is needed. Such devices are often used on private or semiprivate toilet doors. Such doors should not open to backcheck faster than three seconds and require no more than 15 pounds force to stop door movement.

John L. Hogshead, AIA; Perkins & Will; Atlanta, Georgia

14-GA. FRAME

INTERSECT WALL LINING WITH FRAME

1 1/2" X 1 1/2" X 1/8" REINFORCING ANGLE, AND 1/8" PLATE

DOOR LINING MUST INTERSECT LINE OF SIGHT ACROSS FRAME LINING

LEAD-LINED FRAME

Heavy-duty top and bottom pivots carry the weight of lead-lined doors.

DOOR PIVOTS

MAY TRACE OUT FULL STOP

VARIES

45° AND CAPPED

WRAPAROUND (SHOWN) FLUSH OR RECESSED SPAT

HOSPITAL STOP   **SPAT**

FRAME HT.

BASE HT.

FASTEN CLIP TO STRUCTURAL SLAB

CUTOFF FRAME

FLUSH WITH WALL

45° AND CAPPED

CONTINUOUS ROOM BASE

CUTOFF STOP

Door frame stops in health care institutions are designed for ease of mopping.

DOOR STOPS

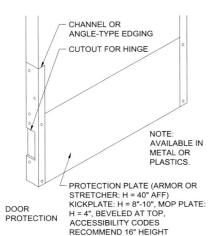

TOP CLAMP

ROLLER STRIKE

BOTTOM FITTING

PLAN

Removable mullions are for use with exit devices on double doors.

REMOVABLE MULLION

DOOR SWING

1/2"

EQ.

EQ.

2 5/8"

DOOR

1 3/8"   5/8"

TYPICAL PROFILE

DOUBLE-EGRESS DOORS

PUSH/PULL PLATE

PUSH/PULL LATCH

EMERGENCY DOORSTOP

LIGHT-DUTY CENTER-HUNG PIVOT

HEALTH CARE RELATED INSTITUTIONAL HARDWARE

DOOR MUTES
Mutes cushion the impact of door against frame, reducing noise.

NO PIN TIP

NO-PIN TIP HINGE PIN
Sloped pin tip minimizes dust accumulation. In psychiatric wards, a protruding hinge pin could be harmful.

CHANNEL OR ANGLE-TYPE EDGING

CUTOUT FOR HINGE

NOTE: AVAILABLE IN METAL OR PLASTICS.

PROTECTION PLATE (ARMOR OR STRETCHER: H = 40" AFF) KICKPLATE: H = 8"-10", MOP PLATE: H = 4", BEVELED AT TOP, ACCESSIBILITY CODES RECOMMEND 16" HEIGHT

DOOR PROTECTION

DOOR PROTECTION

TYPICAL INSTITUTIONAL DOOR HARDWARE

SPECIALTY DOOR DETAILS

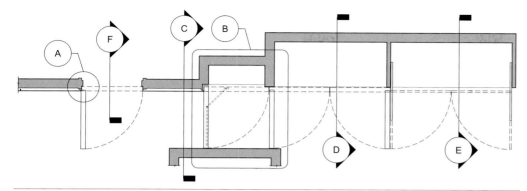

CONCEALED DOORS AND CABINETS IN WOOD VENEER-PANELED WALL

TWO LAYERS 1/2"
GYPSUM BOARD

HOLLOW METAL
DOOR FRAME

DOOR

APPLIED WOOD
PANEL; NOTCH AS
REQUIRED
FOR HINGES

VERIFY SWING
CLEARANCES

1/4"+/-

FULL MORTISE
HINGES

FIXED WOOD
PANEL

(A) MODIFIED STANDARD DOOR AT FRAME AT ENTRY TO SUITE

TWO LAYERS 1/2" OF
GYPSUM BOARD ON
METAL FRAMING

CABINET INTERIORS

WOOD TRIM

VERIFY CLEARANCES
REQUIRED FOR DOOR SWING

PIVOT HINGE
HARDWARE

OFFSET PIVOT HINGE
HARDWARE

FIXED
WOOD
PANEL

1/4"   2"

COORDINATE WITH
HALL WIDTH

WOOD PANEL

OVERHEAD STOP,
HOLD OPEN

VERIFY HALL
WIDTH DIMENSION

WOOD DOOR

CABINET DOOR WITH
WOOD PANEL FACE

(B) BOOKCASE WITH PIVOT HINGE DOOR
In closed position, door appears to part of wall paneling; in open position, it closes off room.

CEILING

GYPSUM BOARD

METAL HANGING
CLIPS

FIXED WOOD
PANELS

GYPSUM BOARD
ON METAL FRAMING

PLYWOOD
SHEATHING

WOOD TRIM
BLOCKING

FINISH FLOORING

(B) FIXED PANEL

CEILING

WOOD TRIM

OFFSET PIVOT
HINGE

ADJUSTABLE SHELF

APPLIED WOOD
PANEL

WOOD DOOR

OFFSET PIVOT
HINGE

FINISH FLOORING

(D) CLOSET WITH OFFSET PIVOT HINGE DOOR

CEILING

WOOD TRIM

ADJUSTABLE SHELF

TV LOCATION

PROVIDE AIR
GRILLES AND
GROMMETS FOR
ELECTRICAL CORDS

PIVOT/SLIDE
WOOD POCKET
DOOR

DRAWERS

4"
MIN.

ELECTRICAL
OUTLET

FINISH FLOORING

(E) TV CABINET

CEILING

WOOD TRIM

1/4"

HOLLOW METAL FRAME

APPLIED WOOD PANEL

WOOD DOOR

THRESHOLD

FINISH FLOORING

(F) ENTRY

ELEVATION

DOOR POCKET AND TRACK

VISIBLE PORTION OF DOOR

C OF DOOR

CENTERING ROLLERS, BOTH SIDES

SOLID BLOCKING

FULLY CONCEALED HALF OF DOOR TO BE SOLID CORE

PARTIALLY EXPOSED HALF OF DOOR TO BE HOLLOW CORE

2'-0" MAX.

3'-0"

FLOOR TO CEILING MINUS 1/2" CLEARANCE TOP AND BOTTOM

WHEELS MOUNTED ALONG CENTER LINE OF DOOR

RECESSED PULL, BOTH SIDES

END ELEVATION

FRAME WALL TO STRUCTURE ABOVE

1'-0"

CENTERING ROLLERS, BOTH SIDES

END PULL

PULL DETAIL

MORTISED METAL PLATE

2"

1 1/2"

1 1/4"

1"

1/2"　1/2"

END DETAIL

SOLID BLOCKING, ALL EDGES

GYPSUM BOARD, PAINTED

1/8" MAX.

METAL TRIM

1/8" MAX.

DOOR FLUSH WITH WALL WHEN CLOSED

1'-0" MAX.

PLAN

CENTERING ROLLERS

HEAVY-DUTY DOOR STOP

DOOR OPENING PLUS 6"

DOOR OPENING

REQUIRED WALL CAVITY

DOOR

CONTINUOUS STEEL ANGLE AT BASE OF CAVITY

FRAME WALL TO STRUCTURE ABOVE

DOOR FLUSH WITH WALL WHEN CLOSED

WHEEL DETAIL

1/2" PLYWOOD, OR MDF FACE BOTH SIDES; FINISH TO MATCH WALLS

SELF-CENTERING WHEELS

CENTERING RAIL, CONTINUOUS STEEL ANGLE

Door is oversized and counterweighted to cantilever out of the pocket to close opening; no ceiling track and/or rollers are visible. This sliding door can also be used in arched openings because there is no overhead track.

CANTILEVERED ROLLING POCKET DOOR

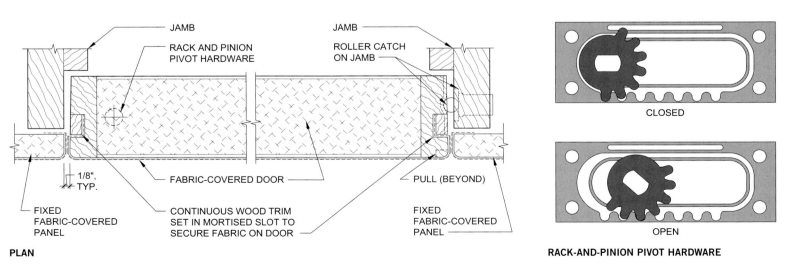

PLAN

JAMB

RACK AND PINION PIVOT HARDWARE

JAMB

ROLLER CATCH ON JAMB

1/8", TYP.

FIXED FABRIC-COVERED PANEL

FABRIC-COVERED DOOR

CONTINUOUS WOOD TRIM SET IN MORTISED SLOT TO SECURE FABRIC ON DOOR

PULL (BEYOND)

FIXED FABRIC-COVERED PANEL

RACK-AND-PINION PIVOT HARDWARE

CLOSED

OPEN

Door sits tight to the adjacent panel when closed, and rotates out and away from adjacent panel when opened, providing tight fit. Door appears to be one in a series of fabric-covered panels when in closed position.

CONCEALED DOOR WITH FABRIC-COVERED PANELS

Tom Bader, AIA; Wheeler Kearns Architects; Chicago, Illinois

PIVOT DOORS AS PORTAL WALLS

In the open position, these doors appear to be paneling in the portal.

PIVOT DOORS RECESSED IN PORTAL WALLS

CONCEALED PORTAL DOORS

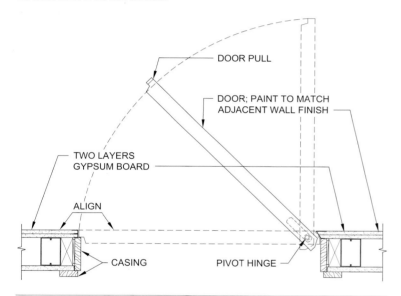

CONCEALED DOOR IN GYPSUM BOARD WALL

ADJACENT CONCEALED DOORS OPENING IN SAME DIRECTION

ADJACENT CONCEALED DOORS OPENING IN OPPOSITE DIRECTION

Wall recess provides light seal and visual privacy. In open position, door does not interrupt the line of the angled wall. This door frame has no jamb.

PIVOT DOOR WITH WALL RECESS

Tom Bader, AIA; Wheeler Kearns Architects; Chicago, Illinois

DOORS ☐ **2**

LOCKSETS

PASSAGE OR CLOSET LOCK	ANSI A156.2, NO. F75

For doors that do not require locking:
Either lever or knob operates latchbolt at all times.
Both levers or knobs are always free.

INSIDE OUTSIDE

PRIVACY OR BATH LOCK	ANSI A156.2, NO. F76

For bathroom or other privacy doors:
Either lever or knob operates latchbolt unless outside lever is locked by push button inside.
Button automatically releases when inside lever is turned or door is closed.
Emergency release is in outside lever.
Inside lever is always active.

INSIDE OUTSIDE

PATIO OR PRIVACY LOCK	ANSI A156.2, NO. F77

For exit doors with limited entry:
Deadlocking latchbolt
Either lever or knob operates latchbolt unless outside lever is locked by push button inside.
Button automatically releases when inside lever is turned or door is closed.
Inside lever is always active.

INSIDE OUTSIDE

COMMUNICATING LOCK	ANSI A156.2, NO. F80

For communicating or store entrance doors:
Deadlocking latchbolt
Either lever operates latchbolt (except when key in either lever locks or unlocks the lever independently of the other).
Should be used only in offices or rooms with multiple entries.

INSIDE OUTSIDE

ENTRANCE OR CORRIDOR LOCK	ANSI A156.2, NO. F81/82

For entrance, general home, or office doors:
Deadlocking latchbolt
Either lever operates latchbolt (except when outside lever is locked inside).
Pushing turn button in inside lever locks outside lever (automatically releases when inside lever is turned or key is rotated in locked outside lever).
Outside lever may be retained in locked position by pushing and rotating turn button 90° clockwise to a horizontal position; it is not released until turn button is manually returned to the vertical position.
Latchbolt is operated by key in outside lever or by rotating inside lever.
Inside lever is always active.

INSIDE OUTSIDE

ENTRY OR OFFICE LOCK	ANSI A156.2, NO. F82

For entrance of office doors:
Deadlocking latchbolt
Either lever or knob operates latchbolt (except when outside lever is locked from inside).
Pushing button in inside lever locks outside lever (automatically releases when inside lever is turned or key is rotated in locked outside lever).
Latchbolt is operated by key in outside lever or by rotating inside lever.
Inside lever is always active.

INSIDE OUTSIDE

CLASSROOM LOCK	ANSI A156.2, NO. F84

For classroom or utility room doors:
Deadlocking latchbolt
Either lever operates latchbolt (except when outside lever is locked by key).
Inside lever is always active.
Key releases outside lever.

INSIDE OUTSIDE

STOREROOM OR CLOSET LOCK	ANSI A156.2, NO. F86

For use on storeroom, utility, or exit doors:
Deadlocking latchbolt
Latchbolt is operated by lever inside, key in outside lever.
Outside lever is always locked.
Inside lever is always active.

INSIDE OUTSIDE

UTILITY, INSTITUTIONAL, OR ASYLUM LOCK	ANSI A156.2, NO. F87

Deadlocking latchbolt
Latchbolt is operated by key in lever from either side.
Both levers are always locked.

INSIDE OUTSIDE

APARTMENT, EXIT, OR PUBLIC TOILET LOCK	ANSI A156.2, NO. F88

For office or apartment building entrance doors or lavatory doors:
Deadlocking latchbolt
Either lever operates latchbolt (except when outside lever is locked by key from within).
Key in outside lever operates latchbolt.
Inside lever is always active.

INSIDE OUTSIDE

SERVICE STATION LOCK	ANSI A156.2, NO. F92

Deadlocking latchbolt
Either lever operates latchbolt.
Push button in inside lever locks outside lever (automatically releases when inside lever is turned, door is closed, or key is rotated in outside lever, except when slotted push button is rotated 90° clockwise to retain outside lever in locked position).
Latchbolt is operated by key in outside lever; inside lever is always active.

INSIDE OUTSIDE

HOTEL OR MOTEL LOCK	ANSI A156.2, NO. F93

For hotel or motel room doors:
Deadlocking latchbolt
Latchbolt is operated by key in outside lever or by rotating inside lever.
Push button on inside lever shuts out all keys except emergency key, and projects visual occupancy indicator in cylinder face.
Push button is released by turning inside lever or closing door.
Inside lever is always active.
Outside lever is always locked.

INSIDE OUTSIDE

EXIT LOCK	**NO ANSI A156.2 NUMBER ASSIGNED**

For exit doors with no entry desired:

Deadlocking latchbolt

Outside lever is always locked.

Inside lever is always active.

INSIDE   OUTSIDE

DORMITORY LOCK	**NO ANSI A156.2 NUMBER ASSIGNED**

Deadlocking latchbolt

Either lever operates latchbolt (except when outside lever is locked by inside push button or key in outside lever).

Inside lever is always active.

When locked by button, the button automatically releases when inside lever is turned or door is closed.

When locked by key, the automatic release is made inoperative and must be manually unlocked by key.

INSIDE   OUTSIDE

PRIVACY LOCK	**NO ANSI A156.2 NUMBER ASSIGNED**

For lavatory or other privacy doors:

Either lever operates latchbolt (except when outside lever is locked by inside push button).

Button automatically releases by turning inside lever or closing door.

Door can be unlocked, when necessary, by operating outside turn button.

No emergency key is required.

Inside lever is always active.

INSIDE   OUTSIDE

EXIT LATCH	**NO ANSI A156.2 NUMBER ASSIGNED**

For twin communicating or exit doors where one-side operation is required; also when space is limited between door and switch panel:

Deadlocking latchbolt

One-lever operation

Blank rose

Should be used only where rooms have more than one entrance.

INSIDE   OUTSIDE

COMMUNICATING OR CLOSET LOCK	**ANSI A156.2, NO. F78**

For twin communicating or close doors where one-side operation or space between doors is limited:

Deadlocking latchbolt

Inside lever operates latchbolt except when lever is locked by key.

INSIDE   OUTSIDE

DUMMY TRIM	**ANSI A156.2, NO. F11/F05**

For nonoperational levers used for decorative trim.

INSIDE   OUTSIDE

KEYED LEVER WITH BLANK PLATE	**NO ANSI A156.2 NUMBER ASSIGNED**

Deadlocking latchbolt by lever, except when lever is locked by key (lever handle is freewheeling when in locked position).

Lever on one side; blank plate on other side

INSIDE   OUTSIDE

PASSAGE LEVER WITH TURNPIECE	**NO ANSI A156.2 NUMBER ASSIGNED**

Latchbolt by lever or by turnpiece

Lever on one side; turnpiece on other side

Lever and turnpiece are always free.

INSIDE   OUTSIDE

KEYED LEVER WITH TURNPIECE	**NO ANSI A156.2 NUMBER ASSIGNED**

Deadlocking latchbolt by lever or turnpiece, except when lever is locked by key.

Whenever lever is locked, latchbolt is operated by key in lever or by turnpiece (lever handle is freewheeling when in locked position).

Lever on outside; turnpiece on other side

Turnpiece is always free.

INSIDE   OUTSIDE

CHANGE KEYS

The purpose of a masterkey system is to provide the convenience of carrying one key to open many—if not all—doors. A masterkey unlocks two or more locks, each of which has its own key that fits no other lock. The number of masterkeys in a system is limited based on the number of different masterkeys, the number of pins in the lock (five, six, or seven), and the steps of variation in the depths of the cuts on the keys.

KEY CODE SYSTEM

FINISHES FOR ARCHITECTURAL HARDWARE

Metals commonly used in architectural hardware are brass, bronze, iron, steel, stainless steel, aluminum, and zinc. The properties of stainless steel, including rust resistance, easy maintenance, and high-luster finish, make it highly suitable for architectural hardware. Aluminum is often alloyed with other metals and can be used instead of cast iron for applications such as doorstops, handrail brackets, and hooks. Forged iron is often used for special decorative trim, such as early-American hand-forged pieces. When selecting metals and their finishes, factors to consider are rust resistance, durability, and appearance.

- *Natural finishes* have the color of the base metal and are low-luster (satin finish) or high-luster (polished finish).
- *Antiqued and distressed finishes* are used to give the appearance of an antique.
- *Oil-rubbed bronze* produces a dark, oxidized finish.
- *Common plated finishes* are chromium or brass, bronze, and nickel plating.

Matching door hardware finishes with other components of a project may be required. One method to ensure a close match is to specify the actual metal alloy number to be provided for plated finishes, for example, UNS No. C32000 for brass (leaded red brass). This method is, however, more costly than using manufacturer's standard finishes, and may not be available for some types of door hardware. Further, even if the metal alloy of a plated finish matches, if the underlying base metal is not the same, the finished appearance will be slightly different. Whether matching finishes or just referencing Builders Hardware Manufacturers Association (BHMA) finish numbers, verify the actual finish by requesting samples from manufacturers. Matchplate samples for some finishes are available from BHMA.

FINISH STANDARDS

The National Institute of Standards and Technology (NIST) originally prepared standards for finishes used for door hardware. These are generally referred to as U.S. Standards (for example, US10B, US26D, and so on). Though these designations are still used by some manufacturers, in recent years, BHMA developed a more complete description of door hardware finish standards. BHMA A156.18, *Materials and Finishes,* gives details of finishes and the closest U.S. Standard number equivalent. BHMA A156.18 takes into account the base metal on which the finish is applied, whereas the U.S. Standard does not. BHMA A156.18 also provides appearance equivalents for various base metals. For example, the BHMA finish number for steel with satin chrome finish is 652; the finish number for the same appearance but with brass base metal is 626; in both cases, the U.S. Standard finish number is US26D. Additional appearance equivalents include plated base metals of stainless steel (654), zinc (682), and aluminum (702 and 713).

MASTERSPEC®; published by ARCOM; Salt Lake City, Utah, and Alexandria, Virginia

BHMA FINISH DESIGNATIONS (PARTIAL LIST)

BHMA CODE NO.	DESCRIPTION	U.S. DESIGNATION
FINISHES FOR ALUMINUM HARDWARE		
627	Satin aluminum, clear-coated	US27
628	Satin aluminum, clear-anodized	US28
666	Bright brass-plated, clear-coated	US3
667	Satin brass-plated, clear-coated	US4
668	Satin bronze-plated, clear-coated	US10
671	Flat-black-coated	US19
672	Bright chromium-plated	US26
FINISHES FOR STAINLESS-STEEL HARDWARE		
629	Bright stainless steel, 300 Series	US32
630	Satin stainless steel, 300 Series	US32D
FINISHES FOR CARBON STEEL HARDWARE		
631	Flat-black-coated	US19
633	Satin brass-plated, clear-coated	US4
637	Bright bronze-plated, clear-coated	US9
639	Satin bronze-plated, clear-coated	US10
640	Oxidized satin bronze-plated, oil-rubbed	US10B
649	Light oxidized statuary bronze-plated, clear-coated	US20
650	Dark oxidized statuary bronze-plated, clear-coated	US20A
651	Bright chromium-plated	US26
652	Satin chromium-plated	US26D
FINISHES FOR BRASS AND BRONZE HARDWARE		
605	Bright brass, clear-coated	US3
606	Satin brass, clear-coated	US4
611	Bright bronze, clear-coated	US9
612	Satin bronze, clear-coated	US10
613	Dark oxidized satin bronze, oil-rubbed	US10B
622	Flat-black-coated	US19
623	Light oxidized statuary bronze-plated, clear-coated	US20
624	Dark oxidized statuary bronze-plated, clear-coated	US20A
625	Bright chromium-plated	US26
626	Satin chromium-plated	US26D
632	Bright brass-plated, clear-coated	US3

FLOOR, WALL, AND CEILING ACCESS DOORS

MOUNTING FRAME WITH ANCHOR STRAPS (TWO ON EACH SIDE)

MOUNTING FLANGE (SURFACE-MOUNTED, DRYWALL BEAD, OR INTEGRAL PLASTER LATH)

DOOR (PAINTED OR RECESSED TO ACCEPT FINISH MATERIAL)

ROUNDED OR SQUARE CORNERS

HINGE (CONCEALED, PIVOTING ROD, PIANO, OR BUTT HINGE)

LATCH (SCREWDRIVER-ACTIVATED CAM, KEYED RING PULL, OR KNURLED KNOB)

6" - 48" (150 - 1220)

6" - 36" (150 - 915)

1 1/4" - 2" (30 - 50) DEPTH, TYP.

WALL OR CEILING ACCESS DOOR CHARACTERISTICS

SLAM LATCH WITH HANDLE

HINGE

FLANGE (WIDTH VARIES)

HOLD-OPEN BAR

TEXTURED PLATE OR 1/8" RECESS IN COVER TO RECEIVE FLOOR FINISH (TILE, CARPET, ETC.)

HINGE ARM

FLOOR HATCH FRAME (ALUMINUM ALLOY OR STEEL)

DETAIL

24" - 48" (610 - 1220)

24" - 42" (610 - 1070)

Floor hatches usually open to 90° and may be single- or double-leaf.

DOOR IN FLOOR

SOCKET HEAD SECURING BOLT, TYP.

HATCH COVER

6" - 48" (150 - 1220)

6" - 48" (150 - 1220)

HATCH FRAME

HATCH COVER

SOCKET HEAD SECURING BOLT

FLOOR FINISH OVER STRUCTURAL CONCRETE FILL

2 1/2" - 3 1/2" (65 TO 90)

ELASTOMERIC DIRT/MOISTURE SEAL

HATCH FRAME ON NONSHRINK GROUT SETTING BED (OR SET ON BEAM)

DETAIL

Hatch cover may be topped with stone, tile, wood, carpet, and the like, over a 1½-in. (40-mm) (minimum) layer of concrete, providing a flat, vibration-free surface. Frame and hatch are fabricated from aluminum steel.

FLOOR ACCESS HATCH

Daniel F.C. Hayes, AIA; Washington, D.C.

CAM LOCK

CONCEALED HINGE

ACOUSTICAL PLASTER WITH CONCEALED HINGE

CAM LOCK

ACOUSTICAL PLASTER SET IN RECESSED DOOR

ACOUSTICAL PLASTER

CONTINUOUS HINGE

ACOUSTICAL PLASTER WITH CONTINUOUS HINGE

ACOUSTICAL TILE

CAM LOCK

ACOUSTICAL TILE SET IN RECESSED DOOR

CONTINUOUS HINGE

ACOUSTICAL TILE

CEILING ACCESS PANELS

CAM LOCK

WALL STUD

FLUSH METAL DOOR

CONTINUOUS (PIANO) HINGE

FLUSH DOORS

CAM LOCK

WALL ANCHOR FOR CMU WALL

GYPSUM BOARD

CONCEALED (PIVOT) HINGE

CONCEALED PIVOT HINGE

SPRING DOOR CLOSURE

LATCH

FIRE-RATED INSULATED DOOR

FIRE-RATED DOOR

Doors may be hinged, set in with clips, or fastened with screws. Hinges may be butt or pivot, separate or continuous, surface or concealed.

The fire rating of access panels should be similar to the ration of the wall in which they occur. Access panels larger than 144 sq in. (930 sq cm) require automatic closers. The minimum size for attic and crawl space often is specified by building tools.

WALL ACCESS DOORS

GLASS

Glass is a hard, brittle amorphous substance made by melting silica (sometimes combined with oxides of boron or phosphorus) with certain basic oxides (notably sodium, potassium, calcium, magnesium, and lead) to produce annealed flat glass by a controlled cooling process. Most glasses soften at 932 to 2,012°F (500 to 1,100°C). Minute surface scratches in manufacturing greatly reduce glass strength.

Glass is considered a liquid, even though it is rigid and behaves like a solid. As is characteristic of a liquid, the atoms in a sheet of glass are randomly arranged. They are frozen in place by rapid cooling during manufacturing. In most other mineral solids, the atoms are arranged in a recognizable geometric pattern and have a crystalline structure.

FLOAT GLASS

Generally accepted as the successor to polished plate glass, float glass has become the quality standard of the glass industry. More than 95% of the glass manufactured in the United States is float glass. It is manufactured by floating molten glass on a surface of molten tin. Because the molten metal is denser than the glass, the two liquids do not mix together. This process produces a glass with very uniform thickness and flatness. After forming, the glass is cooled by a controlled process known as *annealing*.

Annealing relieves internal strains that may have developed during the manufacturing process. It ensures that the glass does not cool and contract at different rates across its surface. If glass is not annealed, it may fracture from differential stresses throughout the sheet when it reaches room temperature. The requirements for float glass are defined in ASTM C1036, *Specification for Flat Glass*. It is available in thicknesses ranging from 3 to 22 mm (⅛ to ⅞ in.).

STRENGTHENED GLASS

There are several types of glass with increased strength: *fully tempered*, *heat-strengthened*, *laminated*, and *wire glass*.

Fully Tempered Glass

Fully tempered glass is produced by heating float glass and then suddenly cooling it with special blowers. The outer surface cools quickly and contracts, constraining the hot inner core as it continues to cool. The surface and edges of fully tempered glass are in compression, while the inner core is in tension. Fully tempered glass is three to five times more resistant to impact, applied pressure, and bending stresses than annealed glass, because the surface tension must be overcome before the glass can be broken. The tempering process is defined by ASTM C1048, *Specification for Heat-Treated Flat Glass—Kind HS, Kind FT, Coated, and Uncoated Glass.*

Cutting or drilling fully tempered glass will destroy the integrity of the skin's compressive strength and will likely cause breakage, therefore, fully tempered glass cannot be field-cut. Fully tempered glass must be fabricated with the required holes or cutouts. It is available in thicknesses from 3 to 25 mm (⅛ to 1 in.).

BASIC GLASS TYPES

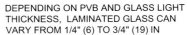

	ANNEALED (REGULAR FLOAT GLASS)	FULLY TEMPERED	HEAT-STRENGTHENED	LAMINATED	WIRED
Safety glass	No	Yes	No	Yes	No
Can be field-cut or drilled	Yes	No	No	Depends on glass type laminated	Yes
Shatter pattern	Shards	Small cubes	Shards	Pieces adhere to interlayer	Pieces held in place by wire
For use in fire-rated assemblies	No	No	No	No	Yes

Heat-Strengthened Glass

The heat-strengthened glass manufacturing process is similar to that of fully tempered, except that the glass is only partially tempered. Annealed glass is heated and cooled in a manner similar to that for fully tempered glass; however, lower surface stresses are produced. Heat-strengthened glass is about twice as resistant to breakage as float glass.

Laminated Glass

Laminated glass consists of two or more layers of glass and an interlayer material sandwiched together to form a single sheet. There are two types of interlayers: *polyvinyl butyral* (PVB) sheets, which are bonded under heat and pressure, and *urethane acrylate resin*, a liquid that is cured under ultraviolet light. PVB interlayers can be colored or patterned and can be combined for a decorative effect. The interlayer blocks a portion of ultraviolet rays, and is a sound barrier, which dampens vibrations between the two pieces of glass. Rice paper and other ornamental sheets can also be used in the lamination process. Cast resin interlayers are clear or custom-colored, and allow more heavily textured glass to be laminated.

Annealed, fully tempered, heat-strengthened, and wire glass types can be laminated. Security glass (bullet- or burglar-resistant) and acoustical glass are types of laminated glass using thicker interlayers. If laminated glass is broken, the glass remains bonded to the interlayer, offering protection from injury, which makes it popular for use in skylights. Laminated glass with an interlayer of .030 in. (.76 mm) minimum thickness meets the Federal Safety Glazing requirements of ANSI Z97.1, *Glazing Materials Used in Buildings—Safety Performance Specifications and Method of Test,* and Consumer Product Safety Commission (CPSC) 16 CFR Part 1201, *Safety Standard for Architectural Glazing Materials,* Category II, similar to tempered glass. Laminated glass with an interlayer thickness of .38 mm (.015 in.) meets the requirements of Category I glass. The standard for laminated glass is ASTM C1172, *Specification for Laminated Architectural Flat Glass.*

DEPENDING ON PVB AND GLASS THICKNESS, LAMINATED GLASS CAN VARY FROM 1/4" (6) TO 3/4" (19) IN THICKNESS

POLYVINYL BUTYRAL (PVB) THICKNESS RANGES FROM 0.03" (0.8) TO 0.09" (2.3)

GLASS THICKNESS RANGES FROM 1/8" (3) TO 3/8" (10)

LAMINATED GLASS

Wire Glass

Wire glass has wire mesh or parallel wires rolled into the center of the glass sheet; it is available in various patterns and pattern sizes such as square-welded mesh, diamond-welded mesh, and linear parallel wire. Pattern sizes range from 13 to 25 mm (½ to 1 in.), depending on pattern type. Some distortion, wire discoloration, and misalignment are inherent. If breakage occurs, the wire helps to hold the glass fragments in the opening, thus preventing personal injuries. This is the standard glass type used for fire-rated doors or partition assemblies.

SAFETY GLASS

Safety glass is glazing material that, if shattered, breaks in a way that reduces the likelihood of cutting and piercing injuries. Fully tempered and laminated glass qualifies as safety glass. Fully tempered glass breaks into small cubical pieces. If laminated glass is shattered, the broken glass adheres to the interlayer.

The requirements for safety glass are defined by two very similar standards: CPSC 16 CFR Part 1201, and ANSI Z97.1. These standards use the same test procedures, with the exception that the CPSC standard uses a greater impact load. Although wired glass does not pass the tests for safety glass described in CPSC 16 CFR Part 1201, it is granted an exemption because it is the only glass type that performs successfully in fire tests.

SECURITY GLASS

Security glass is composed of multilayers of glass and/or polycarbonate plastic laminated together (under heat and pressure) with a polyvinyl butyral (for glass) or polyurethane plastic (for polycarbonate) film. It is available in multilayer laminated glass, insulating, laminated insulating, and double-laminated insulating or spaced configurations. Thicknesses range from 9 to 63 mm (⅜ to 2½ in.) as a laminated product and up to about 120 mm (4¾ in.) for insulating and spaced construction products.

Bullet-resistant glass should meet the requirements of UL 752, *Standard for Bullet-Resisting Equipment* and burglar-resistant UL 972, *Standard for Burglary Resisting Glazing Material*. Consult manufacturers for blast-resistant glass. Security glass products, depending on type, are subject to size limitations; consult with the manufacturer for glazing requirements and restrictions on use.

TINTED GLASS

Tinted glass was developed to control solar heat gain and glare. Float glass is tinted, and is available in green, bronze, gray, and blue, in thicknesses ranging from 3 to 13 mm (⅛ to ½ in.). The glass absorbs a portion of the sun's energy due to its admixture content and thickness; it then dissipates the heat to both the exterior and interior. The thicker the glass, the greater the solar energy absorption. Newer tinted glass types allow more visible light transmission, while blocking a higher percentage of infrared energy than standard tinted glass.

Heat-absorbing tinted glass has a higher temperature when exposed to the sun than clear glass; the central area expands more than the cooler shaded edges, causing tensile stress buildup.

Indoor shading devices such as blinds and draperies reflect energy back through the glass, thus increasing the temperature of the glass. Spaces between indoor shading devices and the glass, including ceiling pockets, should be vented adequately. Heating elements should be located on the interior side of shading devices, directing warm air away from the glass. Consider tilt-limit devices on horizontal blinds to allow for ventilation.

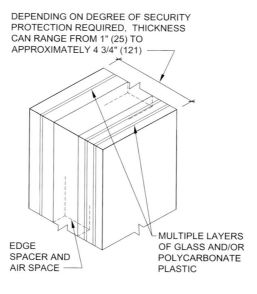

DEPENDING ON DEGREE OF SECURITY PROTECTION REQUIRED, THICKNESS CAN RANGE FROM 1" (25) TO APPROXIMATELY 4 3/4" (121)

EDGE SPACER AND AIR SPACE

MULTIPLE LAYERS OF GLASS AND/OR POLYCARBONATE PLASTIC

INSULATING OR SPACED CONSTRUCTION SECURITY GLASS

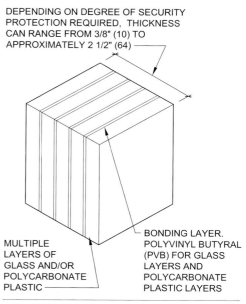

DEPENDING ON DEGREE OF SECURITY PROTECTION REQUIRED, THICKNESS CAN RANGE FROM 3/8" (10) TO APPROXIMATELY 2 1/2" (64)

MULTIPLE LAYERS OF GLASS AND/OR POLYCARBONATE PLASTIC

BONDING LAYER. POLYVINYL BUTYRAL (PVB) FOR GLASS LAYERS AND POLYCARBONATE PLASTIC LAYERS

SECURITY GLASS

REFLECTIVE GLASS

Reflective glass reduces the amount of transmitted, absorbed, and reflective portions of the incident light and energy spectrum, thus improving the energy balance within a building. Typically, pyrolitic or "hard coat" coatings are used on exposed glass surfaces, which are more scratch-resistant than sputtered "soft coat" coatings. Reflective coatings are derived from metals, and are applied to glass, based on the glazing system requirements. Pyrolitic reflective coatings on side 1 (the outside surface) are susceptible to exterior environmental factors. Reflective coatings on sides 2 or 3 are protected from damage, if used in a double-glazed unit.

Reflective glass can be used in interior applications such as shower doors and enclosures, countertops, wall cladding, and furniture.

LOW-EMISSIVITY GLASS

Low-emissivity (Low-E) glass was developed to address energy efficiency concerns for glazing. Hard or soft metallic coatings are applied to the glass, based on application type. Low-E coatings provide more reflectivity for the shortwave solar energy that strikes the glass at a high angle of incidence during the summer, while permitting this warmth to enter during the winter when the angle of incidence is lower. Low-E coatings are applied to side 2 on the first pane of glass in a double-glazed unit. The overall light transmission rate is higher than in tinted and reflective glass types.

INSULATING GLASS

Insulating glass acts as a barrier to conductive heat loss. Insulated glass units are created by sealing an air pocket between two lights of glass, separated by a spacer. The energy efficiency of insulated glass can be increased by adding more lights of glass, or by the use of thin heat-reflecting films suspended between the spacers. New spacer types have been developed that provide a thermal break between the two lights of

glass, for conditions in which there is a large temperature differential between the edges and the center of the glass. Stresses on the seal may cause the eventual deterioration of the sealant, and moisture may appear as condensation between the glass lights. Insulated glass dampens vibrations and sound. Insulated glass units may be created to protect and seal specially treated glass, such as sandblasted glass surfaces.

SPECIALTY GLASS TYPES

Low-Iron Glass

Low-iron glass, or *ultraclear glass*, has high clarity and high visible light transmittance, without the marked greenish tint visible on the edge of standard glass. The clarity in the glass is achieved by the reduction of the iron content by approximately 10%. Thicknesses range from 3 to 19 mm (⅛ to ¾ in.). Low-iron glass can be heat-strengthened, tempered, sandblasted, etched, or assembled into laminated glass. Low-iron glass is used in areas where color rendition is critical, and for furniture, mirrors, museum display cases, signage, and where glass is to be back-coated with light-colored pigments. Trade names for the major manufacturers producing low iron glass are PPG Starphire, Pilkington Opti-White, and Saint Gobain Diamante.

Textured Glass

Textured patterned glass is also known as *rolled* or *figured glass*. It is made by passing molten glass through rollers that are etched to produce the design. Designs include flutes, ribs, grids, and other regular and random patterns, which provide translucency and a degree of obscurity. Usually only one side of the glass is imprinted with a pattern. Patterned glass can be silvered, sandblasted, or have applied colored coatings. A form of textured glass is *impression glass*, in which a clear resin, applied to the glass, is impressed with a pattern. Tempering and sheet size limitations for patterned glass must be verified. Patterning a glass surface may make tempering impossible. Sheet sizes and thicknesses can vary greatly, depending on the type of pattern desired.

FORMED GLASS

Cast Glass

Cast glass, also known as *molded glass*, is formed in molds, using combinations of colors and textures to form the desired product. Cast glass may be molded to precise dimensions and tolerances or it may be formed into art glass units. The casting process allows an unlimited number of glass forms, colors, and textures to be created. Thicknesses and overall sizes are dependent on the design and intended use for the cast glass. Forms of cast glass include glass tiles, stair treads, countertops, artwork, and glass panels.

Translucent Linear Glazing System

Pilkington Profilit manufactures a channel-shaped translucent cast glass product that can be used as an interior wall system. Its most common face dimension is about 10 in. (255 mm) wide, and its structural capabilities allow it to be used in interior application heights of 20 ft (6 m) or more, providing a dramatic linear effect. It is nearly always installed "double-glazed," creating an air space that offers a smooth appearance on both surfaces, and STC reduction of up to 42 dB. It is installed in a system of aluminum channels that can be finished to complement the surrounding conditions, or recessed into the perimeters for a flush appearance. The system can be curved, and glass-to-glass angled corners also can be easily installed, eliminating the necessity of any vertical metal framing at the interior glass area.

Fused Glass

Multiple-layer glass units are formed by fusing compatible glass together under controlled heating. Various glass colors, textures, and compatible three-dimensional materials such as wire, stainless steel, and copper screen can be incorporated into the fused unit. A t*exture* or *tack* fuse maintains a degree of separation between the individual pieces of glass. A *full* fuse melts the various elements and layers into a uniform homogenous form with a smooth surface and rounded edges. Different colors used in a full-fused piece will blend more than in a tack-fused piece. Coated and reflective glass may be fused onto glass substrates. Fused glass is typically used for furniture and decorative accents, glass borders, tiles, panels, light fixtures, and other interior elements.

Slumped Glass

Glass can be molded into various shapes when heated to provide the proper viscosity in a semimolten state. Slumped glass with thicknesses up to 10 mm (⅜ in.) will have the impression of the mold translated to the back side, while thicker glass units will be relatively smooth on the opposite side. Tinted or reflective glass types can be slumped, and processes such as gold leafing, silvering, and airbrushed coloring can be incorporated into the slumped glass texture. Panels up to 4 by 8 ft (1,219 by 2,438 mm) are possible, and the slumped glass can be tempered if required. Molds may be made of materials that can withstand the kiln-slumping temperature of approximately 1,350°F (732°C). Tabletops, shower enclosures, wall panels, and signage can be created from slumped glass.

Bent Glass

A precise, strict tolerance form of slumped glass is known as bent glass. Bent glass is often laminated to meet safety glazing requirements, and may be tempered. Some visual distortion may occur when the radius of the bent glass is tight. Curved shower enclosures, wall partitions, and automobile windshields are applications for bent glass.

PRIVACY GLASS

Blind Glass

Blind glass is float glass that is acid-etched on both sides in a linear, offset pattern, obscuring visibility when viewed perpendicular to the glass. Visibility through the glass is possible when viewing at a 45° angle. Produced in 5-mm (³⁄₁₆-in.) and 8-mm (⁵⁄₁₆-in.) thicknesses, the thicker glass is more effective for a "see-through" effect, while the thinner glass is suited to areas requiring more privacy, such as in doors and in furniture applications.

Electrochromic Glass

Electrochromic glass switchable privacy glazings, identified as polymer dispersed liquid crystal (PDLC), consists of liquid crystals that are enclosed in transparent polymer capsules. The capsules are sandwiched between two sheets of transparent electroconductive film. When voltage is applied, the liquid crystals line up in rows, allowing light to pass freely through the transparent film and glass. Without voltage, the liquid crystals do not line up in rows. This diffuses the light, making the glass appear opaque or obscure.

SURFACE TEXTURING

Surface textures on glass soften transmitted light, add decorative designs, increase obscurity for privacy, or lightly fracture the glass surface for a frosted effect. Surface-texturing processes can be applied to clear, tinted, or reflective glass, prior to tempering.

Sandblasting

Sandblasting is used to create a translucent frosted effect of a desired design on the glass surface. The glass is blasted with small abrasive particles of sand and high-pressure air projected through a nozzle. Different degrees of coarseness are used to achieve varying levels of smoothness. The resulting granular textured surface is susceptible to the absorption of oils. Fingerprints and dirt are typically visible on sandblasted surfaces unless treated with an applied sealer. The sandblasted surface may be protected by enclosing it within an insulated double-glazing unit.

Sandblasting is also the first treatment applied to glass, prior to additional treatments. A sandblasted surface provides improved adhesion for applied sprayed coatings. Laminated glass may be sandblasted, but care should be taken so that the interlayer is not compromised.

Acid Etching

Sandblasted glass is submerged in a bath of hydrofluoric and hydrochloric acids to create a hardened, sealed surface. The glass appears matte, with a soft, light-diffusing quality. Depending on the coarseness of the sandblasting grit, the etched texture may be relatively smooth or grainy. Acid-etched glass may be coated or silvered. It does not show dust, dirt, or fingerprints, and is used in retail residential, and commercial applications for tabletops, counters, shelving, wall cladding, stair treads, and other interior architectural elements. Stencils and etching creams are available to etch smaller areas of glass for signage, mirrors, and windows.

POLYMER DISPERSED LIQUID CRYSTAL PRIVACY GLASS

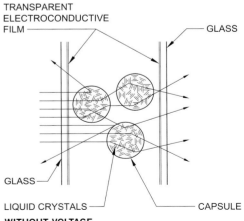

VOLTAGE APPLIED
When voltage is applied (switch is on), the liquid crystals line up in rows, allowing light to pass through.

WITHOUT VOLTAGE
Without voltage (switch is off), the liquid crystals scatter, making the glass appear opaque or obscure.

POLYMER DISPERSED LIQUID CRYSTAL DISPLAY

Glue Chip Glass

To create a fractured, ice-crystal-like frosted effect, hot glue is applied to sandblasted glass, and as it cools, the glue dries and shrinks, removing flakes of glass from the surface. Traditionally, horsehide glue was used for this process, but it has been replaced by synthetic glues. Greater pattern density can be created by a second application of the glue, resulting in a more obscure, frosted appearance. Clear or tinted glass may be glue-chipped, and the glass may be tempered for added strength.

Decorative Silk-Screened (or Frit) Glass

Annealed clear or tinted glass is washed, and ceramic frit paint (in standard or custom colors) is silk-screened on its surface in a standard or custom pattern or design (such as dots, holes, lines, or a logo), then dried in an oven. The frit-coated glass is then subjected to very high temperatures in a tempering furnace to fire the ceramic frit permanently to the glass surface. As a result, silk-screened glass will be either heat-strengthened or tempered after firing. Reflective and low-emissivity coatings can also be applied to the glass surface. Silk-screened glass can be used monolithically or for insulating or laminated glass products. A newer coating process for silk-screened glass uses water-based polymers. This material can be custom-colored or is available in metallic, crackle, frosted, and other custom finishes. This process is much more environmentally friendly than solvent-based coatings. The finish is cured in a low-temperature oven, and the glass may be tempered. Using this process, the glass may be cut, drilled, polished, and postfabricated to suit project needs.

Miscellaneous Coatings

Epoxy coatings are typically applied to the back of glass units. Special printing techniques provide numerous design options on the glass. Coatings may contain glass beads and mica chips, which add a more reflective or metallic appearance. Special metallic coatings can be applied to increase glass reflectivity to light and heat and to carry an electric current.

A form of metallic coating is the dichroic coating, consisting of molecularly thin layers of titanium or zirconium that are highly reflective of one color wavelength of light, while transmitting an entirely different color. Dichroic coatings can be applied to clear or textured glass substrates. Size restrictions may apply due to the dichroic application process limitations. It is used in furniture, accent glass pieces, and art glass. Silicone coatings have been used for decades as a color backing for spandrel glass.

APPLIED MATERIALS

Applied films can be used to modify the appearance or performance of glass. Mylar films can be permanently bonded to the glass with nonyellowing adhesives to create special designs. Tinted films are used as a low-cost alternative to tinted glass in retrofits of existing glass in commercial, residential, and automotive applications. Clear, tough films are available with a Category II safety glazing alternative for glass that is too thin, textured, or shaped so that it cannot be tempered. Applied films are used in jewelry store windows and display cases, where additional protection is needed without affecting the visual quality of the glass. Nylon-fiber-reinforced adhesive-backed films are used on the backs of mirrors for wardrobe doors and wall cladding where safety is a concern but where tempering would cause unacceptable visual distortion.

MIRRORS

Mirrors are created by coating a piece of glass with a reflective coating of silver, with a backing of copper, protected by an epoxy paint top coat. Tinted and clear glass may be silvered with the pyrolitic process to produce mirrors.

One-way mirrors are used for discreet observation, such as in lineup rooms in law enforcement facilities. These mirrors are created by the use of a special reflective coating, which allows approximately 12% transmission and is reflective to the side with the highest light intensity. Light on the observation side is reduced by a 10:1 ratio, which maintains the reflective differential. One-way mirrors should be installed according to the manufacturer's instructions, and the lighting should be coordinated to provide secure one-way visibility.

FIRE-RATED GLASS

Fire-rated glass is a transparent ceramic product. It can be used in fire-rated partitions, in larger areas than typical wire glass locations. Consult local codes and manufacturer's information for limitations. All fire-rated glass is listed and labeled by Underwriter's Laboratories (UL). Fire ratings vary by type of fire-rated glass and thickness, but range from 20 minutes to 2 hours. Three-hour ratings are available with some insulated glass units. Thicknesses range from 5 mm ($\frac{3}{16}$ in.) for nonimpact locations, such as transoms, to 8 mm ($\frac{5}{16}$ in.) for laminated, impact-safety-rated fire-rated glass used in doors. Fire-rated glass may be polished, unpolished, or patterned (obscure).

Fire-rated or fire/impact safety-rated insulated glass units (IGU) are composed of fire-rated glass and either tempered or annealed float glass. These units are available in tinted, low-E, reflective, one-way mirror, and art glass units. Consult manufacturers for specific unit types and applications.

Fire-rated and impact-safety-rated glazing is available that has an intumescent gel layer between two panes of glass. When exposed to heat and light, the gel layer turns opaque and blocks the transfer of radiant heat through the glass for a short period of time.

Special framing is required for fire-rated glazing installations, which must be compatible with the fire rating of the glass. Approved glazing compounds and fire-rated glazing tapes are required to maintain the rating of the installation.

SPECIAL GLASS TYPES

X-ray shielding lead glass, super heat-resistant glass for industrial uses, and other special-use glass types are available for custom applications. Consult manufacturers for information.

WATERJET CUTTING

Waterjet cutting is a precise computer-controlled glass-cutting method. High-velocity water is forced through a small ceramic nozzle, combined with a fine abrasive used as a cutting medium. It is capable of cutting through multiple layers of glass and is useful when dissimilar materials are nested together with the glass, such as metals. Tolerances are .001 in. (.025 mm). Shapes too intricate to be cut by hand or traditional glass-cutting techniques can be waterjet cut.

EDGE TREATMENTS

Polished Edges

Polished edges are created either by machine or by hand, using progressively finer sanding grits with a final polishing with a cork belt, impregnated with a polishing compound. If the glass is to be tempered, the sharp shoulders of the edge are sanded, or "seamed," to remove small cutting nicks, chips, and sharpness. This treatment is necessary to minimize thermal stresses that may occur with small edge fractures. Edge finishing of laminated glass is typically done by hand to protect the soft interlayer, and is typically limited to flat or pencil polishing. If a glass edge is flat-polished, the shoulders are accentuated with a slight polished chamfer known as an *arris* on both sides of the glass.

Beveled Edges

Beveled edges on glass surfaces change the reflection angle of the light and create a framed appearance to the glass. Bevels are ground onto the face of the glass with a succession of diamond-grinding and -polishing wheels. Beveled glass is tempered with the bevel side down toward the horizontal rollers. Thick glass with bevels more than 1 in. (25 mm) wide may slump and warp at the edges, due to the heat required for the glass thickness during the tempering process. Some inconsistencies can be polished out after the tempering process is complete.

Robert Thompson, AIA; Creative Central; Tigard, Oregon
Jana Gunsul, AIA; DES Architects/Engineers; Redwood City, California

GLAZING

HEAD

1/4" TEMPERED GLASS

OPENING

JAMB

1/4" SHIM SPACE
BASE BELOW

1/4" TEMPERED GLASS

GYPSUM BOARD
TRIM, AS REQUIRED
SILICONE SEALANT

SILL

SEALANT
SHIM SPACE
FINISH BASE, AS REQUIRED

FRAMED GLAZING DETAILS

HEAD

METAL OR WOOD SUPPORT; BRACE TO STRUCTURE ABOVE, AS REQUIRED

ALUMINUM ANGLE

CEILING ANGLE
EDGE OF WALL BEYOND
1/4" TEMPERED GLASS

JAMB

1/4" TEMPERED GLASS

GYPSUM BOARD

SILICONE SEALANT

SILL

3/4" X 3/4" CHANNEL

CARPET AND PAD OR OTHER FLOOR FINISH, AS SCEDULED

FRAMELESS GLAZING DETAILS

20-GA. STUDS AT 16" O.C.; ANCHOR TO DECK ABOVE, PROVIDE DIAG. BRACING AT 4'-0" O.C.

CONTINUOUS STRUCTURAL SUPPORT

SHIM, AS REQUIRED

FINISHED CEILING

STRUCTURAL SILICONE (BLACK)

1/2" TEMPERED GLASS

NOTE:
GLASS WILL BE END-BUTTED AT JAMBS AND CAULKED TO GYPSUM BOARD.
HEAD

STRUCTURAL SILICONE (BLACK)

1" X 1" X 1/8" FORMED CHANNEL

BACKER ROD AND SEALANT

1/4" (6)

ALUMINUM TRANSITION AT CARPET

FINISH FLOOR
CONCRETE SLAB

GROUT

3/8" X 1/2" SILICONE COMPATIBLE SETTING BLOCK (BLACK)

EXPANSION ANCHOR

SHIM, AS REQUIRED

SILL

CONCEALED FRAME GLASS PARTITION

1/4" TEMPERED GLASS

3 1/2"
5/8"
2"
3 1/2"

SEE ELEVATION FOR DIMENSION

CONTINUOUS BLOCKING
3 1/2" METAL FRAMING
5/8" GYPSUM BOARD
COUNTER WHERE OCCURS

Sloped sill prevents sitting and the accumulation of debris.

GLASS VISION PANEL WITH SLOPED SILL

(A)
(B)
(C)

AXONOMETRIC VIEW

INTERIOR STOREFRONT

6" METAL STUDS
INSET GLAZED ALUMINUM FRAME

2" (51)

1/4" CLEAR GLASS (TEMPERED, WHERE REQUIRED)

(A) **HEAD**

6" (152)
INSET GLAZED ALUMINUM FRAME

2" (51)

1/4" CLEAR GLASS (TEMPERED, WHERE REQUIRED)

(B) **MULLION**

1/4" CLEAR TEMPERED GLASS
ALUMINUM CHANNEL
WOOD FLOORING
CARPET

(C) **SILL**

SECTION

4" (101)
1 1/2" (38)
ART GLASS
WOOD FRAME
WOOD TOP CAP
1 1/8" (22)
WOOD TRIM
3/4" (19)
BOOTH
TUBE STEEL
SELF-TAPPING SCREWS STAGGERED AT 6" O.C. +/-
WOOD WALL PANELS
WOOD BASE
STONE BASE
4" (101)

ELEVATION

3" (76)
4 1/8" (105)
2'-0" (610)
3" (76)
3'-8" (1118)
4" (102)
SOLID WOOD GLASS FRAME
SOLID WOOD TOP CAP
REVEALS
WOOD WALL PANELS
FLUSH STONE BASE

BASE OF ART GLASS

5/8" (16)
ART GLASS
GLAZING TAPE
GLAZING CHANNEL
1/8" GAP CAULK
1/8" NEOPRENE
1 1/2" (38)
1/2" (13)
SOLID WOOD FRAME
STEEL LEDGE BEYOND
3/4" (19)
3" (76)
STEEL ANGLE BEYOND
1/2" (13)
4" (101)

SECTION AT SUPPORT WALL

LOCATE CENTER OF TUBE ON CENTERLINE BETWEEN BOOTHS
2" X 4" TUBE STEEL SUPPORT; WELD TO PLATE AT FLOOR
WOOD PANELS ON PLYWOOD BACKING
1/2" DIA. EXPANSION ANCHOR WITH 2 1/4" EMBEDMENT
3/4" STEEL PLATE

FRAMING DETAIL

CHANNEL FOR GLASS (BEYOND)
REMOVABLE WOOD TOP FOR GLASS INSTALLATION
3" (76)
2" (51)
18" (457)
4" (102)
ART GLASS
SOLID WOOD GLASS FRAME WRAP ON STEEL SUPPORT
STEEL LEDGE (BEYOND)
CHANNEL FOR GLASS (BEYOND)
STEEL ANGLE WITH FILLET WELD ALL AROUND (BEYOND)
STEEL PLATE; FILLET-WELD TO STEEL TUBE (BEYOND)
WOOD CAP
1/2" REVEALS
STEEL TUBE (BEYOND)

ART GLASS WALL

SECTION

1 1/2" STAINLESS-STEEL RAIL
1 1/2" WOOD RAIL
2" (51)
2" (51)
3 1/2" (89)
2 1/2" (64)
STAINLESS-STEEL SUPPORT, WELD TO COVER PLATE
GLASS PANEL
VERTICAL SUPPORT AT STAIRS
3'-6" (1067)
3'-0 1/2" (927)
2'-10" (867)
WOOD TRIM
VERTICAL SUPPORT WELDED TO EMBEDDED PLATE
FIN. FLR.
2"   7"

PLAN DETAIL

3/8" STAINLESS-STEEL CARRIAGE BOLT
1/2" STAINLESS-STEEL COVER PLATE
1/2" LAMINATED GLASS
RUBBER GASKET
STAINLESS-STEEL VERTICAL POST

ELEVATION

FACE OF WALL OR COLUMN
1 1/2" WOOD RAIL
2" (51)
GLASS PANEL
1/2" GLASS JOINT AT TYPICAL SUPPORT
WOOD TRIM

GLASS GUARDRAIL

Jana Gunsul, AIA; DES Architects/Engineers; Redwood City, California

PLASTER

For centuries, prior to the advent of gypsum board manufacturing, plaster was the primary interior wall and ceiling finish. Conventional plaster provides superior wear resistance to taped gypsum board assemblies. Though it is preferred to attain a uniform, monolithic surface, plaster finishes are more labor-intensive than taped gypsum board assemblies, require greater skill, and can take as long as two days to cure. For these reasons, today, plaster finishes are most commonly used in restoration to match existing conditions and in high-end installations.

Three-coat plaster applications are required on all metal lath and on edge-supported gypsum lath used in ceilings. Three-coat applications are preferred on gypsum lath assemblies, but two-coat applications are acceptable where gypsum lath is properly supported and on masonry plaster bases such as porous brick, clay tiles, and rough concrete masonry units.

Keene's cement plaster is a specialty finish coat of gypsum plaster primarily used where a smooth, dense, vandal-resistant, white finish is desired.

Thickness, proportions of mixes of various plastering materials, and finishes vary. Systems and methods of application also vary widely, depending on local traditions and innovations promoted by the industry.

ORNAMENTAL PLASTER

Molding plaster is used for ornamental trim, running cornices, and other cast plaster pieces. This specialty plaster has a very fine grain and is ideal for sharp detail when used for cast work. Higher-strength molding plaster may be required for ornamental work having thin sections or intricate detail.

FRONT VIEW   SIDE VIEW

DIAMOND MESH EXPANDED METAL

FRONT VIEW   SIDE VIEW

SELF-FURRING DIAMOND MESH

FRONT VIEW   SIDE VIEW

RIB-EXPANDED METAL

METAL LATH TYPES

CONTINUOUS BLOCKING

CONTINUOUS REINFORCING CAST INTO CORNICE

WOOD LATH CAST INTO BACK OF CORNICE

CAST PLASTER CORNICE

WOOD SCREWS INTO BLOCKING; COUNTERSINK HEADS AND FILL

CAST PLASTER ORNAMENT ATTACHED WITH SCREWS

1X BLOCKING CUT TO PROFILE OF CORNICE AND FASTENED TO FRAMING (ALTERNATE SUPPORT: 1" X 3/16" METAL STRAP BENT TO PROFILE OF CORNICE AND FASTENED TO FRAMING)

RUN-IN-PLACE PLASTER CORNICE

BRACKETED CORNICE RUN IN PLACE WITH APPLIED ORNAMENT

TRADITIONAL CAST PLASTER

CONTINUOUS REINFORCING CAST INTO CORNICE

CAST PLASTER CORNICE

METAL STRAP HANGERS

WOOD LATH CAST INTO BACK OF CORNICE

METAL FURRING FOR HUNG CEILING

WOOD LATH CROSS BRACING TO KEEP SIDES OF BEAM SQUARE

CAST PLASTER BEAM

CAST PLASTER CORNICE AND BEAM SCREWED AND HUNG

METAL LATH

CAST PLASTER ORNAMENT APPLIED WITH PLASTER SLIP

DENTILS APPLIED TO PLASTER CORNICE WITH PLASTER SLIP

Definitions

Basecoat: A plaster coat applied before finish coat, scratch coat, and blow coats in three-coat plaster.

Brown coat: In three-coat plaster, the second coat; in two-coat plaster, the first coat.

Fibered plaster: Gypsum plaster containing fibers of hair, glass, nylon, or sisal.

Finish coat: The final coat of plaster, which provides the decorative surface.

Furring: Generally, channels or Z-shapes attached to the underlying wall (or structure for ceilings) for attaching gypsum or metal lath while allowing an air space. Often used on cementitious substrate, resilient furring is used to reduce sound transmission.

Gypsum: Hydrous calcium sulphate, a natural mineral in crystalline form.

Gypsum lath: A base for plaster; a sheet having a gypsum core, faced with paper. Also perforated for interior use.

Hydrated lime: Quicklime mixed with water, on the job, to form a lime putty.

Lime: Obtained by burning various types of limestone, consisting of oxides or hydroxides of calcium and magnesium.

Lime plaster: Basecoat plaster of hydrated lime and an aggregate.

Neat plaster: Basecoat plaster, fibered or unfibered, used for job-mixing with aggregates.

Perlite: Siliceious volcanic glass containing silica and alumina expanded by heat for use as a lightweight plaster aggregate.

Plaster: Cementitious material or combination of cementitious materials and aggregate that, when mixed with water, forms a plastic mass that sets and hardens when applied to a surface.

Portland cement: Manufactured combination of limestone and an argillaceous substance for exterior or wet-atmosphere applications.

Scratch coat: In three-coat plastering, the first coat, which is then scratched to provide a bond for the second, or brown, coat.

Stucco portland cement: Plaster used in exterior application. This plaster requires a waterset; it must not be applied to smooth dense surface or gypsum lath, requires control joints, and cannot have a Keene's cement-lime putty finish.

Three-coat plaster: Preferred application for all substrates; required over metal lath.

Two-coat plaster: Acceptable on lath and on interior face of rough concrete block, clay tile, or porous brick.

Vermiculite: Micaceous mineral of silica, magnesium, and alumina oxides made up in a series of parallel plates or laminae and expanded by heat for use as a lightweight plaster aggregate.

CORNER LATH — 2" OR 3", 105°

STRIP LATH — 4" OR 6"

JOINT REINFORCEMENT

EXPANDED WING — 1 1/4", 2", 2 5/8", 2 7/8", 3 1/2", 1/8"

BULLNOSE — 2 7/8", 3", R= 3/4"

ARCH OR FLEXIBLE — 1/8", 1 1/2"

CORNER BEADS

FLAT — 2", 2 1/4", 2 1/2", 1", 1/4", 3 1/4"

ROUNDED — 2", 3", R = 1 1/2"

SOLID PARTITION TERMINALS

CORNER — 1", 3/4", 1", 3/4"

F-REVEAL AT CEILING — 3/4", 3/4", 1 5/8"

SPECIALTY MOLDINGS

EXPANSION SCREEDS — 5/8", 3/4", 7/8"; 3/4", 1", 1 1/2", 2", 2 1/2", 3/4", 7/8"

ROUNDED — 1/4", 2 1/4", 2"

SQUARE — 3/4"

FASCIA CORNERS

SOLID — 1/2", 3/4", 7/8", 1 3/8"

EXPANDED WING — 1/2", 3/4", 7/8", 1/8", 4 3/4", 5 3/8"

BASE SCREEDS

SQUARE END — 1/2", 5/8", 3/4", 7/8", 1", 1 1/8", 1 1/4", 7/8"

MODIFIED SQUARE END — 1/2", 3/4", 1/4" 45° BREAK, 3 1/8"

EXPANDED-WING CASING BEADS

CONTROL JOINTS — 1/2", 3/4", 7/8", 5 3/8"; 1/2", 3/4", 7/8"

METAL STUD PARTITION WITH PLASTER AND LATH

METAL LATH

PLASTER COATS EACH SIDE

SCRATCH-BROWN FINISH

LATERAL BRACING

HANGER WIRE

CROSS-REINFORCING, AS REQUIRED

45°   45°

MAIN RUNNER CHANNEL

TIE WIRES

3/4" CROSS-RUNNER

PLASTER ON METAL LATH

LIGHT TROFFER

CASING BEAD

SOFFIT

HANGER WIRE

MAIN RUNNER

CROSS-RUNNER

PLASTER ON METAL LATH

PLASTER WALL

EXTERIOR MASONRY WALL

STIFFENER AND FURRING BRACKET

FURRING CHANNEL

INSULATION

CEILING AT FURRED EXTERIOR MASONRY WALL

When interior walls are furred from an exterior masonry wall and insulated, the ceiling should stop short of the furred space. This allows wall insulation to continue above the ceiling line to ceiling or roof insulation, thus forming a complete insulation envelope. In a suspension system that abuts masonry walls, provide 1-in. (25-mm) clearance between ends of main runners or furring channels and wall face.

SUSPENDED PLASTER CEILING DETAILS

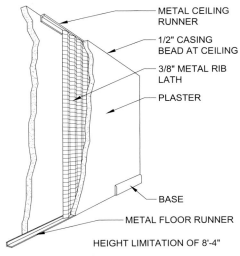

METAL CEILING RUNNER

1/2" CASING BEAD AT CEILING

3/8" METAL RIB LATH

PLASTER

BASE

METAL FLOOR RUNNER

HEIGHT LIMITATION OF 8'-4"

CUTAWAY WALL SECTION

PLASTER

3/8" METAL RIB LATH

PLAN

SOLID METAL LATH

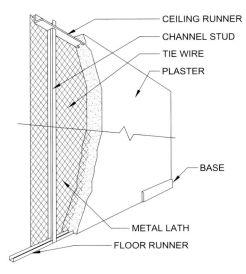

CEILING RUNNER

CHANNEL STUD

TIE WIRE

PLASTER

BASE

METAL LATH

FLOOR RUNNER

CUTAWAY WALL SECTION

CHANNEL STUD

METAL LATH

PLASTER

PLAN

METAL LATH WITH CHANNEL STUD— ONE-HOUR FIRE-RATED

3" BATT INSULATION WITH 2 1/2" STEEL STUDS AT 16" O.C.

3/8" ROCK LATH BASE BOTH SIDES 8" O.C.

5 7/8"

3.4 LB. SELF-FURRING DIAMOND MESH LATH, 8" O.C.

3/4" GYPSUM SAND PLASTER BOTH SIDES

GYPSUM AND PLASTER LATH—TWO-HOUR FIRE-RATED PARTITION

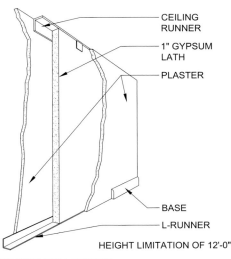

CEILING RUNNER

1" GYPSUM LATH

PLASTER

BASE

L-RUNNER

HEIGHT LIMITATION OF 12'-0"

CUTAWAY WALL SECTION

PLASTER

GYPSUM LATH

PLASTER

PLAN

SOLID GYPSUM LATH

CEILING CHANNEL

METAL LATH

PLASTER

BASE

GYPSUM LATH

STEEL STUD

FLOOR CHANNEL

CUTAWAY WALL SECTION

FLOOR CHANNEL

STEEL STUD

METAL LATH

PLASTER

PLAN

FLOOR CHANNEL

STEEL STUD

GYPSUM LATH

PLASTER

PLAN

METAL STUD

Directions for using tables:
1. Select lath and plaster system.
2. Determine spacing of cross-furring channels from Table 1, "Lath Span."
3. Determine spacing of main runners from Table 2, "Maximum Spacing between Runners."
4. Determine hanger support spacing for main runner from Table 3, "Maximum Spacing between Hangers."
5. Calculate area of ceiling supported per hanger.
6. Select hanger type from Table 4, "Hanger Selection."
7. Select tie wire size from Table 5, "Tie Wire Selection."

TABLE 1. LATH SPAN

	LATH TYPE	WEIGHT LB PER SQ FT	SPAN IN. (MM)
Gypsum Lath	⅜ in. plain	1.5	16 (406)
	½ in. plain	2.0	16 (406)
	½ in. veneer	1.8	16 (406)
	⅝ in. veneer	2.25	16 (406)
	⅜ in. perforated	1.4	16 (406)
Metal Lath	Diamond mesh	0.27	12 (305)
	Diamond mesh	0.38	16 (406)
	⅛ in. flat rib	0.31	12 (305)
	⅛ in. flat rib	0.38	19 (483)
	⅜ in. flat rib	0.38	24 (610)

TABLE 2. MAXIMUM SPACING BETWEEN RUNNERS

CROSS-FURRING TYPE	CROSS-FURRING SPACING IN. (MM)			
	12 (305)	16 (406)	19 (483)	24 (610)
¼-in. dia. pencil rod	24 (610)	—	—	—
⅜-in. dia. pencil rod	30 (760)	—	24 (610)	—
¾-in. CRC*, HRC** (0.3 lb/ft)	—	54 (1,370)	42 (1,070)	36 (915)
1-in. HRC (0.41 lb/ft)	60 (1,520)	—	54 (1,370)	48 (1,220)

*CRC = Cold-rolled channel
**HRC = Hot-rolled channel

TABLE 3. MAXIMUM SPACING BETWEEN HANGERS

MAIN RUNNER TYPE	MAIN RUNNER SPACING FT (MM)				
	3 (915)	3 (1,070)	4 (1,220)	4.5 (1,370)	5 (1,520)
¾-in. CRC (0.3 lb/ft)	2 (610)	—	—	—	—
1½-in. CRC (0.3 lb/ft)	3 (915)	—	—	—	—
1½-in. CRC (0.875 lb/ft)	4 (1,220)	3.5 (1070)	3 (915)	—	—
1½-in. HRC (1.12 lb/ft)	—	—	—	4 (1,220)	—
2-in. CRC (0.59 lb/ft)	—	—	5 (1,520)	—	—
2-in. HRC (1.26 lb/ft)	—	—	—	—	5 (1,520)
½ × ½ × ³⁄₁₆ in. ST1	—	5 (1,520)	—	—	—

For concrete construction only, a 10-gage wire may be inserted in the joint before concrete is poured.

TABLE 4. HANGER SELECTION

MAXIMUM CEILING AREA SQ FT (SQ M)	MINIMUM HANGER SIZE
12 (1.12)	9-gage galvanized wire
16 (1.49)	8-gage galvanized wire
18 (1.67)	³⁄₁₆-in. mild steel rod*
25 (2.32)	¼-in. mild steel rod*
25 (2.32)	³⁄₁₆- × 1-in. steel flat*

*Rods galvanized or painted with rust-inhibitive paint and galvanized straps are recommended under severe moisture conditions.

TABLE 5. TIE WIRE SELECTION

	SUPPORT	MAXIMUM CEILING AREA SQ FT (SQ M)	MINIMUM HANGER SIZE
Cross-Furring		8 (0.74)	14-gage wire
		8 (0.74)	16-gage wire (two loops)
Main Runners	Single hangers between beams	8 (0.74)	12-gage wire
		12 (1.12)	10-gage wire
		16 (1.49)	8-gage wire
	Double-wire loops at supports	8 (0.74)	14-gage wire
		12 (1.12)	12-gage wire
		16 (1.49)	11-gage wire

HANGER (SEE TABLES 4 AND 5)
TABLE 3
TABLE 1
TABLE 2
TABLE 2
CROSS-FURRING
MAIN RUNNER

FURRED AND SUSPENSION SYSTEM COMPONENT SELECTION DETAIL

CONCRETE JOIST
WOOD JOIST
STEEL JOIST
STEEL FLOOR OR ROOF JOISTS
HANGER WIRE
SUSPENSION SYSTEM TIE WIRES, AS REQUIRED
MAIN RUNNER CHANNEL
3/4" CROSS-FURRING CHANNEL
SUSPENSION SYSTEM HANGER WIRE FROM STRUCTURE ABOVE
METAL LATH WIRED TO FURRING CHANNELS 6" O.C.
THREE-COAT PLASTER WITH EXPANSION JOINTS 30'-0" O.C. EACH WAY

METAL LATH SUSPENDED FROM STEEL JOIST

M. Kitty Myers, AIA, and Gabrielle Sapponara;
    Anshen+Allen, Architects; San Francisco, California
James E. Phillips, AIA; Enwright Associates, Inc.;
    Greenville, South Carolina
The Marmon Mok Partnership; San Antonio, Texas

GLASS-REINFORCED GYPSUM (GRG)

CHARACTERISTICS

One of the most important advances in modern plaster technique was the development of glass-reinforced gypsum (GRG), also referred to as *fiberglass-reinforced gypsum* (FRG) or *glass-fiber-reinforced gypsum* (GFRG). GRG is a remarkably lightweight, nontoxic, noncombustible composite of gypsum slurry and glass fiber. It is cast in molds at a manufacturing plant and shipped to the project site.

Since its conception in 1977, GRG has continued to grow in popularity in applications such as column covers, decorative domes, coffered ceilings, and other architectural elements previously available only in plaster. GRG manufacturing techniques can produce thin, high-strength shapes that are inherently flame-resistant.

GRG is suitably lightweight for ceilings or other applications in which weight is a concern. Standard gypsum wallboard finishing techniques are required for the installation of GRG. GRG products can be field-cut for plumbing, electrical, mechanical, or other penetrations with the use of conventional gypsum board tools.

FABRICATION PROCESS

GRG products are cast in polyurethane or latex molds either by hand-laying or spraying. Hand-laying involves layering continuous glass-fiber mats and gypsum slurry in a mold. The spraying process utilizes a nozzle that mixes chopped glass-fiber strands into the gypsum slurry as it is sprayed into a mold. Molds are typically customized for particular projects; however, many proprietary GRG products are available.

The finish face of GRG is smooth and resembles a plaster surface. The back-side appearance is bumpy and irregular, resembling the inside of a fiberglass boat hull, with glass fibers and structural members often visible. When complete, each GRG product is carefully crated and stored to prevent warping or bowing.

Shorter stacking components are used where a smaller mold is needed for producing a series of identical elements. For example, tall columns are often broken into more manageable segments, or "lifts," to reduce installation costs. When pricing columns over 9 ft (3 m) in height, fabricators may propose shorter components. Producing and shipping shorter components may be less expensive, but the installation costs will likely be higher. Fabricators may be required to identify how many lifts will be used when bidding a project.

FINISHING GRG

Because most GRG installations are designed to simulate monolithic plaster systems, a smooth, level finish is of particular concern. In order to ensure the required level of finish, designers should familiarize themselves with the fabrication process and recognize some of the difficulties the fabricator faces. Important questions to ask to determine the cost of fabricating GRG include:

- How can the detail be developed to simplify the installation process?
- Will the fabrication method contribute to simplifying installation?
- Which fastening details does the fabricator offer as standard?
- Which method will offer the required level of finish in the least time?

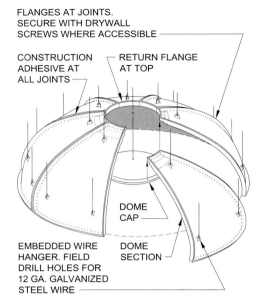

FLANGES AT JOINTS. SECURE WITH DRYWALL SCREWS WHERE ACCESSIBLE

CONSTRUCTION ADHESIVE AT ALL JOINTS

RETURN FLANGE AT TOP

DOME CAP

EMBEDDED WIRE HANGER. FIELD DRILL HOLES FOR 12 GA. GALVANIZED STEEL WIRE

DOME SECTION

Due to its light weight, GRG is popular for use in the fabrication of domed, coffered, and vaulted ceilings. GRG ceilings are suspended from integral fastening points inserted during the casting process. Larger ceiling areas may exploit the casting process by utilizing repeated forms from a limited number of molds.

DOMED CEILING INSTALLATION
Source: Casting Designs, Inc.; Fort Worth, Texas

METAL HANGER

ADHESIVE AND SCREW

26-GA. GALVANIZED METAL REINFORCING AT JOINTS, CAST INTO PANEL

1/8"-DEEP X 3"-WIDE RECESS AT JOINTS

REINFORCED FIBERGLASS TAPE AND JOINT COMPOUND FINISHED TO MATCH PROFILE OF CEILING

ALTERNATE JOINT DETAIL WHEN PANELS ARE NOT ACCESSIBLE FROM THE BACK

JOINT DETAIL

JOINT FINISHING

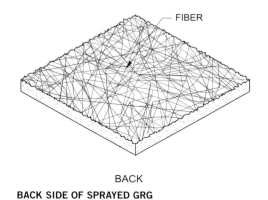

FIBER

BACK
BACK SIDE OF SPRAYED GRG

MAT

BACK
BACK SIDE OF HAND-LAID GLASS-FIBER MAT GRG

FINISH FACE

FRONT
FINISH FACE

GLASS-REINFORCED GYPSUM FABRICATION

WIRE HANGERS

FRAMING
AS REQUIRED

COVE LIGHT
FIXTURE

GLASS-FIBER-REINFORCED
GYPSUM COFFERED PANELS

GLASS-FIBER-REINFORCED
GYPSUM CORNICE

SECTION AT LIGHT COVE

SEPARATE
DOME CAP

GLASS-FIBER-
REINFORCED GYPSUM
COFFERED PANELS

REFLECTED CEILING PLAN

COFFERED CEILING DETAILS

STRUCTURAL
COLUMN

METAL ANGLE
ANCHORS

2 1/2" FLANGES
AT TOP AND
BOTTOM

1/8" DEEP TAPER
FOR JOINT
FINISHING

1 1/2" FLANGES
AT JOINTS

2 1/2" FLANGES
AT TOP AND
BOTTOM

TWO-PIECE COLUMN COVER

STRUCTURAL
COLUMN

CAP INTEGRAL
OR APPLIED AS
SEPARATE
PIECE

ATTACHMENT
BRACKETS

COLUMN SHAFT;
STRAIGHT OR
ENTASIS TAPER

1/8" DEEP
TAPER FOR
JOINT
FINISHING

BASE TO BE
APPLIED AS
SEPARATE
PIECE

ADJUSTABLE CAPITAL AND BASE DETAIL

STRUCTURAL
COLUMN

1 1/2" FLANGES
AT JOINTS

1/8" DEEP TAPER
FOR JOINT
FINISHING

METAL ANGLE
BRACES

2 1/2" FLANGES
AT STACKING
JOINTS

1/8" DEEP TAPER
FOR JOINT
FINISHING

STACKING COLUMN DETAIL

Capitals and bases may be integral to, or separate from, the column casting. The design of capitals often allows for the height to be adjusted, depending on the final ceiling level.

GRG COLUMN COVERS
Source: Casting Designs, Inc.; Fort Worth, Texas

Yon-Hwa Jang; Rhode Island School of Design; Providence, Rhode Island

GYPSUM BOARD ASSEMBLIES

ASSEMBLIES

Gypsum board assemblies are composed of gypsum board panels and the metal support systems to which they are attached. These systems include structural and nonstructural interior partitions, tile backer partitions, and shaft walls.

GYPSUM BOARD PANELS

Gypsum board panels consist of a noncombustible gypsum core, faced with a paper surface. The panels are installed over steel or wood framing, including wall and ceiling assemblies. Certain gypsum board assemblies provide fire resistance of varying degrees and sound transmission reduction. The gypsum board may be finished with paint or other applied finish materials such as wallcovering or tile.

Gypsum board is installed by screwing (and sometimes nailing) it to studs or furring channels. The edges of the gypsum board are tapered to accept a paper-reinforcing tape or a self-adhering fiberglass tape and joint compound.

BEVELED

SQUARE

ROUNDED TAPER

GYPSUM BOARD EDGE TYPES

GYPSUM BOARD TYPES

Gypsum board standard panel size is 4 × 8 ft (1,220 × 2,440 mm). Metric panel size is 1,200 × 3,600 mm. Gypsum board is available for a wide variety of specialty applications, including the following:

- *Type X* is manufactured to achieve fire-resistance ratings.
- *Moisture-resistant* (sometimes called *green board* because of its pale lime green color) has a water-repellant paper face and a moisture-resistant core. Moisture-resistant gypsum board is used as a backing for ceramic tile and in wet areas. It is available with a Type X core.
- *Foil-backed* has a layer of aluminum foil laminated to its backside. The foil surface provides an effective vapor retarder.
- *Gypsum board plaster base* is used as a substrate for veneer plaster and is erected in the same manner as regular gypsum board. It is often referred to as *blue board,* because of the color of its absorptive paper face, designed for a strong bond with plaster materials.
- *Prefinished* is covered with decorative vinyl- or textile-surfaced faces. It is often used in prefabricated demountable partition systems.

METAL STUD PARTITION

WOOD STUD PARTITION

CMU WALL WITH PLUMBING CHASE AND METAL STUD PARTITION

CMU WALL WITH METAL HAT CHANNEL FURRING

DOUBLE-STUD PLUMBING CHASE

CONCRETE WALL WITH METAL HAT CHANNEL FURRING

GYPSUM BOARD ASSEMBLIES

METAL FRAMING

Light-gage steel framing used in interior partitions is cold-formed, meaning that it is fed at room temperature from continuous coils through machines that fold it into stiff shapes. (Much heavier hot-rolled steel shapes are used in structural steel framing.)

Thicknesses

There are three common steel stud thicknesses for nonstructural partitions: 25-, 22-, and 20-gage. These steel studs are nonload-bearing, and cannot support floor loads, but are able to support selected transverse loads, such as wall-mounted shelving, with proper blocking and support. ASTM C645, *Specification for Nonstructural Steel Framing Members,* and ASTM C754, *Specification for Installation of Steel Framing Members to Receive Screw-Attached Gypsum Panel Products,* are helpful in specifying the proper steel stud gage for a given application.

Steel studs are commonly 0.0188-in. (0.48-mm) thick (25-gage) for typical interior partitions. To support cementitious backer units, 0.0346-in.- (0.88-mm-) thick (20-gage) steel studs are recommended; 0.0451 in. (1.115 mm) (18-gage) steel studs are typically used for structural interior partitions.

Steel Stud Spacing and Height

Steel stud spacing and stud height for single- and double-layer gypsum board partitions are identified in ASTM C754, *Standard Specification for Installation of Steel Framing Members to Receive Screw-Attached Gypsum Panel Products,* according to maximum deflection and minimum lateral loading requirements. The *Gypsum Construction Handbook,* published by United States Gypsum, recommends that the deflection limit for gypsum board assemblies be L/240. The maximum allowable deflection is L/120, since greater deflection could cause damage to the gypsum board. Applications of tile or other rigid finish materials to gypsum board partitions may require a deflection limit of L/360 or less. Consult with the applied finish product manufacturer for recommended partition deflection limits.

Steel framing is typically installed at 24 in. (610 mm) on center for partitions. Spacing of 16 in. (406 mm) on center improves the flatness and impact resistance of the partition.

Gypsum board ceilings and soffits are suspended from furring channels. Special profile steel studs are used for interior shaft-wall construction.

GYPSUM BOARD ACCESSORIES

A variety of metal and plastic framing and furring accessories are available, including:

- *Metal angles* are made of 24-gage galvanized steel and are used to secure 1-in. (25-mm) coreboard or liner panels at floor and ceiling in laminated gypsum board partitions.
- *Cold-rolled channels* are made of 16-gage steel and used in furred walls and suspended ceilings.
- *Z-furring channels* are made of 24-gage steel and are used to mechanically fasten insulation blankets, rigid insulation, and gypsum board panels to concrete or masonry walls.

TYPES OF GYPSUM PANEL PRODUCTS

DESCRIPTION	THICKNESS IN. (MM)	WIDTH/EDGE FT (M)	STOCK LENGTH FT (M)
Regular gypsum board used as a base layer for improving sound control; repair and remodeling with double-layer application.	¼ (6)	4 (1.2), square or tapered	8–10 (2.4–3)
Regular gypsum board used in a double wall system over wood framing repair and remodeling.	⅜ (9)	4 (1.2), square or tapered	8–14 (2.4–4.3)
Regular gypsum board for use in single-layer construction.	½, ⅝ (13, 16)	4 (1.2), square or tapered	8–16 (2.4–4.9)
Rounded taper edge system offers maximum joint strength and minimizes joint deformity problems.	⅜ (9.5) ½, ⅝ (13, 16)	4 (1.2), rounded taper	8–16 (2.4–4.9)
Type X gypsum board with core containing special additives to increase fire-resistance ratings. Consult manufacturer for approved assemblies.	½, ⅝ (13, 16)	4 (1.2), tapered, rounded taper, or rounded	8–16 (2.4–4.9)
Aluminum foil-backed board effective as a vapor barrier for exterior walls and ceilings and as a thermal insulator when foil faces ¾ in. (19.1 mm) minimum air space. Not for use as a tile base or in air conditioned buildings in hot, humid climates (Southern Atlantic and Gulf Coasts).	⅜ (9.5) ½, ⅝ (13, 16)	4 (1.2), square or tapered	8–16 (2.4–4.9)
Water-resistant board for use as a base for ceramic tile and other nonabsorbent wall tiles in bath and shower areas. Type X core is available.	½, ⅝ (13, 16)	4 (1.2), tapered	8, 10, 12 (2.4, 3, 3.7)
Prefinished vinyl surface gypsum board in standard and special colors. Type X core is available.	½, ⅝ (13, 16)	2, 2½, 4 (.6, .76, 1.2), square and beveled	8, 9, 10 (2.4, 2.7, 3)
Prefinished board available in many colors and textures. See manufacturer's literature.	⁵⁄₁₆ (8)	4 (1.2), square	8 (2.4)
Coreboard for use to enclose vent shafts and laminated gypsum partitions.	1 (25)	2 (.6), tongue and groove or square	8–12 (2.4–3.7)
Shaft-wall liner core board Type X with gypsum core used to enclose elevator shafts and other vertical chases.	1, 2 (25, 50)	2 (.6), square or beveled	6–16 (1.8–4.9)
Sound underlayment gypsum board attached to plywood subfloor acts as a base for any durable floor covering. When used with resiliently attached gypsum panel ceiling, the assembly meets HUD requirements for sound control in multifamily dwellings.	¾ (19)	4 (1.2), square	6–8 (1.8–2.4)

A large range of adhesives, sealants, joint treatments, and texture products are available from the manufacturers of most gypsum board products.

METAL EDGE TRIM   METAL EDGE TRIM   METAL EDGE TRIM   METAL EDGE TRIM

METAL EDGE TRIM   PREFINISHED CORNER   CONTROL JOINT   METAL THIN-COAT BEAD

Z-FURRING CHANNEL   COLD-ROLLED CHANNEL   METAL RUNNER   METAL STUD

VINYL TRIM   PREFINISHED DIVIDER   METAL FURRING CHANNEL   METAL-RESILIENT CHANNEL

GYPSUM BOARD ACCESSORIES

TYPICAL NONFIRE-RATED PARTITIONS AND CHASES

Nonrated partition.

Ceiling is installed prior to installation of partition.

2½-in. (63-mm) metal stud is adequate for most commercial ceiling height partitions.

3¾-in. (95-mm) partition type may not accommodate back-to-back devices, such as junction boxes.

Sounds such as normal conversation, telephones, and some equipment may be audible.

STC range 35 to 39.

CEILING HEIGHT PARTITION

Nonrated partition. Used where flexibility in the partition is desired to minimize cracking of the gypsum board.

SLIP JOINT AT STRUCTURE ABOVE

Nonrated partition.

Ceilings installed within partitioned space.

Full-height metal studs provide a stable partition. Consult manufacturer's literature for information on allowable heights and transverse loading; for example, shelving.

STC 35.

FULL-HEIGHT STUD PARTITION

Can be used where additional nonfire-rated partition depth is desired.

Lateral bracing must be provided. Above-ceiling space may be used as a plenum.

FULL-HEIGHT DOUBLE-STUD PARTITION

Full-height gypsum board provides moderate above-ceiling security and improved sound attenuation properties.

More stable than ceiling-height double-stud partitions.

FULL-HEIGHT DOUBLE-STUD PARTITION, FULL-HEIGHT GYPSUM BOARD

Suspended acoustical ceiling is installed prior to partition. Fasten head of partition to ceiling suspension system for stability.

Provides lateral bracing.

CEILING-HEIGHT DOUBLE-STUD PARTITION

TYPICAL PERIMETER PARTITIONS

2⅛-IN.-THICK PARTITION

TERMINATES AT CEILING
Gypsum board terminates at the ceiling.

2⅛-IN.-THICK PARTITION

3⅛-IN.-THICK PARTITION

A vapor retarder on the interior of the room (warm side of the partition) may be beneficial.

Metal studs are installed full height to underside of structure above, providing a more stable partition.

Gypsum board extends up above the ceiling, creating a more finished appearance.

Metal stud width allows for installation of selected standard devices, such as shallow junction boxes.

PERIMETER CONDITION WITH FULL-HEIGHT METAL STUD

TERMINATES ABOVE CEILING

Gypsum board extends up above the ceiling, creating a more finished appearance.

A vapor retarder on the interior of the room (warm side of the partition) may be beneficial.

Shallow depth of partition does not allow for installation of some devices, such as junction boxes and receptacles.

PERIMETER CONDITION WITH METAL FURRING CHANNEL

3⅛-IN.-THICK PARTITION

A vapor retarder on the interior of the room (warm side of the partition) may be beneficial.

Fasten metal studs at ceiling track for stability.

Metal stud width allows for installation of most standard devices, such as junction boxes and receptacles.

PERIMETER CONDITION WITH METAL STUD

PLASTER AND GYPSUM BOARD ☐ **2**

METAL-FRAME GYPSUM BOARD PARTITIONS

METAL-FRAME GYPSUM BOARD PARTITIONS

FIRE RATING	STC	WALL THICKNESS IN. (MM)	CONSTRUCTION DESCRIPTION	WALL SECTIONS
1 Hour	35–39	2⅞ (73)	One layer ⅝ in. (16 mm) Type X gypsum board or veneer base applied to each side of 1⅝ in. (41 mm) metal studs 24 in. (610 mm) o.c. with 1 in. (25 mm) Type S gypsum board screws 8 in. (203 mm) o.c. to edges and 12 in. (305 mm) o.c. to intermediate studs. Stagger joints 24 in. (610 mm) o.c. each side.	
	40–44	3⅜ (86)	Base layer ⅜ in. (9 mm) regular gypsum board or veneer base applied to each side of 1⅝ in. (41 mm) metal studs 24 in. (610 mm) o.c. with 1 in. (25 mm) Type S gypsum board screws 27 in. (686 mm) o.c. to edges and 54 in. (1,371 mm) o.c. to intermediate studs. Face layer ½ in. (13 mm) attached on each side to studs with 1⅝ in. (41 mm) Type S gypsum board screws 12 in. (305 mm) o.c. to perimeter and 24 in. (610 mm) o.c. to intermediate studs. Stagger joints 24 in. (610 mm) o.c. each layer and side.	
		4⅞ (124)	One layer ⅝ in. (16 mm) Type X gypsum board or veneer base applied to each side of 3⅝ in. (92.1 mm) metal studs 24 in. (610 mm) o.c. with 1 in. (25 mm) Type S gypsum board screws 8 in. (203 mm) o.c. to vertical edges and 12 in. (305 mm) o.c. to intermediate studs. Stagger joints 24 in. (610 mm) o.c. each layer and side.	
	45–49	3⅛ (79)	Two layers ½ in. (13 mm) regular gypsum board or veneer base applied to each side of 1⅝ in. (41 mm) metal studs 24 in. (610 mm) o.c. Use 1 in. (25 mm) Type S gypsum board screws 12 in. (305 mm) o.c. for base layer and 1⅝ in. (41 mm) Type S gypsum board screws 12 in. (305 mm) o.c. for face layer. Stagger joints 24 in. (610 mm) o.c. each layer and side.	
		3⅛ (79)	Base layer ¼ in. (6 mm) gypsum board applied to each side of 1⅝ in. (41 mm) metal studs 24 in. (610 mm) o.c. with 1 in. (25 mm) Type S gypsum board screws 24 in. (610 mm) o.c. to edges and 36 in. (914 mm) o.c. to intermediate studs. Face layer ½ in. (13 mm) Type X gypsum board or veneer base applied to each side of studs with 1⅝ in. (41 mm) Type S gypsum board screws 12 in. (305 mm) o.c. Stagger joints 24 in. (610 mm) o.c. each layer and side.	
		5½ (140)	One layer ⅝ in. (16 mm) Type X gypsum board or veneer base applied to each side of 3⅝ in. (92 mm) metal studs 24 in. (610 mm) o.c. with 1 in. (25 mm) Type S gypsum board screws 8 in. (203 mm) o.c. to edge and vertical joints and 12 in. (305 mm) o.c. to intermediate stud. Face layer ⅝ in. (16 mm) (same as other layer) applied on one side to stud with laminating compound and attached with 1⅝ in. (41 mm) Type S gypsum board screws 8 in. (203 mm) o.c. to edges and sides and 12 in. (305 mm) o.c. to intermediate studs. 3½ in. (89 mm) glass fiber insulation in cavity. Stagger joints 24 in. (610 mm) o.c. each layer and side.	
	50–54	4 (102)	Base layer ¼ in. (6 mm) regular gypsum board applied to each side of 2½ in. (63 mm) metal studs 24 in. (610 mm) o.c. with 1 in. (25 mm) Type S gypsum board screws 12 in. (305 mm) o.c. Face layer ½ in. (13 mm) Type X gypsum board or veneer base applied to each side of studs with laminating compound and with 1⅝ in. (41 mm) Type S gypsum board screws in top and bottom runners 8 in. (203 mm) o.c. 2 in. (50 mm) glass fiber insulation in cavity. Stagger joints 24 in. (610 mm) o.c. each layer and side.	
		4 (102)	Two layers ½ in. (13 mm) Type X gypsum board or veneer base applied to one side of 2½ in. (63 mm) metal studs 24 in. (610 mm) o.c. Base layer 1 in. (25 mm) and face layer 1⅝ in. (41 mm) gypsum board screws 8 in. (203 mm) o.c. to edge and adhesive beads to intermediate studs. Opposite side layer ½ in. (13 mm) Type X gypsum board or veneer base applied with 1 in. (25 mm) Type S gypsum board screws 8 in. (203 mm) o.c. to vertical edges and 12 in. (305 mm) o.c. to intermediate studs. 3 in. (76 mm) glass fiber insulation in cavity. Stagger joints 24 in. (610 mm) each layer and face.	
	55–59	4¼ (108)	Base layer ¼ in. (6 mm) gypsum board applied to each side of 2½ in. (63 mm) metal studs 24 in. (610 mm) o.c. with ⅞ in. (22 mm) Type S gypsum board screws 12 in. (305 mm) o.c. Face layer ⅝ in. (16 mm) Type X gypsum board or veneer base applied on each side of studs with 1 15/16 in. (49 mm) Type S gypsum board screws 12 in. (305 mm) o.c. 1½ in. (38 mm) glass fiber insulation in cavity. Stagger joints 24 in. (610 mm) o.c. each layer and side.	
2 Hour	40–44	5 (127)	Two layers ⅝ in. (16 mm) Type X gypsum board or veneer base applied to each side of 2½ in. (63 mm) metal studs 16 in. (406 mm) o.c. braced laterally. Use 1 in. (25 mm) for base layer and 1⅝ in. (41 mm) for face layer. Type S-12 gypsum board screws 12 in. (305 mm) o.c. for face layer. 1½ in. (38 mm) glass fiber insulation in cavity. Stagger joints 24 in. (610 mm) o.c. each layer and side.	
	50–54	3⅝ (92)	Base layer ½ in. (13 mm) Type X gypsum board or veneer base applied to each side of 1⅝ in. (41 mm) metal studs 24 in. (610 mm) o.c. Use 1 in. (25 mm) Type S gypsum board screws 12 in. (305 mm) o.c. for base layer and 1⅝ in. (41 mm) Type S gypsum board screws 12 in. (305 mm) o.c. for face layer. 1½ in. (38 mm) glass fiber insulation in cavity. Stagger joints 24 in. (610 mm) o.c. each layer and side.	
	55–59	6¼ (159)	Two layers ⅝ in. (16 mm) Type X gypsum board or veneer base applied to each side of 3⅝ in. (92 mm) metal studs 24 in. (610 mm) o.c. Use 1 in. (25 mm) Type S gypsum board screws 32 in. (812 mm) o.c. for base layer and 1⅝ in. (41 mm) Type S gypsum board screws 12 in. (305 mm) o.c. to edge and 24 in. (610 mm) o.c. to intermediate studs. One side third layer ¼ or ⅜ in. (6 or 9 mm) gypsum board or veneer base applied with laminating compound. Stagger joints 24 in. (610 mm) o.c. each layer and side.	

FIRE-RESISTANCE-RATED ASSEMBLIES

A *fire-resistance rating* denotes the length of time a construction assembly can withstand fire and still serve as a barrier to fire and confine its spread to the area of origin. Fire spreads from one area to another when the barrier collapses, there are openings in the barrier, or sufficient heat is conducted through the bar-

rier to exceed specified temperature limitations. Fire-resistive rating tests are conducted under controlled laboratory conditions by the procedures described in ASTM E119, *Standard Fire Tests of Building Construction Materials*. This test applies to floor- and roof-ceiling assemblies, beams, and columns, as well as partitions. The ratings are expressed in hours.

Fire-rated partitions with hourly ratings are identified in building codes for specific uses. The Underwriter's Laboratory (UL) *Fire Resistance Directory* and other publications are referenced for fire-resistance ratings. Fire-resistance-rated partition types are as follows:

- *Nonrated:* Includes ceiling-height (constructed from floor to ceiling) and full-height partitions (from floor to underside of structure above), not requiring fire-resistance rating. Full-height partitions may have gypsum board facing up to or extending above the ceiling, or fully enclosing the full-height studs.
- *One-Hour:* Separates different uses or occupancies, such as partitions between tenant spaces and public corridors in office buildings, or as indicated by building codes. One-hour partitions are used for smoke separation within a building.
- *Two-Hour:* Encloses vertical openings within a building, including elevator and mechanical shafts, exit stairwells, and mechanical and electrical rooms. Two-hour partitions are used for fire separation and smoke or fire separation within a building.
- *Three-Hour:* Separates and encloses higher-hazard areas.
- *Four-Hour:* Encloses very high-hazard spaces.

Typically used to separate different occupancy types. Consult authorities having jurisdiction for use and restrictions.

Seal all joints, penetrations, and openings with fire-rated sealant when used as a rated partition.

Provide fire dampers where ducts penetrate partitions.

3¾-in. (95-mm) partition type may not accommodate back-to-back devices, such as junction boxes.

Sound attenuation insulation provides improved acoustical properties. STC 45.

FULL-HEIGHT PARTITION—ONE-HOUR FIRE-RATED

Typically used to separate different occupancy types. Consult authorities having jurisdiction for use and restrictions.

Seal all joints, penetrations, and openings with fire-rated sealant when used as a rated partition.

Provide fire dampers where ducts penetrate partitions.

Can be used as a nonrated partition when moderate security and slightly improved acoustical properties are desired.

This partition type may not accommodate back-to-back devices, such as junction boxes.

STC range 35 to 39.

FULL-HEIGHT PARTITION—ONE-HOUR FIRE-RATED

Typically used to separate different occupancy types. Consult authorities having jurisdiction for use and restrictions.

Seal all joints, penetrations, and openings with fire-rated sealant when used as a rated partition.

Provide fire dampers where ducts penetrate partitions.

Two layers of gypsum board on one side provide additional sound attenuation.

FULL-HEIGHT PARTITION—ONE-HOUR FIRE-RATED

PLASTER AND GYPSUM BOARD ☐ **2**

TWO-HOUR FIRE-RATED PARTITIONS

TWO-HOUR-RATED

Type X gypsum board or veneer base (½ in. (13 mm)) applied to gypsum board furring channels. Furring channels 24 in. o.c. (610 mm) attached with 18-gage steel wire ties 48 in. (1,220 mm) o.c. to open web steel joists 24 in. (610 mm) o.c. supporting ⅜ in. (9 mm) rib metal lath or ⁹⁄₁₆-in. (14-mm) deep, 28-gage corrugated steel and 2½ in. (63 mm) concrete slab measured from top of flute. Double channel at board end joints.

STC range 50 to 54.

TWO-HOUR-RATED

Type X gypsum board or veneer base (⅝ in. (16 mm) screw-attached to gypsum board furring channels. Furring channels 24 in. (610 mm) o.c. are suspended from 2½-in. (63-mm) precast reinforced concrete joists 35 in. (889 mm) o.c. with 21-gage galvanized steel hanger straps fastened to sides of joists. Joist leg depth, 10 in. (254 mm). Double channel at board end joints.

STC range 45 to 49.

TWO-HOUR-RATED CEILING OR COLUMN

Two layers of ⅝ in. (16 mm) Type X gypsum board or veneer base around beam. Base layer attached with 1¼ in. (32 mm) Type S gypsum board screws 16 in. (406 mm) o.c., face layer attached with 1¾ in. (44 mm) Type S gypsum board screws 8 in. (203 mm) o.c. to horizontally installed U-shaped steel channels (25-gage steel 1¹¹⁄₁₆ in. (43 mm) wide, and 1 in. (25 mm) legs), located not less than ½ in. (13 mm) from beam flanges. Upper channels secured to steel deck units with ½ in. (13 mm) Type S pan head screws spaced 12 in. (305 mm) o.c. U-shaped brackets formed of steel channels spaced 24 in. (610 mm) o.c. suspended from the upper channels with ½ in. (13 mm) Type S pan head screws and supported steel channels installed at lower corners of brackets. Outside corners of gypsum board protected by 0.020-in. (.5-mm) thick steel corner beads crimped or nailed. (Two-hour restrained or unrestrained beam.)

GYPSUM BOARD AT CEILINGS, BEAMS, AND SOFFITS

SECTION — METAL RUNNER CHANNEL; FASTEN TO UNDERSIDE OF STRUCTURE

FILL ALL VOIDS WITH FIRE-RATED SEALANT AS REQUIRED

BRACE AS REQUIRED

CEILING

PLAN — METAL STUDS @ 2'-0" O.C., MAX.

1/2" GYPSUM BOARD, TWO LAYERS EACH SIDE, FIRE-RATED TYPE X

1 1/2" SOUND INSULATION, FIRE-RATED (SAFB)

SECTION — METAL RUNNER CHANNEL; FASTEN @ 2'-0" O.C., MAX.

4 1/2"
5 5/8"
8"

FIRE-RATED SEALANT BOTH SIDES OF PARTITION

SECTION — CONTINUOUS FIRE-RATED ACOUSTICAL SEALANT, BOTH SIDES

CELL CLOSURE; FILL OPEN CELLS WITH FIRE STOPPING

CEILING

TWO LAYERS 5/8" GYPSUM BOARD EACH SIDE

PLAN — 3 5/8" METAL STUDS @ 2'-0" O.C., MAX.

3" MINIMUM SOUND ATTENUATION INSULATION

RESILIENT CHANNELS @ 2'-0" O.C.

SECTION — WALL BASE

CONTINUOUS FIRE-RATED ACOUSTICAL SEALANT, BOTH SIDES

6 3/4"

SECTION — CONTINUOUS FIRE-RATED SEALANT, BOTH SIDES

CELL CLOSURE; FILL OPEN CELLS WITH FIRE STOPPING

CEILING

PLAN — 3-5/8" METAL STUDS @ 2'-0" O.C., MAX.

3/4" GYPSUM BOARD EACH SIDE

SECTION — FULL BATT INSULATION

WALL BASE

CONTINUOUS FIRE-RATED SEALANT BOTH SIDES

5 1/8"

Two-hour partitions are used at mechanical rooms, electrical closets, and other areas, as required by building codes.

Seal all joints, penetrations, and openings with fire-rated sealant when used as a rated partition.

Provide fire dampers where ducts penetrate partitions.

Can be used as a nonrated partition when increased security and sound attenuation is desired.

STC range 50 to 54.

Double-layer Type X gypsum board partition, two-hour fire-rated.

Can be used as nonrated partition with additional security due to double-layer gypsum board.

Resilient channel provides higher performance sound control.

STC range 55 to 60.

Single-layer ¾ in. (19 mm) Type X gypsum board, two-hour fire-rated.

FULL-HEIGHT PARTITION—TWO-HOUR FIRE-RATED, DOUBLE-LAYER GYPSUM BOARD

TWO-HOUR FIRE-RATED PARTITION, DOUBLE-LAYER GYPSUM BOARD

TWO-HOUR FIRE-RATED PARTITION, SINGLE-LAYER GYPSUM BOARD

FIRE-RESISTIVE COLUMN CONSTRUCTION

ONE-HOUR FIRE-RATED

Base layer ½ in. (13 mm) gypsum board or veneer base tied to column with 18-gage wire 15 in. (380 mm) o.c. Face layer ½ in. (13 mm) gypsum board or veneer base applied with laminating compound over entire contact surface.

TWO-HOUR FIRE-RATED

Base layer ½ in. (13 mm) gypsum board or veneer base against flanges and across web openings fastened to 1⅝ in. (4 mm) metal studs with 1 in. (25 mm) Type S gypsum board screws 24 in. (610 mm) o.c. at corners. Face layers ½ in. (13 mm) Type X gypsum board or veneer base screw-attached to studs with 1 in. (25 mm) Type S gypsum board screws 12 in. (305 mm) o.c. to provide a cavity between boards on the flange. Face layers across the web opening laid flat across the base layer and screw-attached with 1⅝ in. (41 mm) Type S gypsum board screws 12 in. (305 mm) o.c. Metal corner beads nailed to outer layer with 4d nails 1⅜ in. (35 mm) long, 0.067 in. (1.7 mm) shank, ¹³⁄₆₄ in. (5.2 mm) heads, 12 in. (305 mm) o.c.

THREE-HOUR FIRE-RATED

Three layers of ⅝ in. (16 mm) Type X gypsum board or veneer base screw-attached to 1⅝-in. (41-mm) metal studs located at each corner of column. Base layer attached with 1 in. (25 mm) Type S gypsum board screws 24 in. (610 mm) o.c. Second layer with 1⅝ in. (41 mm) Type S gypsum board screws 12 in. (305 mm) o.c. and 18-gage wire tied 24 in. (610 mm) o.c. Face layer attached with 2¼ in. (57 mm) Type S gypsum board screws 12 in. (305 mm) o.c. and 1¼ in. (31 mm) corner beads at each corner nailed with 6d coated nails, 1⅞ in. (47 mm) long, 0.0915 in. (2 mm) shank, ¼ in. (6 mm) heads, 12 in. (305 mm) o.c.

FIRE-RATED COLUMNS

CURVED ASSEMBLIES

Gypsum panels can be applied to cylindrically curved surfaces. Flexible gypsum panels that are ¼-in. (6-mm) thick are designed for this purpose. These panels are more flexible than standard panels of the same thickness. They may be applied dry; or for shorter radii, they may be wet. Typically, the panels are sprayed with a conventional garden hose on the side that will be in tension, then stacked with wet faces together and covered with a plastic sheet for an hour before installation.

For curved walls, installers should be aware of the following:

- To prevent flat areas between framing, shorter bend radii require closer spacing than normal stud and furring spacing.
- Flexible gypsum panels may be applied horizontally or vertically.
- For double-layer applications, panels should be offset by one half of a panel width.
- Cutouts for electrical boxes should not be made until boards have dried and regained their original strength.
- Panels must be allowed to dry completely (about 24 hours under good drying conditions) before joint treatment is applied.

Arches of any radii are easily faced with gypsum board panels. The panels are scored through the backing paper at intervals of 1 in. (25 mm) or less. Joint treatment or veneer plaster can be applied.

MINIMUM BENDING RADII OF DRY GYPSUM BOARD

BOARD THICKNESS		BOARD APPLIED WITH LONG DIMENSION PERPENDICULAR TO FRAMING		BOARD APPLIED WITH LONG DIMENSION PARALLEL TO FRAMING	
in.	mm	ft	m	ft	m
¼	6.4	3	0.9	5	1.8
⅜	9.5	6	1.8	9	2.7
½	13	12	3.7	—	—
⅝	16	18	5.5	—	—

Source: The Gypsum Construction Handbook, *USG Corporation; Chicago, Illinois*

MINIMUM RADII OF ¼-IN. (6-MM) FLEXIBLE PANELS

APPLICATION	CONDITION	LENGTHWISE BEND RADII		MAXIMUM STUD SPACING		WIDTHWISE BEND RADII		MAXIMUM STUD SPACING	
		in.	mm	in.	mm	in.	mm	in.	mm
Inside (concave)	Dry*	32	813	9	229	45	1,143	9	229
Outside (convex)	Dry*	34	864	9	229	20	508	6	152

*75°F (24°C) and 50% relative humidity
Source: The Gypsum Construction Handbook, *USG Corporation; Chicago, Illinois*

FACE LAYER OF GYPSUM PANELS FASTENED TO EACH STUD AT 12" O.C.

BASE LAYER OF GYPSUM PANELS FASTENED TO EACH STUD AT 16" O.C.

SPLICED RUNNER TRACK (TOP AND BOTTOM)

MINIMUM 1'-0" TANGENT TO ARC WITH STUDS SPACED 6" O.C. EACH SIDE

CURVED GYPSUM BOARD ASSEMBLY
Source: The Gypsum Construction Handbook, *USG Corporation; Chicago, Illinois*

ACOUSTICAL PARTITIONS

The reduction of airborne sound transmission, such as normal conversation and other office noise, is identified by Sound Transmission Class (STC) ratings. The STC does not identify reductions of impact or vibration noise, which are classified in the impact insulation class (IIC). Impact and vibration noises may require isolation and sound dampening through means other than the partition.

Partition STC ratings are dependent on the partition mass, resiliency (or isolation), dampening, and sound absorption. Multilayer partitions have more mass than single-layer partitions. Wood studs are less resilient than steel studs and transmit more sound. Isolating wood studs by staggering their placement or using resilient channels improves the resistance to sound transmission. Sound attenuation insulation provides sound dampening and absorption.

Acoustical partitions require sealant at the perimeter edges of the partition assembly, as well as at openings in the gypsum board panel, such as junction boxes and other wall penetrations.

Published sound-rating assembly performance is developed under controlled laboratory conditions. Actual performance may vary from the published STC rating.

RECOMMENDED STC VALUES

RECEIVING ROOM	SOURCE ROOM	STC
Offices Requiring Privacy (e.g., doctor, executive)	Lobby or corridor	50
	General office	45
	Adjacent office	50
	Toilet room	55
Office Areas	Lobby or corridor	45
	Kitchen or dining room	45
Conference and Training Rooms	Other conference room	50
	Adjacent office	50
	General office	50
	Lobby or corridor	50
	Toilet room	55
Hotel Bedrooms	Adjacent bedroom, living room, or bathroom	55
	Lobby or corridor	55
Classrooms (K–12)	Adjacent classroom	45
	Laboratory	50
	Lobby or corridor	50
	Kitchen or dining room	50
	Vocational shop	55
	Music room	55+
	Toilet room	50
All Areas	Mechanical room	60

INTERRUPTED CEILING

PARTITION INTERSECTION

SOUND-ISOLATED ASSEMBLIES

Ceiling is installed prior to installation of partition.

Used when improved acoustical qualities are desired and economy of installation is required.

Not as stable as a full-height partition with studs continuous to the structure above.

STC range 40 to 44.

MODIFIED FULL-HEIGHT PARTITION

Acoustic sealant required for STC rating.

Nonrated or two-hour-rated with Type X gypsum board. Provides additional security due to double-layer gypsum board.

Resilient channel provides higher performance sound control.

STC range 55 to 60.

DOUBLE-LAYER GYPSUM BOARD PARTITION

Nonrated partition.

Ceiling is installed prior to installation of partition.

Commonly used in commercial and high-quality residential construction.

Normal conversation is not audible, but loud sounds may be transmitted through the partition.

STC range 40 to 44.

CEILING-HEIGHT PARTITION WITH SOUND ATTENUATION

MOISTURE-RESISTANT PARTITIONS

Water-resistant gypsum backing board, known as *green board*, consists of a treated core and facings to increase water resistance. The core may soften over time when exposed to moisture. This product is intended for use as a substrate for wall tile or other finish material with a fused, impervious finish, set in adhesive, where wetting of the finish surface is intermittent. This backing board should not be exposed to a direct water flow or excessive moisture, and should not be applied over a vapor retarder. Water-resistant panels tend to sag; do not specify for ceiling installations.

Glass-mat and cementitious backer units are also used as backing panels for areas exposed to moisture. Glass-mat panels contain a gypsum core, covered by a coated glass-fiber mat, which protects the core from moisture. The gypsum core may soften over time when exposed to moisture. Cementitious backer units have a portland cement core, and glass-fiber mesh mats are applied to each face of the units. This product may be used in areas where moisture and direct water flow are present.

VAPOR CONTROL PARTITIONS

Vapor retardation is difficult to control due to the number of penetrations within partitions. Installed more often in colder climates or where air conditioning is used in warmer climates, the vapor retarders are typically installed on the interior side of the exterior wall. Review the installation parameters of a vapor retarder with a mechanical engineer to determine the type and use. Foil-backed gypsum board may be used for vapor control.

GYPSUM BOARD SHAFT-WALL ASSEMBLIES

Gypsum shaft-wall systems are lighter in weight and easier to install than traditional masonry shaft walls. Shaft walls surround multistory vertical chases for elevator or mechanical enclosures. To prevent a fire from quickly spreading to other floors, shaft walls are required to be fire-resistance-rated. Gypsum shaft-wall systems typically consist of floor and ceiling tracks, special studs, special gypsum panels, and Type X gypsum panels.

Gypsum board shaft-wall assemblies are used for elevator hoistway enclosures, return air shafts, chases, and stair enclosures. They are rapidly installed, fire-resistant, and lightweight. Many shaft-wall assemblies are two-hour fire-rated, as required by authorities having jurisdiction.

Shaft-wall assemblies are installed from the exterior of the shaft and utilize proprietary gypsum board liner panels, installed within special profile steel studs. Gypsum board is applied to the studs on the room side of the shaft wall. In stair enclosures, finish panels are also installed on the shaft side of the wall.

Manufactures of shaft walls can provide test data for their assemblies, including fire-resistive, structural, and acoustical characteristics. Not all assemblies have the same test results, so it is recommended that the manufacturer's data be reviewed and compared for a project's specific requirements. Metal stud profiles are specific to a particular proprietary assembly, and therefore cannot be used in an assembly in which it was not tested. Metal stud types from various manufacturers include C-T, I, and C-H profiles, which hold the liner panels in place in the shaft-wall assembly. E-studs are used at corners and termination conditions.

Shaft-Wall Fire Resistance

Fire-resistance requirements and hourly ratings for shaft-wall assemblies are established by building codes based on the construction type and building use group. Consult authorities having jurisdiction for specific code requirements for these assemblies.

Sound Transmission Class

STC ratings of shaft-wall assemblies are developed in laboratory conditions. Field conditions may differ from the manufacturer's published STC data. Acoustical sealant should be included in the assembly construction when subject to positive or negative air pressures. Sealant is installed at the perimeter of the assembly and at voids in which noise, dust, or smoke could pass.

Construction Considerations

Considerations for shaft-wall assemblies include: limiting height and span support capabilities; allowable deflection limits; and intermittent air-pressure loads, which may cause the shaft wall to flex. All openings and devices within the shaft must not compromise the fire-resistance rating. This includes hoistway doors, elevator call buttons, indicator lights, and other items contained within the assembly.

Gypsum board shaft-wall assemblies may crack if subjected to excessive structural movement. Isolate the gypsum finish panels from the structural elements using sealant, installed according to the manufacturer's assembly requirements. Install control joints in large areas of gypsum board panels. Corner reinforcing at openings may be required to minimize cracks in the finish panels.

GYPSUM BOARD ASSEMBLY FINISHES

Gypsum board assemblies are finished with gypsum board tape and joint compounds. Joint compounds include a setting-type compound, formulated from a powder and mixed on-site, to drying-type joint compounds, available in ready-mixed or job-mixed formulations. Taping compounds produce a strong bond between the tape and gypsum board, but are harder to sand and finish than topping or all-purpose compounds. Topping compounds are not suitable for first coat or taping compounds. All-purpose joint compounds have good shrink resistance; however, they are softer than other joint compound types. Shrinkage of the joint compound is not desired, as cracking may result.

Veneer Plaster Finishes

Although conventional plaster is the best system to attain a uniform, monolithic surface with excellent wear resistance, veneer plaster over gypsum board provides a similar performance in days less time. Veneer plaster systems use gypsum board panels (commonly referred to as *blue board*), which improve the speed of installation, while providing better abuse resistance than conventional gypsum board. Plaster thickness is reduced from the standard ½ in. (50 mm) associated with conventional plaster to ⅟₁₆ to ⅛ in. (1 to 3 mm), using high-strength gypsum in the formulation.

TYPICAL SHAFT WALL

Labels on diagram:
- POWER ANCHOR
- SEALANT EACH SIDE
- UNDERSIDE OF STRUCTURE ABOVE
- SCHEDULED CEILING
- TWO LAYERS 5/8" GYPSUM BOARD (FIRE CODE C)
- METAL STUDS (C-H TYPE)
- SCREW-ATTACHED GYPSUM BOARD CANT FOR PROJECTIONS OVER 2"
- WALL BASE
- POWER ANCHOR
- SECTION / PLAN / SHAFT
- 3 3/4"
- 5 1/4"

GYPSUM BOARD FINISH LEVELS

LEVEL	DESCRIPTION
0	Taping, finishing, and corner beads are not required.
1	At joints and angles, embed tape in joint compound. Panel surfaces must be free of excess joint compound, but tool marks and ridges are acceptable.
2	At joints and angles, embed tape in joint compound and apply one separate coat of joint compound over tape, fastener heads, and flanges of trim accessories. Joint compound applied on the face of the tape when the tape is embedded is considered a separate coat. Panel surfaces must be free of excess joint compound, but tool marks and ridges are acceptable.
3	At joints and angles, embed tape in joint compound and apply two separate coats of joint compound over joints, angles, fastener heads, and flanges of trim accessories. Panel surfaces and joint compound must be free of tool marks and ridges.
4	At joints and angles, embed tape in joint compound and apply three separate coats of joint compound over joints, angles, fastener heads, and flanges of trim accessories. Panel surfaces and joint compound must be free of tool marks and ridges.
5*	Finish must be equal to Level 4 (embedding coat and three finish coats) plus a skim coat over the entire gypsum board surface. Surfaces must be smooth and free of tool marks and ridges.

*Level 5 is a high-quality gypsum board finish that is recommended for feature walls with strong lighting or for walls that will receive high-gloss paint. An alternative to the Level 5 finish is gypsum veneer plaster.

Source: MASTERSPEC®; published by ARCOM; Salt Lake City, Utah, and Alexandria, Virginia. Copyright ASTM INTERNATIONAL. Reprinted with permission.

GYPSUM BOARD SHAFT-WALL ASSEMBLIES

SHAFT WALLS AND SOLID GYPSUM BOARD PARTITIONS

FIRE RATING	STC	WALL THICKNESS IN. (MM)	CONSTRUCTION DESCRIPTION	WALL SECTIONS
1-hour	35–39	3⅛ (79)	1 × 24 in. (25 × 610 mm) proprietary Type X gypsum panels inserted between 2½ in. (63 mm) floor and ceiling J-runners with 2½ in. (63 mm) proprietary vented C-H studs between panels. One layer ⅝ in. (16 mm) proprietary Type X gypsum board or veneer base applied parallel to studs on side opposite proprietary gypsum panels with 1 in. (25 mm) Type S gypsum board screws spaced 12 in. (305 mm) o.c. in studs and runners. STC estimate based on 1 in. (25 mm) mineral fiber in cavity (NLB).	FIRE SIDE / FIRE SIDE
	40–44	2⅞ (73)	¾ × 24 in. (19 × 610 mm) proprietary Type X gypsum panels inserted between 2¼ in. (57 mm) floor and ceiling track and fitted to proprietary 2¼ in. (57 mm) slotted metal I-studs with tab-flange. Face layer ⅝ in. (16 mm) Type X gypsum board applied at right angles to studs, with 1 in. (25 mm) Type S gypsum board screws, 12 in. (305 mm) o.c. Sound-tested with 1 in. (25 mm) glass-fiber friction fit in stud space.	FIRE SIDE / FIRE SIDE
2-hour	30–34	2¼ (57)	One layer ⅝ in. (16 mm) Type X gypsum board or veneer base applied vertically to each side of 1 in. (25 mm) gypsum board panels (solid or laminated) with laminating compound combed over entire contact surface. Panel supported by metal runners at top and bottom and horizontal bracing angles of No. 22-gage galvanized steel ¾ in. × 1¼ in. (19 × 31 mm) spaced 5 ft 0 in. (1,524 mm) o.c. or less on shaft side (NLB).	FIRE SIDE
	35–39	4⅛ (105)	Four layers ⅝ in. (16 mm) Type X gypsum board or veneer base applied at right angles to one side of 1⅝ in. (41 mm) metal studs 24 in. (610 mm) o.c. Base layer attached to studs with 1 in. (25 mm) Type S gypsum board screws 12 in. (305 mm) o.c. Second layer attached to studs with 1⅝ in. (41 mm) gypsum board screws using only two screws per board. Third layer attached with 2⅝ in. (66 mm) Type S gypsum board screws similar to second layer. Steel strips 1½-in. (38 mm) wide vertically applied over third layer at stud lines and attached 12 in. (305 mm) o.c. to studs with 2⅝ in. (66 mm) Type S gypsum board screws. Third layer also attached to top and bottom track with 2⅝ in. (66 mm) Type S gypsum board screws placed midway between studs. Face layer attached to steel strips with 1 in. (25 mm) Type S gypsum board screws 8 in. (203 mm) o.c. at each stud. Stagger joints of each layer (NLB).	FIRE SIDE / FIRE SIDE
	40–44	3½ (89)	1 × 24 in. (25 × 610 mm) proprietary Type X gypsum panels inserted between 2½ in. (63 mm) floor and ceiling J-track with T-section of 2½ in. (63 mm) proprietary C-T-metal studs between proprietary gypsum panels. Two layers of ½ in. (13 mm) Type X gypsum board applied to face of C-T-studs. Base layer applied at right angles to studs with 1 in. (25 mm) Type S gypsum board screws 24 in. (610 mm) o.c. and face layer applied at right angles to studs with 1⅝ in. (41 mm) Type S gypsum board screws 8 in. (203 mm) o.c. Stagger joints 24 in. (610 mm) o.c. each layer (NLB).	FIRE SIDE / FIRE SIDE
	45–49	3½ (89)	1 × 24 in. (25 × 610 mm) proprietary Type X gypsum panels inserted between 2½ in. (63 mm) floor and ceiling track with tab-flange section of 2½ in. (63 mm) metal I-studs between proprietary gypsum panels. One layer of ½ in. (13 mm) proprietary Type X gypsum board or veneer base applied at right angles to each side of metal I-studs with 1 in. (25 mm) Type S gypsum board screws 12 in. (305 mm) o.c. Sound-tested using 1½ in. (38 mm) glass-fiber friction fit in stud space (NLB).	FIRE SIDE / FIRE SIDE
	50–54	4 (102)	1 × 24 in. (25 × 610 mm) proprietary Type X gypsum panels inserted between 2½ in. (63 mm) floor and ceiling track with tab-flange section of 2½ in. (63 mm) metal I-studs between proprietary gypsum panels. One layer of ½ in. (13 mm) proprietary Type X gypsum board or veneer base applied at right angles to flanges of I studs adjacent to proprietary gypsum panels with 1 in. (25 mm) Type S gypsum board screws 12 in. (305 mm) o.c. Resilient channels spaced 24 in. (610 mm) o.c. horizontally, screw-attached to opposite flanges of I-studs with 3/8 in. (9 mm) Type S screws, one per channel-stud intersection. ½ in. (13 mm) proprietary Type X gypsum board or veneer base applied parallel to resilient furring channels with 1 in. (25 mm) Type S gypsum board screws 12 in. (305 mm) o.c. Sound-tested using 1 in. (25 mm) glass-fiber friction fit in stud space (NLB).	FIRE SIDE / FIRE SIDE
3-hour	40–44	4⅛ (105)	2 × 24 in. (50 × 610 mm) laminated gypsum board panels installed vertically between floor and ceiling 20-gage J-runners with 25-gage steel H-members between panels. Panels attached at midpoint to 2½ in. (63 mm) leg of J-runners with 2⅜ in. (60 mm) Type S-12 gypsum board screws. H-studs formed from 20- or 25-gage 2 X 1 in. (50 × 25 mm) channels placed back to back and spot-welded 24 in. (610 mm) o.c. Base layer ⅝ in. (16 mm) gypsum board or veneer base applied parallel to one side of panels, with 1 in. (25 mm) Type S gypsum board screws 12 in. (305 mm) o.c. to H-studs. Rigid furring channels horizontally attached 24 in. (610 mm) o.c. to H-studs with 1 in. (25 mm) Type S gypsum board screws. Face layer ⅝ in. (16 mm) gypsum board or veneer base attached at right angles to furring channels with 1 in. (25 mm) Type S gypsum board screws. Face layer ⅝ in. (16 mm) gypsum board or veneer base attached at right angles to furring channels with 1 in. (25 mm) Type S gypsum board screws 12 in. (305 mm) o.c. Stagger joints 24 in. (610 mm) o.c. each layer and side (NLB).	FIRE SIDE
	45–49	5¼ (133)	¾ × 24 in. (19 × 610 mm) proprietary Type X gypsum panels inserted between 2¼ in. (57 mm) floor and ceiling tracks and fitted to 2¼ in. (57 mm) slotted metal I-studs with tab-flange. First layer ⅝ in. (16 mm) Type X gypsum board applied at right angles to studs with 1 in. (25 mm) Type S gypsum board screws 24 in. (610 mm) o.c. Second layer ⅝ in. (16 mm) Type X gypsum board applied parallel to studs with 1⅝ in. (41 mm) Type S gypsum board screws 42 in. (1,066 mm) o.c. starting 12 in. (305 mm) from bottom. Third layer ⅝ in. (16 mm) Type X gypsum board applied parallel to studs with 2¼ in. (57 mm) Type S gypsum board screws 24 in. (610 mm) o.c. Resilient channels applied 24 in. (610 mm) o.c. at right angles to studs with 2¼ in. (57 mm) Type S gypsum board screws. Fourth layer ⅝ in. (16 mm) Type X gypsum board applied at right angles to resilient channels with 1 in. (25 mm) Type S gypsum board screws. Sound-tested with 1 in. (25 mm) glass-fiber friction fit in stud space (NLB).	FIRE SIDE / FIRE SIDE

SPECIAL WALL ASSEMBLIES

NEW WALL ASSEMBLIES

FIRE RATING	STC	WALL THICKNESS IN. (MM)	CONSTRUCTION DESCRIPTION	WALL SECTIONS
1-hour	40	Varies	*Exterior Wall Furring:* One layer ⅝ in. (16 mm) aluminum foil-backed gypsum board applied to ¾ × 1½ in. (19 × 38 mm) Z-furring channel 24 in. (610 mm) o.c., vertically applied with method appropriate to exterior wall. Use 1 in. (25 mm) Type S gypsum board screws 8 in. (203 mm) o.c. to edges and 2 in. (50 mm) o.c. to intermediate Z-channel flange. Insulate cavity with 24 × 1½ in. (610 X 38 mm) rigid foam.	
	40	8⅛ (206)	*Security Wall (15-Minute):* One base layer of 13-gage steel expanded metal mesh with nominal 1 × 2½ in. (25 × 63 mm) grid spacing under one layer of ¾ in. (19 mm) plywood applied to one side of 6 in. (152 mm) metal studs 8 in. (203 mm) o.c. with 1½ in. (38 mm) screws. One face layer of ⅝ in. (16 mm) Type X gypsum board applied to each side with 1 in. (25 mm) Type S gypsum board screws 12 in. (305 mm) o.c. Stagger joints 16 in. (406 mm) o.c. each layer and side.	
	52	10¾ (273)	*Cavity Wall:* One layer ⅝ in. (16 mm) Type X gypsum board applied to outside face of two rows of 1⅝ in. (41 mm) metal studs (air space 9½ in. (241 mm) between inside board faces) 24 in. (610 mm) o.c. with 1 in. (25 mm) Type S gypsum board screws 8 in. (203 mm) o.c. to edges and 12 in. (305 mm) o.c. to intermediate studs. Cross brace at third points vertically with ⅝ in. (16 mm) board gussets 9½ × 12 in. (241 × 305 mm). Use 3½ in. (88 mm) fiberglass insulation in cavity.	
	47	3½ (88)	*Prefinished Gypsum Wall Panels:* One layer, ½ in. (13 mm) Type X prefinished vinyl surface gypsum wall panels (prebowed) applied vertically at joints to each side of 2½ in. (63 mm) metal studs 24 in. (610 mm) o.c. with 1 in. (25 mm) Type S gypsum board screws 30 in. (762 mm) o.c. Attach to intermediate studs with ⅜ in. (9 mm) bead of adhesive. Attach at top and bottom with 1⅜ in. (34 mm) matching finish nails 12 in. (305 mm) o.c. Attach aluminum batten retainer to panels at studs with 1 in. (25 mm) Type S gypsum board screws 12 in. (305 mm) o.c. Install matching finish batten over retainers and 2 in. (50 mm) glass-fiber insulation in cavity. Stagger joints 24 in. (610 mm) o.c. each side.	
	45	5 (127)	*Prefinished Gypsum Wall Panels:* Base layer ½ in. (6 mm) regular gypsum board nailed to 2 × 4 (51 × 102 mm) wood studs 16 in. (406 mm) o.c. with 1⅜ in. (34 mm) 4d coated nails, 12 in. (305 mm) o.c., fire-stopped at midheight. Face layer ½ in. (13 mm) Type X prefinished vinyl surface gypsum wall panels (prebowed) applied vertically to each side with laminating compound and ⅞ in. (22 mm) gypsum board screws, 12 in. (305 mm) o.c. at top and bottom. Stagger joints at 24 in. (610 mm) o.c. each layer and side. Cover exposed fasteners with suitable molding.	
2-hour	50	5¾ (146)	*Water-Resistant Wall (One Side):* One layer ⅝ in. (16 mm) water-resistant gypsum board applied to wet side of 3⅝ in. (92 mm) 20-gage metal studs 16 in. (406 mm) o.c. with 1 in. (25 mm) Type S gypsum board screws 12 in. (305 mm) o.c. Opposite side, two layers ⅝ in. (16 mm) gypsum board installed vertically. Use 3 in. (76 mm) fiber insulation in cavity. Stagger joints 24 in. (610 mm) o.c. each layer and side. For walls not receiving direct and constant water flow. See "Tile Backer Panel" section of Gypsum Board Assemblies.	
	45	8¼ (209)	*Bullet-Resistant Wall (One Side):* Base layer of ¼ in. (6 mm) steel plate bolted to each side of steel tube framed wall with 4 × ¼ in. (101 × 6 mm) steel tube at top, bottom, and 4 ft (1,220 mm) o.c. horizontally. Two layers each side ⅝ in. (16 mm) Type X gypsum board on ⅞ in. (22 mm) furring channels 24 in. (610 mm) o.c. applied with 1 in. (25 mm) Type S gypsum board screws. Stagger joints 24 in. (610 mm) o.c. each layer and side.	

PARTITION ATTACHMENT (SCREW-ATTACHED)

STEEL STUD (2 1/2" MIN.)

METAL FURRING CHANNEL CLIP — 1 1/2" CHANNEL

FURRING CHANNEL

CORNER REINFORCEMENT

PARTITION CEILING RUNNER SCREW ATTACHED TO METAL FURRING CHANNEL

CONTINUOUS CEILING

WIRE TIE

HANGER

1 1/2" CHANNEL

METAL FURRING CHANNEL

FLEXIBLE DUST MEMBRANE

VINYL TRIM

METAL FURRING CHANNEL

GYPSUM BOARD

EXTERIOR WALL

EXTERIOR WALL INTERSECTION

CEILING ASSEMBLIES

SPECIAL CONDITIONS

- STRUCTURE ABOVE
- METAL RUNNER CHANNEL
- 5/8" GYPSUM BOARD
- 3/4" PLYWOOD SUBSTRATE; SECURE TO METAL STUDS AS REQUIRED
- METAL STUDS, SPACING AS REQUIRED TO SUPPORT PLYWOOD SUBSTRATE
- WALL BASE
- METAL RUNNER CHANNEL; FASTEN @ 2'-0" O.C., MAX.

Full-height plywood substrate enables the mounting of wall-hung objects.

EXHIBITION PARTITION

- 1/4" TEMPERED GLASS
- 3 1/2"
- 5/8"
- 2"
- 3 1/2"
- SEE ELEVATION FOR DIMENSION
- CONTINUOUS BLOCKING
- 3 1/2" METAL FRAMING
- 5/8" GYPSUM BOARD
- COUNTER WHERE OCCURS

A sloped sill discourages sitting or the placement of trash.

SLOPED SILL

- POWER ANCHOR
- SEALANT EACH SIDE
- UNDERSIDE OF STRUCTURE ABOVE
- METAL RUNNER CHANNEL; FASTEN @ 2'-0" O.C., MAX.
- 4"
- SCHEDULED CEILING
- METAL STUDS @ 2'-0" O.C., MAX.
- 5/8" GYPSUM BOARD
- LEAD LINING LAMINATED TO 1/2" GYPSUM BOARD
- 5/8" GYPSUM BOARD TWO LAYERS
- WALL BASE
- SEALANT EACH SIDE
- POWER ANCHOR
- VARIES
- 5 1/2"
- 7 7/8"

Lead-lined partitions are used in medical and dental facilities, where exposure to X rays is a concern. Review construction detail with the manufacturer of metal studs to determine proper gage and spacing of metal studs for support of lead sheeting.

Double thickness of gypsum board adds durability. Review wall construction with consulting physicist, who will determine thickness required for lead sheeting and for any shielding required for floor and structure above. Protect any openings in wall with lead sheeting to prevent scatter of X rays, including door frames and receptacles/junction boxes.

LEAD-LINED PARTITION

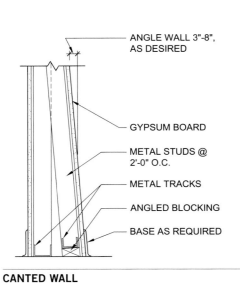

- ANGLE WALL 3"-8", AS DESIRED
- GYPSUM BOARD
- METAL STUDS @ 2'-0" O.C.
- METAL TRACKS
- ANGLED BLOCKING
- BASE AS REQUIRED

CANTED WALL

- PAINT GRADE WOOD TOPCAP
- 1/2" X 1/2" PREFORMED VINYL REVEAL
- CORNER REINFORCEMENT
- 1/2" BLOCKING
- WRAP TOP WITH GYPSUM BOARD
- GYPSUM BOARD ON STUDS @ 2'-0" O.C.
- PARTITION RETURN FOR LATERAL SUPPORT AT END; 3'-0" MAX. RECOMMENDED AT UNATTACHED END
- BASE AS SCHEDULED
- 54" MAX. UNBRACED HEIGHT

PARTIAL-HEIGHT PARTITION

- 1 1/4" APPLIED GYPSUM BOARD PANEL
- PAINTED REVEAL
- 2"
- METAL CORNER BEAD
- 5/8"
- 5/8"

Reveals may be inserted into walls using standard components of varying sizes and configurations.

GYPSUM BOARD PARTITION REVEAL

Jane Clark, AIA; Zimmer Gunzul Frasca Partnership; Seattle, Washington
John Hogshead, AIA; Perkins & Will; Atlanta, Georgia
Justin Estoque; Smithsonian Institution; Washington, D.C.
Douglas Flandro; Rhode Island School of Design; Providence, Rhode Island
Thomas R. Krizmanic, AIA; Studios Architecture; Washington, D.C.

MAXIMUM PARTITION HEIGHTS

TYPICAL LIMITING HEIGHTS: INTERIOR PARTITIONS

STUD WIDTH	STUD SPACING	ALLOWABLE DEFLECTION	PARTITION, ONE LAYER	PARTITION, TWO LAYERS	FURRING, ONE LAYER

25-gage stud (.0179 in. min.) (0.455 mm))

STUD WIDTH	STUD SPACING	ALLOWABLE DEFLECTION	PARTITION, ONE LAYER	PARTITION, TWO LAYERS	FURRING, ONE LAYER
1⅝ (41)	16 (406)	L/120	10 ft 9 in. (3,277)f	10 ft 9 in. (3,277)d	10 ft 3 in. (3,124)d
		L/240	9 ft 6 in. (2,896)d	10 ft 6 in. (3,201)d	8 ft 3 in. (2,515)d
		L/360	8 ft 3 in. (2,515)d	9 ft 0 in. (2,743)d	7 ft 3 in. (2,210)d
	24 (610)	L/120	8 ft 9 in. (2,667)f	8 ft 9 in. (2,667)f	8 ft 9 in. (2,667)f
		L/240	8 ft 3 in. (2,515)d	8 ft 9 in. (2,667)f	7 ft 3 in. (2,210)d
		L/360	7 ft 3 in. (2,210)d	8 ft 0 in. (2,438)d	6 ft 3 in. (1,905)d
2½ (64)	16 (406)	L/120	13 ft 9 in. (4,191)f	13 ft 9 in. (4,191)f	13 ft 9 in. (4,191)d*
		L/240	12 ft 6 in. (3,810)d	13 ft 6 in. (4,115)d	11 ft 0 in. (3,353)d
		L/360	10 ft 9 in. (3,277)d	11 ft 9 in. (3,581)d	9 ft 9 in. (2,972)d
	24 (610)	L/120	11 ft 3 in. (3,429)f	11 ft 3 in. (3,429)f	11 ft 3 in. (3,429)f
		L/240	10 ft 9 in. (3,277)d	11 ft 3 in. (3,429)f	9 ft 9 in. (2,972)d
		L/360	9 ft 6 in. (2,896)d	10 ft 3 in. (3,124)d	8 ft 6 in. (2,591)d
3⅝ (92)	16 (406)	L/120	16 ft 9 in. (5,105)f	16 ft 9 in. (5,105)f	16 ft 9 in. (5,105)f*
		L/240	16 ft 0 in. (4,877)d	16 ft 9 in. (5,105)f	14 ft 6 in. (4,420)d*
		L/360	14 ft 0 in. (4,267)d	14 ft 9 in. (4,496)d	12 ft 9 in. (3,886)d*
	24 (610)	L/120	13 ft 6 in. (4,115)f	13 ft 6 in. (4,115)f	13 ft 6 in. (4,115)f*
		L/240	13 ft 6 in. (4,115)f	13 ft 6 in. (4,115)f	12 ft 9 in. (3,886)d*
		L/360	12 ft 3 in. (3,734)d	13 ft 0 in. (3,962)d	11 ft 0 in. (3,353)d
4 (102)	16 (406)	L/120	17 ft 3 in. (5,208)f	17 ft 3 in. (5,208)f	17 ft 3 in. (5,208)f*
		L/240	17 ft 3 in. (5,208)d	17 ft 3 in. (5,208)f	15 ft 9 in. (4,801)d*
		L/360	15 ft 0 in. (4,572)d	15 ft 9 in. (4,801)d	13 ft 9 in. (4,191)d*
	24 (610)	L/120	14 ft 3 in. (4,343)f	14 ft 3 in. (4,343)f	14 ft 3 in. (4,343)f*
		L/240	14 ft 3 in. (4,343)f	14 ft 3 in. (4,343)f	13 ft 9 in. (4,191)d*
		L/360	13 ft 0 in. (3,962)d	13 ft 9 in. (4,191)d	12 ft 0 in. (3,658)d
6 (152)	16 (406)	L/120	20 ft 0 in. (6,096)f	20 ft 0 in. (6,096)f	20 ft 0 in. (6,096)f*
		L/240	20 ft 0 in. (6,096)f	20 ft 0 in. (6,096)f	20 ft 0 in. (6,096)f*
		L/360	20 ft 0 in. (6,096)f	20 ft 0 in. (6,096)f	18 ft 9 in. (5,715)f*
	24 (610)	L/120	15 ft 0 in. (4,572)v	15 ft 0 in. (4,572)v	15 ft 0 in. (4,572)v*
		L/240	15 ft 0 in. (4,572)v	15 ft 0 in. (4,572)v	15 ft 0 in. (4,572)v*
		L/360	15 ft 0 in. (4,572)v	15 ft 0 in. (4,572)v	15 ft 0 in. (4,572)v*

*Studs exceeding 12 ft (3.6 m) in height require a mid-height anchor to the exterior wall.

The Typical Limiting Heights tables are based primarily on the suggested minimum physical and structural properties (I^x and S^x).

Physical and structural properties may vary by region and manufacturer. Request actual physical and structural property data from your local steel framing manufacturer.

Limiting criteria: d—deflection, f—bending stress, v—end-reaction shear. Consult local code authority for limiting criteria.

Source: United States Gypsum Company SA923, Gypsum Board/Steel Framed Systems

TYPICAL LIMITING HEIGHTS: INTERIOR PARTITIONS

STUD WIDTH	STUD SPACING	ALLOWABLE DEFLECTION	PARTITION, ONE LAYER	PARTITION, TWO LAYERS	FURRING, ONE LAYER

22-gage stud (.0270 in. min.) (0.686 mm))

STUD WIDTH	STUD SPACING	ALLOWABLE DEFLECTION	PARTITION, ONE LAYER	PARTITION, TWO LAYERS	FURRING, ONE LAYER
2½ (64)	16 (406)	L/120	16 ft 6 in. (5,028)d	17 ft 0 in. (5,132)f	15 ft 3 in. (4,648)d*
		L/240	13 ft 0 in. (3,962)d	14 ft 0 in. (4,267)d	12 ft 0 in. (3,658)d
		L/360	11 ft 6 in. (3,505)d	12 ft 3 in. (3,734)d	10 ft 6 in. (3,200)d
	24 (610)	L/120	14 ft 0 in. (4,267)f	14 ft 0 in. (4,267)f	13 ft 3 in. (4,039)d*
		L/240	11 ft 6 in. (3,505)d	12 ft 3 in. (3,734)d	10 ft 6 in. (3,200)d
		L/360	10 ft 0 in. (3,048)d	10 ft 6 in. (3,200)d	9 ft 3 in. (2,819)d
3⅝ (920)	16 (406)	L/120	21 ft 9 in. (6,629)d	22 ft 0 in. (6,706)f	20 ft 3 in. (6,172)d*
		L/240	17 ft 3 in. (5,208)d	18 ft 0 in. (5,486)d	16 ft 0 in. (4,877)d*
		L/360	15 ft 0 in. (4,572)d	15 ft 9 in. (4,801)d	14 ft 0 in. (4,267)d*
	24 (610)	L/120	18 ft 0 in. (5,486)f	18 ft 0 in. (5,486)f	17 ft 9 in. (5,410)d*
		L/240	15 ft 0 in. (4,572)d	15 ft 9 in. (4,801)d	14 ft 0 in. (4,267)d*
		L/360	13 ft 0 in. (3,962)d	13 ft 9 in. (4,191)d	12 ft 3 in. (3,734)d*
4 (102)	16 (406)	L/120	23 ft 9 in. (7,087)f	23 ft 9 in. (7,087)f	21 ft 9 in. (6,629)d*
		L/240	18 ft 6 in. (5,639)d	19 ft 3 in. (5,868)d	17 ft 3 in. (5,258)d*
		L/360	16 ft 3 in. (4,953)d	16 ft 9 in. (5,105)d	15 ft 0 in. (4,572)d*
	24 (610)	L/120	19 ft 0 in. (5,791)f	19 ft 0 in. (5,791)f	19 ft 0 in. (5,791)f*
		L/240	16 ft 3 in. (4,953)d	16 ft 9 in. (5,105)d	15 ft 0 in. (4,572)d*
		L/360	14 ft 0 in. (4,267)d	14 ft 9 in. (4,496)d	13 ft 3 in. (4,039)d*
6 (152)	16 (406)	L/120	29 ft 0 in. (8,839)f	29 ft 0 in. (8,839)f	29 ft 0 in. (8,839)f*
		L/240	25 ft 3 in. (7,696)d	26 ft 0 in. (7,925)d	23 ft 9 in. (7,239)d*
		L/360	22 ft 0 in. (6,705)d	22 ft 9 in. (6,934)d	20 ft 9 in. (6,325)d*
	24 (610)	L/120	23 ft 6 in. (7,163)f	23 ft 6 in. (7,163)f	23 ft 6 in. (7,163)f*
		L/240	22 ft 0 in. (6,705)d	22 ft 9 in. (6,934)d	20 ft 9 in. (6,325)d*
		L/360	19 ft 3 in. (5,867)d	19 ft 9 in. (6,020)d	18 ft 3 in. (5,563)d*

*Studs exceeding 12 ft (3.6 m) in height require a mid-height anchor to the exterior wall.

The Typical Limiting Heights tables are based primarily on the suggested minimum physical and structural properties (I^x and S^x).

Physical and structural properties may vary by region and manufacturer. Request actual physical and structural property data from your local steel framing manufacturer.

Limiting criteria: d—deflection, f—bending stress, v—end-reaction shear. Consult local code authority for limiting criteria.

Source: United States Gypsum Company SA923, Gypsum Board/Steel Framed Systems

MAXIMUM PARTITION HEIGHTS

TYPICAL LIMITING HEIGHTS: INTERIOR PARTITIONS

STUD WIDTH	STUD SPACING	ALLOWABLE DEFLECTION	PARTITION, ONE LAYER	PARTITION, TWO LAYERS	FURRING, ONE LAYER
20-gage stud (.0270 in. min.) (0.686 mm))					
2½ (64)	16 (406)	L/120	17 ft 4 in. (5,283)f	17 ft 11 in. (5,461)f	16 ft 6 in. (5,029)d*
		L/240	13 ft 10 in. (4,216)d	16 ft 1 in. (4,902)d	13 ft 0 in. (3,963)d*
		L/360	12 ft 0 in. (3,658)d	14 ft 0 in. (4,267)d	11 ft 6 in. (3,505)d
	24 (610)	L/120	14 ft 7 in. (4,445)f	14 ft 7 in. (4,445)f	14 ft 6 in. (4,420)d*
		L/240	12 ft 0 in. (3,658)d	13 ft 5 in. (4,089)f	11 ft 6 in. (3,505)d
		L/360	10 ft 6 in. (3,200)d	12 ft 4 in. (3,759)d	10 ft 0 in. (3,048)d
3⅝ (92)	16 (406)	L/120	22 ft 7 in. (6,883)d	23 ft 8 in. (7,214)f	21 ft 9 in. (6,629)d*
		L/240	17 ft 11 in. (5,461)d	20 ft 2 in. (6,147)d	17 ft 3 in. (5,258)d*
		L/360	15 ft 7 in. (4,750)d	17 ft 8 in. (5,385)d	15 ft 0 in. (4,572)d*
	24 (610)	L/120	19 ft 4 in. (5,893)f	19 ft 4 in. (5,893)f	19 ft 0 in. (5,791)d*
		L/240	15 ft 7 in. (4,750)d	17 ft 8 in. (5,385)f	15 ft 0 in. (4,572)d*
		L/360	13 ft 8 in. (4,166)d	15 ft 6 in. (4,724)d	13 ft 3 in. (4,039)d*
4 (102)	16 (406)	L/120	24 ft 3 in. (7,391)d	25 ft 6 in. (7,772)d	23 ft 6 in. (7,163)d*
		L/240	19 ft 2 in. (5,842)d	21 ft 7 in. (6,579)d	18 ft 9 in. (5,715)d*
		L/360	16 ft 10 in. (5,131)d	18 ft 11 in. (5,766)d	16 ft 3 in. (4,953)d*
	24 (610)	L/120	20 ft 9 in. (6,325)d	20 ft 9 in. (6,325)f	20 ft 6 in. (6,248)d*
		L/240	16 ft 10 in. (5,131)d	18 ft 11 in. (5,766)d	16 ft 3 in. (4,953)d*
		L/360	14 ft 8 in. (4,470)d	16 ft 6 in. (5,029)d	14 ft 3 in. (4,343)d*
6 (152)	16 (406)	L/120	32 ft 11 in. (10,033)d	33 ft 11 in. (10,338)f	32 ft 3 in. (9,830)d*
		L/240	26 ft 1 in. (7,950)d	28 ft 6 in. (8,687)d	25 ft 6 in. (7,772)d*
		L/360	22 ft 10 in. (6,960)d	24 ft 11 in. (7,595)d	23 ft 3 in. (7,087)d*
	24 (610)	L/120	25 ft 3 in. (7,696)f	25 ft 3 in. (7,696)f	28 ft 0 in. (8,534)d*
		L/240	22 ft 10 in. (6,960)d	24 ft 11 in. (7,595)d	22 ft 3 in. (6,782)d*
		L/360	19 ft 11 in. (6,071)d	21 ft 10 in. (6,655)d	19 ft 6 in. (5,944)d*

Studs exceeding 12 ft (3.6 m) in height require a mid-height anchor to the exterior wall.

The Typical Limiting Heights tables are based primarily on the suggested minimum physical and structural properties (Ix and Sx).

Physical and structural properties may vary by region and manufacturer. Request actual physical and structural property data from your local steel framing manufacturer.

Limiting criteria: d—deflection, f—bending stress, v—end-reaction shear. Consult local code authority for limiting criteria.

Source: United States Gypsum Company SA923, Gypsum Board/Steel Framed Systems

TYPICAL LIMITING HEIGHTS: INTERIOR PARTITIONS

STUD WIDTH	STUD SPACING	ALLOWABLE DEFLECTION	PARTITION, ONE LAYER	PARTITION, TWO LAYERS	FURRING, ONE LAYER
20-gage stud (.0341 in. min.) (0.866 mm))					
3⅝ (92)	16 (406)	L/120	24 ft 0 in. (7,315)d	25 ft 0 in. (7,620)d	23 ft 0 in. (7,010)d*
		L/240	19 ft 0 in. (5,791)d	19 ft 9 in. (6,020)d	18 ft 3 in. (5,563)d*
		L/360	16 ft 9 in. (5,105)d	17 ft 3 in. (5,258)d	16 ft 0 in. (4,877)d*
	24 (610)	L/120	21 ft 0 in. (6,401)d	21 ft 9 in. (6,629)d	20 ft 3 in. (6,172)d*
		L/240	16 ft 9 in. (5,105)d	17 ft 3 in. (5,258)d	16 ft 0 in. (4,877)d*
		L/360	14 ft 6 in. (4,420)d	15 ft 0 in. (4,572)d	14 ft 0 in. (4,267)d*
4 (102)	16 (406)	L/120	25 ft 9 in. (7,849)d	26 ft 9 in. (8,153)d	24 ft 9 in. (7,544)d*
		L/240	20 ft 6 in. (6,248)d	21 ft 3 in. (6,477)d	19 ft 9 in. (6,020)d*
		L/360	18 ft 0 in. (5,486)d	18 ft 6 in. (5,639)d	17 ft 3 in. (5,258)d
	24 (610)	L/120	22 ft 6 in. (6,858)d	23 ft 3 in. (7,087)d	21 ft 6 in. (6,553)d*
		L/240	18 ft 0 in. (5,486)d	18 ft 6 in. (5,639)d	17 ft 3 in. (5,258)d*
		L/360	15 ft 9 in. (4,801)d	16 ft 3 in. (4,953)d	15 ft 0 in. (4,572)d*

Studs exceeding 12 ft (3.6 m) in height require a mid-height anchor to the exterior wall.

The Typical Limiting Heights tables are based primarily on the suggested minimum physical and structural properties (Ix and Sx).

Physical and structural properties may vary by region and manufacturer. Request actual physical and structural property data from your local steel framing manufacturer.

Limiting criteria: d—deflection, f—bending stress, v—end-reaction shear. Consult local code authority for limiting criteria.

Source: United States Gypsum Company SA923, Gypsum Board/Steel Framed Systems

MAXIMUM PARTITION HEIGHTS BASED ON STUD DEPTH

Stud depth in. (mm)	Gypsum board layers	STRUCTURAL CRITERIA			
		L/120 AT 5 LB/FT[1] SPACING, FT-IN. (MM)		L/240 AT 5 LB/FT[1] SPACING, FT-IN. (MM)	
		16 in.[2] (406)	24 in.[2, 3] (610)	16 in.[2] (406)	24 in.[2] (610)
1⅝ (41.3)	One	11 ft (3,353)	10 ft (3,048)	8 ft 9 in. (2,667)	7 ft 11 in. (2,413)
	Two		12 ft 4 in. (3,759)		9 ft 9 in. (2,972)
2½ (63.5)	One	14 ft 8 in. (4,470)	13 ft 5 in. (4,089)	11 ft 8 in. (3,556)	10 ft 8 in. (3,251)
	Two		15 ft 10 in. (4,826)		12 ft 7 in. (3,835)
3⅝ (92.1)	One	19 ft 5 in. (5,918)	17 ft 3 in. (5,258)	15 ft 5 in. (4,699)	13 ft 8 in. (4,166)
	Two		19 ft 5 in. (5,918)		15 ft 5 in. (4,699)
4 (101.6)	One	20 ft 8 in. (6,299)	18 ft 5 in. (5,613)	16 ft 5 in. (5,004)	14 ft 7 in. (4,445)
	Two		20 ft 8 in. (6,299)		16 ft 5 in. (5,004)

[1]L/120 refers to the maximum allowable deflection based on the length, L, of the stud. Partition heights are the height from the bottom runner to the top runner, not the finished ceiling height.

[2]On center.

[3]Figures shown in bold type are the most common.

Source: ASTM C754, Specification for Installation of Steel Framing Members to Receive Screw-Attached Gypsum Panel Products. Copyright ASTM INTERNATIONAL. Reprinted with permission.

WOOD-FRAME GYPSUM PARTITIONS

Wood studs are not commonly used in commercial construction, as they can shrink after the gypsum panel installation, which can cause nails to loosen and project from the finished surface of the panel, called *nail popping*. This can be minimized by using dried framing lumber and the shortest possible ring-shank nail appropriate for the application. Screws tend to "pop" less than nails.

CORNER REINFORCEMENT

2 X 4 WOOD STUDS AT 2'-0" O.C.

CEILING CONDITION

5/8" TYPE X GYPSUM BOARD

4 7/8"

BASE AS REQUIRED

2 X 4 WOOD PLATE

FLOOR CONDITION

ONE-HOUR FIRE RATING
STC range 35 TO 39.

Base layer ⅝ in. (16 mm) Type X gypsum board applied at right angles to 2 × 10 in. (51 × 254 mm) wood joists with 1 in. (25 mm) Type S gypsum board screws 16 in. (406 mm) o.c. Resilient furring channels spaced 24 in. (610 mm) o.c. and nailed through baseboard into and at right angles to joists. Face layer of ⅝ in. (16 mm) same-type board screwed to furring channel with same-type screws. Tongue-and-groove sub- and finish floor.

TWO-HOUR—DOUBLE-LAYER RESILIENT (WOOD FRAME)

CORNER REINFORCEMENT

PERIMETER SEALANT

5 1/8" TO 5 7/8"

2 X 4 WOOD STUDS AT 2'-0" O.C.

CEILING CONDITION

1/2" OR 5/8" TYPE X GYPSUM BOARD APPLIED TO 1/4" OR 3/8" GYPSUM BOARD

BASE

2 X 4 WOOD PLATE

SEALANT

FLOOR CONDITION

ONE-HOUR FIRE RATING
STC range 45 TO 49.

Proprietary Type X gypsum board electrical radiant heating panels (⅝ in. (16 mm)) attached to resilient furring channels spaced 24 in. (610 mm) o.c. installed to 2 × 10 in. (51 × 254 mm) wood joists 16 in. (406 mm) o.c. 3½ in. (89 mm) glass-fiber insulation friction fit in joist space. Wood floor of nominal 1 in. (25 mm) tongue and groove or ½ in. (13 mm) plywood subfloor and nominal 1 in. (25 mm) tongue and groove or ⅝ in. (16 mm) plywood finish floor.

STC range 45 to 49.

ONE-HOUR—ELECTRIC RADIANT HEAT PANEL

SEALANT

5/8" TYPE X GYP. BD.

FIRE STOP

STAGGERED 2 X 4 WOOD STUDS AT 16" O.C.

CEILING CONDITION

10 3/4"

SOUND INSULATION

FIRE STOP

BASE

2 X 4 WOOD PLATE

SEALANT

FLOOR CONDITION

TWO-HOUR FIRE RATING
STC range 55 TO 59.

WOOD-FRAME, FIRE-RATED WALL SECTIONS

ONE-HOUR FIRE RATING
Type X gypsum board or veneer base (⅝ in. (16 mm)) applied to wood joists 16 in. (406 mm) o.c. Joists supporting 1 in. (25 mm) nominal wood sub- and finish floor or ⅝ in. (16 mm) plywood finished floor with long edges tongue and groove and ½ in. (13 mm) perpendicular to joists with joints staggered.

STC range 35 to 39.

ONE-HOUR FIRE RATING
Type X gypsum board or veneer base (½ in. (13 mm)) applied to gypsum-board-resilient furring channels 24 in. (610 mm) o.c. and nailed to wood joists 16 in. (406 mm) o.c. Wood joists supporting 1 in. (25 mm) nominal tongue and groove wood sub- and finish floor, or ⅝ in. (16 mm) plywood finished floor with long edges tongue and groove and ½ in. (13 mm) interior plywood with exterior glue subfloor perpendicular to joists with joints staggered.

STC range 40 to 44.

ONE-HOUR FIRE RATING
Type X gypsum board or veneer base (½ in. (13 mm)) applied to resilient furring channels. Resilient channels applied 24 in. (610 mm) o.c. to wood joists 16 in. o.c. (406 mm). Wood joists support ½ in. (13 mm) plywood subfloor and 1½ in. (38 mm) cellular or lightweight concrete over felt. 3½ in. (89 mm) glass-fiber batts in joist spaces. Sound-tested with carpet and pad over ⅝ in. (16 mm) plywood subfloor.

STC range 60 to 64.

WOOD-FRAME FLOOR/CEILING ASSEMBLIES

CONTROL JOINTS

Control joints are deliberately created lines of weakness along which cracking will occur. Control joints alleviate the stress that would otherwise cause random cracking as materials shrink, so that cracking is "controlled" to form an orderly pattern of straight lines.

Control joints should be located at geometric discontinuities, such as corners, changes in the height or width of a surface, or openings. In long or large surfaces, control joints should be spaced at intervals that will relieve the expected stresses in the material before those stresses cause damage to the gypsum board.

CONTROL JOINT

GYPSUM BOARD

METAL STUD

COMPRESSIVE GASKET

SEALANT

CONTROL JOINT

WALL CONTROL JOINT

WIRE TIE

CONTROL JOINT

JOINT COMPOUND

CEILING CONTROL JOINT

WOOD-FRAME GYPSUM BOARD ASSEMBLIES

WOOD-FRAME GYPSUM BOARD PARTITIONS

FIRE RATING	STC	WALL THICKNESS IN. (MM)	CONSTRUCTION DESCRIPTION	WALL SECTIONS
1-hour	30–34	4⅞ (124)	One layer ½ in. (13 mm) Type X veneer base nailed to each side of 2 × 4 in. (51 × 102 mm) wood studs 16 in. (406 mm) o.c. with 5d coated nails 8 in. (203 mm) o.c. Minimum ³⁄₃₂ in. (2 mm) gypsum veneer plaster. Joints staggered vertically 16 in. (406 mm) and horizontal joints each side at 12 in. (305 mm).	
		4⅞ (124)	One layer ⅝ in. (16 mm) Type X gypsum board or veneer base nailed to each side of 2 × 4 in. (51 × 102 mm) wood studs 16 in. (406 mm) o.c. with 6d coated nails 7 in. (178 mm) o.c. Stagger joints 24 in. (610 mm) on each side.	
	35–39	5⅛ (130)	Two layers ⅜ in. (9 mm) regular gypsum board or veneer base nailed to each side of 2 × 4 in. (51 × 102 mm) wood studs 16 in. (406 mm) o.c. First layer attached with 4d coated nails, second layer applied with laminating compound and nailed with 5d coated nails 8 in. (203 mm) o.c. Stagger joints 16 in. (406 mm) o.c. each side.	
	45–49	5⅜ (137)	Base layer ⅜ in. (9 mm) regular gypsum board or veneer base nailed to each side of 2 × 4 in. (51 × 102 mm) wood studs 16 in. (406 mm) o.c. Face layer ½ in. (13 mm) (same as base layer). Use 5d coated nails 24 in. (610 mm) o.c. for base layer and 8d coated nails 12 in. (305 mm) o.c. to edge and 24 in. (610 mm) o.c. to intermediate studs. Stagger joints 16 in. (406 mm) o.c. each layer and side.	
		5⅞ (149)	Base layer ½ in. (13 mm) wood fiberboard to each side of 2 × 4 in. (51 × 102 mm) wood studs 16 in. (406 mm) o.c. with 5d coated nails 24 in. (610 mm) o.c. on vertical joints and 16 in. (406 mm) o.c. to top and bottom plates. Face layer ⅝ in. (16 mm) Type X gypsum board or veneer base applied to each side with laminating compound and nailed with 8d coated nails 24 in. (610 mm) o.c. on vertical joints and 16 in. (406 mm) o.c. to top and bottom plates. Stagger joints 24 in. (610 mm) o.c. each layer and side.	
		5⅞ (149)	Both sides resilient channels 24 in. (610 mm) o.c. attached with GWB 54 gypsum board nails to each side of 2 × 4 in. (51 × 102 mm) wood studs 16 in. (406 mm) o.c. One layer ⅝ in. (16 mm) Type X gypsum board or veneer base attached with 1 in. (25 mm) Type S gypsum board screws 12 in. (305 mm) o.c. to each side and vertical joints back-blocked. GWB filler strips along floor and ceiling both sides. Stagger joints 24 in. (610 mm) o.c. each side.	
	50–54	5⅜ (137)	Base layer ¼ in. (6 mm) proprietary gypsum board applied to each side of 2 × 4 in. (51 × 102 mm) wood studs 16 in. (406 mm) o.c. with 4d coated nails 12 in. (305 mm) o.c. Face layer ⅝ in. (16 mm) Type X gypsum board or veneer base applied with laminating compound and nailed with 6d coated nails 16 in. (406 mm) o.c. to each side. 1½ in. (38 mm) mineral fiber insulation in cavity. Stagger joints 24 in. (610 mm) o.c. each side.	
		5⅜ (137)	One side resilient channel 24 in (610 mm) o.c. with 1¼ in. (32 mm) Type S gypsum board screws to 2 × 4 in. (51 × 102 mm) wood studs 16 in. (406 mm) o.c. Both sides ⅝ in. (16 mm) gypsum board or veneer base attached to resilient channel with 1 in. (25 mm) Type S gypsum board screws 12 in. (305 mm) o.c. and GWB to stud with 1¼ in. (3 mm) Type W gypsum board screws. 1½ in. (38 mm) mineral fiber insulation in cavity. Stagger joints 48 in. (1,220 mm) on each side.	
	60–64	6⅞ (175)	One side resilient channel 24 in. (610 mm) o.c. attached with 1 in. (25 mm) Type S gypsum board screws to 2 × 4 in. (51 × 102 mm) wood studs 16 in. (406 mm) o.c. Two layers of ⅝ in. (16 mm) Type X gypsum board or veneer base. First layer attached with 1 in. (25 mm) Type S gypsum board screws, second layer applied with laminating compound. Other side one layer each of ⅝ in. (16 mm) and ½ in. (13 mm) gypsum board or veneer base plus top ⅜ in. (9.5 mm) gypsum board applied with laminating compound. Use 5d coated nails 32 in. (813 mm) o.c. for base, 8d for ½ in. (13 mm) center layer, 2 in. (51 mm) glass fiber insulation in cavity. Stagger all joints 16 in. (406 mm) o.c.	
	40–44	6⅛ (156)	Two layers ⅝ in. (16 mm) Type X gypsum board or veneer base applied to each side of 2 × 4 in. (51 × 102 mm) wood studs 24 in. (610 mm) o.c. Use 6d coated nails 24 in. (610 mm) o.c. for base layer and 8d coated nails 8 in. (203 mm) o.c. for face layer. Stagger joints 24 in. (610 mm) o.c. for each layer and side.	
2-hour	50–54	8 (203)	Two layers ⅝ in. (16 mm) Type X gypsum board or veneer base applied to each side of 2 × 4 in. (51 × 102 mm) wood studs 16 in. (406 mm) o.c. staggered 8 in. (203 mm) o.c. on 2 × 6 in. (51 × 152 mm) wood plates. Use 6d coated nails 24 in. (610 mm) o.c. for base layer and 8d coated nails for face layer. Stagger vertical joints 16 in. (406 mm) o.c. each layer and side.	
	55–59	10¾ (273)	Two layers ⅝ in. (16 mm) Type X gypsum board or veneer base applied to each side of double row of 2 × 4 in. (51 × 102 mm) wood studs 16 in. (406 mm) o.c. on separate plates 1 in. (25 mm) apart. Use 6d coated nails 24 in. (610 mm) o.c. for base layer and 8d coated nails for face layer. 3½ in. (89 mm) glass-fiber insulation in cavity. Stagger joints 16 in. (406 mm) o.c. each layer and side. GWB fire stop continuous in spaces between plates.	

Ted Kollaja, AIA; lauckgroup; Dallas, Texas
Lohan Caprile Goettsch Architects; Chicago, Illinois
Andy Adams; Anshen+Allen, Architects; San Francisco, California
Jim Johnson; Wrightson, Johnson, Haddon & Williams, Inc.; Dallas, Texas
MASTERSPEC®; published by ARCOM; Salt Lake City, Utah, and Alexandria, Virginia

GYPSUM BOARD REVEAL DETAILS

CORNER BEAD

3/4"

5/8"

3/4" H X 5/8" D REVEAL WITH PAINTED WOOD BLOCKING SCRIBED TO WALL

LATERAL FILE CABINET

COORDINATE HEIGHT OF OPENING WITH FURNITURE DEALER

CONTINUOUS WOOD BLOCKING

SHIM TO MAKE CABINET LEVEL

3/4" H X 3/4" D REVEAL, WITH PAINTED WOOD BLOCKING

BASE, DOOR JAMB, AND FILE CABINET ALCOVE REVEAL DETAILS

(A) **FILE CABINET ALCOVE—SECTION**

DOUBLE-LAYER GYPSUM BOARD

METAL WALL FRAMING AND FLOOR CHANNEL

CASING BEAD

WOOD BASE

FLOORING

(B) **WOOD WALL BASE WITH REVEAL**

GYPSUM BOARD

WOOD SILL

CASING BEAD

REVEAL

FLOORING

(B) **NO WALL BASE WITH REVEAL**

REVEAL WALL BASE DETAILS

WIDTH OF FILE CABINETS PLUS 1 1/2" FOR REVEALS PLUS 1/8" MIN. TOLERANCE PER FILE CABINET

COORDINATE WIDTH OF OPENING WITH FURNITURE DEALER

SECTION THROUGH ALCOVE (A)

FILE CABINET ALCOVE—ELEVATION

TAPE AND JOINT COMPOUND

APPLIED GYPSUM BOARD

METAL STUDS

Z-EXTRUDED ALUMINUM REVEAL

BLOCKING

PAINT AS SCHEDULED

1/8" SHIM SPACE

DOOR SILENCER

DOOR STOP ROUTED INTO FRAME

FINISH NAIL SET AND FILLED, TYP.

(C) **WOOD FRAME DETAIL**

TAPE AND JOINT COMPOUND

METAL STUDS

APPLIED GYPSUM BOARD

Z-EXTRUDED ALUMINUM REVEAL

PAINT AS SCHEDULED

DOOR SILENCER

FULLY GROUTED METAL FRAME

(C) **HOLLOW METAL FRAME WITH TWO LAYERS OF GYPSUM BOARD DETAIL**

TAPE AND JOINT COMPOUND

METAL STUDS

APPLIED GYPSUM BOARD

Z-EXTRUDED ALUMINUM REVEAL

PAINT AS SCHEDULED

DOOR SILENCER

FULLY GROUTED METAL FRAME

(C) **HOLLOW METAL FRAME WITH ONE LAYER OF GYPSUM BOARD DETAIL**

REVEAL DOOR JAMB DETAILS

Sarah Bader; Gensler; Chicago, Illinois

TILE-SETTING ACCESSORIES

EDGE PROTECTION

TRANSITION BETWEEN FLOOR COVERINGS OF DIFFERENT HEIGHTS

TRANSITION BETWEEN FLOOR COVERINGS OF SAME HEIGHT

DECORATIVE JOINT

VARIABLE TRANSITION BETWEEN FLOOR COVERINGS OF DIFFERENT HEIGHTS

DECORATIVE JOINT

EDGE PROTECTION AND TRANSITION PROFILES FOR FLOORS

OUTSIDE CORNER PROTECTION AND DECORATION

DECORATIVE PROFILE

OUTSIDE CORNER PROTECTION

FINISHING AND EDGE PROTECTION FOR WALLS

EDGE PROFILE FOR COUNTERTOPS OR STAIRS

SLIP-RESISTANT STAIR NOSING

SLIP-RESISTANT STAIR NOSING WITH REPLACEABLE THERMOPLASTIC TREAD

STAIR NOSING PROFILES

CONTROL JOINT IN THINSET INSTALLATION

EXPANSION JOINT WITH RIGID PVC SIDE SECTIONS

EXPANSION JOINT WITH EDGE PROTECTION

EXPANSION AND CONTROL JOINT PROFILES

CERAMIC TILE

Ceramic tile is fabricated from clay or a mixture of clay and ceramic materials. Natural clay is most commonly used, but porcelain is also available. Porcelain tile is fine-grained and smooth. It can be formed into sharply detailed designs. Tile dimensions are typically nominal. Refer to manufacturer's data for specific tile and trim piece dimensions.

TILE COMPOSITION AND GLAZE

Ceramic tile is made from either natural clay or porcelain, and is glazed or unglazed.

- *Porcelain tile* is a ceramic mosaic or paver tile generally made by the dust-pressed method. It is dense, impervious, fine-grained, and smooth with a sharply formed face.
- *Natural clay tile* is a ceramic mosaic or paver tile with a distinctive, slightly textured appearance. It is made by the dust-pressed or plastic method from clays that have a dense body.
- *Glazed tile* has an impervious facial finish of ceramic materials that is fused to the body of the tile. The body may be nonvitreous, semivitreous, vitreous, or impervious.
- *Unglazed tile* is a hard, dense tile of uniform composition that derives color and texture from the materials used in its fabrication.

TILE TYPES

There are a variety of tile types, including ceramic mosaic, quarry, paver, decorative, mounted, and conductive tile.

Ceramic Mosaic Tile

Ceramic mosaic tile is formed either by the dust-pressed or the plastic method. Usually ¼- to ⅜-in. (6- to 9.5-mm) thick with a facial area of less than 6 sq in. (39 sq cm), it may be made of either porcelain or natural clay and may be plain or have an abrasive mixture throughout.

Quarry Tile

Quarry tile is glazed or unglazed tile made by the extrusion process from natural clay or shale. It usually has a facial area of 6 sq in. (39 sq cm) or more. Quarry tile may be specified with an abrasive grit embedded in the surface for use in areas where slip resistance is a concern.

Paver Tile

Paver tile is glazed or unglazed porcelain or natural clay tile formed by the dust-pressed method with a facial area of 6 sq in. (39 sq cm) or more.

Decorative Thin-Wall Tile

Decorative thin-wall tile is a glazed tile with a thin body that is usually nonvitreous. It is suitable for interior decorative residential use when breaking strength is not a requirement.

Mounted Tile

Mounted tile is assembled into units or sheets to facilitate handling and installation. Tile may be face-mounted, back-mounted, or edge-mounted. Material applied to the face of the tile is usually easily removed, but material bonded to the back is integrated to the tile installation.

Conductive Tile

Conductive tile has specific properties of electrical conductivity but retains other normal physical properties of tile.

WATER ABSORPTION OF CERAMIC TILE

TYPE	WATER ABSORPTION	CERAMIC MATERIAL	USE
Nonvitreous	More than 7.0%	Natural clay	Not for use in continually wet locations
Semivitreous	More than 3.9%, but not more than 7.0%	Natural clay	Not for use in continually wet locations
Vitreous	0.5%–3.0%	Natural clay	For use in continually wet locations
Impervious	0.5% or less	Porcelain	For use in continually wet locations; superior wear resistance

ANSI A 137.1, Specification for Ceramic Tile, quantifies the four levels of water absorption for tile. The density and porosity of the tile determine its capability to absorb moisture. In general, the lower the water absorption level, the better the stain resistance of the tile.

WALL TILE TRIM SHAPES

BULLNOSES FOR THICKSET INSTALLATIONS

BULLNOSES FOR THINSET INSTALLATIONS   **COVE BASE**

SANITARY COVE BASES (ROUND TOP)   **BEADS**

CERAMIC MOSAIC TILE TRIM SHAPES

STRETCHER

OUTSIDE CORNERS

INSIDE CORNERS

TILE INSTALLATION

There are two basic steps in tile installation: setting and grouting. Setting fixes the tile to the substrate with mortar or adhesive. Grouting fills in the spaces between the tiles, binding them into a continuous surface. Tile, mortar, and grout selection are interdependent.

Thickset Installation

Thickset installations use portland cement. A mortar bed, ¾- to 2-in. (19- to 51-mm) thick, is laid. Accurate floor slopes to drains can be installed, and reinforcement with metal mesh or waterproof membranes is possible. Waterproof membranes are flexible sheets or liquids that cure to a seamless membrane and are used in applications that are regularly or continually exposed to water. Both thickset and thinset installations can incorporate waterproof membranes.

Thinset Installation

Thinset installations are most popular (accounting for approximately 90% of installations in the United States) and can be as thin as ³⁄₃₂ in. (2 mm). All methods other than conventional portland cement applications are considered thinset. Bonding materials include dryset mortar, latex portland cement mortar, organic adhesive, epoxy mortar or adhesive, and modified epoxy emulsion mortar. Thinset application requires a continuous, stable, and undamaged surface.

Cementitious backerboards are sometimes used as an underlayment for thinset installations. Cementitious backerboards are made of portland cement or treated gypsum and lightweight aggregate, and are designed to provide a water-resistant base for ceramic tile installations regularly exposed to water; for example, a shower surround.

MORTAR

Mortars are categorized as cementitious and noncementitious. Adhesives are also popular for use in fixing tiles to the substrate.

Cementitious Mortars

Portland cement mortar is a mixture of portland cement and sand (for floors) or lime (for walls) used for thick-bed installation.

Dryset mortar is a mixture of portland cement with sand and additives, imparting water retention that eliminates the need to soak tiles.

Latex portland cement mortar is a mixture similar to dryset, but with latex (an emulsion of polymer particles in water) added to replace all or part of the water in the mortar. It provides better adhesion, density, and impact strength than dryset mortar and is more flexible and resistant to frost damage.

SETTING MATERIALS

TYPE	DESCRIPTION	FEATURES
Cementitious		
Portland Cement Mortar	Portland cement and sand, in proportions of 1:5 for floors; portland cement, sand, and lime, in proportions of 1:5:½ to 1:7:1 for walls	Most surfaces, ordinary installations
Dryset Mortar	Portland cement with sand and additives imparting water retentivity, which is used as a bond coat for setting tile	Thinset installations
Latex-Portland Cement Mortar	Portland cement, sand, and special latex additive, which is used as a bond coat for setting tile	Latex additives improve adhesion, reduce water absorption, and provide greater bond strength and resistance to shock and impact. Required for large-unit porcelain-bodied tile.
Noncementitious		
Epoxy Mortar	Epoxy resin and epoxy hardeners	Chemical-resistant
Modified Epoxy Emulsion Mortars	Emulsified epoxy resins and hardeners with portland cement and silica sand	High bond strength; little or no shrinkage; not chemical-resistant
Furan Resin Mortar	Furan resin and furan hardeners	Chemical-resistant
Epoxy Adhesives	Epoxy resin and epoxy hardeners	High bond strength and ease of application; not optimal chemical resistance
Organic Adhesive	For interior use only; ready to use (no addition of liquid); cures by evaporation	Not suitable for continuously wet applications or temperatures exceeding 140°F

Noncementitious Mortars

Epoxy mortar is a two-part mixture (resin and hardener with silica filler) used where chemical resistance is important. It has high bond strength and high resistance to impact. This mortar and furan mortar are the only two types that can be recommended for use over steel plates.

Modified epoxy emulsion mortars are similar to epoxy mortars. This mixture contains a resin and hardener along with portland cement and sand. Although it is not as chemically resistant as epoxy mortar, it binds well. Compared with mortar created from portland cement exclusively, it allows little or no shrinkage.

Furan mortars are two-part mixtures, composed of furan resin and hardener. Excellent for chemical-resistant uses, they tolerate high temperatures up to 350°F (177°C). *Epoxy adhesive* is a mixture similar to epoxy mortar in bonding capability, but it is not as chemical- or solvent-resistant.

Adhesives

Organic adhesives are one-part mastic mixtures that require no mixing. They remain somewhat flexible (as compared with portland cement mortar) and have good bond strength, but should not be used for exterior or wet applications.

Grout

Grout is used to fill joints between tiles and is selected with a compatible mortar. Grout is either a portland-cement-based mixture or a mixture of other compounds to enhance its performance or ease its installation. The type and size of tile, service level, climatic conditions, tile spacing, and individual manufacturer's recommendations are factors that should be considered when selecting grout.

Portland-cement-based grout is a mixture of portland cement and sand (for floors) or lime (for walls) and is used for thickset installations. Portland-cement-based grouts include commercial portland cement grout, sand-portland, cement grout, dryset grout, and latex portland cement grout.

Nonportland-cement-based grouts include solid epoxy, furan, silicone, and mastic grouts. Mastic grout eliminates the need for mixing on-site.

- *Epoxy grout* is a two- or three-part mixture (epoxy resin hardener with silica sand filler) that is highly resistant to chemicals and has great bond strength. This grout and furan grout are made for different chemical and solvent resistance.
- *Furan resin grout* is two-part furan mixture (similar to furan mortar) that resists high temperatures and solvents.
- *Silicone rubber grout* is an elastomeric mixture of silicone rubber. It has high bond strength, is resistant to water and staining, and remains flexible under freezing conditions.

GROUT GUIDE

	GROUTS CONTAINING PORTLAND CEMENT					OTHERS			
	COMMERCIAL (SANDED)	JOB-SITE MIX (SANDED)	DRYSET (UNSANDED)	COMMERCIAL OR SET WITH LATEX (POLYMER)	MODIFIED EPOXY EMULSION	100% SOLID EPOXY	FURAN	SILICONE OR URETHANE	MASTIC GROUT
W = wall use F = floor use	4		4	4, 9	4	1, 3, 4, 6	1, 3, 4, 6	2, 4	3, 4
TILE TYPE									
Glazed Wall Tile[7]	W		W	W		W		W	W
Glazed Floor Tile[7]	W, F	W, F	W, F	W, F	W, F	W, F			W, F
Ceramic Mosaics	W, F	W, F	W, F	W, F	W, F	W, F		W	W, F
Quarry, Paver, and Packing House Tiles[8]	W, F	W, F		W, F	W, F	W, F	W, F		
Large-Unit Porcelain or Vitreous Tile[8]	W, F	W, F	W, F	W, F	W, F	W, F	F	W	W, F
Dimension Stone[7,8] including agglomerates	W, F	W, F	W, F	W, F	W, F				
USE									
Dry/Limited Water Exposure	W, F	W, F	W, F	W, F	W, F	W, F	W, F	W, F	W, F
Wet Areas[10]	W, F	W, F	W, F	W, F	W, F	W, F	W, F	W, F	
Exteriors[8, 9, 10]	W, F	W, F	W, F	W, F	W, F	W, F 4	W, F 4	W, F	
PERFORMANCE*									
Suggested Joint Widths[5]	$\frac{1}{8}$ to $\frac{5}{8}$ in. (3 to 15 mm)	$\frac{1}{8}$ to $\frac{5}{8}$ in. (3 to 15 mm)	$\frac{1}{8}$ to $\frac{5}{8}$ in. (3 to 15 mm)	$\frac{1}{8}$ to $\frac{5}{8}$ in. (3 to 15 mm)	$\frac{1}{8}$ to $\frac{5}{8}$ in. (3 to 15 mm)	$\frac{1}{8}$ to $\frac{5}{8}$ in. (3 to 15 mm)	$\frac{3}{8}$ to $\frac{5}{8}$ in. (9 to 15 mm)	$\frac{1}{16}$ to $\frac{1}{4}$ in. (1 to 6 mm)	$\frac{1}{16}$ to $\frac{1}{4}$ in. (1 to 6 mm)
Stain Resistance	D	E	D	C	C	A	A	A	B
Crack Resistance	D	E	D	C	C	B	C	A	C
Color Availability	B	D	B	B	B	B	Black only	B	B

*There are five performance ratings, from Best (A) to Minimal (E).

[1] Mainly used for chemical-resistant properties.

[2] Special tools needed for proper application. Silicon, ure-thane, and modified polyvinyl chloride used in pregrouted ceramic tile sheets. Silicone grout should not be used on kitchen countertops or other food preparation surfaces unless it meets the requirements of FDA Regulation No. 21, CFE 177.2600.

[3] Special cleaning procedures and materials are recommended.

[4] Follow manufacturer's directions.

[5] Joint widths are only guidelines. Individual grout manufacturer's products may vary. Consult manufacturer's instructions.

[6] Epoxies are recommended for prolonged temperatures up to 140°F, high-temperature-resistant epoxies and furans up to 350°F.

[7] Some types of glazed ceramic tiles, polished marble, marble agglomerates, and granite can be permanently scratched or damaged when grouted with sanded grout formulas. Do not use sanded grout or add sand to grout when grouting polished marble, marbled agglomerates, and ceramic wall tiles with soft glazes. Check the tile or marble manufacturer's literature and test grout on a separate sample area prior to grouting.

[8] Some types of ceramic tiles and dimensions stone may be permanently stained when grouted with pigmented grout of a contrasting color. WHITE GROUT IS BEST SUITED FOR GROUTING WHITE OR LIGHT-COLORED MARBLE OR GRANITE.

[9] Latex modification may be required in areas subject to freezing temperatures. Consult grout manufacturer for recommended products and methods.

[10] Colored cementitious grouts may darken when wet.

Source: Tile Council of America; Anderson, South Carolina

EPOXY MORTAR AND GROUT
Epoxy mortar and grout are used where leveling of sub-floor is required and where moderate chemical exposure and severe cleaning methods are used, such as in food processing plants.

FURAN RESIN MORTAR AND GROUT
Furan resin mortar and grout are used in kitchens and chemical plants.

EPOXY MORTAR AND GROUT
Epoxy mortar and grout are for use where moderate chemical exposure and severe cleaning methods are used, such as in food processing plants.

CHEMICAL-RESISTANT TILE INSTALLATIONS

MOVEMENT JOINTS

Movement in the structure and the substrate must be accommodated by the ceramic tile installation. For quarry tile and paver tile, a movement joint width should be the same as a grout joint, but not less than ¼ in. (6 mm); for ceramic mosaic tile and glazed wall tile, a movement joint should be not less than ¼ in. (6 mm), but never less than ⅛ in. (3 mm). In addition to expansion joints, there are several types of movement joints, as follows:

- *Control joints or contraction joints* are formed, sawed, or tooled grooves in the concrete substrate, used to create a weakened location where the controlled cracking of the concrete can occur.
- *Construction joints* are located where two separate placements of concrete meet and where reinforcement may be continuous.

- *Isolation joints* are installed where adjoining areas of a concrete substrate may move in three directions and where the formation of cracks is to be avoided.
- *Cold joints* are formed when the size of a concrete slab is too large for one pour, and successive pours are required. Cold joints may crack with movement of the slab. Some slabs are saw-cut at regular intervals to provide controlled cracking locations.

Movement Joint Materials

Backup strips are flexible and compressible types of closed-cell foam polyethylene, butyl rubber, or open-cell and closed-cell polyurethane. These strips should be rounded at the surface that contacts the sealant.

Sealants used are silicone, urethane, or polysulfide. Silicone sealants are used on interior vertical tile surfaces. Mildew-resistant silicone sealants are useful in wet areas. Urethane sealants are used in interior hori-

zontal tile installations. Sealants should comply with ASTM C920, *Standard Specification for Elastomeric Joint Sealants.*

Movement Joint Locations

All expansion, control, construction, cold, and seismic joints in the structure should continue through the tile work, including such joints in vertical surfaces. Joints through tile work directly over structural joints must never be narrower than the structural joint. Expansion joints should be installed in the following circumstances:

- 24 to 36 ft (7.3 to 11 m) in each direction
- Tile work exposed to direct sunlight or moisture, 12 to 16 ft (3.7 to 4.9 m) in each direction
- Where tile work abuts restraining surfaces such as perimeter walls, dissimilar floors, curbs, columns, pipes, ceilings, and where changes occur in backing materials

CONSTRUCTION JOINT

ISOLATION/EXPANSION JOINT

EXPANSION JOINT

MOVEMENT JOINTS
Source: Tile Council of America, Inc.; Anderson, South Carolina

WALL TILE

Wall tile is a glazed tile with a body suitable for interior use. Usually nonvitreous, it is not required or expected to withstand excessive impact or freezing and thawing conditions.

Many tile manufacturers can accommodate custom designs and colors. Minimum orders typically are required.

CEMENT MORTAR
Use cement mortar over masonry, plaster, or other solid backing, to provide firm anchorage for metal lath. This is the preferred method for showers and tub enclosures, and is used in remodeling.

LATEX PORTLAND CEMENT MORTAR
Latex portland cement mortar is used in dry areas in schools, institutions, and commercial buildings. Do not use in areas where temperatures exceed 125°F (52°C).

ONE-COAT METHOD
The one-coat method is used for remodeling or on surfaces that present bonding problems. It is the preferred method of applying tile over gypsum plaster or gypsum board in showers and tub enclosures.

DRYSET MORTAR (CEMENTITIOUS BACKER)
Use dryset mortar in wet areas over well-braced wood or metal studs. Stud spacing should not to exceed 16 in. (405 mm) o.c., and metal studs must be 20-gage or heavier.

COATED GLASS-MAT BACKERBOARD
Coated glass-mat backerboard is used in wet areas over dry, well-braced wood or metal studs. Stud spacing should not exceed 16 in. (405 mm) o.c., and metal studs must be 20-gage or heavier.

WALL DETAILS
Source: Tile Council of America, Inc.; Anderson, South Carolina

CERAMIC TILE DETAILS

CERAMIC TILE
BOND COAT
MORTAR BED 1 1/4"
MIN. TO 2" MAX.
REINFORCING
CLEAVAGE MEMBRANE

CEMENT MORTAR

CERAMIC TILE
BOND COAT
MORTAR BED 1 1/4"
MIN. TO 2" MAX.
REINFORCING
CLEAVAGE MEMBRANE
SUBFLOOR

CEMENT MORTAR

TIE WIRES
1/4" DIA. PENCIL RODS
CERAMIC TILE
BOND COAT
SCRATCH COAT
METAL LATH
EXPANSION JOINT
MORTAR BED 3/4" - 1 1/4"
SLOPE TO DRAIN
BOND COAT
INSULATION
REINFORCED CONCRETE (3" MIN.)

REFRIGERATED ROOM TILE

CERAMIC TILE
DRYSET OR
LATEX-PORTLAND
CEMENT MORTAR
BOND COAT

DRYSET OR LATEX PORTLAND CEMENT MORTAR

CERAMIC TILE
DRYSET OR
LATEX-PORTLAND CEMENT
MORTAR BOND COAT
CEMENTITIOUS BACKER
UNIT "CBU"
DRYSET MORTAR
PLYWOOD
SUBFLOOR

DRYSET MORTAR

INSULATION
TIE WIRES
WATERPROOF MEMBRANE
SEALED SLIP JOINT
1/4" DIA. PENCIL RODS
MORTAR BED
CERAMIC TILE
BOND COAT
3/4" - 1"
SCRATCH COAT
METAL LATH
CERAMIC TILE
EXPANSION JOINT
MORTAR BED
WATERPROOF MEMBRANE
SLOPED TO SUBFLOOR
SLOPE TO DRAIN
3/4" TO 1 1/4"

CEMENT MORTAR STEAM ROOM

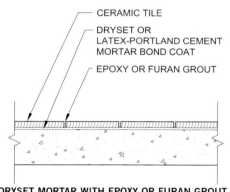

CERAMIC TILE
DRYSET OR
LATEX-PORTLAND
CEMENT MORTAR BOND COAT
EPOXY OR FURAN GROUT

DRYSET MORTAR WITH EPOXY OR FURAN GROUT

EPOXY GROUT
CERAMIC TILE
EPOXY MORTAR BOND COAT
GAP BETWEEN
PLYWOOD SHEETS
DOUBLE WOOD FLOOR

EPOXY MORTAR AND GROUT

WOOD OR
METAL
FRAMING
WATERPROOF
MEMBRANE
CEMENTITIOUS
BACKER UNIT
SEALED SLIP JOINT
CERAMIC TILE
LATEX-PORTLAND
MORTAR BOND COAT
"CBU" ON WOOD OR
METAL STUDS
WATERPROOF MEMBRANE;
SPECIFY LOCATION
EXPANSION JOINT
MORTAR BED
SLOPE TO DRAIN
WATERPROOF
MEMBRANE
SLOPED TO
SUBFLOOR

THIN-BED STEAM ROOM

CERAMIC TILE
ADHESIVE

ORGANIC OR EPOXY ADHESIVE

CERAMIC TILE
ADHESIVE
GAP
DOUBLE WOOD FLOOR

ORGANIC ADHESIVE

FLOORING DETAILS—CONCRETE SUBSTRATE

FLOORING DETAILS—WOOD SUBSTRATE

Source: Tile Council of America, Inc.; Anderson, South Carolina

SPECIAL CONDITIONS

CERAMIC TILE DETAILS

- CERAMIC TILE
- DRYSET OR LATEX-PORTLAND CEMENT MORTAR
- CEMENTITIOUS BACKER UNIT
- MEMBRANE
- FLEXIBLE SEALANT
- TUB HANGER OR END GRAIN WOOD BLOCK
- BATH TUB
- FIREPROOFING WHEN REQUIRED (BY OTHER TRADE)
- WOOD OR METAL STUDS

CERAMIC TILE TUB ENCLOSURE

- EXISTING CERAMIC TILE AND MORTAR BED
- CONTINUOUS SEALANT BEAD
- NEW FLASHING
- NEW CERAMIC TILE AND MORTAR BED
- REPAIR MEMBRANE AND METAL LATH
- NEW WATERPROOF MEMBRANE
- NEW REINFORCED MORTAR BED
- SHOWER PAN OR MEMBRANE
- SLOPED FILL
- CRUSHED STONE*
- WEEP HOLES
- SHOWER DRAIN

* TO PREVENT MORTAR FROM BLOCKING WEEP HOLES

SHOWER RECEPTOR RENOVATION

- FRAMING, WOOD OR METAL
- GYPSUM BOARD
- CERAMIC TILE
- BOND COAT

CERAMIC TILE CEILING

- CERAMIC TILE
- BOND COAT
- MORTAR BED ON SUSPENDED METAL LATH AND SCRATCH COAT, CONCRETE, OR TILE BACKER BOARD

CERAMIC TILE CEILING

CEILINGS AND SOFFITS

- WOOD OR METAL STUDS
- CERAMIC TILE
- DRYSET OR LATEX-PORTLAND CEMENT MORTAR
- CEMENTITIOUS BACKER UNIT
- REINFORCED MORTAR BED 1" TO 1 3/4"
- SHOWER PAN OR MEMBRANE
- SLOPED FILL
- CRUSHED STONE*
- WEEP HOLES
- SHOWER DRAIN

* TO PREVENT MORTAR FROM BLOCKING WEEP HOLES

BACKERBOARD WEEP HOLE CONDITION AT SHOWER

- WOOD OR METAL STUDS
- CERAMIC TILE
- BOND COAT
- REINFORCED MORTAR BED 1" TO 1 3/4"
- SHOWER PAN OR MEMBRANE
- SLOPED FILL
- CRUSHED STONE*
- WEEP HOLES
- SHOWER DRAIN

* TO PREVENT MORTAR FROM BLOCKING WEEP HOLES

MORTAR BED WEEP HOLE CONDITION AT SHOWER

TUBS AND SHOWERS

- ℄ OF OPENING OR DOOR
- RESILIENT HALF THRESHOLD
- THINSET CERAMIC TILE
- VCT

THINSET THRESHOLD CONDITION

- CERAMIC TILE
- MORTAR BED
- BOND COAT
- THRESHOLD
- ADJACENT FLOOR

THICKSET THRESHOLD CONDITION

THRESHOLDS

- CERAMIC TILE
- EPOXY OR ORGANIC ADHESIVE
- PLYWOOD

THINSET COUNTERTOP

- CERAMIC TILE
- BOND COAT
- MORTAR BED
- METAL LATH
- CUT WALL MORTAR AND METAL LATH HERE
- MEMBRANE
- WOOD BASE
- PUNCHED METAL STRIP
- 3/4" TO 1"

CEMENT MORTAR COUNTERTOP

- CERAMIC TILE
- LATEX-PORTLAND CEMENT MORTAR
- CEMENTITIOUS BACKER UNIT
- PLYWOOD
- FIBERGLASS TAPE (THREE PIECES)
- MEMBRANE

CEMENT BACKERBOARD COUNTERTOP

COUNTERTOPS

Tile Council of America, Inc.; Anderson, South Carolina
Winnie Cheng; Rhode Island School of Design; Providence, Rhode Island
Jess McIlvain, AIA, CCS, CSI; Jess McIlvain and Associates; Bethesda, Maryland

TERRAZZO

Terrazzo is a very low-maintenance, seamless floor finish with the luxurious look of stone mosaic and durability comparable to that of concrete. Often selected for its decorative possibilities, terrazzo artistry can produce striking medallions or intricate inlaid patterns.

Terrazzo is a mixture of a binder and crushed aggregate, typically marble. Other aggregate types, such as glass, are available to vary the appearance of the terrazzo. Divider strips of brass, white alloy of zinc, or plastic, are used functionally as control joints, and aesthetically as design elements, to separate fields of color.

AGGREGATE

Aggregate, or stone chips used in terrazzo, includes all calcareous serpentine and other rocks capable of taking a good polish. Marble and onyx are the preferred materials. Quartz, granite, quartzite, and silica pebbles are used for rustic terrazzo and textured mosaics not requiring polishing.

SAND CUSHION TERRAZZO

SAND CUSHION TERRAZZO OVER PRECAST CONCRETE-TYPE DECK

BONDED TERRAZZO

TERRAZZO SYSTEMS

SYSTEM	DESCRIPTION	ADVANTAGES	TOTAL THICKNESS	WEIGHT PSF (kPa)
Sand Cushion	½ in. (13 mm) terrazzo topping over 2½ in. (63 mm) underbed, reinforced with wire mesh, over an isolation membrane over ⅟₁₆ in. (1 mm) of sand, on a concrete slab. For interior use only.	The best available cement terrazzo system, because it is the only system that completely separates the finish from the subfloor. This protects against minor substrate defects telegraphing through to the finish surface.	3 in. (76 mm) including ½ in. (13 mm) terrazzo topping	30 (206)
Bonded	½ in. (13 mm) terrazzo topping over 1¼ in. (32 mm) underbed, on a concrete slab. Interior use only.	Requires less thickness than sand cushion. Can be used for walls.	1¾ to 2¼ in. (44 to 57 mm) including ½ in. (13 mm) terrazzo topping	18 (124)
Monolithic	½ in. (13 mm) terrazzo topping on concrete slab. Performance dependent on the quality of the substrate. A level concrete slab must be provided.	Most economical system. Ideal for large areas such as shopping malls, schools, and stores.	½ in. (13 mm) terrazzo topping	7 (48)
Thinset	¼ to ⅜ in. (4 to 9 mm) terrazzo topping over concrete slab. Thinnest and, typically, most expensive system. Considered to be a resinous flooring type. Epoxy or polyester matrix is used.	Good for renovation work. Both epoxy and polyester resist many types of chemicals, making them suitable for labs, hospitals, and manufacturing facilities.	¼ to ⅜ in. (4 to 9 mm)	4 (27.5)
Precast	Prefabricated custom units for steps, bases, planters, benches, and wall panels.	Variety of uses.	Custom	Varies

Source: Reprinted courtesy of NTMA

STRUCTURAL TERRAZZO SYSTEM

MONOLITHIC TERRAZZO

The National Terrazzo and Mosaic Association (NTMA), an association of terrazzo contractors, material suppliers, and distributors, publishes the *NTMA Technical Manual,* which contains complete specifications for all terrazzo systems.

TERRAZZO SYSTEMS

National Terrazzo and Mosaic Association, Inc.; Terrazzo Specification and Design Guide; *Leesburg, Virginia*

MATRICES

There are two basic types of matrices, or binders: portland cement and resinous chemical binders. Color pigments are added to create special effects. Limeproof mineral pigments or synthetic mineral pigments compatible with portland cement are required. Both white and gray portland cement are used, depending on final color.

Resinous binders are used to install the thinnest possible finish of terrazzo, as thin as ¼ in. (6 mm). Epoxy and polyester binders are two-part formulations, consisting of a resin and a catalyst, to which a dry mix is added. Resinous binders offer increased chemical and abrasion resistance and good impact strength. Resin-based terrazzo requires significantly less maintenance than its cement-based counterpart, and is commonly used in installations where economy and overall weight of the terrazzo system is a concern.

All five types of chemical binders provide excellent chemical and abrasion resistance, except for latex, which is rated good:

- *Epoxy matrix*: Two-component resinous matrix.
- *Polyester matrix*: Two-component resinous matrix.
- *Polyacrylate matrix*: Composite resinous matrix.
- *Latex matrix*: Synthetic latex matrix.
- *Conductive matrix*: Special formulated matrix to conduct electricity with regulated resistance; used in surgical areas and where explosive gases are a hazard.

Divider Strips

White alloy of zinc, brass, or plastic strips are used to control shrinkage of the terrazzo. They vary in width from ⅛ to ½ in. (3 to 13 mm); ⅛ in. (3 mm) is standard.

For systems that adhere to the concrete subfloor, divider strips must also be used precisely above all concrete control joints. The structural engineer must locate control joints in accordance with "ACI Concrete Joint Placement" to prevent random cracking in the slab and terrazzo. Some of the standard requirements include:

- Joints should occur a maximum of three times in feet the depth of the concrete in inches. For example: 4-in. (100 mm) slabs should have concrete joints at a maximum spacing of 12 ft (3.6 m).
- Joints should occur at all corridor intersections and corners.
- Joints should not be spaced more than 1½ times the width of the concrete pour. For example: 6-ft-(2-m-) wide corridors should have joints at a maximum spacing of 9 ft (3 m). In addition, divider strips are typically used to separate colors or designs within the terrazzo.

Control Joints

Plastic zip strips or double-angle strips are used to control cracking due to anticipated shrinkage in the subfloor at construction joints. These are not required in a sand cushion system due to the use of an isolation membrane.

BRASS, PLASTIC, OR ZINC 1/8" - 1/2"

NEOPRENE

STANDARD AND HEAVY TOP

ANGLE AND EXPANSION

DEPTH 3/4", 1", 1 1/4", OR 1 1/2"

DIVIDER STRIPS

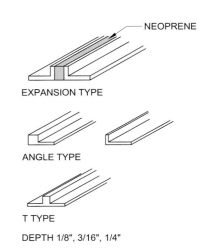

NEOPRENE

EXPANSION TYPE

ANGLE TYPE

T TYPE

DEPTH 1/8", 3/16", 1/4"

DIVIDER STRIPS FOR THINSET TERRAZZO

DIVIDER STRIPS

CAULKING — FOAM STRIP
WALL — UNDERBED
DIVIDER STRIP
1/2"
1 3/4" MIN. TH.
POINT OF BOND — CONCRETE SLAB

RUSTIC TERRAZZO—BONDED TO CONCRETE

TERRAZZO TOPPING — DIVIDER STRIP (PROVIDE ALSO ALONG BEAM CENTERLINE)
6 X 6 X 6 X 8 WIRE MESH WELDED
UNDERBED
1/2"
3" MIN.
STEEL DECK — BEAM

TERRAZZO OVER METAL DECK

INSTALLED DIVIDER STRIPS

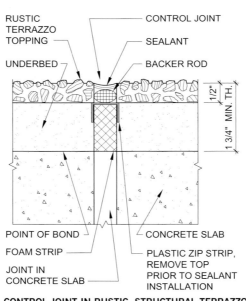

RUSTIC TERRAZZO TOPPING — CONTROL JOINT
SEALANT
UNDERBED — BACKER ROD
1/2"
1 3/4" MIN. TH.
POINT OF BOND — CONCRETE SLAB
FOAM STRIP
JOINT IN CONCRETE SLAB — PLASTIC ZIP STRIP, REMOVE TOP PRIOR TO SEALANT INSTALLATION

CONTROL JOINT IN RUSTIC, STRUCTURAL TERRAZZO

RUSTIC TERRAZZO TOPPING — CONTROL JOINT
SEALANT
4000 PSI CONCRETE UNDERBED — BACKER ROD
PLASTIC ZIP STRIP
1/2"
4" MIN. THICKNESS
WATERPROOF MEMBRANE — CONCRETE SLAB
FOAM STRIP — WIRE MESH, 2" x 2" x 16 OR 18 GA.

UNBONDED RUSTIC TERRAZZO

CONTROL JOINTS

INSTALLATION

In a terrazzo installation, the binder and aggregate mixture are set in place on the prepared floor surface. After the terrazzo surface has cured, it is ground down to a smooth finish. The floor is then grouted to fill any voids, and sealed. A terrazzo floor consists of at least 70% stone. Because porosity can vary among stone types, the pores of both the stone and the binder require the protection of a sealer. For renovation work, terrazzo can be installed over practically any type of existing, stable hard-surface flooring.

SURFACE TREATMENT

Terrazzo systems must be given an application of penetrating type sealer, which fills the pores of the surface to prevent absorption of traffic dirt and stains. Sealers will also highlight the natural colors of the aggregate.

PLAIN TYPE   COVE TYPE

PRECAST TERRAZZO BASE
Precast terrazzo units are routinely available, and almost any shape can be produced. Examples include: straight, coved, and splayed bases; windowsills; stair treads and risers; shower receptors; floor tiles; and wall facings.

FLUSH BASE

REVEAL BASE

POLYACRYLATE TERRAZZO FLOOR AND BASE

RECESSED BASE

CANTED BASE

EPOXY OR POLYESTER TERRAZZO FLOOR AND BASE

POURED-IN-PLACE TERRAZZO BASES

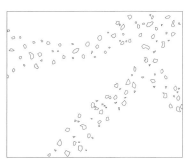

PALLADIANA TERRAZZO
Random fractured slabs of marble up to approximately 15 in. (380 mm) greatest dimension, ⅜ to 1 in. (9 to 25 mm) thick, with smaller chips filling spaces between.

RUSTIC TERRAZZO
Uniformly textured terrazzo in which matrix is depressed to expose chips; not ground or only slightly ground.

VENETIAN TERRAZZO
Larger chips (sizes #3 through #8), with smaller chips filling the spaces between.

STANDARD TERRAZZO
The most common type; relatively small chip sizes (#1- and #2-size chips).

TYPES OF TERRAZZO CLASSIFIED BY APPEARANCE

Trey Klein, AIA; crayfish design; Belmont, Massachusetts
Jason Dickerson; Rhode Island School of Design; Providence, Rhode Island
John C. Lunsford, AIA; Varney, Sexton Syndor Architects; Phoenix, Arizona

STRETCHED CEILING SYSTEMS

CHARACTERISTICS

Stretched ceiling systems utilize lightweight, long-span, continuous sheets of prefinished material to create a large, smooth ceiling plane or a warped, curved ceiling. The maximum span of a stretched ceiling system is dictated by the material. Spans of up to 16 × 40 ft (5 × 12 m) are typical.

Stretched ceiling systems consist of three basic components: a flexible ceiling material, a perimeter rail, and a fitting that attaches the material to the rail. The material is either a polyvinyl chloride (PVC) membrane or a woven fabric, typically made of fire-resistant polyester. The rail is mounted around the perimeter of the space, in either straight or curved configurations. Intermediate supports are not commonly required because of the long spans that are possible with stretched ceiling systems. Rails can be either visible or fully concealed.

CEILING MATERIALS

Translucent and perforated PVC membranes are available. Translucent PVC material can be backlit, creating a luminous appearance. Care should be taken to ensure that the frame profile is not projected onto the backlit surface, creating a shadow.

Photographic-quality artwork can be printed on PVC membranes. PVC systems are available in more than 100 colors. Custom colors are also available, but typically with a large order. Matte, satin, suede, metallic, and reflective finishes are available.

The PVC is recyclable, virtually impermeable to air and moisture (water-staining problems are eliminated), and can easily be cleaned with a soft cloth and liquid cleaner. Polyester-stretched ceiling systems can resemble plaster or gypsum board ceilings.

ANTIMICROBIAL APPLICATIONS

Antimicrobial and antifungal treatments can be integrated into the ceiling material for applications such as hospital operating rooms, cleanrooms, laboratories, and food preparation spaces.

INSTALLATION

Stretched ceiling systems offer a quick, dust-free installation without odors or fumes. These systems are installed relatively quickly; however, experienced installers are required. All forms of penetrations and recessed or surface-mounted fixtures, including lighting, alarms, sprinklers, and ventilation equipment, can be accommodated. Penetrations are all cut in the field to ensure a proper fit. The ceiling material is demountable, providing access to mechanical equipment behind. These systems can be installed over existing ceilings, commonly gypsum board or acoustical tile suspension systems, either with or without acoustical tile installed, depending on the sound characteristics required. For curved installations, wood or metal frames can be used at the perimeter.

Access to mechanical space behind the ceiling is achieved by temporarily removing the flexible material. Lights, sprinklers, and HVAC registers and grills can be incorporated in the ceiling. Penetrations are field-cut.

Andy Adams; Anshen + Allen Architects; San Francisco, California
Brian Tan; Rhode Island School of Design; Providence, Rhode Island

PENETRATION AT LIGHT FIXTURE

FRICTION-FIT PERIMETER ASSEMBLY

INTERMEDIATE SUPPORT

COVE CEILINGS

COVE CEILING WITH LIGHT FIXTURE

COVE CEILING WITH SKYLIGHT

COVE CEILING WITH AIR DIFFUSER

COVE CEILING WITH RETURN AIR GRILLE

(A) DETAIL AT LIGHT FIXTURE

COVE CEILING WITH LIGHT FIXTURE

COVE AT DROPPED CEILING PANEL WITH RETURN AIR GRILLE

SECTION AT CABINETS

COVE CEILING AT WALL HUNG CABINET

Stuart Rehr, RA; GVA Architecture-Interior Design; Columbia, Maryland
Thomas R. Krizmanic, AIA; Studios Architecture; Washington, D.C.

ACOUSTICAL METAL PAN CEILINGS

Acoustical metal pan ceilings are used where aesthetics, durability, and ease of maintenance are desired. Metal pan ceilings are available in many finishes and colors, providing a number of design options and aesthetics. Acoustical metal pan ceiling units enclose sound attenuation pads, which provide varying qualities of acoustical control at the ceiling plane.

Metal pan ceilings are typically snapped or hooked in place on a concealed suspension system or are installed as lay-in units on traditional exposed ceiling suspension systems. Products are now available that incorporate an exposed suspension system and metal pans with special edge details, providing a semiexposed, narrow reveal installation. Metal pan ceilings can be integrated with air diffusers and light fixtures, depending upon the manufacturer's product offerings.

TYPES

Acoustical metal pan ceilings are typically fabricated from steel or aluminum. Options include metal pan sizes, metal coating types, colors, textures, perforation patterns, and acoustical insulation pads.

SIZES

Sizes of metal pans range from 12 × 12 in. (305 × 305 mm) to 24 × 24 in. (610 × 610 mm). Large units are available from some manufacturers in square and plank-type pans. Standard metal pan size offerings vary by manufacturer. Custom sizes are available. Sizes of custom metal pans in general are designated by the suspension method capacity and installation parameters of the project. Metric size equivalents are offered by manufacturers for metal pan units.

THICKNESSES

Thicknesses of metal pans are commonly offered in 20- and 24-gage for steel pans, and 0.032 in. (0.8 mm) and 0.040 in. (1 mm) for aluminum. Sizes of metal pans also determine the metal thickness. Manufacturers offer larger pans in greater thicknesses to provide rigidity and integral strength to the units.

Some manufacturers offer hinged access panels that integrate with the metal pan system; otherwise, the metal pan units are removed for access into the above-ceiling plenum space. Most metal pan systems have downward access or are lay-in units that can be easily removed. For shallow plenum spaces, downward access is a benefit.

The numerous metal finishes available provide various aesthetic and design options. Steel pans can be galvanized, baked enamel, powder-coated, or electroplated. Aluminum pans can be mill-finished, anodized, or painted.

Metal pans are available in standard flat panels, as well as in curved and corrugated units.

INSTALLATION TYPES

Three common installation types are *snap-in, hook-on,* and *lay-in*. Edge details are *square, beveled,* and *reveal,* and are shaped to ensure proper engagement and alignment within the suspension system. Perimeter tiles may be field-cut unless not recommended by the manufacturer. For integration of ceiling fixtures and devices,

factory-provided cutouts can be located in metal pans. This requires the coordination of the entire reflected ceiling plan for areas with metal pan ceilings.

FURRING CHANNEL — WALL MOLDING
FURRING CLIP
SOUND-ABSORBING PAD
METAL PAN — MAIN RUNNER

METAL PAN CEILING

#12 PRESTRAIGHTENED GALVINIZED WIRE AT 4'-0" O.C. ON MAIN TEE; (3) TWISTS IN 1" MIN.; WRAP ANCHOR DEVICE ABOVE AT 100 LBS MIN. PER HANGING POINT; SEISMIC BRACING, SUCH AS COMPRESSION POSTS AND SPLAY WIRING, PER APPLICABLE BUILDING CODE

CROSS TEE — MAIN TEE

TEGULAR EDGE PANEL; FIELD-CUT AS REQUIRED

LAY-IN PANEL SECTION

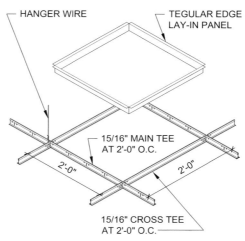

HANGER WIRE — TEGULAR EDGE LAY-IN PANEL

15/16" MAIN TEE AT 2'-0" O.C.

15/16" CROSS TEE AT 2'-0" O.C.

LAY-IN PANEL

METAL PAN FEATURES

SUSPENSION SYSTEMS

Suspension systems for metal pan ceilings are similar to those used for acoustical panel and tile installations. Classifications of the suspension systems are typically intermediate and heavy-duty, depending upon the type and weight of the metal pans. Direct-hung suspension systems are hung from the structure above. In indirect-hung systems, the main tees are attached to carrying channels hung from the structure above. Both types are suspended from hanger wires, with main tees usually located at 48 in. (1,220 mm), on center, maximum. Cross-connector clamps are installed at grid intersections of main and cross tees to provide added strength. Edge trim moldings finish the perimeter of the metal pan ceiling system. Wind-uplift struts, seismic clips, and other devices are available to address the requirements of local codes regarding the installation of metal pan ceilings.

#12 PRESTRAIGHTENED GALVINIZED WIRE AT 4'-0" O.C. ON MAIN TEE; (3) TWISTS IN 1" MIN.; WRAP ANCHOR DEVICE ABOVE AT 100 LBS MIN. PER HANGING POINT; SEISMIC BRACING, SUCH AS COMPRESSION POSTS AND SPLAY WIRING, PER APPLICABLE BUILDING CODE

CROSS TEE — MAIN TEE

RUBBER SPLINE, FIELD-CUT 2" LENGTHS, TWO PIECES AT INTERIOR CORNERS OF EACH PERIMETER PANEL

SNAP-IN PANEL; FIELD-CUT AS REQUIRED

SNAP-IN PANEL SECTION

HANGER WIRE

MAIN TEE AT 2'-0" O.C.

CROSS TEE AT 2'-0" O.C.

SNAP-IN PANEL

SNAP-IN PANEL

ACOUSTIC PROPERTIES

Acoustic qualities vary depending upon the type of metal pan used, perforation quantity and type, and the project conditions. Sound waves are transmitted through the perforations in the metal pan, so the use of sound attenuation pads reduces the sound transmitted. Sound is transmitted through the ceiling plenum if ceiling-height partitions are installed; therefore, sound attenuation panels will improve acoustics. A review with an acoustical consultant and the metal pan ceiling manufacturer for project conditions is recommended.

Fiberglass is the most common material for sound attenuation pads. These pads are typically encapsulated so that no loose fiber can become airborne, thus compromising the indoor air quality. When perforated metal pans are installed without sound attenuation pads, a black backing scrim is installed inside the panel to eliminate any visible elements above the ceiling. Some manufacturers provide mineral fiber inserts in the metal pans to improve the Ceiling Attenuation Class (CAC), which rates the ceiling's capability as a barrier to sound transmission between spaces. Noise Reduction Coefficient (NRC), the capability of an acoustical unit to absorb sound, is greater with fiberglass inserts in the metal panels, but the CAC is lower. Nonperforated metal panels are generally rated with a low NRC range of 0.00 to 0.10. NRLs for perforated metal panels range from 0.65 to 0.90.

FIRE RESISTANCE

Currently, metal pan ceilings are not identified as having specific fire-resistive qualities, and are not listed in the Underwriters Laboratory (UL) Fire Resistance

ROUND ¹⁄₁₆-IN. (1.6-MM) PERFORATIONS, 6% OPEN AREA

ROUND ³⁄₈-IN. (9.4-MM) PERFORATIONS, 9% OPEN AREA

ROUND ³⁄₁₆-IN. (4.7-MM) PERFORATIONS, 5% OPEN AREA

ROUND ¼-IN. (6-MM) PERFORATIONS, 48% OPEN AREA

SQUARE ³⁄₈-IN. (9.4-MM) PERFORATIONS, 11% OPEN AREA

SQUARE ¼-IN. (6-MM) PERFORATIONS, 11% OPEN AREA

Perforated metal pans have a nonperforated border at the perimeter of the unit to provide stiffness and uniformity. A larger percentage of openness generally provides improved acoustics to the panels.

METAL PANEL PERFORATION OPTIONS

Directory. However, the metal pan ceiling products are typically designated as Class A (or Class 1), per ASTM E1264, *Classification for Acoustical Ceiling Products*. Many manufacturers of metal pan ceiling systems identify their products as noncombustible units.

RECYCLED CONTENT

Many manufacturers have integrated recycled material to their metal pan ceiling fabrication, although the percentage of recycled content varies among manufacturers and their products.

ACOUSTICAL TILE CEILINGS

Acoustical tile ceilings are composed of prefabricated ceiling units, which are installed in a concealed or semiexposed metal suspension system. Also known as *concealed spline ceilings,* they are also directly installed on a substrate by stapling or adhesive bonding. While acoustical tile installations provide a monolithic ceiling surface, installation can be more costly, and maintenance of the tile ceiling is more difficult than with acoustical panel installations. An acoustical tile ceiling is not as easily accessible to above-ceiling areas as acoustical panel ceilings with lay-in units. If accessibility is not an issue, an acoustical tile ceiling is an option when the aesthetics and other conditions of the installation are appropriate for the project.

Acoustical tiles are typically 12 × 12 in. (305 × 305 mm); however, larger sizes are available. Thicknesses range from ½ in. (13 mm) to ⅝ in. (16 mm) to ¾ in. (19 mm). Hard metric sizes are available on a more limited basis from manufacturers. Acoustical panels are generally larger than 12 × 12 in. (305 × 305 mm) ceiling tiles, and are installed in exposed or semiconcealed grids.

Fire-resistant acoustical tile assemblies are available when used with applicable UL design criteria. Consult

a manufacturer's product information for specific recommendations on acoustical panel ceiling data.

CEILING TILE COMPOSITION

Composition of the various acoustical tile types used in commercial construction include *mineral fiber base* and *glass fiber base. Cellulose base* is used primarily in residential construction and is not as durable as the commercial-grade panel construction. Construction of the mineral fiber base acoustical panels is cast, wet-

Kerfed-edge acoustic ceiling tile slides into a T- or Z-shaped grid.

KERFED-EDGE ACOUSTIC CEILING TILE

felted, and nodular, and is available in a number of textures and acoustical properties.

Water- or Wet-Felted Tiles

Water- or wet-felted tiles are fabricated from mineral wool, perlite, fillers, and binders, then mixed into a loose slurry that is formed into sheets by draining, compressing, drying, and cutting to size. Fissured, perforated, or stippled textures are added to the tiles prior to painting the units.

Cast or Molded Tiles

Cast or molded tiles are fabricated from mineral fibers, fillers, and binders, then mixed into a pulp and poured into paper or foil-lined molds of the desired size. Surface textures are created by the manipulation of the surface of the molds. Integral colors can be added for a through-color product. The tiles are oven-dried, trimmed, and then painted.

Nodular Tiles

Nodular tiles are fabricated from mineral fibers wound into balls, combined with perlite, fillers, and binders, then mixed into a slurry. The mixture is formed into sheets, oven-dried, and cut to size. The tiles, which are inherently porous, are then textured with fissures and are painted.

TEXTURES AND COLORS

Acoustical tiles are finished with varying textures, typically ranging from fine to heavily fissured. Heavily fissured tiles perform slightly better acoustically, but their appearance at the ceiling plane is more obvious. Medium or fine textures that perform well are available, and are more unobtrusive. Some manufacturers offer special finishes for acoustical panels and tiles, such as vinyl and fabric.

The typical color of acoustical panels is white, although a limited number of standard colors are available for these products. Colors may affect the light reflectance of the ceiling.

EDGE AND JOINT DETAILS

Common edge details are square or beveled shapes. Common joint details are kerfed (grooved or notched-edge, which accepts and conceals the suspension system), rabbeted (cutback), and tongue-and-groove.

Square-edge acoustical tile modules appear more monolithic when installed; however, the joints are sometimes very obvious if the light striking the ceiling is at a low angle of incidence. Acoustical tiles are also subject to edge damage when the tiles are moved.

Beveled edges provide an eased edge, which creates a slight shadow line between the tiles. When moving the tiles after the initial installation, the use of beveled edges can minimize edge damage. Most manufacturers provide beveled edges on ceiling tiles.

SOUND ABSORPTION AND SOUND ISOLATION

In open office areas, the installation of an acoustical tile ceiling will improve the amount of privacy between partial-height partitioned workstations. Within closed areas, an acoustical tile ceiling can improve the transmission of noise from one room to another, if used with appropriate partition types. Manufacturers of acoustical tile ceilings categorize the acoustical features of their products according to industry standard designations for the ratings of sound absorption.

CAC (Ceiling Attenuation Class) and NRC (Noise Reduction Coefficient) both rate sound absorption, but in different ways:

CAC (formerly known as CSTC, Ceiling Sound Transmission Class): Rates a ceiling's efficiency as a barrier to airborne sound transmission between adjacent spaces and from above-ceiling elements. Shown as a minimum value, a ceiling with a high CAC may have a low NRC (Noise Reduction Coefficient).

NRC: Rates average sound absorption coefficient measured at four frequencies: 250, 500, 1,000 and 2,000 Hz, and rates the capability of a ceiling to absorb sound, measured from 0.0 to 1.00. The higher the number, the greater the capability of the tile to absorb sound.

AC: Rates the listener's ability to understand the spoken word within a space, expressed as a decimal, with 1.0 being perfectly intelligible. The AC

PERFORATED, RANDOMLY SPACED HOLES

FISSURED

REVEAL EDGE, STIPPLE FINISH

ROUTED PATTERN, PERFORATED FINISH

SQUARE-EDGE KERFED TILE FOR CONCEALED SUSPENSION SYSTEMS

BEVELED-EDGE KERFED TILE FOR CONCEALED SUSPENSION SYSTEM

CEILING ABSORBS 25% OF LIGHT

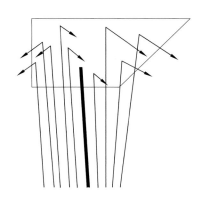

CEILING ABSORBS 11% OF LIGHT

LIGHT REFLECTANCE

rating measures the sound attenuation of a ceiling in open office areas with partial-height partitions and workstation furniture panels, without the use of a sound-masking system.

LIGHT REFLECTANCE

The quantity of light reflected by a surface, defined in ASTM E1477, *Standard Test Method for Luminous Reflectance Factor of Acoustical Materials by Use of Integrating-Sphere Reflectometers,* is known as *light reflectance.* Illuminance is measured in footcandles, or lux (metric measure). One footcandle is approximately 10 lux. A footcandle is the average illumination resulting when one lumen of light falls on 1 sq ft (0.09 sq m) of surface. The total number of lumens on a surface divided by the area of the surface equals footcandles. High Light Reflectance (LR) acoustical tiles provide greater reflected light from the ceiling

plane. LR is measured in values from 0.00 to 1.00. High LR ceiling tiles are particularly effective in open office areas with indirect light sources, where glare is reduced at the work plane and where spaces incorporate daylight as a light source. Usable light is increased and is more evenly distributed. Acoustical ceilings that have a light reflectance above 0.83 are considered to be high light reflectance ceilings, but some products are available that exceed this number and reflect more light. After review of the planned illumination levels, it may be possible to reduce the number of light fixtures within a space, thereby reducing initial installation costs and long-term energy costs.

Light reflectance values are generally lower for those acoustical tiles with textured and embossed patterns. Integrally colored tiles may affect the LR value. Unless the ceiling surface is to be used as a distributor of illumination, lower LR values may not be of concern.

SPECIAL PRODUCT CHARACTERISTICS

Humidity Resistance

Humidity-resistant acoustical tiles are used where sag resistance is desired in high moisture areas, such as locker rooms, shower areas, indoor pools, and laboratories. Commonly made of a ceramic and mineral fiber composite, these tiles can be treated with a coating of an antimicrobial inhibitor to retard the growth of mold and mildew. Humidity-resistant acoustical tiles must be installed with a galvanized-coated steel or aluminum suspension system for moisture resistance.

Fire Resistance

Fire-resistant acoustical ceiling assemblies are composed of UL fire-resistance-rated elements, which form a layer to contain fire within a space. These assemblies are assigned ratings of one, two, three, or four hours. The selection of the acoustical ceiling components for a fire-rated application should be carefully assessed to ensure the proper selection and specification of materials.

Acoustical ceiling tiles typically must have a minimum Class A rating to be installed in a commercial application. ASTM 84 *Standard Test Method for Surface Burning Characteristics of Building Materials,* identifies minimum test standards for the rating of flame spread and smoke developed during exposure to fire. Fire classifications are based on ASTM E1264, *Standard Classification for Acoustical Ceiling Products,* which assigns class ratings based upon performance. For Class A or I ratings, flame spread rating is from 0 to 25; the smoke-developed rating is 0 to 50. Class B or II rating limits flame spread to not more than 75. Current building codes identify the allowable smoke-developed ratings to be 450 or less. Most commercial products are well within these ranges, and most meet Class A or I ratings.

Acoustical tile ceiling products are fire-rated when installed with a fire-resistant suspension system. Fire-resistant acoustical tile ceilings act as a membrane and provide enhanced resistance against flame spread, smoke generation, and structural failure.

The installation of fire-rated assemblies must be coordinated with the fire-rated construction of other components within the space.

SUSPENSION SYSTEMS

General

Concealed acoustical tile ceiling suspension systems are installed at the desired height by hanger wires, which support the metal T- or Z-shaped grid components. The suspension system is typically fabricated from factory-coated steel, as well as galvanized steel systems for improved resistance to moisture.

Concealed suspension systems for acoustical tiles integrate above-ceiling access areas into the system. Access is upward or downward, depending on the system. Care should be taken to prevent damage to the ceiling tile during installation and maintenance of the system and above-ceiling elements.

Structural Performance

Ceiling suspension systems for acoustical tiles are designated as light-, intermediate-, or heavy-duty. Light-duty systems are used where there will be no additional loads other than the acoustical tiles; therefore, these systems are typically used only in residential and light commercial applications. Intermediate-duty systems are capable of supporting a moderate amount of additional load, such as light fixtures and ceiling diffusers. Intermediate-duty systems are commonly used in standard commercial applications. Heavy-duty systems can accommodate additional loads suspended from or installed within the ceiling system. Prior to specifying a suspension system, the anticipated loads on the ceiling should be reviewed to determine the most suitable type.

Components

The concealed suspension system is composed of interlocking 15/16-in.- (24-mm-) wide double-web main beams and cross tees. Main beams are typically installed on hanger wires spaced at 4 ft (1,220 mm), on center, along the beam. Angle or channel-shaped moldings are used for perimeter acoustical tile support. Hanger wires support the main and cross tees from the structure above and are spaced per the manufacturer's recommendations and as project conditions require. Accessory components such as clips and concealed angles are available to allow access to the plenum space above the ceiling.

Other special accessory components of the exposed suspension system include stiffeners, clips, spacers, covers, and adapters. While it may be difficult to identify all of the specific accessory components, the major items anticipated on a project, such as hold-down clips, stiffening braces, partition clip, and so on, should be identified, if possible. Specifications should cover accessories as well as the overall suspension system and acoustical tiles.

CONCEALED GRID

FIRE-RATED GRID (CONCEALED GRID SHOWN)

CONCEALED GRID—UPWARD ACCESS (SIDE PIVOT SHOWN; END PIVOT AVAILABLE)

FIRE-RATED CONCEALED GRID—DOWNWARD ACCESS (END PIVOT SHOWN; SIDE PIVOT AVAILABLE)

ACOUSTICAL CEILING TILE SUSPENSION SYSTEMS

Fastens partition track to ceiling grid.

PARTITION CLIP

Vertical attachment to hanger wire between grid and deck holds suspension system in place during wind uplift and in high-security areas.

STIFFENING BRACE

Attaches to top bulb of grid to hold lay-in tile in place, and helps prevent ceiling tile from fluttering at entryways.

HOLD-DOWN CLIP

ISOLATION HANGERS

HANGER WIRE (12-GA. GALVANIZED STEEL WIRE)

MAIN RUNNER

Isolation hangers isolate ceilings from noise traveling through the building structure. Hangers are also available for isolating ceiling systems to shield spaces from mechanical equipment and aircraft noise.

When it is necessary to isolate a high-noise area from a building, or a "quiet room" from a high surrounding noise level, floors, walls, and ceilings should be built free of rigid contact with the building structure to reduce sound and vibration transmission.

ISOLATION HANGER

ACOUSTICAL CEILING MATERIALS

MATERIALS	SIZES (IN.) 12×12	THICKNESS (IN.) ½	⅝	¾	EDGES T&G	Kerfed and rabbeted	NRC RANGE .45–60	.60–70	.70–80	.80–90	.90–95	USES High humidity	Exterior soffit	High abuse/impact	Scrubbable	Fire rating available
Mineral fiber																
Painted	•	•	•	•	•	•	•	•	•	•						•
Plastic face			•					•					•		•	•
Ceramic face			•				•					•	•			•
Mineral face	•		•	•		•	•							•		•
Mylar face	•		•	•		•	•									

Fire-Resistant Suspension Systems

Fire-rated suspension systems conform to the UL design for fire-rated performance. Expansion points are provided at specific intervals to alleviate stresses on the grid in case of intense heat and fire. Cross-tee end clips and other devices must be used as required by UL and local codes. The acoustical tiles installed within the fire-resistant suspension system must also be of a fire-resistive nature.

ACOUSTICAL CEILING SYSTEMS

CEILING TYPE	COMPONENTS Main, cross tee	Access tees	Z-channel	H-channel	T-spline	Flat spline	Spacer	MATERIALS Bent steel	FINISHES Galvanized	Painted	FIRE RATING AVAILABLE	ACOUSTIC TILE SIZES (IN.) 12×12
Concealed T&G				•	•	•		•	•	•	•	•
Concealed T&G			•					•	•	•	•	•
Concealed Z			•			•		•	•	•	•	•
Concealed access	•	•			•	•	•	•	•	•	•	•

SEISMIC DESIGN

For the installation of an acoustical panel ceiling with seismic design requirement locations, review suspension systems with cross-tee end details that accommodate lateral movement. Check with ceiling suspension system manufacturers to determine the seismic capabilities of a particular system.

ACOUSTICAL PANEL CEILINGS

Acoustical panel ceilings are composed of prefabricated ceiling units, installed in a metal suspension system. They are used where sound attenuation and accessibility to the above ceiling interstitial or plenum space are desired. Acoustical ceilings are large visual elements within a space, and are design elements as well as acoustical features. Partitions, light fixtures, ceiling diffusers, sprinklers, and other devices are attached to or installed within these ceilings, so coordination with the ceiling layout is critical.

Acoustical panels are installed on an exposed metal grid system suspended from the underside of the structure above. In contrast, acoustical tiles are inserted to a concealed suspension system and are generally 12 × 12 in. (305 × 305 mm) and 24 × 24 in. (610 × 610 mm). Common acoustical panel sizes range from 24 × 24 in. (610 × 610 mm) to 24 × 48 in. (610 × 1,220 mm) up to 60 × 60 in. (1,524 × 1,524 mm), and are available in rectangular shapes as well as square. Thicknesses range from ⅝ in. (16 mm) to ¾ in. (19 mm) to 1 in. (25 mm), with other thicknesses available for special applications. Most manufacturers provide hard metric–size acoustical panels to address global needs for their products.

Acoustical panel ceiling products are available to meet special project requirements, including the need for greater durability, light reflectance, and humidity resistance. Fire-resistant acoustical ceiling assemblies are available, when used with applicable UL designs.

Consult a manufacturer's product information for specific recommendations on acoustical panel ceiling data.

CEILING TYPES

ASTM E1264, *Classification for Acoustical Ceiling Products,* provides a classification system for ceiling panels that describes various types of panel faces; however, this system is not typically used by designers to specify ceiling panels.

CEILING PANEL COMPOSITION

Several of the same types of acoustical tile are also employed as acoustical panels: water-felted, cast, or molded and nodular. Special acoustical panels composed of a ceramic and mineral fiber composite are used where increased durability, cleanliness, and resistance to humidity and fumes are required. Mylar-faced acoustical panels are used in cleanroom areas, food service, and other applications where cleanability is important.

Fiberglass panels are processed from a molten state into fibrous glass strands, then formed into sheet/board stock. A separate dimensionally stable facing material is laminated to the fiberglass core to provide texture and pattern. Backings are available to improve acoustical qualities of the fiberglass panels.

Recycled content is increasing within acoustical panel manufacturers' product lines, depending on the product selected. Many manufacturers are addressing the issue of sustainability within the manufacturing process, and recycling of old ceiling panels is becoming more widespread.

EDGE DETAILS

Common edge details are square or tegular (reveal) shapes. Acoustical panels with these edge details are easily dropped in place within the suspension system and are pushed up to access the ceiling plenum.

Square Edge

Square-edge acoustical panels are economical and are installed on the exposed ceiling suspension grid flanges. Square-edge panels do not conceal the suspension grid.

Tegular Edge

Tegular-edge acoustical panels have a reveal edge, which allows the panels to extend below the suspension system, partially concealing the metal grid. Tegular edges can be square, angled, beveled, stepped, or other special shapes, and are generally selected for their aesthetic appearance. When installed within an exposed tee suspension system, the acoustical panels read as modular elements, due to the reveals between the panels. Other suspension system profiles fill the tegular-edge reveal, providing a more flush, monolithic appearance to the ceiling.

Beveled Edge

Beveled edges, often found on tegular-edged units, form an eased-edge condition, which softens the line of the perimeter of the panel. When moving panels after the initial installation, beveled edges can minimize edge damage due to accidental bumping of the panel on the grid.

Combination Edge

Some acoustical panel products are now available with special combination-edge details, allowing for partial or complete concealment of the suspension system. This system provides a more monolithic appearance to the acoustical ceiling.

Dual Edge

Dual-edge treatment allows use of a standard 15/16 in. (24 mm) grid. The system provides the accessibility of a lay-in panel, yet appears monolithic.

Panel Edge

Panel-edge treatments are used for installations such as cleanrooms and other spaces requiring a minimum of particulate emission; sealed edges are available on acoustical panels.

SPECIAL USE

Acoustical ceiling panels are available to address special needs. Food service areas often require products that are accepted by the USDA for food preparation areas. Nonperforated mylar-faced or vinyl-faced acoustical panels with appropriate suspension systems can be installed in food service areas as well as in cleanrooms of certain classes. Acoustical properties of these mylar- or vinyl-faced products are less than those of nonfaced products. A check of the local regulations for these installations is recommended.

Composite ceramic and mineral fiber panel products perform well in areas such as indoor pool areas, hydrotherapy areas, laboratories, and other spaces where corrosive materials may be present. The suspension system grid and hangers should be of a corrosion-resistant material such as aluminum or stainless steel, to minimize deterioration.

SQUARE-EDGE LAY-IN PANEL FOR 15/16 IN. (24 MM) TEE SYSTEM

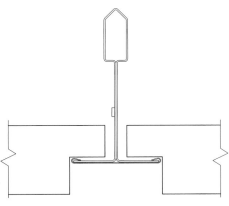

SQUARE TEGULAR EDGE FOR 15/16 IN. (24 MM) EXPOSED TEE SYSTEM

ANGLED TEGULAR EDGE FOR 15/16 IN. (24 MM) EXPOSED TEE SYSTEM

BEVELED TEGULAR EDGE FOR 9/16 IN. (14 MM) EXPOSED TEE SYSTEM

BEVELED TEGULAR EDGE FOR 9/16 IN. (14 MM) BOLT-SLOT TEE SYSTEM

SPECIAL TEGULAR EDGE

PANEL-EDGE CONDITIONS

SUSPENSION SYSTEMS

Exposed acoustical ceiling panel suspension systems are composed of main and cross-tee components, installed at the desired height by hanger wires. The suspension system is typically fabricated from factory-coated steel. Additional types include galvanized steel systems for improved resistance to moisture, and aluminum and stainless steel for other special installation requirements. Fire-rated suspension systems are available, with prenotched expansion relief segments to resist suspension system failure resulting from heat expansion of the grid.

Components

The visible components of an exposed ceiling suspension system include interlocking main beams and cross tees, installed in a prescribed grid to accept the acoustical panels. Main beams are typically installed on hanger wires spaced at 4 ft (1,220 mm), on center, along the beam. Angle or channel-shaped moldings are used for perimeter acoustical panel support. Hanger wires support the main and cross tees from the structure above and are spaced per the manufacturer's recommendations and as project conditions require.

Other special accessory components of the exposed suspension system include stiffeners, clips, spacers, covers, and adapters. While it may be difficult to identify all of the specific accessory components, the major items anticipated on a project, such as hold-down clips, stiffening braces, partition clips, and so on, should be identified, if possible. Specifications should cover accessories as well as the overall suspension system and acoustical panels.

FIRE-RESISTANT SUSPENSION SYSTEMS

Fire-rated suspension systems conform to the UL design for fire-rated performance. Expansion points are provided at specific intervals to alleviate stresses on the grid in case of fire. Cross-tee end clips and other devices must be used as required by UL and local codes. The acoustical panels installed within the fire-resistant suspension system must also be of a fire-resistive nature.

SEISMIC DESIGN

For the installation of an acoustical panel ceiling with seismic design requirement locations, review suspension systems with cross-tee end details that accommodate lateral movement. Check with ceiling suspension system manufacturers to determine the seismic capabilities of a particular system.

$^{15}/_{16}$ **IN. (24 MM) EXPOSED TEE SYSTEM** $^{9}/_{16}$ **IN. (14 MM) EXPOSED TEE SYSTEM** $^{9}/_{16}$ **IN. (14 MM) BOLT-SLOT SYSTEM**

TYPICAL CEILING GRID SYSTEM PROFILES

ACOUSTICAL CEILING SYSTEMS

CEILING TYPE	SUSPENSION SYSTEM COMPONENTS			SUSPENSION SYSTEM MATERIALS				SUSPENSION SYSTEM FINISHES		FIRE RATING AVAILABLE
	Main, Cross tee	T-spline	Spacer	Bent steel	Bent steel, aluminum cap	Bent aluminum	Extruded aluminum	Galvanized	Painted	
Exposed	•			•	•	•	•		•	•
Semiconcealed Grid	•	•	•	•				•	•	•

WALL ANGLE

HANGER WIRE (12-GA. GALVANIZED STEEL WIRE) WRAP THREE FULL TIMES

BUILT-IN EXPANSION SECTION

FIRE-RATED 1 LB/SQ.FT. ACOUSTICAL TILE LAY-IN PANEL

CROSS TEE

MAIN RUNNER

FIRE-RATED EXPOSED GRID

WALL ANGLE

HANGER WIRE (12-GA. GALVANIZED STEEL WIRE) WRAP THREE FULL TIMES

CROSS TEE

ACOUSTICAL LAY-IN PANEL

MAIN RUNNER

EXPOSED GRID

LINEAR METAL CEILINGS

Linear metal ceilings are distinctive in appearance and are used where strong linear aesthetic, durability, and ease of maintenance are desired. Metal surfaces are available with many finishes and colors, which allow for a number of design options for the metal ceiling. Special suspension systems allow custom radius configurations, as well as flat horizontal ceilings, to be installed. Linear metal ceilings are typically installed as snap-in units on a concealed suspension system, and some can accept companion integrated light fixtures.

CEILING TYPES

Linear metal ceilings are fabricated from aluminum, steel, or stainless steel. Options include metal panel (slat) sizes, metal coating types, colors, textures, and acoustical insulation. Linear baffle ceilings are also available, but typically are not installed with acoustical insulation.

SIZES

Linear metal panel dimensions vary by manufacturer, but a common module width range is from 2 in. (51 mm) wide to 8 in. (203 mm) wide. Additional slat panel widths are available from manufacturers. Standard lengths are commonly 12 and 16 ft (3.6 and 4.8 m), but can be tailored to a particular installation with custom lengths. Depths of panels vary, with deeper panels providing a stronger linear effect to the ceiling. Overall size is regulated by the suspension method capacity and installation parameters of the project.

MATERIALS

The most common material for linear metal ceilings is roll-formed aluminum, with typical thicknesses of 0.020 in. (0.5 mm), 0.025 in. (0.6 mm), and 0.032 in. (0.8 mm). Aluminum linear panels are preferred for high-humidity areas and in spaces where the environment fluctuates, as well as for exterior applications. Roll-formed steel linear panels are available, and they can be more economical than aluminum, but are not as commonly used due to concerns about maintenance over time. Stainless steel also performs well, but is typically more costly than aluminum or steel panels.

FINISHES

The numerous metal finishes available provide various aesthetic and design options. Aluminum panels are available mill-finished, anodized, or colored with a baked enamel finish. Steel panels are available with baked enamel, powder coat, or electroplated finishes. Stainless-steel panels are available with brushed or mirror finishes.

Linear metal panel surfaces are available in smooth, perforated, or textured.

Profiles of linear metal ceilings include flat pans and planks, tubular, blade, and baffle shapes. Edge details are formed to ensure proper engagement and alignment within the suspension system. Metal panels intended for interior applications have a roll-finished edge, for strength. Perimeter conditions require special consideration at field-cut panel ends.

For integration of ceiling fixtures and devices, metal panels can be field-cut, unless not recommended by the manufacturer for a particular product installation. Care must be taken when field-cutting the panels, as the rigidity and stiffness of the metal may be compromised.

LINEAR BAFFLE CEILING SYSTEM

LINEAR METAL CEILING

LINEAR METAL CEILING WITH SOUND INSULATION

LINEAR METAL CEILING SYSTEM

TYPICAL BAFFLE PROFILES

TYPICAL PAN CONFIGURATIONS

#12 PRESTRAIGHTENED GALVINIZED WIRE AT 4'-0" O.C. ON MAIN TEE; (3) TWISTS IN 1" MIN.; WRAP ANCHOR DEVICE ABOVE AT 100 LBS MIN. PER HANGING POINT; SEISMIC BRACING, SUCH AS COMPRESSION POSTS AND SPLAY WIRING, PER APPLICABLE BUILDING CODE

LINEAR METAL CEILING PERIMETER CONDITION

ACOUSTIC PROPERTIES

Acoustic properties of linear metal ceilings vary depending upon the type of metal pan used, type of sound attenuation used, and project conditions. Sound waves pass through the reveals between the panels, so the use of sound attenuation will reduce the sound transmitted. Sound passes through the ceiling plenum if ceiling-height partitions are installed in the areas with linear metal ceilings; therefore, sound attenuation batting above the ceiling will improve acoustics slightly. Microperforations are available on some metal panel products, which improve the acoustic qualities of the system, especially if used in conjunction with sound attenuation batting. NRC ratings average around 0.70 to 0.90, depending upon installation conditions.

Fiberglass is the most common material for sound attenuation batting, but it should be wrapped so that the fibers do not escape into the space and compromise the indoor air quality. Reveal filler strips reduce sound transmission. A review with an acoustical consultant and the metal pan ceiling manufacturer may be beneficial when selecting a linear metal ceiling.

SUSPENSION SYSTEMS

Concealed suspension systems for linear metal ceilings are similar to those used for acoustical tile installations. Classifications of the suspension systems are typically intermediate- and heavy-duty, depending upon the type and weight of the linear metal panels. Carrier suspension systems are hung from the structure above by hanger wires, with main tees usually located at 48 in. (1,220 mm), on center, maximum. Special carriers, which require additional support, are available to provide radius configurations of the ceiling. Expansion carriers increase the centerline-to-centerline dimension of the panels to accommodate a nonstandard module installation. Stabilizer bars snap into slots every 4 in. (100 mm), on center, and provide additional strength and rigidity to the suspension system.

ACCESSORIES

Accessories include cross-connector clamps, which are installed at grid intersections of main and cross tees to provide added strength. Wind-uplift struts, seismic clips, and other devices are available to address the requirements of local codes regarding the installation of linear metal ceilings. Trim pieces and moldings are available for perimeter conditions, and access panels provide above-ceiling access.

FIRE RESISTANCE

Some linear metal ceiling systems are listed as UL fire-rated assemblies. Check with manufacturers for specific information regarding the fire resistance of a particular product. Currently, as with metal pan ceilings, linear metal ceilings are not identified as having specific fire-resistive qualities and are not listed in the UL *Fire Resistance Directory*.

RECYCLED CONTENT

Many manufacturers have integrated recycled material to their metal pan ceiling fabrication, although the percentage of recycled content varies among manufacturers and products.

SUSPENDED DECORATIVE GRIDS

Suspended decorative grids are open framework grids, used to provide definition to the ceiling plane and to screen above-ceiling elements. Grids do not enclose the ceiling plenum and are suspended from the structure above.

Decorative grids allow for easy access to lighting, HVAC, and sprinkler systems installed above the ceiling plane.

GRID TYPES

Suspended decorative grids are composed of U-shaped blades roll-formed from sheet metal, formed into modular grid units, and suspended by a ceiling suspension system similar to those used on typical acoustical ceiling installations. Some suspended grid products can support light fixtures, signage, speakers, and other devices typically installed at the ceiling plane.

The suspension of additional elements from the grid must be verified with the manufacturer. Some systems can accommodate the integration of light fixtures and other suspended units within the system. Other systems may require supplemental support for these additional suspended items. Typically, light fixtures are supported from the structure above, independent of the suspended decorative grid system.

GRID MODULE

CELL PANELS

BEAM PROFILE

#12 PRESTRAIGHTENED GALVINIZED WIRE AT 4'-0" O.C. ON MAIN RUNNER THREE TWISTS IN 1" MIN.; WRAP ANCHOR DEVICE ABOVE AT 100 LBS MIN. PER HANGING POINT; SEISMIC BRACING, SUCH AS COMPRESSION POSTS AND SPLAY WIRING, PER APPLICABLE BUILDING CODE

#12 PRESTRAIGHTENED GALVINIZED WIRE AT 4'-0" O.C. ON MAIN RUNNER THREE TWISTS IN 1" MIN.; WRAP ANCHOR DEVICE ABOVE AT 100 LBS MIN. PER HANGING POINT

SPLICE/HANGER OR SEISMIC PLATE; FIELD-FASTEN, AS REQUIRED

COMPRESSION POST PER APPLICABLE BUILDING CODE

SPLAY WIRING AS PER APPLICABLE BUILDING CODE

SEISMIC HANGER CLIP; FIELD-FASTEN, AS REQUIRED

HAIRLINE JOINT

ALIGNMENT CHANNEL

MAIN RUNNER

CROSS RUNNER

MAIN RUNNER

CROSS RUNNER

MAIN AND CROSS-RUNNER INTERSECTION

SEISMIC CLIP DETAIL

SIZES AND COMPONENTS

Grid systems consist of beams or frames, usually 1 in. (25 mm) minimum width. The beams are formed into a larger grid module, typically 2 × 2 ft (610 × 610 mm) or 2 × 4 ft (610 × 1,220 mm). The grid module can be used to form the overall ceiling grid, or can be used as a framework for smaller scale grid inserts. These smaller grids are commonly known as *cells,* which are composed of blades smaller than 1 in. (25 mm) wide. The use of beams, cells, or combinations of the two can provide a ceiling grid with varying openness and visual interest. Beams and cells of differing blade heights can be combined for multiple ceiling plane definition within the suspended grid. Hard metric equivalent sizes are available from most manufacturers.

MATERIALS

Beams are formed from 0.024-in.- (0.6-mm-) thick aluminum or galvanized steel. Ceiling grid blades are fabricated from 0.020-in.- (0.5-mm-) thick aluminum in a U-shaped configuration with square edges. The blades are roll-formed and have top return flanges to provide rigidity for the blade units. In lieu of beams, some grids are composed of steel T-shaped units, with wire mesh inserts instead of cell blades.

FINISHES

Numerous metal finishes are available for varying aesthetic and design options on the grids. Aluminum blades are available anodized or colored with a baked enamel finish. Steel blades are available with colored baked enamel, powder coat, or electroplated finishes. Stainless-steel blades are available with a mirror finish.

CONFIGURATIONS

Suspended decorative grids are typically installed in a right-angled, orthogonal orientation in square and rectangular shapes, but some T-shaped grid types can be installed with curved perimeters and selected custom cell designs. Interlocking components join the beam and cell blades. Moldings and trims are available to finish the ends and perimeter of the grid system.

For access to the ceiling plenum, suspended grids are typically fabricated to provide downward movement of the grid.

ACOUSTIC PROPERTIES

Suspended decorative grids do not have any acoustic value, hence should be used in areas where acoustical performance of the grid is not required or where other sound attenuation is installed within the space.

SUSPENSION SYSTEMS

Suspension systems for decorative grid ceilings are similar to those used for acoustical tile and panel installations. Classifications of the suspension systems for commercial use are typically intermediate- and heavy-duty, depending upon the type and weight of the grid and any approved additional suspended ele-ments. Suspension systems are directly hung from the structure above with hanger wires, with main runners usually located at 48 in. (1,220 mm) on center, maximum. Cross runners are located in the other direction to support each cell module. Accessories such as end clips and seismic clips are available.

FIRE RESISTANCE

Suspended decorative grids are not identified as having specific fire-resistive qualities, and are not listed in the UL *Fire Resistance Directory.* However, some manufacturers identify them as noncombustible items. Check with manufacturers for specific information regarding the fire-resistance ratings of a particular product for a specific installation.

Resources: Armstrong World Industries, Architect's Reference Manual. *Lancaster, PA: Armstrong, 2001.*
American Society for Testing and Materials, ASTM E1374, Guide for Open Office Acoustics and Applicable ASTM Standards. West Conshohocken, PA: ASTM, 1993.
Ceilings & Interior Systems Construction Association. Acoustical Ceilings: Use and Practice. St. Charles, IL: CISCA, 1999.

Pyinerl Chang; Rhode Island School of Design; Providence, Rhode Island
Thitapa Youngcharoen; Rhode Island School of Design; Providence, Rhode Island
Keith McCormack, CCS, CSI; RTKL Associates; Baltimore, Maryland
Setter, Leach & Lindstrom, Inc.; Minneapolis, Minnesota
Blythe + Nazdin Architects, Ltd.; Bethesda, Maryland

ACOUSTICAL CEILING DETAILS

GYPSUM BOARD CEILING

6" MIN.

3/8"

ACOUSTIC CEILING TILE

SHADOW MOLD

FLUSH ACOUSTICAL CEILING TILE AT GYPSUM BOARD CEILING

CONTINOUS METAL TRIM PAINTED TO MATCH GYPSUM BOARD CEILING

ACOUSTIC TILE CEILING

3/4"

1 1/4"

3"

6"

CORNER TRIM

GYPSUM BOARD CEILING

CEILING FRAMING SYSTEM, AS REQUIRED

RECESSED ACOUSTICAL CEILING TILE AT GYPSUM BOARD CEILING

METAL FRAMING AS REQUIRED

GYPSUM BOARD

6"

3 1/2"

3"

ACOUSTIC TILE CEILING

METAL EDGE TRIM

PERIMETER SLOT AIR RETURN

SQUARE-EDGE ACOUSTIC CEILING TILE

EDGE MOLD

FINISH FACE OF WALL

L-MOLD WITH SQUARE-EDGED ACOUSTICAL TILE

3/8"

SQUARE-EDGE ACOUSTIC CEILING TILE

SHADOW MOLD

FINISH FACE OF WALL

SHADOW MOLD WITH SQUARE-EDGED ACOUSTICAL TILE

SQUARE TEGULAR-EDGE ACOUSTIC CEILING TILE

1 1/16"

SHADOW MOLD

FINISH FACE OF WALL

SHADOW MOLD WITH TEGULAR-EDGED ACOUSTICAL TILE

FIELD-CUT TEGULAR-EDGE ACOUSTIC CEILING TILE

EDGE MOLD

FINISH FACE OF WALL

L-MOLD WITH FIELD-CUT TEGULAR-EDGED ACOUSTICAL TILE

3/8"

SQUARE TEGULAR-EDGE ACOUSTIC CEILING TILE

SHADOW MOLD

FINISH FACE OF WALL

SHADOW MOLD WITH TEGULAR-EDGED ACOUSTICAL TILE

Richard Riveire, AIA; DMJM/Rottet; Los Angeles, California

BRICK FLOORING

APPLICATIONS

Brick is a homogenous clay and shale masonry unit, fired at extreme temperatures for a long duration to produce an abrasion-resistant surface material with very high compressive strength. Brick flooring does not require extensive maintenance when properly treated for the application. Interior brick pavers are available in varying sizes and thicknesses to meet the needs of varying installations; they can be specified to meet durability requirements, which range from exterior freeze/thaw exposure to typical indoor environment conditions, including chemical-resistant flooring.

Brick pavers are available in varying sizes and are known by many names. Bricks are available in standard and modular sizes. Nominal dimensions of pavers typically range from (width × length): 4 × 8 in. (102 × 203 mm) to 4 × 12 in. (102 × 305 mm); thickness from 1¼ to 2¼ in. (32 to 57 mm), although the 1¼-in.-

thick brick is less commonly used since thin brick has become available. Thin brick pavers, of ⅜ to ½ in. thick (10 to 13 mm), also known as *brick tiles*, can be installed when material cost and setting depth are of concern. They have been installed in large-scale commercial brick paving projects in lieu of standard brick pavers. Additional brick trim pieces for special conditions such as copings and stair treads are available.

Interior brick paver appearance varies due to manufacturing and firing techniques. Colors range from buff, terra cotta, and darker natural tones to ironspot brick, in smooth to rough textures. Flashed brick is available in a color range featuring black, blue, and brown. Brick pavers are typically available in smooth or wire-cut (also known as *velour*) finishes and are available with chamfered and rounded edges; and special bricks can be fabricated with handicapped-detectable warning features. To add visual interest, brick pavers can be laid up in varying patterns and colors.

SELECTION OF BRICK PAVERS

Brick paver durability is identified by Weathering Classes, defined by ASTM C902, *Pedestrian and Light Traffic Paving Brick*, and ASTM C1272, *Heavy Vehicular Paving Brick*. These standards measure the durability of brick in relation to its compressive strength, 24-hour cold-water absorption, and the saturation coefficient of the brick. Classes SX and MX are suitable for use in exterior installations. Class NX brick pavers are suitable for interior applications, and must be protected from freezing when wet. Most typical interior brick paving installations will not be subjected to freeze/thaw cycles.

The use of salvaged brick is generally not recommended for interior paving, as the durability of the brick is unknown.

Abrasion resistance of paving brick is measured by traffic type classifications, which identify the abrasion index and volume of abrasion loss on the brick, as identified by ASTM C902. Pedestrian traffic, especially from the impact of high-heeled shoes, is typically more abrasive than vehicular traffic.

MORTARED BRICK PAVERS ON WOOD FRAMING

MORTARLESS BRICK PAVERS ON WOOD FRAMING

MORTARLESS BRICK PAVERS ON CONCRETE SLAB

MORTARED BRICK PAVERS ON CONCRETE SLAB

BRICK PAVERS ON STEEL DECK

CONCRETE PAVERS ON CONCRETE SLAB

BRICK FLOORING INSTALLATION

INSTALLATION

Mortar for interior setting beds is typically Type S, which is formulated from 1 part portland cement, ½ part hydrated lime, and 4½ parts sand; or 1 part Type S masonry cement and 3 parts sand. Mortar bed thicknesses vary from ⅜ to 1 in. (10 to 25 mm) thick. Thickset setting beds should be limited to installations where the substrate is a slab on grade or a slab where deflection is minimal to reduce cracking.

Joints between brick pavers may be filled with mortar, sand, or grout. The mortar in joints should be the same as used in the setting bed. For mortarless installations, the joints are hand-tight and filled with mason's sand. Grout composed of cement, lime, sand, and pigment for color is worked into the joints after the pavers have set in the mortar.

Thin brick pavers of ⅜ to ½ in. (10 to 13 mm) thickness may be installed using a thin mortar bed over a rigid substrate, such as concrete. A bond coat is applied to the substrate, prior to the installation of the mortar setting bed. The thin pavers are installed directly on the setting bed.

SEALERS AND PROTECTIVE COATINGS

Sealers and protective coatings, usually in the form of wax, or a combination sealer/finish material, may be applied to interior brick paving to prevent staining. Brick surfaces should be clean and dry prior to the application of any coatings on the flooring. The slip resistance of the brick paving may be affected by the application of the coating.

CHEMICAL-RESISTANT BRICK FLOORING

Chemical-resistant brick flooring has a very low water absorption rate and is fired at higher temperatures than typical interior brick pavers. It is used for industrial, food service, and sanitary areas, which require a chemical- and grease-resistant flooring surface. Chemical-resistant brick is available in varying types, based on the requirements of ASTM C279, *Standard Specification for Chemical-Resistant Masonry Units,* and ASTM C410, *Standard Specification for Industrial Floor Brick.*

Sizes of chemical-resistant brick are similar in length and width to standard brick sizes; however, thicknesses vary based on anticipated use. Bricks range in depth from 1, 1³/₁₆, 1⅜, or 1½ in. (25, 30, 35, or 38 mm) where foot and forklift traffic is anticipated. For heavy traffic areas, brick thickness is 2¼ in. (57 mm); and where severe abuse is anticipated, thickness of 3¾ or 4½ in. (95 or 114 mm) is recommended.

Surfaces of the chemical-resistant brick flooring range from smooth to textured and abrasive surfaces intended to improve slip resistance when wet. Textured surfaces make cleaning more difficult, and chipping/wear on many slip-resistant surfaces may occur. The bottom surface of the bricks is important to consider; use wire-cut or shallow-scored bottoms to minimize the possibility of trapping liquids and bacteria under the brick.

Chemical-resistant brick flooring is typically installed over a reinforced concrete slab. Grouts and resin mortars are usually furan- and epoxy-based. Floor drains are generally installed in chemical-resistant brick floors, and must be compatible with the entire flooring assembly to properly drain any caustic materials. Floors require a minimum slope of ¼ in. per foot (1:50) to drains. Membranes are commonly applied under chemical-resistant brick flooring to provide a barrier to liquids and to act as a cushion between the concrete subfloor and the mortar setting bed.

Any expansion joints required within the installation should be sealed with chemical-resistant sealants. Compatibility with mortars and grouts should be checked.

For specialized industrial chemical-resistant brick flooring installations, such as meatpacking plants and dairies, additional precautions must be taken when installing the chemical-resistant waterproof membrane and the brick flooring, to ensure that local and state health code requirements are met.

Min Kyeny Kang; Rhode Island School of Design; Providence, Rhode Island
Mark Forma; Leo A. Daley Company; Washington, D.C.
MASTERSPEC®; published by ARCOM; Salt Lake City, Utah and Alexandria, Virginia

RUNNING BOND

OFFSET BOND

OFFSET BOND

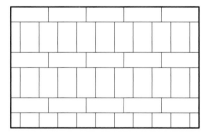

MIXED RUNNING AND STACK BOND

BASKET WEAVE

BASKET WEAVE

DIAGONAL BOND

HERRINGBONE

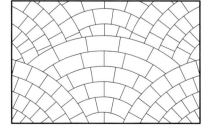

ROMAN COBBLE

BRICK PATTERNS

STONE FLOORING

STONE FLOORING TYPES

Stone flooring, or paving, in interior applications is a durable pedestrian traffic surface. Properly selected and installed, stone flooring wears well over time. Stone flooring can convey a sense of permanence and elegance, and is often used in lobbies and other public spaces.

Numerous types of stones can be used for flooring. The selection of a stone should be appropriate for the intended use. Not all stones are capable of withstanding the traffic of commercial installations, so a review of stone types with the stone fabricator or supplier is recommended.

Stone flooring is available in two basic types: *dimension stone*, which is installed in a thick mortar bed, and *dimension stone tiles*, which is installed in a thick mortar bed or in a thinset installation, similar to ceramic tile installations.

STONE TILE AND PAVER INSTALLATION

Joint width should always be specified; 1/16 to 1/8 in. (1.6 to 3 mm) is considered standard. When installing stone flooring over a wood subfloor, the floor should be reinforced to ensure against deflection.

Lippage is a condition that occurs when tiles are installed with a thin bed over an uneven surface. Tiles may "lip" one edge higher than adjacent tiles, presenting a ragged appearance on the finished surface. In some conditions, a certain amount of lippage is unavoidable. As a general rule, the recommended maximum variation of the finished surface should be no more than 3/16 in. (4.8 mm) cumulative over a 10 ft (3 m) lineal measurement, with no more than 1/32 in. (.8 mm) variation between individual tiles.

DIMENSION STONE

Dimension stone is defined as quarried stone with usually one or more mechanically dressed surfaces. These are thick slabs of stone that are marked as they are cut for matched-pattern installations, such as book-match or end-match configurations.

Dimension stone tiles are less than 3/4 in. (19 mm) thick. They provide the natural beauty of a stone floor without the weight, depth, and expense of dimension stone. However, their thinness makes stone tiles more prone to cracking from impact or normal floor deflection. Stone tiles are installed by either the thick-bed or the thinset installation methods.

Stone flooring dimensions typically range from larger dimension stone paver units with face areas up to 48 sq in. × 3/4, 1 1/4, or 2 in. (1,200 sq mm × 19 (2 cm), 32 (3 cm), or 50 mm) thick. Sizes and shapes are limited to the specific stone's characteristics. Stone tile modules are typically 12 to 24 sq in. × 1/4, 3/8, or 1/2 in. (305 to 610 sq mm × 6, 10, and 13 mm) thick, and typically are furnished with a protective backing to improve the tile strength. Larger stone tile sizes may be available if appropriate for the stone type. Metric sizes for dimension stone and stone tiles are also available from selected manufacturers. Dimension stone for stair and threshold applications are typically custom-sized.

STONE PAVER DURABILITY

Most typical interior stone paving installations will not be subjected to the freeze/thaw cycles of exterior stone paving. Most stones are adequately hard and sound to withstand the rigors of interior pedestrian and light vehicular traffic; however, each stone should be reviewed to determine its appropriateness for a particular paving application.

STONE FINISHES

Stone finishes affect the perception of the color and the slip resistance of stone flooring. Common stone finishes are *polished, honed,* and *thermal.*

- *Polished finishes are the most reflective.* These high-maintenance finishes should be selected with care. For high-traffic public areas, such as lobbies, polished floor finishes are often eventually hidden under nonskid mats.
- *Honed finishes have a dull sheen.* These satin smooth surfaces are often good choices for commercial floors because of their slip resistance.
- *Thermal, sometimes called flamed, finishes are achieved by the application of intense flaming heat to the surface of the stone.* Thermal finishes are usually applied to granite.
- *Waterjet is a newer type of finish for granite, which is between honed and thermal finishes.* Created by high water pressure, the waterjet finish brings out the color of the stone, making it slightly darker than the thermal finish.

TYPICAL FINISHES AND COMMON SIZES OF STONE TILES AND PAVERS

| STONE | FINISH | MINIMUM THICKNESS | | MAXIMUM FACE DIMENSION | | Ha[1] |
		IN	MM	IN	MM	
Granite	Polished Honed Thermal	3/8, 1/2 (tiles) 1 1/4–4 (pavers)	9.5, 13 (tiles) 32–102 (pavers)	12 × 12 (tiles) 15 × 30 (pavers)	305 × 305 (tiles) 381 × 762 (pavers)	N/A
Marble	Polished Honed	1/4–1/2 (tiles) 1 1/4 (pavers)	6–13 (tiles) 32 (pavers)	12 × 12 (tiles) 24 × 24 (pavers)	305 × 305 (tiles) 610 × 610 (pavers)	10
Limestone	Smooth	1 3/4 –2 1/2 (pavers)	44–64 (pavers)	24 × 36 (pavers)	610 × 915 (pavers)	10
Slate	Natural cleft Sand-rubbed	1/4–1	6–25	12 × 12 to 24 × 54	305 × 305 to 610 × 1,372	8
Flagstone	Natural cleft Semirubbed	1/2–4	13–102	12 × 12 to 24 × 36	305 × 305 to 610 × 915	8

[1]Ha, the abrasive hardness value, is the reciprocal of the volume of the material abraded multiplied by 10. A minimum value of 10 is recommended for flooring. Stones with a difference of 5 or more in Ha should not be used together because they will wear differently.

SQUARES

GEOMETRIC

OCTAGON SQUARE

COURSED

DIAMOND

HERRINGBONE

MARBLE AND GRANITE PATTERNS

STONE THRESHOLDS AND TRANSITIONS

The ADAAG states that thresholds are considered changes in level, and are restricted in height and bevel. Vertical changes in level must not exceed ¼ in. (6 mm). Changes in level between ¼ and ½ in. (6 and 13 mm) in height must be beveled with a slope no greater than 1:2. Ramps are required for any changes in level greater than ½ in. (13 mm).

SLIP RESISTANCE

Slip resistance for natural stone flooring is a controversial subject. Slip resistance is a relative measure of the frictional force required to prevent slipping on a paving surface. Various test methods are available to measure the static coefficient of friction (SCOF). ASTM C1028, *Standard Test Method for Determining the Static Coefficient of Friction of Ceramic Tile and Other Like Surfaces by the Horizontal Dynamometer Pull-Meter Method,* measures the static coefficient of friction for ceramic tile and similar surfaces (including stone), and is used under wet and dry conditions. ASTM D2047, *Standard Test Method of Friction of Polish-Coated Floor Surfaces as Measured by the James Machine,* the test for determining the static coefficient of friction for polish-coated floor surfaces, is used to measure slip resistance under dry conditions only. The greater the SCOF number, the less slippery the surface. Currently, there is no test specifically for the slip resistance of stone paving. The appendix to the Americans with Disabilities Act (ADA), *Accessibility Guidelines for Buildings and Facilities (ADAAG),* recommends, but does not require, that stone floors have a minimum static coefficient of friction of 0.6 for level surfaces and 0.8 for ramped surfaces. The ADA does not specify a test method for the static coefficient of friction. These values differ from the Ceramic Tile Institute of America's recommendation of 0.5 or greater. Typically, only a thermal finish will provide the 0.8 SCOF.

When specifying a stone floor, consider the stone finish, application of any topical stone coatings, which may affect the slip resistance, and the type of traffic and use that is anticipated for the installation. Consult the stone fabricator or supplier's test data for SCOF information.

STONE SEALERS

The use of sealers and coatings on interior stone flooring must be carefully considered, as many products are available and the results depend on many factors of the installation and ongoing maintenance of the floor. Sealers can reduce moisture absorption, but require reapplication periodically and may develop an unsightly buildup. Some sealers may change in color over time and may make the floor appear dingy from yellowing and from dirt buildup sticking to the sealer. Coatings are available to improve slip resistance, conceal scratches, and protect the stone from moisture and tracked-in dirt. Consult the product's performance data; use—cautiously—sealers that have been successfully used in the past.

ABRASION RESISTANCE

Abrasion resistance is the capability of the stone to resist wear and absorption, which affects staining and soiling of the stone. Abrasive hardness (Ha) is measured by ASTM C241, *Standard Test Method for Abrasion Resistance of Stone Subjected to Foot Traffic.* Recommended abrasive hardness is 10 for interior flooring. Consult with the stone fabricator or supplier for the selection of appropriate stone types for a particular installation and intended use.

The combination of different stones and different stone finishes may be of concern in interior installations, as the slip and abrasion resistance may differ. Marble and granite in combination will wear unevenly, and may produce additional hazards to pedestrians; moreover, maintenance and refinishing of the floor will be difficult.

DIMENSION STONE INSTALLATION

Installation of interior dimension stone flooring typically uses a mortar setting bed over a structurally sound substrate, usually reinforced concrete. Substrates must support the flooring as well as the intended live and dead loads of the final occupancy. Steel decking systems and wood framing are acceptable if they are stiff enough to limit deflection. Stone can accommodate deflection of approximately 1/720 of the span. In cases where deflection may be a concern, stone tiles may be an option. Uneven substrates intended for thin-set stone tile can be leveled prior to installation. When moisture is a concern, a vapor-retardant membrane should be installed.

OPEN JOINT

THICK-SET–CLOSED JOINT STONE OVER WOOD FLOOR

STONE OVER WOOD FLOOR STONE SANDWICH FLOOR PANEL (PREFAB)

STONE SANDWICH FLOOR PANEL (PREFAB)

STONE FLOORING

SETTING BEDS

Mortar beds are either bonded to the substrate or unbonded, allowing movement between the substrate and the mortar bed. A bonded bed is produced with a 1:3 or 1:4 cement-to-sand mixture, ¾- to 1-in. (19 to 25 mm) thick. Unbonded beds are composed of a semidry 1:3 cement-to-sand mortar mixture laid in thicknesses between 1 to 2½ in. (25 to 64 mm). Thickness of the mortar bed varies based on project conditions. When deflection of the floor is of concern, an isolating membrane should be installed between the substrate and the mortar bed. This bed should be a minimum of 1⅝ in. (40 mm) thick, with steel reinforcing mesh laid midbed for additional strength.

ADHESIVE BEDS

Thinset adhesive beds are approximately ⅛ in. (3 mm) or less and are used for stone tile units. Thin adhesive beds follow the floor plane and cannot accommodate adjustments to the finished floor to become level. Thick adhesive beds range from ⅛ to ¼ in. (3 to 6 mm) in thickness and can accommodate greater adjustments in the level of the finished floor. Refer to the manufacturer's recommendations for suitability of the product to the application and for installation information.

LATEX-MODIFIED PORTLAND CEMENT MORTAR
Use latex-modified portland cement mortar on level, clean slab-on-grade construction where no bending stresses occur and expansion joints are installed.

EPOXY ADHESIVE
Use epoxy adhesive in areas subject to moisture and certain chemicals. It is more costly and difficult to apply than latex portland cement mortar.

THINSET FLOORING DETAILS

STONE STAIRS

Stone may be used on stairs as a finish material or can be supported by stringers to form structural treads. Fully supported treads are typically ¾ to 1¼ in. (19 to 32 mm) thick. Stair substrates may be concrete or steel-framed treads and risers. Treads and risers are installed in a similar manner as stone flooring units, although the thin-set adhesive method is recommended. Based on project conditions, risers may require additional restraint, and treads may be detailed with recessed nonslip strip inserts.

The ADA has established requirements for the configuration and profile of stair elements. Consult the ADA for specific information on design requirements for stairs.

METAL PAN WITH STONE SAFETY TREAD

STONE SUBTREAD AND RISER WITH STONE TREAD

STONE STAIRS WITH STEEL FRAME

JOINTS

Joints between stone flooring pavers are filled with grout. Latex additives in grout are commonly used to increase the flexural strength of the mortar and improve the curing process by retarding the evaporation of water. Dry-set unsanded grouts are used for joints up to ⅛ in. (3 mm) wide. Larger joints are typically filled with sanded grouts, such as portland cement grout, which are used because the sand reduces the shrinkage of the grout as it dries, thus minimizing cracking. Sanded grouts are not recommended for polished stone floors, due to the possibility of scratching by loose sand particles as the grout wears. Marble is more susceptible to scratching than granite.

Control or *expansion joints* are critical to the success of a large area stone floor installation. Dimensional changes in the floor may differ from one installed material to another, and may result from loading settlement and changes in temperature and humidity. Any movement at the substrate level must be reflected in the setting bed and the finish floor to minimize damage to the stone flooring.

Min-Kyung Kang; Rhode Island School of Design; Providence, Rhode Island
Manami Nakabayashi; Rhode Island School of Design; Providence, Rhode Island
MASTERSPEC®, published by ARCOM; Salt Lake City, Utah, and Alexandria, Virginia
Mark Forma; Leo A. Daly Company; Washington, D.C.
Eric. K. Beach; Rippeteau Architects, PC; Washington, D.C.
Building Stone Institute; New York, New York
George M. Whiteside, III, AIA, and James D. Lloyd; Kennett Square, Pennsylvania
Tile Council of America, Inc.; Anderson, South Carolina

CONTROL JOINT AND FULL MORTAR BED

FLEXIBLE JOINT OVER STRUCTURAL MOVEMENT JOINT—HEAVY TRAFFIC

STRINGER DETAIL
Open risers are not allowed in areas under ADA jurisdiction.

WOOD FLOORING

SELECTION CRITERIA

Wood flooring consists of solid or engineered wood products, and is available in strip, plank, and parquet flooring. All wood floors require regular maintenance to maintain their appearance. Wood flooring industry organizations and suppliers provide detailed information on product specifications.

SOLID WOOD FLOORING

Solid wood flooring is available in many hardwood and softwood species. It can be refinished multiple times. Solid wood flooring should not be installed below grade, due to the possibility of moisture damage to the wood floor.

WOOD STRIP FLOORING

Wood strip flooring for normal use is typically a nominal ¾ in. (19 mm) thick, with actual thickness of $^{25}/_{32}$ in. (19.84 mm), in widths ranging from 1½ in. to 2¼ in. (38 to 57 mm). Lengths are random.

WOOD PLANK FLOORING

Wood plank flooring is also typically a nominal ¾ in. (19 mm) thick, in widths ranging from 3 to 10 in. (76 to 250 mm) and is available in random lengths.

WOOD PARQUET FLOORING

Wood parquet flooring consists of small wood strips, available in individual slats, or is formed into panels or tiles that are arranged to form a pattern. Thickness is typically ⁵⁄₁₆ in. (8 mm) for individual strips and square panels. Other thicknesses are available from some parquet flooring manufacturers. Sizes of panels vary according to pattern and availability.

SELECTION OF WOOD FLOORING

Wood flooring should be selected after considering pedestrian and vehicular (cart) traffic, durability required, and potential damage to floors; typical usage, exposure to moisture and sunlight, maintenance, wood floor appearance expectations, and other criteria specific to the project.

The majority of woods specified for commercial flooring are hardwoods such as oak or maple. Best overall appearance, uniformity of color, limited amounts of character marks, and minimal sap marks indicate the most desirable wood flooring.

Flooring can be manufactured from practically every commercially available species of wood. For marketing purposes in the United States, wood flooring is roughly grouped according to species and region. Various grading systems are used with various species, and often specifications differ for boards of different sizes in a given species. For instance, recommended nail size and spacing vary among the several board sizes typically available in oak.

The table below shows typical grades and sizes of boards by species or regional group. Grade classifications vary, but in each case it can be assumed that the first grade listed is the highest quality and that the quality decreases with each succeeding grade. The best grade typically minimizes or excludes features such as knots, streaks, spots, checks, and torn grain, and will contain the highest percentage of longer boards. Grade standards have been reduced in recent years for most commercially produced flooring, hence a thorough review of exact grade specifications is in order when selecting wood flooring.

ENGINEERED WOOD FLOORING

Engineered wood flooring is available in strip, plank, or parquet tiles. Hardwood face veneers are laminated to a dimensionally stable, multiple-ply substrate. Engineered wood floors are not as susceptible to moisture as solid wood flooring, and may be used in below-grade areas, with the proper installation techniques.

TYPICAL GRADES AND SIZES OF BOARDS BY SPECIES OR REGIONAL GROUP

GROUP	INDUSTRY ORGANIZATION	GRADE	THICKNESS IN. (MM)	WIDTH IN. (MM)	NOTES
Oak, ash, black cherry, and walnut; also beech, birch, hard maple, pecan, and hickory	National Oak Flooring Manufacturers Association Memphis, Tennessee Tel: (901) 526-5016 www.nofma.org	Oak, ash, black cherry, and walnut: Clear Select Common (Nos. 1 and 2) Beech, birch, and hard maple: First (including red and white) Second Third (See note for other species)	Strip ¾ (19) ½ (13) Maple, beech, birch only ¾ (19), $^{25}/_{32}$ (20), $^{33}/_{32}$ (26) Plank ¾ (19)	Face 1½ (38), 2 (50), 2¼ (57), 3¼ (82) 1½ (38), 2 (50) 1½ (38), 2 (50), 2¼ (57), 3¼ (82) 3 (76), 4 (101), 5 (127), 6 (152), 7 (177), 8 (203)	Factory-finished oak flooring is available in Prime, Standard, and Tavern grades ¾ in. (19) thick with a face width of 1½ or 2¼ in. (38 or 57 mm). NOFMA grades hickory/pecan as first grade, first grade red, first grade white, second grade, second grade red, and third grade.
Hard maple (*Acer saccharum*—not soft maple); also beech and birch	Maple Flooring Manufacturers Association Northbrook, Illinois Tel: (847) 480-9138 www.maplefloor.org	First Second and Better Third	$^{25}/_{32}$ (20), $^{33}/_{32}$ (26)	Face 1½ (38) 2¼ (57) 3¼ (82)	The Maple Flooring Manufacturers Association states that beech and birch have physical properties that make them fully suitable as substitutes for hard maple. See manufacturer for available width and thickness combinations.
Southern pine	Southern Pine Inspection Bureau Pensacola, Florida Tel: (850) 434-2611 www.spib.org	B and B C C and Better D No. 2	⅜ (9), ½ (13), ⅝ (16), 1 (25), 1¼ (32), 1½ (38)	Nominal Face 2 (50) 1⅛ (28) 3 (76) 2⅛ (54) 4 (101) 3⅛ (79) 5 (127) 4⅛ (104) 6 (152) 5⅛ (130)	Grain may be specified as edge (rift), near-rift, or flat. If not specified, manufacturer will ship flat or mixed-grain boards. Check with manufacturer for available width and thickness combinations.
Western woods (Douglas fir, hemlock, Englemann spruce, Idaho white pine, incense cedar; Lodgepole pine, Ponderosa pine, sugar pine, Western larch, Western red cedar)	Western Wood Products Association Portland, Oregon Tel: (503) 224-3930 www.wwpa.org	All but Idaho white pine: B and Better Select C Select D Select Idaho white pine: Supreme Choice Quality	2 in. (50) and thinner	Nominal 3 (76) 4 (101) 6 (152)	Flooring is machined tongue and groove and may be furnished in any grade. Grain may be specified as vertical (VG), Flat (FG), or mixed (MG). Basic size for flooring is 1 in. × 4 in. × 12 ft (25 mm x 101 mm x 3.6 m); standard lengths are 4 ft (1.2 m) and longer. The moisture content of these grades is 15% MC, with 85% of the pieces less than 12% MC.

Source: National Oak Flooring Manufacturers Association; Memphis, Tennessee

WOOD CHARACTERISTICS

Annual growth rings are visible in the wood and vary in color and density. The inner part of the growth ring is known as *springwood,* and has relatively large cell cavities and thin cell walls. *Summerwood* has smaller cell cavities and thicker, denser cell walls than springwood. Growth rings, when exposed by sawing methods, provide the grain and pattern in the wood flooring.

In hardwoods, plain-sawn lumber generally contains mostly flat-grained wood, while quarter-sawn lumber is nearly all vertically grained.

Figuring is the pattern produced in a wood surface by annual growth rings, rays, knots, and deviations from regular growth.

Medullary rays extend radially from the core of the tree toward the exterior bark. They vary in height from a few cells in some species to 4 in. (100 mm) or more in the oaks; they are responsible for the flake effect common to the quarter-sawn lumber in certain species.

Tangential Grain

Tangential grain is typically called *flat grain;* it is easily recognized by its parabolic (arched) effect. Lumber is considered flat-grained when the annual growth rings make an angle of less than 45° with the wide surface of the board.

Radial Grain

Radial grain is known as *vertical* or *edge grain.* It is generally more stable than flat grain, and is less likely to expand or contract in width with changes in moisture. Lumber is considered vertical grained when the annual growth rings form an angle of 45° to 90° with the wide surface of the board.

Durability

Durability of wood flooring varies with the wood species and the finish selected. Hardwoods such as oak and maple typically perform better than softwoods, such as pine. Not all hardwoods are suitable for wood flooring. The wood species hardness and the cut of the wood flooring affects its ability to resist indentation, wear, and marring.

Wood strip and plank flooring is quarter-sawn (edge grain) or plain-sawn (flat grain) and typically is milled into a tongue-and-groove shape. Quarter-sawn strip flooring is considered to be more durable, due to the exposure of the vertical grain of the wood. It is also more expensive than plain-sawn wood, as more waste wood is generated. Rift-sawn strips are generally associated with oak flooring; it is also costly, as there is more waste than from quarter-sawn wood strips. Jointed, or square-edged flooring is also available. End-grain wood blocks are durable flooring units, installed in a jointed fashion.

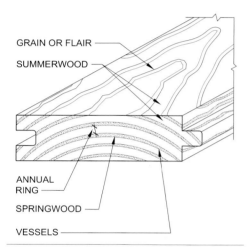

GROWTH RINGS IN WOOD FLOORING
Source: National Wood Flooring Association; Manchester, Missouri

Wood is a hygroscopic material that changes dimensionally with the absorption or release of moisture, causing swelling or shrinking. After manufacturing, wood flooring is kiln-dried at the factory to a 6% to 9% moisture content. At the project site, the flooring must be protected to maintain proper moisture content, and must acclimatize to the space, which should be of the manufacturer's recommended environmental conditions for installation. Prior to installation, provisions should be made for movement of the flooring at the perimeter of the wood floor. The relative humidity of the space and the moisture content of the wood are also factors, as is the moisture content of a concrete substrate.

BLIND-NAILED TONGUE-AND-GROOVE WOOD FLOORING
Source: Maryrose McGowan; Specifying Interiors; John Wiley & Sons, Inc., 1996, p.171.

QUARTER-SAWN, OR EDGE GRAIN

PLAIN-SAWN, OR FLAT GRAIN

CROSS SECTION OF LOG
Source: Maryrose McGowan; Specifying Interiors; John Wiley & Sons, Inc., 1996, p.171.

HOLLOW BACK (EDGE GRAIN)   SCRATCH BACK (FLAT GRAIN)

PLAIN (EDGE GRAIN)   HOLLOW OR SCRATCH BACK (FLAT GRAIN)

The underside of flooring boards may be patterned, and it often contains more defects than are allowed in the top face. Grain is often mixed in any given run of boards. Edge grain is also called vertical grain.

BOARD CHARACTERISTICS

5/16", 3/8", 1/2", AND 5/8"

LIGHT USE

3/4", 25/32"

NORMAL SERVICE

33/32", 1 1/4", AND 1 1/2"

HEAVY USE

Most flooring is available in a variety of thicknesses to suit different wear requirements.

VARIOUS THICKNESSES

NOMINAL OR "COUNTED"

ACTUAL (SOMETIMES NOMINAL)

FACE

ACTUAL

NOMINAL

Cross-sectional dimensioning systems vary among species, patterns, and manufacturers. Trade organizations provide percentage multipliers for computing coverage.

CROSS-SECTION DIMENSIONS

FACE NAIL ALL BOARDS

SUBFLOOR, TYPICAL

JOINTED

+/- 50°

FACE NAIL STARTER BOARD ONLY

TONGUE AND GROOVE

Jointed flooring must be face-nailed, usually with fully barbed flooring brads.

Tongue-and-groove boards are blind-nailed with spiral floor screws, cement-coated nails, cut nails, or machine-driven fasteners; follow the manufacturer's recommendations.

FASTENING

PARQUET FLOOR PATTERNS

INSTALLATION

Wood flooring requires particular care in handling and installation. Prior to installation, the wood flooring should be allowed to acclimate to the space in which it is to be installed, at the humidity level of the final occupancy. Minimize moisture damage to wood floors by avoiding installation in close proximity to wet areas. In addition, to ensure constant temperature and humidity, install wood floors after all "wet" jobs have been completed and after the heating plant and all permanent lighting have been installed.

Wood flooring is subject to expansion and contraction; therefore, perimeter base details that allow for movement and ventilation are recommended. Wood structures require adequate ventilation in basements and crawl spaces. Under a slab on or below grade, moisture control can be further enhanced by use of a vapor barrier; this provision should be carefully considered for each installation.

Wearing properties of wood flooring vary from species to species and should be considered along with appearance when specifying wood floors. In addition, grain pattern affects the durability of a given species. For instance, industrial wood blocks are typically placed with the end grain exposed because it presents the toughest wearing surface. The thickness of the wood above the tongues in tongue-and-groove flooring may be increased for extra service.

Wood floors are installed over a plywood subfloor or over wood sleepers. Strips or planks are blind-nailed in tongue-and-groove installations and face-nailed in butt-jointed installations; parquet floors are commonly set in mastic. Vapor barriers are installed when the installation is slab on grade or below grade. Ventilation is required in certain installation conditions where moisture is a concern. Special conditions require additional detailing for proper installation.

WOOD FLOOR FINISHES

Wood floors must be finished to protect the surface from wear. Applied finishes can be installed in the field or, in the case of engineered wood floors, they can be factory-finished. Floor finishes do not protect the wood from the effects of ultraviolet light, which can alter the appearance of the wood. Some species are more susceptible to change when exposed to sunlight; however, UV inhibitors are available to minimize fading. Color plates C-20 to C-27 illustrate the difference in appearance between water-base urethane and oil-modified polyurethane finishes applied to eight species of wood flooring.

Field Finishes

Unfinished wood flooring can be stained to achieve an exact color match with other design elements or to mimic the appearance of a softer wood that might not have met the performance expectations of the installation.

Before the application of a field finish, wood floors are sanded so that they are level and smooth, then one of several finishes is applied. All of these finishes are subject to wear and must be touched up or removed and reapplied during the life of the floor.

There are basically three types of commercial finishes for wood floors: *acid curing, oil-modified polyurethanes,* and *water-based polyurethanes.*

Acid Curing

Acid-curing finishes, sometimes called Swedish finishes, are hard and durable; they are thicker and less viscous than other types of finishes, making for heavier coats. Acid-curing finishes are solvent-based, two-part formulations requiring on-site mixing. They have a naturally high volatile organic compound (VOC) content, so masks are typically worn because of the noxious odor. These finishes tend to be less expensive than water-based polyurethanes, but more expensive than oil-modified polyurethanes.

Oil-Modified Polyurethane

Oil-modified polyurethanes are easy to apply and the least expensive of the three finishes, but they also have a high VOC content. Oil-modified polyurethanes tend to turn amber-colored (slightly orange) as they age.

Water-Based Polyurethane

Water-based polyurethanes have a low VOC content and do not yellow or change color over time. Because they are thinner, more coats are required to achieve the same depth as produced by an acid-curing finish. Water-based polyurethanes tend to be the most expensive type of wood floor finish.

Tonn Lensment; Rhode Island School of Design; Providence, Rhode Island
Rippeteau Architects, P.C.; Washington, D.C.
Annica S. Emilsson; Rippeteau Architects, P.C.; Washington, D.C.
National Oak Flooring Manufacturers Association; Memphis, Tennessee
National Wood Flooring Association; Manchester, Missouri
MASTERSPEC®; published by ARCOM; Salt Lake City, Utah, and Alexandria, Virginia

TYPICAL BASE SUITABLE FOR MOST WOOD FLOOR SYSTEMS

3/4" EXT. PLYWOOD FASTENED TO SLAB

POLYETHYLENE FILM

VAPOR BARRIER

BUILDING PAPER

NAIL THROUGH TONGUES

CONCRETE SLAB

STRIPS OVER PLYWOOD UNDERLAYMENT

STRIP FLOORING

1/4" POLYETHYLENE FOAM

6-MIL POLYETHYLENE VAPOR BARRIER

TWO LAYERS OF 1 X 6 SLEEPERS PLACED DIAGONALLY 2" APART

STRIPS OVER VENTILATED SLEEPERS

MASTIC

VAPOR BARRIER

RANDOM-LENGTH WOOD SLEEPERS (18" TO 48" LONG) SET IN ROWS 16" O.C.

STRIP FLOORING

POLYETHYLENE FILM

STRIPS OVER STAGGERED TWO-BY-FOUR SLEEPERS

1 X 3 WOOD NAILER

MASTIC

VAPOR BARRIER

STRIP FLOORING

POLYETHYLENE FILM

TREATED 1 X 3

DOUBLE COURSE OF SLEEPER STRIPS

BASE WITH BUILT-IN VENTS

SLEEPER

CUSHION UNDER SLEEPER

POLYETHYLENE FILM

WOOD FLOORING

VAPOR BARRIER

STRIPS OVER CUSHIONED SLEEPERS

PLYWOOD OR BOARD SUBFLOOR MUST BE STURDY AND VENTILATED

STRIP FLOORING

15-LB FELT OR BUILDING PAPER

For parquet flooring, the subfloor must be ¾ in. tongue-and-groove plywood, minimum, with a mastic coating.

STRIPS OVER SUBFLOOR ON WOOD JOISTS

RESILIENT BOARD

STEEL CHANNELS WITH LOCKING CLIPS

6-MIL POLYETHYLENE

EXPANSION SPACE NOT REQUIRED WITH THIS SYSTEM

METAL CHANNEL RUNNERS WITH CLIPS

JAMB

VENTED BASE

METAL THRESHOLD PLATE FIXED TO SLAB, NOT TO FLOORING

WOOD FLOORING

EXPANSION PLATE AT DOORWAY/JOINT WITH DISSIMILAR CONSTRUCTION

END GRAIN WOOD BLOCKS

CONCRETE SLAB

VAPOR BARRIER

PITCH FINISH COATS SQUEEGEED

PITCH SETTING BED

PRIMING OIL

Typical blocks are 3 × 6 in. up to 4 × 8 in., with depths of 2 to 4 in. Urethane finish coats are available for nonindustrial uses.

INDUSTRIAL WOOD BLOCK

Factory Finishes

Acrylic-impregnated (sometimes called *irradiated polymer)* wood flooring is extremely durable. This most recent advance in finishes imparts many of the qualities of resilient flooring to the wood, such as an increased resistance to abrasion and bacterial growth. The process involves removing the air from the pores of dried wood and forcing liquid acrylic into the voids. The plastic-filled wood is then irradiated (exposed to radiation), causing the acrylic to polymerize.

Prefinished wood flooring is also available with multiple coats of polyurethane or other proprietary finishes.

Ecological Issues

The issue of tropical wood use and destruction of the tropical rainforests and other ecologically endangered areas is addressed by many manufacturers of imported wood flooring. Studies have shown that land use changes have actually adversely affected the tropical rainforests more than the lumber industry. Check with wood flooring manufacturers to determine if they are using acceptable means of harvesting imported wood products.

RESILIENT WOOD FLOORING

Resilient wood flooring is commonly used in athletic facilities. The typical wood flooring species for sports facilities is maple, which is preferred due to its density, fineness of grain, and nonsplintering qualities. Beech and birch are also used by some manufacturers for resilient wood floors. Finishes are typically transparent, and supplemental markings may be added with approved materials and techniques for floor striping and logos.

The Maple Flooring Manufacturers Association (MFMA) provides detailed information on the features, installation, and maintenance for maple flooring. Wood sports floor systems vary from one manufacturer to another, and some are engineered for specific purposes, such as aerobics use. Some systems are proprietary and are protected by patents. The information contained in this section refers to typical resilient wood flooring systems. Consult manufacturers for specific information.

Resilient wood flooring is commonly milled into tongue-and-groove-shaped strips of random length. Typical thickness is $^{25}/_{32}$ in. (20 mm) for most general-purpose resilient wood flooring. A $1^{1}/_{32}$ in. (26 mm) thickness is available from selected manufacturers when additional loads are anticipated and where usage is expected to be more severe than normal. Widths range from $1^{1}/_{2}$ in. (38 mm) to $3^{1}/_{4}$ in. (83 mm).

The type of wood sports flooring chosen for a particular situation depends on the following criteria:

- Cost
- Performance of the floor
- Sport(s) to be played on the floor
- Other uses to which floor will be put
- Durability
- Environment in which the floor will be used

Grades of Wood Sports Flooring

Maple, the wood most commonly used for sports flooring in the United States, is available in three grades, which designate only the appearance of the floor and not its performance or durability.

- *First grade:* Nearly free of defects; least color variation, with very little dark hardwood. First grade is used in premier sports venues where appearance is of primary concern.
- *Second and better:* May have tight, sound knots and other slight imperfections and some color variation. This grade of floor has a generally light appearance.
- *Third grade:* All defects and color variations are permitted. This grade of floor is mostly dark heartwood, and is used when cost is a consideration.

Finishes and Game Lines

Wood sports floors are sanded, sealed, and finished with at least two coats of sealer and two coats of finish. Game lines are painted between the last coat of sealer and the first coat of finish. Game line paint must be compatible with sealer and finish.

Karen K. Lindblad; Chicago, Illinois
Jim Swords; HOK Sports Facilities Group; Kansas City, Missouri
Connor/Aga Sports Flooring Corporation; Amasa, Michigan
Robbins Sports Surfaces; Cincinnati, Ohio
Exerflex; Indianapolis, Indiana
Maple Flooring Manufacturers Association; Northbrook, Illinois

Lowest cost
Easy to install
Suitable for multipurpose applications
Use where floor performance is not critical

MASTIC-APPLIED SYSTEM

Good performance characteristics
Relatively low cost
Susceptible to moisture damage

CUSHIONED SYSTEM

Dimensionally stable in all environments
Good multipurpose floor
Limited performance characteristics

CHANNEL AND CLIP SYSTEM

Low cost
Fast installation
Dimensionally stable in all environments
Good multipurpose floor
Limited performance characteristics

NAIL-IN-CHANNEL SYSTEM

AEROBICS STUDIOS

A well-designed aerobics studio will provide a minimum floor space of 5 sq ft (.5 sq m) per person. One wall of full-height mirrors should also be provided. A stretching bar can be incorporated into the mirror wall. A storage closet or built-in wall cabinet for equipment is preferred. If sound transmission will be a problem for rooms located adjacent to the aerobics studio, appropriate partition, floor, and ceiling details should be selected. The ceiling plan should incorporate stereo speakers, ceiling fans, and adequate lighting and ventilating solutions.

The aerobics studio shown includes the essential details and features of a well-designed space.

Sherrie Roach; lauckgroup; Dallas, Texas

ELEVATION

- PAINT AS SCHEDULED
- 22'-0"
- EQ.
- EQ.
- GYPSUM BOARD SOFFIT
- SUSPENDED CEILING
- FIVE EQUAL DOOR PAIRS
- TV
- VCR
- STEREO
- 2'-6"
- 8'-6"
- 6'-0"
- 1'-4" 1'-0" 1'-0"
- PLASTIC LAMINATE STORAGE CABINETS, AS SCHEDULED
- CENTER CABINET DOORS OPEN AND SLIDE INTO POCKETS AT THIS LOCATION ONLY

PLAN

EXAMPLE AEROBICS STUDIO

- MIRROR
- WOOD FLOORING TRANSITION, TYP.
- ELEVATION
- EQUIPMENT STORAGE
- ALLOW 5'-0" SQ. FT. (0.5 SQ. m) PER PERSON
- 5'-0" (1525)
- 5'-0" (1525)
- STRETCHING BAR
- MIRROR

- WALL PARTITION AS SCHEDULED
- BASE AS SCHEDULED
- 1/2" NEOPRENE
- WOOD "SPORT" FLOOR
- 1" VERIFY

FLOOR AT PERIMETER

- DOOR JAMB
- ALUMINUM THRESHOLD TO ALIGN WITH DOOR JAMB
- 1/2" NEOPRENE
- WOOD "SPORT" FLOOR, PREFINISHED WOOD FLOOR SYSTEM WITH SHOCK-ABSORBING FOAM CHANNELS
- FOAM CHANNELS, TYP.
- 1" VERIFY

FLOOR TRANSITION AT DOOR

- 1'-1"
- GYPSUM BOARD SOFFIT
- GYPSUM BOARD
- EQUIPMENT NICHE FOR EXTRA STORAGE ABOVE CABINETS
- 3/4" MDF DOOR CLAD IN PLASTIC LAMINATE
- 3/4" MDF SHELF WITH 1 1/2" LIP, CLAD IN PLASTIC LAMINATE ON STANDARDS AND BRACKETS RECESSED IN SIDE PANELS
- 3/4"
- 5'-11"
- 4"
- 3"
- 3/4" MDF
- INSIDE OF CABINET CLAD IN WHITE MELAMINE

AEROBIC EQUIPMENT CABINET—SECTION

- 2" RADIUS FURNITURE GRADE MAPLE BAR
- CLIP ANGLES, SPACE AS REQUIRED
- WELD STEEL PLATE TO STEEL TUBING
- PAINT FLAT BLACK GYPSUM BOARD THAT IS NOT COVERED BY PLYWOOD
- BLACK GROMMET
- STEEL TUBING CONCEALED IN WALL; GAUGE AS REQUIRED
- 1/4" MIRROR WITH POLISHED EDGES LAMINATED TO 3/4" PLYWOOD
- PAINT FLAT BLACK
- ANCHOR AS REQUIRED
- 2 1/2"
- 3/4", TYP.
- 3'-6" A.F.F.
- 4"

STRETCHING BAR

RESILIENT FLOORING

Resilient flooring provides a dense, nonabsorbent, pliant surface that is generally quiet, comfortable to walk on, and easy to maintain. Resilient flooring types include sheet vinyl, vinyl tile, rubber, linoleum, leather, and cork. Factors the designer may consider in choosing a resilient flooring type include cost, performance, durability, availability, energy and natural resource use, biodegradability, recycled content, recyclability, and toxicity.

VINYL FLOORING

The five basic ingredients used in the manufacture of vinyl flooring are:

- *Polyvinylchloride* (PVC), which imparts wear resistance and durability. PVC is the basis of the binder, which constitutes most of the wear surface. The binder consists of PVC compounded with plasticizers and stabilizers.
- *Plasticizers,* which increase flexibility.
- *Stabilizers,* which provide color permanence and stabilize the pigments against heat and light deterioration.
- *Fillers,* which are added to supplement the bulk and thickness of the flooring. Mineral fillers, the most common, improve fire resistance. Natural fillers increase slip resistance.
- *Pigments,* for color.

Sheet Vinyl

Sheet vinyl flooring, either solid vinyl or backed, forms a continuous finished floor covering. Because sheet vinyl flooring has fewer joints, it is used for applications where spills, dirt, or bacterial growth are of concern. It is commonly specified in hospital operating rooms or other areas where resistance to bacterial growth or water penetration is required.

Sheet Vinyl Seams

There are two types of seams for sheet vinyl installations: *heat-welded* and *chemically welded.* Heat-welded seams are formed by melting a vinyl rod between sheets. Solid-color or patterned welding rods can either accent or camouflage seams. Heat welding requires special equipment and trained installers. Chemical welding is accomplished with the application of a one- or two-part solvent that is mixed on-site. This softens the edges of the vinyl, essentially melting them together. Chemical welding is more economical than heat welding.

GRADES OF SHEET VINYL FLOOR COVERING WITH BACKING*

| TYPE | GRADE | WEAR LAYER THICKNESS, MINIMUM | |
		(IN.)	(MM)
1	1	0.020	0.51
	2	0.014	0.36
	3	0.010	0.25
2	1	0.050	1.27
	2	0.030	0.76
	3	0.020	0.51

*According to ASTM F1303, Standard Specification for Sheet Vinyl Floor Covering with Backing

Type I is defined by a wear layer binder content of not less than 90%. Type II is defined by a wear layer binder content of not less than 34%.

RESILIENT FLOORING SIZES

TYPE	COMPONENTS	THICKNESS IN. (MM)	SIZES
Vinyl sheet	Vinyl resins with fiber back	0.065–0.160 (1.6–4)	6, 10, 12 ft (1.8, 3, 3.6 m) wide
Solid vinyl tile	Vinyl resins	1/16–1/8 (1.5–3)	9 × 9 in. (228 x 228 mm) 12 × 12 in. (305 x 305 mm)
Vinyl composition tile	Vinyl resins with filler	0.050–0.095 (1.2–2.4)	9 × 9 in. (228 x 228 mm) 12 × 12 in. (305 x 305 mm)
Rubber tile	Rubber compound	3/32–3/16 (2.3–4.7)	9 × 9 in. (228 x 228 mm) 12 × 12 in. (305 x 305 mm)
Cork tile	Raw cork and resins	1/8–1/4 (3–6)	6 × 6 in. (152 x 152 mm) 9 × 9 in. (228 x 228 mm)
Cork tile with vinyl coating	Raw cork with vinyl resins	1/8–3/16 (3–4.7)	9 × 9 in. (228 x 228 mm) 12 × 12 in. (305 x305 mm)

SOLID VINYL PARTICLES EXTENDING ALL THE WAY THROUGH FOR UNIFORM APPEARANCE AS FLOORING WEARS

HOMOGENEOUS, OR SOLID, SHEET VINYL
Homogeneous, or solid, sheet vinyl floorings, have no backing. Homogeneous sheet vinyl has superior resistance to indentation, rolling loads, and chemicals, and is suitable for heavy-wear applications because its appearance remains consistent even when worn. It contains much more PVC than backed sheet vinyls, making it more resilient and more expensive.

VINYL CHIPS SUSPENDED IN PURE VINYL

BACKING

BACKED SHEET VINYL
Backed sheet vinyl consists of a vinyl wear layer that is bonded to a backing, with or without an interlayer between the two. Generally, the thicker the wear layer and the higher the binder content, the better the durability and the resistance to abrasion of the vinyl floor covering. The wear layer contains or protects the pattern and consists mainly of a vinyl binder, but may include pigments, fillers, and other ingredients.

CLEAR VINYL

DESIGN PRINTED ON BACKING OR ON UNDERSIDE OF WEAR LAYER

BACKING

TRANSPARENT WEAR LAYER SHEET VINYL
Transparent, or translucent, wear layer sheet vinyl is produced by applying a clear vinyl film over a printed surface. The interlayer may include materials to impart a desired performance attribute.

TYPES OF VINYL SHEET FLOORING

VINYL TILE

Material

Two types of vinyl tile are *solid vinyl tile* and the less expensive *vinyl composition tile* (VCT). Solid vinyl tile, or homogeneous vinyl tile, contains much more PVC than VCT, making it more resilient and resistant to abrasion. Homogeneous vinyl tile has superior indentation and rolling/load resistance. Because the pattern is continuous through the thickness of the flooring, its appearance will remain consistent when worn. Three classes of VCT are defined by ASTM F1066, *Specification for Vinyl Composition Floor Tile:* Type 1, solid color tiles; Type 2, through-pattern tiles; Type 3, surface pattern tiles.

Properties

Vinyl composition tile (VCT) is more brittle than vinyl sheet flooring because it contains much less PVC. VCT is composed mostly of fillers with comparatively small amounts of binder and pigments. Originally, the filler used in vinyl tile contained asbestos and was called *vinyl asbestos tile, VAT.*

Installation

Vinyl tile is less expensive to install than sheet vinyl and easier to replace in damaged areas. Tile layout should consider the center of the room and the size of the last tile that falls at the perimeter. Typically, it is desirable for the perimeter tiles to be as large as possible, and no smaller than half a tile wide.

RUBBER FLOORING

Material

Rubber sheet or rubber tile flooring is composed of natural rubber or synthetic rubber (styrene butadiene), mineral fillers, and pigments.

Types

Two types of rubber floor tile are *homogeneous* and *laminated.* Homogeneous rubber tile has coloring uniform throughout the tile thickness. Laminated rubber tile has coloring or patterning in the wear layer only.

Properties

Durable, resilient, and resistant to a wide variety of harsh chemicals and solvents, rubber flooring is naturally resistant to cosmetic burns. Rubber flooring can tolerate high-traffic public areas.

The slip resistance of homogeneous rubber tile is enhanced by adding raised surface patterns. This material is popular for use as stair treads and nosings.

Rubber flooring is dimensionally stable, sound absorbent, and recyclable. It is resistant to heavy-impact loads, is puncture-resistant, and appropriate for use in indoor playgrounds, health clubs, or off-ice areas at ice skating rinks.

RUBBER TILE WITH RAISED PATTERN

LAMINATED RUBBER TILE

LINOLEUM

LEATHER TILE

COMPOSITION CORK

RESILIENT FLOOR TILES

LINOLEUM

Material

Linoleum (derived from the Latin terms for "flax," *linum,* and "oil," *oleum*) is composed primarily of linseed oil, obtained from the flax plant. The oil is oxidized and mixed with a natural resin, such as rosin tapped from pine trees, and combined with powdered cork for flexibility and limestone for strength and hardness. Wood flour and pigments are added for color and colorfastness. For dimensional stability, this mixture is bonded to a fiber backing (typically burlap) for linoleum sheets or to a polyester backing for tile. Felt backings are used for linoleum countertop or tack surface sheets.

Properties

Linoleum flooring is manufactured in Europe and imported to the United States. There is no American standard for linoleum at this time. Linoleum is biodegradable. Linoleum is a superior thermal and acoustic insulator because of the air pockets found naturally in cork (50% air). Linoleum thickness varies. It is used where superior resilience is required, such as the floors of dance rehearsal studios and health facilities. It is naturally bacteria-resistant and antimicrobial, preventing the growth of dust mites. The antistatic properties of linoleum prevent dust accumulation and reduce the potential for electric shock.

Maintenance

A yellow film forms on the linoleum surface during the drying process when the linseed oil rises to the surface. The film should disappear when exposed to light within no more than six weeks. Linoleum flooring is maintained by damp-mopping. When sheet or tile linoleum is first laid, it is relatively porous, but the oxidization process continues over the life of the floor, during which it becomes progressively more nonporous.

Installation

Linoleum seams can be heat-welded for water resistance, in areas over radiant floors and those exposed to direct sunlight. During the manufacturing process "stove bar marks" occur when the product is looped between suspended poles in the drying room. These deformations are either cut out in the field or eliminated with adhesive and weights during the installation process.

LEATHER TILE

Material

Leather tiles are typically cut from the center of a cowhide (usually a by-product of the food industry), where the fibers are tightest. The leather is vegetable-tanned and colored with penetrating aniline dyes. Leather tiles can be relatively expensive compared to other resilient flooring choices. Leather tiles will have natural grain and color variations. Leather tile flooring develops a patina over time as it wears and oxidizes in light and air.

Maintenance and Installation

Waxing and buffing is required to maintain and protect leather flooring. It is often recommended that the floor be waxed with carnauba wax and buffed at least three times before using to ensure that the leather is properly protected. Plywood is the preferred subfloor for a leather tile installation.

CORK FLOORING

Material

Cork flooring is harvested from the outer layer of cork oak trees grown in Mediterranean regions. The bark becomes loose, approximately every nine years, and is cut away. Composition cork is the most common form of cork flooring. The bark material of the cork oak is granulated, pressed with binders such as synthetic resins, and then baked. The quality of composition cork varies according to the quality and size of granules, the type and quantity of the binder, and the density (compression) of the mix.

Types

Unfinished tile is the standard product form. Also available is prefinished cork with a urethane top coating, vinyl-clad cork, or floating cork floors that either glue or mechanically snap together and float over a thin cork underlayment. Cork sheets and rolls are available with jute backing, but these are difficult to install. Cork is naturally honey-toned but is available in other colors.

Properties

Cork flooring is inherently antistatic, hypoallergenic, and nonslip. Cork provides acoustic and thermal insulation. Cork is also used as an underlayment to increase the resiliency of other types of finish floors. It is temperature-sensitive and should not be used in combination with underfloor heating systems.

Installation

Cork must be glued to a flat smooth surface, either plywood or a moisture-free concrete floor. Seams and depressions should be filled perfectly smooth with a portland-cement-based floor leveler.

Maintenance

Compared to other types of resilient flooring, cork is difficult to maintain. Unless sealed, its appearance can deteriorate from water staining and ingrained dirt. Three to four coats of polyurethane or polymer sealant can prevent surface deterioration. Except for vinyl-finished cork, presealed cork should be sealed after installation to prevent moisture infiltration into the tile joints.

RESILIENT FLOORING INSTALLATION

Preparation

Subfloor preparation is critical to a successful resilient flooring installation. Joints and screw heads must be filled and sanded to prevent telegraphing to the finish floor surface. Also, paper felt can be used over plywood or hardboard (commonly known by the trade

WOOD SUBFLOORS

SURFACE MUST BE CLEAN, DRY, FIRM, AND SMOOTH

DOUBLE-LAYER WOOD FLOOR: PANEL UNDERLAYMENT OF HARDBOARD (1/4" MIN.) OR SANDED PLYWOOD (3/8" MIN.) OR PARTICLEBOARD (3/8" MIN.)

SINGLE-LAYER WOOD FLOOR: COMBINATION SUBFLOOR / UNDERLAYMENT PANELS (3/8" MIN.)

CONCRETE SUBFLOORS

SURFACE MUST BE CLEAN, DRY, FIRM, AND SMOOTH

2"-3" REINFORCED CONCRETE TOPPING OVER PRECAST SLABS

1" CONCRETE TOPPING OVER LIGHTWEIGHT CONCRETE SLABS

PROVIDE A VAPOR BARRIER AND A GRAVEL BASE UNDER SLABS ON GRADE.

FOR SLABS BELOW GRADE, PROVIDE A WATERPROOF MEMBRANE AND A 2" SUBSLAB.

SUBFLOOR PREPARATION FOR RESILIENT FLOORING

name Masonite) to prevent nail or screw heads from showing. Subsurface-water migration and moisture-vapor transmission through concrete slabs can cause resilient floor covering applications to fail. A dampproof membrane is required for moisture protection over slabs on grade.

Adhesives

Adhesives, such as contact cement or mastic, are used to adhere resilient flooring to the substrate. Manufacturers and installers of adhesives are required to comply with the VOC requirements of authorities having jurisdiction. Water-based adhesives are available for many types of installations. Some manufacturers will warranty their flooring only if it is installed with their suggested adhesive.

Faith Baum, AIA, IIDA; Faith Baum Architect; Lexington, Massachusetts
Mia Alwen; Rhode Island School of Design; Providence, Rhode Island
Lerlux Sophonpanich; Rhode Island School of Design; Providence, Rhode Island
MASTERSPEC®; published by ARCOM; Salt Lake City, Utah, and Alexandria, Virginia

WALL

CAP STRIP

SHEET VINYL FLOORING

WOOD OR PLASTIC COVE STICK

Sheet goods, such as linoleum or sheet vinyl, can form an integral, monolithic cove base to simplify maintenance.

COVE BASE

THERMAL CONDUCTIVITY OF FLOORING

| FLOORING | THICKNESS | | THERMAL CONDUCTIVITY (U VALUE) | |
	IN.	MM	BTU/ft²h °F	W/m °K
Cork	1/8	4	0.028	0.050
Linoleum	1/8	4	0.087	0.152
Vinyl	3/16	5	0.427	0.74
Wood	1/4	8	0.119	0.207
Marble	5/8	15	1.598	2.767

Source: Arcobel; Houston, Texas

RESILIENT FLOORING PERFORMANCE ATTRIBUTES

ATTRIBUTE	RESILIENT FLOORING TYPE
Resilience and quietness	Cork tile, rubber tile
Resistance to indentation	Solid vinyl tile
Stain resistance	Vinyl sheet and tile
Alkali resistance	Vinyl sheet and tile
Grease resistance	Vinyl sheet and tile, cork tile with vinyl coating
Durability	Vinyl sheet and tile

STATIC-CONTROL FLOORING

COMMON APPLICATIONS

At one time, conductive floor coverings were used in hospitals where flammable anesthetic gases were used and stored. But this type of anesthesia is no longer used in the United States, and the electronics and computer industries are now the primary markets for static-control flooring. Conductive flooring is also recommended in grain silos and areas where chemicals, munitions, or explosive gases are used or stored.

There are two types of static-control flooring: *static dissipative* and *conductive*. The basic difference is the rate at which an electric charge moves through the floor. The charge moves faster through the conductive flooring because its resistance is lower. The definitions of the two types are based on the measure of electrical resistance as stated in ASTM F150, *Test Method for Electrical Resistance of Conductive and Static-Dissipative Resilient Flooring.*

Static-dissipative flooring has an average electrical resistance greater than 1,000,000 (1.0×10^6) ohms, or 1 megohm, and less than or equal to 1,000,000,000 (1.0×10^9) ohms, or 1,000 megohms, when test specimens are tested surface to ground. It has an average electrical resistance no less than 1,000,000 (1.0×10^6) ohms, or 1 megohm, and less than or equal to 1,000,000,000 (1.0×10^9) ohms, or 1,000 megohms, when installed flooring is tested surface to ground.

Conductive flooring has an average electrical resistance greater than 25,000 (2.5×10^4) ohms and less than 1,000,000 (1.0×10^6) ohms, or 1 megohm, when test specimens and installed floor coverings are tested surface to surface (point to point). It has an average electrical resistance no less than 25,000 (2.5×10^4) ohms with no single measurement less than 10,000 (1.0×10^4) ohms when installed floor coverings are tested surface to ground. Coordinate the exact requirements for the facility with the owner and verify with the manufacturer that the selected product meets those requirements. Require in-place testing of the installed floor to ensure proper performance.

TYPES OF RESILIENT STATIC-CONTROL FLOORING

MATERIAL	THICKNESS IN. (MM)	TILE/ROLL SIZE IN. (MM) (UNLESS OTHERWISE SPECIFIED)	TEXTURE
Vinyl composition tile	0.080 (2.0) and 0.125 (3.2)	12 × 12 (30 × 305)	Smooth
Solid vinyl tile	0.080 (2.0) and 0.125 (3.2)	12 × 12 (305 × 305) 24 24 (610 × 610) or 36 × 36 (915 × 915)	Smooth
Sheet vinyl	0.080 (2.0)	6-ft-6-in.-wide rolls	Smooth
Raised disc rubber tile	0.20 (5.0) overall 0.19 (4.7) base	39.7 × 39.7 (1,000 × 1,000)	Raised Disc
Textured rubber tile	0.14 (3.5)	39.7 × 39.7 (1,000 × 1,000)	Hammered
Sheet rubber	0.080 (2.0) and 0.10 (2.5)	48-in.- (1,220-) wide rolls	Smooth

GROUNDING STATIC-CONTROL FLOORING

Static-control flooring must be grounded to remove the electric charge from the area. A grid of 1- or 2-in.- (25- or 50-mm-) wide copper foil tape is embedded in the primer or base coat for resinous flooring and in the adhesive for resilient flooring. The rate at which the grounding strips are required by the flooring manufacturer varies from one strip every 500 sq ft (46 sq m) to one strip every 2,500 sq ft (232 sq m). This strip is connected to steel columns or some other element in the building grounding system.

RESILIENT STATIC-CONTROL FLOORING

Static-control resilient flooring consists of resilient tiles or sheet material applied to a substrate using static-control adhesive with embedded grounding strips. Joints in the vinyl products can be heat-welded for a seamless installation. They come in various colors, some with a characteristic thin, black thread pattern caused by the encapsulated carbon that provides the electrostatic control. Integral self-cove bases can be constructed from the solid vinyl tiles and sheet vinyl materials.

RESINOUS STATIC-CONTROL FLOORING

Resinous flooring systems provide seamless, durable coatings over concrete and other rigid substrates for commercial, industrial, and institutional applications.

The installation usually includes an integral self-cove base. These systems are harder and denser than resilient flooring, hence they are better for applications that must withstand heavy loads, especially rolling loads. They may also be a better choice where severe acid and chemical spills may occur.

Resinous flooring systems are more expensive than resilient flooring and are not easily repaired or removed after installation. They must be applied by trained, experienced installers recommended or approved by the components' manufacturer. When static control is desired, carbon or other proprietary ingredients are added to the formulation. Consult with manufacturers for final selection of products for specific applications.

Epoxy resin flooring systems are two-component systems that combine liquid resins and hardening/curing agents. Graded aggregates and mineral oxide pigments are added to change the color, finish texture, and performance characteristics of the finished floor. Epoxy resin flooring is available in poured and trowel-applied formulations in thicknesses from $\frac{1}{16}$ to $\frac{1}{2}$ in. (1.6 to 12.8 mm). In a static-control application, the copper foil grounding grid is installed in the primer or base coat layer and connected to the building's grounding system.

Margery Morgan; Symmes Maini & McKee Associates; Cambridge, Massachusetts

STATIC-CONTROL VINYL TILE

- SOLID VINYL TILE
- CONDUCTIVE FIBER
- CONDUCTIVE ADHESIVE
- COPPER FOIL GROUND

STATIC-CONTROL TEXTURED RUBBER TILE

- TEXTURED RUBBER TILE
- CONDUCTIVE ADHESIVE
- COPPER FOIL GROUND

STATIC-CONTROL SHEET RUBBER

- SHEET RUBBER
- CONDUCTIVE CARBON CONES
- CONDUCTIVE ADHESIVE
- COPPER FOIL GROUND

STATIC-CONTROL FLOORING

RESILIENT BASE AND ACCESSORIES

MATERIALS

Resilient wall base and flooring accessories are available in three materials:

- *Vinyl* can be susceptible to shrinking when exposed to heat.
- *Thermoplastic rubber* is a vinyl compound with a comparatively small amount of rubber added for flexibility. Because of the high vinyl content, it performs similarly to vinyl, but is more flexible. It is commonly more expensive than vinyl but less expensive than vulcanized, thermoset rubber.
- *Thermoset rubber* is vulcanized natural rubber. It is the most flexible resilient base material and thus is easier to install and better at hiding surface imperfections in walls and floors. Thermoset rubber base is susceptible to color degradation due to UV exposure; however, it can be specially manufactured with UV inhibitors. White and dark-colored thermoset rubber base tends to hold color best. Lighter colors, especially gray, tend to be prone to color degradation. Thermoset rubber base also tends to be more vulnerable to scuffing than vinyl or thermoplastic rubber. Lighter colors tend not to show scuff marks as much as darker colors.

Although most building codes do not have flammability requirements for wall trim that constitutes less than 10% of the wall surface, the flame-spread ratings and the smoke generated from burning resilient flooring accessories differ among the three materials. Thermoset rubber, when burned, generates less smoke and toxic fumes than vinyl or thermoplastic rubber.

WALL BASE

Wall base conceals the joint where the wall meets the floor. Premolded inside and outside corners are available from some manufacturers, but they may differ in texture and color from straight sections. Straight sections of resilient wall base are available in precut lengths (4 ft (1,219 mm) long) and coils (approximately 100 ft (30 m) long). Coils minimize the number of joints and may reduce installation costs.

There are three basic wall base profiles:

- *Straight base* is meant to be used with carpet.
- *Cove base* is meant to be used with resilient flooring.
- *Butt-to base*, sometimes referred to as *sanitary base*, is available from a limited number of manufacturers. It is installed prior to the finish floor covering. The finish floor covering must be of the same thickness as the butt-to base flange. The base is sealed to the floor and wall, creating an easy-to-clean, more sanitary joint that is popular for health care applications.

Cove moldings support sheet vinyl, sheet linoleum, or other flexible floor coverings when coved up the wall. *Cap moldings* help to finish the exposed edges of coved floor coverings, ceramic tile, or wood paneling.

Ted Kollaja, AIA; lauckgroup; Dallas, Texas

RESILIENT BASE MATERIALS

	RESPONSE TO HEAT	FLEXI-BILITY	RESISTANCE TO GREASE AND OIL	RELATIVE COST
Vinyl	Shrinks	Good	Excellent	$
Thermo-plastic Rubber	Expands	Better	Good	$$
Thermoset Rubber	Expands	Best	Fair	$$$

CARPET ON CUSHION TO FINISH FLOOR

CARPET ON CUSHION TO VCT

CARPET ON CUSHION TO FINISH FLOOR

FINISH FLOOR TO RESILIENT FLOORING

Transition moldings create a smooth transition between different flooring materials or flooring heights and act to conceal seams.

RESILIENT TRANSITION MOLDINGS

DIRECT-GLUE CARPET TO VCT

DIRECT-GLUE CARPET TO VCT

DIRECT-GLUE CARPET TO VCT

DIRECT-GLUE CARPET TO CERAMIC TILE

Snap-in moldings offer the advantage of wear-edge replacement without disrupting the flooring installation.

STRAIGHT BASE

COVE BASE

BUTT-TO BASE

CAP AND MOLDING

WALL BASE

C–1 THE COLOR WHEEL

C–2 MONOCHROMATIC VALUE SCALE: YELLOW

Source: Linda Holtzschue, Understanding Color: An Introduction for Designers, *2nd ed., John Wiley & Sons, Inc., 2002.*

C–3 COMPLEMENTARY COLORS
Adding a small amount of its complement to a pure color reduces its chroma (saturation) and changes its value.

C–4 ANALOGOUS COLORS
Analogy is a relationship between hues no matter what their saturation or value.

Source: Linda Holtzschue, Understanding Color: An Introduction for Designers, *2nd ed., John Wiley & Sons, Inc., 2002.*

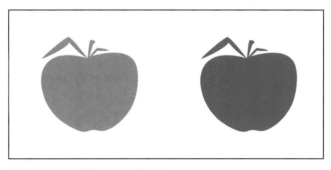

C–5 SPATIAL EFFECTS OF COLORS
Warm colors advance in relation to cool colors, and vivid colors advance in relation to muted ones.
Source: Linda Holtzschue, Understanding Color: An Introduction for Designers, *2nd ed., John Wiley & Sons, Inc., 2002.*

C–7 SIMULTANEOUS CONTRAST—CHANGE OF HUE
Our perception of one color becomes tinged toward the complement (the color directly opposite another on a color wheel) of the color around it.
Source: Wucius Wong, Principles of Color Design: Designing with Electronic Color, *2nd ed., John Wiley & Sons, Inc., 1997, p. 54.*

C–8 SIMULTANEOUS CONTRAST—CHANGE OF VALUE
A change of value occurs when a surrounded color is much lighter or darker than the surrounding color. If the surrounding color is light, the surrounded color appears darker; if the surrounding color is dark, the surrounded color appears lighter.
Source: Wucius Wong, Principles of Color Design: Designing with Electronic Color, *2nd ed., John Wiley & Sons, Inc., 1997, p. 54.*

C–9 SIMULTANEOUS CONTRAST—STRENGTHENED CHROMA
When a color is surrounded by another that is in its complementary hue, this color is strengthened in chroma, because the afterimage of the surrounding color is of the same hue as the surrounded color. For maximum effect, there should be little value contrast.
Source: Wucius Wong, Principles of Color Design: Designing with Electronic Color, *2nd ed., John Wiley & Sons, Inc., 1997, p. 54.*

C–10 SIMULTANEOUS CONTRAST—WEAKENED CHROMA
When two adjacent colors are within 90° of each other on the color wheel, simultaneous contrast can weaken the chroma. For example, orange surrounded by the complementary hue of orange-yellow will be affected by the complementary hue, which is purple-blue. The orange turns slightly grayish, as the purple-blue cast has a neutralizing effect.
Source: Wucius Wong, Principles of Color Design: Designing with Electronic Color, *2nd ed., John Wiley & Sons, Inc., 1997, p. 54.*

DESCRIBING LIGHT-SOURCE COLOR

The pictures are intended, within the limits of modern high-speed printing, to give a good indication of the differences between standard color (older technology), color improved, and high-color rendering fluorescent lamps, at various color temperatures.

Note: Color Rendering (R_a) Index Values in ( ) for F40 lamps.

STANDARD COLOR AND HIGH EFFICIENCY

WARM WHITE (52)	COOL WHITE (60)	LITE WHITE (49)	

GOOD COLOR AND HIGH EFFICIENCY

| 3000K (78) | 3500K (78) | 4100K (78) | 6500K (78) |

VERY GOOD COLOR AND HIGH EFFICIENCY

| 2700K (86) | 3000K (86) | 3500K (86) | 4100K (86) | 5000K (86) |

"WARM"   3000K   3500K   4000K   5000K   "COOL"

C-11 DESCRIBING LIGHT-SOURCE COLOR
The pictures are intended to give an indication of the differences among standard color (older technology), color improved, and high-color-rendering fluorescent lamps at various color temperatures.
Source: General Electric Lighting; Louisville, Kentucky

ANEGRE (FLAT-CUT)

ANEGRE (FLAT-CUT)

ANEGRE (QUARTER-SAWN)

ANEGRE (QUARTER-SAWN)

ASH (FLAT-CUT)

AVODIRE

BIRD'S-EYE MAPLE

BOSSE POMMELLE

BUBINGA (FLAT-CUT)

C–12 WOOD VENEER TYPES

Source: M. Bohlke Veneer Corp.; Cincinnati, Ohio

BUBINGA (QUARTER-SAWN)

BUBINGA (QUARTER-SAWN)

BUBINGA POMMELE

CAMPHOR BURL

CARELIAN BIRCH BURL

CEREJEIRA

DOUGLAS FIR

C–13 WOOD VENEER TYPES

ENGLISH BROWN OAK

ENGLISH SYCAMORE

Source: M. Bohlke Veneer Corp.; Cincinnati, Ohio

ENGLISH SYCAMORE

ETIMOE (FLAT-CUT)

ETIMOE (QUARTER-SAWN)

EUCALYPTUS (QUARTER-SAWN)

EUCALYPTUS

EUROPEAN ASH

EUROPEAN BEECH

C–14 WOOD VENEER TYPES

EUROPEAN BEECH

GABOON

Source: M. Bohlke Veneer Corp.; Cincinnati, Ohio

GONCAL ALVES

HONDURAS

JARRAH

JATOBA

KHAYA (QUARTER-CUT)

KHAYA

LACEWOOD

MACASSAR EBONY

MACORE

C–15 WOOD VENEER TYPES

Source: M. Bohlke Veneer Corp.; Cincinnati, Ohio

MACORE (FIDDLEBACK)

MACORE (FLAT-CUT)

MACORE (QUARTER-SAWN)

MACORE POMMELE

MOVINGUI

MYRTLE BURL

OKOUME

PADAUK

PARANA PINE

C–16 WOOD VENEER TYPES

Source: M. Bohlke Veneer Corp.; Cincinnati, Ohio

PARANA PINE

PEARWOOD

PEROBA

PLANE TREE BURL

PRIMAVERA

RED ELM

RED OAK (FLAT-CUT)

SANTOS ROSEWOOD

SAPELE (FLAT-CUT)

C–17 WOOD VENEER TYPES

Source: M. Bohlke Veneer Corp.; Cincinnati, Ohio

SAPELE (QUARTER-SAWN)

SAPELE (QUARTER-SAWN)

SAPELE POMMELE

SEN

SILVER GREY WOOD

TAMO ASH BURL

TEAK (FLAT-CUT)

C–18 WOOD VENEER TYPES

WALNUT (FLAT-CUT)

WALNUT (QUARTER-SAWN)

Source: M. Bohlke Veneer Corp.; Cincinnati, Ohio

WALNUT BURL

WENGE (FLAT-CUT)

WHITE ASH BURL

WHITE OAK (FLAKEY)

WHITE OAK (FLAT-CUT)

WHITE OAK QUARTER-SAWN)

WHITE OAK (RIFT-CUT)

WILLOW

ZEBRANO

C–19 WOOD VENEER TYPES

Source: M. Bohlke Veneer Corp.; Cincinnati, Ohio

C–20 DOUGLAS FIR WOOD FLOORING
3⅛-in.- (79-mm-) wide strips shown. Durable, but easily dented; somewhat brittle and splinters easily, especially with age.

C–21 HICKORY/PECAN WOOD FLOORING
2¼-in.- (57-mm-) wide strips shown. Combination of strength, hardness, toughness, and stiffness found in no other commercial wood; exceedingly high in shock resistance.

Top portion is finished with water-based urethane; bottom portion is finished with oil-modified polyurethane.
Source: National Wood Flooring Association; Ellisville, Missouri

C–22 RED OAK WOOD FLOORING
2¼-in.- (57-mm-) wide strips shown. Stiff and dense; resists wear, with high shock resistance, though less durable than white oak.

C–23 WHITE OAK WOOD FLOORING
2¼ -in.- (57-mm-) wide strips shown. More durable than red oak. Tannic acid in the wood protects flooring from fungi and insects.

Top portion is finished with water-based urethane; bottom portion is finished with oil-modified polyurethane.
Source: National Wood Flooring Association; Ellisville, Missouri

C–24 SOUTHERN YELLOW PINE WOOD FLOORING
2¼-in.- (57-mm-) wide strips shown. Soft, fairly durable, although not as resistant to scuffs, dents, and abrasions as hardwoods.

C–25 AMERICAN BLACK WALNUT WOOD FLOORING
2¼-in.- (57-mm-) wide strips shown. Moderately dense, very strong, good shock resistance. Not as dent-resistant as oak.

Top portion is finished with water-base urethaned; bottom portion is finished with oil-modified polyurethane.
Source: National Wood Flooring Association; Ellisville, Missouri

C–26 BRAZILIAN CHERRY WOOD FLOORING
1½-in.- (38-mm-) wide strips shown. Dense and very strong.

C–27 MAHOGANY WOOD FLOORING
3¼-in.- (82-mm-) wide strips shown. Excellent durability.

Top portion is finished with water-base urethaned; bottom portion is finished with oil-modified polyurethane.
Source: National Wood Flooring Association; Ellisville, Missouri

FLUID-APPLIED FLOORING

Fluid-applied flooring systems provide seamless, durable coatings over concrete and other rigid substrates for commercial, industrial, and institutional applications. They are usually installed with an integral self-cove base. Consult with manufacturers for final selection of products for specific applications. These systems must be applied by trained, experienced installers who have been recommended or approved by the components' manufacturers.

MEMBRANES

Membranes can be added to the composite of a fluid-applied flooring system to enhance its performance.

Waterproofing membranes may be installed under systems subject to chemical spills and located over occupied spaces. Waterproofing membranes are not necessary over slabs on grade, except in areas where secondary containment is required.

Flexible reinforcing membranes, often containing fiberglass scrim to maximize tensile strength, can be applied over the substrate to help prevent cracks from telegraphing through the fluid-applied flooring. Some manufacturers recommend applying the reinforcement at cracks only; others recommend applying the membrane over the entire substrate. Some systems use the same material for waterproofing membranes as for reinforcing membranes. Verify the compatibility of membranes with the system components.

Margery Morgan; Symmes Maini & McKee Associates; Cambridge, Massachusetts

Polyurethane systems come in trowel-applied and poured, self-leveling formulations in ⅛ to ⅜ in. (3.2 to 9.6mm) thicknesses. They are more expensive than the epoxies, but better able to withstand thermal cycling and thermal shock. Polyurethane is unaffected by freeze/thaw, live steam, and continuous hot water cleaning. Uses include food-processing facilities, commercial kitchens, freezers, and refrigerated storage.

POLYURETHANE FLOORING

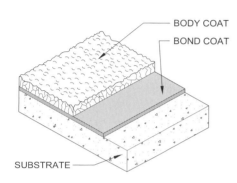

Magnesium oxychloride flooring is a fireproof, trowel-applied, seamless, hard-surface floor that is slip-resistant when wet or dry. Durable and simple to install, it is used primarily in commercial kitchens and manufacturing locations such as welding shops. Its use is not recommended when standing water or mineral corrosives are present. The standard color is red, although some earth tones are available.

MAGNESIUM OXYCHORIDE FLOORING

A methyl methacrylate (MMA) system has two distinct advantages over epoxy: it has a very fast cure time—1 to 2 hours versus 24 to 48 for epoxy—and it can be applied at much lower temperatures than other systems, allowing it to be used in freezers and refrigerated areas. MMA systems cost about 30% more than epoxy systems.

METHYL METHACRYLATE (MMA) FLOORING

Latex resin flooring is trowel-applied and jointless. It offers low absorption and good chemical resistance. Chemical-resistant types are available to handle a variety of anticipated chemical spills. A waterproof membrane may be used to make the floor entirely waterproof, and it may be turned up at the base to form an integral coved base. Uses include showers, laboratories, animal research housing, pharmaceutical plants, and TV studios.

LATEX RESIN FLOORING

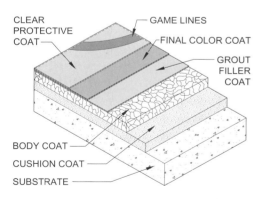

Unlike the other resinous floors described in this section, fluid-applied athletic flooring is a resilient system that replaces wood flooring in gymnasiums and multipurpose rooms. Fluid-applied athletic flooring is much less expensive than suspended wood-floor systems. The system consists of troweled-in-place synthetic rubber latex combined with cements and mineral fillers. Topping this composition are coats of pigmented resin over which game lines and a clear protective resin are applied. A typical installation is ½ in. (13 mm) thick, with the bottom ¼ in. (6.35 mm) being the troweled cushion layer.

FLUID-APPLIED ATHLETIC FLOORING

Epoxy resin flooring comprises two component systems that combine liquid resins and hardening/curing agents. Graded aggregates and mineral oxide pigments can be added to change color, texture, and performance characteristics of the finished floor. Epoxy resin flooring is available in poured and trowel-applied formulations in thicknesses from 1/16 to ½ in. (1.6 to 13 mm). When novolac is added to epoxy resin, the system is more chemically resistant to acids, alkalis, and solvents, and is heat-resistant to 481°F (250° C). (Resins that are produced by employing an acid catalyst and that are reacted with insufficient formaldehyde to completely cure are referred to as *two-stage resins* or *novolac resins.*)

EPOXY RESIN FLOORING

Seamless quartz flooring is seamless decorative flooring that consists of ceramic-coated quartz or colored quartz aggregates in clear epoxy. It may be broadcast or trowel-applied in thicknesses up to ½ in. (13 mm). It is available in a wide range of aggregate colors, and may be slip-resistant. It is typically installed over a concrete substrate and is used in laboratories, locker rooms, and light manufacturing and institutional facilities.

SEAMLESS QUARTZ FLOORING

CARPET AND CARPET TILE

The specification of carpet and carpet tile requires evaluation of the following:

- Carpet construction, which includes tufted, fusion-bonded, woven, hand-tufted, knitted, and needle-punched processes
- Carpet fiber
- Carpet performance characteristics, including face and total weight, pile density, and appearance retention
- Density
- Thermal and acoustic considerations
- Installation
- Carpet cushion

CARPET PERFORMANCE

CHARACTERISTIC	REQUIREMENT (BASED ON FINISHED CARPET)	TEST METHOD
Average pile yarn weight (oz/sq yd)	No less than 6%, as specified	ASTM D418, *Method of Testing Pile Yarn Floor Covering Construction*
Tufts/sq in.	As specified	ASTM D418, *Method of Testing Pile Yarn Floor Covering Construction*
Pile height and/or pile height differential	As specified	ASTM D418, *Method of Testing Pile Yarn Floor Covering Construction*
Tuft bind	10.0 lbf (44.5 N) for loop pile only (minimum average value)	ASTM D1335, *Test Method for Tuft Blind of Pile Floor Coverings*
Dry breaking strength	100 lbf (44.5 N) for loop pile only (minimum average value)	ASTM D2646, *Standard Test Methods for Backing Fabric Characteristics of Pile Yarn Floor Coverings*
Delamination of secondary backing	2.5 lbf per inch (11.1 N per 25.4 mm) (minimum average value)	ASTM D3936, *Standard Test Method for Resistance to Delamination of the Secondary Backing of Pile Yarn Floor Covering*
Resistance to insects (wool only)	"Resistant"	AATCC–24, *Resistance of Textiles to Insects*
Colorfastness to crocking	4 minimum, wet and dry, using AATCC color transference scale	AATCC–165, *Colorfastness to Crocking: Carpets—AATCC Crockmeter Method*
Colorfastness to light	4 minimum, after 40 AFU (AATCC facing units) using AATCC gray scale for color change	AATCC–16E, *Colorfastness to Light*
Electrostatic propensity	3.5 KV (maximum value) for general commercial areas, 2.0 KV (maximum value) for critical environment	AATCC–134, *Electrostatic Propensity of Carpets*
Dimensional tolerance—width	Within 1% of specifications—physical measurements	—

Source: Carpet and Rug Institute; Dalton, Georgia

TESTING REQUIREMENTS FOR FINISHED COMMERCIAL CARPET

CHARACTERISTIC	TEST METHOD/EXPLANATION	REQUIREMENT
Average pile yarn weight (oz/sq yd)	ASTM D418, *Method of Testing Pile Yarn Floor Covering Construction:* Chemically dissolves parts of the finished carpet sample to determine the pile mass or weight. Pile mass or weight includes the pile yarn, both above the primary backing and the amount hidden or buried below the backing.	As specified.
Tufts (per sq in.)	ASTM D418, *Method of Testing Pile Yarn Floor Covering Construction:* Determine the gauge and multiply by the stitches per inch (SPI). ASTM D418 offers instructions on counting the binding sites per unit length or width.	As specified.
Pile thickness or tuft height	ASTM D418, *Method of Testing Pile Yarn Floor Covering Construction:* Determine pile thickness for level loop carpet or tuft height for cut pile carpet. Accurate laboratory determination of height is important for the average pile yarn density determinations.	As specified.
Average pile yarn density	Calculation: Measures the amount of pile fiber by weight in a given area of carpet space. Typically calculated in ounces per cubic yard. Important element in equating quality of carpet to wearabilty, resilience, and appearance retention.	As specified.
Tuft bind	ASTM D1335, *Test Method for Tuft Blind of Pile Floor Coverings:* The amount of force required to pull a single carpet from its primary backing. Determines the capability of the tufted carpet to withstand zippering and snags.	The minimum average value is 10.0 lbf for loop pile.
Delamination strength of secondary backing	ASTM D 335, *Test Method for Delamination Strength of Secondary Backing of Pile Floor Coverings:* Measures the amount of force required to strip the secondary backing from the primary carpet structure. Measured in pounds of force per inch width. Its importance is to predict the secondary delaminating due to flexing caused by traffic or heavy rolling objects.	The minimum average value is 2.5 lbf per inch.
Colorfastness to crocking	Colorfastness to Crocking: Carpet—AATCC-165, *Crockmeter Method:* Transfer of colorant from the surface of a carpet to another surface by rubbing. The transference of color is graded against a standardized scale ranging from 5 (no color transference) to 1 (severe transference).	Rating of 4, minimum, wet and dry, using AATCC color transference scale.
Colorfastness to light	*Colorfastness to Light: Water-Cooled Xenon-Arc Lamp, Continuous Light,* AATCC-16, option E: Accelerated fading test using a xenon light source. After specified exposure, the specimen is graded for color loss using a 5 (no color change) to 1 (severe change) scale.	Rating of 4, minimum, after 40 AATCC fading units using AATCC gray scale for color change.
Electrostatic propensity	AATCC-34, *Electrostatic Propensity of Carpets:* Assesses the static-generating propensity of carpets developed when a person walks across them by laboratory simulation of conditions that may be met in practice. Static generation is dependent upon humidity condition; therefore, testing is performed at 20% relative humidity. Results are expressed as kilovolts (kV). The threshold of human sensitivity is 3.5 kV, but sensitive areas may require that a lower kV product be specified.	Less than 3.5 KV for general commercial areas.
Flammability	*Methenamine Pill Test;* FF 1–70 as found in 16 CFR 1630 and also ASTM D2859: Small-scale ignition test is required of all carpet for sale in the United States.	Seven passes from eight specimens tested.
	Flooring Radiant Panel Test; ASTM E 648, *Test Method for Critical Radiant Flux of Floor Covering Systems Using a Radiant Heat Energy Source:* Depending upon occupancy use and local, state, or other building or fire codes, carpets for commercial use may require panel test classification (class I or II). Class I is considered to be a minimum rating of 0.45 watts per square centimeter; class II is considered to be 0.22 watts per square centimeter or greater. Most codes require only radiant panel testing for carpet to be installed in corridors and exit-way areas.	Per applicable local, state, and federal requirements.
Carpet tile size and thickness	Physical measurements	Typical tolerances are in the range of five thousandths of an inch (5 mils, 0.0005 in.) within 1/32 in. of dimensional specifications.
Carpet tile dimensional stability	*Machine-made Textile Floor Coverings—Determination of Dimensional Changes in Varying Moisture Conditions,* ISO 2551 (Aachen Test)	+/- 0.2% maximum.

Source: Carpet and Rug Institute; Dalton, Georgia

CARPET CONSTRUCTION

Carpet construction refers to the carpet manufacturing method. The three most popular construction methods for commercial carpet construction are tufting, weaving, and fusion bonding. Hand-tufted carpets are often specified for hospitality applications. Knitted and needlepunched carpets are available but less often specified.

- *Tufted carpets* account for as much as 95% of the carpet produced in the United States.
- *Woven carpets* are made on a loom using the original carpet construction method.
- *Fusion-bonded carpet tiles* dominate the carpet tile market in the United States.
- *Knitted carpets* use more face yarn than tufting.
- *Needlepunched carpets* are formed by hundreds of barbed needles punching through blankets of fiber.

TUFTED CARPET

Since its introduction in the early 1950s, tufting has transformed the carpet industry. Compared to other carpet construction methods, tufting does not require skilled labor and requires less expensive equipment to manufacture. It is far less expensive and faster to produce than woven carpet. This process has enabled the mass production of an affordably priced, wide-width textile floor covering.

The tufted construction process is similar to sewing. Hundreds of needles stitch simultaneously through a backing material. To hold the tufted loops in place, the underside of the primary backing is coated with latex adhesive, a rubbery substance that dries hard but remains bendable. A secondary backing material is then applied.

Primary backing materials are the woven or nonwoven fabrics into which the tufts are inserted. They are typically olefin-based, either plain-woven or spunbonded. A thin polymer coating is often applied to bond the warp and weft threads and to minimize unraveling. Spunbonded olefin is inherently resistant to fraying or unraveling. During the tufting process, the olefin fibers are pushed aside, minimizing the distortion of the backing. This helps ensure a uniform pile height. Backings made of olefin are impervious to moisture and are mildew-resistant.

Adhesives used in tufted carpet are usually synthetic latex. Molten thermoplastic compounds are also used. Adhesives permanently anchor the tufts to the primary backing, preventing snags and unraveling.

Secondary backing materials, sometimes referred to as *scrims*, provide dimensional stability to the finished tufted carpet. A secondary backing is added for strength and stability. Secondary backing materials are often made of polypropylene, which is popular because it is moisture-resistant. Alternatives to secondary backings are attached carpet cushions, solid vinyl composites, and coatings referred to as *unitary backings*.

The standard dimension of most manufactured tufted carpet is a 12 ft (36 m) width, although some manufacturers provide 6 ft (1.8 m) and 15 ft (4.5 m) widths for special applications.

CARPET BACKING SYSTEMS

CONSTRUCTION METHOD	TYPICAL BACKING OR BACKING COMPONENTS	TYPICAL BACKCOATING CHEMICAL COMPOUNDS
Tufted	Primary Woven polypropylene slit film Nonwoven polypropylene or polyester	Synthetic SBR latex Polyurethane Polyvinyl acetate Ethylene vinyl acetate Polyvinyl chloride Amorphous resins Thermoplastic polyolefin
	Secondary: Woven leno weave polypropylene Nonwoven polypropylene or polyester Woven jute Fiberglass reinforcement	
Fusion-Bonded	Fiberglass matting	Polyvinyl chloride
Woven	Construction yarns may include: Cotton Jute Polypropylene Polyester Viscose rayon Blends or combinations	Similar materials to tufted, but usually thinner coatings
Hand-Tufted	Cotton canvas	Latex
Needlepunched	(None typically used.)	SBR latex Acrylics Ethylene vinyl acetate SBR latex foam

MANUFACTURING PROCESS

CROSS SECTION

TYPICAL DIMENSIONS

TUFTED CARPET

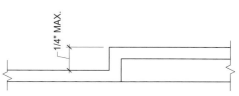

ACCESSIBLE ROUTE CHANGES IN LEVEL UP TO ¼ IN. (6.5 MM)
Changes in level up to ¼ in. (6.5 mm) may be vertical and without edge.

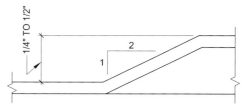

ACCESSIBLE ROUTE CHANGES IN LEVEL BETWEEN ¼ IN. (6.5 MM) AND ½ IN. (13 MM)
Changes in level between ¼ in. (6.5 mm) and ½ in. (13 mm) should be beveled with a slope no greater than 1:2. Changes in level greater than ½ in. (13 mm) should be accomplished by means of a ramp.

ADA CARPET PILE THICKNESS
Carpet having a pile height of ½ in. (13 mm) measured from the bottom of the tuft is allowed. Exposed edges should be secured and have a transition strip. Pile heights over ½ in. (13 mm) must have a transition ramp between the surfaces. Carpet should be securely attached, have a firm cushion or backing, or no cushion, and have a level loop, textured loop, level cut pile, or level cut/uncut pile.

ADA REQUIREMENTS FOR CARPET

CARPET TILE

Carpet tiles provide ready access to a raised floor or easy replacement when soiled or worn. Carpet tile backing systems provide moisture barriers from the base of the pile yarn to the floor, preventing spills from penetrating to the subfloor. Backing materials include polyvinyl chloride (PVC), amorphous resins, and polyurethane cushion. The "hard backs" (PVC and amorphous resin) offer dimensional stability and seam and edge integrity for easy pattern matching. PVC backings are used most often for modular tiles.

Fusion bonding is the most common method of carpet tile construction. It is a thermoplastic process, whereby yarns are attached to a backing material by means of adhesion rather than stitching (as in tufted carpet) or weaving. The adhesive is applied to the backing material, and the yarns are implanted in it. Because the yarn is typically embedded between two parallel backings that must be sliced apart, fusion-bonded carpet is necessarily cut pile.

Fusion-bonded carpet has the greatest percentage of yarn available for wear, but is more expensive than tufted carpet. The cut pile construction of fusion bonding offers greater pile densities at comparable yarn weights than tufted constructions.

Carpet tiles are installed with standard adhesives, releasable adhesives, and mill-applied peel-and-stick adhesives. Carpet tile installation is easier and causes less downtime and productivity loss than traditional carpet installation. Systems furniture divider panels and office furniture do not have to be removed, but are simply lifted with a "jack" system. The tiles are then installed underneath the furniture while it remains in place.

WOVEN CARPET

Weaving, the traditional carpet construction method, produces carpet on a loom, integrating the pile and backing yarns during the carpet construction. Most woven carpet is dimensionally stable as a result of the weaving process and does not require a secondary backing, as tufted carpet does. Weaving accounts for less than 2% of the carpet market in the United States. Its primary use is in the hospitality industry, where long-term durability and intricate pattern detail are primary considerations. There are three basic types of weaving processes: *velvet, Wilton,* and *Axminster.*

I-METHOD MANUFACTURING PROCESS

U-METHOD MANUFACTURING PROCESS

CROSS SECTION

TYPICAL DIMENSIONS

FUSION-BONDED CARPET

TYPICAL DIMENSIONS

AXMINSTER SPECIFICATIONS

APPLICATION	PITCH	ROW	WEIGHT OZ/SQ YD
Guest rooms	7	6	28
	7	7	32
Corridors	8	7	37.75
Ballrooms	8	8	42
Banks	8	9	48
Casino floors	8	9	48
Slot machine areas	8	10	53.5

Source: Soroush Custom Rugs; Kensington, Maryland

VELVET CROSS SECTION
Velvet carpets are made on looms similar to Wilton looms, but without the Jacquard mechanism, so intricate details and elaborate patterns are not available.

WILTON CROSS SECTION
Wilton carpets are limited to about five changes in yarn color. A Wilton carpet is thick and heavy because every color yarn used is carried beneath the pile surface.

AXMINSTER CROSS SECTION
Patterns and colors for Axminster carpets are virtually limitless, because the colored yarns are inserted individually as they are required by the design. Axminsters are cut pile face construction.

WOVEN CARPET

HAND-TUFTED CARPET

Hand-tufted rugs are most often custom-designed for a specific space. They are commonly made of wool and are popular for hospitality and high-end residential applications. Wool yarns are often dyed specifically for the hand-tufted rug. Hand-tufted rugs are made by inserting tufts one at a time by hand, with a tufting gun, into a backing, which is typically cotton canvas. The tufts are not in parallel rows as in machine tufting or weaving. The back of a completed, hand-tufted custom rug is coated with latex. The surface of the rug is finished by one of the following processes:

- *Tip-sheared rugs* are produced by cutting random loops that project beyond the surface of the rug. This process adds texture and visual interest to the level finished surface of the rug.
- *Cut-and-loop rugs* are continuously tufted like single-pile rugs. Those portions of the rug surface that will be cut pile are tufted in a deeper pile height and then cut down to the height of the loop surface.
- *Carved rugs* incorporate three-dimensional designs into the rug surface. After the tufting process is complete, electrically operated shears are used to cut patterns in the rug surface.

Nonrectilinear hand-tufted shapes: Unlike tufted or woven carpets, custom shapes and edge configurations are available in hand-tufted rugs. Hand-tufted rugs are often used in circular or other nonrectilinear applications and on spiral stair treads, where each tread carpet is different. An unlimited number of colors is possible, and intricate custom designs are often incorporated.

KNITTED CARPET

As in the construction of woven carpet, the knitting process integrates pile and backing yarns in one operation. Needles are used to interlace yarns in a series of connecting loops, similar to the hand-knitting process. Knitted carpets are known for their plush piles, because there is more yarn in the wear surface than tufted carpets. Knitted carpet has a tendency to stretch, especially on the diagonal, and is difficult to seam during installation. Knitted carpet represents a very small percentage of the carpet produced in the United States.

NEEDLEPUNCHED CARPET

Needlepunching is achieved by layering thick fiber batts, typically polypropylene, over a support fabric. Hundreds of barbed needles punch through the support fabric, compressing and entangling the fibers. Needlepunched carpets are permeable, which presents a problem when liquids are spilled on a wall-to-wall interior installation. The most common application of needlepunched carpet is outdoor carpet.

HAND-TUFTED CARPET SPECIFICATIONS

TYPICAL APPLICATIONS	PILE	
HIGH-TRAFFIC PUBLIC SPACES AND RESIDENTIAL SPACES		
Standard traffic lobbies	Content	100% semiworsted wool
Board rooms	Face weight	56 oz/yd
Meeting rooms	Total weight	+/- 105 oz/yd
Bar areas	Pile height	15/64 in. (6 mm)
Club rooms	Total thickness	5/16 in. (8 mm)
Royal and presidential hotel suites		
Grand staircases		
VERY HIGH-TRAFFIC PUBLIC SPACES		
Busy hotel lobbies	Content	100% semiworsted wool
Casinos	Face weight	72 oz/yd
Reception areas	Total weight	+/- 125 oz/yd
Lounge areas	Pile height	16/64 in. (7 mm)
Ballrooms	Total thickness	25/64 in. (10 mm)
Main corridors in luxury facilities		
Business service areas in hospitality facilities		
Grand staircases		
EXTREMELY HEAVY-TRAFFIC PUBLIC SPACES		
Hotel lobbies that also function as casino entrances	Content	100% semiworsted wool
	Face weight	88 oz/yd
Main promenade areas	Total weight	+/- 140 oz/yd
	Pile height	16/64 in. (7 mm)
	Total thickness	23/64 in. (9 mm)

Source: Soroush Custom Rugs; Kensington, Maryland

WOOL CARPET PILE WEIGHT DENSITY

TYPE OF TRAFFIC	AMOUNT OF TRAFFIC	LOCATION	PILE WEIGHT DENSITY	PROJECTED LIFE EXPECTATION (IN YEARS)
Light	Up to 1,500 passages/week (250/day)	Hotel guest rooms, private offices, small meeting rooms	80–114	5–7
Medium	1,500–5,000 passages/week (250–750/day)	Hotel guest corridors, conference rooms, small shops, larger offices	115–149	5–7
Heavy	5,000–15,000 passages/week (750–2,500/day)	Restaurants, larger function rooms, open-plan offices, large shops, hotel main corridors	150–199	5–7
Very heavy	15,000+ passages/week (2,500+/day)	Hotel lobbies, office entrance areas, department stores (ground floor), cash register counters, bars	200+	5–7

Source: Soroush Custom Rugs; Kensington, Maryland

For specifying Axminster, Wilton, and hand-tufted wool carpets.

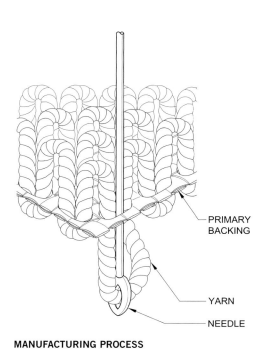

PRIMARY BACKING

YARN

NEEDLE

MANUFACTURING PROCESS

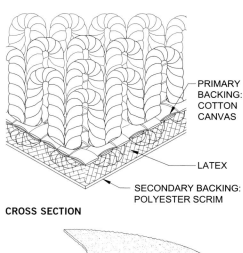

PRIMARY BACKING: COTTON CANVAS

LATEX

SECONDARY BACKING: POLYESTER SCRIM

CROSS SECTION

NO TYPICAL SHAPES
Nonrectilinear shapes are possible with hand-tufted rugs.

HAND-TUFTED CARPET

CARPET FIBERS

A fiber is the fine, hairlike strand that forms the basis of a yarn. Fibers are found in nature or are manufactured (synthetic) and are categorized by their length as either staple or filament.

- *Staple fibers* are short, typically measured in centimeters or inches. All natural fibers except silk are staple fibers.
- *Filament fibers* are long and continuous. Because synthetic fibers are produced by extruding chemical solutions through a showerheadlike device called a *spinerette*, they are filament fibers. However, they can be cut to staple fiber lengths.

Yarns are formed by twisting fibers together to create a continuous strand. Yarns are classified in two types: *spun* and *filament*. Spun yarns are composed of staple fibers twisted together. Filament yarns are composed of continuous strands made from either a spinerette-generated synthetic fiber or from silk. *Bulked continuous filament* (BCF) yarns are continuous strands of synthetic fiber that are formed into yarn bundles without the need for spinning, which is required for all natural and staple synthetic fibers. BCF generally offers better wear, but staple fibers provide the much-sought-after "wool-like" appearance.

Yarn Designations

Yarn designations express the relationship between length and weight. The denier system is used for filament yarns; the yarn count system is used for spun yarns.

Denier

Denier is a unit of yarn measurement equal to the weight in grams of 9,000 meters of the yarn. The higher the denier, the heavier the yarn and generally the better the strength, resiliency, and abrasion resistance. Heavier-filament yarns are designated by higher denier numbers. For example, a 15-denier yarn would be suitable for sheer hosiery; a 2,200-denier yarn would be suitable for carpet.

Yarn Count

The yarn count system is a relative gauge of a spun yarn's weight. Heavier yarns are designated by lower yarn count numbers. For example, a 70-count yarn is quite fine, whereas a 10-count yarn is thick and heavy.

Carpet Fiber Types

Acrylic

Acrylic was one of the first synthetic fibers to be used successfully in the production of carpet. However, because the color and texture of acrylic fiber can be glossy and harsh, and because acrylic carpet pile crushes easily, it is no longer recommended for use as a commercial carpet fiber.

Nylon

Nylon is the most popular carpet fiber. Nylon has excellent wearability, abrasion resistance, and resilience; solution-dyed nylon is also resistant to harsh cleaning chemicals and sunlight fading. However, because of nylon's excellent durability, appearance retention is a concern. Long before a nylon carpet wears out, its appearance can be permanently ruined.

Polypropylene

Polypropylene is the lightest commercial carpet fiber. Polypropylenes are known for their excellent stain and mildew resistance, low moisture absorbency, excellent colorfastness in sunlight, and high strength. They also minimize static electricity. Olefin is a polypropylene. Polypropylene is commonly used in outdoor carpeting.

Polyester

Polyester fibers are known for their color clarity and their capability to retain color. More popular for residential carpet applications than for commercial uses, polyester has a luxurious feel.

Wool

Used for centuries in the manufacturing of carpet, wool is still the standard against which other carpet fibers are judged. It is generally the most expensive carpet fiber and is commonly used in woven carpets. When exposed to flame, wool chars, rather than melting like most synthetic fibers, making it naturally flame-resistant. It dyes well and has good resistance to soil and wear.

Sisal

Sisal is a strong, woody fiber produced from the leaves of the agave plant, which is found in Central America, the West Indies, and Africa. Used mostly in twine and rope, it has become a popular contemporary flooring fiber.

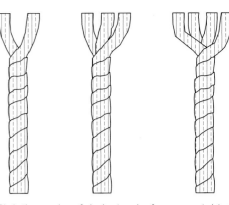

Ply is the number of single strands of spun yarn twisted together to form the yarn. Ply is not a measure of quality, but will affect the appearance of a carpet. Higher-ply counts give a coarser, nubbier texture.

CARPET YARN PLIES

WOOL

NYLON

The outer layer of a wool fiber is scaly, which diffuses light, thus hiding soil. The inner core is composed of long, rounded cells that provide the elasticity essential for excellent appearance retention.

Nylon is extruded through a showerheadlike device called a *spinerette*. Nylon fibers are smooth and tend to be reflective or shiny.

WOOL AND NYLON FIBER

CUT PILE
Cut pile yarns are at the same height.

LEVEL LOOP
Uncut pile yarns are at the same height. Level loop has a pebbled surface texture that hides footprints and chair caster marks.

CUT AND LOOP
Sculptural effect is created.

RANDOM TIP-SHEARED
Tonal contrasts between cut and uncut loops of varying heights are produced in random tip-sheared yarn.

VELVET OR PLUSH
Velvet or plush has a smooth, cut pile. Yarn ends blend together for a consistent surface appearance. This pile type shows footprints and shading marks.

SAXONY
Saxony is similar to velvet pile but has twisted yarn, which gives definition to each tuft. The loops are cut during the construction process. Saxonies are made with heat-set yarn, usually in a dense, low-pile construction. This pile type shows footprints and shading marks.

MULTILEVEL LOOP
Uncut pile yarns are at varying heights.

FRIEZE
Frieze (pronounced *free-zay*) is a tightly twisted, heat-set yarn that hides dirt well.

Pile consists of yarns or fibers projecting from a substrate, acting as a wear surface. The selection of a pile type depends on the desired visual effect and performance expectations.

PILE TYPES

CARPET DENSITY

Density, the amount of pile yarn in unit volume of carpet, is influenced by gauge—stitches per inch across the width—yarn size or thickness, and pile height. A larger yarn can be tufted at a wider gauge and receive the same density as a fine yarn at a small gauge. For areas where heavy foot traffic is likely, a density of 5,000 to 7,000 or more may be necessary. Office spaces with moderate traffic require a density of 4,000 to 6,000. Because of the fundamental differences in the manufacturing processes, different terms are used to describe carpet density for each type of carpet construction.

Density Measurements for Tufted Carpet

Widthwise Density Measurement

Gauge is the measure of the spacing of the tufting needles, center to center, across the width of the carpet. Gauge is measured in fractions of an inch. For example, ⅛-gauge means that the tufting needles are spaced ⅛ in. (3 mm) apart, producing eight yarn ends per inch.

Lengthwise Density Measurement

Stitches define the number of ends tufted by the needles down the length of the carpet. Generally, the number of stitches per inch and the number of needles per inch are approximately the same. *Pile height* is the length of a tuft from the backing surface to the tip of the tuft. It is measured in fractions of an inch. Although a deep pile may provide a more luxurious feel underfoot, it also has a greater tendency to crush and show wear.

Density Measurements for Woven Carpet

Widthwise Density Measurement

Pitch is the number of ends in a 27 in. (685 mm) width of carpet. A yarn loop in the surface of a carpet is referred to as an *end*. The pitch can be divided by 27 to compare widthwise density with that of a tufted carpet. For example, if the pitch is 216, it is divided by 27, which equals eight ends per inch, or ⅛-gauge in a tufted carpet.

Lengthwise Density Measurement

The terms *rows* in Axminster, and *wires* in Wilton and velvet carpets, refer to the number of ends per inch lengthwise. In woven carpet, the pile height is referred to as the *wire height*, referring to the height of the steel blades in the loom on which the tufts are formed. Wire height is stated in decimals of an inch.

CARPET TRAFFIC CLASS RECOMMENDATIONS

AREA	TRAFFIC CLASS
Airports	
Administrative offices	I
Corridors/all public and ticket areas	III
Banks	
Executive offices	I
Lobbies	II–III
Corridors	II–III
Teller windows	III
Convention Centers	
Auditoriums	II–III
Corridors and lobbies	III
Places of Worship	
Churches, synagogues, mosques, etc.	I–II
Meeting rooms	II
Lobbies	II–III
Golf Clubs	
Locker rooms/pro shops	III
Other Areas	II–III
Health Care Areas	
Executive/administrative offices	I–II
Patients rooms/lounges	II
Lobbies/corridors/nurses stations	III
Hotels/Motels/Apartments	
Rooms	I
Corridors	II
Lobbies	III
Libraries/Museums/Art Galleries	
Administrative offices	I
Public areas	II–III
Office Buildings	
Executive or private offices	I
Clerical areas	II
Corridors	II–III
Cafeteria	III
Restaurants	
Dining areas/lobbies	III
Retail Stores	
Windows and display areas	I
Minor aisles/boutiques/specialized departments	II
Major aisles/checkouts/supermarkets, etc.	III
Schools and Colleges	
Administrative offices	I
Classrooms/dormitories	II
Corridors/cafeteria	III

Source: BASF; Dalton, Georgia

CARPET TRAFFIC CLASSIFICATION

CLASS	TRAFFIC	WALK-ONS PER DAY	DESCRIPTION	EXAMPLES
I	Light	Up to 500	Areas that undergo a limited amount of traffic and where there is some soiling	Executive offices, hotel bedrooms
II	Heavy	500–1,000	Areas that undergo frequent traffic flowing in the same direction and where there is heavy dirt, grit, twisting, turning, and spillage	Hotel corridors, auditoriums, school classrooms
III	Extra Heavy	More than 1,000	Areas that are subject to extremely frequent and concentrated traffic flowing in the same direction and where there is severe dirt, grit, twisting, turning, heavy rolling, and spillage	Airports, bank teller window areas

Source: BASF; Dalton, Georgia

CARPET DENSITY GUIDELINES

	CLASS I		CLASS II		CLASS III	
PILE TYPE	WEIGHT OZ/SQ YD	DENSITY OZ/CU YD	WEIGHT OZ/SQ YD	DENSITY OZ/CU YD	WEIGHT OZ/SQ YD	DENSITY OZ/CU YD
Level loop	16	3,600	20	4,200	24	4,800
Cut/loop	20	3,600	24	4,200	28	4,800
Cut pile, not heat-set	28	3,800	33	4,500	38	5,000
Cut pile, heat-set	28	3,800	35	4,500	43	5,000

Source: BASF; Dalton, Georgia

Cut and loop pile type requires 100% latex penetration. Cut and loop with more than 50% cut surface should meet cut pile guidelines.

GAUGE OR PITCH

GAUGE	NEEDLES (ENDS) PER INCH	PITCH
⅜	2.7	73
¼	4	108
3/16	5.3	144
5/32	6.4	173
⅛	8	216
1/10	10	270
5/64	12.8	346
1/16	16	432
1/20	20	540
1/25	25	675

To convert gauge to pitch, multiply needles (ends) per inch by 27; for example, 1/10-gauge is equivalent to 270 pitch, or 10 ends per inch × 27; ⅛-gauge is eight ends of yarn per inch × 27 = 216 pitch.

CARPET PERFORMANCE

Wear resistance of a carpet, like that of other textiles, is affected by many factors, such as the face and total weight, pile density, type and length of the fiber, structure of the yarn, and the construction of the carpet.

Face weight, also referred to as *pile weight* or *yarn weight*, is the weight of the pile yarn in ounces per square yard of carpet. It does not include the weight of the backings or coating. The face weight describes the amount of yarn in the wear surface of the carpet.

Total weight, or *finished weight*, includes the face weight and the weight of backing materials, finishes, and coatings. It is expressed in ounces per square yard of carpet. Total weight is less an indication of quality than of face weight.

Pile density is the weight of pile yarn in a given volume of carpet face. It is determined by the number and size of the carpet tufts. Pile density is the most important selection factor in high-traffic installations. For example, nylon is a very durable fiber; however, if the pile density of a nylon carpet is too low, crushing can occur; and although the nylon may succeed in performance, it can fail in appearance. Average pile density is determined by the following formula:

$$D \text{ (oz/cu yd)} = \frac{36 \times W \text{ (oz/sq yd)}}{T \text{ (in)}}$$

[D (oz/cu yd) ÷ 26,944.67 = g/cu cm], in which D is the density, W is the pile yarn weight, and T is the pile height or thickness.

Pile yarn is the most expensive component in carpet manufacturing. For a given weight, a lower pile height and a higher pile density provide the greatest performance value. The industry standard for measuring average pile yarn weight, tufts per square inch, and average pile density is ASTM D418, *Standard Methods for Testing Pile Yarn Floor Covering Construction.*

Abrasion resistance is sometimes used as a relative measure of a carpet's durability. ASTM D3884, *Standard Test Method for Abrasion Resistance of Textile Fabrics (Rotary Platform, Double-Head Method),* describes the procedures for the Taber Abraser test, named after the company that manufactures the test equipment. In this test, a sample is abraded using a rotary rubbing action. As the sample rotates on a turntablelike platform, two emery wheels rub against the carpet, one rubbing outward and the other inward toward the center of the sample. The results of the test are typically reported in terms of number of cycles (revolutions of the turntable) required to expose the backing material. Because modern synthetic fibers are highly resistant to abrasive wear, wear resistance is not tested for as often as appearance retention.

Appearance retention tests aim to simulate floor traffic with mechanical devices. Pile appearance changes due to wear are commonly tested by either of two methods: the hexapod tumbler test or the Vettermann Drum Test. The Vettermann Drum Test is defined by ASTM D5417, *Standard Practice for Operation of the Vettermann Drum Tester.* A steel ball with 14 rubber studs rolls randomly over a carpet sample mounted inside a rotating drum. ASTM D5252, *Standard Practice for the Operation of the Hexapod Drum Tester,* describes the requirements for the hexapod (meaning six-legged) test. It is similar to the Vettermann Drum Test, except that a 1.97 in. (50 mm) metal cube, with a polyurethane stud screwed into each of its six faces, rolls over the carpet surface.

Watermarking or pooling, a phenomenon in the carpet industry associated primarily with cut pile carpet, is so called because a pool of water appears to be sitting on the carpet. It tends to be most noticeable with solid-color carpets installed in large open areas. Watermarking is not a manufacturer's defect. There is no known cause or remedy for watermarking. One of the theories of watermarking is that of subfloor irregularities, but various other theories exist. Where a cut pile carpet is preferred, the client should be notified in writing that watermarking may occur.

Static control, the electrostatic discharge properties of carpet, may need to be considered where sensitive electronic or computer equipment is in use. Static electricity is created by the friction of rubbing materials together—for example, the sole of a shoe and carpet fiber. Static electricity does not become apparent until the relative humidity drops below 40%. There are two methods for enhancing the electrostatic discharge properties of carpet: the incorporation of a conductive filament, typically carbon-loaded nylon, or the application of topical treatments.

Carpet with integral static-inhibiting fibers should comply with American Association of Textile Chemists and Colorists (AATCC) Test Method–134, *Electrostatic Propensity of Carpets*. This test is a laboratory simulation that assesses the static-generating tendency developed when a person walks across a carpet.

Testing is performed at 20% ±2% relative humidity.

Carpet with static-resistant topical treatments do not generally provide reliable electrostatic discharge under all conditions. Topical finishes may be water-soluble and can lose effectiveness after repeated washings. They can also cause carpet to soil at an accelerated rate.

CARPET STATIC GENERATION

APPLICATION	MAXIMUM STATIC GENERATION
Residential	5.0 KV
General commercial	3.5 KV
Critical commercial	2.0 KV

Carpet in Golf Club Houses and Athletic Facilities

- Specify cut pile rather than loop construction with a minimum pile height of 7/16 in.
- Dense carpet construction is important. Specify a minimum fiber weight of 45 ounces per square yard and a minimum density of 5,000 ounces of pile fiber per cubic yard.
- Contact manufacturers about the appropriateness of any product to be installed in areas where soft spike shoes are allowed. Specifically, always select engineered and tested products.
- Select solution-dyed fiber for colorfastness where there is a concern about fading from sunlight or color loss from chemicals.
- Carpet used outdoors should be designed to resist ultraviolet fading and degradation.

Source: Carpet and Rug Institute; Dalton, Georgia

MINIMUM AVERAGE SPECIFICATIONS FOR CARPET IN SCHOOLS

CARPET PROPERTY/ CHARACTERISTIC	MINIMUM SPECIFICATIONS	TEST METHOD
Type yarn	Solution or yarn-dyed	—
Color	Multicolored products (Select colors complementary to soil type/color in region)	—
Surface/style	Level loop, multilevel loop, textured loop, or cut and loop. Cut pile may be satisfactory for administrative areas.	—
Appearance-retention rating static	≥3.5 (Vetterman 22K cycles or Hexapod 12K cycles) 3.5KV (maximum—not to exceed)	CRI TM–101 AATCC–134 Step Method
Indoor air quality (IAQ)	CRI IAQ Certification	CRI Test Program ASTM D5116

Note: In glue-down installation, include CRI IAQ Testing Program label for installation adhesives. For carpet over cushion, include CRI IAQ Testing Program label for carpet cushion.

Flammability–Radiant Panel Test	Class II (minimum) (Class I in some locations) (or per building code)	ASTM E648
NBS smoke	<450 flaming mode	ASTM E662
Tuft bind (dry)	8 lbs, all products (16–20 lbs suggested for unitary backing)	ASTM D1335
Delamination	Secondary backed products, 3.5 lbs	ASTM D3936
Dimensional stability	Removable modular products, 0.2% or less	ISO 2551
Colorfastness: light	4 or better (60 AFU three cycles)	AATCC–16-E
Colorfastness: ozone	4 or better after two cycles	AATCC–129
Colorfastness: crocking	4 or better (wet and dry)	AATCC–165
Colorfastness: water	4 or better, AATCC Transference Scale (only yarn-dyed carpets)	AATCC–107 (grade change in color and staining)
Soil-resistant treatment	Minimum average of 350 ppm fluorine on pile fiber of three separate tests	CRI TM-102

Source: Carpet and Rug Institute; Dalton, Georgia

CARPET INSTALLATION

There are two types of carpet installation: *stretch-in* and *adhesive*. For broadloom carpet, there are three types of adhesive installation: *direct glue-down, double glue-down,* and the newest installation type, *self-stick*. Releasable adhesives can facilitate carpet repair or replacement.

Stretch-In Installation

Stretch-in installation is the traditional method of carpet installation, whereby the carpet is stretched over a cushion and attached at the perimeter with a tack strip. This is the most common installation method for residential applications and is used commercially for woven wool carpets and in areas where underfoot comfort and luxury are required (for example, hotel lobbies and boardrooms). Stretch-in applications allow for easy removal and replacement of the carpet and cushion. Because stretch-in carpet is secured only around the perimeter, such installations can ripple, causing accessibility problems, hence they may not be appropriate for large areas and heavy commercial or rolling traffic.

Power stretchers are used to put the carpet in tension and stretch it drum-tight. The carpet should be stretched to its fullest to withstand changes in temperature and humidity and other stresses. Cushion selection should be coordinated with the carpet manufacturer to ensure that the carpet warranty is not voided.

Adhesive Installation

Direct Glue-Down

The most common method of commercial installation, direct glue-down is economical and practical. The carpet is glued directly to the floor without a cushion. This is the most dimensionally stable installation method and is often required for stair or ramp applications, even if different installation methods are specified for other areas of the project. Proper substrate conditions are imperative for a successful glue-down installation. Uneven substrates can cause irregular wear patterns.

Double Glue-Down

This installation method combines the underfoot comfort of stretch-in installation with the stability of the direct glue-down method. The carpet cushion is adhered to the floor, then the carpet is glued to the cushion. With either the direct or the double glue-down method, admitting traffic before the adhesive has had time to cure can cause the installation to fail. Hardboard or plywood is typically recommended as protection for an adhesive installation, because covering a new adhesive installation with plastic sheeting may prevent proper curing and cause mold or mildew to develop.

Self-Stick

This is the latest development in carpet installation techniques. A flexible adhesive layer is applied to the carpet backing and is covered with a protective plastic film. The labor involved in adhesive application and the time required to ensure the proper tackiness are eliminated. This type of carpet type typically comes in smaller widths, about 6 ft (1.8 m), for ease of manipulation during layout and installation.

Advantages of Stretch-in Carpet Installation

- Patterned carpet is easier to match.
- It is more resilient than direct glue-down.
- It extends carpet life.
- It is less crushing and packing of pile.
- It adds insulation value (R-value).
- It gives higher sound absorbency (NRC) values.
- It responds better to vacuuming.
- It can be used over floors that may be unacceptable for direct glue-down.
- Removal usually costs less than removal of a direct glue-down installation.
- Corrective measures, such as seam repair, are easier to perform.

Advantages of Direct Glue-Down Carpet Installation

- Cushion cost is eliminated.
- Labor for direct glue-down is usually less expensive.
- It is suitable for rolling traffic and ramp areas.
- Seams are more durable because there is no vertical flex.
- Buckling is minimized in buildings that have heat and air conditioning turned off for extended periods, such as schools, churches, and theaters.
- There are no restretch situations.
- It facilitates access to electrical and telephone lines under the floor.
- Seam peaking is practically eliminated.
- It is unrestricted as to size of area.
- It has intricate border and inlay capabilities.

If carpet with an attached cushion is installed with the direct glue-down method, the following additional considerations apply:
- Improved appearance retention and foot comfort compared to direct glue-down (with no attached cushion) installations
- Increased delamination strength and improved edge ravel resistance
- Functionality as an effective moisture barrier
- Improved thermal and acoustical contribution
- Elimination of second adhesive requirement for double glue-down installation

Advantages of Double Glue-Down Carpet Installation

- The stability of direct glue-down carpet is combined with the cushioning benefits of a separate cushion, stretch-in installation.
- Carpet appearance retention, comfort under foot, and overall performance is improved compared to direct glue-down installations.
- Carpet bordering and inlay is simplified.
- Double glue-down installations are suitabel for wheeled traffic area.
- Size of installation area is not restricted.

CARPET TILE INSTALLATION

There are three methods of carpet tile installation: *free-lay, full-glue,* and with a *tile that has a preapplied pressure-sensitive adhesive coating*. In free-lay installations, a strip of adhesive is applied about every 15 ft (4.5 m) and around the room perimeter. Tiles in those areas are anchored in place, and surrounding tiles are butted snugly against each other. Full-glue installations should be specified where heavy or wheeled traffic is anticipated. In this case, tiles are typically installed with a "stair-step" technique. The installation grows from the center of the room.

COLORING METHODS

Carpet coloring is accomplished by predyeing the carpet fibers before the carpet is manufactured, or *postdyeing* the finished piece of carpet. Most carpet is postdyed, because this process allows manufacturers to respond quickly to the needs of the market.

Predyeing Methods

Solution dyeing is commonly preferred in areas subject to sunlight fading or spills, because the color is integral to the fiber. The dye is combined with the fiber chemicals before the extrusion process. The color of solution-dyed yarn is consistent throughout the fiber. Solution-dyed yarns have excellent colorfastness qualities against both sunlight and crocking, and can withstand cleaning with harsh chemicals. Polyester and nylon are sometimes solution-dyed, but polypropylene is the fiber most commonly dyed in this manner. Solution-dyed yarn holds a large share of the commercial market but only a small portion of the residential market.

Stock dyeing, the oldest method of fiber coloring, is still popular for wool. Staple fibers are placed in large kettles, and the dye is circulated through the fiber. Stock dyeing applies the color to the staple fibers before they are spun into yarn. The color of stock-dyed yarns varies slightly from batch to batch. During the spinning operation, fibers from different dye lots are combined, providing a depth of color not achievable with solution-dyed fibers.

Skein dyeing is a coloring process that applies color after the fibers have been spun into yarn. Skein dyeing is labor-intensive and has limited dye lot capacities. These factors can result in higher dyeing costs than other methods. Skein dyeing is commonly used in dyeing yarn for woven carpets.

Postdyeing Methods

The application of color to greige goods, or undyed carpet, immersed in a dye bath is called *piece dyeing*. After the carpet has been tufted onto its primary backing, and before a secondary backing has been attached, the carpet is dyed. Piece dyeing is generally used for solid-color carpets, but a limited range of patterns are possible by using fibers varying in their propensity to accept different dyes.

PRINTING

Patterns can be applied to carpet (printed) after the finishing process. Printed carpet simulates the intricate patterns of woven carpet at a much lower cost. *Screen printing,* the most widely used printing methods for textiles, is generally faster and more accurate than other printing methods. Color is forced through a perforated plate onto the surface of the carpet as it rolls by. *Jet printing* utilizes rows of very closely spaced jets that spray the carpet with color as it passes by. The texture of jet-printed carpet is often preferred because, unlike screen printing, this process does not crush the carpet pile.

ACOUSTICAL CONSIDERATIONS

Carpet is an important component of the contemporary open office space because of its sound-deadening properties. In office applications, noise created by discussions, office equipment, and furniture movement can effectively be absorbed by the proper selection of carpet and carpet cushion. In hotels, carpeted guest rooms significantly reduce the sound transmissions to the rooms below. In churches and theaters, the noise generated by latecomers can be lessened without altering the carefully engineered acoustics of the space.

One of carpet's most important contributions to the appeal of a space is its acoustical properties. These acoustical properties are measured in three ways:

- Noise Reduction Coefficient (NRC)
- Impact Noise Rating (INR)
- Impact Insulation Class (IIC)

Sound Absorption

The Noise Reduction Coefficient (NRC) is the average of four absorption coefficients measured at frequencies from low- to high-pitched sounds and rounded off to the closest 5%. The NRC is determined by ASTM C423, *Standard Method of Sound Absorption and Sound Absorption Coefficients by the Reverberation Room Method.* The NRC is used in calculating the required amount of sound-absorbing material and can be used to compare the sound-absorption qualities of one material with another. The higher the NRC, the greater the sound absorption.

Cut pile carpets are somewhat more effective in absorbing sound than loop piles. The fiber content of the carpet has little effect on its capability to absorb sound.

Noise Transmission

The Impact Noise Rating (INR) represents the sound insulation provided by a floor-ceiling assembly from an impact noise. Sound levels are measured in an isolated room below. The data are related to a minimum standard of 0 INR. Assembly ratings less than 0 are considered unsatisfactory. Assembly ratings more than 0 are deemed superior.

The Impact Insulation Class (IIC) also measures the sound insulation of a floor-ceiling assembly, but the IIC differs from the INR, not in the test procedure, but in the numerical scale applied. IIC rates floor-ceiling assemblies with positive numbers only in ascending order of efficiency. The higher the value, the less noise transmitted. An IIC value can be estimated by adding 51 to the INR value.

THERMAL CONSIDERATIONS

Carpet contributes to the thermal insulation of a space. The total R-value of a carpet is more dependent on the total thickness of the carpet than the fiber content.

When the carpet R-value is not available, multiply the total carpet thickness measured in inches by a factor of 2.6 to approximate the carpet's R-value. R-values can be considered additive for any combination of materials. For example, a combination of carpet with an R-value of 1.3 and a prime polyurethane cushion with an R-value of 1.6 will yield an overall R-value of 2.9.

INDOOR AIR QUALITY AND CARPET

Some people report allergy or flulike symptoms when exposed to emissions from new construction, including carpet, carpet cushion, and installation adhesives. Limited research to date has found no link between adverse health effects and the levels of chemicals emitted by the installation of new carpet.

To reduce the exposure of these pollutants, however, the Carpet and Rug Institute recommends that the ventilation system in public and commercial buildings be operated at maximum outdoor airflow before, during, and for 48 to 72 hours after new carpet installation. In homes, it is recommended that windows be left open, if possible, and that fans be used to increase the airflow. It is also recommended that carpet be installed when the area is not in use.

CARPET R-VALUES

FIBER TYPE	YARN TYPE	STYLE	PILE HEIGHT (IN.)	PILE WEIGHT (OZ/SQ YD)	GAUGE	STITCHES PER INCH (SPI)	TUFTS/ SQ IN. SPI X GA	R-VALUE
Nylon	CF	LL	.125	10	1/10	8.0	80	0.68
Nylon	CF	LL	.109	20	1/8	6.0	48	0.65
Nylon	CF	LL	.192	28	1/8	8.4	67.2	0.67
Nylon	CF	LL	.125	24	1/10	8.6	86	0.55
Nylon	S	Plush	.250	24	1/8	11.0	88	1.12
Nylon	CF	HLL	—	24	5/32	8.6	55	1.33
Nylon	CF	Shag	1.07	24	3/16	5.2	27.7	1.51
Acrylic	S	LL	.210	42	1/10	8.0	80	0.78
Acrylic	S	LL (FB)	.210	42	1/10	8.0	80	1.03
Polyester	S	Plush	.280	42	5/32	8.5	54.4	0.95
Polyester	S	HLL	—	42	5/32	8.5	54.4	1.66
Nylon	S	Saxony	.552	40	3/16	5.5	29.3	1.96
Nylon	CF	Shag	1.25	43	3/16	4.2	22.4	2.46
Wool	S	Plush	.487	43	5/32	7.0	44.8	2.19
Nylon	S	Plush	.812	58	1/8	10.0	80	1.83
Acrylic	S	Plush	.688	53	5/32	9.0	57.6	1.90
Acrylic	S	Plush	.530	44	3/16	8.25	44	1.71
Olefin	CF	LL	—	20	—	—	—	0.70

Legend: LL = Level Loop; HLL = High-Low Loop (tip-sheared); FB = Attached foam back; S = Spun Yarn; CF = Continuous Filament Yarn

Source: Carpet and Rug Institute; Dalton, Georgia

Study conducted by Georgia Institute of Technology, School of Textile Engineering

CARPET CUSHION R-VALUES

MATERIAL	THICKNESS (IN.)	WEIGHT (OZ/SQ YD)	DENSITY (LBS/CU FT)	R-VALUE
Prime polyurethane	.40	10.3	2.2	1.61
Slab rubber	.23	62.0	—	0.62
Waffled sponge rubber	.43	49.2	—	0.78
Hair- and jute-coated	.44	52.6	—	1.71
Bonded polyurethane	.50	—	4.0	2.09

CARPET ON CUSHION TO CARPET ON PLYWOOD

CARPET ON CUSHION TO DIRECT GLUE-DOWN CARPET

THINSET CERAMIC TILE TO CARPET ON CUSHION

CARPET ON CUSHION TO CARPET ON CUSHION

CARPET ON CUSHION TO EXPOSED CONCRETE FLOOR

THINSET CERAMIC TILE TO DIRECT GLUE-DOWN CARPET, STONE TRANSITION

CARPET TO FINISH FLOOR, SURGED EDGE

CARPET ON CUSHION TO FINISH FLOOR

THINSET CERAMIC TILE TO DIRECT GLUE-DOWN CARPET, RESILIENT TRANSITION

CARPET TO FINISH FLOOR, SEWN EDGE

THICKSET STONE TO DIRECT GLUE-DOWN CARPET

CARPET ON CUSHION TO WOOD

CARPET ON CUSHION TO FINISH FLOOR

DIRECT-GLUE CARPET TO VCT

DIRECT-GLUE CARPET TO VCT

CARPET TRANSITION DETAILS

HIGH-DENSITY JUTE

SYNTHETIC

FIBER CARPET CUSHION

TEXTURED FLAT RUBBER

FLAT RUBBER

SPONGE RUBBER CARPET CUSHION

DENSIFIED POLYURETHANE FOAM

BONDED POLYURETHANE FOAM

POLYURETHANE FOAM CARPET CUSHION

CARPET CUSHION

Carpet cushion can significantly extend the life of a carpet. Environmental conditions, anticipated traffic, and desired feel underfoot should be considered in the selection of a carpet cushion. Carpet cushions can be categorized by three types: *fiber, sponge rubber,* and *polyurethane foam.*

Fiber Cushions

Fiber cushions are made by needlepunching natural fiber, synthetic fiber, or a combination of the two, into a feltlike pad. Antimicrobial treatments are recommended for natural fiber pads because they are susceptible to mold and mildew. Fiber cushions tend to have a firm feel underfoot. Over time, felted fiber cushions may be crushed under heavy wear.

Sponge Rubber

Unlike felted fiber cushions, rubber cushions are highly compressible. Reinforced foam rubber has a smaller cell structure than sponge rubber, thus providing more uniform support. Sponge rubber cushions are generally open-cell foams, which are less resilient than closed-cell foams.

Polyurethane Foam

The chemical compositions of polyurethane foam carpet cushions are similar, but their different cellular structures affect their performance. Bonded polyurethane foam (or *rebond,* as it is sometimes called) is manufactured from scraps of foam bonded together through an adhesive and heat fusion process. Modified prime polyurethane foam is manufactured in a continuous sheet and, unlike densified foam, may contain fillers. Densified foam is denser than modified prime foam and is highly resistant to bottoming out.

Ted Kollaja, AIA; lauckgroup; Dallas, Texas
Kim McGhee; Boston Architectural Center; Boston, Massachusetts
Lilliana Romerz; Boston Architectural Center; Boston, Massachusetts

MINIMUM RECOMMENDATIONS FOR RESIDENTIAL CARPET CUSHION

TYPE	KEY CHARACTERISTICS	CLASS 1[1]			CLASS 2[2]		
		WEIGHT OZ/SQ YD, MIN.	DENSITY LBS/CU FT, MIN.	THICKNESS[3] IN., MIN.	WEIGHT OZ/SQ YD, MIN.	DENSITY LBS./CU FT, MIN.	THICKNESS IN., MIN.
Urethane	Prime		2.2	0.3750	Not recommended for class 2		
	Grafted prime		2.7	0.2500		2.7	0.250
	Densified prime		2.2	0.3130		2.7	0.250
	Bonded		5.0	0.3750		6.5	0.375
	Mechanically frothed		10.0	0.2500		12.0	0.250
Fiber	Rubberized hair jute	40.0	12.3	0.2700	50.0	11.1	0.375
	Rubberized jute	32.0	8.5	0.3125	40.0	8.9	0.375
	Synthetic fibers	22.0	6.5	0.2500	28.0	6.5	0.300
	Resinated recycled textile fiber	24.0	7.3	0.2500	30.0	7.3	0.300
Rubber	Flat rubber	56.0	18.0	0.2200	64.0	21.0	0.220
	Rippled rubber	48.0	14.0	0.2850	64.0	16.0	0.330

[1] *Class 1: Light and moderate traffic such as living and dining rooms, bedrooms, and recreational rooms. Class 2 cushions may be used in Class 1 applications.*
[2] *Class 2: Heavy-duty traffic, such as lobbies and corridors in multifamily facilities, and all stair applications.*
[3] *Maximum thickness for any product is 0.5 in.*

Source: Carpet Cushion Council; Riverside, Connecticut

CLASSIFICATION OF CARPET CUSHION

TYPES OF CUSHION	CLASS I MODERATE TRAFFIC	CLASS II HEAVY TRAFFIC	CLASS III EXTRA-HEAVY TRAFFIC
Commercial Application	Office Buildings: Executive or private offices; conference rooms Healthcare: Executive, administration Schools: Administration Airports: Administration Retail: Windows and display areas Banks: Executive areas Hotels/Motels: Sleeping rooms Libraries/Museums: Administration	Office Buildings: Clerical areas, corridors (moderate traffic) Healthcare: Patient's rooms, lounges Schools : Dormitories, classrooms Retail: Minor aisles, boutiques, specialties Banks: Lobbies, corridors (moderate traffic) Hotels/Motels: Corridors Libraries/Museums: Public areas (moderate traffic) Convention Centers: Auditoriums	Office Buildings: Corridors (heavy traffic), cafeterias Healthcare: Lobbies, corridors, nurses' stations Schools: Corridors, cafeterias Airports: Corridors, public areas, ticketing areas Retail: Major aisles, checkouts, supermarkets Banks: Corridors (heavy traffic), teller windows Hotels/Motels: Lobbies and public areas Libraries/Museums: Public areas Convention Centers: Corridors and lobbies Country Clubs: Locker rooms, pro shops, dining areas Restaurants: Dining areas and lobbies
FIBER			
Rubberized Hair	Wt: 40 oz./sq. yd. Th: .27" D = 12.3	Wt: 40 oz./sq. yd. Th: .3125" D = 12.3	Wt: 50 oz./sq. yd. Th: .375" D = 11.1
Rubberized Jute	Wt: 32 oz./sq. yd. Th: .25" D = 12.3	Wt: 40 oz./sq. yd. Th: .25" D = 12.3	Wt: 40 oz./sq. yd. Th: .34" D = 11.1
Synthetic Fibers	Wt: 22 oz./sq. yd. Th: .25" D = 7.3	Wt: 28 oz./sq. yd. Th: .3125" D = 7.3	Wt: 36 oz./sq. yd. Th: .35" D = 8.0
Resinated Recycled Textile Fiber	Wt: 24 oz./sq. yd. Th: .25" D = 7.3	Wt: 30 oz./sq. yd. Th: .30" D = 7.3	Wt: 40 oz./sq. yd. Th: .375" D = 8.0
SPONGE RUBBER			
Flat Rubber	Wt: 62 oz./sq. yd. Th: .150" CR @ 25% = 3.0 psi min. D = 21	Wt: 62 oz./sq. yd. Th: .150" CR @ 25% = 3.0 psi min. D = 21	Wt: 62 oz./sq. yd. Th: .150" CR @ 25% = 4.0 psi min. D = 26
Rippled Waffle	Wt: 56 oz./sq. yd. Th: .270" CR @ 25% = 0.7 psi min. D = 15	Not recommended for use in this class	Not recommended for use in this class
Textured Flat Rubber	Wt: 56 oz./sq. yd. Th: .220" CR @ 25% = 1.0 psi min. D = 18	Wt: 62 oz./sq. yd. Th: .235" CR @ 25% = 1.5 psi min. D = 22	Wt: 80 oz./sq. yd. Th: .250" CR @ 25% = 1.75 psi min. D = 26
Reinforced Rubber	Wt: 64 oz./sq. yd. Th: .235" CR @ 25% = 2.0 psi min. D = 22 CR @ 65% = 50.0 psi min	Wt: 64 oz./sq. yd. Th: .235" CR @ 25% = 2.0 psi min. D = 22 CR @ 65% = 50.0 psi min	Wt: 54 oz./sq. yd. Th: .200" CR @ 25% = 2.0 psi min. D = 22 CR @ 65% = 50.0 psi min
POLYURETHANE FOAM			
Grafted Prime	D = 2.7 Th: .25" CFD @ 65% = 2.5 psi min.	D = 3.2 Th: .25" CFD @ 65% = 3.5 psi min.	D = 4.0 Th: .25" CFD @ 65% = 5.0 psi min.
Densified	D = 2.7 Th: .25" CFD @ 65% = 2.4 psi min.	D = 3.5 Th: .25" CFD @ 65% = 3.3 psi min.	D = 4.5 Th: .25" CFD @ 65% = 4.8 psi min.
Bonded	D = 5.0 Th: .375" CFD @ 65% = 2.5 psi min.	D = 6.5 Th: .25" CFD @ 65% = 10.0 psi min.	D = 8.0 Th: .25" CFD @ 65% = 8.0 psi min.
Mechanically Frothed	D = 13.0 Th: .30" CFD @ 65% = 9.7 psi min.	D = 15.0 Th: .223" CFD @ 65% = 49.9 psi min.	D = 19.0 Th: .183" CFD @ 65% = 30.5 psi min.

LEGEND:

CFD Compression Force Deflection as measured by ASTM D 3574
CR Compression Resistance in pounds per square inch as measured by ASTM D 3676
D Density in pounds per cubic foot
min. Minimum
Th Thickness
Wt. Weight

Note: All thicknesses, weights, and densities allow a 5% manufacturing tolerance.

Reprinted, by permission, from the Carpet Cushion Council, Commercial Carpet Cushion Guidelines, 1997.

ORIENTAL RUGS

Oriental rugs are produced in a broad geographic region encompassing the Near East, Asia, India, and parts of Eastern Europe. True oriental rugs are handwoven of natural fibers, and are greatly prized for their artistry, patterns, and color. Motifs typically include geometric or floral designs, with striking field and border patterns.

RUG PRODUCTION REGIONS

Sources for modern oriental rugs include the large rug production areas of India, Pakistan, and China. Other oriental rug-weaving centers are located in the countries or regions of Iran (Persia), Turkey (Anatolia), Georgia, Armenia, Azerbaijan (the Caucasus), and the Western and Eastern Turkestan (Afghanistan, Tibet, and Nepal) regions of central Asia. These comprise the seven major geographical groups involved in the production of oriental rugs, each of which has its own style and patterns. Other smaller rug-producing areas include Romania and Spain.

Historically, the Persian Empire (Iran) produced many of the finest rugs; however, the import of Iranian rugs into the United States was prohibited as part of an embargo during the 1970s.

HISTORY

The earliest documented oriental rug dates from 400 to 500 B.C. Tribal nomadic groups were influential in the development of regional rug patterns. During the fifteenth and sixteenth centuries, the art of oriental rugmaking is considered to have reached a peak in Persia. And although popularity diminished in the eighteenth and nineteenth centuries due to the general decline in tribal nomadic groups, increased demand later in the nineteenth century from Western countries boosted production of rugs.

Modern production of oriental rugs continues for many nomadic tribal groups, as well as in the large rug production centers. Many traditional aspects of rugmaking are being revived, such as the use of natural dyes, motifs, and patterns.

MATERIALS

Warp threads are typically made of cotton. Weft yarns are usually wool, but silk, camel wool, and goat hair are used in some rugs. Combinations of silk and wool are available. Historically, accent threads of silver and gold were sometimes used in high-quality rugs.

CONSTRUCTION AND TYPES

Oriental rugmaking principles are consistent: a vertical foundation of threads, called *warps,* is stretched across a loom frame. Rows of horizontal threads, called *wefts,* are applied to the warp threads.

Two types of techniques can be used to develop the carpet pattern: *handknotting* or *flatweaving.*

Handknotted Rugs

Handknotted rugs with face pile and smooth backs are created by wrapping warps with yarns, using specific knot types. The knots are stabilized by the weft threads, which are woven back and forth across the body of the rug.

Flatwoven Rugs

Flatwoven, pileless rugs are created by weaving horizontal warp and vertical weft yarns together in a pattern. They are easier to produce than knotted pile and are less costly. Historically, they were popular due to the more compact size when transported.

Kilims

Kilims are smooth-surfaced, flatwoven rugs found throughout the oriental carpet production area, typically of wool. Kilim patterns are predominately geometric in nature. They are usually reversible due to the nature of the weave.

Soumaks

Soumaks are flatwoven carpets produced with the soumak weave, which produces a herringbone effect. The soumak weave produces many loose yarns on the back.

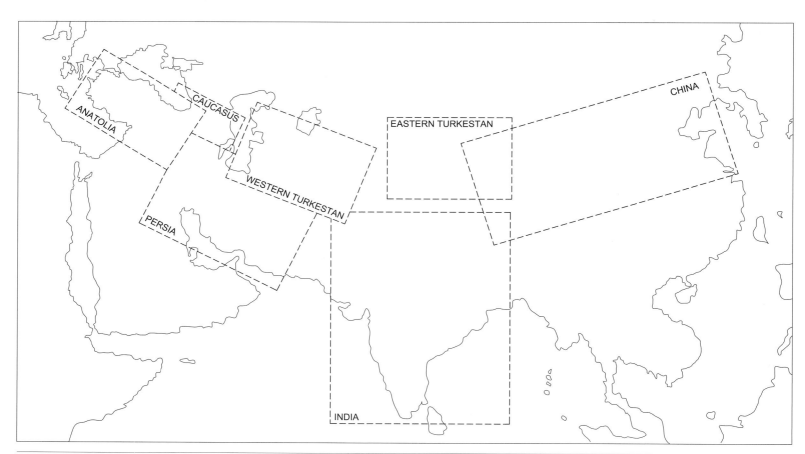

MAP OF ORIENTAL RUG PRODUCTION AREAS
Source: Enza Milanesi, The Bulfinch Guide to Carpets, translated by Jay Hyams (Boston: Little, Brown and Company), 1993.

KILIM TECHNIQUE

SOUMAK TECHNIQUE

FLATWEAVE TECHNIQUES

SLIT TAPESTRY

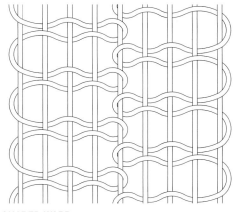

SHARED WARP

FLATWEAVE COLOR CHANGE

In the Turkish, or Ghiordes, knot, the ends of the yarn are pulled forward together between two adjacent warps. It is a symmetrical knot. The Turkish knot is primarily used in Turkey and the Caucasus, a mountain region in the former Soviet Union. This area includes Armenia, Azerbaijan, and Georgia.

TURKISH KNOT

The Persian, or Senneh, knot is an asymmetrical knot, which encircles two warp threads, passing under one and around the other. The ends of the knot can face either left or right. The Persian knot primarily is used in Iran (Persia), India, Pakistan, and China.

PERSIAN KNOT

Dhurries

Dhurries are typically cotton flatwoven rugs from northeastern India. Originally used as an underlayment for beds and carpets, dhurries were woven in vibrant designs and motifs.

Wool dhurries are produced in regions where the climate is severe, and camel hair is often used as the weft yarn.

Druggets

Druggets are flatwoven rugs from India with a heavy weft-faced plain weave.

TAPESTRY

Tapestry is the technique commonly used in the production of flatwoven rugs. Loose ends of weft yarn are buried in the rug construction, but this technique produces slits in the tapestry when vertical columns of color are woven. A technique used by Native American weavers to address this problem is to share a warp between adjacent colors.

RUG KNOTS

Knotted oriental rugs are created by wrapping yarns around warp threads that have been strung on a loom. The two most common types of knots used in pile weaving are the Turkish, or Ghiordes, knot, and the Persian, or Senneh, knot. Knotting techniques vary within some regions, due to local preference. There is no apparent difference in the face appearance and performance of rugs between the two types of knots.

RUG DYES

Traditionally, all natural dyes were used to color the weft yarn. Aniline dyes were introduced in the late nineteenth century, and while easier to produce and use, their colorfastness and color rendition were not as effective as the natural dyes. Currently, the use of natural dyes is increasingly popular in oriental rug production.

RUG FEATURES

1. Outer guard stripe or border
2. Main border
3. Inner guard stripe or border
4. Spandrel
5. Field
6. Medallion

ORIENTAL RUG COMPONENTS

FLAT RUG UNDERLAY

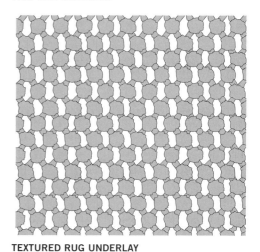

TEXTURED RUG UNDERLAY

OPEN-WEAVE FOAM RUG UNDERLAYS

RUG PATTERNS

Rug patterns are commonly named after the town or region in which they are produced. A central medallion format is one of the most common; however, many carpets have a full-field pattern within the borders. There are many variations to the patterns, colors, and features of oriental rugs. Some rugs are asymmetrical in pattern, and are used as prayer rugs. The directional pattern may be more challenging to use in an installation.

Rug patterns and motifs often reflect tribal influences, such as the Turkoman "gul" emblems, which vary according to the tribal or nomadic group. Symbols were frequently used in oriental rugs with numerous variations.

RUG DENSITY

Typically, the finer the warp, the denser the rug. The density of a pile rug is usually determined by the knots per square inch, or *knot count*. The first number is the number of horizontal knots and the second number is the number of vertical knots. Better-quality rugs have knot counts ranging from $10/20$ to $12/24$.

RUG FINISHING

Upon completion of the weaving, the rug is removed from the loom and is finished by shearing and cleaning. Loose warp ends are usually braided or knotted to form a fringe end. The sides of the rug may be bound or have a selvage border added.

IDENTIFICATION

Rugs can be identified by the style of weaving (Persian), for the tribe or group that produced the carpet (Afshar), the original area in which the rug was first developed (Belouchistan), for its design (tree of life), its use (*yastik*, which means pillow), or the period in which it was produced (Shah Abbas).

Oriental rugs imported into the United States must be labeled with a registration number, the country of origin, and fiber content. Rugs are considered semiantique if over 30 years old, antique if over 60 years old.

INSTALLATION AND MAINTENANCE

The installation of an oriental rug is a function of the rug and flooring type. Hair and jute combination pads or solid sponge-rubber cushions are recommended under the rug to protect the rug and the floor and to stabilize the rug. Open-weave foam pads allow air to circulate under the rug and prevent it from slipping. They also allow dirt to fall through to the floor, reducing the abrasion of the back surface of the rug. Consult with a rug dealer to determine the proper type of pad or cushion, as well as for maintenance information.

Resource: Oriental Rug Importers Association, Inc.; Secaucus, New Jersey

Ted Milligan; Rhode Island School of Design; Providence, Rhode Island

ACOUSTICAL PANELS

PANEL CORE MATERIALS

Core materials can be combined in a panel to achieve the required performance. For example, a nailable surface can be achieved by inserting a plywood nailing strip into a panel with a fiberglass board core material. Common panel core materials:

- *Polyester batting* consists of fibers loosely intertwined and is used to achieve a soft, upholstered appearance.
- *Fiberglass blanket* is a thick sheet of loosely intertwined fiberglass strands. It is often used where acoustical absorption is a concern.
- *Fiberglass board* ranges in density from acoustically absorptive panels with fair tackability to acoustically reflective panels. Tackable, acoustic fiberglass board has a finish face of thin, rigid fiberglass mesh. Fiberglass board heals well and is appropriate for tackable applications. Chemically hardened edges are applied to fiberglass board cores.
- *Mineral fiberboard* (for example, U.S.G. Micore) is a composite of inorganic mineral fibers. Unlike pressed, recycled paper products (for example, Homosote), mineral fiberboard is dimensionally stable. It is more durable and impact-resistant than fiberglass board and can be microperforated where an absorptive acoustic surface is required. The finish face of mineral fiberboard is either sanded or coated. The sanded finish is gray and retains a tighter thickness tolerance. The white latex coating reduces read-through when used with light-colored or transparent fabrics.
- *Particleboard* is a nailable core material. Plywood can warp and is not recommended for use as a core material, but can be used as nailable strips in panels of other core materials.

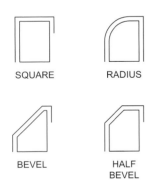

SQUARE   RADIUS

BEVEL   HALF
BEVEL

Extruded panel frames are infilled with a core material. Fiberglass board edges can be chemically hardened to achieve a profile.

PANEL EDGE PROFILES

PANEL INSTALLATION

Common acoustical panel installation methods include:

- *Z-clips,* which are the preferred method for temporary or movable panels. Z-clip panels require a reveal between the top of panel and the ceiling so that the panels can be lifted and lowered into place. The lower clip is fastened to the wall; the upper clip is fastened to the panel.
- *Hook and loop tape* is commonly known by the trade name Velcro. Mechanical fasteners should be used to secure the hook tape to the wall. This method is often used with adhesive to hold panels in place while the adhesive is setting.
- *Impaling clips* are fastened to the wall; the barbed projections of impaling clips are pressed into the panel back. This installation method is not commonly used because of its inability to support substantial weight. It is also more prone to vandalism.
- *Adhesive.* Adhering an acoustical panel to a wall or ceiling is a permanent mounting method. Panels cannot be removed without damaging them and the substrate.

BOTTOM CLIP
FASTENED TO WALL
OR SUBSTRATE

Z-CLIP

METHODS OF ATTACHMENT

PANEL CORE MATERIALS AND PERFORMANCE

PANEL CORE MATERIAL	PANEL PERFORMANCE
Polyester batting	Acoustic absorption
Fiberglass blanket	Acoustic absorption
Mineral fiberboard	Acoustic absorption, tackable
Fiberglass board	Acoustic absorption, tackable
Plywood	Acoustic reflectivity, nailable
Particleboard	Acoustic reflectivity, nailable
Wood board	Acoustic reflectivity, nailable

PANEL TEXTILE SELECTION CONSIDERATIONS

FABRIC ATTRIBUTE	SELECTION CONSIDERATION
Color	Light-colored textiles show soil more readily than dark-colored textiles.
Opacity	Core material should not read through the textile face.
Resilience	Nonbacked textiles ease stretching and do not impair acoustic transparency.
Self-healing	Tackable and nailable panel textiles must be snag-resistant.

IMPALING CLIP WITH ADHESIVE

1/4" 1/2"
3/4"

FINISHED CEILING

Z-CLIPS, TYP.

PLYWOOD STRIP
SECURED TO Z-CLIP
AND PANEL

EASED EDGES AT
PANEL BUTT JOINTS,
TYP.

FACE OF FABRIC

MINERAL FIBERBOARD

Z-CLIPS, TYP.

PLYWOOD STRIP
SECURED TO Z-CLIP
AND PANEL

WALL CONSTRUCTION

WALL BASE AS
SCHEDULED

Z-CLIP MOUNTED PANELS

1/4" 1/2"
3/4"

PAINTED REVEAL,
TYP.

Z-CLIPS, TYP.

PLYWOOD STRIP
SECURED TO Z-CLIP
AND PANEL

3/8"

PAINTED REVEAL,
TYP.

FACE OF FABRIC

MINERAL FIBERBOARD

Z-CLIPS, TYP.

PLYWOOD STRIP
SECURED TO Z-CLIP
AND PANEL

WALL CONSTRUCTION

WALL BASE AS
SCHEDULED

Z-CLIP MOUNTED WITH REVEAL PANEL

1/2"
1/8" +/-

FINISHED CEILING

HOOK AND LOOP TAPE
FASTENER, TYP.

MINERAL FIBERBOARD

EASED EDGES AT
PANEL BUTT JOINTS,
TYP.

FACE OF FABRIC

HOOK AND LOOP TAPE
FASTENER, TYP.

WOOD BLOCKING

WOOD BLOCKING

WALL CONSTRUCTION

WALL BASE AS
SCHEDULED

HOOK AND LOOP TAPE MOUNTED PANELS

SECTION DETAILS *Source: StretchWall Installations, Inc.; Long Island City, New York*

1/4"
1/2"

PAINTED REVEAL   3/8"

PAINTED
REVEAL
BLOCKING

ACOUSTICAL WALL
PANELS ON Z-CLIPS

REVEAL PANELS WITH REVEAL END CONDITION

1/4"
1/2"

ACOUSTICAL WALL
PANELS ON Z-CLIPS

EASED EDGES AT BUTT JOINTS

CLOSED
SIDES

BUTT JOINT PANELS WITH FLUSH END CONDITION

1/4"
1/2"

ACOUSTICAL WALL
PANELS ON Z-CLIPS

BEVELED EDGES, TYP.

CLOSED
SIDES

BUTT JOINT PANELS SET BACK FROM WALL EDGE

PLAN DETAILS *Source: StretchWall Installations, Inc.; Long Island City, New York*

Merve Yoneyman; Rhode Island School of Design;
   Providence, Rhode Island
Robin Staack; Boston Architectural Center; Boston,
   Massachusetts

2 ☐ **WALL FINISHES**

WALLCOVERINGS

Wallcoverings offer improved durability over paint finishes while providing texture and pattern to the wall surface. Wallcovering types include vinyl, textile, wallpapers, fiberglass, and wood veneer. The most popular wallcovering for commercial use is vinyl, favored for its affordability and durability.

VINYL WALLCOVERINGS

The two vinyl wallcovering manufacturing processes are calendering and plastisol methods:

- *Calendering* squeezes liquid vinyl over a series of hot metal rollers, flattening the compound into a sheet. The vinyl is then laminated under heat and pressure to a backing material. Calendered vinyl wallcovering is harder, tougher, and usually much thicker than wallcovering manufactured by the plastisol method.
- The *plastisol* method spreads liquid vinyl onto a backing material, which are then fused together under high temperatures. Plastisol technology is used primarily for residential wallcoverings.

TEXTILE WALLCOVERINGS

Not all textiles are suitable for use as wallcoverings. Textile wallcoverings are not appropriate in applications where wear resistance is a concern.

Textiles must be backcoated to be installed as wallcovering. The backing provides a barrier to prevent adhesives from bleeding through and ruining the finish face of the fabric. Backings also provide the dimensional stability required for a textile to withstand the stretching and smoothing operations of wallcovering installation.

Two types of backcoating treatments are paper backing and acrylic latex backing:

- *Paper backing* involves laminating paper to the reverse side of the textile. This process stiffens the textile for easier installation. The textile assumes properties similar to those of wallpaper.
- *Acrylic latex coating* involves stretching the textile in a frame and applying a latex compound. The textile retains some of its inherent flexibility and is much less dimensionally stable than paper-backed textiles. Latex backings can also improve ravel resistance and seam slippage. The use of latex-coated textile wallcoverings may increase installation costs. Often, this wallcovering's lack of rigidity requires that the adhesive be applied to the wall, rather than to the back of the wallcovering. This process is more labor-intensive and requires a higher degree of skill.

FIBERGLASS WALLCOVERINGS

Fiberglass wallcovering is composed of fiberglass yarns adhered together. Fiberglass wallcovering is inherently flame-resistant and is suitable for use in reinforcing fragile or deteriorating wall surfaces. It is permeable, making it intrinsically mold- and mildew-resistant. Fiberglass wallcoverings must be painted after installation. This wallcovering type provides a textured pattern only, not a color. Typically, a latex paint is selected to maintain the breathability of the wall.

WALLCOVERING DURABILITY CLASSIFICATIONS*

PROPERTY	CATEGORY I: DECORATIVE ONLY	CATEGORY II: DECORATIVE WITH MEDIUM SERVICEABILITY	CATEGORY III: DECORATIVE WITH HIGH SERVICEABILITY	CATEGORY IV: TYPE I COMMERCIAL SERVICEABILITY	CATEGORY V: TYPE II COMMERCIAL SERVICEABILITY	CATEGORY VI: TYPE III COMMERCIAL SERVICEABILITY
Minimum colorfastness		23 h	46 h	200 h	200 h	200 h
Minimum washability		100 cycles	100 cycles	100 cycles	100 cycles	100 cycles
Minimum scrubbability			50 cycles	200 cycles	300 cycles	500 cycles
Minimum abrasion resistance				200 cycles (220 grit)	300 cycles (220 grit)	1,000 cycles (220 grit)
Minimum breaking strength						
MD (machine direction)				40 lb (178 N)	50 lb (222 N)	100 lb (445 N)
CMD (cross machine direction)				30 lb (133 N)	55 lb (245 N)	95 lb (423 N)
Minimum crocking resistance			Good	Good	Good	Good
Minimum stain resistance*			Reagents 1 to 9	Reagents 1 to 9	Reagents 1 to 12	Reagents 1 to 12
Minimum tear resistance				12	25	50
Maximum blocking resistance				2	2	2
Minimum coating adhesion				2 lb/in. (17.8 N/5 cm)	3 lb/in. (26.7 N/5 cm)	3 lb/in. (26.7 N/5 cm)
Minimum cold cracking				No change	No change	No change
Minimum heat aging resistance				Pass	Pass	Pass
Maximum flame spread	25	25	25	25	25	
Maximum smoke developed	50	50	50	50	50	
Maximum shrinkage						

*Per ASTM F793, Standard Classification of Wallcoverings by Durability Characteristics, *Classification Criteria*.

**Reagents: (1) Distilled water, 65° to 75°F; (2) Distilled water, 115° to 125°F; (3) Ethyl alcohol ; (4) Vinegar, 3% acetic; (5) Alkali solution; (6) Hydrochloride, 5%; (7) Soup solution; (8) Detergent solution; (9) Pure orange juice; (10) Butter; (11) Catsup; (12) Tea

THREE GRADES OF WALLCOVERING*

TYPE	BACKING MATERIAL	COMMON COMPOSITION	TOTAL WEIGHT	COATING WEIGHT	USES
I—Light Duty	Scrim (very loose, open weave; similar to cheesecloth; lacks dimensional stability)	Polycotton	Between 7 and 13 oz/sq yd (0.237 and 0.442 kg/sq m)	Between 5 and 7 oz/sq yd (0.17 and 0.237 kg/sq m)	Ceilings, offices, hotel rooms, areas not subject to unusual abrasion or heavy traffic
	Nonwoven (paperlike)	Polyester cellulose			
II—Medium Duty	Osnaburg (loose, open weave)	Polycotton	Between 13 and 22 oz/sq yd (0.442 and 0.748 kg/sq m)	Between 7 and 12 oz/sq yd (0.237 and 0.407 kg/sq m)	Lounges, dining rooms, public corridors, and classrooms
	Nonwoven	Polyester cellulose			
III—Heavy Duty	Drill (denser, firmer weave similar to twill)	Polycotton	22 oz/sq yd (0.748 kg/sq m) or more	12 oz/sq yd (0.407 kg/sq m)	Hospital and food service corridors, wainscot or lower protection for areas of heavy traffic by movable equipment or rough abrasion

*As defined by the Chemical Fabrics and Film Association CFFA-W-101-A, CFFA Quality Standard for Vinyl-Coated Fabric Wallcoverings, and FS CCCW-408C, Wallcovering, Vinyl-Coated.

WOOD VENEER WALLCOVERINGS

Wood veneer wallcovering is made by bonding veneer slices, about 1/64 in. (0.39 mm) thick, to a woven backing material. The resulting wallcovering is thin enough to be pliable along the grain lines but too thick to be flexible in the horizontal direction (perpendicular to the wood grain). The inherent flexibility of wood veneer wallcovering allows easy installation around columns and other curved surfaces.

The thinness of wood veneer wallcovering raises three major concerns: finishing operations after installation, proper substrate preparation, and moisture. Wood veneer wallcovering is too thin to be sanded; therefore, care must be taken during installation so that the surface is not stained or damaged.

Wall surface imperfections tend to telegraph through the thin veneer. In areas where the substrate cannot be prepared to a smooth, level surface, veneered plywood panels are a better choice. Buckling and warpage caused by moisture can be a significant problem for this kind of wallcovering. It is not recommended that wood veneer wallcovering be applied to the interior surface of an exterior wall unless the finish face of the wall is furred out and dampproofed.

Wood veneer wallcoverings are available prefinished or unfinished. Unfinished veneers must be stained and finished after they are installed. Some finishes, for example, penetrating oils, can have an adverse effect on the wallcovering adhesive. Coatings applied to the surface of installed wood veneer should be approved by the wallcovering manufacturer.

The installation of wood veneer wallcovering is similar to the installation of other types of wallcovering; however, the sheets must be butted together and cannot be overlapped and trimmed.

WALL PREPARATION

There are four traditional ways to prepare a wall surface for a wallcovering: prime, seal, size, or apply a wall liner.

- *Primers* assure proper adhesion and are the most commonly required wall preparation for commercial installations.
- *Sealers* are usually oil-based, made either of an alkyd or a shellac. They provide stain-sealing properties; for example, walls that have suffered water damage must typically be sealed before they can be finished with either paint or a wallcovering. Sealers also promote strippability without damage to the wall surface.
- *Sizing* a wall surface lowers the absorbency of the wall by reducing the penetration of the paste. However, sizing does not necessarily improve the bond between the adhesive and the wall surface.
- *Wall liners* are nonwoven sheets; their installation is similar to that of wallcovering. They are sometimes required where wall surfaces cannot be prepared by conventional means. Wall liners can be used to prevent cracks, holes, and gaps from telegraphing through the wallcovering. Wall liners may also be used in lieu of primer/sealers to mask contrasting colors or areas of light and dark on the substrate.

DEFINITIONS OF SIX WALLCOVERING CATEGORIES BASED ON PERFORMANCE*

CATEGORY	DESCRIPTION	USE	COMMENTS
I	Decorative only	For decorative purposes	Wallcoverings are not tested. Wallpaper and other primarily residential wallcoverings fall into this category.
II	Decorative with medium serviceability	Primarily decorative but more washable and colorfast than Category I wallcoverings	In addition to the testing required for minimum washability and colorfastness, wallcoverings are tested for maximum flame spread and smoke development. Primarily for residential use.
III	Decorative with high serviceability	For medium use, where abrasion resistance, stain resistance, scrubbability, and increased colorfastness are necessary	In addition to the testing required for Category II wallcoverings, wallcoverings are tested for minimum scrubbability, stain resistance, and crocking resistance. They meet more stringent requirements for colorfastness than Category II wallcoverings. Primarily for residential use.
IV	Type I Commercial serviceability	For use where higher abrasion resistance, stain resistance, and scrubbability are necessary in heavy consumer and light commercial use	In addition to the testing required for Category III wallcoverings, wallcoverings are tested for maximum shrinkage and minimum abrasion resistance, breaking strength, tear resistance, blocking resistance, coating adhesion, cold-cracking resistance, and heat-aging resistance. All test methods listed in the standard apply to Category III wallcoverings, but the wallcoverings meet more stringent requirements for colorfastness and scrubbability than Category III wallcoverings. Appropriate for private offices, hotel rooms, and areas not subject to unusual abrasion or heavy traffic.
V	Type II Commercial serviceability	For use where better wearing qualities are required and exposure to wear is greater than normal	Tested according to more stringent requirements for scrubbability, abrasion resistance, stain resistance, tear resistance, and coating adhesion than Category IV wallcoverings. Appropriate for public areas such as lounges, dining rooms, public corridors, and classrooms.
VI	Type III Commercial serviceability	For use in heavy-traffic areas	Category VI wallcoverings are tested for the highest scrubbability, abrasion resistance, breaking strength, tear resistance, coating adhesion, and maximum shrinkage. Category VI, Type III wallcoverings are commonly used in high-traffic service corridors where carts may bump into the walls.

* Per ASTM F793, Standard Classification of Wallcoverings by Durability Characteristics.

The backing material, sometimes called the substrate, is the major component in determining the strength and dimensional stability of a wallcovering.

Mildew Resistance

Impermeable wallcoverings such as vinyl can act as vapor barriers under specific climatic conditions. Mildew is a particular problem in warm, humid climates. Moisture migrating through a wall is trapped behind the wallcovering. Gypsum wallboard can become saturated with the condensation, fostering fungal growth. Perforated vinyl or woven fiberglass wallcoverings can be specified to increase the breathability of the wall. Mildew inhibitors can also be added to the vinyl.

Where mildew resistance is required, the wallcovering should have achieved a rating of 0 or 1 when tested according to ASTM G21, *Practice for Determining Resistance of Synthetic Polymeric Materials to Fungi*. A 0 rating means no fungal growth was observed on a wallcovering sample inoculated with spores and incubated for at least 21 days; a 1 rating means less than 10% of the sample surface area was covered with fungal growth.

GUIDELINES FOR CALCULATING ONE LINEAL YARD OF WALLCOVERING

WALLCOVERING WIDTH	SURFACE TO BE COVERED
54 in. (1,370 mm)	13 sq ft (1.2 sq m)
36 in. (910 mm)	9 sq ft (0.8 sq m)

WALLPAPERS

Wallpapers are composed of a paper face and a paper backing. They are not commonly used for commercial applications because of their fragility and poor wear resistance. However, the scratch, stain, and abrasion resistance of wallpaper can be improved by requiring that the finish face be coated with a clear vinyl film.

Typically, residential wallcoverings range from 20½ to 28 in. (521 to 711 mm) wide. A single roll yields 27 to 30 sq ft (2.5 to 2.8 sq m). Single rolls are packaged and sold in double-roll quantities. Double rolls have 56 to 58 sq ft (5.2 to 5.4 sq m) and are approximately 11 yards (10 m) long.

Vinyl-coated papers, consisting of a paper substrate coated with acrylic/vinyl or solid PVC with a total thickness of 2 to 5 mils (0.05 to 0.13 mm), are scrubbable and peelable or strippable. However, they are not suited for commercial applications; they are suitable for use in residential kitchens, bathrooms, and laundry rooms.

Pattern and seam placement may be critical. Large, complicated, dominant pattern repeats may need careful placement to establish a starting point. Dominant pattern repeats are often centered at eye level, with the pattern matching at 72 in. (1,830 mm) above the finish floor.

Carl Henschel; Rhode Island School of Design; Providence, Rhode Island
MASTERSPEC®; published by ARCOM; Salt Lake City, Utah, and Alexandria, Virginia

RANDOM MATCH
Random match is the least wasteful type of pattern matching. Panels do not align horizontally.

DROP MATCH
Drop match patterns do not repeat at the same distance from the ceiling line, creating the greatest potential for waste. Patterns that match every third or fourth panel are referred to as *multiple drop matches*.

DIMENSION OF PATTERN REPEAT —

PATTERN REPEAT

STRAIGHT MATCH
Straight match patterns match with the continuation of the pattern on the next panel. The pattern repeats at the same distance from the ceiling line.

WALLCOVERING PATTERN MATCHING

UPHOLSTERED WALL SYSTEMS

Upholstered wall systems, also referred to as *stretched-fabric wall systems*, combine the luxuriousness of textile wallcoverings and the practicality of a tackable or acoustically absorptive wall surface. Upholstered wall systems are site-constructed coverings that stretch fabric taut over a frame and infill material. They can also be used in ceiling installations.

FRAMING METHODS

The framing material is typically either a plastic extrusion or a wood frame. An extrusion system holds the fabric in place by friction or with concealed fasteners, sometimes aided by an adhesive. Concealed fasteners are used with a wood frame system.

FABRIC SELECTION

Upholstered wall systems require the selection of a highly stable fabric. Upholstery-weight fabrics are good choices. The fabric should be hydrophobic (does not readily absorb moisture); otherwise, seasonal changes in relative humidity may cause sagging and rippling. A fabric that contains more than 30% rayon or viscose or 10% nylon fibers is typically not suitable for use in upholstered wall systems. If the wall system is to perform as a tackable or nailable surface, the selected fabric should be self-healing and snag-resistant. For a seamless appearance, fabrics up to 120 in. (3,050 mm) wide can be specified and installed horizontally (sometimes referred to as *railroading*). Fabric selection considerations include the following:

- *Seams* can be emphasized or deemphasized, depending on fabric weave and color. Seams dis-

CORE MATERIALS

MATERIAL	APPLICATION
Acoustic batting (polyester or fiberglass)	Soft, upholstered appearance; acoustically absorptive
Plywood	Nailable; acoustically reflective surface
Mineral fiberboard	Tackable; acoustically absorptive
Fiberglass board	Durable; impact-resistant

appear in fabric that is vertically directional, yet tend to read as butt joints when the predominant direction of the grain is horizontal. In a nondirectional fabric, seams tend to be more apparent with light-colored fabrics, and less so with dark colors.

- *Joints* between square-edged panels with thin fabrics, tightly butted, tend to read as a monolithic, seamless installation. Wall panel joints are seen more clearly between panels with heavy or thick fabrics or with beveled frame edges.

- *Tackable and nailable surfaces* require fabric that will not easily snag. The heavier the yarn texture, the better for areas where pin-tacking or nailing is required. Linen works well in galleries because of its unobtrusive appearance behind artwork and because it is a hardy, natural fabric that maintains a good appearance through repeated use. Satin and sateen weaves are not recommended for tacking.

- *Weave types* and their dimensional stability must be considered. Taffetas and architectural silks, especially when treated with flame retardants, are subject to greater variance in expansion and contraction. They require limited fluctuation in temperature and humidity. Jacquards, damasks, and basket weaves—regardless of their yarn content—are more dimensionally stable

FIBER MOISTURE REGAIN VALUES

FIBER	MOISTURE REGAIN @ 70°F (21°C) 65% RELATIVE HUMIDITY	ELASTIC RECOVERY FROM A 2–5% STRETCH	
Glass	0%	0%	Hydrophobic (doesn't absorb moisture readily)
Olefin	0%	90%	
Acrylic	1.3–2.5%	92%	
Poyester	.4–.8%	97%	
Nylon	4–4.5%	100%	
Acetate	6%	58%	
Cotton	7–11%	75%	
Silk	11%	92%	
Rayon	15%	54%	
Wool	13–18%	99%	Hydrophilic (absorbs moisture readily)

and can be used in areas where greater variances in temperature and humidity may occur.

- *Light-colored fabrics* (especially white) should be examined to verify that the wall construction will not "read through" the fabric and change its color. The fabric may need to be lined, and the lining may change the appearance of the upholstered wall. By placing the fabric under consideration over a light-colored surface and then over a dark-colored surface, the need for a lining can be determined.

Tanya Nachia; Rhode Island School of Design; Providence, Rhode Island
Robin Staack; Boston Architectural Center; Boston, Massachusetts
MASTERSPEC®; published by ARCOM; Salt Lake City, Utah, and Alexandria, Virginia

STRETCHED FABRIC APPLIED ON SITE
No size limitation.

Labels: RIGID FIBERGLASS INSULATION; STRETCHED FABRIC; CUT OFF HEAD OF BRAD AND SET BELOW FABRIC; FABRIC STAPLED TO BACK OF LOOSE STRIP; WALL CONSTRUCTION

WOOD- OR METAL-EDGED FABRIC-WRAPPED PANELS
Limited in size to core and frame material and the ability to enter building, for example, door opening and elevator cab sizes.

Labels: RIGID FIBERGLASS INSULATION; STRETCHED FABRIC; FABRIC GLUED TO BACK OF ALUMINUM FRAME; EXTRUDED ALUMINUM FRAME; WALL CONSTRUCTION

LIGHTWEIGHT FABRIC PANELS AND FIBERGLASS FOAM CORE
Limited to size of core.

Labels: HOOK-AND-LOOP FASTENERS; RIGID FIBERGLASS INSULATION; STRETCHED FABRIC; HARDENED EDGE OF RIGID FIBERGLASS INSULATION USING HOT RESIN; WALL CONSTRUCTION

PLASTIC TRACK SYSTEM WITH SITE-APPLIED FABRIC
No size limitation.

Labels: STRETCHED FABRIC; SOFT OR RIGID FILLER; TRACK STAPLED AND GLUED TO WALL; HINGED PLASTIC TRACK; WALL CONSTRUCTION

CUSTOM-EDGED COMPOSITE PANEL
Limited to size of core.

Labels: PLYWOOD BACKING; METAL Z-CLIPS; BLOCKING; FABRIC; SOFT OR RIGID FILL; CUSTOM SHAPED EDGE; WALL CONSTRUCTION

UPHOLSTERED WALL—PADDED
Usually stretched from floor to ceiling or between wood trim.

Labels: WALL CONSTRUCTIO; STRETCHED FABRIC; POLYESTER FILL; WELT; WOOD TRIM

STONE FACING

Numerous types of stones can be used for stone facing; however, consideration should be given to the selection of a stone that is appropriate for the intended use. Stone facing typically does not need to meet the rigorous performance criteria of stone flooring, but care should be taken to select a stone that can be cut and dressed to meet the project's design. A review with the stone fabricator or supplier is recommended to minimize the risk of incompatibility of the stone with the intended use.

STONE FACING TYPES

Stone facing is available in two basic types: *dimension stone panels* and dimension *stone tiles*. Marbles and other stones that might be considered too soft for flooring can usually be used for stone facing, with the proper reinforcement and installation.

Dimension Stone Panels

Dimension stone facing panel dimensions typically range from larger-dimension units with face areas up to 48 sq in. (1,200 sq mm) × ¾ in. (19 mm, also known as 2 cm), 1¼ in. to 2 in. (32 mm, also known as 3 cm, to 50 mm) thick. Sizes and shapes are limited to the specific stone's characteristics. A panel that is 2 ft 6 in. × 5 ft 0 in. (762 × 1,524 mm) is a size that stone fabricators can easily handle, and it conforms to the 5 ft (1,524 mm) module of many buildings.

Dimension Stone Tiles

Stone tile modules are dimension stone units that do not exceed 4 sq ft (.37 sq m) and are less than ¾ in. (2 cm) thick. Stone tiles are typically 12 × 12 in. (305 × 305 mm) up to 24 × 24 in. (610 × 610 mm) × ¼, ⅜, and ½ in. (6, 10, and 13 mm) thick, and are usually furnished with a protective backing such as fiberglass to improve the tile strength. Larger stone tile sizes are offered by selected manufacturers.

MARBLE WALL FACING PATTERNS

Stone with distinctive texture and markings, such as certain marbles, lends itself to specific pattern arrangements. The markings vary depending on whether the marble veneer is cut with or across its setting bed.

Blend pattern. Panels of the same variety of stone but not necessarily from the same block are arranged at random.

Side-slip pattern. Panels from the same block are placed side by side or end to end in sequence, to ensure a repetitive pattern and blended color.

End-match pattern. Adjacent panel faces are finished, and one panel is inverted and placed above the other.

Book-match pattern. Adjacent panel faces are finished, and one panel is next to the other.

VENEER CUTTING

Quarry blocks are reduced to slabs by a gang saw. The gang saw consists of a series of parallel steel blades in a frame that moves forward and backward. The most productive and precise gang saws use diamond-tipped blades with individual hydraulic blade tensioners; others are fed a cutting abrasive in a stream of water.

Marble blocks can be sawn either parallel or perpendicular to the bedding plane. The perpendicular cut is referred to as an *across-the-bed* or *vein cut*. The parallel cut is a *with-the-bed* or *Fleuri cut*. Other marbles produce a pleasing surface only when sawn in one direction, and are generally available only in that variety.

VENEER PATTERNS

Only certain marbles lend themselves to specific pattern arrangements, such as side-slip or end-slip, which require a constant natural marking trend throughout the marble block. Formal patterns require selectivity, which usually increases the installed cost of the marble veneer. Usually, material sawn for a vein cut can be matched. Fleuri cuts can only be blended.

Perfection in veneer matching is impossible because a portion of the marble block is lost during the sawing process and because the vein shifts. Ideally, jointing should be planned for groupings of four panels of equal size.

WIRE-TIE ANCHORING SYSTEMS

Wire-tie anchoring systems with plaster or mortar spots are the traditional methods for installing interior stone facing. Wire ties are anchored to the gypsum board, masonry, or concrete wall. In gypsum board construction, wire ties are embedded in plaster-filled metal boxes or are inserted through the gypsum board and are fastened to the partition framing. In masonry walls, the wire ties are embedded in voids filled with mortar or plaster. The disadvantages of wire-tie anchoring systems are twofold: first, fire-rated gypsum board walls require another row of metal studs and another layer of gypsum board if the wire ties are not allowed to penetrate the fire-rated wall; second, seismic restraint for the stone panels is difficult to engineer.

A minimum of four anchors should be provided for stone panels up to 12 sq ft (1.1 sq m), with two additional anchors for each additional 8 sq ft (.74 sq m) of surface area. For stone facing panels over 96 in. (2,400 mm) high, the wire-tie method must be supplemented with intermediate horizontal supports for the vertical stone loads.

BLEND PATTERN

SIDE-SLIP OR END PATTERN

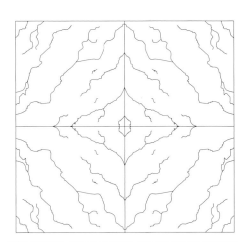

END-MATCH, BOOK-MATCH, OR QUARTER-MATCH PATTERNS

MARBLE WALL FACING PATTERNS

TYPES OF STONE

Granite

Granite can be used on interior walls in many finishes, ranging from highly polished to a rough thermal finish. A waterjet finish is a texture between honed and thermal, and brings out the color of the stone. It is slightly darker than the thermal finish appearance. Granite is much harder than marble, therefore it is more costly to fabricate and finish.

Marble

Marble varieties that are not recommended for exterior use can be successfully used in interior wall panel applications, if properly prepared for vertical installations. Heavily veined marbles, prized for their aesthetic qualities, are examples. Dry seams can be glued together (*sticking*), voids can be filled (*waxing*), and weak areas can be reinforced with metal rods glued into the back of the stone panel (*rodding*). During fabrication, fragile marbles are frequently reinforced with a layer of fiberglass-reinforced plastic prior to final fabrication and polishing of the marble.

Serpentine Marble

Green varieties, called serpentine marble, are sensitive to water and are prone to warping when wet. When installing serpentine stone, use setting materials that do not contain water, such as water-cleanable epoxy adhesives.

Greenstone

Greenstone, a general term for metamorphosed igneous basaltic-type rock, is typically available in honed or cleft finishes, and is not suitable for a highly polished finish, due to the stone structure. Greenstone contains minerals that give it a green appearance: either actinolite, chlorite, or epidote. Sources are usually European, as it is no longer quarried in the United States.

Dolomitic Limestone

Dolomitic limestone is more widely used for interior stone facing, as it is typically not as porous as oolitic limestone, and is often polished similar to marble. It is also available with a smooth-honed finish, a textured sandblasted finish, or a split-face finish.

Slate

Slate is commonly used as a contemporary interior floor or wall finish. It is available in a palette of dark, rich colors including green, black, purple, and red. Slate splits easily into thin sheets. The finish resulting from the natural face is referred to as a *cleft finish*. Slate can also be sand-rubbed to a smooth or honed finish.

Travertine

Travertine is distinguished by its natural cavities, formed by plants embedded during the rock's formation, which must be filled to achieve a smooth surface. Filling materials are typically portland cement, epoxy resins, or polyester resins. Travertine is actually a kind of limestone, but some types that take a polish are classified as marble. It is popular for use as a flooring because its visual texture conceals dirt much better than most other stones.

Stone Tile

Stone tiles are fabricated under different conditions from dimension stone panels and are not typically matched to create patterns, such as book- or end-matching. The greater variation in stone color, pattern, and texture is common in stone tile, and should be factored into the project review prior to installation.

Engineered Composite Stone

New technology has enabled the development of engineered composite stone products. Formulated from stone aggregate and synthetic resin matrix materials, these products are available in sizes ranging from tile units to large panel sheets for horizontal and vertical applications. Composite stone characteristics are strength, nonporosity, durability, and flexibility. Finishes are typically limited to polished; colors range from natural stone tones to vibrant colors. Thicknesses vary, and due to the strength of the composite units, can sometimes be thinner than natural dimension stone. Typical sheet sizes are ¾ in. (2 cm) or 1⅛ in. (3 cm). A manufacturer is currently introducing a ⅜-in.-(1-cm-) thick product for sheet panels. Installation for the sheet panels is similar to natural stone. Tile units are installed with the same thinset methods as for ceramic tile.

STONE FINISHES

The finish of stone flooring affects the perception of its color and the slip resistance. Polished finishes are the most reflective. These high-maintenance finishes should be selected with care. For high-traffic public areas, such as lobbies, polished floor finishes are often eventually hidden under nonskid mats. Honed finishes have a dull sheen. These satin-smooth surfaces are often good choices for commercial floors because of their slip resistance. Thermal, sometimes called *flamed*, finishes are achieved by the application of intense flaming heat to the surface of the stone. Thermal finishes are usually applied to granite.

ABRASION RESISTANCE

Abrasion resistance is the capability of the stone to resist wear and absorption, which affects staining and soiling of the stone. For interior stone facing, abrasion resistance is typically not a factor, unless the stone will be subjected to frequent bumping and scraping. Consult with the stone fabricator or supplier for the selection of appropriate stone types for a particular installation and intended use.

TYPICAL FINISHES AND COMMON SIZES OF INTERIOR STONE WALL PANELS

STONE	GRADE	FINISH	MINIMUM THICKNESS IN. (MM)	MAXIMUM FACE DIMENSION FT (MM)	NOTES
Granite	Building (exterior) Veneer Masonry	Polished Honed	¾–1¼* (19–32)	5 x 5 (1,525 × 1,525)	This very hard and durable surface is not likely to stain. Many colors and grains are available.
Marble	Group A (exterior) Group B Group C Group D	Polished Honed	½–⅞* (13–22)	4 x 7 (1,220 × 2,135)	The most colorful and interesting marbles are in Groups B, C, and D; however, some filling of natural voids may be required. Many colors and patterns are available.
Limestone	Select Standard Rustic Variegated	Smooth Tooled Polished	⅞–3 (22–76)	4 x 9 (1,220 × 2,745)	Soft and easy to shape, but shows wear and may discolor over time. Colors range in the buffs and grays.
Slate	Ribbon Clear	Natural Cleft Sand Rubbed Honed	1–1½ (25–38)	2 ft 6 in. x 5 ft (760 × 1,525)	Ribbon stock is distinguished by its ornamental integral bands, which are usually darker than the rest of the stone. Colors range in the pastel hues.

* ¼ to ½ in. thick (6 to 13 mm) tiles (usually a face dimension of 12 × 12 in. (305 × 305 mm)) are available. Tiles can be directly applied to a wall with adhesive or thin set mortar, similar to flooring applications. Tiles are not recommended for walls over 8 ft (2.4 m) high.

Wire ties are not recommended for Indiana limestone.

WIRE ANCHOR CONNECTION

THREADED
CONCRETE INSERT

WIRE TIE
HANGER

THREADED
DISC HANGER

STONE SOFFIT

SOFFIT DETAIL AT WALL

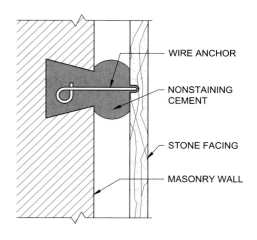

WIRE ANCHOR

NONSTAINING
CEMENT

STONE FACING

MASONRY WALL

WIRE ANCHORED TO MASONRY—SECTION

WIRE ANCHOR

FLOOR

BASE DETAIL

WIRE TIE

PLASTER
SPOTS

2 X 2
BLOCKING

WOOD
STUD

GYPSUM
WALLBOARD

STONE PANEL ON WOOD STUDS

MORTAR

WIRE TIES

SEALANT

Wire anchors can be tied around a dowel inserted vertically into stone.

VERTICAL JOINT DETAIL—PLAN

STONE FACING

DOUBLE-LAYER
GYPSUM BOARD
ON METAL STUDS

VERTICAL CHANNEL
AT EACH STUD

NONSTAINING
CEMENT

1/2"

WIRE ANCHOR

1/2"

HORIZONTAL
CHANNEL

SELF-DRILLING,
SELF-TAPPING
SCREW AT EACH
STUD

1 1/4"

1"   3 1/2"

SELF-DRILLING,
SELF-TAPPING
SCREW AT 2'-0" O.C.

**WIRE ANCHORED TO CHANNEL AND
GYPSUM BOARD—SECTION**

GYPSUM BOARD

WIRE ANCHOR AT
VERTICAL JOINT

NONSTAINING
CEMENT

SEALANT

STONE FACING

STONE LINER
DOWELLED AND
CEMENTED TO
BACK OF STONE
FACING PANEL

ANGLE FASTENED
THROUGH
GYPSUM BOARD
TO METAL STUDS

1 1/2"

2 1/4"

**WIRE ANCHORED TO METAL STUDS AND
GYPSUM BOARD—SECTION**

SELF-DRILLING,
SELF-TAPPING
SCREW

SEALANT

STONE FACING

METAL STUD

NONSTAINING
CEMENT

WIRE ANCHOR

STONE LINER
DOWELLED AND
CEMENTED TO
BACK OF STONE
FACING PANEL

ANGLE FASTENED
TO METAL STUDS

**WIRE ANCHORED TO METAL STUD—
SECTION**

WALL FINISHES ☐ 2

FIRE-RATED METAL STUD WALL—SECTION

Labels: 3/4", 1-5/8" 28-GA. METAL STUDS @ 16" O.C., 3-5/8" 28-GA. METAL STUDS @ 16" O.C., 3/4"± AIR SPACE, 3/4" STONE FACING, BOX ANCHOR, NONSTAINING CEMENT, WIRE ANCHOR, TWO LAYERS 1/2" GYPSUM BOARD (STAGGER JOINTS), 6" ±, 9 1/2"

WIRE LACE ANCHOR—SECTION

Labels: NONSTAINING CEMENT, STONE FACING, WIRE ANCHOR, MASONRY CONSTRUCTION, 1 1/4", 2 1/2"

WIRE TIE AT FIRE-RATED METAL STUD WALL

Labels: WIRE ANCHOR, GYPSUM BOARD, STONE FACING, BOX ANCHOR

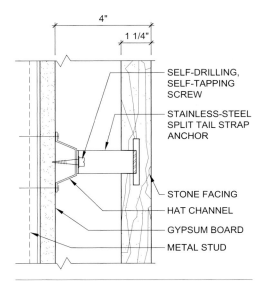

STRAP-ANCHORED SECTION

Labels: 4", 1 1/4", SELF-DRILLING, SELF-TAPPING SCREW, STAINLESS-STEEL SPLIT TAIL STRAP ANCHOR, STONE FACING, HAT CHANNEL, GYPSUM BOARD, METAL STUD

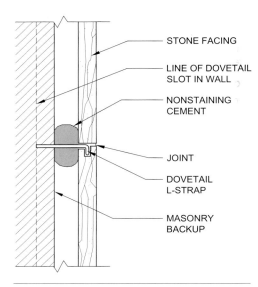

DOVETAIL ANCHOR SECTION

Labels: STONE FACING, LINE OF DOVETAIL SLOT IN WALL, NONSTAINING CEMENT, JOINT, DOVETAIL L-STRAP, MASONRY BACKUP

MECHANICAL ANCHORING SYSTEMS

Mechanical anchoring systems fasten stone directly to the backup wall, eliminating the need for additional studding and gypsum board and providing verifiable seismic restraint. The stone is kerfed on the back side and is restrained by the use of straps or clips. Anchor systems, similar to those used for exterior work over masonry or metal framing, may be fastened to metal studs through gypsum board. Exterior anchors may also be used with metal channel struts, which eliminate the need to coordinate stud location with anchor locations. This type of anchor may still require plaster-setting spots.

GROUT

Grout for interior stone facing is commonly mixed with latex additives, which produces a more flexible and durable joint installation. The stone industry is now referencing ANSI standards for ceramic tile-grouting materials. Dry-set grouts are mixtures of portland cement and water-retentive additives. Unsanded grouts are typically used in joints up to ⅛ in. (3 mm) wide. Wider grout joints are typically sanded, as the sand reduces grout shrinkage and minimizes cracking. When installing sanded grout on polished stone surfaces, protect the stone face to avoid scratching the surface finish.

JOINT SIZES

Joint sizes vary depending on the type of stone and finish selected and whether joints are to be coordinated with exterior or floor joints. For polished stone installations, joints from ¹⁄₁₆ in. (1.5 mm) wide to ⅛ in. (3 mm) wide are used. Currently, the wider joint size is prevalent to allow for more latitude in fabrication dimensions and in backup construction dimensions. For highly textured stone finishes, such as a thermal or cleft finish, a joint width of ¼ to ⅜ in. (6 to 10 mm) wide is common. The larger joint dimension minimizes the visibility of lipping of stone panels. When combining different stone textures, one size joint for the entire installation is recommended, usually the largest required for the different textures.

LIPPAGE

Lippage is the condition where one panel is higher than adjacent panels; it is more common in thinset installations. The recommended maximum variation of the finished stone surface should be no greater than ⅛ in. (3 mm) cumulative over a 10 ft (3 m) lineal measurement, with no greater than a ⅟₃₂ in. (1 mm) variation between individual tiles or panels.

Each interior stone facing project should be reviewed to determine the best method of installation for the installation conditions. Setting space dimensions and project conditions may indicate the use of a particular installation method.

INSTALLATION OF STONE TILE

Stone tile may be installed in a full mortar bed, a thinset mortar bed, or with an adhesive. Thin stone tiles are typically not restrained by ties or anchors, therefore their installation has limitations. Tiles that are installed above 8 ft (2.4 m) high must be additionally restrained with anchors.

Interior stone anchoring systems must be compatible with the stone and substrate. Stone facing may be installed on gypsum board construction, masonry, or concrete walls. Butt joints are not recommended due to potential spalling if movement occurs in the structure.

Mortar Beds

Mortar beds can be used when installing thin stone tiles and thin panels in a thick portland cement mortar system consisting of metal lath, a scratch coat, and a float coat. The stone tile is set into the float coat.

Thinset

Thinset installations are appropriate for vertical application of stone tiles and thin panels up to ½ in. (13 mm) thick. The stone is set in the same manner as ceramic tiles, directly on the substrate of gypsum board or cementitious backer units, using specific thin-bed setting systems. Adhesives should be non-staining, especially when installing light-colored stone.

SPLINE JOINT

LAP JOINT

SET-IN BLOCK

EXPANSION JOINT

CONTROL JOINT

SPLINE EXPANSION JOINT

TYPICAL HORIZONTAL JOINTS

THREADED INSERT AND EYEBOLT

DOVETAIL STRAP WITH HOOK ROD ANCHOR

EYEBOLT AND DOWEL BOLTED TO THREADED CONCRETE INSERT

FLAT HOOK ANCHOR AND DOWEL

TYPICAL SYSTEMS FOR HANGING INTERIOR VENEER STONE

CORNER BUTT

RABBETED CORNER

CORNER L

SLIP CORNER

CORNER BLOCK

QUIRK MITER

TYPICAL CORNER DETAILS

ADHERED STONE BASE

MASONRY OR CONCRETE WALL

STONE FACING

PLASTIC SHIM

NONSTAINING CEMENT

DRY-SET MORTAR FOR FLOOR ONLY

ANCHORED STONE BASE

STONE BASE AND WALL FACING ANCHORED TO MASONRY BACKUP WITH WIRE ANCHORS OR STRAP ANCHORS

WIRE ANCHORS

NONSTAINING CEMENT

DOWEL

GROUT

ANCHORED STONE COVE BASE

MASONRY BACKUP

WIRE ANCHORS

STONE FACING

3/4"

1 1/2"

NONSTAINING CEMENT

1/4"

COVE BASE

MORTAR BED

STONE BASES

Mark Form; Leo Daly Company; Washington, D.C.
George M. Whiteside, III, AIA, and James D. Lloyd; Kennett Square, Pennsylvania
Alexander Keyes; Darrel Downing Rippeteau, Architect; Washington, D.C.
Elizabeth Aukamp; Rhode Island School of Design; Providence, Rhode Island
MASTERSPEC®; published by ARCOM; Salt Lake City, Utah, and Alexandria, Virginia

PAINTS AND COATINGS

COATING SELECTION CRITERIA

Paint has three basic functions: to decorate, to protect, or to modify the performance of the substrate to which it is applied. Paint ingredients, types, and applications all affect a coating's performance. The following criteria are considerations for selecting the appropriate coating for a given application:

Abrasion resistance
Adhesion
Impact resistance
Flexural qualities
Resistance to a given medium (e.g., chemicals)
Resistance to sunlight
Temperature resistance
Drying time (installation criteria)
Appearance
Wetting time
Emissive requirements (reflection and absorption)
Electrical insulation

INGREDIENTS

There are four categories of paint ingredients: pigment, thinner, resin, and additives.

- *Pigment* provides color, hiding, and bulk.
- *Thinner* affects consistency and drying time and carries the pigment and resin to the substrate.
- *Resin* binds the pigment particles together and affects adhesion, durability, and level of protection of the paint film.
- *Additives* enhance the coating's performance with specific desirable characteristics.

The term *paint solids* refers to the resin. The thinner is called the *liquid*. A higher solids content provides a thick, durable, opaque coating. The solids content of paint can be specified by weight or by volume. Volume of solids is the better indicator of performance. Latex paints range from 25% to 40% volume of solids. Alkyd and oil-based paints can exceed 50% volume.

PAINT FORMULATION

Pigments	+	Resin	=	Solids
Solids	+	Liquid	=	Paint
Fused solids	−	Liquid	=	Final coating

Pigments

Pigments provide paints with color or whiteness, opacity, and bulk. Pigments are often the most expensive ingredients in paint. Pigment is added to paint either at the point of sale or in the factory. At the point of sale, colorants are mixed with tint bases or to white paints designed for tinting. Colorants are grounded color pigment particles dispersed in liquid. In the factory, dry powders or colorants are used to make prepackaged colored paints.

Prime pigments provide whiteness and color to paint. White pigment and whiteness in colored paint are predominantly supplied by titanium dioxide. Organic pigments and inorganic pigments supply paint with color. Organic pigments are brighter and not as highly durable as inorganic pigments.

Extender pigments, or inert pigments, impart bulk to coatings and enhance leveling and adhesion. They can negatively affect the final finish, the hiding capacity, and the scrub resistance of paint. Extenders are made from clay, silicates, talc, and zinc oxide.

Thinners

Thinner, also referred to as the *solvent* or *liquid,* reduces coatings to the proper viscosity and provide the means of dispensing the coating from the container to the substrate. It allows the paint to flow and level itself on the substrate. The thinner determines whether paint hardens by oxidation, evaporation, chemical action, or by thermosetting at elevated temperatures. There are two types of thinners, water and solvent. Water is the thinning agent for water-based paints. Oil-based and alkyd paints are thinned by a combustible solvent made from mineral spirits.

Resin

Resin, also referred to as the *binder* or *film former,* is the nonvolatile portion of the paint that binds the pigment particles together, forming the cured paint film. The resin determines the dried paint film's adhesion to the substrate. The resin provides continuity, flow, leveling, and gloss development. It enhances the hardness, toughness, and strength of the paint film.

There are two basic categories of resins: those that are solvent-thinned, such as oil-based and alkyd paints, and those that are water-thinned, such as latex paints. *Solvent-thinned resins* are made from natural or synthetic oils. When exposed to air, the thinner evaporates, leaving the resin oils to harden through the chemical process of oxidation. Oil-based and alkyd paints are made from a solvent, solvent-thinned oil resin, and pigments. Oil-based and alkyd paints have better adhesion and a smoother appearance, and dry much harder than latex paints that are water-thinned. Conversely, oil-based paints can harden to the point at which they become vulnerable to cracking, chipping, and yellowing. *Water-thinned resins* in latex paint are solid plasticlike materials dispersed as microscopic particles in water. This dispersion is a milky-white liquid that the paint industry calls *latex* or *emulsion.* (The *latex* used in the paint industry looks similar to but is not related to the natural latex extracted from rubber trees.) Water-thinned paint dries and hardens through evaporation. Coalescing agents in the paint ensure that the resin particles fuse together as they dry to form a continuous film.

Many types of synthetic polymer are used as resins in latex paint. They vary in terms of their particle size, flow and leveling, hardness, solids types, and price. One hundred percent acrylic and vinyl acrylic (PVA) are the two synthetic polymers most commonly used in North America. For interior applications, 100% acrylic binders are considered to be superior in terms of adhesion under wet conditions and resistance to waterborne stains, to sticking, and to alkaline cleaners. Acrylic latex binders perform well in interior wall paints as drywall primers and in satin and semigloss paints. Styrenated acrylic resins are used in masonry sealers, metal coatings, and in gloss paints.

Additives

Additives are included as needed to enhance the properties of the solids or the liquid ingredients of paint. They can improve paint life within the container and paint application onto the substrate.

PIGMENT VOLUME CONCENTRATION OF PAINT INGREDIENTS FOR INTERIOR COATINGS
Source: Guy Weismantel, Paint Handbook, *McGraw-Hill, New York, 1981.*

PAINT AND COATING TYPES

Alkyd Paint

The solvent-thinned resin in alkyd paint is made from synthetic oils. Alkyd resins are oil-modified polyesters made primarily from alcohol and acid. They are the most common paint resin. Alkyd paints are faster drying, harder, and more durable, and have better color-retention properties than oil-based paints. They are easy to apply, are washable, and have less odor than other paints using solvent thinners. Alkyd paints have poor resistance to alkaline surfaces, such as masonry, and should not be used unless these substrates are properly primed.

Latex Paint

Most water-based paints are referred to as latex paint. Latex paints have very little odor and a fast drying time. Their water-base thinner makes latex paints easy to apply, clean up, and discard. Latex paints are porous; when applied, a latex coating retains microscopic openings that allow it to breathe. Adhesion failure is prevented because moisture that might become trapped beneath the paint's surface can evaporate through these openings. Latex paints have a greater blistering tendency when high levels of tinting color are present.

Oil-Based Paint

The solvent-thinned resin in oil-based paint is made from natural oils, such as linseed oil (from flax seed), soya oil (from soybeans), and tung oil (from china wood tree fruit).

Primers

Primers make a surface more paintable by providing improved adhesion for coatings. Primers are selected in relation to the characteristics of the selected topcoat. Primers serve the following functions:

- Conceal the substrate surface so that the existing coating color does not read through.
- Provide a barrier to prevent moisture from destroying the paint bond.
- Bind substrate surface with the topcoat.
- Limit the paint absorption of a porous substrate, such as a skim coat of plaster.
- Recondition old paint to receive future paint coatings.
- Act as a rust inhibitor.

COMMON PAINT ADDITIVES

ADDITIVE	PURPOSE
Antiskinning Agent	Prevents skin from forming in can prior to use.
Biocide	Prevents spoilage resulting from bacterial growth.
Coalescent	Aids in formation of continuous film in latex paint.
Defoamer	Eliminates air from paint or reduces bubbling upon application.
Drier	Accelerates conversion of solvent paints from liquid to solid state.
Freeze-Thaw Stabilizer	Lowers latex paint freezing point.
Mildewcide	Resists growth of mildew.
Surfactant	Stabilizes mixtures of resins or pigments in solvents or water.
Thickener	Increases consistency of paint and prevents separation of pigment in oil- and water-based paints

PAINTS AND STAINS

Catalyzed Epoxy Paint

Catalyzed epoxy coatings resist chemicals, solvents, stains, physical abrasion, traffic, and cleaning materials. They have good adhesion and color retention. Catalyzed epoxies come in two parts, resin and catalyst. They have limited "pot life," hence are required to be mixed just prior to use. When applied to a substrate, a chemical action occurs that causes a dense hard film to form, similar to baked enamel. Adequate ventilation must be provided during and after application.

Three types of catalyzed epoxies are commonly used in commercial interiors:

- *Polyester epoxies* produce a tough glossy surface.
- *Polyamide epoxies* provide a flexible but durable film.
- *Urethane epoxies* are the most versatile of the epoxy coatings.

Epoxy Ester Paint

Epoxy esters are similar to catalyzed epoxy but have no pot life restrictions and are packaged like conventional paint. The paint film occurs due to oxidation rather than a chemical reaction triggered by a catalyst. Epoxy esters are less durable than catalyzed epoxies.

Flame-Retardant Paints

Flame-retardant paints slow the rate at which fire spreads by delaying the ignition of the surface that has been coated. They are used on combustible materials such as wood to achieve the required flame-spread ratings. These paints delay but do not prevent a fire from spreading. Flame-retardant paints are *intumescent* and protect the substrate from burning by swelling to form a charred layer of blisters when exposed to extremely high heat.

Flame-retardant paint is a foamlike material made with either a water-based thinner or a solvent-based thinner. Requisite fire ratings are achieved with this material based on the number of coatings applied to the substrate at a prescribed thickness. Intumescent paint manufacturers certify painters to ensure that their products are correctly applied.

Fire-Resistant Paints

Fire-resistant paints resist the spread of fire by not contributing to the flame. They are less effective at controlling the spread of fire than intumescent coatings.

Multicolor Coatings

Multicolor coatings are durable and scratch-resistant. They add a three-dimensional quality to a surface, similar to hand-sponge techniques. Multicolor coatings can be water-thinned or solvent-thinned. Traditional solvent-thinned multicolor coatings are composed of tiny bubbles of different sizes and colors suspended in a nonpigmented solution. The separated beads of pigment remain separate until they are spray-applied. They burst upon impact with the surface.

Stains

Stains made from dyes dissolved in either drying oil or water provide translucent or transparent coatings for wood. Pigmented stains are opaque. Oil-based stains use drying oil made from various plants. The oil dries by absorbing oxygen from the surface, and the air creates a tough elastic film that protects a wood. Wood surfaces can be filled before staining in order to affect surface porousness and smoothness, but fillers may cause stains to be absorbed unevenly. Stain may be applied with a brush, spray, roller, or rag pad.

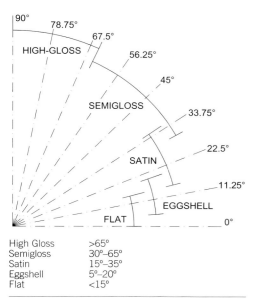

High Gloss	>65°
Semigloss	30°–65°
Satin	15°–35°
Eggshell	5°–20°
Flat	<15°

PAINT SHEENS

The ratio of the volume of pigment to the volume of resin in a paint is called the pigment volume concentration (PVC). Light reflects off a cured paint film with a low PVC for a glossy appearance. Light is diffused by a high PVC paint for a flat finish.

PIGMENT VOLUME CONCENTRATION

DECORATIVE PAINT FINISHES

Decorative paint finishes are used for their aesthetic qualities and for masking minor surface defects. Generally, they provide a surface with a multitoned color and a texture. Decorative paint finishes can be achieved with oil- or water-based paints.

Cobweb Finish

Cobweb finish is provided by a specialty paint that dries into a spiderweb pattern on the painted surface. It is applied with standard spray equipment.

Crackle Finish

This paint technique gives an "alligator" texture to the painted surface. It requires a base coat over which a second specialty paint, crackle coat, is applied.

SHEEN

The presence of pigment reduces the gloss of the cured paint film. By increasing the amount and dimension of the pigment particles in relationship to the amount of resin, the resin's level of gloss or the texture of the paint is reduced. The texture of cured paint is called sheen. Pigment color and sheen determine the light reflectivity of a painted surface, which affects the perception of the color. The more pigment that is present relative to the resin, the rougher-textured, less reflective, and flatter is the paint's appearance. A glossy surface is achieved by a larger volume of resin that encases the pigment.

APPLICATION

Because paint appearance varies depending on its sheen, the color, and the lighting, paint installations typically require mock-ups. Step samples on foam core boards showing progressive layers of coating systems are useful during contract administration. More often, a maximum of three 4 ft by 8 ft (2.1 m by 2.4 m) mock-ups are provided by a contractor for approval before final application is begun. The mock-ups should be applied directly to the substrate to be painted.

Paint adhesion failure appears as peeling, blistering, cracking, or flaking. Paint failure occurs for one or both of the following reasons:

• *The surfaces to be coated have not been properly prepared.* All substrates must be clean, dry, and smooth. All of the products to be coated must be compatible, including patching compounds, sealants, primers, sealers, paints, and other coatings. The paint manufacturer should be consulted for recommendations regarding priming or sealing a substrate and for information describing the proper combination of products to be used.

• *Coatings have not been properly applied.* Optimal temperature application of most paints is crucial. Typically, interior installations require between 50°F (10 C) and 90°F (32°C). The manufacturer will specify. Paint manufacturers specify how much paint should be applied by giving an application rate or a dry film thickness.

$$\text{Application Rate = Sq Ft/Gal}$$

The application rate is the area of substrate in square feet covered by a gallon of paint.

$$\text{Dry Film Thickness = DFT}$$

The dry film thickness is the thickness of the cured paint finish measured in mils. One mil is equal to 0.00245 mm, which is equal to one one-thousandth of an inch.

Faith Baum, AIA, IIDA; Faith Baum Architect; Lexington, Massachusetts

Intumescent paint bubbles and swells when exposed to high heat. The paint film forms a charred layer of blister, insulating the substrate from the fire.

INTUMESCENT PAINT

Volatile Organic Compounds (VOCs)

During the curing process, solvent-thinned coatings (including latex and waterborne coatings) release volatile organic compounds (VOCs) into the atmosphere. The VOCs, in the presence of sunlight, mix with nitrogen oxide in the atmosphere and form the air-pollutant ozone, a component of smog. VOCs are measured in grams of organic solvent per liter of paint or lb/gal (g/l). Each jurisdiction has air pollution control agencies that determine the local VOC requirements. Due to rapidly changing regulations, the Environmental Protection Agency (EPA) should be contacted for current information on VOC regulation.

VISUAL DISPLAY BOARDS

CHALKBOARDS AND MARKERBOARDS

As computers have become more common in class-rooms, chalkboards are often replaced with white dry-erase markerboards that eliminate the chalk dust that can interfere with the computer equipment. Chalk dust can also trigger asthma and other respiratory problems.

Porcelain-enamel markerboards and chalkboards are composed of a porcelain-enamel face sheet laminated to a stabilizing core material with a moisture barrier backing. The backing sheet can be aluminum foil, aluminum sheet, or galvanized steel sheet. The core material can be ¼-in.- (6-mm-) thick hardboard, ⅜-in. (10-mm) thick particleboard or fiberboard in ⅜ or ½ in. (10 or 13 mm) thickness. Aluminum or wood frames and chalk trays can be factory- or field-applied. Map rails and flag holders are also available. Standard sizes are a maximum of 48 in. (1,220 mm) high and 16 ft (4.8 m) long. Combination units that join markerboards, chalkboards, and tackboards in a variety of sizes and configurations within a unifying frame provide versatility in classrooms and meeting rooms.

ELECTRONIC AND INTERACTIVE MARKERBOARDS

Electronic markerboards are capable of recording what is drawn or written on the surface in dry-erase markers to a connected computer for saving, printing, and editing.

Interactive markerboards are products on which an LCD projector displays a computer desktop and allows the user to interact with the information, using special pens designed for laser tracking and automatic color detection.

Some manufactures offer products that can be used either as an electronic markerboard, without a projector, or as an interactive markerboard, with a projector or in conjunction with a plasma display panel.

Interactive plasma display systems utilize flat-screen monitors as interactive computer screens. The units display digital applications without projectors, and transmit handwritten notes or sketches simultaneously.

DRY-ERASE WALLCOVERINGS

This product is similar to a standard vinyl wallcovering in appearance and application. It comes in 75 to 100 ft (230 to 305 m) flexible rolls 48 to 60 in. (1,220 to 1,525 mm) wide. A nonwoven polyester cellulose backing is laminated to a pigmented vinyl with a top surface of Du Pont Teflon thermoplastic film that permits it to be used as a markerboard with dry-erase markers. Ferrous powder can be added to the vinyl during the manufacturing process to produce a surface that will hold magnets. A thin, self-adhesive version is recommended for resurfacing existing chalkboards for use as markerboards.

HUNG ON CLIPS MOUNTED ON ANGLES

CHALKBOARDS AND MARKERBOARDS

CEILING HEIGHT 8 FT (2,400 MM) **CEILING HEIGHT 9 FT (2,475 MM)**

To cover an entire wall, dry-erase wallcovering should be applied horizontally (i.e., railroaded) with the seams out of the main writing and viewing areas of the wall. Seams are practically invisible when double-cut.

DRY-ERASE WALLCOVERING SEAM PLACEMENT

DRY-ERASE WALLCOVERINGS

TYPE	COLOR	USE	SURFACE GLOSS	BACKING	WIDTH* IN. (CM)	WEIGHT OZ/SQ YD (KG/SQ M)
Premium Projection Surface	Matte white	Projection screen Dry-erase writing	Minimal	Nonwoven adhesive	50 (127) or 60 (152)	25 (0.775)
Glare-Free Marker Surface	Matte white	Dry-erase writing Projection screen	Low	Nonwoven adhesive	50 (127) or 60 (152)	25 (0.775)
Magnetic Marker Surface	White or gray	Dry-erase writing that attracts magnets	Moderate	Scrim	48 (122)	40 (1.373)
Premium Marker Surface	White	Dry-erase writing	Moderate	Scrim	48 (122) or 60 (152)	21 (0.712)
Grid Marker Surface	White	Dry-erase writing	Moderate	Scrim	48 (122)	23 (0.780)
Inexpensive Marker Surface	White	Dry-erase writing	High	Nonwoven adhesive	50 (127)	11 (0.373)
Color Surface	Various pastel shades	Dry-erase writing	High	Nonwoven adhesive	60 (152)	18 (0.610) and 30 (0.931)

*Standard roll length; is 100 ft (30.5m), except for grid surface, which is 98 ft (30.0 m), and magnetic surface, which is 75 ft (2.30 m).
Source: Walltalkers; Fairlawn, Ohio

TACKBOARDS

Tackboards are available in a variety of surface materials and manufactured types. For stability, tackable surfaces are usually laminated to substrate. When selecting the backing material, be aware that pushpins can be as long as ½ in. (13 mm), so a hardboard backing may be less desirable than a backing material that will allow the pins to penetrate, such as fiberboard or rigid insulation. As with chalkboards, standard sizes, usually to a maximum of 48 in. (1,220 mm) high and 16 ft (5 m) long, are available from most manufacturers. Wood or aluminum trim is available in various profiles. Tackable surfaces include the following:

- *Natural cork:* Self-healing, resilient surface in a soft, light-brown color. For tackboards, ¼ in. (6 mm) thickness is the most common.
- *Plastic-impregnated cork:* Integrally colored natural cork that has been treated with binders, impregnated with plastic, and surface-sprayed with a plastic coating that provides a washable, durable surface. Usually ¼ in. (6 mm) thick and laminated to a burlap backing. A variety of colors are available.
- *Vinyl fabric:* Type II, medium-duty vinyl fabric, as specified in ASTM F793, Category V, Type II Commercial Serviceability. Can be fire-rated if required by code. A variety of colors and patterns are available.

TACKBOARD SECTION

COMBINATION TACKBOARD/CHALKBOARD OR MARKERBOARD WITH MAP RAIL SECTION

COMBINATION TACKBOARD/CHALKBOARD OR MARKERBOARD ELEVATION

ELECTRONIC MARKERBOARDS

TOILET COMPARTMENTS

SELECTION CRITERIA

When selecting toilet enclosures, screen types, and mounting styles, consider requirements for maintenance, vandal and moisture resistance, supporting construction, and methods for repairing damaged units.

PANEL MATERIALS

Toilet compartments are often categorized by finish or construction. Common finish categories include the following:

- Metal, including baked enamel and stainless steel
- Polymers, including plastic-laminate, phenolic-core, melamine-faced particleboard cores, fiberglass-reinforced panels (FRP) with particleboard cores, solid-surfacing, and solid-surfacing veneers
- Stone

Factory-finished hardwood units (which are generally used for high-cost installations) are also available. Materials may be combined; for instance, compartments may have plastic-laminate doors and panels with stainless-steel pilasters. Baked-enamel and plastic-laminate panels are also available with stainless-steel edge strips.

Metal Toilet Partitions

Metal units include stainless-steel units with sound-deadening honeycomb cores made from resin-impregnated kraft paper, and baked-enamel units. Where grab bars are attached, metal-compartment manufacturers provide wood or particleboard reinforcement or through-bolting kits. Unless specified, manufacturers generally do not reinforce units where small accessories, such as toilet tissue dispensers, are attached. Wood or particleboard reinforcement may result in a slight variation in appearance of baked-enamel finishes at reinforcement locations.

Stainless-Steel Units

Stainless-steel units have excellent long-term durability. They are corrosion-resistant, and stains may be removed with commercial stainless-steel cleaners. They resist denting and marring, but can be scratched with a sharp instrument. Scratches can sometimes be removed by buffing. The fabrication of stainless-steel units is similar to that of baked-enamel units. Alternate core constructions are also offered. Stainless-steel units typically are about two-and-three-fourths to three times more expensive than similar baked-enamel units.

Baked-Enamel Units

The term *baked enamel* is used to describe various pigmented, organic coatings. The baking process is used to accelerate the solvent evaporation or, for thermosetting coatings, to elevate temperatures to the point required to convert the film to a polymerized form. Manufacturers usually describe finishes as *electrostatically applied enamel*, *high-solids*, or *powder coatings*.

Steel units with baked-enamel finishes are the most economical and widely available type of toilet compartment, but they have the least-durable finishes. They are not suitable for areas subject to moisture; although finishes resist corrosion, the panels are susceptible to rust. Finishes are generally adversely affected by chemicals and acids but are resistant to stains made by items such as felt-tip markers or lipstick as long as the staining agent is promptly removed. Units are not prone to warping.

Zinc-coated steel facing sheets are laminated to sound-deadening honeycomb cores of resin-impregnated kraft paper to form doors, panels, and pilasters. Sometimes hardboard can be bonded to the facing sheets for impact resistance. Heavy-duty honeycomb cores, with smaller cells than standard cores, and plywood cores are also available.

Polymer Toilet Partitions

Plastic-laminate, phenolic-core, and fiberglass-reinforced panels (FRP) are the more affordable choices for polymer toilet partitions. Solid-surface and solid-surface veneers are also available.

Taller-than-average doors and panels are used to help ensure privacy. Systems that incorporate a lap joint at doors and pilasters to eliminate vertical sightlines into compartments are available from an increasing number of solid-polymer and phenolic-core unit manufacturers. Some metal units can be modified to include stops and fillers to eliminate vertical sightlines at doors.

INCREASED PRIVACY COMPARTMENTS

OVERHEAD-BRACED COMPARTMENTS
Overhead-braced compartments are the most economical in initial cost; they provide a sturdy installation without the substantial structural connections required for other mounting styles. The majority of installations use this mounting style.

FLOOR-ANCHORED COMPARTMENTS
Floor-anchored compartments are the least stable of the mounting styles when resisting lateral loads; hence, they require substantial connections to a structural concrete slab to provide a rigid installation. They are generally not suitable for schools or other installations subject to high abuse. Manufacturers typically recommend a minimum 2 in. (50 mm) penetration into the structural floor.

CEILING-HUNG COMPARTMENTS
Ceiling-hung compartments cost slightly more than floor-anchored compartments when installed at ceiling heights between 84 and 96 in. (2,134 and 2,438 mm). When used in combination with wall-hung fixtures, this mounting style produces unobstructed floor areas that make maintenance easier. Generally, the maximum ceiling height recommended for this style is 96 in. (2,438 mm). Separate overhead steel support framing is required.

FLOOR-AND-CEILING-ANCHORED COMPARTMENTS
Floor-and-ceiling-anchored compartments are exceptionally strong and are used where vandal resistance is required; however, they are expensive compared to other mounting styles. Most manufacturers limit pilaster heights to 108 in. (2,743 mm). Pilasters are attached to the floor using the same devices as overhead-braced or floor-anchored styles, depending on the manufacturer. Separate overhead support framing is required.

Baked-enamel, stainless-steel, plastic-laminate, and phenolic-core units are generally available in all four mounting styles. Solid-polymer units are generally available in overhead-braced and floor-and-ceiling anchored styles.

MOUNTING STYLES

Plastic-Laminate Units

Plastic-laminate units with particleboard cores are resistant to normal wear, acids, and alkalis, and resist stains made by felt-tip markers, lipstick, and so on. Prompt removal of some staining agents is required to prevent permanent staining. Surfaces are abrasion-resistant but can be scratched with sharp instruments. Vandals can pry the plastic laminate from the particleboard core, and the core will support combustion. Plastic-laminate units are not suitable for areas subject to moisture or high humidity because prolonged exposure can cause delamination of the facing from the core. Plastic-laminate units usually are slightly more expensive than similar baked-enamel units.

Phenolic-Core Units

Phenolic-core panel materials are fabricated by fusing multiple layers of resin-impregnated core sheets or cellulose fibers with thermosetting resins to melamine facing sheets. Panels resist damage from moisture and impacts. The melamine surfaces resist damage from chemicals, urine, stains, and abrasion; however, they can be scratched with hard objects to expose the core. The core is exposed on panel edges and is either black or brown. Phenolic-core units typically are about two-and-one-half to three times more expensive than similar baked-enamel units and are either more or less expensive than solid-polymer units, depending on the manufacturer.

Solid-Polymer Units

Solid-polymer units are fabricated from high-density polyethylene (HDPE) or polypropylene (PP) panels, and resist damage from moisture and impacts. Surfaces resist marking with pens and pencils, and staining. PP panels are harder and more scratch- and dent-resistant than HDPE panels, and are virtually graffiti-proof. Colors and patterns are homogenous through the thicknesses of solid-polymer panels, so scratches may be burnished out.

Solid-polymer panel materials are susceptible to warping, especially at high temperatures, and standard units will support combustion. Metal heat-sink strips, which dissipate heat, should be applied to exposed bottom edges of solid-polymer panels to help prevent burning.

Solid-polymer units typically are about two-and-one-half to three times more expensive than similar baked-enamel units.

Stone Toilet Partitions

The most common varieties of stone used for stone toilet compartments are marble and granite. Limestone that is compact and dense and capable of taking a polish is suitable for use in toilet compartments and can be marketed as either limestone or limestone marble.

Stone varieties with low absorption rates should be specified for use in toilet compartments because they are more resistant to staining. The Marble Institute of America (MIA) recommends marble with an absorption rate of less than 0.2%; however, an absorption rate of less than 0.1% is preferred.

Polished finishes are most commonly specified for marble and granite toilet compartments. Honed finishes are less frequently specified because they more readily absorb stains.

Stone toilet compartments are custom-fabricated. The stone fabricator usually provides product data and shop drawings for only the dimension stone; the door and hardware supplier provides product data and shop drawings for these items. The contractor typically coordinates between the separate sources. Although rare, some marble fabricators provide a complete toilet-compartment package, including doors, hardware, and fittings.

Stone Joint Sealants

Joints between stone and adjacent construction can be sealed with nonstaining urethane sealants. Stone-to-stone joints are usually butted; however, certain varieties of marble and granite tend to warp, making it difficult to maintain tight joints between units. Providing a ⅛-in.-(3-mm-) wide sealant joint between adjacent pieces of stone minimizes the visual effect of joint variations.

FIRE-TEST-RESPONSE CHARACTERISTICS

Toilet compartments and screens are generally considered fixtures; therefore, model building code interior-finish surface-burning-characteristic requirements do not apply. Some local jurisdictions require certain surface-burning characteristics for toilet compartments and screens. Manufacturers also report that owners of high-occupancy buildings impose these requirements; local school systems are often cited as an example. Verify requirements of authorities having jurisdiction and of the owner.

ACCESSIBLE TOILET COMPARTMENTS

Where toilet compartments are provided, at least one must be wheelchair accessible. Where six or more toilet compartments are provided in a toilet room, in addition to the wheelchair-accessible compartment, a 36-in.-(915-mm-) wide ambulatory-accessible compartment is required. Toe clearance 9 in. (230 mm) high and 6 in. (150 mm) deep is required at the front and at least one side of accessible toilet compartments. Toe clearance is not required when the compartment size exceeds the minimum dimension by 6 in. (150 mm) or more. Left- or right-handed configurations are permitted.

MASTERSPEC®; published by ARCOM; Salt Lake City, Utah, and Alexandria, Virginia

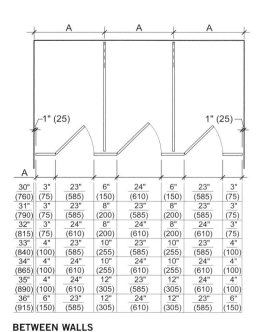

A	A	A	A	A	A	A	A
30" (760)	3" (75)	23" (585)	6" (150)	24" (610)	6" (150)	23" (585)	3" (75)
31" (790)	3" (75)	23" (585)	8" (200)	23" (585)	8" (200)	23" (585)	3" (75)
32" (815)	3" (75)	24" (610)	8" (200)	24" (610)	8" (200)	24" (610)	3" (75)
33" (840)	4" (100)	23" (585)	10" (255)	23" (585)	10" (255)	23" (585)	4" (100)
34" (865)	4" (100)	24" (610)	10" (255)	24" (610)	10" (255)	24" (610)	4" (100)
35" (890)	4" (100)	24" (610)	12" (305)	23" (585)	12" (305)	24" (610)	4" (100)
36" (915)	6" (150)	23" (585)	12" (305)	24" (610)	12" (305)	23" (585)	6" (150)

BETWEEN WALLS

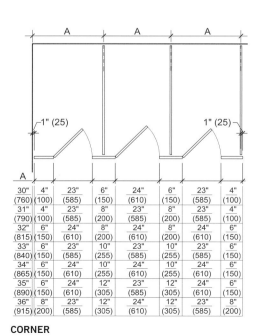

A	A	A	A	A	A	A	A
30" (760)	4" (100)	23" (585)	6" (150)	24" (610)	6" (150)	23" (585)	4" (100)
31" (790)	4" (100)	23" (585)	8" (200)	23" (585)	8" (200)	23" (585)	4" (100)
32" (815)	6" (150)	24" (610)	8" (200)	24" (610)	8" (200)	24" (610)	6" (150)
33" (840)	6" (150)	23" (585)	10" (255)	23" (585)	10" (255)	23" (585)	6" (150)
34" (865)	6" (150)	24" (610)	10" (255)	24" (610)	10" (255)	24" (610)	6" (150)
35" (890)	6" (150)	24" (610)	12" (305)	23" (585)	12" (305)	24" (610)	6" (150)
36" (915)	8" (200)	23" (585)	12" (305)	24" (610)	12" (305)	23" (585)	8" (200)

CORNER

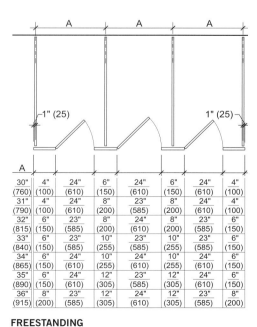

A	A	A	A	A	A	A	A
30" (760)	4" (100)	24" (610)	6" (150)	24" (610)	6" (150)	24" (610)	4" (100)
31" (790)	4" (100)	24" (610)	8" (200)	23" (585)	8" (200)	24" (610)	4" (100)
32" (815)	6" (150)	23" (585)	8" (200)	24" (610)	8" (200)	23" (585)	6" (150)
33" (840)	6" (150)	23" (585)	10" (255)	23" (585)	10" (255)	23" (585)	6" (150)
34" (865)	6" (150)	24" (610)	10" (255)	24" (610)	10" (255)	24" (610)	6" (150)
35" (890)	6" (150)	24" (610)	12" (305)	23" (585)	12" (305)	24" (610)	6" (150)
36" (915)	8" (200)	23" (585)	12" (305)	24" (610)	12" (305)	23" (585)	8" (200)

FREESTANDING

STANDARD COMPARTMENT LAYOUTS
Source: American Sanitary Partition Corporation; Ocoee, Florida

WOMEN'S TOILET ROOM WITH OPEN VESTIBULE
Source: Bobrick Washroom Equipment, Inc.; North Hollywood, California

MEN'S TOILET ROOM WITH DOUBLE-OPEN VESTIBULE
Source: Bobrick Washroom Equipment, Inc.; North Hollywood, California

2   □   COMPARTMENTS AND CUBICLES

WALL AND CORNER GUARDS

INSTALLATION

Wall guards, panels, and trim are typically attached to a finished wall surface with adhesive or screws. For all wall and corner guard installations, it is important to provide backup blocking behind areas where fasteners are attached, particularly for handrail-type guards.

CONTINUOUS METAL RETAINER

1 1/4" - 2"

8" - 12"

VINYL ACRYLIC CRASH RAIL COVER

CONTINUOUS FLEXIBLE CUSHION (OPTIONAL)

SURFACE-MOUNTED

1" - 2"
2"

CONTINUOUS METAL RETAINER

8" - 12"

VINYL ACRYLIC CRASH RAIL COVER

CONTINUOUS FLEXIBLE CUSHION (OPTIONAL)

MOUNTING BRACKET 16" O.C., MAX. HORIZONTAL

WALL-HUNG

CRASH RAILS

PRONOUNCED HANDRAIL EXTRUSION

VINYL ACRYLIC CRASH RAIL COVER

1 1/2"   1 1/2"

5 1/2"

CONTINUOUS METAL RETAINER

CONTINUOUS FLEXIBLE CUSHION

MOUNTING BRACKET, 32" O.C., MAX.

HANDRAIL WITH BUMPER CUSHION

---

1 1/4"

CONTINUOUS METAL RETAINER

VINYL ACRYLIC GUARD COVER

1" TO 4"

FASTENER AT 16" O.C., MAX.

BUMPER GUARD

3/8"
1 3/8"

CONTINUOUS METAL RETAINER

PLASTIC CUSHION

2 3/4"

VINYL ACRYLIC GUARD COVER

FASTENER AT 32" O.C., MAX.

BUMPER GUARD

VINYL ACRYLIC RUB RAIL

DOUBLE-STICK TAPE

7 1/2"

DRILLED AND COUNTER-SUNK FASTENERS AT 16" O.C. (OPTIONAL)

RUB RAIL GUARD

BUMPER GUARDS

METAL STUDS

GYPSUM WALLBOARD

SNAP-ON VINYL ACRYLIC CORNER GUARD

FASTENERS

2" TO 3"

CONTINUOUS METAL RETAINER

2" - 3"

STANDARD

FIRE BARRIER

SNAP-ON VINYL ACRYLIC CORNER GUARD

TYPE-X GYPSUM WALLBOARD

FASTENER

CONTINUOUS METAL RETAINER

1 1/4" RADIUS (OR 1/4" RADIUS)

2" - 3"

FIRE-RATED

SNAP-ON VINYL ACRYLIC CORNER GUARD

1/4" RADIUS (1 1/4" RADIUS ALSO AVAILABLE)

CONTINUOUS METAL RETAINER WITH BULB DESIGN TO DISSIPATE SHOCK

CUSHIONED

Depending on the design of the retainer, corner guards can be mounted to almost any wall angle intersection up to 135°.

FLUSH-MOUNTED CORNER GUARDS

GYPSUM WALLBOARD

METAL FASTENERS (EACH SIDE)

CONTINUOUS METAL RETAINER

CONTINUOUS SPONGE NEOPRENE (FOR CUSHION)

VARIES

2"

WALL-END GUARD

VINYL WAINSCOT

HIGH-IMPACT PRELAMINATED WALL PANEL WITH WALL COVERING

4'-0" TYP.

VINYL LEDGE TRIM

VINYL COVE BASE

GYPSUM BOARD

WAINSCOT PANEL WALL GUARD

GYPSUM WALLBOARD

VINYL ACRYLIC CORNER GUARD

CONTINUOUS METAL RETAINER

BOTTOM AND/OR TOP CAP (OPTIONAL)

2" - 5", TYP.

2" - 5"

SQUARE

GYPSUM WALLBOARD

VINYL ACRYLIC CORNER GUARD

FASTENERS

CONTINUOUS METAL RETAINER

2" - 3", TYP.

2" - 3", TYP.

ROUNDED

GYPSUM WALLBOARD

METAL FASTENERS (ADHESIVE, OPTIONAL)

CLEAR VINYL ACRYLIC CORNER GUARD

3/4" - 2 1/2"

3/4" - 2 1/2"

EXPOSED FASTENER

SURFACE-MOUNTED CORNER UNITS

ACCESS FLOORING

Access flooring creates a chase underneath the floor for wires, cables, and sometimes an air distribution plenum. Access flooring systems are often used in general offices, data centers, computer rooms, and cleanrooms. Multilevel access flooring systems are available that incorporate two or more continuous cavities beneath the floor panels to house wireways and an air distribution plenum. Access flooring consists of panels and an understructure system.

UNDERSTRUCTURES

There are two types of access flooring understructures: low-profile systems and pedestal systems.

- *Low-profile systems* provide a low-height access floor (typically less than 4 in. (100 mm) high)) that does not significantly encroach on space height. In these systems, closely spaced plastic or metal supports incorporate cable management systems and provide support at regular intervals across the panel.
- *Pedestal systems* are composed of either a threaded rod or a telescoping tube, which support the panel at the corners (or at the edge at the floor perimeter). It is considered good practice to adhere pedestal bases to the subfloor to resist horizontal forces.

There are two basic types of pedestal systems: stringlerless and stringer systems.

Stringerless Systems

Stringerless systems consist of pedestals located so that each pedestal head supports four panels at their corners. Stringerless systems provide maximum access to the underfloor cavity. Stringerless understructures can be less stable laterally than those with stringers and are less capable of withstanding lateral forces from earthquakes and other sources; consequently their use is limited to lower finished floor heights.

Two panel types are available for stringerless pedestal systems: *gravity-held* and *bolted-down panels*.

Gravity-Held Panel Systems

Gravity-held panels are secured in place by nesting on an interlocking connection formed in both the panel

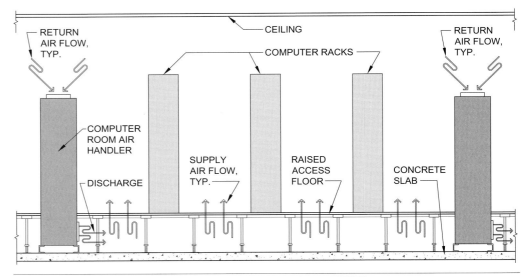

TYPICAL ACCESS FLOORING COMPUTER SPACE AIRFLOW PATTERN

and the pedestal head. This system provides the quickest access because no tools other than a panel lifter are required to remove panels.

Bolted-Down Panels

Bolted-down panels are directly connected to pedestal heads by fasteners located in panel corners. Because the fasteners must be accessible to remove panels, floor coverings must be either removable or permanently attached to panels and of a type that can accommodate exposed countersunk fasteners. Carpet tile is generally selected for the former condition, and either high-pressure plastic laminate or resilient tile for the latter. Bolting panels to pedestals improves the entire system's lateral stability and adds resistance to rocking and overturning. The latter effect can result where partitions are fastened to panels and are subject to unbalanced loads that are not resisted by ceiling connections or other means.

Stringer Systems

Stringer systems are offered with either bolted or snap-on (nonbolted) stringers. The purpose of stringers is to

provide additional lateral support, particularly where panels are frequently removed or where finished floor heights or earthquake loads exceed those that can be accommodated by stringerless systems.

Two panel types are available for stringer systems: *bolted* and *snap-on stringers*.

Bolted Stringer

Bolted stringer systems consist of main stringers, usually two to three modules long, and cross stringers, one module long, which are bolted to pedestals. These stringers may or may not support panel edges.

Snap-On Stringer

Snap-on stringer systems consist of stringers, each one module in length, located under the edge of each panel and interlocking with pedestal heads without using threaded fasteners; this makes the removal of grid members more convenient because no tools are needed. The disadvantage of snap-on stringers is that with frequent use they do not provide the same degree of restraint as bolted stringers.

STRINGER SYSTEMS

STRINGERLESS SYSTEMS

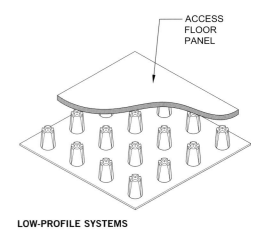

LOW-PROFILE SYSTEMS

ACCESS FLOORING UNDERSTRUCTURE SYSTEMS

DOOR JAMB (BEYOND)

DOOR

THRESHOLD; CENTER ON DOOR JAMB

EXTERIOR PAVING

1/4"

3 1/2" MIN.

ACCESS FLOORING

CONCRETE SLAB

EXTERIOR DOOR AT ACCESS FLOORING

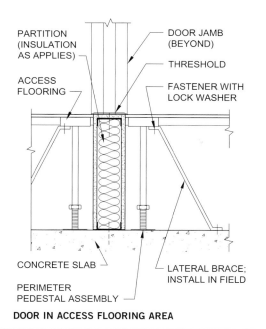

PARTITION (INSULATION AS APPLIES)

DOOR JAMB (BEYOND)

THRESHOLD

ACCESS FLOORING

FASTENER WITH LOCK WASHER

CONCRETE SLAB

PERIMETER PEDESTAL ASSEMBLY

LATERAL BRACE; INSTALL IN FIELD

DOOR IN ACCESS FLOORING AREA

DOOR IN SECTION WITH 1/4" UNDERCUT

DOOR JAMB BEYOND

ACCESS FLOORING

THRESHOLD

CONCRETE SLAB

DOOR AT EDGE OF RECESSED SLAB

THRESHOLDS

THRESHOLD; ATTACH TO PANEL ON ONE SIDE ONLY

ACCESS FLOORING

FASTENER WITH LOCK WASHER

CONCRETE SLAB

LATERAL BRACE; INSTALL IN FIELD

PERIMETER PEDESTAL ASSEMBLY

EXPANSION JOINT

OPEN-CELL NEOPRENE SPONGE GASKET WITH PRESSURE-SENSITIVE TAPE BACKING. USED BETWEEN PANEL JOINTS WHEN DIVIDER IS ON EDGE OF PANEL; CONTINUOUS ON TOP FLANGE OF DIVIDER WHEN DIVIDER IS NOT ON EDGE OF PANEL

ACCESS FLOORING

POP RIVETS

SEAL

PLENUM DIVIDER

PEDESTAL ASSEMBLY

CONCRETE FASTENER

CONCRETE SLAB

PEDESTAL ADHESIVE

PLENUM DIVIDER

FLAT-HEAD SCREW

ALUMINUM FASCIA TOP ANGLE

ALUMINUM FASCIA PLATE

POP RIVETS

PEDESTAL ADHESIVE

RAMP UNDERSTRUCTURE ASSEMBLY

ACCESS FLOORING PANEL

STRINGER

FLAT-HEAD ANCHOR

POP RIVETS

CONCRETE SLAB

RAMP SHOE ASSEMBLY

RAMP SHOE ASSEMBLY

ACCESS FLOORING PANEL

COMBO CORNERLOCK/ STRINGER SCREW

STRINGER SCREW

STRINGER

SWIVEL PEDESTAL HEAD

PEDESTAL ADHESIVE

CONCRETE SLAB

RAMP TRANSITION

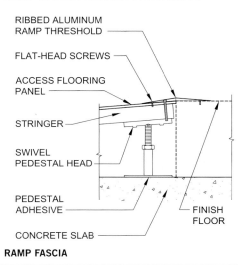

RIBBED ALUMINUM RAMP THRESHOLD

FLAT-HEAD SCREWS

ACCESS FLOORING PANEL

STRINGER

SWIVEL PEDESTAL HEAD

PEDESTAL ADHESIVE

CONCRETE SLAB

FINISH FLOOR

RAMP FASCIA

RAMP AT ACCESS FLOORING

STRUCTURAL PERFORMANCE

Testing for structural performance requirements, except for impact loads and seismic loads, is specified by referencing the Ceilings & Interior Systems Construction Association's (CISCA) CISCA A/F, *Recommended Test Procedures for Access Floors.* This standard is divided into six sections, each covering a different procedure for testing the structural properties of either an individual access flooring component or an access flooring assembly.

- *Section I* contains the test method for determining the maximum deflection and permanent set of access flooring panels when subjected to the rated concentrated design loads. The properties normally measured are top-surface deflection and permanent set, unless the measurements of bottom-surface deflection and set are specified. The latter method is used only with unfilled formed-steel panels, where local deformations on the top surface may produce readings that are not indicative of actual structural performance. Unlike concentrated-load criteria for floors and similar surfaces specified in ASCE 7, *Minimum Design Loads for Building and Other Structures,* which assumes that the load is distributed over an area equal to 6.25 sq ft (0.58 sq

m), the criteria for measuring concentrated load for access flooring involve applying the load through a 1-in.- (25.4-mm-) square or 1.128-in.- (28.6-mm-) diameter steel indentor.

- *Section II* covers the test method for determining the manufacturer's published ultimate-load rating.
- *Section III* covers the test procedure for measuring the durability or deformation, or both, of access flooring systems under exposure to commercially anticipated caster traffic. Two paths and two wheel configurations are included.
- *Section IV* establishes the test method for measuring the permanent set of stringers.
- *Section V* provides the test method for verifying the published axial load that a pedestal assembly can sustain without failure or damage to its components.
- *Section VI* defines the test method for determining the overturning moment that a pedestal assembly and its attachment to the subfloor can resist.

Other loads for which CISCA has not developed standard test methods include impact and earthquake loads. Stringerless systems are less able to resist the higher earthquake loads, particularly when pedestal heights exceed 12 in. (305 mm).

ACOUSTICAL PERFORMANCE

Airborne sound transmitted from one room to another through the access flooring and the underfloor cavity is another consideration when selecting a panel type for partitioned areas requiring acoustic privacy. Currently, no standard test method is designed specifically to measure sound-transmission performance of access flooring.

THERMAL-INSULATING PERFORMANCE

The thermal resistance of various panel types becomes a problem where the underfloor cavity either serves as a plenum to distribute air for cooling purposes or does not serve as a plenum but is over a structural floor whose bottom surface is directly exposed to cold exterior temperatures instead of having an intervening heated and insulated ceiling space. Formed-steel panels and die-cast aluminum panels have lower insulating values than steel-covered, wood-core panels; cementitious-filled, formed-steel panels; and lightweight-concrete-filled panels.

Sarah Bader; Gensler; Chicago, Illinois
Tanya Nachia; Rhode Island School of Design; Providence, Rhode Island
MASTERSPEC®; published by ARCOM; Salt Lake City, Utah, and Alexandria, Virginia

RAIL AT RAMP—ELEVATION

RAIL AT RAMP—PLAN

RAIL AT RAMP

EDGE CONDITION

When access flooring systems are used as plenum air distribution systems, the conditioned air must be delivered at a warmer temperature than overhead systems to ensure comfort underfoot. Air diffusers built into the access flooring panels (sometimes referred to as *salad spinners*) are controlled by hand. Underfloor air systems often do not cool as quickly or as effectively as conventional HVAC systems.

FLOOR DIFFUSER

BANNERS

BANNER TYPES

Traditionally banners have been pole-mounted, wall-mounted, or wall-hung, similar to the way flags are displayed. Today, however, the availability of a wide variety of banner fabrics and innovative graphics-application techniques provide more design opportunities for banner display constructions.

BANNER FABRICS

Common fabrics used for banners include vinyl laminates, vinyl-coated mesh, vinyl-coated polyester, acrylic-coated polyester, nylon, solution-dyed acrylic, solution-dyed modacrylic, and spunbonded polyolefin. Metal and plastic pieces have been made into or sewn onto banners for visual variety. Chain mail, cloth tassels, wooden ornaments, foam, lighting, and many other materials can be incorporated into banners.

Vinyl Laminates

Vinyl laminate fabrics are constructed by sandwiching polyester, nylon, or fiberglass scrims between two layers of vinyl. Technically, they are formed when the scrim is calendered between two layers of thermoplastic film; but generally they are manufactured by applying heat and pressure with an adhesive layer between the film and scrim layers. The scrim provides tensile and tear strength plus dimensional stability.

The vinyl offers a smooth surface for printing graphics. It's relatively easy to make banners from laminates: they can be sewn, heat-sealed, or radio-frequency- (RF) welded. Most laminates have a flame spread rating of 0 to 25. They can be used for nearly any type of banner, except where lightness and translucency are desired. However, they do not have a soft hand, they aren't readily drapeable, and come in limited color choices.

Vinyl-Coated Mesh

From a distance, this material appears to be solid vinyl, but up close, its open-weave design becomes apparent. Meshes, or a combination of solid and mesh fabrics, are often used for outdoor banners, because wind passes through their open weave.

Vinyl-Coated Polyester

Polyester fabrics are woven or knitted polyester fibers that have been coated or treated for durability, smoothness, and printability. Chemical compounds are added to provide pigment; flame retardance; and UV, water, and mildew resistance to the liquid vinyl coating. The coating is applied to the polyester scrim, then cured by passing through a heated chamber. Vinyl-coated polyesters are used most often to create lightweight banners printed on one side.

Acrylic-Coated Polyester

This dimensionally stable fabric is available in a wide range of colors and accepts silk screening, appliqué, and handpainting.

Nylon

Nylon has most of the advantages of polyester, plus it comes in a variety of weights. The translucency and drape of lighter nylons make them popular choices for interior banners. Heavier weights often are used in outdoor applications (nylon and polyester are the fabrics most typically used for flags). Nylon colors can be combined to create new colors. A very versatile fabric, nylon accepts printing, appliqué, handpainting, and vinyl film applications.

Solution-Dyed Acrylic

Acrylic offers the aesthetics of cotton but is resistant to UV light, mildew, and water. Weaving makes the acrylic fabric highly breathable, so hot air and moisture will not be trapped. When solution-dyed, color pigments are added to the acrylic fibers while the fibers are in a semiliquid state. As a result, the color becomes an integral part of the fiber; and unlike piece-dyed acrylic, the color won't wash out. Solution dying reduces fading and deterioration due to UV exposure and is available in more than 100 solid colors, stripes, and patterns.

Solution-Dyed Modacrylic

Although modacrylics share many of acrylic's characteristics, they have significant differences, mainly increased flame resistance and heat sensitivity.

Spunbonded Polyolefin

Spunbonded polyolefin fabrics look and feel much like paper. These fabrics are lightweight, weatherable, and low-cost. They typically are used to create short-term disposable banners.

BANNER FABRICS

FABRIC	DESCRIPTION/USE	ADVANTAGES/DISADVANTAGES
Vinyl laminates	All-purpose	Smooth surface, opaque; for painting.
Vinyl-coated mesh	External	Like vinyl, allows wind to pass through.
Vinyl-coated poly	All-purpose	Many colors; accepts silkscreening graphics.
Nylon	Lightweight	Good translucency; drape-versatile fabric.
Solution-dyed acrylic	Good for UV-exposed areas	Breathable, like cotton; many colors available, and colors won't wash out.
Solution-dyed modacrylic	Like acrylic	Increased flame resistance.
Spunbonded-polyolefin	Short-term banners	Look and feels like paper.
Canvas and drill cloth	Natural fibers	Less expensive, less UV-resistant; may not hold colors well.
Exotic fabrics	For visual appeal	Flammability may be a problem.

SUSPENDED "TOTEM" BANNER

SUSPENDED HORIZONTAL BANNER

SUSPENDED BANNERS

WALL-MOUNTED BANNERS

POLE-MOUNTED BANNERS

WALL-HUNG BANNERS

BANNER TYPES

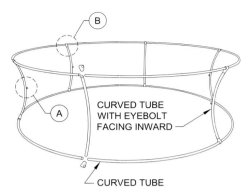

CURVED TUBE
WITH EYEBOLT
FACING INWARD

CURVED TUBE

SUPPORTING STRUCTURE FOR A THREE-DIMENSIONAL BANNER

ALUMINUM
FERNULE

AIRCRAFT-GRADE
STEEL CABLE

1/4" X 2 1/2" STEEL
EYEBOLT

ALUMINUM
TUBING

Ⓐ CONNECTION

1" DIA. ALUMINUM
PIPE INNER SLEEVE
REINFORCEMENT

ALUMINUM
TUBING

CLAMP WITH
HEX NUT
FACING RING
INTERIOR

ALUMINUM
TUBING

Ⓑ SUPPORT

CIRCULAR BANNER

Unsupported Films

Unsupported films, such as polyethylene or vinyl sheeting, are lightweight, inexpensive plastics without any fabric reinforcement (scrim). Their smooth surfaces make them suitable for screenprinting. They do, however, have a finite shelf life as banners, hence should be specified from recent inventory.

Canvas and Drill Cloth

Canvas and drill cloth are natural-fiber fabrics. They perform well for indoor applications and generally are less expensive than synthetics. Despite their lower cost and relative familiarity, canvas and drill cloth are not commonly used. Canvas is less UV-resistant than synthetics, and some believe it is less capable of holding a variety of bright colors. In addition, synthetic options are more economical, have fewer wrinkles, and are easier to print.

Exotic Fabrics

Silk, wool, spandex, linen, satin, nylon netting, metallics, and other fiber types have emerged as alternatives to traditional banner fabrics. Unusual fabrics are often used for their visual appeal in, for example, retail or commercial applications.

Functional concerns also can drive nontraditional fabrics selection. Flammability requirements may dictate that the fabric attached to a ceiling be porous enough to allow water from a fire sprinkler system to pass through it, in which case a nonwoven fabric made from spun fiberglass may prove the best choice.

Metallic Fabrics

Metallized fabrics, such as lamé, have a substrate with a thin covering of metal, often silver, aluminum, or a copper alloy. The substrate may be polyester or nylon, or, when flame retardancy is required, modacrylic. Handling of the fabric, including sewing, laminating, or other processes, depends on the nature of the metal.

Warp-Knit Fabrics

Warp-knit fabrics are gaining interest for banner applications because, if ripped, they resist unraveling at the edges. Spandex, a popular warp-knit fabric, is often used to give a banner a distinctive, tensile-structure shape.

Knit Polyester

Commonly used in outdoor flags and banners, knit polyester requires special automated printing equipment. It is durable, and the knitted construction allows air to pass through, rather than blocking or catching the wind. Knit polyester is longer-lasting and less expensive to manufacture than nylon.

Sheer Fabrics

Satin organza, polyester chiffon, silk taffeta, and other similarly lightweight ethereal materials are popular for use in retail displays and in exhibit halls. When printed, sheer cloths seem to disappear, leaving only the fluttering graphic readily visible. Many sheer fabrics will accept dye sublimation if their polyester content is over 20 percent. Fabrics are preshrunk if dye-sublimated.

ACOUSTICS

The amount of sound a banner absorbs depends on the weight of the fabric, the distance from a wall surface, and how many folds the banner fabric has. Adding banners can help improve acoustic absorption, particularly in hard-surfaced areas or spaces with high ceilings. Banners also can work in conjunction with fabrics used for acoustical panels, speaker covers, or wallcoverings, for additional sound absorption. When improving acoustic absorption is a concern, a nonporous fabric can be specified to enclose a core of fiberglass or similar sound-absorbing material.

GRAPHICS APPLICATION TECHNIQUES

Banner graphics for interior applications tend to be handcrafted, either screenprinted (for multiple runs or particularly sharp graphics), handpainted, airbrushed, or appliquéd by experienced artists and technicians. Some manufacturers of large-run banners have used other methods, such as heated-seal materials and vinyl film. Vinyl film is a quick, inexpensive approach for making identification or advertising banners, especially when only one or two banners are needed.

Graphics application techniques include the following:

- *Cut-out lettering.* Images are cut out of the fabric and replaced from behind with translucent fabric. Excellent for simple graphics when easy readability (and economy) is essential.
- *Eradication.* This graphics process uses chemicals to wipe away a top-coated color from a white vinyl fabric. Eradication is often used for illuminated awnings.
- *Heat transfer.* Images are baked into the fabric using a large vacuum. Bold color separation is possible with heat transfer; however, it doesn't blend colors well and is an expensive process.
- *Ink-jet process.* This process produces photographic-quality images on nearly any material using a computer printer. The images are rich and detailed.
- *Laser printing.* Large-image printing is possible using a laser printer.
- *Pressure-sensitive vinyl.* Vinyl film is cut, peeled from its backing, and applied to the fabric.
- *Sewn-in graphics.* Letters and forms are cut from fabric and sewn to the base fabric.
- *Silkscreening.* Images are transferred onto another material using special screens. Ink is spread over the top of the screen and printed on the fabric face.

ANCHORING SYSTEMS

The size and strength of the necessary hardware, such as the bracket arm's diameter and the anchor bolts' thickness, are selected based on the banner system's dead load. Banners can hang from ceilings on aircraft cable or fishing line, suspended by dowels, which are often made of aluminum tubing. If the banner is more complex and three-dimensional, fiberglass tubing can be used. Frames can be made of steel, aluminum, PVC, or metal-conduit tubing.

To avoid tampering, anchoring hardware should be out of reach of passersby; at the same time, it needs to be accessible enough so banners can be removed easily for maintenance or replacement. To maintain a firm, wrinkle-free appearance, it's often best to have "pole pockets" installed on the top (and sometimes sides) of the banner. Poles slipped into these pockets help maintain a flat, unflappable surface.

Wall-hung banners typically are installed with O-rings or snap hooks. Stick-on corners may be acceptable for smaller banners, where the wall surface cannot be drilled into.

Industrial Fabrics Association International; Roseville, Minnesota

INTERIOR SIGNAGE

Interior signage is a critical element in the success of interior spaces. Signage is used as a means of wayfinding, for room identification, and to depict regulatory conditions and emergency locations, such as stair exits. Emergency exit signage, generally covered under base building interior construction, and governed by code requirements, is not included in this discussion.

Signs may be visual, tactile, or combined. Local codes and ADA guidelines provide information on regulated sign types.

Signs may be freestanding, wall-mounted, floor-mounted, or suspended. Units may be framed or unframed. Custom signs are available.

SIGNAGE PROGRAMS

An interior signage program requires knowledge of the facility or space in which it will be installed. A signage program should identify a sign hierarchy, with different levels and types of signage, and include these steps: Define the scope of the signage project.

1. Assess local codes and regulations.
2. Review ADA requirements.
3. Analyze circulation paths.
4. Review user profile (visitor, staff).
5. Identify key design elements.
6. Develop sign types, locations, and message schedule.

A sign hierarchy allows the user or visitor to quickly recognize major sign types and location points, through consistency of the signage. A flow of information, from general to specific, greatly assists the visitor in wayfinding.

SIGN CATEGORIES

Signs convey four types of information: information, direction, identification, and regulation.

- *Information signs,* including lobby directories and locator maps, provide general location and overall wayfinding information.
- *Direction signs,* such as typical office floor directories, provide more specific local wayfinding information for areas or departments.
- *Identification signs* mark a point of arrival (office, stair) and may be furnished with changeable inserts if the room occupant or function is tempo-

rary. Rooms and spaces having a permanent function, such as restrooms and stairwells, are furnished with permanent graphic information. Local codes and the ADA requirements may determine sign types.

- *Regulation sign types* may be mandated by local codes and regulatory agencies. Many regulation signs are required to address life safety concerns. ADA guidelines apply to many regulation signs.

FREESTANDING MONOLITH INFORMATION SIGN *Source: ASI-Modulex; Dallas, Texas*

TYPICAL FLOOR DIRECTION SIGN
Source: ASI-Modulex; Dallas, Texas

SIGNAGE SYSTEMS

Manufacturers have developed signage systems that address needs for modularity, flexibility, and consistency within a family of signs. Sign types vary within systems for sign hierarchy and application options. Signage systems are available with changeable modular elements for flexibility. Most sign systems include ADA signs. Consult manufacturers for specific product information.

ROOM IDENTIFICATION SIGN

RESTROOM SIGN

OFFICE IDENTIFICATION SIGN

ROOM-IN-USE SIGN

IDENTIFICATION SIGN TYPES
Source: ASI-Modulex; Dallas, Texas

REGULATION SIGNS

WALL-MOUNT UPDATEABLE SIGN— RAIL SYSTEM

SUSPENDED SIGN— RAIL SYSTEM

PROJECTING SIGN— RAIL SYSTEM

WALL-MOUNT SIGN— CHASSIS SYSTEM

CHANGEABLE INSERT SIGN—CHASSIS SYSTEM

SYSTEMS FURNITURE PARTITION MOUNT SIGN—CHASSIS SYSTEM

Text and graphic panels are mounted on the system substructure.

MODULAR SIGNAGE SYSTEMS
Source: ASI-Modulex; Dallas, Texas

ACCESSIBLE SIGNAGE GUIDELINES

The *Americans with Disabilities Act Accessibility Guidelines* (ADAAG) establishes guidelines for accessible signage in Section 4.30. All signage required to be accessible must meet these requirements, as well as any applicable local or state accessibility standards.

Accessible Sign Categories

Accessible signs must be provided in permanent rooms and spaces. Directional, informational, and overhead signs do not require tactile and Braille lettering, but they must meet ADA guideline criteria.

Signs identifying rooms and spaces, whose function will not easily or readily change, must include tactile and Braille text. An office identification sign with a temporary room occupant may include a nonaccessible name plaque in addition to the accessible room identification sign.

Wall-mounted signs that provide direction to or information about functional spaces are not required to include tactile and Braille lettering. However, they must meet requirements for character proportion and height, sign finish, and contrast.

Signs that are projected or suspended overhead must meet requirements for clearance, character proportion and height, sign finish, and contrast.

Building directories, menus, and all other signs that provide temporary information about rooms and spaces, such as the current occupant's name, are not required to comply with ADA guidelines.

Identification of Accessible Facilities and Features

Entrances, Restrooms, and Bathing Facilities

The International Symbol of Accessibility (ISA, or "wheelchair symbol") must be displayed at accessible facility entrances if all entrances are not accessible. Directions must be provided from inaccessible entrances to accessible ones. Similar guidelines apply to restrooms and bathing facilities.

Assembly Areas

The International Symbol of Access for Hearing Loss must be displayed where assistive listening systems are provided, along with a description of the specific listening system.

Areas of Rescue Assistance

Areas of rescue assistance must be identified. If an illuminated exit sign is present, an illuminated sign stating "Area of Rescue Assistance," including the ISA, is required. Instructions must be posted within the area on how to use the area during emergencies. Inaccessible exits must be identified, and signs are required to direct visitors to accessible exits and areas of rescue assistance.

Public Telephones

Text telephones must be identified with the International Telecommunications Device for the Deaf (TDD) Symbol. Volume-control telephones must be identified by the International Symbol of Access for Hearing Loss.

MINIMUM ACCESSIBLE SIGNAGE REQUIREMENTS

	PERMANENT ROOM AND SPACES	DIRECTIONAL-INFORMATIONAL	OVERHEAD	TEMPORARY
Tactile and Braille Characters				
Characters must be raised, minimum 1/32 in. (.8 mm).	•			
Characters must be accompanied by Grade 2 Braille.	•			
Type Styles				
Characters must be uppercase and sans serif or simple serif font.	•			
Characters must have a width-to-height ratio of between 3:5 and 1:1.		•	•	
Characters must have a stroke width-to-height ratio of between 1:5 and 1:10.		•	•	
Character Height				
Tactile characters must be minimum 5/8 in. (16 mm) high, maximum 2 in. (51 mm) high, all uppercase.	•			
Characters must be minimum 3 in. (76 mm) high.			•	
Characters must be sized to viewing distance.		•		
Pictograms (Symbols)				
Equivalent written description must be placed directly below symbol.	•			
Written description cannot be within symbol's background field.	•			
Border dimension of symbol background field must be minimum 6 in. (152 mm) high.	•			
Finish and Contrast				
Characters and background must be eggshell, matte, or other nonglare finish.	•	•	•	
Characters must adequately contrast with background (approximately 70%).	•	•	•	
Mounting Location and Height				
Mounted on wall adjacent to the latch side of the door.	•			
Mounted to avoid door swing and protruding objects.	•			
Mounting height of 60 in. (1,524 mm) from floor to centerline of sign.	•			
Minimum 80 in. (2,032 mm) clearance between overhead sign and floor.			•	

Source: ASI-Modulex; Dallas, Texas

INTERNATIONAL SYMBOL OF ACCESSIBILITY

INTERNATIONAL SYMBOL OF ACCESS FOR HEARING LOSS

INTERNATIONAL TDD SYMBOL

INTERNATIONAL ACCESSIBILITY SYMBOLS
Source: Society for Environmental Graphic Design; Washington, D.C.

TYPICAL PERMANENT ROOM SIGN
Field:
Minimum height ⅝ in. (16 mm), uppercase
Tactile text, raised, minimum ¹⁄₃₂ in. (.8 mm)
Sans serif or simple serif font
Characters must contrast with background.
Grade 2 Braille

Personnel Name Strips:
As temporary signs, are exempt from the ADA design
guidelines.

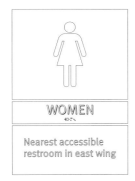

TYPICAL RESTROOM SIGN
Field:
Minimum height 6 in. (152 mm)
Pictogram border or background field
Pictogram not required to be raised.

Room Designation:
Minimum height ⅝ in. (16 mm), uppercase
Tactile text, raised, minimum ¹⁄₃₂ in. (.8 mm)
Sans serif or simple serif font
Text may not be within background field
Grade 2 Braille

Information on nearest accessible restroom required
only when not all restrooms are accessible.

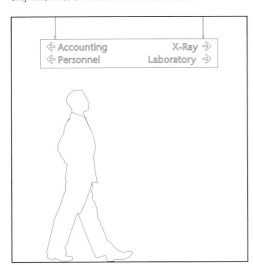

TYPICAL OVERHEAD SIGN
Minimum height 3 in. (76 mm), uppercase
Minimum 80 in. (2,032 mm) from underside of sus-
pended or projecting sign to finished floor

MINIMUM ACCESSIBLE SIGN GUIDELINES
Source: ASI-Modulex; Dallas, Texas

SIGN TYPE AND LOCATION STRATEGY

Review ADAAG requirements, local code, and regulations regarding sign types proposed for a project.
Utilize the signage program results when developing
sign hierarchy, sign types, and location strategies for
the project. Follow these guidelines:

- Be consistent in signage size, location, placement,
  and terminology, to assist visitors in orienting themselves and navigating through the facility.
- Locate directories and maps at main entrances
  and/or lobbies with appropriate information for persons with disabilities.
- Locate directories at elevator or stair lobbies on
  each floor.
- Do not use lightweight, freestanding signs for high-
  traffic areas. Use where specific location requires
  information maneuverability.

Electronic, computer, and videotex technologies can
provide an innovative and highly flexible directory/sign
display system for mapping and routing, information
(facilitywide and local), messages, and information
management capabilities.

Where changeability and flexibility are design priorities, a modular system is recommended. See
manufacturer information for descriptions of types of
available systems, including those meeting ADAAG
requirements. Changeable inserts on nonaccessible
sign components must be managed so that the information system is kept current. Computer files or
specialized software programs provide a means of
tracking signage modifications.

For maximum ease of reading, any given line of an
interior sign should not exceed 30 characters in
length, including upper- and lowercase letters and
spaces between words.

Select the height, visual weight, and font style of text
and symbols for readability. Consider background
materials and contrast when selecting a color scheme.
Refer to the ADAAG and other codes for restrictions on
accessible signage.

Signage readability should always be considered when
selecting text sizes. When signage is required to meet
ADAAG requirements, guidelines have been established to identify minimum requirements for tactile
and visual characters and symbols.

SPECIAL CONDITIONS FOR EMERGENCY EGRESS

Some local jurisdictions require additional signage to
respond to the need for improved egress and area
identification in the event of an emergency for buildings over three stories high. The sign types listed here
are in addition to the code-required signage for these
spaces:

- Stairwell identification
- Additional area of rescue assistance identification
- Elevator car identification
- Evacuation floor plans
- Workspace and office locator maps

SIGNAGE MATERIALS

Signs are available in numerous materials and finishes. Custom materials and finishes are available.
Consult with a manufacturer for material and finish
limitations, particularly when including accessible signage in the signage program.

Typical materials include:

- Photopolymer (for ADA signs), in varying colors
- Acrylic, painted
- Metal (aluminum, steel, stainless steel, brass,
  bronze, copper, etc.), in varying finishes
- Glass

Informational signs, such as main lobby directories,
are also available as illuminated and nonilluminated
units, typically furnished with glass or acrylic covers
and metal frames or housings. Consult with sign manufacturers for information on custom informational
signs and construction requirements.

SIGNAGE GRAPHICS AND TEXT

Signage graphics and text vary based on the sign type,
design, and ADA requirements. Review overall sign
types required for a project to assess ADAAG or other
regulations, which may affect signage graphics or text
aesthetics.

- Silk screened graphics
- Vinyl graphics
- Digital imprinting on vinyl
- Cast, etched, paint-infilled metal
- Sandblasted, silk screened, vinyl-applied glass
- Fused materials

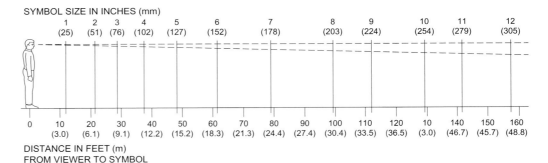

SYMBOL READABILITY

ELECTRONIC INFORMATION SYSTEMS

Changeable signs typically require manual replacement of an insert or other hard copy text or graphic. Computer interfaces for signage addresses the need for flexibility and changing information, mapping, routing, and messages. They may be used at locations where ADA requirements for static signs are not required, such as in main lobby directories. Some sign systems have video technology capabilities integrated into the sign system.

A central computer, which terminates at remote sign locations, controls computerized signs. Changing sign text and graphics is facilitated through the use of the computer. Varying levels of sign hierarchy may be incorporated into this type of system.

DIRECTIONAL SIGNS   **ROOM SIGNS**

Computerized system accommodates varying sign types.

ELECTRONIC INFORMATION SYSTEM *Source: ASI-Modulex; Dallas, Texas*

SURFACE MOUNT   **RECESSED MOUNT**   **SEMIRECESSED MOUNT**   **OVERHEAD MOUNT**   **WALL PROJECTION**

MOUNTING OPTIONS *Source: ASI-Modulex; Dallas, Texas*

ADA SIGN — WALL-MOUNTED DIRECTORY — OVERHEAD SIGN

5'-0" (1524)
4'-0" MIN. (1219)
7'-0" MAX. (2134)
6'-8" MIN. (2032)

SIGNAGE MOUNTING HEIGHTS

FLUSH CEILING   **EYE HOOK**

Conference centers and other facilities facing constantly changing room assignments can integrate this type of signage with an existing room-scheduling system, thus increasing efficiency.

INTERIOR SIGNAGE INSTALLATION

Interior sign installation varies with the application, substrate or mounting surface, weight, and other factors, which should be reviewed with the signage installer. Signage requiring mechanical fastenings may require additional blocking or support to the wall surface to ensure stability.

Wall-mounting options for small signs include:

- Vinyl tape
- Silicone adhesive
- Velcro
- Magnetic tape
- Mechanical fastening

DIRECT BURIAL   **FLANGE-MOUNTED**

HIDDEN POCKET   **TWIST-CLIP FOR SUSPENDED CEILING**

FLOOR-MOUNT OPTIONS
Source: ASI-Modulex; Dallas, Texas

SUSPENSION MOUNTING OPTIONS
Source: ASI-Modulex; Dallas, Texas

LOCKER ROOMS AND SHOWERS

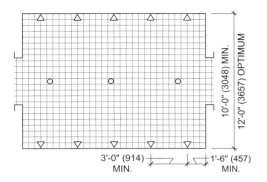

Educational facilities with time constraints should have 10 showerheads for the first 30 persons and one showerhead for every four additional persons. In recreational facilities, one showerhead for each 10 dressing lockers is a minimum. Temperature controls are necessary to keep water from exceeding 110°F (43°C). Both individual and master controls are needed for group showers.

GROUP SHOWERS

| SHOWER PLAN | DRESSING ROOM PLAN |

TYPICAL DIMENSIONS

	MINIMUM	OPTIMUM
Showers	3 ft 0 in. × 3 ft 6 in. (914 × 1,066 mm)	3 ft 6 in. × 3 ft 6 in. (1,066 × 1,066 mm)
Dressing Rooms	3 ft 0 in. × 3 ft 6 in. (914 × 1,066 mm)	3 ft 6 in. × 4 ft 0 in. (1,066 × 1,219 mm)

Individual dressing rooms and showers can be combined in a variety of configurations to obtain 1:1, 2:1, 3:1, and 4:1 ratios

INDIVIDUAL SHOWERS AND DRESSING ROOMS

| WET TOILET AREA | DRYING AREA |

The drying room should have about the same area as the shower room. Provision for drainage should be made. Heavy-duty towel rails, approximately 4 ft (1,220 mm) from the floor, are recommended. A foot-drying ledge, 18 in. (460 mm) high and 8 in. (205 mm) wide, as shown in the drawing, is desirable. An adjacent wet toilet is suggested. Avoid curbs between drying room and adjacent space. Size of towel service area (which can be used for distributing uniforms) varies. Size of area varies with material to be stored; 200 sq ft (18 sq m) is usually sufficient.

DRYING AND WET TOILET AREA

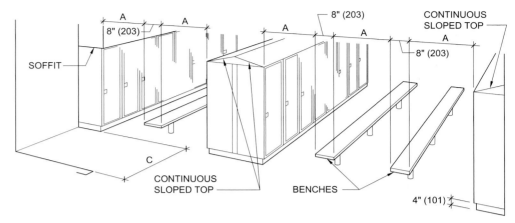

Bench should be, minimally, 8 in. (205 mm) wide and 16 in. (405 mm) high. Traffic breaks of 3-ft (915-mm) minimum width should occur at maximum intervals of 12 ft (3 m). Main traffic aisle should be wider. Avoid lockers that meet at 90° corner.

	A	B	C
Recreation	2 ft 2 in. (660 mm)	1 ft 8 in. (508 mm)	3 ft 6 in. (1,066 mm)
School	2 ft 6 in. (762 mm)	2 ft 6 in. (762 mm)	4 ft 0 in. (1,219 mm)

LOCKER ROOM

Basket racks vary from 7 to 10 tiers in height. Wide baskets require 1 ft (305 mm) shelf space, small baskets 10 in. (255 mm) shelf space; both fit 1- to 1½-ft- (305- to 460-mm-) deep shelf. Back-to-back shelving is 2 ft 3 in. (3,225 mm) wide. Height is 9¼ in. (235 mm).

BASKET ROOM AND BASKET RACK

LOCKER ROOM FACILITIES CHECKLIST

- Fixed benches 16 in. (406 mm) high
- Lockers on raised base
- Locker numbering system
- Hair dryers—one per 20 lockers
- Mirrors at lavatory
- Makeup mirror and shelf
- Drinking fountain (height as required)
- Bulletin board
- Dressing booths, if required
- Full-length mirror
- Clock
- Door signs
- Sound system speaker, if required
- Lighting at mirrors for grooming
- Lighting located over aisles and passages
- Adequate ventilation for storage lockers
- Windows located with regard to height and arrangement of lockers
- Visual supervision from adjacent office

| STORAGE | DRESSING |

STANDARD LOCKER SIZES

WIDTH	9 in. (228 mm)	12 in. (304 mm)	15 in. (381 mm)	18 in. (457 mm)
DEPTH	12 in. (304 mm)	15 in. (381 mm)	18 in. (457 mm)	
HEIGHT	60 in. (1,524 mm)		72 in. (1,828 mm) overall	

For schools, standard storage locker is 9 or 12 in. × 12 × 12 in. to 24 in. (230 or 305 × 305 × 305 mm to 610 mm). Standard dressing lockers are 12 × 12 in. × 60 or 72 in. (305 × 305 mm × 1,525 mm or 1,830 mm). Number of dressing lockers should be equal to the peak period load plus 10% to 15% for expansion.

LOCKER TYPES

| SHOWER HEAD | HAIR DRYER OUTLET | HAND DRYER OUTLET |

6'-6" (MEN) (1981)
6'-0" (WOMEN) (1828)
5'-0" (CHILDREN) (1651)

6'-0" (MEN) (1828)
5'-5" (WOMEN) (1651)
5'-0" (PRETEENS/TEENAGERS) (1529)

3'-8" (MEN) (1117)
3'-6" (WOMEN) (1066)
3'-1" (TEENAGERS) (939)
2'-8" (PRETEENS) (812)

| SHOWER VALVE | ROBE HOOK | CLOCK | TOWEL BAR | FIXED BENCH |

4'-0" (1219)
6'-3" (1905)
6'-6" (MIN.) (1981)
4'-0" (1219)
1'-4" (406)

RECOMMENDED MOUNTING HEIGHTS

LOCKER ROOM DESIGN

The most widely used arrangement of lockers is the *bay system*, with a minimum 4 ft (1,220 mm) circulation aisle at each end of the bays. Ordinarily, the maximum number of lockers in a bay is 16. Locate dry (shoe) traffic at one end of the bays and wet (barefoot) traffic at the other end. For long bays with a single bench, make 3 ft (915 mm) breaks at 15 ft (4.5 m) intervals. Supervision of school lockers is easiest when they are located in single banks along the two walls, providing one or more bays that run the length of the room.

The number of lockers in a locker room depends on the anticipated number of users. For large numbers, separate locker areas should be encouraged. In small buildings, interconnecting doors provide flexibility and allow for the handling of peak loads. Individual dressing and shower compartments and a shower stall for the handicapped may be required.

Locker room entrance and exit doors should have vision barriers. Heavy-duty, moisture-resistant doors at locker room entrances and exits should be of sufficient size to handle the traffic flow and form natural vision barriers. Entrance/exit doors for the lockers should be equipped with corrosion resistant hardware.

Basket storage, if included, generally is self-service. Maximum height is 8 tiers. A dehumidifying system should be provided to dry out basket contents overnight. Separate auxiliary locker rooms for teams, part-time instructors, faculty, or volunteer leaders may be required. A small room for the coach's use may be desirable.

SHOWER ROOM DESIGN

The shower room should be directly accessible to the drying room and locker room that it serves. When a shower room is designed to serve a swimming pool, the room should be located so that all must pass through showers before reaching the pool deck.

Separate wet and dry toilet areas are recommended. Wet toilets should be easily accessible from the shower room. When designed for use with a swimming pool, wet toilets should be located so that users must pass through the shower room after use of toilets.

Finishes

Floors should be of impervious material, such as ceramic or quarry tile, with a Carborundum-impregnated surface, and should slope toward the drains. Concrete floors (nonslip surface), if used, should be treated with a hardener to avoid the penetration of odors and moisture.

Walls should be of materials resistant to moisture and should have surfaces that are easily cleaned. All exterior corners in the locker rooms should be rounded.

Ceilings in shower areas should be of ceramic tile or other material impervious to moisture. Locker room ceilings should be acoustically treated with a material impervious to moisture and breakage. Floor drains should be kept out of the line of traffic, where possible.

GYMNASIUM AND POOL LOCKER ROOM

POOL LOCKER ROOM

GYMNASIUM LOCKER ROOM

BFS Architectural Consulting and Interior Design; YMCA of the USA; Chicago, Illinois

Steel Lockers and Basket Racks

Construction of locker frame and door typically is of 16-gage steel for sides and back. Top and bottom are typically 20- to 24-gage steel. Number plates, a shelf, and coat hooks on back- and sidewalls are generally included. Other construction, such as plastic laminate or wood, is available.

Door types may be solid, perforated (all or part), or louvered (all or part), and ordered in a variety of steel mesh patterns or in special finishes. Doors and locks may be provided with noise-deadening devices. Locking mechanisms include built-in adjustable combination lock,

built-in flat or grooved key, and latching locker handle (for padlock use). All locking mechanisms are available for surface or recessed applications.

Optional locker equipment includes sloping top for nonrecessed locations, with corner miters available, 6 in. (150 mm) legs for open base installation, interior partitions (some models), multiple shelves, coat rods (for models over 18 in. (460 mm) deep), closed base and closed-end base for legs, and attachable bench elements.

Ventilation within locker spaces should provide 15 cu ft (.42 cu m) minimum, air movement for locker.

ADA access may suggest use of some multiple-tier lockers; shelf and coat hooks on single-tier lockers are out of reach of most seated persons.

Benches

Bench arrangements may be attached to locker front or may be freestanding and require a raised installation. Finishes of lockers may be varied as conditions dictate, such as stainless-steel bottoms or sides when used in areas where long-term chemical contamination may affect finishes.

Checking lockers for heavy-duty use are available in enameled steel or stainless steel. Locks are provided with built-in

multiple coin selector, which is owner-adjustable for coins, tokens, or "free" operation. These locks may be installed on

legs, or be recessed, and may be made movable. Overall height is 6 ft (1.8 m) on most models, 5 ft (1.5 m) on some.

LOCKERS

ELEVATION

BASKET RACKS

Basket racks may be arranged in single tier or back to back. Single-tier depth is 1 ft 1¼ in. (335 mm). Optional pilfer guards may be installed on sides, top, and bottom, preventing access into adjacent baskets, and should be considered at the back as well. Basket materials include wire mesh (all surfaces), perforated steel ends and mesh sides and bottom, and louvered ends with perforated steel sides and bottom.

LOCKER SECTION

CHECKING LOCKERS

FILLER PIECE   **FLUSH WALL JOINT**

JAMB   **HEAD AT FASCIA**

RECESSED/FLUSH BASE AT WALL

TWO WOOD SLEEPERS REQUIRED FOR ISLAND INSTALLATION

RECESSED/FLUSH BASE AT ISLAND

INSTALLATION DETAILS

BFS Architectural Consulting and Interior Design; YMCA of the USA; Chicago, Illinois
Frederick C. Krenson, AIA; Rosser Fabrap International; Atlanta, Georgia

WIRE MESH PARTITIONS

Wire mesh partitions are useful where security is needed in combination with visibility and air circulation, for example, storage facilities, computer labs, and payroll distribution areas. The wire mesh typically has 1½ in. (38 mm) openings in a diamond orientation. Smaller openings and square mesh are available at a higher cost.

Standard wire mesh partitions are freestanding panels bolted together and supported by floor anchors. Panels are available in widths from 9 in. (225 mm) to 60 in. (1,500 mm), with a maximum height of 12 ft (3.6 m). Multiple panels can be stacked for greater heights. A variety of hardware and accessories are available, including ceiling panels, trimmed cutouts, hinged and sliding doors, Dutch doors, drop-shelf and slide-up and side-hinged service windows. Components are factory-painted steel.

*Margery Morgan; Symmes Maini & McKee Associates;
   Cambridge, Massachusetts
HMC Group; Ontario, California*

WIRE MESH PARTITION SELECTION GUIDE

USE	MESH OPENING IN. (MM)	WIRE SIZE IN. (MM)	FRAME SIZE IN. (MM)	USES
Standard Duty	1¼ (32)	0.135 (3)	1 (25)	Animal cages
	1½ (38)	0.135 (3)	1 (25)	Elevator pit dividers
	1¾ (44)	0.135 (3)	1¼ (32)	Fire escapes
Heavy Duty	2 (50)	0.162 (4)	1½ (38)	Cashier cages
	2 (50)	0.192 (5)	1½ (38)	Runways Stairway partitions Locker rooms Stockrooms Tool rooms

CHANNEL FRAME

ANGLE, LEG IN

ROD FRAME

ANGLE, LEG OUT

WIRE MESH PARTITION FRAME TYPES

ELEVATION

SECTION A-A

WIRE MESH PARTITION

DEMOUNTABLE PARTITIONS

CHARACTERISTICS

Demountable partitions, also referred to as *relocatable, movable,* or *portable walls,* are factory-fabricated, site-assembled partition systems with unfinished gypsum board or prefinished finish faces. Connectors, bases, and other components are designed as part of the system and are installed with far fewer tools than required for constructed gypsum board partitions.

Flexibility

Demountable partitions are often used in facilities with frequently changing requirements, for their economy and flexibility as compared to traditional, constructed gypsum board partitions. These partitions may be less expensive to install than traditional, constructed gyp-

sum board partitions, and they allow spaces to be reconfigured without extensive renewal or repair of floor and ceiling finishes.

Removable face panels allow wiring in partitions to be easily reconfigured. Demountable partitions can be prewired or have wire chases so that power and communication systems can be easily reconfigured. Taping and sanding (and the dust and debris these operations generate) inherent to standard gypsum board wall construction is eliminated.

Demountable partitions can be reconfigured without extensive renewal or repair of floor and ceiling finishes. Some demountable partition systems are attached to

the flooring and to the ceiling grid, which makes it possible to move the system with virtually no damage to these surfaces.

Economy

Although initial costs are much higher using these systems instead of constructed gypsum board walls, savings are often possible because reconfiguration of the systems is much simpler than standard fixed construction and components, and panels are about 95% reusable. Like furniture, demountable systems are classified by the IRS as portable, tangible, personal property, and may qualify for investment tax credits and depreciation that constructed partitions do not.

DEMOUNTABLE PARTITION TYPES

There are two types of demountable partitions: gypsum panel systems and unitized panel systems.

- *Demountable gypsum panel systems* use gypsum board panels supported by framing that is erected separately. They differ from standard, constructed gypsum board partitions in that the framing and facing panels are installed with concealed fastening devices and pressure-fit members. Specialized installation methods allow for easy disassembly and reuse of components. The faces of these panels can be unfinished for field painting or prefinished with fabric or vinyl wallcovering. Gypsum panel partitions are generally between 3 and 3¾ in. (75 and 95 mm) thick.
- *Demountable unitized-panel partitions* consist of factory-assembled panels with integral internal support that are joined to each other on-site. Connectors and bases may be integral to the panel or separate. The faces of these panels are factory-finished with vinyl wallcovering, fabric, textured steel, or wood veneer. Unitized-panel partitions are thinner than gypsum panel systems, generally between 2 and 3 in. (50 and 75 mm) thick.

REUSE

The reusability of demountable partition components depends on their condition after initial use and the care with which they are dismantled and stored. While unfinished gypsum panels can easily be replaced and matched, it is difficult to anticipate the quantity of factory-finished replacement panels needed for future reconfiguration.

PLANNING

Most demountable partition systems are *nonprogressive* (they do not "creep"); that is, panel widths are nominal and measured from the center of connectors, and panels can be added without disturbing panels already in place. Some partition systems are *progressive,* so that reconfiguring panels may require other panels in a sequence to be shifted. If demountable partitions are used with systems furniture, it is critical to coordinate the dimensions and modules of the panels with the systems furniture.

DOORS AND FRAMES

Doors and frames can be provided within unitized panels or separately. For unitized wall panels and separate door frames to be interchangeable, they must have the same overall dimension. Most unitized panel manufacturers offer standard doors and hardware; however, these components vary among manufacturers, and the number of standard door sizes is limited. For gypsum panel partitions, door frames are provided by the partition manufacturer, but doors and hardware typically are not.

Door operation is either pivoted or hinged. Pivoted door units allow the handing of door units to be changed when they are relocated. Hinged door units are handed and, therefore, less versatile, but can offer greater acoustical privacy.

MASTERSPEC®; published by ARCOM; Salt Lake City, Utah, and Alexandria, Virginia

OPERABLE PANEL PARTITIONS

SELECTION CONSIDERATIONS

Partition weight must be considered in the planning stages. Excessive deflection, particularly when the partition load is concentrated in a stacked position, can damage panels. Panel weight is determined by size, frame material, STC rating, and accessories.

PANEL FINISHES

Panel facing materials include fabric, carpet, paint, plastic laminate, vinyl wallcovering, and wood veneer. Accessories such as chalkboards, markerboards, and tackboards are also available.

PANEL STORAGE CONSIDERATIONS

Panel storage garages must be designed with the panel manufacturers during the design development phase to ensure that adequate space size and configuration are provided. Configuration of the storage garage varies depending on the selected system, as well as the garage door opening width, swing, and closing hardware.

FLOOR TOLERANCES

Flooring irregularities and structural deflection should be anticipated. Panel bottom seals extend 1 to 4 in. (25 to 100 mm) to accommodate floor irregularities. Floor tolerances and bottom seal extension capabilities are especially critical for large, heavy partitions.

Bottom carrier handles about 90% of panel weight. Dirt can accumulate in floor track.

FLOOR-SUPPORTED OPERABLE PARTITION DETAIL

TOP-HUNG OPERABLE PARTITION DETAIL

OPERABLE PARTITION FRAME MATERIALS

OPERABLE PARTITION FRAME MATERIAL	STC RATING	PANEL THICKNESS IN. (MM)
Wood	Up to 51	3–3½ (76–89)
Aluminum (steel-reinforced)	38 to 53	3–4 (76–102)
Steel	38 to 53	3–4 (76–102)

OPERABLE PANEL PARTITION TYPES

	INDIVIDUAL PANELS	HINGED-PAIR PANELS	CONTINUOUSLY HINGED PANELS
System Description	Separate panels	Panels paired and hinged together	All panels hinged together to form a continuous panel train
Maximum Height	Approximately 40 ft (12 m)	Approx. 18 ft (5 m)	Manual: 18 ft (5m) Electric: 30 ft (9 m)
Travel Configurations	Straight run Right-angle intersections Radiused curves	Straight run Radiused curves	Straight run
Operation	Manual	Manual Electric	Manual (total wall weight under 3,700 lb (1,678 kg)) Electric (total wall weight over 3,700 lb (1,678 kg))
Complexity of Operation	May require training to operate	Training required to operate	Simple
Number of Carriers per Panel	Two	One	One or two
Storage	Center or side stacked at the end of the run; remote storage possible	Center or side stacked at the end of the run or at remote storage area	Center stacked at the end of the run
Features	Flexible configurations	Quick setup	Quick setup

OPERABLE PANEL PARTITIONS AND NOISE TRANSMISSION

Reducing noise transmission among spaces separated by operable partitions is a common concern. No partition design can eliminate noise transmission. The manufacturer should be consulted to choose the most appropriate STC rating for the application. Clients should be informed that noise transmissions will vary depending on the functions being held. Noise Isolation Class (NIC) is an indication of the actual-level sound transmission of the built condition (the NIC rating is usually 5 to 12 dB lower than the STC rating). The test is performed after the operable panel partition is installed. Surrounding building materials; "flanking" paths around the partitions; and leaks due to floor, wall, or ceiling deflection can affect the NIC rating.

As a rule of thumb, it is generally not advisable to have a loud music function, such as a wedding or concert, booked for one space while the other side of the partition is holding a quiet conference meeting. In general, the larger the room, the more effectively noise transmission can be controlled. The operable panel partition manufacturer should be consulted to determine the optimum partition type for the size of the space.

FLANKING PATH

The deflection of the end wall to which the operable panel partition is installed can cause sound leaking. Likewise, deflection caused by live loads on the floor or ceiling can contribute to sound leakage. A continuous floor covering under the operable partition can contribute to flanking noise problems. Heavy-duty bottom seals may be required for a textured floor covering, for example, a loop pile carpet. Coordinate with the partition manufacturer early in the design to establish the best ways to reduce flanking noise transmission.

STRUCTURAL CONSIDERATIONS

Coordinate with the operable panel partition manufacturer and the structural engineer to determine the minimum size requirements of the hanger rods, hanger brackets, and track and ball-bearing trolleys. Verify that there is ample ceiling space to accommodate the required minimum dimension.

PATH OF EGRESS

The path of egress is established by the authorities having jurisdiction. Additional means of egress may be needed, as the space is effectively divided into two separate rooms when the operable partition is in place. In this case, ADAAG requirements for the additional means of egress are typically enforced.

ADAAG-compliant pass doors designed for accessibility are available. These pass doors have no thresholds; they open and operate with no more than 5 lbf (22 N), by hardware requiring no gripping or twisting to operate; and they have a clear 32-in.- (813-mm-) wide opening at a 90° swing.

EXPANDABLE JAMB

HINGED JAMB

ANGLE JAMB

EXPANDABLE JAMB WITH BULB SEAL

CLOSURE METHODS

MANUAL SEAL

AUTOMATIC SEAL

BOTTOM SEALS

PANEL WALL WITH PASS DOORS

CENTER STACK

PERPENDICULAR STACK

REMOTE STORAGE

PARALLEL STACK

Dimensions given are for fixed, adjustable, or operable seals. Panels with automatic bottom seals require a wider stack storage area.

STACKED PANEL STORAGE

Margery Morgan; Symmes, Mainee, McKee Associates; Cambridge, Massachusetts
Stephen Luk; Brennan Beer Gorman Architects; New York, New York

TOILET AND BATH ACCESSORIES

ADA requires reach height not to exceed 48 in. (1,219 mm) for forward reach or 54 in. (1,371 mm) for side reach.

All dispensers and disposals can be recessed, semirecessed, or surface- mounted.

COMMERCIAL

RESIDENTIAL AND HOTEL

2 □ **TOILET AND BATH ACCESSORIES**

BANK EQUIPMENT

REQUIREMENTS

Each financial institution sets the standards and defines the requirements for security, equipment, and design, depending on the location and nature of the facility. The designer must coordinate equipment installation with the design of the space. The contract documents should indicate the electrical devices that will be provided by the general contractor (such as open conduits to run wiring for CCTV and burglary wires) and power for those devices, as well as space and millwork for equipment. These items must be coordinated with the financial institution's security equipment vendor.

ROBBERY ALARM SYSTEMS

Robbery alarm systems are commonly provided for banking offices at which the police can ordinarily arrive within five minutes after an alarm has been activated. Other financial institutions should be provided with appropriate devices for promptly notifying the police that a robbery has occurred or is in progress. These systems are typically activated by initiating devices located at each teller's station or window and are safeguarded against accidental transmission.

BURGLARY ALARM SYSTEMS

Burglary alarm systems should be capable of promptly detecting an attack on the outer door, walls, floor, or ceiling of each vault and each safe not stored in a vault. Motion detectors are typically provided. The alarm sys-tem should signal the police, through an intermediary, indicating that a crime against the banking office has occurred or is in progress. Where police cannot arrive within five minutes, a loud bell that is audible inside and 500 ft (152 m) outside should be provided.

WALK-UP AND DRIVE-IN TELLERS' STATIONS OR WINDOWS

Tellers should be effectively protected by bullet-resist-ant barriers from robbery or larceny. Such barriers should be of glass, at least 1³⁄₁₆ in. (30 mm) in thick-ness, or of material of at least equivalent bullet resistance. Pass-through devices should not afford a person outside a direct line of fire.

AUTOMATED TELLER MACHINES (ATMS)

ATMs can weigh 750 lb (340 kg) or more when empty, so structural alterations may be required. ATMs should contain, among other features, a storage chest of cast or welded steel walls, top, and bottom, at least 1 in. (25 mm) thick, with a tensile strength of at least 50,000 psi (344 Mpa). Doors should be constructed of steel at least equivalent in strength to the storage chest and be equipped with a combination lock and a relocking device that will effectively lock the door if the combination lock is punched.

The cash-dispensing control and delivering mecha-nism should be protected by steel, at least ½ in. (13 mm) in thickness, securely attached to the storage chest. An ATM that receives deposits should have a receptacle chest with the same burglary-resistant characteristics as those of a cash-dispensing storage chest and should be designed to protect against the fishing and trapping of deposits.

ATM Accessibility

ADA Accessibility Guidelines (ADAAG), Section 4.34, regulate automatic teller machines; they require that:

- They be accessible per 4.1.3.
- Their controls comply with 4.27 (height of forward reach, 48 in. (1,219 mm); height of side reach, 54 in. (1,371 mm).
- They have clear floor space in compliance with 4.24 (30 by 48 in./762 by 1,219 mm).
- They be usable by persons with impaired vision.

Each ATM must comply, except where two or more are provided at a location; then only one must comply. Drive-up-only ATMs are not required to comply with clear floor space and reach requirements of 4.27 and 4.34.

Local codes may require minimal lighting require-ments at all outdoor ATMs for the protection of the patrons; and some jurisdictions may require planting guidelines for visibility related to safety.

Charles Szoradi, AIA; Washington, D.C.

TELLER STATION

VENDING EQUIPMENT

MONEY CHANGER
$1, 10, 20--2000 BILLS
3400/25/4000/5
115V 180-LB NET

CANDY-SNACK
50 SELECTIONS, 700 ITEMS
115V 3 AMP
500-LB NET

COLD DRINKS
8 SELECTIONS, 350 CANS
115V 10 AMP
650-LB NET

HOT DRINKS
50 SELECTIONS, 900 CUPS
115V 20 AMP
600-LB NET

REFRIGERATED FOOD
11 SHELVES, 150 PRODUCTS
CAROUSEL, 115V 16 AMP
800-LB NET

MICROWAVE
8 CU. FT.
115V 15 AMP
40-LB NET

COMMON VENDING MACHINES

FRONT REACH (ADA)   SIDE REACH (ADA)   FLOOR-MOUNTED   WALL-MOUNTED   TABLE-MOUNTED

EQUIPMENT AND CLEARANCE DIMENSIONS

Design Guidelines for Vending Areas

- Front clearance of 5 ft (1.5 m) is preferred for machines.
- Double door or door larger than 3 ft (1 m) wide is preferred for vending machine area.
- Service access of machines is generally from the front.
- Hot water is not required. Some beverage units require cold water supply with shut-off valve. Overflow waste collects into internal tray.
- Refrigerated vending machines and microwave ovens require a rear wall clearance of up to 8 in. (205 mm) to permit cooling.
- Electric service is 115V. A separate circuit for each machine is preferred. Amperages vary widely from 2 to 20 amps.

VENDING MACHINE ROOM

Charles Szoradi, AIA; Washington, D.C.

FOOD SERVICE EQUIPMENT

STAINLESS-STEEL WORKTABLE WITH SINK

4'-0" TO 4'-6" HIGH WALL (1219 - 1372)

MOBILE BANQUET CABINET

SLOW-COOK OVEN

FOOD CUTTER

TABLETOP WITH SINKS

STAINLESS-STEEL WORKTABLE

TABLE-MOUNTED STEAM-JACKETED KETTLE

FOOD SLICER

FLOOR-MOUNTED FOOD MIXER

STEAM-JACKETED KETTLE

TILTING BRAISING PAN

OVERHEAD POT RACK

CONVECTION STEAMER

COMBINATION OVEN-STEAMER

CONVECTION OVEN

WALL-MOUNTED HAND SINK

BLAST CHILLER AND FREEZER

CONVEYOR OVEN

REACH-IN REFRIGERATOR (OPTIONAL)

REACH-IN FREEZER

UNDERCOUNTER REFRIGERATOR

COLD AREA

GRIDDLE WITH CHEESE MELTER ABOVE

RANGE

HOT AREA

CHARBROILER

CHEF'S TABLE

TO STORAGE AND WALK-INS

PASS-THROUGH REFRIGERATOR

MICROWAVE ON UPPER SHELF

SOUP WELL

STAINLESS-STEEL COUNTER WITH SHELVES BELOW

PASS-THROUGH REFRIGERATOR

DISPLAY REACH-IN REFRIGERATOR

SODA DISPENSER

JUICE DISPENSER

ICE CREAM CABINET

WAIT STATION COUNTER WITH SINK

COFFEE BREWER

TEA MAKER

WALL-MOUNTED HAND SINK

COLD FOOD PREP/BANQUET STAGING   CHEF'S AREA   WAIT STAFF

TYPICAL KITCHEN PLAN

UNDERCOUNTER REFRIGERATOR

MICROWAVE SHELF

DOUBLE SHELF

VARIES

ROLL WARMER

HOT FOOD TABLE

36", TYP.

20", 28", 32"

28", 32"

MICROWAVE SHELF

SOUP WELLS

OPEN SHELVES

TRAY STORAGE

The chef's table is the heart of the kitchen operation. It is where hot and cold foods are arranged on plates for pickup by the wait staff. Since both the kitchen and the wait staff require access, the table is usually designed in an island configuration.

CHEF'S TABLE

COMPARTMENTS MAY HAVE ONE FULL OR TWO HALF-DOORS

DOOR OPENINGS ON EACH SIDE

ONE COMPARTMENT: 30"
TWO COMPARTMENTS: 58"
THREE COMPARTMENTS: 86"

63"

32"

This unit is typically placed either at the end of the chef's table or in the wall separating the service area from the kitchen.

PASS-THROUGH REFRIGERATION

ONE DOOR: 48"
TWO DOORS: 76"
THREE DOORS: 103"

19", 28"

CASTER

PULL-OUT DRAWER

35"

This unit has a capacity of 500 to 1,000 lbs (226 to 453 kg).

UNDERCOUNTER REFRIGERATOR/FREEZER

ONE OR TWO DOORS AVAILABLE

59" TO 71"

ONE DOOR: 30 1/4"
TWO DOORS: 41", 52 1/2", 62 3/4"

PUSH BAR

BUMPER

CASTER

29"

This cabinet is used to keep preplated meals hot.

MOBILE BANQUET CABINET

80"

42"   39"

This unit has cook/chill and cook/freeze options.

BLAST CHILLER AND FREEZER

John Birchfield; Birchfield Enterprises Inc.; Annapolis, Maryland

TEXTILES

FABRIC IN INTERIORS

The immensity of the textile industry is reflected in the vast number of uses of textiles in commercial interior projects. Fabric is used on walls as wallcoverings, stretched-fabric wall and ceiling systems, wall-mounted panels, and systems furniture panels; as vertical hangings for draperies, banners, and vertical louver blinds; as upholstery for seating; and as floor coverings, including carpet and rugs. Leather, commonly used as a luxury upholstery material, can also be used as a floor tile.

FIBERS

Textiles is the term given to any fabric composed of fibers, whether woven, knitted, felted, or manufactured by some other means. A fiber, the basic element of a textile, is a fine, hairlike strand that forms the basis of a yarn. Fibers are found in nature or are manufactured (synthetic). The characteristics that make a given fiber suitable for a particular end-use application are either inherent or engineered by production and processing techniques.

Fiber Types

Fibers range in length from a fraction of an inch to several miles, and can be categorized as *staple* or *filament* fibers. Filament fibers are stronger than staples. Longer fibers typically provide greater strength than shorter ones. The strength of a fiber helps determine the abrasion resistance of the final textile. In addition, yarns made from filaments and longer staples generally seem smoother. All natural fibers except silk are staple fibers. Staple fibers are short and typically measured in centimeters or inches. Most cotton is just over 1 in. (3 cm) in length; wool, between 1 and 8 in. (3 and 20 cm). Filament fibers, such as silk, and synthetic fibers are long and continuous and measured in meters or yards. Silk filaments can approach 2 miles in length, and synthetic fibers can be produced to any continuous length desired. Filament fibers can also be cut to staple fiber lengths.

Natural fibers originate from animal, plant, or mineral sources, and as such are produced seasonally. They can be susceptible to the forces of nature, such as the level of rainfall and attack from insects.

Synthetic, or manufactured, fibers are also produced from natural substances, some of which are inherently fibrous. However, they are not referred to as natural fibers because the usable fiber form is produced through industrial processing. Synthetic fibers are produced by extruding chemical solutions through a showerheadlike device called a *spinneret*. Centuries ago, the silkworm's method of extruding silk was identified as a technique that could possibly be adopted for fiber production. However, commercial production of the first synthetic fiber—rayon—did not begin until 1939. Synthetic fibers are categorized under generic names that refer to their chemical composition. Most are thermoplastic, meaning that they soften and melt when heated.

Natural Fibers

Cotton

Cotton is the most widely used plant fiber, and cotton fabric is used more in the apparel industry than in commercial interiors. Cotton fibers are fairly uniform in comparison with most other natural fibers and are relatively dimensionally stable. Like many cellulosic fibers, cotton has low elasticity and resiliency. It is one of the densest fibers, and wicks away moisture along the fiber and through the fabric. Cotton is, however, flammable and wrinkles easily.

Mercerized cotton is produced by treating cotton yarn under tension to increase its strength and reduce shrinkage. The process causes the fiber to swell slightly, making it appear rounder and smoother. The smoother surface increases the light reflection off the fiber surface, thus giving a more lustrous appearance.

Kapok

Kapok is derived from the seed pod of the Java kapok tree. It is too brittle to be spun into fiber but is soft enough to be used as cushioning material, and was once used for stuffing pillows and seat cushions. It is lightweight and nonabsorbent and can absorb about 30 times its weight in water.

Flax

Derived from the stalk of a plant, flax is referred to as a *bast fiber*. Flax provides a final fiber length of about 12 to 24 in. (300 to 600 mm). Probably the oldest fiber ever woven into fabric, flax was used for mummy wrappings in ancient Egypt.

TEXTILE FIBERS

GENERAL CHEMICAL TYPE	NATURAL			MAN-MADE	
	GENERIC TERM	SOURCE		GENERIC TERM	SOURCE
Cellulose (Plant)	Cotton Kapok	Seed	Cotton plant Kapok tree	Rayon Acetate Triacetate	Wood and cotton
	Hemp Jute Flax (linen) Ramie (China grass)	Stem	Hemp plant Jute plant Flax plant Ramie shrub		
	Sisal Pina	Leaf	Agave plant Pineapple plant		
	Coir	Nut husk	Coconut		
Protein (Animal)	Silk	Silkworm secretion	Moth larvae		
	Wool Mohair Angora Horsehair Alpaca Camel hair Cashmere Llama Vicuna	Hair	Sheep Angora goat Angora rabbit Horse mane and tail Alpaca Bactrian camel Cashmere goat Llama Vicuna		
Mineral	Asbestos	Asbestos rock fibers		Glass Metallic	Silica, sand, and limestone; various metals
Elastomers	Rubber	Rubber tree sap		Synthetic rubber Spandex	Chemicals
Synthesized				Acrylic Aramids Modacrylic Nylon Olefin Polyester Saran Vinyl Vinyon	Petroleum (manufactured polymers)

Source: D. Jackman and M. Dixon, The Guide to Textiles for Interior Designers; *Winnipeg, MB, Canada, Peguis Publishers Limited, 1983.*

Jute

Made from the stem and stalk of the jute plant, its fibers are harsh and brittle; it wrinkles easily and lints badly. These characteristics limit its use in interior finishes primarily to carpet and linoleum backing. Jute reacts to chemicals similarly to cotton and flax and has excellent resistance to microorganisms and insects.

Linen

Linen is derived from flax. It is extremely strong, provides virtually no elasticity, and tends to be brittle. It is not as soft or absorbent as cotton but is more resistant to mildew. Linen does not lint and resists fraying and seam slippage; it does, however, wrinkle and crease easily.

Ramie

Also referred to as *China grass*, ramie is produced from a perennial shrub. It is an exceptionally strong fiber and has a natural luster comparable to that of silk. Thin ramie fiber fabrics resemble fine linen, whereas coarse ramie fiber textiles can resemble canvas. Ramie tends to be stiff, nonelastic, and brittle, and is often blended with softer fibers such as cotton and rayon.

Sisal

Sisal is a leaf fiber named after a Mexican town in the Yucatan peninsula where it is grown. Sisal is also farmed in Africa and South America. It is a stiff and inflexible fiber that tends to stain and crush easily. Uses for sisal include floor mats and rugs.

Silk

The strongest natural fiber, silk varies in length from 1,000 to 1,700 yd (900 to 1,550 m) or longer and is more wrinkle-resistant than the natural cellulosic fibers. Like wool, silk is not degraded by cleaning solvents; however, it does deteriorate under ultraviolet (UV) radiation (sunlight). Silk is comparatively more expensive than other fibers, due to the labor-intensive manufacturing process.

The growth of silk moths for silk production is known as *sericulture*. Liquid silk is excreted from the head of the silkworm to form a cocoon around its body. Cocoons are dried in an oven, killing the pupae inside while preserving the integrity of the cocoons. The silk is then carefully unwrapped and treated for use as a fiber.

WOOL FIBER

WORSTED WOOL FIBER

WOOL

Wool

Wool is sheared primarily from domesticated sheep. Its resiliency and elasticity are exceptional, making it an excellent fiber for use in carpets, upholstery, and apparel. Wool carpet remains the standard by which synthetic fiber carpets are judged. It has good flexibility and can be reshaped by steaming or pressing. Wool burns slowly and is self-extinguishing. Cigarette burns are quickly extinguished with minimal noticeable damage.

Though wool is susceptible to damage by insects, finishing treatments are available to make the fabric unpalatable to moths. Wool fiber has almost no resistance to alkalis (the ingredients found in most detergents); therefore wool must usually be dry-cleaned.

Fiber labeled "wool" may contain unused wool yarn that has been recovered and reconstructed into new yarns. The Wool Products Labeling Act of 1939 was enacted to assist the consumer in understanding the origin of the wool in a fiber or fabric. "Virgin wool" is the designation for wool made into yarn for the first time. "Lamb's wool" is sheared from animals under eight months of age.

Asbestos

The only natural mineral found in fiber form, asbestos is completely fireproof and was used for many years in firefighters' apparel, hazardous industry applications, and domestic applications. Then it was discovered that, when inhaled, the insoluble, barbed-edge fibers become lodged in the lungs and cannot be expelled by coughing. Because lung cancer and other serious diseases have been associated with exposure to asbestos, its use in most applications is no longer legal.

TEXTILE SELECTION CRITERIA

CRITERIA	CHARACTERISTICS
Performance and Safety	
Functional Properties	Insulation, glare reduction, static reduction, fatigue reduction, acoustic control, mobility improvements, safety enhancement
Appearance Retention	Color retention, texture retention, resistance to pilling and snagging, soil hiding, soil repellency, soil shedding, soil release
Durability	Abrasion resistance, tear resistance, dimensional stability, fuzzy fiber loss, repairability, warranty availability
Structural Stability	Tuft bind strength, delamination strength, stability of yarn twist
Flame Resistance	Inherent or applied
Design and Performance Mandates	Flame resistance, indoor air quality, structural stability, colorfastness, wear resistance, functional properties, acoustical value, static reduction
Maintenance	
Cleanability	Washable, dry-cleanable, ease of stain removal, appearance after cleaning
Cleaning Location	On-site versus off-site cleaning
Level of Ironing Required	None, touch-up, extensive
Frequency of Cleaning	Daily, weekly, monthly
Cleaning Products Required	Toxic, biodegradable, readily available
Environmental Product Selection Criteria	
Manufacturing Issues	Effluents produced during manufacturing; products made of recycled materials
Product Issues	Potential for product recycling, potential impact of required cleaning agents
Cost and Installation Product Selection Criteria	
Initial Cost	Product price, accessories prices, fees for design professional, delivery charges, installation charges
Long-Term Costs	Maintenance costs, including equipment, cleaning agents, and labor; warranty costs; insurance costs; energy costs; interest charges
Installation Factors	Site preparation, labor, tools and level of skill needed, permanence: movable, removable, permanent

Source: Jan Yeager and Lura Teter-Justice, Textiles for Residential and Commercial Interiors; *New York, Fairchild Publications, 2000, pp. 15–16.*

Natural Rubber

In the 1920s, it was discovered that latex (liquid rubber) could be extruded into fiber. Its high elasticity, flexibility, and impermeability to water and air make it unique among natural fibers. Rubber fibers lose much of their strength through age, and deteriorate in sunlight, a trait also common to synthetic rubbers such as spandex.

Synthetic Cellulosic Fibers

Rayon

The first manufactured synthetic fiber—rayon—was originally referred to as "artificial silk." Rayon is fabricated principally from wood pulp. Two processes are used in the production of rayon: the *cuprammonium* and the *viscose* methods. The viscose is the major method used today.

The advantages of viscose rayon are that it blends well with other fibers; it is absorbent, and therefore dyes readily; it is economical to produce; and can be made to resemble cotton, linen, silk, or wool. Its disadvantages are that it is not particularly strong and loses strength when wet, has a low resiliency, and wrinkles easily.

Acetate and Triacetate

Although acetate and triacetate have similar chemical compositions, they behave differently as fibers. Acetate has poor resiliency, whereas triacetate has good resiliency. Acetate fibers are flexible, resulting in fabric with excellent draping qualities. It is a thermoplastic fiber, which is easily damaged by heat and wrinkles easily. Triacetate is processed differently from acetate, resulting in a fiber of greater stability and abrasion resistance. It can be heat-treated to prevent the heat sensitivity inherent to acetate. Permanent pleats can be set in triacetate.

Petroleum-Based Synthetic Fibers

Acrylic

First introduced in 1950 under the trade name Orlon, acrylic fiber can be cut into staple lengths and then mechanically bulked for an insulative, fluffy, wool-like effect. It can also be made to simulate the look and feel of silk in filament form. It is exceptionally light, providing bulk without weight, and blends well with other fibers. Acrylic fibers accept dyes well, providing a good selection of colors. However, some acrylics pill easily.

Modacrylics

Although similar to acrylics, modacrylics can withstand higher temperatures, a quality that has made them a popular choice in the manufacture of draperies and casements, as well as industrial products. Modacrylic fibers are also found in a number of specialty applications such as fake furs.

Aramids

Among the various modern synthetic fibers, aramids have unique properties. Alkalis, acids, and solvents have virtually no effect on them. Aramids are marketed under the trade names Nomex and Kevlar. Nomex is a high-temperature-resistant fiber used mostly in apparel such as firefighters' clothing and space suits. Kevlar is also a high-temperature-resistant fiber and is stronger than comparably sized steel. It is also used in bullet-resistant vests. Aramids are difficult to dye, but because they are not used for decorative purposes, usually this is not considered a drawback.

Nylon

Nylon, classified as a polymide, is one of the strongest synthetic fibers. It is highly elastic, with good elongation and recovery properties. Its great strength, high resiliency, and good abrasion resistance make it the most popular carpet fiber. Compared with the moisture absorbency of natural fibers, nylon's is low, so it dries quickly. However, this quality also makes it prone to the buildup of static electricity.

Nylon is available in many formulations. Nylon 6.6, the most widely used type for carpet fibers, has six carbon atoms per individual molecule in each of the two chemicals (hexamethylene diamine and adipic acid) used to make it.

Olefin

Olefin (polypropylene and polyethylene) is relatively inexpensive and very popular for use as a carpet fiber and fabric-type wallcovering. Although today the most widely used olefin fiber is polypropylene, polyethylene was the first olefin fiber to reach commercial importance; for many years it was used as upholstery for airplane seats. Olefin is one of the lightest synthetic fibers and has excellent elastic recovery. Because of its outstanding resistance to stains and crushing and its lack of static generation, olefin continues to increase in popularity as a carpet fiber. Air barriers in buildings, such as Tyvek, are nonwoven olefin textiles.

Vinyon

Vinyon, commonly called *vinyl* or *PVC,* is durable and easy to clean. The most popular application for vinyon in the contract market is as an upholstery fabric, to simulate leather or suede.

Simulated leather fabrics are produced by extruding or expanding polymer solutions. The most commonly used polymers are PVC and polyurethane. Because polymer films have little or no porosity, these fabrics may become uncomfortable in hot or humid weather. The synthetic sheet is bonded to a backing fabric, generally a knit, to give the textile the dimensional stability required for upholstery. Grain markings are embossed into the synthetic film to enhance its appearance as leather.

Simulated suede's surface texture is achieved by one of two processes:

- *Flocking* refers to an electrostatic process whereby charged flock fibers are deposited onto an adhesive coated substrate and then oven-dried.
- *Sueding* or *emerizing* roughens the surface and orients the flock in every direction, unlike brushing and smoothing finishes, which raise the fabric pile in a single direction. This is done by a series of sandpaper-covered disks, which revolve against the flocked surface.

Saran

This relatively expensive fiber is often replaced by olefin fibers in the manufacture of fabric. Saran is, however, stronger and heavier, tough, and durable to maintain. Saran has applications in upholstery, draperies, and some outdoor textile products.

Polyester

The initial research by Du Pont that led to the discovery of nylon also led to the invention of polyester. Among the many outstanding characteristics of polyester is its low moisture absorbency, wrinkle resistance, high strength and resiliency, abrasion resistance, and dimensional stability. Polyester also has excellent crease resistance and is easy to maintain. It is frequently blended with other fibers to enhance its performance.

Mineral Fibers

Glass

Although glass has been used for centuries, it was not until the mid-1800s that it was first produced in fiber form. Glass fiber is unaffected by fire and is sometimes used to stitch upholstery fabrics for seating that complies with California Technical Bulletin 133, a standard commonly used for evaluating the flammability of furniture. Sheer casements are popular applications for fabrics made of glass fibers. Glass fiber has a very low abrasion resistance. Owens-Corning's trade name for its glass fiber product is Fiberglas.

Metallic Fibers

Gold, silver, and aluminum fibers are produced by splitting very thin sheets of metal into narrow ribbons. Because they are weak and soft, they are often combined around a stronger core fiber. The capability of aluminum to be colored makes it the most popular option in this category. In fibers such as Mylar, a polyester coating is applied to the aluminum fiber. In other products, both the polyester and aluminum may be finely ground and combined to produce tarnish-free, washable, but somewhat delicate fibers. Stainless-steel fibers provide strength, tear and abrasion resistance, and prevent static buildup. The fibers can also be used to transmit and radiate heat when connected to a power source.

Elastomeric Fibers

Elastomers are rubberlike substances with fiber forms that offer exceptional elongation. The most common of these is spandex, which is composed of segmented polyurethane. Spandex fibers can be used in the filament form, as a wrapped or core yarn in collaboration with other fibers wrapped around it, or as a core spun yarn, where stable fibers are fed around the spandex core filament to produce a single yarn.

Yarns

The term *yarn* refers to the twisting together of fibers to create a continuous strand. Yarns can have marked differences in their degrees of twist, textural characteristics, complexity, and relative fineness. Simple yarn constructions are common in the structure of carpets and rugs. They are uniform in diameter along their length, and may be composed of a single yarn or a number of single yarns twisted or plied together in different ways.

More complex decorative yarns are applied in textile wallcoverings, upholstery curtains, and drapery fabrics. Complex yarns may contain loops, curls, or other irregular textural effects to add textural and visual interest to the textile. They may contain variations in the level of twist along their length, decorative three-dimensional features, or changes of fiber content.

TWO-PLY YARN

SINGLE YARN

SYNTHETIC FIBER TRADE NAMES

TRADE NAME	FIBER	MANUFACTURER	CHARACTERISTICS	USE
Anso	Nylon	Honeywell	Filament and staple form; soil-resistant	Carpet
Antron III	Nylon	Du Pont	Filament and staple form; trilobal nylon 6.6	Carpet
Cordura	Nylon	Du Pont	High-tenacity; nylon 6.6	Upholstery
Hollofil	Polyester	Du Pont	—	Filling
Kevlar	Aramid	Du Pont	Filament form; bullet-resistant	Upholstery liner (Cal-Tech 133)
Micromattique	Polyester	Du Pont	Microdenier	Draperies
Nomex	Aramid	Du Pont	Filament and staple form; flame-resistant, heat-resistant	Upholstery liner (Cal-Tech 133)
Trevira	Polyester	Treviva GmbH	Flame-resistant	Cubicle curtains
Ultron	Nylon	Monsanto	Nylon 6.6; antistatic	Carpet
Zefstat	Nylon	BASF	—	Carpet
Zeftron	Nylon	BASF	—	Carpet

SPINNERET

Yarns are classified into two types: *spun* and *filament*. Spun yarns are composed of staple fibers twisted together. Filament yarns are composed of continuous strands made from either a spinneret-generated synthetic fiber or from silk.

Smooth, parallel filament yarns may be modified by the use of *throwing* or *texturing*. The great length of silk and filament yarns allow them to be directly twisted together, or "thrown," without the need for spinning. In the texturing process, yarn may be given a more natural appearance, greater elasticity, or a more attractive tactility. The texturing processes may also provide greater bulk or apparent volume in order to achieve greater covering power. Yarns modified in this way are referred to as *bulked continuous filament* (BCF).

Spinning is required for all natural and staple synthetic fibers. BCFs are typical of nylon and polypropylene fibers and generally offer better wear; that said, staple fibers provide the wool-like appearance that is desired in many textiles.

Monofilament yarns, unlike spun and filament yarns, are manufactured directly by the fiber producer. A single filament with a relatively large diameter is drawn and heat-set. Such yarns may be used in the production of lightweight transparent window coverings and as sewing thread for a number of interior textile products.

Yarns are sold by weight, and yarn designations express the relationship between length and weight. The *denier system* is used for filament yarns, and the *yarn count system* is used for spun yarns.

Denier is a unit of yarn measurement equal to the weight in grams of 9,000 meters of the yarn. The higher the denier, the heavier the yarn, and generally the better the strength, resiliency, and abrasion resistance. For example, a 15-denier yarn would be suitable for sheer hosiery; a 2,200-denier yarn would be suitable for carpet.

The yarn count system is a relative gauge of a spun yarn's weight. Heavier yarns are designated by lower yarn count numbers. For example, a 70-count yarn is quite fine, whereas a 10-count yarn is thick and heavy.

PERFORMANCE OF YARNS IN FABRICS

YARN TYPE	DURABILITY	COMFORT	APPEARANCE	CARE
Spun Yarns	Weaker than filament yarns. Ply yarns stronger than simple yarns. Fabrics tend to resist raveling and running.	Warmer, more absorbent.	Fabrics are cottonlike or wool-like in appearance. Fabrics lint and pill.	Yarns do not snag readily.
Filament Yarns	Stronger than spun yarns. Fabrics ravel and run readily.	Cooler; least absorbent.	Fabrics are smooth and lustrous. Fabrics do not lint or pill readily.	Yarns may snag. Resist soiling.
Textured Filament Yarns	Stronger than spun yarns. Fabrics ravel and run less than those made with filament yarns, but more than those made with spun yarns.	Warmer than filament yarns. More absorbent than filament yarns. Stretch more than other yarns.	Fabrics are less lustrous; more similar to those made of spun yarns. Fabrics do not lint, but may pill.	Yarns likely to snag. Soil more readily than filament yarns.
Novelty Yarns	Weaker than filament yarns. Most resist raveling.	Warmer. More absorbent if part is spun.	Interesting texture. Greater novelty effects show wear sooner than smaller novelty effects. Fabrics lint and pill.	Yarns likely to snag. Soil readily.

Source: Norma R. Hollen, Jane Sadler, Anna Langford, Textiles; *New York, Macmillan, 1979, p. 303.*

Yarnlike Structures

A number of elements employed in interior textiles are considered to be yarnlike structures. These components are composed of textile fibers that, although referred to as yarns, are produced with techniques other than throwing or spinning. Included in this group are chenille yarns, felted wool yarns, and metallic yarn. Natural rush, sea grass, and cane, used in handwoven seats and backs of chairs, can also be categorized as yarnlike in their structure.

Woven Fabrics

The majority of textiles used in commercial interiors are woven. Woven fabrics are made by interlacing yarns at right angles to each other on a loom. Woven

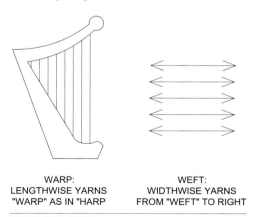

WARP:
LENGTHWISE YARNS
"WARP" AS IN "HARP

WEFT:
WIDTHWISE YARNS
FROM "WEFT" TO RIGHT

WARP AND WEFT

fabrics commonly have one set of lengthwise yarns, referred to as *warps* or *ends*, and one set of crosswise yarns called *weft yarns, woof yarns,* or *filling yarns.*

The fabric count is employed to determine the closeness of the yarn in a material. The count refers to the number of warp and weft yarns in 1 sq in.(6 sq cm).

Special Effects Weaves

Special effects weaves use one or more of the basic weaves for the purposes of creating cut or loop piles, multicolored designs, or particular textures.

Dobby weaves are popular for contract fabrics with small dots, geometric shapes, or florals woven in. They are produced on looms with dobby attachments that mechanically determine which warp threads will be raised or lowered. Piqué, waffle cloth, and huck toweling are dobby weaves.

Matelassés are double cloths in which extra sets of yarns are used to create a puffed or quilted effect.

Crepes are produced by plain or satin weaving. The yarn is twisted so tightly that it has a crinkled or pebbled appearance. Textured yarns are sometimes used to create crepes.

Pile Weaves

Woven pile fabrics are constructed by weaving an additional set of warp or filling yarns into the ground, or basic, yarns. This produces a characteristic three-dimensional effect. The category includes velvet, velveteen, and corduroy fabrics.

Jacquard Weaves

Detailed woven patterns are produced on more complex looms. The Jacquard loom employs a series of punched cards. Each hole in a jacquard card controls the action of one warp yarn. The method is used in tapestries, brocades, and damask. The jacquard process is time-consuming, making this one of the most costly weave types.

Customer's Own Material (C.O.M.)

Seating manufacturers typically supply upholstery fabric options for their chairs. These fabric selections have been tested on their seating and have performed satisfactorily with regard to wear and flammability. Often, however, a designer will find the upholstery selection limiting and will instead select a fabric from a textile manufacturer. Fabric that is not supplied by the fabricator (seating manufacturer, drapery supplier, etc.) is referred to as the *customer's own material* (C.O.M.) or *customer's own leather* (C.O.L.). Written approval from the fabricator is usually required for the use of C.O.M. The fabricator must verify that the material is acceptable as an upholstery fabric. (Note that "customer" in these terms does not refer to the designer's customer; it refers to the manufacturer's customer—the party placing the order—which is the furniture, furnishings, and equipment (FF&E) contractor (furniture dealer, etc.). The material is purchased separately and supplied to the fabricator for application. The FF&E contractor is responsible for the acquisition and coordination of C.O.M.)

APPEARANCE

The following performance factors influence the appearance of a fabric:

- *Luster* is the effect of light rays breaking and reflecting on the surface of a fabric. Silk has a relatively high luster, unlike cotton and wool, which have a low luster. Fabric construction and finishing will have an influence on the final luster of a fabric.
- *Fuzzing* refers to the accumulation of displaced fibers on the surface of a fabric. Pilling occurs as the fibers become tangled and rolled into balls, some of which, depending on the absorbency of the fibers, may be difficult to remove.
- *Electrical attraction of dust, thread, hair, and lint* to a fabric surface affects the appearance of the fabric. Hydrophobic, or nonabsorbent, materials will cling to the surface of a static-prone fabric.
- *Color change* of a fabric can be attributed to fading, crocking, and color loss. *Fading* occurs when dyestuffs are adversely affected by constant exposure to ultraviolet rays, effects of artificial light, or airborne pollutants. *Crocking* refers to the displacement of dyestuff through excessive rubbing or wear. *Color loss* may be attributed to the effects of cleaning agents. If the colorfastness of a particular fabric is unknown or is not guaranteed by the manufacturer, testing should be done on a sample before final selection.
- *Hand* refers to how a textile feels and drapes; it can be affected by the fiber type, yarn, and fabric construction. Hand is a crucial factor in the aesthetic appreciation of a textile. Additional modifications can also be achieved though finishing processes.

BASIC WEAVES

NAME	INTERLACING PATTER	GENERAL CHARACTERISTICS	TYPICAL FABRICS
Plain	Each warp interlaces with each filling.	Most interlacing per square inch. Balanced or unbalanced. Wrinkles most. Ravels most. Less absorbent.	Batiste Voile Percale Gingham Broadcloth Crash Cretonne
Basket	Two or more yarns in either warp or filling or both are woven as one in a plain weave.	Looks balanced. Fewer interlacing than plain weave. Flat looking. Wrinkles less. Ravels more.	Oxford Monk's cloth
Twill	Warp and filling yarns float over two or more yarns from the opposite direction in a regular progression to the right or left.	Diagonal lines. Fewer interlacing than plain weave. Wrinkles less. Ravels more. More pillable than plain weave. Can have higher count.	Serge Surah Denim Gabardine Herringbone
Satin	Warp and filling yarns float over two or more yarns from the opposite direction in a regular progression to the right or left.	Flat surface. Most are lustrous. Can have high count. Fewer interlacing. Long float; subject to slippage and snagging.	Satin Sateen
Crepe	An irregular interlacing of yarns. Floats of unequal lengths in no discernable pattern.	Rough-looking surface. Crepe-looking.	Granite cloth Moss crepe Sand crepe
Dobby	Special loom attachment allows up to 32 different interlacing.	Small figures. Cord-type fabrics.	Shirting madras Huck toweling Waffle cloth Pique
Jacquard	Each warp yarn controlled individually. An infinite number of interlacing is possible.	Large figures.	Damask Brocade Tapestry
Pile	Extra warp or filling yarns are woven in to give a cut or an uncut three-dimensional fabric.	Flush or looped surface. Warm. Wrinkles less. Pile may flatten.	Velvet Velveteen Corduroy Furlike fabrics Wilton rugs Terrycloth
Slack-tension	A type of pile weave. Some warp yarns can be released from tension to form raised areas in the cloth or a pile surface.	Crinkle stripes or pile surface. Absorbent. Nonwrinkling.	Seersucker Terrycloth Frieze
Leno	A doup attachment on the loom causes one of two yarns to be carried over the other on alternating passing of the filling yarns.	Meshlike fabric. Lower thread count fabrics that are resistant to slippage.	Marquisette Curtain fabrics
Swivel	An attachment to the loom. Small shuttles carrying extra filling yarns weave in small dots.	Dots on both sides of fabric as filling floats.	Dotted Swiss

Source: Norma R. Hollen, Jane Sadler, Anna Langford, Textiles; New York, Macmillan, 1979, p. 162.

There are three basic weaves: plain, twill, and satin. Variations and combinations of these types form other weaves.

PROPERTIES OF WOVEN FABRICS

FABRIC TYPE	PROPERTIES
High-thread count	Firmness, strength, cover, body, compactness, stability, wind repellency, water repellency, fire retardancy, reduced raveling of seams.
Low-thread count	Flexibility, permeability, pliability, better drape, higher shrinkage potential, more seam raveling.
Balanced	Less seam slippage; warp and filling wear evenly, resulting in holes.
Unbalanced (usually more warp)	Seam slippage in low count; warp yarns wear out first, leaving strings (common in upholstery fabrics). In plain weave, crosswise ribs give interesting surface.
Floats	Luster, smoothness, flexibility, resiliency, tendency to ravel and snag; seam slippage in low count.

Source: Norma R. Hollen, Jane Sadler, Anna Langford, Textiles; New York, Macmillan, 1979, p. 161.

FABRIC CONSTRUCTION

The plain weave process involves one warp yarn and one weft yarn alternately passing over one another. This results in no particular surface pattern or texture; this makes plain weave textiles ideal backgrounds for printed fabrics. Plain weaves wear well but tend to wrinkle.

PLAIN WEAVE

FIVE-THREAD SATIN WEAVE

Each yarn floats over at least four yarns, resulting in a smooth, lustrous surface. Snagging may pose a problem with the textile because longer lengths of yarn appear on the surface of the textile. Sateen is commonly used in drapery linings.

SATIN WEAVE

FIVE-THREAD SATEEN WEAVE

TWO-TWO TWILL WEAVE

THREE-THREE TWILL WEAVE

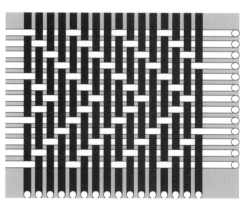

HERRINGBONE WEAVE

In twill weave, each warp yarn passes over and then under the weft yarns as in the plain weave, but the sequence is started slightly higher (or lower) on each successive yarn. A diagonal pattern is created. Herringbone, denim, and gabardine are twill weaves.

TWILL WEAVE

A fabric may also be assessed by the degree of elasticity along a 45° angle between warp and weft, known as the *true bias*. The lengthwise edges of the fabric are called *selvages*.

SELVAGE AND BIAS

WEFT KNIT
Weft knitting is based on the handknitting technique. The process produces flat or tubular goods classified as single or double knits.

WARP KNIT
Warp knitting employs very fast machine techniques capable of producing varying weights of plain or tricot knit fabrics, including fine netting and fabrics intended for industrial use.

KNITTED FABRICS

PERFORMANCE

Abrasion Resistance

Although abrasion resistance is associated with durability, the capability of a fabric to withstand deterioration varies with the application. Abrasion test results are helpful when they are used for purposes of comparison but are not a reliable prediction of actual wear-life.

Abrasion resistance for fabric is often stated in terms of the number of cycles it can endure on a specified machine. The Oscillatory Cylinder Method, commonly called the "Wyzenbeek test" after the man who developed the testing equipment, is the traditional test for abrasion resistance. The Taber Abraser test is sometimes used for fabric but is most often used for testing carpet.

Wear Resistance

The wear resistance of fabric is affected by many factors, including the type and length of the fiber; the structure of the yarn; the construction of the fabric; and the type, kind, and amount of finishing material added to the fibers, yarns, or fabric.

Absorbency

Absorbency refers to the fabric's capability to absorb moisture. Some fibers are stronger when wet, others weaken or show no change; this is an important factor in determining the cleaning methods to use to retain the look of a textile. Absorbency is an important factor in static buildup, stain removal, and dimensional stability should the fabric become wet. Fibers that absorb moisture easily are referred to as *hydrophilic*. Fibers that have difficulty absorbing moisture are known as *hydrophobic*.

Elasticity, Elongation, and Recovery

Elasticity is the capability of the fabric to increase in length when under tension and to return to its original shape when the tension is released, an important factor in maintaining the appearance of upholstered furniture. Elongation addresses the point at which a fabric will break when stretched. Recovery refers to the capability of a fabric to regain its shape after periods of extended elongation, a crucial consideration in upholstery fabrics.

Acoustical Transparency

Occasionally, a fabric will be used for the covering of a speaker or other sound-transmitting device. Hence, the fabric should be acoustically transparent, to minimize sound transmission blockage. Consult with an acoustical engineer and test the fabric to determine if it is suitable for use in this condition. Typically, an open-weave fabric allows sound to pass through more effectively than a more densely woven fabric.

Fire Resistance

Fibers have varying degrees of resistance to heat and flame. In general, lighter, more open fabrics will burn more freely than denser material. Finishing also plays a crucial role in the resistance of a fabric to fire; effectiveness may decrease over time, and cleaning processes may reduce the amount of fire resistance.

ESTIMATING FABRIC YARDAGE

FABRIC WIDTH	PLAIN FABRIC	2–14" (50–355 MM) REPEAT	15"–24" (380–610 MM) REPEAT	25"–27" (635–685 MM) REPEAT	28"–36" (710–915 MM) REPEAT
54" (1370 mm)	+ 0%	+ 10%	+ 15%	+ 20%	+ 25%
50" (1270 mm)	10%	20%	25%	30%	35%
48" (1220 mm)	15%	25%	30%	35%	40%
45" (1145 mm)	40%	50%	55%	60%	65%
36" (915 mm)	50%	60%	65%	70%	75%

Fabrics with a *repeat* (a repeated pattern) or narrower fabric will require more yardage than a standard 54-in.- (1,370-mm-) wide piece.

PROPERTIES OF MAJOR TEXTILES

PROPERTIES	COTTON	FLAX	WOOL	SILK	ACETATE	VISCOSE RAYON	TRIACETATE	ACRYLIC	GLASS	NYLON	OLEFIN	POLYESTER
Abrasion resistance	Good	Fair	Fair	Fair	Poor	Fair	Poor	Fair	Poor	Excellent	Excellent	Good
Absorbency (% M.R.)	8.5	12	13.5	11	6.5	11	3.5	1.5	0	4.5	0.1	1
Drapability	Fair	Poor	Good	Excellent	Excellent	Good	Excellent	Good	Poor	Good	Fair	Fair
Wash or dry-clean	Either	Either	DC	Either	DC	Either	Either	Either	Hand Wash	Either	Either	Either
Sunlight Resistance	Fair	Good	Good	Poor	Good	Fair	Good	Excellent	Excellent	Poor	Good	Good
Hand	Good	Good	Fair–Excellent	Excellent	Excellent	Good	Excellent	Good	Poor	Fair	Fair	Fair
Pilling resistance	Good	Good	Fair	Good	Good	Good	Good	Fair	Excellent	Poor	Good	Very–poor
Resiliency	Poor	Poor	Good	Fair	Fair	Poor	Good	Good	Excellent	Good	Excellent	Excellent
Static resistance	Good	Good	Fair	Fair	Fair	Good	Fair	Poor	Excellent	Poor	Good	Very Poor
Strength (Grams/Denier)	3.0/5.0 Good	6.6/8.4 Excellent	0.8/2.0 Poor	3.9/4.5 Good	0.8/1.5 Poor	0.7/6.0 Poor–Good	0.8/1.4 Poor	1.8/3.5 Fair	6.0/7.0 Excellent	2.5/7.5 Excellent	4.8/7.0 Good	2.5/9.5 Excellent
Thermoplastic	No	No	No	No	Yes	No	Yes	Yes	Yes	Yes	Yes	Yes

Source: A. Cohen; Beyond Basic Textiles; New York, Fairchild Publications, 1982, p. 5.

Microorganism and Insect Resistance

Although some fibers have a natural resistance to mildew, fungi, and bacteria, others are susceptible in certain environmental conditions. Moisture and warmth and the buildup of soil on a fabric may promote microorganic growth. Bacteriostatic finishes are often used to protect vulnerable materials. Particular fibers may also attract insects such as moths, carpet beetles, and weevils. Treatments and finishes that inhibit insect activity should be considered.

FABRIC FINISHING

Surface treatments can be applied to affect the performance of a fabric. Fabrics with applied treatments may stiffen from the resin, decrease in abrasion resistance and absorption, and change color. When considering fabric treatments, apply each to a sample to verify the desired effect.

Water Resistance

A large number of silicone water-repellent finishes are available. Effective alternatives are fluorochemical finishes, which can be applied with other finishing treatments.

Stain Resistance

Stain-resistant treatments make most fabrics resistant to oil- and water-based stains. These treatments are usually spray-applied and rarely have an effect on flame-resistant treatments applied to the same fabric. Fluids bead up on the surface of the treated fabric and do not spread, thus can be easily removed. These finishes are odorless, harmless, and do not alter the hand of the fabric.

Flame Resistance

To comply with building and fire code requirements, fabrics must sometimes be treated with flame-resistant finishes. The type of fabric will determine which process is appropriate. The two types of flame-resistant treatments are polymers and salines.

- *A polymer flame-resistant treatment* is applied through an immersion and heat-setting process. Shrinkage can occur as a result of such a treatment. In some fabrics, there will be a noticeable change in color or stiffness. Although quite durable, most polymer flame-resistant treatments will eventually wash out if the fabric is dry-cleaned.
- *Saline flame-resistant treatments* are less expensive, but are not as durable as polymer solutions. The salt solution has a corrosive effect on metals, such as upholstery tacks and staples, and may leach out.

Flame-resistant backings provide far more protection against the spread of fire than flame-resistant treatments. Aramid fabrics, such as Du Pont's Kevlar, are laminated to the back of upholstery fabric. Lamination reduces the amount of labor involved in applying the barrier fabric between the seat cushion and the finish fabric. Instead of being upholstered twice, first with the aramid and then with the upholstery fabric, the seat is upholstered only once with the laminated fabric.

REACTIONS OF UNMODIFIED FIBERS TO HEAT AND FLAME

FIBER	HEAT RESISTANCE	NEAR FLAME	IN FLAME	REMOVED FROM FLAME	ODOR AND RESIDUE
Cotton	150°C 300°F	No shrinkage; ignites on contact	Burns quickly	Continues burning	Burning paper odor; light fluffy ash
Flax	260°C 500°F	No shrinkage; ignites on contact	Burns quickly	Continues burning	Burning paper odor; light fluffy ash
Wool	132°C 275°F	Curls away from flame	Burns slowly	Self-extinguishing	Burning hair odor; small brittle bead
Silk	135°C 275°F	Curls away from flame	Burns slowly, sputters	Usually self-extinguishing	Burning hair odor; crushable beadlike residue
Rayon	177°C 350°F	No shrinkage; ignites on contact	Burns quickly	Continues burning	Burning paper odor; very little ash
Acetate	177°C 350°F	Fuses and melts away from flame; ignites quickly	Burns quickly	Continues rapid burning	Acrid odor; irregular hard, black bead
Triacetate	232°C 450°F	As acetate	As acetate	As acetate	As acetate
Acrylic	150°C 300°F	Fuses and melts away from flame; ignites quickly	Burns rapidly with hot flame; sputters, melts	Continues burning and molten polymer drops off	Acrid odor; irregular hard, black bead
Modacrylic	150°C 300°F	Fuses and melts away from flame	Burns slowly, if at all; melts	Self-extinguishing	Acrid odor; irregular hard, black bead
Nylon Nylon 6.6	150°C 300°F	Melts away from flame; shrinks, fuses	Burns slowly with melting	Self-extinguishing	Celerylike odor; hard, tough gray or brown bead
Olefin	75°C 165°F	Fuses; shrinks from flame	Melts and burns	Continues burning and melting with sooty smoke	Paraffin wax odor; tough brownish bead
Polyester	120°C 250°F	Fuses, melts, and shrinks from flame	Burns slowly with melting	Self-extinguishing	Chemical odor; dark, tough bead
Saran	115°C 240°F	Fuses, melts, and shrinks from flame	Melts; yellow flame	Self-extinguishing	Chemical odor; crisp tough bead
Glass	315°C 600°F	Will not burn	Softens; glows red	Hardens; may change shape	No odor; hard white bead
Metallic	Variable, dependent on coating, if any	Pure metal: no reaction; coated metal: melts, fuses, and shrinks	Glows red; burns as coating	Hardens as coating	No odor; skeleton outline as coating
Vinyon	65°C 150°F	Fuses and melts away from flame	Burns, melts	Self-extinguishing	Acrid odor; irregular hard, irregular black bead

Source: D. Jackman and M. Dixon, The Guide to Textiles for Interior Designers; *Winnipeg, MB, Canada, Peguis Publishers Limited, 1983, p. 116.*

Antistatic Treatment

The complete removal of static buildup remains a challenge for textile chemists, especially in fabrics that will undergo regular laundering or dry-cleaning operations. Fabric softeners prove effective in reducing static by coating the fibers and restricting electrical conductivity. Finishes incorporated into the fabric fibers are also proving successful.

Mothproofing

Soiled carpets and upholstery are particularly prone to attack by moth larvae. Treatment of the fibers ensures that protection remains despite regular cleaning. New mothproofing systems are being developed to reduce the attraction of the wool to the moth larvae.

Bacterial Protection

Fibers that are exposed to moisture and that contain fungi, microbes, and bacteria lead to a buildup of mildew, mold, and rot. A wide range of materials are prone to bacterial buildup, which can lead to the spread of infection and produce unpleasant odors.

Bacteriostatic and antimicrobial finishes may be applied to the fabric yarn or be added to the fiber during manufacture. Many other finishes contain such repellents, and various products enable the user to maintain a sufficient level of protection.

Insulating Finishes

Plastic and aluminum adhesive coatings are occasionally used to ensure thermal protection. The performance of closely hung drapery panels may be improved. Both may increase heat retention in the winter and reflect the heat of the sun in the summer.

Minimum Care Finishing

Finishing resins provide crease resistance and make it easier to press fabrics. The resins react chemically with the molecular structure of the natural fibers to form a cross-linking system that holds the fabric in a particular configuration. This finishing process is most commonly used in cotton fabrics blended with polyester.

COLORING AND PRINTING

Prior to the middle of the nineteenth century, all dyestuffs were derived from natural sources. With the 1858 discovery of mauve, a coal tar derivative, the development of man-made dyes has made it possible to employ a far greater palette of colored fabrics in interior spaces. A crucial factor in ensuring colorfast fabrics is to match the appropriate dyestuff to the fiber used. Synthetic fibers require very specific dyes, which are often developed with each new fiber type.

Dyeing Methods

Dyeing methods include fiber, yarn, piece, and polychromatic dyeing:

- *Fiber dyeing* ensures greater colorfastness and excellent color penetration. The dye is applied to the natural fiber in its raw state or to the molten polymer or fiber solution. The result is an integrally colored fiber.
- *Yarn dyeing* is one of the oldest methods of fabric coloring. The fibers are spun into yarn prior to the dyeing process.
- *Piece dyeing* refers to the coloration of woven material. The process is the least expensive and easiest way to achieve solid-color fabrics; however, an even distribution of dyestuff can be achieved only if the fabric is made from one fiber type.
- *Polychromatic dyeing* enables random patterns to be dyed into the fabric. Dyestuffs are applied at varying speeds and in different directions through jets or rollers. Computer technology is providing greater options for pattern development.

Printing Methods

In dye bath printing, also known as *resist,* a portion of the fabric is made resistant to the effects of the dye. Three printing techniques for commercial interior finish fabrics are direct, screen, and discharge printing.

Direct Printing

Direct printing, also called *roller, calender,* or *cylinder printing,* is the most common printing method. Colors are deposited on the fabric in the same manner as printing wallpaper or a newspaper. One roller is required for each color. The fabric is passed between the etched color rollers. Most direct-printed fabrics have a white background. Direct-printing types are as follows:

- *Block prints* are produced by stamping the fabric with inked, carved blocks.
- *Flat-bed printing* is an outgrowth of block printing and has been used for more than 200 years. It is especially effective for small runs and large-pattern repeats.

Screen Printing

Screen prints are made by forcing dye through a stencil. A different stencil is used for each color dye required. Screen-printing techniques are as follows:

- *Flat-bed screen printing* uses a squeegee to push dye through a stencil onto fabric that is stretched flat. The process is semiautomatic and can print about 7 yd (6.4 m) a minute.
- *Rotary screen printing* combines roller and screen printing and uses a perforated cylinder screen to apply color. It is a fast, frequently used process, capable of printing 110 yd (100 m) a minute.

Discharge Printing

Discharge printing is a reverse procedure employed to remove dye from a colored fabric in a controlled pattern. A rotary screen-printing device, with bleach or a chemical dye remover, is used to make a design. Polka dot or small floral prints are usually discharge printed. This method can be combined with color printing to simultaneously remove color and print.

Resources: D. Jackman and M. Dixon; The Guide to Textiles for Interior Designers; *Winnipeg, MB, Canada, Peguis Publishers Limited, 1983.*
Jan Yeager and Lura Teter-Justice; Textiles for Residential and Commercial Interiors; *New York, Fairchild Publications, 2000.*

MASTERSPEC®; published by ARCOM; Salt Lake City, Utah, and Alexandria, Virginia

LEATHER

GENERAL

Leather is processed animal skin, primarily from cattle. Three factors contribute to the high cost of leather: the processes used are labor-intensive; the aniline dyes used to color leather are costly; and there is a high rejection rate of the finished hides.

Cattle hide, or cowhide, refers to the skin of a fully grown cow. Such skins are large hides, ranging from 50 to 60 sq ft (4.6 to 5.5 sq m). The center portion of the hide, called the bend, yields the best-quality hide.

Calfskin is the hide of a young animal and is considerably smaller, about 25 sq ft to 35 sq ft (2.3 sq m to 3.2 sq m) Calfskin is characterized by its softness, suppleness, and fine grain.

In calculating the yield of a hide, consider a waste factor of about 10% to 15%. Each yard (0.9 m) of 36-in.-(900-mm-) wide fabric requires about 16 sq ft (1.4 sq m) of leather. Each yard (0.9 m) of 54-in.- (1,370-mm-) wide fabric requires 18 sq ft (1.7 sq m) of leather.

LEATHER PROCESSING

Four steps are required to transform leather hide into a suitable upholstery material: curing and cleaning, tanning, coloring, and finishing.

Curing

Curing involves salting the raw hides to slow down bacterial action that results in the decomposition of the material. Hides are thoroughly cleaned, defleshed, and dehaired.

Tanning

Tanning replaces the natural gelatinous materials found in the skin with tanning solutions; this puts life back into a leather, making it strong, supple, and enduring. There are three primary tanning agents: mineral, vegetable, and a combination of the two:

- *Mineral tanning*. Cured and cleaned hides are immersed in a solution comprising chromium-based salts and oils. About 90% of leather today is tanned by this method. Mineral-tanned hides accept dyes well, allowing rich, vibrant colors to be created.
- *Vegetable tanning*. Vegetable-tanned hides have a heavier feel. They are often left undyed. Vegetable-tanned hides become pliable when wet, yet retain their shape when dry. This tanning solution contains tree bark, typically oak, which provide tannins, which swell the hides. This also gives the leathers a distinct smell.
- *Combination tanning*. This tanning method produces a hide that is quite supple, with a limited acceptance of dyes.

CATTLE HIDE CALF HIDE

HIDE SIZES *Source:* Edelman Leather Handbook, *Teddy and Arthur Edelman, Ltd. Hawleyville, Connecticut*

Hide Coloring

Coloring may be used to camouflage uneven natural color or provide an overall color to the leather.

Aniline dyes are translucent. They do not obscure the natural grain pattern and surface imperfections. The best-quality upholstery leathers are aniline-dyed. The dye penetrates the depth of the hide completely so that as the leather wears, the color remains the same.

Semianiline dyes contain some pigments. The normal variation from one dyed hide to another can be quite noticeable. The use of semianiline dyes helps to ensure uniformity in color among many hides.

Finishing

Finishing refers to the final stages in leather processing. Lubricants and softening agents may be applied to increase suppleness. Imperfections in the hide surface may be removed by shaving or abrasion. Embossing techniques may be employed to increase or unify surface texture. Resins, waxes, and lacquer-based compounds may then be applied and polished to produce a glazed finish.

Leather is categorized by the surface imperfections and how it is processed, as described here:

- *Full-grain leather* (or full-top-grain leather, as it is sometimes called) possesses the genuine original grain of the hide. It has the fewest surface imperfections, hence constitutes the most expensive

SPLIT LEATHER

type of hide. The surface is not embossed or altered in any way; it is the full, natural hide.
- In *top-grain leather*, the original surface pattern, including scars from barbed wire or brands, is removed by abrasion. This skinless surface is embossed with a pattern, typically resembling the grain of the skin that was removed.
- *Split leathers* are made by slicing the hide into two or three thin layers to give uniform thickness to the grain side of the hide. The inside layer is often finished as suede. Inexpensive leathers may be pigmented split leathers with an embossed imitation grain.
- *Suede* is leather with the flesh side exposed. It is rarely used in upholstery or other interior applications. Color may be easily removed by abrasion; this known as *crocking*.

TASK LIGHTING

Task lighting can be defined as lighting that is controlled by the user or that has a specific purpose. Task lights consist of three components: a *light source*, a *reflector* or *diffuser*, and a *support structure*. Task lighting provides one of three types of lighting:

- *Uniform ambient lighting:* These include table and floor fixtures.
- *Local lighting:* These include pendant and portable fixtures.
- *Task-specific lighting:* These include under-shelf and desk fixtures.

UNIFORM AMBIENT LIGHTING

Uniform ambient lighting creates a low-contrast perception. Fixtures should be nonglaring and provide indirect light. This type of lighting works well for senior citizens who have a low-contrast perception and are vulnerable to glare.

LOCAL LIGHTING

Local lighting is specific lighting that requires a different light level than the surrounding space, such as art and object lighting. High-contrast lighting for a specific task, such as a cashier stand or bank transaction counter, is an example of local lighting.

TASK-SPECIFIC LIGHTING

Task-specific lighting allows the users to have the highest level of individual control. The luminaires allow the user to control the optimum angular relationship between the view, task, and light source for specific task. This type of light is ideal when there are inadequate visual conditions or the users have weak eyes.

TASK LIGHTING SELECTION CRITERIA

The quality of the ambient light, daylight, and other light sources in a space will affect the type of task lighting solutions required.

Veiling reflections are produced by light that is reflected off the task into the viewer's eyes. Veiling reflections reduce contrast. Task lights that redirect light to the sides will reduce or eliminate the veiling reflections. Mobile-arm task lights allow the user to position the light for best visibility. *Reflective glare* is caused by highly polished surfaces. Low or indirect light sources can be used when specular surfaces cannot be avoided. *Shadows* can be minimized by light from many directions.

To determine the type of task lighting, consider the following:

- *Activities that will occur in the space.* What light level ranges are required for anticipated tasks? Should they be adjustable by the user?
- *Age of user.* As the eye ages, color discrimination is less accurate. Also, the ability to discern or tolerate extremes of light intensity is reduced, and the aged eye is more sensitive to glare.
- *Control of the lighting system available to the user.* Does the user have individual dimming controls? Is multilevel switching available in the space?

TYPE OF LUMINAIRES

Under-shelf luminaires are frequently supplied by furniture manufactures. Depending on the type of under-shelf luminaires, uniform illuminance and reflected glare may be a problem. *Bare fluorescent lamp strip lights* can produce direct glare if the direct view is not housed with an opaque covering or lip of shelf. *Luminaire strip lights* with an adjustable sleeve can be adjusted to partially block and redirect light. *Luminaires with optics* such as a batwing lens can reduce glare and veiling reflection. An opaque strip with a batwing lens can further reduce the glare of fluorescent lamps.

A portable task light is easy to relocate and allows great flexibility for the user. It can provide more light than an under-shelf product and the angle can maximize visibility. When reading, the portable task light should be positioned to the side rather than the back. The lamp should not be directly visible, to prevent direct glare. The unit should be placed to the left side for right-handed workers and to the right for left-handed workers, to avoid casting a shadow on the task from the person's hand. Some types of portable task lights clip on to the table or desk.

TYPE OF LAMPS

Incandescent and halogen lamps are most commonly used in portable task lights. Incandescent and halogen lamps cover a small area, which makes it easy to direct light but can result in sharp shadows and bright reflections. Incandescent lamps are not as energy-efficient as fluorescent lamps and can become very hot to the touch.

Fluorescent lamps are cooler and more energy-efficient than incandescent. They produce a more diffused light with diffused shadows. The initial cost is higher than incandescent lamps, but the lamps last longer and are less expensive to operate. Approximately one-third less energy is required for fluorescent lamps than incandescent lamps.

Tricia Moore; lauckgroup; Dallas, Texas

Task Lighting Glossary

A-lamp: The incandescent lamp is the most commonly used in North American households. The "A" designation refers to the lamp's bulbous shape.

Compact fluorescent lamp: Single-ended fluorescent discharge light sources with small-diameter tubes.

Direct light: Light emitted by a luminaire in the general direction of the task to be illuminated. The term usually refers to light emitted in a downward direction.

Efficacy: The ratio of light output (in lumens) to input of power (in watts), expressed as lumens per watt (LPW).

Halogen lamp: An incandescent lamp that uses a halogen-fill gas. Halogen lamps have higher-rated efficacies and longer lives than standard incandescent A-lamps.

Illuminance: The amount of light that reaches a surface. Illuminance is measured in footcandles (lux).

Indirect lighting: Light arriving at a surface after reflecting from one or more surfaces that are not part of the luminaire.

Lamp: A radiant light source that emits light.

Luminaire: A complete lighting unit consisting of a lamp or lamps and the parts designed to distribute the light, to position and protect the lamps and to connect the lamps to the power supply.

Luminaire efficiency: The ratio of light emitted by a luminaire to the light emitted by the lamp or lamps within it. Components of a luminaire, such as reflectors and diffusers, absorb some of the light from the lamp. A highly efficient luminaire emits most of the light that the lamp emits.

Prismatic lens: An optical component of a luminaire that is used to distribute the emitted light. It is usually a sheet of plastic with a pattern of pyramid-shaped refracting prisms on one side.

FRISBI
Flos; Huntington, New York

TABLE LAMP
Nessen Lamps, Inc.; Mamaroneck, New York

LOCAL LIGHTING

LUXO DESK LAMP
Luxo Corp.; Port Chester, New York

BERENICE
Artemide; Farmingdale, New York

TASK-SPECIFIC LIGHTING

DUOMO
Koch & Lowy; Avon, Massachusetts

TACCIA
Flos; Huntington, New York

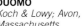

UNIFORM AMBIENT LIGHTING

WINDOW TREATMENTS

Window treatments control light and glare, provide privacy, act as acoustic buffers, and make design statements. Window treatments also play a significant role in the energy performance of a building and must be coordinated with heating and cooling load calculations. The energy efficiency of the building and the comfort of its inhabitants are heavily reliant on the proper selection of window treatments. They can be categorized according to two energy-saving functions: shading from solar heat gain in the summer and insulation from building heat loss in the winter.

SHADING FROM SOLAR HEAT GAIN

Solar radiation is the primary heat source in a commercial building. When sunlight strikes a window, some of the heat energy is reflected and the rest is either absorbed by the glass or transmitted to the interior.

- *Reflected solar radiation* bounces off the surface and does not penetrate the glass.
- *Absorbed solar radiation* is soaked up by the glass and eventually is dissipated by convection or reradiation.
- *Transmitted heat energy* penetrates the glass and heats the building's interior.

Shading coefficient (SC), a term developed by ASHRAE in the 1960s, describes a window system's capability to reduce heat gain. The three solar heat gain factors—reflection, absorption, and transmission—determine a window system's SC. The shading coefficient is a function of the entire window system, including the window treatment. The SC is the ratio between the solar gain through a window system and the gain through ⅛-in.- (3-mm-) thick clear glass under the same conditions. An SC of .22 means that a window system allows 22% of the heat energy transmitted through ⅛-in.- (3-mm-) thick glass into the building's interior. The lower the shading coefficient, the better the window system's capability to reduce incoming solar radiation. Manufacturers typically provide SCs for window systems using blinds or shades.

The effectiveness of a window treatment to protect against solar heat gain depends on its capability to reflect incoming solar radiation back through the window before it can be converted into heat within the building. Because reflectance is the most important property of a window treatment in reducing heat gain, color selection is an important factor. Dark colors tend to absorb heat, and light colors reflect it; thus, white and light-colored window treatments are the first choice for reducing heat gain.

LOW EMISSIVITY GLAZING

Low emissivity can be thought of as the counterpart to high reflectivity. If a surface has high reflectivity, it has low emissivity (low-E). Low-E surfaces allow the visible spectrum of light through while reflecting back a large portion of the thermal radiation, which makes them popular for use as glass coatings. Light comes through, but most of the heat does not. Horizontal louver blind slats and roller shade fabrics are available with low-E coatings that increase the energy performance of a window system.

INSULATION FROM HEAT LOSS

Heat energy moves from a warmer to a colder substance by conduction, convection, or radiation. Most window treatments do not effectively prevent heat loss, because they are inferior insulators.

- *Conduction* is the transfer of heat energy through a substance. Glass is an excellent conductor; heat or cold is quickly and efficiently conveyed through it.
- *Convection* is the transfer of heat energy through air. The human body loses and gains heat primarily through the air.
- *Radiation* is the transmission of energy by invisible light waves independent of a substance or air. For example, solar radiation travels through space (a vacuum) to reach the Earth in this manner.

R-VALUE

Conduction, convection, and radiation determine a material's thermal resistance, referred to as its *R-value*. The R-value measures the insulating effect of a material, the material's resistance to the flow of heat. The larger the R-value, the greater the resistance and the better the insulating value. The effectiveness of a window treatment as an insulator depends on its capability to reduce the conductive transfer of heat to the interior. The R-values of window treatments such as blinds and shades may be quite low. However, in a fully lowered position, they form an insulating airspace next to the window, which somewhat improves the R-value of the window system.

BLINDS

Horizontal Blinds

Horizontal blinds are the traditional, cost-effective solution to controlling glare. Although microblinds have a narrower slat width than miniblinds, they are typically heavier because more slats are required for the same-size blind. This added weight can contribute to a shorter life span for the hardware of microblinds. Blind slats are commonly made of aluminum, PVC, or wood.

Window Treatment Standards

The American Window Covering Manufacturers Association (AWCMA) standard for horizontal blinds calls for the uniform location of the cord lock on the right side of the head channel and the tilting mechanism (typically a wand) on the left side of the head channel. If other locations are required because of inaccessibility, specify the blind-operating hardware location or indicate it on the drawings.

Selection Criteria

If tilt wand and lift cord lengths are not specified, manufacturers typically assume the window sill height to be 36 in. (915 mm) above the finish floor. In commercial applications where pets or children may be involved, accidental strangulation with the traditional end loop and cord equalizer is of concern. Break-through lift cord ends are available as a safety feature. The attached ends of the lift cord separate easily when force is applied.

Perforated slats preserve the view while reducing glare, conserving energy, and providing privacy. Evenly spaced tiny holes allow light through while protecting the interior from solar heat gain. The openness factor for horizontal blinds is typically limited to 6% of the area of the slat so that the strength of the slat is not diminished.

To maintain a uniform appearance in a building's exterior, the base building standard may require blinds with certain features. Top-locking cord locks offer only two blind positions: fully raised and fully lowered. Slat tilt limiters limit the slat angle position, allowing tilt only within a narrow range. A uniform blind color on the building exterior can be maintained, while using a variety of colors on the interior, by specifying slats with different finishes on the concave and convex sides. Where a dark-colored slat is required, the reflectance of the window system can be improved with a light-colored or low-E-coated concave slat side. The color and openness factor of blinds will affect the perception of the view. Perforated, dark window treatments minimize glare and appear to be more transparent.

In comparing horizontal blinds, an increased slat count (number of slats per given dimension) or decreased pitch (rung spacing) usually indicates a better-quality blind.

SOLAR HEAT GAIN

INSULATION FROM HEAT LOSS

MAXIMUM RECOMMENDED SIZES FOR HORIZONTAL ALUMINUM SLAT BLINDS

SLAT SIZE MM	MAXIMUM WIDTH FT (M)	MAXIMUM AREA SQ FT (SQ M)
15–16 (nominally ½ in.)	10 (3)	70 (6.5)
25 (nominally 1 in.)	12 (3.6)	100 (9.2)
50 (nominally 2 in.)	12 (3.6)	135 (12.5)

Vertical Blinds

Vertical blinds are among the easiest window treatments to clean and repair. The vanes collect no more dust than walls or other vertical surfaces. Vertical blind vanes are also easier to replace than horizontal blind slats. Unlike horizontal blinds, vertical blinds can be specified where curved track applications are required. Similar to draperies, *stack-back dimensions* (the width of a window treatment in a fully open position at the side of the window) must be considered if the full window is to be exposed when the blinds are fully opened.

Vane materials for commercial use include fabric, polyvinyl chloride (PVC), and aluminum. The fiber content of fabric vanes is typically polyester; however, cotton, acrylic, fiberglass, and rayon are also available. The fabric can be woven or nonwoven. This vane type can be free-hanging, or the fabric can be inserted into an extruded PVC sleeve to add rigidity and durability. Fabric vanes can be treated with soil repellant or fire-retardant finishes. Sealed or sewn-in bottom weights, or bottom chains linking the vanes together, are often recommended to stabilize this relatively lightweight type of vane.

PVC can be extruded into a variety of vane profiles. These vanes typically contain titanium dioxide (a common light block found in some sunscreen lotions) for opaqueness. PVC vanes should be treated with an antistatic solution to prevent dirt attraction and static cling. Because of PVC's rigidity and weight, bottom chains linking the vanes together are not required. Because the structural integrity of a vane is not as crucial as that of a horizontal blind slat, a much larger openness factor (ranging from about 6% to 13%) is possible for vertical blinds than for horizontal blinds.

ROLLER SHADES

The most effective type of interior protection against heat gain through a window is a light-colored, opaque roller shade. Flat roller shades are categorized by two methods of operation: those that are drawn up onto a roller at the top and those that roll up from the bottom. Bottom-up shades offer privacy while allowing light in. Bead-chain-operated shades are easier to keep clean, because the shades are not touched during operation. They are also ideal for applications where the bottom of a shade is difficult to reach.

REGULAR ROLL SHADE
The roller is installed in front of the shade.

REVERSE ROLL SHADE
The roller is installed behind the shade. Reverse roll should be specified for print shade fabrics, because it allows only the finish face, not the back of the material, to be exposed to the interior.

ROLLER SHADES

ROLLER SHADE
Roller shades can often be fabricated from the same material used for textile wallcoverings or upholstery. Blackout or translucent material is commonly laminated to the back of finish fabrics to change the appearance or performance of the shade. Room-darkening and blackout shades are typically made of fiberglass covered with a PVC film.

PERFORATED ROLLER SHADE
Perforated roller shades utilize a semitransparent shade cloth that permits sun penetration and a view to the outside, while providing heat and UV protection. Shade cloth openness factors range from 1% to 22%. Higher openness factors are achieved with vinyl-covered fiberglass (because of its dimensional stability), as opposed to vinyl-covered polyester.

ROLLER SHADES *Source: KnollTextiles; East Greenville, Pennsylvania; and DFB Sales, Inc.; Long Island City, New York*

DOUBLE ROMAN SHADE
Double Roman shades require from 1½ to 2½ times the vertical fabric fullness of the flat Roman shade. Featuring overlapping folds that cascade down the full height of the shade, a double Roman shade includes horizontal supports at each backfold, which are attached to spacing tapes.

FLAT ROMAN SHADE
Flat Roman shades can be modified for a variety of design statements: for example, a shaped bottom hem, an extra fabric fold at the sill, chrome or brass rods attached to the face of the shade, inverted seams, or the use of horizontal seam spacing. This shade type requires the least amount of fabric.

ROMAN SHADES *Source: KnollTextiles; East Greenville, Pennsylvania; and DFB Sales, Inc.; Long Island City, New York*

Austrian shades are unlined and designed to swoop between vertical shimming tapes. Increasing the number of swoops can create different visual effects, for example, one swoop as opposed to four swoops for the same opening. Austrian shades can be used as stationary top treatments or as valances.

AUSTRIAN SHADE *Source: KnollTextiles; East Greenville, Pennsylvania; and DFB Sales, Inc.; Long Island City, New York*

Pleated shades are typically made from polyester with an antistatic treatment. Pleated shades fabricated from C.O.M. are also available; however, the pleats may deform, sagging at the top and compressing at the bottom. Pleated shades are more commonly used in residential applications, rather than commercial.

PLEATED SHADE *Source: KnollTextiles; East Greenville, Pennsylvania; and DFB Sales, Inc.; Long Island City, New York*

DRAPERIES

Drapery fabric selection should include an evaluation of the drapeability, commonly referred to as the *hand,* of the fabric. By requesting a full-width sample at least 1 yard in length, the appropriateness of the fabric for a hanging application can be determined.

Casements are sheer or semisheer fabrics, often used with operable over-drapes or fixed side panels. Extra-wide fabrics, up to 118 in. (2,997 mm), are available to be "railroaded," thus eliminating the obvious seams inherent in sheer materials.

Linings are fabric backings that enhance the draping qualities of a fabric, increase the energy performance of the window system, or protect the drapery fabric from ultraviolet (UV) radiation. Linings can be sewn to the face fabric if they have compatible cleaning requirements, or they can hang on a separate track. *Metallic linings* in various weights can increase a window system's reflectivity, and *insulating linings* can boost the thermal performance. Ultraviolet inhibitors can be added to lining fabrics to help protect the drapery fabric against deterioration caused by sunlight. Water-repellant finishes protect linings from unsightly staining and streaking from condensation.

Blackout linings are used to darken a room completely. Such linings are popular in hospitality applications or in meeting rooms where the use of projection equipment is anticipated.

Interlinings enhance the performance or appearance of the drapery. For example, an acoustic interlining of heavy cotton flannel increases the sound-absorbing capability of a window treatment. An interlining for a stationary side panel can create more body, eliminating the necessity of a heavier, more expensive drapery fabric. Interlinings hang between the finish fabric and the lining. They require the durability of a lining fabric for protection from UV radiation, moisture, and abrasion.

DRAPERY OPERATION

One-way draw operation describes a drapery panel that opens entirely to one side. A one-way draw is designated as either *full left* or *full right*, indicating the direction in which the drapery stacks as you face it. For example, if you are looking at an open drapery stacked on the right, it is a right draw.

Two-way or *bipart draw* means that the drapery panels meet in the center and open to either side.

Carriers hold the drapery end that traverses the rod. *Butt master carriers* are often used in roll pleat and stack pleat draperies. *Overlap master carriers* are commonly the choice for conventional pleated drapes. Standard overlap for overlap master carriers is 3 in. (75 mm) per panel, and the right panel overlaps the left.

Return is the distance from the traversing rod to the wall or the depth of the projection. When casements and over-drapes are used in the same window opening, the depths of the returns should provide adequate clearance for unencumbered operation. The dimensions of the return and the overlap must be added to the dimension of the opening to determine the drapery panel width. The stack space dimension, or *stack back,* is the drapery width when fully opened. The

stack back must be considered when determining the traversing rod length and may determine the traversing direction.

Manual track operation options for manually operating draperies include wands or pull cords.

BUTT MASTER CARRIER

OVERLAP MASTER CARRIER

DRAW DRAPERIES
Finished drapery panel width for two-way draw draperies = return + stack-back width + one-half of the window opening width + drapery overlap.

DRAPERY CARRIERS

- *Wands* have no mechanized parts compared to other types of track operation hardware, making them the preferred choice for hard-use applications. The wand, also referred to as a baton, is used to drag the drapery into position on its track. Wands are suitable for lightweight draperies.
- *Pull cords* are either free-hanging or strung between a pulley and the drapery heading. The pulley system requires that the pulley be permanently mounted on the wall or floor. Free-hanging pull-cord ends should not be looped because of the strangulation hazard they pose.

Electrical track operation uses motor-operated drapery controls to drive individual or groups of draperies. Timing devices and temperature-sensing controls are available for automatic operation of draperies. Low-voltage motors can be attached to the track, hung below the track, or recessed into the ceiling above the track. Motorized tracks can be controlled remotely by infrared or radio waves or by a wall switch. Radio-controlled remote operation is often preferred because, unlike infrared remote controls, a line of sight is not required between the remote and the motor, and the receiver can be concealed behind the draperies.

Drapery weight affects track-carrying capacity. Carrying capacity decreases if the drapery track is curved. The minimum radius for inside and outside curved tracks varies with hardware type and track configuration.

Fullness is the ratio of the total fabric used, less allowances for side hems and seams, to the finished drapery width. For example, a drapery with 100% fullness is 100% wider than the width of the drapery in a closed position, or twice the finished drapery width.

STACKING WIDTHS FOR PLEATED DRAPERY HEADINGS

OPENING SIZE IN. (MM)	STACKING WIDTHS IN. (MM)			REQUIRED YARDAGE 150% FULLNESS 54-IN.- (137-CM-) WIDE FABRIC	
	PINCH PLEAT	BARREL AND BOX PLEAT	PENCIL PLEAT	FOR DRAPERY LENGTH TO SILL 72 IN. (1,828 MM)	FOR DRAPERY LENGTH TO FLOOR 102 IN. (2,590 MM)
32 (812)	14 (355)	16 (406)	13 (330)	5	7
54 (1,371)	20 (508)	24 (609)	18 (457)	7.5	10.5
76 (1,930)	25 (635)	31 (787)	23 (584)	10	14
98 (2,489)	30 (762)	38 (965)	27 (685)	12.5	17.5
120 (3,048)	36 (914)	46 (1,168)	32 (812)	15	21
142 (3,606)	41 (1,041)	53 (1,346)	37 (939)	17.5	24
164 (4,165)	47 (1,193)	60 (1,524)	42 (1,066)	20	28
186 (4,724)	52 (1,320)	67 (1,701)	47 (1,193)	22.5	31.5
208 (5,283)	58 (1,473)	75 (1,905)	52 (1,320)	25	35

PLEATED DRAPERY PANEL WIDTHS

FULLNESS	MULTIPLIER TO DETERMINE DRAPERY PANEL WIDTH BEFORE PLEATING	CALCULATION (BASED ON 54-IN. (137-CM-) WIDE FABRIC)	PLEATED DRAPERY PANEL WIDTH
100%	2	54 in. ÷ 2 cm = 27	27 in.
125%	2.25	54 in. ÷ 2.25 cm = 24	24 in.
150%	2.5	54 in. ÷ 2.5 cm = 22	22 in.
200%	3	54 in. ÷ 3 cm = 18	18 in.
225%	3.25	54 in. ÷ 3.25 cm = 16.625	16⅝ in.
300%	4	54 in. ÷ 4 cm = 13.5	13½ in.

RECOMMENDED DRAPERY FULLNESSES

	MINIMUM	AVERAGE	MAXIMUM
Unlined Traversing Drapery	100%	150%	200%
Lined Traversing Drapery	100%	125%	150%
Stationary Side Panels	150%	200%	300%

Source: KnollTextiles East Greenville, Pennsylvania; and DFB Sales, Inc.; Long Island City, New York

TRADITIONAL PLEATED HEADING SYSTEMS

The *pleat to dimension* is the width of the drapery after it has been pleated. For example, if a 48 in. (1,220 mm) width of fabric is 19 in. (480 mm) after it has been pleated, it is specified as "pleat to 19 inches." Fullness for a conventional pleated drapery is typically 225% and can range up to 250%, making the stack-back dimension the largest among the drapery types. Pleated headings are reinforced with buckram or other stiffening materials, so special care must be taken in dry cleaning and pressing the pleats. Of all the drapery headings, these are the most readily adaptable at a project site. The required drapery fullness can be accommodated by adjusting the depth and the distance between the pleats.

FESTOONS AND JABOTS
Festoons (A) are deep, horizontal folds with 200% fullness. Jabots (B) are usually self-lined or lined with a contrasting fabric because the back of the fabric is visible. Festoons and jabots are mounted to a valance board prior to installation.

PINCH, OR FRENCH, PLEATS
Pinch pleats, sometimes referred to as French pleats, are typically 4 in. (100 m) high and spaced 4 in. (100 mm) apart. For large windows or a more dramatic appearance, pleats can be extended to 6 in. (150 mm) high. Each pleat has three folds. The amount of fabric in each pleat is determined by the fullness.

BOX PLEATS
Box pleats can be fabricated with heavy-duty buckram, which allows for the support of a great weight. Since the pleats are flat and can produce up to three times the fullness, this heading can be used for stationary side panels in a pocket where there is limited space.

BARREL PLEATS
Barrel pleats are fabricated into cylinder, or barrel, shapes. The pleats can range from small to large (1 to 3½ in. (25 to 90 mm) in diameter). Due to the construction, the stacking ratio is much greater for a given fullness.

PENCIL PLEATS
Pencil pleats provide a soft heading while the uniformity of evenly spaced ⅜ in. (9 mm) pleats creates a structured appearance. This heading makes the drapery appear fuller than it is.

TRADITIONAL PLEATED HEADING SYSTEMS
Source: KnollTextiles; East Greenville, Pennsylvania; and DFB Sales, Inc.; Long Island City, New York

CEILING-MOUNTED DRAPERY

WALL-MOUNTED DRAPERY WITH UPHOLSTERED CORNICE

SINGLE POCKET

DOUBLE POCKET

SINGLE-WINDOW TREATMENT POCKET DIMENSIONS*

	A IN. (MM)	B IN. (MM)
Drapery	6 (152)	6 (152)
Shade	4 (101)	4 (101)
Horizontal Blinds	3 (76)	2 (50)
Vertical Blinds	2 (50)	2 (50)

Add 20% to dimensions if track is motorized.

DOUBLE-WINDOW TREATMENT POCKET DIMENSIONS*

	A IN. (MM)	B IN. (MM)
Drapery with Drapery	12 (304)	12 (304)
Shade with Drapery	10 (254)	6 (152)
Horizontal Blinds with Drapery	8.5 (215)	6 (152)
Vertical Blinds with Drapery	11 (279)	6 (152)

Add 20% to dimensions if track is motorized.

WINDOW TREATMENT POCKET DETAILS
Source: KnollTextiles; East Greenville, Pennsylvania; and DFB Sales, Inc.; Long Island City, New York

LOW-PROFILE TRACK HEADING SYSTEMS

Low-profile track heading systems, sometimes referred to as *architectural heading systems,* appear the same from either side of the window and consequently do not need to be lined for the sake of appearance. These heading styles are popular in installations that require frequent cleaning, for example health care settings, because they can be machine-washed. When installed with a ceiling-mounted, low-profile track, these headings appear to be hanging directly from the ceiling.

WINDOW TREATMENT CLEARANCES

Draperies and venetian blinds of other interior shading devices must be hung so as to provide space at the top and bottom, or on one side and bottom, to permit natural air movement over the room side of the glass. The following criteria must be met to avoid formation of a heat trap:

- Minimum clearance of 1½ in. (38 mm) is required on top and bottom, or on one side and bottom, between shading device and surrounding construction.
- Minimum clearance of 2 in. (50 mm) is required between glass and shading device. Heating/cooling outlets must be to room side of shading device.

If venetian blinds are being used, and these clearances cannot be provided, a two-direction positive stop or lockout that limits the movement of the blinds should be incorporated. For horizontal blinds, the lockout should limit the rotation of the blinds in both directions so that they are not in a position 60° off the horizontal when in the most closed position. For vertical blinds, the lockout should limit movement in both directions so that ½ in. (12 mm) of spacing exists between the blinds when in the closed position. If these guidelines cannot be followed, heat-strengthened glass should be specified in lieu of annealed glass.

Heat-strengthening or full tempering of the glass may be necessary for some installations to offset the effects of the glass size, solar absorption, exterior shading, interior shading, climactic conditions, lack of proper clearances noted above or improper placement, or directing of airflow.

1 1/2" (38) MIN. CLEARANCE

WINDOW FRAME

1 1/2" (38) MIN.

VENETIAN BLIND, DRAPERY, OR ROLLER SHADE

GLAZING

2" (50) MIN. CLEARANCE

1 1/2" (38) MIN.

AIRFLOW

WINDOW TREATMENT CLEARANCES
Source: Glass Association of North America; GANA Glazing Manual; Topeka, Kansas, 1997.

STACK PLEATS
Stack pleats are formed by sewing molded stiffeners to the top of the pleats. The effect at the heading is a well-defined V-shape, which requires a very small stacking width. Stack pleat draperies require the smallest stack-back dimension and can stack as tightly as one-sixth of the drapery width. Fullness and the depth of the pleat are interdependent, which is not the case with traditional pleated headings. The standard fullness for stack pleats is 100%, but fullnesses of 40%, 60%, 80%, and 120% are also available.

ROLL PLEATS
Roll pleats provide a soft, rounded pleating pattern. This drapery type is fabricated from flat panels of fabric. Because there is less fullness, there is also less stack back required for roll pleats than for conventional pleats. Fullness is achieved by varying the spacing between the snaps or grommets on the drapery heading. Standard fullness is 100%, but fullnesses of 60%, 80%, and 120% are also available.

TACKED-ACCORDION PLEATS
Tacked-accordion pleats are formed by sewing molded pleaters to the top of the pleat and then snapping them onto the carriers in the track. The tacked-accordion-pleat heading can be combined with a permanent-pleating process that is applied to the fabric, creating shape creases down the length of the drapery.

ACCORDION PLEATS
Accordion pleats provide the most efficient stacking ratio of the architectural heading systems, but this system produces the largest stacking depth, front to back. This is an excellent system for partitions. The heading can be fabricated with or without buckram, depending on the structure desired.

LOW-PROFILE TRACK HEADING SYSTEMS
Source: KnollTextiles; East Greenville, Pennsylvania; and DFB Sales, Inc.; Long Island City, New York

STACKING WIDTHS FOR LOW-PROFILE DRAPERY HEADINGS

OPENING SIZE IN. (MM)	STACKING WIDTHS IN. (MM)			REQUIRED YARDAGE 150% FULLNESS 54-IN.- (137-CM-) WIDE FABRIC	
	STACK PLEAT	ROLL AND TACKED-ACCORDION PLEAT	ACCORDION PLEAT	DRAPERY LENGTH TO SILL 72 IN. (1,828 MM)	DRAPERY LENGTH TO FLOOR 102 IN. (2,590 MM)
32 (812)	8 (203)	8 (203)	7 (177)	5	7
54 (1,371)	11 (279)	13 (330)	12 (304)	7.5	10.5
76 (1,930)	14 (355)	17.5 (444)	17 (431)	10	14
98 (2,489)	16 (406)	23 (584)	22 (558)	12.5	17.5
120 (3,048)	19 (482)	27.5 (698)	27 (685)	15	21
142 (3,606)	22 (558)	32 (812)	32 (812)	17.5	24
164 (4,165)	25 (635)	38 (965)	42 (1,066)	20	28
186 (4,724)	28 (711)	43 (1,092)	43 (1,092)	22.5	31.5
208 (5,283)	31 (787)	46 (1,168)	54 (1,371)	25	35

Source: KnollTextiles East Greenville, Pennsylvania; and DFB Sales, Inc.; Long Island City, New York

FILE CABINETS

FILE CABINET TYPES

File cabinets are either vertical, which can be used for front-to-back filing configurations only, or lateral, which are wider than they are deep and can be used for either side-to-side or front-to-back hanging file configurations.

Vertical file cabinets are one drawer wide and two to five drawers high. They can only be used for front-to-back hanging file configurations. Common cabinet widths are 15 in. (380 mm), letter size, and 18 in. (460 mm), legal size. Common cabinet depth is 29 in. (710 mm).

Lateral file cabinets are wider than they are deep and can be used for side-to-side and front-to-back hanging file configurations. Common cabinet widths are 30, 36, and 42 in. (760, 915, and 1,065 mm). A 48 in. (1,220 mm) width cabinet is also available and is often used as a systems furniture component. Common cabinet depth is 18 in. (460 mm). Overall cabinet depths and widths vary little among manufacturers, however, drawer height and internal configuration vary to accommodate a wide range of storage materials.

Lateral files require less pull and stand space than vertical files for the amount of material stored. Because lateral files are often a more efficient use of space and because their internal storage can be more easily reconfigured, they are more commonly used than vertical files. Two-drawer file cabinets can be used as credenzas and three-drawer units often serve as space dividers.

SIZE AND CAPACITY

Sizes and capacities of metal file cabinets and components vary. Cabinets with the same nominal dimensions from different manufacturers do not always have the same actual sizes and interior capacities. Some manufacturers differentiate their products from those of other manufacturers by offering cabinets with dimensions that vary from industry standards and that provide increased storage space. Cabinets with shallow drawers can provide more storage space in less overall height. Verify exact dimensions; many manufacturers publish only nominal dimensions in their product literature.

FEATURES

Exterior dimensions and interior capacities of file cabinets vary among manufacturers. Verify exact dimensions; some manufacturers publish nominal dimensions in their product literature.

Finish options provided by some manufacturers include acoustical panels for exposed file cabinet backs; wood drawer fronts; and stone, plastic laminate, and wood tops.

Leveling feet are used to ensure that the file cabinet is level and plumb. Structural damage to the file cabinet can result from twisting if the cabinet is not properly leveled. File cabinets should be leveled after they are fully loaded to compensate for floor deflection.

Enclosed base cabinets may have access to the space for wire and cable routing.

Stackable units offer the flexibility of changing the file cabinet's height in the field. A two-drawer cabinet can grow to three drawers by ordering and connecting another module. Also, the orientation of the drawers can vary in a freestanding group of file cabinets, with some drawers opening to the front and others opening to the back.

PERFORMANCE STANDARDS

ANSI/BIFMA X5.2, *American National Standard for Office Furnishings—Lateral Files Tests,* for lateral file cabinets, and ANSI/BIFMA X5.3, *American National Standard for Office Furnishings—Vertical Files Tests,* for vertical file cabinets, are voluntary standards that include tests for conditions that, if present, may result in injury. The tests addresses static load, dynamic load, and endurance test cycles. Lateral files are tested for

TWO-, THREE-, FOUR-, AND FIVE-DRAWER VERTICAL FILE CABINETS

Anchor bracket attaches to the file cabinet's leveling glide and the floor. To reduce the risk of hazards during earthquakes, the California Office of Statewide Health Planning and Development (OSHPD) requires anchoring file cabinets that have the bottom of their top opening at 60 in. (1,524 mm) or higher.

TIP-OVER PREVENTION METHODS

interlock system performance (tip-over prevention) and retention of drawers or rollout shelves.

FILE CABINET STABILITY

Interlock devices allow only one drawer to be opened at a time, ensuring that the cabinet will not accidentally tip over.

Anchoring file cabinets to the wall, floor, or adjacent cabinets (*ganging*) increases their stability. Seismic considerations may require that file cabinets be anchored. Cabinets that share a common countertop should be anchored to each other. If cabinets are anchored to each other, structural floor-loading limits should be verified; the weight of as few as four or five loaded, ganged cabinets can exceed floor-loading limits.

TWO-, THREE-, FOUR-, AND FIVE-DRAWER LATERAL FILE CABINETS

COUNTERWEIGHTS PLACED IN THE BOTTOM OF THE FILE CABINET

Consider counterweights for applications where top drawers may be used more frequently than bottom drawers, such as two-drawer lateral files adjacent to desks. Some cabinets come with counterweights; in others, they must be specified. If file cabinets are ganged, counterweights may not be necessary.

LOCKS AND KEYS

Some manufacturers offer removable cylinders or locks that can be changed after the cabinets are installed. Two basic lock types are as follows:

- Plunger locks automatically secure themselves when pushed into engagement. They require key action only for unlocking.
- Cam locks require a rotary action for both locking and unlocking.

Three common keying methods are as follows:

- Random keying locks each cabinet with a different key.
- Alike keying locks each cabinet with the same key, providing no in-house security.
- Master keying locks each cabinet with its own key, but a single, master key can access all cabinets. Master keying is usually available for an extra charge. Grand-master and great-grand-master keying are also available.

LOADING AND INSTALLATION

Manufacturers recommend loading file cabinets from the bottom to the top. Weight in the bottom drawer acts to balance the cabinet to prevent tipping.

For file cabinets installed in recesses or alcoves, opening dimensions must include required installation tolerances. Generally, at least an additional ⅛ in. (3 mm) in width per cabinet, for horizontal openings, and an additional ⅛ in. (3 mm) in height is required to allow for cabinet installation without damaging adjacent finishes.

MASTERSPEC®; published by ARCOM; Salt Lake City, Utah and Alexandria, Virginia

DOUBLE SIDE ACCESS WITH CIRCULATION

SIDE ACCESS WITH CIRCULATION

FRONT ACCESS WITH CIRCULATION

SIDE ACCESS ONLY

SIDE ACCESS WITH CIRCULATION AND WORKSTATION

DOUBLE FRONT ACCESS WITH NO CIRCULATION

FILE CABINET ACCESS

SEATING

SELECTION CONSIDERATIONS

Seating selection criteria include *function*—whether for task or lounge seating—and *construction*. Construction considerations include the type of frame, cushions, suspension systems, and whether casters or glides are used on the feet of the seating unit.

SEATING FOR WORK

The chair has been singled out as the most critical comfort factor in the contemporary workplace. Back and arm aches, fatigue, and decreased productivity have all been associated with inadequately designed seating. No other piece of office furniture has been the subject of more lawsuits and insurance claims.

The contemporary office chair is a complicated piece of equipment. It accommodates the movement of its user in one of two ways: with a traditional swivel/tilt mechanism or a synchronized tilt mechanism. The standard swivel/tilt allows the seat to spin on its base and to tilt backward for comfort. In a synchronized tilt chair, the back and seat operate independently at different ratios of motion.

There is no single ideal posture for the performance of work. Each user has to find his or her own individual comfort level. Thus, the most important feature of any chair is adjustability. Separate seat and back assemblies are increasingly popular because they allow for maximum adjustability. There are four basic adjustments that allow the user to customize the fit of a chair: seat height, seat tilt, back height, and back tilt.

- *Seat height* adjustments are made either pneumatically or with a mechanical ratchet. Automatically adjusting chairs use the weight of the user to lower the seat once the pneumatic cylinder is engaged. The ease with which a pneumatic cylinder can be replaced should be considered in selecting this type of chair. Mechanically adjusted seats are twirled clockwise to lower them, and counterclockwise to raise them. An adjustable seat height ensures that the seat is the right height from the floor, the user has enough knee clearance, and the user's eyes and elbows are at the right heights for the work surface.
- *Seat tilt,* in conjunction with back tilt, works to maintain an angle of up to 135° between the torso and the thigh. This angle promotes the natural curvature of the lower spine in which the pressure is evenly distributed on the lumbar vertebrae. The use of a "waterfall" front seat edge helps promote circulation in the lower thigh and leg.
- *Back height* adjustments allow the user to position the backrest to properly and comfortably support the lumbar area. Some chairs allow for the adjustment of the seat depth by moving the backrest inward.
- *Back tilt* flexibility allows the user to lean back in the chair and stretch. The Human Factors Society recommends an adjustable back that ranges from 90° to 105°. The back tilt tension is often adjustable.

THE SPINAL COLUMN

CORRECT LUMBAR SUPPORT
The natural curve of the lower spine is maintained with lumbar support.

INCORRECT LUMBAR SUPPORT
The spine is flattened, exerting excessive pressure on the spinal discs.

THE SITTING SPINE

TYPES OF OFFICE SEATING

Office seating lines are usually available in several design variations. The same visual characteristics are incorporated to a variety of styles that reflect different levels of management. The terms used to describe these differences vary among manufacturers, but the categories generally include a side or guest chair, task chair, one or two levels of seating for managers, and an executive chair.

- A *side chair* or *guest chair* is placed in an office for the use of visitors. It is designed with the expectation that the time a person is seated will be brief and that no tasks requiring posture support will be performed. A side chair does not have casters. A pedestal, four-legged, or glide base are the typical options for the chair base. Side chairs do not have adjustable features.
- *Task seating* (sometimes referred to as *secretarial* or *operational* seating) is designed to support typing and clerical tasks requiring extensive upper body movement, such as filing. A chair of this type usually has detachable arms and a low back.
- A *management chair* may have a low or high back and a wider, thicker seat than one used for task seating. Arms are almost always standard for a management chair. It is designed to support entry-through midlevel managers who spend part of a day working at their desks or keyboards and part of their day conferring.
- An *executive chair* is a larger-scale chair with arms. It has a wider, thicker seat and higher back, to impart an image of authority. Leather is a common upholstery option. Such chairs are not designed for the continuous, repetitive, movements of the average worker; they support computing, conferring, and telephoning. They are also appropriate for use in conference and boardrooms.

PERFORMANCE AND DESIGN STANDARDS

BIFMA X5.1, *Test for General-Purpose Office Chairs,* evaluates the safety, durability, and structural adequacy of office seating. It tests the chair's capability to withstand the load of its user dropping into it, caster durability, swivel cycling, and tilt mechanism. It is a minimum standard: chairs either pass or fail. The standard does not grade or rank chairs.

The Human Factors Society sponsors ANSI 100, *Human Factors Engineering of Visual Display Terminal Workstations.* Among the seating features required by this standard are the following:

- Adjustable task arms to support the user's forearms and a distance between armrests of at least 18.2 in. (462 mm)
- Adjustable seat height range of 16 to 20½ in. (406 to 520 mm)
- Seat depth that permits contact with the seat back in the lumbar region
- Seat cushion at least 18.2 in. (462 mm) wide
- A fixed back angle of 90° or more, or an adjustable back that ranges from 90° to 105°

UPHOLSTERED SEATING

An upholstered armchair, love seat, or sofa can warm a commercial interior with an invitation to sit, spend a moment, and relax. Commonly used in reception areas and executive offices, upholstered seating provides comfort and style. Four construction components must be considered when evaluating upholstered seating: the frame, the suspension system, the cushions, and the upholstery material.

Upholstery Material

The seating frame, suspension system, and cushions form the foundation that is wrapped in an upholstery material. For fabrics with large patterns, the motif should be centered on each seat and back cushion, and should be continuous down the seat front and sides. Fabrics with a *repeat* (a repeated pattern), or narrower-width fabrics, will require more yardage than a standard 54-in.- (1,370-mm-) wide piece of upholstery material.

Customer's Own Material (C.O.M.) and Customer's Own Leather (C.O.L.)

Seating manufacturers typically supply upholstery fabric options for their chairs. The fabric selections have been tested on their seating and have performed satisfactorily with regard to wear and flammability. Often a designer will find the upholstery selection limiting and will select a fabric from a textile manufacturer. Upholstery material that is not supplied by the seating manufacturer is referred to as C.O.M. or C.O.L. Written approval from the furniture manufacturer is usually required for its use. The furniture manufacturer must verify that the material is acceptable as an upholstery fabric.

"Customer" in this sense does not refer to the designer's customer, but to the manufacturer's customer—the party placing the order—which is the furniture, furnishings, and equipment (FF&E) contractor. The material is purchased separately from the seating and supplied to the furniture manufacturer for application. The FF&E contractor (usually the furniture dealer) is responsible for the acquisition and coordination of C.O.M.

Frame

The frame gives an upholstered piece its structure and form. Kiln-dried hardwood provides a dimensionally stable frame foundation. The frame can be assembled with screws, nails, staples, and glue; however, a combination of mortise-and-tenon and double-doweled joints is often used in the most durable seating construction. Seat joints should be reinforced with corner blocks that are glued and screwed in place for added strength. For finer seating units, the portions of the frame that will be exposed are machine-sanded and then hand-sanded to ensure a smooth, scratch-free surface.

Some furniture manufacturers prestain the sanded wood frame to verify that there are no scratches. The prestain must be completely sanded off before the desired stain is applied by hand with either a rag or a brush. Sealer is applied after the wood is stained, preparing the surface to receive the finish coats. Catalyzed urethane is a popular choice for fine wood finishes, because it is extremely hard and resistant to water, alcohol, and scratches. Between each coat, the wood may be scuff-sanded to raise the grain of the wood and to ensure good adhesion.

RUN-RIGHT OR UP-THE-BOLT APPLICATION
This is the traditional method of upholstery application.

"RAILROAD" APPLICATION
This is usually the most efficient use of a fabric. The cushions are upholstered with the selvage edge of the fabric parallel to the seat cushion edge

UPHOLSTERY MATERIAL APPLICATION

Flexible polyurethane foam density is measured in pounds per cubic foot.

FOAM DENSITY CALCULATION

The support factor is the ratio of 65% indentation force deflection (IFD) divided by 25% IFD.

FOAM COMPRESSION MODULUS (SUPPORT FACTOR)

Cushions

Polyurethane foam is the first choice for seating cushions. Multiple grades and densities of foam are usually bonded together to achieve the desired feel. For example, softer foams may be laminated to harder foams to provide surface softness along with firm support. Cushions can be preupholstered in muslin or bonded polyester to increase the life of the upholstery material.

Three basic properties affect the performance of a polyurethane foam: density, the Indentation Force Deflection, and the Compression Modulus.

- *Density* is a measurement of the mass per unit volume, expressed in lb/ft³ (kg/m³). Density is the most important foam property, as it determines the durability and support of the foam. The greater the foam density, the greater the support. Density is not a measurement of firmness; high-density foams can be quite soft. Water, for example, has a high density. Typically, higher-density foams are more expensive than low-density foams.

$$\text{Density} = \frac{\text{Weight (mass)}}{\text{Length} - \text{Width} - \text{Height (volume)}}$$

- *The Indentation Force Deflection (IFD)* is a measure of the foam firmness and is independent of density. It is determined by indenting the foam a percentage of its original height and noting the required force. IFD is an indication of comfort. A 25% IFD (indenting the foam 25% of its original height) is used to measure the surface feel of a foam. The less force required to compress the foam, the softer it is. *The Indentation Force Deflection (IFD)* is a measure of the foam firmness and is independent of density. It is determined by indenting the foam a percentage of its original height and noting the required force. IFD is an indication of comfort. A 25% IFD (indenting the foam 25% of its original height) is used to measure the surface feel of a foam. The less force required to compress the foam, the softer it is. For upholstery, 25% IFD can range from 5 to 50 lb (2.2 to 22 kg).

- *The Compression Modulus*, or support factor, is an indication of the foam's support and is primarily a function of the type of foam. The Compression Modulus is calculated by taking a second IFD measurement by indenting the foam 65% of its original height and dividing it by the 25% IFD. Typically, the greater the difference between the 25% IFD and the 65% IFD, the greater capability the foam has to support weight. To put it another way, the higher the support factor, the better the foam's capability to provide support. In most cases, the higher the foam density, the greater the Compression Modulus.

$$\text{Compression Modulus} = \frac{65\% \text{ IFD}}{25\% \text{ IFD}}$$

SUSPENSION SYSTEMS

Much as a box spring is crucial to the proper support of a mattress, a chair's suspension system provides a firm foundation for the cushions. Several types of springing and webbing systems are combined to achieve the desired support in the seat and back.

Springing systems are used in conjunction with webbing to provide greater resilience and longer wear. There are two common springing systems—*coil spring* and *Marshall units*—each of which is supported by a webbing system. The eight-way hand-tied coil spring system is the most expensive, labor-intensive, and durable. The springs are held together with springing twine that is laced through the top of the spring and tied to adjacent springs in eight directions. This integrates the coils, forming a uniform surface of support. Marshall, or innerspring, units are springs that are contained inside individual pockets of muslin or burlap. Marshall units are purchased joined together, ready to be used as a springing system.

Five webbing systems are commonly used for commercial seating: *woven decking, webbing tape, corrugated steel, wire mesh,* and *sinuous spring.* Rubberized, woven decking is stretched taut across the frame and stapled in place, providing a firm but resilient base for cushions. Interwoven webbing tape, made of jute, cotton, or rubber, provides support directly for cushions or for coil springs. Corrugated steel bands are often used to support coil springs in an eight-way hand-tied suspension system. Plastic-covered wire mesh grids can be stretched across the seating frame for a more affordable suspension system. One of the most popular webbing systems is sagless, or sinuous, springs. This "wiggle wire" is linked together by small helical springs.

CASTER AND GLIDE SELECTION

Two types of casters are popular for use on chair bases: *dual wheel* and *hooded.* The caster wheel is made of either hard or soft plastic, typically nylon. The selection of caster material is based in part on the type of flooring that will be used under the chair.

Hard casters are used on soft floorings such as carpet or carpet tile. The use of a rigid caster increases the chair's mobility on a carpeted surface. When selecting casters that will be used only on carpet floors, keep the following guidelines in mind:

• Hard casters with slightly rounded-wheel edge profiles tend to have better carpet wear characteristics than those with square edges.
• Hard rubber casters tend to mark a carpet more than plastic casters.
• Soft casters are used on hard or resilient floorings to help control the roll of the chair.

Glides are typically specified for chairs that will not be moved repeatedly or are required to remain stationary. Wide-based glides help distribute the weight of the chair and prevent the permanent indentation of a floor finish. Glides may reduce the height of the chair.

INTERWOVEN WEBBING TAPE

EIGHT-WAY HAND-TIED COIL SPRINGS

SAGLESS, OR SINUOUS, SPRINGS

DUAL WHEEL CASTER   **HOODED CASTER**

CASTERS

GLIDES

WOOD-FRAME FURNITURE

CONSTRUCTION

Solid wood is the most commonly used material for structural components of commercial furniture because it is durable, lightweight, and workable. Construction details can determine the useful life and affect the cost of the furniture. When evaluating a piece of wood furniture for the quality of its construction, consider the joinery methods, wood species, and finish.

Joinery Methods

Joinery methods commonly used for wood commercial furniture include *interlocking* and *mechanical* joints. Glue may be used with one of these positive-joint methods; however, glue alone is not adequate to secure commercial furniture joints. In high-quality wood furniture, wood end grain, laminated board edges, and mechanical fasteners (such as screws or nails and joinery methods) are generally not exposed to view.

Interlocking Joints

Interlocking joints include doweled, mortise-and-tenon, dovetail, and dado joints. Dowels are beveled on each end and can be grooved to carry excess glue and allow air to escape as the joint dries. Dowel joints are not as strong or stable as rabbet or mortise-and-tenon joints. Mortise-and-tenon joints are used in high-quality furniture construction to join components such as rails to the legs of tables. Interlocking joints, such as dovetail and dado joints, are used in residential furniture more than in high-quality commercial furniture. Dovetail joints are used to join drawer sides to drawer fronts and backs. Dado joints are used to hold the ends of fixed shelves.

Mechanical Joints

Concealed mechanical fasteners are used to strengthen other carpentry joints. Miter joints are reinforced with corner blocks that are glued and mechanically fastened with screws. Mechanical joints can also permit controlled movement, such as collapsible table legs. Exposed mechanical fasteners are the most contemporary; they are commonly used for affordable furniture that has a limited life span and are popular for use with manufactured board products. Staples, crimped metal fasteners, or clamp nails are not durable enough to be used as commercial furniture fasteners.

WOOD FINISHES

Staining, filling, and sealing, although not required, are often used to improve the appearance or performance of finishes.

Stains

Stains are colorants, not protectants, that are used to make the wood grain more noticeable, change the color of the wood, or imitate a different wood species. After staining, the wood can be filled and sealed.

Stains contain soluble dyes or insoluble pigments as coloring agents that also keep the stains in liquid form.

Water Stains

Water stains are powders that are mixed in water. They provide a fade-resistant, clear, permanent color and are the most difficult stains to apply properly. They raise the grain and usually require light sanding.

DOWEL   **BUTT AND GLUED**   **SPLINE**   **TONGUE-AND-GROOVE**

METHODS OF JOINING BOARDS

DOWEL   **STOP DADO**   **MORTISE-AND-TENON**   **DOVETAIL**

INTERLOCKING JOINTS

GLUED CORNER BLOCK   **SCREWED CORNER BLOCK**

DOVETAIL WITH CORNER REINFORCEMENT   **DOUBLE-SCREWED CORNER BLOCK**

CORNER REINFORCEMENT METHODS

Penetrating Oil Stains

Penetrating oil stains are premixed and are available in a variety of colors. They are likely to fade and bleed into other coats of the finish and are not recommended for most applications.

Pigmented Oil Stains

Pigmented oil stains are the easiest to apply and will not raise the wood grain. Like the penetrating oil stains, they are sold premixed and are available in a variety of colors.

Nongrain-Raising Stains

Nongrain-raising stains are known for their rapid drying time and transparent colors. They are spray-applied.

Fillers

Fillers close the wood grain and pores and are used to produce smooth surfaces on woods with open grains or large pores.

Filler colors can match or contrast with the wood colors. Filler colors and stains can be used together to obtain several appearances.

- *Paste wood fillers* are often used with open-grained woods such as oak, walnut, and mahogany. They differ from wood putty, which is used to fill recesses and defects.
- *Liquid fillers* are used for woods with small pores, such as beech, maple, and cherry.

Sealers

Sealers permeate the wood pores so topcoats are not absorbed into the wood, but adhere to its surface. Sealers are usually applied immediately before the topcoat. They secure the stain and filler and saturate the wood surface. Sealer selection is based on the type of topcoat to be applied. Polyesters, polyurethanes, and other synthetic finishes require specialized sealers.

Topcoats

Topcoats protect the wood from moisture and wear. To prevent the topcoat from yellowing with age, ultraviolet (UV) inhibitors can be added. A clear finish is called *water white* in the furniture-manufacturing industry. Penetrating finishes, like oils and waxes that are often used for residential furniture, soak into the wood and do not build up a protective layer on the wood surface. They are also less durable than topcoats.

Polyesters

Polyesters are the hardest type of topcoat. They are nearly 100% solids when applied and are almost as durable as high-pressure plastic laminates when cured. They also have good filling and leveling characteristics. Polyesters typically have a high gloss but are also available in matte finishes and have characteristics of plastics, such as good resistance to temperature extremes and crazing. Clear and opaque polyester film applications are available. The application of polyesters requires special equipment and skills. These finishes cannot be touched up on-site.

Catalyzed Polyurethanes

Catalyzed polyurethanes are among the most durable finishes and are easier to apply than polyesters. Many consider them the first choice for commercial wood furniture finishing, and they are popular for applications that may be exposed to temperature extremes or UV radiation. Catalyzed polyurethane finishes do not water stain.

Standard Lacquers

Standard lacquers, also called *noncatalyzed lacquers,* are most often used as a residential furniture topcoat. They are easy to apply, polish, and repair; have an unlimited shelf life; and dry quickly for dustproof coats. These lacquers have a high resistance to heat, water, and alcohol, and are available in a full range of sheens. Standard lacquers amalgamate successive coats; each coat partially dissolves previous coats as it is applied to produce a solid, monolithic finish.

CHARACTERISTICS OF WOOD FURNITURE STAINS

STAIN TYPE	CHARACTERISTICS	APPLICATION METHODS	DRYING TIME
Water	Clearest coat, nonbleeding, raises grain; requires light sanding	Wiping, sanding	12 hours
Penetrating oil	Nongrain-raising, likely to bleed, fades	Wiping, brushing	24 hours
Pigmented oil	Easiest to apply, nongrain-raising, hides grain	Wiping, brushing, spraying	3–12 hours
Nongrain-raising	Dries rapidly, nonbleeding, nongrain-raising, clear colors, streaks easily	Spraying	15 minutes–3 hours

Source: William P. Spence and L. Duane Griffiths, Furnituremaking: Design and Construction; Englewood Cliffs, NJ: Prentice Hall, 1991.

ROUND GROMMET
Round grommets are often selected for desks and work surfaces.

RECTANGULAR GROMMET
Rectangular grommets are often selected for credenzas and desk returns.

Grommets are used to organize and conceal electrical and phone line connections beneath the table surface. Dimensions vary among manufacturers.

GROMMETS

SQUARE EDGE

TOP BEVEL - WILL MAKE EDGE APPEAR THICKER

BOTTOM BEVEL - WILL MAKE EDGE APPEAR THINNER

ROUNDED-OVER

TRADITIONAL THUMBNAIL MOLDING

OVOLO

UNDERCUT

SHALLOW-TOP BEVEL

TABLE EDGE PROFILES
Source: Vecta; Grand Prairie, Texas

Catalyzed Lacquers

Catalyzed lacquers have a limited shelf life and are difficult to repair if the finish is damaged. Types of catalyzed lacquers are vinyl, acrylic, and opaque. Vinyl lacquers have a plastic, rather than a nitrocellulose, base. Acrylic lacquers provide a good-quality clear finish. Opaque lacquers are pigmented, alkyd, nitrocellulose lacquers, and dry almost instantly.

Conversion Varnishes

Conversion varnishes provide durable, quick-drying surfaces that resist most common chemicals, but they tend to yellow with age. Opaque conversion varnishes are also available.

Water-Reducible Acrylic Lacquer

Water-reducible acrylic lacquer is not commonly recommended as a finish but may be required to comply with the VOC emission-control standards of authorities having jurisdiction.

MASTERSPEC®; published by ARCOM; Salt Lake City, Utah, and Alexandria, Virginia

CONFERENCE TABLES

SELECTION CRITERIA

Conference room table size and configuration influence the room size as well as the comfort of the occupants. A typical standard table size, which can be used in most conference rooms, improves efficiency in room layout and in furniture storage and retrieval. Accessibility issues for tables are addressed by manufacturers; review for conformance to codes.

Tables in trapezoidal or other shapes permit flexibility in nonstandard table arrangements, which may be useful for situations such as videoconferencing. Modular tables provide greater flexibility in room layout than one large table. Consider room usage and quality level in determining table types and styles. Large tables should be broken into smaller modules for ease of installation.

Table materials and finishes should reflect the function and quality level of the intended conference or training function. High-end quality rooms may be appropriate for custom tables of wood, stone, and glass. Midlevel conference room and training tables should be durable and comfortable, offer the appropriate features, and be cost-effective and easy to store. Tabletop finishes can include plastic laminate, linoleum, wood veneer, and other materials. Edge materials, including wood, rubber, and leather, provide additional protection and/or comfort. Beveled and eased table edges provide greater comfort than squared edges, and are less subject to edge damage. Table edges that are beveled on the underside provide more room for chair arms.

Guidelines for conference and training table design:

- The optimum dimension for each occupant is 30 in. (762 mm), which allows for an average-size chair and space between occupants, without straddling table legs.
- A common table length for two persons is 60 in. (1,524 mm).
- Typical training table size is 30 in. (762 mm) wide, 60 in. (1,324 mm) long, and 29 in. (737 mm) high.
- Table height should allow the armrest to fit under the table without impact. Accessible table heights must accommodate wheelchairs.
- Accessible tables may require special bases for clearance of a wheelchair.
- Table width should allow occupants to work comfortably and have reference space. A common minimum width is 24 in. (610 mm). A 30-in. (762-mm) or greater width can be used if space and function permits and if people are seated across from one another.
- Table bases should be stable, preferably with bearer bars.
- Folding or flip-top tables offer flexibility in room layout and usage.
- Tabletop or recessed power options include plug-in or hardwired capabilities with wire management for LAN, power, and telephone.
- For computer usage, consider recessed computer monitors in special tables to improve sight lines.

SEATING CAPACITY GUIDELINES

ROUND TOPS

DIAMETER IN (MM)	APPROXIMATE CAPACITY
42 (1,067)	4
48 (1,219)	5
54 (1,372)	5
60 (1,524)	6
66 (1,981)	6
72 (1,829)	7
84 (2,134)	8
96 (2,438)	10
108 (2,743)	11
120 (3,048)	12

SQUARE TOPS

DEPTH IN (MM)	WIDTH IN. (MM)	APPROXIMATE CAPACITY
30 (762)	30 (762)	4
36 (914)	36 (914)	4
42 (1,067)	42 (1,067)	4
48 (1,219)	48 (1,219)	4
54 (1,372)	54 (1,372)	4
60 (1,524)	60 (1,524)	8

RECTANGULAR TOPS

DEPTH IN. (MM)	WIDTH IN. (MM)	APPROXIMATE CAPACITY
48 (1,219)	24 (610)	1
60 (1,524)	24 (610)	4
72 (1,829)	24 (610)	4
84 (2,134)	24 (610)	3
36 (914)	30 (762)	4
48 (1,219)	30 (762)	4
60 (1,524)	30 (762)	6
72 (1,829)	30 (762)	6
84 (2,134)	30 (762)	6
96 (2,438)	30 (762)	8
48 (1,219)	36 (914)	4
60 (1,524)	36 (914)	6
72 (1,829)	36 (914)	6
84 (2,134)	36 (914)	6
96 (2,438)	36 (914)	8
72 (1,829)	42 (1,067)	6
84 (2,134)	42 (1,067)	6
96 (2,438)	42 (1,067)	8
108 (2,743)	42 (1,067)	8
120 (3,048)	42 (1,067)	10
72 (1,829)	48 (1,219)	6
84 (2,134)	48 (1,219)	8
96 (2,438)	48 (1,219)	8
108 (2,743)	48 (1,219)	10
120 (3,048)	48 (1,219)	12

RACETRACK TOPS

DEPTH IN. (MM)	WIDTH IN. (MM)	APPROXIMATE CAPACITY
72 (1,829)	36 (914)	6
96 (2,438)	48 (1,219)	6
120 (3,048)	48 (1,219)	8
144 (3,658)	48 (1,219)	10
120 (3,048)	60 (1,524)	10
144 (3,658)	60 (1,524)	10
180 (4,572)	60 (1,524)	12
216 (5,486)	60 (1,524)	14
240 (6,096)	60 (1,524)	16

BOAT TOPS

DEPTH IN. (MM)	WIDTH—CENTER	WIDTH—END	APPROXIMATE CAPACITY
72 (1,829)	36 (914)	30 (762)	6
84 (2,134)	38 (965)	31 (787)	6
96 (2,438)	40 (1,016)	32 (813)	8
120 (3,048)	44 (1,118)	33 (838)	10
144 (3,658)	48 (1,219)	34 (864)	10
168 (4,267)	52 (1,321)	35 (889)	12
192 (4,877)	56 (1,422)	36 (914)	14
216 (5,487)	60 (1,524)	37 (940)	16
240 (6,096)	60 (1,524)	38 (965)	18
264 (6,706)	60 (1,524)	39 (991)	20
288 (7,315)	60 (1,524)	40 (1,016)	20

Source: Vecta; Grand Prairie, Texas

Approximate seating estimates are based on 30 in. (762 mm) per person. Chair widths are assumed to be 25 in. (635 mm), plus 5 in. (127 mm) space between chairs. Adjust these guidelines to accommodate the width of the chair.

BOOTHS AND TABLES

BOOTH CENTERS

CLEARANCES

SEATING
CAPACITY: 6   4-6   4   2-4   2

TABLES SHOULD HAVE ROUNDED ENDS.
TABLES ARE OFTEN 2" (50) SHORTER THAN BOOTH.

Tables should have rounded ends. Tables are often 2 in. (50 mm) shorter than booth.

SEATING CAPACITY

Booth sizes may be determined by local building codes.

BOOTH LAYOUT

Chairmasters Inc.; Bronx, New York

SYSTEMS FURNITURE

TYPES

There are two basic types of systems furniture: *panel-supported* and *freestanding* systems. Many manufacturers offer systems that combine freestanding components with traditional panel-supported units. These systems provide flexibility and function for workplace tasks. High-tech designs, as well as more conservative systems, are available.

Systems furniture is available that addresses the total workplace environment, using walls, panels, post-and-beam construction, work surfaces, filing, storage, raised-floor platforms for wiring and cabling, and other flexible elements. Many systems furniture products are compatible with others from the same manufacturer, allowing greater flexibility and applications.

Panel-Supported Systems

Panel-supported systems, the most popular type of systems furniture, support the work surfaces, accessories, and other furniture components from panels that form the boundaries of the workstation. Wall-mounted slotted standards are also available so that these systems can be hung on a traditional gypsum wallboard wall. BIFMA has authored a standard for panel-based systems furniture; ANSI X5.6, *Standard for Office Furnishings Panel Systems,* tests the safety of panels and panel-mounted components.

Freestanding Systems

Freestanding systems are independent of surrounding panels, and function like floor-supported desks. Furniture components can be attached to the work surface or may be freestanding mobile units. Freestanding systems can be surrounded by panels or installed in a space with constructed walls. New systems furniture types are being developed that integrate technology to the design of the furniture.

PANELS

Panels are used to create workstations, divide work areas, and allow the attachment of work surfaces, storage units, and accessories. Panels must be supported, either by configuration, to create a stable unit, or with freestanding panel support feet. Panel sizes vary by manufacturer and are often described in nominal dimensions. Generic panel widths from major manufacturers are typically based on a 6 in. (152 mm) module: 12-, 18-, 24-, 30-, 36-, 42-, 48-, and 60-in.-(305-, 457-, 610-, 762-, 914-, 1,067-, 1,219-, and 1,524-mm-) wide panel. Common panel heights are 30, 36, 39, 42, 45, 47, 50, 53, 64, 72, 78, and 85 in. (762, 914, 991, 1,067, 1,143, 1,194, 1,270, 1,346, 1,626, 1,829, 1,981, and 2,159 mm). Some panel systems are also based on a 5 in. (127 mm) module: 20- to 60-in.- (508- to 1,524-mm-) wide panel.

Because panel thickness varies with each specific line of systems furniture, from 2 to 6 in. (51 to 153 mm), it should be factored into the overall dimensional footprint when space planning with systems furniture.

Panels are available in acoustical and nonacoustical versions. Other options include tackable surfaces, perforated metal, markerboard panels, and vision panels.

TRADITIONAL PANEL-SUPPORTED SYSTEM
Source: Steelcase Inc., Grand Rapids, Michigan

FREESTANDING SYSTEM
Source: Steelcase Inc., Grand Rapids, Michigan

PLANNING CONSIDERATIONS

Panel widths and heights vary greatly among manufacturers and even among individual lines of furniture provided by the same manufacturer. Allowing for panel progression, if applicable, and careful consideration of a furniture system's capacity for reconfiguration allows the designer to make intelligent decisions in the initial phases of a project.

Low Panels

Lower panel heights, in the 30 to 36 in. (762 to 915 mm) range can be used for desk height panel surrounds, where higher panels would create an obstruction and where communication and supervision may be required. Panels in the 40-in.-(1,016-mm-) high range can be used for transaction height configurations, often supplemented with a countercap transaction work surface. This is useful for reception desks and where an obscured sight line to the interior of the workstation is desired. Panel heights in the 54 to 63 in. (1,371 to 1,600 mm) range provide seated privacy for occupants of the work area, whereas panel heights in the 68 to 80 in. (1,727 to 2,032 mm) range provide standing privacy for the occupants.

Some panels are available with acoustical properties and some offer acoustical and tackable combination panels. Some panels are of perforated metal, to allow ventilation at the backs of equipment or at the base of a station for airflow. Metal and hard-surface panels are also available for ease of maintenance and cleanability and to address static control issues. Many manufacturers also offer open, or *vision,* panels to allow interaction or line of sight between workstations.

Other specialty panels or panel attachments can include markerboards and tool rails, on which to hang essential work tools such as the telephone, paper sorters, calendars, and other supplies, to free up work surface space.

PANEL FABRICS AND FINISHES

Each manufacturer offers a multitude of panel fabrics and frame and component finishes. Confirm the availability of fabric and finishes for each furniture system, especially when combining two or more systems, to allow for finish coordination and compatibility.

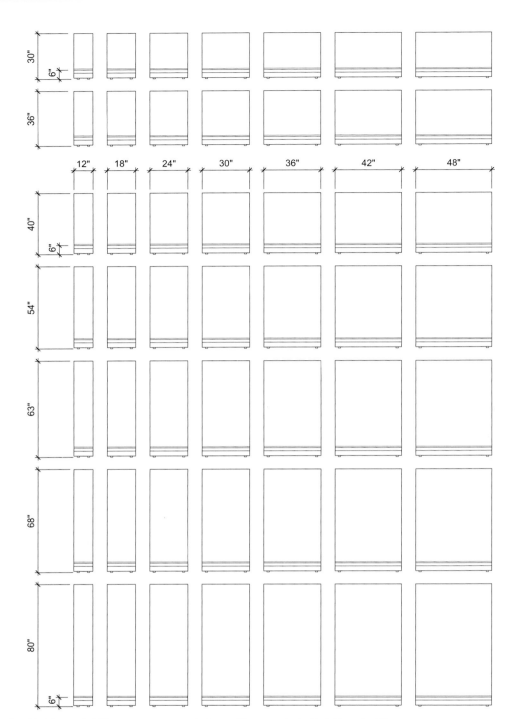

Panel heights and widths vary among manufacturers. Shown are typical heights and widths.

TYPICAL PANEL HEIGHTS AND WIDTHS

PANEL CONSTRUCTION

Most panels are constructed with a steel frame and various types of infill materials, a base, and top cap. Power and data raceways are located at various locations within the panel, most commonly at the base, but also at the belt line, commonly located at desk height. Some manufacturers offer additional horizontal raceways. Panels are typically furnished with slotted standards on the vertical edges, which allow attachment of components at 1 in. (25 mm) increments.

MODULAR PANELS

There are four basic types of panels: *monolithic*, *tiled*, *beltway,* and *stackable*.

Monolithic Panels

Monolithic panels provide one finish surface and one raceway location. This panel type is the most affordable and the least flexible.

Tiled Panels

Tile panels incorporate stacked insert tiles within metal frames. This panel type provides flexibility in tile insert types, finishes, and heights. Different tile types can be combined; for example, a solid panel for modesty at the base and a vision panel above the work surface. Insert tile heights are typically 14 to 16 in. (356 to 406 mm). Other sizes are available to meet installation requirements.

Tiled panels offer the same versatility of material and finish transitions as the stackable panel but without the versatility of height changes, since the frame is integral to the whole panel height. The panel must be removed and replaced with a new height panel in order to achieve height differential. If height flexibility is not an issue for the client, then the tiled panel is a cost-effective way to achieve the look of the stacking panel.

Beltway Panels

Beltway panels offer the convenience of having power, data, and phone receptacles at workstation height. This allows for a more ergonomic approach to equipment changes at the desktop and controls some of the clutter of wires at the base of panel.

Stackable Panels

Some manufacturers offer stackable panels that offer greater versatility in varying the height of panels within a run of workstations, to create a functional and aesthetically pleasing office landscape. The materials and finishes can be changed at each height for function or design purposes, and the final product height can be added to or subtracted from without disruption to each panel or workstation.

MONOLITHIC PANEL

TILED PANEL

BELTWAY PANEL

STACKABLE PANEL

Panel finishes, acoustical ratings, and general performance vary by manufacturer.

PANEL CONSTRUCTION
Source: Knoll, Inc.; East Greenville, Pennsylvania

PANEL CONNECTIONS AND HARDWARE

Each manufacturer provides connecting hardware for panel attachment. Straight-line connectors, or hinges, align and secure straight panels in a row or where a straight panel is attached to a curved panel. Where panels are connected at right angles, hinge connectors are used. Some manufacturers provide special hinge connectors, capable of varying angle connections. T-connectors allow the attachment of the panels to the face of another panel or to a wall. Special connectors allow the attachment of panels of varying height. Off-module connectors are available from selected manufacturers for flexible placement of components independent of the systems furniture module. Consult manufacturers for descriptions of panel connection hardware.

PANEL LOAD CONSIDERATIONS

Special consideration should be given to panel run lengths and panel load restrictions. Each manufacturer has recommended allowances for maximum panel run lengths and panel load tolerances within each system offered. Follow the manufacturer's recommendations to ensure safety within configurations.

DOORS

Most manufacturers offer two types of doors that function in workstations with higher panel heights for privacy: *sliding* and *panel* (sometimes referred to as a *hinge*).

Sliding Doors

Sliding doors are either outside-mounted or inside-mounted, depending on the manufacturer. Most systems provide a sliding door at a 54 to 60 in. (1,372 to 1,524 mm) panel height range, which allows the flexibility of an office atmosphere without sacrificing light or airflow to the general area.

Panel, or Hinge, Doors

Panel doors are usually offered in higher panel heights, in the 72 to 90 in. (1,829 to 2,286 mm) panel height range. They offer the closest approximation to a gypsum board wall office without the cost of such construction. Higher panels should be treated like a gypsum-board-constructed wall in planning considerations since they can block some of the light and airflow to the general area.

COMPONENTS

Most components are panel-hung or work-surface-supported. Balanced loads, such as binder bin storage hung on both sides of a panel, are more stable than a one-sided load.

T-WALL CONNECTOR OR WALL ATTACHMENT BRACKET

STRAIGHT-LINE CONNECTION

L-CONNECTOR, HIGH/LOW PANEL CONDITION

T-CONNECTOR, HIGH/LOW PANEL CONDITION

FOUR-WAY CONNECTOR

PANEL CONNECTIONS
Source: Herman Miller; Zeeland, Michigan

Progressive systems shift, or "creep," when panels are inserted perpendicular to a row of panels.

PROGRESSIVE PANEL SYSTEM

Nonprogressive systems are measured from centerline to centerline of the connector posts. Changes can be made without moving existing panels.

NONPROGRESSIVE PANEL SYSTEM

PROGRESSIVE AND NONPROGRESSIVE PANEL SYSTEMS

The connection methods for panel-supported systems have ramifications in the design and future modification of workstations. Panel-supported systems furniture is considered either *progressive* or *nonprogressive* with regard to the panel-to-panel attachment method.

Progressive Panel Systems

Progressive systems shift, or "creep," when additional panels are added. Panel thicknesses must be accounted for at each connection. Typical panel thickness is a nominal 2 in. (51 mm), although thicker panels are available from various manufacturers. Perpendicular panel connections require the insertion of a connector, resulting in a shift of all subsequent adjacent panels.

Nonprogressive Panel Systems

Changes to the configuration of nonprogressive systems can be made without moving existing panels. Because every panel connection requires a connector post, perpendicular panels can be added or removed without disturbing adjacent workstations. Panel widths in nonprogressive systems are measured from centerline to centerline of the connector posts.

Nonprogressive panel systems are typically powered only at the central spine of a panel run to allow ease of reconfiguration of connecting panels without interruption and additional cost to power and data lines. This should be taken into account when configuring work surface placement, to allow maximum power and data feed from the spine and ensure proper placement of equipment to this proximity.

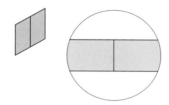

STRAIGHT CONNECTIONS
No creep occurs when panels of the same or varying heights are joined with hinges.

L-CONNECTIONS
A ³⁄₃₂ in. (2 mm) creep occurs at the intersection when panels are joined in an L-configuration.

T-CONNECTIONS
A ³⁄₁₆ in. (4 mm) creep occurs when panels are joined in a T-configuration.

X-CONNECTIONS
A ³⁄₁₆ in. (4 mm) creep occurs in both directions of an X-configuration.

PANEL CREEP CONSIDERATIONS
Source: Steelcase, Inc.; Grand Rapids, Michigan

WORK SURFACES

Horizontal work surfaces are available in various sizes and shapes. They can be attached to panels in panel-hung systems or can be supported by freestanding components, such as file cabinets. Depths are typically 24, 30, or 36 in. (610, 762, or 914 mm); lengths are 24, 30, 36, 45, 60, and 72 in. (610, 762, 914, 1,143, 1,524, and 1,829 mm). Straight, corner, curved, and peninsula-shaped work surfaces are available. Work surface edge profiles vary with each manufacturer but are typically offered in eased, bull-nose, radius, and square edges.

Construction

Construction of work surfaces vary, but many are constructed in a box and cross-member fashion, with a honeycomb core to reduce weight. Finish materials vary, but are commonly plastic laminate or wood veneer. Work surfaces can be provided with grommets for wiring or inserts for attachment of components, such as brackets and pedestals. Custom sizes are available.

Workstation Typicals

When designing workstation *typicals,* or *standards,* for each job function, consider the client's space allocation with regard to footprint dimension allowed for each job title. The requirements of a particular job function—for example, those of a telephone or traveling salesperson—may be minimal with regard to work surface but more extensive with regard to storage capacity for retrieval of, for example, specification and product brochures and client files. In contrast, when planning for a marketing or executive workspace, consider a more expansive work surface, along with additional storage, since these job functions typically require an abundance of both.

Other positions, such as that of administrative assistant, will usually require both ample work surface and storage to accommodate additional equipment. They might also require a transaction top so that workers can be approached without having their workspace invaded by their associates.

Mock-up Workstations

When time and budget allow, a mock-up workstation should be erected by each competing manufacturer to show the client the inherent differences in product lines and to give a realistic sense of spatial relationships. A mock-up also allows for any last-minute revisions to further customize the workstation based on end-user feedback.

WORK SURFACE CONSTRUCTION—WOOD
Source: Knoll, Inc.; East Greenville, Pennsylvania

RECTANGULAR

RECTANGULAR SPLIT TOP

D-PENINSULA

PENINSULA

HALF-ROUND

CORNER WORK SURFACE

SPLIT-TOP CORNER WORK SURFACE

CURVILINEAR WORK SURFACE

The sizes, shapes, and edge details of work surfaces vary greatly with each line of furniture and each manufacturer.

WORK SURFACE TYPES
Source: Knoll, Inc.; East Greenville, Pennsylvania

OVERHEAD STORAGE

Panel-supported open shelves and closed binder bins with flipper doors are typically 12 in. (305 mm) deep, and are available in widths corresponding to most panel widths. Various other storage units and cabinets, both panel-hung and freestanding, are also available.

When selecting closed overhead storage or binder bins, consider ease of door operation. Overhead storage units should have lightweight doors that are easily opened from a seated position, since this is how most operators use their furniture. Some manufacturers offer special bins that enable the user to lightly touch the door to activate an operating mechanism.

KEYING AND LOCKING

Keying and locking functions should also be specified with storage components since some job functions may require maintenance of confidential materials. Refer to specific manufacturer's product guides when making these selections.

FILE CABINETS

Systems furniture file pedestals may be suspended from the work surface or be freestanding fixed or mobile units. They are available in various configurations of file and box drawer combinations, with optional locks. Many systems furniture companies offer separate file cabinet lines that are compatible with the systems furniture.

Some fixed-pedestal file units are mounted to the underside of work surfaces and are part of the support system for that work surface. Usually, these cabinets do not have a file top and are not easy to relocate. Other fixed-pedestal units are freestanding and not attached to the underside of work surfaces. They allow for easy reconfiguration since they are not specifically tied to any one workstation. Most furniture lines offer a few options for drawer pulls to allow for customer preferences.

Many manufacturers offer mobile pedestals with integral cushion tops to act as a guest seat when the workstation footprint is tight and will not allow for the more traditional side chair.

Other storage components include wardrobe and closed freestanding shelving units that add much needed storage space, as well as form, to the interior of a workstation without sacrificing the footprint of the space.

Less traditional components offer an even greater level of storage and flexibility, and should be considered when the application presents itself, such as for group interaction spaces that allow for sharing of components and mobility of these units within a given space. Some of these components include *slip surfaces*, which are small tables on casters that fit easily under fixed work surfaces and can be pulled out when

SHELF   **OVERHEAD CABINET**   **STORAGE CABINET**

BOOKSHELVES   **SHELVING UNIT**   **COAT STORAGE**   **SHELVING/COAT STORAGE**

STORAGE
Source: Knoll, Inc.; East Greenville, Pennsylvania

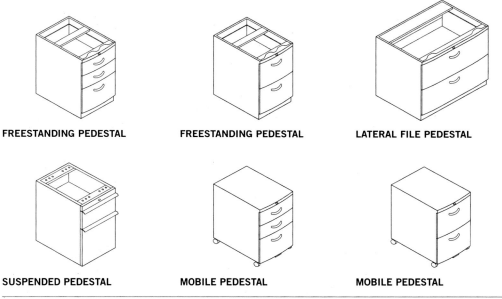

FREESTANDING PEDESTAL   **FREESTANDING PEDESTAL**   **LATERAL FILE PEDESTAL**

SUSPENDED PEDESTAL   **MOBILE PEDESTAL**   **MOBILE PEDESTAL**

FILE CABINETS
Source: Knoll, Inc.; East Greenville, Pennsylvania

needed; special storage taborettes; and flat files that function as both additional storage and work surface space. Tackboards, markerboards, CPU holders, wire managers, pencil drawers, and paper flow and divider units are also available. Check availability of these specialty components with each manufacturer.

KEYBOARD AND MOUSE TRAYS

Keyboard and mouse trays should also be considered for specific end users, to resolve ergonomic issues with regard to repetitive stress injuries. Many types of trays are offered by each manufacturer, from simple adjustable trays to fully articulating tray types.

TASK LIGHTING

Most systems furniture manufacturers offer task-lighting units, which are attached to overhead storage units. Task lights are used in tandem with general office area lighting.

TASK LIGHT
Source: Knoll, Inc; East Greenville, Pennsylvania

POWER AND COMMUNICATIONS

Wire and Cable

Two types of conductors that carry signals are accommodated by systems furniture raceways: *electrical wiring* and *communications cabling*. Electrical wiring and communications cabling are typically separated within the raceway. Wire and cable are distributed from the base building source through the systems furniture to the workstation equipment. This can be accomplished through connections at walls, the floor, or from the ceiling.

Electrical Wiring

Systems furniture manufacturers provide power in assemblies for the hookup of the panel's electrical wiring conduit, commonly called a "pigtail," to the building's electrical supply. Connections between panels are snapped together, making them easy to install and reconfigure. Electrical units are UL-listed. Certain jurisdictions do not accept prewired systems, so an electrician must install the wiring and make the connections from the main building electrical service source.

Systems furniture panels have a capacity of two to four electrical circuits, which vary according to manufacturer and intended use. Some systems furniture manufacturers offer up to six circuits. Panels typically have base raceway capacity for electrical and communications services. Some manufacturers provide *belt-line* power raceways. Others provide even greater flexibility in electrical wiring, dedicated circuits for equipment, and communications cabling placement.

Electrical Disturbances

Some electrical equipment is vulnerable to disturbances or interferences from other electrical sources. Dedicated or designated circuits can be used to help ensure that equipment will not malfunction or be damaged.

Dedicated Circuits

Dedicated circuits are used to keep power "clean," or free from electrical interferences, which can cause problems with sensitive equipment. Although "dedicated" is not defined by the National Electrical Code (NEC), the expression is widely used to describe a circuit that does not share a neutral wire, as many three-phase wiring systems do. The use of common *neutrals* in commercial and industrial situations is standard practice. The neutral return wire carries unbalanced current back to the power source, which can generate interference. These electromagnet fields generate an electric current that flows through wiring, creating electrical "noise."

Designated Circuits

Designated circuits are circuits reserved for use by specific equipment. These circuits are often used for important equipment that requires a heavy electrical load or that is best isolated from other equipment in case of a power outage.

Communications Cabling

Clear communication is an important part of success in the business arena. While phone lines are typically stranded wire, computer systems use a variety of other cable types, including twisted-pair, four-pair, coaxial, fiber-optic, and shielded cable.

Twisted-Pair Cable

Twisted-pair is the traditional, economical type of cable for voice and lower-speed data communication. Each pair of insulated copper wires connects a single signal from one point to another. Twisted-pair cables are not suitable for high-speed and video transmissions.

Four-Pair Cable

Four-pair cable has four sets of copper wire, twisted together and covered with an insulating material. It is inexpensive and is commonly used for voice and data cabling.

Coaxial Cable

Coaxial cable consists of a single copper wire surrounded by an insulator encased in a metal shell, which acts as a ground return. The insulated return is surrounded by a braided wire or foil shield. This shielding makes coaxial cable relatively immune to interference. Coaxial cable transmits a large amount of data at very high speeds with relatively little signal loss. Broadband coaxial cable systems are used by the cable television industry.

Fiber-Optic Cable

Fiber-optic cable consists of a thin glass wire filament, which is used for signal transmission. It is used more commonly in areas with high-tech requirements.

Shielded Cable

Shielded cable is covered with metal foil to keep out electromagnetic interference. Twisted-pair cables are often shielded for improved performance.

LOCAL AREA NETWORK (LAN)

A local area network is a telecommunications network that eliminates the possibility of signal interruption, offering reliable, linked transmission.

Technology continues to evolve, and new developments in communications include wireless networks for radio and infrared transmissions.

WIRING DIAGRAM
8-WIRE/4-CIRCUIT

This circuit is used in areas where power usage is significant and a single isolated circuit is required for sensitive equipment.

WIRING DIAGRAM—EIGHT-WIRE/ FOUR-CIRCUIT
Source: Knoll, Inc.; East Greenville, Pennsylvania

TWISTED-PAIR

COAXIAL CABLE

SHIELDED CABLE

DATA AND COMMUNICATION CABLE TYPES

WIRE AND CABLE CONNECTIONS TO SYSTEMS FURNITURE

Wire and cable connections from the base building source to the equipment at the workstation can be made in a variety of ways, depending on the structure of the base building. Systems furniture panels are typically powered from a base feed, which is connected to the building's electrical and communications systems from a floor monument ("tombstone") or other floor power sources. Modular raised floors provide flexibility in power source locations. Wall connections are used when panels abut building partitions. Power poles provide service from the ceiling.

Wall Receptacles

Wall receptacles connect wire and cable services from the building to the panel raceway. This connection type severely restricts the system's flexibility. Workstation location relies on proximity to power and data supplies. Relocating wall-mounted junction boxes is labor-intensive and generates a comparatively large amount of construction debris.

Cellular Floor System

Cellular floor systems separate wire and cable to protect against electromagnetic interference. Outlets are typically concealed, and the floor finish is level, without the interruption of floor monuments.

Access Floor System

Access flooring is a structural system of removable floor panels above the structural floor. These floor systems, commonly used for computer rooms, can handle the largest capacities. This is the most flexible distribution system, because virtually every inch of wire and cable can be accessed by the removal of a floor panel. However, it requires adequate ceiling heights to allow for a raised floor.

Poke-Through System

Poke-through systems access wire and cable sources in the ceiling cavity below the floor. Modifying a poke-through system requires the disruption of activities on both floors. Fire-rated assemblies and floor monuments must be used to maintain the fire-resistance rating of the floor.

Flat Wire

Flat wire is flexible conductor cable that is so thin it can be placed directly under the finish flooring. It can be folded or easily joined and there is virtually no disruption to the workplace. Carpet tile is the only finish flooring permitted by the National Electric Code (NEC) for use over flat wire.

WALL RECEPTACLE
Underfloor steel ducts are separate, continuous steel channels cast in the concrete floor slab.

UNDERFLOOR STEEL DUCTS

CELLULAR FLOOR
Cellular floor systems incorporate raceways in the structural metal deck.

ACCESS FLOOR
Access floors offer direct access for easy reconfiguration of power and communication system connections.

TOP FEED WITH POWER POLE
*Source: Haworth, Inc.; Holland, Michigan
Illustration from* Designing Commercial Interiors, *by Christine Piotrowski and Elizabeth Rogers; John Wiley & Sons, Inc., 1999, p. 68.*

POKE-THROUGH SYSTEM
Poke-through systems access wire and cable in the ceiling below the floor.

FLAT WIRE
Flat-wire power distribution is installed directly under carpet tile.

WIRE AND CABLE CONNECTIONS TO SYSTEMS FURNITURE

DESIGN CONSIDERATIONS FOR SYSTEMS FURNITURE

When designing a space using systems furniture, consider the following:

- *Building code restrictions.* Local building codes should be reviewed to determine whether the use of systems furniture will impact the code requirements for the space. The requirements for exits will vary according to the type of use, occupancy, and other factors. Panels exceeding a certain height may be considered walls, and therefore will be subject to the minimum width requirements for aisles or corridors formed from these panels. Large areas with open office spaces composed of systems furniture may need to have full-height, rated partitions to meet local codes.
- *Materials* used in systems furniture should meet or exceed minimum code requirements. Vertical surface finishes on panels should have a flame spread index of 25 or less.
- *Lighting* is critical to the success of a systems furniture installation, particularly in an open office area. Systems furniture manufacturers offer task lighting for the immediate work area. General area lighting quality is important to the well-being and comfort of the office worker. The use of computers and the issue of glare has contributed to the development of alternative lighting concepts. Ambient light, which bounces off the ceiling, provides a softer, glare-free overall light in comparison to typical recessed fluorescent or incandescent light fixtures. If using recessed fluorescent fixtures, consider the type of lamp and lens to minimize glare.
- *Acoustics* in open systems furniture installations present unique challenges. Sound travels in all directions and may be difficult to contain. The use of acoustical panels improves sound absorption, but the noise from telephones, conversation, equipment, and other sources may be audible. An acoustical ceiling and carpet on the floor will absorb some of the sound. An acoustical engineer can offer suggestions on how to contain and control noise. Sound-masking systems, utilizing white noise, may be a consideration.

Karen K. Lindblad; Chicago, Illinois
Susan Hardiman; Dorchester, Massachusetts

BASE RACEWAY ELECTRICAL

BELTWAY ELECTRICAL

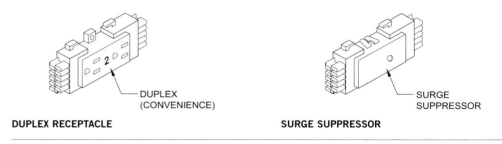

DUPLEX RECEPTACLE   **SURGE SUPPRESSOR**

ELECTRICAL RACEWAY COMPONENTS
Source: Knoll, Inc.; East Greenville, Pennsylvania

INTERIOR PLANTINGS

PLANTS

In order to thrive indoors, plants that are tolerant to interior environmental conditions are often specially chosen. Damage from vandalism and being placed too close to people are also concerns when selecting the hardiness of interior plants.

PLANTING MEDIUM

The medium in which plants are grown is a key element in the healthy interior landscape. The planting medium used for interiors often contains no soil. A planting medium must:

- Be firm enough to support the root structure of a plant and hold it upright (in the case of tall trees or palms, this can be a considerable task).
- Absorb and retain both water and air and provide both to the roots.
- Be compactable, so that it won't settle after the initial installation.
- Discourage the attraction of soil-borne insect pests and diseases.

These criteria can be met by a medium composed primarily of peat and composted bark. Other common ingredients used are perlite and sand. It is highly desirable to use a medium that is sterilized. Although it adds to the expense, sterilization eliminates the possibility of installing a medium that contains insect pests and diseases, a significant advantage for an environment that cannot readily remove such problems once they occur. Outdoors, wind and rain often can keep pests under control, if not eliminate them, while problems such as mold and mildew are also minimized outdoors with good air circulation. Indoors, with no wind, no rain, and planting media designed to retain moisture (to increase watering intervals), these issues become more problematic. Most important, in interior installations, the application of pesticides and fungicides is much more rigidly controlled by law, and in many cases is not allowed at all.

The weight of the plants and planting medium can cause structural design concerns. A typical loam used outdoors may weigh as much as 110 to 120 lb/cu ft (1,762 to 1,922 kg/m³) when saturated with water. The depth necessary to support large plant materials (2½ to 3 ft; 762 mm to 914 mm) may thus generate a dead-load density of more than 300 lb/sq ft (1,464 kg/m³) on the bottom of the planter. Planting media for interior use are generally lighter than standard topsoil, and a lightweight medium can be produced with a density of as little as 70 lb/cu ft (1,121 kg/m³), saturated, by increasing the percentage of perlite. However, the mixed medium must be tested to confirm its density and to ensure its ability to hold up large specimens. The ratio of perlite to other ingredients should not exceed one-third the medium's weight by volume, or its ability to grow plants will be compromised.

BUILT-IN PLANTERS

Consider the following in the design of built-in planters:

- *The angling of the ground bed* allows low plantings to be more visible from afar and creates a look of natural topography.
- *The use of curbs* is essential in design conditions in which the planting bed is flush with the adjoining floor because they will prevent floor-cleaning chemicals from being mopped into the planter.
- *In using tree grates indoors*, provide for a channel around the perimeter of the frame to catch floor-cleaning chemicals.
- *Avoid design conditions where seating is in close proximity to planter beds*, particularly in locations where children are present. Plant vandalism becomes a concern.

Plants can be inadvertently damaged when placed too close to people.

SEATING AT PLANTER

MULCH

INERT FILL

SOIL SEPARATOR

LIP DETAIL

NOTE: FILL MULCH AS SHOWN ABOVE TO PREVENT EXCESSIVE MULCH SPILLING OVER OR TOO LITTLE MULCH EXPOSING THE LIP.

OBSERVATION / SIPHON TUBE

BARK MULCH

SOIL SEPARATOR

PLANT KEPT IN ITS GROW POT

GROW POT

FOAM PELLET FILL

NOTE: INSTEAD OF FOAM PELLET FILL BETWEEN DECORATIVE CONTAINER AND GROW POT, A POLYURETHANE FOAM COLLAR CAN BE WEDGED IN PLACE BENEATH THE MULCH.

FIBERGLASS DECORATIVE CONTAINER

RIGID STYROFOAM SUPPORTS IF NEEDED

Observation tubes allow maintenance staff to check water levels at the bottom of the planter, and if necessary, siphon off excess water.

DECORATIVE CONTAINER INSTALLATION

DECORATIVE PLANTERS

Decorative containers account for the vast majority of interior landscape installations. With the use of plants in built-in planter beds relegated to atrium spaces or other feature locations, the placement of plants in planters is the preferred method of introducing living foliage to commercial spaces.

Decorative container sizes should respond to the shape of the plants they contain. A very wide plant should not be placed in a narrow container, because a wide base may be needed to balance the weight of branches and foliage at the outer extremities of a wide specimen plant. When specifying a decorative container, the interior landscape designer must also be aware of both the overall width and height and the inside width and height of a container, to ensure that the grow pot will fit comfortably within it. Large containers often have lip widths of several inches to help increase the structural strength of the unit. The interior width will thus be significantly less than the overall width. If a plant is to be subirrigated, the additional width or height of the subirrigation unit should be factored into the size specification for the decorative container.

ARTIFICIAL AND PRESERVED PLANTS

Significant recent improvements in the fabrication of artificial and preserved plants have resulted in materials that more closely resemble living plants. The ever-increasing palette of artificial and preserved plants allows designers to specify plants for spaces that are inaccessible or inappropriate for live plants. Large preserved palms, for example, have the favorable trait of being considerably lighter than their live counterparts and can be used in areas where structural limitations prevent the use of large living specimens. Large artificial or preserved plants are, however, considerably more expensive than their live counterparts.

Artificial plants are composed of polyester fabric leaves attached to plastic petioles, which are in turn attached to real or composite wood branches and trunks. The leaves are often photo-embossed with the variegation and venation of live foliage to make them more realistic.

Most preserved plants are palms. They are composed of a PVC trunk core that is hollow, onto which are affixed leaf sheaths that have been cut from real palms. The fronds, also taken from live palm trees, are injected with a chemical that "freeze-dries" their composition to keep them green.

While artificial and preserved plants do not need irrigation, the single most time-intensive and costly maintenance task, they are not maintenance-free, nor are they permanent. Such plants are more prone to vandalism than real plants because they are more brittle, and they become even more brittle with age. They collect dust, and must be cleaned with more care because of their brittleness.

BOTTOMLESS PLANTER

CONCRETE-BOTTOMED PIT PLANTER
The tree is kept in its grow pot.

BUILT-IN PLANTERS WITH TREE GRATE

RECESSED PLANTERS

FEATURE PLANTING

UNDERSTORY PLANTING @ 12" O.C.
(BEHIND FEATURE PLANTING)

REMOVE ALL PLANTS
FROM GROW POTS

4" DIA. OBSERVATION
TUBE WITH CAP

6"

2"

4"

6"

UNHEATED OCCUPIED SPACE

DRAIN WITH WIRE
MESH SCREEN

PLANTING MEDIUM

FLOWERING PLANTS TO REMAIN
WITHIN GROW POTS INSIDE
A LARGER GROW POT

CURB

2" FREEBOARD

SOIL SEPARATOR

CAST-IN-PLACE CONCRETE
STRUCTURAL SLAB

DRAINAGE FILL

2" RIGID INSULATION

WATERPROOFING

Planting bed is mounded and insulated from the unheated space below. Curbing prevents cleaning liquids from infiltrating the planting medium and helps prevent people from stepping into the plant bed.

RECESSED PLANTER WITH CURB AND DRAIN

UNDERSTORY PLANTING

REMOVE ALL PLANTS
FROM GROW POTS

8"

3"

6"

FEATURE PLANTING

PLANTING MEDIUM

CURB

2" FREEBOARD

WATERPROOFING

SOIL SEPARATOR

CAST-IN-PLACE CONCRETE
STRUCTURAL SLAB

STRUCTURAL FILL

VAPOR BARRIER TO FOLLOW
LINE OF COMPACTED SUBGRADE

COMPACTED SUBGRADE

DRAINAGE FILL

Planting bed is mounded and bottomless. Concrete planter walls cast without a bottom can offer substantial cost savings if properly constructed.

RECESSED PLANTER WITH CURB IN SLAB ON GRADE

BUILT-UP PLANTERS

4" DIA. OBSERVATION TUBE WITH CAP

REMOVE ALL PLANTS FROM GROW POTS

8"

2'-6"

4"

PROTECTION BOARD

WATERPROOFING

FEATURE PLANTING

UNDERSTORY PLANTING @ 12" O.C. (BEHIND FEATURE PLANTING)

2" FREEBOARD

2" MULCH

WATERPROOFING

PLANTING MEDIUM

CAST-IN-PLACE CONCRETE PLANTER WALL

SOIL SEPARATOR

DRAINAGE FILL

PROTECTION BOARD OVER WATERPROOFING

CONCRETE KEY JOINT

WATER STOP

CAST-IN-PLACE CONCRETE STRUCTURAL SLAB

DRAIN WITH WIRE MESH SCREEN

HEATED OCCUPIED SPACE

Planting bed is not mounded, and insulation is not required, because the space below is heated.

FLUSH PLANTER WITH FLAT BOTTOM AND DRAIN

OBSERVATION TUBE

UPLIGHT, INSULATED

3"

8"

2'-6"

8"

8"

4" MIN.

OVERLAP SOIL SEPARATOR PORTION OF MIRADRAIN 9000 UP WALL 4" MIN.

SOIL SEPARATOR (TO FILTER DRAINAGE WATER)

PLASTIC DIMPLES (CREATES VOIDS SO DRAINAGE WATER CAN FLOW)

FLAT PLASTIC BASE (TO PROTECT WATERPROOFING)

DETAIL AT MIRADRAIN 9000

FEATURE PLANTING

UNDERSTORY PLANTING @ 12" O.C. (BEHIND FEATURE PLANTING)

2" FREEBOARD

WATERPROOFING

PLANTING MEDIUM

CAST-IN-PLACE CONCRETE PLANTER WALL

WATERPROOFING

MIRADRAIN 9000 (TO RELIEVE HYDRO STATIC PRESSURE)

CONCRETE KEY JOINT

WATER STOP

CAST-IN-PLACE CONCRETE STRUCTURAL SLAB

DRAIN WITH WIRE MESH SCREEN

HEATED OCCUPIED SPACE

Planting bed is not mounded, and insulation is not required, because the space below is heated. Top of planter walls are tapered.

FLUSH PLANTER WITH SLOPED BOTTOM AND DRAIN

BALCONY
GUARD RAIL

GRAB BAR

3'-6"

BALCONY

SECTION

METAL FRAME

BALCONY FLOOR-EDGE-MOUNTED PLANTERS

HOLES
FOR GRAB
BAR

OBSERVATION
TUBE

8" · 4" · 8" · 2"

1 1/2" · 1/2"

8"

1'-0"

1"

1"

PLAN

GLASS PANE

BALCONY RAIL PLANTERS

Balcony rail planters must be detailed to ensure ease of plant installation and maintenance. Balcony plantings can be adapted to manageable maintenance techniques and schedules.

Balcony Floor-Edge-Mounted Planters

If the planter is fitted with a liner that is designed to be removed by hand or via a specially designed hook, the maintenance technician can lift the liner out of the built-in planter and remove the plants that require attention. This method has the advantage of easily replacing individual or groups of plants in the event of plant loss, infestation, or a change of design.

Balcony Rail-Mounted Planters

If plantings are mounted atop a railing, maintenance technicians can readily tend to the plants while they remain in place. The planter itself can serve as the railing for the balcony. However, the rail-top mounted plants can be more easily damaged, inadvertently or by vandalism.

BALCONY
GUARD RAIL

3'-6"

MULCH

GROW POT

SOIL
SEPARATOR

VOID

PLANTER

BALCONY

SECTION

OBSERVATION
TUBE

4"
MIN.

1"

10"

1"

PLAN

ELEVATION

OBSERVATION
TUBE BEYOND

GROW
POT

1" MIN.

GROW POT
WIDTH

1" MIN.

1" FREEBOARD

GROW POT
HEIGHT

PLANTER HEIGHT

2"

MULCH

PERFORATED PLASTIC INSERT
OVER VOID, OR SOIL SEPARATOR
OVER DRAINAGE FILL

WATERPROOFING

PLANTER

BALCONY RAIL

PLANTER DETAIL

BALCONY RAIL-MOUNTED PLANTER

IRRIGATION

Properly designed irrigation systems can greatly reduce maintenance costs because watering is the most time-consuming aspect of interior landscape care. Once the interior landscape is installed, monitoring is required to track changes in the water consumption of individual plants based on their growth and health. Environmental changes in the building (adjustments to air circulation, humidity, cooling, and heating) will also change plant water consumption. There are three methods of watering plants: *by hand*, *automated irrigation systems,* and *subirrigation.*

Domestic water in northern temperate climates is often too cold during the winter months to use for interior landscape irrigation. Water dedicated to irrigation should be tempered by either mixing hot water with cold water, or by heat-tracing supply lines.

Watering by Hand

Hand watering has long been the standard for interior landscape irrigation. This method utilizes a watering can, hose, or a mobile watering device, which consists of a large tank on wheels that delivers water under pressure (battery or pump) from a hose. Top watering compacts the planting medium over time, forcing air out of the root zone and causing the planting medium to settle. The cycle of flooding/drying/flooding is less conducive to optimal plant health than uniform soil moisture. The advantages of hand watering include:

- No cost to design and install.
- Easy to monitor.
- Lack of components to be vandalized.
- Can provide precise water amounts to specific plants.
- Can be used to supply liquid fertilizer or insecticide if needed.
- Flooding to leach the medium of soluble salts can be readily performed.

Plants watered by hand require regular monitoring to determine if the bottom of the root ball is being kept uniformly moist (both continual dryness and continual saturation must be avoided). Technicians must monitor soil moisture levels. Hand-watered plants are most successful when maintained by the same technician. A maintenance technician who services an account on an ongoing basis can familiarize him- or herself with the idiosyncrasies of the plants and planting medium.

WATER RESERVOIR FILL LOCATION

MOISTURE SENSOR

DECORATIVE CONTAINER

WATER RESERVOIR

WATER ENTERS THROUGH SMALL HOLES IN BASE

OVERFLOW DRAINAGE ADAPTER

MOISTURE SENSOR WITH VACUUM SEAL SYSTEM *Source: Planter Technology, Inc., Hayward, California*

WATER INTAKE TUBE

MULCH

ROOT SYSTEM

WATERTIGHT DECORATIVE CONTAINER

FOAM COLLAR

PLANTING MEDIUM

SUBIRRIGATION CONTAINER

VOID

CAPILLARY ACTION

AERATION AND DRAINAGE HOLES

CAPILLARY COLUMN CONTAINS PERLITE

WATER-FERTILIZER RESERVOIR

A subirrigation container can be placed in a decorative, nonwatertight container if it has an impermeable saucer beneath it.

SUBIRRIGATION SYSTEM—WATERTIGHT CONTAINER *Source: Jardinier, Newport Beach, California*

Automated Low-Volume Irrigation Systems

Fabricated soils and drainage systems, controlled climates, limited space, and diminished light intensity and duration combine to require a controlled and concise application of water to interior plants. Advances in automated, low-volume "drip" irrigation systems have expanded their use from agricultural applications to interior irrigation solutions. Automated irrigation systems are typically 10% to 25% more expensive than manual systems.

The advantages of low-volume irrigation include:

- Minimizes the nuisance and liability of overspray onto paved surfaces.
- Exact application of water to the root zone allows for more efficient uptake by the plant.
- Less moisture is available in the planting media for fungi and insects.
- Allows for low-dose pH adjusting, nutrient feeding, and pesticide application via injection pump systems.
- Low-volume equipment is some of the most economical and is installed at or just below grade.
- Water resources are conserved.

The disadvantages of low-volume irrigation are as follows:

- It's more expensive than hand watering.
- System must be routinely monitored and adjusted to promote healthy plants.
- Emitter orifices often clog with debris or mineral deposits and require maintenance.
- There is little leaching of salts from planting medium.
- Visible components can be vandalized.

SUPPLY HEADER

TREE OR FEATURE PLANTING

POLY-TUBING AROUND TREE; INSTALL ADDITIONAL DRIP EMITTERS AS NEEDED FOR TREE WATER REQUIREMENTS

AIR RELIEF VALVE AT HIGHEST POINT

PVC EXHAUST HEADER

DISC-TYPE FILTER (150 MICRON)

REMOTE CONTROL VALVE

FLUSH VALVE

POLY-TUBING IRRIGATION LINES

EDGE OF PLANTER

2" MAIN LINE

PVC SLEEVING INTO PLANTER

LOW-VOLUME DRIP IRRIGATION SYSTEM LAYOUT

SPRAY NOZZLE

1/2" FLEXIBLE PVC PIPE

SEAL SLEEVE PORT

PLANTING AREA

PAVED MATERIAL UNDER PLANTER POT, COORDINATE TO IDENTIFY EXACT POT LOCATIONS AND PAVING SHEDULE FOR SLEEVE INSTALLATION

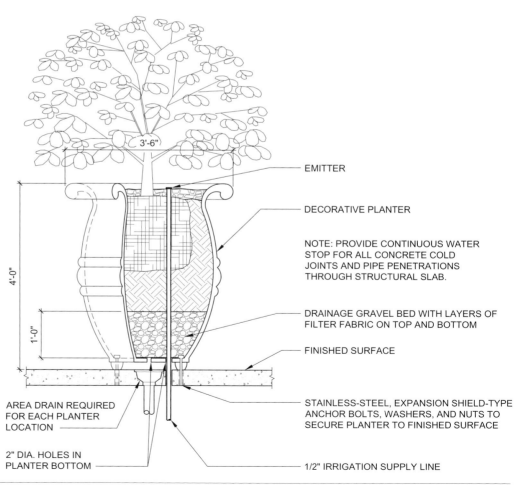

3'-6"

4'-0"

1'-0"

AREA DRAIN REQUIRED FOR EACH PLANTER LOCATION

2" DIA. HOLES IN PLANTER BOTTOM

EMITTER

DECORATIVE PLANTER

NOTE: PROVIDE CONTINUOUS WATER STOP FOR ALL CONCRETE COLD JOINTS AND PIPE PENETRATIONS THROUGH STRUCTURAL SLAB.

DRAINAGE GRAVEL BED WITH LAYERS OF FILTER FABRIC ON TOP AND BOTTOM

FINISHED SURFACE

STAINLESS-STEEL, EXPANSION SHIELD-TYPE ANCHOR BOLTS, WASHERS, AND NUTS TO SECURE PLANTER TO FINISHED SURFACE

1/2" IRRIGATION SUPPLY LINE

DECORATIVE PLANTERS WITH LOW-VOLUME DRIP IRRIGATION

Subirrigation Systems

Subirrigation is a water delivery system in which water is placed in a watertight reservoir beneath or next to the planting medium and is available to the root zone through capillary action or other means. These systems are composed of a watertight container, placed below or adjacent to the root ball of the plant. The water is drawn from the reservoir by one of two methods:

- *Capillary leg* transfers moisture from the reservoir to the planting medium. The capillary leg, filled with planting medium, is placed horizontally adjacent to the reservoir. The planting medium within the root zone draws water up by capillary action from the leg.
- *Moisture sensor with vacuum seal* incorporates a double-walled planter that acts as a water reservoir. A moisture sensor placed in the planting medium near the top creates a vacuum seal when the planting medium is saturated. The water is prevented from exiting the reservoir into the planting medium, unless there is sufficient air in the planting medium to break the seal.

Subirrigation System Considerations

The advantages of a subirrigation system include:

- Allows more water to be applied to a plant or to a planting area than by hand, potentially reducing watering intervals.
- Does not cause settling of the planting medium, so pockets for moisture and air remain in place.
- Plants are generally healthier in a subirrigated environment.

The disadvantages of subirrigation are as follows:

- Higher initial cost than hand watering.
- Neither fertilizer nor insecticide can be added by this method.
- The medium cannot be leached, if necessary. Leaching must be done by hand.
- It is not as easy to monitor, because the bottom, rather than the top, of the medium must be checked for moisture.

Uplights

Ground-mounted uplights are sometimes used to accentuate plant material outdoors during evening hours. Uplights for interior plantings are not recommended for the following reasons:

- *Plant growth.* Uplighting plants is done exclusively for aesthetic purposes; uplights do not contribute to plant growth. A leaf can utilize light for photosynthesis only through the upper side of a leaf.
- *High ambient light levels.* Unlike exterior installations, high interior ambient light levels typically preclude the dramatic contrast of a lighted plant or tree against a dark surrounding.
- *Plant health.* To provide the necessary aesthetic effect desired by uplighting, high-wattage HID lamps are often required. Such lamps and their ballasts give off substantial amounts of heat that must be insulated from surrounding plants to prevent root damage from warm soil temperature.

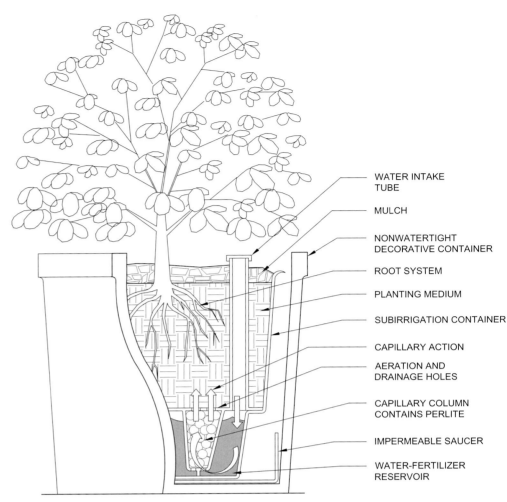

WATER INTAKE TUBE

MULCH

NONWATERTIGHT DECORATIVE CONTAINER

ROOT SYSTEM

PLANTING MEDIUM

SUBIRRIGATION CONTAINER

CAPILLARY ACTION

AERATION AND DRAINAGE HOLES

CAPILLARY COLUMN CONTAINS PERLITE

IMPERMEABLE SAUCER

WATER-FERTILIZER RESERVOIR

NONWATERTIGHT DECORATIVE PLANTER WITH LINER
Source: Jardinier

FILL TUBE

WATER-LEVEL INDICATOR

MULCH

ROOT SYSTEM

PLANTING MEDIUM

WATERTIGHT DECORATIVE CONTAINER

CAPILLARY ACTION

PLATFORM WITH AERATION VENTS

SUBIRRIGATION UNIT

RESERVOIR

CAPILLARY LEG

PLANTING MEDIUM WICK

WATERTIGHT DECORATIVE CONTAINER
Source: MPS

CAPILLARY LEG SUBIRRIGATION SYSTEMS

MANUAL PLANTER TURNTABLE

19'-6" TO 21'-6"
LOBBY FLOOR TO TOP OF PLANT

6'-6"
CLEAR

MANUAL TURNTABLE

GLAZING

For tree grate installations for which sidewall glazing is the only source of light provided, consider the use of a turntable to enable turning the tree to the light. This allows the tree to be turned periodically, preventing uneven growth toward a single light source.

SINGLE LIGHT SOURCE PLANTING

- 2" CLEAR
- DRAIN
- INTERIOR OF PLANT PIT
- STUD PIVOT
- BOLT FLOORPLATE TO FLOOR OF PLANT PIT WITH EXPANSION BOLTS
- 48" DIA., 3/8" STEEL TOP PLATE ABOVE
- 3'-2 1/2 " SQUARE, 1/4" STEEL FLOORPLATE BELOW, PLACED DIAGONAL TO PLANT PIT
- FIXED ROLLER MOUNTED TO TOP PLATE

4'-10"

90°

3'-2 1/2"

3"

9"

TURNTABLE—PLAN

- FEATURE PLANTING
- 1 1/2" DIA. FILL TUBE BEYOND
- METAL TREE GRATE AND FRAME
- PLANTING MEDIUM
- ROOTBALL OF TREE (REMOVED FROM GROW POT)
- FOAM STIFFENERS
- SUBIRRIGATION UNIT
- MOAT WITH PERLITE INFILL
- CUTAWAY FOR STRAPPING
- 3/8" STEEL TOP PLATE OF TURNTABLE ASSEMBLY
- FIXED ROLLER
- 1/4" STEEL FLOORPLATE TURNTABLE ASSEMBLY (BOLTED TO FLOOR OF PLANT PIT)
- CAST-IN-PLACE CONCRETE PLANT PIT

LIGHT LOUVER BEYOND

WELL LIGHT BEYOND

5'-0"

1 5/8"   1'-4"   1/4" MAX OPG.   5/8" TYP.

5 1/4"

3'-7"

2'-11"

5"

2 3/4"

1"

4'-0"

DRAIN   STRUCTURAL FILL   STUD PIVOT   RESERVOIR

CONCEALED MANUAL TURNTABLE

Nelson Hammer, ASLA; Hammer Design, Landscape Architecture; Boston, Massachusetts

CLEANROOMS

CLASSIFICATION

A cleanroom is an environment in which specific particle control must be maintained for manufacturing and aseptic functions. Precise control of temperature, humidity, pressure, noise, and vibration are often part of cleanroom design criteria.

Cleanrooms range in size from mini-environment enclosures to thousands of square feet, as is required for microelectronics fabrication.

.
Cleanrooms are classified by standards that reference particle presence by quantity and size. Federal Standard 209E, *Airborne Particulate Cleanliness Classes in Cleanrooms and Clean Zones,* references the number of 0.5-micrometer (μm or microns) particles per cubic foot. (A micrometer is 10^{-6}m.)

CLEANROOM APPLICATIONS

Cleanroom contamination can originate from workers and materials; contaminants include human skin cells, spittle, hair (100 microns), tobacco smoke, cosmetics, bacteria (0.2 to 0.12 microns), viruses, dust, pollen, solvents, and moisture.

High-efficiency particulate air (HEPA) filters are very efficient (nominally 99.99%) in removing particles down to 0.3 micron in supply air. Ultra-low penetration air (ULPA) filters are very efficient (nominally 99.9995%) down to 0.12 micron particles. Supply air is distributed downward through modular ceiling filters (nominally 2 × 4 ft (610 by 1,220 mm)), which are gel-sealed into tracks.

CLEANROOM AIR FILTRATION COVERAGE

Cleanroom air velocity can range from 10 FPM (10 m/s) in Class 10,000 (M6.5) up to 100 FPM (100 m/s) in Class 1 (M1.5) with up to 600 air changes per hour. The percentage of room filter coverage affects contamination control. Filter coverage is based on the cubic feet per minute (CFM) of air required for the cleanroom classification and the CFM of air delivered per filter.

Class 1 cleanrooms utilize 100% ULPA coverage with air supplied vertically downward with minimal turbulence through a perforated raised-access floor. This airflow pattern is generally known as *vertical laminar flow* (VLF). VLF resists depositing contaminants on surfaces and captures particles in the cleanroom. The free area of floor panels and adjustment dampers below the panels balance the cleanroom airflow.

In higher cleanroom classes, air may be supplied with controlled turbulence for diffused coverage, and returned through low-wall return grilles. Pharmaceutical and food applications require aseptic detailing, with smooth, impervious, and cleanable surfaces. The walls and floor join with a radiused cove and require return air extraction by low-wall return grilles.

Pressurization is a delicate balance between process exhaust and make-up air replenishment. Manufacturing cleanrooms are usually maintained at positive pressure with respect to adjacent areas to resist particle infiltration from the other areas. Cleanrooms with biohazards, how-

CLEANROOM CLASSIFICATION BY INDUSTRY STANDARD OR APPLICATION

HISTORIC ENGLISH CLASSIFICATION		1	10	100	1,000	10,000	100,000
FEDERAL STANDARD 209EM		M1.5	M2.5	M3.5	M4.5	M5.5	M6.5
ISO 14-644-1		3	4	5	6	7	8
INDUSTRY OR APPLICATION	CONTAMINATION FOCUS						
Microprocessor/ semiconductor	Particles/molecules						
Electronics, assembly, controls	Particles						
Aerospace, instrumentation	Particles/molecules						
Fine optics or machine parts	Particles						
Biotechnology and cultures	Particles/microbes						
Medical testing (aseptic)	Particles/microbes						
General medical and operating rooms	Particles/microbes						
General pharmaceutical	Particles/microbes						
Food (beverage filling)	Microbes						
Food (dairy process)	Microbes						
Food (general and meat)	Particles/microbes						

Key
☐ Seldom Used ▨ Frequently Used ■ Commonly Used

ever, are precisely controlled to a negative pressure. As the biohazard increases, the pressure must be maintained at a greater negative pressure.

BIOSAFETY DETERMINATIONS

The Centers for Disease Control and Prevention (CDC) and the National Institutes of Health (NIH) establish practices for biohazard containment including protocol, safety clothing and equipment (primary barrier), and the facility (secondary barrier). CDC/NIH have determined the biosafety levels (BSLs) for materials, which range from BSL-1 (low) to BSL-4 (high). Safety equipment includes classes I, II, and III biological safety cabinets (BSC), which are small cleanroom-type workstations. A class III BSC is completely closed to the room environment; BSL-3 or BSL-4 cannot recirculate any room air, and exhaust air must be treated.

CLEANROOM SPECIAL USE

Portable cleanrooms and component modularity allow workspace reconfiguration for changing processes and equipment. Cleanroom design is supported by operational protocol, including the requirement that

workers wear specified apparel and enter through gowning rooms and air showers. All materials entering or exiting cleanrooms must move through pass-through openings with interlocked doors. Operational protocols must be in place from the beginning of construction through testing and certification of the cleanroom, as well as during use.

Cleanrooms constructed for microelectronics mitigate conductivity and static control interference with special materials and coatings. To minimize airborne molecular contamination, cleanroom construction materials are evaluated and selected for low outgassing characteristics. Vibration control is essential to cleanroom manufacturing processes involving photolithography, optics, and lasers.

IDC Architects, Inc.; Portland, Oregon

SECTION THROUGH BIOTECHNOLOGY CLEANROOM (CLASS 1000/M4.5)

SECTION THROUGH MICROELECTRONICS CLEANROOM (CLASS 1/M1.5) WITH CLEANROOM BAY AND RETURN CHASE

COLD STORAGE ROOMS

MODULAR PANEL FABRICATION

Cold storage rooms are typically constructed of pre-fabricated, 4-in.- (100-mm-) thick insulated panels. An embossed metal finish is often used on the finish panel face to minimize the appearance of fingerprints. Walk-in cooler and freezer compartment heights are typically 8 ft (2.4 m). Drainage requirements for cold storage rooms are stipulated by local building codes. Phase service is required for lights and anticondensate heaters on door panels. Connections are made to the junction box at the light, which is always inside the walk-in, directly opposite the top hinge.

FLOOR CONSTRUCTION

There are three ways to construct the floor of a cold storage room:

- *Floorless cold storage rooms* are appropriate for use in walk-in cooler applications at temperatures above freezing and where there is no space or basement below the floor. The finished concrete slab floor is provided by the general contractor, not the cold storage room fabricator. The wall panels are anchored to the concrete slab.

- *Prefabricated floors for cold storage rooms* are of similar construction to the insulated wall panels. Floor panels are typically designed to withstand a uniformly distributed weight load of 600 lb/sq ft (2,929 kg/sq m). The insulated wall panels are set in a continuous groove of floor panels and are mechanically attached to the floor panels.

- *Insulated concrete slab depressions* can be also be used in cold storage rooms. A subfloor membrane of asphalt emulsion is applied to a smooth and level concrete subfloor depression. This is covered with a waterproof paper (0.01 perm, as determined by ASTM E96, *Standard Test Methods for Water Vapor Transmission of Materials*), which should be installed to extend under the wall panels. The joints should overlap by a minimum 6 in. (150 mm). Two layers of rigid polyurethane board insulation are installed over the moisture barrier. A vapor barrier is then installed over the insulation and flashed up the height of cove and joints overlapped a minimum of 6 in. (150 mm). Finished floor wearing surfaces must be applied.

Cini-Little International, Inc.; Food Service Consultants; Washington, D.C.

SIDE-BY-SIDE PLAN

WALK-THROUGH PLAN

TYPICAL WALK-IN UNITS

DRAIN AND VENT DETAIL

WALK-IN WITH FLUSH METAL FLOOR

WALK-IN WITH FLUSH TILE

WALK-IN FLOOR DETAILS IN NEW CONSTRUCTION

WALK-IN FLOOR OVER BUILDING FLOOR WITH INTERIOR METAL RAMP

WALK-IN FLOOR OVER BUILDING FLOOR WITH EXTERIOR METAL RAMP

WALK-IN DETAILS ON EXISTING SLAB

WALK-IN WITH BUILDING FINISH FLOOR AND EXTERIOR RAMP
Metal flooring is typically made of galvanized steel, stainless steel, or aluminum grating.

SAUNAS

A sauna is a dry heat bath taken in a well-insulated room lined with untreated, kiln-dried softwood and heated by igneous rocks. The purpose of the sauna is to induce perspiration, which cleanses the pores in the skin by removing impurities and lactic acid built up from physical exertion.

Because of the dryness of the air in a sauna (25% humidity, average), the body can accept the higher temperatures a sauna produces (180°F (82°C), average). It is usually better for bathers to lie down than to sit up in a sauna, for the temperature rises about 18°F (7°C) for every foot above the floor level. When a bather is lying down, the heat is equally dispensed over the entire body. Saunas should be located near a shower for the cool-down portion of the sauna.

Wood-framed baseplates should be made of pressure-treated wood; all other framing may be standard wood framing. Metal framing is not recommended because of its high heat-conductance property.

SAUNA CONSTRUCTION

A sauna suite offers a complete heating and cooling cycle with indoor and outdoor cooling areas.

SAUNA SUITE PLAN

Air must be able to flow freely in and out of a sauna and should be changed four to six times per hour. Fresh air is provided through updraft action by combining an air inlet in the sauna wall directly below the heater with an air outlet located at least 6 in. (150 mm) from the ceiling and 24 in. (610 mm) higher than the inlet. A vent space below the door may also be used.

AIR VENT AND TEMPERATURE DIAGRAM

SAUNA BENCH AND FLOORING CONSTRUCTION

SAUNA CONSTRUCTION

Saunas may be prefabricated (precut pieces assembled on the site), modular (factory-built complete panels joined on the site), or custom-built.

The larger the sauna, the more heat is required; hence, the ceiling should be kept as low as possible within the limits imposed by the benches, which generally require 7 ft (2.1 m) clear height.

A 24-in.- (610-mm-) wide, 6-ft-8-in.- (2,030-mm-) high nonlockable door that opens outward is standard in a sauna. This door size maximizes bench space, minimizes heat loss, and provides safe entrance. A 36-in.- (914-mm-) wide door could make a design compatible with ADA guidelines, but wheelchair access is discouraged to protect the metal and plastic components of a wheelchair from excessive heat. Instead, an attendant can assist wheelchair-bound sauna users (taking into consideration liability and safety issues).

Indirect lighting is recommended in a sauna. The best position for the light is above and slightly behind the bather's normal field of view; the switch is always outside the room.

Softwoods like western red cedar and redwood are used in the finish wall surfaces and bench construction of a sauna. Softwoods absorb humidity, keeping the atmosphere dry, and do not absorb heat as readily as hardwoods, keeping the surface comfortable to the touch. Wood should be kiln-dried to a 6% to 11% moisture content.

In private saunas, a water bucket and dipper for creating a burst of steam are common accessories. However, often these are not provided in public saunas to prevent misuse by unknowledgeable bathers, as premature or excessive water application can damage heater parts.

BENCH DIMENSIONS

UPPER BENCH

LOWER BENCH

HEATER

Design benches for a width of 24 in. (610 mm) per person (sitting) and a length of 72 in. (1,830 mm) per person (reclining).

TYPICAL SAUNA PLAN CONFIGURATIONS

STEAMROOMS

STEAM BATHING

Steam bathing has effects similar to the sauna but in a very different climate. Unlike the dry heat of a sauna, a steam bath (or Roman bath) is taken in a warm, moist atmosphere with temperatures up to 125°F (51°C) and humidity near 100%. As with the sauna, the critical factor in steam bathing is the bather's interaction between heat and cold.

STEAMROOM CONSTRUCTION

Steamroom ceilings should be sloped a minimum of 2 in. per ft (16 mm per m) to prevent condensation from collecting and dripping. Sloping from the middle to the edges reduces the height necessary to accomplish this. The ceiling should be no more than 8 ft (2.4 m) high.

Use of vents inside the steamroom is not recommended, but if they are installed, they must be positive-closing with a vaportight seal and waterproof ducts.

Flooring should be skid-resistant, with a floor drain for condensation runoff and cleaning.

The steam generator must be compatible with the construction materials and the volume of the steamroom. Controls for the generator may be located inside or outside the room.

EXTERIOR WALL FINISH
BATT OR RIGID INSULATION
1X2 CORNER CLOSURE TRIM
2X CONSTRUCTION 16" O.C.
3 1/2" TO 5 1/2"
VAPOR BARRIER
1X4 TONGUE-AND-GROOVE CEDAR OR REDWOOD VERTICAL PANELING
1X2 FURRING 24" O.C., MAX.
2X PRESSURE-TREATED WOOD BOTTOM PLATE

CUSTOM

The tongue-and-groove shaped boards used for interior finishes should be at least ⅝ in. (16 mm) thick but no wider than six times their thickness; they are made from softwoods like western red cedar or redwood. Blind-nailing with galvanized, aluminum, or stainless-steel nails is recommended.

SAUNA WALL CONSTRUCTION—DETAILS

EXTERIOR WALL FINISH
BATT OR RIGID INSULATION
1X2 CORNER CLOSURE TRIM
1 1/2"
VAPOR BARRIER
1X4 TONGUE-AND-GROOVE CEDAR OR REDWOOD VERTICAL PANELING
2X2 CONSTRUCTION 16" O.C.
2X PRESSURE-TREATED WOOD BOTTOM PLATE

PREFABRICATED

Vapor barriers under paneling (whether attached to the insulation or separate) must be vaporproof and heat-resistant and act as a heat reflectant. Foil-backed, mineral-based insulation, R-11 minimum, is recommended.

WATERPROOF WALL AND FLOOR FINISH
BACKERBOARD
VAPOR BARRIER
INSULATED WALL CONSTRUCTION
STEAM HEAD FROM HEAT GENERATOR (18" [460] ABOVE FLOOR, LOCATED OPPOSITE SEATING)
SHOWER PAN LINER
MORTAR BED, SLOPED TO DRAIN

Walls, ceiling, floor, and benches must be completely covered with a waterproof finish, such as tile, marble, or acrylic. Exposed gypsum board or plaster is not recommended. All joints must be filled with waterproof sealant.

STEAMROOM WALL CONSTRUCTION

SOUND AND VIBRATION-ISOLATED ROOMS

ISOLATED ROOMS

Isolated rooms incorporate special constructions to reduce intrusive noise and vibration from outside a room or to contain the sound and impact energy generated within a room. Typical applications include music practice rooms, sound studios, testing chambers, mechanical equipment rooms near sensitive areas, spaces exposed to nearby aircraft flyovers, and offices under gymnasiums. Construction of isolated rooms can be very expensive. It is therefore wise to isolate high-noise sources from acoustically critical uses early in the space planning and layout design phase.

The correct design of an isolated room is a "box-within-a-box." The inner box, which comprises the four walls, ceiling, and floor of the isolated room, should be an airtight enclosure constructed of dense, impervious materials; this box must be isolated by resilient supports from the surrounding structure. The base structure that supports the isolated room must be as rigid and massive as possible.

The most effective floor construction is a "floated" concrete pad, which is separated from the base building structure by steel springs, neoprene, or glass-fiber isolation mounts. An isolation mat provides uniform deflection of the floating concrete floor under a wide range of design loads. It consists of 2-in.- (50-mm-) thick, high-density, precompressed molded fiberglass isolation pads, separated by low-density acoustical fiberglass.

Avoid all flanking paths between an isolated room and the base building structure. To ensure that wall penetrations and connections to outside services are as well isolated as the room itself, provide flexible connections in ducts and conduits between the inner and outer box and resilient supports for all piping. Weatherstripped or sound-rated doors and double-glazed, acoustical windows should be part of the continuous, airtight enclosure that defines the inner box.

NOISE REDUCTION

The degree of noise reduction that can be attained by an isolated room depends on the type of construction, its resiliency, the elimination of flanking paths, and the amount of dead airspace surrounding the inner box. A well-built isolated room can achieve field performance ratings of STC 60 to 70 for airborne sound and ratings of IIC 80 to 90 for impact noise. However, even minor flanking paths and acoustical short circuits through nonairtight joints can easily decrease these results by 10 points or more. The sound isolation between spaces will be only as great as the weakest sound path.

PREFABRICATED UNITS

In addition to field-erected isolated rooms as described above, several manufacturers make prefabricated units. These rooms are sold as self-contained music practice rooms, audiometric booths, and control booths for manufacturing plants.

RESILIENT HANGER
Resilient hangers typically are used to isolate duct vibration.

RESILIENT ISOLATOR

DOUBLE CHANNELS FOR RESTRAINT

1/2" +/- SPACE FILLED WITH CLOSED CELL NEOPRENE SPONGE

FLEXIBLE DUCT CONNECTION REQUIRED IF PENETRATION THROUGH STUD WALL IS RIGID

RESILIENT DUCT HANGER

DUCT

6" BATT INSULATION

DUCT PACKED WITH FIBERGLASS AND SEALED WITH NONHARDENING CAULK (1" GAP, MAX.)

TWO LAYERS 5/8" GYPSUM BOARD, BOTH SIDES

INTERIOR WALL (CMU OR GYPSUM BOARD)

BATT INSULATION

CAULK, TYPICAL

FLOATED CONCRETE SLAB ON FORMWORK SYSTEM

PACK PIPE PENETRATION WITH GLASS FIBER AND SEAL WITH NONHARDENING CAULK

RESILIENT NEOPRENE ISOLATOR

LOW-DENSITY FIBERGLASS BATT

BASE BUILDING STRUCTURE

PERIMETER ISOLATION BOARD

DOUBLE CHANNELS FOR RESTRAINT

1/2" +/- SPACE PACKED WITH CLOSED-CELL NEOPRENE SPONGE

RESILIENT CEILING HANGER

1/2"-THICK CLOSED-CELL NEOPRENE TAPE

BATT INSULATION

DOUBLE LAYER OF 5/8" GYPSUM BOARD (STAGGER JOINTS)

RESILIENT SWAY BRACE

EXTERIOR CMU WALL

CAULK

FLOATED CONCRETE SLAB ON JACK-UP FLOOR SYSTEM

SPRING ISOLATOR

PERIMETER ISOLATION BOARD (DENSE GLASS FIBER)

BASE BUILDING STRUCTURE

THREADED ROD, TOP AND BOTTOM

NEOPRENE CUSHION

DEFLECTION SPRING

NEOPRENE SPRING CUP

5 1/2" TO 14 1/2"

HOLE GROUTED FLUSH AFTER FLOOR IS RAISED

FLOATING FLOOR

LIFTING SCREW

RUBBER ISOLATOR

POLYETHYLENE SHEET

CONCRETE SLAB

LIFTING SCREW

SPRING

NEOPRENE SPRING CLIP

SPRING ISOLATOR

ACOUSTICALLY ISOLATED ROOM AT EXTERIOR WALL

ACOUSTICALLY ISOLATED ROOM AT INTERIOR WALL

ISOLATOR DETAILS

2 □ SPECIAL CONSTRUCTION

Don Archiable, SBE, SMPTE; Gensler; Chicago, Illinois
Cerami + Associates; New York, New York

RADIATION-SHIELDED ROOMS

RADIATION PROTECTION

There are three ways to protect humans from harmful exposure to radiation:

- Keep people a sufficient distance from the radiation source.
- Limit length of exposure.
- Contain the radiation source with a protective shield.

Factors to consider in designing a protective shield are the type, characteristics, and amount of radiation; the type of construction; and the properties of the shielding system. It is important to think of an enclosure for a radiation source as a sealed module. Each component in the system must be lined with lead, and all of the connections must overlap to prevent leaks. Joint details are the most important design element once the shielding system has been selected.

Retain a radiation consultant to analyze project requirements and to prescribe the necessary shielding system. The thickness of lead needed is based on the amount of radiation at the site and should be determined by an expert.

LEAD SHIELDING CONSTRUCTION

Lead sheets are available up to 25 mm (1 in.) thick. Specify lead requirements in increments of 0.5 mm (0.019 in.), with a minimum thickness of 1 mm ($\frac{1}{24}$ in.). Adequate physical support is required for sheet lead installations. For health and environmental considerations, lead sheet, plate, and brick are designed to be installed behind other materials.

Door and window frames must be lined with lead equal to the wall shielding level. Lead glass or lead acrylic glazing must be chosen to match wall and frame shielding levels.

Hinges and hardware for lead-lined doors must be designed to carry the weight of the lead.

TYPICAL SHIELDED ROOM DESIGN REQUIREMENTS

CEILING JOINT

WALL-TO-CEILING JOINT

WALL JOINT

WALL-TO-FLOOR JOINT

STEEL STUD AND LEAD-COATED GYPSUM BOARD

WALL-TO-CEILING JOINT

TYPICAL BLOCK JOINT

WALL-TO-CEILING JOINT

LEAD-LINED BLOCK IN CONCRETE FRAME

SEMIPERMANENT RADIATION SHIELDING BARRIER

RADIATION SHIELDING

Lead-lined doors consist of a continuous sheet of lead sandwiched between two wood core panels; they generally measure 1¾ in. (44 mm), plus the thickness of the lead, which is specified by the architect or radiation physicist. Typically, the lead sheet is a minimum 1¾ in. (44 mm) thick and is covered with a flush-type wood veneer or plastic laminate. For lead thicknesses greater than ³⁄₁₆ in. (5 mm), consult the manufacturer for door thicknesses.

Use pivot or continuous hinges specifically designed to carry the weight of lead-lined doors. Depending on the thickness of the lead and the weight of the door, it may be necessary to reinforce the door frame. Steel door frames are lined with lead of the same thickness as walls and doors. Lead-lined doors are available with leaded louvers or view windows.

For lead-lined wallboard and plywood, an unpierced lead sheet is laminated to a sheet of fire-rated wallboard or plywood. Lead thickness is specified by an architect or radiation physicist. Lead joint strips and screw plugs cover any construction gaps or penetrations.

Lead-lined shielding barriers are modular, custom-designed units with clear glazing material on top and a lead-lined opaque panel below. Glazing may be either lead acrylic or lead glass. Check local regulations to ensure that movable radiation shielding is permitted.

View windows are formed from telescoping steel frames (for walls 4½ to 7 in. (115 to 180 mm) thick) with lead. These windows may include voice transmission passages and an adjustable glass stop. The stop permits installation of one to eight pieces of lead glass, as required for radiation protection. Minimum thickness for the glass is 1/4 in., which is equivalent to 2 mm of lead. Windows can be laminated with float glass for increased protection.

An X-ray cassette transfer box installed between diagnostic and film-processing rooms facilitates quick transfer of developed and undeveloped X rays. These boxes are constructed of steel panels lined with a specified lead thickness.

Leaded X-ray glass is used for all windows in X-ray protection rooms. Typical material uses lead-barium glass with more than 60% heavy metal oxide, including at least 55% lead oxide. Glass thickness is 8 mm (.31 in.; lead equivalent 1.8–2.0 mm) to protect against 100 kV X rays, 11 mm (.43 in.; lead equivalent 2.5–2.7 mm) to protect against 150 kV X rays, and 14 mm (.55 in.; lead equivalent 3.0–3.2 mm) to protect against 200 kV X rays.

Jessica Powell; Rippeteau Architects, PC; Washington, D.C.

MEDICAL X-RAY PRODUCT APPLICATION GUIDELINES

APPLICATION	X-RAY COMPONENTS	SHIELDED DOORS	CONTROL WINDOWS
Linear accelerator (LINAC) room	Borated lead walls, lead brick	Borated polyethylene and lead	Telescopic widths typically 4⅞ to 7 in. (124 to 178 mm); larger widths available
X-ray rooms, dental X ray	Stationary or mobile control screens, lead-lined wallboard and plywood	Lead-lined in various lead thicknesses and door sizes	
CAT scan room, PET scan, cardiac catheterization	Lead-lined wallboard and plywood, lead brick (PET scan)	Lead-lined hollow metal and lead-lined solid core wood doors.	
Implant radiology	Interlocking lead brick, lead-lined plywood	Lead-lined doors and frames	

REINFORCED JAMB

HEAD/JAMB

THRESHOLD DETAIL

LEAD-LINED DOOR DETAILS

FIXED LEAD-LINED HOLLOW METAL VIEW WINDOW

ELECTRICAL, PLUMBING, AND HVAC PENETRATION SHIELDING

RADIO FREQUENCY SHIELDING

CONSTRUCTION

Radio frequency (RF) shielding consists of a barrier or shield of electrically conductive materials designed to protect sensitive electronic equipment from the disruptive effects of conducted or radiated electromagnetic interference (EMI).

RF shielding of rooms, large areas, or buildings (called *architectural shielding*) is designed to contain EMI within a given space (e.g., to protect cardiac pacemakers from EMI generated by magnetic imaging resonance (MRI) equipment) or to protect electronic devices from distortion by outside EMI (e.g., to protect computer data or medical ultrasound images from distortion by radio, television, or cellular phone signals).

Shielding from electromagnetic energy is achieved by *metallizing* walls, floors, and ceilings in a room or area. Metallizing isolates a space from energy transmitted through the air (radiated) or through a wire (conducted). Typically, RF shielding is created with knockdown galvanized steel modular rooms or architectural shielding achieved with copper paint or sheeting. Proper shielding requires RF treatment of all mechanical and electrical penetrations into an area, which is achieved by using RF-shielded doors, plumbing components, and HVAC systems, in addition to electrical conductors for power, data, and telephone lines.

SHIELDING EFFECTIVENESS

Rooms or areas may be RF-tested to determine the level of shielding achieved, called *shielding effectiveness.* Shielding effectiveness typically ranges from 40 dB for commercial requirements (99% reduction in radiation) to more than 100 dB (99.999% reduction) for military, government, and hospital MRI enclosures. Shielding effectiveness is always stated in decibels (dB) of reduction over a frequency range expressed in hertz (Hz). The range of frequency that must be shielded varies from 60 Hz for AC power through the kilohertz (kHz) and megahertz (MHz) range for radio, TV, and cellular phones to the gigahertz (GHz) range for microwave energy such as radar.

Solder or use copper to fasten the wall shield to the mesh screen on all four sides.

RF-SHIELDED WINDOW DETAIL (INTERIOR)

COPPER COATING DETAIL FOR WALLS, FLOORS, AND CEILINGS

RF-SHIELDED DOOR AT MODULAR RF-SHIELDED PANEL SYSTEM

RF-SHIELDED DOOR AT STANDARD RF-SHIELDED CONSTRUCTION

FLUSH POCKET THRESHOLD DETAILS

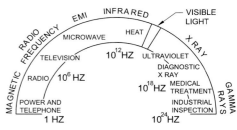

Design for shielding against interference from electromagnetic radiation is based on the electromagnetic frequency spectrum. Since all radiated energy occurs in waveform, interference can be identified by its own frequency, which is expressed in hertz. The diagram above shows where each type of radiated energy occurs in the electromagnetic spectrum. The lowest frequencies are in the range represented by electrical power and AM radio, the highest in the range represented by gamma rays (used in medical linear accelerators).

Each frequency range in the spectrum may require its own shielding design. In many modern projects, the designer and builder must contend with more than one frequency band at a time. A modern hospital, for instance, may require as many as five different shielding solutions, such as magnetic shielding for a 60-Hz power substation, magnetic and EMI shielding for MRI equipment, X-ray shielding for diagnostic X-ray equipment, and gamma ray shielding for a linear accelerator.

ELECTROMAGNETIC SPECTRUM

ROOM CONTAINING RF-EMITTING EQUIPMENT

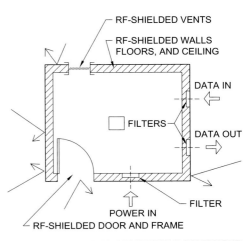

ROOM CONTAINING RF-SUSCEPTIBLE EQUIPMENT

RF-SHIELDED SPACES

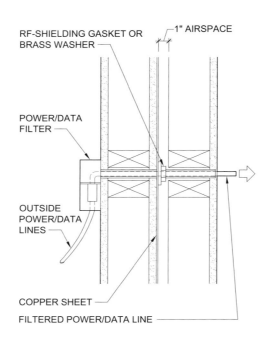

VENT CORE FLANGE

COPPER TAPE (OR SOLDERED SEAM)

3/16" STEEL OR BRASS CELL WAVE GUIDE VENT CORE (1" THICK)

COPPER SHEET

DUCT

2" AIRSPACE

DIELECTRIC (NONCONDUCTIVE) DUCT CONNECTOR

2X4 AND GYPSUM BOARD WALL

Solder seam of vent flange or use copper tape to attach it to copper sheet on all four sides.

RF-SHIELDED DUCT DETAIL

RF-SHIELDING GASKET OR BRASS WASHER

1" AIRSPACE

POWER/DATA FILTER

OUTSIDE POWER/DATA LINES

COPPER SHEET

FILTERED POWER/DATA LINE

POWER AND DATA FILTER DETAIL

4-GAUGE COPPER WIRE TO WATER PIPE OR OTHER GROUND

THREADED ROD

BRASS WASHER AND HEX NUT TIGHTENED AGAINST SHEET

COPPER SHEET

INSIDE OF SHIELDED ROOM

WALL SHIELD GROUNDING DETAIL

1" AIRSPACE

RF SHIELDING-COPPER COATING OR COPPER SHEET ON SHEATHING

BRASS PLATES, ATTACHED TO COPPER WALL SHIELDING AND BRASS DOOR FRAME

BRASS DOOR FRAME WITH HINGE

BRASS KNIFE SLIDES INTO COPPER CONTACTS AT FRAME

RF-SHIELDED DOOR

WOOD CORE DOOR WITH COPPER RF SHIELDING AND LAMINATE FINISH

BRASS SADDLE WITH COPPER CONTACTS AT SILL

BRASS SILL

COPPER RF SHIELDING

FLOOR UNDERLAYMENT

DIELECTRIC HARDBOARD LAYER

VAPOR BARRIER

6"

1/2"

This detail is for construction other than modular panel room systems.

RF-SHIELDED INTERIOR DOOR DETAILS

1/8"-THICK STEEL PLATE BRACKETS, CONTINUOUS AT CEILING-TO-WALL, WALL-TO-WALL, AND WALL-TO-FLOOR JUNCTIONS

SPOT WELD

STRUCTURAL STEEL TUBING

1"±

RF-SHIELDED MODULAR PANELS (WOOD CORE WITH RF-SHIELDING, TYPICALLY 24-GAUGE STEEL SHEET EACH SIDE)

ROOM FLOOR SURFACE

VAPOR BARRIER

DIELECTRIC BASE

FLOOR FINISH

RF PANEL

1/8" SPACER

MODULAR ROOM SECTION
A dielectric (nonconductive) base electrically isolates an RF-shielded structure from a parent room.

RF-SHIELDED MODULAR PANEL ROOM SYSTEM DETAILS

RF-SHIELDED GASKETING

CONTINUOUS THREADED

RF-SHIELDED PANEL

GALVANIZED PIPE PENETRATION

COUPLER

CONTINUOUS THREADED BRASS PIPE

COPPER TUBING

RF-SHIELDED GASKETING

RF-SHIELDED PANEL

COPPER PIPE PENETRATION

John Soltis; Tecknit Shielding Systems; Passaic, New Jersey

BULLET-RESISTANT CONSTRUCTION

CONSTRUCTION NOTES

No construction can be bulletproof. Protected areas should be designed to withstand a level of attack based on the threat at that location and, in particular, the type of arms expected to be used. Each component of the system must be bullet-resistant; there can be no weak links and no gaps.

A truly effective protection plan combines a bullet-resistant system with appropriate detection, alarm, communication, escape, and retaliation capabilities. The complete bullet-resistant environment makes it possible for personnel to escape, retaliate against attack, summon help, and defend themselves against the threat of gunfire, flame, and chemical or mechanical attack.

- BULLET-RESISTANT TRANSFER UNIT
- BULLET-RESISTANT VOICE TRANSMISSION UNIT
- BULLET-RESISTANT DEAL TRAY
- GLASS-MOUNTED GUNPORT
- BULLET-RESISTANT GLASS OR ACRYLIC
- BULLET-RESISTANT DOOR AND FRAME UNIT
- BULLET-RESISTANT STEEL OR FIBERGLASS COMPOSITE WALL

BULLET-RESISTANT WALL DETAILS

STANDARD WALL STUDS

BULLET-RESISTANT STEEL OR FIBERGLASS COMPOSITE (BOTH SIDES, OPTIONAL)

2"-WIDE BULLET-RESISTANT BATTEN (CLOSE BUTT JOINT IN WALL-SHIELD MATERIAL)

BULLET-RESISTANT COMPOSITE WALL PANEL

- STANDARD WALL STUDS
- GYPSUM WALLBOARD COVER (OPTIONAL)
- PREPUNCHED MOUNTING HOLES
- 1/8" TO 1/2" BULLET-RESISTANT STEEL ARMOR LAYER (STAINLESS STEEL OR PAINTED)

BULLET-RESISTANT STEEL WALL PANEL

- BULLET-RESISTANT STEEL, FIBERGLASS, OR CONCRETE
- BULLET-RESISTANT STEEL FRAME
- BULLET-RESISTANT STEEL DOOR WITH THROW BOLT
- FRAME ANCHOR
- BULLET-RESISTANT SPREADER BAR AT SILL

BULLET-RESISTANT DOOR IN CONCRETE WALL

TYPICAL BULLET-RESISTANT MATERIALS

MATERIAL	FUNCTION AND CHARACTERISTICS	THICKNESS IN. (MM)	WEIGHT PSF (KG/SQ M)	REMARKS
Steel	Cost-effective shielding against direct assault Thin	⅛–1 (3–25)	6–24 (29–117)	—
Glass	Cost-effective vision panel shield Scratch-resistant, chemical-resistant Substantial assault can defeat glass	1³⁄₁₆–2 (30–50)	15–31 (73–151)	One-way security glass is available ⅝–1⅝ in. (16–41 mm) thick
Plastics (acrylic)	Relatively high cost Substantial assault can defeat plastic	1¼ (32)	7.8 (38)	Glass-clad polycarbonate is available 1–1¹¹⁄₁₆ in. thick, weight 9.6–17.6 psf.
Composites	Can be opaque or translucent Relatively high cost	¼–1⅛ (6–28)	2.5–11.5 (12–56)	

BULLET-RESISTANT DOOR ASSEMBLIES

Bullet-resistant doors are heavier than regular doors, so the door frame and hinges must be properly reinforced and/or of heavy weight. The it throw on the latchbolt should be thoroughly armored to prevent the door from unlatching after assault.

The door should be equipped with a heavy-duty closer to ensure it closes completely.

Jessica Powell; Rippeteau Architects, P.C.; Washington, D.C.

VAULTS

CONCRETE MODULAR VAULT SYSTEMS

Precast concrete modular vault panels are considerably lighter and thinner than site-poured walls, and provide almost unlimited flexibility when sizing or locating a vault. Modular vaults can be expanded or relocated as required, reusing existing components. Vault panels are typically fabricated from a high-density composite concrete mix with interlacing steel fibers and a welded grid of reinforcement bars. Although manufacturers provide standard vault sizes and configurations, a modular vault design can be custom-fabricated.

Clear spans of up to 19 ft (5.79 m), without the use of support beams, can be achieved by most modular vault systems, simplifying above-ground-level installations.

INSTALLATION

Preengineered panels are site-assembled, typically by welding. Modular vault panels can be disassembled and moved to another location. Existing vaults can be increased or reduced in size by adding or removing panels. Typically, the interior and exterior finishes of the vault are the responsibility of the owner.

Conduit penetrations for alarm and other electrical hookups are cast into the vault panels. Electrical and security wire runs are typically included in a single panel that can be placed almost anywhere within the vault design. HVAC ports with built-in dampers can be specified to provide ductwork to maintain a comfortable environment for vaults that are used as workspaces.

VAULT TYPES

The two types of vaults used to protect valuables are *burglary-resistant* and *fire-resistant*.

Burglary-Resistant Vaults

Underwriter's Laboratories (UL) and Insurance Services Offices (ISO) provide criteria by which the security performance of a vault can be evaluated. UL

performs attack tests on the modular vault systems to ensure that minimum requirements for burglary resistance are met. UL 608, *Standard for Burglary-Resistant Vault Doors and Modular Panels,* classifies vault doors and modular panels by the approximate time it takes to break through the assembly. Test methods used to penetrate the door include expert burglary attack using cutting torches, fluxing rods, portable electric-powered tools, portable hydraulic tools, and common hand tools. The ratings are as follows:

- Class M: one-quarter hour
- Class 1: one-half hour
- Class 2: one hour
- Class 3: two hours

ISO is an organization that is supported by insurance companies and provides a consistent basis for setting standards and rates used in calculating insurance costs. ISO has developed a system for rating security devices, including vaults. Although there are technical

differences between the UL and the ISO standards, certain classifications can be considered comparable.

Fire-Resistant Vaults

Fire-resistant vaults are used primarily to protect vital records. NFPA 232, *Protection of Records,* describes the relative humidity range and maximum temperature requirements for photographic materials, including silver-gelatin, vesicular, color film, and magnetic media. UL 155, *Standard for Tests for Fire Resistance of Vault and File Room Doors,* classifies the fire resistance of vault walls and doors, as follows:

- Class B: two hours
- Class A: four hours
- Class AA: six hours

The hour ratings approximate the time it takes for a fire to penetrate the modular vault system.

Kelsey A. Kruse, AIA; GVA Architecture-Interior Design; Columbia, Maryland

VAULT WALL SECTION

VAULT PANEL PROVIDED AND INSTALLED BY VAULT VENDOR
INSIDE FACE OF VAULT
1/2" STEEL PLATE INSTALLED BY CONTRACTOR
AS REQUIRED
WELD ANGLE TO WELD PADS EMBEDDED IN PANELS
BRACE ANGLE AT ALL INTERIOR CORNERS, PROVIDED BY VAULT VENDOR
REINFORCE CONCRETE SLAB AS REQUIRED FOR RATING
REBAR ANCHORS AT 24" O.C., STAGGERED; WELDED IN PLACE BY CONTRACTOR

SIX-SIDED MODULAR CONCRETE PANEL VAULT

FIVE OR SIX SIDED VAULT, ERECTED ON SITE WITH PREFABRICATED MODULAR CONCRETE PANELS
SAFE DEPOSIT BOXES
FINISH CEILING DETERMINED BY DESIGNER OR OWNER AND PROVIDED BY CONTRACTOR
GATE TYPICALLY PROVIDED BY VAULT VENDOR
CASH VAULT AREA
PARTITION PROVIDED BY CONTRACTOR
GYPSUM BOARD ON METAL OR WOOD FURRING TO FINISH INTERIOR AND EXTERIOR OF VAULT
FINISH FLOOR DETERMINED BY DESIGNER OR OWNER AND PROVIDED BY CONTRACTOR
VAULT DOOR, FRAME AND SILL
SIX SIDED VAULTS INCLUDE PANELS TO FORM FLOOR CONSTRUCTION. PREPARATION OF EXISTING FLOOR IS REQUIRED FOR BOTH FIVE AND SIX SIDED VAULTS

FIRE SUPPRESSION AND ALARM SYSTEMS

FIRE SUPPRESSION SYSTEMS SELECTION CRITERIA

The purpose of a fire suppression system is to extinguish or mitigate the effects of a fire. Selection of the extinguishing medium most appropriate for a project is based on availability, compatibility, cost, and code requirements.

Codes and Standards

Most model, state, and local codes have a separate fire protection section that mandates certain types of fire suppression systems based on occupancy types, potential fire hazards, height, and area of the structure. Insurance companies, such as Factory Mutual, American Risk Insurers, and American Risk Management, have developed design standards to be followed by the clients they insure. In addition, the National Fire Protection Association (NFPA) has developed consensus standards for various suppression systems that are referenced and required to be followed by most codes.

It is important that an adequate code search be made prior to launching the design phase of any project to ensure compliance with the proper codes.

Basic Definitions

Although the exact nature of fire and the combustion process is still not completely understood, it is known that three things are necessary for a fire to be maintained: fuel, oxygen, and a temperature high enough to start ignition or maintain combustion. All fire-extinguishing methods remove one or all of these elements, causing the fire to be extinguished.

Fires are classified as class A, B, C, or D:

- *Class A* fires occur in solid, combustible materials such as wood and paper.
- *Class B* fires occur in combustible liquids such as oil and gasoline.
- *Class C* fires are electrical in nature, such as a short circuit that causes a spark capable of igniting other substances.
- *Class D* fires occur in metals with their own fuel supply.

Building occupancy and other specific areas within a building are classified as *light, ordinary,* or *extra hazard,* according to the potential for fire. Light hazard occurs in office buildings, schools, and public buildings. Ordinary hazard is similar to warehouses and stores with large amounts of combustible material. Extra hazard occurs where there is considerable potential for easily started, large fires. These classifications are more fully explained in the applicable NFPA standards.

The term *automatic* is often used when referring to fire suppression systems. In this context, automatic means operation of the system without human intervention when fire conditions occur.

FIRE SUPPRESSION SYSTEM TYPES

Three general types of systems are used for suppression of fires: water-based, chemical-based (either liquid or powder), and gas-based.

- *Water-based systems* use either water mixed with chemicals that add fire-extinguishing characteristics or undiluted water to cool the fire below ignition temperature or deprive it of oxygen.
- *Chemical-based systems* interfere with the combustion process and deprive the fire of oxygen.
- *Gas-based systems* interfere with the combustion process and deprive the fire of oxygen.

CEILING

DRY OR WET CHEMICAL SYSTEM FOR KITCHENS

TYPICAL GAS DISCHARGE NOZZLES

UNDER FLOOR

TYPICAL FIRE PUMP SCHEMATIC

TYPICAL GAS SYSTEM

Water-Based Systems

The medium most often used to extinguish fires is water. It is readily available, inexpensive, and easy to apply. The most important factor in the use of water-based systems is adequate water pressure. When pressure from the building water supply is inadequate to supply fire standpipe and sprinkler systems, a special fire pump, manufactured and installed specifically for fire suppression systems, is used to increase water pressure. The fire pump is installed in strict conformance with NFPA 20, *Standard for the Installation of Stationary Pumps for Fire Protection.*

There are three types of water-based fire suppression systems: *fire standpipe, foam,* and *sprinkler.*

Fire Standpipe (FSP)

A fire standpipe system is a network of water-filled pipes, hose valves, and fire hose that allows the direct application of water onto a fire. The most common system configuration has hose valves only, which are connected to system piping to allow fire department personnel to connect their hose to the system. Mains are installed in high fire-rated areas such as stairwells. Hose valves are located so that all parts of the building can be reached with a 100 ft (30 m) length of hose and a 20 ft (6 m) water stream from the hose nozzle.

It is accepted practice to supply sprinkler heads from FSP mains in various areas throughout a building. Each connection point is provided with a flow alarm. A test connection is installed at each point to permit authorities to visually verify that the water discharged from one sprinkler head is actually flowing and will initiate an alarm. This test connection is combined with a drain line to permit the entire branch to be drained for maintenance and repair.

Foam

A foam system consists of a water supply, chemical additive injector, piping, and heads placed to discharge foam. The system uses an additive injected to the water supply to produce a soapsudslike discharge. This system is used to extinguish fires in flammable liquids that are lighter than water. The foam floats on top of the liquid and deprives the fire of oxygen.

Sprinkler Systems

A sprinkler system uses water distributed through a network of valves, piping, and nozzles whose primary purpose is to set off an alarm and mitigate the effects of a fire, not necessarily to extinguish it. When a fire condition is present, the heat of the fire melts the element of a closed sprinkler head, allowing water to discharge automatically onto the fire.

The *sprinkler piping system* is sized using one of two methods, *schedule* or *hydraulic.* The schedule method uses pipe sizes based on a minimum available water pressure and the number of heads connected to the piping that appears in NFPA 13, *Standard for the Installation of Sprinkler Systems.* The hydraulic method uses a remote area (that farthest from the water supply source) based on occupancy type, flow of water over the remote area, flow of water at each design point, and pressure available in the system.

The major operating components of a sprinkler system are the operating valve assembly, piping, and nozzles (referred to as heads, for some systems). The operating valve assembly admits water to or sends an alarm upon the flow of water in the system. There are many types of operating valves, and the type of system installed determines the type of valve used. Heads or nozzles distribute water in a special, predetermined pattern based on the requirements of the system. They are available in a wide variety of configurations, including upright, pendant, or sidewall, and can be closed or open. They have different temperature ratings to open the head and various orifice diameters for the discharge of water. Heads provide either standard or quick response, and either standard or extended coverage. They can be installed in a hung ceiling as concealed, flush, or exposed fixtures.

TYPICAL SPRINKLER CONNECTION

FOAM SYSTEM

WET PIPE SYSTEM

DELUGE SYSTEM

WATER MIST SYSTEM

SPRINKLER SYSTEM TYPES

Sprinkler system types include the following:

- *Wet pipe:* This automatic system uses piping filled with water under pressure and closed heads. When a fire condition exsists, the heat melts (fuses) a temperature-sensitive element in the head, causing the head to open and water to flow.
- *Dry pipe:* This automatic system uses piping filled with air under pressure and closed heads. The operating valve assembly is called a *dry pipe valve*. An air compressor is required to make up air lost through leakage. Both water and compressed air are supplied only to the dry pipe valve. When a head fuses due to a fire condition, it lowers the air pressure, opens the valve, and permits water to enter the piping; the water then flows only from the open heads.
- *Preaction:* This automatic system uses closed heads and piping filled with air under atmospheric pressure. Water is supplied to the operating valve assembly, called a *preaction valve*. An ancillary smoke or fire detection system initiates a signal upon detection of heat, fire, or smoke. The signal causes the preaction valve to open, allowing water to enter the piping system. Water will not flow out of the heads unless they fuse due to a fire condition.
- *Deluge:* Used to protect high-hazard areas and specific equipment, this automatic system uses piping filled with air under atmospheric pressure and open heads. An ancillary smoke or fire detection system is required to initiate a signal upon detection of heat, fire, or smoke at the hazard being protected.
- *Antifreeze:* A wet pipe automatic system is filled with an antifreeze solution instead of water to protect areas subject to freezing but too small for a dry pipe system. Operations are similar to those of the standard wet pipe system.
- *Water mist:* This automatic system uses high-pressure water flowing through nozzles designed to discharge very small droplets of water directly onto a fire. A water pump is required to produce the high system pressure.

Chemical-Based Systems

Both wet and dry chemical systems require extensive cleanup after a fire has been extinguished.

Dry Chemicals

This system is used to protect areas for which water is not a suitable extinguishing medium, such as chemi-

cal storage areas and cooking areas with exhaust ductwork that vents grease. A powdered chemical is stored in high-pressure cylinders or tanks connected to a piping system with open heads. The powder is discharged from all of the heads simultaneously.

Wet Chemicals

The recent shift from animal fats to vegetable fats for cooking required a different medium for fighting fires in kitchens. This medium is a wet chemical, which operates in the same manner as the dry chemical system.

Gas-Based Systems

Some gas-based systems use inert gases; others use chemical gases.

Inert Gases

These systems are used when chemicals that may react to water are present or when water will cause unacceptable damage. The gases (generally carbon dioxide or nitrogen) are discharged either directly onto a fire or are used to reduce the oxygen level in a room or area to a point below that required to sustain combustion. This low level also will not sustain life. The gas is stored compressed in high-pressure cylinders or tanks and is connected to a piping system with open heads.

Other Gases (Halon Alternatives)

Chemical gases interfere with the combustion process, and chemical gas systems are often used to protect computer and electronic equipment and areas. The systems operate in the same way as inert gas systems, but usually a lower concentration of gas is required. Halon is no longer permitted because of environmental concerns. Many halon alternatives are available, but their use must be approved by authorities having jurisdiction. Because of the force exerted by the discharging gas, hung ceilings should be reinforced in areas where heads are located, and the heads mounted so they can resist the force of discharge.

Michael Frankel, CIPE; Utility Systems Consultants; Somerset, New Jersey

SPRINKLER HEAD SELECTION CHART

STANDARD COVERAGE	DRY
Upright	Upright
Standard response	Pendant
Quick response	Pendant w/deep escutcheons
Pendant	Recessed pendant
Standard response	Horizontal sidewall
Quick response	
Recessed pendant	
Concealed pendant	
Flush pendant	
Horizontal sidewall	
Recessed horizontal sidewall	
Vertical sidewall	

HIGH PRESSURE: 300 PSI (210,900 KG/SQ M)	FOAM WATER
Upright	Upright
Pendant	Pendant
Recessed pendant	
Horizontal sidewall	
Recessed horizontal sidewall	

EXTENDED COVERAGE	INSTITUTIONAL
Upright	Pendant
Pendant	Horizontal sidewall
Recessed pendant	
Horizontal sidewall	

RESIDENTIAL	EXTENDED COVERAGE
Pendant	Upright
Recessed pendant	Pendant
Concealed pendant	Recessed pendant
Horizontal sidewall	Horizontal sidewall
Recessed horizontal sidewall	

TYPICAL SPRINKLER HEAD SPRAY PATTERNS

SIDEWALL   SUSPENDED CEILING   OPEN SPACE   UPRIGHT   PENDANT

SIDEWALL   CONCEALED   PENDANT

SPRINKLER HEAD TYPES

FIRE ALARM SYSTEMS

The simplest fire alarm system is a self-contained, UL-approved residential smoke detector. It senses products of combustion, sounds an alarm, and signals when the battery needs replacement. Most municipalities require the use of smoke detectors in houses, apartments, and motel or hotel rooms. Check local codes for requirements.

More complex systems are needed in buildings where public safety is an issue, such as schools, hospitals, office buildings, and other commercial establishments or institutions. Although there are still applications for small hard-wired and relay-operated alarm signaling systems, the trend is to use microprocessor-based digital multiplex systems that not only signal the presence of a fire but also initiate other measures, including conditioning fans and dampers for smoke control, closing fire doors and shutters, releasing locked doors, capturing elevators, and transmitting voice messages. Voice communication is required in high-rise buildings of specific group occupancies. It is also recommended for large low-rise buildings to enhance life safety.

Fire alarm systems can either function alone or be integrated with security and building management functions. Processors and their peripheral equipment are generally located in a manned central command center accessible to firefighters. Depending on the degree of reliability desired, redundancy can be provided in wiring and processors, along with battery backup.

Alarm system control cabinets can be 36 in. (914 mm) wide by 8 in. (203 mm) deep. They must have battery backup, be UL-approved, conform to NFPA 72, *National Fire Alarm Code,* and may also require local approval. In small systems where only one cabinet may be required, all the functions required at the command center can be incorporated in the same cabinet and be located in the main entrance lobby. In larger systems, remote cabinets are generally located in wiring closets throughout the building and can be programmed to function independently of the central processor, should it fail.

Audible Alarms

Audible alarms must have an intensity and frequency capable of attracting the attention of those with partial hearing loss. Such alarms should produce a sound

ELECTRONIC FIRE ALARM/COMMUNICATION SYSTEM FUNCTION DIAGRAM

that exceeds either the prevailing sound level in the space by at least 15 dBA or the maximum sound level with a duration of 60 seconds by 5 dBA, whichever is louder. Sound levels should not exceed 120 dbA.

Visual Alarms

Visual alarms should be placed 80 in. (2,032 mm) above the highest floor level within the space, or 6 in. (152 mm) below the ceiling, whichever is lower. In any space required to have a visual alarm, generally all areas

must be within 50 ft (15 m) of the signal (measured horizontally). In large spaces, such as auditoriums, exceeding 100 ft (30 m) across, with no obstructions over 6 ft (2 m) high, devices may be placed around the perimeter, spaced a maximum of 100 ft (30 m) apart, in lieu of suspending devices from the ceiling.

Richard F. Humenn, P.E.; Joseph R. Loring and Associates, Consulting Engineers; New York, New York
JRS Architect; Mineola, New York

A firefighter telephone cabinet should be approximately 12 in. (305 mm) high by 10 in. (255 mm) wide by 3 in. (75 mm) deep, surface or flush. It is provided in lieu of jack plates for a total system. The door can be glass or plastic pane.

FIREFIGHTER TELEPHONE CABINET

A manual pull station should be approximately 7 in. (180 mm) high by 5 in. (130 mm) wide and can be surface- or semirecessed-mounted 54 in. (1,270 mm) above finished floor to lever, per ADA. It can be provided with break-glass rod feature. Operation can be coded or noncoded.

MANUAL PULL STATION

An electronic fire alarm/communication system should be approximately 10 in. (254 mm) high by 7 in. (177 mm) wide, with a xenon strobe visual signal. It should be mounted at 80 in. (2,032 mm) above finished floor or 6 in. (152 mm) below ceiling, whichever is lower, per ADA. Generally, it should be located so that no place in any corridor or hallway is more than 50 ft (15 m) from the signal.

HORN/SPEAKER/VISUAL SIGNAL

2   □   **FIRE SUPPRESSION SYSTEMS**

DUMBWAITERS AND WASTE, LINEN, AND MAIL CHUTES

WASTE AND LINEN CHUTES

Waste and linen chutes should extend full diameter through the roof and be capped with a metal safety vent or glass explosion cap. Sprinklers or flushing spray are recommended at alternate floors. Bottom-hinged hopper doors are commonly used for waste and loose linen. Square side-hinged doors are used for bagged linen. Type "B" doors are recommended. To prevent clogging, door size is restricted in proportion to chute diameter. Type "H" hopper discharge doors are installed when discharge is built into the wall and the receptacle is a cart or bin. Type "A" direct-open discharge doors (not shown) are commonly used when discharge is into a compactor.

MAIL CHUTES

Chutes should be used only for first-class mail. The chute dimensions should be 2×8 in. (50×200 mm) and extend in a vertical line from the beginning point to a receiving box or mailroom. A chute must be accessible for its entire length.

Using the shortest line, receiving boxes may not be placed more than 100 ft (305 m) from the entrance used by the collection person. Locations require local postmaster approval. Receiving boxes must be placed on the same floor the collection person uses to enter the building. Door openings must be at least 12×20 in. (305×510 mm) and not more than 18×30 in. (460×760 mm).

Eric K. Beach; Rippeteau Architects, PC; Washington, D.C.
Wilkinson Company, Inc.; Stow, Ohio
Cutler Manufacturing Corporation; Lakeland, Florida
Atlas Elevator Company; Chicago, Illinois

Floor penetrations may require firestops. Verify with authorities having jurisdiction.

WASTE OR LINEN CHUTE

Installations must comply with USPS requirements and are subject to inspection. USPS provides a list of approved manufacturers. Floor penetrations may require fire stops. Verify with authorities having jurisdiction.

MAIL CHUTE AND COLLECTION BOXES

DUMBWAITERS

ELEVATORS

SELECTION CRITERIA

An elevator system is a major building component, and as such must be carefully considered throughout the design process. Decisions about the number, size, speed, and type of elevators for an installation are based on a number of factors, including the handling capacity and quality of service desired. Proper selection also depends on the type of tenancy, number of occupants, and building design (number of floors, floor heights, building circulation, and other factors). In addition, passenger elevators on accessible routes should comply with the requirements of the *Americans with Disabilities Act Accessibility Guidelines* (ADAAG).

Consult representatives of the elevator industry, or elevator engineers, during the decision-making process to ensure selection of the most suitable elevator system for an application. And because elevator installation is highly regulated, it is also advisable to consult local code officials.

Elevators should be located where they can provide efficient and accessible service. As well, the operational systems (hoistway pit and machine room) and passenger spaces (lobby and elevator car) must be accommodated.

ELEVATOR SYSTEMS

An elevator system includes a *hoistway, machine room, elevator car,* and *waiting lobbies.*

Hoistway

The hoistway is a vertical shaft for the travel of one or more elevators. It includes a pit and usually terminates at the underside of the machine room in a traction system, and at the underside of the roof over the hoistway in a hydraulic system. Access to the elevator car and hoistway is normally through hoistway doors at each floor serviced by the elevator system. Hoistway design is determined by the characteristics of the elevator system selected and by applicable code requirements for fire separation, ventilation, soundproofing, and nonstructural elements.

Machine Room for Traction Elevator

The machine room for a traction elevator is usually located directly above the hoistway, but it may also be situated below, to the side, or to the rear of it. The machine room contains elevator hoisting machinery and electronic control equipment. Adequate ventilation, soundproofing, and structural support for the elevator must be supplied. Also, the machine room must have a self-closing, self-locking access door. Local codes may forbid placement of electrical or mechanical equipment not associated with the elevator in the machine room.

ELEVATOR TYPES BY USE

NEED/USE	PRIVATE RESIDENTIAL	HYDRAULIC	GEARED TRACTION	GEARLESS TRACTION
Private houses	X			
Low-rise, low-speed		X		
Medium-rise, moderate-speed			X	
High-rise, high-speed				X
Low initial cost		X		
No penthouse, lightweight construction		X		
Freight, low-rise		X	X	
Freight, high-rise			X	

Machine Room for Hydraulic Elevator

Normally located near the base of the hoistway, a machine room for hydraulic elevators contains a hydraulic pump unit and electronic controls. Provisions should be made for adequate ventilation and soundproofing, and the room must have a self-closing, self-locking access door. Local codes may forbid placement of electrical or mechanical equipment not associated with the elevator in the machine room.

Elevator Car

Guided by vertical rails on each side, the elevator car conveys passengers or freight between floors. It is constructed within a supporting platform and frame. Design of the car focuses on ceiling, wall, floor, and door finishes, and accompanying lighting, ventilation, and elevator signal equipment.

The car and frame of a *hydraulic elevator system* are supported by a piston or cylinder. The car and frame of a *traction elevator system* are supported by the hoist machine. The elevator and its counterweight are connected with steel ropes.

Waiting Lobbies

Elevator waiting areas are designed to allow free circulation of passengers, rapid access to elevator cars, and clearly visible elevator signals. All elevator lobbies must be enclosed, with the exception of those at the entry level of main buildings.

ELEVATOR TYPES

Hydraulic elevators use an oil hydraulic driving machine to raise and lower the elevator car and its load. Lower speeds and the piston length restrict the

			UNLIMITED HEIGHT MAX. EFFICIENCY UP TO 100' (30m)	
	20' (6m) MAX. HEIGHT	60' (18m) MAX. HEIGHT		UNLIMITED HEIGHT
PRIVATE RESIDENTIAL	HYDRAULIC		GEARED TRACTION	GEARLESS TRACTION

These dimensions are general guidelines for selecting an elevator type, using height as a criterion.

ELEVATOR TYPES

use of this system to heights of approximately 55 ft (16 m). Although it generally requires the least initial installation expense, this elevator type requires more power to operate.

Traction elevators are power elevators in which the energy is applied by means of an electric driving machine. Medium to high speeds and virtually limitless rise allow this elevator type to serve high-rise, medium-rise, and low-rise buildings.

Geared traction elevator systems are designed to operate within the range of 100 to 450 ft (30 to 137 m) per minute, restricting their use to medium-rise buildings.

Gearless traction elevator systems are available in preengineered units with speeds of 500 to 1,200 ft (150 to 365 m) per minute. They offer the advantages of a long life and a smooth ride.

Service elevators in industrial, residential, and commercial buildings are often standard passenger elevator packages modified for service use.

Freight elevators are usually classed as general freight loading, motor vehicle loading, industrial truck, or concentrated loading elevators. General freight loading elevators may be electric drum type or traction or hydraulic elevators.

Private residential elevators may be installed only in a private residence or to serve a single unit in a building with multiple dwelling units. By code, elevators in private residences are limited in size, capacity, rise, and speed.

BUILDING CHARACTERISTICS

Physical building characteristics (such as building height and hoistway location) are considered in conjunction with population characteristics to determine the size, speed, type, and location of elevator systems. Characteristics that particularly affect the elevator systems are:

- *Height:* Determine the distance of elevator travel from lowest terminal to top terminal, the number of floors, and the floor height.
- *Building use:* Identify the location of heavily used building entrance areas, such as those leading to cafeterias, restaurants, auditoriums, and service areas. Typically, plan a building so that no prospective passengers must walk more than 200 ft (610 m) to reach an elevator.

The elevator selection process must begin with a thorough analysis of how people will occupy the building. Four issues are pertinent:

- *Total population and density:* Determine this figure for each floor.
- *Peak loading:* Identify the periods when elevators will carry the highest traffic loads.
- *Waiting time:* Determine the length of time a passenger is expected to wait for the next elevator to arrive.
- *Demand for quality:* Recognize that smooth operation may be as important as fancy finishes.

RESIDENTIAL ELEVATORS

Selection Criteria

Guidelines for selecting an elevator for a private residence can be simplified to a few parameters. By code, residential elevators are limited in size, capacity, rise, and speed, and can be installed only in a private residence or in a multiple dwelling as a means of access to a single residence. Preengineered systems generally offer only a few options for speed, capacity, aesthetic design, and electronic controls.

Elevator Systems for Private Residential Use

Two types of elevator systems are commonly used in private residences: winding-drum machine and hydraulic elevators.

- *Winding-drum machine:* This type of traction elevator employs a grooved drum around which the hoisting cable wraps as it operates. This elevator type does not require a counterweight or a machine room above the hoistway, making it more practical for small places than a standard traction system.
- *Hydraulic elevator:* Hydraulic elevators in private residences employ either a standard holeless arrangement or a roped hydraulic machine. Both types eliminate major construction and drilling, making the system economical and an excellent selection for retrofit applications.

The dimensions given here are appropriate for most applications. For exact dimensions required in specific circumstances, consult manufacturers.

Load Capacity

The load capacity of drum-type machines is 500 lb (226 kg); speed is 30 ft (9 m) per minute. The load capacity of traction and hydraulic machines is 750 lb (340 kg); speed is 36 ft (11 m) per minute.

Guide Rails

Manufacturers usually provide guide rails in 5 ft (1,525 mm) sections, although some manufacturers offer rails that can span the distance from floor structure to floor structure. If an existing structure cannot support guide rails, manufacturers can provide a self-supporting elevator tower that transmits the load to its base. This tower requires increased horizontal clearance in the hoistway.

SINGLE DOOR

ROPED HYDRAULIC

WINDING-DRUM

ELEVATOR TYPES

TWO DOORS—OPPOSITE SIDES

TWO DOORS—ADJACENT SIDES

Standard car size is 36 in. (915 mm) wide × 48 in. (1,220 mm) deep × 80 in. (2,030 mm) high. Other available car depths are 36 in. (915 mm) and 60 in. (1,525 mm).

RESIDENTIAL ELEVATOR PLANS

CONVEYING SYSTEMS □ **2**

TRACTION ELEVATORS

Medium- and high-rise buildings require geared traction and gearless traction elevator systems. The main difference between the two systems is in travel speed. General design considerations involving hoistway, machine room, and elevator planning are similar.

Both geared and gearless drive units are governed by electronic controls, which coordinate car leveling, passenger calls, collective operation of elevators, door operation, car acceleration and deceleration, and safety applications. A broad range of control systems are available to meet individual building requirements.

Structural requirements call for the total weight of the elevator system to be supported by the machine beams and transmitted to the building (or hoistway) structure. Consult with elevator consultants and structural engineers.

Traction Elevator Design Considerations

- Pit depths, overhead clearances, and penthouse sizes should be in accordance with ASME requirements. Local codes may vary from these requirements.
- All overhead dimensions for passenger elevators are based on standard 8-ft- (2.4-m-) high cabs.
- Layout dimensions of the passenger elevator are based on center-opening entrances. Other types are available.
- The machine room for traction elevators is usually located directly above the hoistway. Provide space for the elevator drive, electronic control equipment, and governor; provide sufficient clearance for equipment installation, repair, and removal. Adequate lighting and ventilation (temperature maintained between 65°F and 100°F (18°C and 38°C)) are required by codes, and sound insulation should be provided. Machine room sizes may vary depending on number of cars, type of control, and so on. Check with elevator consultant for requirements.
- Check local codes for required fire enclosures.

This is a very specialized application, so consultation with experts is advised. Traction elevators with basement machine rooms are used in new and existing buildings where overhead clearance is limited.

TRACTION ELEVATOR WITH BASEMENT MACHINE ROOM

GEARLESS ELEVATOR MACHINE ROOM

SIDE-MOUNTED COUNTERWEIGHT
Side-mounted counterweights allow an optional rear entrance door.

REAR-MOUNTED COUNTERWEIGHT

ELEVATOR HOISTWAY TYPES

TRACTION ELEVATOR DIMENSIONS IN FT-IN. (MM)

RATED LOAD LB (KG)	A	B	C	D	E
2,000 (967)	5-8 (1,727)	4-3 (1,295)	7-4 (2,235)	6-11 (2,108)	3-0 (914)
2,500 (1,134)	6-8 (1,828)	4-3 (1,295)	8-4 (2,540)	6-11 (2,108)	3-6 (1,066)
3,000 (1,360)	6-8 (1,828)	4-7 (1,397)	8-4 (2,540)	7-5 (2,260)	3-6 (1,066)
3,500 (1,587)	6-8 (1,828)	5-3 (1,600)	8-4 (2,540)	8-1 (2,463)	3-6 (1,066)
4,500 (2,041)	5-8 (1,727)	7-10 (2,387)	8-2 (2,489)	10-5 (3,175)	4-0 (1,219)

TRACTION ELEVATOR (GEARED)

- ELECTRICAL AND COMMUNICATION WIRING
- MACHINE ROOM PENTHOUSE
- STANDBY POWER SOURCE (MAY BE REMOTE)
- VENTILATION
- SPECIALLY DESIGNED STRUCTURE
- HOISTWAY
- STRUCTURAL BRACKETS FOR GUIDE RAILS
- DOORSILLS, HOISTWAY FRAMES, AND SIGNAL FIXTURE GROUTED
- PIT LADDER
- ELEVATOR PIT
- PIT FOUNDATION

ELEVATOR PLANNING DETAILS

REAR SERVICE CONNECTION

ELEVATOR LOBBY

10'-0" LOBBY WIDTH, MIN.

SINGLE CAR

REAR SERVICE CONNECTION

ELEVATOR LOBBY

10'-0" LOBBY WIDTH, MIN.

PAIRED CARS

REAR SERVICE CONNECTION

X

2X

FOUR-EIGHT CAR ARRANGEMENT

In buildings with several elevator groupings, one group may serve lower floors, while others serve as express elevators to upper floors. When four or more elevators

REAR SERVICE CONNECTION

X

1.75X TO 2.0X

THREE-SIX CAR ARRANGEMENT

serve all or the same part of a building, they must be located in no fewer than two hoistways, but no more than four elevators may be located in one hoistway.

ELEVATOR LOBBY PLANNING

ELEVATOR PLANNING: BUILDING PREPARATION FOR ELEVATOR INSTALLATION

The following base building preparatory work is required to install elevator equipment properly:

- An enclosed elevator equipment room with electrical outlets, adequate lighting, and heating and ventilation sufficient to maintain the room at a temperature between 50°F (10°C), minimum, and 100°F (38°C), maximum
- Temporary enclosures, barricades, or other protection from open hoistways and elevator work areas while the elevator is being installed
- Temporary elevator service prior to completion
- All telephone wiring to machine room control panel, and installation of telephone instruments
- A standby power source when elevator operation from an alternate power supply is required
- A means to disconnect the elevator's main-line power supply automatically to protect the machine room equipment from water damage
- A plumb and legal hoistway; a pit of proper depth with a pit ladder for each elevator; drains, lights, access doors, waterproofing, and hoistway ventilation, as required

- ELEVATOR
- ELEVATOR LOBBY
- "ARA" SIGN
- TWO-WAY COMMUNICATIONS UNIT
- WHEELCHAIR SPACE
- "ARA" SIGN
- "ARA" SIGN
- POSTED INSTRUCTIONS FOR "ARA" SPACE

An *area of rescue assistance* is defined in the ADAAG as "an area which has direct access to an exit, where people who are unable to use stairs may remain temporarily in safety to await further instructions or assistance during emergency evacuation."

The elevator lobby and shaft must be pressurized for smokeproof enclosure, as required by the local building official. The pressurization system must be activated by smoke detectors in locations approved by the local building official. The system's equipment and ducts must be of two-hour fire-resistant construction.

ELEVATOR LOBBY DESIGNED AS AREA OF RESCUE ASSISTANCE

- DECORATIVE HOISTWAY WALL
- GLASS-WALLED ELEVATOR CAB

Observation and glassback elevators travel outside of a hoistway or in a hoistway open on one side. Machinery is concealed or designed to be inconspicuous. Elevators may be engineered for hydraulic, geared, or gearless use. Cabs can be custom-designed with more than 75% of wall area as glass. Only the rear panel is glass in glassback cabs. Safety barriers must be provided at floor penetrations and the ground floor, completely surrounding that part of the elevator not enclosed by the hoistway. This is a very specialized application; consultation is advised.

GLASS-WALLED ELEVATOR CARS

HYDRAULIC ELEVATORS

Operation

Hydraulic elevator systems are used primarily in low-rise installations, where moderate car speed (up to 150 ft (45 m) per minute) is required. A car is connected to the top of a long piston that moves up and down in a cylinder. The car moves up when hydraulic fluid is pumped into the cylinder from a reservoir, raising the piston. The car is lowered when the hydraulic fluid returns to the reservoir. The up and down motions of the elevator car are controlled by the hydraulic valve.

Space Planning

The main space-planning elements of a hydraulic elevator system are the machine room, usually located at the base, and the hoistway, which serves as a fire-protected, ventilated passageway for the elevator car. Adequate structure must be provided at the base of the hoistway to bear the load of the elevator car and its supporting piston or cylinder.

Hydraulic Elevator Design Considerations

- The elevator pit should be reinforced to sustain the vertical forces generated by the system configuration. Consult manufacturer's representatives. All pit depths and overhead clearances should be in accordance with ASME requirements. Local codes may vary from these requirements.
- Car and hoistway dimensions of preengineered units are for reference purposes only. A variety of units are available. Consult manufacturers for dimensions of specific systems.
- Hoistway walls usually serve primarily as fireproof enclosures. Check local codes for required fire ratings.
- Guide rails extend from the floor of the pit to the underside of the overhead (top of hoistway). Consult the elevator manufacturer for the special requirements of excessive floor heights.
- Rail brackets typically are at each floor level. A bracket is required at the top of the hoistway, and an intermediate bracket may be required for certain floor-to-floor heights. Consult the manufacturer.
- Some hydraulic applications may require jack-hole blockouts in the floor of the pit.

PISTON AND CYLINDER DETAIL

(labels: PISTON; CYLINDER SUPPORT PLATE; PIT FLOOR; PRESSURIZATION POINT; PISTON CYLINDER; NONCORROSIVE PROTECTION COVER FOR CYLINDER; EVACUATION TUBE (RELIEVES UNWANTED WATER AND OTHER LIQUIDS FROM CYLINDER))

HOLED HYDRAULIC ELEVATOR

(labels: GUIDE RAILS; ELEVATOR CAB; FIRE-RATED HOISTWAY (BY GENERAL CONTRACTOR); CAB-SUPPORT STRUCTURE; TRAVEL CABLE; RAIL BRACKET ATTACHES TO HOISTWAY WALL; PISTON; PIT LADDER (BY GENERAL CONTRACTOR); 4'-0" PIT DEPTH; CAR BUFFER; WELL HOLE (DEPTH = MAX. RISE + 4'-0", APPROXIMATELY); ELEVATOR PIT; MACHINE ROOM (BY GENERAL CONTRACTOR; APPROXIMATELY 5'-0 X 7'-6"); BOTTOM FLOOR; TOP FLOOR; 12'-3" +/- TOTAL CLEAR HEIGHT; MAX. RISE: 60'-0")

HOLELESS HYDRAULIC ELEVATOR

(labels: ELEVATOR CAB; FIRE-RATED HOISTWAY (BY GENERAL CONTRACTOR); PISTONS; PISTON CYLINDERS; PIT LADDER (BY GENERAL CONTRACTOR); 4'-0" TO 5'-5" PIT DEPTH; CAR BUFFER; ELEVATOR PIT (BY GENERAL CONTRACTOR); MACHINE ROOM (BY GENERAL CONTRACTOR; APPROXIMATELY 5'-0 X 7'-6"); BOTTOM FLOOR; TOP FLOOR; 12'-3" +/- TOTAL CLEAR HEIGHT; MAX. RISE: 20'-0")

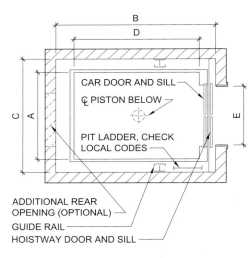

(labels: B; D; C; A; E; CAR DOOR AND SILL; ℄ PISTON BELOW; PIT LADDER, CHECK LOCAL CODES; ADDITIONAL REAR OPENING (OPTIONAL); GUIDE RAIL; HOISTWAY DOOR AND SILL)

HYDRAULIC ELEVATOR DIMENSIONS IN FT-IN. (MM)

RATED LOAD LB (KG)	A	B	C	D	E
2,000 (967)	5-8 (1,727)	4-3 (1,295)	7-4 (2,235)	5-11 (1,803)	3-0 (914)
2,500 (1,134)	6-8 (1,828)	4-3 (1,295)	8-4 (2,540)	5-11 (1,803)	3-6 (1,066)
3,0,00 (1,360)	6-8 (1,828)	4-7 (1,397)	8-4 (2,540)	6-3 (1,905)	3-6 (1,066)
3,500 (1,587)	6-8 (1,828)	5-3 (1,600)	8-4 (2,540)	6-11 (2,108)	3-6 (1,066)
4,500 (2,041)	5-8 (1,727)	7-10 (2,387)	7-5 (2,260)	10-0 (3,048)	4-0 (1,219)

A- and B-dimensions are "clear inside." Rated speeds are 75 to 200 ft (23 to 61 m) per minute.

HYDRAULIC ELEVATOR SIZES

(labels: LIGHTING; VENTILATION; LIGHTING AND MAIN LINE DISCONNECT SWITCH; HYDRAULIC PUMP UNIT; 7'-0" MIN. CLEAR)

A machine room that meets code requirements and is ventilated for temperatures between 65° and 100°F (18° and 38°C) must be provided for all elevators. It is usually located next to the hoistway at or near the bottom terminal landing. Room size may vary depending on the number of cars, capacity, and speed.

Machinery consists of a pump and motor drive unit, hydraulic fluid storage tank, and electronic control panel. Adequate ventilation, lighting, and entrance access (usually 3 ft 6 in. × 7 ft (1,070 × 2,130 mm)) should be provided.

MACHINE ROOM

FREIGHT ELEVATORS

General freight elevators with capacities of 2,000 to 8,000 lb (907 to 3,628 kg) satisfy a variety of material-handling requirements. Industrial truck freight elevators require special design considerations to handle truckloads of 10,000 to 20,000 lb (4,536 to 9,072 kg) or more.

General freight or industrial truck elevators may have either hydraulic or traction drive systems similar to those of other elevator systems. However, the units are usually custom-designed with vertical bipart doors and special structural support to accommodate heavy loads and eccentric loading conditions. Freight elevators usually have simple control systems and operate at slower speeds than other elevators. Their capacity must be sized for the largest expected load.

Freight Elevator Design Considerations

Hoistway walls: Local building codes govern design characteristics; consult with appropriate agencies to determine requirements such as fire rating.

Traction elevators: The hoisting machine may be mounted directly overhead or at the side of the hoistway at any level, including the lowest landing. Special structural design considerations are necessary based on forces created by the use of traction equipment.

Guide rail bracket support: Freight elevators create horizontal forces greater than those created by passenger elevators. Vertical steel is installed within the hoistway to provide bracket support at elevations with bracket locations.

Truckable sills: At the edge of the building floor (leading into the elevator hoistway), a structural steel angle must be in place to avoid deterioration of the building floor through continued use of hand trucks, battery-operated pallet lifts, forklifts, and the like.

Flooring: A variety of materials may be used for flooring in a freight elevator, including checkered steel plate, nonskid materials, galvanized steel, or high-density wood.

Rippeteau Rollins Architecture + Design; Washington, D.C.

TRACTION FREIGHT ELEVATORS

CAPACITY IN LB (KG)	LIGHT- AND MEDIUM-DUTY DIMENSIONS IN FT-IN. (MM)			HEAVY-DUTY POWER TRUCK LOADING		
	A	B	C	D	E	F
2,500 (1,134)	5-4 (1,626)	7-0 (2,134)	5-0 (1,524)	7-10 (2,388)	1-7 (483)	0-11 (279)
4,000 (1,814)	6-4 (1,930)	8-0 (2,438)	6-0 (1,829)	8-10 (2,692)	1-7 (483)	0-11 (279)
8,000 (3,629)	8-4 (2,540)	10-0 (3,048)	8-0 (2,438)	10-10 (3,302)	1-7 (483)	0-11 (279)
12,000 (6,443)	10-4 (3,150)	14-0 (4,267)	10-0 (3,048)	13-6 (4,115)	1-7 (483)	0-11 (279)
20,000 (9,072)	12-4 (3,759)	20-4 (6,196)	12-0 (3,658)	16-6 (5,029)	1-7 (483)	0-11 (279)

HYDRAULIC FREIGHT ELEVATORS

CAPACITY IN LB (KG)	LIGHT- AND MEDIUM-DUTY DIMENSIONS IN FT-IN. (MM)			HEAVY-DUTY POWER TRUCK LOADING	
	A	B	C	D (MANUAL DOORS)	E (POWER DOORS)
2,000 (967)	5-0 (1,524)	6-0 (1,829)	4-8 (1,422)	6-4 (1,930)	6-10 (2,083)
4,000 (1,814)	6-6 (1,981)	8-0 (2,438)	6-2 (1,880)	7-10 (2,388)	8-4 (2,540)
8,000 (3,629)	8-6 (2,591)	12-0 (3,658)	8-2 (2,490)	10-6 (3,200)	10-6 (3,200)
12,000 (5,443)	10-6 (3,200)	14-0 (4,267)	10-2 (3,098)	12-6 (3,810)	12-6 (3,810)
20,000 (9,072)	12-6 (3,810)	20-0 (6,096)	12-2 (3,708)	14-6 (4,420)	14-6 (4,420)

TRACTION FREIGHT ELEVATOR

KEY PLAN

G equals 5 in. (127 mm) for regular counterbalanced hoistway doors and 6¾ in. (172 mm) for pass-type counterbalanced hoistway doors. Pass-type doors are required when floor heights are less than 11 ft (3,350 mm) for 7 ft (2,134 mm) openings and less than 12 ft 6 in. (3,810 mm) for 8 ft (2,458 mm) openings.

HYDRAULIC FREIGHT ELEVATOR

FREIGHT ELEVATOR

ELEVATOR CAB INTERIORS

CHARACTERISTICS

Elevators log more passenger miles than any other means of transportation. The design of elevator cab interiors must respond with durability, safety, and practicality.

Cab Size

Elevator interiors offer unique and challenging design opportunities for designers. Passenger elevator car proportions are wide and shallow to allow efficient movement into and out of the cab. Changing these proportions can be very expensive. A typical size is 35 sq ft (3.2 sq m), with interior cab measurements of 6 ft 8 in. × 5 ft 4 in. (2,032 × 1,625 mm).

Car Capacity

Weight is key in the selection of elevators. Elevator capacity is based on the total expected weight of the car and its contents (suspended load), rather than on allotted area per person, as for other interior spaces in a building. In fact, because the safety cables in the elevator system are designed to accept 6 to 10 times the suspended load of the cab, the weight capacity of an elevator will be far greater than the number of people in a crowded elevator cab.

The designer should determine the total weight of the interior finishes for the cab, as that factor is included in the calculation of the suspended load. Heavy finish materials such as stone or metal can be used in elevator cabs, because elevators can be sized to lift nearly any suspended load. If heavy finish materials are anticipated, the interior designer should alert the elevator consultant early in the design process so that the elevator system can be properly sized to accept the greater weight of those finishes.

Intended Use

Elevator car interiors convey the design concept of the building they serve. An elevator in a corporate business setting will have a very different look from an elevator for a hotel, a hospital, a parking garage, or for high-rise housing. Each particular car should be viewed in its context and with its unique requirements.

REGULATORY REQUIREMENTS

Because elevators are highly used public spaces, the designer must pay particular attention to the codes governing their use. The American Society of Mechanical Engineers (ASME) A17.1, *Safety Code for Elevators and Escalators,* states the following:

- The car and its finishes must be constructed so they will not deform, break, displace, or become damaged in normal use or via an emergency stop.
- Materials used in elevator cars must not be removable with common tools, and they must meet the highest level of smoke and flame spread requirements to protect riding passengers.
- Glass and mirrors must be laminated to avoid injury if they become broken or cracked.
- Nonelevator-related equipment is not allowed in cars.
- Visual displays, graphics, and picture frames are allowed if properly secured. However, no sharp edges are allowed, nor are projections or depressions greater than ¾ in. (19 mm).
- There can be no openings other than the car doors.
- The cars must have ventilation, either natural or forced. Natural ventilation requires openings at the top and bottom of the car totaling 3.5% of the floor area. Forced ventilation requires one air change per minute and auxiliary power for the fan or other air-moving means.

It is critical to the life and safety of all those who use elevators that these requirements be consistently met. With the adoption of the Americans with Disabilities Act (ADA) as law, clearances, rail height requirements, Braille coding, and the location of emergency communications devices are clearly defined. Accessibility standards require minimum widths and depths of cars. The selection and use of interior finish materials must not encroach upon the minimum required cab dimensions.

SELECTION OF FINISHES

The manufacturer's product literature lists a platform size for the car. The steel walls of the cab are fastened to the platform with a 1 in. (25 mm) flange all around, so the empty cab shell is less than the platform size by 1 in. (25 mm) on all four sides. Interior finishes are applied to the inside face of the steel cab walls. Manufacturer's standard cab finishes do not exceed ¾ in. to 1 in. (19 to 25 mm) thickness. The resulting inside clear cab dimensions are measured from the inside face of the finished cab walls. These dimensions, shown on the manufacturer's literature as "cab size," are the minimum clear dimensions governed by code.

If the designer is using custom interior materials in the cab in lieu of the manufacturer's standard finishes, the applied finishes should not exceed a 1 in. (25 mm) thickness. Satin (brushed) stainless steel is the standard finish that most elevator manufacturers offer for fixtures and doors. If other finish materials are desired, the designer should pay close attention to the material thickness for coordination with control panel fixtures and faceplates, and to the material sheet sizes available for use on doors or wall panels. Customizing elevator cab interiors requires careful attention, given that a high-rise elevator has limited space on the control panel and very deliberate, exact dimensioning requirements.

ENTRANCE WALL ELEVATION

SIDE WALL ELEVATION

TYPICAL ELEVATOR CAR INTERIOR

FABRICATION ISSUES

For new construction, or for elevator car renovations, use fabricators who have experience in constructing elevator car interiors, as this is not an enterprise that can be easily taken on by craftspeople who are used to providing finished materials in other interior spaces.

In renovation work, each car will be different because of the wear and tear of many years of use. Elevator cabs are rarely square in any dimension, and in renovation work the differences can be dramatic. An experienced craftsperson specializing in elevator cars will know this and will get exact field measurements of each car on the site. Shop drawings must be reviewed carefully; and discrepancies or problems should be noted by the fabricator, so that the designer and fabricator can work together on an acceptable resolution.

Tolerances between materials need to be greater than typically found in, for example, finished wood paneling in a building interior. Elevator cars can flex, and allowances should be made for that movement. Attention should be paid to how the car will be constructed, giving some flexibility to sizing so that reveals and any special detailing can be accomplished. Simply put, the design should be constructible; for example, a single-piece handrail—side to back to side—may look good, but is nearly impossible to install.

(A) HANDRAIL

(B) CORNER AT WOOD

(C) CORNER AT METAL MESH

(E) HORIZONTAL REVEAL

(F) WOOD-TO-METAL PANEL TRANSITION

PLAN DETAIL AT HANDRAIL

(D) JOINT AT METAL MESH

(G) BASE

These details are indicative of a custom elevator cab in a commercial office building. The materials are heavier than standard cab finishes.

TYPICAL ELEVATOR CAR INTERIOR—DETAILS

DURABILITY

Elevator cars are some of the most heavily trafficked areas in commercial interiors. Therefore, the materials used in elevators must be as durable and tamper-resistant as possible. Floor material selection should consider eventual replacement.

The standard floor recess is ½ in. (13 mm). Deeper recesses are possible, if coordinated early with the elevator consultant for correct sizing of the cab. Hard-surface materials, including tile, terrazzo, and thinset stone, can be used with high initial cost, but very high durability.

When renovating existing elevator car interiors, it is important to be aware that revising materials, such as changing from carpet to tile, is difficult. The materials being removed must be weighed and compared to the weight of the new materials. Added weight must be accommodated in the elevator's lift and balance mechanism.

Vinyl composititon tile (VCT) is often used in cars requiring high durability with low cost—often in parking garage elevators. Diamond-plate metal flooring is a good option for freight elevators due to its hard surface and almost indestructible nature. Carpet is the most widely used flooring material in elevator cars because of its capability to dampen sound and its comfort under foot; moreover, it has a relatively low initial cost when compared to stone, tile, or terrazzo. Carpet in an elevator requires replacement nearly once every six months in areas subject to high traffic. Consequently, it is a good idea when specifying carpet in elevators to provide two sets of carpets for each car. When one carpet is worn or soiled, it can be removed and replaced. Cleaning the carpet in elevator cabs regularly keeps it looking fresh and prolongs its life.

LIGHTING

The lighting for elevator cars requires particular attention, because these are close environments where people, usually strangers, have to stand fairly close to one another for a few seconds up to two minutes. Too much bright light is unflattering to skin and makes people psychologically uncomfortable in such close quarters. To prevent this discomfort, good lighting design requires a balance between having the elevator cab bright enough so that passengers can see into the elevator and feel safe entering it, yet low enough to soften the light within the space.

The light levels in elevators do not need to be as bright as in an office environment or a hotel corridor. Minimum car lighting is 5 fc (50 lux) measured at the car sill. Studies show that using a standard parabolic-type lens fixture in the car ceiling is not a good lighting

MAXIMUM FLOOR TRANSITION AT ELEVATOR THRESHOLD

LEVEL FLOOR TRANSITION AT ELEVATOR THRESHOLD

ELEVATOR THRESHOLD DETAILS *s*
Source: Ted Kollaja, AIA; lauckgroup; Dallas, Texas

solution. The lighting level, while meeting the minimum 5-footcandle requirement, is not enough to adequately illuminate the floor. The result, when the car door opens, is that it can look dark, as if the lights in the car had been turned off and the elevator is out of commission. Placing fixtures that wash the walls of the car with light avoids this problem. A balance of downlighting and sidelighting creates the best environment. Providing a soft wash of light along the walls gives a nice reflected light on the passengers and highlights the handrail, giving focus and sparkle to the car interior. The lights remain on in many cars much of the time, so low-voltage lighting is a good idea for energy savings. Any exposed lamps, whether fluorescent or incandescent, must be shielded to prevent broken glass falling on passengers below; and lamps in elevator cars must be easily accessible for ease in changing them.

CEILINGS AND DOORS

Certain steps may be taken at the early stages of a building's elevator design that add a level of graciousness without adding a lot of cost. Increasing the height of the car interior dramatically improves the feel and is relatively inexpensive. However, increasing the height of the entrances, which are typically 7 or 8 ft (2.1 or 2.4 m), can have significant functional impacts that reduce elevator performance; and higher, heavier doors must be propelled more slowly to be safe.

The ceilings have to be securely fastened to the car-top—they cannot come crashing to the floor during an emergency stop. Top emergency exits are required for use as last-resort removal of trapped passengers. One panel, with an open area of 5 sq ft (.5 sq m) and one dimension no less than 1 ft 4 in. (406 mm), must be provided to meet this requirement. This panel is

locked from the inside, but can be removed from the outside when rescue operations require it. The designer should consider the location and configuration of this required emergency exit when designing the ceiling.

The minimum interior headroom required is 80 in. (2,032 mm), even when movable ceiling panels are used to access the top emergency exit. Often, in buildings where there is no separate freight elevator, passenger cars occasionally serve as the freight elevator. The car should be designed so that the ceiling (which can be much lower than the cartop) can be lifted, allowing the transport of much larger materials. Pad pins on the walls allow users to hang protective coverings inside the cab. Providing pad pins is a good practice in all cabs, regardless of whether there is a freight elevator in the building, because when tenants move in, all elevators may be called upon to carry furniture.

REPAIR AND MAINTENANCE

Elevator users abuse finishes; they stand on handrails, hang from the ceiling, or remove anything not secured. Passengers will stuff trash or other objects anywhere they can. Therefore, avoid designs that include recesses. And because it is difficult to do on-site repairs to elevator finishes when working in such a tight space used by so many people, when using wood or fabric on the car interior, it's a good idea to panelize the interior materials so that a single panel may be removed, replaced, and then repaired off-site.

Karen Gunsul, AIA; Zimmer Gunsul Frasca Partnership; Seattle, Washington
John A. Tornquist Jr., CEI; Lerch Bates and Associates, Inc.; Snohomish, Washington

ESCALATORS AND MOVING WALKS

Escalators are a very efficient form of vertical transportation for very heavy traffic where the number of floors served is limited, normally a maximum of five to six floors. Escalators are not usually accepted as a required exit.

Dimensions are general and will vary somewhat with the manufacturer. Consult manufacturers for structural support, electrical supply, and specific dimensional requirements.

Moving passenger conveyors are particularly useful in transportation terminals, sports arenas, and exposition centers where large numbers of people must move long distances horizontally. The conveyors may be arranged in any combination of horizontal runs and inclines with a practical maximum of 12°.

It is generally not economical to provide moving sidewalks for distances of less than 100 ft (3 m); for distances greater than 300 ft (9 m), their slow operating speed invokes passenger frustration. Narrower units (26 in.; 660 mm) accommodate one adult; 40 in. (1,016 mm) widths allow for both walking and standing passengers.

Alan H. Rider, AIA; DMJM; Washington, D.C.

MOVING PASSENGER CONVEYOR ELEVATION

MOVING PASSENGER CONVEYOR PLAN

MOVING PASSENGER CONVEYORS

SYMBOL	DESCRIPTION	PLANNING DIMENSIONS SCHINDLER IN. (MM)	
A	Nominal width	32 (812)	48 (1219)
B	Width of walk	26 (660)	40 (1016)
C	Overall deck width	4 ft–4½ in. (1333)	5 ft–8½ in. (1740)
W	Top of handrail	2 ft–11⁷⁄₁₆ in. (900)	
X	Depth of truss	3 ft—6½ in. (1079)	
Y	Length of pit	18 ft–10 in. (5740)	
Z	Maximum depth of truss	3 ft–4⁷⁄₁₆ in. (1027)	

ESCALATOR PROFILE

ESCALATORS

SYMBOL	DESCRIPTION	PLANNING DIMENSIONS OTIS IN. (MM)		
A	Nominal width	32 (812)	40 (1016)	48 (1219)
B	Width of strap	24 (609)	32 (812)	40 (1016)
C	Overall deck width	3 ft 11½ in. (1105)	4 ft 7½ in. (1409)	5 ft 3½ in. (1613)
T	Working Point (WP) to end of lower truss	5 ft–9 ⅞ in. (1,774)		
U	Top of handrail	3 ft 2⁹⁄₁₆ in. (979)		
V	Depth of lower pit	3 ft 6 in. (1,066)		
W	Top of handrail	2 ft 8⅛ in. (815)		
X	Depth of truss	3 ft 1⅛ in. (942)		
Y	Length of pit	3 ft 3½ in. (1,003)		
Z	Working Point (WP) to end of upper truss	8 ft 5 in. (2,565)		

BASIC MECHANICAL SYSTEMS

SYSTEM TYPES

The two major considerations in the design of a commercial heating, ventilating, and air conditioning (HVAC) system are the *source of energy* (fuel) to be used and the *method of distribution* within the building. Heat can be distributed in a building by air, water (hydronic systems), or electricity.

AIR SYSTEMS

There are dozens of different all-air comfort conditioning systems, each addressing the complex requirements of larger commercial buildings. In large buildings there is often a simultaneous demand for heating, cooling, and ventilation. Rooms on the sunny side of a building need cooling, rooms on the shaded side need heating, and rooms in the building core require ventilation. Of the many year-round all-air systems in use, the most common are:

- Single-zone
- Multizone
- Single-duct or terminal reheat
- Single-duct variable air volume (VAV)
- Dual-duct

HEATING DISTRIBUTION SYSTEMS

SYSTEM	ADVANTAGES	DISADVANTAGES
Air	Can also perform other functions, such as ventilation, cooling, humidity control, and filtering.	Very bulky ducts require careful planning and space allocation.
	Prevents stratification and uneven temperatures by mixing air.	Can be noisy if not designed properly.
	Very quick response to changes of temperature.	Very difficult to use in renovations.
	No equipment required in rooms being heated.	Zones are not easy to create.
		Cold floors result if air outlets are high in the room.
Hydronic	Compact pipes are easily hidden within walls and floor.	For the most part, can only heat, not cool (exceptions: fan-coil units and valance units).
	Can be combined with domestic hot water system.	No ventilation.
	Good for radiant floor heating.	No humidity control.
		No air filtering.
		Leaks can be a problem.
		Slightly bulky equipment in spaces being heated (baseboard and cabinet convectors).
		Radiant floors are slow to respond to temperature changes.
Electricity	Most compact.	Very expensive to operate (except heat pump).
	Quick response to temperature changes.	Wasteful.
	Very easily zoned.	Cannot cool (except heat pump).
	Low initial cost.	

Source: Norbert Lechner, Heating, Cooling, Lighting: Design Methods for Architects, *2nd Ed.; New York, John Wiley & Sons, Inc., 2001.*

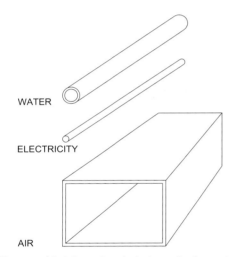

WATER

ELECTRICITY

AIR

Because of their large size, air ducts require the most forethought in design and planning, while electrical heat requires the least. An air heating system requires 1% to 5% of the building's volume for ducts and air-handling equipment.

RETURN

SUPPLY

SUPPLY DUCT

CHIMNEY OR FLUE

SUPPLY DUCT

FURNACE

RETURN DUCT

Air circulates through ducts with the aid of a blower.

THREE METHODS OF HEAT DISTRIBUTION

FROM AIR-HANDLING UNIT (AHU)

SUPPLY DUCT

RETURN DUCT TO AHU

DIFFUSER, TYP.

THERMOSTAT, TYP. (TO AHU)

GRILLE, TYP.

AIR SYSTEM

FLOOR OR ROOF SLAB

CEILING

RETURN AIR

SUPPLY AIR

CONDITIONED SPACE

FLOOR

Single-zone systems are best applied to small residential and commercial buildings. The entire building is treated as a single zone, controlled by a single thermostat and served by a single air-handling unit, which supplies fixed quantities of air to the building spaces. If a change in air volume is required for seasonal changeover (heating to cooling, or vice versa), the duct volume dampers must be reset.

Multiple subzones can be established by thermostatic control of volume dampers in branch ducts feeding different areas. All these zones, however, are in the same mode—heating or cooling. This system has low first cost, simple maintenance, and a long life. However, because it is designed to handle a building as a single zone, often it is not sufficiently flexible to maintain comfort conditions in all rooms. As a result, larger buildings often use multizone systems.

SINGLE-ZONE SYSTEM

Multizone systems are used for medium-sized buildings where different zones have different conditioned air requirements. Hot and cold air are produced centrally and provided to each zone. Therefore, heating and cooling can be provided simultaneously to different zones. Limiting factors include the number of zones and energy costs.

The principal disadvantage of a multizone system is that the ductwork can become enormous. Other disadvantages are that the initial cost of the system is high, it can be difficult to control, and the operation costs can be high because the return air from all the different zones is mixed since there is only one air handler. As a result, warm air is mixed with cold air, resulting in a large waste of energy.

MULTIZONE SYSTEMS

Single-duct reheat systems are not commonly used because of their energy inefficiency. This system uses a single duct that provides air (typically very cold) to the entire building. At each zone, a small reheat coil heats the cold air to the temperature required for that zone. The central system must provide air cold enough (as cold as 40°F (4.4°C)) to meet the maximum cooling load of the building's warmest zone. Though this system has a high first cost and high energy costs, it provides excellent control and constant air volume and does not require a changeover to switch from heating to cooling, or vice versa. This system is often used for laboratories, hospitals, and other facilities requiring accurate temperature control and constant volume for ventilation requirements.

SINGLE-DUCT REHEAT SYSTEMS

VAV systems compensate for variable loads by varying the volume of air supplied, rather than its temperature. The air volume variation is accomplished by a thermostatically controlled variable air-volume box. This box takes main duct air from the single-supply duct and modulates the air quantity supplied to a space to match its load. The central supply will furnish either cold air or warm air depending on outdoor conditions and prevailing indoor needs. This system is better suited for buildings that always need cooling (large interior zones) than to buildings with perimeters requiring constant air changes, such as labs or medical facilities. This system has become the most popular for medium-sized and large buildings because of its low first cost, low energy cost, and small ductwork. These systems cannot, however, simultaneously provide both heating and cooling.

SINGLE-DUCT VARIABLE AIR VOLUME (VAV) SYSTEMS

Dual-duct systems can either be variable-volume or constant-volume. The constant-volume system consists of two complete duct distribution systems—one with hot air and one with cold air. A mixing box at each zone location provides air at the temperature required for the load. Control is excellent with this system. The disadvantages are a high first cost, a high energy cost, and a large volume of building space occupied by a two-duct system.

The variable-volume dual-duct system uses one duct to supply primary air in accordance with the major demand (heating or cooling). This air has variable temperature but constant volume. The second air duct has a fixed temperature but variable volume. The two streams of air are mixed at each zone. This system uses smaller ductwork than the constant-volume system, is cheaper to install, and uses less energy. Control, however, is not as rapid and accurate as with the constant-volume system.

DUAL-DUCT SYSTEMS

DIFFUSERS, REGISTERS, AND GRILLES

The air supply and return devices are often the only element of an HVAC system seen by building occupants. They have a direct impact on thermal and acoustical comfort, and have an indirect impact on indoor air quality. Selection and specification of these devices are important parts of the design process.

Three types of devices are used to supply and return air:

- *Diffusers* are generally intended for ceiling-mounted supply air applications and are designed to provide good mixing of supply air with room air.
- *Registers* are used for supply or return air applications and may be appropriate for ceiling, sidewall, or floor installations.
- *Grilles* are less sophisticated devices primarily intended for return air applications.

Diffusers and registers are selected to deliver a specified airflow with appropriate throw (in terms of both distance and direction) and acceptable noise generation. Diffusers, manufactured of steel or aluminum, are available in a wide range of shapes, sizes, surface appearances, finishes, and installation detailing. Registers come in a more restricted range of shapes and sizes. Grilles are generally square or rectangular in shape.

LOUVERED GRILLE

WALL, TYP.

EGG CRATE GRILLE

PERFORATED GRILLE

RETURN AIR GRILLES

SLOT DIFFUSER

INTEGRAL SLOT DIFFUSER

LINEAR SLOT DIFFUSER

FLOW BAR DIFFUSER

LINEAR LOUVER DIFFUSER

SUPPLY AIR LINEAR DIFFUSERS

PLAN — MODULAR CORE AND PANEL

SECTION

DIRECTIONAL DIFFUSER

PLAN

SECTION

SQUARE CONE DIFFUSER

PLAN

SECTION

COMBINATION SUPPLY/ RETURN DIFFUSER

PLAN — CORE MOVES UP AND DOWN TO VARY AIRFLOW

SECTION

VAV-AUTOMATED DIFFUSER

PLAN

SECTION

MODULAR CEILING DIFFUSER

PLAN

SECTION

ROUND CONE DIFFUSER

PLAN

SECTION

PERFORATED FACE DIFFUSER

PLAN — LIGHT FIXTURE

SECTION — AIR SLOT

AIR SUPPLY LIGHTING TROFFER

PLAN

SECTION

T-BAR LAY-IN DIFFUSER

TWO-WAY SLOT

SUPPLY AIR DIFFUSERS

HYDRONIC SYSTEMS

Active heating and cooling systems for buildings use either air or water as the heat transfer medium. Heating systems that use water are referred to as *hydronic systems*. Cooling systems that use water are often referred to as *chilled-water systems*. Water is a very efficient means of transmitting heat to different areas of a building. Hot water carries almost 3,500 times more heat than the same volume of air. This is the principal advantage of a hydronic system—compactness. Although varied in design, all hydronic heating systems contain the following basic components:

- Hot water boiler and its controls and safety devices
- Expansion tank, also referred to as a compression tank
- Water pump, also called a circulator
- Terminal devices that transfer heat from the circulating water to the various building spaces
- Piping
- Controls that regulate the system

Three types of hydronic heating systems are often commonly referred to by their terminal units, which include the following:

- Fin-tube radiation
- Convectors
- Fan-coil units
- Radiant panels
- Cast-iron radiators
- Steel-panel radiators

Fin-Tube Radiation

Fin-tube radiation units typically consist of a copper pipe on which are mounted square aluminum or copper fins. Hot water passes through the pipe, heating the pipe and, in turn, the fins. This "finned-tube" assembly is installed in a metal enclosure designed to encourage convective air current over the hot pipe and fins. Cool air enters the baseboard enclosure at the bottom, is heated as it passes over the hot-finned pipe assembly, and exits the top of the enclosure to heat the space. The heated air rises, is cooled by the room's heat loss, drops to the floor, and reenters the finned-tube radiator to be reheated.

Convectors

Convectors consist of one or more vertical tiers of finned-tube radiation. They differ from the finned-tube radiators only in that convectors have a much larger capacity. Convector units installed on outside walls should have rear insulation to prevent significant heat loss through the wall. This is especially important for recessed convector units, because the R-value of the wall may be reduced by the recess.

HYDRONIC SYSTEM

FIN-TUBE RADIATORS

CONVECTORS

Fan-Coil Units

Fan-coil units can provide heating, cooling, or both. A fan-coil unit is essentially a cabinet containing a hydronic coil assembly and a motor-driven blower. Hot or cold water is piped to the unit. Control of the blower is often given to the user. Fan-coil units do not usually provide dehumidification. Dehumidification occurs when the room air is cooled below its dew point as it passes over the cooling coil. A condensate pan and drain line is often provided to collect and remove the condensate. Recirculated room air can be filtered as it passes through the return air filter at the base of the unit.

Radiant Panels

Radiant heating systems transfer heat from hot water tubing (or electric cables) embedded in the floor or ceiling to a medium that will distribute heat to the specified space. Hydronic radiant heating is expensive because of the large amount of pipes and valves involved. These systems are more popular in residential projects than in commercial projects.

Radiant floors induce convective air currents in the room because of the natural tendency of heated air to rise. Finish floors should not be made of a thermal insulating material; ceramic tile and wood flooring are suitable. Radiant ceiling installations are less common in commercial interiors because a blanket of heated air forms at the ceiling and remains there, which leads to a condition of stagnant air in a closed room. Overhead radiant panels are often used to heat loading docks and other partially exterior spaces that do not require a fine temperature control.

Cast-Iron Radiators

The classic rib-type cast-iron radiator was originally developed for use in steam systems and later adapted to hydronic hot water systems. Each unit is connected to a water supply and return branch and is normally equipped with an air vent. Hot water passes through the unit and heats the cast-iron ribs, which then heat the room by a combination of radiation and convection. The thermal mass of the radiator itself, plus the contained water, provide a thermal lag that acts to smooth out rapid temperature variations.

Steel-Panel Radiators

The size and unsightliness of the classic ribbed radiator and the hazard of an exposed high heat source were two of the factors that led to the development of flat steel radiators. The "ribs" of these units are flat steel tubes of rectangular cross section, arranged either vertically or horizontally. These units have a smaller thermal mass than cast-iron radiation.

IN-SPACE UNIT   **RECESSED UNIT**   **LOW-PROFILE UNIT**

FAN-COIL UNITS

COMPONENTS OF A FAN-COIL UNIT

CONCRETE TOPPING OVER SUBFLOOR APPLICATION   **SLAB-ON-GRADE APPLICATION**

RADIANT FLOOR SYSTEMS

H-PANEL RADIATOR   **V-PANEL RADIATOR**

RADIATORS

ELECTRIC HEATING SYSTEMS

Electric heating systems for commercial use most commonly produce heat at the point of use. These systems, sometimes referred to as *space heating systems*, have a number of advantages. Installation costs are low because there is no need for a boiler or furnace, and expensive piping or ductwork is not required. Electric heat is also clean and quiet. However, electric heat is expensive in most parts of the United States, and a separate cooling system is required.

Electric energy is ideally suited for local space heating because it is simple to distribute and control. Electric heating systems are widely used in residences, schools, and commercial and industrial facilities. Heating units are placed in individual rooms or spaces and may be combined into zones with automatic temperature controls. Electric in-space heating systems may utilize natural convection, radiant, or forced-air units.

ELECTRIC HEATING SYSTEM

Natural convection units must be installed so that airflow across the resistor will not be impeded.

NATURAL CONVECTION UNITS

Radiant heaters are designed primarily to heat objects rather than space. Current flowing through a high-resistance wire heats up the element or surface of the unit. Heat is transferred from the unit to surfaces or occupants primarily by radiation. For an effective system, it is important to locate radiant heating units carefully in relation to the objects being heated.

RADIANT HEATING UNITS

Forced-air units combine convection heating with fan-powered air circulation. Such units are available in a wide range of capacities to suit a variety of heating loads and occupancy types. Unit ventilations are commonly used on an outside wall, where they have access to outdoor air intake and can prevent cold air downdrafts from window areas.

FORCED-AIR UNITS

COMPUTER ROOM AIR CONDITIONING

Computers generate great quantities of heat in concentrated areas. To ensure proper operation, a precise temperature and humidity environment is required. The range of control may be as narrow as 72°F, ±2°F (22° C, ±1° C) temperature and 50% humidity, ±5%.

The air conditioning equipment should be able to meet the changing conditions created by relocation of equipment, facility expansion, and changes in heat output. Hotspots can result if flexibility is not built into the system.

Downflow and Upflow Systems

Computer room air conditioning systems are either downflow or upflow.

- *Downflow systems* are more commonly used for a number of reasons. Air is returned through the top of the unit and supplied out through the bottom into a raised floor, thereby permitting large quantities of air without disturbing the occupants. Perforated floor outlets can easily be moved, providing flexibility in room layout. The units themselves also form part of the floor grid and can easily be moved.
- *Upflow systems* are used in areas where there is no raised floor (often the case in retrofit situations). They are also used in large rooms when the air is distributed by a ductwork system. Upflow systems are not as flexible as downflow systems for reorganizing equipment in a room.

Redundancy

All systems should be designed with redundancy to provide full, continuous cooling. The degree of redundancy should be weighted against the consequences of downtime of the equipment. A minimum of 25% redundancy is recommended, but 100% may be warranted, depending on future expansion and the degree of backup required.

Vapor Barriers

It is difficult and costly to maintain a computer room at a relative humidity of 50%, ±5%, throughout the year without a vapor barrier. In addition, room partitions should extend beyond the false ceiling to help prevent migration of moisture to and from adjoining areas.

IN-SPACE LOCAL UNIT APPLICATION

DOWNFLOW (OR UPFLOW) SYSTEM WITH RAISED FLOOR

LARGE REMOTE DUCTED SYSTEM

COMPUTER ROOM AIR CONDITIONING TYPES

Large forced-air system is shown with combined heat-rejection systems.

COMPUTER ROOM COOLING UNIT

COMBINED HEAT REJECTION IN MAINFRAME COOLING SYSTEM

Methods of Heat Rejection

Common methods of heat rejection include:

- *Self-contained air-cooled:* Uses air within building return air plenum; limited to small-capacity units.
- *External air-cooled:* Uses outdoor condenser unit; refrigerant lines generally are limited to 100 ft (30 m) above, 30 ft (9 m) below, or 200 total ft (61 m) from computer room to outdoor unit.
- *Water-cooled:* Uses closed-loop condenser water pumped to an external cooling tower to remove heat from condenser within computer room fan-coil unit. Distance from cooling tower to computer room can be longer than that in an external air-cooled system.
- *Glycol-cooled:* Uses closed-loop glycol to carry rejected heat to external dry cooler or cooling tower, which allows greater separation of computer room from outside air. With additional coils, the system can provide "free cooling" during colder weather. This system is preferred in areas where ambient temperature is below –0°F.
- *Chilled water:* Chilled water is pumped from a remote chilled water plant to local fan-coil unit.
- *Combination unit:* May use two or more means of heat rejection to service the system during certain hours of operation or as a backup in case of primary system failure.

Planning Issues

- Evaluate availability of building services and systems, mechanical chases, and electrical power capacities.
- Determine the overall heat load and plan size of system with client and engineer. Design for built-in redundancy with multiple circuits.
- Use qualified engineers to design and engineer the systems and to supervise testing and certification.
- Detail the construction of walls, ceiling, and floors to provide a complete vapor seal and adequate airflow.
- Evaluate energy-efficiency ratios of various kinds of proposed equipment.
- Select a system with high reliability and low noise level.
- Do not ventilate the space when unoccupied.

William R. Arnquist, AIA; Donna Vaughan & Associates, Inc.; Dallas, Texas

Larry O. Degelman, P.E.; Texas A&M University; College Station, Texas

Walter T. Grondzik, P.E.; Florida A&M University; Tallahassee, Florida

PLUMBING FIXTURES

PLUMBING FIXTURE SUPPORTS

When a floor-mounted support cannot be installed, wall-mounted supports can be used if the wall structure is strong enough to support the entire weight of the fixture. In such installations, the support arms are attached to a plate that is bolted directly into the wall structure.

PLUMBING FIXTURE MOUNTING REQUIREMENTS

Off-the-floor plumbing fixtures are often preferred, for the following reasons:

- Installation is done at the floor; floor-mounted installation is done at the ceiling below the fixture, making it more labor-intensive.
- Cleaning costs are lower.
- Horizontal waste reduces the number of core drills required.

A standard width partition (3½ in. (90 mm)) may not be wide enough to support common plumbing fixtures such as lavatories, sinks, and drinking fountains, for the following reasons:

- Placement of pipes prior to construction of the partition may not have been within required tolerances.
- There may be additional plumbing fixtures on the same wall.
- A structural member might be located beneath the chase.
- The fixture is freestanding or does not require a support within the wall.
- The supply pipes for fixtures serve other floors.

SINGLE STUD

Labels: CLEAR SPACE IN WALL CAVITY; HANGER PLATE; HANGER FURNISHED WITH FIXTURE; FIXTURE (LAVATORY OR URINAL); SINGLE STUD; FINISH WALL

DOUBLE STUD OR CMU

Labels: CLEAR SPACE; DOUBLE STUD (OR CMU); FOR PIPE CLEARANCE ADD 1" (25) TO OUTSIDE DIAMETER OF PIPE; FINISH WALL

CLEAR SPACE IN WALL FOR LAVATORY AND URINAL SUPPORTS

SINGLE FIXTURE (DOUBLE CMU WALL)

Labels: CLEAR SPACE; VENT LINE; WATER CLOSET SUPPORT; VERTICAL DISCHARGE WASTE LINE

BACK-TO-BACK FIXTURES (DOUBLE STUD WALL)

Labels: CLEAR SPACE; SOIL STACK FROM ABOVE; VENT LINE; WATER CLOSET SUPPORT; NOTCH WALL PLATE, AS REQUIRED; VERTICAL DISCHARGE WASTE LINE

SINGLE FIXTURE IN FIXTURE GROUP (DOUBLE CMU WALL)

Labels: CLEAR SPACE; VENT LINE; WATER CLOSET SUPPORT; HORIZONTAL WASTE LINE TO REMAINDER OF FIXTURE GROUP

SINGLE-FIXTURE WATER CLOSET SUPPORTS

BACK-TO-BACK FIXTURES IN FIXTURE GROUP (DOUBLE CMU WALL)

Labels: CLEAR SPACE; STACK FOR SOIL PIPE FOR VENT; WATER CLOSET SUPPORT; HORIZONTAL WASTE LINE TO REMAINDER OF FIXTURE GROUP

SUPPORTS FOR WATER CLOSET

This support typically is used with a vitreous china lavatory.

Labels: BASEPLATE (BOLTED FIRMLY TO FLOOR); EXPOSED SUPPORT ARM; STABILIZER ARM; UPRIGHT SUPPORTS WELDED TO BASEPLATE

EXPOSED ARM FIXTURE SUPPORT

When using lavatories of the flat slab type (that is, without a backsplash), manufacturers typically require a 2 to 6 in. (50 to 150 mm) space between the wall finish and the rear of the lavatory to prevent water accumulation.

Labels: EXPOSED ARM EXTENSION IS TYPICALLY COVERED WITH CHROME-PLATED ESCUTCHEON; ESCUTCHEON; CONCEALED SUPPORT ARM; UPRIGHT SUPPORT WITH BASEPLATE (BOLTED FIRMLY TO FLOOR)

CONCEALED ARM FIXTURE SUPPORT

INSTALLATION SPACE REQUIREMENTS FOR PLUMBING FIXTURES

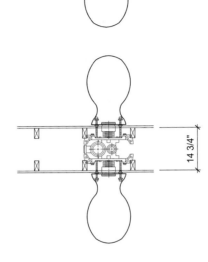

Flush valve
Fixture support independent of wall
Horizontal waste arrangement
No-hub cast-iron pipe

WALL-HUNG WATER CLOSET PLUMBING CHASE SIZES

Wall-hung
Flush valve
Fixture support independent of wall
Horizontal waste arrangement
No-hub cast-iron pipe

URINAL PLUMBING CHASE SIZES

Fixture support independent of wall
No-hub cast-iron pipe

WALL-HUNG LAVATORY PLUMBING CHASE SIZES

TANK-TYPE FLUSH

FLUSH VALVE

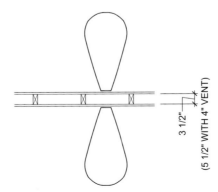

TANK-TYPE FLUSH

FLUSH VALVE

No fixture support
Vertical waste arrangement
No-hub cast-iron pipe

FLOOR-MOUNTED WATER CLOSET PLUMBING CHASE SIZES

Nader Dubestani, P.E.; Sazan Group, Inc.; Bellevue, Washington

WATER CLOSETS, URINALS, AND BIDETS

REVERSE TRAP
Water is introduced to the fixture only through the rim by a gravity flush tank. This action is low cost and used mostly for residential projects. Reverse traps may be used with flush tanks or valves.

BLOWOUT
Water is introduced at high velocity through jets at the bottom of the waterway in a *blowout action*. This action is used for public facilities and industrial projects because of its capability to remove larger objects thrown into the fixture. Blowouts are used with flush valve water supplies only.

SIPHON JET
Water is introduced to the fixture both through the rim and by a jet at the bottom of the waterway. Quiet flushing and moderate cost make this the most commonly used flushing action. Less costly variations include *washout* and *washdown* actions that do not use the jet. The siphon jet can be used with flush valves or tanks.

FIXTURE FLUSHING ACTION TYPES

This low, basinlike plumbing fixture is designed to be straddled, for bathing the posterior of the body.

BIDETS

GRAVITY FLUSH TANK
Water enters the tank through a ball cock and is stopped when the float valve reaches a predetermined level. The handle raises the flapper to release all the water in the tank into the fixture; it stops when the flapper closes. Gravity flush tanks require 10 psi water pressure.

PRESSURE-ASSISTED FLUSH TANK
Water enters a pressure tank installed inside the outer tank, partially filling the tank and compressing the air inside. When flushing is started, the air pressure causes the quick release of water into the fixture. Pressure-assisted flush tanks require 30 psi (2.1 kgf/sq cm) water pressure.

FLUSH VALVE
Flush valves are available in a wide variety of manual and automatic operation fixtures, some with infrared and other proximity sensors. Once flushing has started, a measured quantity of water is quickly introduced to the fixture. Flush valves require 25 psi (1.7 kgf/sq cm) water pressure.

FIXTURE WATER SUPPLY TYPES

WATER CLOSET TYPES

Flush valves and tanks can be installed on either floor-mounted or wall-mounted water closets.

ADA 4.16, *Water Closets,* describes grab bar requirements for water closets. ADA 4.17, *Toilet Stalls,* describes approach, floor space, and grab bar requirements for water closets within toilet stalls. Water closet height should be 17 to 19 in. (430 to 480 mm) to the top of the toilet seat. Seats should not spring up. Mount controls on the wide side of the toilet no more than 44 in. (1,120 mm) above the floor.

For rough-in dimensions, refer to manufacturers' manuals.

Special toilet types are sometimes used, such as vacuum-vented, composting, and chemical toilets.

Current code requires that water closet flush valves and tanks be limited to 1.6 gallon, maximum, per flush of water.

Urinals require flush valves as source of water supply. ADA 4.18, *Urinals,* requires 30 × 48 in. (760 × 1,220 mm) clear floor space in front of urinals to allow a forward approach. Urinals should be wall-hung, with an elongated rim a maximum of 17 in. (430 mm) above the floor. Shields, if provided, should not extend beyond the front of the urinal rim and must have a clearance of 29 in. (740 mm). Flush controls should be accessible and be no more than 44 in. (1,120 mm) above the floor.

If used, urinal tanks should be 92 to 94 in. (2,340 to 2,390 mm) above the floor.

Battery stalls, except accessible ones, should be installed 21 to 24 in. (530 to 610 mm), on center.

WATER CLOSET MOUNTING TYPES AND CLEARANCES

URINALS

BATHTUBS AND SHOWERS: MATERIALS AND FINISHES

Bathtubs are available in many shapes and installation types, and are available in the following materials:

- *Fiberglass:* An economical and common choice, gel-coated fiberglass (also known as FRP) is light-weight and easy to install. Because the material can be molded, fiberglass tubs are available in a variety of shapes. Although not as durable as cast iron or acrylic, fiberglass can easily be repaired.
- *Acrylic:* Acrylic bath fixtures are more readily available than fiberglass, with which it is usually reinforced. Because acrylic is light and easily formed into different shapes, it is a good choice for whirlpools and other large tubs that would be too heavy in cast iron. Acrylic also is a good insulator, thus keeps the water warmer longer.
- *Cast iron:* Very heavy and extremely durable, traditional enamel-coated cast iron resists staining and scratching. It cannot be molded as freely as acrylic or fiberglass, so there are fewer shapes and styles from which to choose.
- *Enameled steel:* This is a lighter-weight, less-expensive alternative to cast iron.

BUILT-IN SHOWER UNITS

SHOWER BASE CONSTRUCTION

SQUARE

RECTANGULAR

CORNER

Materials for bases include acrylic with fiberglass reinforcement, enameled steel, and terrazzo.

SHOWER BASES

RECTILINEAR SHOWER

SQUARE SHOWER WITH SEAT

SITE-BUILT SHOWER PANS

BUILT-IN RECESSED BATHTUB

DROP-IN WHIRLPOOL BATHTUB

FRONT APPROACH

SIDE APPROACH

For tubs with a built-in seat at the head of the tub, the seat must be 15 in. (380 mm) wide, and clear floor space must be provided in front of the seat.

CLEAR FLOOR SPACE FOR ACCESSIBLE BATHTUBS

PLUMBING FIXTURE MOUNTING HEIGHTS AND FIXTURE COUNT

URINAL | PARTITION AT TOILET | PARTITION AT URINAL | SANITARY NAPKIN-TAMPON DISPENSER | SANITARY NAPKIN DISPOSAL UNIT | FRAMED MIRROR WITH SHELF | TOILET PAPER HOLDER | SOAP DISPENSER

HAND/HAIR DRYER | PAPER TOWEL DISPENSER | SHOWERHEAD/ SHOWER CONTROLS | ROBE HOOK | LAVATORY | TOILET | SHOWER ROD | ELECTRIC WATER COOLER

GRAB BAR AT BATHTUB (SEAT AT TUB HEAD)

GRAB BAR AT WATER CLOSET

FIXTURE AND ACCESSORY MOUNTING HEIGHTS

PRELIMINARY PLUMBING FIXTURE COUNT

FACILITY TYPE	WATER CLOSET (PEOPLE)	WATER CLOSET (FIXTURE)	URINAL	LAVATORY	DRINKING FOUNTAIN	SHOWER	SERVICE SINK	NOTES
Stadiums, arenas, convention halls, terminals	1–100	1						
	101–200	2	Note 1	Note 2	1/1,000			Note 4
	201–400	4						
	Additional 300	1						
Churches, auditoriums, theaters	1–50	1						
	51–300	2	Note 1	Note 2	1/1,000			Note 4
	Additional 300	1						
Restaurants	1–50	2						
	51–100	3	Note 1	Note 2	1/200			
	101–200	4						
	Additional 200	1						
Sports clubs, country clubs	1–40	1	Note 1	Note 2	1/75	15/1		Up to 150
	Additional 40	1				30/1		More than 150
Stores, malls, office buildings— employees	1–15	1						
	16–40	2	Note 1	Note 2	1/100		1/floor	
	41–75	3						
	Additional 60	1						
Stores, malls, office buildings— customers	1–15	1						
	16–40	2	Note 1	Note 2				
	41–75	3		Note 3	1/1,000		1/floor	
	Additional 60	1						
Dormitories	1–20	2						One laundry tray

Notes

1. Half of the water closets can be urinals.
2. Half of the lavatories can be water closets.
3. If employee facilities are accessible to customers, no additional fixtures are necessary.
4. Some codes require double or triple the number of water closets for women.
5. Consult local plumbing codes for exact requirements.

American Society of Plumbing Engineers; Westlake, California
Michael Frankel, CIPE; Utility Systems Consultants;
Somerset, New Jersey

ELECTRICAL, DATA, AND TELECOMMUNICATIONS SYSTEMS

ELECTRICAL POWER

The two important concepts in understanding electricity—voltage and current (amps)—can be understood in terms of an analogy to water. The more water in a reservoir (voltage), the greater the flow (current) through the pipe (conductor). Voltage (a "reservoir" of electrons) and current flow (amps) create electrical power. By increasing the size of the pipe, the rate of flow can be increased.

Voltage can be thought of as a reservoir of electrons. The pressure (voltage) in the reservoir causes the electrons to move through the conductor. Voltage is a measure of the electrical "pressure" used to produce a flow of current through a circuit. Current is the amount of electrons flowing through an electrical current. Just as the size of the water pipe restricts how much water will flow, the conductor, typically an electrical wire, offers a specific resistance to the flow of current. The size of the conductor is one factor that determines how much electrical power will be available. The rate of flow of electrons is measured in units called *amperes*, or amps. The conductor carrying that current offers resistance. For example, "20-amp service" means that 20 amps of electrical power are available to that circuit. The term *ohms* describes electrical resistance. If the electrical conductor is too small (high ohms resistance), problems will occur.

VA RATING

Volt/amps, or V/A, is the term used to describe available electrical power. The voltage rating divided by the supply voltage equals amps. For example:

$$\frac{2,400 \text{ (VA rating)}}{120 \text{ (Supply Voltage)}} = 20 \text{ Amps}$$

VA rating is a measure of how much power is available. *Watts* is a measure of how much power an electrical device uses.

WATER POWER
Electrical power can be simply understood as an analogy to water power.

VOLTAGE
Voltage is the potential of electrical power, similar to a reservoir of electrons.

CURRENT
Current can be thought of as the amount of electrons flowing through an electrical conductor.

AMPS, OHMS, AND V/A RATING
The rate of flow of electrons is measured in units called amperes, or amps. Ohms describes electrical resistance. V/A describes available electrical power.

ELECTRICAL POWER

ELECTRICAL AND TELECOMMUNICATIONS SYSTEMS

TYPE	APPEARANCE	DESCRIPTION	USE	RELATIVE CAPACITY
Category 5 (high-capacity telephone/data wire)		Four twisted pairs of high-capacity wire enclosed in an insulated sheath	Telephones, faxes, modems Video Data	Garden hose
RG 6 (coaxial cable)		Heavily shielded and insulated copper core, which carries signal	Video Data	Fire hose
Fiber-optic cable		Glass-lined cable passing laser light pulses, which transmit voice data and image signals at the speed of light	All digital signals	Culvert

STANDARD MOUNTING HEIGHTS FOR ELECTRICAL DEVICES

POKE-THROUGH ELECTRICAL BOX

FLOOR-MOUNTED ELECTRICAL OUTLETS

MONUMENT FLOOR OUTLET

DISTRIBUTION SYSTEMS

Poke-Through Systems

Poke-through systems are used in conjunction with overhead branch distribution systems that run in accessible suspended ceiling cavities to outlets in full-height partitions. When services are required at floor locations without adjacent partitions or columns, as in open office planning, they must either be brought down from a wireway assembly (known as a *power pole*) or up through a floor penetration containing a fire-rated insert fitting and flush or above-floor outlet assembly. To install a poke-through assembly, the floor slab must either be core-drilled or contain preset sleeves arranged in a modular grid. Poke-through assemblies are used in conjunction with cellular deck and underfloor duct systems when the service location required does not fall directly above its associated system raceway.

With one-floor penetration, the single poke-through assembly can serve all the power, communications, and computer requirements of a workstation. Distribution wiring in the ceiling cavity can be run in raceways. The more cost-effective method is to use armored cable (BX) for power and approved plenum-rated cable for communications and data when the ceiling cavity is used for return air. To minimize disturbance to the office space below when a poke-through assembly must be relocated or added, a modular system of prewired junction boxes for each service can be provided, although it is more common to elect this option for power only. A different type of working system must be selected for a floor slab on grade, above a lobby or retail space, above mechanical equipment space, or above space exposed to the atmosphere.

Cellular Deck Systems

The low initial cost of a poke-through system makes it both viable and attractive for investor-owned buildings when tenants are responsible for future changes, and for corporate buildings with limited construction budgets. Poke-through systems are effective when office planning includes interconnecting workstation panels containing provisions (base raceways) to extend wiring above the floor, reducing the number of floor penetrations needed for services.

Based on the projected frequency of changes in office furniture layouts, a corporate or government organization may elect to invest in a permanent raceway system to minimize cost and disturbance to occupants when changes or additions are made. When structural design dictates the use of metal decking, a cellular floor raceway system utilizing trench header ducts is the most likely choice.

Cellular raceways come in a variety of sizes and configurations ranging from ½ to 3 in. (13 to 76 mm) high, with cells 8 or 12 in. (203 or 304 mm) on center, and 2 or 3 cells per section. An overall floor deck can be full cellular, where bottom plates are provided throughout, or blended, as shown.

Trench header ducts come in various sizes and configurations. The height is adjustable for slab depths above cells of 2½ to 4 in. (63 to 101 mm); widths vary from 9 to 36 in. (228 to 914 mm). Cover plates are ¼ in. (6 mm) thick, with lengths from 6 to 36 in. (152 to 914 mm), and can be secured either with spring clips or flush, flathead bolts.

POWER CABLE — COMPUTER DATA CABLE — PRINTER — ZONE JUNCTION BOX FOR ELECTRONICS — CEILING GRID BELOW — CONDUIT TO NEXT ZONE JUNCTION BOX OR UTILITY CLOSET — FLOOR SLAB — CONDUIT AND JUNCTION BOXES SECURED TO UNDERSIDE OF SLAB — FACSIMILE CABLE — TELEPHONE CABLE (VOICE) — POWER CABLE EXTENSION CORD — MONUMENT FLOOR OUTLET OVER POKE-THROUGH ELECTRICAL BOX (CORE DRILLED OR SET INTO PRESET SLEEVES) — FLEXIBLE CONDUIT FOR POWER, ELECTRONICS (COMPUTER/DATA), AND COMMUNICATION (TELEPHONE/FAX) — ZONE JUNCTION BOX FOR POWER — ZONE JUNCTION BOX FOR COMMUNICATIONS — HANGER WIRE FOR CEILING GRID

POKE-THROUGH HARDWARE SYSTEM/ZONE JUNCTION BOX

POWER CABLE — COMPUTER DATA CABLE — PRINTER — 5'-0" O.C. — 2'-6" O.C. — ACCESS COVER — CELLULAR DECKING (THREE CELL) — NONCELLULAR DECKING — ACCESS OPENING TO CELLULAR DECK BELOW — FACSIMILE CABLE — TELEPHONE CABLE (VOICE) — POWER CABLE EXTENSION CORD — ACTIVATED PRESET OUTLET FOR POWER, ELECTRONICS, AND COMMUNICATIONS — CONCRETE FLOOR SLAB — FLUSH CARPETED OR MONUMENT SERVICE FITTINGS PROVIDE ACCESS TO RECESSED POWER AND OTHER OUTLETS — TRENCH DUCT RACEWAY RUNS ACROSS METAL DECK SEE SECTION — ELECTRONICS, POWER, AND COMMUNICATIONS RAN IN SEPARATE CELLS — THREE COMPARTMENT TRENCH DUCT WITH REMOVABLE COVER TO POWER, ELECTRONICS, AND COMMUNICATION UTILITY CLOSETS — 2 1/2" — ACCESS COVER — THREE-COMPARTMENT TRENCH OVER CELLULAR DECK — CELLULAR DECKING — SECTION

CELLULAR DECK SYSTEM WITH TRENCH HEADER DUCTS

Raised Access Floor System

A raised access floor system provides maximum flexibility and lowest cost to relocate or add service. When used in conjunction with a modular system of power, communication and data wiring plug-in receptacles, and cable connector sets, changes can be made without an electrician or wiring technician. Access flooring systems have the highest initial cost of distribution systems.

Access floors can be provided with or without stringers, which are use to minimize the "creep" effect. For a custom installation without ramps or steps, the base floor is depressed.

Access floors do not necessarily require an increase in floor-to-floor height, and if so, the height added is at a much lower per-unit cost than for the rest of the building. When special attention is given to coordinating lighting with other elements in the suspended ceiling, or when lighting is provided below as from the workstations, the cavity can be compressed to compensate for the raised floor.

Flat Cable Wiring System

Flat cable originates at transition boxes located at various intervals along core corridor walls and columns that are individually served from distribution centers in utility closets. Boxes can also be cast in the floor or atop a poke-through insert. Cables are not permitted to pass under fixed partitions and must be carefully mapped out to minimize crossovers and clutter.

To install a service fitting, an interface base assembly must first be secured directly to the concrete floor at the flat cable location. The base assembly stabs into conductors of the flat cable and converts them to round wire. When the service fitting is attached, it is activated and ready for use.

Careful consideration must be given to the application of this system based on limitations that may or may not be acceptable under different conditions. For example, it may be ideal for small areas or renovation of existing buildings where the poke-through or power pole systems are unacceptable or cannot be used. In new construction where poke-through has been chosen as the base building standard system, the flat cable system is a viable solution in areas where poke-through outlets cannot be installed, such as slab on grade.

Carpet tiles are required by most building codes as the floor covering to be used over flat cable installations to facilitate access to the flat cable. Where frequent changes and additions are anticipated, the resulting wear and tear on expensive, glued-down carpet tile may be a disadvantage.

Flat cable systems are labor-intensive to install. Actual installed initial costs and outlet relocation costs are comparable to cellular deck with trench header ducts.

Richard F. Humenn, P.E.; Joseph R. Loring & Associates, Inc.; Consulting Engineers; New York, New York
Gary A. Hall; Hammel Green and Abrahamson; Minneapolis, Minnesota

RAISED-ACCESS FLOOR SYSTEM WITH MODULAR PLUG-IN DISTRIBUTION

FLAT CABLE WIRING SYSTEM

CABLES, BOXES, AND RACEWAYS

ARMORED (BX)

Armored cable is manufactured with two-, three-, and four-conductor insulated wire. Its internal bonds help the armor itself serve as a bonding conductor.

METAL-CLAD (MC)

Manufactured in sizes and specifications similar to armored cable, metal-clad cable is available with a separate insulated ground conductor and in larger sizes.

NONMETALLIC SHEATHED (NM, ROMEX)

Manufactured in two- and three-conductor PVC insulated wire with or without ground wire, nonmetallic sheathed cable is permitted in residential and many other building types up to three stories.

FLAT CABLE

Flat cable has combinations of three, four, and five conductors for easy access under carpet squares. Data, communications, and TV flat cable are available.

CABLES

OCTAGONAL

Commonly used for flush ceiling outlets, octagonal boxes may also be used as floor boxes for monument receptacles.

SQUARE

FLUSH FLOOR

Boxes are mounted to wood floor structures (nonadjustable) or cast-in-place concrete with leveling screws. Concrete boxes include cast-iron, stamped-steel, or nonmetallic materials.

UTILITY   **SWITCH/RECEPTACLE**

Metallic and nonmetallic boxes are available. Flush mounting in concrete requires a concrete tight box and rigid conduit and tubing. In CMU construction, a raceway tubing is threaded through the cavities.

ELECTRICAL BOXES

WALL-MOUNT CABLE RACK

CENTER-HUNG CABLE RACK

CABLE TRAY SYSTEM

Cable trays protect and carry a large number of insulated cables in a limited space. For more protection or where heat buildup is not a problem, perforated or solid bottoms and top covers are available.

CABLE CHANNEL

Cable channel can be used as a branch cable tray to carry a single large cable or conduit or several small ones.

CONDUIT AND CABLE SUPPORTING DEVICES

UNINTERRUPTIBLE POWER SUPPLY SYSTEMS

Uninterruptible power supply (UPS) systems are designed to provide continuous power with specific electrical characteristics by conditioning utility company power, battery power, or generator-supplied power. UPS systems closely control the power supply voltage and frequency to critical equipment such as computers, communications systems, and medical instrumentation.

UPS systems are either online, with power routing through them continuously, or offline, with power routed through them only when the incoming power is interrupted or departs from the design characteristics. The time required for an offline, solid-state UPS to automatically switch on varies with the type of switch selected: in general, the quicker the switch, the more expensive the switching equipment. To prevent loss of data or other problems, the time must be matched to the tolerances of the critical equipment being supplied by the UPS.

Battery backup time is selected to allow a controlled shutdown of equipment or to allow a backup generator to be started and stabilized at full power.

Redundant UPS systems may be required if UPS power loss cannot be tolerated for system maintenance or equipment breakdown.

Charles B. Towles, P.E.; TEI Consulting Engineers; Washington, D.C.

TYPICAL UNINTERRUPTIBLE POWER SUPPLY SYSTEM DIAGRAM

SOLID-STATE UPS

SOLID–STATE UPS SIZES

KVA	WIDTH IN. (MM)	DEPTH IN. (MM)	HEIGHT IN. (MM)	WEIGHT LB (KG)
25	28 (170)	32 (813)	70 (1,780)	1,400 (635)
50	72 (1,830)	36 (915)	72 (1,830)	4,000 (1,814)
125	72 (1,830)	36 (915)	72 (1,830)	5,600 (2,540)
200	72 (1,830)	36 (915)	72 (1,830)	6,000 (2,722)
350	168 (4,267)	32 (813)	76 (1,930)	12,700 (5,761)
500	168 (4,267)	40 (1,016)	76 (1,930)	14,600 (6,623)

Note: Sound level is approximately 65–70 dB. Maintain room temperature at 70–80°F (21–27°C). Some units require clearance for access.

ROTARY UPS

ROTARY UPS SIZES

KVA	WIDTH IN. (MM)	DEPTH IN. (MM)	HEIGHT IN. (MM)	WEIGHT LB (KG)
25	80 (2,030)	24 (610)	62 (1,575)	2,600 (1,179)
50	80 (2,030)	24 (610)	62 (1,575)	3,400 (1,542)
125	125 (3,175)	32 (813)	74 (1,880)	7,000 (3,175)
200	140 (3,556)	32 (813)	80 (2,030)	10,000 (4,536)
350	164 (4,166)	60 (1,524)	84 (2,134)	15,000 (6,804)
500	173 (4,394)	64 (1,626)	98 (2,490)	32,200 (14,606)

Note: Sound level is approximately 60–80 dB. Maintain room temperature at 70–80°F (21–27°C). Some units require clearance for access.

BATTERY CABINET

BATTERY CABINET SIZES

KVA	TIME MIN.	WIDTH IN. (MM)	DEPTH IN. (MM)	HEIGHT IN. (MM)	WEIGHT LB (KG)	NUMBER REQUIRED
75	15	40 (1,016)	32 (813)	76 (1,930)	2,300 (1,043)	2
100	15	40 (1,016)	32 (813)	76 (1,930)	2,300 (1,043)	3
200	15	48 (1,220)	32 (813)	76 (1,930)	2,300 (1,043)	4
400	10	40 (1,016)	32 (813)	76 (1,930)	2,300 (1,043)	8
500	7.5	40 (1,016)	32 (813)	76 (1,930)	2,300 (1,043)	4

36" (915) MIN. CLEARANCE

TWO-TIER BATTERY RACK

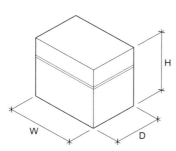

UPS UNDER 10 KVA

UPS UNDER 10 KVA SIZES

WATTS	WIDTH IN. (MM)	DEPTH IN. (MM)	HEIGHT IN. (MM)	TIME MIN.
200	8 (203)	15 (380)	6 (152)	15–20
800	22 (560)	16 (406)	9 (230)	15–20
1,500	22 (560)	16 (406)	18 (457)	15–20
KVA				
3.0	26 (660)	19 (483)	52 (1,320)	10
5.0	36 (914)	19 (483)	52 (1,320)	10
10.0	36 (914)	19 (483)	52 (1,320)	10

Note: A wide variety of UPS systems are available for smaller applications, ranging from desktop models for single microcomputers to floor models that can supply several computers or other equipment.

PART 3

INTERIOR TYPOLOGIES

Commerce

Exhibition

Entertainment

Presentation Technology

Health Care

Hospitality

Athletic Facilities

Education

SPACE MEASUREMENT SYSTEMS

Space measurement of commercial property plays a crucial role in establishing rental rates and space assignment records. These rates are sometimes used to set designer's fees as well.

Several space measurement systems are in use in North America, many of which use identical or similar terms but interpret them in different ways; and sometimes their language is not precise. All systems strive to ensure the utmost fairness to occupants and building owners, but their rules are quite complex, particularly if they must be translated from one system to another. Although several additional regional variations are in use in major North American urban centers, here, six measurement systems are discussed:

- Building Owners and Managers Association (BOMA)—new standard
- Building Owners and Managers Association (BOMA)—former standard
- Real Estate Board of New York, Inc. (REBNY)
- Washington, DC, Association of Realtors (WDCAR)
- General Services Administration (GSA)—former system
- International Facility Management Association (IFMA)

Before 1992, little attempt was made to compare the systems; now, the trend is more toward reconciliation than standardization.

The most recent development in this field has been the promulgation of a major revision by BOMA to its standard. The U.S. General Services Administration has recently decided to classify all future space assignments, including lease actions, in terms compatible with BOMA's new system. The BOMA system is the most widely accepted in commercial real estate transactions, such as leasing. It is also used for tenants' space assignment allocation in many buildings.

NEW BOMA SYSTEM

The BOMA system is tailored to the needs of the commercial office building lessor. It is the oldest and most widely used system. In June 1996, BOMA completed a major revision of its measurement standard ANSI Z65.1, *Standard Method for Measuring Floor Area in Office Buildings.*

As with the previous standard, HVAC convectors, columns, and interior building projections are included

in the measurements. Another aspect that remains the same is that the usable area exclusive to one tenant is still measured from the office (tenant) side of walls separating tenant space from public corridors.

Unlike the old standard, the new standard defines *floor usable area* to include *buildingwide common areas* on that floor. Such areas are prorated to all building tenants on all floors. Areas such as public toilets and electrical and janitorial closets are considered *floor common areas.*

The 1996 standard represents a major departure from the previous edition in the following areas:

- It measures space on a buildingwide basis, rather than exclusively floor by floor.
- Most areas that were formerly amortized or absorbed in the base building cost (and therefore covered in the base rent) are now measured and prorated to all tenants.
- The new standard is much more explicit in naming many of the new building features designed to support all tenants in a building.
- Calculations are more complex, but the results provide a more rational approach to actual contemporary situations.
- Several new definitions have been introduced. Familiar terms like *rentable* and *usable* have been revised to reflect required changes in how they are calculated. The definition of *rentable area* includes office, store, portions of building common areas, and floor common areas prorated to each tenant. Building rentable area almost always remains constant for the life of the building. Usable area changes over the life of the building as tenant space changes. Basement storage and loading dock areas within the building line are considered part of rentable area; parking areas are not.

FORMER BOMA SYSTEM

The former BOMA standard is described here for comparison, as it remains the baseline for rentable areas stated in thousands of leases. Moreover, of the six systems discussed here, it is the most generic, has the simplest set of definitions, and is the easiest to administer—as long as its few categories are specific enough for the intended application. Its major features include:

- Space is measured floor by floor, rather than by the building as a whole.

- Rentable space is constant for the life of the building; usable area changes over the life of the building.
- HVAC convectors are included in measurements.
- Amenities shared by several tenants—such as fitness centers, conference centers, lounges, and vending areas—are not considered rentable. Landlords are expected to factor the costs of such facilities into their basic rental rates. Basement storage and parking areas are not included as part of rentable area.

Except for mechanical penthouses, minimal definition is provided for the allocation of space for central building support operations, such as HVAC, electrical, telephone switch, and UPS systems for the entire building. Common practice is to exclude them all from rentable area, but the standard is not definitive.

Because the old BOMA system measures floor by floor, main lobbies and atrium areas are considered rentable. And because core factors tend to be very high on these floors, BOMA suggests renting usable area in this case.

Usable area exclusive to one tenant is measured from the office (tenant) side of walls separating tenant space and public corridors. Usable space excludes such support areas as public toilets, mechanical rooms, and electrical and janitorial closets.

Three Categories of Commercial Office Space

- *Space rented by measurement.* Represents space in each system that is measured and becomes the basis of the space allocated to a particular tenant and the rent calculation.
- *Space allocated pro rata.* Represents space in each system that is measured, tallied, and allocated pro rata to each tenant, in proportion to its share of space in the building. This share of space, often called the *core,* or *loss factor,* is added to the measured space described above to calculate the total rentable area written into a tenant's lease.
- *Space amortized into the base building cost.* Includes areas that are neither measured nor allocated pro rata in the tenant's lease. Therefore, the costs of such space must be recovered in the base rent charged in relation to measured space in the previous two categories.

This shows a general comparison among the six commercial office space measurement systems.

COMPARISON OF SPACE MEASUREMENT SYSTEMS
Source: BOMI Institute; Facilities Planning and Project Management, 1999; Arnold, Maryland.

REBNY SYSTEM

The REBNY space measurement system is the most landlord-oriented of the six systems described here because it includes the most nonusable space in the rentable area billed to a tenant. From a landlord's viewpoint, this approach has an advantage over the others: the total rentable area of the floor remains constant. In addition, unless space is actually added to or deleted from a tenant's holdings, the tenant's percentage of rentable area of the floor and of the entire building remains constant. This facilitates uniform, consistent allocation of tax increases and operating costs, thereby simplifying administrative procedures.

WDCAR SYSTEM

The WDCAR system was adopted in 1989 by the Washington, DC, Association of Realtors, and supersedes an earlier system used by the Washington, DC, Board of Realtors. It is generally complementary to BOMA's old system, but is more specific. By explicitly excluding more general building support areas, it narrows the range of core factors on unusual floors and simplifies negotiations. Its features closely parallel those of the new BOMA system.

FORMER GSA SYSTEM

GSA is undergoing the most profound change in its relationship with its tenant agencies since its founding in 1949. As a result, the Federal Property Management Regulation (FPMR) 101-17, Temporary Regulation D-76, which included the language of GSA's space measurement system, has expired, leaving no official space measurement system of record.

GSA has also decided to endorse the new BOMA standard as the method referenced in all future leases with private-sector building owners. To embrace this new standard and reconcile it with thousands of existing agency space assignments and leases, GSA has determined that what is called *occupiable space* in its old system equates almost exactly with *floor usable area* in the new BOMA system. The only significant discrepancy concerns HVAC convectors, which are excluded from GSA's *occupiable space* definition but are included in BOMA's *floor usable area*.

IFMA SYSTEM

The IFMA system is the most recently developed. It has been adopted as a standard of the American Society for Testing and Materials (ASTM). It is based on and complements the old BOMA system, but differs in its detail of measurement categories of particular interest to the tenant and to space planners laying out actual furniture and equipment. It is positioned to align with efforts in other countries, particularly through the International Standards Organization (ISO), where the emphasis on space measurement tends to be more tenant-oriented.

Lawrence W. Vanderburgh, RPA, FMA, CFM, RA; BOMI Institute; Arnold, Maryland.

KEY SPACE MEASUREMENT TERMS
Source: BOMI Institute; Facilities Planning and Project Management; 1999, Arnold, Maryland.

COMMERCIAL OFFICE SPACE

The design of commercial office space serves to function appropriately, extend human capability, and enhance productivity. Office space also serves as an aesthetic image of the company's mission.

SPACE SUPPORT FOR WORK PATTERNS

Interaction and autonomy are the two key factors that must be considered together when understanding an organization's work processes. Space plans have a powerful effect on work processes. Performance is enhanced when space layouts support appropriate levels of interaction and autonomy.

ALTERNATIVE OFFICING STRATEGIES

In response to changing business practices and the manner in which different generations work best, a variety of nontraditional strategies have evolved that limit the amount of dedicated office space assigned to each employee. These alternative strategies provide significant benefits to many businesses, including reduced office space rents, higher occupancy ratios, and reduced overhead costs. The term *alternative officing* emerged in the early 1990s to describe the ways businesses are addressing a variety of new work styles and the spaces that support them. *Telecommuting, virtual offices*, and *hoteling* are some of the terms used to describe these alternative officing strategies.

Telecommuting

Telecommuting, which refers to employees who work from home using computers, telephones, and fax machines, has increased in popularity due to reduced overhead costs for employers, increasing demand by employees for flexible schedules, and the expense and inconvenience of commuting. Telecommuting may also be offered as an option for recruiting or retaining employees.

Hoteling

Hoteling is a system of unassigned workspaces that are available to workers by reservation, similar to a hotel. A support person, referred to as a *concierge*, takes reservations and ensures that spaces are equipped when the employee "guest" arrives.

The Chicago office of Ernst & Young is credited with the first application of the term *hoteling*, an alternative officing concept wherein most employees do not have a permanent, assigned desk. Also referred to as *non-territorial space*, hoteling is appropriate for consulting operations where employees spend much of their time on-site at client offices.

Virtual Officing

Virtual officing is an alternative work strategy that describes employees working anywhere at anytime. The use of laptop computers, cell phones, and other portable high-tech tools make the virtual office achievable for the knowledge-based worker.

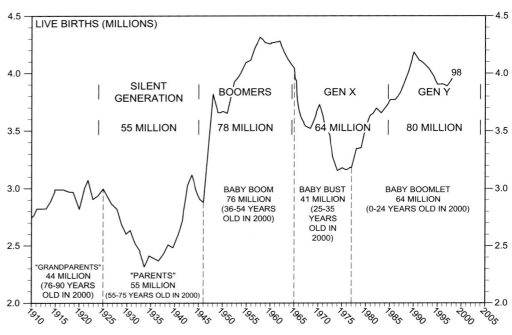

Numbers in parentheses represent the ages of the youngest and the oldest group members in 2000.

U.S. WORKFORCE DEMOGRAPHICS
Source: Steelcase, Inc.; Grand Rapids, Michigan

WORK STYLES OF AMERICANS

	BOOMERS	GEN X	GEN Y
Schooling style/work style	Work alone Structured Unstructured, unsupervised; play with others	Group projects Discussion Team sports for women Mothers worked Computer as a tool	Care-free Need it now Have to be stimulated Can't amuse themselves Multitask
Thought process	Pen and paper	Personal digital assistant (PDA)	Computer
How they get information	Individual research	Internet	Internet; inquiry
What they do with information	"Power is knowledge"; can be knowledge hoarders	Share info across team and individuals	Team comes first; knowledge resides with the team
What they do if they don't like something	Protest, whine	Drop out, withdraw	Circumvent the rules
How they handle interruptions or noise	Close the door	Put on headset	Not bothered by interruptions—"just one more thing"
Expectations for their work environment	Office is a status symbol; need desk credenza, conference table, view	Quick access; not isolated; comfort Community space; like to change environments, people, locations	Do not need to own space; need stimulation
Work hours	8- to 12-hour days	Leave when the job is done	Flexible 24 hours

PATTERN OF WORK: GROUP PROCESS
PROCESS TEAMS TACKLE STRAIGHTFORWARD GROUP WORK THAT REQUIRES A CHANGING BALANCE OF DIFFERENT, INDEPENDENT SKILLS.

TYPE OF SPACE LAYOUT: DEN
OPEN AND SHARED. GROUP SPACES WITH A MEDIUM AMOUNT OF STORAGE. COMPLEX AND CONTINUOUS SPACES INCORPORATE MEETING SPACES AND WORKSPACES.

USE OF IT
PERSONAL COMPUTERS AND SOME SHARED SPECIALIZED GROUP EQUIPMENT.

PATTERN OF WORK: TRANSACTIONAL KNOWLEDGE
HIGH-PERFORMANCE TEAMS MADE UP OF SELF-DIRECTED INDIVIDUALS WORK BOTH COLLABORATIVELY AND INDEPENDENTLY AS WORK PROCESSES ARE CONSTANTLY BEING REDESIGNED.

TYPE OF SPACE LAYOUT: CLUB
OPEN, CLOSED, AND SHARED. DIVERSE, COMPLEX, AND MANIPUTABLE SPACES WITH A RANGE OF SETTINGS THAT SUPPORT A WIDE VARIETY OF TASKS.

USE OF IT
VARIETY OF INDIVIDUAL PERSONAL COMPUTERS ON NETWORKS AND WIDESPREAD USE OF LAPTOPS.

INTERACTION IS THE PERSONAL, FACE-TO-FACE CONTACT THAT IS NECESSARY TO CARRY OUT OFFICE TASKS.

AUTONOMY IS THE DEGREE OF CONTROL, RESPONSIBILITY, AND DISCRETION EACH WORKER HAS OVER THE CONTENT, METHOD, LOCATION, AND TOOLS OF THE WORK PROCESS.

PATTERN OF WORK: INDIVIDUAL PROCESS
DIRECTED CONTRIBUTORS PROCESS WORK THAT HAS BEEN BROKEN DOWN INTO DISCRETE TASKS USING INSTRUCTIONS WITH LITTLE DISCRETION.

TYPE OF SPACE LAYOUT: HIVE
OPEN. CLUSTERED WORK SETTINGS WITH MINIMAL PARTITIONS, MAXIMUM FILING AND IMPOSED SIMPLE SPACE STANDARDS.

USE OF IT
SIMPLE, "DUMB" TERMINALS OR NETWORKED PERSONAL COMPUTERS.

PATTERN OF WORK: CONCENTRATED STUDY
INDEPENDENT AGENTS PERFORM ISOLATED, SELF-DIRECTED WORK.

TYPE OF SPACE LAYOUT: CELL
CLOSED. PRIVATE WORKSPACES, SUCH AS ENCLOSED OFFICES OR INDIVIDUALLY USED, OPEN WORKSTATIONS WITH SCREENS OR PARTITIONS.

USE OF IT
VARIETY OF INDIVIDUAL PERSONAL COMPUTERS ON NETWORKS AND WIDESPREAD USE OF LAPTOPS.

SPACE SUPPORT FOR WORK PATTERNS
Steelcase, Inc.; Grand Rapids, Michigan; and Frank Duffy; DEGW Worldwide; New York, New York

SPACE USAGE IN A HOTELING ENVIRONMENT

Hoteling and other alternative workplace strategies involve the provision of spaces at ratios other than 1:5 for the occupants. This can also be referred to as the *deconstructed workplace,* in which the occupants circulate to a more tailored work environment that is appropriate to the task at hand, instead of providing an exclusive, personal space for each employee. Space is designed to accommodate multiple functions such as meetings, focused work, or equipment-centered tasks. This strategy requires a nonterritorial approach to the

usage of workspaces, and depends on successful sharing of the environment by the occupants, who are not considered permanent residents. By providing tailored work environments and implementing management techniques that support the sharing of such an environment, space efficiencies are realized through maximizing scheduling and usage of each workspace. The occupants go to the space that suits the task at hand, utilizing fewer work settings, hence requiring less leased area.

When studying potential hoteling candidates, the workforce is broken down into general job/type cate-

gories based on the tasks performed by the occupants. The population is divided into three groups: *permanent residents, semipermanent residents,* and *periodic residents.* For the semipermanent and periodic categories, the related work patterns and time spent in the office are surveyed and analyzed to develop the profile of space usage. Based on that information, ratios of the space types for each job type are developed. Usage times are averaged to provide the guidelines for reduced space quantities. Additional workspace can be provided by considering the areas traditionally considered support space, such as break rooms, conference rooms, or other workrooms.

ALTERNATIVE OFFICING STRATEGY

HOTELING

LEGEND

SOLO

COLLABORATIVE

DROP-IN

TEAM LEADERS

Hoteling applications provide one space for more than one employee. Space types are designed to support types of activities, such as solo and collaborative efforts. Spaces are not designed for individual employees; instead, lockers are provided to store employees' materials. The *marketplace exchange* is a communal casual meeting and brainstorming area.

HOTELING STRATEGY

WORKSTATIONS

Office planning frequently uses freestanding, less than full-height, movable system furniture panels. Both traditional and alternative officing strategies can be accommodated by systems furniture workstations. Workstations save space, provide flexibility, and generate less dust and debris than constructed walls when relocated. Although workstation panels often function as walls for visual, acoustic, and wiring purposes, they are considered furniture—not construction—and as such can be depreciated.

CONSIDERATIONS FOR DEVELOPMENT OF WORKSTATION STANDARDS

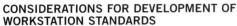

CONSIDERATION	STANDARD
Job Classification or Function	Workstation user and job function: executive, manager, supervisor, professional or technical, clerical
Work Surface Area	Number and size of work surfaces: primary, secondary, tertiary
Machine Use	Amount, types, and sizes of electronic equipment: VDT, PC, printer
Workstation Area	Amount of space to be allocated for the individual task
Conference Requirements	Number of guest chairs required
Storage Requirements	Amount and type or unit size of the material to be stored, and storage locations (under counter or overhead): letter or legal files, computer printouts, binders, bulk
Configuration	Configuration of work surfaces, primary orientation, and opening for the workstation
Wire Management	Type and location of wire management components: baseline wireway, beltline wireway, grommet locations, clips or trays
Accessories	Type and number of accessories: tack surfaces, pencil drawers

OFFICE: 48 SQ FT (4 SQ M)

OFFICE: 64 SQ FT (6 SQ M)

OFFICE: 36 SQ FT (3 SQ M)

OFFICE: 80 SQ FT (7 SQ M)

OFFICE: 120 SQ FT (11 SQ M)

WORKSTATIONS

OFFICE: 65 SQ FT (6 SQ M)

OFFICE: 96 SQ FT (9 SQ M)

OFFICE: 108 SQ FT (10 SQ M)

OFFICE: APPROXIMATELY 45 SQ FT (4 SQ M)

PRIVATE OFFICES

Private, dedicated offices have in the past been strong status symbols to reinforce a business culture's hierarchy or "class differentiation." For knowledge-based workers with high autonomy and limited interaction with coworkers, the dedicated office continues to the most efficient space design to support their efforts. Private offices are especially appropriate for employees involved in concentrated study.

GUEST SEATING

SLIDING DOOR

COAT AND STORAGE TOWER

MOBILE PEDESTAL

MOBILE DESK

LATERAL FILE

OFFICE: 96 SQ FT (9 SQ M)

LATERAL FILE

MOBILE PEDESTAL

MOBILE DESK

SLIDING DOOR

OFFICE: 64 SQ FT (6 SQ M)

GUEST SEATING

SLIDING DOOR

COAT AND STORAGE TOWER

MOBILE PEDESTAL

MOBILE DESK

LATERAL FILE

OFFICE: 100 SQ FT (9 SQ M)

LATERAL FILE

MOBILE PEDESTAL

MOBILE DESK

GUEST SEATING

SLIDING DOOR

OFFICE: 80 SQ FT (7 SQ M)

GUEST SEATING

LATERAL FILE

MOBILE PEDESTAL

MOBILE DESK

COAT AND STORAGE TOWER

OVERHEAD STORAGE

ADJUSTABLE HEIGHT WORK SURFACE

OFFICE: 120 SQ FT (11 SQ M)

PRIVATE OFFICES

LATERAL FILE

MOBILE PEDESTAL

ARTICULATING KEYBOARD TRAY

WORK SURFACE

MOBILE DESK

GUEST SEATING

COAT AND STORAGE TOWER

OFFICE: 150 SQ FT (14 SQ M)

LOUNGE SEATING

GUEST SEATING

LATERAL FILE

MOBILE PEDESTAL

SWIVEL DESKTOP

WORK SURFACE

OFFICE: 225 SQ FT (21 SQ M)

COAT AND STORAGE TOWER

LATERAL FILE

MOBILE PEDESTAL

SLIDING DOOR

GUEST SEATING

MOBILE DESK

OFFICE: 150 SQ FT (14 SQ M)

LOUNGE SEATING

GUEST SEATING

LATERAL FILE

SWIVEL DESKTOP

WORK SURFACE

MOBILE PEDESTAL

OFFICE: 300 SQ FT (28 SQ M)

OFFICE SUPPORT SPACES

Coffee Bars

Accommodations for food and hot beverage service are typically made for general employee use. Conference and training facilities may also require dedicated coffee bars or small kitchenettes.

Copy Rooms

Copy rooms are routinely located throughout large business facilities. Space must be provided for the machine and for storage of supplies. The size of the copier must be determined so that adequate electrical supply can be provided. Large collating copy machines can require 220-volt supply.

PLAN
ELEVATION

- CUP DISPENSERS
- COFFEE
- TRASH CHUTE
- REFRIGERATOR
- CONDIMENT BINS

SMALL COFFEE BAR: 80 SQ FT (7 SQ M)

PLAN
ELEVATION
ELEVATION

- HOT WATER HEATER
- 3'-0" (914) MIN.
- 2'-10" (863)
- ADA-COMPLIANT DISHWASHER
- ADA-COMPLIANT SINK
- REFRIGERATOR
- COFFEE
- ICE MACHINE
- SODA MACHINE
- CUP DISPENSERS
- TRASH
- SODA AND ICE COMPRESSION LOCATION
- CONDIMENT BINS
- SODA BOX STORAGE

LARGE COFFEE BAR: 175 SQ FT (16 SQ M)

- COPIER
- PRINTER
- FAX
- BASE CABINET WITH OVERHEAD STORAGE
- RECYCLE AND TRASH RECEPTACLES

SMALL COPY ROOM: 80 SQ FT (7 SQ M)

- PRINTER
- FAX
- BASE CABINET WITH OVERHEAD STORAGE
- RECYCLE AND TRASH RECEPTACLES
- COPIER

LARGE COPY ROOM: 175 SQ FT (16 SQ M)

CIRCULATION AND LAYOUT GUIDELINES

LIGHTING FOR OFFICE SPACES

Lighting Levels within Workstations

The illumination that reaches a desktop in a direct lighting system is a combination of light arriving directly from the lighting fixture and indirectly via reflectance from various room surfaces. A partition not only interferes with this indirect component of light but can drastically reduce the potential direct component.

A rough approximation of the magnitude of the effect of partition height on lighting levels can be calculated using the following technique. (Note: Do not use this technique for total direct lighting systems unless several luminaires directly contribute light to the cubicle.)

1. Use the coefficient of utilization (CU) table for the fixture to calculate the average illuminance at the top of the partitions. Use the distance from the luminaires to the top of the partitions as the cavity height, and use actual reflectance values, except for the floor; use 0 for the floor cavity reflectance.
2. Determine the transfer coefficient of a virtual ceiling luminaire ("Transfer Coefficients" table). Use the distance from the top of the partition to the desktop as the cavity height. Use the cubicle's partition reflectance as the wall reflectance, and use the effective ceiling cavity reflectance of the actual ceiling cavity above the top of the partitions.
3. Multiply the illuminance from the first step (at the top of the partitions) by the transfer coefficient to find the approximate average illuminance at the desktop.

Illumination Criteria

The lighting levels given are average figures, and assume an empty room.

- *Offices (low to moderate computer use):* 40 to 60 fc (400 to 600 lux), with task lighting as required.
- *Offices (moderate to high computer use):* 20 to 40 fc (200 to 400 lux), with task lighting as required.

42-IN.- (1,066-MM-) HIGH PANELS

60-IN.- (1,524-MM-) HIGH PANELS

PANEL HEIGHT COMPARISON

- *Offices (paper-based tasks only):* 50 to 75 fc (500 to 750 lux), with task lighting at work locations to provide higher lighting levels as required for specific tasks of high difficulty.
- *Conference and meeting rooms:* 30 to 50 fc (300 to 500 lux), with dimming control capabilities when appropriate.
- *Lobbies and hallways:* 10 to 20 fc (100 to 200 lux). Visual Comfort Probability (VCP) is only useful for comparing direct (lensed troffer) lighting systems. A minimum of 70 fc (700 lux) is recommended. (Note that high VCP does not guarantee visual comfort.)

LIGHTING SYSTEM ALTERNATIVES

The following lighting systems, which are appropriate for use in office spaces, use fluorescent sources:

- *Lensed systems* provide adequate basic lighting at the lowest cost, are the easiest to install, and tend to be the most efficient. Many lensed systems exhibit higher-angle (greater than 55°) glare and prove problematic for computer-based offices.
- *Parabolic louvered systems* are low brightness and better for larger rooms where computer work is undertaken. Supplemental lighting for walls is important when using parabolic systems to avoid an overly dim perimeter appearance.
- *Indirect lighting systems,* which provide a comfortable light, must be appropriately spaced to avoid excessively nonuniform brightness on the ceiling. They generally require ceilings of at least 8 ft (2,440 mm) to be feasible, and the use of supplemental task and/or accent lighting. *Direct/indirect lighting systems* must be appropriately spaced and offer a good balance between comfort and efficiency. They require ceilings of at least 8 ft (2,440 mm) to be feasible, and can be more costly than other lighting systems.

CORRIDOR LIGHTING

In office buildings, corridors require reasonably uniform illumination with minimum glare. Since lower lighting levels are recommended in these areas, standard office troffers are not the best or most efficient choices.

Downlighting is the most straightforward solution but tends to create deep shadows and cavelike spaces. Mixing downlights and other lighting fixtures, such as sconces, accent lights, or wallwashers, creates a more visually appealing design with a better balance of brightness among walls, ceiling, and floor.

Wall lighting is an alternative to downlighting and sconces for use in corridors. It can enhance art and graphics, and can reveal wall textures such as those of stone and brick. Grazing lights can highlight polished or specular surfaces such as granite or wood.

SPECIAL LIGHTING ISSUES FOR OFFICES

Lighting for computer use, task lighting, and wall lighting are among the specialized lighting issues in office design.

Computer Lighting

Lighting for computer workspaces is becoming increasingly specialized. There are four distinct approaches to this sort of design:

- *Parabolic troffers optimized for computer spaces:* By meeting specific cutoff and distribution specifications, some parabolic and small-cell-louvered direct lighting fixtures provide lighting acceptable for concentrated computer workspace applications. These lighting systems are generally efficient but tend to create spaces with dark upper walls and ceilings. Supplemental wallwashing, accent lighting, or decorative wall-mounted lighting is needed to offset this shortcoming.
- *Indirect suspended lighting:* Indirect lighting systems that illuminate ceilings in a relatively uniform fashion are also considered good for computer workspaces. General indirect lighting tends to be comfortable but can be flat and uninteresting. Supplemental task lighting, as well as wallwashing and accent lighting, is usually necessary.
- *Direct/indirect lighting:* Some direct/indirect lighting systems have been optimized for illuminating computer workspaces, providing the advantages of the two lighting systems described above. The greatest disadvantage of these direct/indirect systems can be total system cost.
- *Intensive computer-aided design and drawing (CADD) workspaces:* CADD workspaces are the most demanding of all computer workspaces. Neither parabolic nor indirect lighting, even if optimized for computer workspaces, is acceptable unless a dimmable lighting control is used. Task-only lighting systems with very low levels of general light are needed. The unusual requirements of these environments are often best resolved by creating a space where employees can manipulate lighting level intensities with in-line dimmers.

Task Lighting

For use under cabinets or shelves, continuous fluorescent task lights are generally the best choice. Good-quality task lights offer the capability to dim or alter the distribution of light to minimize veiling reflections.

CENTERED DOWNLIGHTS
Each round downlight uses 26 watts of compact fluorescent light (either two 13-watt lamps or one 26-watt lamp). Square downlights use two 16- to 18-watt lamps. Designs produce 10 to 20 fc (100 to 200 lux) at 0.6–0.7 watts/sq ft (6.4–7.5 watts/sq m).

DOWNLIGHTS AND SCONCES
Sconce quantity can be minimized by maintaining a nominal 8 ft (2,440 mm) "either-or" spacing. Sconces and downlights each have two 13-watt lamps or one 26-watt lamp. Designs produce 10 to 15 fc (100 to 150 lux) at 0.6–0.7 watts/sq ft (6.4–7.5 watts/sq m).

WALLWASHERS
Lighting one wall of a corridor can provide effective light and be an attractive design element, highlighting art or graphics. A wall slot is best for textured or polished surfaces and creates a floating ceiling; wallwashers are better for art or graphics. While footcandles (lux) for the wall slots or wallwashers shown are about the same, power use increases to 1.2–1.5 watts/sq ft (13–16 watts/sq m) to illuminate vertical surfaces.

REFLECTED CEILING PLANS CORRIDOR LIGHTING

Table lamps and task lights produce localized task illumination using a portable luminaire. The area of influence is small, but proper location can achieve a successful result, especially if the user can change the lamp's location to suit the task. Use compact fluorescent lamps whenever possible.

Wall Lighting

Office spaces generally require supplemental wall lighting to compensate for the lack of wall lighting provided by most general lighting systems. Wall grazing and wallwashing are two methods used to accomplish this lighting task.

TRANSFER COEFFICIENTS

CEILING	80			50		
WALLS RCR*	**50**	**30**	**10**	**50**	**30**	**10**
0	1.19	1.19	1.19	1.11	1.11	1.11
1	1.03	0.98	0.94	0.96	0.93	0.89
2	0.89	0.81	0.75	0.83	0.78	0.73
3	0.77	0.69	0.62	0.73	0.66	0.60
4	0.68	0.59	0.52	0.64	0.57	0.51
5	0.61	0.51	0.45	0.58	0.50	0.44
6	0.55	0.45	0.39	0.52	0.44	0.38
7	0.49	0.40	0.34	0.47	0.39	0.34
8	0.45	0.36	0.30	0.43	0.35	0.30
9	0.41	0.33	0.27	0.39	0.32	0.27
10	0.38	0.30	0.25	0.36	0.29	0.24

*RCR = room cavity ratio

LIGHTING CRITERIA FOR OFFICES

OFFICE TYPE	CCT[1]	CRI[2]
Most office space	3,500 or 4,100K	>70 CRI
Executive office	3,000 or 3,500K	>70 CRI
Medical office	3,500 or 4,100K	>80 CRI
Art/graphics, dental operatory	5000K	>90 CRI

LIGHTING POWER DENSITY[3]

General office space	0.8 –1.1 watts/sq ft (8.6–11.8 watts/sq m)
Executive office	1.1–1.4 watts/sq ft (11.8–15.0 watts/sq m)
Medical office	1.0–1.8 watts/sq ft (10.7–19.3 watts/sq m)
Drafting/accounting space	1.4–2.0 watts/sq ft (15.0–21.5 watts/sq m)
Meeting rooms	1.0–1.4 watts/sq ft (10.7–15 watts/sq m)
Lobbies and hallways	0.4–0.8 watts/sq ft (4.3–8.6 watts/sq m)

[1]*CCT = correlated color temperature*
[2]*CRI =Color Rendering Index*
[3]*Lighting power density: Approximate design target using fluorescent T8 lamps and electronic high-frequency ballasts (not including task lights) are shown.*

LOBBY LIGHTING

Lobbies offer a primary opportunity for use of dramatic or decorative lighting. Pendants, ceiling fixtures, sconces, and architectural coves are the primary lighting systems, supplemented by downlights, wallwashers, and other architectural light sources. To most easily meet energy code requirements, use fluorescent, compact fluorescent, and/or low-wattage high-intensity discharge (HID) lamps instead of incandescent, whenever possible.

Main lobbies are an important venue for ornamental and decorative lighting design. Wall lighting is especially useful for providing a sense of spaciousness and cheerfulness. Art objects such as paintings or sculpture can benefit from accent lighting.

Architectural and decorative lighting sources are often used in combination in lobbies. Incandescent and halogen lamps may be preferred for specific luminaire types, such as art display lights. When these incandescent sources are used, incorporating a dimming system will help lower energy consumption and extend lamp life. However, whenever possible, use of more efficacious lighting sources such as fluorescent or HID fixtures is recommended.

WALL SLOT LIGHTING **WALLWASHER LIGHTING**

A grazing light such as a wall slot is appropriate for illuminating interior core walls in open spaces, but wallwashers and sconces can be used as well. Wall slot lighting accentuates the wall texture and enhances polished surfaces. Wallwashers accentuate wall pigment and work best for ordinary wall finishes with artwork hanging on them.

WALL LIGHTING

OPEN OFFICE ACOUSTICS

Open offices can provide great flexibility in office arrangements and workflow. However, because workstations or cubicles do not have full-height partitions, noise can be a major problem in such offices. The extent to which speech is distracting depends on the degree to which it is intelligible. An overheard conversation may be annoying or distracting, while an inaudible murmur may not. When designing open offices, the need for communication between workstations should be evaluated in light of work functions and practical separation.

Speech intelligibility and acoustics in an open-plan office can be rated in terms of an articulation index (AI), which is a measure of the ratio between a signal (a neighbor's voice or intrusive noise) and steady background noise (ambient noise from mechanical equipment, traffic, or electronic sound masking). AI values range from near 0 (very low signal and relatively high noise; no intelligibility or good speech privacy) to

ARCHITECTURAL PENDANT

RECESSED ADJUSTABLE ACCENT DOWNLIGHT

RECESSED DOWNLIGHTS OVER SEATING GROUP

Fluorescent pendants and sconces produce general light. Compact fluorescent downlights, wallwashers, and halogen art-accent fixtures provide more specialized lighting that showcases the architecture and artwork and creates an atmosphere.

TYPICAL LOBBY LIGHTING

1.0 (very high signal and low noise; excellent communication or no speech privacy). When communication is desired (for example, in classrooms or teleconference rooms), it is preferable to have a high AI so people can hear well. In an office environment, however, it is preferable to have a low AI, which is more conducive to concentration.

Design Considerations

Low AI ratings for open-plan office spaces can be achieved in three primary ways: by *blocking sound,* by *covering (masking) sound,* and by *absorbing sound.*

Blocking Sound

Partial-height barriers or partitions are necessary to block direct sound transmission between workstations. The barriers must be high enough and wide enough to interrupt the line of sight between a source and a receiver; hence, the first 4 ft (1,220 mm) or so of barrier height do not help speech privacy at all. Barrier heights of 5 ft (1,525 mm) are a minimum requirement for acoustical separation, and heights of 6 ft (1,830 mm) are typical for normal privacy. The barrier should be able to block sound at least as well as the path for sound traveling over the barrier, which means a minimum laboratory sound transmission class value of 24. Barriers or screens should extend to the floor or leave only an inch or so open at the bottom. There should be no open gaps between adjacent panels. Barriers may need to have sound-absorbing facings to reduce reflections to the next workstation.

PLAN

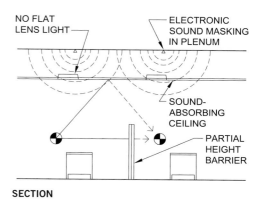

SECTION

ARCHITECTURAL SOLUTIONS FOR SOUND CONTROL IN OPEN OFFICES

Covering Sound

The character and level of background sound is perhaps the most important acoustical design consideration for an open-plan office. A modest level of background or ambient sound will cover, or mask, annoying, intrusive sounds. Masking sound should be neither too loud nor too quiet, between 45 and 50 dBA. Conference rooms and private offices, which require lower levels of background noise, should have plenum treatments so they are shielded from direct exposure to the masking sound.

Sound-masking systems comprise a noise generator, an equalizer to shape the sound spectrum properly, amplifiers, and loudspeakers hidden above an accessible acoustical tile ceiling. Such systems generate a broadband, pleasant-sounding, evenly distributed masking noise. The sound in the plenum filters down through the ceiling and provides an even blanket of sound that will mask the intrusive sound from a neighbor. Avoid untreated sound leaks in the ceiling, such as openings for return air; these become noticeable "hotspots" and draw unwanted attention to the sound from the ceiling. Masking sound from two channels can improve spatial uniformity. Ceiling height and plenum conditions (fireproofing, beams, ducts, etc.) will determine loudspeaker spacing and location. Electronic sound masking should be professionally designed and installed.

POOR LAYOUT

FAIR LAYOUT

PREFERRED LAYOUT

OPEN OFFICE CONFIGURATIONS FOR ACOUSTIC PRIVACY

Absorbing Sound

The ceiling in an open-plan office is the most important surface to treat with highly efficient sound-absorbing material. Glass-fiber ceiling panels often have NRC values of .85 or higher and are the preferred material for open-plan spaces. Regular mineral-fiber acoustical panels have typical NRC values of about .55 to .65. Hard sound-reflective materials such as exposed structure or gypsum board will dramatically reduce privacy and raise annoying sound levels in an office. Most ceiling tile manufacturers provide extensive NRC data for their products and have special products with high absorptive performance for use in open-plan spaces. Materials must also be selected for their capability to reflect light.

Most sound-absorbing materials are measured in a reverberation chamber in accordance with ASTM C423, *Standard Test Method for Sound Absorption and Sound Absorption Coefficients by the Reverberation Room Method,* to determine their random incidence sound-absorption coefficients; and from these data, manufacturers typically report the noise reduction coefficient (NRC). The NRC value is a good first approximation of the capability of a material to absorb sound from the human speech range. For office acoustics, however, a more useful value is the capability of a material to absorb sound at an incident angle of 40° to 60° from a flat ceiling and at frequencies weighted to reflect the relative contribution to speech

Average noise requirements for various office functions are shown.

BACKGROUND SOUND LEVEL FOR OPEN-PLAN OFFICES

intelligibility. Therefore, a more effective tool for evaluating the effectiveness of ceiling materials for sound absorption is the speech absorption coefficient (SAC).

Other Factors

Arrange offices so that entrances are offset, and eliminate direct line of sight or an open view through doorways from one workstation to another. Workstations should be 8 to 10 ft (2,440 to 3,050 mm) apart so voice levels are adequately reduced over distance. Higher ceilings can help reduce noise transfer. Light fixtures in the ceiling plane should not have hard lenses or be placed directly above a partition because the fixture can then act as a mirror for sound across the barrier. Absorptive material may be necessary on some barriers or reflecting surfaces (for example, walls, file cabinets).

Carpet helps reduce footfall and impact noise and is a great benefit in open offices. Finally, voice levels should be kept to a minimum; even the best acoustical treatments cannot prevent disturbances caused by loud voices and hands-off amplified telephone use.

All the factors outlined above are interrelated. For example, doubling the distance between adjacent workstations will reduce a nearby conversation by 5 dBA, while raising the height of a 5 ft (1,525 mm) barrier to 6 ft (1,830 mm) may reduce the sound path over the top by 3 dBA. Changing from a mineral-fiber acoustical ceiling tile to a glass-fiber ceiling tile may reduce reflected noise by 5 dBA. Adding sound masking may change the ambient level by 10 to 20 dBA.

An acoustics consultant can evaluate proposed layouts and materials as part of the design process. The acoustical outcome of a design should be analyzed before construction. As a rough initial guideline, offices in which freedom from distraction is the only criterion will require highly efficient sound-absorbing ceilings and an electronic background masking sound at levels between 45 and 50 dBA. For normal speech privacy,

these conditions should be augmented by keeping workstations 8 to 10 ft (2,440 to 3,050 mm) apart and adding partial-height barriers at least 5 ft (1,525 mm) high, with increased attention to office layout and reflecting sound paths. Confidential privacy requires higher partitions and greater attention to related details; it is extremely difficult to achieve in an open plan.

PRIVACY

Privacy needs vary with the type of work anticipated and, to a lesser extent, with status. Workers with high confidentiality requirements (for example, attorneys, human resources counselors, managers) have high speech privacy requirements (STC 60+). Work groups requiring communication with one another require almost no privacy. Hoteling should offer various levels of privacy consistent with workers' functional requirements.

Privacy not only means not being overheard, but also not being intruded upon so that one's train of thought is interrupted. Workers with tasks requiring concentration (for example, computer programming) need more isolation than people who work in teams. Partitions with STC less than 40 will allow intelligible speech transmission. Partition gaps at window mullions no more than the width of a sheet of paper will transmit intelligible speech no matter how good the partition.

HVAC NC/RC RANGE

NC/RC ranges between 35 and 40 are effective in open office plans, with the higher end useful in larger, more open spaces. Consider an electronic speech-masking (or "white noise") system to augment privacy in open-plan spaces, call centers, and hoteling office areas.

Ted Kollaja, AIA; lauckgroup; Dallas, Texas
Shawn Parks; Rhode Island School of Design; Providence, Rhode Island
Randy J. Burkett, FIALD, IES, LC; Burkett Lighting Design, Inc.; St. Louis, Missouri
Jim Johnson; Wrightson, Johnson, Haddon & Williams, Inc.; Dallas, Texas

ARTICULATION INDEX (AI) FOR OPEN OFFICES

AI VALUE	NOISE REQUIREMENTS	
>.65	Good communication	Necessary when communication is desirable (conference rooms, classrooms, auditoriums, etc.)
.35	Freedom from distraction	Reasonable work conditions not requiring heavy concentration or speech privacy; can hear and understand neighboring conversations
.20	Normal speech privacy	Occasional intelligibility of a neighbor's conversation; work patterns not interrupted
<.05	Confidential speech privacy	Aware of neighbor's conversation but it is not intelligible

RETAIL

DESIGN CRITERIA

Retail design distinguishes itself from other types of interiors because design decisions are made primarily on the basis of generating sales. Successful merchandising creates a cohesive design statement that complements the merchandise and the brand image of the retailer. Presenting merchandise in an appealing manner is imperative.

Understanding the buying behavior and demographics of the targeted shopper, the merchandise category (for example, fashion as opposed to commodity items), and the requirements of the different types of retail space and retail lighting—both general space lighting and display lighting—are key components in successful retail design.

BUYING BEHAVIORS

Buying behaviors are essentially planned or impulse:

- Most impulse purchases can be categorized as emotion-based or a form of entertainment. Impulse buyers enjoy the experience of shopping perhaps as much as they do the goods they purchase. Goods appropriate for impulse buying must be exposed to potential customers and be within easy reach for examination and selection.
- Shoppers who plan purchases may not even enjoy shopping. Because planned-purchase shoppers are often in a hurry, goods appropriate for planned purchases must be easy to find. Efficient circulation, signage, and adequate lighting are important for the shoppers who plan their purchases.

TYPES OF RETAIL SPACES

The three dominant types of retail spaces in the United States are *shopping malls* or *centers, department stores,* and *boutique* and *specialty retail stores.*

Shopping Malls or Centers

Visiting shopping malls has become an American pastime. They are centers of relaxation and entertainment, as well as the most successful sites of sales in the country. Shopping centers rely on excitement, often theatrics, to attract regular and seasonal consumers. Malls often incorporate services and entertainment venues to encourage a more leisurely—and prolonged—stay.

Department Stores

Department stores rely on circulation patterns and signage to draw customers through their store. Hard-flooring aisles, referred to as "hard aisles," provide a primary circulation path. Displays are typically located on carpeted areas to invite the customer to linger and browse, while enjoying the comfort underfoot. Continuity is required throughout the department store, even though each department may be designed separately to give the appearance of a series of boutiques.

The entry floor in department stores is often leased to vendors with high-markup products, such as cosmetics and jewelry. These salespeople receive a commission on each sale made.

Boutiques and Specialty Retail Stores

Specialty stores require an up-to-date design image to attract consumers. Their renovation cycles and budgets are commonly far greater than those of shopping malls or department stores. These spaces rely heavily on window displays, interior finishes, lighting, and acoustics (typically, background music) to entice customers to enter the space. Salespeople are often on commission in boutiques and specialty retail stores.

FIXTURE PLACEMENT

In order to effectively design a merchandising fixture layout, the designer must understand the retailer's merchandise capacity and volume requirements. Fixtures that are placed too close together can make it difficult to for the shopper to review the merchandise and may not comply with ADA requirements. Aisles between or around fixtures should be not less than 36 in. (1,100 mm), including hanger width.

GENERAL SPACE LIGHTING

The lighting levels given here are average figures, and assume an empty room:

- *Grocery store, general light:* 70 to 90 fc (700 to 900 lux), which will result in average center-of-aisle illumination of 50 fc (500 lux), assuming 72 in. (1,830 mm) shelf heights.
- *Wholesale merchandise:* 30 to 50 fc (300 to 500 lux), with display lighting added as needed. For spaces with warehouse-style shelving, empty-room assumptions are not valid; and the 30 to 50 fc (300 to 500 lux) in aisles must account for shadows created by high shelving.
- *General merchandise:* 40 to 60 fc (400 to 600 lux), with display lighting added at key locations to provide 80 to 120 fc (800 to 1,200 lux) for secondary merchandise displays and 200 to 300 fc (2,000 to 3,000 lux) for primary displays.
- *Boutique and specialty retail stores:* 20 to 30 fc (200 to 300 lux) for general lighting. Display lighting is added throughout to provide 60 to 90 fc (600 to 900 lux) for most merchandise and 150 to 300 fc (1,500 to 3,000 lux) for primary displays.
- *Back-of-house storage and stock areas:* 10 to 20 fc (100 to 200 lux), with shadowing impact of high shelving taken into account.

COLOR RENDERING INDEX (CRI) FOR DISPLAY LIGHTING

Wholesale and grocery	3,500 or 4,100K > 70 CRI
Boutique/specialty	3,000 or 3,500K > 80 CRI
General merchandise	3,500 or 4,100K > 70 CRI
Jewelry, art	3,000 or 5,000K > 90 CRI

CRI characteristics are used in the selection of retail light fixtures. See Color Plate C-11 for CRI characteristics for light, to use in the selection of light fixtures.

LIGHTING POWER DENSITY

Grocery	1.4–2.0 watts/sq ft (15–21.5 watts/sq m)
Wholesale	1.0–1.4 watts/sq ft (10.7–15 watts/sq m)
General merchandise	1.2–1.7 watts/sq ft (12.9–18.2 watts/sq m)
Department store	2.0–2.8 watts/sq ft (21.5–30 watts/sq m)
Specialty retail	1.8–3.5 watts/sq ft (19.3–37.6 watts/sq m)
Jewelry, china	2.0–4.5 watts/sq ft (21.5–48.4 watts/sq m)

Listed are approximate design targets for whole stores, including back-of-house. These targets are based on HID (high-intensity discharge) systems and/or T-8/compact fluorescent lamps with electronic high-frequency ballasts, including display lights.

DISPLAY LIGHTING

Track lighting is popular because of its adjustablility and commonly used display lighting system. Use halogen, compact fluorescent, or low-wattage high-intensity discharge (HID) display luminaires.

Recessed display lights are not as flexible as track lights but are concealed from view and generally possess better glare control. This category includes adjustable accent lights and wallwashers. Sources include halogen, low-wattage high-intensity discharge (HID), and compact fluorescent.

CEILING LIGHT FIXTURES
The maximum angle of elevation for lighting is 45°, except when walls are being lighted.

CEILING AND DISPLAY CASE LIGHT FIXTURES
Use wallwashers or accent lighting for walls and shelves; track lights or monopoints for floor displays; and valances in wall niches. Display case lighting is suitable for many applications, from jewelry cases to meat and produce counters.

TYPICAL DISPLAY LIGHTING

SHELVING

STRIP LIGHTING

12'-0" (3657)

GENERAL SALES AREA: 2'-0" X 4'-0" (200 X 400) GRID CEILING, 12'-0" (3657) OR MORE HIGH

12'-0" (3657)

8'-0" (2438)

TROFFER LIGHTING

GENERAL SALES AREA: 2'-0" X 4'-0" (200 X 400) GRID CEILING, 12'-0" (3657) OR MORE HIGH

INDUSTRIAL-STYLE LIGHTING

12'-0" (3657)

12'-0" (3657)

GENERAL SALES AREA: 2'-0" X 4'-0" (200 X 400) GRID CEILING, 14'-0" (4267) OR MORE HIGH

STRIP LIGHTS/STRIP TROUGH LIGHTS

Strip lights and strip trough lights are common in large retail grocery stores and many mass merchandise stores. This layout produces 60 to 80 fc (600 to 800 lux) in an empty room using F96T8 lamps in a strip light or open trough in continuous rows at 1.15 watts/sq ft (12.3 watts/sq m). Lights usually run perpendicular to shelving to allow rearrangement, but parallel lighting is preferable when shelves are fixed.

TROFFER LIGHTING

Troffers in lay-in ceilings are common in the discount retail industry and serve as general-purpose lighting for hardware and general merchandise. The layout above produces 60 to 70 fc (600 to 700 lux) in an empty room using four F32T8 lamps in a lensed or parabolic luminaire at 1.15 watts/sq ft. With high-light-level ballasts, this arrangement produces 80 to 100 fc (800 to 1,000 lux) at 1.58 watts/sq ft.

INDUSTRIAL-STYLE LIGHTING

Industrial-style lights are commonly used for lighting warehouse-style discount stores. The layout shown at left produces 30 to 40 fc (300 to 400 lux) in an empty room using one 100-watt metal halide lamp in an industrial-style luminaire at 0.85 watts/sq ft. Using a 150-watt metal halide lamp, the lighting level is about 40 to 60 fc (400 to 600 lux) at 1.27 watts/sq ft (13.6 watts/sq m).

REFLECTED CEILING PLANS FOR WHOLESALE, GROCERY, AND MERCHANDISE STORES

OTHER DISPLAY LIGHTING TYPES

Monopoint or canopy-mounted accent lights are adjustable lights installed at fixed locations.

Valance lighting is used for merchandise displays along a store's perimeter or confined niche. Linear T-8 and T-5 fluorescent lamps work best for the application from both a color and efficiency standpoint.

Display case lighting is similar to valance lighting except the light is built into the display cases to illuminate the task. Linear fluorescent, compact fluorescent, or low-voltage incandescent or tungsten halogen lamps are used. Fiber-optic end-lighting systems may be useful in certain situations, especially where heat and space are primary considerations. Display case lighting is suitable for many applications, from jewelry cases to meat and produce counters.

Dressing Rooms

Good lighting helps sell clothing. For higher-quality stores, provide attractive light with diffuse illumination of the customer; avoid downlights and track lighting without supplemental wallwashing. In lower-cost and trendy stores, place the emphasis on fixture style and durability.

Store Windows

Use high-wattage track lighting and/or low-voltage accent lighting. Run track vertically along the window sides, across the top of the window, and possibly along the bottom of the window as well. Halogen, compact fluorescent, and HID are all acceptable source types for window display.

Other Specific Applications

Use high-color-rendering or special-purpose fluorescent lamps for meat cases, fabrics, and similar merchandise with special color or visual discrimination needs. For fine jewelry, consider a high CRI, high-color-temperature compact fluorescent lamps, high-color-rendering metal halide lamps, and/or blue-filtered halogen lamps to achieve a flattering 4,100 to 5,000K.

GENERAL LIGHTING FROM 2' X 2' FLUORESCENT

DISPLAY CASES BELOW

PRODUCT HIGHLIGHTING FROM RECESSED ADJUSTABLE ACCENT

BULKHEADS TO FORM "SOFT AISLE"

DOWNLIGHTS IN "SOFT AISLE"

WALLWASHER FROM COMPACT FLUORESCENT

TYPICAL DEPARTMENT STORE LIGHTING—REFLECTED CEILING PLAN

Janis Berglas; White Plains, New York
Randy J. Burkett, FIALD, IES, LC; Burkett Lighting Design, Inc.; St. Louis, Missouri

TRADING ROOMS

ORIGINS

Spaces designed specifically for financial and commodity trading have their origin in postwar America. After World War II, the booming American economy supported the activities of trading floors in private financials institutions and in stock markets.

There are two basic types of trading within financial institutions: *commodity trading* and *financial trading*.

Commodity Trading

Commodity traders are individuals who are not bound to the same financial institution. The commodity trading floor, or *exchange* as it is often called, often features a "pit," with booths located at the periphery of the trading floor. The New York Stock Exchange (NYSE), the New York Board of Trade (NYBOT), Chicago Board of Trade (CBOT), and the New York Mercantile Exchange (NYMEX) are examples of commodity trading institutions. Commodity trading is often done as "open outcry" from a podium, although this is rapidly changing as communications systems continue to advance.

Financial Trading

Financial traders typically represent the same financial institution. Identical trading desks are lined up in rows with clear sight lines to up-to-the-minute financial information. Financial trading is typically done electronically. Market evaluations, and research form the basis of the financial traders decisions.

DESIGN CHARACTERISTICS

Ideally, financial and commodity trading floors are open-plan, column-free spaces with high ceilings (a minimum of 9 ft 6 in. (2,895 mm) is recommended), enabling unrestricted sight lines. Clear lines of sight among traders and electronic displays is critical in both commodity and financial trading.

Raised access flooring is commonly used to accommodate communications cabling and electrical wiring. Power, voice, and data needs are critical in trading rooms. The heat generated by the large amounts of computer equipment must be compensated in the cooling loads for the space. Wire, cable, and cooling are typically accommodated by raised access floors in the trading room.

It is important to minimize travel distances for the traders to minimize the time they spend away from the trading desk. Food service carts are circulated by many financial institutions so that traders need not leave their desks during the day.

Support functions are located at the perimeter of the trading floor.

Acoustics

Conference and meeting rooms require adequate isolation from the noisy activity of the floor. They may have windows to allow monitoring activity. The use of sealed, laminated glazing to minimize speech frequency sound transmission should be considered. Open glazing joints should not be used. Acoustical seals on doors may be warranted.

COMMODITY TRADING

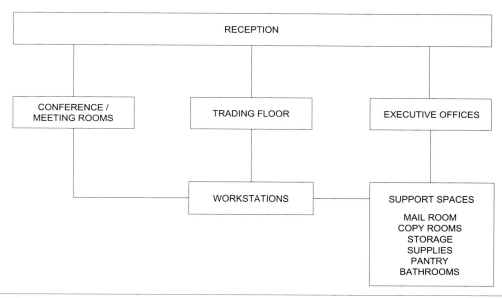

FINANCIAL TRADING

Trading rooms should have interior entrances only; sound-rated door and frame assemblies for exterior egress may be required.

Reverberation

Reverberation can be a major cause of noise buildup, poor speech intelligibility, and ineffective telephone use. The occupied reverberation time for a trading floor should be 1 second or less, to remove speech energy quickly. Acoustical ceiling materials with high Sound Absorption Average (SAA, formerly NRC) rating (0.80 or greater) are required to absorb speech frequencies. Carpeted floors, acoustical wall panels (fabric-wrapped fiberglass, not wood-fiber-based panels), and heavy fabric drapes at windows will also increase sound absorption. Cased openings to adjacent corridors may siphon some sound away from the trading room.

HVAC NC/RC Range

Air conditioning noise decreases speech intelligibility and forces people to raise their voices unconsciously. Fans on computers often exceed the air conditioning noise levels. Quiet computers should be considered. A background noise criterion of RC/NC 30 to 35, similar to private offices, is recommended for trading floors.

TRADING DESKS

Trading desks are typically designed as frames to hold the large amount of very complex equipment required by traders. These desks are often used by other industries that rely on high technology, such as emergency medical call (911) operators.

There are several design elements to consider when selecting and planning trading desks:

- *Layout:* Trading desk layouts depend on the number of central processing units (CPUs) each trader requires, the amount of reference space required, and at-the-desk storage required. Trading strategies that require a limited number of these items can achieve a tighter spline to spline. (The spline is defined as the centerline between face-to-face trading positions.) If the trading room is on a computer network, the number of desks that a space can accommodate is increased.
- *Heat:* Monitors and equipment generate heat that must be vented away from the traders and their desks. Heat builds up both above and below the desk service.
- *Flat-screen power supplies:* Many flat screens have separate power supplies that must be accommodated; others have power supplies built into the trading desk or into the monitor itself.
- *Power requirements:* Each piece of technology on the trading desk requires a power connection. Equipment inventory per desk should be evaluated. Power for critical equipment should be at a minimum on IG (isolated ground) circuits, often this equipment is on UPS (uninterrupted power supply) and generator power. Other peripheral equipment such as PDAs and cell phones are provided with standard power connections.
- *Turrets:* Turrets are phone systems positioned on traders' desks that enable them to have more than one phone line open at the same time. (The term *turret* is a holdover from the early trading floors, where the few telephones that existed on the trading floor were in cylindrical-shaped platforms.)
- *Desktop connectivity:* Accommodations for the connection of personal digital assistants (PDAs) and laptops should be made in each trading desk.

Sarah Bader; Gensler; Chicago, Illinois
Tanya Nachia; Rhode Island School of Design; Providence, Rhode Island

SCHEMATIC TRADING FLOOR

SECTION — 6'-10" (1850)

SECTION — 5'-3" (1600)

PLAN

PLAN

By eliminating CPUs, networked trading desks increase the density of desks on the trading floor by as much as 22% for the overall floor population and 24% for number of trading desks.

TRADING DESKS WITH FLAT PANEL DISPLAY (FPD) AND CPU

TRADING DESKS WITH FPD AND NETWORKED COMPUTERS

CONFERENCE AND TRAINING CENTERS

Today's corporate conference centers offer dedicated meeting facilities, which foster the quick exchange of information and ideas, either in person or by video-conferencing or teleconferencing. Conference centers provide spaces for meetings, presentations, and training functions in a distraction-free environment. Facilities range from nonresidential conference centers to residential conference centers, which include guest rooms and amenities, as well as conference and meeting spaces.

Training centers are designed for the dissemination and presentation of information and may more closely resemble classroom and learning facilities. Corporate training was developed in the United States in the latter half of the twentieth century. As service-oriented businesses became increasingly competitive, corporate training emerged as a way of attracting and maintaining talented employees. Today, many businesses are reliant on skilled workers, and corporate training is seen as an essential component of remaining competitive in business.

Conference center trends include:
- Rapidly changing business requirements
- Increasing workplace diversity
- Technology advancements
- Globalization and overseas competition

Conference and training center facilities have evolved to address current business strategies and programs. Technology has impacted conference and training programs and facility requirements. Videoconferencing, teleconferencing, wireless communications, and computer usage and programs will continue to develop in the near future; therefore, flexibility and planning for future needs should be incorporated into the conference center facility.

CONFERENCE CENTER TYPES

Information contained within this section is for general guideline purposes; each facility is unique and may have different programs and fit-up requirements.

Executive Conference Centers

Executive conference centers typically combine conference and lodging facilities in an independent or hotel-based center. This type of facility is geared toward mid- and upper-level management attendees. Various meeting room sizes accommodate small or large groups for training or management programs. High-end food service and other services support conference and guest needs. Guest rooms are typically larger than standard and are usually provided with work areas and technologically advanced facilities, including computer access, fax, and multiple telephone lines. Amenities such as fitness centers may be included in the facility.

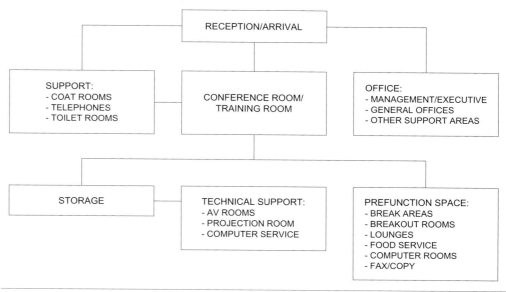

CONFERENCE AND TRAINING CENTERS

Resort conference centers combine executive-level services and facilities with additional recreation or special interest programs. Facilities are similar to executive conference centers.

Corporate Conference and Training Centers

Corporate conference and training centers feature conferencing facilities, as well as employee training areas, for corporate use. Conference and training room types and sizes vary with the individual program requirements.

Corporate conference centers generally provide guest rooms to accommodate extended stays for conference attendees and trainees. Typically, corporate education center guest rooms are furnished with work areas and technologically advanced facilities, including computer access, fax, multiple telephone lines and features, closed-circuit television, and other amenities to support conference and training programs. Amenities such as fitness or recreation areas may be included in the facility.

University Education Centers

University education centers serve a growing market of programs sponsored by universities. Many university education centers offer guest rooms and hotel-like support services.

Executive education centers are often physically connected to the educational facilities that they serve. Executive education centers are similar to conference centers, but are typically smaller in scale and include fewer amenities than executive conference centers.

Conference and executive education rooms average 25% to 35% of a residential university education center.

Ancillary areas include computer rooms for training and as resource areas; office areas for academic use; business center with computer, fax, copier, and other equipment; research areas; and other spaces required to support the university's programs.

Food service facilities may include faculty dining, conference dining, cafeteria-style student dining, and catering services. Conference dining may be incorporated into the classroom area.

Guest rooms for university education centers are typically slightly smaller than corporate conference center guest rooms, depending on the facility type. Levels of amenities vary, but typically include a private bathroom, work area and computer space, good lighting, lounge seating, and other selected appointments.

Continuing education centers provide teaching facilities for in-house and long-distance learning programs. These centers may offer guest rooms, which are typically less luxurious than their executive or corporate center counterparts. The majority of the space is dedicated to conference and classroom space.

University hotel and conference centers serve university-related conference and lodging needs, and may be available for rental for private functions. Facilities are similar to hotels and corporate conference centers.

Nonresidential Conference Centers

Nonresidential conference centers, generally located in metropolitan areas, serve corporate and noncorporate users. Nonresidential conference center facilities are similar to corporate conference centers, but do not include guest rooms for overnight stays. These centers are used for day and evening functions.

Food service is typically limited to refreshments and catered food. Warming kitchens and pantries are preferred in lieu of major preparation kitchens. Conveniently located local lodging, parking, dining, and other amenities are desirable.

For nonresidential conference centers, the ratio of conference and assembly space is approximately half of the total gross area for the facility.

CONFERENCE CENTER PROGRAM

A facility program should be developed in conjunction with the user/owner to determine the proposed requirements for the conference center. The program should identify all room types, sizes, uses, and fit-up requirements, including special construction, mechanical systems, electrical systems, plumbing systems, structural, life safety, acoustical, and other specialty requirements affecting interior design and construction.

CONFERENCE CENTER PLANNING CRITERIA

A conference center program should be developed to determine all facility requirements for the project. An analysis of room types, capacity, layout, usage, and proposed function of each room will assist in the development of an efficient plan.

Issues to review when developing a program for a conference center include, but are not limited to:

- Type of conference center and image proposed
- Adjacencies required
- Traffic flow/circulation
- Lobby/reception area
- Conference and training programs and room types required
- Conference room requirements
- Training room requirements
- Audiovisual and other presentation requirements
- Technology requirements
- Lounge/breakout areas
- Food service types and scope
- Guest room quantity and type
- Fitness and recreation
- Administrative requirements
- Storage needs
- Office area requirements
- Laundry

All rooms and areas should be defined within the conference center program. Conference, amphitheater, and auditorium spaces should be easy to reach from the lobby. Review adjacencies to determine the best means of circulation and layout when planning the conference center.

MULTIPURPOSE ROOMS AND AMPHITHEATERS

CONFERENCE CENTER

TRAINING CENTER

PROTOTYPICAL CONFERENCE CENTERS AND TRAINING FACILITIES
Source: Lohan Caprile Goettsch Architects; Chicago, Illinois

CONFERENCE ROOM DESIGN

Considerations for conference room design include room usage, room size and shape, accessibility, capacity, furniture configuration, privacy and sound attenuation, need for windows/vision panels in doors, movable partitions, HVAC requirements, lighting and controls, accessories, and equipment.

Furniture, materials, and finishes should be appropriate to the quality level of the facility and should be durable and easy to maintain. Casework, such as credenzas, should be adequate to store products frequently used in the conference room.

CONFERENCE ROOM TYPES

Most conference rooms are planned for sophisticated audiovisual presentations, as well as for teleconferencing capabilities. Room size and configuration are critical for the success of certain types of presentations. Consult with equipment manufacturers regarding critical dimensions.

- *Auditorium:* Large capacity of 150 or more, used for formal presentations, theater-type seating arrangement, sloped floor.
- *Amphitheater:* Tiered floor, built-in work surfaces, rounded, horseshoelike seating arrangement.
- *Ballroom:* Large-capacity meeting room and banquet room. Locate prefunction areas adjacent.
- *Boardroom:* Upgraded conference room, seating capacity between 16 and 24, 40 sq ft (4 sq m) per seat, high levels of finishes and furniture. Used by corporate board members; favored by businesses where status is important.
- *Large conference room:* Used for more formal presentations requiring little audience participation. Greater than 1,500 sq ft (139 sq m); room depth generally exceeds 50 ft (15m). May be divided with movable partitions.
- *Medium conference room:* Typically, 1,000 to 1,500 sq ft (93 to 139 sq m), and used for interactive group programs. This is one of the most popular sized conference rooms, and may be divided with movable partitions.
- *Small conference room:* Typically, 300 to 1,000 sq ft (28 to 93 sq m), and used for interactive group programs and small discussion groups. Informal conference areas are generally furnished with flexible, mobile furniture, ranging from modular tables and chairs to lounge-type seating.
- *Breakout room:* Small discussion area or informal meeting space.
- *Classroom/training room:* Varies in size, but generally between 300 and 800 sq ft (28 and 74 sq m).
- *Computer training room:* Workstation configuration requires 30 to 40 sq ft (3 to 4 sq m) per person.
- *Intensive strategy rooms:* Smaller, specialty-use rooms, with high-technology requirements and computer capability.

EXECUTIVE CONFERENCE CENTER CONCEPTUAL REQUIREMENTS

PROJECT ASPECT	AIMS AND REQUIREMENTS
Guest Rooms	Design the rooms for single occupancy during the week. Plan for some double occupancy for the weekend recreational market. Rooms should be similar in feel to first-class hotel rooms, but with special attention to the work area and such work amenities as phone and computer capability; consider the need for common areas.
Lobby	Create character that reinforces the image of the business meeting setting; clearly organize circulation so that visitors can easily locate conference wing, dining, and banquet areas.
Restaurants	Design the conference dining room to allow for expected meeting capacity plus 10%; include a specialty restaurant oriented to the local business community; add a small gourmet restaurant only if a market niche is available locally; lobby lounge should have capability to divide for small private receptions.
Conference Rooms	Provide a multipurpose conference room (flat-floored auditorium or junior ballroom) for full capacity; ballroom or banquet room for special meal functions; amphitheater. Principal focus is 1,000 sq ft (93 sq m) and larger conference rooms and large number of breakout rooms.
Conference Support	Include a large prefunction room near the principal conference room and smaller break areas near each group of meeting rooms; provide access to outdoor terraces, if possible; locate conference services at the conference core; determine need for high-level audiovisual, graphics, and other systems.
Recreation	Provide an indoor pool (outdoor if weather permits), racquetball courts, exercise and aerobics rooms, lockers, and a sauna.

Source: Richard H. Penner; Conference Center Planning and Design; *New York: Watson-Guptill Publications; 1991.*

CORPORATE CONFERENCE CENTER CONCEPTUAL REQUIREMENTS

PROJECT ASPECT	AIMS AND REQUIREMENTS
Guest Rooms	Design the rooms primarily for single occupancy, except in entry-level training centers, where double rooms may be anticipated; rooms require moderate- to high-level furnishings and amenities; minimum per-room area of 250 sq ft (23.2 sq m); provide common area among the guest rooms.
Lobby	Create residential-scale space with the potential to establish image for the center; front desk should be understated; provide only limited seating, as most lounge and social spaces are located elsewhere.
Restaurants	Provide conference dining room for full capacity; consider a second restaurant if center has more than 300 rooms; provide social lounge, game room, library, or reading room, and if corporate policy permits, pub or entertainment lounge.
Conference Rooms	Provide auditorium or banquet room for full capacity; amphitheaters for management development centers should seat up to 100; provide multiple rear-projection conference rooms, breakouts, and specialized training to meet corporate requirements (computers, telecommunications, etc.).
Conference Support	Provide relatively large prefunction room, coffee break room, and flow areas to promote corporate image and opportunities for informal interchange; provide high amounts of audiovisual support, including rear-screen projection; decide whether trainers will be housed at the property, which might add 5,000 sq ft (465 sq m) or more.
Recreation	Provide an indoor pool (outdoor if climate allows), racquetball courts, exercise/aerobics areas, game room and lounge; include team sports facilities such as a gym.

Source: Richard H. Penner; Conference Center Planning and Design; *New York: Watson-Guptill Publications; 1991.*

UNIVERSITY CONFERENCE CENTER CONCEPTUAL REQUIREMENTS

PROJECT ASPECT	AIMS AND REQUIREMENTS
Guest Rooms	Provide designs for single occupancy (double occupancy at campus hotels and continuing education centers); rooms should be of average size; include case discussion room on every floor.
Lobby	Create special space to reinforce image of university; separate circulation to faculty club or other nonconference functions; provide seating area for informal gathering.
Restaurants	Provide single conference dining room with buffet or servery design and with private dining alcoves; design discrete bar areas if required; include additional seating areas for spontaneous meetings.
Conference Rooms	Include 50 person-capacity amphitheaters for case study curricula; provide additional generic classrooms and numerous breakout rooms; add computer classroom if required.
Conference Support	Provide single conference foyer convenient to all rooms; include additional seating; equip with standard audio/visual systems.
Recreation	Provide small fitness center; other sports facilities are elsewhere on campus.

Source: Richard H. Penner; Conference Center Planning and Design; *New York: Watson-Guptill Publications; 1991.*

CONFERENCE ROOM LAYOUTS

THEATER-STYLE SEATING

CLASSROOM LAYOUT

U-SHAPED TABLE ARRANGEMENT

CLUSTER TABLE ARRANGEMENT

Theater-style seating offers the maximum seating capacity. Classroom, U-shaped, and cluster layouts with tables provide similar seating capacity, but are used for various presentation and teaching programs. Seating capacities vary with room dimensions and layout.

CONFERENCE ROOM LAYOUTS
Source: Richard H. Penner, Conference Center Planning and Design; New York: Watson-Guptill Publications, 1991.

CONFERENCE ROOM FOR 4: 150 SQ FT (14 SQ M)

CONFERENCE ROOM FOR 10: 350 SQ FT (33 SQ M)

CONFERENCE ROOM FOR 8: 300 SQ FT (28 SQ M)

U-SHAPED TABLE; CONFERENCE ROOM FOR 10: 350 SQ FT (33 SQ M)

TRAINING ROOM: 675 SQ FT (63 SQ M)

CONFERENCE ROOM FOR 16: 750 SQ FT (70 SQ M)

CONFERENCE ROOM FOR 12: 450 SQ FT (42 SQ M)

TRAINING ROOM: 275 SQ FT (26 SQ M)

CONFERENCE ROOM LAYOUT OPTIONS *Source: lauckgroup; Dallas, Texas*

TRAINING ROOM LAYOUT OPTIONS
Source: lauckgroup; Dallas, Texas

COMPUTER TRAINING ROOM LAYOUTS

Plan demonstrates a combination of a flexible teaming environment that integrates conferencing and workspace for cross-functional teams.

TEAMING AND CONFERENCE ENVIRONMENT
Source: lauckgroup; Dallas, Texas

CONFERENCE ROOM SEATING STANDARDS*

	THEATER STYLE	THEATER STYLE	CLASSROOM STYLE					
	EXECUTIVE SETUP[1]	MAXIMUM SETUP[2]	EXECUTIVE SETUP	MAXIMUM SETUP	HOLLOW SQUARE SETUP	U-SHAPED SETUP	CONFERENCE SETUP	BANQUET SETUP
Ballroom	14 (1.3)	11 (1.0)	22 (2.0)	18 (1.7)	N/A	N/A	N/A	14 (1.3)
Large Conference	16 (1.5)	13 (1.2)	24 (2.2)	20 (1.9)	40–45 (3.7–4.2)	50–55 (4.7–5.1)	N/A	14 (1.3)
Medium Conference	18 (1.7)	15 (1.4)	26 (2.4)	22 (2.0)	34 (3.2)	42 (3.9)	40 (3.7)	N/A
Small Conference	20 (1.9)	15 (1.4)	30 (2.8)	24 (2.2)	32 (3.0)	38 (3.5)	35 (3.3)	N/A
Breakout Room	N/A	N/A	N/A	N/A	N/A	N/A	25 (2.3)	N/A
Boardroom	N/A	N/A	N/A	N/A	32 (3.0)	N/A	40 (3.7)	N/A
Amphi-theater	N/A	N/A	25 (2.3)	N/A	N/A	N/A	N/A	N/A

Figures represent optimum square feet (square meters) per person.
[1]*Executive setup includes executive conference chairs and 24- to 30-in.- (610- to 760-mm-) wide tables.*
[2]*Maximum setup includes stacking banquet chairs and 18-in.- (457-mm-) wide tables.*

Source: Richard H. Penner, Conference Center Planning and Design; *New York: Watson-Guptill Publications, 1991, p 213.*

COMPUTER TRAINING: 725 SQ FT (67 SQ M)

COMPUTER TRAINING—PERIMETER WORK AREAS: 800 SQ FT (74 SQ M)

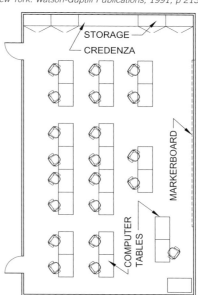

COMPUTER TRAINING FOR 20: 1,410 SQ FT (131 SQ M)

COMPUTER TRAINING ROOM LAYOUT OPTIONS *Source: lauckgroup; Dallas, Texas*

VIDEOCONFERENCE ROOM LAYOUTS

VIDEO CONFERENCE ROOM SIZES

CAPACITY	ROOM SIZE FT (MM)	APPLICATIONS
1–2	Workstation or desk	Informal meetings
		Interviews
		Research
		Development
2–3	9 × 12 (2,745 × 3,660)	General business meetings
		Interviews
		Progress meetings
3–5	11 × 16 (3,350 × 4,880)	General business meetings
		New business development
		Group sales meetings
		Product demonstrations
6–8	15 × 17 (4,570 × 5,180)	General business meetings
		Branch site meetings
		Capabilities demonstrations

SMALL VIDEOCONFERENCING ROOM
Source: Bretford Manufacturing, Inc.; Franklin Park, Illinois

VIDEOCONFERENCING FOR 18: 600 SQ FT (56 SQ M)
Source: lauckgroup; Dallas, Texas

VIDEOCONFERENCE ROOMS

CONFERENCE ROOM SIZE

The room usage, number of occupants in a room, and layout of furniture will establish requirements for the room size and shape. Equipment for presentations may necessitate certain dimensions or clearances. In the programming phase, the designer should inquire about the type of conference or training use for each room type, the desired furniture layout, seating capacity, need for movable partitions, and equipment required.

EGRESS

Most building codes require access to two or more exits when the occupant load is 50 or more; if the occupant loads exceeds 500, access to three or more exits is necessary. Typically, when fixed seating is provided, the occupant load is equal to the number of fixed seats plus wheelchair spaces.

Exit locations must be at least 15 ft (4.5 m) apart. Exit placement is determined by dividing the room in half diagonally and placing an exit within each half of the room, as far apart as possible.

AMPHITHEATERS/TIERED-LEVEL MEETING ROOMS

Accessibility

In order to provide optimum viewing in an amphitheater-style conference room, floors are tiered or sloped. Entries should be provided at the lower and upper levels of the room; and in larger amphitheaters lower and upper entries are required for adequate separation of egress doors, to meet building code requirements. The lower and upper entries must be accessible and located on accessible routes, as described by the *Americans with Disabilities Act Accessibility Guidelines* (ADAAG).

Ceiling Height

The floor-to-floor height is an important factor in tiered-level meeting room design. The greater the rise in a tiered floor system, the greater the floor-to-floor height. A factor of floor-to-floor height is the width of column bays. As the meeting room width is increased, the structural bay dimension is increased; the beam depth then also increases, in order to span between columns. As beam depth increases, either the floor-to-floor height increases or the overall ceiling height within the meeting room is lower.

Clearance is also required beneath the structure for mechanical systems and other elements in the ceiling or plenum space. Coordinate with the structural and mechanical engineers and the audiovisual consultant to determine the appropriate overall height of the meeting room.

Shared Functions

Efficiency and flexibility are heightened by the use of shared functions, which offer facilities for multiple users. Meeting facilities concentrated around dining and prefunction areas are efficient uses of space. Shared, flexible work and conference areas provide additional uses for work areas.

ANCILLARY AREAS

Lobby and Reception Areas in Residential Conference Centers

The lobby is the central registration area for visitors, the center of circulation paths, and the central assembly point for the conference facility. Lobby size may be dependent upon functional requirements, but a rule of thumb is to allow approximately 18 to 22 sq ft (1.6 to 2 sq m) per guest room. The front desk should be adjacent to administrative areas. Lounge seating is generally provided, but the quantity and type may be dependent upon the type of facility and programs offered.

All public areas should be accessible from the lobby and be clearly identified through the use of visual cues or signage. Routes to conference and dining areas should be obvious. Ancillary areas to the lobby include public restrooms, telephone alcoves, coat and luggage areas, security office, and gift shop.

Lobby and Reception Area for Nonresidential Facilities

Nonresidential conference center lobbies may be smaller than those in residential conference centers. A conference service desk, restrooms, large coat and luggage areas for day visitors, and telephone alcoves should be provided. Additional areas, such as security offices, business center for visitors, and other amenities may be desirable.

Routes to conference and dining areas should be obvious and clearly marked.

Prefunction Areas

Prefunction areas allow visitors to assemble and converse outside of the large meeting room, banquet room, or ballroom. The prefunction area may be significant, depending upon the number of people anticipated for the major function. To support a large meeting room or banquet room, the prefunction area may be at least 25% of the meeting room area. Other conference room areas in the same facility may have smaller prefunction spaces to allow for multiple events at one time.

Lounges/Break Areas

Many conference centers have satellite lounges, which serve as break areas for the conference functions. Seating may be all lounge-type, or mixed, with tables and chairs. Refreshments are typically located at break areas.

Business Center

A business center is provided to support the business needs of the visitor. Furnished with computer access, fax, copier, and other office-related amenities, the business center may be located adjacent to the conference services administrative offices.

SUPPORT SERVICES

Food Service and Dining Facilities

Conference center dining options vary with the type of facility. Executive and corporate conference centers may have several types of dining, ranging from formal dining rooms with wait staff service to self-service casual dining. Some conference centers may receive their food from a separate kitchen, as in a hotel-based conference center. Preparation kitchens are required for all in-house food service programs. Conference and training centers offering a limited refreshment menu and catered meals may require only smaller pantries and warming kitchens. Provide refreshment areas at or near breakout spaces and at other locations, as required, to accommodate a group on a limited break period without crowding.

The type and scope of dining service should be discussed in the programming phase. A significant amount of square footage is dedicated to food service within the conference center.

Fitness Center

A fitness center may be provided in some conference centers. These may be large facilities with swimming pools, gyms, and exercise areas, or may be limited to a small workout room. Any type of fitness area requires special construction; noise, odors, and vibration should be isolated from the rest of the conference center and residential areas. Avoid locating wet areas such as swimming pools or steamrooms at or near building expansion joints or other locations where the watertightness of the construction may be jeopardized. Laundry facilities should also be isolated, due to vibration, noise, and humidity. Review program requirements with consultants to determine the accommodation of the fitness and recreation areas within the facility.

Storage

Adequate storage space for a conference center is critical. An area of at least 5% to 10% of the conference and training areas should be dedicated to storage space. Furniture and equipment such as tables, chairs, lecterns, display material, audiovisual equipment, carts, dollies, and other items should be stored in easily accessible areas. Additional space may be required if there is a large amount of furniture that does not stack or nest, including tables and chairs.

Signage

Signage is critical in a conference or training facility. Clear, obvious signage assists first-time and repeat visitors with wayfinding and room identification. Directories and maps provide general locations; informational signs identify room functions. Flexibility is advantageous for signage when user groups and room functions change. Changeable inserts provide an easily maintained system for room identification. Electronic signage is gaining popularity in conference centers, as is computer software maintenance of conference and training center scheduling and room assignment.

FURNITURE AND CASE GOODS

Conference and training room furniture types range from traditional tables and chairs to more informal arrangements. Current trends in informal meeting rooms have influenced furniture types, including modular tables for flexible arrangements, special table sizes and shapes, lounge seating with attached tablet arms for use with laptop computers, and mobile accessories such as presentation boards and easels. Some manufacturers have developed conference modules within their systems furniture products, integrating conference spaces to open office areas.

CONFERENCE ROOM SEATING

Seating comfort for meetings of long duration is critical. Conference room seating types may differ depending on the type of room and function. A related or compatible series of seating will unify the image of the conference facility. Consider the following when selecting seating for conferences:

- *Ergonomics* should be considered when selecting seating for a conference center. Adjustments for seat height, seat tilt, back height and positions, tilt posture controls, and arms are desirable, depending on the type of chair under consideration.
- *Upholstered seat and back cushions* should be firm and comfortable.
- *Chair shape and adjustment features* should accommodate the contours of the body.
- *Streamlined, lightweight chairs* allow for easier movement.
- *Five casters,* minimum, on a chair are desirable for stability. Caster type should be appropriate for the floor material used.
- *Upholstery selection* should reflect chair usage: leather is a high-end material; wool and wool/natural fiber blends wear well and reduce static electricity; polyester and other synthetic fiber blends are suitable for frequent use and durability. Some chairs have an open-weave upholstery fabric, which allows air circulation and provides a streamlined appearance.

Executive or corporate conference rooms may have mid- or high-back upholstered executive chairs on casters; training rooms may have task chairs or tablet armchairs; and typical conference rooms may have low-back upholstered swivel/tilt chairs on casters. Lounge-type seating with tablet arms may be used for informal meetings, facilitating laptop computer usage. Four-leg guest chairs are not as flexible as chairs on casters, but can be a cost-effective alternative. Many four-leg chairs are available as stacking chairs, which may be acceptable for banquet functions and short-term meetings. Stacking chairs are more easily and compactly stored than conventional seating.

BUILT-IN CASEWORK

A built-in credenza or shelf complements the meeting or training room by providing additional storage or serving space. Built-in casework enhances the visual unity of the room and can be used to frame windows and enclose convector covers.

CONFERENCE ROOM ACCESSORIES

Conference room accessories and equipment should be planned into the room design. Permanent equipment includes whiteboards, projection screens, hanging-rail systems, shelving, clocks, and other devices fastened to the partitions or ceiling. Movable fixtures and equipment include easels, lecterns, carts, equipment cabinets, and portable screens.

SITTING ZONES—SQUARE TABLE, FOUR PEOPLE

SITTING ZONES—CIRCULAR TABLE, FOUR PEOPLE

WORK ZONE AND CIRCULATION ZONE—SQUARE TABLE

ANTHROPOMETRICS

Anthropometrics should be considered when designing conference and training areas. Sitting and working zones, as well as comfortable sight lines in various configurations, enhance the comfort of the users.

AUDIOVISUAL CONFERENCE TABLE SIGHT LINES

AUDIOVISUAL CONFERENCE TABLE SIGHT LINES

U-SHAPED TABLE

CONFERENCE TABLE ANTHROPOMETRICS
Source: Julius Panero and Martin Zelnik, Human Dimension and Interior Space; *New York: Whitney Library of Design; 1979.*

LIGHTING FOR CONFERENCE AND MEETING ROOMS

Conferencing facilities have become a vital part of the modern office environment, and appropriate lighting to support their function is critical. A lighting system must provide general illumination, task lighting, perimeter wallwashing or accent lighting, and, often, audiovisual presentation support lighting. Additionally, decorative or architectural enhancement lighting may be appropriate.

A combination of lighting types is generally best in meeting rooms. Uplights from sconces or pendants produce ambient light, while recessed downlights illuminate the table. Wallwashers can light presentation or art walls, with adjustable accent lights providing flexibility in highlighting podiums and lecterns. Lighting controls should be employed to orchestrate the various lighting conditions through preset dimming, whenever possible.

CONFERENCE CENTER AUDIOVISUAL PRESENTATION ROOMS

The construction of conference center audiovisual presentation rooms requires special consideration.

Locations of the rooms, privacy, acoustics, and other concerns should be addressed.

Exterior light and noise should not interfere with presentations. If walls are glazed, provide blackout shades to eliminate glare. Noise from the exterior should be reduced to less than 35 dBA to minimize distractions.

Reverberation should be maintained at less than 0.8 seconds for improved acoustics. A gypsum board ceiling in the front half of the space may be a useful sound reflector, amplifying sound to the audience. Nonrectilinear room shapes, especially circular and elliptical forms, may affect acoustics; consult with an acoustical engineer.

The HVAC NC/RC range should be kept as low as possible for greater speech intelligibility: 20 to 25 is a desirable range, 30 is acceptable if the project faces budget constraints.

Allow sufficient space above ceilings for ductwork to be in round or nearly square cross sections. Flat, wide ductwork may be noisy if the wide sections of sheet metal vibrate.

CONFERENCE CENTER COMMUNICATIONS

Conference center communications, including long-distance learning, videoconferencing, television distribution, telephone, and Internet connections are commonly employed. Special features are required for functions such as videoconferencing, and future needs should be considered when designing for future technology. A control room may be required for receiving outside signals, recording, and transmitting programs throughout the facility and to other locations.

Source: Richard H. Penner, Conference Center Planning and Design: A Guide for Architects, Designers, Meeting Planners, and Facility Managers; New York: Watson-Guptill Publications, 1991.

Ted Kollaja, AIA; lauckgroup; Dallas, Texas
Ted Milligan; Rhode Island School of Design; Providence, Rhode Island

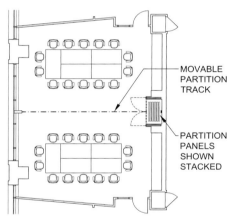

Plan illustrates the operable partition track (shown dotted) and panel stacking position in wall pocket with swing door closure. Panels are hung from overhead tracks. Fasten tracks to structure above for stability.

CONFERENCE ROOM WITH OPERABLE PARTITION *Source: lauckgroup; Dallas, Texas*

TYPICAL CONFERENCE ROOM LIGHTING PLAN *Source: Randy J. Burkett, FIALD, IES, LC; Burkett Lighting Design, Inc.; St. Louis, Missouri*

SECTION—MULTIMEDIA CONFERENCE ROOM

TELEVISION BROADCAST FACILITIES

BROADCAST STUDIO DESIGN

There are several key considerations in the design of a broadcast facility: the aspect ratio of the camera being used, the set design, electrical conditioned power HVAC system selection, and acoustics. The aspect ratio refers to the size, configuration, and format of the signal being broadcast.

TELEVISION BROADCAST SIGNALS

There are two types of television broadcast signals: NTSC (analog) and digital.

NTSC TV

During the wide acceptance of television in the period between 1948 and 1998, broadcast transmissions remained virtually unchanged. The analog signals of traditional television (referred to as NTSC TV after the governing body, the National Television Standards Committee) transmitted one signal, one direction. Because digital broadcast technology (DTV) enables up to eight signals to be transmitted and returned, television networks can initiate a variety of businesses, as well as offer traditional television programming.

Digital TV

Digital television (DTV), which includes high-definition, or HDTV, and standard-definition television, or SDTV, provides greater picture sharpness, a larger, wider picture, and a greater depth and variety of color. Because of the high picture quality provided by DTV, flaws in the studio set can be detected. Unlike the theatrical quality of construction and trompe l'oeil finishes used in NTSC TV sets, DTV requires the use of real finish materials as well as finished-carpentry-quality craftsmanship.

TRANSITION TO DTV

In the United States, the Federal Communication Commission (FCC) set deadlines by which stations must have completed the transition from NTSC TV to DTV. Commercial television stations were required to complete construction of DTV facilities by May 1, 2002, and public stations by May 1, 2003, although analog transmissions (NTSC TV) will continue for some time after that. Since extensions are granted based on individual circumstances, the discussion of NTSC TV is included.

Throughout the transition period, analog transmissions will be able to be received. After the switch to DTV, regular television sets will need to be converted to receive

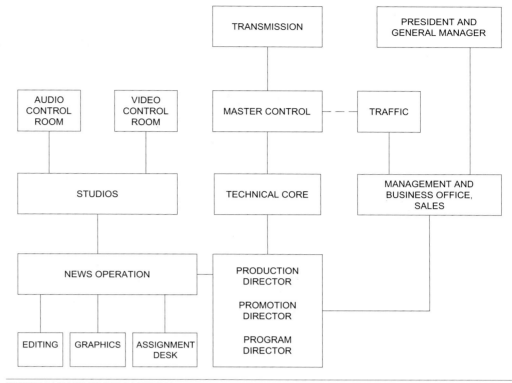

BROADCAST FACILITY DIAGRAM

broadcasts, although the sets will remain functional indefinitely.

AUDIO

Typically, the audio for DTV is AES (an abbreviation of Audio Engineering Society, the organization that sponsors the defining standard). AES is sometimes referred to as AC-3, which is the transmission audio component version 3 5.1 SS (Surround Sound audio). Surround Sound is digital sound created by Dolby labs. It is a multichannel audio system. This is the CD-quality audio complement to digital TV.

STUDIO LAYOUT

DTV studios are never square, due to the aspect ratio of the camera. Popular studio sizes are 60 × 80 ft (18 × 24 m) and 80 × 100 ft (24 × 30.5 m). Studios can be as large as 100 × 120 ft (30.5 × 36.5 m), which is the largest practical size.

NTSC TV (ANALOG) PICTURE
A 4:3 aspect ratio.

DTV (DIGITAL) PICTURE
A 16:9 aspect ratio.

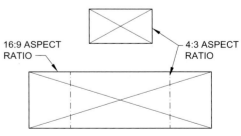

16:9 ASPECT RATIO —   — 4:3 ASPECT RATIO

ASPECT RATIO COMPARISON
The aspect ratio refers to the height-to-width ratio of a television screen. For traditional television (NTSC), the aspect ratio is 4:3; for high-definition television (DTV), the aspect ratio is 16:9. The camera aspect ratios are logarithmic, not linear, calculations.

ASPECT RATIO COMPARISON

TYPICAL STUDIO SECTION WITH AUDIENCE

ELEVATION

PLAN

A smaller studio for blue- or green-screen video broadcasts is often included in a larger news or production facility. The "hard syke wall" curves where it intersects the floor so that no transition can be seen.

TYPICAL HDTV BROADCAST STUDIO (16:9 ASPECT RATIO)

SET DESIGN

Two types of set design are commonly employed: a *cyc,* short for *cyclorama,* which is the wall and whatever construction of images appear on it behind the talent, and a *virtual set,* which uses two-dimensional, chromakey screens (commonly referred to as *blue screens*) onto which images are projected. There is no constructed set in a virtual studio. Virtual sets require much greater communication among the production designer, virtual creator, and the control room.

The major design components of a broadcast studio are the suspended lighting grid (referred to as the "grid") and the mechanical equipment it supports and conceals, and acoustic considerations.

Grid

The grid supports lighting equipment and scenic elements. It is typically made of structural steel black iron pipe that is 1½ in. (38 mm) O.D. Rigging for the pipe an either be fixed or motorized. It is mounted at a height that corresponds to the aspect ratio of the television broadcast system used by the facility. For NTSC television news broadcasts, the minimum grid height is 18 ft (5.5 m); for other productions, the minimum grid height is 22 ft (6.7 m), with a 24 ft (7.3 m) height preferred. For DTV news broadcasts, a minimum grid height of 20 ft (6 m) is recommended; and for productions, a minimum grid height of 50 ft (15.2 m) is suggested. Grid heights are logarithmic, not linear, calculations. All lighting-level calculations are logarithmic as well.

HVAC Systems

Because of the heat generated by studio lighting, HVAC systems are kept on full operation at all times. These systems are required to be quiet as well as efficient. High-volume/low-velocity distribution systems are commonly used to prevent hissing and other low-frequency sounds that a microphone might pick up.

SECTION

PLAN

STUDIO: 90 × 110 FT (2,743 × 3,353 MM)

Grid height, skid prop size, or available square footage can determine a broadcast studio's size.

TYPICAL STUDIO SIZES

HVAC equipment is isolated or decoupled from the studio. HVAC units should never be placed on the roof or floor because of vibrations that can transmit through the structure, carrying low-frequency sound to the broadcast studio. Prevention of this is often accomplished with the use of acoustic traps and tuned ductwork.

SECTION

PLAN

STUDIO: 60 × 80 FT (1,828 × 2,438 MM)

Standard grid height for news: 18 ft (548 mm) AFF
Standard grid height for production: 24 ft (731 mm) AFF

ACOUSTICS

Privacy

Studios use live microphones for audio pickup, so noise intrusion must be avoided. Sound-rated door and frame assemblies (STC 50 to 55) and thick double glazing at control rooms (if glazed; not all TV studios use glass) should be required. Acoustical window assemblies (STC 50-plus) are the most reliable sound isolation for glazed units.

SINGLE-DECK VIDEO CONTROL ROOM

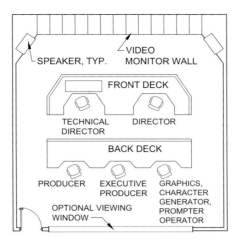

The control room layout considers the sight lines of the viewer in relation to the monitors. A viewing window is often placed between the video and audio control rooms when they are adjacent to each other.

TWO-DECK VIDEO CONTROL ROOM

Controls and monitors for robotic-controlled cameras can also be located in the studio.

Plumbing walls and mechanical chases must be isolated from studio partitions. Carpeting of adjacent corridors and offices is also recommended so that footfall impact noise does not transmit under partitions into the studio.

SINGLE-PERSON ROBOTIC CAMERA CONTROL ROOM

The shape of the room is determined by the number of speakers. There are no flat, reflective surfaces in an AES audio studio.

AES (AC-3) AUDIO STUDIO

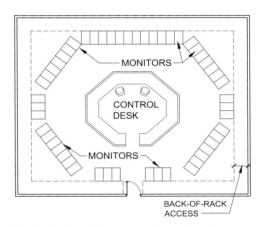

The Master Control Room (sometimes referred to as Network Operations Control Room (NOC) or Integration and Release) monitors all incoming and outgoing signals for multicasting; 360° visibility is required.

MASTER CONTROL ROOM

Exterior Noise Insulation

The acoustical design concept for television broadcast studios is a "box-inside-a-box." Avoid placing the studio under an exposed roof deck. Potential helicopter and other urban or mechanical noise sources should be evaluated. Buffer the studio by surrounding it with storage and other quiet support spaces. Masonry construction should be considered if transportation or mechanical noise sources are a concern.

Reverberation

Sound reverberation has to be controlled, but not to the extent required in audio recording studios. This is due to the use of close microphone placement on talent and low background noise level. A reverberation time of 0.75 second or less is desirable.

The use of 1 in. (25 mm) cementitious wood fiber panels over fiberglass insulation and velour drapes on tracks supported from the lighting grid should be considered. Ceiling options for reducing reverberation time include sprayed cellulose insulation for hard-deck surfaces, suspended acoustical ceiling grid (this can be awkward because of required HVAC penetrations), fiberglass on impaling pins, or efficient sound-absorbing steel deck (not ribbed type with perforations on vertical sides of flutes, but flat-deck profile with perforations on horizontal surfaces with insulation behind).

HVAC Acoustics

HVAC RC/NC values should be 20 or less. Both supply and return air pathways must be adequately attenu-ated to meet this criterion. Sufficient vertical space for larger-than-usual supply and return ducts above lighting grid must be provided in order to keep air velocity and consequent noise very low. Keep noise-producing fittings such as mixing boxes and sharp duct bends outside the studio footprint. Good HVAC design introduces already-quiet air into the studio. Supply diffusers and return air grilles, if used, should be rated NC/RC 15 or less at maximum design airflow.

Don Archiable, SBE, SMPTE; Gensler; Chicago, Illinois
Jim Johnson; WJHW Acoustical Consultants; Dallas, Texas
Natasza Naczas; Rhode Island School of Design;
*   Providence, Rhode Island*

DISTRIBUTION AND WAREHOUSE FACILITIES

Distribution facilities are highly efficient operations in which products are stored and from which orders are filled and shipped to meet customer demand. Distribution facilities house raw materials, parts, or finished products, most commonly at the manufacturing or distribution level. This storage, all along the supply chain, from raw material to product delivery, adds cost, which can be reduced by efficient distribution practices and facilities.

Distribution facilities are designed from the inside out. That is, the size and shape of the product determines how the facility will be operated and what form the building will take. Storage volume can be increased much more cheaply by increasing the height of a building than by increasing its footprint. Column layouts must accommodate a combination of rack types and allow for changes in rack type. Mixed-rack types may be placed together in one storage area.

In addition to storage areas, distribution facilities require a battery-charging area, a maintenance area, shipping and receiving offices, other business offices, utility equipment spaces, and truck and rail docks.

Most new facilities are built so it will be easy to double the storage area at a later date. Expansion requirements usually direct the organization of storage areas, as it is difficult to expand through a loading dock, and disruptive and expensive to expand through utility spaces or offices.

STORAGE DESIGN CRITERIA

The store product is the module that determines an efficient warehouse size. To provide uniformity in the industry, a common unit load format has developed, using a *pallet* as the tool for shipping, storing, and receiving product. The *palletized unit load* is now the modular building block from which 90% of warehouse dimensions are derived.

The most common method of handling products uses a standardized Grocery Manufacturers Association pallet. Different product combinations can be packed on a single pallet. For identification, each product is called a *stock-keeping unit* (SKU), although the same product in different packaging or with different cost structures can be identified as distinct SKUs.

When a unit load is stackable, and large amounts of the same SKU are stored in one place (typically at a manufacturing facility), unit loads can be stacked on the floor. Typically, these stacks are no higher than 3 ft (915 mm) in lanes deeper than 12 unit loads from front to back. Unit loads are also stored in pallet racks. Typically made of steel (cold-rolled or formed), racks are available in numerous types. The type of pallet rack appropriate for any application depends on the variety, quantity, and movement (velocity) of the unit loads being stored and retrieved.

In a typical distribution facility, the contents are rotated 10 to 20 times a year. However, depending on many factors, this *inventory turn* number may vary from 2 to 52 turns for perishable products (52 turns means an average product storage time of about a week).

OFFICES OVER LOADING DOCK

ONE-STORY CORE

Illustrated are four types of schematic grocery distribution facilities. Grocery facilities exemplify distribution to retail outlets, demonstrating the complexity involved in storing products with varying requirements. Grocery facilities often require five or more coolers with different temperatures, as well as heated storage areas and special fruit-ripening rooms. The building configuration is determined by the temperature-conditioned space requirements.

Each schematic is designed around the facility operation. The storage rooms, with their varying conditions,

TYPICAL DISTRIBUTION FACILITIES

Distribution center management seeks to minimize construction costs by increasing product movement times and choosing storage layouts that minimize the building footprint. It is less expensive to build taller buildings for vertical storage than to increase the building footprint; however, it may be more labor-intensive to access very high storage areas. Moving unit loads in and out of pallet racks is very different from selecting cases or individual items from unit loads.

Most distribution centers receive product in full-unit loads. Some ship full-unit loads, while others ship smaller numbers of cases or less-than-case quantities. Most distribution centers ship a combination of full-unit loads and smaller quantities.

TWO-STORY CORE

STORAGE WAREHOUSES ROTATED ABOUT ADMINISTRATION AREA

complicate the space layout. Also, because each space may expand independently, planning for future expansion must consider each space individually.

Refrigerated space is a specialized single-use space and, as such, can double the cost of constructing warehouse space. Refrigerated rooms, particularly freezers, should not open directly into unconditioned environments. Typically, a refrigerated dock serves as a buffer between these rooms and nonrefrigerated spaces.

[Image: TYPICAL WAREHOUSE CIRCULATION PATTERN diagram with labels: MULTIPLE DEEP RACK (BACK-TO-BACK), SINGLE DEEP RACK (BACK-TO-BACK), VERY NARROW AISLE (VNA) PICK PATH, LOADING DOCK AREA, PICK PATH, DOCK OFFICE]

The rack layout is based on the building column spacing. Often the column spacing accommodates combinations of different rack types.

An even number of selection aisles is preferred so the selection path begins and ends on the dock or at the order assembly area.

TYPICAL WAREHOUSE CIRCULATION PATTERN

LIGHTING FOR INDUSTRIAL SPACES

Industrial high-intensity discharge (HID) downlight systems provide good acceptable light at low cost, and thus are frequently used in industrial spaces. High-bay downlights are specifically suited for mounting heights greater than 20 ft (6 m). Low-bay downlights generally have lower wattage and are best for mounting heights less than 20 ft (6 m). Aluminum reflectors and prismatic glass or acrylic reflectors direct most light downward, although some light is directed upward in certain luminaires. Special aisle-lighters and other types are available.

Fluorescent systems are useful for mounting heights up to about 20 ft (6 m). They require more fixtures than HID systems but provide more uniform light with softer shadows. Use electronic ballasts to eliminate stroboscopy. Fluorescent systems make good task lights for workstations.

Special-application luminaires come in hundreds of different types, each optimized for a specific job, workstation, environment, or hazard. Examples include explosion-proof, vapor-tight, and paint-booth luminaires.

Illumination Criteria

The lighting levels given are average figures:

- *Industrial manufacturing—general:* 30 to 50 fc (300 to 500 lux) in an empty room with task lighting as needed.
- *Industrial manufacturing—assembly and rough inspection:* 50 to 70 fc (500 to 700 lux) in an empty room.
- *Industrial manufacturing—fine assembly and moderate inspection:* 50 to 70 fc (500 to 700 lux) in an empty room with task lighting as needed to achieve 100 to 200 fc (1,000 to 2,000 lux), depending on type of work.
- *Industrial manufacturing—specialized:* Refer to the IESNA *Lighting Handbook.*
- *Lunchrooms and break areas:* 20 to 30 fc (200 to 300 lux) in an empty room.
- *Hallways and circulation areas (excluding workspaces):* 10 to 20 fc (100 to 200 lux) in an empty room.
- *Warehouses:* With high stacks, 20 fc (200 lux), minimum, vertical illumination on stacks; for general use, 20 to 40 fc (200 to 400 lux) in an empty room. General illumination of 5 to 10 fc (50 to 100 lux).

The amount and type of dirt and other airborne particles present in an application can affect luminaire selection. For spaces where hazardous, corrosive, or explosive vapors or dust are present, special lighting equipment is generally required.

Safety

Backup quartz auxiliary lamps are needed for HID systems. Where rotating machinery is used, take precautions to prevent stroboscopic problems by using fluorescent lighting systems or rotating phases of power.

St. Onge, Ruff and Associates, Inc.; York, Pennsylvania

SECTION

NORMAL X SPACING BETWEEN INDUSTRIAL FLUORESCENT LUMINAIRES SHOULD NOT EXCEED 1.4 TO 1.6 TIMES THE MOUNTING HEIGHT, Z; AND NORMAL Y SPACING SHOULD NOT EXCEED 1.2 TO 1.4

TYPICAL 8'-0" (2438) INDUSTRIAL FLUORESCENT FIXTURE

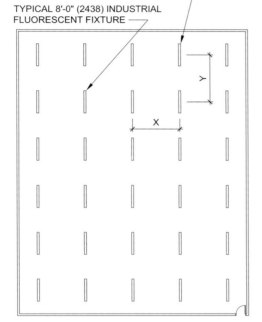

REFLECTED CEILING PLAN

TYPICAL FLUORESCENT GENERAL LIGHTING FOR INDUSTRIAL APPLICATIONS

SUSPENSION CABLES

FLUORESCENT LAMP — — APERTURED REFLECTOR

FLUORESCENT

SECTION

NORMAL X AND Y SPACINGS BETWEEN HIGH-BAY INDUSTRIAL LUMINAIRES SHOULD NOT EXCEED 1.5 TO 1.8 TIMES THE MOUNTING HEIGHT, Z

TYPICAL INDUSTRIAL HID FIXTURE

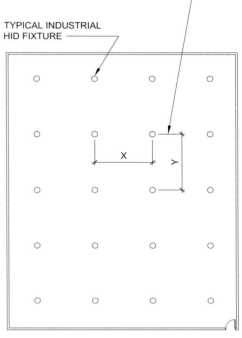

REFLECTED CEILING PLAN

TYPICAL HID GENERAL LIGHTING FOR INDUSTRIAL APPLICATIONS

BALLAST HOUSING

REFLECTOR

HID LAMP

CLEAR GLASS LENS

HID

COMMON DOWNLIGHTING FOR DISTRIBUTION FACILITIES

COLOR RENDERING INDEX (CRI) FOR DISTRIBUTION AND WAREHOUSE FACILITIES

FACILITY TYPE	COLOR RENDERING INDEX
Heavy industry, storage	2,100–5,000K>20 CRI
Most industrial	3,000–5,000K>50 CRI
Most warehouse	2,100–5,000K>20 CRI
Precise assembly	4,100–5,000K>70 CRI

LIGHTING POWER DENSITY FOR DISTRIBUTION AND WAREHOUSE FACILITIES

FACILITY TYPE	LIGHTING POWER DENSITY
Warehouse	0.2–0.5 W/sq ft (2.1–5.3 W/sq m)
Light industrial	0.8–1.2 W/sq ft (8.6–12.9 W/sq m)
Precision industrial and inspection areas	1.2–1.8 W/sq ft (12.91–19.3 W/sq m)
Storage areas	0.1–0.3 W/sq ft (1–3.2 W/sq m)
Lunchrooms and hallways	0.6–1.0 W/sq ft (6.4–10.7 W/sq m)

MUSEUMS AND EXHIBIT SPACES

MUSEUM TYPES

The defining characteristic of any modern museum is its collection. Each museum has its own special character and requirements. The more common types of museums include:

- Art museums
- Children's museums
- College and university museums
- History museums
- Nature centers
- Park museums and visitor centers
- Science and natural history museums
- Specialized museums: aeronautics and space, agriculture, architecture, forestry, and military

MUSEUM SPACE RELATIONSHIPS AND SPACE TYPES

Museums consist of discrete blocks of space that must be kept separate for secure and efficient operations. Typically, the main departments include: public services, galleries, educational facilities, temporary exhibition support facilities, general staff services, collections management, collections storage, and curatorial and administrative offices.

PROGRAMMING

The development of a thorough program for museum planning is critical. Museums are composed of many different spaces, each accommodating a particular function. Each anticipated function must be analyzed and accommodated individually. In addition, the future growth of museum collections and facilities must be addressed.

ACCESSIBILITY

Compliance with the principles of the Americans with Disabilities Act (ADA) enhances the museum experience for disabled visitors and staff. Accommodation for special needs include:

- Ramps and elevators
- Large-print labeling and signage with good contrast and lighting
- Captioned film, video, and audio

Ramps and elevators may reduce accidents, and are preferred by persons in wheelchairs, families with strollers, the elderly, and those with limited mobility.

Place exhibit objects in positions that are visible from both seated and standing positions.

Large-print labeling and captioning encourages the visitor to read the informative text, while aiding those with some sight restrictions. Audio narration also assists visitors with sight impairment.

PUBLIC SERVICE SPACES

Public nongallery spaces should be located together near the public entrance. They include vestibules, public lobby, information desk, coat and parcel checkroom, museum shop, auditorium, meeting rooms, A/V presentation/orientation room, public toilets, drinking fountains, and telephones.

SPACE RELATIONSHIPS

Public Lobby

The lobby has many practical functions: orientation and access to all public service functions within the museum and a setting for social functions. Size is often governed by the capacity needed for banquet dinners and/or receptions. During receptions, visitors may be dispersed throughout the galleries, depending on the kinds of events taking place in the museum's public spaces.

Meeting Rooms and Auditoriums

These will vary widely according to the particular events program. Smaller museums usually have either a sloped-floor auditorium or a multipurpose room. Larger museums may have both. Rooms may be used for museum events or be rented to other public and private groups, depending on museum policy. For security and operating economy, auditoriums and meeting rooms must be accessible when the galleries are closed.

Museum Shop and Bookstore

The retail shop should open to the lobby where it will be visible and attractive as visitors leave the museum. An adjacent office and inventory space are required.

Public Restrooms

Restrooms should be sized to accommodate the largest anticipated exhibition openings or auditorium audiences. Plumbing fixture counts should be at least the code minimum, but greater if large groups are anticipated on a regular basis. Interpretations in plumbing fixture counts should be clarified with appropriate building code officials.

PUBLIC SERVICE RELATIONSHIPS

VIEWING AND BEHAVIOR

Exhibit viewing heights are influenced by the average standing person's eye level and comfortable viewing range. Some displays are visible from a seated position, which enables persons of smaller stature and those in wheelchairs to view the objects on display.

SITTING AND LEANING BEHAVIOR

People naturally gravitate toward surfaces at comfortable heights to lean against, perch, or sit. Galleries may be provided with some seating for visitors. Seating may affect the duration of the rest period. Hard benches provide places for short rest periods; comfortable chairs encourage longer periods of sitting.

VIEWING HEIGHT AND COMFORTABLE VISUAL SPACE

VIEWING DISTANCE

VIEWING HEIGHT AND COMFORTABLE VISUAL SPACE

SITTING AND LEANING BEHAVIOR

INFERRED FLOW

UNSTRUCTURED FLOW

STRUCTURED FLOW

EXHIBIT CIRCULATION

EXHIBIT GALLERY TYPES

Museum gallery types include:

- Art galleries
- Interpretive galleries
- Science center galleries
- Visible storage galleries
- Changing exhibition galleries

GALLERY CHARACTERISTICS

Galleries should be isolated spaces conducive to concentrating on the objects exhibited. When the museum is closed, the galleries should become secure, dark vaults.

Gallery Flexibility

Galleries must provide flexibility to house various exhibit types. This is achieved in traditional art museums by providing a variety of well designed, proportioned, and organized gallery rooms of different sizes and characters. Flexibility within gallery spaces is maintained with open floor space, a modular ceiling system, and movable exhibition walls, so the space can be reconfigured based on exhibition requirements. A level of physical changeability provides flexibility within the context of fixed gallery rooms.

Proportions

A rectangular floor plan is generally desirable for gallery spaces. Ceiling heights should be proportional to the plan size of the room and to the objects to be exhibited: 11 to 14 ft (3.4 to 4.3 m) is appropriate. Lower ceilings may be acceptable in certain intimate galleries such as those exhibiting old master prints, photographs, or other very small objects. Very high ceilings may be desirable in feature areas of galleries, when exhibiting large artifacts.

Finish Materials

Floors, walls, and (ideally) ceilings should be capable of supporting considerable weight through the use of fasteners. Floors and walls should have securely attached ¾ in. (19 mm) tongue-and-groove plywood substrates. Suitable flooring materials are tongue-and-groove hardwood strip flooring, stone, terrazzo, or carpet. Suitable wall materials are thin (¼ or ⅜ in.; 6 or 10 mm) drywall or stretched fabric. Ceilings may be painted drywall or acoustical ceiling panels. If the flooring is a hard-surface material, an acoustical ceiling is desirable.

EXHIBIT CASEWORK AND DISPLAY UNITS

Most museum artifacts are exhibited in protective display cases. The artifacts are secured, while allowing visitors to view the objects within a sealed display environment. Temperature, relative humidity, contamination, and outside chemical pollutants are controlled within the sealed case.

Case Construction

Cases may be constructed of wood or metal. Wood construction is less stable than metal, and should be treated with vapor barrier products to seal the wood surfaces. Metal cases provide dimensional stability. They may be fabricated from steel, which requires a protective coating to prevent corrosion, or aluminum. Case construction materials or finishes should be composed of conservation-appropriate materials that do not outgas any chemical substances.

Display cases may require ventilation and air filtration to remove contaminants from the air within the case. Provide power to cases as required; freestanding cases may require power feeds from the floor.

Case Security and Seals

Display case security should be discussed with a security consultant before selecting secure construction type, case materials, glazing, and locking systems. Locking options include: pneumatic, electronic, and manual locking devices. Specify tamper-resistant screws that are exposed. Consider electronic detection sensors in high-security areas.

Cases may require seals to contain the internal environment within the unit. Gaskets are typically employed to seal the display case glazing in place.

Case Lighting

Incandescent, fluorescent, or fiber-optic illuminator sources may be used for integral display case lighting. Provide ventilation to dissipate heat generated from lamps; fans may be required to evacuate hot air.

INDIVIDUAL GALLERY SIZES AND CEILING HEIGHTS

GALLERY TYPE	FLOOR AREA SQ FT (SQ M)	CEILING HEIGHT FT (M)
Intimate Galleries		
Old master prints and drawings Archival documents Jewelry Small decorative arts Miniature dioramas Gems and minerals Insects, small animals	300–900 (28–84)	9–11 (2.7–3.4)
Medium Galleries		
Fourteenth- to nineteenth-century paintings Traditional sculpture Furniture Decorative arts Small historical exhibits Medium-sized artifacts Most scientific exhibits Interactive galleries Most temporary exhibits	1,000–2,000 (93–186)	11–14 (3.4–4.3)
Large Galleries		
Central gallery among smaller galleries Large Baroque paintings Twentieth-century paintings and sculpture Temporary exhibitions Industrial history Architectural reconstructions Historical reconstructions Large dioramas Large natural history exhibits (dinosaurs, etc.)	2,000–5,000 (186–465)	14–20 (4.3–6.1)

PLATFORMS/CASES

MOVABLE EXHIBIT WALLS

FLEXIBLE OPEN-PLAN GALLERY

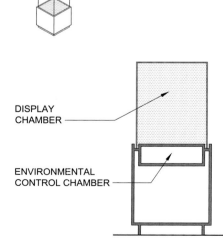

DISPLAY CHAMBER

ENVIRONMENTAL CONTROL CHAMBER

VITRINE PEDESTAL CASE

LIGHT ATTIC

DISPLAY CHAMBER

ENVIRONMENTAL CONTROL CHAMBER

BACK WALL CASE

DISPLAY CASE CONSTRUCTION
Source: National Park Service, "Exhibit Conservation Guidelines," Division of Conservation, 1999.

MUSEUM SUPPORT SPACES

Scientific Research Laboratories

Science museums often support significant research programs, which require various laboratory types, including clean, dirty, and wet laboratories, and special storage and equipment rooms. The requirements for these rooms must be programmed in close cooperation with the scientists involved.

Education Spaces

Many museums offer active educational programs, ongoing A/V presentations, and orientation talks for groups of both children and adults. Museum education spaces include:

- Holding areas for children's coats and personal belongings
- Orientation rooms
- Studio classrooms
- Lecture classrooms
- Staff and docent offices

Administrative and Curatorial Offices and Workspaces

Offices for museum administrators and curators are similar to business or academic offices. Future office and work area space needs should be addressed when designing the museum. Curators may need larger-than-usual offices if museum objects are stored in them for examination and research. Security and special HVAC may be required.

General Staff Services

Back-of-the-house facilities include: shipping and receiving area, sallyport, central security station, shops, graphics studio, exhibition preparation room, isolation room, specimen room, X-ray laboratory, photography studio, A/V storage and workrooms, and other specialized museum support spaces. Security guards' toilets, showers, and dressing rooms should be provided. Other areas may be required to support museum programs.

Temporary Exhibition Storage and Staging

Adequate spaces must be provided for receiving and handling exhibition materials. These materials consist of museum objects borrowed from other institutions and/or individuals. Conservation-standard climate control and security must be provided in order to avoid liability for damage and to meet the strict requirements sophisticated modern lenders often impose on borrowing institutions.

Shipping and Receiving Facilities

Receiving and sending traveling exhibitions require access to a shipping and receiving room, adjacent to a loading dock. Immediate access to the crating/uncrating room and to the freight elevator is suggested. Very close monitoring of this space by security personnel is essential. Security monitoring may include the use of X rays, similar to those used for airport security.

Crating/Uncrating Room

A large room must be provided as a workspace for crating and uncrating borrowed museum objects, for temporarily storing both the objects and their crates, and for examining, photographing, and organizing the objects in preparation for gallery installation. Space may be required to handle several exhibitions simultaneously. The space must be secure, clean, and climate-controlled to museum conservation standards. Provide work surface areas and storage units as required.

Temporary Collections Storage

After objects are removed from their crates, they must be examined, organized, and securely stored prior to installation. After the exhibition closes, they must be stored and prepared for crating. Provide workspace and storage units as required.

Temporary Crate Storage

While the objects are in the museum, the crates must be stored and maintained under proper humidity conditions.

Collections Management

Collections management facilities accommodate the handling, care, storage, and conservation of the museum's own collections. Clear unobstructed passageways are essential between the shipping dock to the carpentry shop, crating/uncrating room, galleries, and collections storerooms. Door openings, freight elevators, and corridor heights, widths, and corner configurations must be uniformly large to accommodate movement of exhibit materials. Placement of ducts and piping must be carefully coordinated to avoid bottlenecks.

Registration

The registrar generally is responsible for handling all museum objects, keeping track of their location within the museum, and maintaining records about each object, whether owned by the museum or loaned as part of a temporary exhibition. These activities require office and workspace, facilities for extensive paper files and computer operations, and sometimes space for temporary object storage.

Matting and Framing

The matting and framing area must be a cleanroom furnished with work tables and storage for materials. Minor conservation procedures also may take place here if the museum does not have a conservation laboratory.

Conservation Laboratories

Most small museums do not have conservation labs. Larger museums, however, may have extensive facilities, including separate laboratories for specialized conservation procedures such as those required for paintings, sculpture, three-dimensional decorative arts, textiles, cars, industrial machinery, fossils, taxidermy, or anthropological artifacts. Each kind of conservation requires special facilities and equipment.

Museum Storage

Collections storage and general storage serve different functions within the museum. General storage space can be located in back-of-the-house areas. Collections storage, however, must meet the most exacting security and climate control requirements and must be correctly located.

General Storage

Museums require large amounts of miscellaneous material that must be stored. General storage areas accommodate building and office supplies, museum store inventory, furniture, exhibition casework, equipment, and other items relating to the museum operation.

Collections Storage

Collections storerooms must be clean, dry, secure, well lighted, free of overhead pipes containing liquids, and properly air conditioned to meet conservation climate control standards. They must be located conveniently near shipping and receiving, curatorial offices, registration, and other collections management facilities. Minimizing the possibility of flooding or other water damage is essential. Whether collections storage is separated into discrete rooms or centralized in large open vaults depends on the nature of the collections and on administrative policies about staff responsibilities. Provision for growth of the collections is critical. Security for collections storage is a priority.

Collections Storage Equipment

Types and quantities of storage units and the required floor area must be determined by analysis of the collections in conjunction with the collections management staff. Space must be provided for storage of materials-handling equipment and shelving, files, specialized racks, specimen cabinets, and oversized objects storage areas. Many museum objects are kept in containers, such as acid-free boxes, solander boxes, textile screens, and rolled textile tubes, which are placed in or on the storage units.

High-Density Storage Systems

High-density storage systems, also referred to as *compact storage systems,* are composed of rolling shelving units. A substantially higher density of objects may be stored than in traditional storage units. These systems, though efficient, are costly, and may inhibit the capability of fire suppression systems to extinguish flames inside the collections storage units when in the closed position. They require either depressed floor construction, for built-in recessed floor tracks, or ramps, for the surface installation of tracks. Structural systems will be impacted due to the weight of potential stored materials. If future compact storage systems are anticipated, the design of the storage space, materials to be stored, and structural loading capacity should be reviewed.

MUSEUM LIGHTING

Public Areas

Lighting in museum public areas differs from lighting in gallery areas. The hours of operation may affect lighting types; evening functions may require lighting effects and levels not utilized during daylight hours. Public areas generally do not contain exhibits, so the use of natural light is acceptable if the galleries are distinctly separate from these spaces.

Lighting for Art

The two principal methods for lighting art are uniform illumination and nonuniform illumination.

- *Uniform lighting* for all vertical surfaces that will receive art allows viewers to select their own focus. It is possible to change objects without readjusting the lighting equipment.
- *Nonuniform lighting* focuses light on individual objects while leaving the surround in comparative darkness, creating a dramatic environment. Every time the art changes, the lighting equipment requires readjustment.

In a space that will have frequently changing exhibits and nonuniform illumination, a flexible lighting system is appropriate. Track systems are often used due to the ease of locating and aiming the track luminaries.

Excellent color rendering is essential for the proper appreciation of the objects. Continuous-spectrum, high-color-rendering sources allow the art to be viewed under spectral distribution conditions similar to those under which it was created.

The artwork medium, surface texture, type of frame, and enclosure (glass or plastic) of an object are considered in artwork lighting. For flat works mounted on a horizontal surface, the optimum placement for a light source is usually at an angle of 30° from nadir (straight down) to eye level (5 ft 6 in. [1,676 mm] above the finished floor, on average).

An aiming angle of less than 30° (more nearly vertical) causes shadows from the frame and distortion of the object due to exaggeration of the texture. An aiming angle greater than 30° (more nearly horizontal) results in reflected glare from the surface of the object, washing out the detail. This greater angle will also cause viewers to be standing in their own shadow and will cause the luminaire to be a source of glare to others.

The way three-dimensional objects are lighted also affects the viewer's perception of the piece. Concentrated beams create higher contrast and deeper shadows, emphasizing form and texture. Frontal lighting between 30° and 45° from horizontal, and between 30° and 45° from vertical, models objects in a manner that best replicates sunlight.

Lighting a vertical surface behind an object provides a luminous backdrop that serves to separate the object visually from its background. Lighting the object from the side as well as from above provides added dimension to the piece.

Reversing the expected relationship of highlight and shadow, and lighting an object from a less conventional angle, disturbs perception. Uplighting creates an ominously ghoulish impression; backlighting leaves an object in silhouette.

CONSERVATION OF MATERIALS

Conservation of materials is a fundamental concern in the lighting of art. All organic material is susceptible to pigment change and weakening of strength from exposure to light and heat. These materials include paper, cotton, linen, parchment, leather, silk, wool, feathers, hair, dyes, oils, glues, gums, and resins; and because of similarities in chemical structure, most synthetic dyes and plastics.

Damage is related to wavelength. Ultraviolet (UV) radiation causes more damage, but more visible radiation is present in all light sources, including daylight. A material that is fairly "fast" (more stable), such as the oil in paintings, will be changed mainly by UV radiation. More sensitive dyes and pigments, which are damaged either by UV or visible radiation, will be changed mainly by the visible radiation, since it is more plentiful.

Design tips for artwork conservation include:

- Minimize daylight exposure and apply UV filter films to windows where necessary.
- Ensure that all electric sources are fitted with UV filters, especially those other than incandescent.
- Maintain general display lighting levels for moderately sensitive materials, such as oil and tempera paintings, lacquers, undyed leathers, ivory, and bone, at 15 fc (150 lux) or less.
- Maintain general display lighting levels for extremely sensitive materials such as pen-and-ink drawings, prints, watercolors, tapestries, textiles, costumes, and manuscripts, at 5 fc (50 lux) or less.
- Minimize display exposure time whenever practical to lessen any potential degradation.
- Carefully control the intensity of all forms of light. Discuss lighting intensities with a qualified conservator.

Lighting in Collections Storerooms

Lighting in collections storerooms should provide adequate illumination for handling and examination of objects, while protecting them from unnecessary exposure to ultraviolet light and visible radiation. Lighting may be switched so that general light is provided for safe passage in aisles; additional light can be switched on when required.

Fluorescent lighting must be provided with UV shielding. Indirect systems that reflect light from a painted white ceiling containing titanium dioxide will greatly reduce the UV component and result in even light distribution. Light from high-pressure sodium bulbs contains almost no ultraviolet light; however, color discrimination is difficult in this light.

MUSEUM EXHIBIT OBJECT MAXIMUM LIGHTING LEVELS

OBJECTS SENSITIVE TO LIGHT MAXIMUM 5 FC (50 LUX*)	OBJECTS LESS SENSITIVE TO LIGHT MAXIMUM 20 FC (200 LUX)	OBJECTS INSENSITIVE TO LIGHT MAXIMUM 30 FC (300 LUX)
Textiles	Oil and tempera paintings	Metal
Tapestries	Undyed leather	Stone
Costumes	Horn	Glass
Watercolors	Bone	Ceramics
Gouache	Ivory	Jewelry
Prints	Oriental lacquer	Enamel
Drawings		
Manuscripts		
Miniatures		
Paintings in distemper media		
Wallpapers		
Dyed leather		
Most natural history exhibits, including botanical specimens, fur, and feathers		

*Lumen: Measured light striking a display surface; 1 footcandle = 1 lumen = 10.76 lux.

Source: Gary R. Steffy, Architectural Lighting Design, 2nd Ed.; New York: John Wiley & Sons, Inc., 2001.

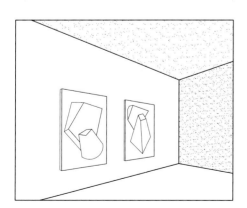

UNIFORM WALLWASHING FOR ARTWORK

NONUNIFORM ACCENT LIGHTING FOR ARTWORK

AVERAGE EYE HEIGHT 5'-6" (1676)   30°

OPTIMUM AIMING ANGLES

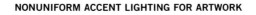

GALLERY LIGHTING
Source: Gary Gordon, and James L. Nuckolls, Interior Lighting for Designers, 3rd Ed.; New York: John Wiley & Sons, Inc., 1995.

MUSEUM ACOUSTICS

Museum acoustics vary within the different space types. Acoustics in museums may be less of a consideration than light control, flexibility, and ease of maintenance. Isolate noisy back-of-the-house spaces from the public areas of the museum. Isolate areas that are susceptible to vibration as well as noise.

The HVAC NC/RC range for mechanical equipment noise should be 25 in small to medium-sized spaces, and up to 30 in large galleries. Reverberation is generally well tolerated, unless the space is to be used for seminars or meetings. For auditorium spaces, reverberation time should be 0.8 seconds or less.

MUSEUM SECURITY

Effective museum security is the result of thorough museum planning, quality lock and alarm systems, and vigilant professional and security staff practices. A specialized museum security consultant can assist the museum staff and the designer with these issues.

Security for the museum building and exhibit space should be achieved by:

• Physically resistant construction
• Electronic systems to deter and detect theft and vandalism
• Constant human presence or a rapid human response if alarms are triggered

Planning for security involves understanding the zones that must be kept separate, and how public, staff, and objects will move through the museum. When entering and leaving the galleries, the public should be required to pass through one easy-to-monitor checkpoint. Nongallery public functions (such as auditoriums, museum shops, or toilets) should not be accessible through the galleries. When closed, galleries should function as secure vaults. Emergency fire exits from galleries should be minimal, alarmed, and easy to locate.

SECURITY STATION AT SHIPPING AND STAFF ENTRANCE

Staff areas should be clearly separated from galleries and public services. Shipping and receiving and staff entrances must be tightly monitored and easily controlled by the security staff. Collections storerooms should be treated as vaults and should not contain any mechanical or electrical equipment that might require access for maintenance or in emergencies. Mechanical ductwork and grilles must be designed to prevent access by burglars to locked galleries and collection storerooms.

Alarm Systems

Electronic alarm systems should be designed by professionals who specialize in museum security systems. Such specialized professionals also should be consulted with regard to locking systems. Often, alarm system work is not part of the general construction contract for reasons of confidentiality. A source of backup power may be desirable. The issue of security should be reviewed with appropriate museum authorities.

Public and Staff Access

Public and staff movement through the museum must be carefully separated. There should be only one public and one staff/shipping entrance to the museum. Public and staff areas will be open at different times, and each should be securable when not open. Public service areas, such as the lobby, museum store, restrooms, and food service areas, should be easily accessible during open hours.

Ideally, there should be only one point of access to the galleries from the public services area. Access from public to staff areas should be strictly limited and easily monitored. Staff should not need to move through galleries when they are closed. The staff entrance and shipping and receiving dock should be together and be easy to monitor and control by security personnel.

Ancillary Spaces

Auditoriums, theaters, and food service facilities present special service access problems because they operate on different schedules from other museum functions, and these operations may conflict with the museum's needs for security and cleanliness. Separate service access for these facilities may be appropriate.

Security Station

In most small and medium-sized museums, the central security station should be located at the service entrance with secure windows opening to the outdoors, to the shipping and receiving room, and to a staff entrance sallyport. In large museums, the central station may be in a more secure location away from all entrances, with a shipping clerk's station at the service entrance.

CLIMATE CONTROL

Determine whether the entire building or only areas containing collections items (galleries and collections storerooms) will be maintained at conservation standards. If the conservation-standard areas are limited, the rest of the building can be treated like any other public building. Adequate physical separations, including vapor barriers, must be provided between conservation and human comfort zones.

Humidity Control

Control of relative humidity (RH) is the single most critical factor in museum environments. Although ideal conditions vary for different kinds of collections, desirable RH for most museum objects is approximately 50%. This level must be held constant at all times. However, maintenance of 50% relative humidity throughout the winter months in cold climates tends to produce severe condensation on windows and within the exterior wall construction. Prevention of condensation requires installation of vapor barriers and insulation systems. A completely continuous *zero perm* vapor barrier system is essential. In this context, zero perm means a permeability rating of less than .01 grains of water per square foot per hour per inch of mercury vapor pressure, in accordance with ASTM E96, *Standard Test Methods for Water Vapor Transmission of Materials,* test procedure A, B, or BW.

In cold-climate situations, it may be determined that installation of zero perm vapor barriers and required mechanical equipment is impossible or impractical. The alternate approach is to design the wall and roof systems to permit one slow, controlled cycle per year, varying from about 25% RH in winter to about 50% in summer. Hourly, daily, or weekly fluctuations must be avoided under any circumstances.

Air Filtration

Requirements for air filtration vary depending on the quality of the outside air and the conservation demands of the museum objects to be housed. Generally, an acceptable choice would be bag filters with disposable prefilters, UL Rating Class 1; that is, particulates removed to 95% efficiency on ASHRAE 52/76. Electrostatic filters must not be used because they produce destructive ozone. Activate carbon filters are effective in removing gaseous pollutants, but they are expensive and require active maintenance.

Operating Cycles

Heating and cooling loads vary greatly between occupied galleries (with lights and people) and unoccupied ones (closed and dark). When unoccupied, systems should be designed to operate at a low maintenance level.

Location of Piping, Outlets, Switches, and Controls

All piping containing liquids should be kept out of areas containing museum objects. Plumbing should not be located above galleries and collections storerooms.

All convenience outlets, switches, HVAC thermostats, humidistats, and other control devices must be kept off gallery walls. Outlets should be in the base and in the floor. Switches should be remote. Thermostats and humidistats can be located in return air ducts.

Tim Shea, AIA; Richard Meier & Partners; Los Angeles, California
Douglas Flandro; Rhode Island School of Design; Providence, Rhode Island
Tam Youngcharoen; Rhode Island School of Design; Providence, Rhode Island
John D. Hilberry, AIA; John D. Hilberry & Associates, Inc., Architects and Museum Planners; Detroit, Michigan

FIRE SUPPRESSION

Options for fire suppression systems for museum use that cause limited or no damage to artifacts have increased thanks to technological advances and innovations. Recent technologies, including *water mist systems* and *gaseous agents,* were originally designed to protect expensive electronic devices in demanding industrial or military environments. Traditional *deluge systems* have an exemplary reliability and effectiveness record, although their discharge can result in significant damage to artifacts. In addition, *fire detection systems* are now available that can detect a fire in its incipient precombustion phase.

Deluge Systems

Deluge systems include wet pipe, dry pipe, preaction, and other traditional systems. The more simple systems, such as wet pipe and dry pipe, have a high degree of reliability and are effective in extinguishing fires as long as a fire suppression head can direct a water stream onto a flame. These systems, though effective, can create significant collateral damage to artifacts as the water stream drenches a surface, because most materials are susceptible to water damage. In addition, iron oxides found in piping are discharged when the system is activated. Dry pipe systems discharge more iron oxide than wet pipe systems. Deluge systems operate under relatively low water pressure.

Mist Systems

Mist systems include both fog and water mist. They atomize relatively small amounts of water into fine mist or dense fog; the difference between them is the size of the water droplet. The atomized water droplets act more like a gas than a liquid and are induced to combustion sources; that is, the heads do not need to point at a combustion source as in deluge systems; the mist will move to a combustion source. These systems release much less water and cause significantly less damage than deluge systems. However, dissolved salts found in water can dry onto artifacts and require removal.

Mist systems cool fires primarily by the latent heat of vaporization; that is, the water droplets turn to steam and cool a fire. In addition, the steam helps to smother a fire by displacing fire in the vicinity of the fire. The discharge of a mist system must result in enough fog to extinguish a fire, hence can be disorienting to the people who are seeking exit from the room. The efficacy of the systems is difficult to predict when multiple rooms open onto one another or when a door or window is open.

Mist systems operate under relatively high water pressure. They are typically more expensive to install than deluge systems. However, their piping is much smaller in diameter than those found in deluge systems and may cause less disruption to an existing structure than the piping found in deluge systems.

Gaseous Agents

Gaseous agents, also known as *clean agents,* are effective in extinguishing fires, especially in a contained environment. In part, they have been developed as a substitute for halon. The systems include FM-200, inergen, FE-13, and carbon dioxide. Combined with a sensitive air-sampling smoke detection system, these systems can extinguish a fire in its incipient phase. Gases used in this type of suppression continue to be developed and tested. These systems typically do not cause damage to artifacts when discharged, which makes them particularly attractive for museum and curatorial environments. FM-200 absorbs large amounts of heat energy from the surface of a burning material. Inergen consists of nitrogen, argon, and carbon dioxide; it lowers the oxygen content below the level that supports combustion, but is appropriate for use in occupied areas. Carbon dioxide systems displace oxygen, so their use is not appropriate for occupied areas.

The system components include gas storage tanks, pressurization tanks, piping, and heads. Many of these systems are relatively large and bulky. The gas storage tanks must be refilled after discharge, and the cost varies among systems. FM-200, for example, is much more expensive than inergen to recharge. In addition, FM-200 cannot be valved to serve multiple rooms, while inergen can. FM-200 tends to cost less to install if it is serving one enclosed room. FE-13 nozzles can be installed up to 25 ft (7.6 m) high, compared with 12 ft (3.6 m) for FM-200. FE-13 is also effective at temperatures down to 40°F (4.4°C); inergen is effective to 32°F (0°C). The installation cost of these systems is about two to three times that of deluge systems.

Fire Detection Systems

Fire detection systems include standard ionization smoke detectors, rate-of-rise heat detection, beam detectors, and sensitive air-sampling detection systems. Air-sampling systems can detect fire in their incipient phase prior to ignition, and this characteristic has two primary benefits: They can provide an early warning and prevent deluge systems from discharging prematurely, and they can activate mist or gaseous systems to extinguish a fire before significant damage occurs. The system includes PVC piping and some type of spectrum analyzer. The piping must be installed to each air-sampling location, and this can be a relatively cumbersome process in comparison with wired or wireless detection heads found in ionization smoke detection systems.

COMPARISON OF FIRE SUPPRESSION SYSTEMS SERVING CURATORIAL STORAGE

SYSTEMS	DELUGE SYSTEMS			MIST SYSTEMS		GASEOUS AGENTS			
DESCRIPTION OF FIRE SUPPRESSION	WET PIPE	DRY PIPE	PREACTION SYSTEMS	FOG SYSTEMS	MIST SYSTEMS	FM 200 SYSTEM	INERGEN	CO₂	FE-13
Selection Criteria: Damage to Artifacts									
Organic									
Cellulose	High	High	High	Moderate	Moderate	None	None	None	None
Inorganic									
Ferrous Metal	High	High	High	Moderate	Moderate	None	None	None	None
Mixed Media	High	High	High	Moderate	Moderate	None	None	None	None
System Complexity	Simple	Moderate	Complex	Moderate	Moderate	Moderate	Moderate	Moderate	Moderate
Effectiveness in Enclosed Room	High	High	High	High	High	Moderate	Moderate	Moderate	Moderate
Effectiveness in Open Room	High	High	High	High	High	High	High	High	High
Effectiveness in Multiple Open Rooms	High	High	High	Difficult to predict	Difficult to predict	Low	Low	Low	Low
Installation Cost	Low	Low	Moderate	High	High	High	High	High	High
Maintenance and Recharge Cost	Low	Low	Moderate	Moderate	Moderate	High	Moderate	Moderate	Moderate
Comments	Relatively simple to install; water is under pressure.	Piping must slope to drain. Initial water output contains iron oxides. Must drench surfaces.	Requires two sources of detection to alarm simultaneously. Can be wet or dry pipe.	Leaves dissolved salt deposits. Seeks combustion source.	Leaves dissolved salt deposits. Seeks combustion source.	Does not displace oxygen. Separate systems required to protect multiple rooms. Very expensive to recharge. Acceptable for use in occupied areas.	Displaces oxygen but safe for human exposure. Can be valved for multiple rooms. Acceptable for use in occupied areas.	Displaces oxygen. Not for use in occupied areas.	Does not displace significant amounts of oxygen. Acceptable for use in occupied areas.

Jeffrey Meese, AIA; Cambridge, Massachusetts

PERFORMANCE THEATERS AND REHEARSAL HALLS

PLANNING CRITERIA

The term *theater* originates from the Greek verb *theatai,* meaning to see or behold. Originally places of social ceremony as well as entertainment, modern theaters are designed to support the type of performances presented within the space. Some theaters are used for one purpose, but more commonly, multiple presentation styles must be accommodated within one space.

Theaters for music and dramatic performances are among the most complex building types, particularly with regard to the interior functions and acoustics. Audience sight lines, layout, seating capacity, aisles, exiting, size and type of performance areas, and acoustical volume guidelines determine interior design constraints.

Acoustics and lighting are of primary importance, and accommodation must be made for audiences that may be seated for several hours. Acoustical and lighting consultants are typically involved in theater projects. Testing of the acoustical design properties of the theater is critical to ensure that the acoustical calculations are appropriate to the actual space.

The circulation flow in a theater must be obvious and easy to navigate. Public spaces, including the lobby and auditorium, are separate from performance/back-of-house areas.

Life Safety

Theaters are considered assembly spaces, therefore emergency exiting and general life safety issues are critical in theaters. Consult applicable building codes for local jurisdiction requirements.

Interior Construction

Box-in-a-box construction may be used for the most critical spaces, with lobbies, galleries, promenades, and so on, acting as buffer zones between the interior envelope and the exterior building skin. Interior construction should attempt to reach STC 60-plus if the exterior construction is at least STC 50.

Heavy concrete and masonry construction tends to be more forgiving of noise and vibration transmission problems than lightweight, long-span steel construction. A more successful acoustically isolated theater is generally a result of a more substantial structure and partitioning system.

The circulation flow in a theater must be obvious and easy to navigate. Public spaces, including the lobby and auditorium, are separate from performance/back-of-house areas.

THEATER ADJACENCY DIAGRAM

PRINCIPAL WESTERN THEATER FORMS AND CHRONOLOGY
ANCIENT

PRIMITIVE

GREEK ARCHAIC
(IKRIA)

GREEK CLASSICAL

GRECO-HELLENISTIC

ROMAN

GRECO-ROMAN
ODEUM

CLASSICAL: UP TO 400 AD

MODERN

SINGLE-VISTA STAGE
(SERLIO)

MULTIPLE-VISTA
STAGE (PALLADIO)

PROSCENIUM STAGE
(ALLIOTTI)

THEATER OF
SHAKESPEARE

GRANDE SALLE

☐ AUDITORIUM

▨ ORCHESTRA

▦ STAGE

LATE RENAISSANCE: 1550 TO 1650

HORSESHOE-SHAPED
AUDITORIUM
PROSCENIUM STAGE

THEATER OF THE
RESTORATION

FAN-SHAPED
AUDITORIUM
PROSCENIUM STAGE

FAN-SHAPED AUDITORIUM
PROSCENIUM, APRON,
CALIPER STAGE

PARTIALLY ENVELOPING
AUDITORIUM
THRUST STAGE

FULLY ENVELOPING
AUDITORIUM
IN-THE-ROUND STAGE

BAROQUE, NEO-BAROQUE: 1650 TO 1870   CONTEMPORARY: 1870 TO 1970

Source: George C. Izenour, Theatre Design, *2nd Ed.; New Haven, CT: Yale University Press; 1996, p. 33.*

THEATER VIEWING ANGLE

Orientation of Seated Spectator

Orienting chairs or rows of chairs so that the spectators face the center of action of the performing area minimizes head strain.

Angle of Vision of Spectator

The human eye has a peripheral spread of vision of about 130°. This angle of view from chairs in the front rows will define the outer limits of the maximum-sized performing area.

Angle of Encounter

The angle of encounter is defined by the 130° peripheral spread of vision of a single performer standing at the "point of command." Patrons seated outside the spread of this angle will not have eye contact with the performer.

Distance between Performance and Last Row of Spectators

Minimizing this distance while satisfying the preceding parameters enhances achievement of visual and sound communication.

130°

ANGLE OF ENCOUNTER

POINT OF
COMMAND

ANGLE OF ENCOUNTER

VIEWING ANGLE

STAGE

APRON

AISLE   SEATING   SEATING   AISLE

AMERICAN SEATING

STAGE

APRON

AISLE   AUDIENCE
SEATING   AISLE

CONTINENTAL SEATING

PROSCENIUM ARCH

PROSCENIUM THEATER SECTION

Source: J. Michael Gillette, Theatrical Design and Production; *Mountain View, CA: Mayfield Publishing Company, 1992.*

THEATER CONFIGURATIONS

The plan configuration of a theater should respond to the type of performances anticipated. The basic types of theater configurations include those planned for projected images, a proscenium stage (zero encirclement), 90° to 130° encirclement, 180° to 270° encirclement, and 360° encirclement. The same seating area is shown for each of the theater configurations on this page.

ZERO ENCIRCLEMENT

180° TO 270° ENCIRCLEMENT

SCREEN PROJECTION

90° TO 130° ENCIRCLEMENT

360° ENCIRCLEMENT

Screen Projection

The following design considerations apply to a theater configured for images projected on a screen:

- The minimum distance between the first row and the screen (D$_F$) is determined by the maximum allowable angle between the sight line from the first row to the top of the screen and the perpendicular to the screen at that point. A maximum angle of 30° to 35° is recommended.
- The maximum distance between the screen and the most distant viewer (MDV) should not exceed eight times the height of the screen image. An MDV two to three times the screen width is preferred.
- Screen width (W) is determined by the use of the appropriate aspect ratio between the screen image width and height.
- Curvature of screens may reduce the amount of apparent distortion for a larger audience area. Curvature of larger screens may help to keep the whole of the image in focus and may provide a more uniform distribution of luminance.

Zero Encirclement (Proscenium Stage, Picture Frame Stage, End Stage)

The following design considerations apply to a theater configured for zero encirclement:

- The angle of audience spread in front of a masking frame is determined by the maximum size of the corner cutoff from a rectangular-shaped performing area that can be tolerated by seats at the side.
- Audience may not fill angle of encounter from point of command.
- Audience is farthest from performing area.
- There is a large range in size of performing area.
- Provides for a large amount of scenic wall surfaces without masking sight lines.
- Horizontal movement of scenery is possible, perpendicular and parallel to centerline.
- Possibility exists of short differences in arrival time between direct and reflected sound at the spectator, which may be beneficial to music performances.

90° to 130° Encirclement (Pictorial Open Stage, Wide Fan, Hybrid, Thrust Stage)

The following design considerations apply to a theater configured for 90° to 130° encirclement:

- Audience spread is defined and limited by angle of encounter from point of command.
- Performing area shape is trapezoidal, rhombic, or circular.
- Audience is closer to performing area than with zero encirclement.
- Picture frame is less dominant.
- There is a range in choice of size of performing area.
- Provision for an amount of scenic wall surfaces is possible without obscuring the performing area.
- Horizontal movement of scenery is possible in directions at 45° to and parallel to centerline.
- Shape of seating area places maximum number of seats within the directional limits of the sound of the unaided voice, which is beneficial for speech performance.

180° to 270° Encirclement (Greek Theater, Peninsular, Three-Sided, Thrust Stage, Three-Fourths Arena Stage, Elizabethan Stage)

The following design considerations apply to a theater configured for 180° to 270° encirclement:

- Audience spread is well beyond angle of encounter from point of command in order to bring audience closer to performing area.
- Simultaneous eye contact between performer and all spectators is not possible.
- There is a minimum range of choice in size of performing area.
- Provision of small amount of scenic wall surfaces is possible without masking sight lines.
- Horizontal movement of scenery is only possible parallel to centerline.
- Large encirclement by audience usually demands actor vomitory entrance through or under audience.

360° Encirclement (Arena Stage, Theater-in-the Round, Island Stage, Center Stage)

The following design considerations apply to a theater configured for 360° encirclement:

- Performer is always seen from rear by some spectators.
- Simultaneous eye contact between performer and all spectators is not possible.
- Audience is closest to performance.
- No range of choice is available in size of performing area.
- No scenic wall surfaces are possible without obscuring the view of the performing area.
- Horizontal movement of scenery is not readily possible.
- Encirclement by audience demands actor vomitory entrance through audience area.

LIVE PERFORMANCE THEATERS

7'-0" CLEAR

2 1/2 TO 3 TIMES OPENING RECOMMENDED FROM FLOOR TO GRID

GRID IRON

STAGEHOUSE NEEDED FOR CHANGING AND STORAGE OF SCENERY

CONVEX AND IRREGULAR SURFACES AID SOUND DIFFUSION; DOMES, VAULTS, AND OTHER LARGE CONCAVE SURFACES MAY CAUSE ACOUSTICAL PROBLEMS

HIGHER CEILING FOR LONGER REVERBERATION TIME AS REQUIRED FOR CONCERTS: TYP. HALL VOLUME 220-380 CU FT PER AUDIENCE SEAT

LOWER CEILING FOR SHORTER REVERBERATION TIME AS REQUIRED FOR DRAMA AND SPEECH: TYP. HALL VOLUME 80-150 CU. FT. PER AUDIENCE SEAT

PROJECTION BOOTH

MONAURAL SOUND REINFORCEMENT SYSTEM SPEAKER CLUSTER-LOCATE ON CENTERLINE OF HALL

LOW-FREQUENCY ENCLOSURE

HIGH-FREQUENCY DRIVERS AND HORNS

LIGHTING CATWALKS

BORDERS

45° TYP.

ALLOW ROOM FOR ACOUSTICAL TREATMENT

ACOUSTICAL TRANSPARENT SPEAKER ENCLOSURE

HARD ENCLOSURE FOR CONCERTS

SEE INDEX FOR "THEATER SITE LINES"

TYP. LIMITS OF SPACE REQUIRED FOR DRAMA

D

H

TYP. STAGE OPENING FOR OPERA AND DANCE 18'-30'

8'-0" MAX.

ORCHESTRA PIT AREA 10-14 SQ. FT. PER MUSICIAN

LAST ROW UNDER BALCONY SHOULD HAVE CLEAR SIGHT LINE TO SPEAKER CLUSTER

TYP. STAGE OPENING FOR DRAMA 12'-18'

TYP. STAGE OPENING FOR CONCERTS 24'-40'

3'-0" TO 8'-0" TYP.

EDGE OF APRON TO BE THIN AS POSSIBLE

In performance halls used for concerts, the stage and audience seating area should be treated as one volume. In multiple-use halls, this condition is achieved with a hard orchestra shell, which must be demountable to allow for full use of the stage for scenery and stage sets. Acoustical requirements may dictate that reflective surfaces at the ceiling of the orchestra enclosure extend out above audience seating.

CONFIGURATIONS FOR LIVE PERFORMANCES

PROSCENIUM STAGES

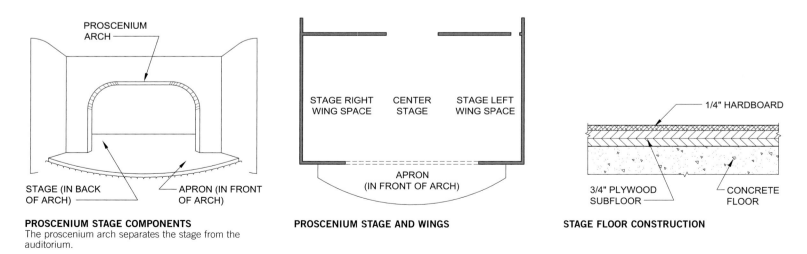

PROSCENIUM ARCH

STAGE (IN BACK OF ARCH)

APRON (IN FRONT OF ARCH)

PROSCENIUM STAGE COMPONENTS
The proscenium arch separates the stage from the auditorium.

STAGE RIGHT WING SPACE   CENTER STAGE   STAGE LEFT WING SPACE

APRON (IN FRONT OF ARCH)

PROSCENIUM STAGE AND WINGS

1/4" HARDBOARD

3/4" PLYWOOD SUBFLOOR

CONCRETE FLOOR

STAGE FLOOR CONSTRUCTION

PROSCENIUM STAGE

HEATER SIGHT LINES

C = 5" C = 2 1/2"

$H_E = 44"$ (TYP.)

BALCONY - CONSTANT RISE PER ROW

$R = \frac{T}{D_B}[E_B + (N - 1) C] + C$

$D_B = \frac{T}{R-C}[E_B + (N - 1) C]$

$E_B = \frac{D_B}{T}(R - C) - C (N - 1)$

E_B

D_B

30° MAX.

NOTE: BALCONY MAY ALSO BE DESIGNED WITH AN ISCIDOMAL SLOPE

D_6
D_5
D_4
D_3
D_2
D_1

T

H_E

E_6
E_5
E_4
E_3
E_2
E_1

C

n = 6
n = 5
n = 4
n = 3
n = 2
n = 1

R_5
R_2

APS 2" ABOVE STAGE

$E_n = D_n[\frac{E_1}{D_1} + C (\frac{1}{D_1} + \frac{1}{D_2} + \frac{1}{D_3} + \ldots + \frac{1}{D_{n - 1}})]$

$R_n = E_n - E_{n - 1}$

MAXIMUM STAGE HEIGHT FOR LIVE PERFORMANCES = 42" ($E_1 = 0$)

APS = Arrival of point of sight (focal point or intersection of highest sight line with focal plane)
N = Number of rows in seat bank
n = Row number for which computations are being made
D_1 = Horizontal distance from APS to first-row eye position
D_n = Horizontal distance from APS to eye position at row n

D_b = Horizontal distance from APS to eye position at front of row of balcony
L = Horizontal distance from first-row eye position to a vertical focal plane
E_1 = levation of eye level at first row above APS
E_n = Elevation of eye level at row n above APS
H_E = Eye height of seated person (44 in. typical; 1,117 mm)

H_{APS} = Height of APS above first-row floor level
C = Sight line head clearance, 2½ in. (63 mm) to see over two rows in front; 5 in. (127 mm) to see over one row in front
T = Row-to-row spacing (tread)
R = Riser height between rows
R_n = Riser height at front of row n
P = Percent slope

ISCIDOMAL (EQUAL SEEING) FLOOR SLOPE

SEE LOCAL CODE FOR REQUIRED HEIGHT (26" TO 30" TYP.)

KEEP HEIGHT OF SOLID RAILING BELOW SIGHT LINE FROM FRONT-ROW

BALCONY RAILING

T

T

20" MAX.

DATUM OR CHAIR SIZE LINE

VARIES

3'-8" EYE LEVEL

PLUMB LINE CLEARANCE (SEE NOTE)

8 1/2" ±
15 1/2" ±
6" ±
17" ±

ANGLE VARIES

PITCH VARIES
8 1/4" TYP. MAX.
5 1/4" TYP. MIN.
6 3/4", 7 1/2" STANDARD

END PANEL AVAILABLE FOR MOST CHAIRS

1" RECOMMENDED FROM BACK WALL OR RAIL FOR STANDEE

CHAIR WIDTH

FLOOR MOUNTED CHAIR

RISER-MOUNTED CHAIR

VARIES

SEAT SPACING

THEATER SIGHT LINES

FLOOR SLOPE WITH CONSTANT RISE PER ROW

SLIGHTLY SLOPED FLOOR—VERTICAL FOCAL PLANE

SEATING AREA DESIGN

Seating Area Efficiency

The floor area efficiency in square feet per seat is a function of the row spacing, the average chair width, and the space allocation per seat for aisles.

Efficiency (F) = seat factor + aisle factor

$$F \text{ [sq ft/seat]} = (W_sT)/(144) + (IT)/(144) \times (1)/(S_{avg})$$

where:

W_s = average seat width (in.)
T = row-to-row spacing (tread) (in.)
I = average aisle width (in.) (42 in. (1,067 mm) width is typical)
S_{avg} = average number of seats in a row per single aisle: 8 or fewer—inefficient layout; 14 to 16—maximum efficiency (multiple-aisle seating); 18 to 50 and more—continental seating.

Seating Capacity and Audience Area

Audience area = capacity × efficiency

SEATING CAPACITY AND AUDIENCE AREA TYPE

SEATING CAPACITY	THEATER TYPE
35–75	Classroom
75–150	Lecture room, experimental theater
150–300	Large lecture room, small theater
300–750	Average drama theater in educational setting
750–1,500	Small commercial theater, repertory theater, recital hall
1,500–2,000	Medium-large theater, large commercial theater
2,000–3,000	Average civic theater, concert hall, multiple-use hall
3,000–6,000	Very large auditorium
More than 6,000	Special assembly facilities

PERFORMING AREA

	MINIMUM SQ FT (SQ M)	AVERAGE SQ FT (SQ M)	MAXIMUM SQ FT (SQ M)
Lectures (single speaker)	150 (13.9)	240 (22.3)	500 (46.5)
Revue, nightclub	350 (32.5)	450 (41.8)	700 (65)
Legitimate drama	250 (23.2)	550 (51.1)	1,000 (92.9)
Dance	700 (65)	950 (88.3)	1,200 (111.5)
Musicals, folk opera	800 (74.3)	1,200 (111.5)	1,800 (167.2)
Symphonic concerts	1,500 (139.4)	2,000 (185.8)	2,500 (232.3)
Opera	1,000 (92.9)	2,500 (232.3)	4,000 (371.6)
Pageant	2,000 (185.8)	3,500 (325.2)	5,000 (464.5)

THEATER SEATING

Standard Seating Materials

Standard seating frame types include cast iron or steel, riser-mounted, or floor-mounted standards. Pedestal-mounted standards using continuous beam support or cantilevered standards are also available, and a folding tablet arm is usually available.

Chair arms may be of upholstered fabric, wood, plastic, or metal. Chair backs may be constructed of plastic, molded plywood, or rolled-stamped metal, or be upholstered front and rear. Higher backs and bottom extensions for scuff protection are also available. Chair seats may be upholstered, or of plywood, plastic, metal pan, coil or serpentine springs, or polyurethane foam.

Row to Row Spacing Criteria

Consult local codes for required minimum row spacing. Codes typically stipulate a minimum clear plumb line distance measured between the unoccupied chair and the rear of the back of the chair in front, as follows:

- 32 to 33 in. (813 to 838 mm): Typical minimum for multiple-aisle seating.
- 34 to 37 in. (864 to 940 mm): Typical minimum for modified continental seating.
- 38 to 42 in. (965 to 1,067 mm): Typical minimum for continental seating.

Comfort for the Seated Person

Guidelines for enough leg room to provide seated comfort are as follows:

- 32 in. (813 mm): Knees will touch chair back; uncomfortable
- 34 in. (864 mm): Minimum spacing for comfort.
- 36 in. (914 mm): Ideal spacing for maximum comfort.
- 38 in. (965 mm) and up: Audience cohesiveness may suffer.

Ease of Passage in Front of Seated Persons

Guidelines for spacing seats to provide comfortable passage in front of seated patrons are as follows:

- 32 to 34 in. (813 to 864 mm): Seated person must rise to allow passage.
- 36 to 38 in. (914 to 965 mm): Some seated persons will rise.
- 40 in. (1,016 mm) and up: Passage in front of seated persons possible

Safety

Excessive plumb line distance may entice exiting persons to squeeze ahead and cause a jam. Consult applicable codes for aisle and exit path widths.

Efficiency

Minimum seat row spacing reduces maximum distance to stage.

MULTIPLE-AISLE SEATING

CONTINENTAL SEATING

THEATER ACOUSTICS

Acoustical Considerations

Theaters and performance spaces are rooms in which good hearing conditions are critical to the use of the space and exchange of aural information. The design of a performance space generally requires input from an acoustical consultant.

Loudness

Sound generated by speakers or musicians should be projected efficiently to the audience and captured within the space. The *sending end* of the room (i.e., the stage) should be acoustically hard. Walls near the performer should be angled or splayed to enhance projection and prevent *flutter echoes* at the stage. Walls and ceilings in the audience area should be hard so they can reflect sound, unless absorptive treatment is needed to eliminate problematic reflections or focusing or to reduce reverberation time (RT) for particular program needs.

Quiet

Good hearing environments should maximize the signal-to-noise ratio. In addition to the desired signal being well projected, unwanted noise should be eliminated. To accomplish this requires very low background sound levels (NC-20 range) from mechanical equipment. Sound-lock vestibules eliminate intrusive noise from a lobby and allow latecomers to enter without acoustical interference to the show. Carpeted aisles help reduce footfall noise. Noise from exterior environmental sources should also be considered. Avoid lightweight roofs, which will transmit rain noise.

Spaciousness

Because of the lateral configuration of the human ear, sound signals that are slightly different in each ear allow the listener to hear an acoustical quality called *spaciousness*, which is usually highly desired, especially for classical music. This sense of spaciousness can be enhanced if the distribution of sound through a large hall is diffused, enabling the ear to literally hear reflections from many facets of the side and rear walls. This diffusion can be enhanced by protrusions and angled surfaces on the sidewalls.

Reverberation Time (RT)

Refer to the accompanying tables on optimum reverberation times and preferred volume/seat ratios. Room volume and area of absorption can be calculated to predict RT. The design factor affecting RT the most is ceiling height. The relationship between the volume of a hall and the number of seats is often a good approximation of sound quality in the room.

In wide halls with high ceilings, seats in the center of the orchestra often suffer from lack of early reflections. Reflecting canopies or arrays over the front rows can bring reflected sound to these seating areas, which

otherwise may suffer from poor articulation. Often, seating at the rear of the balcony does not experience this problem, and these seats have excellent acoustics.

Articulation

Much of the clarity of sound that audiences need for speech intelligibility and clear musical attacks comes from the sound reflected off hard surfaces that reaches listeners within 50 to 80 milliseconds of the direct sound (which always reaches the listener first). To enhance articulation of acoustics in a hall, the design must ensure there are enough surfaces to reduce the time gap between the initial (direct) sound and these early reflections; the initial time delay gap should be less than 50 milliseconds. Sound travels 1,120 ft/second (333 m/second), so the initial time delay gap for prime seating locations should not exceed 50 ft (13 m).

Tim Shea, AIA; Richard Meier & Partners; Los Angeles, California
Leonor de Lope Friedeberg; Rhode Island School of Design; Providence, Rhode Island
Peter H. Frink; Frink and Beuchat: Architects; Philadelphia, Pennsylvania

PREFERRED VOLUME/SEAT RATIOS

VOLUME/SEAT		SOUND QUALITY OF SPACE
CU FT	CU M	
Less than 200	Less than 6	Quite "dead"; suitable for speech and cinema
300 to 350	8–10	Good for music
Greater than 500	Greater than 14	Good for organ music only; too reverberant for speech

OPTIMUM REVERBERATION TIMES AT MIDFREQUENCIES (500–1000 Hz) FOR PERFORMANCE SPACES

The breadth of RT range for each room type is a function of the room volume: the larger the room volume, the closer to the longer end of the range. The smaller the room volume, the closer to the shorter end of the range.

PERFORMANCE SPACE ACOUSTICS

Focusing

Focusing concentrates sound waves in one area, causing hotspots where the sound is louder or unnatural in quality. Concave surfaces either in plan or section can present major focusing problems if they are not identified and treated.

Seats

The largest area of sound-absorbing surface in a performance hall is the seating. Absorptive properties will change dramatically when they are occupied, since a person introduces about 5 sabins for each seat, which significantly affects reverberation time. Use of upholstered seats makes the RT similar whether the seats are empty or fully occupied.

Balconies

Balconies bring additional persons into the performance space and create more intimacy between audience and performer. But if the balcony overhang is too great, seating under a balcony can be cut off from the main volume of sound. A reasonable rule of thumb is that the overhang depth should not exceed the height of the opening (greater ratios are acceptable where live music is not part of the program).

Orchestra Pit

The surface over the orchestra pit should be angled to project sound out to the audience, but diffuse so that some energy is reflected back to the performers onstage. The front wall of the orchestra pit should be a hard surface so the front rows of the audience do not hear direct sound and so that more energy is reflected back to the performers onstage. Front and back walls may require drapery to vary and control the degree of sound reflected off these surfaces.

Sound System

Electronic sound systems may be used for amplification or for playback or recorded material. Depending on the source, the loudspeakers used to distribute the sound should be located at the center slightly in front of the speaker (for speech amplification) or on the left and right sides (for musical stereo playback or amplification of the orchestra pit). Additional loudspeakers may be needed under a balcony or at the rear of the hall to cover the upper balconies. The sound control location must be well placed within the audience area covered by the loudspeakers. Additional transmitters using infrared signals or FM radio signals can be used to meet ADA requirements.

STAGE LIGHTING SYSTEMS

System Design

A stage lighting system provides a flexible arrangement of dimmers, lighting positions, and outlet devices. Stage lighting fixtures may be placed where needed and controlled individually or in groups, according to the differing requirements of each production.

Stage Lighting System Terms

Dimmer. A device that controls the intensity of stage lighting fixtures; a remotely controlled electronic device in current practice. Standard sizes are 1.2 kW, 2.4 kW, 6.0 kW, 12.0 kW, and 120V.

Circuit. A grounded stage lighting circuit; usually no common neutrals are permitted. Load sizes depend in part on local codes—20 A is average, 15 A is maximum in some areas; some 50 A are often also provided. Circuits are distributed throughout the theater for fixture plug-in; they terminate at a dimmer rack, patch panel, or transfer panel.

Dimmer-per-circuit. A configuration whereby every stage lighting circuit home-runs to an independent dimmer.

Patch panel. A custom-made device for interconnecting a large number of stage lighting circuits to a small number of dimmers.

Transfer panel. A custom-made device enabling permanent circuits to be disconnected from the theater's dimming system and connected to a show's touring dimming system. Front-of-house circuits are generally made "transferable" in this way in large multipurpose theaters that must accommodate tours.

Front-of-house (FOH). In a proscenium theater, the audience side of the proscenium.

Followspot. A very bright manually operated spotlight used to "follow" a performer around the stage. Light source can be incandescent, carbon arc, xenon, or HMI.

Leko, fresnel, ellipsoidal, parcan, scoop, floodlights. Theatrical lighting fixtures.

Striplight. A continuous fixture containing a number of lamps and used for downlight, backlight, footlight, and cyclorama lighting—usually 6 or 8 ft long (1.8 or 2.4 m) with 12 lamps in three or four circuits.

Control console. Often called the *light board,* a computerized, manual, or hybrid control device for stage lighting dimmers. Generic types include 2-, 5-, or 10-scene *preset consoles* (manual) and *memory consoles* (computerized).

Connector strip. A type of outlet device for stage lighting circuits; essentially, a continuous wireway with outlets or "pigtails."

Cyclorama (cyc, for short). A large seamless white or pale-blue backdrop, used scenically to represent the sky or provide a surface on which abstract colors and patterns can be projected with stage lighting fixtures. Usually cloth; plaster is difficult to repair, and is not recommended.

Outlet box. An outlet device for stage lighting circuits. Box size and circuit quantities vary. Surface-mounted or recessed styles are available. Circuit numbers must appear on the faceplate (with adhesive labels or engraved).

Box boom. An important front-of-house sidewall lighting position in a proscenium theater.

Cove, beam, slot, truss. A front-of-house lighting position located at the auditorium ceiling.

Followspot booth. Houses the followspots. Enclosed, if possible, and ventilated per code. Usually at or near the rear of the house and quite high; 30° to 45° to the edge of the stage is preferred. Four spots require a booth, nominally 24 ft (7.3 m) wide × 10 ft (3 m) deep; two spots require one, 12 ft (3.6 m) wide × 10 ft (3 m) deep.

Control booth. Primary location for control console. Good view of stage preferred. Often located on the main level at the rear of the house. Houselighting controls should be duplicated here as well as backstage.

Dimmer room. Location for dimmer racks. Can be remote from the stage. Locate for efficiency of load and feed-wire conduit runs. Ventilate to accommodate heat load (approximately 5% connected load). Control humidity to protect equipment.

Booms, ladders, tormentors (side pieces such as flats or drapes placed just upstage of the proscenium to adjust the width of the opening). Onstage sidelighting positions. Nonarchitectural; located temporarily for each production, as required.

Pipes, battens, electrics. Onstage overhead lighting positions. Usually rigging pipes or pipe grid members. In a proscenium theater, often one or more rigging pipes will be permanently designated as "electrics" and served with connector strips attached directly to the pipe.

The planning of a stage lighting system should address the following considerations:

- Type of use
- Size of performing area
- Size of theater, location of stage lighting positions
- Budget

Determine requirements for the following subjects:

- Dimmer-per-circuit or patched circuit system
- Quantity of dimmers
- Quantity of distribution of stage lighting circuits
- Electrical feed size
- Type of stage lighting outlet devices
- Type of control console
- Type and quantity of stage lighting fixtures and accessories

STAGE LIGHTING POSITIONS

It is crucial that a theater be provided with adequate, easily accessible stage lighting positions, served with an adequate quantity of circuits. Accessibility is a key issue. Lighting positions in an active theater require daily access for maintenance purposes and to focus and color the fixtures. Safety and ease must be kept in mind, as well as crew size, which is crucial to theater economics. Using a ladder is both time-consuming and dangerous and requires more than one stage-hand. A catwalk is much safer, less time-consuming, and requires only one stagehand.

In a proscenium theater, lighting is done from a variety of positions and angles. Frontlighting is provided by sidewall positions called *box booms,* the balcony railing, and ceiling positions, which can be recessed within the ceiling or exposed as catwalks. Followspots are generally located in a booth at the top rear of the theater. Onstage, rigging sets with dedicated stage lighting outlet devices (connector strips or drop boxes) and portable vertical floor-mounted pipes called *booms* provide positions for downlighting, sidelighting, and backlighting. These positions are all-important, and every attempt should be made to provide them.

In flexible studio or black-box theaters, a pipe grid or a system of catwalks should be provided over the entire floor area of the theater to which lighting equipment (and scenery) can be attached. This grid should be well served by stage lighting circuits in boxes or connector strips. A two-way grid of 1½ in. (38 mm) diameter pipe, nominally 4 to 6 ft (1,210 to 1,830 mm) o.c. should be adequate in most cases, accessed by ladder from the floor. The catwalk system is preferable, but requires a taller room.

In a thrust or arena theater, a grid of a series of cat-walks should be provided over the main stage area to accommodate downlighting, sidelighting, and back-lighting. Catwalks, ceiling slots, or ceiling-mounted pipes should be provided for frontlight and low washes, similar to the balcony rail or second cove in a proscenium theater. If there is a conventional stage-house behind the thrust, it should be served in the same way as a proscenium theater's stagehouse, with overhead pipes and side booms.

Joshua Dachs; Jules Fisher Associates Inc., Theater Consultants; New York, New York
Carl Rosenberg, AIA; Acentech, Inc.; Cambridge, Massachusetts

RECOMMENDED PARAMETERS FOR STAGE LIGHTING SYSTEMS

THEATER TYPE	NUMBER OF SEATS	FEED SIZE*	CIRCUIT QUANTITY	DIMMER QUANTITY
Elementary school	Varies	100	24–36	18–361
Junior high or middle school	Varies	300	75–100	75–100
High school	Varies	400	100–150	100–150
Studio theater	75–300	400	150–200	36–200**
Educational drama theater	300–750	800	200–400	200–400
Small professional theater	750–1,500	1,200	300–500	300–500
Medium-size theater	1500–2,000	1,600	400–600	400–600
Large multipurpose theater, civic theater, roadhouse	More than 2,000	2,400	600–800	600–800

Feed size is shown in amps, 3-phase, 120/208 VY.

**A simple patch system, where the circuits terminate in male "pigtails," which can be plugged directly into a small quantity of portable dimmer jacks, is generally more economical for small installations with limited budgets than a dimmer-per-circuit scheme.*

PLAN

SECTION

PROSCENIUM THEATER

THEMED ENVIRONMENTS

HISTORY

Themed environments are a contemporary typology, whose roots can be traced back to London's Crystal Palace (1851), the first example of Europe's expositions in which large places were devoted to the display of new ideas in architecture and innovations in the industrial field. Such fairs promoted a culture of enthusiasm about the advancement and ability of the human race, idealizing what was anticipated in the next century.

At the turn of the century, amusement parks in America brought forth a new kind of entertainment. For the first time, storybook and pulp fiction fantasies were experienced in real-life form, as these environments exemplified what was once merely a fantasy.

Themed environments can typically be described as either *plot-driven,* providing a fantasy immersion entertainment experience for the patron, or as *branding,* which bolsters product sales and promotes a company's image.

Plot-Driven Environments

What has become commonly known as a theme park is best exemplified in Disneyland, conceived by filmmaker Walt Disney. His intention of enabling people to experience his characters in real time and place yielded a unique architecture, one driven by plot. Today, Disney's Imagineering group embarks on a process that involves writing a script for the environment, consulting with producers, storyboarding, researching, architectural planning, and design.

Similarly, consumers are lured by other environments that provide total immersion and adventure, as in the case of casinos such as Caesar's Palace, the Venetian, the Luxor, and the Aladdin, in Las Vegas, Nevada, where the customer's participation in a fantasy is encouraged and constantly reinforced. Such experiences provide consumers with immediate gratification that otherwise would be inaccessible.

Branding Environments

The built environment communicates image. People have preconceived notions about the companies that provide goods and services, which may not be based on personal experience. A successful, well-designed brand paints an image of a company and generates trust and respect. It is created with full knowledge of the marketing campaign launched for that company or its products.

Theme design has become a tool for creating brands and bolstering commercial markets. For example, Hard Rock Café, a theme restaurant, creates an environment that gives a taste of celebrity, using autobiographical mementos and musical artifacts. Likewise, Niketown strengthens the Nike brand by plunging its clients in an environment that ushers them into awareness of all Nike products.

The corporate branding process affects all forms of communication, including advertising, public relations, product packaging, sales force training, and environmental design.

Corporate branding deliberately creates a predetermined overall impression of the company to all parties that are integral to the company's success, including customers, employees, stockholders, and the media.

THEMED ENVIRONMENT DESIGN TYPES

DESIGN PROCESS

Unlike the design of many other typologies, themed environments often begin with three-dimensional sketches, models, and storyboards, which tell a fictitious story about the type of experience a patron might have. These interiors are heavily dependent on the artist's conceptions and constructions.

The first aspect considered by the designers of Disney theme parks and themed environments is what the camera would capture if the guest experience were a movie being filmed. Each environment is considered as a film set, hence scale, proportion, and perspective are evaluated.

The design process starts with a *blue sky* phase, followed by conceptual design, feasibility studies (the reality of the storyboard ideas are tested), schematic design, design development, construction documents, and construction administration.

The blue sky phase is the presentation and development of the *big idea*. Many people from different disciplines brainstorm the big idea, and then create a story to support it. For example, for the Blizzard Beach feature at Walt Disney World in Orlando, Florida, an image of a woman snow skiing in a bikini was seen and approved by Michael Eisner; then a story was created to support that image: a freak snowstorm hits Florida. The story is developed just as it is in the moviemaking process, by the use of storyboards. The story is illustrated on 3-by-5-in. (76-by-127-mm) or 5-by-7-in. (127-by-177-mm) cards and assembled on 4-by-8-in. (101-by-203-mm) boards in a presentation format similar to that used to pitch ideas to movie producers. The artists and creative people start by rendering their vision before programming or feasibility studies are done. The story and its details are then researched, and an art director (who may be an architect or interior designer) follows the project all the way through to completion, to ensure that the integrity of the story is maintained.

Extensive use of three-dimensional and computer models is made during the design process. All aspects of the project and finishes are modeled and scrutinized.

Scale

The psychological impact of a themed experience includes the manipulation of scale and the perception of the patron.

Scaling is determined on the evaluation of the three-dimensional models. For example, the second floor of building facades is often three-quarter scale to effectively shrink the environment. Effects created by manipulating the scale of design elements are often determined by approaching the design process as if designing a movie set and evaluating what a movie camera would capture.

Character Finishes

Character finishes or scenic treatments are often suggested, not specified, by the designer. Character finishes include trompe l'oeil finishes, theatrical finishes, or actual construction materials.

Wood and metal can be distressed in various ways, depending on the theme of the design. For example, metal is beaten with sledges and hammers until the correct level of denting is achieved, while wood is usually sandblasted and cut with knives to bring out texture. Cement plaster mock-ups are used to attempt to replicate finishes that are adapted from visual research and the storyboards.

Art direction during construction is required to give the construction contractor guidance. The construction contractor is often required to match a sample panel. Mock-ups are commonly done on most finishes. The base paint is often much different from the final *character paint* color and finish. The character paint gives personality to a surface, such as rust, light aging, or peeling paint to old, rundown facades.

ACOUSTICS

Acoustics in themed environments are of concern where noise generated within one theme area has to be isolated from another nearby. Noise sources may include amplified sound, hydraulically actuated equipment, motor-driven rides, and the like. In sports-themed venues, patrons may be able to play basketball or other sports on suspended floors above dining or other less noisy areas, so impact-isolating construction may be required.

Tim Shea, AIA; Richard Meier & Partners; Los Angeles, California
Anna Rosete; Rhode Island School of Design; Providence, Rhode Island
Brian Tan; Rhode Island School of Design; Providence, Rhode Island

AUDIOVISUAL PRESENTATION FACILITIES

DESIGN DETERMINANTS

Audiovisual (A/V) presentation facilities include training rooms, lecture halls, classrooms, boardrooms, and auditoriums. The size, type, and location of displayed images must be determined so that the space supports the presentation for the intended audience. For instructional material, legibility of displayed characters and symbols is of critical importance.

A/V EQUIPMENT

Presentation furnishings include easels, lecterns, and portable sound systems. An audiovisual presentation system often includes the following equipment:

- Video display (video projector, "flat-screen" plasma display, or video monitor)
- Loudspeakers and amplifier
- Routing switcher
- Remote control system
- A computer, for presentations or to browse the Internet
- Hookup for a portable notebook computer
- Document/object camera, for use with printed documents or small objects
- Video equipment, including TV monitors, plasma/flat/data monitors, VCRs, DVD players, TV/VCR combo units, professional camcorders

Typically, each of these components is provided by a different manufacturer. A/V dealers, referred to as *integrators,* combine these various components and ensure that they are properly installed.

LARGE-SCREEN DISPLAYS

For large-screen display of video images, LCD, DLP, and D-ILA projectors are commonly used. Flat-panel displays (plasma displays) are available in limited sizes, with the largest current models limited to about 61 in. (1,549 mm) diagonal. For the legible display of instructional material where the viewing distance exceeds 15 to 20 ft (4.5 to 6 m), video projection technology is required to produce an adequate size image. For instructional uses, video display technology is supplanting film-based display technology (slides, motion fixture film, and overhead transparencies) because the newest film-to-video transfer devices preserve the resolution of the film media.

Digital echo cancellers are used with the microphones and loudspeaker system to help provide an echo-free and nonreverberant sound quality. In distance learning applications, a camera that can automatically track the movements of the instructor is often employed.

FRONT- AND REAR-PROJECTED IMAGES AND MARKING SURFACES

TRADITIONAL BLACKBOARD MODE

TRANSPARENCY OVERHEAD MODE

VIDEOCONFERENCE MODE

DIFFERENT PRESENTATION MODES

VIDEOCONFERENCE AND DISTANCE LEARNING FACILITIES

Videoconference and distance learning systems are typically designed for the audiovisual presentation to the local audience. Common industries and applications include the following:

- *Education:* Distance learning classes, links with other schools, access to remotely located experts, preliminary employment interviews
- *Offices:* Staff, project, marketing and board meetings, employee
- *Health care:* Evaluation of X rays, charts, and other data; remote consultations; staff meetings
- *Government and military:* Strategic and network meetings, command center communications, training
- *Manufacturing:* Production meetings, product quality analysis, process review, collaboration, remote supplier meetings, training
- *Legal:* Remote depositions and arraignments, judicial proceedings

PLAN

ELEVATION—FRONT PROJECTION MODE

SECTION AT EQUIPMENT ROOM

ELEVATION—VIDEOCONFERENCE MODE

CONFERENCE ROOM FOR A/V PRESENTATIONS AND VIDEOCONFERENCES

TIER-STYLE CLASSROOM FOR DISTANCE LEARNING

OPTIMAL VIEWING AREA UP TO 45° HORIZONTAL VIEWING ANGLE

GOOD TO MARGINAL VIEWING AREA BETWEEN 45° AND 60° HORIZONTAL VIEWING ANGLES

FV = FARTHEST VIEWER

60° VIEWING ANGLE

45° VIEWING ANGLE

W = WIDTH OF PROJECTED IMAGE

CV = CLOSEST VIEWER

IDEALLY, VIEWERS SHOULD NOT HAVE TO TURN THEIR HEADS MORE THAN 15° TO VIEW THE PROJECTED IMAGE. IN A WIDE ROOM, SEATS THAT ARE ARRANGED IN CURVED ROWS HELP TO ACHIEVE THIS GOAL.

VA = Horizontal viewing angle; measured from perpendicular to screen surface
W = Width of the projected image
H = Height of the projected image
FV = Distance from the center of the projection screen to the farthest viewer
CV = Distance from the center of the projection screen to the closest viewer

DETERMINING OPTIMUM VIEWING AREA

OPTIMUM VIEWING AREAS

	COMPUTER VIDEO	HDTV	STANDARD (NTSC) VIDEO	35MM SLIDES	16MM MOTION PICTURE FILM	OVERHEAD TRANSPARENCIES
Image Aspect Ratio (W:H)	4:3	16:9	4:3	1:1.493	4:3	1:1
H	0.75 x W	0.5626 x W	0.75 x W	M	0.4255 x W	—
W	1.33 x H	1.78 x H	1.33 x H	—	2.35 x H	—
FV	≤ 4 x W	≤ 6 x H	≤ 8–10 x H	≤ 6 x H	≤ 4 x W	≤ 6 x H
CV	≥ 1.5–2 x W	≥ 1.5 –2 x W	≥ 1.5–2 x W	≥ 1.5–2 x W	≥ 1.5–2 x W	≥ 1.5–2 x W

35° TO 60° BEND ANGLE

D = .9 TO 1.2 X W

W = WIDTH OF PROJECTED IMAGE

REAR PROJECTION PLAN, NO MIRROR

LIMIT OF VIEWING AREA DEPENDS ON SCREEN TYPE

OPTIMAL VIEWING AREA SHOWN WITH SHADING

OFF-AXIS VIEWING OF REAR PROJECTION IMAGES

VIEWING AREA

The acceptable viewing area for most rear projection screen facilities is limited by the image brightness variation across the screen. The maximum acceptable *bend angle* (BA) depends on the optical characteristics of the screen. For diffusion screens, the BA is typically in the range of 35° to 50°. Beyond this range, either the image will have an unacceptable hotspot or the image brightness variation will be too great for the eye to handle.

Screens that incorporate *lenticular lens* elements typically provide broad horizontal viewing areas, accompanied by restricted vertical viewing angles. This requires the viewers to be seated in the same plane.

Screens that incorporate *both diffusion and fresnel lens* elements typically provide the most uniformly illuminated image—side-to-side, top-to-bottom, and corner-to-corner.

SECTION—REAR PROJECTION, NO MIRROR

SECTION—REAR PROJECTION, WITH MIRROR

CEILING-MOUNTED FRONT PROJECTION SCREEN

IMAGE HEIGHT

TWO-ROW OVERVIEW
SIGHT LINE (NOTE 2)

35° MAX.

RAISED PLATFORM OR STAGE IMPROVES SIGHT LINES TO SPEAKER

SIGHT LINES WITH FLAT FLOOR

IMAGE HEIGHT

TWO-ROW OVERVIEW
SIGHT LINE (NOTE 2)

30° - 35° MAX.

SIGHT LINES WITH SLOPED FLOOR

CEILING-MOUNTED VIDEO PROJECTOR

ALTERNATE
LOCATION FOR
VIDEO PROJECTOR
(SEE NOTE 3)

TWO-ROW OVERVIEW SIGHT LINE (NOTE 2)

IMAGE HEIGHT

30° - 35°
(NOTE 1)

SIGHT LINES WITH STEPPED FLOOR

5" (127)
TYP.

3'-8" (1118) TYP.

Minimum sight lines should be based on a two-row overview. This assumes that viewers can see between the heads of the people seated in the row directly in front of them.

SIGHT LINES FOR TWO-ROW OVERVIEW

SIGHT LINES

The vertical viewing angle is the angle from the viewer's eyes to the top of the image. For optimum sight line, it should not exceed 30° to 35° above the horizontal.

Many video projectors are available with optional lenses that allow placement toward the front or at the center or rear of the room. The majority of video projectors are designed to be elevated so that the lens is approximately aligned with the top or bottom of the image. For rear projection, the lenses are often designed to allow the projector to be on the axis of the screen center.

VIEWING ANGLES

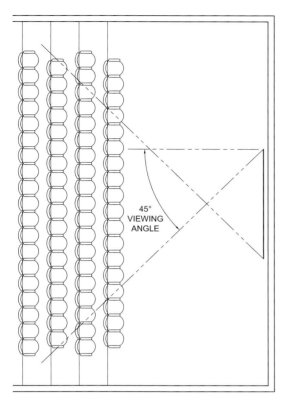

A single flat screen provides poor viewing for front corner seats.

VIEWING ANGLES FOR A SINGLE FLAT SCREEN

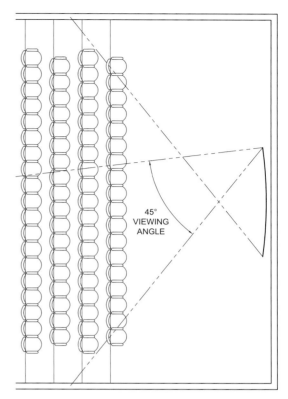

Viewing is improved for front corner seats by using a curved projection screen. Screen radius is one to two times the distance from the screen to the farthest viewer.

VIEWING ANGLES FOR A SINGLE CURVED SCREEN

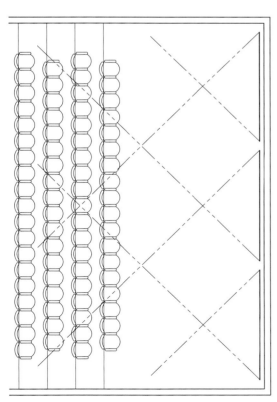

All projection screens are mounted parallel to front wall. This results in poor viewing for seats on the opposite side of the room from the screens.

VIEWING ANGLES FOR MULTIPLE SCREENS

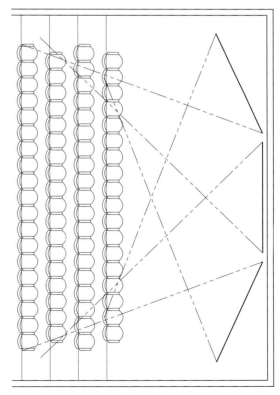

Side projection screens are angled toward the audience. This results in improved viewing for people across the room from the screen.

VIEWING FOR MULTIPLE SCREENS

*Jeffrey E. Bollinger and Jason Martinez; Acentech, Inc.;
Cambridge, Massachusetts*

HEALTH CARE FACILITIES

HISTORY OF HEALTH CARE

The practice of Western medicine predates the life of Hippocrates, an influential Greek physician during the fifth century BC. To this day, individuals entering the field of medicine are required to honor the Hippocratic Oath, which embodies the code of medical ethics.

During the early Roman Empire, facilities designed to serve the needs of the Roman military were commonly found. However, health care for the general public was very limited; the temple and the home were the principal places of healing. These Roman facilities were required to be compact and efficient in terms of their layout of functional spaces.

Open Nursing Wards

Monasteries were typically arranged with guesthouse functions for the rich and infirmaries for the poor. The nursing ward in the infirmary was usually aisled with patient beds on each side; it also had a chapel at the end so that the sick could see the altar and hear the services. During the Middle Ages, medical treatment was so inadequate that these wards were essentially places where patients waited to die, hopefully in closer communication with God. Efficient layout of functional spaces continued to be an important part of the design.

In her book *Notes on Nursing* (written in 1859) and in a paper, "Notes on Hospitals," Florence Nightingale described the importance to the health of patients of adequate ventilation, noise control, light, cleanliness, and variety. The single greatest influence upon hospital architecture for more than 100 years was the Nightingale Pavilion, which consisted of open, cross-ventilated nursing wards connected by corridors.

Private Rooms

In the twentieth century, with the advent of advanced pharmaceuticals, new diagnostic technologies, and the erection of high-rise hospitals, health care became more patient-focused. While the importance of Nightingale's basic concepts of nursing care are still relevant, the open nursing wards have given way to patient rooms that afford more privacy.

U.S. Health Care Delivery

The U.S. health care delivery system has changed radically since the early 1980s. The federal government now attempts to control health care costs for patients receiving Medicare and Medicaid benefits by assigning fixed costs to hundreds of standard diagnoses (called *diagnostic related groups,* or DGRs) and reimbursing health care facilities only this amount for each patient stay. The result has been a substantial shift to outpatient treatment for many diagnoses, including surgery. Consequently, hospitals now face a surplus of inpatient beds and great pressures to revise physical plants to accommodate many more outpatients. At the same time, health insurance companies have cut benefits for inpatient care. All of this has changed the way hospitals are planned and has stimulated new conceptual responses to the new functional challenges. In addition, hospitals are no longer the only building types responding to health care needs.

Codes and Regulations

Hospitals are also reviewed periodically by national organizations. The Joint Commission on Accreditation

1. ENTRANCE HALL
2. ROOMS FOR NURSES AND ADMINISTRATORS
3. PATIENT ROOMS (TYP.)
4. CORRIDOR
5. ANTEROOM
6. SUPPORT ROOMS
7. PASSAGEWAYS

This Roman military hospital was constructed in the first century AD in Switzerland.

ROMAN MILITARY HOSPITAL: VINDONISSA

HALL OF THE POOR

PROJECT: HOTEL-DIEU, c. 1444
BEAUME, FRANCE

Hôtel-Dieu is considered to be the oldest existing example of a hospital. It was designed by Jehan Wisecrere and constructed in 1443, in Beaune, France.

HALL OF THE POOR, HÔTEL-DIEU

of Healthcare Organizations (JCAHO) is responsible for review of compliance with environment of care regulations and currently reviews hospitals based on the 1997 Life Safety Code. The Centers for Medicare and Medicaid Services (CMS), formerly known as the Health Care Financing Administration (HCFA), reviews hospitals for compliance with Medicare/Medicaid regulations and conditions of participation. It currently reviews under the 1985 Life Safety Code.

Defend in Place

Hospital patients may have limited or no ability to seek safety without assistance in the case of fire or smoke. In the Defend in Place life safety approach, patients

are not completely evacuated from the building but are moved to an adjacent smoke compartment or through a *horizontal exit,* which is an adjacent compartment separated by a partition of two-hour fire resistance. In this concept, the hospital is divided into compartments to limit fire spread.

Another life safety measure used in the modern hospital is the engineered smoke removal system. The primary cause of death in building fires is smoke, either through inhalation or through disorientation due to poor visibility. The engineered smoke removal system reduces injury and death by utilizing the hospital ventilating system to remove the products of combustion.

HOSPITAL BUILDING TYPES

Primary Care/Community

Like the family doctor, for many people, the community hospital is the first contact with the health care system. Hospital primary care provides general treatment and diagnostic services within a limited, well-defined geographic area. Such services usually include general surgery, standard radiography, and fluoroscopic imaging, routine laboratory tests, and emergency care, as well as general medicine, maternity, and pediatrics. A small unit usually serves as a combined intensive care unit (ICU) and cardiac care unit (CCU). The number of inpatient beds can range from 25 to 50 for small rural hospitals to 100 to 150 for facilities in developed areas.

Regional Referral Hospitals

Compared to primary care hospitals, referral hospitals serve larger, less well-defined areas and provide not only basic care but also more specialized care, including orthopedics; eye, ear, nose, and throat (EENT); urology; cardiology; oncology; and neurology. Computerized tomography (CT), scanning, magnetic resonance imaging (MRI), ultrasonography, and nuclear medicine imaging are also present to support these specialties. Cardiac catheterization, open-heart surgery, and cancer treatment programs are sometimes available. The emergency department has a heavier workload because of the specialty capabilities available. The number of inpatient beds can range from 150 to 200 to 300 to 350 or more.

Tertiary Care/Teaching

Because many tertiary care teaching hospitals have world-class reputations and provide extremely specialized services, they may attract patients from all over the world. Such facilities seek to provide not just health care but also a setting (and patients) for medical research and education. Balancing these objectives is an important consideration in the design of such hospitals. All the specialties are represented, as well as some state-of-the-art diagnostic and treatment modalities, which frequently are still in development. Imaging devices such as positron emission tomography (PET) scan, procedures such as "gamma knife" treatment for cancer, and "cleanrooms" for patients recovering from bone marrow transplants must all be housed in specially designed facilities. Tertiary care hospitals may be physically linked to a medical school's basic science and clinical research laboratories, academic offices, classrooms, and very large outpatient facilities. The number of inpatient beds can vary from 400 to 450 to 800 to 900 or more.

Specialty Hospitals

Specialty hospitals, such as rehabilitation, psychiatric, and pediatric hospitals, treat only one kind of patient. Other specialty hospitals include those devoted to women's and children's health. While they contain most of the treatment and diagnostic areas of a standard hospital, they also have special design needs: patient privacy, appropriate scale, and nonthreatening environments.

PRIMARY CARE/COMMUNITY HOSPITAL

REGIONAL REFERRAL HOSPITAL

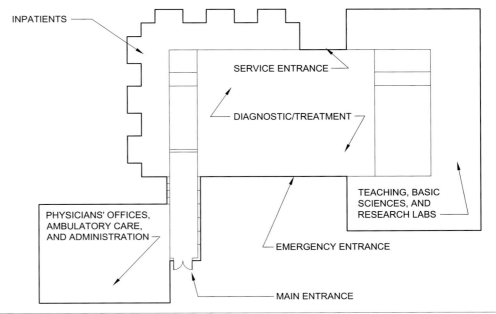

TERTIARY CARE/TEACHING HOSPITAL

Urgicenters

The movement toward outpatient care has stimulated the development of freestanding facilities, not necessarily associated with a hospital, for patients to use as they might a family doctor—frequently on a walk-in basis, without an appointment. Urgicenters can relieve overburdened hospital emergency rooms of nonemergency work. To compete with freestanding urgicenters, hospitals are starting urgicenters contiguous to their own emergency departments; a triage nurse can direct walk-in patients to appropriate treatment in the hospital, but in a less-intensive, nonemergency setting.

Surgicenters

The increase in outpatient surgery has also prompted the development of freestanding surgical facilities, where doctors perform surgery that might otherwise be done in a hospital. State regulations limit patient stays to 24 hours, so the surgery performed must not require the potential support of hospital services. To compete with surgicenters, hospitals are providing outpatient surgery as well: up to 80% of all surgery in some hospitals is outpatient.

Birthing Centers

The movement to limit hospital stays, combined with an increasing desire to deliver babies in a less institutional setting, has resulted in the development of freestanding birthing centers. Such centers provide for normal deliveries, which accounted for 75% to 80% of births in the United States in 1990. Complicated and cesarean-section (C-section) deliveries, which require special support, may remain in the hospital setting. Whether in a hospital or freestanding birthing center, the trend is to reduce the average maternity stay. Consequently, a new planning theory simplifies and accelerates the functional flow of the maternity patient. Labor, delivery, and postpartum stays are now routinely combined in one room (called LDRP). The design of the LDRP room must balance the needs for special air conditioning, medical gas outlets, and monitoring capability with the desire to create a homelike atmosphere. To compete with birthing centers, hospitals are providing LDRP suites contiguous to C-section operating rooms.

Ambulatory Care Facilities

Increased demand for outpatient care has stimulated the development of freestanding ambulatory care facilities—large outpatient clinics operated by groups of physicians or health maintenance organizations (HMOs). These facilities can combine versions of the urgicenter, surgicenter, and birthing center with full diagnostic support; the resulting functional grouping has been called a "hospital without beds." Ambulatory care planning modules must be flexible. Scheduling each clinic module by hours of use is the most important programming and planning factor in designing functional outpatient clinics. To compete with such centers, hospitals are providing on-site ambulatory care facilities, ranging from contiguous office buildings for physicians to large outpatient clinics.

John L. Hogshead, AIA; John Elledge, AIA; Leisa Hardage, AIA; Marcia Knight, RID; Debbie Heitzman; Katrina Evans; Rey Perez; Joseph Fain; Perkins & Will; Atlanta, Georgia

SURGICENTER FLOW DIAGRAM

BIRTHING CENTER—TYPICAL LDRP ROOM

TYPICAL AMBULATORY CARE/OUTPATIENT CLINIC MODULE

PROGRAMMING

Strategic Plans

Health care facilities periodically attempt to identify strategies for satisfying probable future needs. Such strategies may involve adding a new treatment or diagnostic service or expanding to capture a larger market share of a particular service and to encourage physicians to use the facilities. A long-range strategic plan documents such goals.

Master Facility Plans

Master facility plans are derived from the strategic plan and consist of (1) a projection of future space needs, (2) a comparison of those needs to available existing space, (3) an analysis of existing functional deficiencies, (4) an analysis of existing mechanical and electrical systems and their capacity, (5) block plan diagrams proposing directions for growth and areas of renovation, (6) prioritization and phasing of proposed construction projects, and (7) preliminary construction and project cost estimates based on the proposed phasing.

A reasonable rule of thumb for converting construction cost estimates to project costs is to add 40%. This percentage includes major movable equipment and furnishings, design fees, and design and construction contingencies.

Functional Space Programming

Functional space programming is often developed in two consecutive levels of detail. The first level is conceptual and is expressed in departmental gross square feet (DGSF). This level of programming is used to develop master facility plans. It consists of a department-by-department calculation of the areas within the overall boundaries of each department, including internal departmental circulation and partitions. DGSF is directly derived from projected departmental workloads or personnel numbers. Earlier popular programming methods, which link the size of a department to the numbers of beds in a hospital, are no longer valid because of the large shift to outpatient workloads.

The conceptual program must be completed by adding estimated mechanical/electrical spaces as DGSF, plus an overall factor (in the range of 1.10 to 1.15) to convert all DGSF to total building gross square feet (BGSF), which adds all general circulation, both vertical and horizontal, and exterior walls.

The second level of detail is a space-by-space program listing in usable net square feet (NSF) of all the functions in the facility. Major mechanical and electrical spaces should also be treated as NSF. These areas can then be factored variously at approximately 1.20 to 1.65 (depending on circulation and partitioning needs) to get DGSF; that result factored by 1.10 to 1.15 yields BGSF. If the assumptions used in the conceptual program are still valid, the DGSF of both conceptual and detailed programs should be approximately the same.

Source: Stephen Kliment (ed.), Building Type Basics for Healthcare Facilities; *New York: John Wiley & Sons, Inc., 2000.*
Donald W. Wesley, AIA; Ellerbe Becket; Washington, D.C.
Charles F.D. Egbert, AIA; Egbert, Clarens, and Associates, PC Architects; Washington, D.C.

DIAGRAMMATIC MASTER FACILITY PLAN

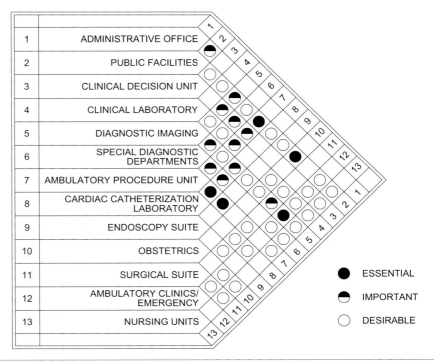

ADJACENCY MATRIX

INPATIENT HOSPITALS

The modern inpatient hospital is a city in microcosm. The basic activities found in the city—birth, work, sleep, eating, and dying—all occur in the hospital. Consequently, even a small hospital is a complex organizational structure. Complicating the organizational structure are the systems required in the hospital. This complexity can be made easier to understand by dividing the hospital into its hierarchical component parts, just as a city can be understood through the hierarchy of its neighborhoods.

The most basic division in the hospital organization is between the *patient tower* and the *diagnostic/treatment and support chassis.*

Patient Tower

The patient tower is composed of nursing units in which a group of patients receive care from a nursing team. In days of old, multibed wards were standard; these were replaced by two-patient semiprivate rooms. More recently, the private room has become the norm. Present-day surgery techniques, improvements in pharmacology, limits on cost imposed by HMOs, together with the recognition that patients may more comfortably convalesce at home have reduced the length and need for inpatient hospital stays. This has resulted in a smaller but sicker inpatient population and a blurring of the difference between "regular" inpatients and ICU patients.

The future trend is toward the *universal room,* a private room large enough to accommodate the equipment normally seen in an intensive care unit and therefore capable of accommodating patients of all acuities. The use of computerized bedside charting improves the observation capabilities of the nursing staff, helping to make this possible. A typical nursing unit comprises approximately 32 beds, the nursing station, and support space. Each patient floor of a large hospital may have two such units, or about 64 beds.

Diagnostic/Treatment and Support Chassis

The other major component in the hospital organization is the diagnostic/treatment and support chassis. If the nursing units form a tower, then this component is commonly referred to as a *pancake.* The requirement for windows in patient rooms limits the size of a patient floor. However, the relatively large diagnostic and treatment departments and their desired adjacencies result in a somewhat larger floorplate, hence the analogy to a pancake. As the term *diagnostic/treatment and support chassis* suggests, there are two principle divisions: the medical servicese and the ancillary services.

Diagnostics consists primarily of radiology and laboratories. The treatment component is composed of: surgery, cardiac catheterization, physical therapy, respiration therapy, labor and delivery, the pharmacy, and the emergency department. The ancillary support component consists broadly of: administration, admissions, medical records, dietary, material management, central sterile supply, morgue, housekeeping, and the energy plant.

Each department can be thought of as a neighborhood within the hospital "city."

INPATIENT HOSPITAL PATIENT TOWER AND DIAGNOSTIC/TREATMENT CHASSIS (THE "PANCAKE")
Perkins and Will; Atlanta, Georgia

OUTPATIENT HOSPITALS

Outpatient hospitals provide a simplified and less costly environment to deliver diagnostics and treatment to ambulatory patients. Compared to an inpatient hospital, an outpatient hospital is relatively simple, as there are neither patient nursing floors nor food preparation areas. Since long-term recovery and convalescence cannot be provided, the level of surgery that can be performed is limited. Recent developments in minimally invasive surgery, however, allow increasing numbers of procedures to be safely performed on an outpatient basis. A patient coming in for such surgery is prepped, undergoes surgery, recovers, and is sent home the same day. The outpatient hospital can offer several benefits to the patient: ease of access, streamlined registration, increased family member access, and a less institutional feel, especially compared to a large urban hospital.

Conceptually the outpatient hospital may be considered as similar to the diagnostic and treatment component of an inpatient hospital. Typically, surgery, noninvasive treatments such as lithotripsy (kidney stone treatment), physical therapy, and pain management may be provided, as well as diagnostic modalities such as radiography, fluoroscopy, computerized tomography, and magnetic resonance imaging. Because there are no patient sleeping rooms, a number of preop/postop patient holding rooms or cubicles are provided adjacent to the surgery suite. Depending on the level of recovery, they may be equipped with either a stretcher or recliner.

Specialized outpatient care may be provided, such as cancer care or orthopedics/sports medicine. A cancer center will offer radiation therapy and chemotherapy to the cancer patient. An orthopedics and sports medicine center will focus on problems of, and injury to, bones and muscles. Radiographic diagnostics and treatment through surgery, physical therapy, and hydrotherapy would be accommodated.

An outpatient center may be attached to an inpatient hospital and provide all the benefits of a stand-alone facility, but also allow for operational efficiency. A surgery suite can be laid out such that the inpatient and outpatient points of entrance are separated. The outpatient side can be designed much as it might be for a freestanding facility, but the operating rooms would be used for both inpatient and outpatient cases. The fact that OR staff, equipment, instruments, and central sterile supply are not duplicated enables greater efficiency, yet remains "invisible" to the patient and family.

Project: Joan Glancy-Howell Station Outpatient Facility, Lawrenceville, Georgia
Designer: Perkins and Will; Atlanta, Georgia

OUTPATIENT HOSPITAL

MEDICAL OFFICE BUILDINGS: GENERAL

Medical office buildings (MOBs) fall under the general health care heading of "Outpatient" or "Ambulatory Care." MOBs are most commonly constructed to support the need for physician office space of one of the following health care providers: hospitals, health maintenance organizations, and private physician practices.

The typical MOB provides office space for individual physicians, physician groups, and ambulatory ancillary services that either complement the services provided by the hospital or that are not normally provided within the hospital itself.

While MOBs accommodate the spatial needs of the providers of ambulatory health care services, they are not considered as health care or institutional occupancies. MOBs are considered to be business occupancies by the various model codes.

MEDICAL OFFICE BUILDINGS: HEALTH MAINTENANCE ORGANIZATION (HMO)-AFFILIATED

Health maintenance organizations (HMOs) fall under the general health care heading of "Managed Care." Most HMOs consist of a collection of health care professionals and business administrators who together, in an effort to manage the escalating costs of health care, provide health care insurance coverage to individuals and groups. HMOs provide low-cost, ongoing health care services to individuals and groups that become members of the HMO by paying regular, fixed monthly installments to the HMO system. Once enrolled as members, individuals may take advantage of the HMO's services, including its staff of nurses, general practitioners, specialists, and the HMO's buying power relative to prescription drug purchases. Members are encouraged to maintain their health by visiting the doctor on a regular basis, thus, the term "health maintenance."

HMOs deliver health care services through a variety of building types, which include hospitals, clinics, pharmacies, urgent care centers, and medical office buildings (MOBs).

Typically, HMO MOBs differ from hospital/developer-affiliated MOBs because most HMOs have their MOBs custom-designed based on a previously established clinical space and functional program, which depend on the particular medical services being offered. The design of each clinical space is typically based on previously established design standards for size and configuration of each particular space, HVAC requirements, lighting levels, quality of finishes, and so on.

A typical HMO MOB would include a typical general practice/internal medicine suite, ancillary departments, and an administrative area. Typical general practice/internal medicine suites include a waiting room/reception area, height/weight stations, exam room, procedure room, holding room, nurse station, patient toilets, physicians' offices, clean supply, and soiled utility. Administrative and support areas include an administration/business office, medical records, technical support, imaging, urgent care, laboratory, pharmacy, and central supply.

Programmatic functions and services are housed in adjacent hospital.

EXAMINATION FUNCTION AND SERVICES
Project: Cannaday Building, Mayo Clinic; Jacksonville, Florida
Perkins and Will; Atlanta, Georgia

MEDICAL OFFICE BUILDING—HMO-AFFILIATED
Project: Henry Towne Center, Kaiser Permanente; McDonough, Georgia
Perkins and Will; Atlanta, Georgia

MEDICAL OFFICE BUILDINGS: HOSPITAL/DEVELOPER-AFFILIATED

Historically, both new and existing hospital facilities have been faced with limited project budgets and limited land availability within the hospital campus. Therefore, most hospitals are restricted to project budgets that will accommodate only the essential clinical, diagnostic, and support functions and equipment required to provide the much-needed inpatient health care services. In many cases, project budgets are not adequate to accommodate physician office space or space for various ancillary support services.

As a result, the hospitals themselves or medical real estate developers may eventually construct one or more medical office buildings (MOBs) near the campus to supplement the office space needs and services provided by the hospital.

MOBs are generally very similar to a typical commercial speculative office building in their architectural layout:

- Efficient "skin" or building envelope
- Common building core elements (entrance lobby; elevators; exit stairs; toilets; mechanical, electrical, and plumbing; fire protection; and so on)
- "Racetrack" public corridor, which wraps the building core and provides access to potential medical office suites
- Common parking and loading facilities based on code minimum requirements

But where MOBs differ from commercial speculative office buildings most notably is in the manipulation of their architectural components. Size of the building floorplate, structural bay spacing, core-to-glass depths, space planning module, use of stretcher elevators, and so on are all dependent on the programmatic intent of the hospital/developer. Multiple small medical suites (800 to 1,500 sq ft (74 to 139 sq m)), multiple large medical suites (3,000 to 6,000 sq ft (278 to 557 sq m)), or a mixture of small and large medical suites, all will, in their own ways, influence the final architectural layout.

Layout Parameters for MOBs

Typical architectural layout parameters for planning new or evaluating existing MOBs are as follows:

Building floorplate: 12,000 net sq ft (1,114 sq m) minimum

Structural bay spacing: 24 by 25 ft (7.3 by 7.6 m) and 30 by 32 ft (9.1 by 9.7 sq m)

Core-to-glass depth varies:

- 33 ft (10 m) nominal (for small medical suites)
- 37 ft (11.2 m) nominal (most common)
- 49 to 85 ft (14.9 to 25.9 m) nominal (for large medical suites)

Space planning module: 4 ft (1,229 mm), 4 ft 6 in. (1,370 mm) or 5 ft (1,525 mm)

REGIONAL HOSPITAL
Project: Florida Hospital—Heartland Medical Center; Sebring, Florida
Perkins and Will; Atlanta, Georgia

1900s: DOUBLE-LOADED CORRIDOR

1930s TO 1950s: CROSS SHAPE

1940s: RACETRACK

1950s: COMPACT CIRCLE

1950s: COMPACT SQUARE

1970s: COMPACT TRIANGLE

N = NURSING STATION

COMMON NURSING UNIT FORMS
Source: Stephen Kliment (ed.), Building Type Basics for
Healthcare Facilities; *New York: John Wiley & Sons,
Inc., 2000, pp. 139–141.*

NURSING UNIT PLANS AND ORGANIZATION

A clear recognition of each nursing unit's organizational pattern is required to ensure a floor plan that will support the unit. One of the most critical aspects is the variation in size, location, and makeup of the staff during shifts. A scheme with support space fully dispersed, with a close patient-nurse link during the day shift, may be very inefficient with reduced staffing at night and a consequent repositioning of the nurses to a location accessible to a larger number of beds.

Maximum and minimum travel distances from the center of the activity are as important as the average distance. With great distance variations, some patients may receive closer observation by nurses than others. Analysis of the maximum distance between patient rooms is an indicator of the inefficiency generated during lower staffing hours.

Current trends have eliminated inpatient care for patients who, 10 years ago, would have been admitted to the hospital. This means that patients who are admitted are in far greater need of observation. Therefore, the primary goal is to minimize distance—the average distance of travel, the range of distance between the nearest and the farthest patient rooms and the nurse work core, and the distances between all patient rooms. These distance calculations must be tempered by the number of beds per unit.

NURSING UNIT PLAN TYPES

Having evolved from the open ward model of the Nightingale Pavilion, nursing units have continued to strive for improved nursing operational efficiencies, improved patient care, and the integration of technological advancements. Reducing travel distances for nursing staff is the primary planning objective for architects and designers. Reduced travel distances results in an increase in nurse/patient contact. The *distance-to-bed factor* is a summation of the distance from the nursing work center (nurse station) to the patient bed divided by the number of patient beds.

Double-Loaded Corridor

The double-loaded corridor model was the standard design for many years because of the need for cross-ventilation and natural lighting. However, it made for very long distances between the nurse station and the end rooms of the unit. The core still contains space unrelated to nursing (elevator space, for example) and is thus less compact than it could be.

Cross Shape

The cross shape unit is an early attempt at creating operational efficiencies by modifying the basic elements of the double-loaded model. Nurse stations and support areas remain at the center of the plan. Travel distances between the nurse stations and the most

remote patient rooms are kept to a minimum; however, the round-trip travel distance remains similar to that of the double-loaded unit.

Racetrack

This design demonstrated a far more efficient unit than the single, double-loaded corridor plan: it placed the nursing support core between two corridors in what has been called the *double corridor* plan. This unit shows a combination of one central work core with dispersal of support functions in the form of a pass-through "nurse server" adjacent to the door of each room to provide patient supplies for the convenience of the staff. Although this design was highly efficient during the day, the distances from the ends of the floor created problems when staffing was limited at night. The support core also contains space unrelated to nursing (elevators, stairs, HVAC) and is thus less compact than it could be.

Compact Circle

This circular unit removed elevators, stairs, and HVAC components from the support core and located them where they could also serve additional nursing towers in the future. All patient beds are arrayed around the nursing support core, and travel distances are minimal. Another means of reducing nurse travel results from providing "redundant" circulation; that is, by providing more than one route from point to point.

Working within a circle has a number of built-in problems, however. The number and sizes of patient rooms dictated by program requirements control the diameter of the circle. It is strictly a coincidence when the resulting space in the center provides the required area to accommodate the program for nursing support.

Constructability issues associated with curved and angled partitions, odd-shaped spaces, and so on usually result in an increase in overall construction costs.

Compact Square

This model is conceptually identical to the compact circle. However, the compact square, or rectangular, unit is much more flexible than the circular unit in terms of the ratio of patient rooms to the amount of support space, thanks to the ease of changing the exterior dimensions on each side while maintaining the same bed count. Most compact rectilinear plans have an efficiency rating close to that of the circular plans and provide a higher degree of flexibility in planning the units.

Due to the efficiency of the rectilinear plan, constructability issues are limited and economical construction costs are more easily achieved.

Compact Triangle

This model is conceptually identical to the compact square.

INPATIENT HOSPITALS: PATIENT TOWER/NURSING UNIT

An inpatient hospital nursing unit consists primarily of the patient rooms. However, there are activities that must be accommodated to support care given to the patients: nurse's station, soiled utility room, clean supply area, nourishment station, staff lounge, and medicine station.

Nurse's Station

The traditional nurse's station accommodates the work area for the unit clerk, with chart makeup material, chart storage, and nurses' charting work counters. It may also provide nonnursing support staff work areas to a respiratory therapist, social service personnel, and a nutritionist. The work areas accommodate a computer and monitor and printers. A physician's dictation station may also be included. Recent trends in the use of computers in bedside charting have dispersed some of these functions away from a central nurse station toward the group of patient rooms served by each nurse. This reduces the congestion created by a number of staff members working in the same area.

Soiled Utility Room

The need to provide an aseptic environment in the hospital requires that dirty instruments, linen, waste, and spent material be separated from clean. That is the purpose of the soiled utility room, which usually contains a sink and work counter, soiled linen hampers, and trash containers for waste and "red bag" waste. It may also contain a clinical service sink, or "hopper," to dispose of the contents of bedpans where bedpan washers are not installed on the patient toilets.

Clean Supply Area

The clean supply area provides storage for clean linen, supplies, and equipment. It may also contain a sink and work counter, in which case it is known as a *clean utility room*. Equipment or linen may alternately be stored in rooms specific to them.

Nourishment Station

Meals are served to inpatients from carts brought up to the floor from the kitchen at mealtimes. At other times, juice, coffee, ice, and snacks will be provided from a nourishment station. The equipment usually found in the nourishment station includes a sink and counter, refrigerator, ice machine, and a microwave oven, as well as storage cabinets.

Staff Lounge

Since nursing staff members must remain near their unit during their shift, a lounge is provided in the nursing unit. Lunch and bathroom breaks are taken here. A staff lounge will typically contain a table and chairs, a sink and counter, refrigerator, microwave oven, and personnel lockers, where a separate locker room is not provided. A staff toilet room may be located adjacent to the lounge.

Medicine Station

The medicine station provides space for drug and IV storage and dispensing. Drugs and medicines are typically prepared in the central pharmacy and delivered to the nursing unit by cart or pneumatic tube carrier. A medicine station will contain a sink, refrigerator, and double-locked narcotics locker, as well as nonsecured storage cabinets. In recent years, computer-controlled dispensing units have become common, allowing more precise tracking of inventory and staff access. Such units may replace the narcotics locker and are about 28 in. (710 mm) square and 4 ft (1,220 mm) high. Where many drugs are kept in inventory, multiple units may be used, including units designed to dispense IV fluids.

Historically, each of the functions would have been in a separate room near the central nurse's station. But with the trend toward decentralizing nurse-station functions, these units may be duplicated within a unit to allow ready access to these functions. A couple of decentralized larger secure rooms with, for example, material and linen storage and medicine and nourishment stations developed as separate alcoves within them, will decrease the steps and time needed to provide caregiving to each patient.

NURSE'S STATION

SOILED/CLEANROOM

PLAN

Ⓐ **ELEVATION—ISLAND**

Ⓑ **ELEVATION—FORM STORAGE**

Ⓒ **ELEVATION—WORKSTATIONS**

Station is centrally located within nursing unit and has clearly defined work zones. Good circulation between the work zone and the nursing unit is essential.

NURSE'S STATION
Project: Gwinnett Medical Center; Lawrenceville, Georgia
Designer: Perkins and Will; Atlanta, Georgia

John L. Hogshead, AIA; John Elledge, AIA; Leisa Hardage, AIA; Marcia Knight, RID; Debbie Heitzman; Katrina Evans; Rey Perez; Joseph Fain; Perkins & Will; Atlanta, Georgia

HOSPITAL PATIENT ROOMS

General Acute Care

Patient rooms must be accessible, easy to maintain, and spacious enough to contain high-tech life-support and monitoring equipment. Entry doors should be a minimum of 48 in. (1,219 mm) wide. Wider openings are sometimes required to accommodate large equipment and surgical teams during emergency situations. A clear area of 48 in. (1,219 mm) should be maintained at the foot of patient beds. Equip patient rooms with basic amenities such as a patient chair, visitor chair, television set (VCR optional), wardrobe for full-length garments and luggage, drawers for clothing and personal items, and a countertop for flowers and cards.

Patient rooms should include toilet facilities, though central bathing areas may be provided in lieu of individual showers. Doors to accessible toilet rooms must provide a clear opening of 32 in. (812 mm), minimum. If doors swing in, equip them with hardware that permits emergency access. Universal precautions require a lavatory in, or near the entrance to, each patient room and a place to store gloves, masks, and gowns. Space for electronic equipment, such as a patient data terminal and printer, may be required. Semiprivate patient rooms should contain cubicle curtains for visual privacy.

Intensive Care

Patients in an intensive care unit are under continuous observation. Each room should be visible from the nurse's station or a staffed corridor workstation. Each unit must contain equipment for continuous monitoring. Provide a nurse call at each bed for summoning assistance. Beds should be within view of an exterior window, preferably an operable window. Provide bedside space for visitors and a curtain for visual privacy. Doors should be a minimum of 48 in. (1,219 mm) wide. Sliding doors may be used for access to rooms or cubicles within a suite. Provide at least one private room or cubicle in each ICU for patients requiring isolation and/or separation. Toilet units can be provided in each bed area, along with a sink, countertop for preparing medications, and universal precautions storage. IV tracks and exam lights are typically placed above each bed.

Because of the acuity of illness of these patients, rolling life-support equipment often occupies space at the side and foot of the bed. Maintain a minimum of 48 in. (1,219 mm) on three sides of each bed. Utility columns allow 360° access around the patient.

Finishes and Headwalls

Finishes in patient rooms should be durable and easy to maintain. Epoxy paint is sometimes used at wet or medication preparation areas. Consult local codes for restrictions on finishes in patient rooms. Depending on the room type, bed headwalls may include a nurse call button, reading light, room light switches, television controls, electrical outlets, central monitoring capabilities, and suction, vacuum, and various medical gas outlets. Headwalls are available as prefabricated units or can be built into the partition.

Timothy J. Cowan; Burt Hill Kosar Rittelmann Associates; Pittsburgh, Pennsylvania

SEMIPRIVATE PATIENT ROOM

PRIVATE PATIENT ROOM

INTENSIVE CARE UNIT PATIENT ROOM

OPERATING ROOM

SURGICAL SUITES

General-purpose operating rooms must be extremely flexible due to widely varying spatial requirements of surgical procedures and personal preferences of the surgical staff. Public health codes limit the minimum size of operating rooms to 360 sq ft (33 sq m), exclusive of casework. Certain procedures can require significantly more space. Operating rooms should be roughly square in plan and free of columns, with the operating room table located in the approximate center of the room to allow for maximum flexibility in positioning of equipment and personnel. Delivery rooms may be a minimum of 300 sq ft (27 sq m), exclusive of casework, for noncesarean births, and 360 sq ft (33 sq m) for cesarean. In delivery rooms, the operating room table is typically shifted from the center of the room to provide more space at the foot end. Operating room finished ceiling height should be no lower than 9 ft (2.7 m), with an ample ceiling cavity for service space above. Because of the extreme complexity of these areas, extensive participation by doctors, technicians, equipment manufacturers, and engineers is required throughout the design process.

Finishes

The primary concern in surgical room finishes is cleanliness. Flooring materials should be seamless and have an integral base for ease of maintenance. Walls should be finished with a scrubbable epoxy base paint or with vitreous ceramic tile and bacteria-resist-

ant grout. Ceiling finishes should be either plaster or gypsum board. Built-in casework, countertops, sinks, and similar items should be stainless steel.

In operating rooms where flammable gases will be used, an antistatic flooring surface must be specified to avoid sparks that could cause an explosion. Finishes throughout the operating room should be of light, neutral colors to avoid any distortion in skin color.

Environmental Controls

Temperature and humidity in operating rooms must be strictly regulated to maintain a suitable environment for surgery. Positive air pressure must be maintained with respect to other areas to avoid infiltration of contaminants from outside the operating room. Air should be supplied at low velocities, with diffusers positioned to avoid formation of air eddies. Return registers should be near floor level, adjacent to medical gas columns, and at furthest points from each other for evacuation of anesthetic gases, dust, and microbes. In areas where flammable gases will be used, electrical outlets must be explosionproof or be placed 5 ft (1,525 mm) above finished floor; high-hazard fire protection systems should be installed.

Dental Operatories

The dental chair base is equipped with hot and cold water, wet suction, compressed air, drainage if required for cuspidor, and power. In addition, a chair-

DENTAL OPERATORY

mounted operating light may be used in lieu of a ceiling-mounted fixture. The wall-mounted medical gas console typically includes nitrogen, oxygen, and nitrous oxide. If nitrous oxide gas is included, a scavenging system should be provided. Medical gases can be supplied by tanks on movable carts. While room finishes are not as critical in dental operatories as in operating rooms, all surfaces should be washable.

Deborah Hershowitz and Frank Giese; Rogers, Burgun, Shahine and Deschler Architects; New York, New York Blythe + Nazdin Architects, Ltd.; Bethesda, Maryland

DIAGNOSTIC AND TREATMENT CHASSIS

Diagnostics—Imaging

The imaging or radiology department contains modalities using X rays and other means to "see inside" the body without opening it up. These modalities are: radiography, fluoroscopy, computed tomography (CT), nuclear medicine, ultrasound, magnetic resonance imaging (MRI), and in some instances, positron emission tomography (PET).

The support spaces for an imaging department are: processing space (including darkrooms for film development), viewing rooms with both film illuminators and high-resolution monitors for digital images, and film storage space.

Clinical Laboratory

The primary source of information about the health of a human body is the clinical laboratory and its related pathology service. The analysis of bodily fluids and tissues can reveal the presence of disease-causing agents or chemical imbalances. The principal sections of a clinical laboratory are: chemistry (urinalysis), hematology (blood studies), immunology (immune system), blood bank (blood typing and cross-matching), and microbiology (presence of microorganisms). Anatomical pathology focuses primarily on the study of disease in and condition of bodily tissue. The divisions of the pathology lab are: gross tissue (large specimen examination), histology (examination of gross tissue by microscope), cytology (examination of fluid cells for abnormality), frozen section (examination of a thin slice of tissue by microscopy), and autopsy (postmortem examination).

Treatment

Surgery

The surgery suite consists of general and specialty operating rooms (OR), the postoperative recovery unit (PACU), central sterile supply, outpatient prep/postholding rooms, and staff/surgeon dressing rooms. Many procedures can be performed in a general OR. In a smaller hospital, all of the rooms may be considered such, allowing scheduling flexibility. In a larger hospital, offering more sophisticated forms of surgery, specialty rooms devoted to specific kinds of procedures may be provided, such as for cardiac, neurological, and orthopedic services. Other types of procedure rooms not requiring the level of sterility of the operating room but that are located in or near the surgery suite are cystoscopy (providing fluoroscopic studies of the urinary system) and endoscopy (noninvasive procedures using endoscopes to study the gastrointestinal and respiratory tracts).

Cardiac Catheterization Laboratory

Cardiac catheterization has both diagnostic and therapeutic applications. The cardiac catheterization laboratory (cath lab) uses special radiographic and fluoroscopic equipment together with minimally invasive procedures to capture images of the heart and circulatory system.

IMAGING DEPARTMENT

CLINICAL LABORATORY

Pharmacy

The pharmacy has three main functions: prescription preparation, dispensing, and clinical consulting. It provides prescription medications, IV solutions, and investigational drugs to patients. The pharmacy utilizes space in several areas of the hospital. The main pharmacy may be near the materials management department to facilitate receiving of bulk shipments. Outpatient prescriptions will be delivered from this location. Inpatient medication is supplied from medication stations at the nurse station on patient floors. Satellite pharmacies may be operated in specific departments, such as the OR suite or emergency room in the larger hospital. Automated vending stations are now used to secure and monitor drug dispensing.

Emergency Department

The emergency department provides diagnosis and treatment to patients requiring immediate care due to injury, sudden illness, poisoning, and so on. It is typically subdivided according to severity of the case. The principal divisions are trauma, emergent, and fast-track. Each area will have appropriately sized treatment rooms. A trauma room is not unlike a surgical operating room, and a fast-track room is similar to an exam room in a physician's office. Patients arrive at the emergency department by ambulance or as "walk-ins." Accordingly, two points of entry should be provided. When the patient arrives, he or she is triaged to determine acuity and is then taken to the appropriate area. A principal diagnostic requirement is imaging, so adjacency with the radiology department can prevent duplication of radiographic equipment in the emergency department.

Labor and Delivery/Obstetrics

The obstetrics department serves the needs of the pregnant woman prior to, during, and after the delivery of the infant. Labor, delivery, recovery, and postpartum (LDRP) rooms in some combination with nursery and support space are its principal components.

In the traditional model, each of the phases of delivery takes place in a room specific to it. The patient is moved from room to room as birthing proceeds. More recently, the labor/delivery/recovery (LDR) model has been ascendant. The patient stays in one room for labor, delivery, and recovery, and is then moved to a postpartum unit; the infant is moved to the nursery. Thus, the patient is moved, but only one time. A further development of this concept avoids moving the patient at all. The patient may remain in the same room in which she has delivered for the postpartum period, and is thus the LDRP model. While this minimizes patient movement, it does so at the expense of efficiency of space utilization. The delivery period requires a larger room than a postpartum room, with space for the obstetrician and nurses, as well as a bassinet/warmer space for the infant. For a given number of births, this model will require more space.

These models are for normal deliveries. High-risk/cesarean deliveries take place in a delivery room equipped like an operating room, a C-section room. A specialized nursery for premature or other at-risk infants is the neonatal intensive care unit (NICU).

The labor/delivery suite may be part of a larger women's services department in a larger hospital. Such a department would make available the full spectrum of medical services specific to women.

Physical Therapy/Rehabilitation

After skeletal or muscular injury or disease, a patient may require therapy to regain strength, flexibility, and motion. The physical therapy department is the setting for this on an inpatient or outpatient basis. Typical areas within the department are: gymnasium, individual treatment rooms or cubicles, and a hydrotherapy area. The gymnasium will have specialized equipment for exercise. The individual therapy cubicles allow for massage, electrical stimulation, manipulation, and other treatments. Tanks of circulating water in several sizes allow for limb or total body submersion. Larger physical therapy departments may include occupational therapy, speech pathology, and audiology.

Respiratory Therapy

Respiratory care has both diagnostic and treatment aspects. Pulmonary function tests and blood gas analysis detect problems or diseases of the lungs. Inhalation therapy, with supplemental oxygen or ventilators, is the treatment side. Inhalation therapy is typically provided at the patient's location, while diagnostics occur in the department.

(A) ELEVATION—ISLAND

(B) SECTION AT COUNTER

ONE-HOUR-RATED WALL TO UNDERSIDE OF DECK

FIRE SHUTTER TIED TO FIRE ALARM SYSTEM

LIGHT FIXTURE

COUNTER PRIVACY WALL BY MILLWORK FABRICATOR

MILLWORK BY VENDOR (INSTALLED BY VENDOR)

8" METAL STUD

PLAN

PHARMACY

HEALTH CARE FURNITURE AND EQUIPMENT

History

The first chair designed specifically for use in a health care environment is most often attributed to the Mayo Clinic in Rochester, Minnesota. First developed in 1954, the Mayo Chair was designed to accommodate a wide variety of patient body types and medical conditions, and to provide comfort for long periods of sitting.

Important design considerations evident in the initial Mayo Chair include open back and sides for cleaning, eight-way hand-tied springs in the seat cushion for comfort and aesthetics, wide seat depth and width for added comfort, and sloped seats and arms to accommodate the wide range of body types, ailments, and the elderly. Today, several manufacturers offer health care furniture product lines that incorporate many of these initial design features, along with many design improvements that have been developed over the years.

Sanitation Practices

Sanitation practices include sterilization, disinfection, and cleaning.

- *Sterilization*: The destruction of microbial life. Instruments used in invasive (surgical) procedures are sterilized and wrapped until needed. Sterilization is carried out in the health care facility with steam under pressure, liquid or gaseous chemicals, or dry heat.
- *Disinfection*: The intermediate measure between sterilization and cleaning, carried out with pasteurization (hot water disinfection) or chemical germicides.
- *Cleaning*: The process of making something free of filth. Patient room furniture is not routinely disinfected; it is cleaned.

There is no protocol for cleaning patient room furniture. However, the Occupational Safety and Health Administration (OSHA) requires each health care provider to implement an infection-control plan. Each facility is given the latitude to define its own program and cleaning procedures and to identify the cleaning products it will use. It is important to verify that the cleaning agents used by the health care facility will not adversely affect the appearance or performance of furniture finishes.

Patient Room Furniture

A hospital patient room is typically furnished with a bed, over-bed table, patient chair, guest chair, bedside cabinet, wardrobe cabinet, chest of drawers, and sometimes a desk. Hospital beds and over-bed tables are usually purchased from the same manufacturer to ensure compatibility. They are bought by the health care institution as equipment, and seldom is a specifier involved in their selection except for the possibility of participating in color selection. The primary concerns for selecting patient room furniture include the comfort of the patient and the mobility and cleanability of the furniture.

Materials

High-pressure decorative laminates provide durable and easily sanitized bedside cabinet-top and tabletop surfaces. Uniform throughout, solid wood edges provide superior wear resistance to veneers and are easy to maintain and restore. Radiused or beveled edges retain their appearance longer than sharp corners. Because wood-veneered finishes are more expensive to restore after exposure to impact, scratches, or heat, they are often limited to use on the vertical surfaces of patient room furniture. All components of patient room furniture should be treated with a moisture-resistant sealer.

Bedside Cabinets

Some manufacturers provide perforated back panels for patient room case goods. These ventilated backs reduce odor buildup. Backs and sides should be flush so the unit can fit tight against a wall for space-saving efficiency. Unnecessary protrusions into the room can inhibit the caretaker's work area around the patient's bed. Protective bumpers can protect both the edges on cabinets and the finishes on adjacent wall surfaces, furniture, and equipment. Pull-out shelves, under tabletop surfaces, are convenient places for medicines and meal trays. They provide an immediate, clean surface without disturbing items on top of the bedside cabinet. Casters allow quick and easy relocation of the bedside cabinet when full access to the bed is required.

Slide-mounted glides for drawers should be used because they are the easiest to open with one hand. Caretakers or patients may have to open a drawer with only one hand. Full-length, finger-pull drawer pulls allow a grasp at any point along the drawer. Drawers should not be so wide that two drawer pulls are necessary. Drawer extensions with positive stops should be required for the safety of patients and their guests. One-piece plastic drawers with rounded interior corners are easy to clean. In conventional drawer construction, fluids can seep into the seams between sides and bottom.

Headboards and Footboards

Headboards and footboards are often available to match other patient room furniture pieces and can be prepared to accommodate the bed being used.

Seating

Safety, comfort, and hygiene are the primary design considerations in the selection of patient and patient room seating. Patient seating is designed to persuade recovering patients to get out of bed as soon as possible and for as long as possible. Getting out of bed can lift spirits, increase circulation, and reduce the risk of decubitus ulcers, or bed sores. Sleeper chairs that convert into beds for overnight visitors are appropriate for use as guest seating. Some manufacturers offer innerspring mattresses in their sleeper chairs. Many sleeper chairs extend to the side, rather than into the center of the patient's room. The sideways spread saves valuable floor space in the middle of the room, which the health care staff may need to occupy while tending to the patient.

Chair Seats

Seating with rounded edges and radius corners does not create pressure points or restrict blood circulation. If blood circulation is cut off, the patient's legs may become numb and the patient could fall when rising out of the chair. A waterfall-front seat edge aids circulation in the patient by reducing pressure at the back of the knees. A chair with a slight rocking motion provides the opportunity to get a little exercise and may help dissipate anxiety. The shifting and redistribution of body weight that rocking provides can increase blood circulation and give comfort.

Rising and sitting are difficult if the seating is too low, too deep, or too soft. Chairs used for the partially disabled or infirm must be easy to get into and out of with dignity. Swing-away or drop chair arms make access to seating and transfers to wheelchairs easier. Lift chairs help users while they are rising from or sitting in the seat. Floor space under the front of the chair is essential, to allow users to position their feet under their center of gravity when preparing to stand. Seating with a higher seat (usually about 20 in. (490 mm)) are available for hip replacement patients.

Chair Stability

Stability and mobility are important features for seating used in patient rooms. Health care seating must be stable, to prevent the chair from tipping or slipping out from underneath the person being seated. However, the seating should not be bulky or heavy, so it can be relocated easily without damaging floor finishes. A handle or ledge built into the top of the chair back can make moving the chair easier. Transport casters or skid glides can protect floor finishes. Rear chair legs that extend beyond the back of the chair can protect wall finishes from damage.

Chair Arms

Chair arms must support the weight of the rising or sitting person. While a person is seated, chair arms should be full length to support the entire forearm of the patient and to take the weight off the patient's shoulders. The armrest should be high enough to provide optimum leverage and offer a secure grip. Armrests that extend beyond the front of the seat and angle upward offer additional support to a rising person in an almost standing position.

Chair Backs

Supportive backs add to the comfort and safety of users. They should ensure the safety of patients, who may slump forward during semiconscious states of sleep. There must also be sufficient lumbar and lordotic-curvature support to reduce the stress and fatigue caused by long periods of sitting. Removable headrest pillows are available from some manufacturers for additional support and comfort.

Health Care Seating Maintenance

Keeping seating clean and disinfected is easier if it does not have recesses, inside corners, molding, trim, and surface-attached decoration. Cracks, crevices, and joints can trap dirt, crumbs, and body fluids, encouraging bacterial growth. The hospital staff must be able to wipe chair surfaces clean of spilled medications, food, and unhygienic fluids. A "crumb space," or gap between the seat and the chair back and arms, is commonly incorporated into chair designs for easy cleaning. Some manufacturers provide removable seat cushions for more complete cleaning. Open or closed arm panels in half or three-quarter height permit easy access to all sides of the seat cushion during cleaning.

Solid wood chairs are easy to maintain and restore. Because solid wood is homogeneous throughout, scratches are easy to repair, unlike plastic laminate or wood veneers. The primary advantage of metal chairs is that many of them can be sanitized in an autoclave, like other pieces of hospital equipment.

Upholstery Considerations

For routine maintenance, easy and economical reupholstering of seating is a necessity. When upholstery fabric is torn or punctured, the exposed foam cushion can absorb fluids and odors, rendering the chair unusable. Reupholstering and replacement are easier if seat cushions are removable and replaceable on-site. Cushion covers should be also removable. To discourage vandalism, cushion-cover closures should be inaccessible when the cushion is attached to the chair frame. Some manufacturers provide removable chair seats for on-site cleaning.

Upholstery materials with heavy naps are inappropriate for patient seating because they inhibit the patient's ability to slide in and out of the chair. Although upholstering with vinyl has been the traditional answer to the moisture problems in health care applications, newer materials are available that reduce body heat buildup and skin irritations often associated with impervious vinyls.

Fluid-barrier fabrics protect chair seat cushions from moisture and can extend a cushion's useful life. They can be upholstered onto the cushion and covered with upholstery fabric or laminated to the back of the upholstery material. Bacteriostatic agents are often used in fluid-barrier fabrics.

Fabric treatments for common contaminants in the health care environment, including bacteria and fungi, are available. Gram-positive bacteria typically dwell on skin and in dry environments and can be associated with food poisoning and strep infections. Gram-negative bacteria are associated with water supplies and can cause bacterial pneumonia and skin and eye irritations. Fungi accelerate product deterioration and are associated with eye, nose, and throat irritations. These fabric treatments reduce the risk of microbiological contamination and premature product deterioration.

MEDICAL EQUIPMENT PLANNING

Medical equipment planning is an integral part of the overall planning process and commences at the onset of a project. It is a vital component to any new construction or renovation of an existing facility; it is key in departments that are equipment-focused (such as operating rooms, critical care environments, and imaging departments), and is crucial to successful project completion and seamless transition and occupancy of a health care facility.

Planning procedures are determined within the restraints of schedules, budgets, and logistical requirements.

Traditionally, the equipment planning role was designated to departmental staff as an addition to their existing responsibilities. But this has proven to be unsatisfactory because medical staff members lack the architectural and engineering knowledge necessary to the task, potentially leading to project delays or requiring costly changes to be made.

Some architectural/interior design firms specializing in the design of health care facilities utilize in-house medical equipment planners or employ the services of medical equipment planning consultants; other facility owners prefer to contract the medical equipment planner directly.

It is important to note that while equipment vendors provide important design and planning information to the health care designer, their role is different from that of an equipment planner. The equipment vendors' planning information supports their primary goal, which is to sell equipment, and their planning information is specific to their own line of equipment. In contrast, equipment planning consultants do not recommend one brand of equipment over another, although they might assist owners in selecting equipment by helping them understand differences among available brands.

Services provided by medical equipment planners include, but are not limited to, inventory of existing equipment, equipment planning and budget analysis, equipment specifications and layouts, system planning, schedule development, equipment and furniture expediting and coordination, warehouse and installation/relocation management, milestone schedules, occupancy planning, regulatory compliance, coordination of in-service education, and an asset management inventory program.

Medical equipment is classified as to its impact on the project and whether there are costs associated with the building budget. A broad classification divides equipment into three classes or groups: *fixed, major movable,* and *minor movable* equipment.

Class (Group) 1 Medical Equipment

Class (Group) 1 Medical Equipment is defined as equipment that is attached to the facility or structure and/or services, such that modification of the facility and/or services is required for installation or removal. These items are usually acquired and installed by the contractor based on the specifications and require-

ments of the construction documents. Radiographic imaging, radiation therapy, and patient monitoring are the most notable exceptions to the rule. To avoid contractual confusion, these exceptions are sometimes (with the assent of contracting parties) reclassified as Class 2.

Class 1 equipment would include (but not be limited to): walk-in environmental chambers, sterilizers, surgical lights, anesthesia gas columns, steam generators, and fume hoods.

Class (Group) 2 Medical Equipment

Class (Group) 2 Medical Equipment is defined as equipment that is capable of relocation without modification to facility or structure or services. It has characteristics (size, electrical service, access, weight, heat production, and so on) significant enough to warrant facility design attention.

Class 2 equipment would include (but not be limited to): portable radiographic imaging systems, cardiopulmonary bypass pumps, defibrillators, hypo/hyperthermia blankets, refrigerators, diathermy machines, camera or insufflator (a device used to blow gas into the body cavity, most commonly air in laparoscopic sugeries) towers, patient monitoring, and blood gas analyzers.

Class (Group) 3 Medical Equipment

Class (Group) 3 Medical Equipment is defined as equipment that also is capable of relocation without modification to facility structure or services; however, it does not have characteristics other than size or work function significant enough to warrant facility design attention.

Class 3 equipment would include (but not be limited to): plinth tables, IV stands, stretchers, wheelchairs, chart racks, carts, waste containers, and linen hampers.

A system of classifying equipment is found in "Guidelines for Construction and Equipment of Hospital and Medical Facilities," published by the American Institute of Architects, Washington, D.C.

MEDICAL EQUIPMENT PLANNERS

The expertise of a medical equipment planner provides in-depth technical knowledge of all aspects of facilities equipment requirements. Medical equipment planners with a clinical background serve as liaison between the health care designer and the users, providing an open channel of communication and incorporating the users' requirements into the facility design.

Research and education ensures the medical equipment planner has knowledge of current equipment and its usage, as well as what will be available in the future; recommendations must always be made with a thorough knowledge of the equipment and the needs of the department.

John L. Hogshead, AIA; John Elledge, AIA; Leisa Hardage, AIA; Marcia Knight, RID; Debbie Heitzman; Katrina Evans; Rey Perez; Joseph Fain; Perkins & Will; Atlanta, Georgia
Nancy Vayo; Rhode Island School of Design; Providence, Rhode Island
Meryl Grant; Rhode Island School of Design; Providence, Rhode Island

CONTINUING CARE RETIREMENT COMMUNITIES

HISTORY

The roots of the continuing care concept can be traced to the social programs of England, Germany, and Scandinavia. Among the precursors of the senior housing communities were the medieval guilds, which enabled self-reliant people, through prior contributions, to insure themselves against losses arising from death, sickness, injury, or old age.

In the United States, special types of housing with health care provisions have been developing for more than a hundred years. *Continuing care retirement communities* (CCRCs) evolved from the life care communities started by religious and fraternal organizations. CCRCs are private-sector ventures (most often, but not necessarily, nonprofit) that depend financially on entrance and monthly fees, incorporating features of pooled risk.

AGING IN PLACE

CCRCs provide both housing and health care for the elderly, in addition to emphasizing social involvement and community life. A CCRC is intended to provide a continuum of care throughout the lifetime of its residents, allowing them to "age in place." It does so by maintaining an assortment of on-site medical, social, and residential services. This allows residents to enter into the community while still relatively active and then to take advantage of more intensive care as it becomes necessary.

There are three main stages of care:

- *Independent living units (ILUs)* provide a sense of independent living for older adults who are capable of doing the basic chores of everyday life, but who may need occasional help from others. Units come in a variety of forms, including studio apartments, one- and two-bedroom units, and larger units having full kitchens. Residential services are often available, such as meals, housekeeping, and laundry service.
- *Assisted living* provides assistance for residents who have chronic care needs and require some assistance with activities of daily living. Assisted living facilities are an intermediate step between independent living and nursing care. They provide assistance for residents with chronic care needs, excluding complete 24-hour skilled nursing care. Assisted living services include helping a resident with bathing, dressing, taking medications, and other daily activities. Facilities often have scaled-down kitchens.
- *Skilled nursing care* provides short-term, long-term, or rehabilitative nursing care. This stage of care provides round-the-clock nursing services. Nursing care is often located within the CCRC or at a related facility nearby. Some CCRCs provide nursing or assisted living units that are designed for people with special medical needs, such as those with Alzheimer's dementia.

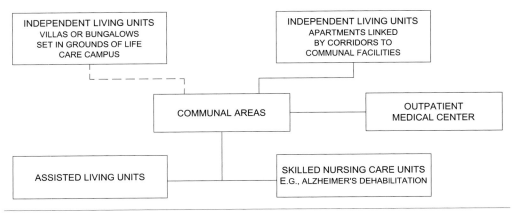

CCRC FACILITY FUNCTION DIAGRAM

EFFECTS OF AGING

Most CCRCs have a minimum age requirement, most commonly 65 years of age. Resident safety is an important consideration because the older adult experiences decreased muscle mass and other physiological changes due to aging. These changes affect vision, hearing, taste, smell, touch, body structure, strength, dexterity, balance, mobility, and memory and/or mental capabilities. In short, the body's ability to function properly and efficiently decreases.

One implication of decreased muscle strength is that residents cannot move doors as easily. This, coupled with the loss in dexterity that comes with arthritis, suggest design modifications to facilitate easy access to the building and its components. Grab bars and a monitored emergency call system are usually available in all levels of CCRCs.

The aged may experience impairment to balance, fine motor movements, and gait, so a prominent safety element in design decisions is addressing these issues, such as by reducing the risk of falls caused by poor balance by providing soft landing surfaces and secure footing, both of which are features of carpeting. Flooring should be composed of nonslip surfaces, and should be level, with no protruding seams, cracks, or joints. Patterns that can be perceived to vibrate should be avoided, as they can trigger vertigo, dizziness, and nausea. Support railings are valuable aids for individuals who lack stability when walking.

Declining motor skills directly affect the elderly resident's options in getting around and in performing simple activities of daily living. Thus, whenever possible, stairs should be replaced by elevators and ramps. The elderly may also require more space to get around because of their general instability, and to accommodate their locomotion aids. The types of pulls and levers used should be easier for older adults to grasp than regular knobs or the various kinds of currently popular finger pulls. A zero- or minimal-resistance

hinge is desirable for cabinets. Kitchen and bathroom drawers should be capable of supporting an individual's weight. In public areas, chairs should be provided at regular intervals for resting, and should appear to be naturally decorative.

One key reason that older adults reside in group settings is to avoid being alone, so it is also important to design sociability into the environment. Amenity areas where people congregate should be situated where residents naturally pass by. For some seniors, mail and meals are the only activities that draw them out of their private living spaces, so mailboxes should be placed where people may socialize if they wish. It is also important that the design include private space where residents can go to gracefully avoid social involvement or to observe rather than participate directly. It is beneficial to place smaller social or reading rooms near the larger social gathering points, so that people can be by themselves or with one or two companions yet not feel isolated. The concept of choice should be considered, so that the senior residents have personal options in creating private and public space to promote their independence. Residents should be allowed to personalize their new environment by furnishing their living space with their own furniture, personal items, paintings, and knick-knacks.

REGULATORY AND ACCREDITING AGENCIES

Often, community care licensing laws govern physical plant accommodations, care, supervision, and quality of services; also, state health and safety codes often must be followed when designing a CCRC. In skilled nursing units, nursing stations must meet state and local regulatory requirements. The Continuing Care Accreditation Commission (CCAC) is the nation's only accrediting body for CCRCs. Aging services continuums (ASCs), which can be licensed or otherwise authorized to operate by different states in varying ways, are accredited by the CCAC.

RESIDENTIAL UNIT FLOOR PLAN

ASSISTED LIVING LAYOUT

SKILLED NURSING LAYOUT

CCRL
Project: The Meridian; Wall Township, New Jersey
Designer: Hillier Group; Princeton, New Jersey

SPACE FUNCTIONS

SPACE	FUNCTIONS
Lobby (plan space 2)	Clearly define the space to orient the organization of the different functions that occur within it. Communicate the identity of the building to the residents and visitors as a main circulation space; the lobby should be conveniently located near elevators, restrooms, and all other secondary areas.
	Consider acoustics, lighting, and access to the restroom facilities.
Lounges/Courtyard (plan space 3)	Orient the residents and visitors physically, and provide visual cues for the different functions within the space.
	Design for flexibility, to accommodate multiple activities simultaneously (e.g., beverage service, entertainment, and social gathering).
	Provide a variety of seating zones.
Central Dining Rooms (plan space 9, 10)	Install sturdy yet easily movable seating.
	Install flexible lighting to enhance the ambience and to provide visual cues.
Independent Living Units (plan space 13)	Design self-contained apartment units for active or young elderly people.
	The area per unit may vary, but an average independent living unit is usually between 1,000 and 2,000 sq ft (93 and 185 sq m) and includes a bedroom, bathroom, living room area, and kitchenette/dining area.
	Promote independence and individuality among residents.
Assisted Living Units (plan space 11)	Usually, design in the form of single bedrooms intended for frailer, older elderly.
	Possibly, include scaled-down kitchens.
	Enable residents to have their own private apartments or to share living space.
	Aid individuals in maintaining as much independence and freedom as possible, except for periodic assistance with such specific tasks as bathing, dressing, medication dosage, transportation, and similar needs.
Skilled Nursing Units (plan space 12)	Maintain the lifestyle quality and health care needs of multiple individuals within a setting of commonly shared services.
	Usually, provide private (single-occupancy) and semiprivate (double-occupancy) rooms.
	Furnish rooms with facility furniture.
	Compose each unit of a bedroom with an attached toilet room, which often contains a shower for bathing, depending on the abilities of each resident (a common bathing room should also be available).

DESIGN CONCEPTS

DESIGN CONCEPT	DESIGN REQUIREMENTS
Independence	Provide barrier-free design to accommodate persons using wheelchairs and walking aids.
	Install safety features such as handrails and nonslip surfaces in an unobtrusive fashion.
	Provide repetitive visual cues through the use of graphics, color, or planting to aid in orientation.
Social Interaction	Provide spaces for informal social contact; for example, entrance lobbies, mailboxes, and alcoves interspersed along corridors.
	Increase the potential for social interaction by developing smaller-size units and by using smaller arrangements.
	Facilitate opportunities for viewing on- and off-site activities generated by residents, staff, visitors, and family members.
	Design activity rooms to be small in scale, with furniture arranged to encourage small group formation.
Interaction with the Community	Provide residents with access to shops and services, either by proximity or a transportation service.
	Enable the on-site amenities to serve the neighborhood elderly as well as the current residents.
Aging in Place	Provide different levels of shelter and care units. During tenure, a resident could conceivably occupy in succession a rental apartment in the independent living unit, a room for the semidependent in an assisted living unit, and a double-occupancy room in a skilled nursing care unit.
	Design site plans of CCRCs to reflect this segmentation of shelter and care; skilled nursing and assisted living units are separated from independent living units, frequently hidden in the rear of the property, far away from the main entrance.
	Make independent living units flexible and adaptable over time, to address any number of impairments/disabilities that accompany the aging process.
Residential Characteristics	Make the scale, the material selections, interior design treatments, furniture and accessory selections, and room dimensions consistent with the residential environment, rather than commercial or institutional settings.
	Avoid mandatory meal services. Each unit should have a kitchen so residents have the option for personal or group dining.
Individual Choice	Harmonize the size and scale of the development to fit into the neighborhood.
Opportunities for Individual Choice	Provide a variety of types of living units, such as one- or two-bedroom independent apartments, as well as congregate arrangements.
	Permit residents to furnish their dwelling units to suit their personal tastes.
Safety and Security	Install emergency call systems in individual units and at various public areas in and around the buildings.
	Ensure safe pedestrian access to neighborhood units.

CCRC COMMON AREAS AND ADMINISTRATION SPACES

DESIGN CONSIDERATIONS

Corridors as Rooms

Typically, long-term care facilities are dominated by corridors. When resident or social rooms open from a corridor, they are generally discrete spaces joined by a single door. This pattern of corridors and rooms lacks a hierarchy and is both boring and disorienting. Minimizing the impact of these long, narrow, dark passageways is necessary to achieve success in this type of building. One of the most effective ways to minimize the corridor is to make these spaces more like destinations (rooms) and less like narrow extrusions of space (passages).

Civilizing the Corridor

Corridors should vary in width, rather than be one size. Corridors that are the same width for more than 35 to 40 ft (10.6 to 12 m) begin to look monotonous. In contrast, when a corridor is increased to a width of 12 to 14 ft (3.6 to 4.2 m), it starts to look and feel like a room, not a hallway. The corridor width doesn't have to be equal or symmetrical on both sides. In fact, the more asymmetrical it is, the more informal it appears. A corridor that is 12 to 14 ft (3.6 to 4.2 m) wide and 20 to 25 ft (6 to 7.6 m) long can accommodate furniture and become a well-scaled, intimate sitting area. Making part of the corridor a living room provides a convenient place for residents to sit on their way back and forth to their units, adding variety, interest, and the possibility of social exchange. Corridor heights, like corridor widths, should also vary.

Creating a Spine Circulation Connection

Clerestory windows or skylights add to the drama by introducing natural light. Nursing homes with a minimum corridor width of 8 ft (2.4 m) are often uniform. Because regulations affecting the exiting of residents in gurneys allow little, if any, furniture to be placed in an 8 ft (2.4 m) corridor, they often appear plain and monotonous. In assisted living, where this is not required, varying the corridor width from 6 to 12 ft (1.8 to 3.6 m) can often be done without adding much additional space to the corridor.

LIVING UNITS

COMMUNITY, DINING, AND RECREATION SPACES

LOBBY, ACTIVITIES, RECREATION, AND RETAIL SPACES

FLOOR PLANS OF PRIMARY CCRC SPACES

Creating a Compact Footprint

Because older residents must go from their dwelling units to the dining room, it is important that corridor distance be minimized. The maximum length from the portal of the furthest unit to the elevator should not be much more than 100 ft (30 m). If it is longer than this, frail residents with ambulatory difficulties will have a hard time maintaining their independence. In fact, the first residents who move to an elevator-assisted building often select rooms that are on the first floor or closest to the elevator. There should be a place with a bench or chair on which to rest every 35 to 40 ft (10.6 to 12 m). This gives residents the chance to recharge before they continue to walk to the elevator. Corridors should be no longer than 35 to 40 ft (10.6 to 12 m) without an offset. The single-point perspective of a 100-ft- (30-m-) long corridor can be overwhelming.

Daylighting the Corridor

Another way of reducing the drabness of a corridor is by introducing light. In some buildings, single- and double-loaded corridors alternate, giving the user a periodic connection with a courtyard or an external view. Creating greenhouse-style glass enclosures along a corridor introduces natural light and provides an expanded view to the surrounding landscape. Single-loaded corridors also provide easy access to balconies or patios where residents can take in a breath of fresh air. In the Netherlands, exterior non-conditioned corridors are often faced with a three-quarter-height window wall that acts as a wind break but preserves the exterior nature of the corridor. Large skylights are also wonderful sources of light in corridors. In a one- or two-story building, they can bring natural light into the darkest area of the building.

Corridors and Social Spaces

Opening a corridor to a social space with a view outside reduces the feeling of enclosure. Asymmetrical corridor plans are more interesting than an orthogonal square courtyard and often aid orientation. Residents use corridors to walk for exercise in the winter and during inclement weather. Therefore, the system of corridors should be arranged to link pathways with destinations so that walking can be a more enjoyable experience. Seating in corridors allows residents to rest, while providing opportunities for spontaneous conversation. Corridors should have handrails or, better yet, lean rails that are at least 3½ in. (90 mm) deep to help steady residents. Lean rails have proven to be very effective in hundreds of installations and are far more visually attractive than handrails.

Decorating the Corridors

Artwork and wall-mounted accessories break up continuous wall surfaces and animate them with visually stimulating content. Furniture in corridors, which leaves a minimum of 5 ft (1.5 m) for passage, can add three-dimensional interest. Corridors can take on different characteristics by varying the wallcoverings, artwork, furniture, and accessories. Baseboard trim and cove moldings add decorative interest, as do wallpaper borders. Some facilities develop themes that give each corridor a unique character. This adds interest, promotes wayfinding, and creates visual continuity that many residents find intriguing.

Older frail residents often require a long time to get from their units to common spaces. Corridors with artwork and accessories make these long trips shorter by giving residents something to look at. Corridors that end with a painting or a piece of furniture can skillfully terminate the view down a corridor. In Europe, corridors are often used to display artwork that residents have collected. Decorated in this way, the corridor takes on a more personal and eclectic character.

USING AN OPEN PLAN TO CREATE DEFINITION AND AMBIGUITY

An open plan has the advantage of defining the extent of a room in more than one way. It is the ambiguity of the extent of a space that often makes it interesting. Rooms that visually lead into one another provide opportunities for visual stimulation while also helping the older person preview the next space. The ability to link one room to another visually is even more valuable in a communal setting such as assisted living, where opportunities to preview the activities of a space give residents a greater sense of control over their environment. When looking into an open-plan room, they perceive multiple layers of space, which is in stark contrast to the "what you see is what you get" dining room commonly used in nursing homes.

Defining the Extent of a Space

Changing floor material is a common approach to defining the spatial extent of a room. Older people typically have a downward gaze and, as a result, notice the floor more than they do the ceiling. However, even subtle changes in floor materials can cause level differences or surface friction differences that could lead to tripping. Ceiling treatments like soffits, recesses, and applied wood trim create spaces within larger volumes and thereby add to spatial variety.

PROGRESSION OF ALZHEIMER'S DISEASE

	PHASE	BEHAVIORAL/FUNCTIONAL	COGNITIVE	EMOTIONAL
Stage 1	Forgetfulness 2–4 years	No observable deficits	Difficulty remembering names	Anxiety and appropriate concern about symptoms
			Word-finding deficit that becomes obvious to intimates	Loss of spontaneity
				Irritability
Stage 2	Confusion	Difficulty with complex tasks and demanding employment situations	Poor concentration	Anxiety about symptoms
		Nocturnal restlessness	Impairment of reason and judgment	Denial of symptoms
			Possible episodes of getting lost	Flat affect
			Difficulty recalling recent events and aspects of own history	Withdrawal from challenging situations
			Difficulty traveling	
			Financial incompetence	
			Impairment of abstract thought	
Stage 3	Dementia 2–10 years	Inability to initiate or complete purposeful tasks	Severe memory loss; inability to recall major aspects of life, names of close family members	Denial and shame
		Nocturnal confusion and wandering	Loss of ability to understand written texts and numbers	Catastrophic incidents: irritability, agitation, and violent episodes
			Loss of appetite	Personality changes
				Paranoia, hallucinations, delusions
				Obsessive behavior
	Terminal 1–3 years	Incontinence	Lack of awareness of time, space, and events	Catastrophic incidents: irritability, agitation, and violent episodes
		Dependence for all care	Loss of speech	
		Loss of basic psychomotor skills (e.g., walking)	Abulia (loss of intentionality)	
			Difficulty swallowing	
			Significant weight loss	
			Inability to recall own name	
			Seizures	

- SMOOTH WALL TEXTURE TO PREVENT SCRAPED KNUCKLES
- FINGER HOLD
- LOW-VOLTAGE LIGHT TO ENHANCE CONTRAST BETWEEN HANDRAIL AND WALL
- CHASER-TYPE EGRESS EMERGENCY LIGHTING, CONTINUOUS TO EXIT

Handrails should be located on both sides of the corridor and should return back to the wall to prevent clothing from catching on an open end. Stair and ramp handrails should be distinct from adjacent wall surfaces so they can be quickly identified. Metal finishes that feel cold or reflect glare should be avoided.

HANDRAIL

UNIT CLUSTERS THAT ENCOURAGE SOCIAL EXCHANGE

Clustering units around a common space is normally employed to reduce the perceived length of a corridor and to create opportunities for social interaction and friendship formation. Clusters occur in different configurations that depend on the number of units grouped together. The simplest approach is to locate two doors next to one another, or four doors that all open onto a corridor alcove. The simple juxtaposition can create many opportunities for social exchange. Propinquity strongly influences friendship formation. The chances are that at least two of the four residents will develop an informal friendship or even a deeper, more substantive bond. Usually no more than 8 to 10 rooms can be comfortably situated around a corridor lounge.

Components of Unit Clusters

When clustering units, the nature of the connection between the unit and the corridor is a key to its social success. The following techniques can be utilized to better connect a unit with the corridor and the entry doors of surrounding neighbors:

- *Interior window:* Privacy can be ensured by installing curtains that can be opened or closed by residents when they want to socialize or be alone.
- *Dutch doors:* Opening the upper half of a barn-style door to the corridor is a friendly gesture common in northern Europe.
- *Display shelf:* A space outside the door for displaying items can make the unit appear more friendly and personal from the corridor.
- *Alcove:* An entry alcove off the corridor creates a buffer space where personalization can take place.
- *Furniture, artwork, or other accessories:* A flower pot, painting, wreath, or artwork accessory located next to the door can make the setting unique.
- *A light fixture:* This can extend the idea of the "front stoop" and act as an informal signal to others regarding the residents' interest in socializing.

A window provides a powerful connection between the unit and the corridor. It also allows the unit to be daylighted on the corridor side if a skylight or window introduces natural light into the cluster. In one-hour, fire-rated corridors, the window glass may be reduced in size or may need to be rated. Dutch doors also make this kind of social connection more viable because residents can choose to leave them partially open. Dutch doors are common in northern European CCRC facilities.

COLORS AND PATTERNS

Selecting colors and patterns for the interior applications of assisted living environments is influenced by taste and physiology. Physiologically, during normal aging, the lens of the eye yellows, so the eye requires more light and greater contrast for visual clarity. Creating contrast is one of the easiest things a designer can do to enhance visual function. In general, lighter colors make a room appear larger, while darker colors make it appear smaller. Light-colored letters on a dark background are generally the easiest to read.

Colors

Keep in mind that everyone perceives colors differently, not just because of their age, but also because of their culture and background. Colors and patterns have symbolic and cultural meanings that differ for everyone. Generally, warm colors in the red/orange/yellow range energize a space, while cool colors in the blue/turquoise/green range are more soothing. Cool colors are often associated with tranquility and contentment. The yellowing of the cornea turns blue into grays and whites to yellow. Purple also appears grayer, and blue and green often become less distinctive and run together. Pastels are frequently harder to read, especially blues, lavenders, and pinks; therefore, brighter colors are sometimes best. The easiest colors to read are red, orange, and yellow.

Color perception is also affected by the color of lighting. Under incandescent light, fabrics appear more yellow. This generally is preferable to fluorescent light, which often has a blue-green cast. However, full-spectrum fluorescent lighting creates a reflection that is more like incandescent and natural light.

Another way to create contrast is to select colors from the opposite sides of the color wheel. The designer who selects a green carpet might likely select furniture or fabrics with a red coloration. Ceilings should have high reflectance, in the 70% to 90% range. Walls should be on the light side, varying from 40% to 60% reflectance, while floors can be darker, in the 30% to 50% range, which is the density of light wood.

Patterns

Patterned fabrics and wallcoverings can add variety to an otherwise bland environment, but they can also be overwhelming. Subtle patterns in wallcoverings, with colors in the lighter pastel yellow-to-light-brown range are usually safe. Fabric patterns should be rich and should match the scale of a room. A large pattern for a chairback might do well in a large dining room but would be less successful in a small office space.

REDUCING OFFENSIVE NOISE AND SMELLS

In most traditional skilled nursing environments, the two most common complaints of family members are offensive odors and noise.

Odor Problems

The smell of urine is the greatest odor problem. Fortunately, today, there are a number of new products and practices to address this:

- *Moisture-barrier fabrics for seating*, as well as the moisture-proofing protocols and products available today, keep urine from soaking into furniture coverings.
- *Antimicrobial carpets* with attached resilient backing and concrete sealing protocols also make carpet absorption less problematic.
- *Ventilation systems* used today introduce continuous fresh air under positive pressure to common spaces and corridors. This air migrates through the units then exits the building via ventilation shafts in the bathroom. When the system is designed this way, it constantly moves foul air away from common areas, where it is most likely to be noticed by guests.
- *Various personal incontinence products* also reduce the problem of urine spillage.

Noise Problems

The other major complaint about institutional environments is the high noise level, often related to the large amount of hard-surface material that is commonly used because it is easy to clean. Walls, floors, and ceiling are often hard, as well, and are frequently coated with reflective semigloss paint. In some rooms, there is very soft material for sound absorption. Vinyl flooring is often mistakenly used in place of carpeting because it is considered more sanitary.

A high-quality loop or cut pile carpet with an integrated pad remains the cheapest and most effective way of reducing noise in a building. In addition to reducing noise, carpets are softer surfaces that cushion falls more effectively than a hard-surface floor covering. Other noise sources can simply be avoided. For example, the use of a public address system, common in older nursing facilities, creates an obnoxious, unwanted sound. Finally, furniture fabrics can also be helpful. In a dining room where chairs require vinyl seats, chairbacks can be padded, and heavy window fabrics can be used to absorb noise.

USING RESILIENT MATERIALS

Because of the safety that carpeting provides, it is commonly used throughout a facility as the dominant floor material. In dining areas and entry vestibules, where food spills and dirt can cause problems, a loop carpet is often a better solution than a cut pile carpet because it is sturdier and somewhat easier to clean. In some dining areas, like those used by memory-impaired residents, a hard surface is sometimes a better choice. Sheet vinyl with resilient backing is available in a number of attractive patterns. Wood-grain patterns are among the most interesting because they are realistic and come in a variety of colors and patterns.

Reducing Injuries from Falls

Bathroom floors should be covered with nonslip sheet vinyl for easy cleaning. Numerous tile patterns are available today that resemble residential applications. Smoking rooms and elevator floors often benefit from something other than carpet. Fire stairs are often overlooked, but staff often use them to rush to a resident's room, so for safety purposes, carpeting makes great sense here because of the risk of falling. Another possible risk associated with falling is injury from sharp edges and corners. All counters and casework should be rounded, and hard-edged surfaces like glass and metal tabletops should be avoided.

REDUCING GLARE

Glare, especially from clear bulbs with visible filaments, is particularly troublesome to CCRC residents. A frosted globe or shade reduces glare by spreading the intensity of light to a larger surface, thus reducing contrast. The aging eye is more susceptible to glare because of changes associated with the hardening and yellowing of the cornea. Cataracts, which are common in old age, also exacerbate problems caused by glare.

Glare can often result from a contrast in light level from one room to another or from a dark wall color against a window wall. Increasing the amount of light inside a room or lightening the color of the wallcovering can reduce glare by balancing the light more effectively. Skylights located in the darkest portion of a room can introduce a large amount of light that "balances" an exterior window wall.

PERSONALIZATION AT THE UNIT EDGE

Personalizing the area adjacent to the entrance to residents' units is a common strategy. It is often accomplished by incorporating artwork or a shadow box to help a resident identify his or her room and to serve as a device for introducing the staff to the person's background and life experiences. Though there is not much empirical evidence to support the idea that personal items placed at the unit edge help in identification or orientation, shadow boxes, memory walls, and cases have become a common feature in most assisted living and dementia units.

Wayfinding Devices

Items that are unusual in size, shape, and color are likely to attract more attention and be more effective as wayfinding devices. For example, a wreath on one door, twinkle lights on another, and a window box with plants on a third are more likely to be effective orientation devices because they are very different from one another. Large, differentiated, and distinct items often appear to be the most effective. Shadow boxes filled with meaningful memorabilia, although they may not be effective as orientation devices, serve to decorate the hallway. They also help to make the corridor much more personal and expressive.

Personalizing Corridors

In northern Europe, it is not uncommon for residents to hang personal photographs and paintings on the corridor walls adjacent to their units. This makes the corridor more interesting, because it reflects the lifestyles, tastes, and interests of residents. The items utilized to personalize an entry can include:

- Plant or package shelf for display items
- Door knocker
- Mailbox
- Window to the corridor
- Custom-made decorative door
- Sconce or can light mounted near the door
- Name tag
- Room number
- Shadow box or memory wall

These are just a few of the items that can be combined to create a unique and personal statement at each door. Corridors that do not utilize any of these ideas appear undifferentiated and dull. One of the more effective features is an internal window that connects the unit with the corridor. This is often identified by residents and family members as a device that can provide staff with an early warning of an impending problem.

THE 100 PERCENT CORNER

There is often one place within a building where the opportunity exists to create a powerful social nexus. This place is referred to as a *successful 100 percent corner* because its unique physical connection to views and activities naturally attracts residents. It often embodies a combination of the following: external and internal views of interesting activities, access to food or snacks, proximity to a major circulation pathway, and comfortable seating for sitting and talking.

MEMORY WALL AT UNIT ENTRY

A 100 percent corner can be created by design or it can occur naturally. It usually results from a unique cluster of attributes and activities. Every building should contain interesting and engaging places where residents can interact with one another or use passively by themselves. Having a 100 percent corner facilitates meaningful activity as well as social exchange.

Use of the 100 Percent Corner

The activities in this space can vary from hour to hour. Different groups might use it for reading the morning paper, having a midmorning snack, waiting for mail delivery, playing cards, or socializing after dinner. There can be more than one of these places in a building, but a single setting is more likely to be more heavily used. If the 100 percent corner is constituted properly, it needs no assistance from an activity director to work. It becomes a naturally occurring place of interest to interact with or to observe others. The most likely furniture configuration for a 100 percent corner is a table with six to eight chairs.

Attributes of a Successful 100 Percent Corner

The creation of this type of place involves physical and visual linkages to other people and places in the building. The following factors enhance the success of a 100 percent corner:

- *View to the outside:* This is preferably to an entry porch, the parking lot, or an active area of the site.
- *View to a major circulation pathway:* This should be a heavily trafficked pathway such as the circulation route from the front door to the elevator or from the elevator to the dining room.
- *Access to a public restroom:* A restroom should be located within 25 to 35 ft (7.5 to 10.5 m).
- *Access to snacks:* This includes informally provided food and drink.
- *Visual and physical access to mailboxes:* Some residents want a place to sit in anticipation of mail delivery.
- *Good lighting:* Lighting should be adequate for reading and card playing.
- *View of staff activities:* This includes the activities of

nurses, caregivers, the activity director, and the executive administrative staff.

- *iew of any internal resident activities:* These include activities taking place in the building's activity room, library, lounge, or outdoors.
- *Several comfortable chairs around a table:* These should be in a space that is large enough to sit six to eight people at the table.
- *Access to storage and supplies:* A nearby storage cabinet should contain cards, table games, puzzles, or other amusements.

SOCIOPETAL DESIGN

Sociopetal Space

A sociopetal space is an inwardly oriented shared area that is accessible from surrounding perimeter rooms. Any space can be sociopetal if it attracts residents, who use it to interact with one another. Because one of the main purposes of group housing is to stimulate social exchange, sociopetal spaces play an important role in connecting individuals with one another. In many buildings designed with cluster units, residents' unit doors open onto a furnished living room. This shared space allows residents to become acquainted with one another. Furniture arranged to optimize interaction can also encourage residents to come together and interact.

CCRCs are often designed so that every resident room has a door that opens onto a large central space, which stages a range of social and therapeutic activities, including dining, exercise, and social interaction. Atrium- and mews-style enclosed streets can attract residents, who socialize with one another as they walk through these centrally located spaces.

Sociopetal Furniture

Overstuffed chairs located around a 48 in. (1,220 mm) circular ottoman is an example of a sociopetal furniture arrangement. When older residents sit here, they place their feet on the ottoman, relax, and converse with one another. Social interaction is stimulated by the physical closeness of the setting and by the fact that they can speak privately to one another in a relaxed atmosphere.

FURNITURE FOR CCRCS

Several furniture layout and planning issues should be considered in the design of CCRCs:

- *The distance between pieces of furniture* should be increased by one-quarter to one-third the standard space planning dimensions, to accommodate people with physical differences, specifically anyone with reduced vision and general mobility impairment.
- *Furniture colors* should contrast with the floor and with other surrounding colors.
- *Mirror-finish surfaces or glass tops* can produce glare and blend with the surroundings, which is a hazard for people with reduced vision.
- *Furniture drawers* require horizontal C-grip handles or pulls that can be operated with a slightly closed hand, to aid people with reduced dexterity.
- *Furniture legs* should not protrude further than the seat or top surface, to avoid tripping people with reduced vision.

SEATING

Considerations

A comfortable chair should allow the user to place both feet flat on the floor. Most of the sitter's weight should be on the buttocks, and there should be a space between the thigh and front edge of the seat. Pressure behind the thigh over an extended period of time can aggravate circulation problems.

The deeper the seat, the more slant needed on the backrest for comfort. An open space between the seat and the back is often more comfortable, as it allows extra room for the buttocks. Seat heights should always be 17 to 18 in. (430 to 460 mm) above the floor and should be relatively horizontal from front to back. The width of the seat should be no less than 16 in. (405 mm) and the depth no less than 15 in. (380 mm). The back of the chair should be adjustable from 8 to 13 in. (203 to 330 mm) above the seat surface. The seat may have to be adjusted in height (between 13⅔ and 20⅔ in. (345 to 525 mm) above the finish floor). The angle of the seat and backrest should also be adjustable.

Rounded seat edges and radiused corners that will not create pressure points that restrict circulation will prolong comfort. The chair should have sufficient lumbar support to reduce the stress and fatigue inherent with long periods of sitting. Cleanliness and disinfection are facilitated by installing furniture that does not incorporate recesses, inside corners, molding, trim, and surface-attached decoration. A "crumb space," or gap between the seat and the chairback and arms, is commonly incorporated into chair designs for easy cleaning.

Chairs should not tilt forward or backward too easily. Legs should be widely spaced to improve stability for people with reduced balance. Chairs with armrests allow the user to rest naturally on the arms. They offer a sense of security and provide support in rising from the chair. The armrests should be 8 to 9 in. (205 to 230 mm) above the seat surface and 1 to 2 in. (25 to 50 mm) below the table apron, to avoid pinching the fingers. Armrests that extend out slightly beyond the front edge of the seat offer better leverage for sitting and rising. Wide armrests are easier to grip. Low bracing interferes with rising from a chair if the user's feet are tucked under the seat to push off. Instead of brac-

SEATING FOR THE ELDERLY *Source: Berryann Raschko,* Housing Interiors for the Disabled and Elderly; *New York, Van Nostrand Reinhold, 1991.*

ing, stretchers can be used to provide support, stabilizing a chair for transfer from a wheelchair.

A seat cushion is helpful where the spine meets the seat, and proper cushioning prevents skin ulcers. Seat cushions must be firm but comfortable. Soft cushions impede transfer from a wheelchair. If the deck is also soft, plywood can be added under the cushion for support. Loose seat cushions and back cushions should be secured with Velcro or snaps to prevent slippage. Firm, secure cushions aid stability when rising from a sitting position. Removable cushion covers without welting, ridges, and tufts are easier to maintain. Welting at the front of the seat may hamper circulation to the legs. Cushion covers should be removable, with final closures that are inaccessible when the cushion is reattached to the chair frame, to discourage vandalism. Seating surfaces where skin or clothing make contact with the furniture should be upholstered or smoothed with at least a ⅛ in. (3 mm) radius edge. Special attention should be given to all rattan and wicker surfaces, which can cut skin or prick clothing and skin.

Upholstery fabrics that allow the skin to breathe and prevent slipping also make chairs more comfortable. Textured fabrics with corrugation give more friction. Nylon upholstery can be used for abrasion resistance, polypropylene for stain and sun resistance (but not resistance to heat or stretching), and wool for porosity and comfort. Vinyl and plastic covering on chairs may become hot, slippery, and uncomfortable, and should not be used on upholstery planned for long-term seating. Shiny vinyl is associated with institutional use and makes an interior appear sterile.

A head support must be provided on deeply reclining chairs. An adjustable cushion is appropriate. The height from seat to headrest is 27½ to 34 in. (700 to 865 mm). Headrests are beneficial for elderly persons who nap in their chairs. Locking casters on furniture make it easy to rearrange the room and allow furniture to be pushed out of the way by people who use strollers, luggage wheels, or mobility assistance devices. A footrest that is high enough to keep the knees bent at a height slightly above the waist can be helpful for people with back problems. They should be easy to remove and be kept well away from high-traffic areas.

Seating Types

There are four common types of seating found in CCRCs:

- *Rockers* facilitate the shifting of weight in the rocking process and make prolonged sitting more comfortable. Rockers also aid muscle tone, digestion, and circulation. They should be lockable to aid in transferring.
- *Swivel chairs* make it easier for people to maintain eye contact and to read body language more easily in a group situation. This chair type must have a locking mechanism for easy transfer and stability.
- *A high-back chair* can provide protection from drafts and promote a feeling of greater security. Lightweight, open chairs usually occupy less floor space and are easy to move.
- *Shower chairs* with arms provide greater comfort and safety than fold-up shower seats. The lightweight frame makes it easy to lift the chair in and out. The seat should allow soap and water to pass through and should be slip-resistant. Rubber feet prevent chair slippage.

BEDS

Size

A shorter bed provides additional space for people who use strollers, luggage wheels, or mobility assistance devices. Many older people are comfortable with a 66 in. (1,675 mm) youth bed. The narrow width of a twin-size mattress allows the user to grip the edge of the mattress for leverage, to assist in turning over in bed.

Electrically operated height-adjustable beds enhance independent mobility. Low height allows easy entry, to address the nonrestraint consideration for wheelchair users. High height assists exit from the bed and allows caregivers easy access.

Mattresses

A mattress should provide good heat retention, offer sufficient absorption to allow ventilation, and be flame-retardant. Mattress underlayments should be firm, to prevent sag. Examples of good underlayment are: plywood panels, open coil springs with little side play, and pocket coil springs. Flat springs are rejected because of sag that results from prolonged use. People who are not susceptible to pressure sores can elevate their knees to relieve lumbar pressure. Elevated beds can also be helpful to people with respiratory ailments or nausea.

Accessories

Siderails keep users safe by preventing them from rolling out of bed and helping them to sit up. They also protect users in the sitting position. They should be removable for ease of entry and exit. Latches for the siderails should be within reach, not at the foot of the bed.

Source: Victor Regnier, Design for Assisted Living: Guidelines for Housing the Physically and Mentally Frail; *New York, John Wiley & Sons, Inc., 2002, pp 70–109.*

Jan Bishop, AIA, and Elizabeth Niedzwiecki, AIA; Hillier Group; Princeton, New Jersey
Noreen McGing, RNC, BSN, MJ; West Suburban Health Care; Oak Park, Illinois
Sunyoung Kwon; Rhode Island School of Design; Providence, Rhode Island
Soyploy Phanich; Rhode Island School of Design; Providence, Rhode Island

HOTELS

THE HOTEL GUEST

The words "hotel," "hospital," and "hospice" all are derived from the same Latin root, *hospitalitas,* meaning "of a guest." In the Middle Ages, monasteries provided food and lodging for travelers and pilgrims; the infirm would be kept comfortable, which was all that could be offered them due to inadequate medical care. Today, the business traveler and technology define the contemporary hotel guest's expectations of amenities in every area. Communication technologies such as fax, high-speed Internet accesses, and teleconferencing facilities are widely used in hotel guest rooms.

DESIGN CONSIDERATIONS

The primary design considerations for hotel spaces include the following:

- Main lobby
- Circulation
- Guest rooms, including standard rooms and suites
- Guest room bathrooms
- Guest room corridors
- Food and beverage outlets
- Function rooms, including ballrooms, meeting rooms, and exhibition spaces
- Structural bay determinants

HOTEL CLASSIFICATION

Hotels are often classified by a symbol or "star" system to distinguish their level of service, space, and facilities available, but the system varies in different countries and by hospitality association standards. Therefore, it is advisable to first establish the desired grade of the hotel with the operator before doing a detailed program. The required grade of the hotel will give a good indication of the required number of rooms, room sizes, number of public spaces and functions, staff-to-guests ratio, and the respective back-of-house spaces and sizes.

HOTEL SPACES AND RELATIONSHIPS DIAGRAM

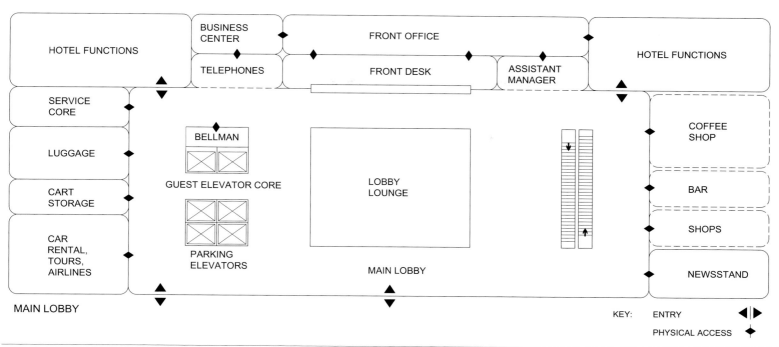

MAIN LOBBY SPACES AND RELATIONSHIPS DIAGRAM

MAIN LOBBY: PLANNING AND DESIGN

The main lobby is the principal space around which the hotel is formed; it is the "heart" of the hotel. Functionally, it serves as the guest's point of orientation; all hotel functions radiate from the lobby; guest and visitor circulation begin and end here. This central space is the focus of many hotel operations and guest activities and conceptually serves as the organizing principle for the entire design.

Circulation

The general circulation layout should facilitate movement and provide for the separation of guests, staff, and maintenance personnel, to avoid disturbing the guests and to enable efficient service. The designer should separate the circulation of resident and nonresident guests by providing direct access to, for instance, restaurants and banquet halls, to avoid congestion in the main reception area and provide better control and supervision. The quality of the design and practicality of the layout must satisfy four diverse functions:

- Guest services
- Social activities
- Guest Circulation
- Visitor Circulation

The arriving hotel guest's first concern is registration, therefore, the front desk should be accessible and highly visible from the entrance, along with the telephones, assistant manager's desk, concierge station, and the bell captain's station. The following facilities are often required in the registration area: standing-height counter, for guests to write on; house telephone; space for public transit timetables and tourist brochures; U.S. Postal Service mailbox and stamp dispenser; clocks and calendars, visible by staff and guests; a safe for guests' use; and luggage storage.

Other guest services that should be near, but not necessarily in, the lobby are the information desk; newsstand; luggage room; and airlines, car rental, and theater ticket concessions.

Social Activities

The lobby is often the site of a lounge, bar, tea service, or restaurant. Even without food and beverage service as the focal point, however, groupings of furniture are typically arranged to facilitate conversation. A successful lobby design accommodates waiting, relaxing, and meeting both for residential and nonresidential guests.

Guest Circulation

Guest arriving with baggage should receive assistance at the main entrance of the hotel by the doorman. Registration occurs at the front desk, with two excep-

tions: VIP guests may register on a special VIP floor, and large groups that have preregistered may use a meeting room to receive room keys and instructions. Direct access must be possible for all guests from the main entrance to the point of registration and to their individual guest rooms without passing through any ancillary spaces. Parking access to the hotel should connect to the main registration level and, for security reasons, be completely separate from guest floor circulation.

Visitor Circulation

Visitors arriving at the hotel to browse, dine, or attend a scheduled function should be encouraged to pass through the main lobby. Certain hotel functions may, however, have separate entrances depending on the hotel's location and specific programmatic objectives. Frequently, a separate ballroom entrance is used where large-scale events may occur.

HOTEL CIRCULATION AND RELATIONSHIP DIAGRAM

GUEST ROOMS

Guest rooms comprise between 50% and 80% of the total hotel area. The form of the guest floors has an impact on the entire design. Natural light, exiting, and circulation requirements must be satisfied by the guest floor layout.

Tower and atrium solutions adapt well to urban and restricted sites, while larger sites allow greater design flexibility in clustering guest units into courtyard schemes and other arrangements, such as triangular, C-, H-, L-, O-, T-, X-, and Y-shaped plans.

Hotel operators establish the types of guest expected, approximate length of stay, amount of luggage they anticipate, as well as specific guest requirements, such as work surfaces, special electrical outlets, task lighting, security needs, and special seating. A balance must be attained between the operational requirements, the quality of finishes, guest room dimensions, and the construction budget. Each hotel operator should prepare a typical guest room FF&E budget forecast at the beginning of the project to serve as a design guide.

Access points between public levels, service levels, and guest floors will have a direct effect on the typical guest floor layout. All floors, even low-rise walk-ups, must be accessible by elevator to provide for service, the elderly, and the handicapped. In low-rise schemes, elevator cores may be dispersed to allow greater design flexibility. In tower schemes, both guest and service elevator cores should be located within the mid-third of the guest floor, not at the extremities.

The dimensional requirements of the guest room module and guest corridor are set by the hotel operator. These dimensions establish the depth of the guest floor *bay,* which is approximately 60 ft (18 m) for double-loaded floors and 30 ft (9 m) for single-loaded floors. The double-loaded guest floor is the most efficient layout; however, due to the popularity of the atrium scheme, single-loaded corridor schemes are often planned.

Guest Room Design

Guest room design is directly affected by construction and hotel operation costs. Design techniques other than size may be used to achieve cost-effective objectives. For example, variations in ceiling heights, larger foyers, or larger bathrooms can create a feeling of spaciousness. The careful selection of finishes and furniture is also necessary to achieve an appropriate guest room décor.

Guest Room Size

In comparing the guest room requirements of the largest U.S. hotel operators serving the business and tourist market, the areas and dimensions of guest rooms fall within a narrow range. The minimum guest room width for double occupancy is 12 ft (3.60 m); the average width varies between 12 ft 6 in. and 14 ft (3.75 and 4.20 m). Guest rooms over 14 ft (4.20 m) in width are considered luxurious. The overall depth of an average room, including bath and foyer, is between 25 ft and 30 ft (7.5 and 9 m).

T-SHAPED PLAN

TRIANGULAR-SHAPED PLAN WITH ATRIUM

LINEAR PLAN

L-SHAPED PLAN

SCHEMATIC GUEST FLOOR PLANS

GUEST ROOM SIZES

HOTEL TYPE	AVERAGE LOW			AVERAGE HIGH			LUXURY		
	AREA SQ FT (SQ M)	WIDTH FT (M)	LENGTH FT (M)	AREA SQ FT (SQ M)	WIDTH FT-IN. (M)	LENGTH FT (M)	AREA SQ FT (SQ M)	WIDTH FT (M)	LENGTH FT (M)
Room*	200 (18)	12 (3.7)	17 (5.2)	240 (22)	13-6 (4.1)	18 (5.5)	270 (24)	15 (4.6)	18 (5.5)
Bath**	40 (4)	5 (1.5)	8 (2.4)	48 (4.5)	6 (1.8)	8 (2.5)	54 (5)	6 (1.8)	9 (2.7)
Guest room	300 (27)	12 (3.7)	25 (7.6)	380 (34)	13-6 (4.1)	26 (8)	400 (36)	15 (4.6)	27 (8.2)
Factor	80 (7)	—	—	90 (8)	—	—	100 (9)	—	—
Gross Area per Floor***	380 (35)	—	—	470 (42)	—	—	500 (45)	—	—

Note: Width and length of interior room dimensions noted.
Room sized for twin beds.
**For four-fixture bath, add 12 sq ft (1.1 sq m).*
***Add additional corridor factor for single-loaded corridors.*

BEDROOM AREAS BY HOTEL CLASS FOR PRELIMINARY DESIGN

START RATING	SIZE SQ FT (SQ M)
Two-star	215–237 (20–22)
Three-star	269–290 (25–27)
Four-star	323–366 (30–34)
Five-star/exclusive	388+ (36+)

Star rating systems vary among countries.

GUEST ROOMS

12'-6" TO 14'-6"
(3810 - 4420)

25'-0" TO 31'-0" (7620 - 9450)

LUGGAGE
BENCH

WELCOME
BAR

STORAGE

WORK/
BUSINESS
AREA

SLEEPING
AREA

PERSONAL
AREA

ROOM CONFIGURATIONS FOR STANDARD ROOM SIZE

32'-4" (9850)

8'-8" (2640) 8'-8" (2640) 8'-8" (2640)

14'-9" (4500) 14'-9" (4500) 14'-9" (4500)

STANDARD ROOM COMBINATIONS

GUEST ROOM ADAPTED AS MEETING ROOM

STANDARD SUITES

14'-9" (4500)   29'-6" (9000)

32'-4" (9850)

TWO-BEDROOM SUITE

14'-5 1/2" (4407)   22'-5 1/2" (6842)   14'-9" (4500)

29'-1 1/2" (8875)

TWO-BEDROOM LUXURY SUITE

29'-1 1/2" (8875)

14'-7 1/2" (4460)   14'-1 1/2" (4308)

32'-4" (9850)

22'-1 3/4" (6750)

PAIR ROOMS WITH ENTRY VESTIBULE

SUITE WITH FIVE-FIXTURE BATHROOM

Guest Room Mix Analysis

The guest room floor plans illustrate the procedure for analyzing planning and room layout for a hypothetical hotel. The plans show the typical and suite floors, the latter with five different room types. The number of different room types is increased further by handicapped-accessible rooms and by various suites. The following describes the necessary steps for designing layout, including key plans for each floor, labeled with room shape (I, II, etc.), bed type (K, DD, etc.), room number, and connecting doors, and a comprehensive tally of the guest room mix.

1. *Architectural shape.* Identify each room of a different shape or configuration (primarily different dimensions or bathroom layout) and assign it a number. Different room types are identified by a Roman numeral in the top half of the circular code in each room.
   - Room I is the most typical.
   - Room II is similar but has a different configuration at the entry vestibule.

- Room III is the corner guest room with a wider bay and different bathroom.
- Room IV is a two-bay conference suite (only one key).
- Room V is a two-bay living room that connects to two standard guest rooms.

2. *Bed type.* Label each room by its bed type (king, queen, double-double, twin, king-studio, parlor, accessible, etc.) and place an abbreviation on the plan. Note that the standard room type may be furnished in a variety of ways.

3. *Connecting rooms.* Mark interconnecting rooms with an open circle, for example, between rooms 15 and 17. Hotel operators seek a specific number of connecting pairs of particular types (for example, half the pairs connect K to DD).

4. *Suites.* Position suites, combinations of a living room and one or more adjoining bedrooms, within the typical room configuration. Two suites are shown in the example: a conference suite in the corner that connects to a standard double-double room, and a VIP suite that connects to two bed-

rooms. The VIP suite also counts as a "key," or rentable unit, because it has a full bathroom and a convertible sofa. Often, the suites are grouped together on the top guest room floors.

5. *Room numbers.* Assign room numbers to the bays to meet the management company's eventual operating requirements. Doing this in schematic design greatly aids communication among the various design professionals and reduces confusion later if the hotel operator modifies the room numbering system. Determine room numbers to simplify directional and destination signage; maintain corresponding numbers on different floors.

6. *Key and bay analysis.* Develop a summary table to tally the number of rentable "keys" and room modules for each floor by architectural shape or bed type. The table next to each plan cross-references the number of room types (I to V) and the bed types for each floor. Frequently, a larger chart is developed for the entire hotel showing the stacking of typical and suite floors and providing totals of the number of rooms for each type.

TYPICAL FLOOR

SUITE FLOOR

GUEST ROOM ANALYSIS

TYPE	BED	NUMBER	BAYS
I	K	7	7
	DD	5	6
II	DD	3	3
III	K	3	3
IV	CS	1	2
Totals		20	21

SUITE ROOM ANALYSIS

TYPE	BED	NUMBER	BAYS
I	K	2	2
	DD	4	4
	P	1	1
III	K	2	2
IV	CS	1	2
V	VIP	2	4
VI	VIP	1	2
CL		0	4
Totals		13	21

Source: Walter A. Rutes, Richard H. Penner, and Lawrence Adams, Hotel Design, Planning, and Development, "Guestroom Mix Analysis," Table 15.4; New York: W.W. Norton, 2001, p. 256.

GUEST ROOM BATHROOMS

Design Considerations

For many hotels, the guest room bathrooms are an important element in defining the level of luxury for the hotel. For high-end hotels, bathrooms may feature the separation of wet and dry areas and the compartmentalization of toilets and bidets. Consider the following for incorporation into the bathroom design:

- Durable hardware and finishes
- Adequate vanity lighting and a large mirror
- Sufficient counter/shelf area for cosmetics
- Adequate overhead lighting to allow reading in tub
- Number of fixtures

Typical U.S. guest room baths have three fixtures: toilet, sink, and tub. Luxury U.S. baths have four fixtures: toilet, sink, shower stall, and tub. European and Middle-Eastern suites generally have four fixtures; toilet, bidet, sink, and tub. Deluxe suites will have large bathrooms with custom-designed tubs and two sinks. Occasionally, separate showers, sauna, or steamrooms are provided.

Bathtubs are usually 5 ft (1.5 m) in length, although the 5 ft 6 in. (1.65 m) tub is popular in first-class hotels. All bathroom fixtures should have individual shut-off valves accessible within bathroom for easy maintenance. Countertops should be a minimum of 4 ft (1,220 mm) in length, with backsplashes against all adjacent walls. Bathroom hardware usually includes the following:

- Shower rod 1¼ in. (30 mm) in diameter and 6 ft 2 in. (1.85 m) above the floor
- Towel shelf for clean towels
- Towel bar near sink
- Towel bar near tub
- Grab bar in tub
- Dual toilet paper holder
- Recessed soap dishes beside tub
- Robe hooks
- Facial tissue container, which may be built in
- Convenience outlet for shavers and hair dryers near sink

FOUR-FIXTURE BATHROOM

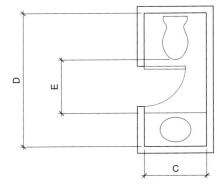

TOILET ROOM

BATHROOM DIMENSIONS

BATHROOM DIMENSIONS

	MINIMUM	COMFORTABLE	IDEAL
A	4'-1" (1.25 m)	4'-4" (1.32 m)	4'-7" (1.40 m)
B	7" (0.18 m)	8" (0.2 m)	10" (0.25 m)
C	2'-8" (0.81 m)	3'-0" (0.91 m)	3'-0" (0.91 m)
D	5'-10" (1.78 m)	6'-6" (1.98 m)	6'-8" (2.03 m)
E	1'-6" (0.46 m)	1'-10" (0.56 m)	2'-0" (0.61 m)
F	8'-7" (2.62 m)	8'-10" (2.69 m)	9'-1" (2.77 m)

40 SQ FT
(3.7 SQ M)

54 SQ FT
(5.0 SQ M)

72 SQ FT
(6.7 SQ M)

THREE-FIXTURE BATHROOMS

56 SQ FT
(5.2 SQ M)

78 SQ FT
(7.2 SQ M)

96 SQ FT
(8.9 SQ M)

110 SQ FT
(10.2 SQ M)

FOUR-FIXTURE BATHROOMS

220 SQ FT
(20.4 SQ M)

FIVE-FIXTURE BATHROOM

SHOWER

BATHTUB

8'-8" (2640)

SINK

D A B C

TOILET

BIDET

9'-7 1/2" (2932)

PLAN

SHOWER ENCLOSURE
AND EXPOSED FIXTURES

GRAB BAR

CLOTHES HOOKS

BATHTUB

Ⓐ **ELEVATION AT SHOWER AND TUB**

WALL-MOUNTED
MAGNIFYING
MIRROR

LIGHT
FIXTURE

SOAP DISH

BATHTUB

TELEPHONE

GFI OUTLET

SINK

Ⓒ **ELEVATION AT TUB AND SINK**

WALL-MOUNTED
MAGNIFYING MIRROR

LIGHT FIXTURE

COUNTER AND
BACKSPLASH

MIRROR

TOWEL
SHELF

RECESS

BATHTUB   SINK   TOILET   BIDET

Ⓑ **ELEVATION AT TUB, SINK, BIDET, AND TOILET**

TOWEL
SHELF

RECESS

TOWEL BAR

MULTIROLL
TOILET TISSUE
HOLDER

BIDET

SHOWER
ENCLOSURE

GRAB BAR

Ⓓ **ELEVATION AT TOILET AND SHOWER**

FIVE-FIXTURE BATHROOM

GUEST ROOM CORRIDOR DESIGN

Public corridor design should be a continuation of the quality, style, and ambiance established in both the public space and the guest rooms. The guest room corridor bridges the transition from the public space to the private space. Confluence of design can be achieved through imaginative repetition of basic design elements.

Long double-loaded corridors are typical for hotel guest room floors. The corridor is usually restricted to the minimum width and height. Large mechanical ducts typically run in the ceiling space of the public corridor and limit the ceiling height to the minimum of 7 ft (2,130 mm). The minimum corridor width is usually 8 ft (2,440 mm) for a double-loaded corridor.

A variety of design elements can be employed to break down the homogeneity of a long corridor. Door groupings and locations can be varied to create varying rhythms. Repetitive door recesses, altered ceiling heights, pilasters, repetitive light fixtures, and variations in carpet patterns, wall finishes, and color schemes can be used to add interest to a long, double-loaded corridor.

A maid's closet should be located in the corridor near the service elevator. Plan for one maid's closet for every 15 to 30 rooms, depending upon the level of service the hotel intends to provide.

CORRIDOR ELEVATION

CORRIDOR PLAN

OFFSET GUEST ROOM ENTRIES

CORRIDOR ELEVATION

CORRIDOR PLAN

ALIGNED GUEST ROOM ENTRIES AT REGULAR INTERVALS, FORMING NODAL POINTS

CORRIDOR ELEVATION

CORRIDOR PLAN

ALIGNED GUEST ROOM ENTRIES AT ALTERNATING INTERVALS

CORRIDOR ELEVATION

CORRIDOR PLAN

OFFSET GUEST ROOM ENTRIES AT REGULAR INTERVALS

FOOD AND BEVERAGE OUTLETS

Restaurants, bars, and nightclubs generate a major portion of a hotel's revenue, so it is important that the food and beverage program suit the expected clientele and the hotel's location. Equal concern must be given to the relationship between the menu, interior design statement, and location of the outlet within the hotel.

Design Considerations

Design considerations for some common types of food and beverage outlets are as follows:

• *Coffee shops* are the most basic, and often the busiest, hotel outlets. They are the meeting place for guests and should be centrally located, highly visible, and open for service 80% of the day. Coffee shops are generally in or adjacent to the main lobby.

• *Restaurants and specialty dining rooms* are formal, enclosed spaces with theme décors that reflect the menu. Many hotels offer both a first-class restau-

rant and one or more specialty restaurants. Holding bars are generally designed as part of these restaurants.

• *Fast-food outlets* are seldom provided in hotels because they attract an economically undesirable crowd. However, where extensive commercial and exhibition areas are planned within the hotel, or where the hotel in part of large mixed-use development, fast-food outlets may be suitable.

• *Bars and lounges* may be considered "magnets" to attract guests and visitors, and their location and design should reinforce these objectives. Open and visually attractive bars include lobby bars, cocktail lounges, terrace bars, and poolside bars. Enclosed bars and lounges provided as part of restaurants are appropriate within entertainment facilities and private clubs.

• *Entertainment facilities* such as a disco, casino, or nightclub are planned for local clientele as well as hotel guests. When outlets are planned to accommodate large crowds, a street-level entrance should be considered.

Locating Food Outlets

All food and beverage outlets should be visible and easy to reach. Directing guests through attractive portions of the hotel, for example, along courtyards or through atria, provides a pleasurable experience for the guest. As long as the food outlets are not isolated, a certain travel distance may be desirable. Guests and visitors should, however, never have to pass through guest floor corridors or prefunction areas to reach a food or beverage outlet.

As many food and beverage outlets as possible should radiate off one main kitchen. In large hotels with expansive food and beverage programs, more than one kitchen becomes necessary. This allows some flexibility in locating the various outlets, but may be less efficient in terms of food service and control. Achieving an appropriate food and beverage location for the guest while maintaining an efficient food and beverage operation is often a challenge.

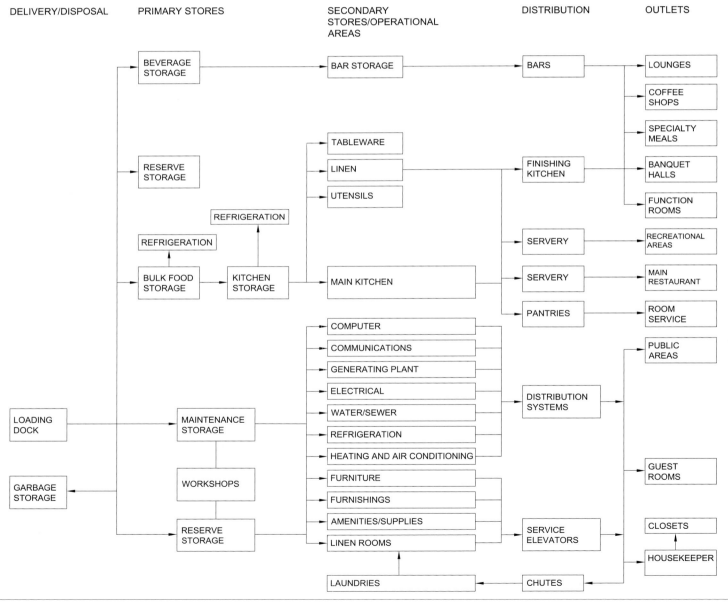

HOTEL MAINTENANCE AND RESTAURANT SUPPORT AREAS
Source: David Adler, ed., Metric Handbook: Planning and Design Data, *2nd Ed.; Oxford: Architectural Press, 1999.*

HOTEL DINING FACILITIES

Wide circulation aisles are required to accommodate luggage and lobby traffic.

LOBBY LOUNGE

FORMAL DINING ROOM WITH VESTIBULE AND WAITING AREA

FORMAL DINING ROOM WITH ADJACENT LOUNGE

Views, luxurious finishes, and areas that enable conversational privacy are often provided in formal dining rooms.

FORMAL DINING ROOMS

Casual dining is characterized by more closely spaced tables and efficient service.

CASUAL DINING

Visibility of various food options should be considered. Proper ventilation is imperative for the comfort of the diner.

DISPLAY DINING

FUNCTION ROOMS

Ballrooms

Ballrooms are used for formal entertainment and as banquet and meeting spaces. The décor is typically formal with quality finishes, carpeting, and decorative lighting. The adjacent prefunction space complements the ballroom décor and serves as a place to gather to have cocktails or to register for meetings.

Because ballrooms attract guests sometimes in evening attire, separation of circulation from exhibition traffic and more casual areas of the hotel is desirable. Direct and formal access from the main lobby is important because ballrooms are often used for community functions. Under certain circumstances, separate access to the street may be desirable. Ballrooms require expansive column-free space, which readily subdivides into two or three rooms, often in the proportion of one-third or two-thirds.

Meeting Rooms

Meeting rooms are semiformal spaces used for lectures, conferences, meetings, and an occasional cocktail party. Direct access from the main lobby and guest rooms is desirable. An internal connection with the ballroom is important as well, to increase the flexibility in programming meetings and breakout sessions.

Meeting rooms should be planned as flexibly as possible to accommodate various size groups between 30 and 200 persons. Large meeting rooms need prefunction corridors to allow guests to congregate prior to meeting. Boardrooms and private dining rooms may function better when designed as fixed rather than as flexible space.

Exhibition Spaces

Exhibition areas provide display space for various trade shows attended by guests, community members in the trade, and, on occasion, the general public. Direct access from the street is practical because of the number of visitors expected. Guest access, however, should be through the main lobby, for security reasons. Exhibition area finishes may be considered "serviceable," as these spaces must be designed for heavy traffic and constantly changing exhibits. Exhibition space is rarely provided in smaller or upscale properties.

Exhibition areas have columns located on a grid to accommodate display booths that are, maximum, 8 × 10 ft (2.4 × 3 m) and/or 10 × 10 ft (3 × 3 m), and aisles that are 8 to 10 ft (2.4 to 3 m) in width. Ceilings heights should be in comfortable proportion to the overall space. Division of the exhibition space is sometimes desirable to allow for different-size shows.

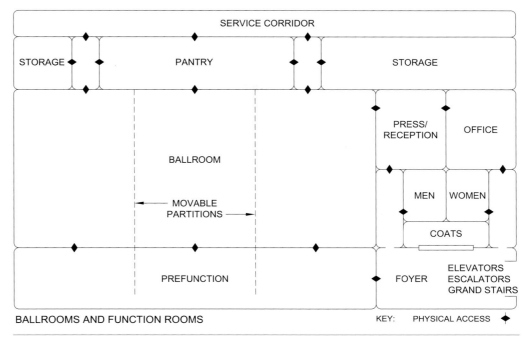

BALLROOMS AND FUNCTION ROOMS   KEY: PHYSICAL ACCESS ◆

BALLROOM ADJACENCIES DIAGRAM

TABLE SEATING FOR SIX
Banquet module: 7 ft 9 in. by 7 ft 9 in. (2,360 by 2,360 mm)
Area: 60 sq ft (5.5 sq m)

TABLE SEATING FOR EIGHT
Banquet module: 8 ft 11 in. by 8 ft 11 in. (2,720 by 2,720 mm)
Area: 80 sq ft (7.4 sq m)

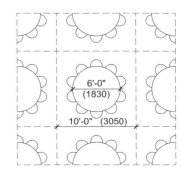

TABLE SEATING FOR TEN
Banquet module: 10 ft by 10 ft (3,050 by 3,050 mm)
Area: 100 sq ft (9.2 sq m)

BANQUET SEATING—10 SQ FT (.9 SQ M) PER PERSON

Food and Service Considerations

Ballrooms, if not backed up to a main kitchen, require a full service pantry. Meeting rooms require small pantries or coffee service, while boardrooms and private dining rooms need adjacent pantries. Exhibition areas may occasionally have in-house food and beverage service. In general, vending machines are provided and operated by an independent company.

Dock and Elevator Considerations

Exhibition areas and ballrooms may be used to exhibit large bulky items, even automobiles. Direct, same-level access with the loading dock is both efficient and economical, especially for exhibition areas. Having at least one major function on the dock level eliminates the need for additional large-freight elevators.

CLASSROOM SEATING—18 SQ FT (1.6 SQ M) PER PERSON

THEATER SEATING—9 SQ FT (.8 SQ M) PER PERSON

MEETING SEATING

STRUCTURAL BAY DETERMINANTS

Guest rooms and ballrooms are the primary areas to be considered in establishing the structural span requirements for a hotel. Other hotel areas that require large spans (for example, recreational areas or nightclubs) may be located either on the roof level or within the ballroom's structural bay. Atrium and lobby spaces are generally located outside the guest tower footprint and have a separate framing system. Parking, when introduced to the building, should not determine, but rather be adjusted to fit within, the overall structural system.

Ballrooms and other areas requiring long spans or special structures should be located outside the footprint of the guest tower to alleviate major and expensive structural design problems required in transferring loads. Often these elements are placed adjacent to the guest tower, in the crux of an L- or between the legs of the H- and U-shaped guest towers.

Ballrooms must have column-free interiors, which necessitates long-span structural bays. Clear width requirements vary between 35 and 95 ft (10 and 28 m), depending on the programmed area specified by the hotel operator. Ballrooms spans are based on ballroom areas established from banquet seating requirements of 12 sq ft per person (1 sq m per person). The clear ceiling height for ballrooms is between 16 and 34 ft (1.5 and 3.1 m).

ACOUSTICS

Isolate guest rooms from elevator shafts, ice and beverage dispenser rooms, and major duct chases. "Buffer spaces" such as janitorial services, storage, and stair towers can be placed between guest rooms and sources of noise. Avoid locating guest rooms over bars and live (amplified) entertainment spaces. Minimize glazing on exterior walls facing freeways, airports, rail lines, and other major sources of noise. Locate laundries, pool equipment, central plant equipment, and outdoor equipment, such as cooling towers, where noise is least likely to cause conflicts with guest activities or neighboring properties (local noise zoning ordinances may need to be reviewed).

Guest Rooms

An STC of 50 or greater should be used for guest rooms. Place TVs in cabinets for better sound isolation from the adjacent wall. Insulate corridor doors to at least B-label standards. Use solid-core doors at bath. Locations near freeways, rail lines, airports, and racetracks may require special exterior skin design noise assistance from a consultant. Carpet floors for impact noise control. Use flat-slab construction for economy and ease of sealing demising partitions to overhead structure. Air conditioning background noise levels should be limited to NC 35.

Meeting Rooms and Ballrooms

Enclose meeting rooms and ballrooms with STC 55 to 60 partitions. Use heavy doors with frame seals. Use corridors to buffer meeting rooms from kitchen noise. Movable partitions should provide STC 52 to 55; avoid accordion-style partitions if speech privacy is required. Specify carpet, especially if meeting room or ballroom is over occupied spaces. Portable dance floors can be set up on carpet when required. Mixes of drywall, wood, fiberglass-reinforced gypsum elements, and acoustical panels are acceptable for ceilings, if sound-absorbing area can be at least 50% of ceiling area.

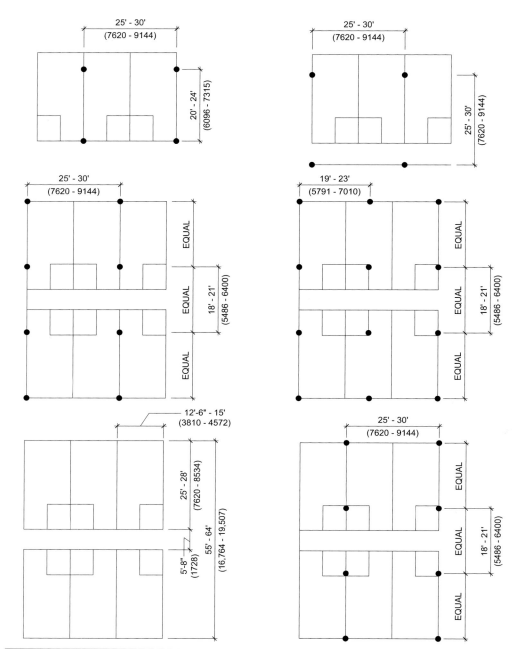

TYPICAL STRUCTURAL BAYS AND COLUMN LOCATIONS FOR GUEST TOWERS

BALLROOM DIMENSIONS*

	AREA	LENGTH	×	WIDTH
OCCUPANCY	SQ FT (SQ M)	FT (M)		FT (M)
200 persons	2,400 (216)	70 (21)	×	35 (10)
400 persons	4,800 (432)	100 (30)	×	48 (14)
600 persons	7,200 (648)	120 (36)	×	60 (18)
800 persons	9,600 (864)	138 (41)	×	70 (21)
1,000 persons	12,000 (1,080)	150 (45)	×	80 (24)
1,500 persons	18,000 (1,620)	190 (57)	×	95 (29)

*Based on a proportion of 2:1 (width being clear span).

The minimum recommended ceiling NRC is 0.60. Sound-absorbing fabric-wrapped fiberglass panels on walls with an NRC of 0.80 are useful at reducing reverberant noise buildup during events. Treat 20% to 50% of available wall surface area with acoustical panels. Panels can be spaced up to a few feet apart for aesthetic purposes. For panels that are below door-head height, specify an impact-resistant construction, available from most panel manufacturers. HVAC rating should not exceed NC 35.

SOM; New York, New York
Michael L. Blankenship; Rhode Island School of Design; Providence, Rhode Island
May Sophonpanich; Rhode Island School of Design; Providence, Rhode Island

RESTAURANTS

Restaurant interiors offer designers the opportunity to create a distinctive environment, which reinforces the restaurant concept. For restaurants, an inviting interior space is as desirable as a reputation for good food and service. A strong restaurant concept is essential for the design and operation of the restaurant to attract diners. The well-designed restaurant transcends restaurant type; an appealing fast-food café may be as successful as an upscale establishment.

RESTAURANT TYPES

Fast-Food Restaurants

Fast-food restaurants provide a limited menu that is inexpensive, cooked quickly, and served with little or no waiting. There is no table service in fast-food restaurants, and beverage, condiment, and trash receptacles may be located in the dining area. Often, eating utensils, such as spoons or forks, are not required to consume the food. Seating in fast-food restaurants, often molded fiberglass or other nonupholstered selections, is designed for ease of cleaning and maintenance. The seating is also limited in comfort, to encourage brief stays. The comfort of the seating arrangement is often related to the amount of money spent on a meal.

Full-Service Restaurants

In a full-service restaurant, a wait staff serves seated patrons. Full-service restaurants range from casual dining establishments to upscale, fine dining restaurants. The level of comfort, refinement, and service reflects the type of restaurant. Full-service restaurants may include bars, private dining areas, banquet facilities, and possibly live entertainment areas. An upscale restaurant may contain higher-maintenance materials and finishes, and tables may be larger and more widely spaced than in a casual family restaurant. Comfortable chairs with arms might be used in a restaurant that anticipates a diner's stay to be over an hour.

PLANNING AND DESIGN

Restaurant planning and design commences with the development of a restaurant program. The restaurant concept determines the type of design and the operation of the restaurant. The concept or dining experience desired, menu, type of clientele, hours of operation, and operations concerns all contribute to the success of the restaurant design.

A restaurant program incorporates subjective design criteria, which affect space allocation and design. For example, many restaurants prefer to have a small waiting area, which, when full, promotes the impression that the restaurant is popular. If a general dining room is planned to be a noisy, energetic space, then secluded or private dining areas might be incorporated as a bal-

ance. The number of dining seats is an important consideration in determining waiting area and kitchen space requirements. Each restaurant presents unique challenges, which must be addressed by the owner and operations staff, designer, and food service consultant.

Front of House and Back of House

The *front-of-the-house* operations (areas the patron utilizes, such as entry area, waiting room, dining room, and bar) must be carefully coordinated with the *back-of-the-house* facilities (kitchen, food and beverage storage, offices, trash removal). Typically, the back of the house is designed by food equipment consultants. The design of the patron area must support the functions of the service areas; the service areas must carry out the concept of the patron area.

Acoustic Considerations

Acoustic privacy is generally not an issue in large public dining spaces. Secluded banquettes and private dining rooms can be set apart for better acoustic and visual separation. Food preparation noise can be isolated by careful placement of kitchen entries or the use of a vestibule, double-entry doors, or serpentine staging areas.

Some restaurants are intentionally designed to be noisy to hasten departures and increase table turnaround, thus increasing profitability. The NC/RC range can be up to 40 for a noisy, quick turnaround restaurant. An NC/RC of 35 is more appropriate for a general-purpose service restaurant. For a quiet conversational environment, an NC/RC of 30 is desirable.

Adjacencies

Restaurant adjacencies typically follow a prescribed flow, with public front-of-the-house spaces separated from the functional back-of-the-house areas. Consider waiting area, traffic to the dining and bar spaces, restroom locations, and service staff flow throughout the restaurant.

In the back of the house, separate the food preparation from the soiled dish and trash pickup. Traffic should not cross between the preparation food line and the soiled food/dishwashing areas. Consider adjacencies and circulation from the receiving area into the back-of-the-house spaces; food and supply deliveries, staging, and storage should not impede the flow of staff.

RELATIONSHIP BETWEEN TIME AND MONEY SPENT ON MEALS

TIME SPENT IN RESTAURANT	AMOUNT SPENT ON MEAL
< 45 minutes	Less than $15
45–90 minutes	Between $15 and $25
> 60 minutes	More than $25

Source: National Restaurant Association; Washington, D.C., 1993

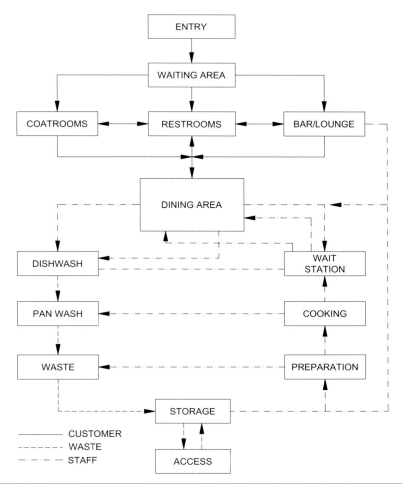

RESTAURANT ADJACENCY DIAGRAM

PROTOTYPICAL RESTAURANT PLANS

BRASSERIE, NEW YORK, NEW YORK *Source: Diller & Scofidio; New York, New York*

Compressed entry area transitions to an open dining space.

RESTAURANT, CHICAGO, ILLINOIS *Source: Aria Group Architects, Inc.; Oak Park, Illinois*

3   □   HOSPITALITY

SPACE ALLOCATION

The dining room and bar must be efficiently planned to ensure revenue potential. However, having more tables does not necessarily lead to increased revenue. Upscale restaurants generally require more space between tables for privacy. The restaurant concept, menu, and operation style influences space allocation. Depending on the type of restaurant and menu, kitchen areas range from 30% to 45% of the total restaurant area.

PRELIMINARY GUIDE FOR FRONT-OF-HOUSE AREAS

FOOD SERVICE VENUE	SUGGESTED AREA PER PATRON SQ FT (SQ M)
Banquet Facility	10–11 (.9–1.0)
Fast-Food	11–14 (1–1.3)
Full-Service	15–18 (1.4–1.7)
Cafeteria	6–18 (1.5–1.7)
Upscale Gourmet	17–22 (1.6–2.0)

CODE REQUIREMENTS

Building codes identify restaurants as assembly spaces. Comply with local code requirements for construction, including plumbing fixture counts.

The *Americans with Disabilities Accessibility Guidelines* (ADAAG) defines requirements for accessible construction and furniture. These include handicapped accommodations in restrooms; counter, bar, and food service line-critical dimensions; furniture clearance requirements; and minimum dimensions for access aisles.

The local Department of Health reviews restaurants for compliance with regulations for general sanitation in food handling and proper food storage. Construction that is easily and readily cleanable, such as floor, wall, and ceiling surfaces, and equipment that is sanitary and cleanable is required. A food service consultant designs and specifies back-of-the-house stainless-steel equipment and installation methods.

INTERIOR FINISHES

Restaurant interior finishes and materials vary from the front of the house to the back of the house. The public area interior finishes and materials should support the quality level and maintenance effort desired for the restaurant concept.

Interior materials are typically required to be flame-retardant. The selection of interior finishes and materials durability is dependent on the restaurant concept and desired life of the products. Restaurant interiors are often scheduled to be redesigned or refurbished on a five-year cycle, as not only do concepts become stale, but finishes become worn and stained.

The food-handling area finishes must be sanitary, easily cleaned, and durable. Flooring should be impervious and slip-resistant; bases should be coved or as defined by the local health department; wall surfaces should be FDA-approved fiberglass-reinforced plastic (FRP) panels or other acceptable material, such as tile or other impervious product; ceilings should be cleanable, such as Mylar-faced panels.

LIGHTING

Lighting in restaurants establishes mood and ambiance. Lighting levels may vary based on hours of operation; a restaurant that is open only during the day may have different lighting requirements from an establishment open for evening dinner service. Restaurants typically utilize incandescent lighting, which provides a warm-quality light. Incandescent lamps are less energy-efficient than fluorescent lamps. The quality of fluorescent light is generally not desirable in restaurant public spaces; however, it is acceptable for back-of-the-house areas. Light fixtures located in food preparation areas should be equipped with a cleanable prismatic or other lens that covers the unit.

Consider the dramatic effect of local lighting or ambient lighting, which provides soft illumination. Multiple light source types may be appropriate.

Review the materials and finishes proposed for a restaurant, under conditions that replicate the space and under day and evening lighting conditions.

RESTAURANT PATRON AREAS

Dining and Bar Area

Restaurant patrons typically develop their first impressions of the restaurant from the main dining room and bar areas. The interior design and overall ambiance of the restaurant signal the type of dining experience for the patron. The restaurant concept may offer a variety of space types, including open or multilevel dining areas, secluded alcoves, private dining rooms, or features such as display cooking areas. A mix of seating and table types, adequate aisle and serving areas, and well-chosen materials and lighting combine to create a comfortable, inviting dining environment.

Flexibility in dining spaces is an asset. Private dining and compartmentalization of the main dining areas provide a means of accommodating large or small groups of diners without disrupting the general dining area.

Bar areas may be open to the dining area or separate, possibly with a different design aesthetic from the main dining area. Consider the hours of use, smoking areas (if allowed), and other elements that may influence the location and adjacency of the bar to the dining area, such as the noise generated with the use of televisions.

Restrooms

Restrooms should be placed in a convenient location for restaurant patrons. Due to odors and noise, it may be prudent to locate the restrooms away from the entrance and waiting areas. Consider screening the restroom entrance from the dining area.

The design of the restrooms is as important as that for the dining areas. Patrons should be confident that the restrooms are clean, well maintained, and adequate for peak-time needs. Building codes identify minimum plumbing fixture counts; however, it may be advantageous to increase the fixture count to accommodate the patrons at peak occupancy times. Refer to the ADAAG for accessible restroom requirements.

WAIT STAFF SERVICE STATIONS

Wait staff service stations are located between the front of the house and the back of the house. Service stations should be fabricated from stainless steel or other cleanable materials, and are typically furnished with equipment, supplies, and selected beverages. Many service stations include a point-of-service (POS) terminal to calculate patron bills and process credit card receipts, depending on the operations preference of the restaurant owner.

The size and configuration of the space may determine the number of wait staff stations/POS terminals.

FURNITURE AND FURNISHINGS

Different table sizes and shapes offer variety in seating arrangements. Table sizes are known as *tops*—two-top, four-top—and reflect the number of seats at that table type. The mix of table sizes is dependent on the target clientele, menu, and general operational goals. Two-top tables are popular in urban areas for efficiency in seating; 36-in. (915-mm) square tables may be more desirable for two diners, but this table size occupies more area.

Table options include flip-up corners or edges to increase table size or to change shape (square table to a round table).

Chair selections reflect the type of comfort level desired; a fast-food restaurant may provide hard-surface chairs and nonupholstered seats to discourage lingering, while a full-service restaurant may provide comfortable, upholstered dining chairs. Chair arms assist diners in standing, and may be used more frequently in higher-end restaurants. Arms may not be desired in a casual dining area with tighter aisle clearances.

Banquettes can be used to provide comfortable, flexible seating arrangements and midheight privacy screens. The table size mix can vary at banquette areas by locating tables next to one another or separately. Two-tops, for instance, can be combined to create a table for four or more diners. Booths are desirable for comfort, privacy, and intimacy.

RESTAURANT FURNITURE DESIGN CRITERIA

SERVICE AISLES

- For square seating, allow 72 in. (1,830 mm) minimum between tables (30 in. (760 mm) aisle plus two chairs back to back).
- For diagonal seating, allow 36 in. (915 mm) minimum between corners of tables.
- For wall seating, allow 30 in. (760 mm) minimum between wall and seat back.
- Allow a minimum of 30 in. (760 mm) for bus cart and service cart access.

PATRON AISLES

- Refer to local codes for restrictions on requirements.
- For wheelchair access, allow 36 to 44 in. (915 to 1,120 mm) in aisles.
- For wall seating, allow 30 in. (760 mm) minimum between walls and table.
- Provide clear floor space for table access. Such clear floor space cannot overlap knee space by more than 19 in. (485 mm).

TABLE PLACEMENT

- Allow circulation space adjacent to doors and food service areas.
- Provide an adequate number of table types for seating flexibility.
- Consider restaurant type when designing table layouts; generally, upscale restaurants have a more generous table spacing than casual full-service restaurants.

TABLE AND COUNTER CRITERIA

- The tops of accessible tables and counters should be 28 to 34 in. (711 to 864 mm) high. A portable raised leaf may be provided to adapt lower tables.
- If seating for people in wheelchairs is provided at tables or counters, knee space at least 27 in. (685 mm) high, 30 in. (760 mm) wide, and 19 in. (485 mm) deep must be provided.
- Where food and drink are served at counters exceeding 34 in. (864 mm) in height, a portion of the main counter, 60 in. (1,524 mm) in length, should be made accessible; or accessible tables must be located in the same area.
- Corners and edges of table and countertops should be rounded for safety.

SEATING CRITERIA

- Chair seat height is usually 18 in. (457 mm). Seat heights should be slightly higher at wheelchair-accessible tables.
- Seats should be a minimum of 16 in. (406 mm) deep and 16 in. (406 mm) wide.
- Padding and cushions should be firm.
- Armrests aid diners in rising from the seat.
- Table or counter supports should not interfere with seat knee space so the feet can be positioned for rising.

RECTANGULAR TABLE

ROUND TABLE

STANDARD TABLE DIMENSIONS

SQUARE TABLES

PERSONS	A OR B
Two	2 ft–2 ft 6 in. (610–760 mm)
Four	3 ft–3 ft 6 in. (915–1,065 mm)

RECTANGULAR TABLES

PERSONS	A	B
Two (on one side)	3 ft 6 in.–4 ft (1,065–1,220 mm)	
Six (three on each side)	5 ft 10 in.–7 ft (1,778–2134 mm)	2 ft 6 in.–3 ft (760–915 m)
Eight (four on each side)	7 ft 6 in.–9 ft (2,285–2,745 mm)	

SQUARE TABLE

Round tables are usually recommended for seating four or more persons.

Dimension "A" depends on the perimeter length required per seat (1 to 2 ft; 560 to 610 mm) per person. For cocktails, 1 ft 6 in. (460 mm) is sufficient.

Tables 3 ft (915 mm) and wider will seat at least one person at each end.

Smaller table sizes are satisfactory for drink service; larger sizes are needed for dining. Tables with center bases accommodate ganged table arrangements better than four-legged tables.

The type and style of service affects tables and arrangements. Consider the use of service carts and high chairs, as well as accessibility for the disabled.

ROUND TABLES

PERSONS	A
Four to five	3 ft–3 ft 6 in. (915–1,065 mm)
Six to seven	3 ft 6 in.–4 ft 6 in. (1,065–1,370 mm)
Seven to eight	4 ft 6 in.–5 ft (1,370–1,525 mm)
Eight to ten	5 ft–6 ft (1,525–1,830 mm)

CHAIR

STOOL

TYPICAL DIMENSIONS

ACOUSTICS

Acoustical requirements vary within a restaurant. The level of noise can be controlled with the use of sound-absorptive materials and finishes and by compartmentalization of areas. Certain restaurant types may desire noisier dining and bar areas. In these cases, a noisy, bustling, energetic environment is part of the restaurant concept.

Privacy

Privacy is not an issue in large public dining areas. Secluded banquettes and private dining rooms can be set apart for more privacy, if desired.

Isolate kitchen noise through judicious placement of entrances and use of vestibules or serpentine staging areas to buffer against kitchen noise when doors are open.

Reverberation and Reflection

Avoid creating areas that are too quiet, or "dead," to avoid connotation of little traffic or unpopularity. Many restaurants are designed to be loud and reverberant to create a vibrant atmosphere, discourage lingering, and increase "table turns" and, thus, profitability. Hard surfaces promote this philosophy.

Adding carpet, acoustical ceiling areas, and upholstered walls gives a plush, quiet atmosphere that is conducive to conversation, if that is the goal of the restaurant. High-backed, semienclosed banquettes can promote a sense of privacy even in a relatively noisy establishment.

HVAC NC/RC Range

The NC/RC range may reach 40 or even 45 if a noisy, quick-turnaround atmosphere is desired. In general:

• 30 for a quiet, conversation-friendly and upscale environment.
• 40 for bars associated with restaurants.
• 35 for restaurants with quiet live music or piano bars; with amplified groups, 40 to 45.

Exterior Noise Insulation

This is seldom an issue unless the restaurant is located in an extremely high noise environment. Vestibule entries and a central waiting area can buffer dining areas from exterior noise intrusion. Minimize glass area or increase its sound isolation rating, if required to reduce outdoor noise.

BAR DIMENSIONS

A = 8'-4" TO 11'-7" (2.5 m - 3.5 m)
B = 1'-6" TO 2'-0" (457 - 610)
C = 2'-4" TO 3'-2" (711 - 965)
D = 2'-6" TO 3'-0" (762 - 914)
E = 2'-0" TO 2'-6" (610 - 762)
F = 6" - 7" (152 - 178)
G = 1'-10" TO 2'-2" (559 - 660)
H = 2'-6" TO 2'-10" (762 - 864)
I = 11" TO 1'-10" (279 - 559)
J = 7" - 9" (178 - 229)
K = 6" - 9" (152 - 229)
L = 2'-6" (762)
M = 3'-6" TO 3'-9" (1067 - 1143)
N = 3'-0" TO 3'-6" (914 - 1067)
O = 5'-0" TO 5'-9" (1524 - 1753)

BAR DIMENSIONS
Ratio of counter seating to servers is 10:1 to 12:1.

LOW COUNTER DIMENSIONS

A = 4'-11" TO 5'-6" (1499 - 1676)
B = 3'-1" TO 3'-3" (940 - 991)
C = 1'-10" TO 2'-0" (559 - 610)
D = 1'-7" MINIMUM (483)
E = 1'-6" TO 2'-0" (457 - 610)
F = 2'-4" TO 2'-8" (711 - 813)
G = 2'-3" MINIMUM (686)
H = 4" - 8" (102 - 203)
I = 5'-0" MINIMUM (1524)

LOW COUNTER DIMENSIONS
A continental bar with low seating is one means of achieving accessibility. The bartender's area can be lowered or the seating area can be on a raised platform accessed by a ramp.

BARS AND COUNTERS

1'-7" MIN (483)

ARMREST 7" - 8" (179 - 203) ABOVE CHAIR SEAT

27" MIN. (686) KNEE SPACE FOR WHEELCHAIR CLEARANCE

10 1/2" - 11 1/2" (267 - 292)

1'-6" (457) TO COORDINATE WITH ACCESSIBLE TABLE

ACCESSIBLE FURNITURE

SEATING ARRANGEMENTS FOR PERSONS USING WHEELCHAIRS

CLEARANCES:
A = 6" (152) MINIMUM (NO PASSAGE)
B = 1'-6" (457) (LIMITED PASSAGE)
C = 1'-7" (483)
D = 2'-6" (762)
E = 3'-0" (914)
F = 3'-6" (1067)
G = 4'-0" (1219)
H = 4'-6" (1372)
I = 6'-0" (1829)

All dimensions are minimum clearances. Seating layouts indicate general configurations and are not intended to depict any specific type of operation. Tables may be converted from square to round to enlarge seating capacity. Booth seating makes effective use of corner space. A wheelchair-accessible route, at least 36 in. (914 mm) wide, is required to connect the entrance, accessible fixed seating, and restrooms.

TYPICAL SEATING ARRANGEMENTS

RESTAURANT SYSTEMS

Mechanical

The mechanical system in a restaurant must function consistently to provide a comfortable environment for patrons. In the dining and bar areas, the heating and air conditioning needs may fluctuate with different occupancy levels and according to the changing seasons. Smoking areas (where allowed) in restaurants and bars are difficult to ventilate and may need to be in a different zone from other dining areas.

In kitchen, dishwashing, and other back-of-the-house areas, the heat and humidity generated will affect the overall mechanical system. Cooking areas require hoods to draw smoke and odors out of the kitchen area, and may tie into black-iron ducts. Certain cooking fuels, such as mesquite wood, can generate tarry substances, which may adhere to the inside of the ductwork. All grease-laden exhausts require cleanouts for access.

Some restaurants operate on a negative-pressure system, which helps in drawing heat, odors, and smoke out of the food service area. Consultation with mechanical engineers, code officials, and food service consultants is of utmost importance when designing exhaust hoods.

Plumbing

Efficient, trouble-free plumbing is required for a restaurant operation. Dining area wait staff stations, bar areas, restrooms, food preparation areas, and dishwashing are all dependent on plumbing. Grease traps are required in kitchen/dishwashing areas.

Coordination

Coordination of the food service equipment and the kitchen service supplies is critical. Rough-ins for plumbing, electrical, and gas service must be precisely located to ensure proper placement at equipment locations and coordination with finish materials.

FOOD SERVICE EQUIPMENT

Food service equipment is typically specified by the food service consultant. All food service equipment must meet the sanitation and construction standards of the National Sanitation Foundation. Most equipment is located in the back of the house; however, some food serving display units are located in the public dining areas, in areas such as salad bars. Sneeze guards are required at open food displays, and refrigeration is required to store and serve perishable food.

Exhaust hoods remove air, water vapor, grease, and food odors from the kitchen area, and air and water vapor from dishwashing areas. Ovens and steam-jacketed kettles only require hoods that remove air, heat, and water vapor; but if large amounts of grease from a broiler, charbroiler, fryer, or grill are present, the hood system must extract this pollutant before the air is drawn outside by fans. This is done with grease "cartridges" or with stainless-steel extractors, both of which violently blow the exhausted air around. The grease particles are collected in a trough for easy removal, or are run out a drain.

- The length of the hood and the equipment types underneath determines CFM requirements for exhaust hoods. Typical requirements range from 150 to 450 CFM (4.2 to 12.7 cu m per minute) per linear foot (305 mm) of hood.
- Some codes may require a higher exhaust rate. To make up this air differential and to prevent more air from being drawn from surrounding areas, introduce air through a supply duct. The supplied air should make up 50% to 85% of the total exhaust.

TYPICAL KITCHEN PLAN

HEAVY COOKING EQUIPMENT SIDE (250 CFM / LINEAR FT) | **LIGHT COOKING EQUIPMENT SIDE** (150 CFM / LINEAR FT)

Single exhaust hoods are available for single cooking lines. Dimensions and capacities of exhaust hoods vary with particular kitchen cooking requirements.

TYPICAL EXHAUST HOOD REQUIREMENTS

COUNTER WITH SNEEZE GUARD

Source: Cini-Little International, Inc.; Schaumburg, Illinois

Tim Shea, AIA; Richard Meier & Partners; Los Angeles, California
Ji-Seong Yun; Rhode Island School of Design; Providence, Rhode Island
Jim Johnson; Wrightson, Johnson, Haddon & Williams, Inc.; Dallas, Texas
Janet B. Rankin, AIA; Rippeteau Architects; Washington, D.C.
Cini-Little International, Inc., Food Service Consultants; Washington, D.C.

ATHLETIC FACILITIES

TENNIS

Visibility in Indoor Courts

Locate light fixtures outside the playing lines, preferably parallel to the alley lines.

A highly reflective ceiling surface and indirect lighting reduce shadows and provide the most even lighting conditions.

For optimum color contrast between the court, background, and ball, medium-dark colors are best up to 8 ft (2.4 m) along the sides of the court and 12 to 14 ft (3.6 to 4.2 m) high behind the court area. Above these zones, white or light matte finish is best.

Perimeter curtains and dividing nets can also be used to provide a background that reduces distractions and keeps the ball from going into adjacent courts. These are generally black or green and are hung so the top of the divider is 12 ft (3.6 m) above the floor, stopping ½ to 2 in. (13 to 50 mm) above the court surface.

American with Disabilities Act

The Americans with Disabilities Act (ADA) requires that tennis courts be accessible to both players and spectators in wheelchairs. At least one court must be fully accessible in a small facility; more may be required in a large facility. Curb cuts, walkways to and from the courts, gateways, drinking fountains, restrooms, locker rooms, and other spectator and player amenities must comply with federal, state, and local codes on accessibility.

Kathleen O'Meara; OM Architecture; Baltimore, Maryland
U.S. Tennis Court and Track Builders Association; Ellicott City, Maryland
National Federation of State High School Associations; Kansas City, Missouri

FABRIC FRAME COURT BUILDING—SECTION

LONG-BAY STRUCTURE—SECTION

AIR-SUPPORTED STRUCTURE—SECTION

INDOOR COURT BUILDING ENCLOSURES

TYPICAL MULTIPLE TENNIS COURT LAYOUT

INDIVIDUAL TENNIS COURT

BASKETBALL

10'-0" (3048) LENGTH (L) 10'-0" (3048)

10'-0" (3048)

3'-0" (914)

1'-0" (305) TYP.

7'-0" (2134)

3'-0" (914)

DIVISION LINE

2" (51) WIDE X 8" (203) DEEP

6'-0" (1829) RADIUS

16'-0" (4877)

12'-0" (3658)

WIDTH (W)

4'-0" (1219) PLANE OF GOAL

14" (356) SPACES 16" (406) MARKS, TYP.

19'-0" (5791)

2'-0" (610) RADIUS

6'-0" (1829) RADIUS

3'-0" (914)

THREE-POINT LINE

28'-0" (8.5 m) COACH'S BOX

10'-0" (3048) MIN. UNOBSTRUCTED CLEARANCE AROUND COURT

10'-0" (3048)

PLAN

11'-4" (3454) FOLDED

SAFETY LOCKING BAR

HYDRAULIC CYLINDER

MOVABLE GOAL RING

1" HIGH-DENSITY FOAM PADDING

2" HIGH-DENSITY FOAM PADDING

9'-0" (2743)

10'-0" (3048)

6'-6" (1981)

COURT LINE

COUNTERWEIGHTS (BUILT INTO FRAME)

6'-0" (1829)

4'-0" (1219)

4'-0" (1219)

3'-6" (1067)

PORTABLE HYDRAULIC GOAL—ELEVATIONS

MANUAL PUMP OR ELECTRICAL CONTROL LOCATION

3'-6" (1067)

14'-0" (4267) PLAYING POSITION

PORTABLE HYDRAULIC GOAL—PLAN

1/2" (13) TEMPERED GLASS

3" (76) WHITE BORDER

2" (51) WHITE BORDER

1'-3" (381)

5" (127)

5" (127)

3'-6" (1067)

4'-0" (1219)

6" (152)

2 1/16" (52.4)

5'-1 7/8" (1572)

6'-0" (1829)

9'-2 7/8" (2816) TO FLOOR

FULLY PADDED

BACKBOARD—ELEVATION AND SECTION

BASKETBALL COURT DIMENSIONS

TYPE	LENGTH FT (M)	WIDTH FT (M)	THREE-POINT LINE RADIUS FT-IN (M)
NBA	94 (28)	50 (15)	23-9 (7.2)
International	94 (28)	50 (15)	20-7 (6.3 m)
NCAA (men)	94 (28)	50 (15)	19-9 (6)
WNBA, NCAA (women)	94 (28)	50 (15)	19-9 (6)
High school (women)	84 (25)	50 (15)	19-9 (6)
High School (men)	84 (25)	50 (15)	19-9 (6)

Dean Cox, AIA; Collins Rimer Gordon Architects; Cleveland, Ohio

RACQUETBALL AND HANDBALL

4'-0" X 8'-0" X 7/8" TONGUE-AND-GROOVE PARTICLEBOARD WITH LAMINATED FINISH

1 3/4" SOLID CORE WOOD DOOR WITH LAMINATED FINISH

FIRE-RETARDANT SOUNDPROOF MATERIAL

ADJUSTABLE ALUMINUM DOOR FRAME

GYPSUM BOARD

4" 18-GA. METAL "C" STUD AT 16" O.C.

DOOR AT JAMB—DETAIL

SWING-OUT MOUNTING LUG

TEMPERED GLASS LENS

5-1/2"

LIGHT FIXTURE—DETAIL

6" 16-GA. METAL JOIST AT 12" O.C.

4'-0" X 8'-0" X 5/8" TONGUE-AND-GROOVE PARTICLEBOARD WITH LAMINATED FINISH

WIRE HANGER TO SUPPORT METAL TEE

20'-0" AFF

8'-0" TO BACK WALL

CEILING CONDITION—DETAIL

1"

TRACK INSERT 8'-0" LENGTH, STANDARD

MOVABLE COURT WALL FRAME

COURT WALL

MOVABLE WALL ASSEMBLY FOR COURT CONVERSION—DETAIL

Racquetball and Handball Courts

Racquetball and handball use essentially the same-size court; however, handball may be played on courts with one, three, or four walls, and either indoors or outdoors. For a standard one-wall handball court, the wall should be 20 ft (6 m) from the outside edge of one sideline to the outside edge of the other sideline, and be 16 ft (4.8 m) high, including any top line. For three-wall handball, the sidewalls should be 44 ft (13.4 m) long, but the court should be marked for 40 ft (12 m) long.

Temperature and humidity requirements for racquetball courts must be maintained during storage,

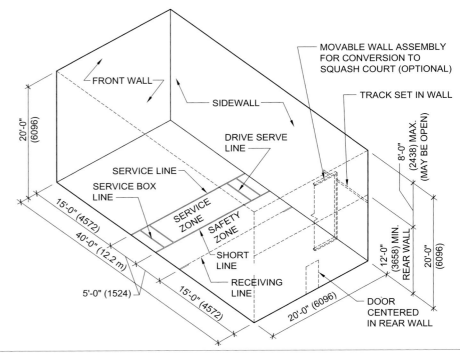

FRONT WALL

SIDEWALL

MOVABLE WALL ASSEMBLY FOR CONVERSION TO SQUASH COURT (OPTIONAL)

TRACK SET IN WALL

DRIVE SERVE LINE

SERVICE LINE

SERVICE BOX LINE

SERVICE ZONE

SAFETY ZONE

SHORT LINE

RECEIVING LINE

DOOR CENTERED IN REAR WALL

20'-0" (6096)

8'-0" (2438) MAX. (MAY BE OPEN)

12'-0" MIN. (3658) REAR WALL

20'-0" (6096)

15'-0" (4572)

40'-0" (12.2 m)

5'-0" (1524)

15'-0" (4572)

20'-0" (6096)

RACQUETBALL COURT

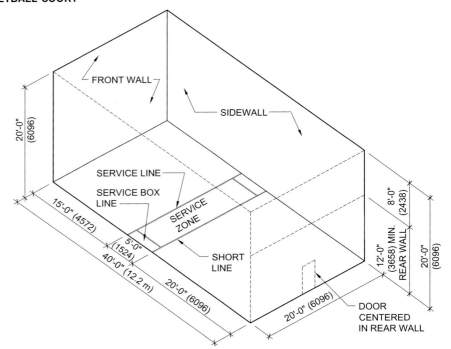

FRONT WALL

SIDEWALL

SERVICE LINE

SERVICE BOX LINE

SERVICE ZONE

SHORT LINE

DOOR CENTERED IN REAR WALL

20'-0" (6096)

8'-0" (2438)

12'-0" MIN. (3658) REAR WALL

20'-0" (6096)

15'-0" (4572)

5'-0" (1524)

40'-0" (12.2 m)

20'-0" (6096)

20'-0" (6096)

HANDBALL COURT

installation, and operation. The range for temperature is 65°F to 78°F (18°C to 25°C) and for humidity is 40% to 60%.

All lines should be 1½ in. (38 mm) wide, painted red. Racquetballs are 2 in. (50 mm) in diameter; handballs are 1⅞ in. (47 mm) in diameter.

Materials and installation of glass wall systems must comply with the safety and performance standards for walls established by the appropriate court sport association, the manufacturer, and local building codes. For this and other guidelines, contact the U.S.

Handball Association or the U.S. Racquetball Association.

A movable rear wall unit may be specified to convert a racquetball court that is 40 ft (12 m) long into a 32-ft- (9.7-m-) long squash court. The World Squash Federation sanctions the use of a 20-ft- (6-m-) wide racquetball court for squash, which normally has a court 21 ft (6.4 m) wide.

U.S. Racquetball Association; Colorado Springs, Colorado
U.S. Handball Association; Tucson, Arizona

SQUASH

6" 18-GA. METAL STUD AT 16" O.C.

7/8" TONGUE-AND-GROOVE PARTICLEBOARD WITH LAMINATED FINISH

3/4" CORK AROUND PERIMETER

2 5/8"

POLYETHYLENE VAPOR BARRIER

25/32" HARDWOOD MAPLE FLOORING

COMMON SIDEWALL—SECTION

STEEL OR WOOD FRAMING AT 16" O.C.

1" NOMINAL TONGUE-AND-GROOVE PARTICLEBOARD WITH LAMINATED FINISH

COURT WALL—DETAIL

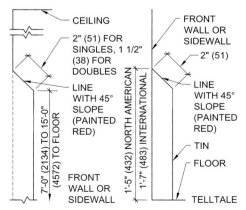

MATTE FINISH OR UNFINISHED MAPLE OR ASH FLOORING OVER WOOD SLEEPERS AT 12" O.C.

SEALANT JOINT

1/2" TEMPERED STRUCTURAL GLASS

2 5/8" THICKNESS

METAL BRACKET, FASTENED TO FLOOR

GLASS WALL SYSTEM—DETAIL

CEILING

2" (51) FOR SINGLES, 1 1/2" (38) FOR DOUBLES

LINE WITH 45° SLOPE (PAINTED RED)

7'-0" (2134) TO 15'-0" (4572) TO FLOOR

FRONT WALL OR SIDEWALL

1'-5" (432) NORTH AMERICAN

1'-7" (483) INTERNATIONAL

FRONT WALL OR SIDEWALL

2" (51)

LINE WITH 45° SLOPE (PAINTED RED)

TIN

FLOOR

TELLTALE

All playing walls of the court should be constructed of the same materials, with a hard, smooth finish, and strength and deflection characteristics as defined by the World Squash Federations or the United States Squash Racquets Association.

A squash court may be constructed from a number of materials, as long as they have suitable ball-rebound characteristics and are safe for play as recommended by the governing squash association.

COURT MARKINGS

Kenneth D. Jaffe; U.S. Squash Racquets Association; Bala-Cynwyd, Pennsylvania

FRONT WALL LINE

TOP OF COURT

SERVICE LINE

TELLTALE

SIDEWALL LINE

BACK WALL LINE

18'-6" (5639) MIN.

15'-0" (4572) TO BOTTOM OF LINE

3'-6" (1067) MIN.

5'-10" (1778) TO BOTTOM OF LINE

1'-7" (483)

SHORT LINE

HALF-COURT LINE

SERVICE BOX

7'-0" (2134) TO BOTTOM EDGE OF LINE

5'-3" (1600) INSIDE DIMENSION

SERVICE BOX

32'-0" (9.8 m)

INSIDE DIMENSION

5'-3" (1600)

14'-0" (4267)

10'-6" (3200)

10'-6" (3200)

21'-0" (5401)

10'-6" (3200)

DOOR CENTERED IN REAR WALL (3'-0" X 7'-0" MAX. SIZE)

All lines on a singles court should be 50 mm (2 in.) wide, painted red.

INTERNATIONAL SINGLES SQUASH COURT (SOFT BALL)

TOP OF COURT

SERVICE LINE

FRONT WALL

TELLTALE

SIDEWALL

31'-0" (9.5 m)

14'-0" (4267)

REAR WALL

DOOR IN REAR WALL (3'-0" X 7'-0" MAX.)

20'-0"

8'-2" (2489) TO TOP OF LINE

1'-5" (432)

SERVICE QUARTER-CIRCLE

SHORT LINE

HALF-COURT LINE

℄ DOOR AND WALL

5'-0" (1524)

15'-0" (4572)

7'-0" (2134)

4'-6" (1372) RADIUS

30'-0" (9.1 m)

45'-0" (13.7 m)

15'-0" (4572)

12'-6" (3810)

12'-6" (3810)

12'-6" (3810)

25'-0" (7.6 m)

Lines on a doubles court should be 1 in. (25.4 mm) wide, except the upper game line, which should be a 1½-in.- (38-mm-) wide bevel.

The ceiling height of the doubles court should be minimum of 24 ft. (7.3 m) high, with the lighting at that height.

NORTH AMERICAN DOUBLES SQUASH COURT (HARD BALL

AMATEUR BOXING

3" - 4" (76 - 102) DIAMETER CORNER POST

ROPES WRAPPED IN SOFT MATERIAL

PADDED FLOOR OF RING

2'-0" (610) MIN.

24'-0" (7.3 m)
16'-0" TO 20'-0" (4877 - 6096)

2'-0" (610) MIN.

1'-0" (305)
4" (102)
4'-10" (1473)
1'-6" (457)
3'-0" TO 4'-0" (914 - 1219)

AMATEUR BOXING RING

KARATE

0.05-m-(2"-) WIDE LINE, TYP.
12 m (39'-4 1/2")
8 m (26'-3")
2 m (6'-6 3/4")
2 m (6'-6 3/4")
2 m (6'-6 3/4")
2 m (6'-6 3/4")

SAFETY AREA

1.5 m (4'-11")
2 m (6'-6 3/4")
8 m (26'-3")
12 m (39'-4 1/2")

UNMARKED CENTER OF COURT

2 m (6'-6 3/4")

CORNER JUDGE
COURT CLERKS

COMPETITORS' SEATING (RED)
COMPETITORS' SEATING (WHITE)

Ceilings should be a minimum of 10 ft (3 m) high to accommodate the swinging of swords and bows. Structural support is needed in the ceiling for the heavy bags used in karate. Eight 100-lb (45-kg) bags are located approximately 4 ft (1.2 m) on center. Doors should not open into the mat area, and no mirrors or windows should be nearby.

KARATE MAT

WEIGHT LIFTING

12 m (39'-7 1/2") (COMPETITION)
4 m (13'-1 1/2") (COMPETITION)
SCORER'S TABLE
COMPETITION

8'-0" (2438) TRAINING
3'-0" (914)
2'-0" (610)
2'-0" (610)
4'-0" (1219)
8'-0" (2438) TRAINING
4 m (13'-1 1/2")
4 m (13'-1 1/2") (COMPETITION)
4 m (13'-1 1/2")
4 m (13'-1 1/2") (COMPETITION)
12 m (39'-7 1/2") (COMPETITION)

6 m (19'-8 1/4")

PLATFORM
STAGE (COMPETITION ONLY)

SIDE REFEREE
SIDE REFEREE
JURY
HEAD REFEREE

PLAN

WRESTLING

38'-0" (11.6 m)
5'-0" (1524)
28'-0" (8.5 m) DIAMETER
38'-0" (11.6 m)

10'-0" (3048) CIRCLE
2"- (51-) WIDE LINE
MAT PERIMETER

5'-0" (1524)

TYPICAL MAT

JUDO

14 m - 16 m (45'-11 1/4" TO 52'-6")
3 m (9'-10")

MAT PERIMETER
SCOREBOARD
SCORER'S TABLE

RED COMPETITOR
REFEREE
WHITE COMPETITOR

1 m TYP. (3'-3 3/8")
8 m - 10 m (26'-3" TO 32'-9 3/4")
14 m - 16 m (45'-11 1/4" TO 52'-6")

3 m (9'-10")

JUDGE
TIMER'S TABLE
DANGER AREA
SAFETY AREA

JUDO MAT

BOWLING

82'-0 3/16" (25 m) MIN.
15'-0" (4572) MIN. (APPROACH)
62'-10 3/16" (19.15 m) (BOWLING LANE)
4'-2" (1270)
5'-0 1/8" (152?)

GUTTERS
BOWLING LANE
TAIL PLANK
FOUL LINE (3/8" TO 1" WIDE)
RETURN BALL GUTTER
PIT FLOOR

PLAN

3'-5 1/2" (1054) (LANE WIDTH)
9 1/4" (235)
ROUND-TYPE GUTTER
9 1/4" (235)

FLAT-TYPE GUTTER
1 7/8" (47.6) MIN.

SECTION THROUGH LANE

GYMNASTICS

3'-3 1/4" (1000)
39'-4 1/2" (12 m)
39'-4 1/2" (12 m)
6'-6 1/2" (2000) MIN. SURROUNDING FLOOR AREA

PLAN

MAT OVER SPRING TYPE FLOOR
FOAM BORDER
6" (152) MAX
3'-3 1/4" (1000)

MAT EDGE SECTION

FLOOR EXERCISE MAT

LANDING MAT
VAULTING HORSE
VAULTING BOARD
RUNWAY
3'-0" (914)
6'-0" (1829)
78'-0" (23.8 m) MIN.
82'-0" (25 m) MAX.
18'-0" (5.5 m)

VAULTING RUNWAY

ADJUSTABLE POMMELS (ADJUSTS FROM 15 3/4" - 18 1/2" (400 - 470) IN WIDTH)
5'-3 1/2" (1600)
ADJUSTS FROM 3'-1 1/2" TO 4'-5" (950 - 1350)
11" (275)

A practice vaulting buck is similar to a vaulting horse but is only 2 ft 9 in. (835 mm) long.

VAULTING AND POMMEL HORSE

7'-10 1/2" (2400 MM)
6'-10 3/4" (2100 MM) TO 9'-2 1/4" (2800 MM)
GUY CABLES
FLOOR PLATE ANCHOR, TYP.

Bar height adjusts in 50-mm (2 in.) increments.

HORIZONTAL BAR

3" - 9"
FINISH FLOOR
ANCHOR SET INTO CONCRETE SLAB

Floorplates, installed flush with the top of the floor finish, are used to anchor horizontal bars, ring frames, and so on to the floor. Plates must be used with eye-screw attachments.

FLOORPLATE DETAIL

HIGH BAR, 1 9/16" (39) DIAMETER
LOW BAR, 1 9/16" (39) DIAMETER
3'-3 1/2" TO 5'-3" (1000 - 1600)
4'-9" TO 5'-5" (1450 - 1650)
7'-4" TO 8'-0 1/2" (2250 - 2450)
GUY CABLES
FLOORPLATE ANCHOR, TYP.

Bar height typically adjusts in 50-mm (2 in.) increments.

UNEVEN BARS

9'-0 1/4" (2750)
9'-2 1/4" (2800)
FLOORPLATE ANCHOR, TYP.

RINGS AND RING FRAME

Gymnastics Apparatus

The dimensions and specifications on this page are for general reference only. Refer to the appropriate safety manual for specific requirements for recreational or training gymnastics or for state, regional, national, and international competitions: Federation Internationale de Gymnastique (FIG); U.S.A. Gymnastics (USAG); National Collegiate Athletic Association (NCAA); and National Federation of State High School Associations (NFSH).

A clearance of 5 to 6 ft (1.5 to 1.8 m) is recommended from one apparatus to another, including corresponding mat area or obstructions such as other apparatus, walls, or columns. Each competitive area must have its own physical space, which may not overlap another competitive area. The floor exercise area must be free of obstructions. Leave room for mounting, dismounting, and vaulting areas.

16'-5" (5004)
3'-3 1/2" TO 3'-11 3/4" (1003 - 1213)
4" (102)

BALANCE BEAM

BILLIARDS, POCKET BILLIARDS, AND SNOOKER

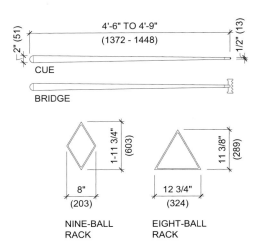

CUE

BRIDGE

NINE-BALL RACK

EIGHT-BALL RACK

Flooring must be permanently level and able to withstand point loads.

Traditionally designed billiard tables weigh about 1.5 tons (680 kg) spread over eight legs.

Lighting must not produce harsh shadows, but some modeling of the ball is desirable. Avoid direct or reflected glare. True-color rendering is important in snooker. An overall bright light is needed for each table; natural lighting is not essential. Fluorescent lamps are unacceptable.

Some sound insulation is required to prevent distractions from outside the playing area.

GAME PIECES

DARTS

PLAN

DARTBOARD

DART

DARTBOARD

TABLE DIMENSIONS

TYPE OF TABLE	PLAYING SURFACE		TABLE SIZE	
	WIDTH FT (M)	LENGTH FT (M)	WIDTH FT (M)	LENGTH FT (M)
English (Snooker)	7–2 (2.2)	14–4 (4.4)	8–2 (2.5)	15–4 (4.7)
Standard 9 ft (2.7 m)	4–2 (1.3)	8–4 (2.5)	5–2 (1.6)	9–4 (2.8)
Standard 8 ft (2.4 m)	3–8 (1.1)	7–4 (2.2)	4–8 (1.4)	8–4 (2.5)
Standard 7 ft (2.1 m)	3–2 (9.6)	6–4 (2)	4–2 (1.3)	7–4 (2.2)
Oversized 8 ft (2.4 m)	3–10 (1.2)	7–8 (2.3)	4–10 (1.5)	8–8 (2.6)

BILLIARDS AND SNOOKER TABLE

TABLE TENNIS

Flooring should be level and slightly resilient; do not use nonskid material.

Walls should provide a uniformly dark, matte background with enough contrast to help players follow the ball.

Lighting often varies for different standards of play, but 15 to 50 fc (150 to 500 lux) at table height is the acceptable range. Do not use fluorescent or natural lighting; tungsten halogen lighting is preferable.

Sectional tables are stored upright when not in use.

TABLE DIMENSIONS

SWIMMING

164'-0 3/16" (50 m)

LINE INDICATES SLOPE AT POOL BOTTOM

STARTING PLATFORM FOR 25-YD COMPETITION

ADD TO LENGTH TO ACCOMMODATE DIMENSIONS FOR TOUCHPADS, TILE FACING, ETC.

25-YD BACKSTROKE FLAG STANCHION, TYP.

DARK TILE LANE MARKINGS, 12" (305) MIN. WIDTH

54'-0" TO 75'-1" (16.4 m - 22.9 m)

6'-7" TO 9'-0" (2007 - 2743)

POOL DRAINS

15'-0" (4572)

8" TO 1'-6" (203 - 457)

BACKSTROKE FLAG LINE, SUSPENDED ABOVE WATER

LIFEGUARD CHAIR, TYP.

FALSE START/ RECALL LINE

TURNING END FOR 25-YD COMPETITION

REMOVABLE FLOATING LANE DIVIDERS (4" (102) DIAMETER, TYP.)

STARTING PLATFORM

6" - 12" (152 - 305) BETWEEN WATER LEVEL AND POOL DECK, TYP.

25-YD COMPETITION END WALL TARGET

GUARD CHAIR

5'-0" (1524) MIN.

4'-0" TO 6'-7" (1219 - 2007)

DRAIN

A 25 m (82 ft) pool width will provide 10 lanes for training or competition and accommodate international meets of any distance. An economical alternative for pool length is 70 m (229 ft) with at least one bulkhead to separate training and competition.

50 M (164 FT) COMPETITION SWIMMING POOL

Pool Design

The information on this page is based on current standards and rules for swimming races, competition diving, and other aquatic competitions stipulated by the following aquatic sport organizations:

- FINA (Federation Internationale de Natation Amateur) governs international competition, including the Olympic Games.
- U.S. Swimming (United States Swimming, Inc.) governs open and age group levels in the United States.
- U.S. Diving (United States Diving, Inc.) governs open and age group levels in the United States.
- NCAA (National Collegiate Athletic Association) governs all collegiate competition.
- NFHS (National Federation of State High School Associations) governs all high school competition.

Consult the *Official Swimming Pool Design Compendium* (Merrick, NY: National Swimming Pool Foundation) for specific rules of all the governing bodies.

Swimming pool dimensions must be measured from the inside walls or from the tile or timing devices attached to the walls. Touchpads for automatic timing may be used if they do not shorten the race course beyond minimum specifications. Markings on the finish pad and bulkheads must conform to required markings on the end walls. Visible numbers identifying lanes must be provided.

End walls and movable bulkheads serving as end walls must be parallel and vertical for a distance of 3 ft 6 in. (1 m) below the overflow level of the water. No protrusions are permitted below the surface. End walls should be finished with a nonslip surface.

All ladders, steps, or stairs must be recessed into sidewalls or be easily removable for competition.

Lighting at water level should be 100 fc (1,000 lux). (FINA standards dictate 60 fc (600 lux) at water level.)

50 M (164 ft) Pool Dimensions

When a range of dimensions is given, consult the appropriate governing organization (FINA, USS, NCAA, or NFHS) for specific dimensions.

Depending on the governing organization, pool size, and competition type, the following information applies for dimensions from the starting platform end of the pool:

- To the backstroke flag line, the dimension ranges from 15 ft (4.5 m) to 16 ft 4 in (4.9 m).
- For 50 m (164 ft) pools, the dimension to the false start/recall stanchion ranges from 42 ft (11 m) to 65 ft 7 in. (20 m).
- For 25 yd and 25 m pools, the dimension to the false start/recall stanchion ranges from 33 ft 1 in. (10 m) to 60 ft 1 in. (18.3 m).

BOTTOM AND SIDES OF POOL TO BE WHITE OR LIGHT COLOR

WATER SURFACE LEVEL

END WALL TARGET

12" (305)

3'-6" (1067)

3'-6" (1067) MIN.

5'-0" (1524)

2'-8" TO 3'-0" (813 - 914)

12" (305)

12" (305)

LANE DIVISIONS, TYP.

LINES, DARK COLOR, TYP.

8" - 12" (203 - 305)

For end wall target design, verify with authorities having jurisdiction.

LANE END MARKINGS

PLAN

SECTION

25 M AND 25 YD COMPETITION SWIMMING AND DIVING POOL

DIVING POOL ATTACHED TO SWIMMING POOL

COMBINED 25 M AND 25 YD SWIMMING POOL

25 M and 25 Yd Pool Dimensions

When a range of dimensions is given, consult the appropriate governing organization (FINA, USS, NCAA, or NFHS) for specific dimensions.

Depending on the governing organization, pool size, and competition type, the following information applies for dimensions from the starting platform end of the pool:

- To the backstroke flag line, the dimension ranges from 15 ft (4.5 m) to 16 ft 4¾ in. (5 m).
- To the false start/recall stanchion, the dimension ranges from 33 ft 1 in. (10 m) to 60 ft 1 in. (18.3 m).

ALTERNATE POOL LAYOUTS

3 ☐ **ATHLETIC FACILITIES**

Pool Platforms, Ladder, Bulkheads, and End Wall Targets

SIDE ELEVATION

PLAN

In pools with a water depth of 3 ft 6 in. to 4 ft (1,065 to 1220 mm) at the starting end (measured at the end wall or any point within 12 in. (305 mm) of the end wall, starting platforms may be no more than 18 in. (460 mm) above the water surface. Otherwise, the swimmers must start from the deck or in the water.

In pools with a water depth less than 3 ft 6 in. (1,065 mm) in the starting end, the swimmers must start in the water.

STARTING PLATFORM REQUIREMENTS

PLAN

POOL LADDER

ALTERNATE STARTING PLATFORMS

PLAN

BUILT-IN STEPS WITH GRAB RAILS

FLOATING FLOOR   **SCISSOR JACK**

SECTIONS SHOWING MOVABLE FLOORS

PLAN—BULKHEAD

SECTIONS SHOWING BULKHEAD IN VARIOUS STORAGE POSITIONS

BULKHEADS AND MOVABLE FLOORS

Pool Perimeter Overflow

ROLL-OUT GUTTER SYSTEM

SEMIRECESSED OPEN GUTTER SYSTEM

SEMIRECESSED GUTTER SYSTEM

In addition to the stainless-steel system shown, gutters may be designed as an integral part of the concrete deck edge.

FULLY RECESSED GUTTER SYSTEM

The zero-depth gutter system is typically used for walk-in or leisure-type pools.

ZERO-DEPTH GUTTER SYSTEM

Surface skimmers are not recommended for use in competitive pools.

SKIMMER DETAIL

Perimeter Overflow Systems

A perimeter overflow system must be provided on all public swimming pools. The system must be designed and constructed to maintain the water level of the pool at the operating level of the overflow rim or weir device. Applicable codes determine the dimension from the deck to the water level.

When used as the only overflow system on a pool, a perimeter overflow system must extend around a minimum of half the swimming pool perimeter. Perimeter overflow systems must be connected to the circulation system.

The perimeter overflow system in combination with the upper rim of the pool must constitute a handhold. It must be designed to prevent entrapment of a swimmer's arms, legs, or feet, and to permit inspection and cleaning.

Roll-out and/or zero-depth flush perimeter overflow systems are most commonly used in recreational pools and walk-in shallow areas. Competitive pools that have

semirecessed gutters along their length to trap wave surge and prevent reflected waves must have fully recessed gutters at the ends or provide a visual barrier that can be seen by competing swimmers.

Metal swimming pool systems with built-in perimeter overflow are available. In addition to the overflow channel, the metal liner may contain the return waterline from the filtration system. A metal liner that incorporates a cove between wall and floor is desirable to facilitate cleaning.

Deck areas adjoining an overflow system are generally required to slope away from it to separate drains. When a deck is sloped to the pool overflow, provide for diverting the overflow to waste during deck cleaning.

Return water may enter the gutter through a series of skimming weirs spaced around the pool perimeter or by overflow into the gutter. For normal recreational use, the water level is kept at the center of the skimmer face, allowing the pool to act as a surge chamber and absorb water displacement caused by swimmers. For competitive use, the water level is raised to the gut-

ter lip. Waves then flow over the lip and are returned through the surge tank without rebound.

Surface Skimmers

If surface skimmers are used, provide one for each 500 sq ft or fraction thereof of the pool surface. When two or more skimmers are used, they must be located so they maintain effective skimming action over the entire surface of the pool. To obtain the most effective skimming action, locate the skimmers with regard to the prevailing wind and drift, shape of the pool, and water circulation pattern. Use of directional inlet fittings will help ensure a proper circulation pattern.

Skimmers may not be permitted in larger pools; see local health department codes for limitations on public pool use. Skimmers are not recommended for use in competitive pools.

Robert D. Buckley, AIA; Robert D. Buckley Architect; Kalamazoo, Michigan
D. J. Hunsaker; Counsilman/Hunsaker & Associates; St. Louis, Missouri
National Swimming Pool Foundation; Merrick, New York

ARENA FOOTBALL

ARENA FOOTBALL FIELD

GOALPOST AND REBOUND NET

INDOOR SOCCER

CONTINENTAL INDOOR SOCCER
LEAGUE (CISL) FIELD MARKINGS

Indoor soccer, in both the USSF and the FIFA, is typically played in hockey arenas within the existing rink walls, on an artificial playing surface affixed to the rink surface.

INDOOR SOCCER FIELD

SOCCER GOAL

TARGET SHOOTING

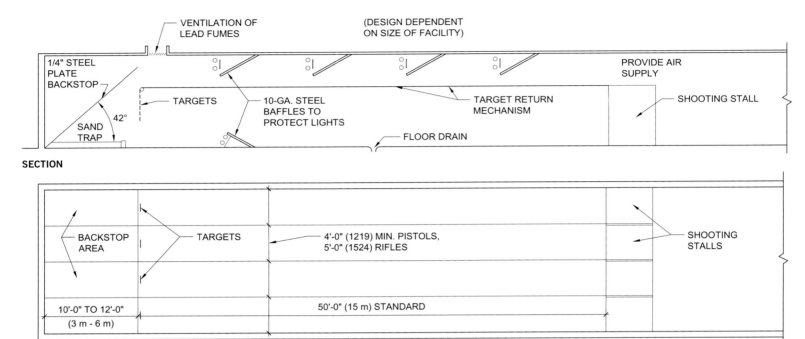

SECTION

PLAN

TARGET SHOOTING RANGE

Shooting Range Design Considerations

When planning a firearms range, consider the following:

- Placement of traps; use of stalls, and placement of firing line; provision for space for spectators; protection from ricochet; prevention of spilled powder explosions
- Ventilation adequate to dissipate lead fumes
- Noise abatement
- Lighting
- The use of range design consultants is advisable. Contact the National Rifle Association for information.

FENCING

STRIP

WEAPONS

Fencing Design Considerations

Wooden nonskid flooring is ideal. A rubber piste is used on slippery floors. When a special metallic piste is used, a rubber mat must be placed beneath it to prevent hits on the floor being registered by the electronic scoring device. In competitive fencing, the score is kept by an electronic apparatus, which records each hit, and is linked to the fencers by wires. The wires are kept from trailing the ground by a spring-loaded spool. These spools often are recessed in a pit at each end of the piste.

Mary Bilodeau Klinoff; Concord, Massachusetts

ICE HOCKEY

Ancillary Spaces at Ice Rinks

The design of an ice rink must include planning for the ancillary space requirements described here:

- Large hinged swing gates that open into the ice rink, usually at one end, are needed to accommodate the Zamboni, a machine used for resurfacing the ice.
- An area is needed outside the main ice rink for disposal of ice removed by the Zamboni. This space customarily is large enough to allow ½ to 1 cu yd (.4 to .8 m³) of ice to melt into a drainage sump. However, some smaller indoor facilities simply remove the scraped ice to the exterior of the building.

- A header trench 3 ft wide × 3 ft deep (915 mm by 915 m) should be located at one side of the ice rink to accommodate piping connections to underfloor systems.
- Floor surfaces for which access to the rink is required for skaters and a Zamboni normally consist of a rubber belting assembly or similar material.

Rink Design and Planning

The details shown on this page represent typical systems. Actual details must be modified as appropriate for individual projects.

The details shown indicate options for seasonal and year-round operations. Choice of design, detailing, underfloor

heating, insulation, and other features depends on the anticipated operation of a particular rink.

Considerations affecting ice rink design and planning include requirements for underfloor drainage, ventilation, and humidity control; subsoil conditions at the site; the requirements of refrigeration plants, the ice-making system, and lighting and other electrical features; and maintenance and operational needs.

It is recommended that a qualified consultant be involved in the design and planning of ice rink systems.

Dean Cox, AIA; Collins Rimer Gordon Architects; Cleveland, Ohio

SECTION AT RINK'S EDGE WALL

YEAR-ROUND RINK (NATURAL SAND FLOOR WITH INSULATION)

ICE HOCKEY GOAL

ICE HOCKEY RINK SIZE

ICE HOCKEY RINK SIZE

RINK TYPE	LENGTH FT (M)	WIDTH FT (M)
NHL	200 (61)	85 (26)
Olympic	200 (61)	100 (30)
NCAA	200 (61)	85 (26)
College and High School	200 (61)	85 (26)

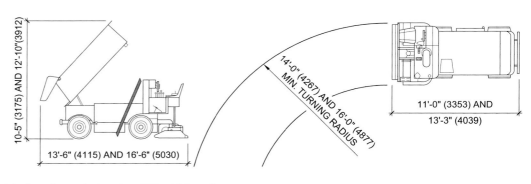

Vehicle dimensions shown represent two of the available models. Consult manufacturer for additional information.

ZAMBONI ICE RESURFACER

CURLING

CURLING

LIBRARIES

HISTORY

The word "library" is derived from the Latin word *liber,* for book. The earliest libraries were privately owned collections of books and scrolls, to be viewed only by the wealthy and the religious or political elite. As societies developed and economies expanded, centers of learning shifted from monasteries to schools and universities, where library collections were made available to scholars and students. With the invention of the printing press, the expansion of economic development, and, later, the establishment of more democratic governments, libraries began to open their doors to the public.

Early libraries housed their collections in simple cabinets. Books were opened upon lecterns for viewing and, often, were chained to the lectern to prevent thefts. Modern libraries today contain many different media and provide space for widely varying activities, from public lectures to private study, and from viewing film, video, DVDs, or other visual media to listening to audio collections on records, tapes, or CDs. With the advent of electronic information technologies, libraries are no longer simply repositories for physical collections of information, but are also portals of access to the enormous network of information on the Internet.

CONCEPTUAL PLANNING

Conceptual planning for libraries begins with an assessment of the intended users of the facility. For example, a community or public library should respond to the wide range of ages and interests of the expected user groups. In contrast, an academic library designed only for upper-level collegiate work or private research will focus on the needs of a more specialized user group and inventory of library materials. In the programming phase, a set of spatial requirements is generated. This design program is written to reflect the specific needs of the facility and the materials that will be stored, accessed, and checked out.

Area calculations are made for these spatial requirements with a projected growth for the future. These calculations are based on formulas that differ for library types. The library staff and administration will contribute greatly to the design parameters that are outlined during the programming phase, since each library has unique operational procedures. If the facility will be a public library, often the design team will lead public meetings in order to understand the needs and goals of the community and to help the library board garner public support for the project. For larger libraries and academic libraries, often a library consultant is retained for this part of the design process.

PROGRAM SPACES FOR LIBRARIES

The program for every library will differ in the content and layout of spaces. The diagram on this page is an example of interior spaces that may be included in the program for a small to medium-sized public library. A brief description of each of the major components is given in the following subsections.

Auditorium

Some library boards desire an auditorium space in their program, for use in public presentations, readings, or other community events. This kind of space is generally adjacent to the public lobby, but is separate from the rest of the spaces that house the library's inventory of materials, to allow after-hours or separate use of the auditorium. The designer should determine early in the programming phase whether food or beverage vending is desired, and plan accordingly.

Checkout

This is the central point in the flow of library materials and visitor traffic into and out of the facility. In addition to providing a desk where patrons check out materials, this area serves as a focal point for visitor inquiries and a source of initial wayfinding information for the facility. The library staff will have important input on the function and details for the design of this area, since the number of staff members and their duties will determine much of the programmatic direction for the space. Larger libraries may separate the checkout area from the control or inquiry functions for smoother traffic flow.

Children's Area

For a community library, including a children's area will build enthusiasm for reading among children and for support of the library's reading programs. The children's area should be near the checkout desk to provide a visual connection between library staff and the area. Restrooms nearby are a basic requirement. Ideally, library visitors will be able to see the children's area from the lobby. Colorful signage and wall or ceiling materials will attract children's attention and provide a good signpost to guide them directly to the place designed just for them.

Catalogue

Most libraries today have their collections catalogued on a database that is viewed from computer terminals. Some libraries, however, still utilize a paper card catalogue system, so the designer should confirm which system the library staff intends to use. Generally, this area should be located near the checkout desk so that staff members are available for inquiries, but it could be located separately if a staff desk is nearby so that patrons can conveniently seek assistance. Some libraries provide catalogue terminals within the stacks.

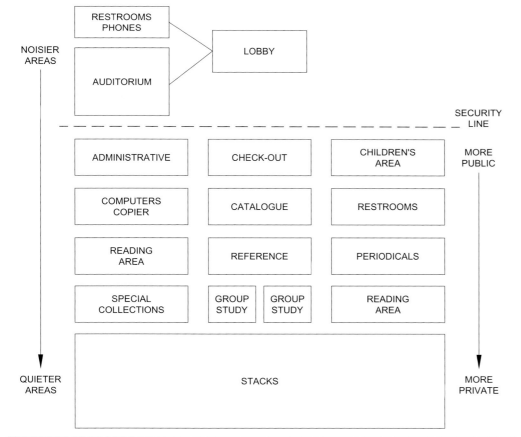

CONCEPTUAL DIAGRAM FOR A SMALL PUBLIC LIBRARY

DESIGN CONSIDERATIONS

Structural Elements

The layout of the grid for the structural columns should be developed to correlate with the layout of the stacks and aisles. It is desirable for the columns to be sized or furred out to match the width of the stacks, to provide one continuous face along the front of the stacks. This eliminates setbacks from the face of the shelving that could collect trash or inhibit convenient floor maintenance in these areas. For similar reasons, columns that protrude beyond the face of the stacks should be avoided, so as not to interfere with minimum aisle widths.

Two ways to maximize storage area for the collections are decreasing the floor-to-floor height in the stack area and using high-density sliding storage systems. In libraries with large collections, the stacks may be housed in a separate wing of the building, with shorter floor-to-floor heights than the more public spaces. In some large libraries, though using high-density sliding storage systems for stacks may be desirable, this will increase the dead and live loads for which the structural system was designed. Because high-density shelving systems allow for almost twice the storage of the typical stacks system, they are often considered when an increase in book storage capacity is desired. Such systems have various uses, including to archive periodicals or infrequently used items. High-density sliding shelving systems are accessed only by trained library staff; they are not open to the public.

Acoustics

Appropriate acoustical separation begins in the schematic layout of spaces, with the segregation of noisier activities from quieter activities. In the conceptual diagram figure shown above right, note that the more public areas—including the lobby, auditorium, checkout desk, children's area, and the restrooms—are grouped apart from the more private areas—the reference and periodicals areas, reading areas, and the stacks. When considering the schematic layout of interior spaces, the designer should also identify potential outside noise sources, such as trucks at the loading dock or traffic on adjacent roads. Additional acoustical separation of spaces can be achieved with sound partitions and doors and acoustically absorptive material on the ceilings and floors.

While noise in a library can be obtrusive, silence can also be a distracting aspect of the environment. Therefore, some amount of low-level white noise is acceptable, particularly in the reading areas. The sound of air traveling through the HVAC system can provide adequate masking noise, if the system is designed properly. However, the designer should work closely with the mechanical consultant to reduce noticeable or obtrusive noise from the HVAC system, such as whistling or rattling sounds from ducts or air diffusers. The designer should also work with the lighting designer to avoid the selection of light fixtures that require noisy ballasts.

In this example, column spacing 22 ft 6 in. × 22 ft 6 in. (6.8 × 6.8 m) with standard shelving provides a very efficient arrangement (especially as shown to the right of this illustration). However, the next bay of shelving to the left (or right) is somewhat less efficient, depending upon the particulars of the layout. To be clear about the efficiency of any module for other than a small library, more than one structural bay must be considered.

COLUMN NARROWER THAN STACK WIDTH CREATES NICHE THAT MAY COLLECT TRASH

COLUMN LARGER THAN STACK WIDTH CREATES PINCH POINT IN AISLE WIDTH

STRUCTURAL ELEMENTS FIGURE GRID LAYOUT

FLOOR-TO-FLOOR HEIGHT AT STACKS CAN BE SHORTER THAN AT PUBLIC AREAS

Aisles

The aisles parallel to the stacks are called *range aisles;* those perpendicular to the stacks are called *cross aisles*. The minimum aisle width at accessible stacks is 36 in. (914 mm), to meet the requirements of the *Americans with Disabilities Act Accessibility Guidelines* (ADAAG); but 42 in. (1,066 mm) is preferred, to allow wheelchair access and enough space for an ambulatory person to pass. In some instances, the Building Code requires 44 in. (1,117 mm) aisles for adequate exiting, depending on whether the aisles are open to the public and the occupant load expected. The designer should review with the library staff where the more popular or frequently used collections will be positioned among the stacks, so that additional range aisle width can be provided to accommodate higher traffic in those areas. Range aisles are generally designed for the minimum required width in order to achieve maximum efficiency for the stack layout, with greater cross aisle width to handle the tributary loads of the range aisles. In all cases, the designer should review with the local code authority the minimum aisle and exit clearances at the stacks.

Shelving

The shelving chosen for the stacks will depend on the size of materials in the library's collection. Standards in the United States for shelf depths are generally 7, 9, and 11 in. (177, 228, and 279 mm) actual dimension, or 8, 10, and 12 in. (203, 254, and 304 mm) nominal dimension, with deeper shelves available for oversize collections. Manufactured metal shelving is the most common product specified for new libraries because of its modularity, ease of adjustability, and cost-effectiveness. A variety of accessories are available, such as solid or wire bookends, slanted display shelves for periodicals, and placard holders. In regions where seismic concerns are important, shelving should be braced to the building structure to prevent overturning in an earthquake.

STANDARD AISLE WIDTH

AISLE WIDTH AT SHELVING

Human dimensions in very large aisles are clearly intended for very heavy use. The figure at the far right assumes a file cabinet that is 17½ in. (444 mm) deep, which is shallower than most. Even the typical card catalog cabinet is about 20 in. (508 mm) deep, including the handles.

AISLE WIDTH AT CARD CATALOG

PERIODICAL DISPLAY SHELVING

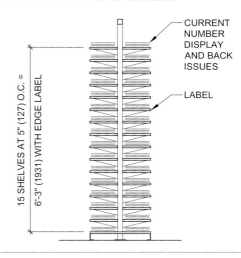

Lighting

Adequate lighting, without glare, is the goal for most interior spaces in a library. Some collections may contain light-sensitive pieces, and these should be located in designated areas with lighting designed specifically for the parameters of the materials being stored and viewed.

Lighting at reading areas can be from overhead ambient sources, as well as from floor lamps or task lights on tabletops. Design of task lighting should be detailed to reduce glare on the table surface and to prohibit a direct view of the lamp source. Fixtures should be selected without a wide range of flexibility for the angle of the shade, to prevent users from inadvertently shining the fixture directly at those seated opposite.

Ambient Lighting

Ambient lighting at the stacks can be provided with overhead fixtures, positioned in rows parallel to the shelving. This offers good light quality at the shelving, since the light shines directly on the face of the shelves. However, this limits flexibility in changing stack locations later, since the new stack location could be positioned directly below a fixture, resulting in shadows and dimly lit shelving.

Overhead Lighting

Overhead fixtures positioned perpendicular to the stacks provide an even light quality in the space, but will result in slightly less direct light onto the shelving than if positioned parallel to the stacks. However, a perpendicular arrangement offers greater flexibility for layout or repositioning the stacks in the future than is possible with the parallel lighting arrangement.

Indirect Lighting

The use of indirect fixtures provides an effective ambient light source, while reducing glare and shadows. These fixtures direct the light to the ceiling instead of the floor, which results in bounce-light off the surface of the ceiling for general illumination. The designer may choose to have the shelf units at the stacks outfitted with indirect fixtures on top that point up to the ceiling; an alternative is to select fixtures that are separate from the stacks, either ceiling-suspended above the stacks or mounted on the columns or walls. This type of lighting will require a ceiling surface that is light-colored for good reflectivity and that is near enough to the stacks to be feasible as a reflective surface for the light.

Mounted Lighting

For spaces with very high ceilings, where ceiling-mounted light fixtures would be too far above the stacks, another option is to affix lighting to the shelving unit itself or to a system of struts that span between the shelf units. This offers the benefits of lighting parallel to the stacks, with flexibility for moving the stacks later.

Daylighting

Designing for natural light in libraries creates inviting spaces that encourage people to come to the library and settle in with a good book. Skylights that are posi-

LIGHTING PARALLEL TO STACKS

INDIRECT LIGHTING AFFIXED TO STACKS

LIGHTING PERPENDICULAR TO STACKS

STRUTS AFFIXED TO STACKS WITH PARALLEL LIGHTING

LIGHTING CONFIGURATIONS

tioned to capture direct sunlight are best located in areas such as primary circulation spaces or public lobbies. The designer considering skylights over the stacks or reading areas should detail them to prevent direct sunlight on the library collections and to control glare. North-facing glass or sun-shading devices that deflect direct light are preferable in these situations. Individual reading alcoves near exterior windows offer patrons cozy places for reading, and often become the most popular spots in the building.

Security Devices

The central location of the checkout area provides a point of visual observation of library visitors entering or leaving the facility. Electronic security devices, using radio frequency identification equipment to detect the presence of a coded tag on the library materials, are typically located at building exits. To prevent unauthorized removal of library materials, these devices emit an audible and/or visual alarm when the tag is within a specified range of the device. Library staff desensitize the tag at the checkout desk, which allows the visitor to exit without setting off the alarm.

The designer should refer to the manufacturer's data for system requirements to properly locate the devices in plan; but, in general, they should be positioned to encourage a traffic pattern that will allow visitors to enter and exit to the right. Minimum separation of the devices is 36 in. (914 mm), though some manufacturers produce units that can be up to 48 in. (1,219 mm) apart. If the library handles a large volume of patrons, it may be necessary to include turnstiles at the exits to guide visitors, single-file, past the security devices. The use of other security devices such as cameras and monitors should be discussed during the programming phase to determine the level of security and sophistication of devices appropriate for the facility.

Wiring

Now that electronic information technologies are commonly used, the planning of a library must address the accommodation of the wiring required for these technologies. While the design of the system and its capacity differ for each library, the accommodation of these systems is the same. The designer should consider the arrangement of electrical and data wiring, the placement of the wiring within the infrastructure, the placement of wiring within the casework and the furniture, the accessibility of these systems, the management of these systems, and the possibility for future growth. While future technological advancement will bring wireless technology to the forefront (some libraries already utilize it in limited areas), present-day library design requires the resolution of these wiring issues. For larger libraries, an information technology consultant is often retained for the design and installation of these systems.

Library Furniture

Durability, functionality, and comfort are fundamental characteristics of good library furniture. Providing custom casework at the checkout desks or other furniture pieces offers an opportunity to bring continuity to interior spaces by incorporating finish materials used elsewhere in the space into the casework design. Alternatively, several manufacturers offer furniture systems designed specifically for library use. Often, by combining prefabricated pieces (such as tables, chairs, study carrels, or shelving at the stacks) with custom-designed casework (such as the checkout desk or other specialty pieces) the designer can be a good steward of the budget, while incorporating custom quality design features into the interior space.

Seating

Comfortable soft seating, such as upholstered chairs and sofas, is generally best for informal reading or lounge areas. Pull-up chairs with metal or wood arms are typically used at reading tables and carrels. That said, it's important to note that these furniture pieces are subject to extremely heavy wear, and frequent reupholstery is indicated; thus, fabrics should be of the heaviest duty, because they may have a life span of only four to five years. Chairs with mechanically adjustable features are rarely selected for libraries because they are subject to heavy use, hence, potentially frequent maintenance.

Tables

Reading tables and study carrels often incorporate power outlets and possibly data outlets, depending on the extent of Internet access deemed appropriate in the program, to allow patrons to plug in their laptop computers or other electronic devices. Reading tables and study carrels should be sized large enough for library patrons to spread out their materials, particularly in areas where oversized materials are viewed. The recommended height of study carrel partitions is at least 52 in. (1,320 mm) above the floor to provide privacy within the carrel. Tables or podiums with slanted tops are designed for more convenient reading by slanting the table top toward the viewer. This type of slanted-top table is useful for viewing oversized materials or newspapers.

The selection and arrangement of both seats and tables should be made to meet the requirements of the *Americans with Disabilities Act Accessibility Guidelines* and those of the local codes.

The seminal work of Keyes D. Metcalf, *Planning Academic and Research Library Buildings* (Chicago, IL: American Library Association Editions, 1999), and updated editions of his original work will provide readers with an exhaustive investigation of library design issues.

The designer of a new library can also contact the many library associations for publications and articles on current thinking for planning libraries and their interior spaces. These include the American Library Association (ALA), the Association of College and Research Libraries (ACRL), the Library Administration and Management Association (LAMA), and the International Federation of Library Associations and Institutions (IFLA).

Jane Clark, AIA; Zimmer Gunsul Frasca Partnership; Seattle, Washington
Natasa Jelic; Rhode Island School of Design; Providence, Rhode Island
Jim Johnson; Wrightson, Johnson, Haddon & Williams, Inc.; Dallas, Texas

Round tables are not normally recommended for research purposes, but they may be desired in a staff room or in an area designed for light reading.

LIBARARY READING ROOM TABLE LAYOUT

LOUNGE CHAIRS, TABLES, AND SHELVING LAYOUT

CHILD CARE CENTERS

FIRST CHILD CARE CENTERS

As of the mid-1990s, 30% of all children under the age of five in the United States were enrolled in a child care center. In *Child Care Design Guide*, Anita Rui Olds has calculated that these children "may have spent as many as 12,500 hours in a child care center—the amount of time that most adults have spent in elementary and high school combined." Yet the impact of these environments and this type of care is still not fully understood. Many of the first child care centers were located in renovated buildings and educational wings or basements of churches and synagogues. Structures constructed for the sole purpose of housing child care still comprise a relatively new building type; it is only recently that designers who themselves experienced these environments as children are beginning to bring their perceptions and insights to the planning and design of these facilities.

DESIGNING ENVIRONMENTS FOR CHILDREN

Designing spaces for children requires an awareness of and sensitivity to the uniqueness of the child as the user within the space. There are both obvious and obscure differences between the perceptions of adults and children regarding spaces, as well as their use of them.

The most obvious difference between adults and children is physical size. An environment whose elements are scaled to the size of the children who will make up the primary user group communicates that their needs were important in the design of the space. For example, windows set at the eye level of children, and lavatory handles that can be reached without standing on stools, indicate that the environment has been designed with children in mind, as opposed to one in which children are forced to adapt to a space that has been designed for adults. Not only does a child-scaled environment help to generate children's sense of control and comfort, it also leads to a higher degree of safety by reducing their need to, for example, stretch awkwardly to reach objects or stand precariously on the edge of furnishings to see over or out.

In the creation of children's spaces, it is also important to remember the very limited experience that children have had with built environments. Whereas adults automatically assume many relationships between and within spaces because they're familiar with the design repetition used in similar spaces, newborns and toddlers cannot, for example, always understand the difference in behavior that is appropriate for the airport and behavior that is appropriate for a religious setting. Likewise, most young children do not always understand the function or purpose of waiting rooms. Children's perceptions of space are also unique. To an adult, a long narrow corridor can be understood as an expedient means of organizing spaces. To the child, it may appear to be a great opportunity for running with no obstructions. Obviously, with repeated exposure and maturity, children become familiar with the organization of spaces, their functions, and expected behaviors within certain types of spaces; but for the designer of children's spaces, it is important to remember the relatively small amount of experience children have engaging with and understanding the built environment.

It is also important that designers remember that signage that is often used in public buildings to orient adults is of little or no value to young children, who lack the ability to read or to understand unfamiliar words. Thus, the use of visual architectural elements and graphics that delineate a course of travel may give a child, even when accompanied by an adult, some sense of control and may help the child to create a means to find his or her way within the built environment.

As users of space, children also represent a vulnerable population. They typically have no power in shaping their environments and, therefore, can only respond to them. Consequently, it is important that they be provided with sensitively designed spaces that will allow them a degree of understanding and sense of control over their surroundings.

Scale

The prevailing thought of many child care and design professionals is that the child care center environment should present a homelike atmosphere in terms of its organization of spaces and use of building materials, interior furnishings, and finishes. Children often suffer anxiety when separated from their parents, and this anxiety may be alleviated to some degree by environments that engender a feeling of familiarity. Some research has indicated that there may even be a direct relationship between the degree of "homelikeness" of a facility and the tendency for caregivers to respond to the children in a more familial manner.

The optimum maximum size for child care centers is between 60 to 75 children. Centers of this size often feature radial organizations with a commons or multipurpose area that can be shared by the surrounding group rooms placed in the center.

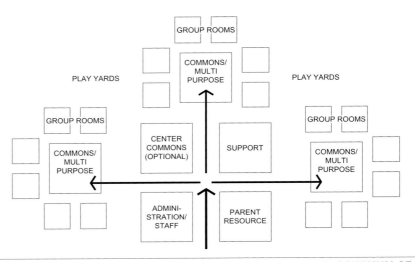

RADIAL ORGANIZATION OF SPACES FOR A SMALL CHILD CARE CENTER (MAXIMUM OF 60 TO 75 CHILDREN)

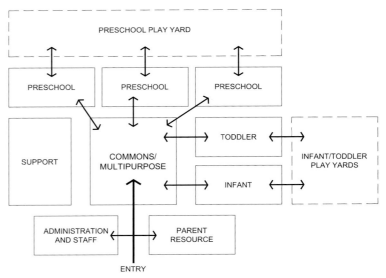

This arrangement features smaller buildings located around a central organizing space. Security at entry to the campus and at each building must be considered. Parent resources and some staff support areas may be duplicated within each building for ease of access.

CAMPUS PLAN FOR A CHILD CARE CENTER (MORE THAN 75 CHILDREN)

Campus-Type Plan

Designers of facilities destined to service more than 75 children should consider using a campus-type plan in an effort to reduce the scale of the facility and the massing of the structures. Smaller-scale environments are more apt to appear homelike and are thought to be less intimidating to a child than larger unfamiliar environments. A campus plan that comprises multiple buildings, each housing fewer children and featuring separate identities and individual entries, is highly desirable. This type of campus plan does, however, require that a mechanism and procedure be developed to ensure security for the entire campus and at each entry to prevent unauthorized and undocumented entry by visitors. If a campus plan is not possible, a building plan that incorporates smaller clusters or pods within a larger building is encouraged.

Within the center of the "campus," great attention should be given to the design of administrative and staff support areas to ensure that they do not overtake or diminish the prominence of the children's areas. This, too, helps to create a warm and exciting child-friendly environment by downplaying those areas that do not directly serve the child.

SPACES

The day-to-day operations that take place in, as well as the number of children who use, a child care center can greatly impact the type, size, and organization of the required space. The objective of the center can also play a role in the design, hence should be completely understood by the designer prior to beginning design. The sole purpose of some centers is to care for children during the absence of their parents, while other center programs may include an educational objective. The hours of service can also greatly impact the design, especially if the center provides child care for children whose parents may work during night hours. In consultation with the center's owner or director, a list of building area requirements can provide a starting point for discussions that will lead to the delineation of spatial needs and relationships for centers of most any size and program.

An integral part of the design of a child care center is the development of outdoor spaces. Outdoor spaces function best when they are accessible directly from the group rooms. This strengthens the relationship between the indoor and outdoor spaces because it makes them readily available. Both the group room and the outdoor play yard should consist of spaces with many different qualities: spaces that are quiet, spaces that are noisy, spaces that are messy, spaces that are neat, spaces that are cozy, and spaces that are open.

Group Rooms

The design of group rooms within a child care facility is of great importance, as it is in these spaces that children will spend most of their time. Many activities and functions occur simultaneously within group rooms. It is important to note that the programs of some child care centers will feature multiage groupings, as opposed to a group of same-age children.

BUILDING AREA REQUIREMENTS FOR CHILD CARE FACILITIES

	MINIMUM	ADEQUATE	EXCELLENT
Group Rooms	55 sq ft/child (5.1 sq m/child)	65 sq ft/child (6 sq m/child)	72 sq ft/child (6.7 sq m/child)
Support Areas	15 sq ft/child (1.4 sq m/child)	20 sq ft/child (1.9 sq. m/child)	24 sq ft/child (2.2 sq m/child)
Circulation/ Service Areas	18 sq ft/child (1.7 sq m/child)	25 sq ft/child (2.3 sq m/child)	29 sq ft child (2.7 sq m/child)
Total Building Area	88 sq ft/child (8.2 sq m/child)	110 sq ft/child (10.2 sq m/child)	125 sq ft/child (11.6 sq m/child)
Outdoor Play Areas	75 sq ft/child (7 sq m/child)	125 sq ft/child (11.6 sq m/child)	200 sq ft/child (18.6 sq m/child)

State and local agencies that regulate and license child care centers typically have established minimum space requirements; they should be contacted for more precise calculations of required areas.

THE COPPER HOUSE, HUSKY CHILD DEVELOPMENT CENTER; HUSKY INJECTION MOLDING SYSTEMS, LTD.; BOLTON, ONTARIO, CANADA
Source: Jacob, Silverstein, Winslow and Deyenhardt Architects; Berkeley, CA

Regions and Zones

Within each group room, certain activities function more efficiently when grouped together. These groupings also tend to influence the finishes that may be selected within each area. Group rooms should be divided into two areas: a *wet region* and a *dry region*.

Within the wet region, it is best to create an *entry zone* and a *messy zone*. The entry zone may serve as a "front porch," or transitional area, where the child enters the room; it may be furnished with individual "cubby" storage units for the children, as well as other types of storage. It is also helpful to provide a bench for children to sit on, to, for example, remove rain boots, or for adults, to assist children putting on coats and shoes.

The messy zone should support activities that involve water or where children otherwise cause messes during use, such as art areas and sand play tables. The messy zone is also the best area in which to locate the access to the outdoor play area since dirt and mud may be tracked in on the bottom of shoes. Flooring for the wet region is typically a hard flooring that is durable and easy to maintain.

The dry region supports activities that are not as potentially damaging to interior finishes; thus it can be designed to appear much softer in its presentation. The dry region can be further divided into an *active zone* and a *quiet zone*, reflecting the level of energy

and noise that may be generated by children playing in each of these areas. The dry region may feature carpeted floors or area rugs that help to further define different play areas.

PLAN SHOWING RELATIONSHIPS OF REGIONS AND ZONES WITHIN A TYPICAL TODDLER GROUP ROOM

ADA Accessibility Guidelines for Building Elements Designed for Children's Use

In 1998, the Architectural and Transportation Barriers Compliance Board (the "Access Board") issued a document (Publication S-30, "Building Elements Designed for Children's Use Final Rule") to provide guidance in the establishment of alternatives for building elements for use by children with disabilities. The document is currently awaiting adoption by the U.S. Justice Department; until it has been formally adopted, the guidelines included in the document are advisory only and are not required or enforceable.

Publication S-30 contains specifications that are based on children's dimensions and anthropometrics and that may be applied to building elements designed specifically for use by children ages twelve and younger. Presently, architects and designers who wish to incorporate these alternatives into their designs for environments may do so through provision 2.2 (Equivalent Facilitation) of the existing *Americans with Disabilities Act Accessibility Guidelines* (ADAAG). This provision permits departures from ADAAG requirements in order to provide equal or greater access. The document not only offers alternatives to various configurations and dimensions of building elements, it also includes, in the appendix, various charts that further break down the information into what is most appropriate according to the age group served.

It is important to note that once the decision has been made to adopt one of the alternative provisions offered by the ADAAG for use in the design of a space for children, all of the alternate provisions must be observed. For example, the decision to use a toilet with a seat height that is allowed under the alternates for children requires that the toilet stall depth, placement of grab bars, and so on, also conform to the alternate provisions for children set for these elements.

The ADAAG provisions that offer child-related alternatives and additional recommendations within the document's appendix include:

    4.15 Drinking Fountains and Water Coolers

    4.16 Water Closets

    4.17 Toilet Stalls

    4.19 Lavatories and Mirrors

    4.24 Sinks

    4.32 Fixed or Built-in Seating or Tables

Additionally, the ADAAG appendix contains helpful information about the following provisions in order to provide more comfortable accessibility for children with disabilities:

    4.2.5 and 4.2.6 Forward and Side Reach

    4.8.5 Handrails

PLAYGROUND DESIGN

As in the group rooms, the playground in a child care center will be divided into zones; the most typical are described in the following subsections.

Entry Zone

The entry zone in the playground should feature a distinctive sense of introduction to the playground area, either by the use of a physical element, such as a gate or entry arch, or via some distinctive change from the surrounding areas. It should provide a neutral zone in which the child can observe the entire playground, gather a sense of its layout, assess the available play opportunities, and make decisions as to when and which activity to engage in first.

This zone may also feature signage that lists rules for playground use and expected behavior, and perhaps any donor boards that list the names of those whose support has made the playground possible. Bike racks should also be located within or near this zone.

Active/Noisy Play (Gross Motor Play) Zone

The gross motor play zone is where all of the activities traditionally associated with playgrounds take place, such as swinging, sliding, and climbing. It is important to offer a mix of activities that exercise both the lower body (legs) and the upper body (arms). Activities should offer a range of challenge levels. These activities may be provided through manufactured play equipment or custom-designed elements. All equipment should be designed to meet ASTM F1487, *Standard Consumer Safety Performance Specification for Playground Equipment for Public Use,* and this zone should meet the requirements of the ADAAG for play areas.

Natural Elements Zone

The purpose of including this zone in the playground program is to reduce the tendency to overdevelop the play area. An open grassy area where children can run and play informal ball games is an important part of a successful playground. These large open areas can also provide space for use of large *manipulatives.* Other natural elements, such as gardens, may be located throughout the playground, but plantings should be set in raised planters or located in areas that will not be vulnerable to children running through them to get from one part of the playground to another.

Additional landscaping, such as trees located throughout the playground, can provide desirable shade and, with the addition of seating such as tree benches, encourage social interaction. The natural topography of the site should be taken advantage of whenever possible. Varying levels or terraces within a playground can give children a variety of enjoyable perspectives and views. That said, it is important to ensure that the view of responsible adults on-site is not impaired as they supervise the children at play. This is especially important in playgrounds that are to be used by young children.

SPACES FOR CHILD CARE CENTERS

Group Rooms	Infants Toddlers Preschoolers After-schoolers
Indoor Multipurpose	Common Area
Administration	Director's Office Secretary's Office Receptionist Reception Area Conference Room Sick Child Room Restrooms
Parent Resource Area	Information Center (books, videos, etc.) Seating Area
Staff Area	Workroom Break Room Personal Storage (Personal storage and restroom areas may be located in or within close proximity to the group rooms for convenience and continuity of supervision.)
Circulation/ Maintenance/Utility Areas	Laundry Kitchen Maintenance Mechanical/Electrical Areas
Storage	Curriculum Materials Art/Craft Materials Indoor Play Equipment Buggies/Carriages
Outdoor Areas	Infants' Play Toddlers' Play Preschoolers' Play After-schoolers' Play Outdoor Storage

GROUP ROOMS FOR CHILD CARE CENTERS

Infant Room Activities	Sleeping Rocking Swinging Playing Crawling Food preparation Eating Diapering Listening Watching
Infant Room Furnishings	Cribs Adult rocking chairs Swing seats Shelf units for toy storage Crawling mats Audiovisual equipment and storage High chairs Food prep and storage units (including refrigerator) Adult chairs Changing tables Personal infant storage units Two adult sinks (diapering and food prep) Adult toilet
Toddler Room Activities	Book looking Rocking Playing Building Arts/crafts Dramatic play Food prep Eating Diapering and toileting Sand play Water play Music Listening Napping
Toddler Room Furnishings	Adult rocking chairs Book stand (front of book visible) Toy/block shelves Dramatic play furnishings (e.g., play kitchen, doll furnishings, dress-up, etc.) Tables and chairs Changing table Child-sized toilets (two per 10 to 14 children) Child hand sinks Two adult sinks (diapering and food prep) Easels Sand table Water table Individual cubby storage units Audiovisual equipment and storage Food storage and prep units Art supply storage Cots (typically stackable) Audiovisual equipment and storage
Preschool Room Activities	(Same as toddler room but without diapering)
Preschool Room Furnishings	(Same as toddler room with the following possible additions: Loft Woodworking table

Source: Anita Rui Olds, Child Care Design Guide; *New York, McGraw-Hill, 2001.*

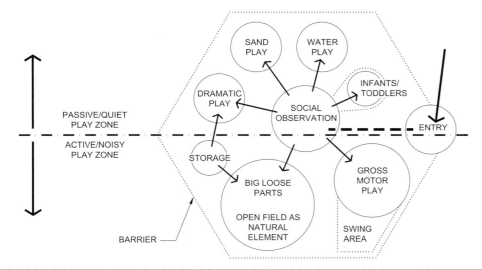

PLAYGROUND ZONE RELATIONSHIPS

Big Loose Parts Zone

Enabling children to build and manipulate an environment to their own design facilitates physical, cognitive, and social development. This zone, therefore, should consist of large so-called manipulatives that can be organized and reorganized by the children in a large open area to create new and different play events at will. Boxes, crates, planks, and boards can be arranged in many configurations, allowing the children to create their own play environment. Big loose parts can consist of found objects such as pieces of wood boards and planks, crates, or large refrigerator boxes. Of course, before such objects are allowed for use by children, responsible adults must check such objects for any safety hazards such as splinters, nails, and staples. Although more costly, manufactured products are also available, and these offer a higher degree of safety and durability.

Notably, the big loose parts zone requires a high degree of supervision to ensure that the children do not create dangerous or unstable constructions, while keeping in mind that the developmental benefits of this type of play are invaluable. Adequate storage should be available in close proximity to store the equipment between uses.

Passive/Quiet (Dramatic) Play Zone

At the ages of five and six, role-playing in children is at its peak. Whether playing house, store, or fast-food restaurant, reenacting roles that they have seen adults perform is, for many children, the first type of interactive play with other children. This zone, therefore, will feature structures or props that can encourage and enrich this type of play. Built structures can range from the very abstract or generic designs, which allow the children to pretend the structure to be whatever they choose, to the more definitive, such as playhouses. Dramatic play can be further enhanced through the provision of small-scale props such as dress-up clothes, tables and chairs, and empty food boxes. A storage area in close proximity for these items must be available.

It is important to design the dramatic play structures so that children in wheelchairs can access and maneuver within any interior spaces. Many manufactured gross motor play structures include spaces beneath the decks that can be developed as dramatic play areas. However, as a type of passive play, dramatic play is often incompatible with the active and noisy activities of children on the play structure, hence it is best located in a separate area.

Social Spaces

Areas that support social interaction between children and between children and adults should be located throughout the playground. Social areas should accommodate a range of group sizes from small (two to three) to larger groups of six or more. These areas are often successfully integrated into the playground's landscaping or gardens. If the playground serves a facility, such as a school or child care center, it may be useful to provide an area within the playground that can accommodate a typical class size (12 to 24 children).

Sand Play Zone

Sand play is a favorite activity, especially for young children. It provides a tactile and creative activity that can be enjoyed by a child playing alone or with other children. Sand play also has high educational value while providing an excellent means of developing manual dexterity.

The sand play area may be contained within a box that is built above grade. For ease of access by children who may have difficulty climbing over a barrier around the sand box, a recessed sand play area that places the top of the sand at grade level and can be walked into may be desirable. For greater play value, locate the sand play area beside or in close proximity to a source of water. For children confined to wheelchairs, sand play may be provided through the use of an elevated table with raised edges. Provisions must be made for the sand to be covered nightly or inspected daily to keep it free from litter, debris, and feline feces.

Water Play Zone

Children are highly attracted to water. Water play, like sand play, offers children opportunities for play that change with each encounter. Water play facilities can range from a water table that can be filled and drained between each use to large water play structures, similar to those found in water parks. Depending on the extent of water play activities and the type of play anticipated, this area may be located in the active/noisy play zone. However, for playgrounds in which water play is limited to activities during which only the hands and arms get wet, this activity is more suited to the quiet/passive play zone.

The decisions regarding the degree and intensity of water play in the design of a playground should be based on the amount of supervision that will be provided when water play is available and the degree to which caregivers are prepared to allow children and their clothing to become wet. This activity is often located adjacent or near to the sand play area creating the possibility of mixing the two elements together. A nonslip surface should be specified beneath any water play area.

Hard Surface Zone

Certain activities, such as games that require ball dribbling (e.g., basketball and four-square) and riding wheeled toys, such as tricycles, or propelling toy vehicles, require a hard surface. "Roadways" may function as part of the dramatic play area through the creation of drive-through structures, such as restaurants and banks, and parking spaces. Storage for these vehicles may also be required.

The hard surfaces made be constructed of packed earth, concrete, or asphalt. Packed earth has the advantage of being easier on knees and elbows in the event of falls; however, puddles may form that make the area unusable for long periods of time until it dries out. Concrete, though unforgiving when fallen on, is durable and can be made safer with a light slip-resistant finish. Concrete also causes less strain on knee joints, stays cooler in hot weather than asphalt, and offers a surface on which sidewalk games can be painted and sidewalk chalk can be used. Although the most costly option, rubber-safety surfaces offer the highest degree of safety and comfort.

Infant and Toddler Zone

If it is anticipated that infants and toddlers (ages two to five) will be using the playground, it is recommended that equipment specifically designed to a smaller scale be used and that activities and surfaces appropriate for crawling babies be included. Separation from zones used by older children is also recommended.

Playground Amenities for Support, Comfort, and Safety

The playground design also has to incorporate areas for storage, comfort, and safety, as described in the following subsections.

Storage

Storage areas that either are accessible directly from the playground or are in close proximity to it eliminate the need for a supervising adult to leave the play area in order to retrieve play equipment and items that support the various types of play on the playground. A single storage area may be located in a central location, or multiple, smaller storage areas may be located in direct relationship to the areas of the playground that they serve. Storage is typically required for the dramatic play, big loose parts, and hard surface zones.

Lockable storage is especially critical for playgrounds that will be used in conjunction with a facility such as a school or child care center during the day, and then revert to community use during after-school hours and on weekends. Also important in planning for storage is the location of trash receptacles in the areas of the playground that tend to generate trash, such as around picnic tables and seating areas.

Comfort and Safety Amenities

Amenities that will provide for the safety of the children and the comfort of both the children and the adult supervisors may include water fountains, misters, seating that offers unobstructed views of the various play areas, and restrooms that either are included in the playground area or are within close proximity. Creating a relaxing setting for the supervising adults, such as a shaded area with tables and comfortable seating that is centrally located for easier supervision, may result in their allowing the children to play for longer periods of time.

Barriers

In the design of a playground, it is often necessary or desirable to erect physical barriers that either direct a child's movement around certain pieces of playground equipment or that discourage or prevent a child from traveling from one part of the playground to another or from leaving the playground area. These barriers can be made "hard," by the use of fencing, or "soft," with the use of dense landscaping and berms, depending on the degree of separation that is needed. The adult supervisor will be more likely to give children freedom to play and run when there is a barrier that surrounds the play area; also, supervision of the entry and exit areas to the playground will provide confidence that children stay within the confines of the playground.

Within the playground it is also advisable to separate infant and toddler play areas from those of older children for the safety of the younger children. The separation between the two areas does not necessarily have to be a physical barrier. These areas can often be separated simply by creating a sense of passage from one space to the other, so that older children do not accidentally enter the infant/toddler area, and vice versa.

Barriers should also be considered around swings areas to dictate entry into the area from the front, facing the swings, as opposed to from the side, where a child may pass in the trajectory of a swinging child to reach an unoccupied swing seat.

Guidelines for Floor Finish Selection

- The floor is furniture in child care centers; therefore, make floors warm and inviting to provide many physical and programmatic benefits.
- Use carpet to introduce softness (a prime indicator of center quality) to children's spaces. Good-quality, thick, dense carpet is more durable and responds better to cleaning than thinner carpets of lesser quality. Cut piles are more residential than loop piles.
- Vinyl-backed "peel-and-stick" carpets, which are 100% washable, are ideal for children's group rooms. Installation of carpet squares, as opposed to sheet goods, sometimes facilitates replacement of heavily soiled areas. Large remnants of scrap or mill-end carpets, bound at the edges, can be used to delineate areas in the quiet and active zones if installed carpet is not desired.
- Use 1-in.-sq ceramic tiles to create a nonslippery, water-resistant surface in wet play bays. Large ceramic tiles (12 to 14 in. sq) are slippery in wet areas but excellent for high-use entries and corridors. Scored and colored concrete is equally durable, resists slipping, and lends itself to custom artistic treatment.
- Always choose a carpet tile or linoleum that is mottled or flecked, since solid colors reveal every stain, scratch, and scuff mark. Subdued patterns and colors are preferable to dominant and geometric designs.

Source: Anita Rui Olds, Child Care Design Guide; *New York, McGraw-Hill, 2001.*

Guidelines for Ceiling Design

- Ceiling design is an important contributor to the spirit of a place. Avoid suspended ceilings with 2 ft × 4 ft (200 × 400) grids, which are associated with institutional settings. Vary ceiling heights to signal changes in space use and different levels of intimacy, to provide variety and area definition, and to vary the quality of light and sound. In narrow corridors and small rooms, a high ceiling can minimize feelings of entrapment. Group rooms benefit from two to four different ceiling heights corresponding to the activity levels of the four zones.
- Shape the ceiling to help define the space below. A vaulted ceiling creates a "center" and "edges" to the activities that take place below it.
- Consider incorporating various materials; for example, using plaster, wood, mosaic tile, stucco, and stained glass. Ceiling treatment is especially important where children (infants) will be lying down and looking up.
- Consider a change in ceiling height, coupled with a change in ceiling material; this is particularly powerful in creating a unique sense of "place."
- Where cost is a factor, make creative use of banners to vary ceiling heights and afford aesthetic interest.

Source: Anita Rui Olds, Child Care Design Guide; *New York, McGraw-Hill, 2001.*

HEIGHT (INCLUDING INFANT LENGTH)

STANDING EYE LEVEL

VERTICAL REACH TO GRIP

ANTHROPOMETRIC DATA FOR CHILDREN

STANDING WORKTOP HEIGHTS

SEATED WORKTOP HEIGHTS

SEAT HEIGHTS

ANTHROPOMETRIC DATA FOR CHILDREN

3 ☐ **EDUCATION**

Guidelines for Wall Finish Selection

- Consider enlivening walls in selected locations by adding wood, stucco, stone, carpet, cork, and brick to enhance their color and tactile qualities.
- Consider glass and glass block walls, in limited quantities, where acoustic but not visual separation is desired.
- Use textures on walls to help control sound clue boundaries and to assist in wayfinding and area definition (as texture and color changes are used on floors).
- Discourage cinder block walls because of their abrasiveness, unfinished feel, and institutional look.
- Incorporate curved walls or curved portions of a wall to break the monotony of straight lines and invite people into a space. This is especially effective in public areas: corridors, stairwells, entrances, and around corners. That said, carefully evaluate the use of curved walls in group rooms because rectangular furniture does not easily fit against a curve.
- Add wood, carpet or handwoven rugs, mirrors, and mosaic tile to architectural elements, such as protruding and freestanding columns, to soften them and add interest.
- Consider using wood in a variety of forms for wall surfaces, baseboards, bumper guards, and handrails.
- Add cove bases at the juncture of walls and floors as another prominent design element. Choose colors and materials that match the walls to make them less prominent and reduce the institutional feel of a space.
- Keep in mind that half-walls and partitions in children's spaces can do most things full walls do: provide platforms, tables and seats, plant ledges, display surfaces, and façades for dramatic play. Remember that partitions need to be stable and nonflammable and should not block any means of egress. Some states require them to be screwed or otherwise affixed to the floor. It is helpful if they have some acoustic insulation properties as well.
- Paint walls; paint is inexpensive and easy to apply and change. Vinyl-covered walls provide a slightly more curable surface, but at greater cost and with less flexibility.
- Provide plenty of display space in group rooms and corridors by covering large portions or entire walls with materials such as linoleum, cork, hook-and-loop tape, or fabric that is capable of receiving tape and staples.
- Install mirrors of tempered glass, not plastic, at child height; these resist scratching and clouding.

Sources: Anita Rui Olds, Child Care Design Guide; *New York, McGraw-Hill, 2001.*
Linda Cain Ruth, Design Standards for Children's Environments; *New York, McGraw-Hill, 2000.*

Linda Cain Ruth, AIA; College of Architecture Design and Construction; Auburn University, Alabama

Conceptual Design: Anita Rui Olds; Anita Olds and Associates; Woodacre, California
Architectural Design: Barbara Winslow; Jacobson, Silverstein, Winslow/Degenhardt Architects; Berkeley, California
Interior Design: Carla Mathis; Carla Mathis Designs; Menlo Park, California
Architect of Record: J.H. Rust; J.H. Rust, Architect; Toronto, Ontario, Canada
Landscape Design: Ruedi Hofer; PMA Landscape Architects; Etobicoke, Ontario, Canada

ELEMENTARY AND SECONDARY SCHOOLS

PROGRAMMING AND PLANNING GUIDELINES

Most state departments of education, as well as many organizations, have developed standards to guide the planning, design, and construction of school facilities. These standards vary, reflecting the learning process and curricula for different age groups, as well as for children with special needs. Representative program guidelines for the four most common types of school are included:

- Kindergarten and preschool
- Elementary school
- Middle (or junior high) school
- High school

DESIGN STANDARDS

In the United States, the primary source of standards—other than state or local regulatory departments—is the National Association for the Education of Young Children (NAEYC) in Washington, DC. NAEYC issues the most widely used accreditation standards for programs for children from birth to eight years, standards that are often higher than state licensing standards.

Kindergarten and Preschool

Kindergarten typically is a child's first introduction to school, or marks a transition from another preschool program, nursery school, Head Start, certain forms of day care, or any of the many other types of early childhood programs. In most school systems children enter this program at age five or six, but a growing number of states are mandating early childhood programs for younger ages.

Kindergarten generally is defined as a form of preschool education in which children are taught through creative play, social contacts, and natural expression. The concept was originated in Germany in 1837 by Fredrich Froebel. *Kindergarten,* "child's garden," was based on the idea that children's play was significant. Froebel employed games, songs, and stories to address the needs of children (at that time generally ages three to seven). The kindergarten served as a transitional stage from home to school and often was a child's first formal learning experience. In 1861, American educator Elizabeth Palmer Peabody opened the first kindergartens in the United States, in Boston. By the 1920s, kindergartens were included in public schools in most parts of the United States.

Historically, a child's first day at kindergarten was often his or her first formal learning experience away from home, but today more children have been exposed to other forms of preschool programs or child care. Thus, the issue of separation from home and parents must be considered, as well as the transition to a group social environment in which the child usually does not know the other members.

CLUSTER MODEL—FOCUS ON THE INTERIOR
The interior cluster model is organized around open play space.

CLUSTER MODEL—FOCUS ON THE OUTDOORS
The outdoors cluster model is organized around common services and corridor.

LINEAR MODEL
The linear model is organized along an interior spine; focus on the outdoors and covered porches at each classroom.

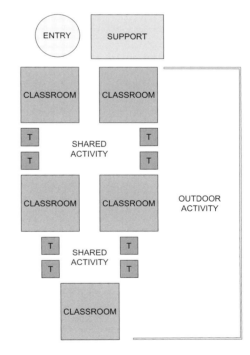

HYBRID LINEAR MODEL
The hybrid linear model is organized along a complex spine made up of a series of activity and play spaces.

KINDERGARTEN AND PRESCHOOL PLAN ORGANIZATIONS

DEVELOPMENTAL GUIDEPOSTS FOR CHILDREN AND ADOLESCENTS

AGE RANGE	PHYSICAL	EMOTIONAL	SOCIAL
Early Childhood (ages 3–5)	• Body growth slows, more adult proportions develop. • At 6, neural development 90% complete. • From 4 to 8 years, lymphoid development increases from 40 to 90%. • Most children are farsighted. • Muscle development begins at 4 years, but larger muscles dominate.	• Tendency to fear imaginary or anticipated dangers. • Crying and tantrums diminish; anger can be expressed in words (often by threatening or yelling). • Anger directed at cause of frustration, retained for longer periods of time; but 4-year-olds begin to seek ways to hide it from others. • Channeling anger and frustration is important.	• Begin to understand concept of taking turns and tend to imitate adults. • 4-year-olds prefer to spend time playing and cooperating with others and can pick up social cues from surroundings. • 5-year-olds prefer to play with others. • May create imaginary playmates if deprived of contact with other children, but most will outgrow these playmates by age 5.
Middle Childhood (ages 6–9)	• Apparent difference between growth rate of girls and boys (girls closer to end growth states, boys taller and heavier). • Nearsightedness may begin to develop at 8 years. • 6-year-olds use whole bodies for activities, and large muscles are more developed; 7-year-olds more cautious and show ease with fine motor skills; 8-year-olds develop fine motor skills and have increased attention spans. • Nervous habits begin to appear at age 7.	• 6-year-olds begin to assert independence and demonstrate confidence. • 6-year-olds fear the supernatural. • 7-year-olds are more stable, narcissistic, polite, responsive, empathetic, less aggressive, and can draw connections between cause and effect. • 8-year-olds demonstrate greater independence, vacillate between moods, and begin to sense how others feel about them. • 7- and 8-year-olds discover some of their limitations and may hesitate to try new tasks, but 8-year-olds seek to create an external image of competence and confidence.	• Family influence decreases, peers are more important, teachers become authority figures. • 6-year-olds have many internal conflicts, resulting in capriciousness. • 6-year-olds choose playmates on qualities of age and size (not gender or ethnicity); 7-year-olds are more aware of social status or ethnicity differences among themselves. • 7-year-olds are self-critical and often disassociate themselves from frustrations. • 7-year-olds are well mannered unless bored; 8-year-olds are more developed socially. • 7-year-olds are more conscious of position among peers; boys and girls play separately. • 8-year-olds prefer company and approval of peers, and exhibit more self-control and modesty.
Late Childhood (ages 9–11)	• More resistance to disease. • Steady increases in body measurements: height and weight (girls more than boys), and muscle growth. • Have fine motor skills. • May feel uncomfortable with scrutiny. • Many girls begin showing signs of puberty.	• Fear exclusion from peers. • Prone to outbursts but try to control them. • 10-year-olds are mild tempered, seek reassurance from others; anger comes and goes quickly. • 10-year-olds fear heights and dark. • 11-year-olds fear school, friends, for parents' welfare, strange animals, threatening world events; are more easily angered, often resulting in physical violence, but can control outbursts more appropriately.	• Socialize in exclusive groups with own sex (boys' groups gravitate toward shows of bravado and competition; girls' groups are well structured and more concerned with maturity). • Develop important individual friendships, which are often fluid. • Ties to family less important than ties to peers; adult shortcomings looked at critically, often leading to conflicts.
Early Adolescence (ages 12–14)	• Enter pubescence, puberty, and postpubescence. • Activate primary and secondary sex characteristics.	• Emotions vacillate; responses are inconsistent. • 12-year-olds may develop a derogatory sense of humor to control emotions. • 13-year-olds withdraw from others, tending toward secrecy and sullenness. • 14-year-olds use derogatory humor as defense and primary form of communication.	• Motivated by desire to fit in with peers, which prevents individual expression but emboldens adolescents to assert independence from home. • Peer groups are exclusive and develop from single-sex to coed. • Intensely drawn to a best friend, believing that only this other person understands.
Late Adolescence (ages 15–18)	• Height and weight stabilize. • Girls generally physically mature by 18, boys by 19.	• Feel restrained or controlled by adults. • Have insecure self-image; may fear inadequacy. • Focus attention on opposite sex or close peers. • Feel challenged to find comfortable self-image.	• Assert independence; have power struggles with parents; are most concerned about social life. • If uncomfortable with adulthood, may withdraw to former behaviors.

As a child grows, he or she typically learns in different ways, and the physical environment of the school should reflect this characteristic.

KINDERGARTEN DESIGN CONCEPT

The design of schools for early childhood education has always been geared toward comfortable, supportive, and adaptive settings that are conducive to a learning process derived from familiar play and hands-on activities. Specific features associated with home, as well as school, are considered in developing an appropriate transitional setting. The type, size, scale, and variety of more public and private spaces underlie appropriate design and planning.

Much like a house, containing public spaces (living room, parlor, foyer, family room) and more private spaces (kitchen, upstairs bedrooms, bathrooms, etc.), a school should create spaces for comfortable retreat and quiet, reflective play, as well as for small and large group activities. Today, the typical age of children in kindergarten programs ranges from four to six years.

Among the general goals that all early childhood and kindergarten programs should strive to achieve are the following:

- Create a visually rich, fun, and surprising environment.
- Provide spaces and surfaces for display of children's work.
- Provide a variety of settings for work-in-progress.
- Introduce a variety of social settings for small and large groups.
- Make strong connections between the indoors and the outdoors; above all, use daylighting as much as possible.
- Connect spaces to promote communication, orientation, and flexible programming and staffing.
- Build in flexibility of space to accommodate evolving teaching practices.
- Create a distinctive, pleasing entrance.
- Pay special attention to the scale and height of typical elements such as windows, doors, doorknobs and pulls, sinks, toilets, counters, furnishings, mirrors, steps, shelving and storage, light switches, towel dispensers, and other accessories.

Access to kindergarten programs typically is through the public elementary school system, but there are many other options, such as child care centers, day schools, and private elementary schools. Minimum space standards for early childhood education and kindergarten programs have historically been determined by state regulation, often by the U.S. Department of Public Welfare, for child care centers and day schools, or by the U.S. Department of Education, for programs that are components of public schools. Most minimum space standards are based on a square-foot allowance per child, but these standards can vary from state to state.

This classroom (1,000 sq ft (92.9 sq m); 24-student capacity) accommodates a variety of group and individual activities with specific areas for instruction, group reading, wet projects, and small groups.

KINDERGARTEN AND GRADE 1 CLASSROOM

The Physical Environment

The indoor and outdoor environments must be safe, clean, attractive, and spacious. There should be enough usable space indoors so children are not crowded (a minimum of 35 sq ft (3.2 sq m) of usable playroom floor space indoors per child and a minimum of 75 sq ft (6.9 sq m) of play space outdoors per child). Program staffs must have access to the designated space and sufficient time to prepare the environment before children arrive.

Activity areas should be clearly defined by spatial arrangement. Space is arranged so that children can work individually, together in small groups, or in a large group. Clear pathways must be provided for children to move from one area to another and to minimize distractions.

Preschool Design Concept

The space for children three years and older should be arranged to facilitate a variety of small group and individual activities, including block-building, sociodramatic play, art, music, science, math, manipulatives, and quiet reading and writing. Other activities such as sand play and woodworking are also often accommodated. Carpeted spaces as well as hard surfaces, such as wood floors and ample crawling and toddling areas, are typically provided for infants and young toddlers. Sturdy furniture is required to enable nonwalkers to pull themselves up or balance themselves while walking. School-age children should be provided separate space that is arranged to facilitate a variety of age-appropriate activities and permit sustained work on projects.

Children's Equipment

Age-appropriate materials and equipment of sufficient quantity, variety, and durability should be readily accessible to children and arranged on low, open shelves to promote independent use. Individual spaces for children to store their personal belongings should be provided.

Private Areas

Private areas should be made available indoors and outdoors so that children can have occasional solitude. Soft elements such as rugs, cushions, or rocking chairs should be provided for the comfort of the child, in addition to sound-absorbing materials to minimize noise.

Outdoor Areas

Outdoor areas include a variety of surfaces, including soil, sand, grass, hills, flat sections, and hard areas for wheeled toys. Outdoor spaces include shaded, open, and digging area; outdoor equipment should enable riding, climbing, balancing, and individual play. The outdoor area is protected by fences or by natural barriers from access to streets or other dangers.

Staff Work Area

The work environment for staff should include a place for adults to take a break or work away from children, an adult-size bathroom, a secure place for staff to store their personal belongings, and an administrative area that is separated from the children's areas for planning or preparing materials.

KINDERGARTEN AREA REQUIREMENTS

The required space standards for kindergartens often fall short of those recommended by social and behavioral research, in both quantity and arrangement of space. Facilities with too little space (less than 35 usable sq ft (3.2 sq m) of space per child) may lead to more aggressive and destructive behavior, fewer friendly contacts, and less solitary learning and play. Conversely, too much space (more than 50 usable sq ft (4.6 sq m) of space per child) can result in reduced attention spans, more supervision required by staff, and an increase in aimless, random behavior.

Outdoor Activities

The amount of recommended space for outdoor activity can vary significantly. It is best to provide at least the minimum required space, rather than no outside space at all. Compensation for lack of outdoor space with additional indoor activity space, in equal proportion to the outdoor requirement, is acceptable. Given the constraints of building sites, particularly in urban or inner-city locations, outdoor space may not be possible. In such situations, designers must find inventive solutions to enable access to fresh air and sunlight. Any outdoor space, however small, can be important, providing release to the children and offering a broad range of educational opportunities, even if they do not satisfy requirements for an outdoor area.

Entrance

The main entrance should be a welcoming, spacious area with adequate seating and places for informal visiting. It should be large enough to accommodate small groups of children and adults. This is often the place where children exhibit signs of anxiety over separation from parents. Display areas for bulletins and children's projects can be provided at both adults' and children's eye level. Ideally, the entrance should be close to administrative areas to provide security and to accommodate parent-teacher meetings.

Administrative Space

Administrative areas should be located near the entrance for easy access by families and for view of the main entrance. Administrative areas usually include a director's office with adequate space for a small meeting table, staff mailboxes, a small meeting room, space for records storage and supplies, space for a small quiet room and first-aid room, and a staff workroom and break area with bathroom.

Corridors and Transition Spaces

Corridors can be viewed as extensions of activity space. Avoid long, straight hallways by providing nooks and alcoves for sitting, play, and display. Provide space for wall and ceiling-hung projects, and display cases for various art objects. Design open corridor spaces with interior glass windows looking into adjacent classroom and activity spaces; take advantage of borrowed natural light. Avoid designing corridors to have no other use but circulation. Use carpeting or other acoustic materials to reduce noise.

Classrooms

A well-designed classroom environment is safe for children, supports their emotional well-being, stimulates their senses, and challenges their skills. Subdividing the classroom into well-defined "activity pockets" identifies physical spaces each of which is functionally limited to one activity but not completely closed off from the rest of the classroom or instructor supervision. Observation of preschool children at play suggests that they have a tendency to cluster into small groups of fewer than five, with a mean of about two children. If activity areas are sized for two to five children and an instructor, they should range between 40 and 60 sq ft (3.7 and 5.5 sq m) each. In addition, space should be provided either within the classroom or in a nearby area to allow for an entire class to meet as a single group.

The optimum class size is approximately 20 children per classroom. Select finishes to help reduce noise (think in terms of 20 children at active play). Create areas for distinct activities: for example, group meetings; quiet individual concentration; laboratory and semiactive spaces; workshop and studio spaces for art, drama, blocks, games, and so on. These areas are best created through the use of movable furnishings, shelves, bookcases, and so forth, to promote flexibility and the individual character of each classroom. Rectangular spaces are typically easier to configure than square or oddly shaped areas.

Design space to meet both children's and adult's physical needs. Be sure to provide seating, tables, workspace, and storage suited to both. Provide space for cubbies and lockers, either between classrooms or within classrooms; allow for adult assistance. Provide for display of plants and objects. Take advantage of areas below windows for quiet seating nooks or play areas. Provide a play area specifically suited to wet or messy activities.

Personalization, Display, and Storage

Providing inventive and creative ways to display the work and projects of the children is essential to support their "habitation" of the space. Every part of the architecture should be thought of as potential display space; use walls, ceilings, floors, and furnishings throughout the facility. Care should be taken to provide a variety of display spaces for two-dimensional flat work and three-dimensional pottery, mobiles, sculpture, and small crafts. The display area should be flexible and allow for quick and easy alteration. A display space should be designed for viewing by both adults and children. Appropriate lighting should emphasize the displays and should be adjustable in both position and intensity. The following are suggestions for display spaces:

- Install picture rails or shelves along walls. Give particular attention to corridor areas, where walls may become repetitive.
- Arrange closed display cases for viewing from one side or from all sides.
- Make use of windowsills or areas in front of windows where natural light and the interplay of light and shadow can enhance the objects viewed.

RECOMMENDED MINIMUM SPACE REQUIREMENTS FOR KINDERGARTEN AND PRESCHOOL

Direct activity/classroom space	42 sq ft (3.9 sq m)/child
Staff support/storage space	38 sq ft (3.5 sq m)/child
Observation space (often used by parents or staff)	9 sq ft (.83 sq m)/child
Subtotal assignable space	89 sq ft (8.26 sq m)/child
Nonassignable space, "multiplier"*	20 sq ft (1.8 sq m)/child
Total facility space/child	109 sq ft (10 sq m)/child
Outdoor activity space	75–200 sq ft (6.9–18.5 sq m)/child

*The multiplier is applied to the program area to account for circulation, wall thickness, miscellaneous support spaces, and so forth, but may not include adequate space for mechanical/electrical equipment depending on the system selected.
Source: Campus Child Care News 11(1), January 1996.

SPACES IN SAMPLE FACULTY PROGRAM FOR KINDERGARTEN

PROGRAM SPACE	AREA SQ FT (SQ M)
Entry area	200 (18.5)
Program assistant's/reception area	120 (11.1)
Administrative assistant's office	120 (11.1)
Director's office	160 (14.8)
Administration copy/supply room	100 (9.3)
Staff workroom/break area/toilet	350 (32.5)
Meeting/parent conference room	200 (18.5)
Quiet room/first aid	100 (9.3)
Kindergarten classrooms (5 @ 800 sq ft (74.3 sq m) each) (Classroom area includes storage, cubbies, kitchen, etc.)	4,000 (371)
Classroom bathrooms (5 @ 80 sq ft (7.4 sq m) each)	400 (37.2)
Central activity/dining area	1,500 (139.3)
Central activity storage	200 (18.5)
Art studio (with kiln)	500 (46.4)
Art studio storage	60 (5.5)
Kitchen/food storage	600 (55.7)
General facility storage	200 (18.5)
Subtotal usable space	8,810 (818.5)
Multiplier for circulation, mechanical area, etc. @ 1.2	1,760 (163.5)
Total Facility Program (average @ ±106 sq ft (9.8 sq m)/child)	10,570 (981.9)

Kindergarten program for 100 children

Kitchen and Pantry

A kitchenette can serve a group of classrooms or the entire school area, with counters and cabinets at heights for both children and adults. Locking cabinets should be specified. Locate the kitchenette for easy and secure delivery access and so that it is adjacent to the dining area. If possible, allow for a clear view from the dining area with interior windows, to promote child-staff interaction and learning. Arrange space to allow for display cooking. Ensure that adequate ventilation is provided.

ELEMENTARY SCHOOLS

Elementary schools typically are defined as including grades 1 through 5 and, sometimes, grade 6. The program criteria set here for grades 1 through 5 can also be used for grade 6, if included in the elementary program. Elementary schools often also include prekindergarten and kindergarten.

Major Program Elements

The program elements of an elementary school can be categorized in three major areas:

- *Classrooms:* General-purpose classrooms, special education classrooms
- *Specialized program areas:* Music room, science room, art room, computer lab, gymnasium, cafeteria, auditorium, library
- *Administrative and resource areas:* General office, principal's office, guidance office, nurse's office, faculty room, teachers' resource room, specialized resource areas for remediation

It is these three areas that determine the net square footage needed for an elementary school. However, the amount of square footage dedicated to each of these categories can vary greatly from building to building. The number of classrooms is dependent on class size, the applicable standards, and the enrollment projections for each grade level. The amount of square footage dedicated to specialized program areas is somewhat discretionary and depends on how many special programs will be offered. The number of such programs depends, in turn, on the operating budget, the size of the student body, and other factors. However, many school spaces are designed with shared functions, such as a single space used for the gymnasium, auditorium, and cafeteria. The special program areas should not be considered in computing the student capacity of an elementary school. In elementary schools, classroom space determines school capacity. Administration and resource areas are programmed on a school-by-school basis and are dependent on staffing, operating budgets, and other factors.

TYPICAL MINIMUM CLASSROOM SIZES FOR U.S. ELEMENTARY SCHOOLS

STATE	REQUIREMENTS
New York	The minimum standard for an elementary classroom is 770 net sq ft (71.5 net sq m), based on 27 students.
California	Grades 1 through 12 require not less than 960 net sq ft (89.1 net sq m) or an equivalent space that provides not less than 30 sq ft (2.7 sq m) per student.
Virginia	Requires 975 sq ft (90.5 sq m) for first grade and 800 sq ft (74.3 sq m) for grades 2 through 5.
Florida	Recommends 25 students per classroom for grades 1 through 3, at a range of 36 to 40 net sq ft (3.3 to 3.7 net sq m) per student, and 28 students per classroom for grades 4 through 6, at a range of 30 to 34 net sq ft (2.7 to 3.1 net sq m) per student.

Classrooms

For general-purpose classrooms, it is typical to size rooms for approximately 28 students. Note that most schools attempt to keep the number of students per classroom lower than that, usually 22 to 24 students. Nonetheless, unless otherwise established, it is prudent to design for 28 to account for population growth, unbalanced section sizes, and similar contingencies. Classroom sizes typically range from 750 to 1,000 net sq ft (69.6 to 92.9 sq m).

Many states have minimum standards for classroom size. Elementary-age students need to sit either at individual tables and chairs or at group tables. Project areas within the classroom are also needed, which may include areas for science, computer clusters, and other equipment-intensive spaces. In addition, adequate space must be allowed for classroom materials and student storage. Storage should be sized for coats, briefcases, purses, backpacks, and so on. Most elementary schools do not have lockers in corridors, so storage areas must be accommodated within the classroom.

Specialized Program Areas

The quantity of specialized program areas is determined by the offerings at the school, and varies from school to school. In some cases, multiple functions can be accommodated in a single space, such as a cafeteria and auditorium or a science and art room.

Community Use

Elementary schools are community facilities—cafeterias, auditoriums, and gyms are commonly used after normal school hours. Therefore, separate entrances, security, and mechanical zones should be considered.

This classroom (1,000 sq ft (29.9 sq m); 24-student capacity) is smaller than the pre-K and K-1 classroom. It accommodates a variety of group and individual activities with specific areas for instruction, group reading, wet projects, and small groups.

CLASSROOM FOR GRADES 2 THROUGH 5

PERFORMANCE ART SPACE

ART AND MEDIA SPACE

SPECIALIZED PROGRAM AREAS

MIDDLE SCHOOL AND JUNIOR HIGH SCHOOL

The first middle school emerged as a separate entity early in the twentieth century. Middle schools were established in many areas to provide a mix of vocational and secondary education for the majority of students who quit formal schooling by grade 9. Middle schools are defined here as grades 6 through 8.

Today, for most school districts in the United States, the middle school is still evolving. The middle school experience is intended to provide a transition from the self-contained, nurturing environment of the elementary school to the departmental configuration of the high school. Students are introduced to departmental teaching, interdisciplinary teaching, flexible scheduling, block scheduling, collaborative learning, and flexible groupings.

Program Elements

The program elements of a middle school can be categorized into four major areas:

- *Classrooms:* General-purpose classrooms, clusters of classrooms (commonly referred to as the "house"), and special education classrooms.
- *Student resource centers:* Technology center, music instruction area, flexible laboratory space, art instruction room, gymnasium, cafeteria, auditorium, library, special-use and club meeting rooms, video technologies, and exhibition space.
- *Teacher support areas:* Conference rooms, common faculty (team teaching) planning and workrooms, faculty dining room, and adult toilet and telephone rooms.
- *School administration:* General offices and waiting area, principal's and assistant principal's suite; guidance, nurse, and custodial offices; and specialized resource rooms for remediation.

Typically, fundamental instruction spaces include general classrooms, library, and gymnasium spaces. In the case of a middle school, 156 sq ft (14.4 sq m) per student is a reasonable planning number for a student population ranging from 500 to 700 students. To deal with financial and other constraints, many school programs include large common areas that have been developed to offer flexible and multifunction opportunities within the same space. Typically, the gymnasium, auditorium, and cafeteria are combined in some fashion (sometimes for two of these functions only). This savings in construction cost must be weighed against the appropriateness of the resultant finishes, acoustic properties, lighting, and scheduling for each of the functions proposed in the multipurpose space.

Classrooms

General-purpose classrooms typically are designed to accommodate a maximum of 28 students. The permitted maximum number of students per classroom may vary somewhat from state to state. At the middle school level, the typical average class size for both new construction and building additions ranges from 23 to 25 students. This average allows for an increase in the student population of three to five students per classroom without requiring new construction. Extra capacity within the classroom can also accommodate varying class sizes.

SPACE REQUIREMENTS FOR MIDDLE SCHOOL ADMINISTRATION

PROGRAM ELEMENT	TYPICALLY REQUIRED BY CODE	NET SQ FT (NET SQ M) RANGE
General Office		
Waiting area	No	200–400 (18.5–37.1)
Secretary's space	No	75–150 (6.9–13.9)
Principal's office	Yes	250 (23.2)
Assistant principal's office	No	200 (18.5) (requirement based on school population) 600–800 (55.7–74.3) (mail, duplications, processing, etc.)
Work area	No	200–400 (18.5–37.1)
Guidance office	Yes	120 (11.1) per counselor, plus waiting area if clustered (one per 75 students)
Nurse's suite		
Waiting room	No	100–200 (9.2–18.5)
Nurse's office	Yes	150 (13.9)
Nurse's assistant area	No	100 (9.2) (recommended if student population is over 500)
Examination area	Yes	80 (7.4) per station (recommend 1 station/150 students)
Rest area	No	150 (13.9)
Toilet room	Yes	80 (7.4)
Specialized resource rooms for remediation	No	450 (41.8)
Custodial space	No	Depends on function; may include paper supply/storage, shop area, cleaning equipment, grounds equipment, etc.

SPACE REQUIREMENTS FOR COMMON MIDDLE SCHOOL PROGRAM ELEMENTS

PROGRAM ELEMENT	TYPICALLY REQUIRED BY CODE	NET SQ FT (NET SQ M) RANGE
Computer center	No	850–1,200 (78.9–111.5) (1 per 250 students)
Music instruction room	No	850–1,200 (78.9–111.5) (1 per 250 students)
Laboratory spaces	No	1,000–1,200 (92.9–111.5) (1 per 125 students)
Art instruction room	No	1,000–1,200 (92.9–111.5) (1 per 250 students)
Gymnasium	Yes	3,500 (325) (= one station) (1 station per 250 students)
Cafeteria	Yes	School population × 50% × 10 (.92) (recommended) (provides two lunch periods total)
Kitchen	No	Depends on food program and equipment; typically equal to one-third the size of dining area
Auditorium	No	School capacity × 50% × 7 (.65) (recommended) (based on seating one half of the school population)
Library	Yes	10 (.92) per student (recommended)
Special use rooms	No	500–750 (46.4–69.6) per use
Media/video center	No	750–1,000 (69.6–92.9)
Exhibition/display areas	No	Standards developed on a school-by-school basis

LARGE GROUP SPACES

SMALL GROUP SPACES

Classrooms are planned to have integrated technology available in a variety of configurations to enable simulations research and streaming videos. Small group rooms are designed as breakout areas for the shared use of the middle school.

STUDENT LEARNING SPACES

Middle School Design Issues

The middle school experience is intended to provide a transition for students from the self-contained class-rooms and nurturing environment of the elementary school to the departmental configuration of the high school. School design has historically been based on the notion that subject-specific classrooms accommodate one teacher, perhaps an assistant, and a group of students for designated periods during the school day. This "cells and bells" approach centers on the idea that the student goes (physically) to the subject.

Teaming

The increasingly popular middle school educational philosophy of *teaming* has developed as an alternative to the subject-specific classroom. The teaming methodology supports the notion that instructional spaces are flexible and functionally specific. In essence, the subject comes to the student. Cooperative learning, group projects, and team teaching are the main tools that educators use to foster the team philosophy.

The House Model

Middle school teaming can be defined as an educational program that allows a subset (or house) of students in a specific grade to receive the core of their scholastic instruction from one group of teachers within a small group of flexible classrooms and support spaces. These flexible classrooms are deliberately designed to be function-specific rather than subject-specific.

In this concept, a grade level typically is a *team*. The team is composed of *houses*. A common example of the teaming strategy for a grades 6 to 8 middle school is three teams (one each for sixth, seventh, and eighth grade) of two houses each.

House Size

Each house in a large middle school may accommodate approximately four classrooms or 100 students. Educators suggest that this diversity in the number of students per grade and other physical discontinuities adds to the middle school experience.

The house approach offers a smaller-size environment within the whole in which a core group of students and teachers can gather, chat, and grow. The house is often the architectural building block of new middle school design.

The great majority of the existing middle schools in the United States were planned and built before the teaming and house methodologies were conceived. As many school districts built new high schools, the old high school was often retrofitted to accommodate the middle school program.

SINGLE LABORATORY SUPPORTING SEPARATE AND DISTINCT CLASSES WITH SHARED SUPPORT SPACES

MERGED LABORATORY SUPPORTING SEPARATE AND DISTINCT CLASSES WITH SEPARATE SUPPORT SPACES

LABORATORIES SUPPORTING TWO CLASSES WITH SHARED SUPPORT SPACES

SINGLE LABORATORY SUPPORTING SINGLE MERGED CLASS WITH SHARED SUPPORT SPACES

A variety of configurations can be supported by the house model, while responding to site and architectural issues. A house includes three or four flexible classrooms, a flexible lab space, a computer and technology area, a conference area, and other support spaces.

HOUSE CONCEPT

House Planning Considerations

Among the planning considerations for the house school model are the following:

- The relationship of the house to other houses and student resource centers must be carefully considered.
- Lockers are typically located in the corridor. This is part of the transition from the elementary level, where cubbies (individual open storage units with coat hook and shelf) are often located within the classroom.
- An enclosed courtyard may be less desirable at the middle and high school levels, in contrast to the elementary level, where containment and supervision are handled differently. Rather than containing the school population, the design must provide students easy and safe access to the site and to athletic facilities.

Community Use

The school should be perceived as a community resource. Any opportunity to involve the community with the school is considered a benefit, and ultimately serves to increase awareness about the school and its ongoing needs and contributions to the community as a whole.

Community access should be considered in the location of principal common areas. Typically, the gymnasium and auditorium also serve as meeting places for parents who come to the school to see their children in athletic and performance events. Likewise, local community groups often use these spaces for their functions.

Community use of any of the school's spaces is involved with the issue of proper security for the school. Security relies on the proper design and adjacency of spaces within the plan of the school. The location and configuration of entry vestibules, adjacency of main common area spaces to parking, and other considerations are important in planning the school.

Circulation

The configuration of common area circulation elements should provide opportunities for students to mix and to hold impromptu meetings. Most new plans allow for generously proportioned stairs and landings, window openings that define a space, corridors with nodes, and so on. As with most other grade levels, middle school design should reflect several general considerations as well:

- Cafeterias, kitchens, and auditoriums require service access.
- The main administration suite should be located adjacent to the main entrance of the school. Visitors should not have to struggle to find the main office. The administration should be aware of the comings and goings at the school.
- Specialized program areas shared by all students should be central to the building plan.
- Direct access for students, from the school bus into the school building, reduces the chance of injury and mishap. The plan should be configured so that once students are in the school, access to the outside common areas and athletic facilities are away from vehicular traffic.

This space accommodates distance learning, interactive foreign language studies, language arts programs, graphic design, independent study, and after-school activities (for example, school newspaper editing).

RESOURCE CENTER

LECTURE AND WET LAB

SCIENCE LAB

LECTURE AND DRY LAB

LECTURE AND DRY LAB

A laboratory that support exercises or experiments in technology, research, and simulation are referred to as a dry lab. A laboratory that support exercises or experiments in chemistry or physics are referred to as a wet lab. These room arrangements can be accommodated by the science lab shown above.

SCIENCE LAB OPTIONS

HIGH SCHOOL

The emergence of the dedicated high school building in the late 1800s and early 1900s occurred as a response by school districts to the ever-increasing pressure from the public to provide more, and better, education to the masses. Society was experiencing a major economic boom because of the Industrial Revolution, and both adults and children were hired as cheap labor to work in factories. Many parents concluded that this was no life for their children and demanded that more education be provided beyond the eighth grade.

Early High School Design

The typical early high school consisted of classrooms, a gymnasium, a cafeteria, an auditorium, and vocational shop classrooms. The shops were intended to provide the knowledge necessary for the student to go out into the workforce and gain employment among the more skilled laborers, an idea similar to the apprenticeship concept popular in European countries. High schools have continued to change throughout the twentieth century.

Contemporary High School Design

Today's high schools are still dedicated to the concept of group instruction; however, there is now greater emphasis on the importance of individual learning than in years past. Many campuses today are considered "open," allowing students to move freely on and off campus and to have flexible scheduling of classes and independent studies.

Many new courses of study are offered today, thus creating the need for more specialized rooms and often requiring larger, more flexible spaces. As a result, the square footage requirements of today's high school continue to grow beyond those of the traditional high school of the 1920s.

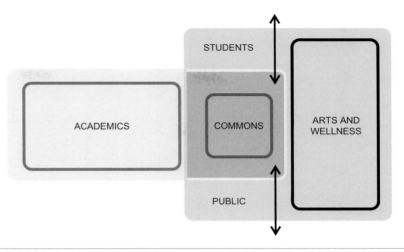

CONTEMPORARY HIGH SCHOOL PLANNING MODEL

Space Requirements

Many states have developed space standards for high school facilities to ensure equality among the many school districts within a state. New York State is among these states; it requires all new construction, including additions, to meet minimum state standards, which are included below.

General Classroom

General classrooms (770 sq ft (71.5 sq m) minimum) are ever increasing in size because of the use of computers and the additional space required for new technology. A larger room, if affordable, is strongly recommended. The recommended size is 900 sq ft (83.6 sq m).

Views to the exterior are highly recommended, and in many areas are required. Adequate artificial lighting levels are critical and should be closely coordinated with the placement of blackboards, marker boards, and computers, to avoid excessive glare. Flooring materials, typically vinyl composition tile or carpeting, should be easy to maintain.

Art Room and Storage Space

One art room should be provided for every 500 students (1,200 sq ft (111.5 sq m) minimum). All necessary electrical facilities must be provided for kilns, computers, and any other special equipment. Plumbing for sinks and cleanup areas is also required. At these grade levels, art rooms are often provided for specific art concentrations such as drawing and painting, ceramics and pottery, photography, and jewelry making. Each will have its own special requirements.

Space is provided to students to create art projects with a two-dimensional focus.

VISUAL ART SPACE

Classrooms should be planned so that integrated technology is available in a variety of configurations.

GENERAL CLASSROOM

Special Education Classrooms

Special education classroom requirements vary greatly, depending on the level of care given in these spaces and the student-teacher ratio. For classrooms that serve students who have severe mental disabilities, it is recommended that private toilet facilities, including showers and changing stations, be provided directly adjacent to or within the classrooms. A special education suite can be created, whereby one toilet facility for every two or three classrooms is adequate.

- If the student-teacher ratio is 12 to 15 students per teacher, 770 sq ft (71.5 sq m) minimum is recommended.
- If the student-teacher ratio is six students per teacher, 450 sq ft (41.8 sq m) minimum is recommended.
- If the student-teacher ratio is eight students per teacher, 550 sq ft (51 sq m) minimum is recommended.
- Resource rooms should be a minimum size of 300 sq ft (27.8 sq m).

Ancillary space should also be provided, equal to at least one-quarter the size of the special education classroom. This should be directly adjacent to or within the classroom. It is often recommended to locate these classrooms near the nurse and health suite.

Business Classroom

A business classroom generally is larger (1,000 sq ft (92.9 sq m) minimum) than a typical classroom because of technology used today. Special attention must be given to the requirements of the school district and its planning for future technology infrastructure. Some school districts will choose to disperse computers throughout a school, enabling students to access a computer in many locations, eliminating the need for a specific room dedicated to business studies.

Computer Classroom

A computer classroom (1,000 sq ft (92.9 sq m) minimum) has requirements similar to those for the business classroom. Special mechanical requirements, including air conditioning and ventilation, often make such rooms more costly than general classrooms. Views to the exterior, though not necessary, are recommended; however, care must be exercised in the placement of computers to avoid excessive screen glare.

Office and Secretarial Practice Room

The requirements of an office practice classroom (840 sq ft (78 sq m) minimum) are similar to those for a computer classroom. The space requirement is less because the typical number of students is smaller.

Home and Careers (Homemaking) Classrooms

One space should be provided for every 500 students, of 1,200 sq ft (111.5 sq m) minimum. Such classrooms often have complete residential kitchens; therefore, special attention must be given to plumbing, natural gas, and electrical requirements. A separate instruction area is often provided away from the kitchen area, where sewing may be taught; or another room may have to be provided, depending on the school curriculum. If another room is needed, it is sized according to specific school needs.

Industrial Arts Space

One space (2,000 sq ft (185.8 sq m) minimum) should be provided for every 500 students. An industrial arts room also requires an additional 200 sq ft (18.6 sq m) minimum for storage.

SPECIAL EDUCATION SUITE

Vocational and technology education is supported in a flexible space to allow changes in programs.

BUSINESS CLASSROOM

Program activities in a digital production classroom include high-powered graphic 2D design and 3D animation and rendering.

COMPUTER CLASSROOM

Music Room

A music room (770 sq ft (71.5 sq m) minimum) is often much like a general classroom; however, special attention must be given to the acoustics. The use of acoustic wall padding and/or acoustic concrete masonry units is suggested. One classroom should be provided for every 500 students.

Instruments and Band Space

The placement of this space (1,400 sq ft (130 sq m) minimum) and the surrounding adjacencies is critical because of the acoustic considerations. Often a separate wing or dedicated area is designated to create a music suite that includes music classrooms, band rooms, auditorium, choir rooms, and music practice rooms. Substantial storage is required for this space, considering the sizes and types of instruments. As a general rule, the space requirements for this area are 15 sq ft (1.4 sq m) per student. One such area should be provided for every 500 students. Daylight is not necessary, but recommended. Sometimes a tiered floor is desirable, but incorporating this feature will result in a space that is less flexible and that requires a greater square footage per student.

Vocal and Chorus Space

The design of this space (1,200 sq ft (111.5 sq m) minimum) should follow the same guidelines as for a band room. Storage requirements for this space, however, are less than those for a band room. A piano, depending on its size, may increase the required area. As a general rule, the space requirements for this area are 7 sq ft (.65 sq m) per student. One classroom should be provided for every 500 students. As in a band room, a tiered floor may be included, again resulting in less flexibility and requiring a greater square footage per student.

Music Practice Rooms

Music practice rooms vary in size, depending on whether they are used for instrument or vocal practice. Daylight is not necessary, but increased ventilation for these spaces may be appropriate. As a general rule, the space requirement for a practice room is no less than 25 sq ft (2.3 sq m) total.

Vocational Shop

The space requirements for vocational shops vary greatly with the program requirements. Special mechanical and electrical systems may be needed for such spaces as automotive repair shops, woodworking shops, and machinist shops.

Mechanical Drawing and Computer-Aided Design (CAD) Classrooms

Classrooms for mechanical drawing and CAD have requirements similar to those for a computer classroom (840 sq ft (78 sq m) minimum). But the space requirement is less because the number of students in these rooms is typically smaller. The increased use of computers may necessitate air conditioning these spaces.

Earth Science Classroom

Although an earth science room (1,000 sq ft (92.9 sq m) minimum) is similar to a general classroom, the space needed for storage is much greater. Storage for rocks, soil, microscopes, and so forth, must be provided. Moreover, students often perform experiments that must be stored for days or weeks, so space should be provided for these situations.

Biology Classroom

A biology classroom (1,200 sq ft (111.5 sq m) minimum) often requires separate student work areas and a general instruction space. The designer should plan for an increased need for storage space.

Chemistry Classroom

The instruction space in a chemistry classroom (1,200 sq ft (111.5 sq m) minimum) is usually more elaborate in its furnishings than the earth science and biology classrooms.

It is often desirable to provide an instruction space in which students sit at desks while the teacher instructs at the blackboard or lab table. This space is separate from the lab spaces provided for student lab work and experiments.

Natural gas or propane is provided, as well as sinks with hot and cold water. Emergency shutoffs and eye-washing stations are required. Chemical storage facilities should be provided in locked cabinets or rooms. Fume hoods and special ventilation requirements are often mandated for this room. Preparation areas or rooms should be provided; their size will depend on the amount of casework provided in the main room.

Durable materials, resistant to chemical and flame damage, should be used for flooring, casework, and countertops.

Physics Classroom

The requirements for a physics classroom (1,200 sq ft (111.5 sq m) minimum) are very similar to those for biology and chemistry rooms. The school should develop requirements for a specific physics curriculum that can be incorporated into the final design of the room.

Study Hall

The size varies for study halls, but as a general design aid, assume that 25 percent of the student population will be out of class at a given time. Space will have to be provided for these students. Depending on the scheduling of classes, it is sometimes possible to accommodate most of the students attending study hall by using the cafeteria, auditorium, library, or unused classrooms. If a further need is anticipated beyond the use of these spaces, plan to provide 15 sq ft (1.4 sq m) per student.

SMALL
PRACTICE ROOM

PIANO

GROUP
PRACTICE ROOM — MARKER/TACK BOARD

Music practice rooms provide a soundproof setting for individual and small group rehearsals.

MUSIC PRACTICE ROOMS

PORTABLE RISERS

DIRECTOR'S STAND

STEREO

MARKER/TACK BOARD

Program activities for the band include learning and practicing.

PERFORMANCE BAND ROOM

PORTABLE RISERS

DIRECTOR'S STAND

PIANO

STEREO

MARKER/TACK BOARD

Program activities for the choir and the orchestra include learning and practicing.

CHOIR AND ORCHESTRA ROOM

Library and Reading Areas

The space requirements for libraries vary greatly, depending on the existing number of books and other periodicals and the anticipated growth of these materials. The number of stored periodicals and paperback books must also be considered. Some schools incorporate in this space computer labs, teaching and gathering areas for small group instruction, separate workspaces, and private offices. Many schools provide air conditioning in the library because, increasingly, this space is used as a community resource.

Because the library is a multiuse space, care must be given to acoustics and lighting. Visual access to every area of the space by the librarian and staff is important, to maintain ongoing supervision. To achieve this, careful placement of the reception area, book stacks, reading areas, and computer areas is critical. Visual supervision of the computer areas is especially important, because most schools now provide Internet access.

The amount of space dedicated to reading areas within a library can be generally calculated, given that 10% of the school population will occupy the space at one time. For this 10% figure, 25 sq ft (2.3 sq m) per person should be provided. The placement of reading areas of various sizes throughout the library is recommended. This arrangement will, however, make the task of enabling adequate visual supervision from the reception area more difficult, but not impossible.

Gymnasium

The space for a gymnasium varies in size, but should be no smaller than 48 × 66 ft (14.6 × 20.1 m). One gymnasium should be provided for every 500 students. If a school intends to play in official tournaments, the designer of the gymnasium should plan for the official high school basketball court size, which measures 50 ft × 84 ft (15.2 × 25.6 m). Note, however, that these decisions do not take into consideration the recommended 10 to 15 ft (3 to 4.5 m) safety zones behind each main backboard.

Bleacher seating for spectator sports is often incorporated in the design of a gymnasium, as well. The capacity of bleacher seating can be calculated by dividing the length of a bleacher row by 18 linear in. (457 mm) per person and multiplying by the number of rows to be provided.

Careful attention must be given to acoustic and mechanical systems. Because the intended use of the space is for increased physical activity, its mechanical requirements usually surpass those of a general-use space. Lighting is critical in such a space, often requiring an increase in footcandles (lux). Sound systems and sports equipment, such as scoreboards, time clocks, volleyball nets, and the like, will affect the design of the space.

Special provisions must be incorporated for the protection of equipment, such as fire alarms and strobes, scoreboards, time clocks, lighting, and speakers. Wire mesh covers can be placed over these items to protect them from basketballs, volleyballs, and the like. Protection of the lighting is particularly important to prevent shattered pieces of glass from showering the floor and anyone on it. Shatterproof protective safety lenses should be provided for all lighting fixtures.

The media center should be extremely flexible, to accommodate dramatically changing uses. For example, by locating the media center adjacent to the dining area, opportunities are created for informal information, making the media center a hub for student activity, similar to a "cybercafé."

LIBRARY AND MEDIA CENTER

LAYOUT FOR MAIN GYM AND PRACTICE GYM

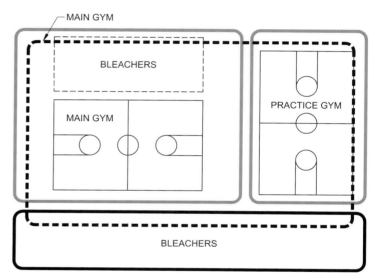

LAYOUT FOR THREE PRACTICE GYMS
Larger gymnasiums are often designed to be split into two or more sections, with either a folding wall or a retractable curtain. In these cases, special attention must be given to exiting requirements and acoustics.

GYMNASIUM LAYOUTS

Auditorium (Fixed Seating)

The size of fixed-seating auditoriums vary, but as a general design rule, this type of auditorium requires 7 sq ft (.6 sq m) per person. If fixed seating is provided, the space will be dedicated to the specific use of auditorium, lecture hall, or general assembly space for large groups. This type of space will most likely have a stage. The design of a stage varies greatly, depending on the district needs. A true stage, by definition, has fly space to allow for movable scenery, lighting, and other required equipment. This type of stage most often has a curtain system, requiring equipment to control curtain movement. Sloped floors with fixed seats in these spaces will enhance the viewing sight lines.

Acoustics, sound equipment, and lighting equipment are critical to the design. Usually, specialists are consulted by the design professional. General house lighting and special theater lighting are often provided, including a dimmer system for control.

Careful attention should be given to building codes concerning fire protection, seating capacity, and seating placement, as well as aisle widths and lengths. Some auditoriums may include a balcony level, which requires additional code analysis with respect to exiting requirements.

Depending on the amount and type of equipment included, these spaces often cost more to construct than most other spaces in a high school.

Auditorium (Loose Seating)

A school district desiring greater flexibility may choose to have an auditorium with movable (loose) seating. These auditoriums, whose size varies, often have the same or similar requirements as those with fixed seats: as a general design rule, 15 sq ft (1.4 sq m) per person are required. In this type of space, floors are not sloped, and folding partitions can be added to increase flexibility. Acoustical design is even more critical if the space is used for multiple purposes. To save money and space, a stage can be provided in a gymnasium or cafeteria to form a "gymtorium" or "cafetorium." This arrangement accomplishes the goal of cost and space savings, but limits the activities that can be successfully accommodated in this multipurpose space.

Nurse and Health Suite

The nurse and health suite is generally located near, or within, the main offices of the school. The size of this area will vary greatly depending on the total population

STAGE

Auditoriums are multipurpose performance spaces for student and community presentations. Students practice presentation skills, expression, and public speaking in these spaces.

AUDITORIUM (500 SEATS)

of the building. There should be a waiting area for students and staff. A private office should be directly adjacent to the waiting area and should allow direct visual contact for supervision. This office should also have direct visual contact with a "resting room," which should have cots or beds; the number included will depend on the level of service provided by the nurse, but as a general rule, there should be one bed for every 200 students.

Toilet Facilities

Toilet facilities are often the least supervised areas in a school; hence, all materials and equipment should be vandal-resistant. Ceiling construction assemblies should be specified to withstand the anticipated level of abuse. Metal stud and gypsum wallboard and acoustic tile ceilings with hold-down clips are among the common choices. Special ventilation is required.

Storage and Property Control Facilities

Adequate storage facilities must be provided to accommodate the mass quantities of reading materials, paper goods, and other materials and equipment that are not used on a daily basis. The amount of space required varies from one school to another. As a general rule, one-tenth the total gross area of the facility will be required. Storage areas should be placed throughout the building to allow proper access from areas that will use these facilities. Storage room sizes vary according to what will be stored.

The nurse and health suite functions as a clinic for the distribution of prescription medications to students and for medical treatment.

NURSE AND HEALTH SUITE

Delivery, storage, and distribution of goods throughout the school are supported by this space.

STORAGE AND PROPERTY CONTROL AREA

MATERIAL SELECTION FOR SCHOOLS

Many schools in use today across the country are housed in buildings more than 50 years old. The need for these buildings to withstand the wear and tear from decades of accommodating schoolchildren and various educational programs should be a major factor in the selection of materials. The materials used to construct a school building should be durable and maintainable. They should be capable of withstanding years of use and abuse while continuing to provide an atmosphere conducive to learning.

Common Material Selections for Primary Spaces

The decisions made regarding material selections, as well as the accessories to protect them, will possibly have the most profound effect on the physical environment and its familiarity to children. We often associate the most institutional and, unfortunately, intimidating settings with endless vinyl tile floors, painted concrete-block walls, cold fluorescent lighting, and numerous wall and corner protection accessories. Although these materials will last a long time, they convey a stronger sense of factory than of home. There are, however, many new products on the market that can provide the durability and maintainability needed without significant compromise of the environment.

Walls

The use of gypsum board for walls is more than likely, given today's budget considerations, but this material does not provide very suitable impact resistance. Highly susceptible to gouging, dents, and corner damage, standard gypsum products must be enhanced or protected. The use of new high-impact gypsum products now on the market (more commonly specified in public housing projects) or the addition of a "skim coat" of diamond-hard plaster to at least a height of 4 ft (1.2 m), can help to improve the durability of the walls. Painted or ground-face block is a common alternative.

Floors

Consideration should be given to new carpet materials for use in classrooms and large play areas both to enhance acoustic quality and to reduce injuries associated with slippery, harder surfaces. In many schools, area rugs are used so that they can be moved, replaced, and quickly cleaned. Solution-dyed products with integral moisture backing should be specified to ensure color retention and easy cleanup of soils and spills. In toilet rooms and in areas used for artwork or wet or messy activities, consider the use of VCT or sheet-vinyl products, which provide long-term durability and maintainability as well as many aesthetic options. Some products offer an attractive wood-flooring appearance with 6-ft- (1.8-m-) wide sheets capable of welded seaming and flash cove base details for watertightness.

CONSIDERATIONS FOR MATERIAL SELECTIONS IN SCHOOLS

AREA	CONSIDERATIONS
Administration	Soft flooring for comfort and acoustics Acoustical barrier walls Cleanable surfaces in workrooms Ventilation for copying area
Offices	Acoustical barrier walls for privacy Proper air change and ventilation Durability (not as critical as in student environments)
Nurse's area	Sanitary conditions Germ-resistant environment Easy to clean and disinfect Hard, nonporous flooring Smooth, cleanable surfaces Disinfectable sick cots Nonpollutant, nonallergenic environment Proper ventilation, humidity, and temperature levels Fluid-impervious materials
Library	Quiet environment Nonglare, nonreflective surfaces for computer use Indirect lighting Controlled moisture and humidity levels
Classrooms	Easily cleaned flooring Hard flooring, with a throw-rug option Environment conducive to concentration Glare from windows controlled Work surface/furnishing durability reflective of classroom function Durable shelving and casework Water-resistant walls, cabinets, floors around sink and toilet areas
Kitchen	Adherence to sanitation regulations Hard, nonporous, nonslip flooring Ability to withstand heavy daily cleaning with chemicals and disinfectant Seamless surfaces for food preparation and cooking Splash-guard surfaces at sink area Floor and wall surfaces resistant to oil and cooking residues Heat-resistant finishes Smooth surfaces resistant to the growth of bacteria
Cafeteria	Hard, nonporous flooring Smooth surfaces resistant to the growth of bacteria Finishes that can be cleaned with disinfectants Hard, smooth wall surfaces for cleaning (at least as a wainscot)
Gymnasium	Resilient floor surface that allows true bounce and spring action Hard, durable wall surfaces for ball play Padded wall sections located strategically for game play Noise reduction via acoustical block, ceiling treatments, etc. Durability of all products used: lights, scoreboard, doors, clocks, etc. Vandal-resistant materials
Locker Rooms	Nonporous, nonslip flooring Ability to withstand heavy cleaning and student abuse Water- and humidity-resistant materials Mildew-resistant curtains Vandal-resistant materials Proper ventilation at clothing and equipment storage areas Durable lockers and furnishings Moisture-resistant wall surfaces
Auditorium	Ease of cleaning beneath the seating area Soft floor finish on walking surfaces to reduce noise Hard and soft wall surfaces placed to achieve the best acoustical properties Vandal-resistant materials Hard surface or cushioned seating, as defined by client Flame-resistant finishes and curtains Resilient stage flooring
Technology	Nonglare or antiglare surfaces Static-resistant materials Quiet environment Ability to control exterior light
Science	Chemical- and acid-resistant materials Hard, cleanable floor finish Proper ventilation for chemical and gas use Water-resistant work surfaces, cabinetry, walls, and floors Chemical storage
Art	Cleanable walls, floors, and ceilings (seamless preferred) Hard, smooth flooring Natural light Heavy-duty storage shelving Fire-resistant kiln area Water-resistant work surfaces, cabinetry, walls, and floors

Ceilings

Acoustics should be addressed for each area designed. The use of acoustic ceiling tile in most areas is important, and carpeting should be considered wherever possible. In areas with harder surfaces, such as large expanses of glass wall or hard-tile flooring, acoustic tile ceilings will not be enough. Consideration should be given to the use of acoustic wall treatments such as fabric-wrapped panels. Care should be taken not to locate these panels in high-impact areas, which generally extend up to 4 ft (1.2 m) above the floor.

Wall Protection

The protection of openings and corners, always a consideration, will ultimately help the facility maintain its appearance. The use of corner guards at key impact areas is recommended; and consideration should be given to recessed guards with carefully coordinated coloring, which helps to blend them with the interior design.

Trim and Casework

The use of natural wood to enhance the quality of a space is often desirable and can provide a very durable low-maintenance alternative to painted trim and cabinets. Among the common woods used for their durability and affordability are maple and oak. Many manufacturers producing children's furnishings work in maple or other light woods, such as birch or beech. These woods are worth considering in determining the color and aesthetic for trim and casework. If painted cabinets are desired, factory polyester or vinyl paint coatings offer good durability as well as easy cleanup. Unfortunately, colors are often limited to white or almond. Countertops of plastic laminate are quite functional, but cabinet fronts, doors, and drawer fronts on lower cabinetry may peel and delaminate over time. Melamine materials should be used on concealed surfaces only.

The materials selected for a school building should support the educational programs and objectives of the client. The environment should be comfortable for the activities within the space, and the materials chosen should add to the comfort in the children's environment. For example, kindergarten children spend much of their day on the floor, working as groups or in centers, and require a soft play surface such as carpeting. In a high school science classroom, students work at a lab station with chemicals that could be damaging to certain materials. The lab space should have hard, smooth work surfaces; and floor finishes should be easy to clean and chemically resistant.

OPERATION AND MAINTENANCE

A well-designed school will withstand the expected impacts and abuse from its student populations. The building should be easy for its caretakers to operate and maintain and, ultimately, preserve the financial investment made by the community that authorized its construction. Operations and maintenance issues are different for new construction and existing buildings.

New School Construction

A new school assignment is an ideal opportunity for an owner and a design team to develop a building that is operations- and maintenance-friendly. The design of the building should be tailored to the requirements of its educational program, consider the abilities of its caretaker, and be easy to operate and maintain. Common sense is usually the best tool for making design decisions that result in a school that is easy to operate and maintain. The designer should consider the following factors related to operations and maintenance:

- The design team's responsibility to advise the community on the best life-cycle strategy for any school construction program
- Sophistication of the building's caretakers
- Durability of building products and equipment
- Special considerations for specific program areas

Throughout the twentieth century, a large percentage of schools used masonry materials for the exterior, in conjunction with masonry, glazed tile, hardwood trim, plaster, and other durable materials for major interior corridors and common areas. The use of robust materials continues to offer the soundest approach for school design today. It is critical for the designer to understand the client's ability to maintain the building and to operate the proposed systems. The skills of a school's staff vary greatly from district to district, and the size of the caretaking staff can range from a single custodian to a team of custodial and facility management people. The size of the staff is, of course, no indicator of its sophistication.

Protection against Vandalism

The durability of building products and equipment is directly related to the expenditure of maintenance staff hours and the subsequent life-cycle costs of the building's systems. The designer must specify building products that anticipate vandalism, graffiti, and heavy use. The building design should make supervision as easy as possible for the adults who will work in the building. Such a plan includes simple sight lines and provides adult use areas throughout the building—staff meeting rooms and educational resource areas. Sensible location of staff use areas (e.g., closer to the classrooms) can reduce adults' travel time to these spaces and ensure that an adult is always present or nearby in every area of the school. This arrangement can increase adult supervision and reduce vandalism and abuse of the school.

Durability of Materials

It is common for corridor and classroom partition walls to be built of painted concrete block or glazed masonry units. Because gypsum surfaces are easily scarred, these more durable walls have proven to be easier to maintain. Similarly, terrazzo flooring products have historically provided an attractive and durable floor surface in areas of heavy traffic. Owing to their cost, however, these products have virtually disappeared from new school construction in recent decades. Alternate products such as vinyl composition tile, epoxy tile, and the much more durable media carpet fibers, where appropriate, are typically used today.

Existing School Buildings

Renovation of an existing school typically involves the correction of existing maintenance and operations problems. For obvious reasons, school districts generally tend to invest most of their financial resources in teaching staff and educational materials (books, technology, athletic equipment, etc.) The physical condition of the school is typically ignored until a problem occurs. Student overcrowding, a leak in the roof, and continuous shorting-out of the electrical power system are examples of such problems. Operations and maintenance considerations for new buildings, as discussed above, should be applied in renovations of existing buildings whenever possible. The designer should consider the following additional factors as they relate to operations and maintenance of an existing school:

- Condition of the mechanical, electrical, and plumbing systems
- Energy conservation through replacement and upgrade of systems
- Sophistication of the building's caretakers
- Typical points of failure
- Identification and mitigation of toxic substances

Existing Conditions

The design team must survey the school's mechanical, electrical, plumbing, and fire-protection systems. Part of the conditions assessment phase must include estimates of the remaining life of existing equipment. This phase should also include detailed interviews of the caretakers, teaching staff, and administration of the school. These interviews can identify problems that are unique to the particular school building and that recur throughout the school year.

Mechanical and Electrical Systems

A study of the existing mechanical and electrical systems and the building envelope (windows and typical wall and roof section) can suggest upgrades of the systems through more efficient energy use. The design team will have to compare first costs with savings in utility costs through the payback period. Another area of study includes the building's heating system. Again, the design professional will be asked to determine the cost of a system upgrade in contrast to future utility cost savings.

Thermal and Moisture Failures

Typical points of failure in the exterior envelope include brick joints, brick joints at windows, and roofing materials. These three areas are among the most neglected in school buildings throughout the country.

Hazardous Materials

Identification and mitigation of toxic substances are critical to both the project budget and the schedule. It is essential that a qualified environmental engineer complete thorough tests of an existing school as early as possible in the design process. Only the written report by a qualified engineer should be relied upon for determinations in this area. If left undetected until late in the design or construction process, the presence of asbestos or other toxic substances can undermine the construction budget and cause serious delays in the schedule. It can also undermine the architect's credibility with the school board and the community.

Raymond C. Bordwell, AIA, Peter Brown, AIA, and Kathie Engelbrecht; Perkins & Will; Educational Facilities Planning and Research Group; Chicago, Illinois
Text excerpted from: Bradford Perkins (Stephen Klimnet, ed.); Building Type Basics for Elementary and Secondary Schools; New York, John Wiley & Sons, Inc., 2001, pp. 15–217.

LIGHTING FOR SCHOOLS

Troffer systems, lensed or parabolic, provide good, acceptable light at low cost and are commonly used in schools. Recessed lighting minimizes vandalism and is efficient.

Suspended direct/indirect and indirect systems are favored for better lighting comfort, and are suited for spaces with ceilings higher than 9 ft (2.7 m).

Industrial-style lighting systems are often used in industrial education, arts, gymnasium, and other spaces requiring plentiful, inexpensive, durable lighting. If using high-intensity discharge (HID) sources, provide quartz auxiliary lamps on some fixtures or an independent instant-on lighting system. Choose luminaires carefully, making note of manufacturer's recommendations.

Randy J. Burkett, FIALD, IES, LC; Randy Burkett Lighting Design, Inc.; St. Louis, Missouri
James Robert Benya, PE, FIES, IALD; Pacific Light Works; Portland, Oregon
Robert Sardinsky; Rising Sun Enterprises; Basalt, Colorado

16'-0" TO 22'-0"
(4876 TO 6705)

16'-0" TO 22'-0" (4876 TO 6705)

In a 10,000 sq ft (929 sq m) gymnasium, average lighting would be a 40 to 50 fc (400 to 500 lux) at 0.95 watts/sq ft provided b 400-watt metal halide fixtures.

REFLECTED CEILING PLAN—GYMNASIUM

COLOR RENDERING INDEX (CRI) CHARACTERISTICS FOR LIGHT

Most classrooms	3,500 or 4,100K > 70 CRI
Commons, lunchrooms	3,000 or 3,500K > 80 CRI
Gymnasiums (primary–secondary)	3,500 or 4,100K > 70 CRI
Art/graphics classrooms	3,500–5,000K > 80 CRI

LIGHTING POWER DENSITY

Classrooms	0.8–1.1 W/sq ft
Lecture halls	1.2–2.0 W/sq ft
Arts and industrial education	1.2–1.6 W/sq ft
Gymnasiums (primary–secondary)	1.2–1.5 W/sq ft
Commons and hallways	0.4–0.8 W/sq ft

Listed are approximate design targets using T8 lamps and electronic high-frequency ballasts or HID systems (not including task lights).

RECESSED (OR SURFACE MOUNTED) DIRECT LIGHTING SYSTEM (TROFFER) USED FOR MOST CLASSROOMS, ESPECIALLY FOR ROOMS WHERE TRADITIONAL PAPER-BASED TASKS ARE ROUTINELY PERFORMED

STANDARD 2' X 4' (200 X 400) CEILING GRID

TYPICAL DESK LOCATION

DIRECT LIGHTING FIXTURE (TROFFER)

WINDOW WALL

A layout with four F32T8 lamps and an electronic ballast in each suspended classroom fixture produces 40 to 50 fc (400 to 500 lux) in the seating area and 20 to 30 vertical fc (200 to 300 lux) on the chalkboard at 0.97 watts/sq ft. The direct/indirect fixtures are designed for traditional classrooms. An indirect lighting system might be used in a computer classroom.

REFLECTED CEILING PLAN—SUSPENDED DIRECT/INDIRECT CLASSROOM LIGHTING

LIGHT ABOVE CHALKBOARD

SUSPENDED INDIRECT/DIRECT LIGHTING SYSTEM USED FOR GENERAL STUDIES WITH LIMITED COMPUTER WORK

STANDARD 2' X 4' (200 X 400) CEILING GRID

TYPICAL DESK LOCATION

SUSPENDED DIRECT/INDIRECT LIGHTING FIXTURE, MINIMUM 15" (367) SUSPENSION

WINDOW WALL

This layout, suitable for traditional classrooms, produces 50 to 60 fc (500 to 600 lux) in an empty room using three F32T8 lamps in a lensed or parabolic luminaire at 1.29 watts/sq ft. With a low light-level ballast, it can also produce 40 to 50 fc (400 to 500 lux) at 1.09 watts/sq ft. For computer classrooms, use computer-optimized parabolics and dimming.

REFLECTED CEILING PLAN—TROFFER CLASSROOM LIGHTING

LECTURE HALLS

PLANNING CRITERIA

The primary program elements for planning lecture halls are class size, traffic patterns to and from the space, the functional requirements specific to the course material to be presented, and the presentation technology used to present it. Important supporting features include acoustics, lighting, and equipment storage.

Class Size

The number of students in the class will determine the room size and the arrangement of egress doors. The designer should request information about expected class sizes at the beginning of the programming phase of the project. Most building codes require access to a minimum of two exits when the occupant load is 50 or more; if the occupant load exceeds 500, access to three or more exits is necessary. Typically, when fixed seating is provided, the occupant load is equal to the number of fixed seats plus wheelchair spaces.

In order to provide optimum viewing for the students, most lecture halls are designed with floors that are tiered or sloped. Entries should be provided at the lower and upper levels of the room; and in larger lecture halls, lower and upper level entries are necessary for adequate separation of egress doors to meet building code requirements. The lower and upper entries must be accessible and located on accessible routes, as described by the *Americans with Disabilities Act Accessibility Guidelines* (ADAAG). If the class is structured such that interaction between students and presenters is expected (requiring students to move to the front, or lower level, to participate in the presentation or demonstration), an accessible route should be provided within the room, between the lower and upper levels of the lecture hall. This is best achieved with ramped aisles. If ramped aisles are not feasible, a mechanical lift within the space can be provided.

Traffic Patterns

When several large lecture halls are grouped together in a building, the resulting number of people traveling to and from the lecture halls between class periods can range into the hundreds. In addition, equipment that is used for class demonstrations but stored outside the lecture hall will require a planned route between the storage area and the lecture hall. Appropriately sized hallways that can handle these heavy traffic loads must be accommodated. As a secondary function to providing an adequate traffic route, hallways can also serve as waiting areas outside the lecture halls for those students who arrive early and wait for their class to begin. The designer should consider making these hallway spaces as useful and pleasant as the lecture halls themselves.

Functional Requirements of Curricula

The subject matter of the course is an important aspect of lecture hall design. For example, science classes may require a laboratory demonstration bench with gas and water service, or a computer science class may necessitate power and data hookups at each student station. The designer should discuss

SIGHT LINES

9'-6" (2900)   4'-0" (1220)   13'-6" (4115)   4'-0" (1220)

SECTION

PROJECTION ROOM

PLAN

TYPICAL LECTURE HALL

course-specific design parameters early in the programming phase and incorporate them in the design of the lecture hall.

Structural Bay Size

The selection and design of the structural system should be based on providing a space that is as free of columns as possible. Lecture hall sizes and column bays for new construction should be coordinated between the designer and the structural engineer so that columns are located within the perimeter walls. Walls should be flush with the column face to avoid protrusions into the lecture hall. This is particularly important at side aisles, for a constant aisle width, and for flush wall surfaces where handrails and wall base run along the sidewalls.

Ceiling Heights

Floor-to-floor heights are an important factor in lecture hall design. The greater the riser height in a tiered floor

system, or degree of slope in a sloped floor system, the greater the floor-to-floor height. Although steeper slopes provide better viewing angles, the result is higher construction costs in building a taller room. Another factor in floor-to-floor heights is the width of column bays. As the lecture hall width is increased, the structural bay dimension is increased. Generally speaking, as the structural bay is increased, the beam depth will also increase, in order to span between columns. As beam depth increases, either the floor-to-floor height will be increased or the overall ceiling height within the lecture hall will be lower. This is due in part to the size of the structural members, but also to the clearance required beneath the beams for mechanical systems and other elements in the ceiling space. The designer should carefully coordinate with the structural engineer, mechanical engineer, and the audiovisual consultant to determine the appropriate overall height of the lecture hall.

PRESENTATION TECHNOLOGY

Images can be viewed on a screen at the front of the room, using equipment that is located at the rear of the lecture hall, in a separate projection room at the front of the lecture hall, or at the ceiling at the approximate center of the lecture hall. Selecting the location of the projection equipment will affect the area required, particularly if a separate projection room is desired.

Rear Screen Projection

Using a separate projection room at the front is called *rear screen projection*. Rear projection screens provide higher-contrast ratios than front projection because they absorb rather than reflect the ambient room light falling on the front of the screen. The advantage that rear screen projection offers is the capability

to project higher-contrast images on the screen with the room lights at a higher ambient level than is possible with front projection. The disadvantage is that rear screen projection is more expensive than front projection, considering both the area required for the separate projection room and the technology used in rear screen projection.

Front Projection

Front projection can be accomplished with equipment located in a cabinet at the rear of the lecture hall or in a separate projection room. This choice depends on the amount of equipment to be used, the ability of the projection technologists who manage the room, and the desire for tighter security offered by a separate equipment room.

Ceiling-Mounted Projection Equipment

Projection equipment located at the ceiling can provide front projection and eliminate the need for a separate projection room or cabinet. In this scenario, the equipment is either permanently mounted at the ceiling or mounted on a platform that retracts into the ceiling cavity when not in use. Access for maintenance of the equipment requires planning since the equipment is not conveniently accessed from the floor of the lecture hall.

Often, the presentation or course material will require freestanding equipment that is brought to the room for a demonstration. This type of equipment may require a storage room outside of the lecture hall. It is important for the designer to determine the technological program elements early in the design process, including whether to use front or rear projection, in order to properly locate and provide for the equipment.

EGRESS AT FRONT OF ROOM
Projection equipment is within room.

EGRESS AT FRONT AND REAR OF ROOM
Projection equipment is at rear of room.

EGRESS AT FRONT AND REAR OF ROOM
Rear projection room is located in the front the room.

CONCEPTUAL LECTURE HALL DIAGRAMS

TIERED AND SLOPED FLOORS

Lecture halls with tiered or sloped floors offer better viewing angles for the students than lecture halls with flat floors. Most building codes allow risers at the aisles in tiered floors to be as low as 4 in. (100 mm) or as high as 8 in. (205 mm). Riser heights must be equal for the entire flight in the aisle. Where increased tier height is desired for better viewing angles, secondary treads can be incorporated into each tier. In this case, tread depth can be as little as 11 in. (280 mm), but 12 to 18 in. (305 to 460 mm) treads allow a more comfortable gait when ascending or descending the aisles. Risers should be located parallel to and at the front edge of the tier, rather than at the end of a seat row (i.e., perpendicular to the edge of the tier), to avoid tripping hazards when exiting the row. Seating specifications will affect the way risers and treads are configured at tiered floors.

Overall rise and run dimensions for sloped floors are determined by desired viewing angles. Most building codes limit the slope of ramped aisles to one unit vertical in eight units horizontal (12.5% slope) in lecture halls with sloped floors.

AISLES

Ramped aisles require a slip-resistant floor surface. *Stepped aisles* require a contrasting marking stripe at the nosing to make the treads apparent when descending the aisle. Most building codes require the marking stripe to be 1 to 2 in. (25 to 50 mm) wide and to extend across the length of the nosing.

When wall base is provided at the walls alongside stepped aisles, the designer can either step the base to match the rise and run of the steps for a uniform base height, or slope the top of the base and vary the height of the base at the steps.

HANDRAILS

Most building codes require a wall-mounted handrail at the side aisles and at stepped aisles where there are two or more adjacent steps. A handrail is required at center aisles as well. The requirements of the ADAAG and most building codes require that handrails be 1½ in. (38 mm) in diameter with a minimum of 1½ in. (38 mm) clear space between the handrail and the wall. The handrails should not extend more than 3½ in. (89 mm) into the required aisle width. Handrails should be mounted at a height of 34 to 38 in. (865 to 965 mm) above the floor or above the tread at stepped aisles, as measured from the edge of the nosing. At the end of the run, handrails should extend 12 in. (305 mm) plus the depth of one tread at stepped aisles, or 12 in. (305 mm) beyond the end of the ramp for sloped aisles. At the top of the run, the handrail should extend 12 in. (305 mm) beyond the top riser at tiered floors, or the top of the ramp at sloped floors. A handrail, curb, or fixed counter should be provided at the leading edge of the riser at wheelchair spaces at tiered floors to prevent falling hazards.

RECTILINEAR PLAN FORM
Rectilinear room shapes can provide optimal seat count per unit of net floor area. It is also easier to arrange rectilinear room shapes together within the rest of the building plan than nonrectilinear shapes. However, the greater the seat count in a rectilinear plan, the farther the last row of seats will be from the presenter, as compared to the fan-shaped plan.

FAN-SHAPED PLAN FORM
Fan-shaped lecture halls are useful if class dialogue or debate is desired, since students can see one another more easily than in a rectilinear lecture hall design. Room shapes where seats are arranged around the front of the lecture hall can provide optimal viewing for the students. However, fan-shaped rooms can be more challenging to arrange efficiently within the building plan.

LECTURE HALL PLAN LAYOUTS

STEPPED WALL BASE
For a staggered appearance, 8 in. (203 mm) base steps up with each riser.

STEPPED WALL BASE
An 8 in. (203 mm) base at tiers, but not at secondary treads. Recessed wall light can be located in the taller portion of the base over the secondary treads.

SLOPED WALL BASE
Sloped at uniform distance from tread nosings. Flat section required at main treads (tiers).

SLOPED WALL BASE
Sloped relative to nosings at main treads (tiers).

WALL BASE AT STEPPED AISLES

SEATING

It is recommended that seating in lecture halls with tiered or sloped floors be fixed, rather than movable. Student seating that offers an individual writing surface at each seat is called *tablet arm seating*. Student seating that offers a continuous fixed counter along the front of each row is called *counter seating*. Often, the course material will determine whether counter or tablet arm seating is desired. Counter seating provides more surface area for student materials or laptop computers, whereas tablet arm seating provides only a small surface suitable for note taking. Either seating type can be outfitted with data and power connections for student computers, but the counter style provides space for a broader range of laptop sizes. Tablet arm seats can be spaced more closely along a row than counter seating; as a result, a lecture hall with tablet arm seating will accommodate more seats per unit of net floor area than with counter seating. Fixed student seating can be either tablet arm or counter seating.

Tablet Arm Seating

The tablets can be specified in three configurations: the tablet can be fixed in place, the tablet can swing up for easier access into the seat, or the tablet can swing up and rotate back to rest vertically between seats. The latter is the most convenient for user egress from the seat. Tablets are available in large or small sizes, offering more or less surface area for note taking, and can be ordered in left- or right-hand configurations. The number of left-hand tablets should be about 5% to 10% of the total seat count. It is useful to locate the left-hand tablets at the ends of rows so that the user's left elbow is toward the aisle rather than toward the neighboring seat. Tablet arm seating can be specified as individually post-mounted, or several seat systems can be mounted on a steel beam. It is easier to clean beneath the steel beam type, but the beam can transmit vibrations from one seat to another.

TABLET ARM SEATING WITH EQUIDISTANT SEAT STAGGER

TABLET ARM SEATING WITH OFFSET SEAT STAGGER

STAGGERED SEATS

Counter Seating

Counter seating provides a more ample writing surface than tablets. It is a popular choice in many lecture halls, but it can be more expensive and requires more space per seat count. The seats can be individually postmounted, or they can be grouped in twos and mounted on a central post beneath the counter, in which case each seat swivels on its fitting and swings out away from the counter. This provides the means of getting into and out of the seat and offers comfortable seating for a broad range of body sizes. Singular swivel seat posts are available for rows with an uneven num-

ber of seats. When single seats are needed, the designer should not arrange the post such that the seat will swing into the side aisle. When selecting counter seating, the designer should specify modesty panels for the front edge of the counter.

Power and Data Outlets

Power and data outlets can be provided in the sidepost of tablet arm seats or at the counter for students who use laptop computers at their station. Manufacturers have several options available, including recessed or concealed outlets. Removable outlet covers are discouraged since they can be broken or lost.

Calculating the Number of Seats

To determine the number of seats allowed per row before reaching an aisle, the designer should consult the authorities having jurisdiction, since several factors must be considered in calculating maximum permissible seat count per row. Building codes prescribe the minimum row depth (as measured front to back of the row) based on the selection of seat type. Generally, the designer should consider whether providing the minimum row depth allowed by the building code will be too narrow, since students often carry and use several books and other materials in class.

Staggered Seating

Staggering the seats from row to row, so they are not aligned directly behind one another, will improve sight lines. However, the degree of seat stagger can affect the ability of those seated in an upper row to view the work of those in the row below (a potential problem during an exam). A mock-up of tier height and seat stagger may be useful to determine optimal viewing angles and appropriate seat stagger.

When tablet arm seats are staggered, the width of the tread at the end of the row should be increased, to prevent tripping hazards at shorter rows. With counter seating, the treads should be a uniform width, and the counter should extend to the riser edge, regardless of the degree of seat stagger.

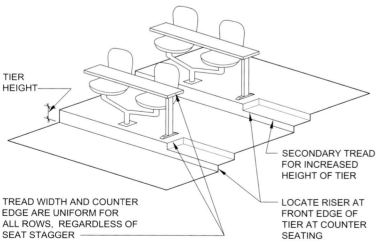

TIER HEIGHT

TREAD WIDTH AND COUNTER EDGE ARE UNIFORM FOR ALL ROWS, REGARDLESS OF SEAT STAGGER

SECONDARY TREAD FOR INCREASED HEIGHT OF TIER

LOCATE RISER AT FRONT EDGE OF TIER AT COUNTER SEATING

RISERS AT COUNTER SEATING
For counter seating, the first riser is located in line with the raised tier to align with the counter.

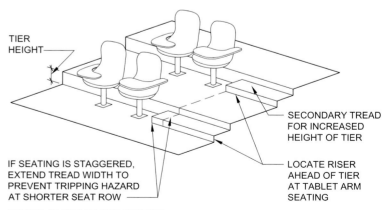

TIER HEIGHT

IF SEATING IS STAGGERED, EXTEND TREAD WIDTH TO PREVENT TRIPPING HAZARD AT SHORTER SEAT ROW

SECONDARY TREAD FOR INCREASED HEIGHT OF TIER

LOCATE RISER AHEAD OF TIER AT TABLET ARM SEATING

RISERS AT TABLET ARM SEATING
For tablet arm seating, the first riser is located in front of the raised tier to align the tread with the row of seats.

Riser configuration at lecture halls with tiered floors will vary depending on whether the seating is tablet arm or counter seating.

TIERED SEATING

FURNITURE

In addition to the student seating, lecture halls need other furniture such as podiums, demonstration tables, freestanding chairs for presenters, and other pieces as necessary by program. There are many manufacturers that specialize in these products.

PODIUMS

Podiums can be simple, movable tabletop units that serve as a place to locate the speaker's paperwork, or complex units that serve several technical functions in the lecture hall. Many podiums have built-in control panels for managing the audiovisual media, lighting, draperies, and other technological instruments. These podiums can be custom-made, or a control panel can be specified for the manufacturer to install in a prefabricated unit. Some provide space for mounting equipment, such as computers, VCRs, and DVD players. Podiums can also be designed to be height-adjustable.

WHEELCHAIR SPACES

ADAAG specifies the minimum number of wheelchair spaces according to the following table. The designer should verify requirements with the authorities having jurisdiction. In addition, 1% (but not less than 1%) of all fixed seats are required to be aisle seats without armrests on the aisle side.

The minimum space needed for a wheelchair user for a straight-in approach is 33 in. (840 mm) wide by 48 in. (1,220 mm) long, and for a side approach is 33 in. (840 mm) wide by 60 in. (1,524 mm) long. Wheelchair spaces should be provided with good lines of sight comparable to the lines of sight provided for general seating. Typically, in lecture halls that are large enough to have entries at the front and back, or in multiple locations of the room, wheelchair spaces are provided at each of these levels; in fact, the ADAAG specifies that if the seating capacity exceeds 300, wheelchair spaces must be provided in more than one location. A writing surface should be provided at wheelchair spaces. This can be a movable table or a fixed counter that wheelchair users pull up to.

ACCESSORIES

There are several accessory items that may be useful or required in lecture halls, including: a clock, a wastebasket, a stick or laser pointer, map rails, hooks, a fire extinguisher located near the laboratory demonstration table, and storage for marking pens, chalk, erasers, and stickpins.

WHEELCHAIR SEATING CAPACITY

SEATING CAPACITY	WHEELCHAIR SPACES
4–25	1
26–50	2
51–300	4
301–500	6
More than 500	6, plus one for each additional 100 seats

VIEWING PROJECTED IMAGES

The minimum, maximum, and optimal viewing angles and distances for projected images depend significantly on the type of images being shown and on the tolerance of users. Design goals should be established in coordination with the audiovisual consultant, taking the project specifics into account. In general, the optimal *view cone* for viewing the image without distortion is bounded by the area at a 45° angle from each side of the screen to the opposite seating area. Viewers outside this angle will have a hard time reading text (especially of smaller size) or discerning accurate geometry of the image. Aisles can be located outside the view cone.

For each viewer, ideally, the screen should be big enough for the full resolution of the image to be visible,

but not so big that the artifacts (scan lines, pixels, noise) are visible. In general, the maximum viewing distance should not exceed four to five times the image height for computer images; however, video images (DVDs or videotapes) may be viewed at up to six to seven image heights; and high-resolution workstation-type graphics should be viewed at three heights or fewer. The minimum viewing distance should be at least one and a half image heights for computer images and at least two to two and a half heights for video, which has lower resolution. It is obviously impossible to meet these criteria for all seats and all types of images without greatly reducing space efficiency, so an important step in initial design is to establish an appropriate compromise for the specific project. Seats may be located outside this optimal range, but image clarity will be reduced.

IMAGES VIEWED FROM SEATS LOCATED OUTSIDE THE OPTIMAL VIEW CONE MAY NOT BE AS CLEAR OR MAY DISTORT

FARTHEST ROW OF SEATS FOR OPTIMUM VIEWING 6 TO 7 TIMES SCREEN HEIGHT FOR VIDEO IMAGES

FARTHEST ROW OF SEATS FOR OPTIMUM VIEWING 4 TO 5 TIMES SCREEN HEIGHT FOR COMPUTER IMAGES

NEAREST ROW OF SEATS FOR OPTIMUM VIEWING 2 TO 2.5 TIMES SCREEN HEIGHT FOR VIDEO IMAGES

NEAREST ROW OF SEATS AT 1.5 TIMES SCREEN HEIGHT FOR COMPUTER IMAGES

OPTIMAL VIEW CONE AT 45°

RECTILINEAR LECTURE HALL WITH 6-FT- (1,830-MM-) HIGH SCREEN

IMAGES VIEWED FROM SEATS LOCATED OUTSIDE THE OPTIMAL VIEW CONE MAY NOT BE AS CLEAR OR MAY DISTORT

FARTHEST ROW OF SEATS FOR OPTIMUM VIEWING 6 TO 7 TIMES SCREEN HEIGHT FOR VIDEO IMAGES

FARTHEST ROW OF SEATS FOR OPTIMUM VIEWING 4 TO 5 TIMES SCREEN HEIGHT FOR COMPUTER IMAGES

NEAREST ROW OF SEATS FOR OPTIMUM VIEWING 2 TO 2.5 TIMES SCREEN HEIGHT FOR VIDEO IMAGES

NEAREST ROW OF SEATS AT 1.5 TIMES SCREEN HEIGHT FOR COMPUTER IMAGES

OPTIMAL VIEW CONE AT 45°

FAN-SHAPED LECTURE HALL WITH 4-FT- (1220-MM-) HIGH SCREEN

OPTIMUM VIEW CONE

AUDIOVISUAL EQUIPMENT

Many presenters still prefer traditional projection equipment, including slide projectors and overhead projectors. In fact, these technologies can provide brighter and more detailed images than video projectors at much lower cost. However, the convenience of instant display of computer images, Web pages, DVDs, and videotapes is making the video projector the standard equipment in most rooms. Lecture halls should also accommodate optical slide and overhead projectors, to be flexible for all presentation media and styles. Overhead projectors are generally located at the front of the room on a table or cart. They can be stored in the room or in a separate equipment room. Slide projectors are usually located at the rear of the room, either in a separate projection booth or on an equipment rack in a media alcove behind the back row of seats. And because slide projectors generate heat, the equipment cabinet should provide a means of ventilation.

Projection Screens

Projection screens can be *fixed, motorized,* or *manual.* Motorized screens are more expensive and require some maintenance, but are less prone to jamming than manual screens. Fixed screens are generally mounted above a fixed chalkboard or markerboard. Screens are available that have tensioning cables along the sides that keep the screen flat, in order to avoid distortion of the image—these are especially useful for larger rolldowns or for critical imagery. The location of projection screens should be coordinated with lighting locations to avoid light spills onto the screen.

An efficient way of utilizing an overhead projector is to project onto a side screen while other images are simultaneously projected on a center screen. This allows the presenter to sketch on the overhead while discussing the image from the center of the room. However, it can be difficult to achieve good sight lines for all seats when using dual screens. Dual slide presentations will affect screen size and projection booth parameters.

Ceiling-Mounted Projectors

With ceiling-mounted or ceiling-recessed projectors, video signals are transmitted to the projector through one or more coaxial cables. The projector can be remotely controlled, so access to the projector is required only for maintenance. Several manufacturers of retractable projector mounts provide a recessed ceiling installation. These are more costly than exposed projector installations and require access for maintenance, but offer a clean-looking ceiling when the projector is not in use. Exposed installations will require some space below the ceiling, to permit the lens to be at the same height as the top of the image on the screen. The distance required for the projector to be hung below the ceiling is a function of the height of the top of the image area of the screen relative to the ceiling. This must be considered when determining ceiling heights and sight lines.

Rear Screen Projection

Rear screen projection will allow the lecture hall's ambient lighting to have higher contrast (which will be perceived as brighter, although the actual brightness is the same) than front projection technology. A general rule for room sizing is that the room depth behind the screen be equal to the width of the screen, although exact dimensions must be determined as a function of the chosen projector or lens, and whether mirrors are used. Screens for rear projection can be more expensive than front projection screens.

Projection Booths

Separate projection booths, whether for rear screen or forward screen projection, generally require more space than if the projector is located in the lecture hall. An enclosed projection booth provides a quieter environment in the lecture hall because the projector and other equipment that has cooling fans are enclosed separately from the hall. It also offers some advantage for equipment security since the equipment is not exposed within the lecture hall and does not move around on carts within the building. The booth may, however, require an operator within the room, as well as a means of communication between the operator and the presenter.

If a separate projection booth is not provided for the lecture hall, a secured area is necessary to house the amplifiers, switching mechanism, VCRs, and other equipment needed to route the signals and remotely control the equipment. This can be a simple locked closet that is wide enough to accept an equipment rack. A standard rack is approximately 2 sq ft (610 sq mm), and requires front and rear access for servicing (unless a pull-out or swing-out style is used). It can be located near the front of the room if access by the presenter (e.g., for loading video tapes or disks) is required.

Chalkboards and Markerboards

Other visual media used in lecture halls include chalkboards, markerboards or whiteboards, and interactive electronic media boards. These are generally installed at the front and center of the room. Chalkboards and markerboards are available that slide vertically to take advantage of higher ceilings in tall lecture halls. This vertical sliding arrangement offers more writing surface for the presenter and allows panels to be visible above one another. Tackboards are useful when placed to the side of the central chalkboard or markerboard.

Equipment Selection

Systems should be designed by an audiovisual engineer and should take into account the room size, shape, lighting, optics, and acoustic properties. The designer should coordinate carefully with the audiovisual engineer for the location and visibility of screens and loudspeakers in the lecture hall. Additionally, the location of video and microphone jacks should be reviewed in conjunction with the arrangement of the podium or demonstration bench so that the presenter is allowed full range of movement in the front of the room. Wireless technology offers solutions to the tripping hazards caused by microphone cords.

Projection Screen Sizes

Recommended screen shapes (aspect ratio) should be based on a width-to-height ratio of 4:3 for computer images and standard video, 16:9 for high-definition

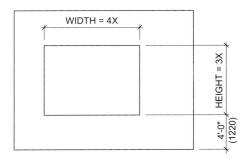

SCREEN SIZE FOR VIDEO
Ratio of screen size is 4:3.

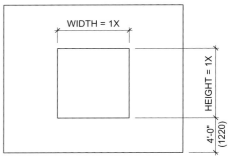

SCREEN SIZE FOR SINGLE SLIDES
Ratio of screen size is 1:1.

SCREEN SIZE FOR DUAL SLIDES
Ratio of screen size is 2:1.

PROJECTION SCREEN SIZES

video (such as wide-screen DVDs), and 1:1 for slides (where both vertical and horizontal orientations will be used). For dual images side by side, the width should double, with the height remaining the same. In a flat-floor space, the bottom of the projection screen (or interactive display board) should be located no lower than 4 ft (1,220 mm) from the bottom of the image to the floor, to avoid the lower part of the image being blocked by persons seated in front of the viewer. Where seating is tiered, conventional sight-line analysis should be used to determine minimum image height. In addition, for viewing comfort, no part of the image should be more than 30° above or below the "horizon" for any viewer. In practice, the ceiling height is often the limiting factor in screen size and height.

LIGHTING

It is appropriate to provide differing light sources and light levels within lecture halls. During the programming phase, the designer should inquire about the lighting requirements for various class activities and for the instructional media required by the course material. For example, certain science demonstrations may require lighting with features such as specific color temperature, or Variac controlled dimmers, to avoid changing the outcome of the experiment. (Variac controlled dimmers do not create electrical interference in other systems and are used primarily in science and laboratory applications.)

Lighting Controls

In most lecture halls, the lighting at the front of the room is switched separately from the lighting at the audience portion of the room. Often, there is a light source directly over the podium that is switched separately from the rest of the lighting at the front of the room, so that the speaker is visible when the room is darkened. Lighting at the audience portion of the room can be on dimmers so that students can take notes when the lights are dimmed for presentations. More complex lighting control scenarios can be provided to meet program requirements. However, as control systems become more sophisticated, the control panel should remain as easy to use as possible, so that new users can easily understand the different lighting scenarios. Often, the lighting controls can be integrated with the audiovisual control system for greater ease of use.

The location of lighting controls is an important consideration, since the presenter should have control over the degree of dimming for the lighting in the room. Often there is an integral control panel at the speaker's podium. These controls should monitor all systems in the room, such as lighting, speakers, projection equipment, and window draperies. If there is no podium, the control panel should be provided at another location that is convenient to the presenter. If a separate projection room is provided in the design, the same controls should be located in the projection room so that A/V personnel who operate equipment for the presentation can monitor the lighting and other systems from within the projection room. At least one switch for lighting should be available at the primary presenter entrance so that the presenter can turn on the lights upon entering the room to prepare for a lecture or presentation.

Daylighting

Generally, daylight sources are discouraged in lecture halls because of the complexities of controlling daylight. If exterior windows or other daylight sources are provided in the room, the designer should determine whether the presentation equipment or course material will require blackout conditions. Design for blackout draperies or screens must be customized to the window profile to prevent light leaks.

CONTRASTING STRIP AT NOSING

STEP LIGHT CAST INTO CONCRETE STAIR NOSING

LIGHT CAST ONTO TREAD BELOW

PATHWAY LIGHTING RECESSED AT STAIR TREAD

Emergency Lighting

If blackout conditions are necessary for the operation of certain presentation equipment or by the instructional media of the course, the lighting designer should consult with code authorities to determine the emergency lighting requirements. In some jurisdictions, blackout conditions are permitted if the emergency lighting is circuited to automatically activate when the fire alarm system is tripped. Typically, pathway lighting is provided along the aisles and is not switched off at any time when the room is occupied. Pathway lighting can be incorporated into the seating at the end of each seat row, recessed in the walls along the side aisles, or incorporated into the design of the risers of a tiered floor system.

ACOUSTICS

Privacy

Acoustically, the opposite of privacy is communication. Communication is central to the education process. Good communication within the classroom or lecture hall is crucial, which is why privacy from unwanted sounds from outside the learning space is central to its design.

The goal is freedom from intruding sound in order to minimize distraction and to maintain classroom attentiveness. STC between classrooms and around lecture halls should be a minimum of 55; over 60 is recommended. Partitions must extend to the structural floor above to achieve this rating. Applied door frame seals are recommended with minimal undercut. Sound-rated door assemblies are not typically required.

Larger lecture halls may utilize voice amplification as an effective adjunct to an audiovisual presentation system.

Exterior Noise Insulation

Noise from outside the lecture hall can reduce speech intelligibility. For those with hearing impairments, exterior noise can further degrade the ability to extract a useful signal from a noisy environment.

The windows and building skin should be able to reduce intermittent exterior noise peaks to 40 dBA or less, and the continuous exterior noise ambient level to less than that produced by HVAC inside the unoccupied indoor space.

Reverberation

The human brain treats reverberant sound as noise, which masks or hides the useful "signal" content of speech; that is, reverberant sound makes it harder to understand what is heard.

Specify ceiling, floor, and wall finishes that will absorb sound efficiently enough to reduce reverberation time to 0.5 to 0.8 second. The reverberation range is proportional to classroom capacity. A Sound Absorption Average (SAA, previously NRC) rating of 0.75 or greater for ceiling materials is recommended. An SAA of 0.90 or greater is recommended for acoustical wall panels. Most classrooms and lecture halls surveyed in United States and Canada were found to exhibit excessive reverberation.

HVAC NC/RC Range

NC/RC range of 20 to 25 or 30 to 35 dBA is recommended for the unoccupied classroom or lecture hall, to help achieve a signal-to-noise ratio of at least +15 dB.

Industry Standard

ANSI Standard S12.60, *Acoustical Performance Criteria, Design Requirements and Guidelines for Schools,* is under development and will be the technical basis for federal regulations and building codes governing acoustics in classrooms.

OTHER SERVICES

Each lecture hall should have adequate power and data outlets at the front of the room for use by the presenter and for the necessary equipment. The designer should take care in locating outlets so that power cords do not become trip hazards. Power and data outlets can also be provided in student furniture. A telephone is useful in a lecture hall for convenience and for emergencies.

Jane Clark, AIA; Zimmer Gunsul Frasca Partnership; Seattle, Washington
Mayura Dhume; Rhode Island School of Design; Providence, Rhode Island
Mark A. Rogers, P.E.; Sparling; Seattle, Washington
Jim Johnson; Wrightson, Johnson, Haddon & Williams, Inc.; Dallas, Texas

PART 4

APPENDIX

Plane and Solid Geometry

Metric System

Uniform Commercial Code

CSI MasterFormat

Industry Directory

PLANE AND SOLID GEOMETRY

TRIANGLE
AREA = ½ any altitude × its base
(altitude is perpendicular distance
to opposite vertex or corner.)

$A = ½ \ b \times h$

TRAPEZOID
AREA = ½ sum of parallel
sides × altitude

$A = \dfrac{h(a+b)}{2}$

CIRCLE
$AREA = \dfrac{\pi D^2}{4} = \pi R^2$

$CIRCUMFERENCE = 2\pi R = \pi D$
$(\pi = 3.14159265359)$

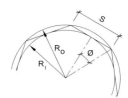

REGULAR POLYGON
$AREA = \dfrac{nSR_1}{2}$
(n = number of sides)

$ANY \ \ SIDE \ \ S = 2\sqrt{R_0{}^2 - R_1{}^2}$

$R = \dfrac{S}{2 \ TAN \ \emptyset} \qquad R_0 = \dfrac{S}{4 \ SIN \ \emptyset}$

TRAPEZUM (IRREGULAR QUADRILATERAL)
AREA = Divide figure into two
triangles and find areas as above.

PARALLELOGRAM
AREA = either side × altitude

CIRCULAR SEGMENT
$AREA = \dfrac{(\text{Length of arc a}) \times R - \alpha \ (R - y)}{2}$

$CHORD \ \alpha \ = 2\sqrt{2yR - y^2}$

$= 2R \ SIN \dfrac{A°}{2}$

CIRCULAR SECTOR
$AREA = \dfrac{aR}{2}$

$= \text{Area of circle} \times \dfrac{A°}{360}$

$= 0.0087 \ R^2 A°$

$ARC \ a = \dfrac{\pi R A°}{180°} = 0.0175 \ R A°$

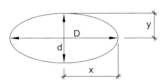

ELLIPSE
AREA = .7854 Dd
Approx. perimeter

$= \pi \sqrt{2(x^2 + y^2)}$

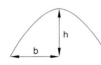

PARABOLA
$AREA = \dfrac{4hb}{3}$

GEOMETRIC PROPERTIES OF PLANE FIGURES

GEOMETRIC PROPERTIES OF CIRCULAR PLANE FIGURES

SPHERE
$VOLUME = \dfrac{4\pi R^3}{3}$

$= 0.5236 \ D^3$

$SURFACE = 4\pi R^2$

$= \pi D^2$

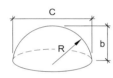

SEGMENT OF SPHERE
$VOLUME = \dfrac{1\pi b^2 (3R - b)}{3}$

(or sector − cone)

$SURFACE = 2\pi Rb$
(not including surface
of circular base)

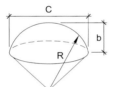

SECTOR OF SPHERE
$VOLUME = \dfrac{2\pi R^2 b}{3}$

$SURFACE = \dfrac{\pi R(4b + c)}{2}$

(or: segment + cone)

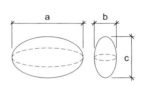

ELLIPSOID
$VOLUME = \dfrac{\pi abc}{6}$

SURFACE: No simple rule

PARABOLOID OF REVOLUTION
VOLUME = Area of circular
base × ½ altitude

SURFACE: No simple rule

CIRCULAR RING OF ANY SECTION
R = Distance from axis of
ring to true center of section

VOLUME = Area of
section × 2πR

SURFACE = Perimeter of
section × 2πR (consider the
section on one side of axis only)

VOLUMES AND SURFACES OF DOUBLE-CURVED SOLIDS

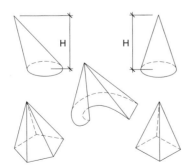

h = ALTITUDE
OF CUT-OFF

H = ALTITUDE
OF WHOLE

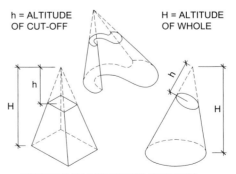

SURFACES OF SOLIDS

The area of the surface is best
found by adding together the areas
of all the faces.

The area of a right cylindrical surface = perimeter of base x length
of elements (average length if other
base is oblique).

The area of a right conical surface
= perimeter of base x ½ length of
elements.

There is no simple rule for the area
of an oblique conical surface or for
a cylindrical one where neither base
is perpendicular to the elements.

PRISMS AND CYLINDERS, RIGHT OR OBLIQUE, REGULAR OR IRREGULAR
Volume = area of base × altitude

Altitude = distance between parallel bases,
measured perpendicular to the bases.
When bases are not parallel, then:
Altitude = perpendicular distance from
one base to the center of the other.

PYRAMIDS OR CONES, RIGHT OR OBLIQUE, REGULAR OR IRREGULAR
Volume = area of base × ⅓ altitude

Altitude = distance from base to apex,
measured perpendicular to base.

FRUSTUM OR TRUNCATED PORTIONS OF THE SOLIDS SHOWN
Volume = From the volume of the whole
solid; if complete, subtract the volume of
the portion cut off.

The altitude of the cutoff part must be
measured perpendicular to its own base.

Source: J.R. Hoke, Jr., ed.;
Architectural Graphic Standards;
New York, John Wiley & Sons, Inc.

VOLUMES AND SURFACES OF TYPICAL SOLIDS

METRIC CONVERSIONS IN CONSTRUCTION

This appendix assimilates metric conversion information to address the appropriate presentation of metric units of measure in construction specifications.

The applicable international metric standard is the International System of Units (SI). The purpose of this appendix is to provide guidance in converting U.S. customary weight and measure units, referred to as inch-pound (IP) units, to metric, and to assist in the proper presentation of metric units in construction documents. Within *Interior Graphic Standards*, text and conceptual drawings provide both IP and SI units, determined by SI conversion standards in order to provide a proportional frame of reference.

Use the tables below to convert the IP units to SI for use in construction documents. In addition, use common sense and professional judgment when converting IP to SI units, as not all conversions are logical or intuitive. Moreover, product manufacturers may have their own policies and procedures for producing metric-sized and IP-sized products.

CONVERSION RULES

In a *soft conversion*, an exact inch-pound measurement is mathematically converted to its exact (or near-exact) metric equivalent. In a *hard conversion,* a new, rounded, rationalized metric number is created that is convenient to work with and remember.

When converting numbers from inch-pound to metric, round the metric value to the same number of digits as there were in the inch-pound number. In all cases, use professional rounding to determine the exact value.

With professional rounding, the basic module of metric design is 100 mm. Make every effort to keep design dimensions in this increment. Additional multimodules and submodules, in preferred order, are 6,000, 3,000, 1,200, 600, 300, 50, 25, 20, and 10. Example: 1,990 BOCA Article 514.7 requires 36 in. (914 mm) of unobstructed pedestrian walkway width. However, 914 mm is not a clean and rational number, so should be rounded to facilitate the easiest construction possible. Since anything less than 914 mm would not meet the code requirements, the preferred number would be 1,000 mm. Submodules will produce a rounding of 950, 925, or 920 mm.

Soft Metric

Soft metric means "no physical change." This implies the product need not be physically modified to be used in a metric project. More than 95% of currently used building products will not change. In the future, as standard international metric product sizes are developed by the International Standards Organization (ISO) or another standards organization, these products may undergo modification to be compatible in the world market. Custom products, often made by computer-controlled machinery, can be specified in any size.

Hard Metric

Hard metric means "product requires physical change." The product must be physically modified to be efficiently used in a metric project, which is planned on a metric grid. A handful of current products must undergo hard metric conversion to new metric sizes.

HARD METRIC PRODUCTS

PRODUCT	SIZE (MM)
Brick	90 × 57 × 190[1]
Concrete masonry unit	190 × 190 × 390[1]
Drywall	1,200 × 2,400[2]
Raised access flooring	600 × 600
Suspended ceiling tiles and grids	600 × 600 and 600 × 1,200
Fluorescent lighting fixtures (lay-in type only)	600 × 600 and 600 × 1,200
Air diffusers and grilles (lay-in type only)	600 × 1,200 widths

[1]Three vertical courses of metric modular brick with a joint of 10 mm equals 201 mm, which is rounded to 200. Three vertical rows of 200 equal 600 mm; 600 x 600 mm is a preferred nominal module for masonry.
[2]Drywall thicknesses remain the same to minimize production impact. The standard thicknesses are 12.7 and 15.9 mm. Standard stud spacing is 400 mm.

METRIC PRODUCTS

Construction product manufacturers will determine actual product dimensions and values. Their decisions involve economics and practicality. Factors in their decision include the following:

- Cost of plant and manufacturing conversion, including changes in tooling, retesting and recertification, new literature, and additional marketing
- Economics of single versus double product inventory
- Demand for products from the industry in either system of measure

USING METRIC UNITS IN SPECIFICATIONS

Metric specifications should use mm for almost all measurements. The use of mm is consistent with the dimensions specified in major codes, such as BOCA and NEC. With the use of mm, the decimal point is used when extreme precision is indicated. Meters may be used only where large, round metric sizes are specified. Centimeters must not be used in specifications. This is consistent with the recommendations of the AIA and ASTM.

RULES FOR WRITING METRIC SYMBOLS AND NAMES

The following are suggested formats for use in metric terms:

- Print the unit symbol in upright type and in lowercase except for liter (L) or unless the unit name is derived from a proper name.
- Print decimal prefixes in lowercase for magnitudes 10^3 and lower; print the prefixes in uppercase for magnitudes 10^6 and higher.
- Leave a space between the numeral and symbol (example: 12 mm).
- Do not use the degree mark with kelvin temperatures.
- Do not leave a space between a unit symbol and its decimal prefix (example: km).
- Do not use the plural of unit symbols, but do use the plural of written unit names (example: kg, kilograms).
- For technical writing, use symbols in conjunction with numerals (example: 10 m²) and write out unit names if numeral is not used (example: square meters).
- Indicate the product of two or more units in symbolic form by using a dot positioned above the line (example: kg.;m·s²).

TABLE COMPARISON OF DRAWING SCALES

INCH-FOOT SCALES	INCH-FOOT RATIO	METRIC SCALE[1]
Full size	1:1	1:1
Half size	1:2	1:2
4 in. = 1 ft 0 in.	1:3	
3 in. = 1 ft 0 in.	1:4	1:5
2 in. = 1 ft 0 in.	1:6	
1½ in. = 1 ft 0 in.	1:8	1:10
1 in. = 1 ft 0 in.	1:12	
¾ = 1 ft 0 in.	1:16	1:20
½ in. = 1 ft 0 in.	1:24	1:25
¼ in. = 1 ft 0 in.	1:48	1:50
1 in. = 5 ft 0 in.	1:60	
⅛ in. = 1 ft 0 in.	1:96	1:100
1 in. = 10 ft 0 in.	1:120	
1⁄16 in. = 1 ft 0 in.	1:192	1:200
1 in. = 20 ft 0 in.	1:240	1:250
1 in. = 30 ft 0 in.	1:360	
1⁄32 in. = 1 ft 0 in.	1:384	
1 in. = 40 ft 0 in.	1:480	1:500
1 in. = 50 ft 0 in.	1:600	
1 in. = 60 ft 0 in.	1:720	
1 in. = 80 ft 0 in.	1:960	1:1,000

[1] Metric drawing scales are expressed in nondimensional ratios. Metric scales 1:2, 1:25, and 1:250 have limited use.

DRAWING SHEET DIMENSIONS[1]

SIZE	SHEET SIZE
A0[2]	1,189 × 841 mm (46.8 × 33.1 in.)
A1	841 × 594 mm (33.1 × 23.4 in.)
A2	594 × 420 mm (23.4 × 16.5 in.)
A3	420 × 297 mm (16.5 × 11.7 in.)
A4	297 × 210 mm (11.7 × 8.3 in.)

[1]The ISO's A-series drawing sizes are preferred metric sizes for design drawings.

[2]A0 is the base size with an area of one square meter. Smaller sizes are half the long dimension of the previous size. All A-sizes have a height-to-width ratio of 1 to the square root of 2. Use a 35-mm microfilm frame to reduce these sizes.

- Do not mix names and symbols (example: N meter).
- Do not use a period after a symbol except when it occurs at the end of a sentence, or for inches (in.) for clarity, so it does not read as the preposition 'in.'
- Always use decimals, not fractions.
- Use a zero before the decimal marker for values less than 1.
- When preparing documentation for use outside the United States, use spaces instead of commas to separate blocks of three digits for any number over four digits (example: 45 138 kg or 0.004 46 kg). In the United States, the decimal marker is a period; in other countries, a comma usually is used.

USING MEASUREMENT CONVERSION TABLES

These tables present a summary listing of those measurement units normally encountered in construction specifications and drawings. They provide a compilation of a variety of measures from inch-pound (IP) to metric (SI) notations. Generally, the designations identify (from left to right) the following:

- IP measurement unit customarily used
- Exact numerical factor that will derive the exact SI measurement
- SI measurement unit traditionally used

The following listings do not differentiate between soft, hard, or rationalized hard conversions. These listings are examples of customary IP and SI measurement units with the pertinent numerical multiplier.

METRIC PREFIXES

MULTIPLES	PREFIXES	SYMBOLS
$1\ 000\ 000\ 000\ 000 = 10^{12}$	tera	T
$1\ 000\ 000\ 000 = 10^{9}$	giga	G
$1\ 000\ 000 = 10^{6}$	mega	M
$1\ 000 = 10^{3}$	kilo	k*
$100 = 10^{2}$	hecto	h
$10 = 10$	deka or deca	da
$0.1 = 10^{-1}$	deci	d
$0.01 = 10^{-2}$	centi	c
$0.001 = 10^{-3}$	milli	m*
$0.000\ 001 = 10^{-6}$	micro	m
$0.000\ 000\ 001 = 10^{-9}$	nano	n
$0.000\ 000\ 000\ 001 = 10^{-12}$	pico	p

Commonly used with base units in design and construction

CONVERSION FACTORS

QUANTITY	FROM INCH-POUND UNITS	TO METRIC UNITS	MULTIPLY BY
Length	mile	Km	1.609344*
	yard	M	0.9144*
	foot	M	0.3048*
		mm	304.8*
	inch	mm	25.4*
Area	square mile	km²	2.59000
	acre	m²	4046.87
		ha (10 000m²)	0.404687
	square yard	m²	0.83612736*
	square foot	m²	0.09290304*
	square inch	mm²	645.16*
Volume	acre foot	m³	1233.49
	cubic yard	m³	0.764555
	cubic foot	m³	0.0283168
		cm³	28316.85
		L (1000 cm³)	28.31685
	100 board feet	m3	0.235974
	gallon	L (1000 cm³)	3.78541
	cubic inch	cm³	16.387064*
		mm³	16387.064*
Mass	lb	kg	0.453592
	kip (1,000 lb)	metric ton (1,000 kg)	0.453592
Mass/unit length	plf	kg/m	1.48816
Mass/unit area	psf	kg/m²	4.88243
Mass density	pcf	kg/m³	16.0185
Force	lb	N	4.44822
Force/unit length	plf	N/m	14.5939
Pressure, stress, modulus of elasticity	psf / psi	Pa / kPa	47.8803 / 6.89476
Bending moment, torque, moment of force	ft-lb	N·m	1.35582
Moment of mass	lb ft	kg·m	0.138255
Moment of inertia	lb ft²	kg·m²	0.0421401
Second moment of area	in4	mm⁴	416231
Section modulus	in3	mm³	16387.064*
Mass/area (density)	lb/ft²	kg/m²	4.882428
Temperature	°F	°C	5/9(°F-32)
Energy, work, quantity of heat	KWh	MJ	3.6*
	Btu	J	1055.056
	ft lbf	J	1.35582
Power	ton (refrig)	kW	3.517
	Btu/s	kW	1.055056
	hp (electric)	W	745.700
	Btu/h	W	0.293071
Heat flux	Btu/f²h	W/m	3.152481
Rate of heat flow	Btu/s	kW	1.055056
	Btu/h	W	0.2930711
Thermal conductivity (k value)	Btu/ft·h·°F	W/m·K	1.73073
Thermal conductance (U value)	Btu/ft²·h·°F	W/m²·K	5.678263

BASE UNITS

PHYSICAL QUALITY	UNIT	SYMBOL
Length	Meter	m
Mass[1]	Kilogram	kg
Time	Second	s
Electric current	Ampere	A
Thermodynamic temperature[2]	Kelvin	K
Luminous intensity	Candela	cd
Amount of substance[3]	Mole	mol

[1]*"Weight" is often used to mean "mass."*

[2]*Celsius temperature (°C) is more commonly used than kelvin (K), but both have the same temperature gradients. Celsius temperature is simply 273.15° warmer than kelvin.*

[3]*Mole is the amount of molecular substance and is used in physics.*

DERIVED UNITS

QUANTITY	NAME	SYMBOL	EXPRESSION
Frequency	hertz	Hz	$Hz = s^{-1}$
Force	newton	N	$N = kg \cdot m/s^{2}$
Pressure, stress	pascal	Pa	$Pa = N/m^{2}$
Energy, work, quantity of heat	joule	J	$J = N \cdot m$
Power, radiant flux	watt	W	$W = J/s$
Electric charge, quantity	coulomb	C	$C = A \cdot s$
Electric potential	volt	V	$V = W/A$ or J/C
Capacitance	farad	F	$F = C/V$
Electric resistance	ohm	W	$\Omega = V/A$
Electric conductance	siemens	S	$S = A/V$ or Ω^{-1}
Magnetic flux	weber	Wb	$Wb = V \cdot s$
Magnetic flux density	tesla	T	$T = Wb/m^{2}$
Inductance	henry	H	$H = Wb/A$
Luminous flux	lumen	lm	$lm = cd \cdot sr$
Illuminance	lux	lx	$lx = lm/m^{2}$

DECIMAL EQUIVALENTS

FRACTION	DECIMAL OF AN INCH	DECIMAL OF A FOOT
1/64	0.15625	
1/32	0.3125	
3/64	0.046875	
1/16	0.0625	0.0052
5/64	0.078125	
3/32	0.09375	
7/64	0.109375	
1/8	0.125	0.0104
9/64	0.140625	
5/32	0.15625	
11/64	0.171875	
3/16	0.1875	0.0156
13/64	0.203125	
7/32	0.21875	
15/64	0.234375	
1/4	0.250	0.0208
17/64	0.265625	
9/32	0.28125	
19/64	0.296875	
5/16	0.3125	0.0260
21/64	0.328125	
11/32	0.34375	
23/64	0.359375	
3/8	0.375	0.0313
25/64	0.390625	
13/32	0.40625	
27/64	0.421875	
7/16	0.4375	0.0365
29/64	0.453125	
15/32	0.46875	
31/64	0.484375	
1/2	0.500	0.0417
33/64	0.515625	
17/32	0.53125	
35/64	0.546875	
9/16	0.5625	0.0469
37/64	0.578125	
19/32	0.59375	
39/64	0.609375	
5/8	0.625	0.0521
41/64	0.640625	
21/32	0.65625	
43/64	0.671875	
11/16	0.6875	0.0573
45/64	0.703125	
23/32	0.71875	
47/64	0.734375	
3/4	0.750	0.0625
49/64	0.765625	
25/32	0.78125	
51/64	0.796875	
13/16	0.8125	0.0677
53/64	0.828125	
27/32	0.84375	
55/64	0.859375	
7/8	0.875	0.0729
57/64	0.890625	
29/32	0.90625	
59/64	0.921875	
15/16	0.9375	0.0781
61/64	0.953125	
31/32	0.96875	
63/64	0.984375	
1	1.00	0.0833
2	2.00	0.1667
3	3.00	0.2500
4	4.00	0.3333
5	5.00	0.4167
6	6.00	0.5000
7	7.00	0.5833
8	8.00	0.6667
9	9.00	0.7500
10	10.00	0.8333
11	11.00	0.9167
12	12.00	1.0000

LINEAR MEASURE

IP UNIT	MULTIPLY BY	SI UNIT
mils (1/1,000 in.)	0.0254	millimeters (mm)
inches	25.4	millimeter (mm)
feet	304.8	millimeter (mm)
feet	0.3048	meter (m)
yards	914.4	millimeter (mm)
yards	0.9144	meter (m)
miles	1.609 344	kilometer (km)
gage[1]	—	millimeter (mm)
picks per inch (textiles)	0.3937	picks per centimeter (cm)

[1]Gage here is a designation for sheet metal thickness or wire diameter. This designation must be transposed from gage to inch thickness or diameter and then converted to an SI unit. There are many gage "standards" used in the metals industry;

consult the appropriate gage table for the applicable inch measurement before converting. For galvanized and electroplated zinc-coated steel, the thickness to be used includes the coating; for galvanized metal deck and other structural applications, the thickness of the base metal before coating may need to be specified instead.

MASS AND DENSITY

IP UNIT	MULTIPLY BY	SI UNIT
grains	64.79891	milligram (mg)
	0.06479891	gram (g)
ounces (oz)	28.349523	gram (g)
	0.028349523	kilogram (kg)
pounds (lb)	0.45359237	kilogram (kg)
tons	0.90718474	tonne
	907.18474	kilogram (kg)
ounces per linear inch (oz/in.)	1.11612	gram/millimeter (g/mm)
	1.11612	kilogram/meter (kg/m)
pounds per linear foot (lb/ft)	1.48816	kilogram/meter (kg/m)
ounces per square inch (oz/sq in.)	439.4189	gram per square millimeter (g/sq mm)
	0.4394189	kilogram per square meter (kg/sq m)
ounces per square foot (oz/sq ft)	305.15426	gram per square meter (g/sq m)
	0.3052	kilogram per square meter (kg/sq m)
ounces per square yard (oz/sq yd)	33.91	gram per square meter (g/sq m)
pounds per square inch (lb/sq in.)	703.0696	kilogram per square meter (kg/sq m)
pounds per square foot (lb/sq ft)	4.88243	kilogram per square meter (kg/sq m)
pounds per cubic inch (lb/cu in.)	27.67990	gram per cubic centimeter (g/cu cm)
pounds per cubic foot (lb/cu ft)	16.01846	kilogram per cubic meter (kg/cu m)
pounds per cubic yard (lb/cu yd)	0.5933	kilogram per cubic meter (kg/cu m)

VELOCITY AND RATE OF FLOW

IP UNIT	MULTIPLY BY	SI UNIT
inches per minute (in./min.)	1524	millimeter per second (mm/s)
feet per second (fps)	0.3048	meter per second (m/s)
feet per minute (fpm)	0.00508	meter per second (m/s)
miles per hour (mph)	0.44704	meter per second (m/s)
	1.609344	kilometer per hour (km/h)
cubic feet per second (cfs)	28.31685	liters per second (L/s)
cubic feet per minute (cfm)	0.471947	liters per second (L/s)
cubic feet per hour (cfh)	7.87	milliliters per second (mL/s)
U.S. gallons per minute (gpm)	0.06309	liters per second (L/s)
U.S. gallons per hour (gph)	0.001052	liters per second (L/s)
revolutions per minute (rpm)	Do not convert	
steam flow rate (lb/h) at 212 deg F	0.284	kilowatts (kW)

AREA MEASURE

IP UNIT	MULTIPLY BY	SI UNIT
square inches (sq in.)	6.4516	square centimeter (sq cm)
square feet (sq ft)	0.0929034	square meter (sq m)
square yards (sq yd)	0.8361274	square meter (sq m)
acres	4046.87	square meter (sq m)
	0.404687	hectare (ha)
square miles (sq mi)	2.589988	square kilometer (sq km)
	2.59	hectare (ha)
quantity per square foot (/sq ft)	10.764	quantity per square meter (/sq m)
quantity per square yard (/sq yd)	1.196	quantity per square meter (/sq m)

CUBIC MEASURE

IP UNIT	MULTIPLY BY	SI UNIT
cubic inches (cu in.)	16.387064	milliliter (mL)
cubic feet (cu ft)	0.02831685	cubic meter (cu m)
cubic feet (cu ft) (volume)	28.32	liter (L)
cubic yards (cu yd)	0.76455	cubic meter (cu m)

LIQUID MEASURE

IP UNIT	MULTIPLY BY	SI UNIT
U.S. gallons (gal)	3.785412	liter (L)
U.S. quarts	0.946353	liter (L)
U.S. pints	0.473176	liter (L)
U.S. fluid ounces (oz)	29.57353	milliliter (mL)

ENERGY, HEAT, AND WORK

IP UNIT	MULTIPLY BY	SI UNIT
British thermal unit (Btu)	1055.06	joule (J)
	1.05506	kilojoule (kJ)
Equivalent direct radiation (EDR)—hot water	44.0	watt (W)
Equivalent direct radiation (EDR)—steam	70.3	watt (W)
ft-lbf/in.	53.38	joule per meter (J/m)
foot-pound force (ft × lbf)	1.355818	joule (J)
	0.001355818	kilojoule (kJ)
inch-pound force (in. × lbf) (torque or moment)	0.1130	N × m
kilowatt-hour (kWh)	3600	kilojoule (kJ)
	3.6	megajoule (MJ)
horsepower-hour	2684.52	kilojoule (kJ)
	2.684	megajoule (MJ)
Btuh (heat)	0.2930722	watt (W)
ton (refrigeration)	3.517	kilowatt (kW)
lb(steam)/h at 212 deg F	0.284	kilowatt (kW)
Btuh × sq ft (heat flow rate)	3.154591	watt per square meter (W/sq m)
Btu × ft/h × sq ft × deg F (thermal conductivity, k-value)	1.730735	W/m × K
Btu × in./h × sq ft × deg F (thermal conductivity, K-value)	0.1442279	W/m × K
Btu/sq ft × h × deg F (thermal conductance, U- or C-value)	5.678263	W/sq. m × K
deg F × h × sq ft/Btu × in. (thermal resistivity, R-value)	6.933471	K × m/W
deg F × h × sq ft/Btu (thermal resistance, R-value)	0.176110	K × sq m/W
perms (23 deg C) (grains/h × sq ft × in. Hg) (vapor permeance)	57.4525	ng/Pa × s × sq m
perm inches (grains/h × ft × in. Hg) (vapor permeability)	1.459 29	ng/Pa × s × m
cfm/sq ft of surface area	5.080	L/s × sq m
	0.00508	cu m/s × sq m

POWER

IP UNIT	MULTIPLY BY	SI UNIT
horsepower (550 ft × lbf/s) (hp)	745.6999	watt (W)
horsepower (electric)	746.000	watt (W)
horsepower (boiler)	9.81	kilowatt (kW)
horsepower (water)	746.043	watt (W)
foot-pounds force per second	1.355818	watt (W)
foot-pounds force per minute	0.02259697	watt (W)

TEMPERATURE

IP UNIT	MULTIPLY BY	SI UNIT
Fahrenheit (deg F)	Actual temperature: Subtract 32 degrees then multiply by 5/9 (0.5556)	Celsius (deg C)
	Temperature differential: Multiply by 5/9 (0.5556) (Do not subtract 32)	Celsius (deg C) or Kelvin (deg K)

ELECTRICITY AND ILLUMINATION

IP UNIT	MULTIPLY BY	SI UNIT
candela per square foot (cd/sq ft)	10.76391	candela per square meter (cd/sq m)
candela per square inch (cd/sq in.)	1550.0	candela per square meter (cd/sq m)
foot-lamberts	3.42626	candela per square meter (cd/sq m)
lumens (lm) per square foot	10.76391	lux (lx)
foot-candles (fc)	10.76391	lux (lx)
ohms/1,000 feet (wire resistance)	3.28	ohms/km
degrees (plane angles)	0.0174	radians

FORCE, PRESSURE, AND STRESS

IP UNIT	MULTIPLY BY	SI UNIT
ounces force	0.278014	newton (N)
pounds force (lbf)	4.448222	newton (N)
pounds force per foot (lbf/ft)	14.59	newton per meter (N/m)
kip force	4448.222	newton (N)
	4.448222	kilonewton (kN)
tons force	8896.444	newton (N)
	8.896444	kilonewton (kN)
tons force per foot	29187.81	newton per meter (N/m)
pounds force per square inch (lbf/sq in.) (psi) (psig)	6894.757	pascal (Pa) or N/sq m
	6.894757	kilopascal (kPa) or kN/sq m
	0.006894757	megapascal (MPa) or MN/sq m
pounds force per square foot (lbf/sq ft)	47.88026	pascal (Pa) or N/sq m
	0.047880	kilopascal (kPa) or kN/sq m
	0.000047880	megapascal (MPa) or MN/sq m
tons force per square inch	13789.514	kilopascal (kPa)
	13.789514	megapascal (MPa)
tons force per square foot	95760.513	pascal (Pa)
	95.760513	kilopascal (kPa)
	0.095760513	megapascal (MPa)
inch water gage (inch wg) at 60 deg F (16 deg C)	248.84	pascal (Pa)
feet of water column at 60 deg F (16 deg C)	2.9861	kilopascal (kPa)
inch of mercury column at 0 deg C (32 deg F)	3386.38	pascal (Pa)
inch of mercury column at 60 deg F (16 deg C)	3376.85	pascal (Pa)

CONSTRUCTION MATERIAL UNITS OF MEASURE CONVERSION TABLES

Construction Material Unit-to-Unit Conversions

These tables offer construction material subject listings (organized by MasterFormat division) of sizes and measurement units normally encountered in construction specifications and drawings. The listings include only those units that need special attention and are not conventional in terms of typical dimensions or expressions. Simple linear, area, or volume units are not illustrated unless the conversion is unusual.

The following tables present material and product subjects with inch-pound (IP) and metric (SI) notations. SI units are either soft or hard conversions or represent products manufactured to metric sizes. It is not necessary for the specifier using this document to discern between them. The determination for the converted unit is based on the following:

- Construction experience and practice
- Recommendations by interested U.S. metric assistance agencies
- The stated intentions of North American manufacturers and industry groups associated with construction product manufacturing
- Logical and rational use of dimensions

Reading Conversion Tables

- The subjects within a division (usually referring to a MasterFormat subject heading or specification section category)
- The specific product (usually referring to a subject or material found within that subject heading or specification section)
- The customary IP unit used
- The SI unit recommended by industry or preferred by designer (In a few instances, the SI size or dimension may be the same as the IP unit.)
- The rounding and precision rule that applies

DIVISION 1—GENERAL REQUIREMENTS

SUBJECT	PRODUCT	IP UNIT	SI UNIT	ROUNDING/PRECISION RULES
Temporary lighting	Project site temporary lighting	fc	lm	
Quality assurance	Tolerances	inches per unit measurement	mm per unit measurement	Round to easily measured units.
	(Example)	⅛ in. in 10 ft	3 mm in 3 m	

DIVISION 2—SITE CONSTRUCTION

SUBJECT	PRODUCT	IP UNIT	SI UNIT	ROUNDING/PRECISION RULES
Earthwork	Soil and aggregate materials compacted	% density	% density	
	Aggregate materials	Sieve sizes by screen number	mm and micrometer	See ASTM E11, *Standard Specification for Wire Cloth and Sieves for Testing Purposes.*
	Grand slope	ratio	ratio	
		in./ft	mm/m	
		%	%	
Paving and surfacing	Concrete unit	psi	MPa	
	Concrete reinforcing	ksi (kips/sq in.)	MPa	
	Concrete mix	psi	MPa	
Utility piping	Drainage pipe	inch NPS	DN	See Tables of Standard Sizes.
	Slope on piping	%	%	
Landscaping	Irrigation pressure pipe	psi	MPa	
	Seeding	lb/1,000 sq ft	kg/100 sq m	

DIVISION 3—CONCRETE

SUBJECT	PRODUCT	IP UNIT	SI UNIT	ROUNDING/PRECISION RULES
Reinforcement	Steel yield strength	psi	MPa	See ASTM A615/A615M, *Standard Specification for Deformed and Plain Billet-Steel Bars for Concrete Reinforcement.*
	Bar diameter	inches	M (numbers that assimilate mm)	
Concrete	Concrete mix	psi	MPa	Round to nearest 10th of an MPa.
	Floor flatness	inches/foot or FF/FL numbers	mm/m	Do not convert FF/FL numbers.
Precast concrete units	Unit thickness	inches	mm	Modular

DIVISION 4—MASONRY

SUBJECT	PRODUCT	IP UNIT	SI UNIT	ROUNDING/PRECISION RULES
Mortar	Mortar and grout strength	Types M, S, N, O	Do not convert.	
	Joint height	inches	mm	Modular coursing
Masonry units	Brick coursing: three bricks, three joints	8 in.	200 mm	Modular coursing
	Block coursing: one block, one joint	8 in.	200 mm	Modular coursing

DIVISION 5—METALS

SUBJECT	PRODUCT	IP UNIT	SI UNIT	ROUNDING/PRECISION RULES
Structural steel	Rolled sections	height in inches by weight in lb/ft	height in mm by weight in kg/m	
Steel deck	Profile height	inches	mm	See SDI standards for flute sizes.
	Metal thickness	inches	mm	See Tables of Standard Sizes.
	Metal yield strength	Grades A to F	same designation	
Cold-formed metal framing	Load-bearing studs	inches	mm	See Tables of Standard Sizes.
	Applied loads	lbf/sq ft	kN/sq m	
Galvanized (zinc) coatings	Zinc coating on steel	G-series designations	Z-series designations	See Tables of Standard Sizes.
Steel stairs	Stair and landing loads	lbf/sq ft	kN/sq m	
	Lateral load on handrail	lb	N	

DIVISION 6—WOOD AND PLASTICS

SUBJECT	PRODUCT	IP UNIT	SI UNIT	ROUNDING/PRECISION RULES
Wood framing materials	Wood studs	2 × 4 in. nominal, 1½ × 3½ in. actual	38 × 89 mm actual	See Tables of Standard Sizes.
	Stud spacing	16 in.	400 mm	Modular
			406 mm (for work using 48-in. panels)	
	Plywood thickness	5⁄16 in.	8 mm	
		3⁄8 in.	9.5 mm	
		½ in.	12.7 mm	
		5⁄8 in.	16 mm	
		¾ in.	19 mm	
	Plywood sheet size	24 × 48 in.	600 × 1,200 mm	Modular
Finish lumber materials	Wood trim	inches	mm	Generally, round to nearest mm.

DIVISION 7—THERMAL AND MOISTURE PROTECTION

SUBJECT	PRODUCT	IP UNIT	SI UNIT	ROUNDING/PRECISION RULES
Waterproofing	Cotton-fabric reinforcement	oz/sq yd	g/sq m	
	Bitumen application	gal/100 sq ft	L/sq m	
	Membrane thickness	mils	mm	
Vapor retarders	Vapor permeability	perms (grains/h × sq ft × inches Hg)	ng/Pa × s × sq m	
	Sheet thickness	mils	mm	
Air barriers	Maximum air leakage by area (infiltration or exfiltration)	cfm/sq ft (reference pressure of 1.57 lbf/sq ft)	L/s × sq m (reference pressure of 75 Pa)	
Board insulation	Board thickness	inches	mm	
	Board sizes	width by length—inches	width by length—mm	
	Board density	lb/cu ft	kg/cu m	
Batt insulation	Batt sizes	friction fit to stud space	friction fit to stud space	Modular stud spacing
Asphalt shingles	Individual shingle weight	lb/100 sq ft	kg/sq m	
Wood shingles	Shingle length	inches	mm	Round to even dimensions.
Metal siding	Metal thickness (uncoated)	inches	mm	See Tables of Standard Sizes.
Roofing	Gypsum sheathing	½ in.	12.7 mm	See ASTM C79, *Standard Specification for Treated Core and Nontreated Core Gypsum Sheathing Board.*
	Rate of bitumen application	lb/100 sq ft	kg/sq m	
Traffic membrane	Application thickness	mils	mm	
Metal roofing, flashings, gutters	Copper thickness	oz/sq ft	mm (thickness)	See Tables of Standard Sizes.
	Steel thickness	inches	mm	See Tables of Standard Sizes.
	Aluminum thickness	inches	mm	See Tables of Standard Sizes.
	Lead	lb/sq ft	mm (thickness)	
	Underlay (roll felt paper)	#15, #30 (# does not mean lb)	#15, #30	

DIVISION 8—DOORS AND WINDOWS

SUBJECT	PRODUCT	IP UNIT	SI UNIT	ROUNDING/PRECISION RULES
Doors	Thickness, width, height	inches	mm	Modular sizes
Steel frames	Metal thickness	inches	mm	See Tables of Standard Sizes.
Aluminum-framed wall systems	Aluminum mullions	inches	mm	Soft converted
	Finish coatings	mils	mm	
Glass	Thickness	—	mm	Metric sizes per ASTM C1036, *Standard Specification for Flat Glass.*
	Wire glass thickness	—	6.4 mm	Metric sizes per ASTM C1036, *Standard Specification for Flat Glass.*

DIVISION 9—FINISHES

SUBJECT	PRODUCT	IP UNIT	SI UNIT	ROUNDING/PRECISION RULES
Gypsum board systems	Gypsum sheathing thickness	⅜ in.	9.5 mm	Per ASTM C 36
		½ in.	12.7 mm	Per ASTM C 36
		⅝ in.	15.9 mm	Per ASTM C 36
Floor and wall tile (ceramic and quarry)	Tile thickness	⅜ in.	10 mm	Rounded dimensions
		½ in.	13 mm	
	Tile size for domestic and imported	inches	mm	Rounded to modular dimensions
Terrazzo	Terrazzo chip size	MTMA #	(same)	
Acoustic ceilings	Acoustic panel and tile sizes	inches	mm	Modular sizes
Resilient flooring	Tile and sheet thickness	inches	mm	
	Tile size	inches	mm	
Carpet	Carpet weight	oz/sq yd	g/sq m	
	Stitches	no./inch	no./cm	
Synthetic flooring	Material thickness	mils	mm	
Coatings	Material thickness	mils	mm	

DIVISION 10—SPECIALTIES

SUBJECT	PRODUCT	IP UNIT	SI UNIT	ROUNDING/PRECISION RULES
Access flooring	Panel size	inches	mm	Modular sizes
	Design-imposed concentrated loads	lbf	N	
Fire extinguishers	Capacity	gal (or units and class)	L (or units and class)	

DIVISION 11—EQUIPMENT

SUBJECT	PRODUCT	IP UNIT	SI UNIT	ROUNDING/PRECISION RULES
Included in other divisions.				

DIVISION 12—FURNISHINGS

SUBJECT	PRODUCT	IP UNIT	SI UNIT	ROUNDING/PRECISION RULES
Included in other divisions.				

DIVISION 13—SPECIAL CONSTRUCTION

SUBJECT	PRODUCT	IP UNIT	SI UNIT	ROUNDING/PRECISION RULES
Integrated ceilings	Grid size	inches	mm	Modular sizes
	Illumination levels	fc	lx	
	Air supply and return	cfm at a reference pressure	L/s at a reference pressure	
Cold storage rooms	Design temperature	deg F	deg C	
Radiation protection	Sheet lead	lb/sq ft	kg/sq m or mm thickness	

DIVISION 14—CONVEYING SYSTEMS

SUBJECT	PRODUCT	IP UNIT	SI UNIT	ROUNDING/PRECISION RULES
Vertical transportation	Travel speed	fpm	m/s	

DIVISION 15—MECHANICAL

SUBJECT	PRODUCT	IP UNIT	SI UNIT	ROUNDING/PRECISION RULES
Pipe sizes	Fire-protection, plumbing, hydronic, steam, and refrigeration piping systems. Materials include cast iron, vitrified clay, aluminum, DWV, ABS, PVC, copper tubing, copper pipe, brass, steel, CPVC, PB, concrete, polyethylene.	inch NPS	DN	See Tables of Standard Sizes.
	Gasket thickness	inches	mm	Exact
Meters and gauges	Sizes, lengths, and diameters	inches	mm	
	Pressures	psig	kPa	
	Vacuum	inches Hg	kPa	Different measurement value
Pumps	Flow	gpm	L/s	
	Total dynamic head	feet (or psig)	kPa	Different measurement value
	Speed	rpm	Do not convert.	
	Motor	hp	Do not convert.	
Power	Electric motor	hp	Do not convert.	
Tanks	Capacity	gal	L	
	Pressure rating	psig	kPa	
Vibration isolation	Isolator loading	psig	kPa	
	Spring deflection	inches	mm	
Insulation	Rated service temperature	deg F	deg C	
	Density	lb/cu ft	kg/cu m	
	Water-vapor transmission	perms	ng/Pa × s × sq m	
	Tie wire	inches	mm	See Tables of Standard Sizes.
	Moisture barrier	mils	mm	
	Jacket thickness	inches (or mils)	mm	
Fire-hose cabinets	Tub, door	inches	mm	See Tables of Standard Sizes.
	Static-pressure limits	psig	kPa	
Fire extinguishers	Pump tank	gal	L	
	Carbon dioxide, dry chemical	lb	kg	
Plumbing piping	Pipe slopes	%	%	(Example: ¼ in./ft = 2%)
	Polyethylene pipe-casing thickness	mils	mm	
	Sewer pipe test pressure	feet of water	kPa	
Interceptors	Unit rating	gpm	L/s	
	Grease or oil capacity	lb	kg	
Catch basins	Cover waterflow capacity	cfs	cu dm/s	
Plumbing fixtures	Water-closet rim height	inches	mm	
	Flush-valve flush volume	gal	L	
	Fixture outside dimensions	inches	mm	
	Lavatory drilling	inches o.c.	mm o.c.	Modular dimensions
	Fixture waterflow	gpm	L/s	
Water heaters	Storage capacity	gal	L	
	Input	Btuh	kW	
	Recovery rate	gph	L/s	
	Temperature rise	deg F	deg C	
	Maximum working pressure	psig	kPa	
Water softeners	Softening capacity	grains	grams	
	Service flow	gpm	L/s	
	Pressure drop	feet (or psig)	kPa	
	Casing working pressure	psig	kPa	
	Resin capacity	cu ft	cu m	
	Salt capacity	lb	kg	
Sump pumps and sewage ejectors	Flow	gpm	L/s	
	Head	feet	kPa	
	Speed	rpm	Do not convert.	
	Motor	hp	Do not convert.	
Compressors (air)	Airflow	scfm	L/s	
	Operating or discharge pressure	psig	kPa	
	Altitude	feet	m	
Receivers	Capacity	gal	L	
Compressed cylinders	Pressure	psig	kPa	
	Temperature	deg F	deg C	
Water treatment, bypass (pot) feeders	Capacity	qt or gal	L	
	Working pressure	psig	kPa	
Water treatment, solution tanks	Capacity	gal	L	
Water treatment, cleaning compounds	Concentration	lb/100 gal	kg/1,000 L	
	Cartridge filter	None	mm (SI is standard)	
Heating appliances	Gas input	Btuh	W	
	Oil input	Btuh	W	
	Heating output	Btuh	W	
	Gas initial pressure	inches wg	Pa	
	Gas flow	cfh	L/s	
	Hot water or steam boilers, pressure-relief valves	psig	kPa	

(Table continued)

DIVISION 15—MECHANICAL (CONTINUED)

SUBJECT	PRODUCT	IP UNIT	SI UNIT	ROUNDING/PRECISION RULES
Breechings	Flue sizes	inches	mm	
	Metal sizes	inches	mm	See Tables of Standard Sizes.
Induced-draft fans	Capacity	cfm	L/s	
	Static pressure	inches wg	Pa	
Direct-fired furnaces	Supply air temperature, temperature rise	deg F	deg C	
	Airflow	cfm	L/s	
	External static pressure	inches wg	Pa	
	Fan motor	hp	Do not convert.	
Refrigeration compressors	Capacity, refrigeration	tons	kW	
Air-cooled condensing units	Heat rejection	Btuh	W	
	Coil airflow	cfm	L/s	
	Compressor input	kW	kW	
Water chillers	Safety-relief valve, waterside working pressure	psig	kPa	
	Refrigeration capacity	tons	kW	
	Waterflow	gpm	L/s	
	Water pressure drop	feet (or psig)	kPa	
	Working steam pressure	psig	kPa	
	Steam flow rate	lb/h	kg/h	
	Natural gas input	MBh	kW	
Cooling towers	Waterflow	gpm	L/s	
	External static pressure	inches wg	Pa	
Heat exchangers	Tubes, OD	inches	mm	
	Working pressure	psig	kPa	
	Working temperature	deg F	deg C	
	Heat transfer	Btuh	kW	
	Waterflow	gpm	L/s	
	Steam	psig	kPa	
	Steam heating capacity (and flow rate)	lb/h	kW	
	Pressure drop, working pressure	psig	kPa	
Air conditioning units	Cooling output	Btuh	W	
	Coil and unit conditions	deg F DB and deg F WB	deg C DB and deg C WB	
	Unit input	kW	kW	
Air coils	Airflow	cfm	L/s	
	Air pressure drop	inches wg	Pa	
	Tubes, OD	inches	mm	
	Casing frame	inches	mm	
	Test or working pressure	psig	kPa	
	Fin spacing	fins per inch	mm o.c.	
Humidifiers	Airflow	cfm	L/s	
	Air pressure drop	inches wg	Pa	
	Saturation efficiency	%	%	
	Rated capacity	lb/h	kg/h	
	Steam pressure	psig	kPa	
Terminal heat-transfer units	Heat output	Btuh	kW	
	Unitary heat output	Btuh per foot	kW/m	
	Casing	inches	mm	See Tables of Standard Sizes.
	Tubing, coils, and fin diameter	inches	mm	
Air handling	Airflow	cfm	L/s	
	Air velocity	fpm	m/s	
	External static pressure	inches wg	Pa	
	Casing, pressure class	inches wg	Pa	
	Insulation density	lb/cu ft	kg/cu ft	
Fans	Airflow	cfm	L/s	
	Static pressure	inches wg	Pa	
	Fan speed	rpm	Do not convert.	
Filters	Face and air velocity	fpm	m/s	
	Resistance to airflow	inches wg	Pa	
	Rated airflow capacity	cfm	L/s	
Filter gauge	Diameter	inches	mm	
	Range	inches wg	Pa	
Ducts	Galvanized coating on steel	G-series	Z-series	See Tables of Standard Sizes.
	PVC coating	mils	mm	
	Maximum velocity	fpm	m/s	
	Duct, pressure class	inches wg	Pa	
	Duct liner, density	lb/cu ft	kg/cu m	
Air-terminal units	System pressure ratings	inches wg	Pa	
Air outlets and inlets	Dimensions	inches	mm	
Controls	Pneumatic pressures	psig	kPa	
	Electric actuator resistance	ohms	ohms	
	Actuator torque	inch-pounds	N × m	

DIVISION 16—ELECTRICAL

SUBJECT	PRODUCT	IP UNIT	SI UNIT	ROUNDING/PRECISION RULES
Conduits	Electrical metallic tubing (EMT), intermediate metal conduit (IMC), and galvanized steel conduit (GRC) nominal size	inches	# EMT, IMC, GRC	See Tables of Standard Sizes.
	Flexible metallic conduit nominal size	inches	Do not convert.	
	Nonmetallic conduit nominal size—all types, including flexible conduit and tubing	inches	Do not convert.	
Outlet, junction, and pull boxes	Capacity	cu in.	cu cm	
Metallic cable trays	NEMA standard spans	feet	m	
	NEMA standard loads	lb/ft	kg/m	
	NEMA standard lengths	feet	m	
	NEMA standard widths	inches	mm	
	Standard rail height	inches	mm	
Underfloor raceways	Linear dimensions	feet and inches	mm	
Wires and cables	Conductor size	AWG	Do not convert.	
	Insulation and shielding thickness	mils	mm	
	Capacitance per unit length	pF/ft	pF/m	
	Attenuation per unit length	dB/100 ft	dB/100 m	
	Resistance per unit length	ohms/1,000 ft	ohms/km	
Transformers	Insulation class	None	SI is standard.	
	Insulation temperature rise	None	SI is standard.	
Lighting fixtures	Luminous intensity	SI is standard.	cd	
	Luminous flux	SI is standard.	lm	
	Luminous-flux density	fc	lx	
	Luminous efficacy	SI is standard.	lm/W	
	Luminance	foot-lamberts	cd/sq m	
	Luminous energy	SI is standard.	lm × s	
	Lamp bulb size	⅛ of an inch	Do not convert.	
	Compact fluorescent lamp lengths	inches	mm	Soft converted
	Fluorescent lamps—U.S. sizes	inches	Do not convert.	
Engine generators	Piston speed	fpm	mm/s	
	Coolant hose pressure rating	psig	KPa	
	Engine size	hp	kW (may be hp' for the interim)	
	Air requirement	cfm	cu m/min.	
	Liquid consumption	gal/h	L/h	
	Altitude	feet	m	
	Fuel-gas energy content	Btu/cu ft	MJ/cu m	
	Fuel-gas energy consumption	cfh	cu m/h	
Lightning protection	Air-terminal and ground rod sizes	inches	mm	
	Cable size	kcmil or AWG	sq mm or AWG	

TABLES OF STANDARD SIZES

METRIC EQUIVALENTS OF STEEL SHEET METAL GAGES

| | UNCOATED STEEL | | | | GALVANIZED STEEL | |
| | NOMINAL THICKNESS | | MINIMUM THICKNESS | | NOMINAL THICKNESS | |
NO.	IN.	MM	IN.	MM	IN.	MM
8	0.164	4.18	0.156	3.96	0.168	4.27
9	0.150	3.8	0.142	3.61	0.153	3.89
10	0.134	3.42	0.126	3.20	0.138	3.50
11	0.120	3.04	0.112	2.84	0.123	3.12
12	0.105	2.66	0.097	2.46	0.108	2.74
14	0.075	1.90	0.067	1.70	0.079	2.01
16	0.060	1.52	0.053	1.35	0.064	1.63
18	0.048	1.21	0.043	1.09	0.052	1.32
20	0.036	0.91	0.033	0.84	0.040	1.02
22	0.030	0.76	0.027	0.69	0.034	0.86
24	0.024	0.61	0.021	0.53	0.028	0.71
25	0.021	0.53	0.018	0.46	0.025	0.64
26	0.018	0.46	0.016	0.41	0.022	0.56
28	0.015	0.38	0.013	0.33	0.019	0.48

Uncoated steel sheet sizes (nominal) are based on the Manufacturers' Standard of the American Iron and Steel Institute (AISI), which is based on the U.S. Standard Gage (a weight gage).

Minimum uncoated steel sizes (inch) are determined by subtracting the tolerances listed in ASTM A568 from nominal sizes. For No. 18 gage and thicker, the tolerances for hot-rolled sheet were used; and for No. 20 gage and thinner, those for cold-rolled sheet were used.

Electrolytic zinc-coated steel is measured by gage listed for uncoated steel not for galvanized steel. The thickness includes the coating, according to ASTM A591, Standard Specification for Steel Sheet, Electrolytic Zinc-Coated, for Light Coating Weight [Mass] Applications.

Galvanized steel thicknesses include the coating (ASTM A653/A653M, Standard Specification for Steel Sheet, Zinc-Coated (Galvanized) or Zinc-Iron Alloy-Coated (Galvannealed) by the Hot-Dip Process, calls for thickness to include the coating). For structural applications, such as metal deck, galvanized steel sheet may be specified by minimum uncoated base metal thickness; in this case, use minimum sizes designated for uncoated steel rather than for galvanized steel.

SHEET ALUMINUM SIZES

in.[1]	0.020	0.024	0.032	0.040	0.050	0.063	0.080	0.1	0.125	0.160
mm[2]	0.51	0.61	0.81	1.02	1.27	1.60	2.03	2.54	3.18	4.06

[1]*The preferred inch thicknesses have been established for use in specifying sheet aluminum.*
[2]*Sizes given in mm are rounded equivalents of the preferred inch thicknesses. For additional preferred thicknesses, see ANSI B32.1 and ANSI B32.3.*

METRIC EQUIVALENTS OF WIRE GAGES

| | U.S. STEEL WIRE GAGE OR WASHBURN & MOEN | | AMERICAN WIRE GAGE OR BROWN & SHARPE | |
NUMBER	IN.	MM	IN.*	MM*
8	0.162	4.11	0.1285	3.264
9	0.148	3.76	0.1144	2.906
10	0.135	3.43	0.1019	2.588
11	0.120	3.05	0.0907	2.304
12	0.106	2.69	0.0808	2.052
14	0.080	2.03	0.0641	1.628
16	0.062	1.57	0.0508	1.290
18	0.048	1.22	0.0403	1.024
20	0.035	0.89	0.0320	0.813
22	0.029	0.74	0.0253	0.643
24	0.023	0.58	0.0201	0.511

Sizes listed in ASTM B3.

PIPE AND TUBE SIZE DESIGNATIONS

NPS[1]	DN[2]	NPS	DN	NPS	DN
½	15	2	50	5	125
⅝	18	2½	65	6	150
¾	20	3	80	8	200
1	25	3½	90	10	250
1¼	32	4	100	12	300
1½	40	4½	115		

[1]*NPS is the inch-pound designation for nominal pipe size.*
[2]*DN is the metric designation for diameter nominal.*
For pipe sizes more than 12 in., use the conversion factor of 25 mm per inch.

STAINLESS-STEEL AND NONFERROUS SHEET METAL SIZES

| | STAINLESS STEEL | | NONFERROUS METALS | |
GAGE	IN.	MM	IN.	MM
8	0.172	4.37	0.128	3.26
9	0.156	3.97	0.114	2.91
10	0.141	3.57	0.102	2.59
11	0.125	3.18	0.091	2.30
12	0.109	2.78	0.081	2.05
14	0.078	1.98	0.064	1.63
16	0.062	1.59	0.051	1.29
18	0.050	1.27	0.040	1.02
20	0.038	0.95	0.032	0.81
22	0.031	0.79	0.025	0.64
24	0.025	0.64	0.020	0.51
26	0.019	0.48	0.016	0.40
28	0.016	0.40	0.012	0.32

For copper flashing and sheet metal, 10 oz = 0.34 mm, 12 oz = 0.41 mm, 14 oz = 0.48 mm, 16 oz = 0.55 mm, 18 oz = 0.62 mm, 20 oz = 0.7 mm, 24 oz = 0.8 mm, and 32 oz = 1.1 mm.

GALVANIZED COATING WEIGHTS

| | TRIPLE SPOT TEST (TOTAL BOTH SIDES) | | |
IP DESIGNATION	OZ/SQ FT	G/SQ M	SI EQUIVALENT*
G01	N.R.	N.R.	Z001
G30	0.30	90	Z90
G40	0.40	120	Z120
G60	0.60	180	Z180
G90	0.90	275	Z275
G115	1.15	350	Z350
G140	1.40	450	Z450
G165	1.65	500	Z500
G185	1.85	550	Z550
G210	2.10	600	Z600
G235	2.35	700	Z700
G300	3.00	900	Z900
G360	3.60	1,100	Z1100

*SI equivalents for coating weights are approximate only; they are the SI designations that are the most nearly equal to the corresponding IP designations.

SCREW SIZES

NO.	INCH DIAMETER	METRIC DIAMETER	SI SIZE
2	0.086	2.18 mm	M2 × 0.4
3	0.099	2.51 mm	M2.5 × 0.45
4	0.112	2.84 mm	M3 × 0.5
6	0.138	3.51 mm	M3.5 × 0.6
8	0.164	4.17 mm	M4 × 0.7
10	0.190	4.83 mm	M5 × 0.8
12	0.216	5.49 mm	—
14	0.242	6.15 mm	M6 × 1.0
16	0.268	6.81 mm	—

Number sizes apply to machine, wood, and sheet-metal screws. SI sizes are for machine screws only.

Standard lengths for SI machine screws are 5, 6, 8, 10, 13, 16, 20, 25, 30, 35, and 40 mm.

LUMBER SIZES

| | NOMINAL SIZE | | ACTUAL SIZE | |
| | DRY | | GREEN | |
IN.	IN.	MM	IN.	MM
1	¾	19	²⁵⁄₃₂	20
1¼	1	25	1¹⁄₃₂	26
1½	1¼	32	1⁹⁄₃₂	33
2	1½	38	1⁹⁄₁₆	40
3	2½	64	2⁹⁄₁₆	65
4	3½	89	3⁹⁄₁₆	90
6	5½	140	5⅝	143
8	7¼	184	7½	190
10	9¼	235	9½	241
12	11¼	286	11½	292

COPPER TUBE OD AND SIZE DESIGNATIONS*

ASTM B88 NOMINAL OR STANDARD SIZE, IN.	ASTM B88M NOMINAL OR STANDARD SIZE, MM	DN DESIGNATION
⅛	6	6
3/16	8	7
¼	10	8
⅜	12	10
½	15	15
⅝	18	18
¾	22	20
1	28	25
1¼	35	32
1½	42	40
2	54	50
2½	67	65
3	79	80
3½	—	90
4	105	100
5	130	125
6	156	150
8	206	200
10	257	250
12	308	300

*Correspondence is not exact on any designation. ASTM B88M, Standard Specification for Seamless Copper Water Tube (Metric), presents nominal or standard sizes of 6 mm, 8 mm, and 10 mm that do not correspond with nominal or standard sizes in ASTM B88, Standard Specification for Seamless Copper Water Tube. Sizes 15 mm and larger correspond roughly to the above sizes in ASTM B88.

METAL ELECTRICAL CONDUIT SIZES TC "METAL ELECTRICAL CONDUIT SIZES"*

TRADE SIZE (IN.)	METRIC SIZE DESIGNATIONS FOR EMT, IMC, AND GRC		
½	16 EMT	16 IMC	16 GRC
¾	21 EMT	21 IMC	21 GRC
1	27 EMT	27 IMC	27 GRC
1¼	35 EMT	35 IMC	35 GRC
1½	41 EMT	41 IMC	41 GRC
2	53 EMT	53 IMC	53 GRC
2½	63 EMT	63 IMC	63 GRC
3	78 EMT	78 IMC	78 GRC
3½	91 EMT	91 IMC	91 GRC
4	103 EMT	103 IMC	103 GRC
5	—	—	129 GRC
6	—	—	155 GRC

*Type of conduit must appear regardless of units of measure selected.

PLASTIC ELECTRICAL CONDUIT SIZES TC "PLASTIC ELECTRICAL CONDUIT SIZES" *

IP SIZE (IN.)	METRIC SIZE (MM)	IP SIZE (IN.)	METRIC SIZE (MM)
½	16	2½	63
¾	21	3	78
1	27	3½	91
1¼	35	4	103
1½	41	5	129
2	53	6	155

*Type of conduit must appear regardless of units of measure selected.

SPECIFICATION WRITING RULES

When producing construction specifications and drawings using metric units, address the following:

- Consistent use of terms, abbreviations, and notations
- Standard use of correct terms that properly express the IP and the SI notation
- Guidelines for written statements and numeric expressions

SUBJECTS NOT ADDRESSED

Several subjects of concern to the specifier, but not included in this appendix, are:

- Building codes and regulations may not contain metric units of measure exclusively. New editions may initially offer dual notation of units and later include only metric units. SI units expressed in codes may not be stated in the unit preferred by product manufacturers or expressed in specifications.
- Fire-tested assemblies and materials that comprise those assemblies are now represented in IP units. When manufacturers change products to standard metric units, those assemblies may need to be retested.
- Land surveys will require conversion from current IP to SI units. Elevations (and inverts) once converted may be expressed in meters above sea level, including the datum. Land title registrations for some states may require descriptions and site or property drawings to be dually annotated depending on their progress of conversion.

ABBREVIATIONS, SYMBOLS, AND PUNCTUATION OF UNITS OF MEASURE

To standardize both IP and SI units in construction documents:

- Insert a space between the measurement value and the measurement unit except when used as a compound modifier.

  Example: Use 20 MPa, not 20MPa.
  Use 10 lb, not 10lb or 10-lb.

- Use uppercase letters for SI units for the following:

  A for ampere
  C for Celsius
  F for farad
  G for giga
  H for Henry
  J for Joule
  K for Kelvin
  L for liter
  M for mega
  N for Newton
  T for tera
  V for volt
  W for watt

- Do not use exponents to indicate square or cube. Use the abbreviations (sq or cu) in formulas or numeric expressions.

  Example: Use 36 sq ft, not 36 ft².
  Use 36 sq m, not 36 m².
  Example: Use 36 cu ft, not 36 ft³.
  Use 36 cu m, not 36 m³.

- Do not indicate a plural by adding an "s" to metric symbols or names.

  Example: 8 kilograms is 8 kg, not 8 kgs.

- Do not use centimeters (cm) except for square and cubic centimeters. Some metric products, such as imported ceramic tile, may express sizes in cm.

  Example: 10-cm tile should be stated as 100-mm tile.

- Do not mix symbols with words in the same compound expression.

  Example: The correct expression is L/s, not L/second or liter/s.

- When expressing dimensions in IP units, use inch for measurements less than or equal to 1 inch and inches for measurements more than 1 inch. Do not use the inch (″) symbol.

  Example: ⅞ inch, 1 inch, 1⅛ inches, 4 inches, unless used as a compound modifier. A 12-inch-high curb compared to a curb that is 12 inches high. Do not use symbols for feet and inches in IP units.

  Example: 3′6″ should be stated as 3 ft 6 in.

- Use millimeters (mm) for linear (length, width, and thickness) dimensions.

  Example: 0.0625 in. sheet metal thickness converts to 1.59 mm.

- Avoid using compound numbers, such as the feet and inches designation, in specifications. Use all inches when possible and practical. This will result in like units between IP and SI.

  Example: Use 40 in. (1,016 mm) instead of 3′4″, 96 in. (2,438 mm) instead of 8 ft.

- Use millimeter (mm) instead of meter (m) or centimeter (cm). Use millimeters for imported ceramic tile even though manufacturers use centimeters in their product literature. Large linear dimensions, such as building length, may use feet and meters instead of inches and millimeters.

- When using whole numbers plus fractions in IP units, use a hard hyphen between the whole number and numerator of the fraction to keep the terms together.

  Example: 10-5/16 or 2-1/2

- In IP units, do not use keyboard characters for ¼, ½, or ¾; use 1/4, 1/2, or 3/4.
- Express values less than 1 in decimal form with a preceding 0.

  Example: Use 0.25, not .25.

- Express decimals only to the degree of accuracy required (unless necessary for consistency).

  Example: Use 29 in., not 29.00 in., unless the value is intended to have a precision of 0.01 in. Use 6 mm, not 6.00 mm, unless the value is intended to have a precision of 0.01 mm.

To delimit numeric expressions:

- For IP units to the left of the decimal, do not delimit whole numbers of four or fewer digits. Use commas in whole numbers having five or more digits by delimiting the digits in groups of three digits with a comma. For SI units, the same rule applies, except use a hard space instead of a comma.

  Example: IP: 1727 ft or 10,000 ft
  SI: 3000 m or 10 000 m

- For IP units to the right of the decimal, do not delimit the digits.

  Example: 0.0004 in. or 0.00055 in.

- For SI units, use prefixes such as kilo or mega to keep values between 0.1 and 9999.
- A few measurement units are common to both IP and SI, such as volts, amperes, and resistance in ohms. Express these values using the SI rules stated above.
- Use a hard space within any numeric expressions to inhibit word-processing software's automatic word wrap.

MANUSCRIPT RULES

In compound notations, use "by" to indicate the multiplier; do not use a lowercase x. Express multiplication in formulas with a lowercase multiplication symbol "×."

  Example: 12 by 24 in. (300 by 600 mm)
  cfm × sq ft (L/s × sq m)

Exercise care in the proper presentation of IP and SI formulas by using the correct symbols.

  Example: Thermal resistance is expressed in IP units as deg F × h × sq ft/Btu; and in SI units as K × sq m/W.

There are three rules for referencing standards:

If there are two separate standards for inch-pound and metric units, cite them separately, as follows:

  ASTM C 478 (ASTM C 478M)
  (Use hard spaces *both* before and after the C.)

If one standard covers both inch-pound and metric units, and has a slash in the title, cite it as follows:

  ASTM A 366/A 366M

If the reference *also* cites a specific grade, type, class, or other designation, group the information according to units, as follows:

  ASTM A 525/A 525M, G60 (Z180)
  ASTM A 526/A 526M, G60 (Z180)

DRAWINGS

When converting weight and measure units, consider the relationship of selected units to drawing notes, measurement dimensions, and other expressed units. This relationship is of concern in computer programming developments that will electronically link with specification text. Drawing coordination checklists will address this issue as they are updated or as new ones are created.

An overview of the highlights of metric conversion for construction drawings and specifications comprises the following:

- All linear dimensions are expressed in millimeters (mm) except on-site and civil drawings, where meters (m) with up to three digits to the right of the decimal may be used. Each drawing set should have a definition for the use of SI units to clearly indicate how to differentiate between millimeters and meters.
- Survey elevation measurements use meters (m) above mean sea level, usually with 1 or more digits to the right of the decimal. Floor slab elevations may also use meters (m) above a benchmark or some other reference elevation point.
- Plane angles in surveying are expressed in degrees, minutes, and seconds; or degrees and decimals of a degree.

  Example: 84 degrees 12 minutes 8 seconds or 68.435 degrees. Express slopes as a ratio or percentage. In a ratio, the vertical unit is always to the left of the colon; the horizontal unit is to the right of the colon.

- For slopes less than 45 degrees, the vertical component should be a unitary value.

  Example: A roof slope of 3 in 12 becomes 1:4.

- For slopes greater than 45 degrees, the horizontal component should be a unitary value.

  Example: A steep embankment of 2.5:1.

- For slopes on piping, present as a percentage. List only the percentage with no IP or SI codes and no IP units (percentage is neither IP nor SI).

  Example: ¼ in. in 10 ft becomes 0.2%.

- Express drawing scale to a unitary base.

  Example: ⅛ in. per foot (converts exactly to 1:96) becomes 1:100. (Drawing scales are available in metric divisions.)

- Mechanical and electrical drawings often indicate values and capacities in a variety of single or combined IP units:

  Example: Ceiling diffusers identify cubic feet per minute (cfm) for intended air supply. The metric equivalent liters per second (L/s) must follow the proper metric convention and be consistent with the specification SI (metric) notations.

Converting drawing measurement units, addressing nondimensional issues, and recognizing their effect on drawings are described more thoroughly in NIBS's *Metric Guide for Federal Construction*.

SOURCES

American Society for Testing and Materials. ASTM E 380: Practice for Use of the International System of Units (SI) (the Modernized Metric System) *(West Conshohocken, PA: ASTM), 1993, PCN 03–543189, pp. 34, 35.*

———. ASTM E 62I: Practice for Use of Metric (SI) Units in Building Design and Construction (Committee E–6 Supplement to E 380), *1994, p. 30.*

American Society of Heating, Refrigerating and Air-Conditioning Engineers. SI for HVAC&R; ASHRAE Policy on Units. *7th ed. (Atlanta, GA: ASHRAE), 1992, p. 6.*

General Services Administration, Office of Design and Construction. Metric Design Guide. *Draft, 2nd ed. (Washington, DC: GPO), 1992.*

Institute of Electrical and Electronics Engineers. IEEE 268: American National Standard for Metric Practice *(ANSI) (New York: IEEE, 1992), p. 64.*

International Organization for Standardization; Technical Committee 12. International Standard ISO 1000: SI Units and Recommendations for the Use and Their Multiples and of Certain Other Units. *3rd ed. (Geneva: ISO 1000), 1992(E), p. 22.*

National Institute of Building Sciences; the Construction Subcommittee of the Metrication Operating Committee of the Interagency Council on Metric Policy. Metric Guide for Federal Construction *(Washington, DC: NIBS), 1991, p. 34.*

MASTERSPEC®; published by ARCOM; Salt Lake City, Utah, and Alexandria, Virginia.

UNIFORM COMMERCIAL CODE – ARTICLE 2 SALES

PART 1. SHORT TITLE, GENERAL CONSTRUCTION AND SUBJECT MATTER

PART 2. FORM, FORMATION AND READJUSTMENT OF CONTRACT

PART 3. GENERAL OBLIGATION AND CONSTRUCTION OF CONTRACT

PART 4. TITLE, CREDITORS AND GOOD FAITH PURCHASERS

PART 5. PERFORMANCE

PART 6. BREACH, REPUDIATION AND EXCUSE

PART 7. REMEDIES

2-101. SHORT TITLE.

This Article shall be known and may be cited as Uniform Commercial Code-Sales.

2-102. SCOPE; CERTAIN SECURITY AND OTHER TRANSACTIONS EXCLUDED FROM THIS ARTICLE.

Unless the context otherwise requires, this Article applies to transactions in goods; it does not apply to any transaction which although in the form of an unconditional contract to sell or present sale is intended to operate only as a security transaction nor does this Article impair or repeal any statute regulating sales to consumers, farmers or other specified classes of buyers.

2-103. DEFINITIONS AND INDEX OF DEFINITIONS.

(1) In this Article unless the context otherwise requires
  (a) "Buyer" means a person who buys or contracts to buy goods.
  (b) "Good faith" in the case of a merchant means honesty in fact and the observance of reasonable commercial standards of fair dealing in the trade.
  (c) "Receipt" of goods means taking physical possession of them.
  (d) "Seller" means a person who sells or contracts to sell goods.
(2) Other definitions applying to this Article or to specified Parts thereof, and the sections in which they appear are:

  "Acceptance". Section 2-606.
  "Banker's credit". Section 2-325.
  "Between Merchants". Section 2-104.
  "Cancellation". Section 2-106(4).
  "Commercial unit". Section 2-105.
  "Confirmed credit". Section 2-325.
  "Conforming to contract". Section 2-106.
  "Contract for sale". Section 2-106.
  "Cover". Section 2-712.
  "Entrusting". Section 2-403.
  "Financing agency". Section 2-104.
  "Future Goods". Section 2-105.
  "Goods". Section 2-105.
  "Identification". Section 2-501.
  "Installment contract". Section 2-612.
  "Letter of Credit". Section 2-325.
  "Lot". Section 2-105.
  "Merchant". Section 2-104.
  "Overseas". Section 2-323.
  "Person in position of Seller". Section 2-707.
  "Present sale". Section 2-106.
  "Sale". Section 2-106.
  "Sale on approval". Section 2-326.
  "Sale or return". Section 2-326.
  "Termination". Section 2-106.

(3) The following definitions in other Articles apply to this Article:

  "Check". Section 3-104.
  "Consignee". Section 7-102.
  "Consignor". Section 7-102.
  "Consumer Goods". Section 9-109.
  "Dishonor". Section 3-507.
  "Draft". Section 3-104.

(4) In addition Article 1 contains general definitions and principles of construction and interpretation applicable throughout this Article.

2-104. DEFINITIONS: "MERCHANT"; "BETWEEN MERCHANTS"; "FINANCING AGENCY".

(1) "Merchant" means a person who deals in goods of the kind or otherwise by his occupation holds himself out as having knowledge or skill peculiar to the practices or goods involved in the transaction or to whom such knowledge or skill may be attributed by his employment of an agent or broker or other intermediary who by his occupation holds himself out as having such knowledge or skill.
(2) "Financing agency" means a bank, finance company or other person who in the ordinary course of business makes advances against goods or documents of title or who by arrangement with either the seller or the buyer intervenes in ordinary course to make or collect payment due or claimed under the contract for sale, as by purchasing or paying the seller's draft or making advances against it or by merely taking it for collection whether or not documents of title accompany the draft. "Financing agency" includes also a bank or other person who similarly intervenes between persons who are in the position of seller and buyer in respect to the goods (Section 2-707).
(3) "Between Merchants" means in any transaction with respect to which both parties are chargeable with the knowledge or skill of merchants.

2-105. DEFINITIONS: TRANSFERABILITY; "GOODS"; "FUTURE" GOODS; "LOT"; "COMMERCIAL UNIT".

(1) "Goods" means all things (including specially manufactured goods) which are movable at the time of identification to the contract for sale other than the money in which the price is to be paid, investment securities (Article 8) and things in action. "Goods" also includes the unborn young of animals and growing crops and other identified things attached to realty as described in the section on goods to be severed from realty (Section 2-107).
(2) Goods must be both existing and identified before any interest in them can pass. Goods which are not both existing and identified are "future" goods. A purported present sale of future goods or of any interest therein operates as a contract to sell.
(3) There may be a sale of a part interest in existing identified goods.
(4) An undivided share in an identified bulk of fungible goods is sufficiently identified to be sold although the quantity of the bulk is not determined. Any agreed proportion of such a bulk or any quantity thereof agreed upon by number, weight or other measure may to the extent of the seller's interest in the bulk be sold to the buyer who then becomes an owner in common.
(5) "Lot" means a parcel or a single article which is the subject matter of a separate sale or delivery, whether or not it is sufficient to perform the contract.
(6) "Commercial unit" means such a unit of goods as by commercial usage is a single whole for purposes of sale and division of which materially impairs its character or value on the market or in use. A commercial unit may be a single article (as a machine) or a set of articles (as a suite of furniture or an assortment of sizes) or a quantity (as a bale, gross, or carload) or any other unit treated in use or in the relevant market as a single whole

2-106. DEFINITIONS: "CONTRACT"; "AGREEMENT"; "CONTRACT FOR SALE"; "SALE"; "PRESENT SALE"; "CONFORMING" TO CONTRACT; "TERMINATION"; "CANCELLATION".

(1) In this Article unless the context otherwise requires "contract" and "agreement" are limited to those relating to the present or future sale of goods. "Contract for sale" includes both a present sale of goods and a contract to sell goods at a future time. A "sale" consists in the passing of title from the seller to the buyer for a price (Section 2-401). A "present sale" means a sale which is accomplished by the making of the contract.
(2) Goods or conduct including any part of a performance are "conforming" or conform to the contract when they are in accordance with the obligations under the contract.
(3) "Termination" occurs when either party pursuant to a power created by agreement or law puts an end to the contract otherwise than for its breach. On "termination" all obligations which are still executory on both sides are discharged but any right based on prior breach or performance survives.
(4) "Cancellation" occurs when either party puts an end to the contract for breach by the other and its effect is the same as that of "termination" except that the canceling party also retains any remedy for breach of the whole contract or any unperformed balance.

2-107. GOODS TO BE SEVERED FROM REALTY: RECORDING.

(1) A contract for the sale of minerals or the like (including oil and gas) or a structure or its materials to be removed from realty is a contract for the sale of goods within this Article if they are to be severed by the seller but until severance a purported present sale thereof which is not effective as a transfer of an interest in land is effective only as a contract to sell.
(2) A contract for the sale apart from the land of growing crops or other things attached to realty and capable of severance without material harm thereto but not described in subsection (1) or of timber to be cut is a contract for the sale of goods within this Article whether the subject matter is to be severed by the buyer or by the seller even though it forms part of the realty at the time of contracting, and the parties can by identification effect a present sale before severance.
(3) The provisions of this section are subject to any third party rights provided by the law relating to realty records, and the contract for sale may be executed and recorded as a document transferring an interest in land and shall then constitute notice to third parties of the buyer's rights under the contract for sale.
[Note: *As amended in 1972.*]

2-201. FORMAL REQUIREMENTS; STATUTE OF FRAUDS.

(1) Except as otherwise provided in this section a contract for the sale of goods for the price of $500 or more is not enforceable by way of action or defense unless there is some writing sufficient to indicate that a contract for sale has been made between the parties and signed by the party against whom enforcement is sought or by his authorized agent or broker. A writing is not insuffi-

cient because it omits or incorrectly states a term agreed upon but the contract is not enforceable under this paragraph beyond the quantity of goods shown in such writing.

(2) Between merchants if within a reasonable time a writing in confirmation of the contract and sufficient against the sender is received and the party receiving it has reason to know its contents, it satisfies the requirements of subsection (1) against such party unless written notice of objection to its contents is given within 10 days after it is received.

(3) A contract which does not satisfy the requirements of subsection (1) but which is valid in other respects is enforceable

(a) if the goods are to be specially manufactured for the buyer and are not suitable for sale to others in the ordinary course of the seller's business and the seller, before notice of repudiation is received and under circumstances which reasonably indicate that the goods are for the buyer, has made either a substantial beginning of their manufacture or commitments for their procurement; or

(b) if the party against whom enforcement is sought admits in his pleading, testimony or otherwise in court that a contract for sale was made, but the contract is not enforceable under this provision beyond the quantity of goods admitted; or

(c) with respect to goods for which payment has been made and accepted or which have been received and accepted (Sec. 2-606).

2-202. FINAL WRITTEN EXPRESSION: PAROL OR EXTRINSIC EVIDENCE.

Terms with respect to which the confirmatory memoranda of the parties agree or which are otherwise set forth in a writing intended by the parties as a final expression of their agreement with respect to such terms as are included therein may not be contradicted by evidence of any prior agreement or of a contemporaneous oral agreement but may be explained or supplemented

(a) by course of dealing or usage of trade (Section 1-205) or by course of performance (Section 2-208); and

(b) by evidence of consistent additional terms unless the court finds the writing to have been intended also as a complete and exclusive statement of the terms of the agreement.

2-203. SEALS INOPERATIVE.

The affixing of a seal to a writing evidencing a contract for sale or an offer to buy or sell goods does not constitute the writing a sealed instrument and the law with respect to sealed instruments does not apply to such a contract or offer.

2-204. FORMATION IN GENERAL.

(1) A contract for sale of goods may be made in any manner sufficient to show agreement, including conduct by both parties which recognizes the existence of such a contract.

(2) An agreement sufficient to constitute a contract for sale may be found even though the moment of its making is undetermined.

(3) Even though one or more terms are left open a contract for sale does not fail for indefiniteness if

the parties have intended to make a contract and there is a reasonably certain basis for giving an appropriate remedy.

2-205. FIRM OFFERS.

An offer by a merchant to buy or sell goods in a signed writing which by its terms gives assurance that it will be held open is not revocable, for lack of consideration, during the time stated or if no time is stated for a reasonable time, but in no event may such period of irrevocability exceed three months; but any such term of assurance on a form supplied by the offeree must be separately signed by the offeror.

2-206. OFFER AND ACCEPTANCE IN FORMATION OF CONTRACT.

(1) Unless otherwise unambiguously indicated by the language or circumstances

(a) an offer to make a contract shall be construed as inviting acceptance in any manner and by any medium reasonable in the circumstances;

(b) an order or other offer to buy goods for prompt or current shipment shall be construed as inviting acceptance either by a prompt promise to ship or by the prompt or current shipment of conforming or non-conforming goods, but such a shipment of non-conforming goods does not constitute an acceptance if the seller seasonably notifies the buyer that the shipment is offered only as an accommodation to the buyer.

(2) Where the beginning of a requested performance is a reasonable mode of acceptance an offeror who is not notified of acceptance within a reasonable time may treat the offer as having lapsed before acceptance.

2-207. ADDITIONAL TERMS IN ACCEPTANCE OR CONFIRMATION.

(1) A definite and seasonable expression of acceptance or a written confirmation which is sent within a reasonable time operates as an acceptance even though it states terms additional to or different from those offered or agreed upon, unless acceptance is expressly made conditional on assent to the additional or different terms.

(2) The additional terms are to be construed as proposals for addition to the contract. Between merchants such terms become part of the contract unless:

(a) the offer expressly limits acceptance to the terms of the offer;

(b) they materially alter it; or

(c) notification of objection to them has already been given or is given within a reasonable time after notice of them is received.

(3) Conduct by both parties which recognizes the existence of a contract is sufficient to establish a contract for sale although the writings of the parties do not otherwise establish a contract. In such case the terms of the particular contract consist of those terms on which the writings of the parties agree, together with any supplementary terms incorporated under any other provisions of this Act.

2-208. COURSE OF PERFORMANCE OR PRACTICAL CONSTRUCTION.

(1) Where the contract for sale involves repeated occasions for performance by either party with

knowledge of the nature of the performance and opportunity for objection to it by the other, any course of performance accepted or acquiesced in without objection shall be relevant to determine the meaning of the agreement.

(2) The express terms of the agreement and any such course of performance, as well as any course of dealing and usage of trade, shall be construed whenever reasonable as consistent with each other; but when such construction is unreasonable, express terms shall control course of performance and course of performance shall control both course of dealing and usage of trade (Section 1-205).

(3) Subject to the provisions of the next section on modification and waiver, such course of performance shall be relevant to show a waiver or modification of any term inconsistent with such course of performance.

2-209. MODIFICATION, RESCISSION AND WAIVER.

(1) An agreement modifying a contract within this Article needs no consideration to be binding.

(2) A signed agreement which excludes modification or rescission except by a signed writing cannot be otherwise modified or rescinded, but except as between merchants such a requirement on a form supplied by the merchant must be separately signed by the other party.

(3) The requirements of the statute of frauds section of this Article (Section 2-201) must be satisfied if the contract as modified is within its provisions.

(4) Although an attempt at modification or rescission does not satisfy the requirements of subsection (2) or (3) it can operate as a waiver.

(5) A party who has made a waiver affecting an executory portion of the contract may retract the waiver by reasonable notification received by the other party that strict performance will be required of any term waived, unless the retraction would be unjust in view of a material change of position in reliance on the waiver.

2-210. DELEGATION OF PERFORMANCE; ASSIGNMENT OF RIGHTS.

(1) A party may perform his duty through a delegate unless otherwise agreed or unless the other party has a substantial interest in having his original promisor perform or control the acts required by the contract. No delegation of performance relieves the party delegating of any duty to perform or any liability for breach.

(2) Unless otherwise agreed all rights of either seller or buyer can be assigned except where the assignment would materially change the duty of the other party, or increase materially the burden or risk imposed on him by his contract, or impair materially his chance of obtaining return performance. A right to damages for breach of the whole contract or a right arising out of the assignor's due performance of his entire obligation can be assigned despite agreement otherwise.

(3) Unless the circumstances indicate the contrary a prohibition of assignment of "the contract" is to be construed as barring only the delegation to the assignee of the assignor's performance.

(4) An assignment of "the contract" or of "all my rights under the contract" or an assignment in similar

general terms is an assignment of rights and unless the language or the circumstances (as in an assignment for security) indicate the contrary, it is a delegation of performance of the duties of the assignor and its acceptance by the assignee constitutes a promise by him to perform those duties. This promise is enforceable by either the assignor or the other party to the original contract.

(5) The other party may treat any assignment which delegates performance as creating reasonable grounds for insecurity and may without prejudice to his rights against the assignor demand assurances from the assignee (Section 2-609).

2-301. GENERAL OBLIGATIONS OF PARTIES.

The obligation of the seller is to transfer and deliver and that of the buyer is to accept and pay in accordance with the contract.

2-302. UNCONSCIONABLE CONTRACT OR CLAUSE.

(1) If the court as a matter of law finds the contract or any clause of the contract to have been unconscionable at the time it was made the court may refuse to enforce the contract, or it may enforce the remainder of the contract without the unconscionable clause, or it may so limit the application of any unconscionable clause as to avoid any unconscionable result.

(2) When it is claimed or appears to the court that the contract or any clause thereof may be unconscionable the parties shall be afforded a reasonable opportunity to present evidence as to its commercial setting, purpose and effect to aid the court in making the determination.

2-303. ALLOCATION OR DIVISION OF RISKS.

Where this Article allocates a risk or a burden as between the parties "unless otherwise agreed", the agreement may not only shift the allocation but may also divide the risk or burden.

2-304. PRICE PAYABLE IN MONEY, GOODS, REALTY, OR OTHERWISE.

(1) The price can be made payable in money or otherwise. If it is payable in whole or in part in goods each party is a seller of the goods which he is to transfer.

(2) Even though all or part of the price is payable in an interest in realty the transfer of the goods and the seller's obligations with reference to them are subject to this Article, but not the transfer of the interest in realty or the transferor's obligations in connection therewith.

2-305. OPEN PRICE TERM.

(1) The parties if they so intend can conclude a contract for sale even though the price is not settled. In such a case the price is a reasonable price at the time for delivery if

(a) nothing is said as to price; or
(b) the price is left to be agreed by the parties and they fail to agree; or
(c) the price is to be fixed in terms of some agreed market or other standard as set or recorded by a third person or agency and it is not so set or recorded.

(2) A price to be fixed by the seller or by the buyer means a price for him to fix in good faith.

(3) When a price left to be fixed otherwise than by agreement of the parties fails to be fixed through fault of one party the other may at his option treat the contract as cancelled or himself fix a reasonable price.

(4) Where, however, the parties intend not to be bound unless the price be fixed or agreed and it is not fixed or agreed there is no contract. In such a case the buyer must return any goods already received or if unable so to do must pay their reasonable value at the time of delivery and the seller must return any portion of the price paid on account.

2-306. OUTPUT, REQUIREMENTS AND EXCLUSIVE DEALINGS.

(1) A term which measures the quantity by the output of the seller or the requirements of the buyer means such actual output or requirements as may occur in good faith, except that no quantity unreasonably disproportionate to any stated estimate or in the absence of a stated estimate to any normal or otherwise comparable prior output or requirements may be tendered or demanded.

(2) A lawful agreement by either the seller or the buyer for exclusive dealing in the kind of goods concerned imposes unless otherwise agreed an obligation by the seller to use best efforts to supply the goods and by the buyer to use best efforts to promote their sale.

2-307. DELIVERY IN SINGLE LOT OR SEVERAL LOTS.

Unless otherwise agreed all goods called for by a contract for sale must be tendered in a single delivery and payment is due only on such tender but where the circumstances give either party the right to make or demand delivery in lots the price if it can be apportioned may be demanded for each lot.

2-308. ABSENCE OF SPECIFIED PLACE FOR DELIVERY.

Unless otherwise agreed
(a) the place for delivery of goods is the seller's place of business or if he has none his residence; but
(b) in a contract for sale of identified goods which to the knowledge of the parties at the time of contracting are in some other place, that place is the place for their delivery; and
(c) documents of title may be delivered through customary banking channels.

2-309. ABSENCE OF SPECIFIC TIME PROVISIONS; NOTICE OF TERMINATION.

(1) The time for shipment or delivery or any other action under a contract if not provided in this Article or agreed upon shall be a reasonable time.

(2) Where the contract provides for successive performances but is indefinite in duration it is valid for a reasonable time but unless otherwise agreed may be terminated at any time by either party.

(3) Termination of a contract by one party except on the happening of an agreed event requires that reasonable notification be received by the other party and an agreement dispensing with notification is invalid if its operation would be unconscionable.

2-310. OPEN TIME FOR PAYMENT OR RUNNING OF CREDIT; AUTHORITY TO SHIP UNDER RESERVATION.

Unless otherwise agreed
(a) payment is due at the time and place at which the buyer is to receive the goods even though the place of shipment is the place of delivery; and
(b) if the seller is authorized to send the goods he may ship them under reservation, and may tender the documents of title, but the buyer may inspect the goods after their arrival before payment is due unless such inspection is inconsistent with the terms of the contract (Section 2-513); and
(c) if delivery is authorized and made by way of documents of title otherwise than by subsection (b) then payment is due at the time and place at which the buyer is to receive the documents regardless of where the goods are to be received; and
(d) where the seller is required or authorized to ship the goods on credit the credit period runs from the time of shipment but post-dating the invoice or delaying its dispatch will correspondingly delay the starting of the credit period.

2-311. OPTIONS AND COOPERATION RESPECTING PERFORMANCE.

(1) An agreement for sale which is otherwise sufficiently definite (subsection (3) of Section 2-204) to be a contract is not made invalid by the fact that it leaves particulars of performance to be specified by one of the parties. Any such specification must be made in good faith and within limits set by commercial reasonableness.

(2) Unless otherwise agreed specifications relating to assortment of the goods are at the buyer's option and except as otherwise provided in subsections (1)(c) and (3) of Section 2-319 specifications or arrangements relating to shipment are at the seller's option.

(3) Where such specification would materially affect the other party's performance but is not seasonably made or where one party's cooperation is necessary to the agreed performance of the other but is not seasonably forthcoming, the other party in addition to all other remedies

(a) is excused for any resulting delay in his own performance; and
(b) may also either proceed to perform in any reasonable manner or after the time for a material part of his own performance treat the failure to specify or to cooperate as a breach by failure to deliver or accept the goods.

2-312. WARRANTY OF TITLE AND AGAINST INFRINGEMENT; BUYER'S OBLIGATION AGAINST INFRINGEMENT.

(1) Subject to subsection (2) there is in a contract for sale a warranty by the seller that
(a) the title conveyed shall be good, and its transfer rightful; and
(b) the goods shall be delivered free from any security interest or other lien or encumbrance of which the buyer at the time of contracting has no knowledge.

(2) A warranty under subsection (1) will be excluded or modified only by specific language or by circumstances which give the buyer reason to know that the person selling does not claim title in himself or that he is purporting to sell only such right or title as he or a third person may have.

(3) Unless otherwise agreed a seller who is a merchant regularly dealing in goods of the kind warrants that the goods shall be delivered free of the rightful claim of any third person by way of infringement or the like but a buyer who furnishes specifications to the seller must hold the seller harmless against any such claim which arises out of compliance with the specifications.

2-313. EXPRESS WARRANTIES BY AFFIRMATION, PROMISE, DESCRIPTION, SAMPLE.

(1) Express warranties by the seller are created as follows:

    (a) Any affirmation of fact or promise made by the seller to the buyer which relates to the goods and becomes part of the basis of the bargain creates an express warranty that the goods shall conform to the affirmation or promise.

    (b) Any description of the goods which is made part of the basis of the bargain creates an express warranty that the goods shall conform to the description.

    (c) Any sample or model which is made part of the basis of the bargain creates an express warranty that the whole of the goods shall conform to the sample or model.

(2) It is not necessary to the creation of an express warranty that the seller use formal words such as "warrant" or "guarantee" or that he have a specific intention to make a warranty, but an affirmation merely of the value of the goods or a statement purporting to be merely the seller's opinion or commendation of the goods does not create a warranty.

2-314. IMPLIED WARRANTY: MERCHANTABILITY; USAGE OF TRADE.

(1) Unless excluded or modified (Section 2-316), a warranty that the goods shall be merchantable is implied in a contract for their sale if the seller is a merchant with respect to goods of that kind. Under this section the serving for value of food or drink to be consumed either on the premises or elsewhere is a sale.

(2) Goods to be merchantable must be at least such as

    (a) pass without objection in the trade under the contract description; and

    (b) in the case of fungible goods, are of fair average quality within the description; and

    (c) are fit for the ordinary purposes for which such goods are used; and

    (d) run, within the variations permitted by the agreement, of even kind, quality and quantity within each unit and among all units involved; and

    (e) are adequately contained, packaged, and labeled as the agreement may require; and

    (f) conform to the promise or affirmations of fact made on the container or label if any.

(3) Unless excluded or modified (Section 2-316) other implied warranties may arise from course of dealing or usage of trade.

2-315. IMPLIED WARRANTY: FITNESS FOR PARTICULAR PURPOSE.

Where the seller at the time of contracting has reason to know any particular purpose for which the goods are required and that the buyer is relying on the seller's skill or judgment to select or furnish suitable goods, there is unless excluded or modified under the next section an implied warranty that the goods shall be fit for such purpose.

2-316. EXCLUSION OR MODIFICATION OF WARRANTIES.

(1) Words or conduct relevant to the creation of an express warranty and words or conduct tending to negate or limit warranty shall be construed wherever reasonable as consistent with each other; but subject to the provisions of this Article on parol or extrinsic evidence (Section 2-202) negation or limitation is inoperative to the extent that such construction is unreasonable.

(2) Subject to subsection (3), to exclude or modify the implied warranty of merchantability or any part of it the language must mention merchantability and in case of a writing must be conspicuous, and to exclude or modify any implied warranty of fitness the exclusion must be by a writing and conspicuous. Language to exclude all implied warranties of fitness is sufficient if it states, for example, that "There are no warranties which extend beyond the description on the face hereof."

(3) Notwithstanding subsection (2)

    (a) unless the circumstances indicate otherwise, all implied warranties are excluded by expressions like "as is", "with all faults" or other language which in common understanding calls the buyer's attention to the exclusion of warranties and makes plain that there is no implied warranty; and

    (b) when the buyer before entering into the contract has examined the goods or the sample or model as fully as he desired or has refused to examine the goods there is no implied warranty with regard to defects which an examination ought in the circumstances to have revealed to him; and

    (c) an implied warranty can also be excluded or modified by course of dealing or course of performance or usage of trade.

(4) Remedies for breach of warranty can be limited in accordance with the provisions of this Article on liquidation or limitation of damages and on contractual modification of remedy (Sections 2-718 and 2-719).

2-317. CUMULATION AND CONFLICT OF WARRANTIES EXPRESS OR IMPLIED.

Warranties whether express or implied shall be construed as consistent with each other and as cumulative, but if such construction is unreasonable the intention of the parties shall determine which warranty is dominant. In ascertaining that intention the following rules apply:

    (a) Exact or technical specifications displace an inconsistent sample or model or general language of description.

    (b) A sample from an existing bulk displaces inconsistent general language of description.

    (c) Express warranties displace inconsistent implied warranties other than an implied warranty of fitness for a particular purpose.

2-318. THIRD PARTY BENEFICIARIES OF WARRANTIES EXPRESS OR IMPLIED.

[Note: If this Act is introduced in the Congress of the United States this section should be omitted. (States to select one alternative.)]

Alternative A

A seller's warranty whether express or implied extends to any natural person who is in the family or household of his buyer or who is a guest in his home if it is reasonable to expect that such person may use, consume or be affected by the goods and who is injured in person by breach of the warranty. A seller may not exclude or limit the operation of this section.

Alternative B

A seller's warranty whether express or implied extends to any natural person who may reasonably be expected to use, consume or be affected by the goods and who is injured in person by breach of the warranty. A seller may not exclude or limit the operation of this section.

Alternative C

A seller's warranty whether express or implied extends to any person who may reasonably be expected to use, consume or be affected by the goods and who is injured by breach of the warranty. A seller may not exclude or limit the operation of this section with respect to injury to the person of an individual to whom the warranty extends.

[Note: As amended in 1966.]

2-319. F.O.B. AND F.A.S. TERMS.

(1) Unless otherwise agreed the term F.O.B. (which means "free on board") at a named place, even though used only in connection with the stated price, is a delivery term under which

    (a) when the term is F.O.B. the place of shipment, the seller must at that place ship the goods in the manner provided in this Article (Section 2-504) and bear the expense and risk of putting them into the possession of the carrier; or

    (b) when the term is F.O.B. the place of destination, the seller must at his own expense and risk transport the goods to that place and there tender delivery of them in the manner provided in this Article (Section 2-503);

    (c) when under either (a) or (b) the term is also F.O.B. vessel, car or other vehicle, the seller must in addition at his own expense and risk load the goods on board. If the term is F.O.B. vessel the buyer must name the vessel and in an appropriate case the seller must comply with the provisions of this Article on the form of bill of lading (Section 2-323).

(2) Unless otherwise agreed the term F.A.S. vessel (which means "free alongside") at a named port, even though used only in connection with the stated price, is a delivery term under which the seller must

    (a) at his own expense and risk deliver the goods alongside the vessel in the manner usual in that port or on a dock designated and provided by the buyer; and

    (b) obtain and tender a receipt for the goods in

exchange for which the carrier is under a duty to issue a bill of lading.

(3) Unless otherwise agreed in any case falling within subsection (1)(a) or (c) or subsection (2) the buyer must seasonably give any needed instructions for making delivery, including when the term is F.A.S. or F.O.B. the loading berth of the vessel and in an appropriate case its name and sailing date. The seller may treat the failure of needed instructions as a failure of cooperation under this Article (Section 2-311). He may also at his option move the goods in any reasonable manner preparatory to delivery or shipment.

(4) Under the term F.O.B. vessel or F.A.S. unless otherwise agreed the buyer must make payment against tender of the required documents and the seller may not tender nor the buyer demand delivery of the goods in substitution for the documents.

2-320. C.I.F. AND C.& F. TERMS.

(1) The term C.I.F. means that the price includes in a lump sum the cost of the goods and the insurance and freight to the named destination. The term C. & F. or C.F. means that the price so includes cost and freight to the named destination.

(2) Unless otherwise agreed and even though used only in connection with the stated price and destination, the term C.I.F. destination or its equivalent requires the seller at his own expense and risk to
(a) put the goods into the possession of a carrier at the port for shipment and obtain a negotiable bill or bills of lading covering the entire transportation to the named destination; and
(b) load the goods and obtain a receipt from the carrier (which may be contained in the bill of lading) showing that the freight has been paid or provided for; and
(c) obtain a policy or certificate of insurance, including any war risk insurance, of a kind and on terms then current at the port of shipment in the usual amount, in the currency of the contract, shown to cover the same goods covered by the bill of lading and providing for payment of loss to the order of the buyer or for the account of whom it may concern; but the seller may add to the price the amount of the premium for any such war risk insurance; and
(d) prepare an invoice of the goods and procure any other documents required to effect shipment or to comply with the contract; and
(e) forward and tender with commercial promptness all the documents in due form and with any indorsement necessary to perfect the buyer's rights.

(3) Unless otherwise agreed the term C. & F. or its equivalent has the same effect and imposes upon the seller the same obligations and risks as a C.I.F. term except the obligation as to insurance.

(4) Under the term C.I.F. or C. & F. unless otherwise agreed the buyer must make payment against tender of the required documents and the seller may not tender nor the buyer demand delivery of the goods in substitution for the documents.

2-321. C.I.F. OR C. & F.: "NET LANDED WEIGHTS"; "PAYMENT ON ARRIVAL"; WARRANTY OF CONDITION ON ARRIVAL.

Under a contract containing a term C.I.F. or C. & F.

(1) Where the price is based on or is to be adjusted according to "net landed weights", "delivered weights", "out turn" quantity or quality or the like, unless otherwise agreed the seller must reasonably estimate the price. The payment due on tender of the documents called for by the contract is the amount so estimated, but after final adjustment of the price a settlement must be made with commercial promptness.

(2) An agreement described in subsection (1) or any warranty of quality or condition of the goods on arrival places upon the seller the risk of ordinary deterioration, shrinkage and the like in transportation but has no effect on the place or time of identification to the contract for sale or delivery or on the passing of the risk of loss.

(3) Unless otherwise agreed where the contract provides for payment on or after arrival of the goods the seller must before payment allow such preliminary inspection as is feasible; but if the goods are lost delivery of the documents and payment are due when the goods should have arrived.

2-322. DELIVERY "EX-SHIP".

(1) Unless otherwise agreed a term for delivery of goods "ex-ship" (which means from the carrying vessel) or in equivalent language is not restricted to a particular ship and requires delivery from a ship which has reached a place at the named port of destination where goods of the kind are usually discharged.

(2) Under such a term unless otherwise agreed
(a) the seller must discharge all liens arising out of the carriage and furnish the buyer with a direction which puts the carrier under a duty to deliver the goods; and
(b) the risk of loss does not pass to the buyer until the goods leave the ship's tackle or are otherwise properly unloaded.

2-323. FORM OF BILL OF LADING REQUIRED IN OVERSEAS SHIPMENT; "OVERSEAS".

(1) Where the contract contemplates overseas shipment and contains a term C.I.F. or C. & F. or F.O.B. vessel, the seller unless otherwise agreed must obtain a negotiable bill of lading stating that the goods have been loaded in board or, in the case of a term C.I.F. or C. & F., received for shipment.

(2) Where in a case within subsection (1) a bill of lading has been issued in a set of parts, unless otherwise agreed if the documents are not to be sent from abroad the buyer may demand tender of the full set; otherwise only one part of the bill of lading need be tendered. Even if the agreement expressly requires a full set
(a) due tender of a single part is acceptable within the provisions of this Article on cure of improper delivery (subsection (1) of Section 2-508); and
(b) even though the full set is demanded, if the documents are sent from abroad the person tendering an incomplete set may nevertheless require payment upon furnishing an indemnity which the buyer in good faith deems adequate.

(3) A shipment by water or by air or a contract contemplating such shipment is "overseas" insofar as by usage of trade or agreement it is subject to the commercial, financing or shipping practices characteristic of international deep water commerce.

2-324. "NO ARRIVAL, NO SALE" TERM.

Under a term, "no sale no arrival" or terms of like meaning, unless otherwise agreed,

(a) the seller must properly ship conforming goods and if they arrive by any means he must tender them on arrival but he assumes no obligation that the goods will arrive unless he has caused the non-arrival; and
(b) where without fault of the seller the goods are in part lost or have so deteriorated as no longer to conform to the contract or arrive after the contract time, the buyer may proceed as if there had been casualty to identified goods (Section 2-613).

2-325. "LETTER OF CREDIT" TERM; "CONFIRMED CREDIT".

(1) Failure of the buyer seasonably to furnish an agreed letter of credit is a breach of the contract for sale.

(2) The delivery to seller of a proper letter of credit suspends the buyer's obligation to pay. If the letter of credit is dishonored, the seller may on seasonable notification to the buyer require payment directly from him.

(3) Unless otherwise agreed the term "letter of credit" or "banker's credit" in a contract for sale means an irrevocable credit issued by a financing agency of good repute and, where the shipment is overseas, of good international repute. The term "confirmed credit" means that the credit must also carry the direct obligation of such an agency which does business in the seller's financial market.

2-326. SALE ON APPROVAL AND SALE OR RETURN; CONSIGNMENT SALES AND RIGHTS OF CREDITORS.

(1) Unless otherwise agreed, if delivered goods may be returned by the buyer even though they conform to the contract, the transaction is
(a) a "sale on approval" if the goods are delivered primarily for use, and
(b) a "sale or return" if the goods are delivered primarily for resale.

(2) Except as provided in subsection (3), goods held on approval are not subject to the claims of the buyer's creditors until acceptance; goods held on sale or return are subject to such claims while in the buyer's possession.

(3) Where goods are delivered to a person for sale and such person maintains a place of business at which he deals in goods of the kind involved, under a name other than the name of the person making delivery, then with respect to claims of creditors of the person conducting the business the goods are deemed to be on sale or return. The provisions of this subsection are applicable even though an agreement purports to reserve title to the person making delivery until payment or resale or uses such words as "on consignment" or "on memorandum". However, this subsection is not applicable if the person making delivery
(a) complies with an applicable law providing for a consignor's interest or the like to be evidenced by a sign, or
(b) establishes that the person conducting the business is generally known by his creditors to be substantially engaged in selling the goods of others, or

(c) complies with the filing provisions of the Article on Secured Transactions (Article 9).

(4) Any "or return" term of a contract for sale is to be treated as a separate contract for sale within the statute of frauds section of this Article (Section 2-201) and as contradicting the sale aspect of the contract within the provisions of this Article on parol or extrinsic evidence (Section 2-202).

2-327. SPECIAL INCIDENTS OF SALE ON APPROVAL AND SALE OR RETURN.

(1) Under a sale on approval unless otherwise agreed
  (a) although the goods are identified to the contract the risk of loss and the title do not pass to the buyer until acceptance; and
  (b) use of the goods consistent with the purpose of trial is not acceptance but failure seasonably to notify the seller of election to return the goods is acceptance, and if the goods conform to the contract acceptance of any part is acceptance of the whole; and
  (c) after due notification of election to return, the return is at the seller's risk and expense but a merchant buyer must follow any reasonable instructions.

(2) Under a sale or return unless otherwise agreed
  (a) the option to return extends to the whole or any commercial unit of the goods while in substantially their original condition, but must be exercised seasonably; and
  (b) the return is at the buyer's risk and expense.

2-328. SALE BY AUCTION.

(1) In a sale by auction if goods are put up in lots each lot is the subject of a separate sale.

(2) A sale by auction is complete when the auctioneer so announces by the fall of the hammer or in other customary manner. Where a bid is made while the hammer is falling in acceptance of a prior bid the auctioneer may in his discretion reopen the bidding or declare the goods sold under the bid on which the hammer was falling.

(3) Such a sale is with reserve unless the goods are in explicit terms put up without reserve. In an auction with reserve the auctioneer may withdraw the goods at any time until he announces completion of the sale. In an auction without reserve, after the auctioneer calls for bids on an article or lot, that article or lot cannot be withdrawn unless no bid is made within a reasonable time. In either case a bidder may retract his bid until the auctioneer's announcement of completion of the sale, but a bidder's retraction does not revive any previous bid.

(4) If the auctioneer knowingly receives a bid on the seller's behalf or the seller makes or procures such a bid, and notice has not been given that liberty for such bidding is reserved, the buyer may at his option avoid the sale or take the goods at the price of the last good faith bid prior to the completion of the sale. This subsection shall not apply to any bid at a forced sale.

2-401. PASSING OF TITLE; RESERVATION FOR SECURITY; LIMITED APPLICATION OF THIS SECTION.

Each provision of this Article with regard to the rights, obligations and remedies of the seller, the buyer, purchasers or other third parties applies irrespective of title to the goods except where the provision refers to such title. Insofar as situations are not covered by the other provisions of this Article and matters concerning title become material the following rules apply:

(1) Title to goods cannot pass under a contract for sale prior to their identification to the contract (Section 2-501), and unless otherwise explicitly agreed the buyer acquires by their identification a special property as limited by this Act. Any retention or reservation by the seller of the title (property) in goods shipped or delivered to the buyer is limited in effect to a reservation of a security interest. Subject to these provisions and to the provisions of the Article on Secured Transactions (Article 9), title to goods passes from the seller to the buyer in any manner and on any conditions explicitly agreed on by the parties.

(2) Unless otherwise explicitly agreed title passes to the buyer at the time and place at which the seller completes his performance with reference to the physical delivery of the goods, despite any reservation of a security interest and even though a document of title is to be delivered at a different time or place; and in particular and despite any reservation of a security interest by the bill of lading
  (a) if the contract requires or authorizes the seller to send the goods to the buyer but does not require him to deliver them at destination, title passes to the buyer at the time and place of shipment; but
  (b) if the contract requires delivery at destination, title passes on tender there.

(3) Unless otherwise explicitly agreed where delivery is to be made without moving the goods,
  (a) if the seller is to deliver a document of title, title passes at the time when and the place where he delivers such documents; or
  (b) if the goods are at the time of contracting already identified and no documents are to be delivered, title passes at the time and place of contracting.

(4) A rejection or other refusal by the buyer to receive or retain the goods, whether or not justified, or a justified revocation of acceptance revests title to the goods in the seller. Such revesting occurs by operation of law and is not a "sale".

2-402. RIGHTS OF SELLER'S CREDITORS AGAINST SOLD GOODS.

(1) Except as provided in subsections (2) and (3), rights of unsecured creditors of the seller with respect to goods which have been identified to a contract for sale are subject to the buyer's rights to recover the goods under this Article (Sections 2-502 and 2-716).

(2) A creditor of the seller may treat a sale or an identification of goods to a contract for sale as void if as against him a retention of possession by the seller is fraudulent under any rule of law of the state where the goods are situated, except that retention of possession in good faith and current course of trade by a merchant-seller for a commercially reasonable time after a sale or identification is not fraudulent.

(3) Nothing in this Article shall be deemed to impair the rights of creditors of the seller
  (a) under the provisions of the Article on Secured Transactions (Article 9); or
  (b) where identification to the contract or delivery is made not in current course of trade but in

satisfaction of or as security for a pre-existing claim for money, security or the like and is made under circumstances which under any rule of law of the state where the goods are situated would apart from this Article constitute the transaction a fraudulent transfer or voidable preference.

2-403. POWER TO TRANSFER; GOOD FAITH PURCHASE OF GOODS; "ENTRUSTING".

(1) A purchaser of goods acquires all title which his transferor had or had power to transfer except that a purchaser of a limited interest acquires rights only to the extent of the interest purchased. A person with voidable title has power to transfer a good title to a good faith purchaser for value. When goods have been delivered under a transaction of purchase the purchaser has such power even though
  (a) the transferor was deceived as to the identity of the purchaser, or
  (b) the delivery was in exchange for a check which is later dishonored, or
  (c) it was agreed that the transaction was to be a "cash sale", or
  (d) the delivery was procured through fraud punishable as larcenous under the criminal law.

(2) Any entrusting of possession of goods to a merchant who deals in goods of that kind gives him power to transfer all rights of the entruster to a buyer in ordinary course of business.

(3) "Entrusting" includes any delivery and any acquiescence in retention of possession regardless of any condition expressed between the parties to the delivery or acquiescence and regardless of whether the procurement of the entrusting or the possessor's disposition of the goods have been such as to be larcenous under the criminal law.
[Note: If a state adopts the repealer of Article 6-Bulk Transfers (Alternative A), subsec. (4) should read as follows:]

(4) The rights of other purchasers of goods and of lien creditors are governed by the Articles on Secured Transactions (Article 9) and Documents of Title (Article 7).
[Note: If a state adopts Revised Article 6-Bulk Sales (Alternative B), subsec. (4) should read as follows:]

(5) The rights of other purchasers of goods and of lien creditors are governed by the Articles on Secured Transactions (Article 9), Bulk Sales (Article 6) and Documents of Title (Article 7).
[Note: As amended in 1988.]

2-501. INSURABLE INTEREST IN GOODS; MANNER OF IDENTIFICATION OF GOODS.

(1) The buyer obtains a special property and an insurable interest in goods by identification of existing goods as goods to which the contract refers even though the goods so identified are non-conforming and he has an option to return or reject them. Such identification can be made at any time and in any manner explicitly agreed to by the parties. In the absence of explicit agreement identification occurs
  (a) when the contract is made if it is for the sale of goods already existing and identified;
  (b) if the contract is for the sale of future goods

other than those described in paragraph (c), when goods are shipped, marked or otherwise designated by the seller as goods to which the contract refers;

(c) when the crops are planted or otherwise become growing crops or the young are conceived if the contract is for the sale of unborn young to be born within twelve months after contracting or for the sale of crops to be harvested within twelve months or the next normal harvest reason after contracting whichever is longer.

(2) The seller retains an insurable interest in goods so long as title to or any security interest in the goods remains in him and where the identification is by the seller alone he may until default or insolvency or notification to the buyer that the identification is final substitute other goods for those identified.

(3) Nothing in this section impairs any insurable interest recognized under any other statute or rule of law.

2-502. BUYER'S RIGHT TO GOODS ON SELLER'S INSOLVENCY.

(1) Subject to subsection (2) and even though the goods have not been shipped a buyer who has paid a part or all of the price of goods in which he has a special property under the provisions of the immediately preceding section may on making and keeping good a tender of any unpaid portion of their price recover them from the seller if the seller becomes insolvent within ten days after receipt of the first installment on their price.

(2) If the identification creating his special property has been made by the buyer he acquires the right to recover the goods only if they conform to the contract for sale.

2-503. MANNER OF SELLER'S TENDER OF DELIVERY.

(1) Tender of delivery requires that the seller put and hold conforming goods at the buyer's disposition and give the buyer any notification reasonably necessary to enable him to take delivery. The manner, time and place for tender are determined by the agreement and this Article, and in particular

(a) tender must be at a reasonable hour, and if it is of goods they must be kept available for the period reasonably necessary to enable the buyer to take possession; but

(b) unless otherwise agreed the buyer must furnish facilities reasonably suited to the receipt of the goods.

(2) Where the case is within the next section respecting shipment tender requires that the seller comply with its provisions.

(3) Where the seller is required to deliver at a particular destination tender requires that he comply with subsection (1) and also in any appropriate case tender documents as described in subsections (4) and (5) of this section.

(4) Where goods are in the possession of a bailee and are to be delivered without being moved

(a) tender requires that the seller either tender a negotiable document of title covering such goods or procure acknowledgment by the bailee of the buyer's right to possession of the goods; but

(b) tender to the buyer of a non-negotiable document of title or of a written direction to the bailee to deliver is sufficient tender unless the buyer seasonably objects, and receipt by the bailee of notification of the buyer's rights fixes those rights as against the bailee and all third persons; but risk of loss of the goods and of any failure by the bailee to honor the non-negotiable document of title or to obey the direction remains on the seller until the buyer has had a reasonable time to present the document or direction, and a refusal by the bailee to honor the document or to obey the direction defeats the tender.

(5) Where the contract requires the seller to deliver documents

(a) he must tender all such documents in correct form, except as provided in this Article with respect to bills of lading in a set (subsection (2) of Section 2-323); and

(b) tender through customary banking channels is sufficient and dishonor of a draft accompanying the documents constitutes non-acceptance or rejection.

2-504. SHIPMENT BY SELLER.

Where the seller is required or authorized to send the goods to the buyer and the contract does not require him to deliver them at a particular destination, then unless otherwise agreed he must

(a) put the goods in the possession of such a carrier and make such a contract for their transportation as may be reasonable having regard to the nature of the goods and other circumstances of the case; and

(b) obtain and promptly deliver or tender in due form any document necessary to enable the buyer to obtain possession of the goods or otherwise required by the agreement or by usage of trade; and

(c) promptly notify the buyer of the shipment.

Failure to notify the buyer under paragraph (c) or to make a proper contract under paragraph (a) is a ground for rejection only if material delay or loss ensues.

2-505. SELLER'S SHIPMENT UNDER RESERVATION.

(1) Where the seller has identified goods to the contract by or before shipment:

(a) his procurement of a negotiable bill of lading to his own order or otherwise reserves in him a security interest in the goods. His procurement of the bill to the order of a financing agency or of the buyer indicates in addition only the seller's expectation of transferring that interest to the person named.

(b) a non-negotiable bill of lading to himself or his nominee reserves possession of the goods as security but except in a case of conditional delivery (subsection (2) of Section 2-507) a non-negotiable bill of lading naming the buyer as consignee reserves no security interest even though the seller retains possession of the bill of lading.

(2) When shipment by the seller with reservation of a security interest is in violation of the contract for sale it constitutes an improper contract for transportation within the preceding section but impairs neither the rights given to the buyer by shipment and identification of the goods to the contract nor the seller's powers as a holder of a negotiable document.

2-506. RIGHTS OF FINANCING AGENCY.

(1) A financing agency by paying or purchasing for value a draft which relates to a shipment of goods acquires to the extent of the payment or purchase and in addition to its own rights under the draft and any document of title securing it any rights of the shipper in the goods including the right to stop delivery and the shipper's right to have the draft honored by the buyer.

(2) The right to reimbursement of a financing agency which has in good faith honored or purchased the draft under commitment to or authority from the buyer is not impaired by subsequent discovery of defects with reference to any relevant document which was apparently regular on its face.

2-507. EFFECT OF SELLER'S TENDER; DELIVERY ON CONDITION.

(1) Tender of delivery is a condition to the buyer's duty to accept the goods and, unless otherwise agreed, to his duty to pay for them. Tender entitles the seller to acceptance of the goods and to payment according to the contract.

(2) Where payment is due and demanded on the delivery to the buyer of goods or documents of title, his right as against the seller to retain or dispose of them is conditional upon his making the payment due.

2-508. CURE BY SELLER OF IMPROPER TENDER OR DELIVERY; REPLACEMENT.

(1) Where any tender or delivery by the seller is rejected because non-conforming and the time for performance has not yet expired, the seller may seasonably notify the buyer of his intention to cure and may then within the contract time make a conforming delivery.

(2) Where the buyer rejects a non-conforming tender which the seller had reasonable grounds to believe would be acceptable with or without money allowance the seller may if he seasonably notifies the buyer have a further reasonable time to substitute a conforming tender.

2-509. RISK OF LOSS IN THE ABSENCE OF BREACH.

(1) Where the contract requires or authorizes the seller to ship the goods by carrier

(a) if it does not require him to deliver them at a particular destination, the risk of loss passes to the buyer when the goods are duly delivered to the carrier even though the shipment is under reservation (Section 2-505); but

(b) if it does require him to deliver them at a particular destination and the goods are there duly tendered while in the possession of the carrier, the risk of loss passes to the buyer when the goods are there duly so tendered as to enable the buyer to take delivery.

(2) Where the goods are held by a bailee to be delivered without being moved, the risk of loss passes to the buyer

(a) on his receipt of a negotiable document of title covering the goods; or

(b) on acknowledgment by the bailee of the buyer's right to possession of the goods; or

(c) after his receipt of a non-negotiable document of title or other written direction to deliver, as provided in subsection (4)(b) of Section 2-503.

(3) In any case not within subsection (1) or (2), the risk of loss passes to the buyer on his receipt of the goods if the seller is a merchant; otherwise the risk passes to the buyer on tender of delivery.

(4) The provisions of this section are subject to contrary agreement of the parties and to the provisions of this Article on sale on approval (Section 2-327) and on effect of breach on risk of loss (Section 2-510).

2-510. EFFECT OF BREACH ON RISK OF LOSS.

(1) Where a tender or delivery of goods so fails to conform to the contract as to give a right of rejection the risk of their loss remains on the seller until cure or acceptance.

(2) Where the buyer rightfully revokes acceptance he may to the extent of any deficiency in his effective insurance coverage treat the risk of loss as having rested on the seller from the beginning.

(3) Where the buyer as to conforming goods already identified to the contract for sale repudiates or is otherwise in breach before risk of their loss has passed to him, the seller may to the extent of any deficiency in his effective insurance coverage treat the risk of loss as resting on the buyer for a commercially reasonable time.

2-511. TENDER OF PAYMENT BY BUYER; PAYMENT BY CHECK.

(1) Unless otherwise agreed tender of payment is a condition to the seller's duty to tender and complete any delivery.

(2) Tender of payment is sufficient when made by any means or in any manner current in the ordinary course of business unless the seller demands payment in legal tender and gives any extension of time reasonably necessary to procure it.

(3) Subject to the provisions of this Act on the effect of an instrument on an obligation (Section 3-802), payment by check is conditional and is defeated as between the parties by dishonor of the check on due presentment.

2-512. PAYMENT BY BUYER BEFORE INSPECTION.

(1) Where the contract requires payment before inspection non-conformity of the goods does not excuse the buyer from so making payment unless

(a) the non-conformity appears without inspection; or

(b) despite tender of the required documents the circumstances would justify injunction against honor under the provisions of this Act (Section 5-114).

(2) Payment pursuant to subsection (1) does not constitute an acceptance of goods or impair the buyer's right to inspect or any of his remedies.

2-513. BUYER'S RIGHT TO INSPECTION OF GOODS.

(1) Unless otherwise agreed and subject to subsection (3), where goods are tendered or delivered or identified to the contract for sale, the buyer has a right before payment or acceptance to inspect them at any reasonable place and time and in any reasonable manner. When the seller is required or

authorized to send the goods to the buyer, the inspection may be after their arrival.

(2) Expenses of inspection must be borne by the buyer but may be recovered from the seller if the goods do not conform and are rejected.

(3) Unless otherwise agreed and subject to the provisions of this Article on C.I.F. contracts (subsection (3) of Section 2-321), the buyer is not entitled to inspect the goods before payment of the price when the contract provides

(a) for delivery "C.O.D." or on other like terms; or

(b) for payment against documents of title, except where such payment is due only after the goods are to become available for inspection.

(4) A place or method of inspection fixed by the parties is presumed to be exclusive but unless otherwise expressly agreed it does not postpone identification or shift the place for delivery or for passing the risk of loss. If compliance becomes impossible, inspection shall be as provided in this section unless the place or method fixed was clearly intended as an indispensable condition failure of which avoids the contract.

2-514. WHEN DOCUMENTS DELIVERABLE ON ACCEPTANCE; WHEN ON PAYMENT.

Unless otherwise agreed documents against which a draft is drawn are to be delivered to the drawee on acceptance of the draft if it is payable more than three days after presentment; otherwise, only on payment.

2-515. PRESERVING EVIDENCE OF GOODS IN DISPUTE.

In furtherance of the adjustment of any claim or dispute

(a) either party on reasonable notification to the other and for the purpose of ascertaining the facts and preserving evidence has the right to inspect, test and sample the goods including such of them as may be in the possession or control of the other; and

(b) the parties may agree to a third party inspection or survey to determine the conformity or condition of the goods and may agree that the findings shall be binding upon them in any subsequent litigation or adjustment.

2-601. BUYER'S RIGHTS ON IMPROPER DELIVERY.

Subject to the provisions of this Article on breach in installment contracts (Section 2-612) and unless otherwise agreed under the sections on contractual limitations of remedy (Sections 2-718 and 2-719), if the goods or the tender of delivery fail in any respect to conform to the contract, the buyer may

(a) reject the whole; or

(b) accept the whole; or

(c) accept any commercial unit or units and reject the rest.

2-602. MANNER AND EFFECT OF RIGHTFUL REJECTION.

(1) Rejection of goods must be within a reasonable time after their delivery or tender. It is ineffective unless the buyer seasonably notifies the seller.

(2) Subject to the provisions of the two following sections on rejected goods (Sections 2-603 and 2-604),

(a) after rejection any exercise of ownership by

the buyer with respect to any commercial unit is wrongful as against the seller; and

(b) if the buyer has before rejection taken physical possession of goods in which he does not have a security interest under the provisions of this Article (subsection (3) of Section 2-711), he is under a duty after rejection to hold them with reasonable care at the seller's disposition for a time sufficient to permit the seller to remove them; but

(c) the buyer has no further obligations with regard to goods rightfully rejected.

(3) The seller's rights with respect to goods wrongfully rejected are governed by the provisions of this Article on seller's remedies in general (Section 2-703).

2-603. MERCHANT BUYER'S DUTIES AS TO RIGHTFULLY REJECTED GOODS.

(1) Subject to any security interest in the buyer (subsection (3) of Section 2-711), when the seller has no agent or place of business at the market of rejection a merchant buyer is under a duty after rejection of goods in his possession or control to follow any reasonable instructions received from the seller with respect to the goods and in the absence of such instructions to make reasonable efforts to sell them for the seller's account if they are perishable or threaten to decline in value speedily. Instructions are not reasonable if on demand indemnity for expenses is not forthcoming.

(2) When the buyer sells goods under subsection (1), he is entitled to reimbursement from the seller or out of the proceeds for reasonable expenses of caring for and selling them, and if the expenses include no selling commission then to such commission as is usual in the trade or if there is none to a reasonable sum not exceeding ten per cent on the gross proceeds.

(3) In complying with this section the buyer is held only to good faith and good faith conduct hereunder is neither acceptance nor conversion nor the basis of an action for damages.

2-604. BUYER'S OPTIONS AS TO SALVAGE OF RIGHTFULLY REJECTED GOODS.

Subject to the provisions of the immediately preceding section on perishables if the seller gives no instructions within a reasonable time after notification of rejection the buyer may store the rejected goods for the seller's account or reship them to him or resell them for the seller's account with reimbursement as provided in the preceding section. Such action is not acceptance or conversion.

2-605. WAIVER OF BUYER'S OBJECTIONS BY FAILURE TO PARTICULARIZE.

(1) The buyer's failure to state in connection with rejection a particular defect which is ascertainable by reasonable inspection precludes him from relying on the unstated defect to justify rejection or to establish breach

(a) where the seller could have cured it if stated seasonably; or

(b) between merchants when the seller has after rejection made a request in writing for a full and final written statement of all defects on which the buyer proposes to rely.

(2) Payment against documents made without reservation of rights precludes recovery of the payment for defects apparent on the face of the documents.

2-606. WHAT CONSTITUTES ACCEPTANCE OF GOODS.

(1) Acceptance of goods occurs when the buyer
   (a) after a reasonable opportunity to inspect the goods signifies to the seller that the goods are conforming or that he will take or retain them in spite of their non-conformity; or
   (b) fails to make an effective rejection (subsection (1) of Section 2-602), but such acceptance does not occur until the buyer has had a reasonable opportunity to inspect them; or
   (c) does any act inconsistent with the seller's ownership; but if such act is wrongful as against the seller it is an acceptance only if ratified by him.
(2) Acceptance of a part of any commercial unit is acceptance of that entire unit.

2-607. EFFECT OF ACCEPTANCE; NOTICE OF BREACH; BURDEN OF ESTABLISHING BREACH AFTER ACCEPTANCE; NOTICE OF CLAIM OR LITIGATION TO PERSON ANSWERABLE OVER.

(1) The buyer must pay at the contract rate for any goods accepted.
(2) Acceptance of goods by the buyer precludes rejection of the goods accepted and if made with knowledge of a non-conformity cannot be revoked because of it unless the acceptance was on the reasonable assumption that the non-conformity would be seasonably cured but acceptance does not of itself impair any other remedy provided by this Article for non-conformity.
(3) Where a tender has been accepted
   (a) the buyer must within a reasonable time after he discovers or should have discovered any breach notify the seller of breach or be barred from any remedy; and
   (b) if the claim is one for infringement or the like (subsection (3) of Section 2-312) and the buyer is sued as a result of such a breach he must so notify the seller within a reasonable time after he receives notice of the litigation or be barred from any remedy over for liability established by the litigation.
(4) The burden is on the buyer to establish any breach with respect to the goods accepted.
(5) Where the buyer is sued for breach of a warranty or other obligation for which his seller is answerable over
   (a) he may give his seller written notice of the litigation. If the notice states that the seller may come in and defend and that if the seller does not do so he will be bound in any action against him by his buyer by any determination of fact common to the two litigations, then unless the seller after seasonable receipt of the notice does come in and defend he is so bound.
   (b) if the claim is one for infringement or the like (subsection (3) of Section 2-312) the original seller may demand in writing that his buyer turn over to him control of the litigation including settlement or else be barred from any remedy over and if he also agrees to bear

all expense and to satisfy any adverse judgment, then unless the buyer after seasonable receipt of the demand does turn over control the buyer is so barred.
(6) The provisions of subsections (3), (4) and (5) apply to any obligation of a buyer to hold the seller harmless against infringement or the like (subsection (3) of Section 2-312).

2-608. REVOCATION OF ACCEPTANCE IN WHOLE OR IN PART.

(1) The buyer may revoke his acceptance of a lot or commercial unit whose non-conformity substantially impairs its value to him if he has accepted it
   (a) on the reasonable assumption that its non-conformity would be cured and it has not been seasonably cured; or
   (b) without discovery of such non-conformity if his acceptance was reasonably induced either by the difficulty of discovery before acceptance or by the seller's assurances.
(2) Revocation of acceptance must occur within a reasonable time after the buyer discovers or should have discovered the ground for it and before any substantial change in condition of the goods which is not caused by their own defects. It is not effective until the buyer notifies the seller of it.
(3) A buyer who so revokes has the same rights and duties with regard to the goods involved as if he had rejected them.

2-609. RIGHT TO ADEQUATE ASSURANCE OF PERFORMANCE.

(1) A contract for sale imposes an obligation on each party that the other's expectation of receiving due performance will not be impaired. When reasonable grounds for insecurity arise with respect to the performance of either party the other may in writing demand adequate assurance of due performance and until he receives such assurance may if commercially reasonable suspend any performance for which he has not already received the agreed return.
(2) Between merchants the reasonableness of grounds for insecurity and the adequacy of any assurance offered shall be determined according to commercial standards.
(3) Acceptance of any improper delivery or payment does not prejudice the aggrieved party's right to demand adequate assurance of future performance.
(4) After receipt of a justified demand failure to provide within a reasonable time not exceeding thirty days such assurance of due performance as is adequate under the circumstances of the particular case is a repudiation of the contract.

2-610. ANTICIPATORY REPUDIATION.

When either party repudiates the contract with respect to a performance not yet due the loss of which will substantially impair the value of the contract to the other, the aggrieved party may
   (a) for a commercially reasonable time await performance by the repudiating party; or
   (b) resort to any remedy for breach (Section 2-703 or Section 2-711), even though he has notified the repudiating party that he would await the latter's performance and has urged retraction; and

   (c) in either case suspend his own performance or proceed in accordance with the provisions of this Article on the seller's right to identify goods to the contract notwithstanding breach or to salvage unfinished goods (Section 2-704).

2-611. RETRACTION OF ANTICIPATORY REPUDIATION.

(1) Until the repudiating party's next performance is due he can retract his repudiation unless the aggrieved party has since the repudiation cancelled or materially changed his position or otherwise indicated that he considers the repudiation final.
(2) Retraction may be by any method which clearly indicates to the aggrieved party that the repudiating party intends to perform, but must include any assurance justifiably demanded under the provisions of this Article (Section 2-609).
(3) Retraction reinstates the repudiating party's rights under the contract with due excuse and allowance to the aggrieved party for any delay occasioned by the repudiation.

2-612. "INSTALLMENT CONTRACT"; BREACH.

(1) An "installment contract" is one which requires or authorizes the delivery of goods in separate lots to be separately accepted, even though the contract contains a clause "each delivery is a separate contract" or its equivalent.
(2) The buyer may reject any installment which is non-conforming if the non-conformity substantially impairs the value of that installment and cannot be cured or if the non-conformity is a defect in the required documents; but if the non-conformity does not fall within subsection (3) and the seller gives adequate assurance of its cure the buyer must accept that installment.
(3) Whenever non-conformity or default with respect to one or more installments substantially impairs the value of the whole contract there is a breach of the whole. But the aggrieved party reinstates the contract if he accepts a non-conforming installment without seasonably notifying of cancellation or if he brings an action with respect only to past installments or demands performance as to future installments.

2-613. CASUALTY TO IDENTIFIED GOODS.

Where the contract requires for its performance goods identified when the contract is made, and the goods suffer casualty without fault of either party before the risk of loss passes to the buyer, or in a proper case under a "no arrival, no sale" term (Section 2-324) then
   (a) if the loss is total the contract is avoided; and
   (b) if the loss is partial or the goods have so deteriorated as no longer to conform to the contract the buyer may nevertheless demand inspection and at his option either treat the contract as avoided or accept the goods with due allowance from the contract price for the deterioration or the deficiency in quantity but without further right against the seller.

2-614. SUBSTITUTED PERFORMANCE.

(1) Where without fault of either party the agreed berthing, loading, or unloading facilities fail or an agreed type of carrier becomes unavailable or the

agreed manner of delivery otherwise becomes commercially impracticable but a commercially reasonable substitute is available, such substitute performance must be tendered and accepted.

(2) If the agreed means or manner of payment fails because of domestic or foreign governmental regulation, the seller may withhold or stop delivery unless the buyer provides a means or manner of payment which is commercially a substantial equivalent. If delivery has already been taken, payment by the means or in the manner provided by the regulation discharges the buyer's obligation unless the regulation is discriminatory, oppressive or predatory.

2-615. EXCUSE BY FAILURE OF PRESUPPOSED CONDITIONS.

Except so far as a seller may have assumed a greater obligation and subject to the preceding section on substituted performance:

(a) Delay in delivery or non-delivery in whole or in part by a seller who complies with paragraphs (b) and (c) is not a breach of his duty under a contract for sale if performance as agreed has been made impracticable by the occurrence of a contingency the non-occurrence of which was a basic assumption on which the contract was made or by compliance in good faith with any applicable foreign or domestic governmental regulation or order whether or not it later proves to be invalid.

(b) Where the causes mentioned in paragraph (a) affect only a part of the seller's capacity to perform, he must allocate production and deliveries among his customers but may at his option include regular customers not then under contract as well as his own requirements for further manufacture. He may so allocate in any manner which is fair and reasonable.

(c) The seller must notify the buyer seasonably that there will be delay or non-delivery and, when allocation is required under paragraph (b), of the estimated quota thus made available for the buyer

2-616. PROCEDURE ON NOTICE CLAIMING EXCUSE.

(1) Where the buyer receives notification of a material or indefinite delay or an allocation justified under the preceding section he may by written notification to the seller as to any delivery concerned, and where the prospective deficiency substantially impairs the value of the whole contract under the provisions of this Article relating to breach of installment contracts (Section 2-612), then also as to the whole,

(a) terminate and thereby discharge any unexecuted portion of the contract; or

(b) modify the contract by agreeing to take his available quota in substitution.

(2) If after receipt of such notification from the seller the buyer fails so to modify the contract within a reasonable time not exceeding thirty days the contract lapses with respect to any deliveries affected.

(3) The provisions of this section may not be negated by agreement except in so far as the seller has assumed a greater obligation under the preceding sections.

2-701. REMEDIES FOR BREACH OF COLLATERAL CONTRACTS NOT IMPAIRED.

Remedies for breach of any obligation or promise collateral or ancillary to a contract for sale are not impaired by the provisions of this Article.

2-702. SELLER'S REMEDIES ON DISCOVERY OF BUYER'S INSOLVENCY.

(1) Where the seller discovers the buyer to be insolvent he may refuse delivery except for cash including payment for all goods theretofore delivered under the contract, and stop delivery under this Article (Section 2-705).

(2) Where the seller discovers that the buyer has received goods on credit while insolvent he may reclaim the goods upon demand made within ten days after the receipt, but if misrepresentation of solvency has been made to the particular seller in writing within three months before delivery the ten day limitation does not apply. Except as provided in this subsection the seller may not base a right to reclaim goods on the buyer's fraudulent or innocent misrepresentation of solvency or of intent to pay.

(3) The seller's right to reclaim under subsection (2) is subject to the rights of a buyer in ordinary course or other good faith purchaser under this Article (Section 2-403). Successful reclamation of goods excludes all other remedies with respect to them. [Note: *As amended in 1966.*]

2-703. SELLER'S REMEDIES IN GENERAL.

Where the buyer wrongfully rejects or revokes acceptance of goods or fails to make a payment due on or before delivery or repudiates with respect to a part or the whole, then with respect to any goods directly affected and, if the breach is of the whole contract (Section 2-612), then also with respect to the whole undelivered balance, the aggrieved seller may

(a) withhold delivery of such goods;

(b) stop delivery by any bailee as hereafter provided (Section 2-705);

(c) proceed under the next section respecting goods still unidentified to the contract;

(d) resell and recover damages as hereafter provided (Section 2-706);

(e) recover damages for non-acceptance (Section 2-708) or in a proper case the price (Section 2-709);

(f) cancel.

2-704. SELLER'S RIGHT TO IDENTIFY GOODS TO THE CONTRACT NOTWITHSTANDING BREACH OR TO SALVAGE UNFINISHED GOODS.

(1) An aggrieved seller under the preceding section may

(a) identify to the contract conforming goods not already identified if at the time he learned of the breach they are in his possession or control;

(b) treat as the subject of resale goods which have demonstrably been intended for the particular contract even though those goods are unfinished.

(2) Where the goods are unfinished an aggrieved seller may in the exercise of reasonable commercial judg-

ment for the purposes of avoiding loss and of effective realization either complete the manufacture and wholly identify the goods to the contract or cease manufacture and resell for scrap or salvage value or proceed in any other reasonable manner.

2-705. SELLER'S STOPPAGE OF DELIVERY IN TRANSIT OR OTHERWISE.

(1) The seller may stop delivery of goods in the possession of a carrier or other bailee when he discovers the buyer to be insolvent (Section 2-702) and may stop delivery of carload, truckload, planeload or larger shipments of express or freight when the buyer repudiates or fails to make a payment due before delivery or if for any other reason the seller has a right to withhold or reclaim the goods.

(2) As against such buyer the seller may stop delivery until

(a) receipt of the goods by the buyer; or

(b) acknowledgment to the buyer by any bailee of the goods except a carrier that the bailee holds the goods for the buyer; or

(c) such acknowledgment to the buyer by a carrier by reshipment or as warehouseman; or

(d) negotiation to the buyer of any negotiable document of title covering the goods.

(3)

(a) To stop delivery the seller must so notify as to enable the bailee by reasonable diligence to prevent delivery of the goods.

(b) After such notification the bailee must hold and deliver the goods according to the directions of the seller but the seller is liable to the bailee for any ensuing charges or damages.

(c) If a negotiable document of title has been issued for goods the bailee is not obliged to obey a notification to stop until surrender of the document.

(d) A carrier who has issued a non-negotiable bill of lading is not obliged to obey a notification to stop received from a person other than the consignor.

2-706. SELLER'S RESALE INCLUDING CONTRACT FOR RESALE.

(1) Under the conditions stated in Section 2-703 on seller's remedies, the seller may resell the goods concerned or the undelivered balance thereof. Where the resale is made in good faith and in a commercially reasonable manner the seller may recover the difference between the resale price and the contract price together with any incidental damages allowed under the provisions of this Article (Section 2-710), but less expenses saved in consequence of the buyer's breach.

(2) Except as otherwise provided in subsection (3) or unless otherwise agreed resale may be at public or private sale including sale by way of one or more contracts to sell or of identification to an existing contract of the seller. Sale may be as a unit or in parcels and at any time and place and on any terms but every aspect of the sale including the method, manner, time, place and terms must be commercially reasonable. The resale must be reasonably identified as referring to the broken contract, but it is not necessary that the goods be in existence or that any or all of them have been identified to the contract before the breach.

(3) Where the resale is at private sale the seller must give the buyer reasonable notification of his intention to resell.

(4) Where the resale is at public sale

    (a) only identified goods can be sold except where there is a recognized market for a public sale of futures in goods of the kind; and

    (b) it must be made at a usual place or market for public sale if one is reasonably available and except in the case of goods which are perishable or threaten to decline in value speedily the seller must give the buyer reasonable notice of the time and place of the resale; and

    (c) if the goods are not to be within the view of those attending the sale the notification of sale must state the place where the goods are located and provide for their reasonable inspection by prospective bidders; and

    (d) the seller may buy.

(5) A purchaser who buys in good faith at a resale takes the goods free of any rights of the original buyer even though the seller fails to comply with one or more of the requirements of this section.

(6) The seller is not accountable to the buyer for any profit made on any resale. A person in the position of a seller (Section 2-707) or a buyer who has rightfully rejected or justifiably revoked acceptance must account for any excess over the amount of his security interest, as hereinafter defined (subsection (3) of Section 2-711).

2-707. "PERSON IN THE POSITION OF A SELLER".

(1) A "person in the position of a seller" includes as against a principal an agent who has paid or become responsible for the price of goods on behalf of his principal or anyone who otherwise holds a security interest or other right in goods similar to that of a seller.

(2) A person in the position of a seller may as provided in this Article withhold or stop delivery (Section 2-705) and resell (Section 2-706) and recover incidental damages (Section 2-710).

2-708. SELLER'S DAMAGES FOR NON-ACCEPTANCE OR REPUDIATION.

(1) Subject to subsection (2) and to the provisions of this Article with respect to proof of market price (Section 2-723), the measure of damages for non-acceptance or repudiation by the buyer is the difference between the market price at the time and place for tender and the unpaid contract price together with any incidental damages provided in this Article (Section 2-710), but less expenses saved in consequence of the buyer's breach.

(2) If the measure of damages provided in subsection (1) is inadequate to put the seller in as good a position as performance would have done then the measure of damages is the profit (including reasonable overhead) which the seller would have made from full performance by the buyer, together with any incidental damages provided in this Article (Section 2-710), due allowance for costs reasonably incurred and due credit for payments or proceeds of resale.

2-709. ACTION FOR THE PRICE.

(1) When the buyer fails to pay the price as it becomes due the seller may recover, together with any inci-

dental damages under the next section, the price

    (a) of goods accepted or of conforming goods lost or damaged within a commercially reasonable time after risk of their loss has passed to the buyer; and

    (b) of goods identified to the contract if the seller is unable after reasonable effort to resell them at a reasonable price or the circumstances reasonably indicate that such effort will be unavailing.

(2) Where the seller sues for the price he must hold for the buyer any goods which have been identified to the contract and are still in his control except that if resale becomes possible he may resell them at any time prior to the collection of the judgment. The net proceeds of any such resale must be credited to the buyer and payment of the judgment entitles him to any goods not resold.

(3) After the buyer has wrongfully rejected or revoked acceptance of the goods or has failed to make a payment due or has repudiated (Section 2-610), a seller who is held not entitled to the price under this section shall nevertheless be awarded damages for non-acceptance under the preceding section.

2-710. SELLER'S INCIDENTAL DAMAGES.

Incidental damages to an aggrieved seller include any commercially reasonable charges, expenses or commissions incurred in stopping delivery, in the transportation, care and custody of goods after the buyer's breach, in connection with return or resale of the goods or otherwise resulting from the breach.

2-711. BUYER'S REMEDIES IN GENERAL; BUYER'S SECURITY INTEREST IN REJECTED GOODS.

(1) Where the seller fails to make delivery or repudiates or the buyer rightfully rejects or justifiably revokes acceptance then with respect to any goods involved, and with respect to the whole if the breach goes to the whole contract (Section 2-612), the buyer may cancel and whether or not he has done so may in addition to recovering so much of the price as has been paid

    (a) "cover" and have damages under the next section as to all the goods affected whether or not they have been identified to the contract; or

    (b) recover damages for non-delivery as provided in this Article (Section 2-713).

(2) Where the seller fails to deliver or repudiates the buyer may also

    (a) if the goods have been identified recover them as provided in this Article (Section 2-502); or

    (b) in a proper case obtain specific performance or replevy the goods as provided in this Article (Section 2-716).

(3) On rightful rejection or justifiable revocation of acceptance a buyer has a security interest in goods in his possession or control for any payments made on their price and any expenses reasonably incurred in their inspection, receipt, transportation, care and custody and may hold such goods and resell them in like manner as an aggrieved seller (Section 2-706).

2-712. "COVER"; BUYER'S PROCUREMENT OF SUBSTITUTE GOODS.

(1) After a breach within the preceding section the buyer may "cover" by making in good faith and without unreasonable delay any reasonable purchase of or contract to purchase goods in substitution for those due from the seller.

(2) The buyer may recover from the seller as damages the difference between the cost of cover and the contract price together with any incidental or consequential damages as hereinafter defined (Section 2-715), but less expenses saved in consequence of the seller's breach.

(3) Failure of the buyer to effect cover within this section does not bar him from any other remedy.

2-713. BUYER'S DAMAGES FOR NON-DELIVERY OR REPUDIATION.

(1) Subject to the provisions of this Article with respect to proof of market price (Section 2-723), the measure of damages for non-delivery or repudiation by the seller is the difference between the market price at the time when the buyer learned of the breach and the contract price together with any incidental and consequential damages provided in this Article (Section 2-715), but less expenses saved in consequence of the seller's breach.

(2) Market price is to be determined as of the place for tender or, in cases of rejection after arrival or revocation of acceptance, as of the place of arrival.

2-714. BUYER'S DAMAGES FOR BREACH IN REGARD TO ACCEPTED GOODS.

(1) Where the buyer has accepted goods and given notification (subsection (3) of Section 2-607) he may recover as damages for any non-conformity of tender the loss resulting in the ordinary course of events from the seller's breach as determined in any manner which is reasonable.

(2) The measure of damages for breach of warranty is the difference at the time and place of acceptance between the value of the goods accepted and the value they would have had if they had been as warranted, unless special circumstances show proximate damages of a different amount.

(3) In a proper case any incidental and consequential damages under the next section may also be recovered.

2-715. BUYER'S INCIDENTAL AND CONSEQUENTIAL DAMAGES.

(1) Incidental damages resulting from the seller's breach include expenses reasonably incurred in inspection, receipt, transportation and care and custody of goods rightfully rejected, any commercially reasonable charges, expenses or commissions in connection with effecting cover and any other reasonable expense incident to the delay or other breach.

(2) Consequential damages resulting from the seller's breach include

    (a) any loss resulting from general or particular requirements and needs of which the seller at the time of contracting had reason to know and which could not reasonably be prevented by cover or otherwise; and

(b) injury to person or property proximately resulting from any breach of warranty.

2-716. BUYER'S RIGHT TO SPECIFIC PERFORMANCE OR REPLEVIN.

(1) Specific performance may be decreed where the goods are unique or in other proper circumstances.

(2) The decree for specific performance may include such terms and conditions as to payment of the price, damages, or other relief as the court may deem just.

(3) The buyer has a right of replevin for goods identified to the contract if after reasonable effort he is unable to effect cover for such goods or the circumstances reasonably indicate that such effort will be unavailing or if the goods have been shipped under reservation and satisfaction of the security interest in them has been made or tendered.

2-717. DEDUCTION OF DAMAGES FROM THE PRICE.

The buyer on notifying the seller of his intention to do so may deduct all or any part of the damages resulting from any breach of the contract from any part of the price still due under the same contract.

2-718. LIQUIDATION OR LIMITATION OF DAMAGES; DEPOSITS.

(1) Damages for breach by either party may be liquidated in the agreement but only at an amount which is reasonable in the light of the anticipated or actual harm caused by the breach, the difficulties of proof of loss, and the inconvenience or nonfeasibility of otherwise obtaining an adequate remedy. A term fixing unreasonably large liquidated damages is void as a penalty.

(2) Where the seller justifiably withholds delivery of goods because of the buyer's breach, the buyer is entitled to restitution of any amount by which the sum of his payments exceeds

(a) the amount to which the seller is entitled by virtue of terms liquidating the seller's damages in accordance with subsection (1), or

(b) in the absence of such terms, twenty per cent of the value of the total performance for which the buyer is obligated under the contract or $500, whichever is smaller.

(3) The buyer's right to restitution under subsection (2) is subject to offset to the extent that the seller establishes

(a) a right to recover damages under the provisions of this Article other than subsection (1), and

(b) the amount or value of any benefits received by the buyer directly or indirectly by reason of the contract.

(4) Where a seller has received payment in goods their reasonable value or the proceeds of their resale shall be treated as payments for the purposes of subsection (2); but if the seller has notice of the buyer's breach before reselling goods received in part performance, his resale is subject to the conditions laid down in this Article on resale by an aggrieved seller (Section 2-706).

2-719. CONTRACTUAL MODIFICATION OR LIMITATION OF REMEDY.

(1) Subject to the provisions of subsections (2) and (3) of this section and of the preceding section on liquidation and limitation of damages,

(a) the agreement may provide for remedies in addition to or in substitution for those provided in this Article and may limit or alter the measure of damages recoverable under this Article, as by limiting the buyer's remedies to return of the goods and repayment of the price or to repair and replacement of nonconforming goods or parts; and

(b) resort to a remedy as provided is optional unless the remedy is expressly agreed to be exclusive, in which case it is the sole remedy.

(2) Where circumstances cause an exclusive or limited remedy to fail of its essential purpose, remedy may be had as provided in this Act.

(3) Consequential damages may be limited or excluded unless the limitation or exclusion is unconscionable. Limitation of consequential damages for injury to the person in the case of consumer goods is prima facie unconscionable but limitation of damages where the loss is commercial is not.

2-720. EFFECT OF "CANCELLATION" OR "RESCISSION" ON CLAIMS FOR ANTECEDENT BREACH.

Unless the contrary intention clearly appears, expressions of "cancellation" or "rescission" of the contract or the like shall not be construed as a renunciation or discharge of any claim in damages for an antecedent breach.

2-721. REMEDIES FOR FRAUD.

Remedies for material misrepresentation or fraud include all remedies available under this Article for non-fraudulent breach. Neither rescission or a claim for rescission of the contract for sale nor rejection or return of the goods shall bar or be deemed inconsistent with a claim for damages or other remedy.

2-722. WHO CAN SUE THIRD PARTIES FOR INJURY TO GOODS.

Where a third party so deals with goods which have been identified to a contract for sale as to cause actionable injury to a party to that contract

(a) a right of action against the third party is in either party to the contract for sale who has title to or a security interest or a special property or an insurable interest in the goods; and if the goods have been destroyed or converted a right of action is also in the party who either bore the risk of loss under the contract for sale or has since the injury assumed that risk as against the other;

(b) if at the time of the injury the party plaintiff did not bear the risk of loss as against the other party to the contract for sale and there is no arrangement between them for disposition of the recovery, his suit or settlement is, subject to his own interest, as a fiduciary for the other party to the contract;

(c) either party may with the consent of the other sue for the benefit of whom it may concern.

2-723. PROOF OF MARKET PRICE: TIME AND PLACE.

(1) If an action based on anticipatory repudiation comes to trial before the time for performance with respect to some or all of the goods, any damages based on market price (Section 2-708 or Section 2-713) shall be determined according to the price of such goods prevailing at the time when the aggrieved party learned of the repudiation.

(2) If evidence of a price prevailing at the times or places described in this Article is not readily available the price prevailing within any reasonable time before or after the time described or at any other place which in commercial judgment or under usage of trade would serve as a reasonable substitute for the one described may be used, making any proper allowance for the cost of transporting the goods to or from such other place.

(3) Evidence of a relevant price prevailing at a time or place other than the one described in this Article offered by one party is not admissible unless and until he has given the other party such notice as the court finds sufficient to prevent unfair surprise

2-724. ADMISSIBILITY OF MARKET QUOTATIONS.

Whenever the prevailing price or value of any goods regularly bought and sold in any established commodity market is in issue, reports in official publications or trade journals or in newspapers or periodicals of general circulation published as the reports of such market shall be admissible in evidence. The circumstances of the preparation of such a report may be shown to affect its weight but not its admissibility.

2-725. STATUTE OF LIMITATIONS IN CONTRACTS FOR SALE.

(1) An action for breach of any contract for sale must be commenced within four years after the cause of action has accrued. By the original agreement the parties may reduce the period of limitation to not less than one year but may not extend it.

(2) A cause of action accrues when the breach occurs, regardless of the aggrieved party's lack of knowledge of the breach. A breach of warranty occurs when tender of delivery is made, except that where a warranty explicitly extends to future performance of the goods and discovery of the breach must await the time of such performance the cause of action accrues when the breach is or should have been discovered.

(3) Where an action commenced within the time limited by subsection (1) is so terminated as to leave available a remedy by another action for the same breach such other action may be commenced after the expiration of the time limited and within six months after the termination of the first action unless the termination resulted from voluntary discontinuance or from dismissal for failure or neglect to prosecute.

(4) This section does not alter the law on tolling of the statute of limitations nor does it apply to causes of action which have accrued before this Act becomes effective.

MASTERFORMAT

LEVEL TWO NUMBERS AND TITLES

Introductory Information
00001	Project Title Page
00005	Certifications Page
00007	Seals Page
00010	Table of Contents
00015	List of Drawings
00020	List of Schedules

Bidding Requirements
00100	Bid Solicitation
00200	Instructions to Bidders
00300	Information Available to Bidders
00400	Bid Forms and Supplements
00490	Bidding Addenda

Contracting Requirements
00500	Agreement
00600	Bonds and Certificates
00700	General Conditions
00800	Supplementary Conditions
00900	Addenda and Modifications

Facilities and Spaces
Systems and Assemblies
Construction Products and Activities
Division 1 General Requirements
01100	Summary
01200	Price and Payment Procedures
01300	Administrative Requirements
01400	Quality Requirements
01500	Temporary Facilities and Controls
01600	Product Requirements
01700	Execution Requirements
01800	Facility Operation
01900	Facility Decommissioning

Division 2 Site Construction
02050	Basic Site Materials and Methods
02100	Site Remediation
02200	Site Preparation
02300	Earthwork
02400	Tunneling, Boring, and Jacking
02450	Foundation and Load-Bearing Elements
02500	Utility Services
02600	Drainage and Containment
02700	Bases, Ballasts, Pavements, and Appurtenances
02800	Site Improvements and Amenities
02900	Planting
02950	Site Restoration and Rehabilitation

Division 3 Concrete
03050	Basic Concrete Materials and Methods
03100	Concrete Forms and Accessories
03200	Concrete Reinforcement
03300	Cast-in-Place Concrete
03400	Precast Concrete
03500	Cementitious Decks and Underlayment
03600	Grouts
03700	Mass Concrete
03900	Concrete Restoration and Cleaning

Division 4 Masonry
04050	Basic Masonry Materials and Methods
04200	Masonry Units
04400	Stone
04500	Refractories
04600	Corrosion-Resistant Masonry
04700	Simulated Masonry
04800	Masonry Assemblies
04900	Masonry Restoration and Cleaning

Division 5 Metals
05050	Basic Metal Materials and Methods
05100	Structural Metal Framing
05200	Metal Joists
05300	Metal Deck
05400	Cold-Formed Metal Framing
05500	Metal Fabrications
05600	Hydraulic Fabrications
05650	Railroad Track and Accessories
05700	Ornamental Metal
05800	Expansion Control
05900	Metal Restoration and Cleaning

Division 6 Wood and Plastics
06050	Basic Wood and Plastic Materials and Methods
06100	Rough Carpentry
06200	Finish Carpentry
06400	Architectural Woodwork
06500	Structural Plastics
06600	Plastic Fabrications
06900	Wood and Plastic Restoration and Cleaning

Division 7 Thermal and Moisture Protection
07050	Basic Thermal and Moisture Protection Materials and Methods
07100	Dampproofing and Waterproofing
07200	Thermal Protection
07300	Shingles, Roof Tiles, and Roof Coverings
07400	Roofing and Siding Panels
07500	Membrane Roofing
07600	Flashing and Sheet Metal
07700	Roof Specialties and Accessories
07800	Fire and Smoke Protection
07900	Joint Sealers

Division 8 Doors and Windows
08050	Basic Door and Window Materials and Methods
08100	Metal Doors and Frames
08200	Wood and Plastic Doors
08300	Specialty Doors
08400	Entrances and Storefronts
08500	Windows
08600	Skylights
08700	Hardware
08800	Glazing
08900	Glazed Curtain Wall

Division 9 Finishes
09050	Basic Finish Materials and Methods
09100	Metal Support Assemblies
09200	Plaster and Gypsum Board
09300	Tile
09400	Terrazzo
09500	Ceilings
09600	Flooring
09700	Wall Finishes
09800	Acoustical Treatment
09900	Paints and Coatings

Division 10 Specialties
10100	Visual Display Boards
10150	Compartments and Cubicles
10200	Louvers and Vents
10240	Grilles and Screens
10250	Service Walls
10260	Wall and Corner Guards
10270	Access Flooring
10290	Pest Control
10300	Fireplaces and Stoves
10340	Manufactured Exterior Specialties
10350	Flagpoles
10400	Identification Devices
10450	Pedestrian Control Devices
10500	Lockers
10520	Fire Protection Specialties
10530	Protective Covers
10550	Postal Specialties
10600	Partitions
10670	Storage Shelving
10700	Exterior Protection
10750	Telephone Specialties
10800	Toilet, Bath, and Laundry Accessories
10880	Scales
10900	Wardrobe and Closet Specialties

Division 11 Equipment
11010	Maintenance Equipment
11020	Security and Vault Equipment
11030	Teller and Service Equipment
11040	Ecclesiastical Equipment
11050	Library Equipment
11060	Theater and Stage Equipment
11070	Instrumental Equipment
11080	Registration Equipment
11090	Checkroom Equipment
11100	Mercantile Equipment
11110	Commercial Laundry and Dry Cleaning Equipment
11120	Vending Equipment
11130	Audio-Visual Equipment
11140	Vehicle Service Equipment
11150	Parking Control Equipment
11160	Loading Dock Equipment
11170	Solid Waste Handling Equipment
11190	Detention Equipment
11200	Water Supply and Treatment Equipment
11280	Hydraulic Gates and Valves
11300	Fluid Waste Treatment and Disposal Equipment
11400	Food Service Equipment
11450	Residential Equipment
11460	Unit Kitchens
11470	Darkroom Equipment
11480	Athletic, Recreational, and Therapeutic Equipment
11500	Industrial and Process Equipment
11600	Laboratory Equipment
11650	Planetarium Equipment

11660	Observatory Equipment
11680	Office Equipment
11700	Medical Equipment
11780	Mortuary Equipment
11850	Navigation Equipment
11870	Agricultural Equipment
11900	Exhibit Equipment

Division 12 Furnishings

12050	Fabrics
12100	Art
12300	Manufactured Casework
12400	Furnishings and Accessories
12500	Furniture
12600	Multiple Seating
12700	Systems Furniture
12800	Interior Plants and Planters
12900	Furnishings Restoration and Repair

Division 13 Special Construction

13010	Air-Supported Structures
13020	Building Modules
13030	Special Purpose Rooms
13080	Sound, Vibration, and Seismic Control
13090	Radiation Protection
13100	Lightning Protection
13110	Cathodic Protection
13120	Pre-Engineered Structures

13150	Swimming Pools
13160	Aquariums
13165	Aquatic Park Facilities
13170	Tubs and Pools
13175	Ice Rinks
13185	Kennels and Animal Shelters
13190	Site-Constructed Incinerators
13200	Storage Tanks
13220	Filter Underdrains and Media
13230	Digester Covers and Appurtenances
13240	Oxygenation Systems
13260	Sludge Conditioning Systems
13280	Hazardous Material Remediation
13400	Measurement and Control Instrumentation
13500	Recording Instrumentation
13550	Transportation Control Instrumentation
13600	Solar and Wind Energy Equipment
13700	Security Access and Surveillance
13800	Building Automation and Control
13850	Detection and Alarm
13900	Fire Suppression

Division 14 Conveying Systems

14100	Dumbwaiters
14200	Elevators
14300	Escalators and Moving Walks
14400	Lifts
14500	Material Handling

14600	Hoists and Cranes
14700	Turntables
14800	Scaffolding
14900	Transportation

Division 15 Mechanical

15050	Basic Mechanical Materials and Methods
15100	Building Services Piping
15200	Process Piping
15300	Fire Protection Piping
15400	Plumbing Fixtures and Equipment
15500	Heat-Generation Equipment
15600	Refrigeration Equipment
15700	Heating, Ventilating, and Air Conditioning Equipment
15800	Air Distribution
15900	HVAC Instrumentation and Controls
15950	Testing, Adjusting, and Balancing

Division 16 Electrical

16050	Basic Electrical Materials and Methods
16100	Wiring Methods
16200	Electrical Power
16300	Transmission and Distribution
16400	Low-Voltage Distribution
16500	Lighting
16700	Communications
16800	Sound and Video

INDUSTRY DIRECTORY

PART 1—GENERAL PLANNING AND DESIGN DATA

HUMAN FACTORS

ACE
Association of Canadian Ergonomists
1304–2 Carlton St.
Toronto, ON
CANADA M5B 1J3
(888) 432-2223
Fax: (416) 979-1144
http://www.ace.ergonomist.ca

DoD
Department of Defense
Ergonomics W Group
http://chppm-
www.apgea.army.mil/ergowg/default.htm

Ergoweb, Inc.
P.O. Box 1089
93 West Main St.
Midway, UT 84049
(888) ERGOWEB
Fax: (435) 654-5433
http://www.ergoweb.com

HFES
Human Factors and Ergonomics Society
P.O. Box 1369
Santa Monica, CA 90406-1369
(310) 394-1811
Fax: (310) 394-2410
http://www.hfes.org

IEA
International Ergonomics Association
Laboratoire d'Érgonomie, CNAM
41 rue Gay Lussac
75005 Paris
FRANCE
+33-1-44-107802
Fax: +33-1-43-253614
http://www.iea.org

Usernomics
1153 Foster City Blvd., #4
Foster City, CA 94404
(650) 349-3252
Fax: (650) 349-8560
http://www.usernomics.com

ACCESSIBILITY

Americans with Disabilities Act
Information Office
U.S. Department of Justice
Civil Rights Division
P.O. Box 66738
Washington, DC 20035-998X
(202) 514-0301
http://www.ada.ufl.edu

AHA
American Health Care Association
1201 L St., NW
Washington, DC 20005
(202) 842-4444
Fax: (202) 842-3860
http://www.ahca.org

BOCA
Building Officials and Code
Administrators International
4051 W. Flossmoor Rd.
Country Club Hills, IL 60478-5795
(800) 214-4321
Fax: (708) 799-4981
http://www.bocai.org

CAH
The Center for Accessible Housing
School of Design
North Carolina State University
P.O. Box 8613
Raleigh, NC 27695-8613
(919) 515-3082
Fax: (919) 515-3023

CIDEA
The Center for Inclusive Design and
Environmental Access
School of Architecture & Planning
University of Buffalo
Buffalo, NY 14214-3087
(716) 829-3485 x329
Fax: (716) 829-3861
http://www.ap.buffalo.edu

CIL
The Center for Independent Living
2539 Telegraph Ave.
Berkeley, CA 94704
(510) 841-4776
Fax: (510) 841-6168
http://www.cilberkeley.org

CUD
The Center for Universal Design
College of Design
North Carolina State University
50 Pullen Rd., Brooks Hall, Room 104
Campus Box 8613
Raleigh, NC 27695-8613
(800) 647-6777
Fax: (919) 515-7330
http:/www.design.ncsu.edu

Fair Housing Information Clearinghouse
P.O. Box 6091
Rockville, MD 20850
(800) 343-3442 (V) or (800) 877-8339
(TDD)
http://circsol.com/fairhousingNorth
Carolina

SBCCI
Southern Building Code Congress
International, Inc.
900 Montclair Rd.
Birmingham, AL 35213-1206
(800) 877-2224
Fax: (205) 592-7001
http://www.sbcci.org

COLOR THEORY

AATCC
American Association of Textile Chemists
and Colorists
P.O. Box 12215
Research Triangle Park, NC 27709
(919) 549-8141
Fax: (919) 549-8933
http://www.aatcc.org

CII
Colour & Imaging Institute
University of Derby
Kingsway House East
Kingsway, Derby DE22 3HL, England
+44 (0) 1332-622217
Fax: +44 (0) 1332-622218
http://colour.derby.ac.uk

CMG
Color Marketing Group
5904 Richmond Hwy, #408
Alexandria, VA 22303
(703) 329-8500
Fax: (703) 329-0155
http://www.colormarketing.org

ISCC
Inter-Society Color Council
11491 Sunset Hills Rd.
Reston, VA 20190
(703) 318-0263
Fax: (703) 318-0514
http://www.iscc.org

Society of Dyers and Colourists
P.O. Box 244, Perkin House
82 Grattan Rd.
Bradford BD1 2JB, England
+44 (0) 1274-725138
Fax: +44 (0) 1274-392888
http://www.sdc.org.uk

ACOUSTICS

ASA
Acoustical Society of America
2 Huntington Quadrangle, Suite 1N01
Melville, NY 11747-4502
(516) 576-2360
Fax: (516) 576-2377
http://asa.aip.org

Audio Engineering Society
60 East 42nd St., Rm 2520
New York, NY 10165
(212) 661-8528
Fax: (212) 682-0417
http://www.sdc.org.uk

NCAC
National Council of Acoustical Consultants
66 Morris Ave., Suite 1A
Springfield, NJ 07081-1409
(973) 564-5859
Fax: (973) 564-7480
http://www.ncac.com

NIBS
National Institute of Building Sciences
1090 Vermont Ave., NW, Suite 700
Washington, DC 20005-4905
(202) 289-7800
Fax: (202) 289-1092
http://www.nibs.org

INTERIOR LIGHTING DESIGN

American Lighting Association
2050 Stemmons Freeway, Suite 10046
Dallas, TX 75207
(800) 605-4448
Fax: (214) 698-9899
http://www.americanlightingassoc.com

AEIC
Association of Edison Illuminating
Companies
600 North 18th St.
P.O. Box 2641
Birmingham, AL 35291-0992
(205) 257-2530
Fax: (205) 257-2540
http://www.aeic.org

Certified Ballast Manufacturers
Association
355 Lexington Ave., 17th Fl.
New York, NY 10017-6603
(212) 297-2122
Fax: (212) 370-9047
http://www.certbal.org

DOE
Department of Energy
1000 Independence Ave., SW
Washington, DC 20585
(800) DIAL-DOE
Fax: (202) 586-4403
http://www.energy.gov

EEI
Edison Electric Institute
701 Pennsylvania Ave., NW
Washington, DC 20004
(202) 508-5000 or (800) EEI-4688
Fax: (202) 508-5794
http://www.eei.org

IALD
International Association of Lighting
Designers
The Merchandise Mart
200 World Trade Center, Suite 487
Chicago, IL 60654
(312) 527-3677
Fax: (312) 527-3680
http://www.iald.org

IESNA
Illuminating Engineering Society of North
America
120 Wall St., 17th Floor
New York, NY 10005-4001
(212) 248-5000
Fax: (212) 248-5017
http://www.iesna.org

LBL
Lawrence Berkeley National Laboratory
Lighting Systems Research Group
Mail Stop 46-125
1 Cyclotron Rd.
Berkeley, CA 94720
(510) 486-5388
Fax: (510) 486-6940
http://www.lbl.gov

LRC
Lighting Research Center
Rensselaer Polytechnic Institute
21 Union St.
Troy, NY 12180
(518) 687-7100
Fax: (518) 687-7100
http://lighting.lrc.rpi.edu

LRI
Lighting Research Institute
P.O. Box 1550
Hendersonville, NC 28793-1550
(828) 692-1904
Fax: (828) 692-6820
http://www.arcat.com/arcatcos/cos37
/arc37375.cfm

NIBS
National Institute of Building Sciences
1090 Vermont Ave., NW, Suite 700
Washington, DC 20005-4905
(202) 289-7800
Fax: (202) 289-1092
http://www.nibs.org

NLB
National Lighting Bureau
8811 Colesville Rd., Suite 6106
Silver Spring, MD 20910
(301) 587-9572
Fax: (301) 589-2017
http://www.nlb.org

SBCCI
Southern Building Code Congress
International, Inc.
900 Montclair Rd.
Birmingham, AL 35213-1206
(800) 877-2224
Fax: (205) 592-7001
http://www.sbcci.org

CONTRACT ADMINISTRATION

AIA
The American Institute of Architects
1735 New York Ave., NW
Washington, DC 20006
(800) 212-3837
Fax: (202) 626-7547
http://www.aia.org

IREM
Institute of Real Estate Management
430 North Michigan Ave.
Chicago, IL 60611-4090
(800) 837-0706
Fax: (800) 338-4736
http://www.irem.org

The Construction Specifications Institute
601 Madison St.
Alexandria, VA 22314-179156
(703) 684-0300
Fax: (703) 684-0465
http://www.csinet.org

SECURITY

BOMA
Building Owners and Managers
Association International
1201 New York Ave. NW, Suite 300
Washington, DC 20005
(202) 371-0181
Fax: (732) 544-2515
http://www.boma.org

CTBUH
Council on Tall Building and Urban
Habitat
c/o Bursar's Office
Lehigh University
177 ATLSS Dr.
Bethlehem, PA 18015
(610) 758-3515
Fax: (610) 758-4522
http://www.ctbuh.org

IAPSC
International Association of Professional
Security Consultants
2402 Vista Nobleza
Newport Beach, CA 92660
(949) 640-9918
Fax: (949) 640-9911
http://www.iapsc.org

IFCI
International Fire Code Institute
5360 Workman Mill Rd.
Whittier, CA 90601-2298
(562) 699-0124
Fax: (562) 699-8031
http://www.ifci.org

NAAA
National Alarm Association of America
P.O. Box 3409
Dayton, OH 45401
(800) 283-6285
Fax: (513) 461-4759
http://www.naaa.org

NBFAA
National Burglar and Fire Alarm
Association
8300 Colesville Rd., Suite 750
Silver Spring, MD 20910-6225
(301) 585-1855
Fax: (301) 585-1866
http://www.alarm.org

NCPI
National Crime Prevention Institute
University of Louisville, Shelby Campus
Burhans Hall, Rm 266
9001 Shelbyville Rd.
Louisville, KY 40292
(502) 852-6987
Fax: (502) 852-6990
http://www.louisville.edu/a-s/ja/ncpi

SSC
Skyscraper Safety Campaign—A Project
of Parents & Families of Firefighters & WTC
Victims
P.O. Box 70
Woodlawn Station
Bronx, NY 10470
http://www.skyscrapersafety.org

SBCCI
Southern Building Code Congress
International, Inc.
900 Montclair Rd.
Birmingham, AL 35213-1206
(800) 877-2224
Fax: (205) 592-7001
http://www.sbcci.org

INTERIOR LANDSCAPE DESIGN

American Nursery & Landscape
Association
1000 Vermont Ave., NW, Suite 300
Washington, DC 20005
(202) 789-2900
Fax: (202) 789-1893
http://www.anla.org

ALCA
Associated Landscape Contractors of
America
150 Elden St., Suite 270
Herndon, VA 20170
(703) 736-9666
Fax: (703) 736-9668
http://www.alca.org

ASLA
American Society of Landscape Architects
636 Eye St., NW
Washington, DC 20001-3736
(888) 999-2752
Fax: (202) 898-1185
http://www.asla.org

ENVIRONMENTAL QUALITY

IAQ
American Indoor Air Quality Council
P.O. Box 11599
Glendale, AZ 85318-1599
(800) 942-0832
Fax: (623) 581-6270
http://www.iaqcouncil.org

ANSI
American National Standards Institute
1819 L St. NW, Suite 600
Washington, DC 20036
(212) 642-4980
Fax: (212) 642-4900
http://www.ansi.org

ASSE
American Society of Safety Engineers
1800 East Oakton
Des Plaines, IL 60018
(847) 699-2929
Fax: (847) 768-3434
http://www.asse.org

Alternative Technology Association
P.O. Box 2001
Lygon St. North
Brunswick East, VIC 3057
+61-3-9388-9311
Fax: +61-3-9388-9322
http://www.ata.org.au/main.htm

BFRL
Building and Fire Research Laboratory
National Institute of Standards and
Technology (NIST)
100 Bureau Dr., Stop 8600
Gaithersburg, MD 20899
(301) 975-6850
http://www.bfrl.nist.gov

BOMA
Building Owners and Managers
Association International
1201 New York Ave. NW, Suite 300
Washington, DC 20005
(202) 371-0181
Fax: (732) 544-2515
http://www.boma.org

CRBT
Center for Resourceful Building
Technology
P.O. Box 100
Missoula, MT 59806
(406) 549-7678
Fax: (406) 549-4100
http://www.crbt.org

CREST
Center for Renewable Energy &
Sustainable Technology
1612 K St., NW, Suite 202
Washington, DC 20006
(202) 293-2898
Fax: (202) 293-5857
http://www.crest.org

CTBUH
Council on Tall Building and Urban
Habitat
c/o Bursar's Office
Lehigh University
177 ATLSS Dr.
Bethlehem, PA 18015
(610) 758-3515
Fax: (610) 758-4522
http://www.ctbuh.org

EEBA
Energy and Environmental Building
Association
10740 Lyndale Ave. South, 10W
Bloomington, MN 55420-5615
(952) 881-1098
Fax: (952) 881-3048
http://www.eeba.org

Environmental Building News/Building
Green, Inc.
122 Birge St., Suite 30
Brattleboro, VT 05301
(802) 257-7300
Fax: (802) 257-7304
http://www.buildinggreen.com

Environmental Design and Construction
755 West Big Beaver Rd., Suite 1000
Troy, MI 48084
(248) 244-6258
http://www.edcmag.com

EPA
Environmental Protection Agency
Ariel Rios Building
Washington, DC 20004
(202) 260-0279
Asbestos Information Hotline:
(800) 368-5888
Tools for Schools Hotline: (866) 837-3721
Resource Center: (202) 260-5922
Indoor Air-Quality Information:
 (800) 438-4318
http://www.epa.gov

Greenguard (Indoor Air Quality Certified)
1337 Capital Circle, Suite A
Atlanta, GA 30067
(800) 427-9681
Fax: (770) 980-0072
http://www.greenguard.org

IAAM
International Association of Assembly
Managers
635 Fritz Dr., Suite 100
Coppell, TX 75019-4442
(800) 935-4226
Fax: (972) 255-9582
http://www.iaam.org

ICBO
International Conference of Building
Officials
5360 S. Workman Mill Rd.
Whittier, CA 90601-2298
(800) 423-6587
http://www.icbo.org

LEAD
Leadership for Environment and
Development
LEAD International
48 Prince's Gardens
London SW7 2PE
Great Britain
+44-870-220-2900
Fax: +44-870-220-2910
http://www.lead.org

LEED
Leadership in Energy and Environmental
Design
US Green Building Council
1015 18th St., NW, Suite 805
Washington, DC 20036
(202) 828-7422
Fax: (202) 828-5110
http://www.usgc.org/LEED

NFPA
National Fire Protection Association
International
One Batterymarch Park
P.O. Box 9101
Quincy, MA 02269-9101
(617) 770-3000
Fax: (617) 770-0700
http://www.nfpa.org

NIBS
National Institute of Building Sciences
1090 Vermont Ave., NW, Suite 700
Washington, DC 20005-4905
(202) 289-7800
Fax: (202) 289-1092
http://www.nibs.org

OPPT
Office of Pollution Protection and Toxics
US EPA
1200 Pennsylvania Ave., NW
Washington, DC 20460
(202) 564-3810
Toxic Substances Information Hotline:
(202) 554-1404
http://www.epa.gov/opptintr

OSHA
Occupational Safety and Health
Administration
200 Constitution Ave.
Washington, DC 20210
(800) 321-OSHA
http://www.osha.gov

RecycleNet Corporation
P.O. Box 24017
Guelph, ON
CANADA N1E 6V8
(519) 767-2913
http://www.recycle.net

Smart Communities Network
3040 Continental Dr.
P.O. Box 3838
Butte, MT 59701
(406) 494-4572
Fax: (406) 494-2905
http://www.sustainable.doe.gov

USGBC
United States Green Building Council
1015 18th St., NW,
Suite 805
Washington, DC 20036
(202) 82-USGBC
Fax: (202) 828-5110
http://www.usgbc.org

LIFE SAFETY CONSIDERATIONS

BOCA
Building Officials and Code Administrators
International
4051 W. Flossmoor Rd.
Country Club Hills, IL 60478-5795
(800) 214-4321
Fax: (708) 799-4981
http://www.bocai.org

IBHS
Institute for Business and Home Safety
4775 East Fowler Ave.
Tampa, FL 33617
(813) 286-3400
Fax: (813) 286-9960
http://www.ibhs.org

ICBO
International Conference of Building
Officials
5360 S. Workman Mill Rd.
Whittier, CA 90601-2298
(800) 423-6587
http://www.icbo.org

ICC
International Code Council
5203 Leesburg Pike, Suite 600
Falls Church, VA 22041
(703) 931-4533
Fax: (703) 379-1546
http://www.intlcode.org

IFCI
International Fire Code Institute
5360 Workman Mill Rd.
Whittier, CA 90601-2298
(562) 699-0124
Fax: (562) 699-8031
http://www.ifci.org

SBCCI
Southern Building Code Congress
International, Inc.
900 Montclair Rd.
Birmingham, AL 35213-1206
(800) 877-2224
Fax: (205) 592-7001
http://www.sbcci.org

SEISMIC CONSIDERATIONS

BSSC
Building Seismic Safety Council
National Institute of Building Sciences
1090 Vermont Ave., Suite 700
Washington, DC 20005-4905
(202) 289-7800
Fax: (202) 289-1092
http://www.nibs.org

FEMA
Federal Emergency Management Agency
500 C St., SW
Washington, DC 20472
(202) 566-1600
www.fema.gov

Office of Urban Rehabilitation
Department of Housing and Urban
Development
451 Seventh St., SW
Washington, DC 20410
(202) 708-1422
http://www.hud.gov

SSC
Skyscraper Safety Campaign—A Project
of Parents & Families of Firefighters &
WTC Victims
P.O. Box 70
Woodlawn Station
Bronx, NY 10470
http://www.skyscrapersafety.org

BUILDING SYSTEMS

LGSI
Light Gage Structural Institute
5150 Paige Rd., P.O. Box 560746
The Colony, TX 75056
(972) 370-0967 or (800) 406-7387
Fax: (800) 944-6884

SSMA
Steel Stud Manufacturers Association
8 S. Michigan Ave., Suite 1000
Chicago, IL 60603
(312) 456-5590
Fax: (312) 580-0165
http://www.arcat.com/arcatos/cos41/arc41
600.cfm

PART 2—INTERIOR BUILDING COMPONENTS

CONCRETE

ACI
American Concrete Institute
P.O. Box 9094
Farmington Hills, MI 48333-9094
(248) 848-3700
Fax: (248) 848-3701
http://www.concrete.org

APA
Architectural Precast Association
6710 Winkler Rd., Suite 8
Fort Meyers, FL 33919
(941) 454-6989
Fax: (941) 454-6787
http://www.archprecast.org

CRA
Concrete Repair Association
99 West St.
Farnham GU9 7EN, United Kingdom
44-1252-739145
http://www.concreterepair.org.uk

CSDA
Concrete Sawing and Drilling Association
10901 D Roosevelt Blvd. North,
Suite 100-A
St. Petersburg, FL 33716
(727) 577-5004
Fax: (727) 577-5012
http://www.csda.org

ICRI
International Concrete Repair Institute
c/o Milton J. Collins
3166 South River Rd., Suite 132
Des Plaines, IL 60018
(847) 827-0830
Fax: (847) 827-0832
http://www.icri.org

NPCA
National Precast Concrete Association
10333 N. Meridian St., Suite 272
Indianapolis, IN 46290-1081
(800) 366-7731
Fax: (317) 571-0041
http://www.precast.org

NRMCA
National Ready-Mixed Concrete
Association
900 Spring St.
Silver Spring, MD 20910
(301) 587-1400
Fax: (301) 585-4219
http://www.nrmca.org

PCI
Precast/Prestressed Concrete Institute
209 West Jackson Blvd., No. 500
Chicago, IL 60606
(312) 786-0300
Fax: (312) 786-0353
http://www.pci.org

PTI
Post-Tensioning Institute
1717 West Northern Ave., Suite 114
Phoenix, AZ 85021
(602) 870-7540
Fax: (602) 870-7541
http://www.post-tensioning.org

TCA
Tilt-Up Concrete Association
113 First St., West
P.O. Box 204
Mount Vernon, IA 52314
(319) 895-6911
Fax: (319) 895-8830
http://www.tilt-up.org

MASONRY

BIA
Brick Industry Association
11490 Commerce Park Dr.
Reston, VA 20191-1525
(703) 620-0010
Fax: (703) 620-3928
http://www.bia.org

ILI
Indiana Limestone Institute of America, Inc.
Stone City Bank Building, Suite 400
Bedford, IN 47421
(812) 275–4426
Fax: (812) 279-8682
www.iliai.com

MHA
Masonry Heater Association of North
America
1252 Stock Farm Rd.
Randolph, VT 05060
(802) 728-5896
Fax: (802) 728-6004
http://www.mha-net.org

NBGQA
National Building Granite Quarries
Association, Inc.
1220 L. St., NW, Suite 100–167
Washington, DC 20005
(800) 557–2848
http://www.nbgqa.com

PCA
Portland Cement Association
5420 Old Orchard Rd.
Skokie, IL 60077-1083
(847) 966-6200
Fax: (847) 966-8389
http://www.portcement.org

STONE

ASI
Allied Stone Industries
8632 N. Foothills Hwy
Boulder, CO 80302
(614) 228-5489
http://www.alliedstone.com/index.htm

BSI
Building Stone Institute
P.O. Box 507
Purdys, NY 10578
(914) 232-5725
Fax: (914) 232-5259
http://www.buildingstone.org

CSI
Cast Stone Institute
10 West Kimball St.
Winder, GA 30680
(770) 868-5909
Fax: (770) 868-5910
http://www.caststone.org

ILI
Indiana Limestone Institute of America
Stone City Bank Building, Suite 400
Bedford, IN 47421
(812) 275-4426
Fax: (812) 279-8682
http://www.iliai.com

MIA
Marble Institute of America
30 Eden Alley, Suite 301
Columbus, OH 43215
(614) 228-6194
Fax: (614) 461-1497
http://www.marble-institute.com

NSSGA
National Stone, Sand and Gravel
Association
2101 Wilson Blvd., Suite 100
Arlington, VA 22201
(703) 525-8788
Fax: (703) 525-7782
http://www.nssga.org

METALS

AAI
Aluminum Association
900 19th St., NW
Washington, DC 20006
(202) 862-5100
Fax: (202) 862-5164
http://www.aluminum.org

AISC
American Institute of Steel Construction, Inc.
1 East Wacker Dr., Suite 3100
Chicago, IL 60601-2001
(312) 670-2400
Fax: (312) 670-5403
http://www.aisc.org

AISI
American Iron & Steel Institute
1101 17th St., NW, Suite 1300
Washington, DC 20036
(202) 452-7100
Fax: (202) 463-6573
http://www.steel.org

AWS
American Welding Society
550 NW LeJeune Rd.
Miami, FL 33126
(800) 443-9353
Fax: (305) 443-7559
http://www.aws.org

BBII
Brass and Bronze Ingot Manufacturers
200 South Michigan Ave., Suite 1100
Chicago, IL 60604-2404
(312) 372-4000
Fax: (312) 939-5617

CDA
Copper Development Association, Inc.
260 Madison Ave.
New York, NY 10016
(212) 251-7200
Fax: (212) 251-7234
http://www.copper.org

CFSBI
Cold Finished Steel Bar Institute
11 Park Place
Falls Church, VA 22046
(703) 538-3543
Fax: (703) 241-5603
http://www.cfsbi.com

ICA
International Copper Association, Ltd.
260 Madison Ave., 16th Floor
New York, NY 10016
(212) 251-7240
Fax: (212) 251-7245
http://www.copper.org/centers

IPA
Industrial Perforators Association
5157 Deerhurst Crescent Circle
Boca Raton, FL 33486
(561) 447-7511
http://www.iperf.org

LIA
Lead Industries Association
13 Main St.
Sparta, NJ 07871
(973) 726-5323
Fax: (973) 726-4484
http://www.leadinfo.com

MBMA
Metal Building Manufacturers Association
c/o Thomas Associates, Inc.
1300 Sumner Ave.
Cleveland, OH 44115-2851
(216) 241-7333
Fax: (216) 241-0105
http://www.mbma.com

MPC
Materials Properties Council
3 Park Ave., 27th Floor
New York, NY 10016-5902
(212) 591-7693
Fax: (212) 591-7183
http://www.forengineers.org/mpc

MTI
Metal Treating Institute
1550 Roberts Dr.
Jacksonville Beach, FL 32250
(904) 249-0448
Fax: (904) 249-0459
http://www.metaltreat.com

NAAMM
National Association of Architectural Metal
Manufacturers
8 South Michigan Ave., Suite 1000
Chicago, IL 60603
(312) 332-0405
Fax: (312) 332-0706
http://www.naamm.org

NiDI
Nickel Development Institute
214 King St. West, Suite 510
Toronto, ON
CANADA M5H 3S6
(416) 591-7999
Fax: (720) 554-0909
http://www.nidi.org

NISD
National Institute of Steel Detailing
7700 Edgewater Dr., Suite 670
Oakland, CA 94621-3022
(510) 568-3741
Fax: (510) 568-3781
http://www.nisd.org

NOMMA
National Ornamental and Miscellaneous
Metals Association
532 Forest Parkway, Suite A
Forest Park, GA 30297
(404) 363-4009
Fax: (404) 366-1852
http://www.nomma.org

EXPANSION CONTROL

AMA
Adhesives Manufacturers Association
2300 North Barrington Rd., Suite 400
Hoffman Estates, IL 60195
(847) 490-5377
http://www.adhesive.org/ama

ASC
Adhesive and Sealant Council
7979 Old Georgetown Rd., Suite 500
Bethesda, MD 20814
(301) 986-9700
Fax: (301) 986-9795
http://www.ascouncil.org

NPCA
National Paint and Coatings Association
1500 Rhode Island Ave., NW
Washington, DC 20005-5597
(202) 462-6272
Fax: (202) 462-8549
http://www.paint.org

SWRI
Sealant, Waterproofing, and Restoration
Institute
14 West 3rd St., Suite 200
Kansas City, MO 64105
(816) 472-7974
Fax: (816) 472-7765
http://www.swrionline.org

WOOD

AF&PA
American Forest and Paper Association
1111 19th St., NW, Suite 800
Washington, DC 20036
(202) 463-2700
Fax: (202) 463-2471
http://www.afandpa.org

AWC/NFPA
American Wood Council
National Forest Products Association
1111 19th St., NW, Suite 800
Washington, DC 20036
(202) 463-2766
Fax: (202) 463-2791
http://www.afandpa.org/WoodDesign/index
.html

CRA
California Redwood Association
405 Enfrente Dr., Suite 200
Novato, CA 94949
(888) 225-7339
Fax: (415) 382-8531
http://www.calredwood.org

CWC
Canadian Wood Council
1400 Blair Place, Suite 210
Ottawa, ON
CANADA K1J 9B8
(613) 731-7800
Fax: (206) 731-7899
http://www.cwc.ca

FPS
Forest Products Society
2801 Marshall Court
Madison, WI 53705-2295
(608) 231-1361
Fax: (608) 231-2152
http://www.forestprod.org

LMA
Laminating Materials Association
116 Lawrence St.
Hillsdale, NJ 07642-2730
(201) 664-2700
Fax: (201) 666-5665
http://www.lma.org

NAHB
National Association of Home Builders
Home Builder Press/NAHB Bookstore
1201 15th St., NW
Washington, DC 20005
(202) 822-0200
Fax: (202) 822-0559
http://www.nahb.org

NELMA
Northeastern Lumber Manufacturers
Association, Inc.
272 Tuttle Rd., P.O. Box 87A
Cumberland Center, ME 04021
(207) 829-6901
Fax: (207) 829-4293
http://www.nelma.org

SCMA
Southern Cypress Manufacturers
Association
400 Penn Center Blvd., Suite 530
Pittsburgh, PA 15235-5605
(412) 829-0770
Fax: (412) 829-0844
www.cypressinfo.org

Southern Forest Products Association
P.O. Box 641700
Kenner, LA 70064-1700
(504) 443-4464
Fax: (504) 443-6612
http://www.sfpa.org

The Engineered Wood Association
P.O. Box 11700
Tacoma, WA 98411-0700
(253) 565-6600
Fax: (253) 565-7265
http://www.apawood.org

WRCLA
Western Red Cedar Lumber Association
1200-555 Burrard St., P.O. Box 275
Vancouver, BC V7X 1S7
(604) 684-0266
Fax: (604) 687-4930
http://www.wrcla.org

WWPA
Western Wood Products Association
522 SW 5th Ave., Suite 500
Portland, OR 97204-2122
(503) 224-3930
Fax: (503) 224-3934
http://www.wwpa.org

World Forest Institute
4033 SW Canyon Rd.
Portland, OR 97221
(503) 228-0819
Fax: (503) 228-3624

PLASTICS

APC
American Plastics Council
1300 Wilson Blvd.
Arlington, VA 22209
(800) 2-HELP-90
http://www.americanplasticscouncil.org

PIA
Plastics Institute of America
333 Aiken St.
Lowell, MA 01854-3686
(508) 934-3130
Fax: (508) 459-9420
http://www.pia.caeds.eng.uml.edu

RMA
Rubber Manufacturers Association
1400 K St., NW, Suite 900
Washington, DC 20005
(800) 220-7620; or (202) 682-4800
http://www.rma.org

SPI
Society of the Plastics Industry
1801 K St., NW, Suite 600K
Washington DC, 20006
(202) 974-5200
Fax: (202) 296-7005
http://plasticsindustry.org

VI
Vinyl Institute
1300 Wilson Boulevard, Suite 800
Arlington, VA 22209
(703) 741-5670
Fax: (703) 741-5672
http://www.vinylinfo.org

FINISH CARPENTRY

AWI
Architectural Woodwork Institute
1952 Isaac Newton Sq. West
Reston, VA 20190
(703) 733-0600
Fax: (703) 733-0584
http://www.awinet.org

CRA
California Redwood Association
405 Enfrente Dr., Suite 200
Novato, CA 94949
(888) 225-7339
Fax: (415) 382-8531
http://www.calredwood.org

CWC
Canadian Wood Council
1400 Blair Place, Suite 210
Ottawa, ON
CANADA K1J 9B8
(613) 731-7800
Fax: (206) 731-7899
http://www.cwc.ca

HPVA
Hardwood Plywood and Veneer
Association
1825 Michael Faraday Dr.
P.O. Box 2789
Reston, VA 20195-0789
(703) 435-2900
Fax: (703) 435-2537
http://www.hpva.org

NELMA
Northeastern Lumber Manufacturers
Association, Inc.
272 Tuttle Rd., P.O. Box 87A
Cumberland Center, ME 04021
(207) 829-6901
Fax: (207) 829-4293
http://www.nelma.org

NHLA
National Hardwood Lumber Association
P.O. Box 34518
Memphis, TN 38184-0518
(901) 377-1818
Fax: (901) 382-6419
http://www.natlhardwood.org

Southern Forest Products Association
P.O. Box 641700
Kenner, LA 70064-1700
(504) 443-4464
Fax: (504) 443-6612
http://www.sfpa.org

The Engineered Wood Association
P.O. Box 11700
Tacoma, WA 98411-0700
(253) 565-6600
Fax: (253) 565-7265
http://www.apawood.org

WIC
Woodwork Institute of California
3164 Industrial Blvd.
PO Box 980247
West Sacramento, CA 95798
(916) 372-9943
Fax: (916) 372-9950

WMMPA
Wood Moulding & Millwork Producers
Association
507 First St.
Woodland, CA 95695
(530) 661-9591 or (800) 530-7889
Fax: (530) 661-9586
http://www.wmmpa.com

WRCLA
Western Red Cedar Lumber Association
1200-555 Burrard St., P.O. Box 275
Vancouver, BC V7X 1S7
(604) 684-0266
Fax: (604) 687-4930
http://www.wrcla.org

WWPA
Western Wood Products Association
522 SW 5th Ave., Suite 500
Portland, OR 97204-2122
(503) 224-3930
Fax: (503) 224-3934
http://www.wwpa.org

CASEWORK

AWI
Architectural Woodwork Institute
1952 Isaac Newton Sq. West
Reston, VA 20190
(703) 733-0600
Fax: (703) 733-0584
http://www.awinet.org

WIC
Woodwork Institute of California
3164 Industrial Blvd.
PO Box 980247
West Sacramento, CA 95798
(916) 372-9943
Fax: (916) 372-9950

DOORS

AHMA
American Hardware Manufacturers
Association
801 N. Plaza Dr.
Schaumberg, IL 60173-4977
(847) 605-1025
Fax: (847) 605-1093
http://www.ahma.org

American Hardboard Association
1210 W. Northwest Hwy.
Palatine, IL 60067
(847) 934-8800
Fax: (847) 934-8803
http://www.hardboard.org

BHMA
Builders Hardware Manufacturers
Association
355 Lexington Ave., 17th Floor
New York, NY 10017
(212) 297-2122
Fax: (212) 370-9047
http://www.buildershardware.com

DHI
Door and Hardware Institute
14150 Newbrook Dr., Suite 200
Chantilly, VA 20151-2232
(703) 222-2010
Fax: (703) 222-2410
http://www.dhi.org

IWFA
International Window Film Association
P.O. Box 3872
Martinsville, VA 24115-3871
(276) 666-4932
Fax: (276) 666-4933
http://www.iwfa.com

National Fire Protection Association
International
One Batterymarch Park
P.O. Box 9101
Quincy, MA 02269-9101
(617) 770-3000
Fax: (617) 770-0700
http://www.nfpa.org

NFRC
National Fenestration Rating Council
P.O. Box 7031
Silver Spring, MD 20907
(717) 428-3125
Fax: (301) 588-6342
http://www.nfrc.org

NRHA
National Retail Hardware Association
5822 West 74th St.
Indianapolis, IN 46278
(317) 290-0338
Fax: (317) 328-4354
http://www.nrha.org

WDMA
National Wood Window and Door
Manufacturers Association
1400 E. Touhy Ave.
No. 470
Des Plaines, IL 60018
(847) 299-5200
Fax: (847) 299-1286
http://www.wdma.com

SDI
Steel Door Institute
30200 Detroit Rd.
Cleveland, OH 44145-1967
(440) 899-0010
Fax: (440) 892-1404
http://www.steeldoor.com

SWI
Steel Window Institute
c/o Thomas Assoc. Inc.
1300 Sumner Ave.
Cleveland, OH 44115-2851
(216) 241-7333
Fax: (216) 241-0105
http://www.steelwindows.com

WINDOWS

IWFA
International Window Film Association
P.O. Box 3872
Martinsville, VA 24115-3871
(276) 666-4932
Fax: (276) 666-4933
http://www.iwfa.com

NFRC
National Fenestration Rating Council
P.O. Box 7031
Silver Spring, MD 20907
(717) 428-3125
Fax: (301) 588-6342
http://www.nfrc.org

NRHA
National Retail Hardware Association
5822 West 74th St.
Indianapolis, IN 46278
(317) 290-0338
Fax: (317) 328-4354
http://www.nrha.org

SGCC
Safety Glazing Certification Council
P.O. Box 9
Henderson Harbor, NY 13651
(315) 646-2234
Fax: (315) 938-7453
http://www.arcat.com/arcatos/cos37/
arc37798.cfm

SWI
Steel Window Institute
c/o Thomas Assoc. Inc.
1300 Sumner Ave.
Cleveland, OH 44115-2851
(216) 241-7333
Fax: (216) 241-0105
http://www.steelwindows.com

WCMA
Window Covering Manufacturers
Association
355 Lexington Ave., Suite 1700
New York, NY 10017-6603
(800) 506-4653; or (212) 661-4261

WDMA
National Wood Window and Door
Manufacturers Association
1400 E. Touhy Ave.
No. 470
Des Plaines, IL 60018
(847) 299-5200
Fax: (847) 299-1286
http://www.wdma.com

GLAZING

AGSA
Art Glass Suppliers Association
1100-H Brandywine Blvd.
P.O. Box 3388
Zanesville, OH 43702-3388
(614) 452-4541
Fax: (614) 452-2552
http://www.agsa.org

GANA
Glass Association of North America
2945 SW Wanamaker Dr., Suite A
Topeka, KS 66614
(785) 271-0208
Fax: (785) 271-0166
http://www.glasswebsite.com

GICC
Glazing Industry Code Committee
2945 SW Wanamaker Dr., Suite A
Topeka, KS 66614
(785) 271-0208
http://www.glazingcodes.org

IGMA
Insulating Glass Manufacturers Alliance
27 Goulburn Ave.
Ottawa, ON
CANADA K1N 8C7
(613) 233-1510
Fax: (613) 233-1929
http://www.igmaonline.org

IWFA
International Window Film Association
P.O. Box 3872
Martinsville, VA 24115-3871
(276) 666-4932
Fax: (276) 666-4933
http://www.iwfa.com

NGA
National Glass Association
8200 Greensboro Dr., 3rd Floor
McLean, VA 22102-3881
(800) DIAL-NGA
Fax: (703) 442-0630
http://www.glass.org

SGAA
Stained Glass Association of America
10009 East 62nd St.
Raytown, MO 64133
(816) 737-2090
Fax: (816) 737-2801
http://www.stainedglass.org

SGCD
Society of Glass and Ceramic Decorators
4340 East-West Hwy., Suite 200
Bethesda, MD 20814
(301) 951-3933
Fax: (301) 951-3801
http://www.sgcd.org

SIGMA
Sealed Insulating Glass Manufacturers
Association
401 N. Michigan Ave.
Chicago, IL 60611-4267
(312) 644-6610
Fax: (312) 527-6783

PLASTER AND GYPSUM BOARD

FWCI
Foundation of the Wall and Ceiling
Industry
803 West Broad. St., Suite 600
Falls Church, VA 22046
(703) 534-8300
Fax: (703) 534-8307
http://www.awci.org

GA
Gypsum Association
810 First St., NE, #510
Washington DC, 20002
(202) 289-5440
Fax: (202) 289-3707
http://www.gypsum.org

IILP
International Institute for Lath and Plaster
1043 Stuart St., No. 2
P.O. Box 1663
Lafayette, CA 94549
(612) 645-0208
Fax: (612) 645-0209
http://www.lilp.org

TILE

CTIOA
Ceramic Tile Institute of America
12061 West Jefferson Blvd.
Culver City, CA 90230
(310) 574-7800
Fax: (310) 821-4655
http://www.ctioa.org

ITC
Italian Trade Commission
33 East 67th St.
New York, NY 10021
(212) 980-1500
Fax: (212) 758-1050
http://www.italtrade.com

TCA
Tile Council of America
100 Clemson Research Blvd.
Anderson, SC 29625
(864) 646-8453
Fax: (864) 646-2821
http://www.tileusa.com

TERRAZZO

NTMA
National Terrazzo and Mosaic Association
110 E. Market St., Suite 200-A
Leesberg, VA 20176-3122
(703) 779-1022
Fax: (703) 779-1026
http://www.ntma.com

CEILINGS

ASA
Acoustical Society of America
2 Huntington Quadrangle, Suite 1N01
Melville, NY 11747-4502
(516) 576-2360
Fax: (516) 576-2377
http://asa.aip.org

CISCA
Ceilings and Interior Systems Construction
Association
1500 Lincoln Hwy, No. 202
St. Charles, IL 60174
(630) 584-1919
Fax: (630) 584-2003
http://www.cisca.org

WA
Wallcoverings Association
401 N. Michigan Ave.
Chicago, IL 60611-4267
(312) 644-6610
Fax: (312) 527-6705
http://www.wallcoverings.org

WOOD FLOORING

HMA
Hardwood Manufacturer's Association
400 Penn Center Blvd., Suite 530
Pittsburgh, PA 15235-5605
(412) 829-0770
Fax: (412) 829-0844
http://www.hardwood.org

NOFMA
National Oak Flooring Manufacturers
Association
P.O. Box 3009
Memphis, TN 38173-0009
(901) 526-5016
Fax: (901) 526-7022
http://www.nofma.org

NWFA
National Wood Flooring Association
16388 Westwoods Business Park
Ellisville, MO 63021
(800) 422-4556
Fax: (636) 391-6137
http://www.woodfloors.org

WWPA
Western Wood Products Association
522 SW 5th Ave., Suite 500
Portland, OR 97204-2122
(503) 224-3930
Fax: (503) 224-3934
http://www.wwpa.org

RESILIENT FLOORING

RFCI
Resilient Floor Covering Institute
401 Jefferson St., Suite 102
Rockville, MD 20850-2617
(301) 340-8580
Fax: (301) 340-7283
http://www.rfci.com

CARPET

CCC
Carpet Cushion Council
P.O. Box 546
Riverside, CT 06878
(203) 637-1312
Fax: (203) 698-1022
http://www.carpetcushioncouncil.org

CRI
Carpet and Rug Institute
310 Holiday Ave.
P.O. Box 2048
Dalton, GA 30722
(706) 278-3176
Fax: (706) 278-883
http://www.carpet-rug.com

JCBC
Jute Carpet Backing Council and Burlap
and Jute Association
c/o Textile Bag and Packaging Association
Drawer 8
322 Davis Ave.
Dayton, OH 45401-0008
(937) 476-8272
Fax: (937) 258-0029

PAINTS AND COATINGS

PDCA
Painting and Decorating Contractors of
America
3913 Old Lee Hwy, Suite 33B
Fairfax, VA 22030
(800) 332-7322; or (703) 359-0826
Fax: (703) 359-0826
http://www.pdca.org

INTERIOR SIGNAGE

ISA
International Sign Association
801 North Fairfax St., Suite 205
Alexandria, VA 22314
(703) 836-4012
Fax: (703)-836-8353
http://www.signs.org

Marking Device Association International
222 Wisconsin Ave., Suite 1
Lake Forrest, IL 60045
(847) 283-9810
Fax: (847) 283-9808
http://www.mdai.org

SEGD
Society for Environmental Graphic Design
100 Vermont Ave., No. 400
Washington, DC 20005
(202) 638-5555
Fax: (202) 638-0891
http://www.segd.org

WBDG
Whole Building Design Guide
1095 Vermont Ave., NW, Suite 700
Washington, DC 20005
(202) 289-7800
Fax: (202) 289-1092
http://www.wbdg.org

WSA
World Sign Associates
8774 Yates Dr., No. 120
Westminster, CO 80031-6906
(303) 427-7252
Fax: (303) 427-7090

PREFABRICATED PARTITIONS

CPA
Composite Panel Association
18928 Premiere Ct.
Gaithersburg, MD 20879-1569
(301) 670-0604
Fax: (301) 840-1252
http://www.pbmdf.com/index.asp

EJMA
Expansion Joint Manufacturers
Association, Inc.
25 North Broadway
Tarrytown, NY 10591
(914) 332–0040
Fax: (914) 332-1541
www.ejma.org

TOILET AND BATH ACCESSORIES

CTFA
Cosmetic, Toiletry, and Fragrance
Association
1101 17th St., NW, Suite 300
Washington, DC 20036
(202) 331-1770
Fax: (202) 331-1969
http://www.ctfa.org

ISSA
International Sanitary Supply Association
7373 North Lincoln Ave.
Lincolnwood, IL 60646-1799
(847) 982-0800
Fax: (847) 982-1012
http://www.issa.com

NAMN
North American Association of Mirror
Manufacturers
2495 SW Wanamaker St.
Topeka, KS 66611
(785) 271-0208
Fax: (785) 271-0166

PEI
Porcelain Enamel Institute
P.O. Box 920220
Norcross, GA 30010
(770) 281-8980
Fax: (770) 281-8981
http://www.porcelainenamel.com

BANK EQUIPMENT

National Alarm Association of America
P.O. Box 3409
Dayton, OH 45401
(800) 283-6285
http://www.naaa.org

NBFAA
National Burglar and Fire Alarm
Association
8300 Colesville Rd., Suite 750
Silver Spring, MD 20910-6225
(301) 585-1855
Fax: (301) 585-1866
http://www.alarm.org

NIBESA
National Independent Bank Equipment
and Systems Association
1411 Peterson St.
Park Ridge, IL 60068
(847) 825-8419
Fax: (847) 825-8445
http://www.nibesa.com

UL
Underwriters Laboratories
333 Pfingsten Rd.
Northbrook, IL 60062
(847) 272-8800
http://www.ul.com

VENDING EQUIPMENT

NAMA
National Automatic Merchandising
Association
20 N. Wacker Dr., Suite 3500
Chicago, IL 60606
(312) 346-0370
Fax: (312) 704-4140
http://www.vending.org

NBVA
National Bulk Venders Association
200 N. LaSalle St.
Room 2100
Chicago, IL 60601-1095
(312) 621-1400
Fax: (312) 621-1750
http://www.nbva.org

NCUSA
National Coffee Association of USA, Inc.
15 Maiden Lane, Suite 1405
New York, NY 10038
(212) 766-4007
Fax: (212) 766-5815
http://www.ncausa.org

FOOD SERVICE EQUIPMENT

National Association of Food Equipment
Manufacturers
401 N. Michigan Ave.
Chicago, IL 60611-4267
(800) 336-0019
Fax: (312) 245-1566
http://www.nafem.org

WI
Wine Institute
c/o Librarian
425 Market St., Suite 1000
San Francisco, CA 94105
(415) 512-0151
Fax: (415) 442-0742
http://www.wineinstitute.org

FABRICS

AFMA
American Fiber Manufacturers
Association
1530 Wilson Boulevard, Suite 690
Arlington, VA 22209
(703) 875-0432
Fax: (703) 875-0907
http://www.fibersource.com

APC
American Plastics Council
1300 Wilson Blvd.
Arlington, VA 22209
(800) 2-HELP-90
http://www.americanplasticscouncil.org

ATMI
American Textiles Manufacturers
Institute, Inc.
1130 Connecticut Ave., NW, Suite 1200
Washington, DC 20036-3954
(202) 862-0500
Fax: (202) 862-0570
http://www.atmi.org

CFFA
Chemical Fabrics & Film Association, Inc.
1300 Sumner Ave.
Cleveland, OH 44115-2851
(216) 241-7333
Fax: (216) 241-0105
http://www.chemicalfabricsandfilm.com

ITMF
International Textile Manufacturers
Federation
Am Schanzengraben 29
Postfach
CH-8039 Zurich
+41-1-283-63-80
Fax: +41-1-283-63-89
http://www.itmf.org

OTEX
US Department of Commerce Office of
Textiles and Apparel
U.S. Dept. of Commerce
International Trade Administration
Office of Textiles and Apparel
Room H3100
14th and Constitution Ave., NW
Washington, DC 20230
(202) 482-5078
Fax: (202) 482-2331
http://www.otexa.ita.doc.gov

VI
Vinyl Institute
1300 Wilson Bld., Suite 800
Arlington, VA 22209
(703) 741-5670
Fax: (703) 741-5672
http://www.vinylinfo.org

TASK LIGHTING

ALA
American Lighting Association
World Trade Center, Suite 10046
2050 Stemmons Freeway
P.O. Box 420288
Dallas, TX 75342-0288
(800) 274-4484
Fax: (214) 698-9899
http://www.americanlightingassoc.com

IALD
International Association of Lighting Designers
The Merchandise Mart
200 World Trade Center, Suite 487
Chicago, IL 60654
(312) 527-3677
Fax: (312) 527-3680
http://www.iald.org

FURNITURE

AASA
American Association of School Administrators
1801 N. Moore St.
Arlington, VA 22209
(703) 528-0700
Fax: (703) 841-1543
http://www.aasa.org

AATCC
American Association of Textile Chemists and Colorists
P.O. Box 12215
Research Triangle Park, NC 27709-2215
(919) 549-8141
Fax: (919) 549-8933
http://www.aatcc.org

AFMA
American Furniture Manufacturers Association
P.O. Box HP-7
High Point, NC 27261
(336) 884-5000
Fax: (336) 884-5303
http://www.afma4u.org

American Library Association
50 East Huron St.
Chicago, IL 60611
(800) 545-2433
Fax: (312) 440-9374
http://www.ala.org

Americans with Disabilities Act Information Office
U.S. Department of Justice
Civil Rights Division
P.O. Box 66378
Washington, DC 20035-998
(202) 514-0301 or (202) 514-0383
http://www.ada.ufl.edu

ASFD
American Society of Furniture Designers
144 Woodland Dr.
New London, NC 28127
(910) 576-1273
Fax: (910) 576-1573
http://www.asfd.com

ASID
American Society of Interior Designers
608 Massachusetts Ave., NE
Washington, DC 20002
(202) 546-3480
Fax: (202) 546-3240
http://www.interiors.org

AWFS
Association of Woodworking and Furnishings Suppliers
5733 Rickenbacker Rd.
Commerce, CA 90040
(800) 946-AWFS
Fax: (323) 838-9443
http://www.awfs.org

BIFMA
Business and Institutional Furniture Manufacturers Association International
2680 Horizon Dr., S.E., Suite A1
Grand Rapids, MI 49546-7500
(616) 285-3963
Fax: (616) 285-3765
http://www.bifma.org

CFC
Contract Furnishings Council
1190 Merchandise Mart
Chicago, IL 60654
(312) 321-0563

CPSC
Consumer Product Safety Commission
4330 East-West Hwy.
Bethesda, MD 20814-4408
(800) 638-2772; or (301) 504-0990
Fax: (301) 504-0124
http://www.cpsc.gov

IFDA
International Furnishings and Design Association
191 Clarksville Rd.
Princeton Junction, NJ 08550
(609) 799-3423
Fax: (609) 799-7023
http://www.ifda.com

IFAI
Industrial Fabrics Association International
1801 Country Rd. BW
Roseville, MN 55113-4601
(800) 225-4324
Fax: (651) 631-9334
http://www.ifai.com

IOPFDA
Independent Office Products and Furniture Dealers Association
301 North Fairfax St.
Alexandria, VA 22314
(703) 549-9040
Fax: (703) 683-7552
http://www.iopfda.org

KCMA
Kitchen Cabinet Manufacturers Association
1899 Preston White Dr.
Reston, VA 20191-5435
(703) 264-1690
Fax: (703) 620-6530
http://www.kcma.org

NASFM
National Association of Store Fixture Manufacturers
3595 Sheridan St., Suite 200
Hollywood, FL 33021
(954) 893-7300
Fax: (954) 893-7500
http://www.nasfm.org

National Kitchen and Bath Association
687 Willow Grove St.
Hackettstown, NJ 07840
(908) 852-0033
http://www.nkba.org

National School Supply and Equipment Association
8300 Colesville Rd., Suite 250
Silver Spring, MD 20910
(301) 495-0240
Fax: (301) 495-3330
http://www.nssea.org

NHFA
National Home Furnishings Association
P.O. Box 2396
High Point, NC 27261
(919) 883-1650
Fax: (919) 883-1195
http://www.homefurnish.com/NHFA

OPMA
Office Products Manufacturers Association
5024-R Campbell Blvd.
Baltimore, MD 21236
(410) 933-3454
Fax: (410) 931-8111
http://www.opmassn.org

SEFA
Scientific Equipment and Furniture Association
7 Wildbird Lane
Hilton Head Island, SC 29926-2766
(843) 689-6878

State of California, Department of Consumer Affairs
Bureau of Home Furnishings and Thermal Insulation
Technical Information
400 R St.
Sacramento, CA 95814
(800) 952-5210; or (916) 445-1254
http://www.dca.ca.gov

UFAC
Upholstered Furniture Action Council
P.O. Box 2436
High Point, NC 27261
(336) 885-5065
Fax: (336) 884-5072
http://www.ufac.org

FURNITURE MARTS

Americas Mart
240 Peachtree St., NW, Suite 2200
Atlanta, GA 30303
(404) 220-3000
Fax: (404) 220-3030
http://www.americasmart.com

Boston Design Center
One Design Center Place
Boston, MA 02210
(617) 338-5062
http://www.bostondesign.com

Dallas Design Center
1025 N. Stemmons Freeway, Suite 605A
Dallas, TX 75207
(214) 747-2411

Denver Design Center
595 South Broadway
Denver, CO 80209
(303) 733-2455
http://www.denverdesign.com

International Market Square
275 Market St.
Minneapolis, MN 55405
(612) 338-6250

Los Angeles Mart
1933 S. Broadway, Suite 244
Los Angeles, CA 90007
(213) 749-7911
http://www.lamart.com

Marketplace Design Center
2400 Market St.
Philadelphia, PA 19103
(215) 561-5000
http://www.marketplacedc.com

Merchandise Mart
222 Merchandise Mart Plaza, Suite 470
Chicago, IL 60654
(800) 677-6278
http://www.mmart.com

Miami International Merchandise Mart
777 NW 72nd Ave.
Miami, FL 33126
(305) 261-2900, ext. 169
Fax: (305) 261-3659
http://www.mimm.com

Pacific Design Center
8687 Melrose Ave., M-60
Los Angeles, CA 90069
(310) 657-0800
http://www.pacificdesigncenter.com

San Diego Design Center
6455 Lusk Blvd.
San Diego, CA 92121
(619) 452-7332

San Francisco Mart
1355 Market St.
San Francisco, CA 94103
(415) 552-2311
http://www.sfmart.com

Washington Design Center
300 D St., SW
Washington, DC 20024
(202) 554-5053

INTERIOR PLANTINGS

ANLA
American Nursery & Landscape Association
1000 Vermont Ave., NW, Suite 300
Washington, DC 20005
(202) 789-2900
Fax: (202) 789-1893
http://www.anla.org

ASLA
American Society of Landscape Architects
636 Eye St., NW
Washington, DC 20001-3736
(888) 999-2752
Fax: (202) 898-1185
http://www.asla.org

Associated Landscape Contractors of America
150 Elden St., Suite 270
Herndon, VA 20170
(703) 736-9666
Fax: (703) 736-9668
http://www.alca.org

SPECIAL CONSTRUCTION

IES
Institute of Environmental Sciences
940 East Northwest Hwy
Mount Prospect, IL 60056
(708) 255-1561
Fax: (708) 255-1699
http://www.nspi.org

NSPI
National Spa and Pool Institute
2111 Eisenhower Ave.
Alexandria, VA 22314
(703) 838-0083
Fax: (703) 549-0493
http://www.nspi.org

SEFA
Scientific Equipment and Furniture
Association
7 Wildbird Lane
Hilton Head Island, SC 29926-2766
(843) 689-6878

FIRE SUPPRESION SYSTEMS

Building and Fire Research Laboratory
National Institute of Standards and
Technology
Building 226 Room B216
Gaithersburg, MD 20899
(301) 975-6850
http://www.bfrl.nist.gov

FEMA
Fire Equipment Manufacturers
Association
1300 Sumner Ave.
Cleveland, OH 44115-2185
(216) 241-7333
Fax: (216) 241-0105
http://www.yourfirstdefense.com

Fire Suppression Systems Association
5024-R Campbell Blvd.
Baltimore, MD 21236
(410) 931-8100
Fax: (410) 931-8111
http://www.podi.com/fssa

FM Global
1151 Boston-Providence Turnpike
P.O. Box 9102
Norwood, MA 02062-9102
(781) 762-4300
Fax: (781) 762-9375
http://www.factorymutual.com/engr.htm

FRS/NRCC
Fire Research Section
National Research Council Canada
Ottawa, Canada KIA OR6
(613) 993-9101
http://www.nrc.ca

NAFED
National Association of Fire Equipment
Distributors
401 North Wabash Ave., No. 732
Chicago, IL 60601
(312) 245-9300
Fax: (312) 245-9301
http://www.nafed.org

National Fire Sprinkler Association
Route 22 and Robin Hill Corporate Park
Box 1000
Patterson, NY 12563
(914) 878-4200
Fax: (914) 878-4215
http://www.nfsa.org

NFPA
National Fire Protection Association
International
One Batterymarch Park
P.O. Box 9101
Quincy, MA 02269-9101
(617) 770-3000
Fax: (617) 770-0700
http://www.nfpa.org

SFPE
Society of Fire Protection Engineers
7315 Wisconsin Ave., Suite 1225W
Bethesda, MD 20814
(301) 718-2910
Fax: (301) 718-2242
http://www.sfpe.org

UL
Underwriters Laboratories
333 Pfingsten Rd.
Northbrook, IL 60062
(847) 272-8800
Fax: (847) 272-8129
http://www.ul.com

ULC
Underwriters Laboratories of Canada
7 Crouse Rd.
Scarborough, ON
CANADA MIR 3A9
(416) 757-3611
http://www.ulc.ca

CONVEYING SYSTEMS

EIA
Elevator Industries Association, Inc.
233-43 Bay St.
Douglaston, NY 11363
(718) 279-3859
Fax: (718) 423-6576

Elevator Escalator Safety Foundation
P.O. Box 6273
Mobile, AL 36660
(334) 479-2199
http://www.eesf.com

Elevator World, Inc.
P.O. Box 6507
Mobile, AL 36660
(334) 479-4514
Fax: (334) 479-7043
http://www.elevator-world.com

IUEC
International Union of Elevator
Constructors
Suite 310, Clark Building, Suite 310
5565 Sterrett Place
Columbia, MD 21044
(410) 997-9000

MHIA
Material Handling Industry of America
8720 Red Oak Blvd., Suite 201
Charlotte, NC 28217-3992
(800) 345-1815; or (704) 676-1190
Fax: (704) 676-1199

NAEC
National Association of Elevator
Contractors
1298 Wellbrook Circle N.E.
Conyers, GA 30207
(404) 496-1270
Fax: (404) 496-1272
Email: naec@mindspring.com
http://www.naec.org

National Association of Elevator Safety
Authorities
67 East Weldon, Suite 103
P.O. Box 15643
Phoenix, AZ 85012
(602) 760-9660
Fax: (602) 760-9714
http://www.pcslink.com/~naesa

NAVTP
National Association of Vertical
Transportation Professionals
P.O. Box 636
Bowie, MD 20718
(301) 262-3150
Fax: (301) 262-3194

NEI
National Elevator Industry, Inc.
185 Bridge Plaza North
Room 310
Fort Lee, NJ 07024
(201) 944-3211
Fax: (201) 944-5483

NEIEP
National Elevator Industry Educational
Program
11 Larson Way
Attleboro Falls, MA 02763
(508) 699-2200
Fax: (508) 699-2495

MECHANICAL SYSTEMS

ADC
Air Diffusion Council
104 South Michigan Ave., Suite 1500
Chicago, IL 60603
(312) 201-0101
Fax: (312) 201-0214

ASHRAE
American Society of Heating, Refrigerating
and Air-Conditioning Engineers
1791 Tullie Circle, NE
Atlanta, GA 30329-2305
(800) 527-4723; or (404) 636-8400
Fax: (404) 321-5478
http://www.ashrae.org

Air Conditioning Contractors of America
1712 New Hampshire Ave., NW
Washington, DC 20009
(202) 483-9370
Fax: (202) 234-4721
http://www.acca.org

Air Conditioning and Refrigeration
Wholesalers Association
1650 South Dixie Dr.,
5th Floor
Boca Raton, FL 33432
(561) 338-3495
Fax: (561) 338-3496
http://www.arw.org

Air Distributing Institute
4415 West Harrison St.,
Suite 242C
Hillside, IL 60162
(708) 449-2933

Air Movement and Control Association
International, Inc.
30 West University Dr.
Arlington Heights, IL 60004
(847) 394-0150
Fax: (847) 394-0066
http://www.amca.org

ARI
Air-Conditioning and Refrigeration Institute
4301 Northwest Fairfax Dr.,
Suite 425
Arlington, VA 22203
(703) 524-8800
Fax: (703) 528-3816
http://www.ari.org

ASME
American Society of Mechanical
Engineers
1828L St., NW, Suite 906
Washington, DC 20006
(202) 785-3756
Fax: (202) 429-9417
http://www.asme.org

Cooling Tower Institute
Box 73383
Houston, TX 77273
(713) 583-4087
http://www.cti.org

HI
Hydronics Institute, Division of GAMA
P.O. Box 218
Berkeley Heights, NJ 07922-0218
(908) 464-8200
Fax: (908) 464-7818
http://www.gamanet.org

NAPHCC
National Association of Plumbing-Heating-
Cooling Contractors
180 South Washington St.
P.O. Box 6808
Falls Church, VA 22046-1148
(703) 237-8100
Fax: (703) 237-7442
http://www.naphcc.org

SMACNA
Sheet Metal and Air Conditioning
Contractor's National Association
4201 Lafayette Center Dr.
Chantilly, VA 20151-1209
(703) 803-2980
Fax: (703) 803-3732
http://www.smacna.org

PLUMBING SYSTEMS

American Society of Plumbing Engineers
3617 Thousand Oaks Blvd.,
Suite 210
Westlake Village, CA 91362-3649
(805) 495-7120
Fax: (805) 495-4861
http://www.aspe.org

ASSE
American Society of Sanitary Engineering
28901 Clemens Rd., Suite 100
Westlake, OH 44145
(440) 835-3040
Fax: (440) 835-3488
http://www.asse-plumbing.org

CIPSI
Cast Iron Soil Pipe Institute
5959 Shallowford Rd., Suite 419
Chattanooga, TN 37421
(423) 892-0137
Fax: (423) 892-0817
http://www.cispi.org

IAPMO
International Association of Plumbing and
Mechanical Officers
20001 Walnut Dr. South
Walnut, California 91789-2825
(909) 595-8449
Fax: (909) 594-3690
http://www.iapmonet.org

PMI
Plumbing Manufacturers Institute
1340 Remington Rd., Suite A
Schaumberg, IL 60173
(847) 884-9764
Fax: (847) 884-9775
http://www.pmihome.org

ELECTRICAL SYSTEMS

ACEEE
American Council for an Energy-Efficient
Economy
100 Connecticut Ave., NW, Suite 801
Washington, DC 20036
(202) 429-8873
http://www.aceee.org

AEIC
Association of Edison Illuminating
Companies
600 North 18th St.
P.O. Box 2641
Birmingham, AL 35291-0992
(205) 257-2530
Fax: (205) 257-2540
http://www.aeic.org

EEI
Edison Electric Institute
701 Pennsylvania Ave., NW
Washington, DC 20004
(202) 508-5000 or (800) EEI-4688
Fax: (202) 508-5794
http://www.eei.org

Electric Power Research Institute
Box 10412
Palo Alto, CA 94303-0813
(415) 855-2000
Fax: (415) 855-2954
http://www.epri.com

IEEE
Institute of Electrical and Electronics
Engineers
Headquarters
445 Hoes Lane
P.O. Box 1331
Piscataway, NJ 08855-1330
(908) 562-3800
Fax: (908) 562-1571
http://www.ieee.org

IESNA
Illuminating Engineering Society of North
America
120 Wall St., 17th Floor
New York, NY 10005-4001
(212) 248-5000
Fax: (212) 248-5017
http://www.iesna.org

NCTA
National Cable Television Association
1724 Massachusetts Ave., NW
Washington, DC 20036
(202) 775-3669
http://www.ncta.com

NECA
National Electrical Contractors Association
3 Bethesda Metro Center, Suite 1100
Bethesda, MD 20814-3299
(301) 657-3110
Fax: (301) 215-4500
http://www.necanet.org

NEMA
National Electrical Manufacturers
Association
1300 N 17th St., Suite 1847
Rosslyn, VA 22209
(703) 841-3200
Fax: (703) 841-3300
http://www.nema.org

NETA
International Electrical Testing Association
106 Stone St.
Morrison, CO 80465
(303) 697-8441
Fax: (303) 697-8431
http://www.electricnet.com/neta

TIA/EIA
Telecommunications Industry
Association/Electronic Industries Alliance
2500 Wilson Blvd., Suite 300
Arlington, VA 22201-3834
(703) 907-7700
http://www.tiaonline.org

UL
Underwriters Laboratories
333 Pfingsten Rd.
Northbrook, IL 60062
(847) 272-8800
http://www.ul.com

SECTION 3—INTERIOR TYPOLOGIES

OFFICE

OPUG
Office Planners and Users Group
Box 11182
Philadelphia, PA 19136
(215) 335-9400

RETAIL

NASFM
National Association of Store Fixture
Manufacturers
3595 Sheridan St., Suite 200
Hollywood, FL 33021
(954) 893-7300
Fax: (954) 893-7500
http://www.nasfm.org

NRF
National Retail Federation
325 7th St., NW, Suite 1100
Washington, D.C. 20004
(800) NRF-HOW2
Fax: (202) 737-2849
http://www.nrf.com

EXHIBITION

AAM
American Association of Museums
1225 Eye St., NW, Suite 200
Washington, D.C. 20005
(202) 289-1818
Fax: (202) 289-6578
http://www.aam-us.org

PERFORMANCE THEATERS AND REHEARSAL HALLS

LHAT
League of Historic American Theatres
1511 K St., NW, Suite 923
Washington, DC 20005
(202) 783-6966
http://www.lhat.org

National Endowment for the Arts
1100 Pennsylvania Ave., NW
Washington, DC 20506
(202) 682-5400
http://arts.endow.gov

USITT
US Institute for Theatre Technology
6443 Ridings Rd.
Syracuse, NY 13206-1111
(800) 938-7488
Fax: (315) 463-6525
http://www.usitt.org

THEMED ENVIRONMENTS

TEA
Themed Entertainment Association
175 East Olive Ave., Suite 304
Burbank, CA 91502-0126
(818) 843-8497
Fax: (818) 843-8477
http://www.themeit.com

PRESENTATION TECHNOLOGY

AEA
American Electronics Association
601 Pennsylvania Ave., NW, Suite 600
Washington, DC 2004
(202) 682-9110
Fax: (202) 682-9111
http://www.aenet.org

AMPAS
Academy of Motion Picture Arts and
Science
8949 Wilshire Boulevard
Beverly Hills, CA 90211-1972
(310) 247-3000
Fax: (310) 859-9351
http://www.ampas.org

ATAS
Academy of Television Arts & Sciences
5220 Lankershim Boulevard
North Hollywood, CA 91601
(818) 754-2800
http://www.emmys.org

AVIA
Audio Video Intelligent Association
2219 West Oliver Ave., #238
Burbank, CA 91506
(818) 562-1997
http://www.avia.org

CEDIA
Custom Electronic Design & Installation
Association
9202 North Meridian St., Suite 200
Indianapolis, IN 46260-1810
(800) 669-5329
Fax: (317) 571-5603
http://www.cedia.net

CABA
Continental Automated Buildings
Association
1200 Montreal Rd.
Building M-20
Ottawa, ON
K1A 0R6, CANADA
(888) 798-CABA
Fax: (613) 991-9990
http://www.caba.org

EIA
Electronic Industries Alliance
2500 Wilson Boulevard
Arlington, VA 22201
(703) 907-7500
http://www.eia.org

USA INCE
Institute of Noise Control Engineering
of the Iowa State University
College of Engineering
212 Marston Hall
Ames, IA 50011-2353
(515) 294-6142
Fax: (515) 294-3528
http://www.inceusa.org

HEALTH CARE

AAHA
American Association of Homes for the
Aging
901 E St., NW, Suite 500
Washington, DC 20004-2011
(202) 783-2242
Fax: (202) 783-2255
http://www.aahsa.org

AHA
American Hospital Association
1 North Franklin, Suite 2700
Chicago, IL 60606
(312) 422-3000
http://www.aha.org

HHS/DHFP
U.S. Department of Health and Human
Services
Division of Health Facilities Planning
200 Independence Ave., SW
Washington, DC 20201
(202) 619-0257
http://www.hhs.gov

USVA/AS
U.S. Veterans Administration Architectural
Services
810 Vermont Ave., NW
Washington DC, 20420
(202) 273-5400
http://www.va.gov

HOSPITALITY

AH&LA
American Hotel & Lodging Association
1201 New York Ave., NW, #600
Washington, DC 20005-3931
(202) 289-3100
Fax: (202) 289-3199
http://www.ahma.com

ARDA
American Resort Development
Association
1201 15th St., NW, Suite 400
Washington, D.C. 20005-2842
(202) 371-6700
Fax: (202) 289-8544
http://www.arda.org

IHRA
International Hotel & Restaurant
Association
251 rue du Faubourg
St. Martin 75010
Paris, France
+33 (0) 1-44-899400
Fax: +33 (0) 1-40-367330
http://www.ih-ra.com

NSF
National Sleep Foundation
1522 K St., Suite 500
Washington, DC 20005
(202) 347-3471
Fax: (202) 347-3472
http://www.sleepfoundation.org

TEA
Themed Entertainment Association
175 East Olive Ave., Suite 304
Burbank, CA 91502-0126
(818) 843-8497
Fax: (818) 843-8477
http://www.themeit.com

ATHLETIC FACILITIES

AAU
Amateur Athletic Union of the United
States
c/o Walt Disney World Resorts
P.O. Box 10000
Lake Buena Vista, FL 32830-1000
(407) 934-7200
http://www.aausports.org

Billiard and Bowling Institute of America
200 Castlewood Dr.
North Palm Beach, FL 33408
(561) 840-1120
Fax: (561) 863-8984
Email: sdsgma@aol.com

International Racquet Sports Association
263 Summer St.
Boston, MA 02110
(617) 951-0055
Fax: (617) 951-0056
http://www.ihrsa.org

National Collegiate Athletic Association
6201 College Blvd.
Overland Park, KS 66211
(913) 339-1906
Fax: (913) 339-1950
http://www.ncaa.org

National Swimming Pool Foundation
10803 Gulfdale, Suite 300
San Antonio, TX 78216
(210) 525-1227
http://www.nspf.com

NBA
National Basketball Association
645 Fifth Ave., 10th Floor
New York, NY 10022
(212) 407-8000
Fax: (212) 832-3861
http://www.nba.com

NRPA
National Recreation and Park Association
22377 Belmont Ridge Rd., Suite 300
Ashburn, VA 20148
(703) 858-0784
Fax: (703) 858-0794
http://www.nrpa.org

NSPI
National Spa and Pool Institute
2111 Eisenhower Ave.
Alexandria, VA 22314
(703) 838-0083
Fax: (703) 549-0493
http://www.nspi.org

U.S. Professional Tennis Association
1 USPTA Center
3535 Briarpark Dr.
Houston, TX 77042
(713) 978-7782
Fax: (713) 978-7780
http://www.uspta.org

U.S. Tennis Association
70 West Red Oak Lane
White Plains, NY 10604
(914) 696-7000
Fax: (914) 696-7167
http://www.usta.com

U.S. Tennis Court and Track Builders
Association
3525 Ellicott Mills Dr., Suite N
Ellicott City, MD 21043
(410) 418-4875
Fax: (410) 418-4805
http://www.ustctba.com

YMCA-USA
National Council of Young Men's Christian
Association
101 N. Wacker Dr.
Chicago, IL 60606
(312) 977-0031
Fax: (312) 977-9063
http://www.ymca.net

EDUCATION

OPUG
Council of Educational Facility Planners
641 Chatham Lane, Suite 217
Columbus, OH 43221
(614) 792-8103
http://www.cefpi.com

National Child Care Association
1029 Railroad. St., NW
Conyers, GA 30207-5275
(800) 543-7161
Fax: (404) 388-7772
http://www.nccanet.org

NSBA
National School Boards Association
1680 Duke St.
Alexandria, VA 22314
(703) 838-6722
Fax: (703) 683-7590
http://www.nsba.org

SCUP
Society for College and University
Planning
339 East Liberty, Suite 300
Ann Arbor, MI 48104
(734) 998-7832
Fax: (734) 998-6532
http://www.scup.org

INDUSTRY ORGANIZATIONS

ABC
Associated Builders and Contractors
1300 North 17th St., Suite 800
Rosslyn, VA 22209
(703) 812-2000
Fax: (703) 812-8200
http://www.abc.org

ADDA
American Design Drafting Association
P.O. Box 11937
Columbia, SC 29211
(803) 771-0008
Fax: (803) 771-4272
http://www.adda.org

AGC
Associated General Contractors of
America
333 John Carlyle St., Suite 200
Alexandria, VA 22314
(703) 548-3118
Fax: (703) 548-3119
http://www.agc.org

AIBD
American Institute of Building Design
2505 Main St., Suite 209B
Stratford, CT 06615
(800) 366-2423
Fax: (203) 378-3568
http://www.aibd.org

ASFD
American Society of Furniture Designers
144 Woodland Dr.
New London, NC 28127
(910) 576-1273
Fax: (910) 576-1573
http://www.asfd.com

ASLA
American Society of Landscape Architects
636 Eye St., NW
Washington, DC 20001-3736
(888) 999-2752
Fax: (202) 898-1185
http://www.asla.org

CCA
Canadian Construction Association
Albert St.
Ottawa, ON
K1P 5E7 CANADA
(613) 236-9455
Fax: (613) 236-9526
http://www.cca-acc.com

DMI
Design Management Institute
29 Temple Place, 2nd Floor
Boston, MA 02111
(617) 338-6380
Fax: (617) 338-6570
http://www.dmi.org

FHS
Furniture History Society
c/o Dr. Brian Austen
1 Mercedes Cottages
St. John's Rd.
Haywards Heat
RH16 4EH, UK
44-1444-413845
Fax: 44-1444-413845

GAS
Glass Art Society
1305 4th Ave., Suite 711
Seattle, WA 98101-2401
(206) 382-1305
Fax: (206) 382-2630
http://www.glassart.org

ISO
International Organization for
Standardization
1, rue de Varembe, Case postale 56
CH-1211 Geneva 20, Switzerland
+41-22-749-01-11
Fax: +41-22-733-34-30
http://www.iso.org

IWPA
International Wood Products Association
4214 King St. West
Alexandria, VA 22302
(703) 820-6696
Fax: (703) 820-8550
http://www.iwpawood.org

NAHBRC
National Association of Home Builders
Research Center
400 Prince George's Boulevard
Upper Marlboro, MD 20774
(301) 249-4000
Fax: (301) 430-6180
http://www.nahbrc.org

NARI
National Association of the Remodeling
Industry
780 Lee St., Suite 200
Des Plaines, IL 60016
(800) 611-NARI
Fax: (847) 298-9225
http://www.nari.org

NAWIC
National Association of Women in
Construction
327 South Adams St.
Fort Worth, TX 76104
(800) 552-3506
Fax: (817) 877-0324
http://www.nawic.org

NCARB
National Council of Architectural
Registration Boards
1801 K St., NW, Suite 1100K
Washington, DC 20006
(202) 783-6500
Fax: (202) 783-0290
http://www.ncarb.org

NCIDQ
National Council for Interior Design
Qualification
1200 18th St., NW, Suite 1001
Washington, DC 20036
(202) 721-0220
Fax: (202) 721-0221
http://www.ncidq.org

NIST
National Institute of Standards and
Technology
Public Inquiries Unit
100 Bureau Dr., Stop 3460
Gaithersburg, MD 20899-3460
(301) 975-6478
Fax: (301) 975-8295
http://www.nist.gov

RAIC
Royal Architectural Institute of Canada
330-55 Murray St.
Ottawa, ON
K1N 5M3 CANADA
(613) 241-3600
Fax: (613) 241-5750

U.S. Access Board
1331 F St., NW, Suite 1000
Washington, DC 20004-1111
(202) 272-0080
Fax: (202) 272-0081
http://www.access-board.gov

USGBC
U.S. Green Building Council
1015 18th St., Suite 805
Washington, DC 20036
(202) 828-7422
Fax: (202) 824-5110
http://www.usgbc.org

WCAA
Window Coverings Association of America
3550 McKelvey Rd., No. 202C
Bridgeton, MO 63044-2535
(314) 770-0263
http://www.wcaa.org

U.S. INTERIOR DESIGN REGULATING AGENCIES

Alabama State Board of Registration for
Interior Designers
P.O. Box 11026
Birmingham, AL 35202
(205) 879-6785
http://www.alabamaadministrativecode.
state.al.us/UpdatedMonthly/VolXIXN9/
w2wtoc.htm

Arkansas State Board of Residential
Interior Designers
1023 Whitewood
Benton, AR 72015
(501) 315-7482
http://www.state.ar.us/directory/detail2.
cgi?ID=1148

California Council for Interior Design
Certification
1605 Grand Ave., Suite 4
San Marcos, CA 92069-2440
(760) 761-4734
Fax: (760) 761-4736
http://www.ccidc.org

Colorado Board of Examiners of Architects
1560 Broadway, Suite 1340
Denver, CO 80202
(303) 894-7801
Fax: (303) 894-7802

Connecticut Department of Consumer
Protection Professional Licensing
Division—Interior Design
165 Capitol Ave.
Hartford, CT 06106
(800) 842-2649
Fax: (860) 566-7630
http://www.state.ct.us/dcp

Florida Department of Business and
Professional Regulation
Board of Architecture and Interior Design
Norwood Center
1940 North Monroe St.
Tallahassee, FL 32399-0751
(850) 488-6685
Fax: (850) 922-2918
http://www.state.fl.us/dbpr/pro/arch/
arc_index.shtml

Georgia State Board of Architects and
Interior Designers
237 Coliseum Dr.
Macon, GA 31217-3858
(912) 207-1400
Fax: (912) 207-1410
http://www.sos.state.ga.us/plb/architects/
default.htm

Illinois Board of Interior Design
Professionals
320 West Washington, 3rd Floor
Springfield, IL 62786
(217) 785-0080
Fax: (217) 782-7645
http://www.dpr.state.il.us/who/intd.asp

Louisiana State Board of Examiners of
Interior Design
8017 Jefferson Hwy, Suite B-3
Baton Rouge, LA 70809
(225) 298-1283
Fax: (225) 298-1284
http://www.state.me.us/pfr/olr/categories/
cat04.htm

Maine Board of Architects, Landscape
Architects and Interior Designers
35 State House Station
Augusta, ME 04333-0035
(207) 624-8522
Fax: (207) 624-8367
http://www.dllr.state.md.us/license/
cert_int_des/cidintro.html

Maryland Board of Certified Interior
Designers
500 North Calvert St., Room 308
Baltimore, MD 21202-2272
(410) 230-6262
Fax: (410) 333-0021

Michigan Department of Consumer and
Industry Services
Interior Designers Certification Program
P.O. Box 30018
Lansing, MI 48909-7518
(517) 241-9253
http://www.aelslagid.state.mn.us

Minnesota Board of Architecture,
Engineering, Landscaping, Landscape
Architects, Geosciences and Interior Design
133 7th St. East
St. Paul, MN 55101-2333
(612) 296-2388
Fax: (651) 297-5310
http://www.aelslagird.state.mn.us

Missouri Interior Design Council
360 Missouri Blvd.
P.O. Box 1335
Jefferson City, MO 65102-1335
573) 522-4683
Fax: (573) 536-3469
http://www.ded.state.mo.us/
regulatorylicensing/professionalregistration/
interior

Nevada State Board of Architecture,
Interior Design and Residential Design
2080 East Flamingo Rd., Suite 225
Las Vegas, NV 89119
(702) 486-7300
Fax: (702) 486-7304
http://www.nsbaidrd.state.nv.us

New Mexico Board of Interior Design
2055 South Pacheco, Suite 400
Santa Fe, NM 87504
(505) 476-7077
Fax: (505) 476-7087
http://www.rld.state.nm.us/b&c/
interior_design_board.htm

New York State Education Board of
Interior Design
Interior Design Consumer Brochure
89 Washington Ave., 2nd Floor
Albany, NY 12234
(518) 474-3817
Fax: (518) 474-6382
http://www.op.nysed.gov/interior.htm

Puerto Rico State Department
Examining Board of Interior Designers
P.O. Box 3271
San Juan, Puerto Rico 00902
(787) 722-2121
Fax: (787) 722-4818

Tennessee Department of Commerce and
Insurance
Board of Architectural and Engineering
Examiners
500 James Robertson Parkway, 3rd Floor
Nashville, TN 37243-1142
(615) 741-3221
Fax: (615) 532-9410
http://www.state.tn.us/commerce/ae.html

Texas Board of Architectural Examiners
P.O. Box 12337
Austin, TX 78711-2337
(512) 305-9000
Fax: (512) 305-8900
http://www.tbae.state.tx.us

Virginia APELSCIDLA Board for Architects,
Professional Engineers, Land Surveyors,
Certified Interior Designers and
Landscape Architects
Department of Commerce
3600 West Broad St.
Richmond VA 23230-4917
(804) 367-8512
Fax: (804) 367-6946
http://www.state.va.us/dpor/ape_main.htm

Washington D.C. Board of Architecture
and Interior Design
914 North Capitol St., NE, Suite 7200
Washington, D.C. 20002
(202) 442-4461
Fax: (202) 442-4258

Wisconsin Department of Regulation and
Licensing
P.O. Box 8935
Madison, WI 53708
(608) 266-5439

INTERIOR DESIGN EDUCATION

C²Ed
Center for Collaboration and Education in
Design
c/o CLARB
144 Church St. NW, Suite 201
Vienna, VA 22180
(866) 464-2233
http://www.c2ed.net

FIDER
Foundation for Interior Design Education
Research
146 Monroe Center NW, Suite 1318
Grand Rapids, MI 49503-2822
(616) 458-0400
Fax: (616) 458-0460
http://www.fider.org

NASAD
National Association of Schools of Art and
Design
11250 Roger Bacon Dr., Suite 21
Reston, VA 20190
(703) 437-0700
Fax: (703) 437-6312
http://www.arts-accredit.org

INTERNATIONAL PERIODICALS

Abitare
Editrice Segesta s.p.a.
15 c.so Monfrote 20122
Milan, Italy
http://www.abitare.it

Architectural Design
42 Leicester Gardens
London W2 3AN
England
(071) 402-2141

Architectural Record
1221 Ave. of the Americas
New York, NY 10020
(212) 512-2594
http://www.archrecord.com

Architectural Review
Architectural Press, Ltd.
33-35 Bowling Green Lane
London EC1R ODA
England
(071) 837-1212
http://www.arplus.com

Architecture
1130 Connecticut Ave., NW,
Suite 625
Washington, DC 20036
(202) 828-0995

A & U
Architecture + Urbanism
A & U Publishing Co., Ltd.
30-8 Yushima 2-chome
Bunkyo-ku
Tokyo 113, Japan
(03) 816-2935

Architecture d'Aujourd'hui
Group Expansion
67 ave. de Wagram
75017 Paris, France
763-12-11

Blueprint
26 Cramer St.
London W1M 3HE
England
(071) 486-7419

Contract
VNU Business Publications USA
770 Broadway, 4th Floor
New York, NY 10003

Daidalos
Bertelsmann Druck + Dienstlheistung
Berlin GmbH
Schlusterstrasse 42
D-1000 Berlin 15 Germany

Design Book Review
1418 Spring Way
Berkeley, CA 94708
(415) 486-1956

Domus
Editoriala Domus
Ufficio Abbonamenti
via A Grandi 5-7
20089 Rozzano
Milano, Italy

El Croquis
Barcelo 15
28004 Madrid, Spain
(91) 445-2194
http://www.elcroquis.es/default.asp

House and Garden
Conde Naste Publications
350 Madison Ave.
New York, NY 10017
(212) 880-8800
http://condenet.com/mags/hg

Harvard Architecture Review
Harvard University
Graduate School of Design
Gund Hall
48 Quincy St., #301
Cambridge, MA 02138
(617) 495-2591

IS
L.C. Clark Publishing Co.
840 U.S. Hwy. One, Suite 330
North Palm Beach, FL 33408–3834

Interior Design
Reed Business Information
360 Park Avenue South
New York, NY 10010

Japan Architect
Japan Architect Co., Ltd.
31-2 Yushima 2-chome
Bunkyo-ku
Tokyo 113, Japan
(03) 811-7101
http://www.japan-architect.co.jp

L'Arca
L'Arca edizioni SpA
Ufficio Abbonamenti
viale Bianca Mariall
20122 Milan, Italy
(02) 790240

Lotus International
Electa Periodici Srl
via D. Trentacoste 7
20134 Milan, Italy
(02) 215631

ARCHITECTURAL COLLECTIONS

American Institute of Architect's
Knowledge Center
1735 New York Ave., NW
Washington, DC 20006
(202) 626-7492

American Planning Association Library
122 S. Michigan Ave.
Chicago, IL 60603
(312) 431-9100
http://www.planning.org

Architectural Woodwork Institute Library
P.O. Box 1550
Centreville, VA 22020
(703) 222-1100
http://www.awinet.org

Arizona State University
Architecture and Environmental Design
Library
College of Architecture
Tempe, AZ 85287
(602) 965-6400
http://www.asu.edu/caed/RESOURCES/
AEDLIBRARY/html/AEDLibrary.htm

Art Institute of Chicago
Ryerson & Burnham Libraries
Michigan Ave. at Adams St.
Chicago, IL 60603
(312) 443-3666
http://www.artic.edu/aic/libraries

Athenaeum of Philadelphia
219 S. Sixth St.
Philadelphia, PA 19106
(215) 925-2688
http://www.philaathenaeum.org

Atlanta Historical Society
Archives/Library
3101 Andrews Dr., NW
Atlanta, GA 30305
(404) 261-1837

Auburn University Archives
Ralph Brown Draughon Library
Auburn, AL 36849
(205) 844-1705
http://www.lib.auburn.edu/architecture/
buildings/ralph_brown_draughon_library.
htm

Avery Architectural and Fine Arts Library
Columbia University
New York, NY 10027
(212) 854-3501
http://www.columbia.edu/cu/lweb/
indiv/avery

Boston Architectural Center Library
320 Newbury St.
Boston, MA 02115
(617) 536-9018
http://www.the-bac.edu/library

Boston Public Library
Fine Art Department
Copley Square
P.O. Box 286
Boston, MA 02117
(617) 536-5400
http://www.bpl.org

California Polytechnic State University
Environmental Design Resource Library
3801 W. Temple Ave., Bldg. 7
Pomona, CA 91768
(714) 869-2665

California Polytechnic State University
Robert E. Kennedy Library
San Luis Obispo, CA 93407
(805) 756-2344
http://www.lib.calpoly.edu

California State University, Fresno
Henry Madden Library
Department of Special Collections
Fresno, CA 93740
(209) 278-2595
http://www.lib.csufresno.edu

Chicago Public Library
Visual and Performing Arts, Art
Information Center
Harold Washington Library Center
400 S. State St.
Chicago, IL 60605
(312) 747-4800
http://www.chipublib.org/CPL.html

Cleveland Public Library
Fine Arts and Special Collections
Department
Fine Arts Section
325 Superior Ave.
Cleveland, OH 44114
(216) 623-2848
http://www.cpl.org

Colonial Williamsburg Foundation Library
Special Collections
415 N. Boundary St.
Williamsburg, VA 23187
(804) 220-7420
http://www.history.org/history/jdrlweb/
index.cfm

Cornell University
Fine Arts Library
Sibley Dome
Ithaca, NY 14853
(607) 255-3710
http://www.library.cornell.edu/finearts

Detroit Public Library
Art and Literature Department
5201 Woodward Ave.
Detroit, MI 48202
(313) 833-1470
http://www.detroit.lib.mi.us

El Paso Public Library
Southwest Collection
501 N. Oregon St.
El Paso, TX 79901
(915) 543-5440
http://www.ci.elpaso.tx.us/library/
epplmain.htm

Engineering Societies Library
United Engineering Center
345 E. 47th St.
New York, NY 10017
(212) 705-7611

Frank Lloyd Wright School of Architecture
Library
Taliesin West
Scottsdale, AZ 85261
(602) 860-2700

Free Library of Philadelphia
Art Department
Logan Square
Philadelphia, PA 19103
(215) 686-5403
http://www.library.phila.gov

Furniture Library Association Library
1009 N. Main St.
High Point, NC 27262
(919) 883-4011

General Services Administration
GSA Library
General Services Bldg., Rm. 1033
18th F St. NW
Washington, DC 20405
(202) 501-0788

Georgia Institute of Technology
Price Gilbert Memorial Library
Architecture Library
Architecture Library
225 North Ave., NW
Atlanta, GA 30332
(404) 894-4877
http://www.gatech.edu/libraries

Getty Center for the History of Art and the
Humanities
Resource Collections
401 Wilshire Blvd., Suite 400
San Monica, CA 90401
(310) 458-9811

H2M Group (Holzmacher, McLendon &
Murrell, P.C.)
575 Broad Hollow Rd.
Melville, NY 11747
(516) 756-8000

Harrington Institute of Interior Design
Design Library
410 S. Michigan Ave.
Chicago, IL 60605
(312) 939-4975
http://www.interiordesign.edu/about.
asp#dl

Harvard University
Graduate School of Design
Frances Loeb Library
Gund Hall
Cambridge, MA 02138
(617) 495-2574
http://www.gsd.harvard.edu/library

Hellmuth, Obata & Kassabaum, Inc.
HOK Library
1831 Chestnut St.
St. Louis, MO 63103
(314) 421-2000

Illinois Institute of Technology
Paul V. Galvin Library
35 W.33rd St.
Chicago, IL 60616
(312) 567-6844
http://www.gl.iit.edu

Library of Congress
Humanities and Social Sciences Division
Microform Reading Room Section
Thomas Jefferson Building, LJ-140B
Washington, DC 20540
(202) 707-5471
http://www.loc.gov/rr/microform/guide

Library of Congress
Prints & Photographs Division
James Madison Memorial Building
LM 339
Washington, DC 20540
(202) 707-5836
http://lcweb.loc.gov/rr/print

Massachusetts Institute of Technology
Rotch Library of Architecture and
Planning
Rm. 7-238
Cambridge, MA 02139
(617) 258-5599
http://libraries.mit.edu/rotch

Massachusetts Institute of Technology
Rotch Library of Architecture and
Planning
Visual Collections
Rm. 7-304
Cambridge, MA 02139
(617) 253-7098
http://libraries.mit.edu/rotch

Metropolitan Museum of Art
Photograph and Slide Library
1000 Fifth Ave.
New York, NY 10028
(212) 879-5500
http://www.metmuseum.org

Montana State University Library
Special Collections
P.O. Box 173320
Bozeman, MT 59717
(406) 994-4242
http://www.lib.montana.edu

National Archives & Records
Administration
Cartographic & Architectural Branch
8th & Pennsylvania Ave., NW
Washington, DC 20408
(703) 756-6700

National Association of Home Builders
National Housing Library
1201 15th St., NW
Washington, DC 20005
(800) 368-5242
http://www.nahb.org

National Gallery of Art
Gallery Archives
Washington, DC 20565
(202) 842-6614
http://www.nga.gov

National Gallery of Art Library
6th & Constitution Ave., NW
Washington, DC 20565
(202) 842-6511
http://www.nga.gov

New York Public Library
Miriam and Ira D. Wallach Division of Art,
Prints & Photographs
Art and Architecture Collection
Fifth Ave. & 42nd St., Rm. 313
New York, NY 10018
(212) 930-0834
http://www.nypl.org/research/chss/spe/art/
photo/photo.html

Newark Public Library
New Jersey Reference Division
5 Washington St.
Box 630
Newark, NJ 07101
(201) 733-7776
http://www.npl.org

Oak Park Public Library
Local Author and Local History Collections
834 Lake St.
Oak Park, IL 60301
(708) 383-8200
http://www.oppl.org

Oberlin College
Clarence Ward Art Library
Allen Art Bldg.
Oberlin, OH 44074
(216) 775-8635
http://www.oberlin.edu/library/libncollect/
art/Default.html

Payette Associates, Inc. Library
28 S. Summer St.
Boston, MA 02210
(617) 342-8201

Princeton University
Marquand Library
McCormick Hall
Princeton, NJ 08544
(609) 258-5860
http://libweb.princeton.edu/libraries/
marquand.php

Princeton University
Rare Books and Special Collections
Firestone Library
Princeton, NJ 08544
(609) 258-3184
http://libweb.princeton.edu/libraries/
firestone.php

Princeton University
School of Architecture Library
Princeton, NJ 08544
(609) 258-3256
http://libterminal.princeton.edu/ues/
UES_PAGE/index.htm

Robert Scott Small Library
Special Collections
College of Charleston
Charleston, SC 29401
(803) 953-8016
http://www.cofc.edu/~library/cofclib.html

Smithsonian Institution Libraries
Cooper-Hewitt Museum of Design
2 E. 91st St.
New York, NY 10128
(212) 860-6887
http://www.si.edu/archives/archives/
2ba19.htm

Society for the Preservation of New
England Antiquities Library
141 Cambridge St.
Boston, MA 02114
(617) 227-3956
http://www.spnea.org/visit/coll.htm

Society of the Four Arts Library
Four Arts Plaza
Palm Beach, FL 33480
(407) 655-2766
http://www.fourarts.org

Syracuse University
E.S. Bird Library
Fine Arts Department
Syracuse, NY 13244
(315) 443-2440
http://libwww.syr.edu

Theatre Historical Society Archives
York Theatre Bldg., 2nd Floor, Suite 200
152 N. York Rd.
Elmhurst, IL 60126
(708) 782-1800
http://www.historictheatres.org

Tulane University
Howard-Tilton Memorial Library
Southeastern Architectural Archive
New Orleans, LA 70118
(504) 865-5697
http://www.tulane.edu/~html

Tuskegee University, Architecture Library
Wilcox Building A
Tuskegee, AL 36088
(205) 727-8351
http://www.tusk.edu/library/libraries

U.S. Department of Housing and Urban
Development Library
451 7th St., SW, Rm. 8141
Washington, DC 20410
(202) 708-2370
http://www.hud.gov/library/index.cfm

University of California, Berkeley
Environmental Design Library
210 Wurster Hall
Berkeley, CA 94720
(510) 642-4818
http://www.lib.berkeley.edu/ENVI

University of California, Los Angeles
Arts Library
2250 Dickson Art Center
Los Angeles, CA 90024
(310) 825-3817
http://www.library.ucla.edu/libraries/arts

University of Kansas
Kansas Collection
220 Spencer Research Library
Lawrence, KS 66045
(913) 864-4274
http://spencer.lib.ku.edu/kc

University of Maryland
National Trust for Historic Preservation
Library Collection
College Park, MD 20742
(301) 405-6320
http://www.lib.umd.edu/NTL/ntl.html

University of Minnesota
Manuscripts Division
826 Berry St.
St. Paul, MN 55114
(612) 627-4199
http://special.lib.umn.edu/manuscripts

University of Missouri–Kansas City
Western Historical Manuscript Collection
302 Newcomb Hall
Kansas City, MO 64110
(816) 235-1543
http://www.umkc.edu/whmckc

University of Nevada, Reno
Special Collections Department/University
Archives
University Library
Reno, NV 89557
(702) 784-6538
http://www.library.unr.edu

University of Oregon Library
Architecture & Allied Arts Library
Eugene, OR 97403
(503) 346-3637
http://libweb.uoregon.edu/index.php

University of Pennsylvania
Architectural Archives
Furness Building
220 S. 34th St.
Philadelphia, PA 19104
(215) 898-8323
http://www.upenn.edu/gsfa/archives/
archives/index.html

University of Pennsylvania
Fisher Fine Arts Library
Furness Building
220 S. 34th St.
Philadelphia, PA 19104
(215) 898-8325
http://www.library.upenn.edu/finearts/
finearts.html

University of Southern California
Helen Topping Architecture & Fine Arts
Library
800 Watt Way, Rm. 4
Los Angeles, CA 90089
(213) 740-1956
http://artscenter.usc.edu/afa

University of Southern California
School of Architecture
Greene and Greene Library
c/o Huntington Library
1151 Oxford Rd.
San Marino, CA 91108
(818) 405-2232

University of Texas Libraries
Humanities Research Center
Austin, TX 78713
(512) 471-9119
http://www.lib.utexas.edu

University of Utah
Special Collections Department
Marriott Library
Salt Lake City, UT 84112
(801) 581-8863
http://www.lib.utah.edu

University of Virginia
Fiske Kimball Fine Arts Library
Bayly Dr.
Charlottesville, VA 22903
(804) 924-7024
http://www.lib.virginia.edu/fine-arts

University of Washington
Collections & Preservation Division
Seattle, WA 98195
(206) 543-1929
http://www.lib.washington.edu

Urban Land Institute
Information Center
625 Indiana Ave., NW
Washington, DC 20004
(202) 624-7117
http://www.uli.org

Virginia Historical Society Library
428 North Blvd.
Box 7311
Richmond, VA 23221
(804) 358-4901
http://www.vahistorical.org/research/
main.htm

Virginia Polytechnic Institute
International Archive of Women in
Architecture
Special Collections Department
P.O. Box 90001
Blacksburg, VA 24062
(703) 231-6308
http://spec.lib.vt.edu/IAWA

Yale University
Art and Architecture Library
Yale Station, Box 1650A
New Haven, CT 06520
(203) 432-2640
http://www.library.yale.edu/art/aa.html

GLOSSARY

above-base building standard Materials and constructions that are not included in the base building standard.

absorption The process of soaking up energy.

acid-curing finish A solvent-based wood floor finish.

acknowledgment A confirmation of the purchase order, in regard to the purchase orders.

acrylic (1) A clear, transparent plastic material widely used for skylights and security glazing. (2) A manufactured fiber composed primarily of acrylonitrile.

addenda Contract modifications made to the bidding documents.

additive Substance added to another in relatively small amounts to impart or improve desirable characteristics.

administrative law That body of law, including decrees and legal decisions, generated by administrative agencies, boards, and commissions. Involves the administration of law by nonjudicial agencies created by the executive or legislative branches of the government.

agency A legal agreement between two persons, whereby one is designated the agent of the other.

agent A person authorized to act on behalf of another and subject to the other's control in dealing with third parties.

agreement The contract document that briefly states the work of the contract, the project time, and the contract sum. It includes other contract documents by reference.

alkaline A material having a pH greater than 7.0 in water.

alkyd A resin formed by the combination of alcohol and acid.

alloy A metal made from mixing various metals to combine their desirable properties.

annealed glass Glass cooled under conditions to minimize internal stresses.

anodize A finish applied principally to aluminum, which involves passing an electrical current across a solution, most commonly sulfuric acid, in which the aluminum is immersed.

application rate The amount of paint that must be applied to a surface to achieve the desired performance, given as the area of substrate in square feet that should be covered by a gallon of paint, or sq ft/gal. For example, an intumescent paint may have to be applied at a rate of 190 sq ft/gal to achieve the required coating thickness, whereas a regular paint may have an application rate of 300 sq ft/gal.

aramid A manufactured fiber with low flammability and high strength used in firefighter's apparel, barrier fabrics between upholstery cushions and fabric, and in bullet-resistant vests.

austenitic A process by which steel is heated above a certain temperature causing certain components to transform to austentite, making the steel nonmagnetic; named after Sir William Roberts-Austen who invented the process.

Axminster A woven carpet in which successive weft-wise rows of pile are inserted during the weaving process according to a predetermined arrangement of colors.

base building The commercial office building shell and core, including essential services such as the elevator, HVAC system, and toilet rooms.

base building standard A package of typical tenant improvements provided by, and sometimes required by, the landlord. Sometimes called the *building standard*.

beck dyeing A textile dye method consisting of advancing a continuous loop of textile through a dye bath.

bill of lading A document evidencing the receipt of goods for shipment and issued by a person engaged in the business of transporting or forwarding goods.

bill of sale A written statement evidencing the transfer of personal property from one person to another.

blackout lining A fabric backing used with a drapery to darken a room completely.

book match The back of the top wood veneer leaf is matched to the face of the lower leaf, creating a mirror image and continuity in grain, much like the open leaves of a book.

brass A copper-zinc alloy.

bronze Originally, a copper-tin alloy; today the term is used to identify other alloys with a bronze color.

building code A set of laws that set forth the minimum requirements for design and construction to protect public health and safety.

building gross area The floor area within the exterior face of the building, including the thickness of the exterior wall.

bulked continuous filament (BCF) Continuous strands of synthetic fiber that are formed into yarn bundles without the need for spinning.

butt master carrier A drapery carrier that holds the drapery end traversing the rod and joins it to the other drapery end with no overlap. Butt master carriers are often used in roll pleat and stack pleat draperies.

calendering A process used to manufacture vinyl wallcovering that squeezes vinyl to the consistency of dough over a series of hot metal rollers, flattening the compound into a sheet.

calfskin The hide of a young animal.

carbon steel Steel containing up to 1.20% carbon with, generally, no other alloying elements added.

carrier A business that undertakes to transport persons or goods or both.

cascade A lined window treatment with folds of fabric hanging from the top of a drapery heading.

casement A sheer or semisheer fabric window treatment, often used with operable over-drapes or fixed side panels.

casework Cabinets, cases, fixtures, or other storage units that are built in or attached to the building.

cast Produced by pouring molten material into a mold.

catalyzed lacquer A lacquer containing nitrocellulose that dries harder and faster than noncatalyzed lacquer, but cannot be easily touched up.

cattle hide The skin of a fully grown cow.

Ceiling Sound Transmission Class (CSTC) A value that correlates with the reduction of sound, expressed in increments of 5. The higher the CSTC, the better the sound reduction capability of the ceiling system.

cementitious backerboard Smooth, lightweight boards made of portland cement or treated gypsum and lightweight aggregate, and reinforced with glass fiber, that are sometimes used as an underlayment for thinset installations. They are designed to provide a water-resistant base for ceramic tile installations regularly exposed to water (for example, in a shower surround).

ceramic mosaic tile Tile with a face area of less than 6 sq in. (150 sq mm).

change directive A written contract modification when the consequent alteration of the contract sum or schedule has not yet been agreed upon.

change order A written contract modification altering the contract sum. Only the owner can authorize a change order.

chemical finish For metals, a finish produced by the reaction of a metal surface to various chemical solutions.

C.I.F. Cost, insurance, and freight. Terms instructing a carrier to collect the cost of goods shipped, insurance, and freight charges.

code A compilation of statutes; a set of laws.

C.O.L. Customer's own leather. Leather that is not supplied by the product manufacturer.

colorfastness The capability of a material to retain its original hue.

color through A term used to describe high-pressure decorative laminates that are a uniform color throughout the thickness of the sheet.

colorway A set of colors for a given pattern or texture. Fabric or wallcovering manufacturers offer a pattern in a variety of colorways to suit different color schemes.

C.O.M. Customer's own material. Material, typically fabric, that is not supplied by the product manufacturer.

common areas Corridors, lavatories, elevator vestibules, and other areas that tenants share in common.

common carrier A company that transports goods or persons for compensation and offers its facilities to the general public without discrimination. Compare *contract carrier*.

common law The body of recorded court decisions that courts refer to and rely upon when making legal decisions. Past judicial decisions and reasoning; involves the application of precedent in applying the law.

compression modulus An indication of a foam's support, calculated by indenting the foam to 65% of its original height and dividing it by the IFD.

concealed grid ceiling system A suspended ceiling system where the grid supporting the ceiling tiles is not visible in the finished ceiling. Also referred to as a *concealed spline system*.

conditions of the contract The document that establishes the duties and responsibilities of the construction or FF&E contractor, the owner, and the designer. The conditions of the contract consist of the general conditions and the supplementary conditions.

conduction The transfer of heat energy through a substance.

consideration In contract law, the mutual promise to exchange benefits and sacrifices between the parties.

constitution The basic law of a nation or state.

constitutional law That body of law that involves a constitution and its interpretation.

continuous piece dyeing A textile dye method in which the greige goods travel through a long production line. First, an applicator spreads dye on the greige goods, then the dye is fixed in a steamer, and the piece is washed and dried.

contract An agreement between two or more component parties, based on mutual promises to do or to refrain from doing some particular thing that is neither illegal nor impossible. The agreement results in an obligation or a duty that can be enforced in a court of law.

contract carrier A carrier that provides transportation for compensation only to those people with whom it desires to do business. Compare *common carrier*.

contract documents The documents that describe the work included in the contract. Contract documents consist of the contract forms (including the agreement, bonds, and certificates) the conditions of the contract, the specifications, the drawings, and the addenda.

contract for construction An agreement between the owner and the construction contractor to provide expertise and service.

contract for FF&E An agreement between the owner and the FF&E contractor to provide services such as warehousing, delivery, and installation. It is primarily a sale-of-goods contract.

contract modifications Changes to the construction or FF&E documents, including addenda, change orders, change directives, and supplemental instructions.

convection The transfer of heat energy through air.

cork The outer layer of the cork oak tree that is harvested for use as, among other things, resilient flooring.

crocking Rubbing off.

curtain A hanging textile window treatment. Usually refers to an unlined treatment with a gathered or shirred heading.

dealer The local or regional presence of a manufacturer that processes sales and provides various support and follow-up services to the consumer.

dedicated circuit An electrical circuit with three conductors, consisting of hot, neutral, and ground, between the final overcurrent device protecting the circuit and the outlets that are reserved for use only with specific equipment.

delamination The separation of two materials that had been bonded together.

delivery The transfer of possession from one person to another.

demised premises That portion of a property covered by a lease agreement, usually defined by the walls and other structures that separate one tenant's space from that of another.

demising walls The partitions that separate one tenant's space from another.

denier A unit of yarn measurement equal to the weight in grams of 9,000 meters of the yarn.

density The mass-per-unit volume.

descriptive specification Specifications that detail the requirements for products, materials, and workmanship.

design-award-build The traditional approach to a construction contract whereby the designer prepares the contract documents, the contract is awarded to a construction contractor, and the project is built.

design/build A construction contract process wherein one party is responsible for both the design and the construction.

destination contract A contract under which the seller is required to deliver goods to a place of destination. Title passes to the buyer when the seller delivers the goods.

dimension stone Quarried stone with usually one or more mechanically dressed surfaces.

dimension stone tile Dimension stone that is less than ¾ in. (19 mm) thick.

direct glue-down The most common method of commercial carpet installation, whereby the carpet is glued directly to the floor without a cushion. This is the most dimensionally stable carpet installation method and is often required for stair or ramp applications.

direct sales force A selling team that represents the product's manufacturer, not the manufacturer's dealer.

double glue-down A carpet installation method whereby the carpet cushion is adhered to the floor and the carpet is then glued to the cushion.

drapery A hanging, textile window treatment. Usually refers to lined treatments with a stiffened, constructed heading requiring a traversing rod and carriers.

drawings Graphic representations describing the shape and form of the space and the quantities, sizes, and locations of materials and goods. Part of the contract documents.

drop shipment A shipment whereby goods are shipped to a destination different from that of the party who ordered and paid for them.

dry film thickness (DFT) The thickness of the cured paint or coating finish measured in mils (1/1000 in.).

electrolyte A liquid that conducts electricity.

emissivity No or low reflectivity. If a surface has high reflectivity, it has low emissivity.

end A yarn loop in the surface of a carpet.

end match Wood veneers are book matched, then the ends of the sheets are matched, creating a long and wide matching veneer piece.

exposed grid ceiling system A ceiling suspension system of square or rectilinear frames that are visible in the finished ceiling and hold attached or loose laid panels.

express warranty An oral or written statement, promise, or other representation about the quality of a product.

extruded Produced by forcing semimolten material through a die.

face weight The weight of the carpet pile yarn in ounces per square yard; also referred to as *pile weight* or *yarn weight*.

fast-track A construction contract process whereby construction begins before the project design is complete. Separate construction contracts are defined, and contract documents are prepared for each phase. Fast-tracking often increases construction cost due to decreased labor efficiency.

ferrous Consisting mostly of iron; from the Latin *ferrum*, meaning iron.

FF&E Furniture, furnishings, and equipment. Those items included in a project that are considered removable and not part of the construction.

fiber A fine hairlike strand that forms the basis of a yarn.

fiber cushion A carpet cushion made by needlepunching natural fiber, synthetic fiber, or a combination of the two, into a feltlike pad.

fiberglass Glass in fibrous form used in making various products.

filament fiber A long, continuous fiber measured in meters or yards.

filament yarn Continuous strands of silk or of synthetic fiber from a spinerette, twisted together.

fire-resistant A substance that resists the spread of fire by not contributing to the flame.

flame-retardant A substance that slows the rate at which a fire spreads.

flammability The capability to support combustion.

flammability standard A specified level of flammability performance.

flammability test method A group of procedures carried out by a testing laboratory to measure whether a product conforms to the stated acceptance criteria or classification cited by the flammability standard.

flash cove An integral, monolithic wall base for finish flooring.

flitch (1) The section of the wood log ready to be sliced into leaves; (2) the bundle of leaves stacked in sequence after slicing.

float glass Glass sheet manufactured by cooling a layer of liquid glass on a bath of molten tin.

F.O.B. Defined by the UCC as "free on board." It is the place where the title to the goods and risk of loss pass from the seller to the buyer. The buyer pays the transportation costs from the point named in the F.O.B. "place." (UCC 2-319).

F.O.B. factory-freight prepaid Term indicating that the buyer has title to the goods during transit, but the supplier pays the transportation charges to the destination. In this way, the buyer has the convenience of not having to arrange for transportation and the supplier reduces its liability.

F.O.B. place of destination Term indicating the seller is responsible for delivering the goods. The cost of the goods includes shipping charges. If the goods are stolen, damaged, or destroyed in transit, it is the seller's responsibility to recover damages from the carrier (UCC 2-319).

F.O.B. place of shipment Term indicating that the buyer owns the goods at the place of shipment (typically, the manufacturer's factory loading dock). The goods are given to the carrier (typically, a truck), and the seller is no longer responsible for the delivery of the goods or their condition upon arrival. The buyer pays for shipping. If the goods are stolen, damaged, or destroyed in transit, it is the buyer's responsibility to recover damages from the carrier. When the terms of shipment do not specify shipping point or destination, it is assumed to be F.O.B. place of shipment.

French pleat A traditional, folded and stitched drapery heading, sometimes referred to as a *pinch pleat*.

full-grain leather Leather with the original, genuine grain of the hide; the most expensive type of hides.

fullness In reference to draperies and curtains, fullness is the ratio of the total fabric used, less allowances for side hems and seams, to the finished drapery width. For example, a drapery with 100% fullness is 100% wider than the width of the drapery in a closed position, or twice the finished drapery width.

full warranty Under the Magnuson-Moss Warranty Act, a defective product will be fixed or replaced free within a reasonable time after a complaint has been made about the product.

furnish To supply and deliver to the project site, ready for unloading, unpacking, assembly, installation, and similar operations.

furniture dealer The local or regional presence of the furniture manufacturer that processes furniture sales and provides various support and follow-up services.

fusion-bonded carpet A thermoplastic carpet tile manufacturing process whereby yarns are attached to a backing material by means of adhesion rather than tufting or weaving.

gage Measurement according to some standard or system. Also spelled "gauge."

galvanic corrosion Metal corrosion caused by an electrolyte.

galvanize The application of zinc to the surface of cast iron, steel, or steel alloys to prevent corrosion.

gauge (carpet) The measure of the spacing of the tufting needles, center to center, in a tufted carpet.

gel coat A pigmented polyester coating that is applied to the inside surface of a mold and becomes an integral part of a finished piece; for example, a cultured marble countertop.

general conditions of the contract Standardized documents establishing the duties and responsibilities of the construction or FF&E contractor, the owner, and the designer. The general conditions are modified through the supplementary conditions of the contract. See *conditions of the contract*.

glass-reinforced gypsum (GRG) A high-strength, high-density gypsum, reinforced with extruded glass fibers, that is molded to the required shape.

glazed tile A ceramic tile with an impervious finish composed of ceramic materials fused to the face of the tile. The body of a glazed tile may be nonvitreous, semivitreous, vitreous, or impervious.

gloss The relative luminous reflectance. Defined by ASTM D523, *Standard Test Method for Specular Gloss*.

goods All things (including specially manufactured goods) which are movable at the time of identification to the contract for sale other than the money in which the price is to be paid, investment securities, and things in action. (UCC 2-105).

greige goods An unfinished fabric just off the loom or knitting machine.

gypsum Hydrous calcium sulfate.

gypsum board An interior facing panel made from a gypsum core sandwiched between paper faces; also called *drywall*, *sheet rock*, or *plasterboard*.

hand A fabric's tactile qualities, for example, softness, firmness, drapability, and resiliency.

hardboard A very dense panel product manufactured in a manner similar to medium-density fiberboard (MDF) but under higher pressure, often without adhesive.

hardwood Wood from a deciduous tree.

heat-strengthened glass Glass that has been strengthened by heat treatment, but not to the extent of fully tempered glass.

heat-treated glass Glass that has been strengthened by heat treatment; either fully tempered glass or heat-strengthened glass.

honed A satin smooth stone finish with a dull sheen.

high-pressure decorative laminate (HPDL) Plastic laminate; commonly used for countertops.

hygrometer A device that measures relative humidity.

Impact Noise Rating (INR) A measurement of the sound insulation of a floor and ceiling assembly.

implied warranty A warranty imposed by law rather than by statements, descriptions, or samples given by the seller.

Indentation Force Deflection (IFD) A measure of foam firmness.

install To set up for use or service, including unloading, unpacking, assembly, erection, placing, anchoring, applying, working to dimension, finishing, curing, protecting, cleaning, and similar operations.

Interzone Attenuation and Articulation Class (AC) A single-figure rating measuring the sound-reflective characteristics of ceiling systems in spaces with partial-height walls.

intumescent Swelling and charring when exposed to flame. An intumescent substance expands to form an insulating char when exposed to fire.

Jacquard loom A loom used for figured fabrics such as tapestries, brocades, and damask weaves. Jacquard weaving uses a series of punched cards. Each card perforation controls the action of one warp yarn.

lacquer A coating that dries extremely quickly through the evaporation of a volatile solvent.

lamb's wool Wool sheared from sheep under eight months of age.

laminated glass A glazing material consisting of outer layers of glass laminated to an inner layer of plastic.

landlord A person who owns real property and who rents or leases it to someone else; a lessor.

law A set of rules created by the governing body of a society to ensure the orderly maintenance of that society.

lease A contract granting the use of certain real property to another for a specified period of time in return for payment of rent.

leaves Individual wood veneer slices cut from a log section.

limited warranty Under the Magnuson-Moss Warranty Act, a warranty that is not a full warranty.

lining A fabric backing used to enhance certain qualities of a fabric, for example, drapability, energy performance, and protection from ultraviolet (UV) radiation.

linoleum A resilient flooring material composed of oxidized linseed oil or other resins, mixed with cork or wood flour, mineral fillers, and pigments; derived from the botanical terms for "flax," *linum,* and "oil," *oleum.*

MasterFormat A list of six-digit numbers and titles that classify the materials and requirements of construction and FF&E projects, promulgated by the Construction Specification Institute (CSI).

mastic A pastelike adhesive.

mechanical finish For metals, a finish accomplished by buffing, grinding, polishing, or otherwise texturing the metal surface.

medium-density fiberboard (MDF) A panel product manufactured by breaking down wood particles into fibers by steam pressure, mixing them with adhesive resins, and pressing them into panels.

mercerization A treatment of cotton yarn or fabric to increase its luster and affinity for dyes. The material is immersed under tension in a cold sodium hydroxide solution and is later neutralized in acid. The process causes a permanent swelling of the fiber and thus increases its luster.

merchant A person who deals in goods of the kind sold in the ordinary course of business or who otherwise claims to have knowledge or skills peculiar to those goods.

mineral tanning A leather tanning process using a tanning solution based on chromium salts. Mineral-tanned hides accept dyes well, including rich, vibrant colors. About 90% of leather today is tanned by this method.

natural fiber Textile fiber from animal, plant, or mineral sources.

needlepunched carpet A method of manufacturing carpet by layering tick fiber batts (typically polypropylene) over a support fabric and punching barbed needles through the support fabric.

Noise Reduction Coefficient (NRC) A rating of the sound-absorbing efficiency of a material.

noncatalyzed lacquer An easy-to-apply, touch-up, and recoat solvent-based lacquer, forming a monolithic finish. Sometimes referred to as *standard lacquer.*

nonferrous Containing little or no iron.

nonvitreous An absorption of 7.0% or more when used to describe ceramic tile.

nonvolatile Does not readily evaporate.

oil-modified polyurethane An easy-to-apply, affordable wood floor finish that tends to amber (turn slightly orange) as it ages.

olefin A manufactured fiber of light weight, high strength, and good abrasion resistance. It is used primarily in the manufacture of indoor-outdoor carpet.

on center Spacing measured from the center of one component to the center of the next.

one-way draw A drapery or curtain operation that opens entirely to one side, designated as either *full left* or *full right,* indicating the direction in which the drapery stacks as you face it. For example, if you are looking at an open drapery stacked on the right, it is a right draw.

ordinance A statute or regulation enacted by a municipal (city or town) government.

oriented strand board (OSB) A panel product manufactured from thin, narrow strands of both hardwood and softwood that are blended with adhesive and formed into a multilayer panel.

overlap master carrier A drapery carrier that holds the drapery end traversing the rod and joins it to the other drapery end with an overlap. Overlap master carriers are often used in conventional pleated draperies.

PageFormat A page organization for specifications promulgated by the Construction Specification Institute (CSI).

panel When referring to window treatments, a panel is a single drapery unit of one or more fabric widths.

parquet Wood flooring consisting of small lengths of wood strips, either individual slats or preconfigured into tiles, that are arranged to form patterns.

particleboard A panel product manufactured from wood particles and fibers that are bonded under heat and pressure with an adhesive resin.

patina A thin layer of corrosion resulting from oxidation.

paver tiles Ceramic tiles with a face size of 6 sq in. (1,150 sq mm) or more.

performance specification Specifications that describe the required results.

pH A numeric scale used to indicate how acidic or basic (alkaline) a solution is.

piece dyeing The dyeing of fabrics after weaving or knitting, as opposed to dyeing in the form of yarn.

pigment An insoluble substance used as coloring.

pile In carpets, the face yarn, as opposed to the backing yarn.

pile density The weight of the pile yarn in a given volume of carpet face.

pile height The length of a carpet tuft from the backing to the tip of the tuft.

pile weight See *face weight.*

pinch pleat A traditional, folded and stitched drapery heading, sometimes referred to as a *French pleat.*

pitch The number of ends (yarn loops) in a 27 in. (685 mm) width of carpet.

plain sawn Cuts made tangentially to the annual growth ring of a tree. This sawing method produces the least waste and requires the least labor.

plain weave One of the three fundamental weaves: plain, satin, and twill. Each weft yarn passes successively over and under each warp yarn, alternating each row.

plastisol A method of manufacturing vinyl wallcovering that spreads liquid vinyl onto a backing material as it is rolled by. The materials are then fused together under high temperatures.

pleat to The width of the drapery after it has been pleated. For example, if a 48 in. (121.92 cm) width of fabric is 19 in. (48.26 cm) after it has been pleated, it is specified as "pleat to 19 in. (48.26 cm)."

plenum The space between a finished ceiling and the structure above.

plywood A sandwich of wood or wood products between two layers of wood veneer, top and bottom.

polyester A manufactured fiber of high strength that is resistant to shrinking and stretching; a quick-drying fiber with good crease retention and wrinkle resistance.

polymer A giant molecule composed of many identical simple molecules.

polymerization The process by which polymers are formed; the basic formation of plastics.

polyurethane A large group of resins and plastic compounds used in varnishes, insulation foam, and sealants.

precedent A model case that a court can follow when facing a similar situation.

prescriptive specifications Specifications that delineate product or material attributes.

primer A substance that prepares a surface for the application of a finish by increasing the surface adhesion.

private carrier A company that transports goods or persons under individual contract with those seeking its service. A private carrier is not required to serve all requests, unlike a common carrier.

project site The space available to the construction or FF&E contractor for performance of construction or installation activities. The extent of the project site should be shown on the drawings.

proprietary specifications Specifications requiring a specific product from a specific manufacturer.

pro rata Proportionately.

provide To furnish and install, complete and ready for the intended use.

purchase order The form used to order goods. It contains a description of the goods, the supplier's catalog identification code, the number of items required, and the price.

purchase order acknowledgment A confirmation of the purchase order.

quarry tile A tile that is extruded from either natural clay or shale.

quarter sawn Cuts made with the growth rings at 60° to 90° angles to the face of the board. This sawing method is not available for all species of wood.

R-value The insulating effect of a material; a material's resistance to the flow of heat.

radiation The transmission of energy by invisible light waves independent of a substance or air.

railroading Fabric applied in a horizontal manner, the way in which it is unrolled from the bolt, with the selvage edge parallel to the seat cushion edge.

rayon A manufactured fiber composed of regenerated cellulose; originally known as artificial silk.

real property The ground and anything permanently attached to it, including land, buildings, and growing trees and shrubs; the air space above it and the land.

receipt Taking physical possession of goods (UCC 2-103).

reducing strip An extruded piece that creates a smooth transition and connection between floorings of different types and, possibly, heights.

reference standard specifications Specifications based on the requirements set by an accepted authority.

reflection Energy bending back from and not penetrating a surface.

regulation A governmental order with the force of law.

rentable area The floor area that a tenant pays rent on; usually defined as the interior floor area excluding vertical penetrations through the floor, for example, air shafts, elevators, and stairways.

repeat Distance between two identical patterns in a length of material, typically fabric or wallcovering.

resilient flooring A manufactured sheet or tile of polyvinyl chloride, linoleum, cork, or other material with resilience.

resin A nonvolatile (does not readily evaporate) component of paints, coatings, and plastics.

return In reference to window treatments, the return is the distance from the traversing rod to the wall or the depth of the projection.

rift sawn Cuts made with growth rings at 30° to 60° angles to the face of the board.

roll pleat A soft, rounded, uncreased drapery heading.

rotary cutting A wood veneer slicing method that produces wide sheets of veneer. The log is mounted on a lathe and the veneer is sliced off as the log spins around.

rows The number of ends (yarn loops) per inch in a lengthwise section of Axminster carpet.

safety glass Glazing material that complies with ANSI Z97.1, *Safety Glazing Materials Used in Buildings.*

sale The passing of title to goods from the seller to the buyer for a price.

samples Examples of materials or workmanship.

satin weave One of the three fundamental weaves: plain, satin, and twill. The face of the fabric consists almost completely of floating warp yarns. Satin-weave fabrics have a characteristic smooth, lustrous surface.

SectionFormat A three-part format for the organization of specification sections, promulgated by the Construction Specification Institute (CSI).

selvage (also *selvedge*) The narrow edge of woven fabric that runs parallel to the warp. It is made with stronger yarns in a tighter construction than the body of the fabric, to prevent raveling.

semivitreous An absorption of more than 3.0%, but not more than 7.0%, when used to describe ceramic tile.

sericulture The growth of silk moths for their silk production.

setting material A substance used to fix tile; includes the traditional mortars and the relatively new adhesives.

shading coefficient (SC) A measure of a window systems capability to reduce heat gain.

sheen The reflectance of a surface.

shop drawings Detailed drawings prepared by a fabricator to guide the production of the item, for example, casework.

silicone A polymer used for high-range sealants and water repellents.

skein dyeing The dyeing of yarn in the form of skeins.

slip match Adjacent wood veneer leaves are laid side by side in sequence, in a repeating pattern with no continuity in grain.

softwood Wood from a coniferous tree.

solid surfacing material A thick, dense synthetic sheet, uniform through the depth of the material; known by the trade name Corian, manufactured by Du Pont.

specifications Written contract documents that describe the quality of materials and their construction or installation.

split leather Leather made by slicing the hide into two or three layers. The inside layer is often finished as suede.

sponge rubber cushion A carpet cushion made of flat sponge, ripple (waffle) sponge, or reinforced foam rubber. Sponge rubber cushions are generally open-cell forms.

spun yarn Staple fibers twisted together to form a continuous strand.

stack back The width of a window treatment in a fully open position beside the window.

stack pleat A creased drapery heading with the pleat crease sewn front and back for the length of the drapery.

stain A transparent or opaque coating that penetrates and colors a wood surface without masking its inherent grain.

standard A material specification, practice, or test method based on technical research and testing by industry experts.

staple fiber A short fiber, typically measured in centimeters or inches. All natural fibers except silk are staple fibers.

static generation The tendency of a substance to generate static electricity.

statute A law passed by legislature.

statutory law The body of law that includes statutes and ordinances.

stitches The number of ends sewn by the needles down the length of a tufted carpet.

stretch-in installation The traditional method of carpet installation whereby the carpet is stretched over a cushion and attached at the perimeter with a tack strip.

strike off A small printed sample of a custom order for the designer's review and approval.

stock dyeing The dyeing of fibers in staple form.

subfloor The load-bearing surface beneath the finish surface.

supplemental instructions An interpretation or clarification of the contract documents by the designer that does not alter the contract sum or schedule.

supplementary conditions of the contract Customized document modifying the duties and responsibilities of the construction or FF&E contractor, the owner, and the designer, as described in the general conditions. See *conditions of the contract.*

swag A textile window treatment heading with draped soft folds at the tops of drapery.

synthetic fiber Textile fibers that are man-made.

tempered glass Glass that has been heat-treated to increase its toughness and its resistance to breakage.

tenant A person who has temporary possession of an interest in the real property of another.

tenant improvement Materials and construction that form the infill responding to the tenant's needs.

tenant improvement allowance A sum of money allowed for tenant improvements, typically including standard items that will be installed at no cost to the tenant. The quantity of tenant improvements in the allowance is usually described per square foot of rentable space.

tender An offer or performance by one party to a contract which, if unjustifiably refused, places the other party in default and permits the party making the tender to exercise remedies for breach of contract.

terrazzo A floor finish material consisting of concrete with an aggregate of marble chips selected for color and size, which is ground and polished smooth after curing.

testing laboratory An independent entity engaged to perform specific inspections or tests, either at the project site or elsewhere, and to report on and, if required, to interpret the results.

textile Fabric made of fibers, whether woven, knitted, felted, or manufactured by some other means.

thermal finish A stone finish achieved by the application of intense flaming heat to the surface of the stone. Thermal finishes are usually applied to granite.

thermoplastics Plastics that become soft when heated and can be remolded repeatedly without affecting the properties of the plastic.

thermosets Plastics that are permanently hardened after undergoing an irreversible chemical change during processing.

thick-set A ceramic tile setting method using a thick bed of portland cement mortar.

thinner That portion of a paint or coating that is volatile (readily evaporates); the thinner does not become part of the cured film.

thin-set A ceramic tile setting method using a thin layer of dry-set mortar or latex-portland cement mortar.

title The right of ownership to goods. A subdivision of a code containing all the statutes that deal with a particular area of law.

top-grain leather Leather in which the original surface pattern, including scars from barbed wire or brands, is removed by abrasion. This skinless surface is embossed with a pattern, typically resembling the grain of the skin that was removed.

transmission The penetration of energy through a substance.

tuft A cluster of yarns drawn through a fabric or backing and projecting from the surface in the form of cut yarns or loops.

tuft bind The force required to pull a tuft out of a finished carpet. The industry standard for measuring tuft bind is ASTM D 1335, *Standard Test Method for Tuft Bind of Pile Floor Covering.*

tufted carpet Carpet produced by a tufting machine instead of a loom; much as in sewing, the needles are forced through a backing material forming loops, or tufts.

twill weave One of the three fundamental weaves: plain, satin, and twill. A weave characterized by diagonal lines produced by a series of staggered floating warp threads.

two-way draw A drapery or curtain operation that parts drapery panels that meet in the center, opening to either side.

underlayment A panel laid smooth over a subfloor to create a smooth, stiff surface for the application of the finish flooring.

Uniform Commercial Code (UCC) A set of statutory laws relating to certain commercial transactions, including the sale of goods, commercial paper, bank deposits and collections, letters of credit, bulk transfers, warehouse receipts, bills of lading, and secured transactions. Sales law is contained in the UCC.

upholstered wall system A site-constructed wallcovering that stretches fabric taut over a frame and infill material.

up-the-bolt Fabric applied in a vertical manner, with the selvage edge perpendicular to the seat cushion edge.

usable area The floor area that is inhabitable by the tenant.

variance An exemption or an exception permitting a use that differs from those permitted under the existing zoning law.

varnish A slow-drying transparent coating.

vegetable tanning A leather tanning method using a tanning solution based on tree bark, typically oak. The hides are submerged in the solution, and the tannins (tanning materials) from the bark swell the hides.

vehicle That portion of a paint or coating that conveys the ingredients that remain on the substrate after the paint or coating has cured.

velvet (1) A woven carpet in which the pile ends are lifted over wires that are inserted in the same manner as the weft and that cut the pile as they are drawn. (2) A fabric with a short, dense cut pile that produces a rich appearance and soft texture.

vinyl composition tile (VCT) Resilient flooring tiles composed mostly of fillers with a comparatively small amounts of binder and pigments.

virgin wool Wool made into yarn for the first time.

vitreous Glasslike; ceramic tile with an absorption of 0.5% or less.

volatile Readily evaporates.

volatile organic compounds (VOC) Those components of paints and coatings that evaporate readily. VOCs adversely affect human health and the environment.

wall base A strip of material that conceals the joint where a wall meets the floor.

wall liner A nonwoven sheet used under wallcovering where wall surfaces cannot be prepared by conventional means. Wall liners can be used to prevent cracks, holes, and gaps from telegraphing through the wallcovering.

warehouse A building in which any goods, particularly wares or merchandise, are stored.

warp Yarns that run lengthwise and parallel to the selvage in woven fabrics.

warranty A statement, promise, or other representation that an item has certain qualities; also, an obligation imposed by law, that an item will have certain qualities. Warranties made by means of a statement or other affirmation of fact are called *express warranties;* those imposed by law are *implied warranties.*

warranty of fitness for a particular purpose An implied warranty that goods will be fit for a particular purpose. This warranty is given by the seller to the buyer of goods whenever the seller has reason to know of any particular purpose for which the goods are needed, and the buyer relies on the seller's skill and judgment to select the goods.

warranty of merchantability An implied warranty that the goods are fit for the ordinary purpose for which such goods are used. Unless excluded, this warranty is always given by a merchant who sells goods in the ordinary course of business.

water-based polyurethane A low-VOC, nonyellowing, expensive wood floor finish.

weft Yarns that run from selvage to selvage at right angles to the warp in woven fabrics.

Wilton A woven carpet in which the pile yarns are an integral part of the carpet, being held in place by the weft, usually made on a Jacquard loom.

wire The number of ends (yarn loops) per inch in a lengthwise section of Wilton or velvet carpet.

wired glass Glass in which a wire mesh is embedded during the manufacturing process.

wire height The pile height of woven carpet.

work letter A document that describes the improvements to the leased space. It is attached to, and a part of, the lease.

wrought Produced by rolling semimolten material into sheets and punching or cutting out the required shape.

yarn A continuous strand formed by twisting fibers together.

yarn count A relative gauge of a spun yarn's weight; heavier yarns are designated by lower yarn count numbers.

yarn weight See *face weight.*

zoning law A local regulation or ordinance that restricts certain areas to specific uses; for example, areas zoned for residential, commercial, agricultural, industrial or other uses.

INDEX